The
Chambers
Paperback Dictionary

CHAMBERS
An imprint of Chambers Harrap Publishers Ltd
338 Euston Road, London,
NW1 3BH

Previous editions published 1998, 2003 and 2007
This edition published by Chambers Harrap Publishers Ltd 2007

© Chambers Harrap Publishers Ltd 2012

A CIP catalogue record for this book is available from the British Library.

ISBN 9780550105462

Designed and typeset by Chambers Harrap Publishers Ltd, Edinburgh and Sharon McTeir, Creative Publishing Services
Printed and bound by CPI Group (UK) Ltd, Croydon, CR0 4YY

Contents

Contributors to the last edition

Editors
Ian Brookes
Lorna Gilmour
Lucy Hollingworth
Mary O'Neill
Howard Sargeant

Data Management
Patrick Gaherty

Prepress
Heather Macpherson

Contributors to this edition

Editorial Director
Sarah Cole

Commissioning Editor
Robert Williams

Editor
Martin Manser

Production Controller
Georgina Cope

Preface

In *The Chambers Paperback Dictionary* you will find all you need to know about words in daily use – how to spell them, what they mean, what their different forms are and, if the words are unusual or particularly difficult, how to pronounce them. To help distinguish between meanings, many words are illustrated by phrases in which they may occur.

To provide further practical help, words which present special problems or are often confused with each other (eg *complement* and *compliment*; *flounder* and *founder*) have a warning note at the end of their entry.

In updating the dictionary, a full survey of the contents has been made and many additional words that are now in common use have been added. The system for indicating pronunciation has also been overhauled to make it easier to use for all speakers of English.

For this new edition of the dictionary, we have also included a good writing guide designed to inform and entertain. It contains a wealth of useful information on clear writing style, commonly misspelt words, global English and spelling memory prompts.

Up-to-date, modern and easy to use, we hope you will find this book a reliable and helpful companion.

How to use the dictionary

Main word entry	**teacup** *noun* a medium-sized cup for drinking tea • **a storm in a teacup** *see* **storm**
	teak *noun* **1** a hardwood tree from the East Indies **2** its very hard wood **3** a type of African tree
Definition	**teal** *noun* a small water bird like a duck
	team *noun* **1** a side in a game: *a football team* **2** a group of people working together **3** two or more animals working together: *team of oxen* • **team spirit** *noun* willingness to work as part of a team • **team up with** join together with, *usu* in order to do something
Warning about easily confused words	Do not confuse with: **teem**
	tear¹ *noun* **1** a drop of liquid from the eye **2** (**tears**) a state or spell of crying • **tear gas** *noun* gas that causes the eyes to stream with tears, used in crowd control *etc* • **in tears** weeping
Tense forms of verb	**tear²** *verb* (**tearing, tore, torn**) **1** pull with force: *tear apart/tear down* **2** make a hole or split in (material *etc*) **3** hurt deeply **4** *informal* rush: *tearing off down the road* ◇ *noun* a hole or split made by tearing
Usage information	
	tearful *adj* **1** inclined to cry **2** in tears; crying • **tearfully** *adv*
Part of speech: *noun, verb*, etc	**tease** *verb* **1** irritate and upset on purpose **2** pretend to upset or annoy for fun: *I'm only teasing* **3** untangle (wool *etc*) with a comb **4** sort out (a problem or puzzle) ◇ *noun* someone who teases
	teasel *noun* a type of prickly plant
	teaser *noun* a difficult problem or puzzle

techie /tek-i/ *noun, informal* someone who is an expert in or very enthusiastic about new technology

> Pronunciation guidance

technical *adj* 1 relating to a particular art or skill, *esp a mechanical or industrial one: what is the technical term for this?/a technical expert* 2 according to strict interpretations or rules: *technical defeat* • **technically** *adv* according to a strict interpretation or rule; strictly speaking

> Example of use

technicality *noun* (*plural* **technicalities**) a technical detail or point

technician *noun* someone trained in the practical side of an art

technique *noun* the way in which a process is carried out; a method

technology *noun* 1 science applied to practical (*esp* industrial) purposes 2 the practical skills of a particular civilization, period, *etc* • **technological** *adj* • **technologically** *adv* • **technologist** *noun*

teddy *noun* (*plural* **teddies**) 1 a stuffed toy bear (also called **teddy bear**) 2 a one-piece woman's undergarment

> Plural form of noun

tedious *adj* boring • **tediously** *adv* • **tedium** *noun*

> Related words, listed alphabetically

tee *noun* 1 the square of level ground from which a golf ball is driven 2 the peg or sand heap on which the ball is placed for driving • **tee up** place (a ball) on a tee

> Set phrases containing the entry word

teem *verb* 1 be full: *teeming with people* 2 rain heavily

Do not confuse with: **team**

teenage *adj* suitable for, or typical of, people in their teens

Abbreviations used in the dictionary

The dictionary also has some labels in full (for example *informal* and *music*) which show you the manner or the subject area in which a word or meaning is used.

abbrev	abbreviation
adj	adjective
adv	adverb
Aust	Australian English
Brit	British English
comput	computing
conj	conjunction
derog	derogatory
E	East
eg	for example
esp	especially
etc	and so on, and other things
exclam	exclamation
hist	history
ie	that is
med	medicine
N	North
orig	originally
prep	preposition
S	South
Scot	Scottish English
sing	singular
TV	television
UK	United Kingdom
US	United States (and often Canadian) English
USA	United States of America
usu	usually
W	West

Pronunciation guide

The dictionary gives you help when the pronunciation of a word is particularly tricky. Pronunciations are given in slashes after the entry word, for example:

acquiesce /ak-wee-*es*/

The way the pronunciations are shown is designed to be easily understandable. The syllables are separated by hyphens, and the stressed syllable (that is, the syllable pronounced with most emphasis) is shown in italic type.

Here is a guide to the letters and letter combinations that are used to show different sounds:

Vowels

/a/	shows the sound in *bat*
/ah/	shows the sound in *far, dance*
/ai/	shows the sound in *my, pine*
/air/	shows the sound in *care*
/aw/	shows the sound in *all, saw*
/e/	shows the sound in *pet*
/ee/	shows the sound in *bee*
/eh/	shows the sound in *same*
/i/	shows the sound in *bid*
/o/	shows the sound in *got*
/oh/	shows the sound in *note, though*
/oo/	shows the sound in *moon, lose*
/ow/	shows the sound in *house, now*
/oy/	shows the sound in *boy, soil*
/u/	shows the sound in *cup*
/uh/	shows the sound in *thorough*
/ur/	shows the sound in *bird*
/uu/	shows the sound in *foot*

Pronunciation guide

Consonants

/ch/	shows the sound in *cheap*
/dh/	shows the sound in *then*
/ng/	shows the sound in *sing*
/sh/	shows the sound in *shine*
/th/	shows the sound in *thin*
/xh/	shows the sound in *loch*
/zh/	shows the sound in *measure*

The consonant letters b, d, f, g, h, j, k, l, m, n, p, r, s, t, v, w and z are pronounced as in standard English.

Additional sounds

/anh/ and /onh/ represent French vowels that are pronounced nasally, as in **impasse** /*anh*-pas/ and **blancmange** /bluh-*monhzh*/.

Aa

a *or* **an** *adj* **1** one: *a knock at the door* **2** any: *an ant has six legs* **3** in, to or for each: *four times a day*

The form *a* is used before words beginning with a consonant, *eg* knock; *an* is used before words beginning with a vowel, *eg* ant

---

aardvark *noun* a long-nosed S African animal that feeds on termites

aback *adv*: **taken aback** surprised

abacus *noun* (*plural* **abacuses**) a frame with columns of beads for counting

abandon *verb* **1** leave, without meaning to return to **2** give up (an idea *etc*) ◇ *noun* lack of inhibition • **abandonment** *noun*

abase *verb* make (someone) respected less • **abasement** *noun*

abashed *adj* embarrassed, confused

abate *verb* become less strong or intense • **abatement** *noun*

abattoir /ab-uh-twah/ *noun* a (public) slaughterhouse

abbess *noun* (*plural* **abbesses**) the female head of an abbey or a convent

abbey *noun* (*plural* **abbeys**) **1** a monastery or convent ruled by an abbot or an abbess **2** the church now or formerly attached to it

abbot *noun* the male head of an abbey

abbreviate *verb* shorten (a word, phrase, *etc*)

abbreviation *noun* a shortened form of a word *etc* used instead of the whole word, *eg maths* for *mathematics*

abdicate *verb* give up (a position, *esp* that of king or queen) • **abdication** *noun*

abdomen *noun* the part of the human body between the chest and the hips • **abdominal** *adj*

abduct *verb* take away by force • **abduction** *noun*

abet *verb* (**abetting, abetted**) help or encourage to do wrong

abeyance *noun*: **in abeyance** undecided; not to be dealt with for the time being

abhor *verb* (**abhorring, abhorred**) look on with horror, hate • **abhorrence** *noun*

abhorrent *adj* hateful • **abhorrently** *adv*

abide *verb* put up with, tolerate • **abiding** *adj* lasting • **abide by** keep, act according to

ability *noun* (*plural* **abilities**) **1** power or means to do something **2** talent

abject *adj* miserable, degraded

ablaze *adj* **1** burning fiercely **2** gleaming like fire

able *adj* **1** having the power or means (to do something) **2** clever • **ably** *adv*

able-bodied *adj* not disabled

ablutions *plural noun, formal* washing of the body

abnormal *adj* **1** not normal (in behaviour *etc*) **2** unusual • **abnormal-**

ity *noun* • **abnormally** *adv*

aboard *adv & prep* on(to) or in(to) (a ship or aeroplane)

abode *noun, formal* a home

abolish *verb* do away with (eg a custom) • **abolition** *noun* • **abolitionist** *noun* someone who tries to do away with anything, *esp* slavery

abominable *adj* **1** hateful **2** very bad, terrible • **abominably** *adv* • **the Abominable Snowman** (*also called* **Yeti**) a large animal believed to exist in the Himalayas

abominate *verb* hate • **abomination** *noun* **1** something you hate **2** hatred

Aboriginal *or* **Aborigine** *noun* a member of the native people of Australia • **Aboriginal** *adj*

abort *verb* **1** not develop (eg a plan), not complete (eg a mission) **2** remove (a foetus) to end a pregnancy • **abortive** *adj* coming to nothing, useless: *an abortive attempt*

abortion *noun* the removal of a foetus so that a baby is not born

abound *verb* exist in large numbers or amounts • **abounding in** full of, having many

about *prep* **1** near (in time, size, *etc*): *about ten o'clock* **2** on the subject of: *a book about fishing* **3** here and there in: *scattered about the room* ◇ *adv* **1** in a place: *stood about waiting* **2** to different parts of a place: *running about* • **about to** on the point of (doing something)

above *prep* **1** over, in a higher position than: *above your head* **2** greater than: *above average* **3** feeling yourself too good for something: *she was not above getting her hands dirty* ◇ *adv* **1** overhead **2** earlier on (in a letter *etc*) • **above board** open and honest

abrasion *noun* **1** a graze on the body **2** the action of rubbing off

abrasive *adj* **1** rough and used for

rubbing down **2** having a rude manner ◇ *noun* something rough used for rubbing • **abrasively** *adv*

abreast *adv* side by side • **abreast of** up to date with: *abreast of current affairs*

abridge *verb* shorten (a book, story, *etc*) • **abridgement** *or* **abridgment** *noun*

abroad *adv* **1** in or to another country

abrupt *adj* **1** sudden, without warning **2** bad-tempered, short, curt • **abruptly** *adv*

abscess *noun* (*plural* **abscesses**) a pus-filled swelling on the body

abscond *verb* run away secretly: *absconded with the money*

abseiling /ab-sehl-ing/ *noun* the sport of sliding down a rope from a high place • **abseil** *verb*

absent *adj* away, not present • **absence** *noun* the state of being away • **absentee** *noun* someone who is absent • **absently** *adv* • **absent-minded** *adj* forgetful • **absent yourself** stay away

absolute *adj* complete, not limited by anything: *absolute power* • **absolutely** *adv* completely

absolve *verb* pardon • **absolution** *noun* forgiveness, pardon

absorb *verb* **1** soak up (liquid) **2** take up the whole attention of • **absorbed** *adj*

absorbent *adj* able to soak up liquid • **absorbency** *noun*

absorption *noun* **1** the act of absorbing **2** complete mental concentration

abstain *verb* **1** refuse to cast a vote for or against **2** (with **from**) choose not to do or have something enjoyable • **abstention** *noun*

abstemious *adj* choosing not to eat, drink or enjoy yourself much • **abstemiousness** *noun*

abstention see abstain

abstinence noun not drinking alcohol etc • **abstinent** adj

abstract adj existing only as an idea, not as a real thing ◇ noun a summary • **abstraction** noun

abstruse adj difficult to understand

absurd adj clearly wrong; ridiculous • **absurdity** noun

abundance noun a plentiful supply • **abundant** adj plentiful • **abundantly** adv

abuse verb 1 use wrongly 2 insult or speak unkindly to; treat badly ◇ noun 1 wrongful use 2 insulting language or behaviour • **abusive** adj

abysmal adj, informal very bad; terrible • **abysmally** adv

abyss noun (plural **abysses**) a bottomless depth

AC abbrev alternating current (compare with: **DC**)

a/c abbrev account

acacia /uh-keh-shuh/ noun a thorny shrub or tree with white or yellow flowers

academic adj 1 to do with formal study, not practical skills: academic subjects 2 theoretical: purely of academic interest 3 of a university etc ◇ noun a university or college teacher • **academically** adv

academy noun (plural **academies**) 1 a college for special study or training 2 a society for encouraging science or art 3 in Scotland, a high school

acanthus noun a Mediterranean shrub

ACAS abbrev Advisory, Conciliation and Arbitration Service, an organization that runs negotiations in industrial disputes

accede verb: **accede to** agree to

accelerate verb increase in speed • **acceleration** noun

accelerator noun a lever or pedal used to increase the speed of a car etc

accent noun 1 the way in which words are pronounced in a particular area etc: a Scottish accent 2 a mark used in some languages to show the sound of a vowel 3 (a mark indicating) stress on a syllable or word 4 emphasis: the accent must be on hard work • **accentuate** verb make more obvious; emphasize

accept verb 1 take (something) offered 2 agree or submit to • **acceptable** adj satisfactory; pleasing • **acceptance** noun the act of accepting

---

Do not confuse with: **except**

---

access noun right to enter, or way to enter ◇ verb get (information from a computer)

Do not confuse with: **excess**

---

accessible adj 1 easily approached 2 easily understood • **accessibility** noun

accessory noun (plural **accessories**) 1 a piece of jewellery, a handbag, etc that goes with clothes 2 an additional piece of equipment: car accessories 3 a criminal's helper

accident noun 1 an unexpected event causing injury 2 a mishap • **accidental** adj happening by chance • **accidentally** adv • **by accident** by chance and unintentionally

acclaim verb praise enthusiastically ◇ noun enthusiastic reception: met with critical acclaim • **acclamation** noun enthusiastic praise

acclimatize verb accustom to another climate or situation • **acclimatization** noun

accommodate verb 1 find room for 2 give or do (what someone wants) • **accommodating** adj obliging • **accommodation** noun lodgings

accompany verb (**accompanying**, **accompanied**) 1 go or be with 2 play music for (a singer) • **accompaniment** noun 1 something that accompanies 2 the music played while a singer sings • **accompanist** noun someone who plays an accompaniment

accomplice noun someone who helps a criminal

accomplish verb 1 complete 2 bring about • **accomplished** adj 1 completed 2 skilled, talented • **accomplishment** noun 1 completion 2 a personal talent or skill

accord verb 1 give, grant 2 have the same opinion ◇ noun agreement • **accordingly** adv therefore • **according to** 1 as told by 2 in relation to: paid according to your work • **in accordance with** following (a rule etc) • **of your own accord** of your own free will

accordion noun a musical instrument with bellows, a keyboard and metal reeds • **accordionist** noun an accordion player

accost verb approach and speak to

account noun 1 a record of finances 2 a description of events etc; an explanation ◇ verb give a reason (for) • **accountable** adj answerable, responsible • **accountant** noun a keeper or inspector of accounts • **on account of** because of

accoutrements /uh-koo-truh-munts/ plural noun equipment or clothes

accredited adj having official status or authority

accrue verb 1 be given or added to 2 accumulate, collect: the account accrued no interest • **accrued** adj

accumulate verb 1 collect 2 increase • **accumulation** noun 1 a collection 2 a mass or pile

accurate adj correct, exact • **accu-**

racy noun • **accurately** adv

accursed adj, formal hateful

accuse verb bring a (criminal) charge against • **accusation** noun a charge brought against anyone • **accuser** noun • **the accused** the person charged with a crime

accustomed adj 1 used to: accustomed to travel 2 usual

ace noun 1 the one on playing-cards 2 an expert: a computer ace 3 tennis an unreturned serve

acetylene /uh-set-uh-leen/ noun a gas used for giving light and heat

ache noun a continuous pain ◇ verb be the source of or be in continuous pain

achieve verb 1 get (something) done, accomplish 2 win • **achievement** noun

acid adj 1 of taste: sharp 2 sarcastic ◇ noun a chemical containing hydrogen, able to dissolve metals (contrasted with: **alkali**) • **acidity** noun the state of being acid • **acid rain** noun rain containing sulphur and nitrogen compounds and other pollutants

acidify verb (**acidifying**, **acidified**) make or become acid

acknowledge verb 1 admit the truth of 2 write to say you have received (something) • **acknowledgement** or **acknowledgment** noun

acme noun the stage of being most successful

acne noun a common skin disease with pimples

acorn noun the seed of the oak tree

acoustic /uh-koo-stik/ adj 1 of hearing or sound 2 of a guitar or other musical instrument: not electric • **acoustics** noun 1 sing the study of sound 2 plural the characteristics of a room etc that affect the hearing of sound in it

acquaint verb make (someone)

familiar (with) • **acquaintance** *noun* **1** someone whom you know slightly **2** knowledge

acquiesce /ak-wee-es/ *verb* (often with **in**) agree (to) • **acquiescence** *noun* • **acquiescent** *adj*

acquire *verb* obtain, get • **acquired** *adj* gained; not innate or inherited • **acquisition** *noun* **1** the act of getting **2** something got

acquisitive *adj* eager to get more possessions • **acquisitiveness** *noun*

acquit *verb* (**acquitting, acquitted**) declare (someone) innocent of a crime • **acquittal** *noun* a legal judgement of 'not guilty' • **acquit yourself well** do well, be successful

acre *noun* a land measure containing 4840 square yards or about 4000 square metres • **acreage** *noun* the number of acres in a piece of land

acrid *adj* harsh, bitter

acrimony *noun* bitterness of feeling or speech • **acrimonious** *adj*

acrobat *noun* someone who performs gymnastic feats, tightrope-walking, *etc* • **acrobatic** *adj*

acronym *noun* a word formed from the initial letters of other words, *eg* *radar* from *radio detecting and ranging*

across *adv & prep* to or at the other side (of): *jumped into the river and swam across/winked at him across the table* • **across the board** involving everyone or everything; sweeping

acrostic *noun* a poem *etc* in which the first or last letters of each line, taken in order, spell a word or words

acrylic *noun* a synthetically produced fibre ◇ *adj* made with this material

act *verb* **1** do something **2** behave in a particular way: *act foolishly* **3** play a role on stage, in film, *etc* ◇ *noun* **1** something done **2** a government law **3** a section of a play

action *noun* **1** something done **2** dramatic events portrayed in a film, play, *etc* **3** a law case • **actionable** *adj* likely to cause a law case: *actionable statement*

active *adj* **1** busy; lively and energetic **2** closely involved in an organization **3** *grammar* describing the form of a verb in which the subject performs the action of the verb, *eg* 'the dog bit the postman' • **activate** *verb* start (something) working • **activity** *noun*

actor *noun* someone who acts in a play or film

actress *noun* (*plural* **actresses**) a female actor

actual *adj* real, existing in fact • **actuality** *noun* • **actually** *adv* really

actuary *noun* (*plural* **actuaries**) someone who works out the price of insurance • **actuarial** *adj*

actuate *verb* **1** make (a machine *etc*) start working **2** motivate

acumen *noun* quickness of understanding

acupressure *noun* a method of treating illness by applying pressure to certain key points on the body

acupuncture *noun* a method of treating illness by piercing the skin with needles • **acupuncturist** *noun* a practitioner of acupuncture

acute *adj* **1** quick at understanding **2** of a disease: severe, but not lasting very long **3** of an angle: less than a right angle (*contrasted with*: **obtuse**) • **acute accent** *noun* a forward-leaning stroke (´) placed over letters in some languages to show their pronunciation • **acuteness** *noun*

AD *abbrev* in the year of our Lord, *eg* AD 1900 (from Latin *anno Domini*)

ad *noun, informal* an advertisement

adage *noun* an old saying, a proverb

adagio *noun* a slow-paced piece of music

adamant *adj* unwilling to change an opinion or decision • **adamantly** *adv*

Adam's apple *noun* the natural lump that sticks out from a man's throat

adapt *verb* make suitable; alter so as to fit • **adaptable** *adj* easily altered to suit new conditions • **adaptation** *noun*

adaptor *noun* a device allowing an electrical plug to be used in a socket for which it was not designed, or several plugs to be used in the same socket

add *verb* 1 make one thing join another to give a sum total or whole 2 mix in: *add water to the dough* 3 say further • **addition** *noun* 1 the act of adding 2 something added • **additional** *adj* • **additive** *noun* a chemical *etc* added to another substance

adder *noun* the common name of the viper, a poisonous snake

addict *noun* someone who is dependent on something, often on a drug or alcohol, either physically or mentally • **addiction** *noun* dependence • **addictive** *adj* creating dependence, habit-forming • **addicted to** dependent on (a drug, alcohol, *etc*)

addition and **additive** *see* add

address *noun* (*plural* **addresses**) 1 the name of the house, street, and town where someone lives *etc* 2 speech ◇ *verb* 1 speak to 2 write the address on (a letter *etc*)

adenoids *plural noun* glandular tissues at the back of the nose

adept *adj* very skilful

adequate *adj* sufficient, enough • **adequacy** *noun* • **adequately** *adv*

adhere *verb* 1 stick (to a surface *etc*) 2 keep to a rule, agreement, *etc* • **adherence** *noun*

adherent *noun* a follower or supporter of a cause *etc* ◇ *adj* sticking (to)

adhesion *noun* the act of sticking (to a surface *etc*)

adhesive *adj* sticky, gummed ◇ *noun* something that makes things stick to each other

ad hoc *adj* set up for a particular purpose only

ad infinitum *adv* for ever

adjacent *adj* (with **to**) next to

adjective *noun, grammar* a word that gives information about a noun, *eg* 'the *black* cat', 'times are *hard*' • **adjectival** *adj*

adjoin *verb* be joined to • **adjoining** *adj*

adjourn *verb* 1 stop (a meeting *etc*) with the intention of continuing it at another time or place 2 (with **to**) go to another place: *adjourn to the lounge* • **adjournment** *noun*

adjudicate *verb* 1 give a judgement on (a dispute *etc*) 2 act as a judge at a competition • **adjudication** *noun* • **adjudicator** *noun* someone who adjudicates

adjunct *noun* something joined or added

adjust *verb* rearrange or alter to suit the circumstances • **adjustable** *adj* • **adjustment** *noun*

adjutant *noun* a military officer who assists a commanding officer

ad-lib *verb* (**ad-libbing, ad-libbed**) speak without preparation ◇ *adj* without preparation

administer *verb* 1 give (help, medicine, *etc*) 2 carry out (the law *etc*) 3 manage or govern

administration *noun* 1 management 2 (the body that carries on) the government of a country *etc* • **administrate** *verb* manage or govern • **administrative** *adj* • **administrator** *noun* someone involved in the administration of a country *etc*

admiral *noun* the commander of

a navy • **admiralty** *noun* the government office that manages naval affairs

admire *verb* **1** think very highly of **2** look at with pleasure • **admirable** *adj* worthy of being admired • **admirably** *adv* • **admiration** *noun* • **admirer** *noun*

admit *verb* (**admitting**, **admitted**) **1** acknowledge the truth of, confess **2** let in **3** (with **of**) leave room for, allow: *admits of no other explanation* • **admissible** *adj* allowable • **admission** *noun* **1** (the price of) being let in **2** anything admitted • **admittance** *noun* the right or permission to enter

admonish *verb* **1** tell off, scold **2** warn • **admonition** *noun* **1** a telling-off **2** a warning • **admonitory** *adj*

ad nauseam *adv* to a boring degree

ado *noun* trouble, fuss

adobe /uh-*doh*-bi/ *noun* clay used to make bricks for building

adolescent *noun* someone between a child and an adult in age ◇ *adj* of this age • **adolescence** *noun*

adopt *verb* **1** take as your own (*esp* a child of other parents) **2** start doing or using • **adoption** *noun* • **adoptive** *adj* adopted, taken as your own: *her adoptive country*

adore *verb* **1** love (someone) very much **2** like (something) very much • **adorable** *adj* very loveable • **adorably** *adv* • **adoration** *noun* **1** worship **2** great love

adorn *verb* decorate (with ornaments *etc*) • **adornment** *noun* ornament

adrenaline *noun* a hormone produced in response to fear, anger, *etc*, preparing the body for quick action

adrift *adv* **1** drifting, floating **2** lagging behind others

adroit *adj* skilful

adulation *noun* great praise • **adulatory** *adj*

adult *adj* grown up ◇ *noun* a grown-up person

adulterate *verb* make impure by adding something else • **adulteration** *noun*

adultery *noun* unfaithfulness to a husband or wife • **adulterer** *or* **adulteress** *noun*

advance *verb* **1** go forward **2** put forward (a plan *etc*) **3** help the progress of **4** pay before the usual or agreed time ◇ *noun* **1** movement forward **2** improvement **3** part of a payment given early as a loan • **advanced** *adj* well forward in progress • **advancement** *noun* progress • **in advance** beforehand

advantage *noun* **1** a better position, superiority **2** gain or benefit ◇ *verb* help, benefit • **advantageous** *adj* profitable; helpful • **take advantage of** make use of (a situation, person, *etc*) in such a way as to benefit yourself

advent *noun* **1** coming, arrival: *before the advent of television* **2** (**Advent**) in the Christian church, the four weeks before Christmas

adventure *noun* a bold or exciting undertaking or experience

adventurer *noun* **1** someone who takes risks, *esp* in the hope of making a lot of money **2** a mercenary soldier

adventurous *adj* taking risks, liking adventure • **adventurously** *adv* • **adventurousness** *noun*

adverb *noun* a word that gives more information about the meaning of a verb, adjective, or other adverb, *eg* 'eat *slowly*', '*extremely* hard', '*very* carefully' • **adverbial** *adj* of or like an adverb

adversary *noun* (*plural* **adversaries**) an enemy; an opponent

adverse *adj* unfavourable: *adverse criticism* • **adversity** *noun* when bad things happen

---

Do not confuse with: **averse**

---

advert *noun, informal* an advertisement

advertise *verb* **1** make known to the public **2** stress the good points of (a product for sale)

advertisement *noun* a photograph, short film, *etc* intended to persuade the public to buy a particular product

advice *noun* **1** something said as a help to someone trying to make a decision *etc* **2** a formal notice

---

Do not confuse with: **advise**

---

advisable *adj* wise, sensible • **advisability** *noun* • **advisably** *adv*

advise *verb* **1** give advice to **2** recommend (an action *etc*) • **adviser** *noun* • **advisory** *adj* giving advice: *advisory body*

Do not confuse with: **advice**

---

advocate *noun* **1** someone who pleads for another **2** in Scotland, a court lawyer ◇ *verb* **1** plead or argue for **2** recommend

adze *or US* **adz** *noun* a kind of axe used by a carpenter

adzuki *or* **azuki** *noun* a kind of kidney bean grown in China and Japan

aegis /ee-jis/ *noun*: **under the aegis of** in the name of, and with the protection and authority of

aeon *or* **eon** /ee-on/ *noun* a very long period of time, an age

aerate *verb* put air or another gas into (a liquid)

aerial *adj* **1** of, in or from the air: *aerial photography* **2** placed high up or overhead: *aerial railway* ◇ *noun* a wire, rod or dish that receives or sends radio or television signals

aerobatics *plural noun* stunts performed by an aircraft

aerobics *sing noun* a system of rhythmic physical exercise that aims to strengthen the heart and lungs

aerodrome *noun* a small private airport

aeronautics *sing noun* the science or art of flight

aeroplane *or US* **airplane** *noun* an engine-powered flying vehicle with wings

aerosol *noun* a container of liquid and gas under pressure, from which the liquid is squirted as a mist

aesthetic *adj* **1** of beauty or its appreciation **2** artistic, pleasing to the eye • **aesthetically** *adv*

affable *adj* pleasant, easy to speak to • **affability** *noun* • **affably** *adv*

affair *noun* **1** events *etc* connected with one person or thing: *the Watergate affair* **2** (**affairs**) personal concerns, transactions, *etc*: *his affairs seemed to be in order* **3** business, concern: *that's not your affair* **4** a romantic relationship, *esp* an illicit one

affect *verb* **1** influence or change **2** make emotional **3** pretend to feel *etc* • **affectation** *noun* pretence • **affected** *adj* **1** not natural, sham **2** made emotional • **affecting** *adj* moving the feelings

---

Do not confuse with: **effect**

---

affection *noun* a strong liking • **affectionate** *adj* loving • **affectionately** *adv*

affidavit /af-i-*deh*-vit/ *noun, law* a written statement made on oath

affiliated *adj* (with **with** or **to**) officially connected • **affiliation** *noun*

affinity *noun* (*plural* **affinities**) **1** a liking or taste for something **2** a close likeness

affirm verb state firmly • **affirmation** noun a firm statement • **affirmative** adj saying 'yes'

affix verb attach to

afflict verb give continued pain or distress to • **afflicted** adj suffering • **affliction** noun great suffering, misery

affluent adj wealthy • **affluence** noun wealth

afford verb 1 be able to pay for 2 give (a benefit etc) • **affordable** adj

afforestation noun the mass planting of trees • **afforest** verb

affray noun a fight, a brawl

affront verb insult openly ◇ noun an insult

afloat adv & adj floating

afoot adv happening or about to happen: I could tell something was afoot

aforesaid adj mentioned before: the aforesaid person

afraid adj 1 feeling fear, scared 2 informal sorry to have to admit that: I'm afraid there are no tickets left

afresh adv once again

aft adv at or towards the back of a ship

after prep 1 later in time than: after dinner 2 following: arrived one after another/day after day 3 in memory or honour of: named after his father 4 in order to catch: run after the bus 5 about: asked after her health 6 despite: after all my efforts, it still didn't work ◇ adv later in time or place: we left soon after ◇ conj later than the time when: after she arrived, things improved • **after-** prefix later in time or place: aftertaste/afterthought • **after all** 1 all things considered: after all, he's still young 2 despite everything said or done before: I went after all

afterbirth noun the placenta and membranes expelled from the uterus after giving birth

afterlife noun the existence of the soul or spirit after the body dies

aftermath noun the bad results of something: the aftermath of the election

afternoon noun the time between noon and evening ◇ adj taking place in the afternoon

aftershave noun a lotion used on the face after shaving

afterthought noun a later thought

afterwards adv later, after that

again adv 1 once more: say that again 2 in or into the original state, place, etc: there and back again 3 on the other hand: again, I might be wrong 4 informal at another later time: see you again

against prep 1 in opposition to: against the law/fight against injustice 2 in the opposite direction to: against the wind 3 close to, touching: lean against the wall 4 as protection from: guard against infection 5 on a background of: against the sky

agate /a-git/ noun a kind of precious stone

age noun 1 the time someone or something has lived or existed 2 a long period of time ◇ verb (**ageing, aged**) become or make visibly older • **aged** adj 1 old 2 of the age of: aged five • **of age** legally an adult

ageism noun discrimination on grounds of age • **ageist** adj discriminating on grounds of age

agency noun (plural **agencies**) 1 the office or business of an agent 2 the means by which something is done

agenda noun 1 a list of things to be discussed at a meeting 2 a list of things to be done

agent noun 1 someone who arranges things 2 someone appointed to decide for another 3 a spy 4 a substance used for something

agent provocateur /a-zhonh pro-vo-ka-*tur*/ noun someone who deliberately incites others to violence, illegal action, *etc*

aggrandize verb make more important or powerful • **aggrandizement** noun

aggravate verb 1 make worse 2 *informal* annoy • **aggravating** adj • **aggravation** noun

aggregate noun a total

aggressive adj 1 ready to attack first 2 quarrelsome • **aggression** noun • **aggressively** adv • **aggressor** noun

aggrieved adj angry about unfairness

aggro /a-groh/ noun, informal aggression, hostility

aghast adj shocked by something bad

agile adj moving quickly and easily, nimble • **agility** noun

agitate verb 1 stir up political feeling 2 make nervous or upset • **agitation** noun • **agitator** noun someone who stirs up political feeling

AGM abbrev annual general meeting

agnostic noun someone who believes it is impossible to know whether God exists or not • **agnosticism** noun

ago adv in the past: *that happened five years ago*

agog adj eager, excited

agony noun (*plural* **agonies**) great pain • **agonize** verb worry a lot about a decision • **agonizing** adj causing great pain • **agony aunt** noun someone who gives advice in an agony column • **agony column** noun a regular column in a newspaper or magazine in which readers submit and receive advice about personal problems

agoraphobia noun great fear of open spaces • **agoraphobic** noun & adj (someone) suffering from agoraphobia

agrarian adj of farmland or farming

agree verb 1 have the same opinion 2 say that you will do something, consent • **agreeable** adj 1 pleasant 2 ready to agree • **agreeably** adv • **agreement** noun 1 sameness of opinion 2 an arrangement based on a joint decision • **agree with** 1 approve of 2 cause no problems in digestion: *the fish didn't agree with me*

agriculture noun the cultivation of the land, farming • **agricultural** adj

aground adj & adv stuck on the bottom of the sea or a river: *run aground*

ahead adv in front; in advance: *a roadblock ahead of us/finishing ahead of time*

AI abbrev 1 artificial intelligence 2 artificial insemination

aid verb help, assist ◇ noun 1 help 2 money and supplies given to developing countries

aide-memoire noun something to help you remember; a reminder

AIDS or **Aids** abbrev Acquired Immune Deficiency Syndrome, a serious illness that destroys the body's resistance to diseases of all kinds

ail verb 1 be ill 2 worry (someone)

ailment noun a trouble, disease

aim verb 1 point at (*esp* with a gun) 2 intend to do 3 have as your purpose ◇ noun 1 the act of, or skill in, aiming 2 the thing you intend to achieve, goal • **aimless** adj without aim or purpose • **aimlessly** adv

air noun 1 the mixture of gases (mainly oxygen and nitrogen) that we breathe, the atmosphere 2 space overhead 3 pleasantly cool outdoor conditions, fresh air 4 a person's look or manner 5 a tune ◇ verb 1 expose to the air in order to freshen or dry 2 make known (an opinion *etc*) • **airbag** noun a bag that automatically inflates inside a car on impact to protect the driver from injury • **airbed**

noun a mattress that can be inflated • **airborne** *adj* in the air, flying • **air-conditioned** *adj* equipped with a system for filtering and controlling the temperature of the air • **airfield** *noun* an expanse of land where aircraft can land and take off • **air force** *noun* the branch of the armed forces using aircraft • **air-gun** *noun* a gun worked by means of compressed air • **airing** *noun* the act of exposing to the air • **airless** *adj* unpleasantly lacking in air, stuffy • **airlock** *noun* **1** a bubble in a pipe obstructing the flow of a liquid **2** a compartment with two doors for entering and leaving an airtight spaceship *etc* • **airmail** *noun* mail carried by air • **air miles** *plural noun* credits for buying air tickets • **air-raid** *noun* an attack by aeroplanes • **airship** *noun* a large balloon which can be steered and driven • **airtight** *adj* made so that air cannot get in or out • **on the air** broadcasting

aircraft *noun* (*plural* **aircraft**) a flying vehicle

airline *noun* a company providing air transport services

airplane *US for* **aeroplane**

airport *noun* a place where aircraft land and take off, with buildings for customs, waiting rooms, *etc*

airy *adj* (**airier**, **airiest**) **1** well supplied with fresh air **2** light-hearted • **airily** *adv*

aisle /ail/ *noun* **1** a passage between seats in a theatre *etc* **2** the side part of a church

ajar *adv* partly open: *leave the door ajar*

aka *abbrev* also known as: *Stevens, aka The Fly*

akimbo *adv* with hand on hip and elbow bent outward

akin *adj* similar

à la *prep* in the style of

à la carte *adj & adv* with each dish

chosen and priced separately

alacrity *noun* eagerness and speed of action

à la mode *adj & adv* **1** fashionable **2** *US* served with ice-cream: *apple pie à la mode*

alarm *noun* **1** a loud signal that warns of danger **2** an alarm clock **3** sudden fear ◇ *verb* frighten • **alarm clock** *noun* a clock that makes a noise to wake you up • **alarming** *adj* frightening or worrying • **alarmist** *noun* someone who frightens others needlessly • **raise the alarm** warn people that something bad is happening

alas! *exclam* a cry showing grief

albatross *noun* (*plural* **albatrosses**) a large sea-bird

albino *noun* (*plural* **albinos**) a person or animal with no natural colour in their skin, hair and eyes

album *noun* **1** a book with blank pages for holding photographs, stamps, *etc* **2** a set of musical recordings issued under one title

albumen *noun* the white of eggs

alchemy *noun* an early form of chemistry aimed at changing other metals into gold • **alchemist** *noun* someone who practised alchemy

alcohol *noun* **1** drinks that can make people drunk **2** the spirit contained in such drinks • **alcoholic** *adj* of or containing alcohol ◇ *noun* someone addicted to alcohol • **alcoholism** *noun* addiction to alcohol

alcopop *noun* an alcoholic drink bought ready-mixed with lemonade *etc*

alcove *noun* a recess in a room's wall

al dente *adj & adv* cooked so as to retain some firmness in texture

alder *noun* a type of tree that grows beside ponds and rivers

alderman *noun* **1** *hist* a councillor

next in rank to the mayor of a town *etc* **2** *US* a member of the governing body of a city

ale *noun* beer, *esp* when brewed and stored using traditional methods

alert *adj* **1** watchful **2** quick-thinking ◇ *noun* a signal to be ready for action ◇ *verb* make alert, warn • **on the alert** on the watch (for)

alfalfa *noun* a kind of grass, often used for animal fodder (*also called:* **lucerne**)

alfresco *adj & adv* in the open air

algae /al-gee/ or /al-jee/ *plural noun* simple plants that live in or near water and have no roots or leaves, *eg* seaweed

algebra *noun* a type of mathematics that uses letters and symbols to represent quantities

algorithm *noun* a series of steps followed to solve a mathematical equation or create a computer program *etc*

alias *adv* also known as: *Mitchell alias Grassic Gibbon* ◇ *noun* (*plural* **aliases**) a false name

alibi *noun* **1** the plea that someone charged with a crime was elsewhere when it was done **2** the state or fact of being elsewhere when a crime was committed

alien *adj* **1** from another planet **2** foreign ◇ *noun* **1** a being from another planet **2** a foreigner • **alienate** *verb* make (someone) feel left out, uninterested or discontented • **alien to** not in keeping with: *alien to her nature*

alight *verb* (**alighting, alighted**) **1** get off or out of a vehicle **2** of a bird *etc*: settle or land somewhere ◇ *adj & adv* on fire, burning

align /uh-lain/ *verb* **1** put (things) in line with each other **2** take sides in an argument *etc* • **alignment** *noun* arrangement in a line

alike *adj* like one another, similar ◇ *adv* in the same way, similarly

alimentary *adj* of food • **alimentary canal** *noun* the passage through the body that begins at the mouth

alimony *noun* an allowance paid by a husband to his wife, or a wife to her husband, to provide support when they are legally separated

alive *adj* **1** living **2** full of activity • **alive to** aware of

alkali *noun* a substance that reacts with an acid to form a chemical salt (*contrasted with:* **acid**) • **alkaline** *adj* • **alkalinity** *noun*

all *adj & pronoun* **1** every one (of): *we are all invited/all letters will be answered* **2** the whole (of): *painted all the house* ◇ *adv* wholly, completely: *dressed all in red* • **all-rounder** *noun* someone skilled in many kinds of work, sport, *etc* • **all in** with everything included: *£10 all in* • **all over 1** over the whole of **2** everywhere **3** finished, ended

Allah *noun* in Islam, God

allay *verb* **1** make less, relieve: *tried to allay my fears* **2** calm

allege *verb* say without proof • **allegation** *noun*

allegiance *noun* loyalty

allegory *noun* (*plural* **allegories**) a simple story that suggests a deeper, more serious subject • **allegorical** *adj*

allergen *noun* a substance that causes an allergic reaction

allergy *noun* (*plural* **allergies**) abnormal sensitivity of the body to something • **allergic** *adj*

alleviate *verb* make less severe or extreme • **alleviation** *noun*

alley *noun* (*plural* **alleys**) **1** a narrow passage or lane **2** an enclosure for bowls or skittles

alliance *see* **ally**

alligator *noun* a large reptile like a crocodile

alliteration *noun* the repetition of a sound at the beginning of two or more words close together, *eg* 'round and round the rugged rock' • **alliterative** *adj*

allocate *verb* give to each a share • **allocation** *noun*

allot *verb* (**allotting**, **allotted**) give each person a share of, distribute • **allotment** *noun* **1** a small plot of ground for growing vegetables *etc* **2** the act of distributing

allow *verb* **1** let (someone do something) **2** (with **for**) take into consideration in plans *etc* **3** give, *esp* at regular intervals: *she allows him £40 a week* **4** admit, confess • **allowable** *adj*

allowance *noun* a fixed sum or amount given regularly • **make allowances for** treat differently because of taking into consideration special circumstances *etc*

alloy *noun* a mixture of two or more metals

allude to *verb* mention in passing

Do not confuse with: **elude**

---

allure *noun* feature or quality that makes something attractive or tempting • **alluring** *adj*

allusion *noun* an indirect reference

Do not confuse with: **delusion** and **illusion**

---

ally *noun* (*plural* **allies**) someone in alliance with another; a friend ◇ *verb* (**allies**, **allying**, **allied**) join yourself to by treaty *etc* • **alliance** *noun* a joining together of two people, nations, *etc*, for a common cause • **allied** *adj*

alma mater *noun* someone's former university or school

almanac *noun* an annual book listing events in a particular year, or giving a timetable of natural events, *eg* the phases of the moon

almighty *adj* extremely powerful or forceful • **the Almighty** God

almond *noun* a flattish oval nut from a small tree of the peach family

almost *adv* very nearly but not quite: *almost five years old/almost home*

alms *plural noun* money given to poor people

aloe /a-loh/ *noun* a South African plant of the lily family with thick succulent leaves that yield a juice with cosmetic and medicinal uses

aloft *adv* high in the air

alone *adj* not accompanied by others, solitary: *alone in the house* ◇ *adv* **1** only, without anything else: *that alone is bad enough* **2** not accompanied by others: *do you live alone?* • **leave alone** not touch or disturb

along *prep* over the length of: *walk along the road* ◇ *adv* with you: *bring your friends along!* • **alongside** *prep* beside ◇ *adv* near a ship's side • **along with** together with

aloof *adj* regarding others as unimportant and uninteresting • **aloofness** *noun*

aloud *adv* so as to be heard

alpha *noun* the first letter of the Greek alphabet • **alpha test** *noun, comput* an initial test of software during development (*compare with*: **beta test**)

alphabet *noun* letters of a language given in a fixed order • **alphabetic** or **alphabetical** *adj* in the order of the letters of the alphabet • **alphabetically** *adv*

alpine *adj* of the Alps or other high mountains

already *adv* **1** before this or that time: *I've already done that* **2** now, before the expected time: *you can't have finished already*

Alsatian *noun* a German shepherd dog

also *adv* in addition, besides, too: *I also need to buy milk* • **also-ran** *noun* a competitor in a race or contest who was not among the winners

altar *noun* **1** a raised place for offerings to a god **2** in Christian churches, the communion table

alter *verb* change • **alteration** *noun*

altercation *noun* an argument or quarrel

alter ego *noun* **1** a second, secret side to someone's personality **2** a trusted friend, a confidant(e)

alternate *verb* do two things in turn; happen in turn ◊ *adj* happening *etc* in turns • **alternately** *adv* • **alternation** *noun*

Do not confuse: **alternate** and **alternative**

---

alternative *noun* a second possibility, a different course of action: *I had no alternative but to agree* ◊ *adj* offering a second possibility: *an alternative solution* • **alternative medicine** *noun* the treatment of diseases and disorders using procedures not traditionally practised in orthodox medicine

although *conj* in spite of the fact that

altimeter *noun* in an aircraft, an instrument that shows how high you are flying

altitude *noun* height above sea level

alto *noun* (*plural* **altos**) *music* **1** the male voice of the highest pitch **2** female voice of lowest pitch

---

An alternative term for the female *alto* voice is **contralto**

---

altogether *adv* **1** considering everything, in all: *there were 20 of us altogether* **2** completely: *not altogether satisfied*

altruism *noun* unselfish concern for others • **altruistic** *adj* • **altruistically** *adv*

aluminium or *US* **aluminum** *noun* an element, a very light metal

alumnus *noun* (*plural* **alumni**) a former student or pupil

always *adv* **1** for ever: *he'll always remember this day* **2** every time: *she always gets it wrong*

AM *abbrev* amplitude modulation (*compare with*: **FM**)

am *abbrev* before noon (from Latin *ante meridiem*)

am *see* be

amalgam *noun* a mixture (*esp* of metals)

amalgamate *verb* **1** join together, combine **2** mix • **amalgamation** *noun*

amanuensis *noun* an assistant to an author

amaretto *noun* an Italian liqueur flavoured with almonds

amass *verb* collect in large quantity

amateur *noun* someone who takes part in a thing for the love of it, not for money (*contrasted with*: **professional**)

amateurish *adj* not done properly; not skilful • **amateurishly** *adv*

amaze *verb* surprise greatly • **amazement** *noun* • **amazing** *adj* • **amazingly** *adv*

Amazon *noun* **1** one of a nation of mythological warrior women **2** a tall, athletic, physically strong woman

ambassador *noun* **1** a government minister who looks after the interests of one country in another country **2** a representative

amber *noun* a hard yellowish fossil resin used in making jewellery ◇ *adj* **1** made of amber **2** of a yellowish-orange colour

ambidextrous *adj* able to use both hands with equal skill • **ambidexterity** *noun*

ambience *noun* the atmosphere in a room, at an event, *etc* • **ambient** *adj*

ambiguity *noun* (*plural* **ambiguities**) uncertainty in meaning

ambiguous *adj* **1** having two possible meanings **2** not clear • **ambiguously** *adv*

Do not confuse with: **ambivalent**

---

ambition *noun* the desire for success, power, fame, *etc* • **ambitious** *adj* • **ambitiously** *adv*

ambivalent *adj* having two contrasting attitudes towards something • **ambivalence** *noun* • **ambivalently** *adv*

Do not confuse with: **ambiguous**

---

amble *verb* walk without hurrying ◇ *noun* an unhurried walk

ambrosia *noun* the food of the ancient Greek gods, which gave eternal youth and beauty

ambulance *noun* a vehicle for taking ill or injured people to hospital

ambush *noun* (*plural* **ambushes**) a surprise attack made from a hiding-place ◇ *verb* attack suddenly from a position of hiding

amen *exclam* said at the end of a prayer, hymn, *etc*: so be it

amenable *adj* open to advice or suggestion • **amenably** *adv*

amend *verb* **1** correct, improve **2** alter slightly • **amendment** *noun* a change, often in something written

• **make amends** make up for having done wrong

Do not confuse with: **emend**

---

amenity *noun* (*plural* **amenities**) a pleasant or convenient feature of a place *etc*

amethyst *noun* a precious stone of a bluish-violet colour

amiable *adj* likeable; friendly • **amiability** *noun* • **amiably** *adv*

amicable *adj* friendly • **amicably** *adv*

amid or **amidst** *prep* in the middle of, among: *staying calm amidst all the confusion*

amiss *adv* wrongly; badly

amity *noun, formal* friendship

ammonia *noun* a strong-smelling gas consisting of hydrogen and nitrogen

ammunition *noun* bullets, bombs, *etc*

amnesia *noun* loss of memory • **amnesiac** *noun & adj* (someone) suffering from amnesia

amnesty *noun* (*plural* **amnesties**) a pardon for criminals

amniocentesis *noun, med* a test of the health of a foetus using a sample of fluid drawn from the uterus

amoeba /uh-mee-buh/ *noun* (*plural* **amoebas** or **amoebae**) a very simple form of animal life found in ponds *etc*

amok or **amuck** *adv*: **run amok** go mad and do a lot of damage, run riot

among or **amongst** *prep* **1** in the midst or in the middle of: *among friends* **2** in shares, in parts: *divide amongst yourselves* **3** in the group of: *among all her novels, this is the best*

amoral *adj* incapable of distinguishing between right and wrong • **amorality** *noun* • **amorally** *adv*

Do not confuse with: **immoral**

amorous adj 1 loving 2 involving loving or sexual behaviour • **amorously** adv

amount noun 1 total, sum 2 a quantity • **amount to** 1 add up to 2 be equivalent to: *a statement that amounts to an apology*

amp noun 1 an ampère 2 *informal* an amplifier

ampère noun the standard unit of electric current

ampersand noun the character (&) representing *and*

amphetamine noun a type of drug used as a stimulant

amphibian noun 1 an animal that lives on land and in water 2 a vehicle for use on land and in water • **amphibious** adj amphibian

amphitheatre noun a theatre with seats surrounding a central arena

ample adj 1 plenty of 2 fairly large

amplify verb (**amplifies, amplifying, amplified**) 1 make louder 2 make more pronounced • **amplification** noun • **amplifier** noun an electrical device for increasing loudness

amplitude noun the size of a radio wave

amputate verb cut off a human limb • **amputation** noun • **amputee** noun someone who has had a limb amputated

amuck another spelling of **amok**

amulet noun a small object worn to protect the wearer from witchcraft, disease, *etc*

amuse verb 1 make (someone) laugh 2 give (someone) pleasure • **amusement** noun • **amusing** adj 1 funny 2 giving pleasure

an see **a**

anabolic steroids plural noun steroids used to increase the build-up of body tissue, *esp* muscle

anachronism noun something in a story, film, *etc* that seems odd because it does not belong to the period in which the story, film, *etc* is set • **anachronistic** adj

anaconda noun a large South American water snake

anaemia or US **anemia** noun a shortage of red cells in the blood

anaemic or US **anemic** adj 1 suffering from anaemia 2 pale or ill-looking

anaerobic adj not requiring oxygen to live

anaesthesia or US **anesthesia** noun loss of feeling or sensation

anaesthetic or US **anesthetic** noun a drug given to a patient before an operation to cause temporary lack of feeling in a part of the body, or cause unconsciousness • **anaesthetist** noun a doctor trained to administer anaesthetics • **anaesthetize** verb

anagram noun a word or sentence formed by reordering the letters of another word or sentence, *eg veil* is an anagram of *evil*

anal adj of the anus

analgesic noun a pain-killing drug ◇ adj pain-killing

analogous adj similar, alike in some way • **analogously** adv

analogue or US **analog** adj 1 showing time or another measurement by means of a pointer on a dial (*compare with*: **digital**) 2 storing or presenting information in a form that can be processed by a computer (*compare with*: **digital**)

analogy noun (*plural* **analogies**) a description that explains what something is like by comparing it to something similar

analyse or US **analyze** verb **1** examine in detail **2** break down, separate into parts

analysis noun (plural **analyses**) **1** a detailed examination (of something) **2** a breaking up of a thing into its parts

analyst noun **1** someone who analyses **2** a psychiatrist or psychologist

analyze US spelling of **analyse**

anarchy noun **1** a situation in which there is no government and no laws **2** disorder or confusion • **anarchic** or **anarchical** adj • **anarchist** noun someone who wants a society without government or laws

anathema noun a hated person or thing: opera is anathema to him

anatomy noun **1** the study of the parts of the body **2** the body • **anatomist** noun

ancestor noun a member of an earlier generation of someone's family; a forefather • **ancestral** adj • **ancestry** noun line of ancestors

anchor noun a heavy piece of iron with hooked ends, for holding a ship fast to the bed of the sea etc ◇ verb **1** fix firmly in position **2** let down the anchor • **anchorman, anchorwoman** noun the main presenter of a news programme • **cast anchor** let down the anchor • **weigh anchor** pull up the anchor

anchorage noun a place where a ship can anchor

anchorite noun a hermit, a recluse

anchovy noun (plural **anchovies**) a small fish of the herring family

ancient adj **1** very old **2** from a much earlier period of history

ancillary adj serving or supporting something more important

and conj **1** joining two statements, pieces of information, etc: black and white film/add milk and stir **2** in addition to: 2 and 2 make 4

android noun a robot in human form

anecdote noun a short, interesting or amusing story, usually true • **anecdotal** adj

anemometer noun an instrument for measuring the speed of the wind

anemone noun a type of woodland or garden flower

aneroid barometer noun a barometer that measures air pressure without the use of mercury

aneurism /an-yoo-rizm/ noun a swelling in a blood vessel

angel noun **1** a messenger or attendant of God **2** a very good or beautiful person • **angelic** adj • **angelically** adv

angelica noun a plant whose candied leaf-stalks are used as cake decoration

anger noun a bitter feeling against someone, annoyance, rage ◇ verb make angry

angina noun a form of heart disease causing acute pains

angle noun **1** the V-shape made by two lines meeting at a point **2** a corner **3** a point of view ◇ verb try to get by hints etc: angling for a job

angler noun someone who fishes with a rod and line • **angling** noun the sport of fishing

Anglican adj of the Church of England ◇ noun a member of the Church of England

anglicize verb **1** turn into the English language **2** make English in character • **anglicization** noun

Anglo-Saxon adj & noun **1** (of) the people of England before the Norman Conquest **2** (of) their language

angora noun very soft wool made from the hair of the Angora goat or rabbit

angry adj (**angrier, angriest**) feeling

or showing anger • **angrily** adv

anguish noun very great pain or distress

angular adj 1 having many straight edges and corners 2 to do with angles 3 thin, bony • **angularity** noun

animal noun 1 a living being that can feel and move of its own accord 2 an animal other than a human ◇ adj of or like an animal

animate verb 1 make lively 2 give life to ◇ adj living • **animated** adj 1 made using the techniques of animation 2 lively

animation noun 1 a film made from a series of drawings or computer-generated images that give the illusion of movement when shown in sequence 2 the techniques used to produce such films 3 liveliness • **animator** noun an artist who works in animation

animosity noun bitter hatred, enmity

aniseed noun a seed with a flavour like that of liquorice

ankh /angk/ noun a cross in the shape of a T with a loop at the top

ankle noun the joint connecting the foot and leg

annals plural noun yearly historical accounts of events

anneal verb toughen glass or metal by heating it strongly and cooling it slowly

annex noun (also spelled **annexe**) a building added to another ◇ verb 1 take possession of (esp a territory) 2 add, attach • **annexation** noun

annihilate /uh-nai-uh-leht/ verb destroy completely • **annihilation** noun

anniversary noun (plural **anniversaries**) the day of each year when a particular event is remembered

annotate verb 1 add notes giving information or explanation 2 write notes on • **annotation** noun

announce verb make publicly known • **announcement** noun • **announcer** noun someone who announces programmes on TV or radio

annoy verb make rather angry; irritate • **annoyance** noun

annual adj yearly ◇ noun 1 a plant that lives only one year 2 a book published yearly • **annually** adv

annuity noun (plural **annuities**) a yearly payment made for a certain time or for life

annul verb (**annulling**, **annulled**) 1 declare (eg a marriage) no longer legally valid 2 put an end to • **annulment** noun

anodyne adj 1 so inoffensive as to be boring 2 soothing, relieving pain ◇ noun something that soothes pain

anoint verb 1 smear (someone) with ointment or oil 2 give (someone) an important position, title, etc

anomaly noun (plural **anomalies**) something unusual that does not follow rules or expectations • **anomalous** adj

anon abbrev anonymous ◇ adv, old or informal soon

anonymous adj without the name of the author, giver, etc being known or given • **anonymously** adv

anorak noun a hooded waterproof jacket

anorexia noun 1 (also called: **anorexia nervosa**) an emotional illness that makes the sufferer not want to eat, sometimes resulting in a dangerously low body weight 2 lack of appetite • **anorexic** adj of or suffering from anorexia ◇ noun someone suffering from anorexia

another adj 1 a different (thing or person): moving to another job 2 one more of the same kind: have another *biscuit* ◇ *pronoun* an additional thing of the same kind: *do you want another?*

answer *verb* **1** speak, write, *etc* in return or reply **2** find the result or solution (of a sum, problem, *etc*) **3** (with **for**) be responsible **4** (with **for**) suffer, be punished ◇ *noun* something said, written, *etc* in return or reply; a solution • **answerable** *adj* **1** able to be answered **2** responsible: *answerable for her actions*

ant *noun* a very small insect that lives in organized colonies • **ant-hill** *noun* a mound of soil built by ants as a nest • **have ants in your pants** be impatient or restless

antagonist *noun* **1** an enemy **2** an opponent • **antagonism** *noun* hostility, opposition, enmity • **antagonistic** *adj* opposed (to), unfriendly, hostile

antagonize *verb* make hostile; cause dislike in

Antarctic *adj* of the South Pole or regions round it

ante /an-ti/ *noun* a stake in poker *etc* • **up the ante** *informal* increase the costs or risks involved

ante- *prefix* before

anteater *noun* a long-nosed American animal that feeds on ants and termites

antecedent *noun* **1** someone who lived at an earlier time; an ancestor **2** (**antecedents**) previous conduct, history, *etc* ◇ *adj* going before in time

antedate *verb* **1** put a date on (*eg* a document) that is earlier than the real date **2** be earlier in date than; predate

antediluvian /an-ti-di-*loo*-vi-un/ *adj* very old or old-fashioned

antelope *noun* a graceful, swift-running animal like a deer

antenatal *adj* **1** before birth **2** relating to pregnancy: *antenatal clinic*

antenna *noun* (*plural* **antennas** or

antennae) **1** an insect's feeler **2** an aerial

anteroom *noun* a room leading into another larger room

anthem *noun* **1** a piece of music for a church choir **2** any song of praise

anthology *noun* (*plural* **anthologies**) a collection of specially chosen poems, stories, *etc*

anthracite *noun* coal that burns with a hot, smokeless flame

anthrax *noun* an infectious disease of cattle, sheep, *etc*, sometimes transferred to humans

anthropoid *adj* of apes: resembling humans

anthropology *noun* the study of human behaviour and society • **anthropological** *adj* • **anthropologist** *noun*

anti- *prefix* against, opposite: *anti-terrorist*

antibiotic *noun* a medicine taken to kill disease-causing bacteria

antibody *noun* (*plural* **antibodies**) a substance produced in the human body to fight bacteria *etc*

anticipate *verb* **1** look forward to, expect **2** realize in advance **3** act before (someone or something) • **anticipation** *noun* **1** expectation **2** excitement • **anticipatory** *adj*

anticlimax *noun* a dull or disappointing ending

anticlockwise *adj* & *adv* in the opposite direction to the movement of the hands of a clock

antics *plural noun* amusing or annoying behaviour

anticyclone *noun* a circling movement of air round an area of high air pressure, causing calm weather

antidote *noun* **1** a medicine that fights the effect of poison **2** something that has the effect of preventing something unpleasant from happening

antifreeze noun a chemical with a low freezing-point, added to a car radiator to prevent freezing

antihistamine noun a medicine used to treat an allergy

antipathy noun extreme dislike

antiperspirant noun a substance applied to the body to reduce sweating

antipodes /an-*tip*-uh-deez/ plural noun places on the earth's surface exactly opposite each other, esp Australia and New Zealand in relation to Europe • **antipodean** adj

antique noun an old, interesting or valuable object from earlier times ◇ adj 1 old, from earlier times 2 old-fashioned • **antiquarian** noun a dealer in antiques • **antiquated** adj very old or old-fashioned

antiquity noun (plural **antiquities**) 1 ancient times, esp those of the Greeks and Romans 2 (**antiquities**) objects from earlier times

antiseptic noun a chemical that destroys germs ◇ adj destroying germs

antisocial adj 1 annoying or harmful to other people 2 disliking the company of other people

antithesis /an-*tith*-uh-sis/ noun (plural **antitheses**) the exact opposite: the antithesis of good taste • **antithetical** adj

antler noun the horn of a deer

antonym noun a word that means the opposite of another word

anus /*eh*-nus/ noun the opening between the buttocks through which faeces leave the body

anvil noun a metal block on which blacksmiths hammer metal into shape

anxiety noun (plural **anxieties**) 1

worry about what may happen, apprehensiveness 2 a worrying thing

anxious adj worried, apprehensive • **anxiously** adv

any adj 1 some: is there any milk? 2 every, no matter which: any day will suit me ◇ pronoun some: there aren't any left ◇ adv at all: I can't work any faster • **anybody** pronoun any person • **anyhow** adv 1 in any case: I think I'll go anyhow 2 carelessly: scattered anyhow over the floor • **anyone** pronoun any person • **anything** pronoun something of any kind • **anyway** adv at any rate • **anywhere** adv in any place • **at any rate** in any case, whatever happens

AOB abbrev (written on agendas etc) any other business

apart adv 1 in or into pieces: came apart in my hands 2 in separate places: they now live apart ◇ adj 1 with a space between: with legs apart 2 living in separate places: they've been apart for years • **apart from** 1 separate, or separately, from 2 except for: who else knows apart from us?

apartheid /uh-*pah*-taid/ noun the political policy of keeping people of different races apart

apartment noun 1 a set of rooms for living in, a flat 2 a room in a house

apathy noun lack of interest or enthusiasm • **apathetic** adj • **apathetically** adv

ape noun a large, tailless, upright-walking animal of the group that includes chimpanzees, gorillas and orang-utans ◇ verb imitate

aperitif /uh-pe-ri-*teef*/ noun a drink taken before a meal

aperture noun an opening, a hole

APEX abbrev 1 advance purchase excursion, a reduced fare for travel booked in advance 2 Association of Professional, Executive, Clerical and Computer Staff, a trade union

apex noun (plural **apexes** or **apices**) 1 a point formed where two sloping lines or surfaces meet 2 the highest point of anything

aphasia noun inability to speak or express thoughts verbally

aphid /eh-fid/ noun a small insect that feeds on plants

aphrodisiac noun a drug, food, etc that increases sexual desire ◇ adj causing increased sexual desire

apiary noun (plural **apiaries**) a place where bees are kept • **apiarist** noun someone who keeps an apiary or studies bees

apiece adv to or for each one: three chocolates apiece

aplomb /uh-plom/ noun calm self-assurance

apocalypse noun the destruction of the world • **apocalyptic** adj

apocryphal /uh-pok-rif-ul/ adj unlikely to be true

apogee /ap-uh-jee/ noun 1 a culmination, a climax 2 the point of an orbit furthest from the earth

apologize verb express regret, say you are sorry

apology noun (plural **apologies**) an expression of regret for having done wrong • **apologetic** adj expressing regret

apoplexy noun sudden loss of ability to feel, move, etc, a stroke • **apoplectic** adj

apostle noun 1 one of the disciples of Christ 2 an advocate for a cause 3 a preacher

apostrophe noun 1 a mark (') indicating possession: the minister's cat 2 a similar mark indicating that a letter etc has been missed out, eg isn't for is not

apothecary noun (plural **apothecaries**) old a chemist

appal verb (**appalling**, **appalled**) horrify, shock • **appalling** adj shocking

apparatus noun 1 instruments, tools or material required for a piece of work 2 an instrument or machine

apparel noun, formal clothing

apparent adj 1 easily seen, evident 2 seeming to be the case • **apparently** adv

apparition noun 1 a mysterious object that appears suddenly 2 a ghost

appeal verb 1 be pleasing or attractive (to) 2 ask earnestly (for help etc) 3 law take a case that has been lost to a higher court ◇ noun 1 a request for help 2 law the taking of a case to a higher court

appealing adj 1 pleasing or attractive 2 asking earnestly • **appealingly** adv

appear verb 1 come into view 2 arrive 3 seem • **appearance** noun

appease verb make (someone) less hostile or angry, esp by giving what was asked for

appendage noun something joined or hanging on (to something)

appendectomy noun, med surgical removal of the appendix

appendicitis noun, med inflammation of the appendix

appendix noun (plural **appendices** or **appendixes**) 1 a part added at the end of a book 2 a small worm-shaped part of the bowel

appertain verb, formal have something to do with, relate (to)

appetite noun 1 desire for food 2 taste or enthusiasm (for): no appetite for violence

appetizer noun a snack, or a first course, eaten before a main meal

appetizing adj of food: looking or smelling tasty

applaud *verb* show approval of by clapping the hands

applause *noun* clapping that shows approval

apple *noun* a round firm fruit with red or green skin

appliance *noun* a machine, *esp* one with a domestic use

applicable *adj* 1 relevant, suitable 2 able to be applied

applicant *noun* someone who applies for a job, grant, *etc*

application *noun* 1 a formal request to be considered for something, *eg* a job or a grant 2 the act of applying for a job, grant, *etc* 3 a computer program 4 something applied to a surface, *eg* an ointment 5 hard work, close attention

appliqué *noun* needlework in which cut pieces of fabric are sewn onto a background to form patterns

apply *verb* (**applies, applying, applied**) 1 ask formally to be considered (for) a job, grant, *etc* 2 be relevant, have an effect: *the rule doesn't apply in this case/that criticism doesn't apply to you* 3 put (paint *etc*) on a surface 4 use • **apply yourself** work hard

appoint *verb* 1 give a job: *she was appointed manager* 2 fix (a date, time, etc) for something

appointment *noun* 1 an arrangement to meet someone 2 a job, a post 3 the act of appointing

apportion *verb* divide in fair shares

apposite /ap-uh-zit/ *adj* suitable, appropriate

appraise *verb* estimate the value or quality of • **appraisal** *noun* • **appraising** *adj* quickly summing up

appreciate *verb* 1 see or understand the good points, beauties, *etc* of: *appreciate art* 2 understand: *I appreciate your point* 3 rise in value

• **appreciable** *adj* noticeable, considerable • **appreciation** *noun*

apprehend *verb* 1 arrest 2 *formal* understand

apprehension *noun* worry or fear

apprehensive *adj* worried or afraid
• **apprehensively** *adv*

apprentice *noun* someone who is learning a trade • **apprenticeship** *noun* the time during which someone is an apprentice

appro *noun, informal* approval

approach *verb* 1 come near 2 be nearly equal to 3 speak to in order to ask for something ◇ *noun* (*plural* **approaches**) 1 a coming near to 2 a way leading to a place • **approachable** *adj* 1 easy to speak to, friendly 2 able to be reached

approbation *noun* approval, good opinion

appropriate *adj* right in the circumstances, suitable ◇ *verb* 1 take possession of 2 set (money *etc*) apart for a purpose • **appropriately** *adv* • **appropriation** *noun*

approve *verb* 1 have a good opinion (of), like: *did he approve of the new curtains?* 2 give official agreement to or permission for • **approval** *noun*
• **on approval** on trial, for return to a shop if not bought

approx *abbrev* 1 approximate 2 approximately

approximate *adj* more or less accurate ◇ *verb* be or come near (to)
• **approximately** *adv* • **approximation** *noun* a rough estimate

APR *abbrev* annual percentage rate

après-ski /ap-reh-*skee*/ *adj* taking place after a day's skiing

apricot *noun* an orange-coloured fruit like a small peach

April *noun* the fourth month of the year

a priori /eh-prai-aw-rai/ *adj, formal* based on things already known, proved or experienced

apron *noun* **1** a garment worn to protect the front of the clothes **2** the hard surfaces next to an airport building where aircraft stand **3** the part of the stage in front of the curtains in a theatre

apropos /ap-ruh-*poh*/ *adv*: **apropos of** in connection with, concerning

apse *noun* a rounded wall at the east end of a church, behind the altar

apt *adj* **1** likely (to): *apt to change his mind* **2** suitable, fitting ● **aptness** *noun* suitability

aptitude *noun* talent, ability

aqualung *noun* a breathing apparatus worn by divers

aquamarine *noun* **1** a type of bluish-green precious stone **2** a bluish-green colour ◇ *adj* bluish-green

aquarium *noun* (*plural* **aquaria**) a tank for keeping fish or marine animals, or a building with such tanks

aquatic *adj* living or growing in water

aqueduct *noun* a bridge for taking a canal *etc* across a valley

aquiline *adj* **1** of a nose: curved or hooked **2** like an eagle

arable *adj* of land: used for growing crops

arbiter *noun* **1** someone who sets a standard or has influence: *arbiter of good taste* **2** someone chosen to decide a dispute ● **arbitrage** *noun* the practice of buying goods *etc* in one market and selling in another to make a profit

arbitrary *adj* **1** decided or chosen at random, rather than according to a system or rule **2** placed or arranged haphazardly ● **arbitrarily** *adv* ● **arbitrariness** *noun*

arbitrate *verb* act as a judge in a dispute ● **arbitration** *noun* the settlement of a dispute by an impartial person ● **arbitrator** *noun* someone who arbitrates

arboreal *adj* **1** of trees **2** living in trees

arbour *noun* a seat in a garden shaded by trees or climbing plants

arc *noun* **1** a curve **2** part of the circumference of a circle ● **arc-lamp** or **arc-light** *noun* a bright lamp lit by a special kind of electric current

arcade *noun* a covered walk, *esp* one with shops on both sides

arch *noun* (*plural* **arches**) **1** the curved overhead part of a doorway, gateway, *etc* **2** a curved support for a bridge, roof, *etc* ◇ *adj* mischievous, roguish ◇ *verb* raise or curve in the shape of an arch

arch- *prefix* chief, main: *arch-enemy*

archaeology or US **archeology** *noun* the study of the people of earlier times from the remains of their buildings *etc* ● **archaeological** *adj* ● **archaeologist** *noun*

archaic *adj* **1** belonging to an earlier period and no longer used **2** old-fashioned ● **archaism** *noun* an old word or custom that is no longer used

archangel *noun* a chief angel

archbishop *noun* a chief bishop

archdeacon *noun* a clergyman next in rank below a bishop

archduke *noun, hist* the title of the ruling princes of Austria

archer *noun* someone who shoots arrows from a bow ● **archery** *noun* the sport of shooting with a bow and arrows

archetype /*ahk*-i-taip/ *noun* **1** a perfect example **2** an original model ● **archetypal** *adj*

archipelago   /ah-ki-*pel*-uh-goh/

noun (*plural* **archipelagoes** *or* **archipelagos**) a group of small islands

architect *noun* someone who plans and designs buildings

architecture *noun* **1** the study of building **2** the style of a building • **architectural** *adj*

archive *noun* **1** a collection of historical documents, broadcast recordings, *etc* kept as a record and for research purposes **2** a building or room in which such a collection is kept

archway *noun* a passage or road beneath an arch

Arctic *adj* of the region around the North Pole • **arctic** *adj* very cold

ardent *adj* eager, enthusiastic, passionate • **ardently** *adv* • **ardour** *noun*

arduous *adj* requiring great effort, determination or strength; testing • **arduously** *adv* • **arduousness** *noun*

are *see* **be**

area *noun* **1** the space covered by a surface, measured in square units **2** a region, a piece of land or ground

arena *noun* **1** any place for a public contest, show, *etc* **2** *hist* the centre of an amphitheatre *etc* where gladiators fought

arguable *adj* that can be argued as being true • **arguably** *adv*

argue *verb* (**arguing**, **argued**) **1** quarrel in words **2** try to influence people by giving reasons for or against

argument *noun* **1** a heated discussion, quarrel **2** reasoning (for or against something) • **argumentative** *adj* fond of arguing

aria /ah-ri-uh/ *noun* a song for solo voice in an opera

arid *adj* dry • **aridity**, **aridness** *nouns*

arise *verb* (**arising**, **arose**, **arisen**) **1** start to exist, happen **2** stand up or rise up

aristocracy *noun* people of high social class whose social titles are inherited; nobility • **aristocrat** *noun* a member of the aristocracy • **aristocratic** *adj* of the aristocracy

arithmetic *noun* a way of counting and calculating by using numbers • **arithmetical** *adj*

ark *noun* the covered boat used by Noah in the Biblical story of the Flood

arm *noun* **1** the part of the body between the shoulder and the hand **2** anything jutting out like an arm **3** (**arms**) weapons ◇ *verb* equip with weapons • **armchair** *noun* a chair with arms at each side • **armed** *adj* carrying a weapon, *esp* a gun • **armpit** *noun* the hollow under the arm at the shoulder

armada *noun* a fleet of armed ships

armadillo *noun* (*plural* **armadillos**) a small American animal whose body is protected by bony plates

armageddon *noun* a final battle or devastation, an apocalypse

armaments *plural noun* equipment for war, *esp* the guns of a ship, tank, *etc*

armistice *noun* a halt in fighting during war, a truce

armorial *adj* of a coat-of-arms

armour *noun, hist* a protective suit of metal worn by knights • **armoured** *adj* of a vehicle: protected by metal plates • **armoury** *noun* an arms store

army *noun* (*plural* **armies**) **1** a large number of soldiers armed for war **2** a great number of anything

aroma *noun* a pleasant smell • **aromatic** *adj* sweet-smelling, perfumed

aromatherapy *noun* a healing therapy involving massage with plant oils • **aromatherapist** *noun*

arose *past tense of* **arise**

around *prep* **1** on all sides of, surrounding: *the wall around the gar-*

den **2** all over, at several places in: *papers scattered around the room* **3** near in time, place, amount: *I left him somewhere around here/come back around three o'clock* ◇ *adv* **1** all about, in various places: *people stood around watching* **2** so as to face the opposite direction: *turn around slowly* • **get around 1** of a story: become known to everyone **2** be active

arouse *verb* **1** cause to have a feeling **2** make sexually excited **3** awaken • **arousal** *noun*

arpeggio /ah-*pej*-i-oh/ *noun, music* a chord with the notes played in rapid succession, not at the same time

arraign /uh-*rehn*/ *verb* charge officially with an offence

arrange *verb* **1** put in some order **2** plan (an event *etc*) • **arrangement** *noun* **1** a plan or agreement to do something **2** the way things are set out

arras *noun* a screen of tapestry

array *noun* **1** order, arrangement **2** an impressive number or collection ◇ *verb* **1** arrange (things) **2** dress (someone) or decorate (something)

arrears *plural noun*: **in arrears** not up to date; behind with payments

arrest *verb* **1** seize, capture, *esp* by power of the law **2** stop **3** catch (the attention *etc*) ◇ *noun* **1** capture by the police **2** stopping • **arresting** *adj* striking, capturing the attention

arrival *noun* **1** the act or time of arriving **2** someone or something that arrives

arrive *verb* reach a place • **arrive at** reach, come to (a decision *etc*)

arrogant *adj* proud, self-important • **arrogance** *noun* • **arrogantly** *adv*

arrow *noun* **1** a straight, pointed weapon shot from a bow **2** an arrow symbol, *eg* on a road-sign, showing direction

arrowroot *noun* a starch used in powdered form for thickening liquids

arse *noun, taboo slang* the buttocks • **arse around** fool about, waste time

arsenal *noun* a factory or store for weapons, ammunition, *etc*

arsenic *noun* an element that, combined with oxygen, makes a strong poison

arson *noun* the crime of setting fire to a place on purpose • **arsonist** *noun*

art *noun* **1** drawing, painting, sculpture, *etc* **2** cleverness, skill; cunning **3** (**arts**) non-scientific subjects of study **4** an activity that involves skill and judgment: *the art of conversation* • **artful** *adj* cunning • **artless** *adj* not sneaky or deceitful; frank

artefact *or* **artifact** *noun* a human-made object

arteriosclerosis *noun* hardening of the arteries

artery *noun* (*plural* **arteries**) a tube that carries blood from the heart through the body • **arterial** *adj* of or like arteries • **arterial road** *noun* a main road

artesian well *noun* a well in which water rises to the surface by natural pressure

arthritis *noun* inflammation of a joint, causing pain and stiffness • **arthritic** *noun & adj*

artichoke *noun* a ball-shaped vegetable with spiky, fleshy leaves that grows on a tall plant • **Jerusalem artichoke** a vegetable that is the knobbly brown root of a type of sunflower

article *noun* **1** a thing, object **2** a piece of writing in a newspaper, journal, *etc* **3** a numbered section of a long legal document **4** (**articles**) an agreement made up of clauses: *articles of apprenticeship* **5** *grammar* the name of the words *the, a, an*

articulate *adj* expressing thoughts or

words clearly ◇ *verb* express clearly
● **articulated lorry** *noun* a lorry with a cab which can turn at an angle to the main part of the lorry, making cornering easier ● **articulation** *noun*

artifact another spelling of **artefact**

artificial *adj* 1 not natural; human-made 2 not sincere; affected ● **artificial insemination** *noun* the insertion of sperm into the uterus by means other than sexual intercourse ● **artificiality** *noun* ● **artificially** *adv*

artillery *noun* 1 big guns 2 an army division that uses these

artisan *noun* a skilled worker

artist *noun* 1 someone who paints pictures 2 someone skilled in anything 3 an artiste ● **artistry** *noun* skill as an artist

artiste /ah-*teest*/ *noun* a performer in a theatre, circus, *etc*

artistic *adj* 1 having or showing a talent for art 2 of artists: *the artistic community* ● **artistically** *adv*

as *adv & conj* in phrases expressing comparison or similarity: *as good as his brother/the same as this one* ◇ *conj* 1 while, when: *happened as I was walking past* 2 because, since: *we stayed at home as it was raining* 3 in the same way that: *he thinks as I do* ◇ *adv* for instance ● **as for** concerning, regarding ● **as if** *or* **as though** as it would be if ● **as to** regarding ● **as well (as)** too, in addition (to)

ASAP *abbrev* as soon as possible

asbestos *noun* a thread-like, fire-resistant mineral used in the past as a building material but now avoided because of the dangers of asbestosis ● **asbestosis** *noun* a lung disease caused by inhaling asbestos dust

ASBO *abbrev* Anti-Social Behaviour Order

ascend *verb* 1 climb, go up 2 rise or slope upwards ● **ascendancy** *or* **ascendency** *noun* control (over)

● **ascendant** *or* **ascendent** *adj* rising
● **ascent** *noun* 1 an upward move or climb 2 a slope upwards; a rise
● **ascend the throne** be crowned king or queen

ascertain *verb* 1 find out 2 make certain

ascetic /uh-*set*-ik/ *noun* someone who avoids all kinds of pleasure

ascribe *verb* 1 think of as belonging to: *ascribing the blame* 2 say that (a book, painting, *etc*) is the work of someone: *a poem ascribed to Shakespeare*

ash *noun* (*plural* **ashes**) 1 a hardwood tree with silvery bark 2 (**ashes**) what is left after anything is burnt

ashamed *adj* feeling shame

ashen *adj* very pale

ashore *adv* on or onto the shore

aside *adv* on or to one side; apart ◇ *noun* words spoken which those nearby are not supposed to hear

asinine *adj* stupid

ask *verb* 1 request information about: *asked for my address* 2 invite: *we've asked some friends over for dinner*

askance *adv*: **look askance at** be disapproving or suspicious of

askew *adv* not properly straight or level

asleep *adj* 1 sleeping 2 of limbs: numb

ASLEF *abbrev* Associated Society of Locomotive Engineers and Firemen, a trade union

asp *noun* a small poisonous snake

asparagus *noun* a vegetable that is the young spear-shaped shoots of a plant

aspect *noun* 1 element, feature 2 look, appearance 3 view, point of view 4 side of a building *etc* or the direction it faces in

aspen *noun* a kind of poplar tree

asperity noun 1 harshness, sharpness of temper 2 bitter coldness

asphalt noun a tarry mixture used to make pavements, paths, etc

asphyxia /as-fik-si-uh/ noun suffocation by smoke or other fumes • **asphyxiate** verb suffocate • **asphyxiation** noun

aspidistra noun a pot-plant with large leaves

aspire verb (with to or after) hope or try to achieve (something difficult, ambitious, etc) • **aspiration** noun • **aspiring** adj hoping or trying to be: an aspiring director

aspirin noun a pain-killing drug

ass noun (plural **asses**) 1 a donkey 2 a stupid person 3 US slang the buttocks

assail verb attack • **assailant** noun an attacker

assassin noun someone hired to kill (esp a politically important person) • **assassinate** verb murder (esp a politically important person) • **assassination** noun

assault noun 1 an attack, esp a sudden one 2 the crime of attacking someone physically or sexually ◇ verb attack

assegai noun a long South African spear tipped with metal

assemblage noun a collection, a gathering

assemble verb 1 put together the parts of (a machine etc) 2 bring (people) together 3 of people: come together

assembly noun (plural **assemblies**) 1 the activity of fitting pieces together 2 a gathering of people for a special purpose 3 a parliament or other legislative body • **assembly line** noun a series of machines and workers that manufacture an article in separate stages

assent verb agree ◇ noun agreement

assert verb 1 state firmly 2 insist on (a right etc) • **assertion** noun • **assertive** adj not shy, inclined to assert yourself • **assert yourself** make yourself noticed, your opinions heard, etc

assess verb 1 estimate the value, worth or quality of 2 fix an amount (to be paid in tax etc) • **assessment** noun • **assessor** noun someone who assesses

asset noun 1 a good feature, an advantage 2 (**assets**) the property of a person, company, etc

assiduous adj hard-working, conscientious • **assiduously** adv

assign /uh-sain/ verb 1 give to someone as a share or task 2 fix (a time or place) • **assignation** /as-ig-neh-shun/ noun an appointment to meet • **assignment** noun 1 a task given 2 an act of assigning

assimilate verb 1 take in (information) 2 adapt to a new culture or new surroundings • **assimilation** noun

assist verb help • **assistance** noun • **assistant** noun 1 someone who helps a more senior worker 2 someone who serves in a shop

assizes plural noun the name of certain law courts in England

associate verb 1 keep company with 2 join (with) in partnership or friendship 3 connect in thought: I don't associate him with hard work ◇ noun a friend, partner, companion

association noun 1 a club, society, union, etc 2 a partnership, friendship 3 a connection made in the mind

assorted adj various, mixed • **assortment** noun a variety, a mixture

assuage /uh-swehj/ verb ease (pain, hunger, guilt, etc)

assume verb 1 take to be true without proof or certainty 2 take (a responsibility etc) upon yourself 3 put on (a disguise *etc*) • **assumed** *adj* **1** adopted **2** pretended: *assumed air of confidence*

assumption *noun* **1** something taken to be true without proof or certainty **2** the act of assuming

assure *verb* **1** make (someone) sure **2** state positively (that) • **assurance** *noun* **1** a feeling of certainty; confidence **2** a promise **3** insurance • **assured** *adj* certain; confident

asterisk *noun* a star (*) used in printing for various purposes, *esp* to point out a footnote or insertion

astern *adv* at or towards the back of a ship

asthma *noun* an illness causing difficulty in breathing • **asthmatic** *adj* suffering from asthma ◊ *noun* someone with asthma

astonish *verb* surprise greatly • **astonishing** *adj* • **astonishment** *noun* amazement, wonder

astound *verb* surprise greatly, amaze • **astounding** *adj*

astrakhan /as-truh-kan/ *noun* woollen fabric with a curly pile

astral *adj* of the stars

astray *adv* • **go astray** become lost • **lead astray** encourage to behave badly

astride *adv* with legs apart ◊ *prep* with legs on each side of

astringent *noun* a lotion *etc* used for closing up the skin's pores ◊ *adj* **1** used for closing the pores **2** of manner: sharp, sarcastic

astrology *noun* the study of the stars and their supposed power over people's lives • **astrologer** *noun*

astronaut *noun* someone who travels in space

astronomer *noun* someone who studies astronomy

astronomical *adj* **1** of astronomy **2** of a number: very large

astronomy *noun* the study of the stars and their movements

astute *adj* having a lot of knowledge from experience; shrewd • **astutely** *adv* • **astuteness** *noun*

asunder *adv, formal* apart, into pieces

asylum *noun* **1** protection from persecution or danger given to someone fleeing another country **2** *old* a home for mentally ill people

at *prep* **1** showing position, time, *etc*: *I'll be at home/come at 7 o'clock* **2** costing: *cakes at 25 pence each* • **at all** in any way: *not worried at all*

ate *past tense of* eat

atelier /a-tul-yeh/ *noun* an artist's studio, a workshop

atheism *noun* belief that there is no God • **atheist** *noun* someone who does not believe in a God • **atheistic** *adj*

athlete *noun* someone good at sport, *esp* running, gymnastics, *etc*

athletic *adj* **1** physically fit, agile and good at sport **2** of athletics

athletics *plural noun* running, jumping, *etc* or competitions in these events

atlas *noun* (*plural* **atlases**) a book of maps

ATM *abbrev* automatic teller machine, a machine used for withdrawing cash from a bank account

atmosphere *noun* **1** the air round the earth **2** the mood in a place or among people: *friendly atmosphere*

atmospheric *adj* **1** of the atmosphere **2** with an impressive atmosphere • **atmospheric pressure** *noun* the pressure exerted by the atmosphere at the earth's surface, due to the weight of the air • **atmospherics** *plural noun* air disturbances causing crackling noises on the radio *etc*

atoll /a-tol/ noun a coral island or reef

atom noun 1 the smallest part of an element 2 anything very small • **atomic** adj 1 relating to atoms 2 using atomic energy • **atomic bomb** or **atom bomb** noun a bomb in which the explosion is caused by nuclear energy • **atomic energy** noun nuclear energy • **atomic number** noun the number of protons in the nucleus of an atom of an element

atone verb make up for doing something bad • **atonement** noun

atrocious adj 1 informal very bad 2 cruel or wicked • **atrociously** adv • **atrociousness** noun

atrocity noun (plural **atrocities**) 1 a terrible crime 2 informal something very ugly

attach verb 1 fasten or join (to) 2 think of (something) as having: don't attach any importance to it • **attached** adj 1 fastened 2 (with **to**) fond (of) • **attachment** noun 1 something attached 2 a joining by love or friendship

attaché /uh-tash-eh/ noun a junior member of an embassy staff • **attaché case** noun a small briefcase

attack verb 1 use violence to harm someone physically 2 criticize very strongly 3 approach an opponent's goal etc in an attempt to score ◇ noun 1 an act of attacking someone physically or with words 2 a fit of an illness 3 an approach on an opponent's goal etc 4 the players in a team whose role is to attack

attain verb achieve • **attainable** adj able to be attained • **attainment** noun 1 an achievement or accomplishment 2 the act of attaining

attempt verb try ◇ noun 1 a try or effort: first attempt 2 an attack: an attempt on the president's life

attend verb 1 be present at 2 (with **to**) wait on, look after 3 formal pay attention to 4 formal accompany

attendance noun 1 the fact of being present: my attendance was expected 2 the number of people present: good attendance at the first night

attendant noun someone employed to look after a public place, shop, etc: cloakroom attendant ◇ adj accompanying, related: stress and its attendant health problems

attention noun 1 careful notice: pay attention 2 concentration 3 care 4 military a stiffly straight standing position: stand to attention

attentive adj 1 giving or showing attention 2 politely looking after someone • **attentively** adv • **attentiveness** noun

attic noun a room just under the roof of a house

attire verb, formal dress ◇ noun, formal clothing

attitude noun 1 a way of thinking or feeling: positive attitude 2 a confident or defiant way of behaving or dressing considered impressive in youth culture 3 a position of the body

attorney noun (plural **attorneys**) 1 someone with legal power to act for another person 2 US a lawyer

attract verb 1 arouse liking or interest: what attracted you to him? 2 draw to or towards: magnets attract iron

attraction noun 1 the feeling of liking someone or something 2 the power of attracting: magnetic attraction 3 something which attracts visitors etc: tourist attraction

attractive adj 1 good-looking, likeable 2 pleasing: attractive price

attribute /uh-trib-yoot/ verb 1 say or think that something is the cause of: attribute the accident to human error 2 say that something was written, painted, etc by: a painting attributed to Rembrandt ◇ noun /a-trib-yoot/ 1 a personal quality or feature 2 a characteristic that goes with something: *attributes of power* • **attributable** *adj* • **attributive** *adj*

attrition *noun* a gradual but relentless wearing down

aubergine /*oh*-buh-zheen/ *noun* an oval vegetable with dark purple skin

auburn *adj* of hair: reddish-brown in colour

auction *noun* a public sale in which articles are sold to the highest bidder ◊ *verb* sell by auction • **auctioneer** *noun* someone who sells by auction

audacious *adj* daring, bold • **audaciously** *adv* • **audacity** *noun*

audible *adj* loud enough to be heard • **audibility** *noun* • **audibly** *adv*

audience *noun* **1** a number of people gathered to watch or hear a performance *etc* **2** a formal interview with someone important: *an audience with the Pope*

audio *noun* the reproduction of recorded or radio sound ◊ *adj* relating to such sound: *an audio tape*

audio-visual *adj* involving a combination of sound and images

audit *verb* examine accounts officially ◊ *noun* **1** an official examination of a company's accounts **2** a detailed assessment: *an environmental audit of the area* • **auditor** *noun* someone who audits accounts

audition *noun* a short performance in which a performer's ability or suitability is judged

auditorium *noun* (*plural* **auditoria** or **auditoriums**) the part of a theatre *etc* where the audience sits

auditory *adj* of hearing

au fait /oh *feh*/ *adj* familiar with

augment *verb* increase in size, number or amount • **augmentation** *noun* • **augmentative** *adj*

augur *verb*: **augur well** or **auger ill**

be a good or bad sign for the future

August *noun* the eighth month of the year

august /aw-*gust*/ *adj* full of dignity, stately

aunt *noun* a father's or a mother's sister, or an uncle's wife

au pair /oh *pair*/ *noun* a foreign girl who does domestic duties in return for board, lodging and pocket money

aural *adj* relating to the ear or to hearing • **aurally** *adv*

Do not confuse with: **oral**

---

aurora borealis /aw-*raw*-ruh baw-ri-*ah*-lis/ *noun* the appearance of bands of coloured light in the night sky in Northern regions

auspices *plural noun*: **under the auspices of** under the control or supervision of

auspicious *adj* promising to be good or successful; favourable • **auspiciously** *adv*

austere *adj* **1** severe in manner **2** without luxury; simple, sparse • **austerity** *noun*

authentic *adj* true, real, genuine • **authentically** *adv* • **authenticity** *noun*

authenticate *verb* show to be true or real • **authentication** *noun*

author *noun* the writer of a book, poem, play, *etc*

authoring *noun* composing, writing, compiling, *etc* using information technology

authoritarian *adj* insisting on strict authority ◊ *noun* an authoritarian person

authoritative *adj* **1** providing reliable information **2** stated by an expert or someone in authority • **authoritatively** *adv*

authority noun (plural **authorities**) 1 power or right 2 someone whose opinion is reliable, an expert 3 a local council or other body that runs something 4 (**authorities**) people in power

authorize verb 1 give (a person) the power or the right to do something 2 give permission (for something to be done) • **authorization** noun

autism noun a disability that affects a person's ability to relate to and communicate with other people • **autistic** adj affected with autism

autobahn /aw-toh-bahn/ noun a motorway in Germany

autobiography noun (plural **autobiographies**) the story of someone's life, written or told by himself or herself • **autobiographer** noun the writer of an autobiography • **autobiographical** adj

autocrat noun a ruler who has complete power • **autocracy** noun government by such a ruler • **autocratic** adj expecting complete obedience

autograph noun 1 the signature of a famous person 2 someone's own signature or handwriting ◇ verb of a famous person: write your own name on: autograph the book

automate verb make (a process) automatic by getting machines to do it • **automation** noun the use of machines to control processes in factories etc

automatic adj 1 of a machine etc: self-working 2 of an action: done without thinking ◇ noun 1 something automatic (eg an automatic washing-machine) 2 a kind of self-loading gun • **automatically** adv • **automatic pilot** noun 1 a device which can be set to control an aircraft on a course 2 the state of mind of doing things unthinkingly

automaton /aw-tom-uh-tun/ noun (plural **automatons** or **automata**) 1 a mechanical toy or machine made

to look and move like a human 2 someone who acts mindlessly, like a machine

automobile noun, US a car

autonomy noun the power or right of a country to govern itself • **autonomous** adj • **autonomously** adv

autopsy noun (plural **autopsies**) an examination of a body after death

autoteller noun an ATM

autumn noun the season of the year following summer, when leaves change colour and fruits are ripe • **autumnal** adj 1 relating to autumn 2 like those of autumn: autumnal colours

auxiliary adj supplementary, additional ◇ noun (plural **auxiliaries**) a helper, an assistant

AV abbrev 1 audio-visual 2 Authorized Version (of the Bible)

avail verb & noun • **avail yourself of** make use of • **to no avail** without any effect, of no use

available adj able or ready to be used or had • **availability** noun

avalanche noun 1 a mass of snow and ice sliding down from a mountain 2 a great amount: an avalanche of work

avant-garde /av-onh-gahd/ adj writing, painting, etc in a style that is ahead of its time: an avant-garde writer

avarice noun greed, esp for money • **avaricious** adj greedy

avatar /av-uh-tah/ noun a Hindu god in visible form

avenge verb (**avenging**, **avenged**) take revenge for (a wrong) • **avenger** noun

avenue noun 1 a wide tree-lined street 2 a means, a way: avenue of escape

average noun the result obtained by

adding several amounts and dividing the total by this number, *eg* the average of 3, 7, 9 and 13 is 8 (32 ÷ 4) ◇ *adj* **1** of medium size, ability, quality, *etc* **2** obtained by working out an average: *the average cost will be £10 each* ◇ *verb* **1** form an average **2** find the average of

averse *adj* not fond of, opposed (to)

Do not confuse with: **adverse**

---

aversion *noun* **1** extreme dislike or distaste: *an aversion to sprouts* **2** something that is hated

avert *verb, formal* **1** turn away or aside: *avert your eyes* **2** prevent from happening: *avert the danger*

aviary *noun* (*plural* **aviaries**) a place for keeping birds

aviation *noun* the practice of flying or piloting aircraft

aviator *noun* an aircraft pilot

avid *adj* extremely enthusiastic: *an avid reader* • **avidity** *noun* • **avidly** *adv*

avocado *noun* (*plural* **avocados**) **1** a pear-shaped vegetable with a rough peel and rich, creamy flesh **2** a light, yellowish green colour

avoid *verb* escape, keep clear of • **avoidable** *adj* • **avoidance** *noun*

avoirdupois /av-wah-doo-*pwah*/ *noun* the system of measuring weights in pounds and ounces (*compare with*: **metric**)

avow *verb, formal* declare openly or state sincerely • **avowal** *noun* • **avowed** *adj* • **avowedly** *adv*

await *verb* **1** wait for **2** be going to happen to: *the terrible fate that awaited them*

awake *verb* **1** rouse from sleep **2** stop sleeping ◇ *adj* not asleep

awaken *verb* **1** awake **2** arouse (interest *etc*) • **awakening** *noun*

award *verb* **1** give (a prize *etc*) **2** grant (a benefit *etc*) legally ◇ *noun* something that is awarded

aware *adj* **1** having knowledge (of), conscious (of): *aware of the dangers* **2** alert • **awareness** *noun*

away *adv* **1** to or at a distance from the speaker or person spoken to: *throw that ball away/a village five miles away* **2** not here; not at home or work: *she is away all this week* **3** in the opposite direction: *he turned away and left* **4** into nothing: *the sound died away* **5** constantly; diligently: *working away* • **do away with** abolish, get rid of • **get away with** do (something) without being punished • **make away with** steal and escape with • **right away** immediately

awe *noun* wonder or admiration mixed with fear ◇ *verb* affect with awe: *awed by the occasion* • **awestruck** *adj* full of awe

awesome *adj* **1** causing wonder or admiration mixed with fear **2** *informal* remarkable, admirable

awful *adj* **1** *informal* bad or unpleasant: *an awful headache* **2** *informal* very great: *an awful lot* **3** terrible: *I feel awful about what happened* • **awfully** *adv, informal* very, extremely: *awfully good of you* • **awfulness** *noun*

awkward *adj* **1** clumsy, not graceful **2** difficult to deal with: *awkward customer* • **awkwardly** *adv* • **awkwardness** *noun*

awl *noun* a hand tool for boring small holes

awning *noun* **1** a canvas canopy over a shop front **2** a tent-like extension fitted to a caravan

AWOL /eh-wol/ *abbrev* absent without leave

awry /uh-*rai*/ *adj & adv* **1** not according to plan, wrong **2** not straight or level, crooked

axe *noun* (*plural* **axes**) a tool for chopping ◇ *verb* **1** cancel (a plan *etc*) **2** reduce greatly (costs, services, *etc*)

axiom *noun* a truth, an accepted principle

axis *noun* (*plural* **axes**) **1** the line, real or imaginary, on which a thing turns **2** the North-South line around which the earth appears to turn **3** a fixed line from which points are measured on a graph

axle *noun* the rod on which a wheel turns

ayatollah *noun* a religious leader of the Shiite branch of Islam

azalea *noun* a flowering plant related to the rhododendron

azimuth *noun* the angle of the imaginary line between the horizon and the position of a star, the sun, *etc*

azure *adj* sky-coloured, clear blue

Bb

BA abbrev **1** Bachelor of Arts **2** British Airways

babble verb talk indistinctly or foolishly ◇ noun indistinct or foolish talk

babe noun **1** a baby **2** informal an attractive young woman

baboon noun a large monkey with a dog-like snout

baby noun (plural **babies**) a very young child; an infant ◇ verb (**babies**, **babying**, **babied**) treat like a baby • **babyhood** noun the time when someone is a baby • **babysitter** noun someone who stays in the house with a child while its parents are out

bachelor noun an unmarried man • **Bachelor of Arts**, **Bachelor of Science**, etc someone who has passed examinations at a certain level in subjects at a university

bacillus /buh-sil-us/ noun (plural **bacilli**) a rod-shaped bacterium

back noun **1** the rear part of the human body from the neck to the base of the spine **2** the upper part of an animal's body **3** the part of anything situated behind: sitting at the back of the bus **4** football etc a player positioned behind the forwards ◇ adj of or at the back ◇ adv **1** to or in the place from which someone or something came: back at the house/walked back home **2** to or in a former time or condition: thinking back to their youth ◇ verb **1** move backwards **2** (often with **up**) help or support **3** bet on (a horse etc) • **back down** stop insisting or asserting an opinion • **back out 1** move out backwards **2** excuse yourself from keeping to an agreement • **back to front** the wrong way round • **back up** comput copy a file of work to another disk, for security reasons • **put your back into** work hard at • **put someone's back up** irritate someone • **with your back to the wall** in desperate difficulties

backbone noun **1** the spine **2** the main support of something **3** courage and determination

backdate verb make (eg a payment) apply from an earlier date

backer noun a supporter

backfire verb **1** of a vehicle: make an explosive noise in the exhaust pipe **2** of a plan: go wrong

backgammon noun a game similar to draughts, played with dice

background noun **1** the space behind the main figures or objects in a picture **2** details that explain something **3** someone's family and upbringing

backhand noun, tennis a stroke played with the back of the hand facing the ball • **backhanded** adj of a compliment: with an additional, unflattering meaning

backing noun **1** support **2** a musical accompaniment on a recording **3** material used on the back of a picture etc

backlash noun a violent reaction against something

backside noun, informal the buttocks

backstroke noun a stroke used in swimming on the back

backup noun a copy of computer data, stored on another disk

backward adj 1 to or towards the back: *backward glance* 2 slow in learning or development

backwards adv 1 towards the back: *walked backwards out the door* 2 in a reverse direction; back to front: *written backwards* 3 towards the past

backwater noun 1 a remote, dull or unsophisticated place 2 a river pool separate from the main stream

bacon noun salted and dried meat from a pig

bacteria plural noun (sing **bacterium**) tiny organisms found in air, water and in the body, many of which cause disease; germs • **bacterial** adj

bacteriology noun the study of bacteria • **bacteriologist** noun

bad adj 1 unpleasant, negative, upsetting: *bad news/bad publicity/ a bad day at the office* 2 (often with **for**) harmful: *smoking is bad for you* 3 of food: rotten, decaying 4 immoral; wicked 5 severe, serious: *bad dose of flu* 6 injured: *a bad back* 7 guilty or regretful: *I still feel bad about teasing him* • **bad language** noun swearing • **badly** adv 1 not well 2 severely; very much • **badness** noun

bade past tense of **bid**

badge noun a small sign or brooch-like ornament worn to identify the wearer or express support or an opinion

badger noun a burrowing animal of the weasel family that comes out at night ◇ verb pester or annoy

badminton noun a game in which players use rackets to hit a shuttlecock over a high net

badmouth verb, informal say unpleasant or negative things about; criticize

baffle verb be too difficult for; puzzle, confound ◇ noun a device that reduces noise, *eg* fitted on an engine's exhaust • **baffling** adj

BAFTA abbrev British Academy of Film and Television Arts

bag noun 1 a container made of soft flexible material 2 a suitcase or hold-all: *don't leave your bags unattended* ◇ verb (**bagging, bagged**) 1 put in a bag 2 secure possession of; claim: *bag a seat* 3 kill (animals) in a hunt • **bag lady** noun a homeless woman who carries her belongings with her in shopping bags • **bags of** many, plenty of

bagatelle noun a board game in which balls are struck into numbered holes

bagel /beh-gul/ noun a ring-shaped bread roll with a dense texture

baggage noun 1 luggage 2 experiences, attitudes, *etc* from the past that adversely affect future relationships

baggy adj (**baggier, baggiest**) of clothes: large and loose ◇ noun (**baggies**) informal wide, knee-length shorts • **bagginess** noun

bagpipes plural noun a wind instrument made up of a bag, a pipe for blowing into, a chanter with finger-holes, and several pipes through which the sound is released

bail noun 1 money given to secure the temporary release of an untried prisoner 2 cricket one of the pieces across the top of the wickets • **bail out** 1 obtain temporary release of (an untried prisoner) by giving money that will be forfeited if they do not return for trial 2 bale out

---

Do not confuse with: **bale**

---

bailie noun, hist a burgh magistrate in Scotland

bailiff noun 1 an officer who works for a sheriff 2 a landowner's agent

bairn *noun, Scot* a child

Baisakhi /bai-*sak*-i/ *noun* the annual Sikh festival held at the Hindu New Year

bait *noun* **1** food put on a hook to make fish bite, or in a trap to attract animals **2** something tempting or alluring ◇ *verb* **1** put bait on a hook *etc* **2** provoke to anger; tease

baize /behz/ *noun* woollen cloth like felt

bake *verb* **1** cook in an oven **2** dry or harden in the sun or in an oven • **baking powder** *noun* a raising agent added to flour in cake-making *etc*

baker *noun* someone who bakes or sells bread *etc* • **bakery** or **bakehouse** *noun* a place used for baking in

baklava /*bak*-luh-vuh/ *noun* a Middle-Eastern pastry filled with nuts and honey

balaclava /bal-uh-*klah*-vuh/ *noun* a knitted covering for the head and neck

balalaika /ba-luh-*lai*-kuh/ *noun* a traditional Russian musical instrument like a guitar

balance *noun* **1** steadiness: *lost my balance and fell over* **2** an amount of money left over or still needing to be paid **3** a traditional device for weighing, with two hanging pans ◇ *verb* **1** be the same in weight **2** make both sides of an account the same **3** make or keep steady: *balanced it on her head*

balcony *noun* (*plural* **balconies**) **1** a platform built out from the wall of a building **2** an upper floor in a theatre *etc*

bald *adj* **1** without hair **2** plain, frank: *a bald statement*

balderdash *noun* nonsense

bale *noun* a large tight bundle of cotton, hay, *etc* • **bale out 1** escape by parachute from an aircraft in an emergency **2** (also **bail out**) scoop water out of a boat

---

Do not confuse with: **bail**

---

baleful *adj* harmful, malevolent: *baleful influence*

balk *verb* (with **at**) refuse to do something

ball¹ *noun* **1** anything round: *ball of wool* **2** the round object used in playing many games • **ball bearings** *plural noun* small steel balls that sit loosely in grooves and ease the revolving of one machinery part over another • **on the ball** *informal* in touch with a situation, alert • **play ball** *informal* play along, co-operate

ball² *noun* a formal party with dancing • **have a ball** *informal* have a great time; enjoy yourself

ballad *noun* **1** a slow love song **2** a narrative poem with a simple rhyme scheme, *usu* in verses of four lines

ballast *noun* sand, gravel, *etc* put into a ship to steady it

ballerina *noun* a female ballet dancer

ballet *noun* a form of stylized dancing that tells a story by mime

ballistic missile *noun* a long-range missile that has no guidance system but simply falls onto its target

balloon *noun* a bag filled with gas to make it float in the air, *esp* one made of thin rubber used as a toy *etc* ◇ *verb* puff or swell out

ballot *noun* a way of voting in secret by marking a paper and putting it into a special box ◇ *verb* gather the opinions of by ballot

ballpark *noun, US* a sports field for ball-games ◇ *adj* approximate, estimated: *ballpark figure*

ballpoint *noun* a pen with a tiny ball as the writing point

ballroom noun a large room used for public dances etc

balls plural noun, taboo slang **1** testicles **2** courage **3** rubbish, nonsense • **balls-up** noun a disorganized situation caused by mistakes or misunderstandings

balm noun **1** a sweet-smelling healing ointment **2** something soothing

balmy adj **1** gentle, soothing: balmy air **2** sweet-smelling • **balminess** noun

balsam noun an oily sweet-smelling substance obtained from certain trees

balsawood noun a lightweight wood obtained from a tropical American tree

balti noun a style of Indian cooking in which food is cooked and served in a wok-like pan

balustrade noun a row of pillars on a balcony etc, joined by a rail

bamboo noun the woody, jointed stem of a very tall Indian grass

bamboozle verb confuse, puzzle • **bamboozling** adj

ban noun an order forbidding something ◊ verb (**banning**, **banned**) forbid officially (the publication of a book etc)

banal adj lacking originality or wit; dull and ordinary • **banality** noun • **banally** adv

banana noun the long yellow fruit of a tropical tree

band noun **1** a group of musicians playing together **2** a strip of some material to put round something **3** a stripe (of colour etc) **4** a group of wavelengths for radio broadcasts **5** a group of people ◊ verb join together

bandage noun a cloth dressing for a wound

bandana noun a strip of cloth tied round the head for decoration or as a hairband

B and B abbrev bed and breakfast

bandit noun a member of a gang of robbers

bandolier or **bandoleer** noun a belt for carrying gun cartridges, worn across the body

bandwagon noun an activity or movement that suddenly becomes fashionable • **jump on the bandwagon** join an activity or movement when it becomes fashionable or likely to succeed

bandwidth noun **1** the spread of the range of frequencies used for transmitting TV or radio signals **2** the capacity for transmitting information over a link between computers

bandy adj of legs: bent outward at the knee • **bandy words** argue

bane noun a cause of trouble or annoyance: the bane of my life

baneful adj destructive, poisonous

bang noun **1** a sudden loud noise **2** a heavy blow ◊ verb **1** close with a bang; slam **2** hit forcefully or painfully; bump: banged his head on the door • **banger** noun, informal **1** a sausage **2** an old car

bangle noun a bracelet

banish verb **1** order to leave a country **2** force yourself to get rid of (doubts, fear, etc) • **banishment** noun

banister noun the posts and handrail of a staircase

banjo noun (plural **banjoes** or **banjos**) a stringed musical instrument like a guitar, with a long neck and a round body

bank noun **1** an organization that offers saving, lending and other financial services **2** a mound or ridge of earth etc **3** the edge of a river **4** a place where blood etc is stored till needed **5** a public bin for collecting items for recycling: bottle bank • **banker** noun someone who manages a bank • **bank**

holiday noun a day on which all banks and many shops etc are closed • **banknote** noun a piece of paper money issued by a bank • **bank on** depend on, count on

bankrupt noun someone who does not have enough money to pay their debts ◇ adj **1** unable to pay debts **2** utterly lacking in: bankrupt of ideas • **bankruptcy** noun

banner noun **1** a large flag carried in processions etc, often hung between two poles **2** any flag

banns plural noun a public announcement of a forthcoming marriage

banquet noun a ceremonial dinner

banshee noun a female spirit that wails to warn of approaching death in Scottish and Irish folk tales

bantam noun a small kind of hen

banter noun friendly teasing and joking

baptize verb **1** dip in, or sprinkle with, water as a sign of admission into the Christian church **2** give a name to; christen • **baptism** noun • **baptismal** adj

bar noun **1** a room or counter where drinks are served in a pub, hotel, etc **2** a pub, esp in a town **3** a rod of solid material: iron bars **4** a solid block: bar of soap/chocolate **5** something that prevents something; a hindrance: poverty should be no bar to education **6** a time division in music **7** the lawyers who plead in a court **8** the rail at which prisoners stand for trial **9** a broad line or band **10** a bank of sand etc at the mouth of a river ◇ prep except: all the runners, bar Ian, finished the race ◇ verb (**barring**, **barred**) **1** exclude, shut out: barred from the competition **2** obstruct: our exit was barred • **barcode** noun a series of thick and thin printed lines representing product information that can be read by a scanner • **barring** prep except for, but for

barb noun the backward-pointing spike on an arrow, fish-hook, etc

barbarian noun an uncivilized person ◇ adj uncivilized • **barbaric** adj **1** uncivilized **2** extremely cruel • **barbarity** noun

barbecue noun **1** a structure or piece of equipment for grilling food over heat **2** an outdoor party with food cooked on a barbecue ◇ verb cook (food) on a barbecue

barbed adj **1** of a comment: intended to be hurtful; caustic **2** of a hook: having a barb or barbs • **barbed wire** noun wire with regular clusters of sharp points, used for fencing etc

barber noun a men's hairdresser

barbiturate noun a type of sedative drug

bard noun, formal a poet

bare adj **1** uncovered, naked **2** plain, simple **3** empty ◇ verb uncover, expose • **barefaced** adj showing no shame or embarrassment; unabashed: barefaced lie • **barefoot** adj with no shoes or socks on • **barely** adv hardly, scarcely

bargain noun **1** something bought cheaply **2** an agreement, esp about buying or selling ◇ verb argue about a price etc • **bargain for** expect: more than he bargained for • **into the bargain** in addition, besides

barge noun a flat-bottomed boat used on rivers and canals ◇ verb **1** rush clumsily **2** push or bump (into): a man barged right into me **3** push your way (into) rudely: you can't go barging in without knocking

baritone noun **1** a male singing voice between tenor and bass **2** a singer with this voice

bark[1] noun the noise made by a dog ◇ verb **1** of a dog: give a bark **2** speak sharply or angrily

bark[2] noun the rough outer covering of a tree's trunk and branches

barley *noun* a grain used for food and for making malt liquors and spirits • **barley sugar** *noun* sugar candied by melting and cooling to make a sweet • **barley water** *noun* a drink made from pearl barley

bar mitzvah /bah mits-vuh/ *noun* a Jewish ceremony to mark a boy's coming of age

barmy *adj* (**barmier, barmiest**) *informal* foolish or stupid

barn *noun* a building in which hay, grain, *etc* is stored

barnacle *noun* a type of shellfish that sticks to rocks, ships' hulls, *etc*

barometer *noun* an instrument that measures air pressure as an indicator of weather

baron *noun* **1** a man who has a low rank in British nobility **2** a powerful person, *esp* in a business: *drug baron* • **baronial** *adj*

baroness *noun* (*plural* **baronesses**) a woman who has a low rank in British nobility

baronet *noun* a man who has the lowest rank in British nobility • **baronetcy** *noun* the rank of baronet

baroque /buh-*rok*/ *adj* in a very flamboyant style popular in the 17th century

barracks *plural noun* a place for housing soldiers

barracuda *noun* a large fierce West Indian fish

barrage *noun* **1** heavy gunfire against an enemy **2** an overwhelming number: *barrage of questions* **3** a bar across a river built to make the water deeper

barrel *noun* **1** a wooden cask with curved sides **2** the metal tube of a gun through which the shot is fired

barren *adj* **1** of land: dry and empty, with very few plants **2** not able to have babies; infertile • **barrenness** *noun*

barricade *noun* a barrier put up to block a street *etc* ◇ *verb* **1** block or strengthen against attack **2** shut behind a barrier

barrier *noun* **1** a strong fence *etc* used for keeping people out or controlling entry **2** something that prevents something; an obstacle: *his age was not a barrier to success*

barrister *noun* a lawyer who pleads cases in English or in Irish courts

barrow *noun* **1** a small hand-cart **2** a mound built over an ancient grave

barter *verb* give one thing in exchange for another ◇ *noun* trading by exchanging goods without using money

basalt *noun* hard black rock formed when lava cools

base *noun* **1** something on which a thing stands or rests **2** the bottom or underside of something **3** a place from where an expedition, military action, *etc* is carried out ◇ *verb* **1** use as a foundation: *based on the facts* **2** have as a home or headquarters: *a company based in Glasgow* ◇ *adj* immoral, wicked • **baseless** *adj* without foundation; untrue • **basement** *noun* a storey below ground level in a building

baseball *noun* a North American ball game in which players make a circuit of four bases on a field

bash *verb* hit hard ◇ *noun* a heavy blow • **have a bash** *informal* make an attempt

bashful *adj* shy • **bashfully** *adv*

basic *adj* **1** dealing with what is simplest or most fundamental: *basic training/knowledge* **2** providing only essentials, not comfort or luxury: *rather basic accommodation* • **basically** *adv* fundamentally, essentially

basil *noun* an aromatic herb used in cooking

basilica *noun* a church with a large

central hall and a rounded wall behind the altar

basilisk noun **1** a mythological reptile with a deadly look and poisonous breath **2** a type of American lizard

basin noun **1** a wide, open dish **2** a washhand basin **3** the land drained by a river and its tributaries

basis noun (plural **bases**) **1** something on which a thing rests, a foundation: the basis of their friendship **2** the main ingredient

bask verb **1** lie in warmth **2** feel great pleasure (in): basking in glory

basket noun **1** a container made of strips of wood, rushes, etc woven together **2** a related group or collection: basket of currencies

basketball noun a team game in which goals are scored by throwing a ball into a raised net

basque /bask/ noun a woman's close-fitting under-bodice

bas-relief /bah-ruh-leef/ noun sculpture carved to stand slightly out from a background

bass[1] /behs/ noun (plural **basses**) **1** the low part in music **2** a deep male singing voice **3** a singer with this voice ◇ adj low or deep in tone ● **bass clef** see **clef**

bass[2] /bas/ noun (plural **bass** or **basses**) a fish of the perch family

bassoon noun a musical wind instrument with low notes

bastard noun **1** informal a general term of abuse **2** a child born to parents who are not married to each other

baste[1] verb spoon fat over (meat) while roasting to keep (it) from drying out

baste[2] verb sew loosely together with big stitches; tack

bastion noun **1** something that preserves a situation: the last bastions of male power **2** a tower on a castle etc

bat[1] noun a shaped piece of wood etc for hitting a ball in some games ◇ verb (**batting**, **batted**) use the bat in cricket etc ● **batsman, batswoman** noun (plural **batsmen, batswomen**) someone who bats in cricket etc

bat[2] noun a mouse-like flying animal

bat[3] verb (**batting, batted**) flutter (eyelids etc)

batch noun (plural **batches**) a quantity of things made or done at one time

bated adj: **with bated breath** anxiously

bath noun **1** a container that holds water in which to wash the body **2** the water in a bath **3** a washing of the body in a bath **4** (**baths**) a public building with an artificial pool for swimming ◇ verb wash in a bath ● **bathchair** noun an old-fashioned wheelchair ● **bathroom** noun a room containing a bath, lavatory, etc

bathe verb **1** wash gently: bathe your eyes **2** swim in water **3** take a bath ● **bathed in** covered with

bathos /beh-thos/ noun a sudden change from a serious subject to a silly one

batik noun a method of dyeing patterns on cloth by waxing certain areas so that they remain uncoloured

baton noun **1** a light stick used by a conductor of music **2** a stick carried by an athlete in a relay race

---

Do not confuse with: **batten**

---

battalion noun a part of a regiment of foot soldiers

batten noun **1** a small piece of timber fixed as a support **2** a strip of wood used to fasten down a ship's hatches during a storm ◇ verb (with **down**) fasten down firmly

Do not confuse with: **baton**

batter *verb* hit repeatedly ◇ *noun* a beaten mixture of flour, milk and eggs, for cooking ● **battered** *adj* **1** treated violently; abused **2** worn out by use ● **battering-ram** *noun, hist* a weapon in the form of a heavy beam for breaking through walls *etc*

battery *noun* (*plural* **batteries**) **1** a device for storing and transmitting electricity **2** a number of large guns **3** a series of cages in which hens are kept for egg-laying

battle *noun* **1** a fight between armies **2** a struggle to achieve something or defeat someone ◇ *verb* fight ● **battle-axe** *noun* **1** *hist* a kind of axe used in fighting **2** *informal* a fierce, domineering woman ● **battlefield** *noun* the site of a battle ● **battleship** *noun* a heavily armed and armoured warship

battlement *noun* a wall on the top of a building, with openings or notches for firing through

batty *adj* (**battier**, **battiest**) *informal* crazy, eccentric

bauble *noun* a brightly-coloured piece of jewellery of little value

baud *noun* a measure of the speed at which computer information is transmitted along a telephone line *etc*

bawdy *adj* (**bawdier**, **bawdiest**) referring to sex in a humorous or vulgar way

bawl *verb* shout or cry out loudly ◇ *noun* a loud cry

bay *noun* **1** a wide inlet of the sea in a coastline **2** a space in a room *etc* set back; a recess **3** a laurel tree ◇ *verb* of dogs: bark ● **bay window** *noun* a window that sticks out from a room, forming a recess inside the room ● **hold at bay** fight off

bayonet *noun* a steel stabbing blade that can be fixed to the muzzle of a rifle ◇ *verb* stab with a bayonet

bazaar *noun* **1** a sale of goods for charity *etc* **2** a marketplace in the Middle East

bazooka *noun* a weapon, held on the shoulder, that fires shells over a short range

BB *abbrev* Boys' Brigade, a Christian youth organization similar to the Scout Association

BBC *abbrev* British Broadcasting Corporation, a television company funded by the UK government

BC *abbrev* before Christ: 55 *BC*

be *verb* (*present forms* **am**, **are**, **is**; *past tense* **was**, **were**; *past participle* **been**) **1** live, exist: *there may be some milk left* **2** have a position, quality, *etc*: *she wants to be a dentist/if only you could be happy*

be is also used to form tenses of other verbs, eg I *was* running for the bus/when *will* you *be* arriving?, and to form the passive voice, eg the car *is being* repaired

beach *noun* (*plural* **beaches**) a sandy or pebbly strip of shore ◇ *verb* drive or haul a boat up on the beach ● **beachcomber** *noun* someone who searches beaches for useful articles

beacon *noun* **1** a flashing light or other warning signal **2** *hist* a fire on a hill used as a signal of danger

bead *noun* **1** a small pierced ball of glass, plastic, *etc*, used in needlework or jewellery-making **2** a drop of liquid: *beads of sweat*

beadle *noun* an officer of a church or college who looks after buildings

beagle *noun* a small hound used in hunting

beak *noun* **1** the hard, horny part of a bird's mouth with which it gathers food **2** a pointed part that sticks out

beaker noun a tall cup or glass, usually without a handle

beam noun 1 a long straight piece of wood or metal 2 a shaft of light 3 a radio signal 4 the widest part of a ship's hull ◇ verb 1 shine 2 smile broadly 3 send by radio waves

bean noun 1 a seed of various plants whose seeds come in pods 2 any of various plants whose seeds come in pods

bear noun a large powerful animal with shaggy fur and hooked claws ◇ verb (**bearing**, **bore**, **borne** or **born**) 1 put up with (something unpleasant); endure 2 produce (fruit, children, etc) 3 formal carry (something) • **bearable** adj able to be endured; tolerable • **bearer** noun someone employed to carry equipment on an expedition • **bearskin** noun the high fur cap worn by the Guards in the British Army • **bear in mind** remember, take into account • **bear out** confirm: this bears out my suspicions • **bear with** be patient with • **bring to bear** bring into use

---

born is used for the past participle when referring to the birth of a child, idea, etc: when were you born?; otherwise the form is **borne**: I couldn't have borne it any longer

---

beard noun the hair that grows on a man's chin and cheeks

bearing noun 1 way of walking, standing or behaving 2 direction 3 connection: it has no bearing on the issue 4 part of a machine that supports a moving part

beast noun 1 a four-footed animal 2 a brutal person

beastly adj 1 extremely cruel or unpleasant 2 informal nasty • **beastliness** noun

beat verb (**beating**, **beat**, **beaten**) 1 hit repeatedly 2 defeat 3 of your heart: throb in the normal way 4 stir (a mixture etc) with quick movements ◇ noun 1 a regular pattern of sounds 2 the heart's regular throbbing 3 the regular round of a police officer etc • **beaten** adj 1 defeated 2 of metal: shaped by hitting with a hammer 3 of earth: worn smooth by treading • **beat up** injure by repeated hitting, kicking, etc

beatific /beh-uh-tif-ik/ adj of, or showing, great happiness

Beaufort scale /boh-fut/ noun a scale used for measuring the speed and strength of wind

beautician noun someone who provides beauty treatments such as manicures and hair removal

beautiful adj very attractive or pleasing • **beautifully** adv

beauty noun (plural **beauties**) 1 the quality of being very attractive or pleasing 2 a very attractive woman

beaver noun 1 a very large North American rodent with a flat tail that builds a den of sticks on a stream that it dams 2 a member of the most junior branch of the Scout Association

becalmed adj of a sailing ship: unable to move because of lack of wind

because conj for the reason that: we didn't go because it was raining ◇ adv (with **of**) on account of: because of the holiday, the bank will be shut

beck noun: **at someone's beck and call** always ready to carry out someone's orders or requests

beckon verb make a sign with the finger to summon (someone)

become verb 1 come to be: she became angry 2 formal suit (someone): that colour becomes you • **becoming** adj 1 suiting someone well and making them look attractive 2 of behaviour: appropriate, suitable

bed noun 1 a place on which to rest

or sleep **2** a plot for flowers *etc* in a garden **3** the bottom of a river *etc* ◇ *verb* (**bedding, bedded**) **1** plant in soil *etc* **2** provide a bed for **3** *informal* have sex with • **bed and breakfast** *noun* **1** a room for the night with breakfast provided the following morning **2** a private house that offers a bed and breakfast service to paying guests • **bedclothes** *plural noun* bedcovers • **bedding** *noun* **1** bedcovers, pillowcases, *etc* **2** straw *etc* for cattle to lie on • **bedridden** *adj* kept in bed by weakness, illness, *etc* • **bedrock** *noun* **1** the solid rock under the soil **2** the principles or people that provide the foundation for something: *friendship is the bedrock of a good marriage* • **bedroom** *noun* a room for sleeping • **bedspread** *noun* a top cover for a bed • **bedstead** *noun* a frame supporting a bed

bedlam *noun* a place full of uproar and confusion

bedraggled *adj* wet and untidy-looking after being caught in rain *etc*

bee *noun* **1** a winged insect that makes honey in wax cells **2** a gathering to take part in a particular activity: *quilting bee* • **beehive** *noun* a dome or box in which bees are kept • **make a beeline for** go directly towards

beech *noun* (*plural* **beeches**) a forest tree with grey smooth bark

beef *noun* meat from a cow, bull or ox • **beefy** *adj* stout, muscular

beefeater *noun* **1** a guardian of the Tower of London **2** a member of the Queen's or King's Guard

Beelzebub *noun, old* the Devil, Satan

been *past participle of* be

beer *noun* an alcoholic drink *usu* made from barley or wheat, often flavoured with hops

beet *noun* a plant with a carrot-like root, one type (**sugar beet**) used as a

source of sugar, the other (**beetroot**) used as a vegetable

beetle *noun* an insect with four wings, the front pair forming hard covers for the back pair

beetling *adj* **1** of cliffs *etc*: overhanging **2** of eyebrows: heavy, frowning

beetroot *see* beet

befall *verb* (**befalling, befell, befallen**) *formal* happen to: *a disaster befell them*

befit *verb* (**befitting, befitted**) *formal* be suitable or right for

before *prep* **1** earlier than: *before three o'clock* **2** in front of: *the man standing before me* **3** rather than, in preference to: *I'd die before telling him* ◇ *adv* **1** on a previous occasion **2** in front ◇ *conj* earlier than the time that: *before he was born* • **beforehand** *adv* previously, before the time when something else is done

befriend *verb* act as a friend to

beg *verb* (**begging, begged**) **1** ask for money *etc* from others **2** ask earnestly: *he begged her to stay* • **beg the question** take as being proved the very point that needs to be proved

began *past tense of* begin

beget *verb* (**begetting, begat, begotten**) *formal* **1** be the father of **2** cause

beggar *noun* **1** someone who begs for money **2** a very poor person • **beggarly** *adj* poor; worthless • **beggar belief** be beyond belief; be incredible

begin *verb* (**beginning, began, begun**) **1** start to do something **2** start to happen • **beginner** *noun* • **beginning** *noun*

begone *exclam, formal* go away!

begrudge *verb* be annoyed about or envious of (something good that someone has): *he begrudged me my success*

beguiling *adj* charming • **beguile** *verb*

begun past participle of **begin**

behalf noun: **on behalf of 1** as the representative of: on behalf of my client **2** in aid of; collecting on behalf of the homeless

behave verb **1** act (in a certain way): he always behaves badly at parties **2** conduct yourself well: can't you behave for just a minute? • **behaviour** noun • **badly-behaved** adj with bad manners • **well-behaved** adj with good manners

behead verb cut off the head of, as a punishment

behemoth /bee-uh-moth/ noun a huge monster

behest noun: **at someone's behest** formal because someone has ordered or demanded it

behind prep **1** at or towards the back of: behind the door **2** the cause of: what's behind this strange decision? **3** in support of; encouraging: behind him in his struggle ◇ adv **1** at the back **2** not up to date: behind with his work

behold verb (**beholding, beheld**) formal look (at); see

beholden adj: **beholden to** grateful to because of a good turn

behove verb: **it behoves you to** formal you ought to

beige noun a pale yellowish-brown colour ◇ adj of this colour

being noun **1** a living person or thing **2** existence

belabour verb hit (someone) repeatedly; thrash • **belabour the point** discuss a subject at too great length

belated adj arriving late

belch verb **1** bring up wind from the stomach through the mouth **2** of a fire etc: send up (smoke etc) violently ◇ noun a short escape of air from the stomach through the mouth

beleaguered /bi-lee-gud/ adj **1** in a situation in which many people are criticizing or opposing **2** under attack by an enemy; besieged

belfry noun (plural **belfries**) the part of a steeple or tower in which the bells are hung

belie verb (**belying, belied**) formal **1** show that (something) previously believed or claimed is false **2** create an impression that is different from reality: her youthful energy belies her advanced age

belief noun **1** what someone thinks to be true **2** faith

believe verb **1** think of as true or as existing **2** trust (in) **3** think or suppose • **believable** adj • **make believe** pretend

belittle verb cause to appear foolish or unimportant

bell noun **1** a hollow metal object that gives a ringing sound when hit **2** the sound made by a bell or other ringing device

bellicose adj inclined to fight or argue; aggressive • **bellicosity** noun

belligerent adj angrily and forcefully stating opinions or disagreeing; quarrelsome • **belligerence** or **belligerency** noun

bellow verb roar like a bull ◇ noun a deep roar

bellows plural noun an instrument for making a blast of air, eg to increase a fire

belly noun (plural **bellies**) **1** the abdomen **2** the underpart of an animal's body **3** the bulging part of anything • **bellyache** noun **1** a stomach pain **2** a persistent whine or complaint • **belly button** noun, informal the navel • **belly dance** noun a sensuous dance performed by women with circling movements of the stomach and hips • **belly flop** noun an inexpert dive landing face down on the water • **bellyful** noun more than enough (of something) • **belly laugh** *noun* a deep laugh

belong *verb* **1** be someone's property: *this book belongs to me* **2** be a member of (a club *etc*) **3** be born in or live in: *I belong to Glasgow* **4** of an object: have its place in: *those glasses belong in the kitchen* • **belongings** *plural noun* what someone owns or carries with them; possessions

beloved *adj* much loved, very dear ◇ *noun* someone who is much loved

below *prep* **1** closer to the ground than: *her skirt reached below her knees* **2** lower in rank than: *a captain is below a major* ◇ *adv* in a lower position: *looking down at the street below*

belt *noun* **1** a strip of leather, cloth, *etc* worn around the waist **2** a loop of rubber *etc* that is turned by an engine or motor and turns something else itself **3** a broad strip of land ◇ *verb* **1** put a belt round **2** *informal* hit with a fist *etc* • **belted** *adj* wearing or having a belt

bemoan *verb* complain about

bemused *adj* confused, puzzled

bench *noun* (*plural* **benches**) **1** a long seat **2** a table at which practical work is done **3** (**the bench**) the judges of a court

bend *verb* (**bending, bent**) **1** curve **2** stoop ◇ *noun* **1** a curve **2** a turn in a road

beneath *prep* **1** directly under something; underneath: *sitting beneath the tree reading a book* **2** covered by: *wearing a black dress beneath her coat* **3** considered too low a task *etc* for: *sweeping floors was beneath him* ◇ *adv* below: *the hills and the village beneath*

benediction *noun* a blessing

benefactor *noun* someone who gives others money or does good to others

beneficial *adj* having a positive effect on; advantageous • **beneficially** *adv* • **beneficiary** *noun* someone who receives something good, *esp* money or property in a deceased person's will

benefit *noun* **1** something good that you receive or experience **2** money received from social security or insurance schemes: *unemployment benefit* ◇ *verb* (**benefiting, benefited**) **1** do good to **2** gain advantage: *benefited from the cut in interest rates*

benevolence *noun* **1** tendency to do good; kindliness **2** a kind act • **benevolent** *adj* kindly • **benevolently** *adv*

benign /bi-*nain*/ *adj* **1** gentle, kindly **2** of disease: not causing death (*contrasted with*: **malignant**)

bent *verb* past form of **bend** ◇ *adj* **1** curved, crooked **2** *informal* dishonest **3** *informal, derog* homosexual ◇ *noun* a natural liking or aptitude (for something) • **be bent on** be determined on

bequeath *verb* leave by will

bequest *noun* money, property, *etc* left in a will

berate *verb* scold very angrily

bereaved *adj* suffering from the recent death of a relative or friend • **bereavement** *noun*

bereft *adj* lacking, deprived (of)

beret /*be*-reh/ *noun* a flat, round hat of soft cloth

Bermuda shorts *plural noun* loose-fitting shorts reaching almost to the knees

berry *noun* (*plural* **berries**) a small round juicy fruit

berserk *adj* in a frenzy; mad

berth *noun* **1** a room for sleeping in a ship *etc* **2** the place where a ship is tied up in a dock ◇ *verb* moor (a ship) • **give a wide berth to** keep well away from

beryl *noun* a type of precious stone

such as an emerald or aquamarine

beseech verb (**beseeches, beseeching, besought** or **beseeched**) formal ask earnestly

beset verb (**besetting, beset**) 1 make very worried 2 attack from all sides; surround

beside prep 1 by the side of, near: the building beside the station 2 compared with: beside her sister she seems quite shy 3 away from, wide of: beside the point • **be beside yourself** lose self-control • **beside the point** irrelevant

besides prep 1 in addition to: he has many other friends, besides me 2 other than, except: nothing in the fridge besides some cheese ◇ adv 1 also, moreover: besides, it was your idea 2 in addition: plenty more besides

besiege verb (**besieging, besieged**) 1 surround (a town etc) with an army 2 crowd round: besieged by fans

besmirch verb 1 spoil the reputation of 2 make dirty; stain

besotted adj: **besotted with** foolishly fond of

bespoke adj of clothes: made to measure

best adj good in the most excellent way ◇ adv in the most excellent way ◇ verb defeat • **best man** noun someone who attends a man who is being married • **best part** noun the largest or greatest part • **bestseller** noun a book etc that sells exceedingly well • **at best** under the most favourable circumstances • **do your best** try as hard as you can • **make the best of** do as well as possible with

bestial adj disgustingly crude or cruel; beastly

bestow verb give

bestride verb stand or sit across; straddle

bet noun money put down to be lost or kept depending on the outcome of a race etc ◇ verb (**betting, bet** or **betted**) place a bet

beta test comput noun a second test of software before its release (compare with: **alpha test**)

bête noir /bet nwar/ noun a particular dislike

betray verb 1 give up (secrets, friends, etc) to an enemy 2 show signs of: his face betrayed no emotion • **betrayal** noun

betrothed adj, formal engaged to be marriage • **betrothal** noun

better adj 1 good to a greater degree; of a more excellent kind 2 healthier 3 completely recovered from illness: don't go back to work until you're better ◇ adv in a more excellent way ◇ verb improve • **better off** 1 in a better position 2 richer • **get the better of** defeat, overcome • **had better** ought to, must • **think better of** change your mind and decide not to do

between prep 1 in the space dividing two things or the period separating two times: there was an empty seat between us/between 3 o'clock and 6 o'clock 2 in shares to; among: divide the chocolates between you 3 from one thing to another: the road between Edinburgh and Glasgow 4 comparing one to the other: the only difference between them is the price

bevel noun a slanting edge ◇ verb (**bevelling, bevelled**) give a slanting edge to • **bevelled** adj

beverage noun a drink

bevy[1] noun (plural **bevies**) 1 a group of women or girls 2 a flock of quails

bevy[2] or **bevvy** noun (plural **bevies** or **bevvies**) Brit informal 1 an alcoholic drink 2 a drinking session

bewail verb complain loudly about

beware verb watch out for (something dangerous)

bewilder verb puzzle, confuse • **bewildering** adj • **bewilderment** noun confusion

bewitch verb put under a spell; charm • **bewitching** adj charming; very beautiful

beyond prep 1 on the far side of: beyond the next set of traffic lights 2 later than: beyond January 3 more than: beyond the call of duty 4 too far gone for: beyond repair 5 too difficult or confusing for: it's beyond me! ◇ adv on or to the far side, further away

bhaji /bah-jee/ noun an Indian appetizer of vegetables in batter, fried in a ball

bhangra /bang-gruh/ noun music combining Western rock and traditional Punjabi styles

bi- prefix 1 having two: biped/bipolar 2 occurring twice in a certain period, or once in every two periods: bi-monthly

biannual adj happening twice a year

Do not confuse with: **biennial**

bias noun 1 the unfair favouring of one person or thing over others that are equally good 2 a tendency to move in a particular direction 3 a weight on or in an object making it move in a particular direction ◇ verb (**biases**, **biasing** or **biassing**, **biased** or **biassed**) give a bias to

bib noun 1 a piece of cloth put under a child's chin to protect their clothes from food stains etc 2 a part of an apron, overalls, etc above the waist, covering the chest

Bible noun the holy book of the Christian Church • **Biblical** adj

bibliography noun (plural **bibliographies**) 1 a list of books (about a subject) 2 the art of classifying books

• **bibliographer** noun someone who compiles bibliographies, or who studies book classification

bibliophile noun a lover of books

bicentenary noun (plural **bicentenaries**) the two-hundredth year after an event, eg someone's birth

biceps sing noun the muscle at the front of the upper part of the arm

bicker verb argue over small matters

bicycle noun a simple vehicle with two wheels, driven by pedals

bid verb (**bidding**, **bade** or **bid**, **bidden** or **bid**) 1 offer a price (for) 2 tell, say: bidding her farewell 3 command or invite: the queen bids you join her ◇ noun 1 an offer to buy something, esp in an auction 2 a bold attempt: a bid for freedom

bide verb: **bide your time** wait patiently for the right moment to do something

bidet /bee-deh/ noun a low wash-basin for washing the genital area

biennial adj lasting two years; happening once every two years ◇ noun a plant that flowers only in its second year • **biennially** adv

Do not confuse with: **biannual**

bier /bee-uh/ noun a carriage or frame for carrying a dead body

bifocals plural noun glasses or contact lenses with one section for near vision and another for viewing distant objects

big adj (**bigger**, **biggest**) 1 large in size, amount, extent, etc 2 important

bigamy noun the crime or fact of having two wives or two husbands at once • **bigamist** noun • **bigamous** adj

bight noun a small bay

bigot noun someone with narrow-minded, prejudiced beliefs • **bigoted**

adj prejudiced • **bigotry** *noun*

bike *noun, informal* a bicycle

bikini *noun* (*plural* **bikinis**) a woman's brief two-piece bathing suit

bilateral *adj* involving two groups, nations, *etc*: *bilateral agreement* • **bilaterally** *adv*

bilberry *noun* (*plural* **bilberries**) an edible dark-blue berry

bile *noun* **1** fluid from the liver **2** bad temper

bilge *noun* **1** the widest part of a ship's bottom **2** bilgewater **3** *informal* nonsense • **bilgewater** *noun* water that lies in a ship's bottom

bilingual *adj* **1** written in two languages **2** able to speak two languages fluently

bilious *adj* **1** feeling the urge to vomit; nauseous **2** of a sickening greenish-yellow colour • **biliousness** *noun*

bill *noun* **1** a statement of money owed **2** an early version of a law before it has been passed by parliament **3** a bird's beak **4** a printed sheet of information

billboard *noun* a large board on which advertisements are pasted, erected in a public place

billet *noun* a lodging, *esp* for soldiers ◇ *verb* lodge (soldiers) in private houses

billiards *noun* a game played with a cue and balls on a table

billion *noun* **1** a million millions (1,000,000,000,000) **2** *US* (now often in Britain) a thousand millions (1,000,000,000)

billow *verb* **1** of clothes, sails, *etc*: be bulging because filled with wind **2** of smoke: rise in huge clouds • **billowy** *adj*

billy *or* **billycan** *noun* (*plural* **billies** *or* **billycans**) a container for cooking, making tea, *etc* outdoors

billy goat *noun* a male goat

bimbo *noun* (*plural* **bimbos**) *derog* an attractive but not very intelligent young woman

bin *noun* a container for rubbish or goods ◇ *verb* (**binning, binned**) **1** put in a bin **2** throw away

binary *adj* made up of two • **binary system** *noun* a mathematical system in which numbers are expressed by two digits only, 1 and 0

bind *verb* (**binding, bound**) **1** tie up or tie together **2** make (someone) feel strongly connected (to) **3** make (someone) promise • **binding** *noun* **1** anything that binds **2** the cover, stitching, *etc* which holds a book together

binge *noun* a spell of over-eating or drinking too much ◇ *verb* eat and drink too much

bingo *noun* a popular gambling game using numbers

binoculars *plural noun* a device for looking at distant objects, using both eyes

biodegradable *adj* able to be broken down naturally by bacteria

biodiversity *noun* the fact that there is a healthy variety of animal and plant life in an area

biography *noun* (*plural* **biographies**) a book about someone's life • **biographer** *noun* someone who writes a biography • **biographical** *adj*

biology *noun* the study of living things • **biological** *adj* • **biologist** *noun*

biopsy *noun* (*plural* **biopsies**) an examination of diseased cells carried out to identify or assess the disease

bipartisan *adj* involving people from two groups working together

biped *noun, formal* an animal with two feet, *eg* a bird

birch *noun* (*plural* **birches**) **1** a type of hardwood tree **2** a bundle of birch twigs used for beating as a punishment ◇ *verb* beat with a birch

bird *noun* a feathered egg-laying creature, most species of which can fly • **bird of prey** *noun* a bird (*eg* a hawk) that kills and eats small animals or birds • **bird's-eye view** *noun* a good view of something from above • **bird-watching** *noun* the study of birds in their natural surroundings • **get the bird** *slang* be booed or hissed at

birdie *noun* a score of one stroke under par for a hole in golf

biretta *noun* a square cap worn by Roman Catholic clergy

biriyani *noun* an Indian dish of spiced rice

birl *verb, Scot* spin round; whirl

Biro *noun, trademark* a type of ballpoint pen

birth *noun* the very beginning of someone's life • **birthday** *noun* **1** the day on which someone is born **2** the date of this day each year • **birthmark** *noun* a mark on the body from birth • **birthright** *noun* a right that someone may claim because of their parentage

biscuit *noun* dough baked hard in small cakes

bisect *verb* cut into two equal parts

bisexual *adj & noun* **1** (a person who is) sexually attracted to both males and females **2** (an animal) having both male and female sex organs

bishop *noun* a high-ranking member of the clergy in the Roman Catholic Church and the Church of England • **bishopric** *noun* the district ruled by a bishop

bison *noun* (*plural* **bison**) a large wild ox with shaggy hair and a fatty hump

bisque /bisk/ *noun* a rich shellfish soup

bistro /bee-stroh/ *noun* (*plural* **bistros**) a small informal restaurant

bit¹ *noun* **1** a small piece or amount **2** a small tool for boring **3** the part of the bridle that a horse holds in its mouth **4** *comput* the smallest unit of information • **bitty** *adj* piecemeal, scrappy • **a bit** to a small extent; a little: *I feel a bit tired* • **bit by bit** gradually • **do your bit** do your required share • **to bits** apart, in pieces

bit² *past tense of* **bite**

bitch *noun* (*plural* **bitches**) **1** *slang* a term of abuse for a woman **2** a female dog, wolf, *etc*

bitchy *adj* of a woman: spiteful, malicious • **bitchily** *adv* • **bitchiness** *noun*

bite *verb* (**biting**, **bit**, **bitten**) grip, cut or tear with the teeth ◇ *noun* **1** a grip with the teeth **2** a part or amount bitten off **3** a wound caused by an animal's or insect's bite **4** a fish's nibble at an angler's bait

bitmap *noun, comput* a method of screen display where each pixel is assigned one or more bits of memory ◇ *verb* (**bitmapping**, **bitmapped**) • **bitmapped** *adj* • **bitmapping** *noun*

bitten *past participle of* **bite**

bitter *adj* **1** unpleasant to the taste; sour **2** harsh: *bitter cold* **3** angry about something disappointing or unfair; resentful • **bitterly** *adv* • **bitterness** *noun* • **bittersweet** *adj* happy or pleasant in some respects and sad or unpleasant in others

bittern *noun* a bird resembling a heron

bitty *see* **bit¹**

bitumen *noun* tar used for road surfaces

bivouac *noun* an overnight camp outdoors without a tent ◇ *verb* (**bivouacking**, **bivouacked**) sleep outdoors without a tent

bi-weekly *adj* happening twice a week or once every two weeks

bizarre adj odd, strange • **bizarrely** adv

blab verb (**blabbing, blabbed**) **1** talk a lot **2** let out a secret

black adj of the darkest possible colour ◇ noun the darkest possible colour • **black-and-blue** adj badly bruised • **blackball** verb exclude from (a club etc); ostracize • **black belt** noun an award for a high level of skill in martial arts • **black economy** noun unofficial business or trade, not declared for tax • **black eye** noun a bruised area round the eye as a result of a blow • **blackhead** noun a small black spot on the skin • **black hole** noun a region in space with such a strong gravitational pull that nothing can escape from it • **black ice** noun a thin transparent layer of ice on a road etc • **blackleg** noun someone who works when other workers are on strike • **black market** noun illegal or dishonest buying and selling • **black pudding** noun sausage made from pig's blood • **black sheep** noun someone who is considered a failure or outsider in a group • **black tie** noun formal evening dress • **black widow** noun a very poisonous American spider, the female of which often eats her mate • **black out** become unconscious

blackberry noun (plural **blackberries**) a blackish-purple soft fruit that grows on a prickly stem

blackbird noun a medium-sized thrush-like bird, the male of which is black

blackboard noun a dark-coloured board for writing on in chalk

blackcurrant noun a small round black fruit

blacken verb **1** make black or dark **2** dishonour, defame: blackening his name

blackguard /blag-ahd/ noun, old a dishonourable or wicked person

blacklist noun a list of people to be refused credit, jobs, etc ◇ verb put on a blacklist

blackmail noun the crime of threatening to reveal secrets unless money is paid ◇ verb threaten by blackmail • **blackmailer** noun

blackout noun **1** total darkness caused by putting out or covering all lights **2** a temporary loss of consciousness

blacksmith noun someone who makes or repairs iron goods, esp horseshoes

bladder noun the organ in which urine collects in the body • **bladderwrack** noun a common seaweed with air bladders on its strands

blade noun **1** the cutting part of a knife, sword, etc **2** a leaf of grass or wheat

blag verb (**blagging, blagged**) slang scrounge, get for nothing: blagging his way into the club

blame verb find fault with; consider responsible for something bad ◇ noun fault; responsibility for something bad • **blameless** adj • **blameworthy** adj deserving blame

blancmange /bluh-monzh/ noun a jelly-like pudding made with milk

bland adj **1** mild, not strong or sharp: bland taste **2** uninteresting or unexciting; dull

blandishments plural noun flattering words or acts

blank adj **1** clear, unmarked: blank sheet of paper **2** expressionless: a blank look ◇ noun **1** an empty space **2** a cartridge without a bullet • **blank verse** noun non-rhyming poetry in a metre of 5 feet per line

blanket noun **1** a bedcovering of wool etc **2** a widespread, soft covering: blanket of snow ◇ adj covering a group of things: a blanket agreement ◇ verb cover widely or thickly

• **blanket bombing** noun bombing from the air over a widespread area

blare verb sound unpleasantly loud ◇ noun a loud unpleasant sound, eg on a trumpet

blarney noun flattery or persuasive talk

blasé /blah-zeh/ adj not impressed or concerned, esp because of being already familiar with something

blaspheme verb 1 speak irreverently of a god 2 swear, curse • **blasphemer** noun • **blasphemous** adj • **blasphemy** noun

blast noun 1 a sudden strong gust of wind 2 an explosion or its force 3 a loud note, eg on a trumpet ◇ verb 1 break (stones, a bridge, etc) by explosion 2 produce a loud noise 3 formal cause (plants) to wither ◇ exclam damn! • **blast furnace** noun a furnace into which hot air is blown, used in iron-smelting • **blast-off** noun the moment of the launching of a rocket • **at full blast** as quickly, strongly, etc as possible

blatant adj very obvious and often shameless: blatant lie • **blatantly** adv

blaze noun 1 a bright flame 2 a large destructive fire ◇ verb 1 burn with a strong flame 2 throw out a strong light

blazer noun a light jacket often worn as part of a uniform

blazon verb 1 make known publicly 2 display openly

bleach noun a strong chemical substance used for cleaning, whitening clothes, etc ◇ verb whiten or remove the colour from

bleak adj 1 giving little hope of success or survival 2 exposed to harsh weather • **bleakly** adv • **bleakness** noun

bleary adj (**blearier**, **bleariest**) of eyes: tired and inflamed • **blearily** adv

bleat verb 1 cry like a sheep 2 complain in an irritating or whining way ◇ noun 1 a sheep's cry 2 an irritating whine

bleed verb (**bleeding**, **bled**) 1 lose blood 2 draw blood from • **bleeding** noun a flow of blood

bleep noun a high-pitched intermittent sound ◇ verb give out such a sound

blemish noun (plural **blemishes**) 1 a stain 2 a fault or flaw ◇ verb 1 stain 2 spoil

blend verb mix together ◇ noun a mixture • **blender** noun an electric machine that mixes or liquidizes food

bless verb 1 wish happiness to 2 make happy 3 make holy • **blessed** or **blest** adj 1 happy or fortunate 2 made holy; consecrated • **blessing** noun 1 a wish or prayer for happiness 2 a source of happiness or relief: the extra money was a blessing to them • **blessing in disguise** something unexpectedly useful or beneficial

blether verb, Scot 1 chatter 2 talk nonsense

blight noun 1 a disease that makes plants wither 2 a cause of harm or destruction ◇ verb destroy

blimp noun a small airship used for observation, advertising, etc

blind adj unable to see ◇ noun 1 a window screen 2 a deception or trick ◇ verb 1 make blind 2 dazzle • **blind alley** noun 1 a street open only at one end 2 a method or process that produces no useful result • **blindfold** adj with the eyes bandaged or covered, so as not to see ◇ verb apply a blindfold to • **blindman's buff** noun a game in which a blindfold person tries to catch others • **blindness** noun

bling noun, slang showy jewellery

blink verb 1 close the eyes for a moment 2 shine intermittently ◇ noun the action of blinking

• **blinkers** *plural noun* pieces of leather over a horse's eyes to prevent it seeing in any direction except in front

blip *noun* a short interruption or pause in a regular pattern

bliss *noun* very great happiness • **blissful** *adj*

blister *noun* a thin bubble on the skin full of watery matter ◇ *verb* rise up in a blister

blithe *adj* happily unconcerned • **blithely** *adv*

blitz *noun* (*plural* **blitzes**) **1** an air attack **2** a sudden violent attack

blizzard *noun* a fierce storm of wind and snow

bloated *adj* swollen, puffed out • **bloater** *noun* a type of smoked herring

blob *noun* **1** a drop of liquid **2** a round spot

bloc /blok/ *noun* an alliance of countries for trade *etc*

block *noun* **1** a large heavy piece of wood, stone, *etc* with a regular shape **2** a connected group of buildings **3** an obstruction: *road block* **4** an engraved piece of wood or metal for printing **5** *hist* the piece of wood on which people were beheaded ◇ *verb* prevent from making progress; hinder • **blockbuster** *noun, informal* a highly successful film, book, *etc* • **blockhead** *noun* a stupid person • **block letters** *plural noun* capital letters

blockade *verb* surround a fort or country so that food *etc* cannot reach it ◇ *noun* the surrounding of a place in this way

blockage *noun* something that causes an obstruction

blog *noun, comput* short for **weblog** ◇ *verb* (**blogging, blogged**) write a weblog • **blogger** *noun* • **blogging** *noun*

bloke *noun, Brit informal* a man

blond *adj* **1** of a man's hair: light-coloured **2** of a man: with light-coloured hair

blonde *adj* **1** of a woman's hair: light-coloured **2** of a woman: with light-coloured hair ◇ *noun* a woman with light-coloured hair

blood *noun* **1** the red liquid that flows in the bodies of human beings and animals **2** someone's descent or parentage: *royal blood* • **blood donor** *noun* someone who gives blood that is stored and given to others in transfusions *etc* • **blood group** *noun* any one of the types into which human blood is divided • **bloodhound** *noun* a breed of large dog with a good sense of smell • **bloodless** *adj* without bloodshed: *bloodless revolution* • **bloodshed** *noun* violent loss of life; slaughter • **bloodshot** *adj* of eyes: inflamed with blood • **bloodthirsty** *adj* eager to kill • **blood vessel** *noun* a vein or artery in which the blood circulates

bloody *adj* (**bloodier, bloodiest**) **1** covered with blood **2** extremely violent **3** *informal* used to describe something annoying • **bloodily** *adv*

bloom *verb* **1** of a plant: produce flowers **2** be in good health ◇ *noun* **1** a flower **2** a rosy colour **3** freshness **4** a powder on the skin of fresh fruits

bloomers *plural noun* **1** women's loose underpants with legs gathered above the knee **2** *hist* a woman's outfit of a jacket, skirt and baggy knee-length trousers

blossom *noun* **1** a flower **2** the flowers on a fruit tree ◇ *verb* **1** produce flowers **2** develop or flourish

blot *noun* **1** a spot of ink **2** a stain ◇ *verb* (**blotting, blotted**) **1** stain **2** dry (writing) with blotting paper • **blotting paper** *noun* thick paper for absorbing spilled or excess ink • **blot out** remove from sight or memory

blotch *noun* (*plural* **blotches**) a spot

or patch of colour *etc* ◇ *verb* mark with blotches • **blotched** *adj* • **blotchy** *adj*

blotto *adj, Brit slang* drunk

blouse *noun* a loose piece of clothing for the upper body

blouson /bloo-zonh/ *noun* a loose-fitting blouse gathered at the waist

blow *noun* 1 a hard stroke or knock, *eg* with the fist 2 *informal* a sudden piece of bad luck ◇ *verb* (**blowing**, **blew**, **blown**) 1 of wind: move around 2 force air out of your mouth 3 play (a wind instrument) by forcing air from your mouth into it 4 breathe hard or with difficulty • **blowfly** *noun* a fly that lays its eggs in dead flesh • **blowlamp** *or* **blowtorch** *noun* a tool for aiming a very hot flame at a particular spot • **blowy** *adj* windy • **blow over** pass and be forgotten • **blow up** 1 destroy by explosion 2 fill with air 3 enlarge (a photograph)

BLT *abbrev* bacon, lettuce and tomato (sandwich)

blubber *noun* the fat of whales and other sea animals

bludgeon *verb* cause serious injury to by beating with a heavy object

blue *noun* the colour of a clear sky ◇ *adj* 1 of this colour 2 *informal* unhappy, depressed 3 containing sexual material: *blue film* • **bluebell** *noun* 1 the wild hyacinth 2 in Scotland, the harebell • **blue blood** *noun* royal or aristocratic blood • **bluebottle** *noun* a large fly with a blue abdomen • **bluechip** *adj* of a business company: reliable for investment; prestigious • **Blue Peter** *noun* a blue flag with white centre, raised when a ship is about to sail • **blueprint** *noun* a plan of work to be done • **out of the blue** unexpectedly • **the blues** 1 slow simple music with a sad theme that originated in the black communities of 1920s America 2 low spirits, depression

bluff *adj* 1 rough and cheerful in manner 2 frank, outspoken ◇ *verb* try to deceive by pretending self-confidence ◇ *noun* 1 a steep cliff overlooking the sea or a river 2 deception, trickery

blunder *verb* make a bad mistake ◇ *noun* a bad mistake

blunderbuss *noun* (*plural* **blunderbusses**) *hist* a short handgun with a trumpet-shaped barrel

blunt *adj* 1 having an edge or point that is not sharp 2 honest or direct to the point of rudeness ◇ *verb* make less sharp or less painful • **bluntly** *adv* frankly, straightforwardly • **bluntness** *noun*

blur *noun* something seen or remembered unclearly ◇ *verb* (**blurring**, **blurred**) make unclear • **blurred** *adj*

blurb *noun* the publisher's brief description of a book, printed on the jacket

blurt *verb*: **blurt out** speak suddenly and without thinking

blush *noun* (*plural* **blushes**) 1 a red glow on the face caused by embarrassment *etc* 2 a reddish glow ◇ *verb* go red in the face

bluster *verb* 1 blow strongly 2 boast loudly ◇ *noun* 1 a blasting wind 2 empty boasting

BMA *abbrev* British Medical Association, the organization that controls the UK medical profession

BMus *abbrev* Bachelor of Music

boa *noun* a long scarf of fur or feathers • **boa constrictor** *noun* a large snake that kills its prey by winding itself round it and crushing it

boar *noun* 1 a wild pig 2 a male domestic pig

board *noun* 1 a sheet of wood 2 a group of people who run a business: *board of directors* 3 stiff card used to bind books 4 food: *bed and board* ◇ *verb* 1 cover with boards 2 supply with food in return for payment **3** get on (a ship, aeroplane, *etc*) ● **boarder** *noun* someone who receives food and lodging ● **boarding house** *noun* a private house where paying guests receive meals and accommodation ● **boarding school** *noun* a school in which the pupils live all or part of the time

boast *verb* speak too proudly about yourself; brag ◇ *noun* something said in a boasting manner ● **boastful** *adj* fond of boasting ● **boastfully** *adv* ● **boastfulness** *noun*

boat *noun* **1** a vehicle that travels on water **2** a boat-shaped dish: *sauce-boat*

boater *noun* a straw hat with a flat top and a brim

boatswain *or* **bosun** /boh-sun/ *noun* an officer who looks after a ship's boats, rigging, *etc*

bob[1] *verb* (**bobbing, bobbed**) **1** move up and down rapidly **2** cut (hair) to about neck level ◇ *noun* a bobbed haircut

bob[2] *noun* a bobsleigh

bobbin *noun* a reel or spool on which thread is wound

bobble[1] *noun* **1** a small ball of tufted wool **2** a small ball on the surface of fabric

bobble[2] *verb* bob continuously ◇ *noun* a bobbing motion

bobby *noun* (*plural* **bobbies**) *Brit informal* a police officer

bobsleigh *noun* a long sledge with a thin body, used for racing

bode *verb*: **bode well** *or* **bode ill** be a good or bad sign

bodhisattva /bo-di-*sat*-vuh/ *noun* a future Buddha

bodhran /bo-*ran*/ *noun* a hand-held Irish or Scottish drum, beaten with a short stick

bodice *noun* the close-fitting part of

a woman's or girl's dress above the waist

bodkin *noun, old* a large blunt needle

body *noun* (*plural* **bodies**) **1** the whole of a human being or animal, or the torso only **2** a corpse **3** the main part of anything **4** a mass of people **5** *informal* a bodystocking ● **bodily** *adj* of the body ◇ *adv* with the whole body off the ground: *carried bodily out of the room* ● **bodyguard** *noun* someone whose job is to protect another person from physical attack ● **body language** *noun* communication by means of conscious or unconscious gestures, attitudes, facial expressions, *etc* ● **bodystocking** *noun* a one-piece woman's undergarment ● **bodyswerve** *verb, informal* avoid deliberately ● **bodywarmer** *noun* a padded sleeveless jacket

boffin *noun, informal* a scientist

bog *noun* **1** a marsh **2** *slang* a toilet ● **boggy** *adj* marshy ● **bog-standard** *adj* of the ordinary kind or lowest grade ● **bog down** prevent from making progress

bogey[1] *noun* something greatly feared

bogey[2] *noun* a score of one stroke over par for a hole in golf

boggle *verb* be astonished at

bogus *adj* false

bohemian *noun* someone who lives outside social conventions, *esp* an artist or writer ◇ *adj* of the lifestyle of a bohemian

boil *verb* **1** of a liquid: reach the temperature at which it turns to vapour **2** bubble up owing to heat ◇ *noun* a kind of inflamed swelling ● **boiling** *adj* extremely or unpleasantly hot ● **boiling point** *noun* the temperature at which a liquid turns to vapour (*eg* for water, 100°C)

boiler *noun* a container in which

water is heated or steam is produced

boisterous *adj* noisy and rough • **boisterously** *adv* • **boisterousness** *noun*

bold *adj* **1** full of courage; daring **2** full of defiance or impudence; cheeky **3** striking: *bold colours* **4** of printing type: thick and clear • **boldly** *adv* • **boldness** *noun*

bolero /buh-*lair*-roh/ *noun* **1** a traditional Spanish dance **2** a very short, open jacket

bollard *noun* **1** a short post on a street used for traffic control **2** a post to which ropes are fastened on a ship or quay

bollocks *plural noun, slang* **1** the testicles **2** rubbish, nonsense • **bollocking** *noun, slang* a severe reprimand

Bolshevik *noun* **1** *hist* a member of the Extreme Socialist Party in revolutionary Russia **2** *derog* a communist

bolshy *adj* (**bolshier, bolshiest**) *informal* awkward, uncooperative • **bolshiness** *noun*

bolster *noun* a long cylindrical pillow or cushion • **bolster (up)** support

bolt *noun* **1** a small sliding metal bar used to fasten a door *etc* **2** a large screw with a flat end **3** a roll of cloth ◇ *verb* **1** fasten with a bolt **2** swallow (food) hurriedly **3** rush away, escape • **bolt upright** sitting with a very straight back

bomb *noun* **1** a case containing explosive or other harmful material thrown, dropped or timed to go off automatically **2** (**the bomb**) a nuclear bomb ◇ *verb* drop bombs on • **bomber** *noun* **1** an aeroplane built for bombing **2** someone who plants bombs • **bombshell** *noun* **1** a startling piece of news **2** a stunningly attractive woman

bombard *verb* **1** attack with artillery **2** overwhelm (with): *bombarded with letters* • **bombardment** *noun*

bombast *noun* pompous language • **bombastic** *adj* using pompous language

bona fide /boh-nuh *fai*-deh/ *adj* real, genuine: *bona fide excuse*

bonanza *noun* **1** an unexpected and sudden source of wealth **2** a large amount of something desirable

bond *noun* **1** something that brings people together: *music was a bond between them* **2** an investment that pays a fixed rate of return, or the certificate given to the investor **3** a rope or chain used for tying someone or fastening something

bondage *noun* **1** sexual practices that involve tying up one of the participants **2** slavery

bone *noun* **1** a hard material forming the skeleton of animals **2** one of the connected pieces of a skeleton: *the hip bone* ◇ *verb* take the bones out of (meat *etc*)

bonfire *noun* a large fire in the open air

bonk *verb* **1** hit with a hollow sound **2** *slang* have sex

bon mot /bon *moh*/ *noun* a saying

bonnet *noun* **1** the hinged covering over a vehicle engine **2** a woman's decorative hat that fastens under the chin

bonny *adj* good-looking; pretty

bonsai /*bon*-zai/ *noun* a miniature or dwarf tree created by special pruning

bonus *noun* (*plural* **bonuses**) **1** an extra payment in addition to wages **2** something desirable extra

bony *adj* (**bonier, boniest**) **1** full of bones **2** unattractively thin; skinny **3** made of bone or bone-like substance

boo *verb* make a sound of disapproval ◇ *noun* a sound of disapproval

boob *noun* **1** *informal* a mistake **2** *slang* a woman's breast

booby *noun* (*plural* **boobies**) an idiot • **booby prize** *noun* a prize for the person who is last in a competition • **booby trap** *noun* a device hidden or disguised as something harmless, intended to injure the first person to come near it

boogie *verb* dance to pop music ◇ *noun* dancing to pop music

book *noun* 1 a number of pages bound together 2 a written work which has appeared, or is intended to appear, in the form of a book ◇ *verb* order (places *etc*) beforehand • **book group** *noun* a group of people who meet regularly to discuss a book • **book-keeping** *noun* the keeping of accounts • **booklet** *noun* a small paperback book • **bookmaker** *noun* someone who takes bets and pays winnings • **bookmark** *noun* 1 a strip of card or leather used to mark a particular page in a book 2 a record of the address of a website • **bookworm** *noun* 1 an avid reader 2 a grub that eats holes in books

bookie *noun*, *informal* a bookmaker

boom *verb* 1 make a hollow sound or roar 2 increase in prosperity, success, *etc* ◇ *noun* 1 a loud, hollow sound 2 a rush or increase of trade, prosperity, *etc*: *oil boom/property boom* 3 a pole along which a sail is stretched

boomerang *noun* a curved piece of wood that when thrown returns to the thrower, a traditional hunting weapon of Australian Aboriginals

boon *noun* something to be grateful for; a blessing

boor *noun* an annoyingly rough or rude person • **boorish** *adj*

boost *verb* increase or improve (something): *boost the sales figures* ◇ *noun* an increase

booster *noun* 1 a device for increasing the power of a machine *etc* 2 the first of several stages of a rocket

boot *noun* 1 a heavy shoe covering the foot and lower part of the leg 2 *Brit* a place for stowing luggage in a car 3 *comput* the starting of a computer from its start-up programs 4 a kick ◇ *verb* kick • **bootee** *noun* a knitted boot for a baby • **boot up** *comput* start (a computer) by running its start-up programs • **to boot** in addition, as well

booth *noun* 1 a covered stall, *eg* at a market 2 a small compartment for telephoning, voting, *etc*

bootleg *adj* of alcohol, recorded music, *etc*: made illegally • **bootlegger** *noun* a dealer in illegal drink, recordings, *etc*

booty *noun* valuable objects taken in war; plunder

booze *noun*, *slang* alcoholic drink ◇ *verb* drink a lot of alcohol • **booze-up** *noun* an occasion when a lot of alcohol is drunk

border *noun* 1 the edge of anything 2 the boundary of a country 3 a flowerbed in a garden ◇ *verb* (with **on**) be near to: *bordering on the absurd* • **borderline** *adj* midway between one category and another, *esp* between being considered satisfactory or unsatisfactory

bore¹ *verb* 1 make a hole by piercing 2 be tiresome to: *this book bores me* ◇ *noun* 1 a pierced hole 2 the size across the tube of a gun 3 a tiresome person or thing 4 a wave that rushes up a river mouth at high tide • **boring** *adj*

bore² *past tense of* **bear**

boredom *noun* lack of interest or enthusiasm

born *adj* by birth, natural: *a born actor* • **be born** 1 of a baby: come out of the mother's womb 2 come into existence

Do not confuse: **born** and **borne**

borne *past participle of* **bear**

borough /buh-ruh/ *noun* **1** *hist* a town with special privileges granted by royal charter **2** a town that elects Members of Parliament

borrow *verb* have or use temporarily with permission from the owner

borsch or **borscht** /bawsh/ *noun* an East European beetroot soup

borzoi *noun* a breed of long-haired dog

bosh *noun, old* nonsense

bosom *noun* **1** breasts **2** the midst or centre: *bosom of her family* ◇ *adj* of a friend: close, intimate

boss *noun* (*plural* **bosses**) someone in charge; a manager or supervisor ◇ *verb* order about in a high-handed way

bossy *adj* (**bossier, bossiest**) tending to boss others; domineering • **bossily** *adv* • **bossiness** *noun*

bosun *see* **boatswain**

botany *noun* the study of plants • **botanic** or **botanical** *adj* • **botanist** *noun* someone who studies botany • **botanic garden** *noun* a large public garden containing plants and trees from different countries

botch *verb* do, deal with, or repair clumsily ◇ *noun* a badly done repair or piece of work

both *adj & pronoun* the two, the one and the other: *we're both going to Paris/both the men are dead* ◇ *adv* equally, together: *both willing and able*

bother *verb* **1** be a nuisance to: *stop bothering me!* **2** take time or trouble over: *don't bother with the dishes* ◇ *noun* trouble, inconvenience

bothy *noun* (*plural* **bothies**) **1** in Scotland, a hut to give shelter to hillwalkers **2** a simply furnished hut for farm workers

Botox treatment *noun, trademark* a procedure where a substance is injected into the skin to make wrinkles less apparent

bottle *noun* a hollow narrow-necked container for holding liquids ◇ *verb* put in a bottle • **bottle bank** *noun* a container for depositing glass for recycling • **bottle up** keep in, hold back (feelings)

bottleneck *noun* **1** a narrow part of a road leading to become crowded with traffic **2** a stage in a process where progress is held up

bottom *noun* **1** the lowest part or underside of anything **2** the buttocks • **bottomless** *adj* extremely deep

botulism *noun* food-poisoning caused by bacteria in infected tinned food *etc*

boudoir /bood-wah/ *noun* a lady's bedroom or private room

bough /bow/ *noun* a branch of a tree

bought *past form of* **buy**

boulder *noun* a large stone

boulevard *noun* a wide street lined with trees

bounce *verb* **1** rise into the air after hitting the ground *etc* **2** make (a ball *etc*) do this **3** of a cheque: be sent back because of insufficient money in the account to pay it ◇ *noun* a rising into the air after hitting the ground • **bouncing** *adj* full of life; lively • **bounce back** recover after a setback or trouble

bouncer *noun* someone employed to force troublemakers to leave a club *etc*

bound¹ *noun* **1** a leap, a jump **2** (**bounds**) borders, limits ◇ *verb* **1** jump, leap **2** enclose, surround • **boundless** *adj* having no limit, vast • **bound for** intending to go to, or on the way to • **bound to** certain to • **out of bounds** beyond the permitted limits

bound[2] *past form of* **bind**

boundary *noun* (*plural* **boundaries**) **1** an edge, a limit **2** a line *etc* marking an edge

bountiful *or* **bounteous** *adj* **1** existing in large amounts; plentiful **2** giving a lot; generous

bounty *noun* (*plural* **bounties**) **1** a plentiful supply **2** generosity in giving money or help • **bounty hunter** *noun* someone who tracks down people wanted by the authorities to collect the rewards offered

bouquet /boo-*keh*/ *noun* **1** a bunch of flowers **2** a scent, *eg* of wine • **bouquet garni** *noun* a bunch of herbs put in a stew *etc*

bourbon /*bur*-bun/ *noun* American whisky made from maize

bourgeois /*bawzh*-wah/ *adj* of the middle class • **bourgeoisie** *noun* the middle class

bout *noun* **1** a round in a contest **2** an attack of illness; a spell: *bout of flu*

boutique *noun* a small shop selling fashionable clothes *etc*

bovine *adj* **1** of or like cattle **2** stupid

bow[1] /bow/ *verb* **1** bend **2** nod the head or bend the body in greeting **3** give in: *bow to pressure* **4** weigh (someone) down ◇ *noun* **1** a bending of the head or body **2** the front part of a ship

bow[2] /boh/ *noun* **1** anything in the shape of a curve or arch **2** a weapon for shooting arrows, made of a stick of springy wood bent by a string **3** a looped knot **4** a wooden rod with horsehair stretched along it, by which the strings of a violin *etc* are played • **bow-legged** *adj* having legs curving outwards • **bow window** *noun* a window built in a curve

bowdlerize *verb* cut out large passages from (a piece of writing), *esp* spoiling it

bowel *noun* **1** intestine **2** (**bowels**) the innermost or deepest part of anything: *in the bowels of the earth*

bower /*bow*-uh/ *noun* a shady spot in a garden

bowl *noun* **1** a basin for holding liquids **2** a heavy wooden ball, used in skittles *etc* **3** (**bowls**) a game played on a green with specially weighted bowls ◇ *verb* **1** play bowls **2** move speedily like a bowl **3** *cricket* throw the ball towards the wicket **4** *cricket* put (a player) out by knocking the wicket with the ball • **bowl over 1** knock down **2** surprise greatly

bowler *noun* **1** someone who plays bowls **2** someone who bowls in cricket **3** a man's hat with a rounded top

box *noun* (*plural* **boxes**) **1** a case of wood, card, *etc* for holding anything **2** a panel of printed information, or a place on a printed page for filling in information **3** an evergreen shrub or small tree used for hedging **4** an enclosure of private seats in a theatre ◇ *verb* **1** put in a box **2** confine in a small space **3** engage in the sport of boxing **4** punch: *I'll box your ears!* • **box office** *noun* an office where theatre tickets *etc* may be bought

boxer *noun* **1** someone who boxes as a sport **2** a breed of large smooth-haired dog with a head like a bulldog's • **boxer shorts** *plural noun* loose-fitting men's underpants

boxing *noun* the sport of fighting with the fists wearing padded gloves • **Boxing Day** *noun* the first weekday after Christmas Day

boy *noun* **1** a male child **2** *old* a male servant • **boyfriend** *noun* a regular male companion, especially in a romantic relationship • **boyhood** *noun* the time of being a boy • **boyish** *adj* • **boyishly** *adv*

boycott *verb* refuse to attend (an event) or do business with (a company, nation, *etc*) ◇ *noun* a refusal to attend or do business

bpi *abbrev, comput* bits per inch

bps *abbrev, comput* bits per second

bra *noun, informal* an article of women's underwear for supporting the breasts

brace *noun* **1** a piece of wire fitted over teeth to straighten them **2** a pair of pheasant, grouse, *etc* when shot **3** a carpenter's tool for boring **4** (**braces**) shoulder-straps for holding up trousers ◇ *verb* give support to • **brace yourself 1** press your body against a hard surface to prepare for an impact **2** prepare to hear bad news

bracelet *noun* a circular ornament for the wrist

bracing *adj* making you feel healthy and full of energy

bracken *noun* a coarse kind of fern

bracket *noun* **1** a support for something fastened to a wall **2** each of a pair of written or printed marks, eg ( ), [ ], used to group together several words **3** a grouping or category: *in the same age bracket* ◇ *verb* **1** enclose in brackets **2** group together

brackish *adj* of water: rather salty

brag *verb* (**bragging, bragged**) boast ◇ *noun* a boast

braggart *noun* someone vain and boastful

braid *verb* plait (the hair) ◇ *noun* **1** a plait of hair **2** decorative ribbon used as trimming

braille /brehl/ *noun* a system of raised marks on paper which blind people can read by feeling

brain *noun* the part of the body that is the centre of feeling and thinking, inside the skull ◇ *verb* hit hard on the head • **brainchild** *noun* something successful invented or thought up by a particular person • **brainwashing** *noun* forceful persuasion or training that makes someone have particular views • **brainwave** *noun* a good idea • **brainy** *adj, informal* clever

braise *verb* stew (meat) in a small amount of liquid

brake *noun* a part of a vehicle used for stopping or slowing down ◇ *verb* slow down by using the brake(s)

bramble *noun* **1** the blackberry bush **2** its fruit

bran *noun* the inner husks of wheat *etc*, separated from flour after grinding

branch *noun* (*plural* **branches**) **1** an arm-like limb of a tree **2** one of several shops or offices owned by a large company or organization ◇ *verb* go out from a central line or path • **branch out** become involved in additional new activities

brand *noun* **1** a make of goods with a special trademark **2** a permanent mark made by a red-hot iron ◇ *verb* **1** mark with a brand **2** mark with disgrace: *branded as a thief* • **brand-new** *adj* absolutely new

brandish *verb* wave (a weapon *etc*) about

brandy *noun* (*plural* **brandies**) an alcoholic spirit made by distilling grape juice

brass *noun* (*plural* **brasses**) **1** metal that is an alloy of copper and zinc **2** *music* brass wind instruments ◇ *adj* **1** made of brass **2** playing brass musical instruments: *brass band* • **brassy** *adj* **1** like brass **2** of a woman's voice or appearance: unrefined, coarse

brassière *noun, formal* a bra

brat *noun* **1** a badly behaved or unpleasant child **2** *derog* any child

bravado /bruh-*vah*-doh/ *noun* a silly or unconvincing show of bravery

brave *adj* ready to meet danger, pain, *etc* without showing fear; courageous, noble ◇ *verb* face or meet (something) boldly and without fear

◇ *noun, hist* a Native American warrior • **bravely** *adv* • **bravery** *noun*

bravo /brah-*voh*/ *exclam* well done!

bravura /bruh-*vyaw*-ruh/ *noun* impressive confidence or courage; spirit

brawl *noun* a noisy, wrestling fight ◇ *verb* fight in a noisy wrestling way

brawn *noun* muscle power • **brawny** *adj* big and strong

bray *noun* a donkey's cry ◇ *verb* make a donkey's cry

brazen *adj* 1 showing no shame or modesty: *brazen hussy* 2 of or like brass • **brazenly** *adv* • **brazen it out** face a difficult situation with bold impudence

brazier *noun* an iron basket for holding burning coals

brazil nut *noun* the large three-sided nut of a Brazilian tree

breach *noun* (*plural* **breaches**) 1 a place where a wall, fence, *etc* has been broken; a gap 2 a breaking of a law, a promise, *etc* ◇ *verb* make a gap or opening in • **breach of the peace** a breaking of the law by noisy, offensive behaviour

bread *noun* food that is a baked mixture of flour and water, *usu* risen with yeast • **breadwinner** *noun* someone who earns a living for a family

breadth *noun* 1 distance from side to side; width 2 impressive extent: *breadth of knowledge*

break *verb* (**breaking**, **broke**, **broken**) 1 (cause to) fall to pieces or apart 2 act against (a law, promise, *etc*) 3 interrupt (a silence) 4 tell (news) 5 soften the effect of (a fall) 6 cure (a habit) 7 of a boy's voice: drop to a deep male tone ◇ *noun* 1 an opening 2 a pause 3 *informal* a lucky chance • **breakable** *adj* • **breakage** *noun* 1 the act of breaking 2 something broken • **breakdown** *noun* 1 a division into parts 2 a collapse from nervous exhaustion *etc*

• **breaker** *noun* a large wave • **break-in** *noun* illegal forced entry of a house *etc* with intent to steal • **breakthrough** *noun* a sudden success after some effort • **breakwater** *noun* a barrier built to break the force of waves • **break down** 1 divide into parts 2 of an engine: fail 3 be overcome with crying or nervous exhaustion • **break in** 1 tame, train (a wild horse *etc*) 2 enter a place by force with the intention of stealing • **break into** enter (a place) by force with the intention of stealing • **break out** 1 appear suddenly 2 escape 3 (with **in**) become covered (with a rash *etc*) • **break up** 1 (cause to) fall to pieces or apart 2 end a relationship; split up

breakfast *noun* the first meal of the day ◇ *verb* eat this meal

bream *noun* a small silvery freshwater fish

breast *noun* 1 either of the milk-producing glands on a woman's body 2 the front part of a human or animal body between neck and belly; the chest 3 a part of a jacket or coat that covers the breast • **breastbone** *noun* the bone running down the middle of the breast • **breastplate** *noun* a piece of armour for the breast • **make a clean breast** make a full confession

breath *noun* 1 the air drawn into and then sent out from the lungs 2 an instance of breathing 3 a very slight breeze

Do not confuse: **breath** and **breathe**

breathalyser *noun* a device into which someone breathes to indicate the amount of alcohol in their blood

breathe *verb* (**breathing**, **breathed**) 1 draw in and send out air from the lungs 2 whisper

breather *noun, informal* a rest or pause

breathless adj 1 breathing very fast; panting 2 excited • **breathlessly** adv • **breathlessness** noun

breathtaking adj 1 extremely impressive 2 extremely fast • **breathtakingly** adv

bred past form of breed

breech noun the back part of the barrel of a gun • **breech birth** noun the birth of a baby feet first from the womb

breeches plural noun trousers reaching to just below the knee

breed verb (**breeding**, **bred**) 1 produce (children or a family) 2 mate and rear (animals) 3 cause: dirt breeds disease ◇ noun 1 a group of animals etc descended from the same ancestor 2 type, sort: a new breed of salesmen

breeding noun 1 act of producing or rearing animals 2 good manners; education and training

breeze noun a gentle wind

breezy adj (**breezier**, **breeziest**) 1 windy, gusty 2 full of energy; lively • **breezily** adv

brethren plural noun, old brothers

breve /breev/ noun a musical note (𝄺) equivalent to double a whole note or semibreve

brevity noun the use of only a few words to express something; conciseness

brew verb 1 make beer 2 make (tea etc) 3 be gathering or forming: there's trouble brewing 4 plan (something unpleasant): brewing mischief • **brewer** noun someone who brews beer

brewery noun (plural **breweries**) a place where beer is made

briar or **brier** noun 1 a wild rose 2 a heather plant whose wood is used for making tobacco pipes

bribe noun a gift of money etc given to persuade someone to do something ◇ verb give a bribe to • **bribery** noun

bric-à-brac /brik-uh-brak/ noun small odds and ends

brick noun 1 a block of baked clay for building 2 a toy building-block of wood etc

bride noun a woman who is about to be married, or is newly married • **bridal** adj of a bride or a wedding • **bridegroom** noun a man who is about to be married, or is newly married • **bridesmaid** noun an unmarried woman who attends the bride at a wedding

bridge¹ noun 1 a structure built to carry a road or railway line across a river etc 2 the captain's platform on a ship 3 the bony part of the nose 4 a thin piece of wood holding up the strings of a violin etc ◇ verb (**bridging**, **bridged**) 1 build a bridge over 2 extend from one end to the other; span

bridge² noun a card game for two pairs of players

bridle noun the harness on a horse's head to which the reins are attached ◇ verb 1 put a bridle on (a horse) 2 of a horse: toss the head indignantly 3 object or refuse angrily • **bridle path** noun a path for people on horses

Brie /bree/ noun a soft cheese with a yellowish centre and white rind

brief adj 1 lasting a short time 2 expressed in a few words only; concise ◇ noun a set of notes giving information or instructions, esp to a lawyer about a law case ◇ verb instruct or inform in advance • **briefly** adv • **in brief** in a few words

briefcase noun a slim case for carrying documents

briefs plural noun close-fitting underpants

brier another spelling of briar

brigade noun a large group of soldiers, usually two battalions

brigadier noun a senior army officer

brigand noun, old a robber

bright adj 1 full of light; shining 2 clever 3 cheerful

brighten verb make or become bright

brilliant adj 1 very clever 2 informal very good, excellent 3 sparkling • **brilliance** noun • **brilliantly** adv

brim noun 1 the edge of a cup etc: filled to the brim 2 the protruding lower edge of a hat or cap ◊ verb (**brimming**, **brimmed**) be full • **brimful** adj full to the brim

brimstone noun, old sulphur

brine noun salt water • **briny** adj

bring verb (**bringing**, **brought**) 1 fetch, lead or carry (to a place) 2 cause to exist or arrive: the medicine brings him relief • **bring about** cause • **bring home to** make (someone) realize (something) • **bring off** do (something) successfully • **bring to** bring back to consciousness • **bring up 1** rear, feed and educate: brought up three children single-handed 2 mention: I'll bring it up at the meeting 3 informal vomit

brink noun the edge of a cliff etc • **brinkmanship** noun the pursuit of a policy to the very edge of disaster • **on the brink of** almost at the point (of, on the verge of): on the brink of tears

brioche /bree-osh/ noun a rich bread made with egg dough

briquette /bri-ket/ noun a small brick of compressed charcoal etc used as fuel for barbecues

brisk adj 1 moving quickly: a brisk walk 2 lively and efficient: a brisk manner • **briskly** adv • **briskness** noun

bristle noun a short, stiff hair on an animal, a brush, etc ◊ verb 1 of hair or fur: stand on end 2 show anger and indignation: he bristled at my remark • **bristly** adj having bristles; rough

brittle adj hard but easily broken

broach verb 1 begin to talk about: broached the subject 2 begin using (eg a case of wine); open

broad adj 1 wide 2 covering many subjects or areas; extensive 3 of an accent etc: strong, obvious • **broaden** verb make or become broader • **broadly** adv

broadband noun a fast Internet connection provided via a dedicated cable, not an ordinary phone line

broadcast verb transmit (a programme etc) on radio or television ◊ noun a programme transmitted on radio or television

broadsheet noun a large-format newspaper reporting news extensively (compare with: **tabloid**)

broadside noun 1 a strong attack in an argument etc 2 a shot by all the guns on one side of a ship

brocade /brohk-ehd/ noun a silk cloth on which fine patterns are sewn

broccoli noun a hardy variety of cauliflower with small green or purple flower-heads

brochure /broh-shaw/ or /brohshuh/ noun a booklet giving details of available goods or services: holiday brochure

brogue¹ /brohg/ noun a strong shoe

brogue² /brohg/ noun a broad accent in speaking: Irish brogue

broil verb, US grill

broke past tense of **break** ◊ adj, informal having no money

broken past participle of **break**

broker noun someone who buys and sells stocks and shares for clients ◊ verb 1 act as a broker 2 negotiate on behalf of others: broker a deal

bromide noun 1 a chemical used as a sedative 2 a dull person 3 an overused expression; cliché **4** a black-and-white photographic print

bronchitis *noun* an illness affecting the windpipe, causing difficulty in breathing • **bronchial** *adj* having to do with the windpipe

bronco *noun* (*plural* **broncos**) *US* a half-tamed horse

brontosaurus *noun* a large plant-eating dinosaur with a long neck, now *usu* called an **apatosaurus**

bronze *noun* a metal that is an alloy of copper and tin ◇ *adj* of the dark yellowish-brown colour of bronze • **bronzed** *adj* suntanned

brooch /brohch/ *noun* (*plural* **brooches**) a piece of jewellery worn pinned to the clothing

brood *verb* **1** of a hen *etc*: sit on eggs **2** think anxiously for some time ◇ *noun* **1** a number of young birds hatched at one time **2** young animals or children of the same family

brook *noun* a small stream ◇ *verb* put up with; endure

broom *noun* **1** a long-handled brush for sweeping **2** a type of shrub with yellow flowers • **broomstick** *noun* the handle of a broom

Bros *abbrev* Brothers

broth *noun* soup, *esp* one made with vegetables

brothel *noun* a house where prostitution is practised

brother *noun* **1** a man or boy who has the same parents as another person **2** a male comrade • **brotherhood** *noun* **1** comradeship between men **2** a men's association • **brother-in-law** *noun* **1** the brother of someone's husband or wife **2** the husband of someone's sister or sister-in-law • **brotherly** *adj* of a brother, or showing the affection or comradeship of a brother

brought *past form of* **bring**

brow *noun* **1** a forehead **2** an eyebrow **3** the edge of a hill

browbeat *verb* bully

brown *noun* a dark colour made by mixing red and green ◇ *adj* **1** of this colour **2** *informal* suntanned • **brownfield site** *noun* an area of new building on a site on which the previous buildings have been demolished • **brownnose** *verb, slang* be insincerely eager to please someone in authority in order to get benefits; fawn

brownie *noun* **1** a helpful fairy or goblin **2** a Brownie Guide • **Brownie Guide** *noun* a junior member of the Guide Association

browse *verb* **1** glance through a range of books, shop merchandise, *etc* **2** feed on the shoots or leaves of plants • **browser** *noun* a computer program for searching for and managing data from the World Wide Web

bruise *noun* a discoloured area on the skin, the surface of fruit *etc*, where it has been hit ◇ *verb* cause bruises to appear on

brunch *noun* (*plural* **brunches**) a meal combining breakfast and lunch

brunette *noun* a woman with dark brown hair

brunt *noun*: bear *or* take the brunt take most of the strain or impact

brush *noun* (*plural* **brushes**) **1** a tool with tufts of bristles for smoothing hair, cleaning, painting, *etc* **2** a disagreement, a brief quarrel **3** the tail of a fox **4** undergrowth ◇ *verb* **1** tidy (hair) with a brush **2** remove by sweeping **3** touch lightly in passing • **brushwood** *noun* **1** broken branches, twigs, *etc* **2** undergrowth

brusque /broosk/ *adj* sharp in manner; rude • **brusquely** *adv* • **brusqueness** *noun*

Brussels sprouts *plural noun* vegetables that look like small cabbages

brut /broot/ *adj* of sparkling wine: dry

brutal *adj* extremely violent or cruel
• **brutality** *noun* • **brutally** *adv*

brute *noun* 1 an animal 2 a cruel person • **brute strength** *noun* pure physical strength • **brutish** *adj* extremely violent or cruel

BSc *abbrev* Bachelor of Science

BSE *abbrev* bovine spongiform encephalopathy, a brain disease of cattle

BST *abbrev* British Summer Time

BT *abbrev* British Telecom

bubble *noun* a thin ball of liquid blown out with air ◇ *verb* of liquid: rise in bubbles

bubbly *adj* (**bubblier**, **bubbliest**) 1 full of bubbles 2 lively, vivacious ◇ *noun, informal* champagne or sparkling wine

buccaneer *noun, old* a pirate

buck *noun* 1 a male deer, goat, hare or rabbit 2 *US informal* a dollar ◇ *verb* of a horse *etc*: attempt to throw a rider by rapid jumps into the air

bucket *noun* a container for water *etc*

buckle *noun* a clip for fastening straps or belts ◇ *verb* fasten with a buckle • **buckler** *noun* a small shield

buckshot *noun* large lead shot fired from a shotgun

buckwheat *noun* a plant whose seed is used to feed animals and is ground into flour

bucolic /byoo-*kol*-ik/ *adj* of the countryside; rural

bud *noun* a round part on a plant that develops into a flower or leaves ◇ *verb* (**budding**, **budded**) produce buds • **budding** *adj* showing signs of becoming: *budding author*

Buddhism *noun* a religion whose followers worship Buddha, the title of the 6th-century religious leader Gautama Siddhartha • **Buddhist** *noun & adj*

budge *verb* (**budging**, **budged**) move slightly; stir

budgerigar *noun* a kind of small parrot often kept as a pet

budget *noun* 1 a government plan for the year's spending 2 an amount of money available to spend, or any plan of future spending ◇ *verb* allow for in a budget: *the project has been budgeted for*

budgie *noun, informal* a budgerigar

buff *noun* 1 a light yellowish-brown colour 2 an enthusiast: *film buff* ◇ *verb* polish

buffalo *noun* (*plural* **buffaloes**) 1 a large Asian ox, used to pull heavy loads 2 the North American bison

buffer *noun* 1 something that lessens the force of a blow or collision 2 something that provides protection against possible unpleasantness

buffet¹ /*buf*-it/ *verb* knock about violently ◇ *noun* a violent impact

buffet² *noun* /*buuf*-eh/ a range of dishes set out at a party *etc* for people to serve themselves

buffoon *noun* a ridiculous person • **buffoonery** *noun*

bug *noun* 1 a small insect 2 a disease germ: *a tummy bug* 3 a tiny hidden microphone for recording conversations 4 a problem in a computer program causing errors in its execution ◇ *verb* (**bugging**, **bugged**) 1 conceal a microphone in (a room *etc*) 2 record with a hidden microphone 3 *informal* annoy or harass

bugbear *noun* something annoying

bugger *noun, taboo slang Brit* a general term of abuse ◇ *verb* 1 have anal intercourse with 2 *Brit slang* make a mess of; ruin

buggy *noun* (*plural* **buggies**) a child's pushchair

bugle *noun* a small military trumpet

• **bugler** noun someone who plays the bugle

build verb (**building, built**) 1 put together the parts of anything 2 cause to develop ◇ noun physique: a man of heavy build • **builder** noun • **built-up** adj of an area: containing houses and other buildings

building noun 1 a house or other structure with walls and a roof 2 the act or trade of building (houses etc) • **building society** noun an institution like a bank which accepts investments and whose main business is to lend people money to buy a house

bulb noun 1 the rounded part of the stem of an onion, tulip, etc , in which they store their food 2 a glass globe surrounding the element of an electric light • **bulbous** adj bulb-shaped

bulge noun a swelling ◇ verb (**bulging, bulged**) swell out

bulghur /bul-guh/ noun a kind of wheat

bulimia noun an eating disorder in which bingeing is followed by self-induced vomiting or purging • **bulimic** adj suffering from bulimia

bulk noun 1 large size 2 the greater part: the bulk of the population • **bulkhead** noun a wall in the inside of a ship, meant to keep out water in a collision

bulky adj taking up a lot of room • **bulkily** adv

bull noun the male of animals of the ox family, also of the whale, elephant and some other large animals • **bulldog** noun a breed of strong, fierce-looking dog • **bullfight** noun a public entertainment in Spain in which a bull is angered and usually killed • **bullfinch** noun a small pink-breasted bird • **bullfrog** noun a type of large frog • **bullring** noun the arena in which bullfights take place • **bull's-eye** noun 1 the mark in the middle of a target 2 a striped sweet

bulldozer noun a large vehicle for levelling land and clearing away obstacles • **bulldoze** verb 1 use a bulldozer on 2 force: bulldozed his way into the room

bullet noun the piece of metal fired from a gun • **bullet-proof** adj not able to be pierced by bullets

bulletin noun a report of current news, someone's health, etc • **bulletin board** noun 1 a noticeboard 2 comput a service on an electronic network providing messages and information

bullion noun gold or silver in the form of bars

bullock noun a young bull

bully noun (plural **bullies**) someone who unfairly uses their physical strength or senior position to hurt or frighten others ◇ verb (**bullies, bullying, bullied**) act like a bully

bulrush noun (plural **bulrushes**) a large strong reed that grows on wet land or in water

bulwark /buul-wurk/ noun 1 a strong defensive wall 2 a person or thing that provides protection or defence

bum[1] noun, Brit slang the buttocks • **bumbag** noun a carrying pouch strapped round the waist

bum[2] noun, US slang 1 a homeless person, esp one who lives by begging 2 a lazy or useless person ◇ adj useless, dud • **give someone the bum's rush** get rid of them quickly

bumble-bee noun a type of large bee

bumf or **bumph** noun, Brit informal miscellaneous uninteresting papers, leaflets, etc

bummer noun, slang something extremely annoying or disappointing

bump verb 1 hit with a heavy blow 2 knock by accident ◇ noun 1 the sound of a heavy blow 2 an accidental knock **3** a raised lump

bumper *noun* a bar round the front and back of a car's body to protect it from damage ◇ *adj* large: *bumper crop*

bumph *another spelling of* **bumf**

bumpkin *noun, derog* a person from the country, *esp* when considered awkward or unsophisticated

bumptious *adj* self-important

bun *noun* **1** a sweet roll made of egg dough **2** hair wound into a rounded mass

bunch *noun* (*plural* **bunches**) a number of things tied together or growing together ◇ *verb* crowd together

bundle *noun* a number of things loosely tied together ◇ *verb* **1** tie in a bundle **2** push roughly: *bundled the children into the car*

bung *noun* the stopper of the hole in a barrel, bottle, *etc* ◇ *verb* stop up with a bung

bungalow *noun* a single-storey detached house

bungle *verb* **1** do badly or clumsily **2** mishandle, mismanage ◇ *noun* a clumsy or mishandled action

bunion *noun* a lump or swelling on the joint of the big toe

bunk *noun* a narrow bed, *eg* in a ship's cabin • **bunk bed** *noun* one of a pair of narrow beds one above the other

bunker *noun* **1** a sandpit on a golf course **2** an underground shelter **3** a large box for keeping coal

bunkum *noun* nonsense

bunny *noun* (*plural* **bunnies**) a child's name for a rabbit

Bunsen burner *noun* a gas-burner used in laboratories

bunting[1] *noun* **1** thin cloth used for making flags **2** flags

bunting[2] *noun* a bird of the finch family

buoy /boy/ *noun* **1** a floating mark acting as a guide or warning for ships **2** a float, *eg* a lifebuoy

buoyant *adj* **1** able to float **2** cheerful • **buoyancy** *noun* • **buoyantly** *adv*

bur *another spelling of* **burr**

burden *noun* **1** a load **2** something difficult to bear, *eg* poverty or sorrow **3** *old* the chorus of a song • **burdensome** *adj*

burdock *noun* a type of plant with hooked leaves

bureau /byaw-roh/ *noun* (*plural* **bureaux** *or* **bureaus**) **1** a writing table **2** an office

bureaucracy /byaw-rok-ruh-si/ *noun* government by officials

bureaucrat /byaw-ruh-krat/ *noun* an administrative official • **bureaucratic** *adj* • **bureaucratically** *adv*

burgeoning *adj* rapidly expanding or developing

burger *noun* a flat, round cake of meat, cooked by frying or grilling

burgh /buh-ruh/ *noun* in Scotland, a borough

burglar *noun* someone who breaks into a house to steal • **burglary** *noun* the crime of breaking into a house to steal

burgle *verb* commit burglary

burial *noun* the placing of a body under the ground after death

burlesque *noun* a piece of writing, acting, *etc* that makes fun of somebody

burly *adj* (**burlier**, **burliest**) with a broad, strong-looking body

burn[1] *verb* (**burning**, **burnt** *or* **burned**) **1** set fire to **2** be on fire **3** injure by burning **4** *comput* copy data onto a compact disc ◇ *noun* an injury or mark caused by fire • **burner** *noun* the part of a lamp or gas-jet from which the flame rises

burn² noun, Scot a small stream

burnish verb & noun polish

burnt past form of **burn¹**

burp verb bring up wind noisily from the stomach through the mouth ◊ noun a loud escape of wind from the mouth

burr or **bur** noun the prickly head of certain plants

burrito noun (plural **burritos**) a Mexican flour tortilla with a filling of meat, beans, etc

burrow noun a hole or passage in the ground dug by certain animals for shelter ◊ verb make a passage beneath the ground

burst verb (**bursting, burst**) 1 break suddenly (after increased pressure) 2 move, speak, etc suddenly or violently

bury verb (**buries, burying, buried**) 1 place (a dead body etc) under the ground 2 cover, hide

bus noun (plural **buses**) a large road vehicle used for public transport ● **bus stop** noun an official stopping place for buses

busby noun (plural **busbies**) a tall fur hat worn by certain soldiers

bush noun (plural **bushes**) 1 a large woody plant smaller than a tree 2 wild, unfarmed country in Africa or Australia ● **bushbaby** noun a type of small lemur ● **bushranger** noun in Australia, an outlaw living in the wilds ● **bush telegraph** noun the quick passing on of news from person to person; the grapevine

bushy adj (**bushier, bushiest**) 1 growing thickly: bushy hair 2 full of bushes ● **bushily** adv ● **bushiness** noun

business /biz-nis/ noun (plural **businesses**) 1 someone's work or job 2 trade, commerce: business is booming 3 a matter of personal interest or concern: none of your business

● **businesslike** adj practical, methodical, alert and prompt ● **businessman, businesswoman** noun someone who works in commerce

busk verb play or sing in the street for money ● **busker** noun

bust noun 1 a woman's breasts 2 a sculpture of someone's head and shoulders

bustard noun a large, fast-running bird similar to a turkey

bustier /bus-ti-eh/ noun a woman's strapless under-bodice

bustle verb busy oneself noisily ◊ noun 1 noisy activity, fuss 2 hist a stuffed pad worn under a woman's full skirt

busy adj (**busier, busiest**) having a lot to do ● **busily** adv ● **busybody** noun someone who is nosey about others ● **busy yourself with** occupy yourself with

but conj 1 showing a contrast between two ideas etc: my brother can swim but I can't/that paint isn't black but brown 2 except that; without that: it never rains but it pours ◊ prep with the exception of; except: no one but Tom had any money/take the next road but one (ie the second road) ◊ adv only: we can but hope ● **but for** were it not for: but for your car, we would have been late

butane /byoo-tehn/ noun a gas commonly used for fuel

butch adj of a woman: looking or behaving in a masculine way

butcher noun someone who prepares and sells meat ◊ verb 1 kill and carve up (an animal) for food 2 kill cruelly ● **butchery** noun great or cruel slaughter

butler noun a man who is the most senior servant in a household

butt noun 1 a large barrel or similar container 2 someone of whom others make fun 3 the part of a rifle or shotgun that you hold **4** the end of a finished cigarette or cigar **5** a violent blow with the head **6** *US slang* the buttocks ◇ *verb* strike with the head • **butt in** interrupt or interfere • **butt out** *slang* stop interfering

butter *noun* a fatty food made by churning cream ◇ *verb* spread with butter • **buttercup** *noun* a wild plant with a cup-like yellow flower • **buttermilk** *noun* the milk that is left after butter has been made • **butterscotch** *noun* hard toffee made with butter • **butter up** flatter with a view to persuading

butterfly *noun* (*plural* **butterflies**) a flying insect with large, often patterned wings

buttock *noun* one of the two fleshy parts of the body on which you sit

button *noun* **1** a knob or disc of metal, plastic, *etc* used to fasten clothing **2** a knob pressed to work an electrical device ◇ *verb* fasten by means of buttons • **button it** be quiet

buttonhole *noun* a hole through which a button is passed ◇ *verb* catch the attention of (someone) and force them to listen

buttress *noun* (*plural* **buttresses**) a support on the outside of a wall ◇ *verb* support, prop up

buxom *adj* plump and pretty

buy *verb* (**buying**, **bought**) get in exchange for money ◇ *noun* a purchase: *a good buy* • **buyer** *noun*

buzz *verb* **1** make a humming noise like bees **2** of aircraft: fly threateningly close to ◇ *noun* **1** a humming sound **2** *informal* a phone call • **buzzer** *noun* a signalling device that makes a buzzing noise • **buzzword** *noun* a word well-established in a particular jargon, its use suggesting up-to-date specialized knowledge

buzzard *noun* a large brown and white bird of prey

by *adv* **1** near: *a crowd stood by, watching* **2** past: *people strolled by* **3** aside: *money put by for an emergency* ◇ *prep* **1** next to or near: *standing by the door* **2** past: *going by the house* **3** through, along, across: *we came by the main road* **4** indicating the person who does something: *written by Burns/played by a young actor* **5** of time: not after: *it'll be ready by four o'clock* **6** during the time of: *working by night* **7** by means of: *by train* **8** to the extent of: *taller by a head* **9** used to express measurements, compass directions, *etc*: *6 metres by 4 metres/ north by northwest* **10** in the quantity of: *sold by the pound/paid by the week* • **by-election** *noun* an election held in a parliamentary constituency for a special reason, *eg* because the local MP has died • **bygone** *adj* past • **bygones** *plural noun* old grievances or events that have been, or should be, forgotten • **by-law** *or* **bye-law** *noun* a law that applies in a local area only • **bypass** *noun* a road built round a town *etc* so that traffic need not pass through it • **by-product** *noun* something useful obtained during the manufacture of something else • **byroad** *or* **byway** *noun* a side road • **bystander** *noun* someone who stands watching an event or accident • **byword** *noun* someone or something well-known for a particular quality

bye *noun* **1** *cricket* a run scored from a ball that the batsman does not hit **2** the right to proceed to the next round of a competition without playing a game, *usu* because there is no available opponent

byte /bait/ *noun, comput* a unit used to measure data or memory

Cc

C *abbrev* degree(s) Celsius or centigrade

c *or* **ca** *abbrev* about (from Latin *circa*)

CAB *abbrev* Citizen's Advice Bureau

cab *noun* **1** a taxi **2** *hist* a hired carriage

cabaret /kab-uh-reh/ *noun* **1** an entertainment consisting of variety acts **2** a restaurant with a cabaret

cabbage *noun* a round firm vegetable with densely packed leaves

caber /kehb-uh/ *noun* a heavy pole tossed in competition at Highland games

cabin *noun* **1** a wooden hut **2** a small room used for living quarters in a ship **3** the part of a commercial aircraft containing passenger seating • **cabin crew** *noun* the flight attendants on a commercial airline

cabinet *noun* **1** a cupboard with shelves and glass doors for displaying objects **2** a similar container for storage *etc* **3** a wooden case with drawers **4** a selected number of government ministers who decide on policy • **cabinetmaker** *noun* a maker of fine furniture

cable *noun* **1** a strong rope or thick metal line **2** an underground wire **3** *informal* cable television **4** a line of covered telegraph wires laid under the sea or underground **5** a telegram sent by such a line ◇ *verb* telegraph by cable • **cable television** *noun* a service transmitting television programmes to individual subscribers by underground cable

cacao /kuh-kah-oh/ *noun* a tree from whose seeds cocoa and chocolate are made

cache /kash/ *noun* **1** a store or hiding place for ammunition, treasure, *etc* **2** things hidden **3** *comput* part of a computer's memory that stores data that is frequently accessed

cachet /kash-eh/ *noun* **1** prestige **2** an official stamp or seal

cackle *noun* **1** the sound made by a hen or goose **2** a laugh that sounds like this

cacophony /kuh-kof-uh-ni/ *noun* (*plural* **cacophonies**) an unpleasant noise • **cacophonous** *adj* • **cacophonously** *adv*

cactus *noun* (*plural* **cactuses** *or* **cacti**) a type of prickly plant

CAD *abbrev* computer-aided design

cad *noun, old* a dishonourable, despicable man

cadaver /kuh-dav-uh/ *noun* a human corpse

cadaverous *adj* unhealthily pale and thin • **cadaverously** *adv* • **cadaverousness** *noun*

caddie *noun* an assistant who carries a golfer's clubs

caddy *noun* (*plural* **caddies**) a box for storing tea

cadence *noun* **1** a fall of the voice, *eg* at the end of a sentence **2** a group of chords ending a piece of music

cadenza *noun* a musical passage at the end of a movement, concerto, *etc*

cadet /kuh-*det*/ noun **1** an officer trainee in the armed forces or police service **2** a school pupil who takes military training

cadge verb (**cadging**, **cadged**) obtain by lazily or unfairly depending on other people's generosity • **cadger** noun

Caesarean /siz-*air*-ri-un/ adj of a birth: delivered by cutting through the walls of the mother's abdomen ◇ noun a Caesarean birth or operation

caesura /siz-*yaw*-ruh/ noun **1** a pause in the middle of a line of poetry **2** any pause or break

café noun a small restaurant serving coffee, tea, snacks, etc

cafeteria noun a self-service restaurant

cafetière /kaf-i-ti-*air*/ noun a coffee pot with a plunger mechanism

caffeine noun a stimulating drug found in coffee and tea

caftan noun a long-sleeved, ankle-length Middle-Eastern garment

cage noun **1** a barred enclosure for birds or animals **2** a lift used by miners ◇ verb (**caging**, **caged**) close up in a cage

cagey or **cagy** adj (**cagier**, **cagiest**) unwilling to speak freely; wary • **caginess** noun

cagoule noun a lightweight anorak

cahoots plural noun: **in cahoots with** working closely with in planning something bad; in collusion with

cairn noun **1** a heap of stones marking a grave or the top of a mountain **2** a breed of small terrier

cairngorm noun a brown or yellow variety of quartz used in jewellery

cajole verb persuade by flattery • **cajolery** noun

cake noun **1** a baked piece of dough made from flour, eggs, sugar, etc **2** something pressed into a lump: cake of soap ◇ verb become dry and hard • **have your cake and eat it** enjoy both of two alternative things

calamine noun a pink powder containing a zinc salt, used to make a skin-soothing lotion

calamity noun (plural **calamities**) a great disaster • **calamitous** adj • **calamitously** adv

calcium noun a chemical element that is a constituent of chalk, lime, bones and teeth

calculate verb **1** work out by mathematics **2** think out in an exact way • **calculable** adj able to be counted or measured • **calculating** adj thinking cleverly and selfishly • **calculation** noun a mathematical reckoning; a sum • **calculator** noun a machine that does mathematical calculations

calculus noun a branch of mathematics dealing with changing amounts

Caledonian adj belonging to Scotland

calendar noun a table or list showing the year divided into months, weeks and days

calendula noun a preparation of marigold flowers used in herbal medicine

calf¹ noun (plural **calves**) **1** the young of a cow or ox **2** the young of certain other mammals, eg an elephant or whale **3** calf's skin cured as leather

calf² noun (plural **calves**) the back of the lower part of the leg

calibrate verb **1** mark the scale on (a measuring instrument) **2** check or adjust the scale of (a measuring instrument)

calibre or US **caliber** noun **1** the diameter of a tube or the barrel of a gun **2** of a person: quality of character or ability

calico noun a patterned kind of cotton cloth

call verb 1 shout 2 give a name to: what is your cat called? 3 order to come; summon 4 make a short visit (on) 5 telephone ◊ noun 1 a shout 2 a short visit 3 a telephone conversation 4 a demand for something: no call for classics teachers 5 a bird's song ● **call centre** noun a building where workers provide services to a company's customers by telephone ● **call off** cancel, or decide not to take part in (something arranged) ● **call up** 1 call on the telephone 2 order to join the armed forces; conscript

calligraphy noun the art of handwriting ● **calligrapher** noun ● **calligraphic** adj

calling noun a vocation or career

callipers or **calipers** noun 1 plural an instrument like compasses, used to measure thickness 2 sing a splint to support the leg, made of two metal rods

callous adj cruel, hard-hearted ● **callously** adv ● **callousness** noun

---

Do not confuse with: **callus**

---

callow adj young and inexperienced or naive ● **callowly** adv ● **callowness** noun

callus noun (plural **calluses**) an area of thickened or hardened skin

---

Do not confuse with: **callous**

---

calm adj 1 still or quiet 2 not anxious or flustered ◊ noun 1 absence of wind 2 quietness, peacefulness ◊ verb make peaceful ● **calmly** adv ● **calmness** noun

calorie noun 1 a measure of the energy-giving value of food 2 a measure of heat ● **calorimeter** noun an instrument for measuring heat

calumny noun (plural **calumnies**) a false accusation or lie about a person

calve verb give birth to a calf

calypso noun (plural **calypsos**) a West Indian improvised song

calyx /keh-liks/ noun (plural **calyces** or **calyxes**) the outer covering that protects a flower bud before it opens

calzone /kal-tsoh-ni/ noun a type of folded-over pizza

CAM abbrev computer-aided manufacturing

camaraderie noun the affection and support that friends give each other; fellowship

camber noun a curve that makes the middle of a road higher than the sides

camcorder noun a hand-held device that records events on videotape

came past tense of **come**

camel noun an animal with one or two fatty humps on its back, native to Asia and Africa

cameo noun (plural **cameos**) 1 a brief film appearance by a well-known actor 2 a gem or stone with a figure carved in relief (contrasted with: **intaglio**)

camera¹ noun an instrument for taking photographs

camera² noun: **in camera** in private

camisole /kam-i-sohl/ noun a woman's undervest with thin shoulder straps

camomile noun a plant with pale yellow flowers, used as a medicinal herb

camouflage /kam-uh-flahzh/ noun 1 the disguising of the appearance of something to blend in with its background 2 a pattern of green and brown blotches used for combat clothing and casual clothes made in imitation of it 3 natural protective colouring in animals ◇ *verb* disguise by camouflage

camp[1] *noun* **1** a group of tents, caravans, *etc* forming a temporary settlement **2** fixed military quarters ◇ *verb* **1** pitch tents **2** set up a temporary home • **camp bed** *noun* a small portable folding bed • **campsite** *noun* an area for pitching tents, setting up caravans, *etc*

camp[2] *adj* exaggeratedly affected, effeminate or vulgar for comic effect • **campness** *noun*

campaign *noun* **1** organized action in support of a cause or movement **2** a planned series of battles or movements during a war ◇ *verb* **1** organize support: *campaigning against the poll tax* **2** serve in a military campaign

campanile /kam-puh-*nee*-li/ *noun* a bell-tower

campanology *noun* bell-ringing • **campanologist** *noun*

camphor *noun* a pungent solid oil obtained from a cinnamon tree, or a synthetic substitute for it, used to repel insects *etc*

campion *noun* a plant with pink or white star-shaped flowers

campus *noun* (*plural* **campuses**) the grounds and buildings of a university or college

can[1] *verb* (**could**) **1** be able to (do something): *can anybody here play the piano?* **2** have permission to (do something): *asked if I could have the day off* • **can but** can only: *we can but hope*

can[2] *noun* a sealed tin container for preserving food or liquids ◇ *verb* (**canning**, **canned**) seal in a tin to preserve • **canned music** *noun* prerecorded bland music

canal *noun* an artificial waterway for boats

canapé /*ka*-nuh-peh/ *noun* a small

piece of savoury food served as an appetizer

canary *noun* (*plural* **canaries**) a songbird with yellow plumage, kept as a pet

canasta *noun* a card game similar to rummy

cancan *noun* a high-kicking dance of French origin, performed by women

cancel *verb* (**cancelling**, **cancelled**) **1** decide that (a planned event) will not happen: *cancel all engagements for the week* **2** mark for deletion by crossing with lines • **cancellation** *noun* • **cancel out** make ineffective by balancing each other

cancer *noun* a malignant growth in the body • **cancerous** *adj*

candelabrum *noun* a decorative candle-holder for several candles

candid *adj* frank, open, honest • **candidly** *adv*

candida /kan-*did*-uh/ *noun* an infection caused by a yeastlike fungus

candidate *noun* **1** someone applying for a job or entered in a competition **2** an entrant in a political election • **candidacy** *or* **candidature** *noun*

candied *adj* cooked or coated in sugar

candle *noun* a stick of wax containing a wick, used for giving light • **candlestick** *noun* a holder for a candle • **candlewick** *noun* a cotton tufted material, used for bedspreads *etc* • **not worth the candle** not worth the effort or expense needed

candour *or US* **candor** *noun* frankness, honesty

candy *noun* **1** sugar crystallized by boiling **2** *US* (*plural* **candies**) sweets, chocolate • **candyfloss** *noun* a mass of spun sugar

cane *noun* **1** the woody stem of bamboo, sugar cane, *etc* **2** a walking stick ◇ *verb* beat with a cane • **cane**

sugar *noun* sugar extracted from sugar cane

canine *adj* of dogs • **canine tooth** *noun* a pointed tooth found on each side of the upper and lower jaw

canister *noun* a metal container, *esp* cylindrical and containing gas or liquid

canker *noun* **1** a spreading sore **2** a disease in trees, plants, *etc*

cannabis *noun* a narcotic drug obtained from the hemp plant

cannelloni *plural noun* wide hollow tubes of pasta, stuffed with meat, cheese, vegetables, *etc*

cannery *noun* (*plural* **canneries**) a factory where food is canned

cannibal *noun* **1** someone who eats human flesh **2** an animal that eats its own kind • **cannibalism** *noun* • **cannibalistic** *adj* • **cannibalize** *verb* take parts from a broken machine *etc* for use in repairing or building something else

cannon *noun* a large gun mounted on a wheeled carriage

Do not confuse with: **canon**

---

cannonball *noun* a solid metal ball shot from a cannon

cannot *verb* **1** used with another verb to express inability to do something: *I cannot understand this* **2** used to refuse permission: *he cannot see me today*

canny *adj* (**cannier**, **canniest**) **1** wise, shrewd **2** cautious • **cannily** *adv* • **canniness** *noun*

canoe *noun* a light narrow boat moved by paddles

canon *noun* **1** a rule used as a standard to judge by **2** a member of the Anglican clergy connected with a cathedral **3** a list of saints **4** an accepted or established list: *not in the liter-*

ary canon **5** a piece of music in which parts follow each other repeating the melody

---

Do not confuse with: **cannon**

---

cañon *another spelling of* **canyon**

canonical *adj* part of an accepted canon: *canonical text*

canonize *verb* put on the list of saints • **canonization** *noun*

canopy *noun* (*plural* **canopies**) a piece of heavy cloth suspended overhead for shade or decoration

cant[1] *noun* **1** the slang or vocabulary of a particular group: *thieves' cant* **2** insincere talk

cant[2] *noun* a slope, an incline ◇ *verb* tilt from a level position

can't *short form of* **cannot**

cantankerous *adj* crotchety, bad-tempered, quarrelsome • **cantankerously** *adv* • **cantankerousness** *noun*

cantata *noun* a short piece of music for a choir

canteen *noun* **1** a dining room in a factory or other workplace **2** a flask for water **3** a case for storing cutlery

canter *verb* move at an easy gallop ◇ *noun* an easy gallop

cantilever *noun* a large projecting bracket used to support a balcony or staircase • **cantilever bridge** *noun* a bridge consisting of upright piers with cantilevers extending to meet one another

canton *noun* a federal state in Switzerland

canvas *noun* (*plural* **canvases**) **1** coarse, strong cloth used for sails, tents, *etc* **2** a piece of this cloth stretched and used for painting on

canvass *verb* go round asking for votes or opinions • **canvasser** *noun*

canyon *noun* a deep, steep-sided

river valley • **canyoning** noun a sport where people travel along fast-flowing natural watercourses without a boat

cap noun **1** a peaked soft hat **2** a lid on a container; a top **3** a contraceptive diaphragm ◇ verb (**capping**, **capped**) **1** put a cap on **2** set a limit to (a budget etc) **3** do better than; improve on: no-one can cap this story **4** select for a national sports team

capable adj able to cope with difficulties without help • **capability** noun • **capably** adv • **capable of** able or likely to achieve, produce, etc: capable of a better performance

capacious adj roomy • **capaciously** adv • **capaciousness** noun

capacitor noun a device for collecting and storing electricity

capacity noun (plural **capacities**) **1** ability to do something: capacity for growth **2** the amount that something can hold **3** post, position: capacity as leader • **to capacity** to the greatest extent possible: filled to capacity

cape¹ noun a thick shawl or covering for the shoulders

cape² noun a point of land running into the sea

caper¹ verb leap, dance about ◇ noun **1** a leap **2** informal a prank or adventure

caper² noun the bud of a Mediterranean shrub, pickled or salted for eating

capercaillie or **capercailzie** /kap-uh-keh-li/ or /keh-puh-keh-li/ noun a kind of large grouse

capillary noun (plural **capillaries**) **1** a tiny blood vessel **2** a very fine tube ◇ adj very fine, like a hair • **capillary action** noun the force that makes liquid in a thin tube rise up the tube

capital noun **1** the chief city of a country: Paris is the capital of France **2** a letter in its large form **3** money for running a business **4** money invested, or accumulated wealth ◇ adj **1** most important; main **2** of a letter: written or printed in upper case, eg A, B or C **3** punishable by death: capital offence **4** informal excellent • **capital punishment** noun punishment by death • **make capital out of** turn to your advantage

capitalism noun a system in which a country's wealth is owned by individuals, not by the State • **capitalist** noun someone who supports or practises capitalism • **capitalistic** adj

capitalize verb **1** use to your advantage **2** write in capital letters • **capitalization** noun

capitulate verb give in to an enemy • **capitulation** noun

capon noun a young castrated cock fattened for eating

cappuccino noun coffee with frothy hot milk added

caprice /kuh-prees/ noun a sudden, impulsive change of mind or mood

capricious adj tending to change opinion or mood suddenly; fickle • **capriciously** adv • **capriciousness** noun

capsize verb overturn in the water, or cause to overturn

capstan noun a device used for winding in heavy ropes on a ship or quay

capsule noun **1** a small gelatine case containing a dose of medicine etc **2** a self-contained, detachable part of a spacecraft **3** a dry seed-pod on a plant

Capt abbrev captain

captain noun **1** the commander of a company of soldiers, a ship or an aircraft **2** the leader of a sports team ◇ verb lead • **captaincy** noun the rank of captain or period of being captain

caption noun a heading for a newspaper article, photograph, *etc*

captious *adj* quick to find fault; judgemental

captivate *verb* charm, fascinate

captive *noun* a prisoner ◇ *adj* **1** taken or kept prisoner **2** not able to get away: *captive audience*

captivity *noun* **1** the state of being a prisoner **2** the situation of a wild animal kept in a zoo *etc*, not in the wild

captor *noun* someone who takes a prisoner

capture *verb* **1** take by force **2** get hold of; seize: *capture the imagination* ◇ *noun* **1** the act of capturing **2** something captured

car *noun* **1** a private motor vehicle with *usu* four wheels **2** *US* a train carriage • **car park** *noun* a place where cars may be left for a time • **car pool** *noun* an arrangement between car owners to take turns at driving each other to work *etc*

carafe /kuh-*raf*/ *noun* a bottle-shaped container for serving wine, water, *etc*

caramel *noun* **1** sugar melted and browned **2** a sweet made with sugar and butter • **caramelize** *verb* cook slowly in butter and sugar

carat *noun* **1** a measure of purity for gold **2** a measure of weight for gemstones

---

Do not confuse with: **carrot**

---

caravan *noun* **1** a covered vehicle with living accommodation, pulled by a car **2** a number of travellers and their animals crossing the desert together

caravanserai /ka-ruh-*van*-suh-rai/ *noun* a shelter or simple inn in the desert where caravans stop

caraway *noun* a plant with spicy seeds used in cooking

carbine *noun* a short light automatic rifle

carbohydrate *noun* a compound of carbon, hydrogen and oxygen, *eg* sugar or starch

carbon *noun* an element of which charcoal is one form • **carbonated** *adj* of a drink: made fizzy by the addition of carbon dioxide • **carbon copy** *noun* **1** a copy of a document made using carbon paper **2** an exact copy • **carbon dioxide** *noun* a gas present in the air and breathed out by humans and animals • **carbonic** *adj* of or made with carbon • **carbon-iferous** *adj* producing or containing coal or carbon • **carbon monoxide** *noun* a poisonous gas with no smell • **carbon paper** *noun* paper coated with black ink, interleaved between ordinary paper when typing to produce exact copies

carbuncle *noun* **1** a fiery-red precious stone **2** an inflamed swelling under the skin

carburettor *or US* **carburetor** *noun* the part of a vehicle engine that changes the petrol into vapour

carcass *noun* the dead body of an animal

carcinogen *noun* a substance that encourages the growth of cancer • **carcinogenic** *adj* causing cancer

carcinoma /kah-si-*noh*-muh/ *noun* (*plural* **carcinomas** *or* **carcinomata**) a cancerous growth

card *noun* **1** very thick paper or thin cardboard **2** an illustrated, folded piece of paper sent in greeting *etc* **3** a credit card or debit card: *can I pay with a card?* **4** (**cards**) any of the many types of games played with a pack of special cards ◇ *verb* comb (wool) to untangle it and prepare it for spinning into yarn

cardboard *noun* stiff board made from paper

cardiac *adj* of the heart: *cardiac failure*

cardigan *noun* a knitted woollen jacket

cardinal *adj* principal, important ◇ *noun* the highest rank of priest in the Roman Catholic Church • **cardinal number** *noun* a number that expresses quantity, *eg* 1,2,3 (*contrasted with*: **ordinal number**)

care *noun* **1** close attention **2** worry, anxiety **3** protection, keeping: *in my care* ◇ *verb* be concerned or worried: *I don't care what happens now* • **carefree** *adj* having no worries • **careworn** *adj* worn out by anxiety • **care for 1** look after **2** feel affection or liking for • **care of** at the house of (often written as **c/o**) • **take care** be careful; watch out

career *noun* **1** life's work **2** profession ◇ *verb* run rapidly and wildly: *careering along the pavement*

careful *adj* taking care to avoid danger or mistakes • **carefully** *adv* • **carefulness** *noun*

careless *adj* paying little attention; not taking care • **carelessly** *adv* • **carelessness** *noun*

caress *verb* touch gently and lovingly ◇ *noun* (*plural* **caresses**) a gentle touch

caretaker *noun* someone who looks after a building ◇ *adj* in charge temporarily; interim: *caretaker government*

cargo *noun* (*plural* **cargoes**) the goods carried by a ship or plane

caribou *noun* the North American reindeer

caricature *noun* a picture of someone that exaggerates certain of their features ◇ *verb* draw a caricature of • **caricaturist** *noun*

caries /*kair-eez*/ *noun* tooth decay • **carious** *adj* decaying

carillon /kuh-*ril*-yun/ *noun* **1** a set of bells on which tunes can be played **2** a tune played with bells

carmine *noun* a bright red colour ◇ *adj* of this colour

carnage *noun* slaughter, killing

carnal *adj* involving sexual or physical pleasure

carnation *noun* a type of pink, red or white garden flower

carnival *noun* a celebration with processions, parties, *etc*

carnivore *noun* a flesh-eating animal

carnivorous *adj* eating meat • **carnivorously** *adv* • **carnivorousness** *noun*

carol *noun* a hymn or song sung at Christmas • **caroller** *noun* • **carolling** *noun*

carouse *verb* take part in a bout of noisy drinking • **carousal** *noun*

carousel /ka-ruh-*sel*/ *noun* **1** *US* a merry-go-round **2** a rotating conveyor belt for luggage at an airport *etc*

carp[1] *noun* a freshwater fish found in ponds

carp[2] *verb* find fault with small errors; complain about nothing

carpe diem /*kah*-peh *dee*-em/ *exclam* seize the day; make the most of the present

carpel *noun* the female part of a flower that carries the seeds

carpenter *noun* someone who makes the wooden parts of buildings and other structures; a joiner • **carpentry** *noun* the trade of a carpenter

carpet *noun* the woven covering of floors, stairs, *etc* ◇ *verb* cover with a carpet

carriage *noun* **1** a comfortable horse-drawn vehicle **2** a passenger vehicle pulled by a locomotive **3** the cost of delivering a parcel **4** a way of walking; bearing

carriageway *noun* one side of a road, on which traffic is travelling in a single direction and which may consist of several lanes

carrier *noun* **1** someone who carries goods **2** a machine or container for carrying **3** someone who passes on a disease • **carrier bag** *noun* a plastic bag for carrying shopping • **carrier pigeon** *noun* a pigeon used to carry messages

carrion *noun* rotting animal flesh

carrot *noun* a vegetable in the form of an orange-coloured root

---

Do not confuse with: **carat**

---

carry *verb* (**carries, carrying, carried**) **1** pick up and take to another place **2** contain and take to a destination: *cables carrying electricity* **3** have as a mark; bear: *carry a scar* **4** of a voice: be able to be heard at a distance **5** win, succeed: *carry the day* **6** keep for sale: *we don't carry cigarettes* • **carry-on** *noun* a fuss • **carry-out** *noun, Scot* a take-away meal or alcoholic drink • **carried away** overcome by emotion; overexcited • **carry on** continue (doing) • **carry out** accomplish; succeed in doing • **carry the can** accept responsibility for an error • **carry weight** have force or authority

cart *noun* **1** a horse-drawn vehicle used for carrying loads **2** a small wheeled vehicle pushed by hand ◇ *verb* **1** carry by cart **2** drag, haul: *carted off the stage* • **cart-horse** *noun* a large, heavy work-horse • **cartwright** *noun* someone who makes carts

carte blanche /kaht *blonhsh*/ *noun* freedom to take action or make decisions; a free hand

cartel *noun* a group of firms that agree on similar prices for their prod-

ucts to reduce competition

cartilage *noun* a strong elastic material in the bodies of humans and animals; gristle

cartography *noun* the science of map-making • **cartographer** *noun*

carton *noun* a small container for food or drink made of cardboard, plastic, *etc*

cartoon *noun* **1** a comic drawing, or strip of drawings, often with a caption **2** an animated film **3** a drawing used as the basis for a large painting *etc* • **cartoonist** *noun* someone who draws cartoons

cartridge *noun* **1** a case holding the powder and bullet fired by a gun **2** a spool of film or tape enclosed in a case **3** a tube of ink for loading a pen **4** the part of a record-player that holds the stylus

cartwheel *noun* **1** the wheel of a cart **2** a sideways somersault with hands touching the ground

carve *verb* **1** make or shape by cutting **2** cut up (meat) into slices

cascade *noun* **1** a waterfall **2** an abundant hanging display: *cascade of curls* ◇ *verb* fall like or in a waterfall

case *noun* **1** a container or outer covering **2** something that happens; an occurrence **3** a statement of facts; an argument **4** what is true: *if that is the case* **5** a trial in a law court: *murder case*

casement *noun* a window that opens on hinges

cash *noun* money in the form of coins and notes ◇ *verb* turn into, or change for, money • **cashback** *noun* **1** a facility where a person paying for goods by debit card may also withdraw cash **2** money offered as an incentive to enter into a financial agreement • **cash card** *noun* a card issued by a bank *etc* that allows the holder to use a cash dispenser • **cash dis-**

penser noun a machine that allows money to be withdrawn from a bank account; an ATM ● **cash register** noun a machine for holding money that records the amount put in ● **cash in on** profit from

cashew noun a kidney-shaped nut produced by a tropical tree

cashier noun someone who looks after the receiving and paying of money, esp in a shop ◇ verb, military dismiss in disgrace

cashmere noun fine soft goat's wool

casino /kuh-see-noh/ noun (plural **casinos**) a building in which gambling takes place

cask noun a barrel containing wine etc

casket noun 1 a small box for holding jewels etc 2 US a coffin

cassava noun a tropical plant with roots from which tapioca is obtained

casserole noun 1 a covered oven-proof dish for cooking and serving food 2 food cooked in a casserole

cassette noun 1 a small case for film, magnetic recording tape, etc 2 the magnetic tape itself

cassock noun a long robe worn by priests

cassowary /kas-uh-wuh-ri/ noun (plural **cassowaries**) a large flightless bird of Australia and New Guinea

cast verb (**casting**, **cast**) 1 throw 2 shed (a skin, hair, etc) 3 shape in a mould 4 choose actors for (a play or film) 5 give a part to (an actor etc) ◇ noun 1 something shaped in a mould 2 plaster encasing a broken limb 3 the actors in a play 4 a small heap of earth thrown up by a worm 5 an eye squint 6 a type: cast of mind ● **cast down** adj depressed ● **cast iron** noun unpurified iron melted and moulded into shape ● **cast-off** adj used by someone else; second-hand

castanets plural noun hollow shells of ivory or hard wood, clicked together to accompany a dance

castaway noun a deserted or ship-wrecked person

caste noun a class or rank of people, esp one of the four social classes into which people are divided in Hindu society

castellated adj having walls, towers, etc like those of a castle

caster another spelling of **castor**

castigate verb scold severely ● **castigation** noun ● **castigator** noun

castle noun a fortress or fortified house

castor or **caster** noun a small wheel, eg on the legs of furniture ● **castor sugar** or **caster sugar** very fine granulated sugar

castor oil noun a kind of palm oil used medicinally

castrate verb remove the testicles of

castrato noun (plural **castrati**) a male singer who has been castrated to preserve a high voice

casual adj 1 happening by chance: casual encounter 2 informal: casual clothes 3 not careful or concerned: casual attitude to work 4 not regular or permanent; temporary: casual labour

casualty noun (plural **casualties**) 1 someone who is killed or wounded 2 a casualty department ● **casualty department** noun a hospital department for treating accidental injuries etc

cat noun 1 a sharp-clawed furry animal kept as a pet 2 an animal of the family that includes lions, tigers, etc ● **cat burglar** noun a burglar who breaks into houses by climbing walls etc ● **cat flap** noun a small door set in a larger door to allow a cat entry and exit ● **cat-o'-nine-tails** noun a whip with nine lashes • **cat's cradle** noun a children's game of creating patterns by winding string around the fingers • **Cat's-eye** noun, trademark a small mirror fixed in a road surface to reflect light at night

cataclysm noun 1 a violent change; an upheaval 2 a great flood of water

catacombs plural noun an underground burial place

catalogue noun an ordered list of names, books, objects for sale, etc ◇ verb 1 list in order 2 compile details of (a book) for a library catalogue

catalyst noun 1 a substance that speeds up or prevents a chemical reaction without itself changing 2 something that brings about a change

catalytic converter noun a device designed to reduce toxic emissions from a vehicle engine

catamaran noun a boat with two parallel hulls

catapult noun 1 a small forked stick with a piece of elastic attached, used for firing small stones 2 hist a weapon for throwing heavy stones in warfare

cataract noun 1 a disease of the outer eye 2 formal a waterfall

catarrh /kuh-tahr/ noun inflammation of the lining of the nose and throat causing a discharge

catastrophe /kuh-tas-truh-fi/ noun a sudden disaster • **catastrophic** adj • **catastrophically** adv

catch verb (**catches, catching, caught**) 1 take hold of; capture 2 become affected by (a disease): catch a cold 3 get on, or be in time to get on: catch the last train 4 surprise (someone doing something bad): caught him stealing ◇ noun 1 a haul of fish etc 2 something you are lucky to have got or won 3 a hidden flaw or disadvantage: where's the catch? 4 a fastening: window catch • **catching** adj infectious • **catchphrase** or **catchword**

noun a phrase or word that is popular for a while • **catch-22** noun an absurd situation with no way out • **catchy** adj of a tune: easily remembered • **catch on** become popular • **catch up on** 1 draw level with after being behind 2 get up to date with (work etc)

catchment area noun 1 an area from which the pupils in a school are drawn 2 an area from which a river or reservoir draws its water supply

catechism /kat-uh-kizm/ noun 1 a religious book that teaches by asking questions to which it gives the answers 2 a series of searching questions • **catechize** verb ask many questions

categorical adj allowing no doubt or argument: categorical denial • **categorically** adv

category noun (plural **categories**) a class or group of similar people or things • **categorize** verb divide into categories

cater verb 1 provide food 2 supply what is required: cater for all tastes • **caterer** noun

caterpillar noun the larva of an insect that feeds on plant leaves ◇ adj, trademark (**Caterpillar**) moving on rotating metal belts: Caterpillar tractor

caterwaul verb howl or yell like a cat

catgut noun cord made from sheep's stomachs, used to make strings for violins, harps, etc

catharsis /kuh-thah-sis/ noun a pleasant and necessary release of strong emotions • **cathartic** adj

cathedral noun 1 the church of a bishop 2 the chief church in a bishop's district

Catherine wheel noun a firework that rotates as it burns

catheter noun a tube put into the body to remove urine when the bladder is not working properly

cathode ray tube noun a device in a television set that causes a narrow beam of electrons to strike against a screen

Catholic adj of the Roman Catholic Church • **Catholicism** ◇ noun

catholic adj wide, comprehensive: a catholic taste in literature

catkin noun a tuft of small flowers on certain trees, eg the willow and hazel

CAT scan noun computer-assisted tomography scan, a form of X-ray that produces a three-dimensional image from a sequence of passes

cattle plural noun animals that eat grass, eg cows, bulls and oxen

Caucasian noun a White person ◇ adj White

caucus /kaw-kus/ noun, US a meeting of members of a political party to nominate candidates for election etc

caught past form of **catch**

caul noun a membrane sometimes covering a baby's head at birth

cauldron noun a large cooking pot

cauliflower noun a vegetable of the cabbage family with an edible white flower

caulk verb make (a wooden boat) watertight by filling in the gaps between the boards ◇ noun a paste used in the building trade to fill gaps, eg between a window frame and a wall

cause noun 1 that which makes something happen: the cause of death 2 a reason for action: cause for complaint 3 an aim for which a group or person works: the cause of peace ◇ verb make happen

cause célèbre /kawz seh-lebr/ noun a notorious controversy or controversial person

causeway noun a raised road over wet ground or shallow water

caustic adj 1 burning, corroding 2 very sarcastic or critical; biting: caustic wit • **caustically** adv

cauterize verb burn away flesh with a hot implement in order to make a wound heal cleanly • **cauterization** noun

caution noun 1 carefulness because of potential danger: approach with caution 2 a warning ◇ verb warn • **cautionary** adj giving a warning

cautious adj showing caution; careful • **cautiously** adv

cavalcade noun a procession on horseback, in cars, etc

cavalier noun, hist a supporter of the king in the Civil War of the 17th century ◇ adj offhand, careless: cavalier attitude

cavalry noun soldiers mounted on horses

cave noun a hollow place in the earth or in rock • **caveman**, **cavewoman** noun a prehistoric cave-dweller • **cave in** fall or collapse inwards

caveat /kav-i-at/ noun a warning about the limits of an earlier statement or agreement

cavern noun a deep hollow place in the earth

cavernous adj 1 huge and hollow 2 full of caverns • **cavernously** adv

caviar noun the pickled eggs of the sturgeon

cavil verb (**cavilling**, **cavilled**) make objections over small, unimportant details

cavity noun (plural **cavities**) 1 a hole or hollow 2 a decayed hollow in a tooth

cavort verb dance or leap around

caw verb call like a crow ◇ noun a crow's call

cayenne noun a type of very hot red pepper

cayman noun (plural **caymans**) a South American alligator

CBE abbrev Companion of the Order of the British Empire, a civilian award for achievement

CBI abbrev Confederation of British Industry, an organization that represents employers

cc abbrev cubic centimetre(s)

CD noun a compact disc, a thin plastic disc on which digital information is stored

CD-R abbrev compact disc recordable, a CD on which a user can record digital information

CD-ROM abbrev compact disc read-only memory, a pre-recorded CD on which a user cannot record new information

cease verb come or bring to an end

ceasefire noun a pause in fighting between armies or armed groups

ceaseless adj continuing without stopping • **ceaselessly** adv

cedar noun a large evergreen tree with a hard sweet-smelling wood

cede verb allow someone else to have

ceilidh /keh-li/ noun an event involving traditional Scottish dancing, sometimes combined with musical performances

ceiling noun 1 the inner roof of a room 2 an upper limit

celandine noun a small yellow wild-flower

celebrate verb commemorate an event (eg a birthday or marriage) by going out, having a party, etc • **celebrated** adj famous • **celebration** noun

celebrity noun (plural **celebrities**) 1 a famous person; a star 2 fame

celery noun a vegetable in the form of fibrous stalks

celestial adj 1 of outer space or the sky: celestial bodies 2 heavenly

celibate adj abstaining from sexual intercourse • **celibacy** noun

cell noun 1 the smallest, fundamental part of living things 2 a small room in a prison, monastery, etc 3 the part of an electric battery containing electrodes

cellar noun an underground room used for storing things, esp wine or coal

cellist /chel-ist/ noun someone who plays the cello

cello /chel-oh/ noun a large stringed musical instrument played upright in a seated position, with a bow

Cellophane noun, trademark a thin transparent wrapping material

cellphone noun, US a mobile phone

cellular adj made of or having cells

cellulite noun fatty deposits that give the skin a dimpled appearance

Celluloid noun, trademark a very hard elastic substance used for making photographic film etc

cellulose noun a substance found in plants and wood, used to make paper, textiles, etc

Celsius /sel-si-us/ adj 1 of a temperature scale: consisting of a hundred degrees, on which water freezes at 0° and boils at 100° 2 of a degree: measured on this scale: 10° Celsius

Celtic /kelt-ik/ adj 1 belonging to the ancient people of Europe or their descendents eg in Scotland, Wales and Ireland 2 belonging to a group of languages that includes Gaelic, Breton and Welsh

cement noun 1 a powdered mixture of clay and lime used to make concrete 2 strong glue ◇ verb 1 put together with cement **2** establish firmly: *cemented their friendship*

cemetery *noun* (*plural* **cemeteries**) a place where the dead are buried

cenotaph /sen-uh-taf/ *noun* a monument to a person or group buried elsewhere

censer *noun* a container for burning incense in a church

Do not confuse: **censer**, **censor** and **censure**

---

censor *noun* someone who officially assesses the content of books, films, *etc* and decides if it breaks rules about offensiveness ◊ *verb* delete or withhold on the grounds of offensiveness, political sensitivity, *etc*

censorious *adj* finding fault; judgemental • **censoriously** *adv*

censure *noun* expression of disapproval; blame ◊ *verb* blame or criticize

census *noun* (*plural* **censuses**) a periodical official count of the people who live in a country

---

Do not confuse with: **consensus**

---

cent *noun* a coin that is the hundredth part of a larger unit of currency, *eg* of a US dollar

centaur *noun* a mythological monster, half man and half horse

centenary *noun* (*plural* **centenaries**) a hundredth anniversary • **centenarian** *noun* someone a hundred or more years old

centennial *adj* **1** having lasted a hundred years **2** happening every hundred years ◊ *noun* a centenary

centigrade *adj* on the Celsius scale

centigram *noun* a hundredth part of a gram

centilitre *noun* a hundredth part of a litre

centimetre *noun* a hundredth part of a metre

centipede *noun* a small crawling animal with many legs

central *adj* **1** located in or belonging to the centre **2** chief, main: *central point of the argument* • **central heating** *noun* heating of a building by water, steam or air from a central point • **central locking** *noun* a system whereby all the doors of a vehicle are locked by locking the driver's door • **central processing unit** *noun* the main control unit of a computer

centralize *verb* **1** group in a single place **2** bring under one central control • **centralization** *noun*

centre or *US* **center** *noun* **1** the middle point or part **2** a building used for some special activity: *sports centre/shopping centre* ◊ *verb* (**centring, centred**) put in the centre

centrifugal *adj* moving away from the centre

centripetal *adj* moving towards the centre

centurion *noun, hist* a commander of 100 Roman soldiers

century *noun* (*plural* **centuries**) **1** a hundred years **2** *cricket* a hundred runs

ceramic *adj* **1** made of pottery **2** of pottery-making ◊ *noun* **1** something made of pottery **2** (**ceramics**) the art of pottery

cereal *noun* **1** grain used as food **2** a breakfast food prepared from grain

cerebral *adj* **1** of the brain **2** appealing to highly educated people; intellectual • **cerebrally** *adv*

ceremonial *adj* done with ceremony or as part of a ceremony • **ceremonially** *adv*

ceremonious *adj* full of ceremony

• **ceremoniously** adv • **ceremoniousness** noun

ceremony noun (plural **ceremonies**) the formal acts that accompany an important event: marriage ceremony

cerise /suh-rees/ adj & noun cherry-red

certain adj 1 sure; not to be doubted 2 fixed, settled 3 particular but unnamed: stopping at certain places/ a certain look • **certainly** adv • **certainty** noun

certificate noun a written or printed statement giving official information, eg details of a birth or passed examinations

certify verb (**certifies**, **certifying**, **certified**) put down in writing as an official promise or statement etc

cervical /sur-vi-kul/ adj of the cervix • **cervical smear** noun a collection of a sample of cells from the cervix for examination under a microscope

cervix noun the neck of the womb

cessation noun a ceasing or stopping; an ending

cesspool noun a pool or tank for storing liquid waste or sewage

CET abbrev central European time

cf abbrev compare (from Latin confer)

CFC abbrev chlorofluorocarbon

CGI abbrev computer generated imagery, used in animated films

chador /chud-uh/ noun a veil worn by Islamic or Hindu women, covering the head and shoulders

chafe verb 1 make sore by rubbing 2 wear away by rubbing 3 become annoyed

chaff noun 1 husks of corn left after threshing 2 something of little value 3 good-natured teasing ◇ verb tease jokingly

chaffinch noun (plural **chaffinches**) a small songbird of the finch family

chagrin /shuh-grin/ noun annoyance, irritation • **chagrined** adj annoyed

chain noun 1 a number of metal links or rings passing through one another 2 (**chains**) these used to tie a prisoner's limbs; fetters 3 a number of connected things: a chain of events 4 a group of shops owned by one person or company 5 a number of atoms of an element joined together ◇ verb fasten or imprison with a chain • **chain letter** noun a letter containing promises or threats, requesting the recipient to send a similar letter to several other people • **chain mail** noun armour made of iron links • **chain reaction** noun a chemical process in which each reaction in turn causes a similar reaction • **chainsaw** noun a power-driven saw with teeth on a rotating chain • **chain-smoker** noun someone who smokes continuously • **chain store** noun one of several shops under the same ownership

chair noun 1 a seat for one person with a back to it 2 a university professorship: the chair of French literature 3 a chairman or chairwoman • **chairlift** noun a row of chairs on a rotating cable for carrying people up mountains etc • **chairman**, **chairwoman** or **chairperson** noun someone who is in charge of a meeting

chakra noun in yoga, a centre of spiritual power in the body

chalet /shal-eh/ noun a small wooden house

chalice noun a cup for wine, used eg in church services

chalk noun 1 a type of limestone 2 a compressed stick of coloured powder used for writing or drawing ◇ verb mark with chalk • **chalky** adj 1 of chalk 2 white, pale

challenge verb 1 question another's right to do something 2 ask (someone) to take part in a contest, eg to settle a quarrel ◇ noun 1 a difficult but stimulating task that tests ability or determination **2** a questioning of another's right **3** a call to a contest • **challenger** noun • **challenging** adj difficult but stimulating

chamber noun **1** a room **2** a place where a parliament meets **3** a room where legal cases are heard by a judge **4** an enclosed space or cavity **5** the part of a gun that holds the cartridges • **chamber music** noun classical music for a small group of players, suitable for performance in a room rather than a large hall

chamberlain noun an officer appointed by the crown or a local authority to carry out certain duties

chamberpot noun a portable container used as a toilet in the bedroom

chameleon /kuh-*meel*-yun/ noun a small lizard able to change its colour to match its surroundings

chamois /*sham*-wah/ noun **1** a goat-like deer living in mountainous country **2** (*also called*: **shammy**) a piece of soft leather made from its skin, used for cleaning windows, polishing, *etc*

champ verb chew noisily • **champing at the bit** impatient to act

champagne /sham-*pehn*/ noun sparkling wine from the Champagne region of northern France

champion noun **1** someone who has beaten all others in a competition **2** a strong supporter of a cause: *champion of free speech* ◇ verb support the cause of

championship noun **1** a contest to find a champion **2** the title of champion **3** the act of championing a cause

chance noun **1** an opportunity **2** a risk, a possibility **3** something unexpected or unplanned ◇ verb **1** risk **2** happen by accident ◇ adj happening by accident • **by chance** not by arrangement; unexpectedly • **chance upon** meet or find unexpectedly

chancel noun the part of a church where the altar is and where the choir sits

chancellor noun **1** the Chancellor of the Exchequer **2** the head of government in some European countries **3** the head of a university • **Chancellor of the Exchequer** the minister in the British cabinet in charge of government spending • **Lord Chancellor** the head of the English legal system

chancery noun (in England) the Lord Chancellor's court

chancy adj (**chancier**, **chanciest**) risky

chandelier /shan-duh-*leer*/ noun a fixture hanging from the ceiling with branches for holding lights

change verb (**changes**, **changing**, **changed**) **1** make or become different **2** give up or leave (a job, house, *etc*) for another **3** put on different clothes **4** give (money of one kind) in exchange for (money of another kind) ◇ noun **1** the act of making or becoming different **2** money returned when a buyer gives more than the price of an article **3** money in the form of coins **4** another set of clothing • **change of life** the menopause

changeable adj likely to change or often changing • **changeably** adv

changeling noun a child secretly taken or left in place of another

channel noun **1** a narrow sea **2** a band of frequencies for radio or television signals **3** a passage along which water flows **4** a way of doing or achieving something: *make your complaint through official channels* ◇ verb (**channelling**, **channelled**) direct into a particular course

chant verb recite in a singing manner ◇ noun a singing recitation • **chanter** noun a pipe with finger holes on a set of bagpipes, on which the melody is played

chanterelle /shonh-tuh-*rel*/ noun a yellowish edible mushroom

chaos /*keh*-os/ noun disorder, confusion

chaotic adj disordered, confused • **chaotically** adv

chap noun, informal a man

chapati /chuh-*pat*-i/ noun a round of unleavened Indian bread

chapel noun 1 a small church 2 a small part of a larger church 3 Brit a Catholic or Nonconformist church

chaperone noun a woman who attends a younger one when she goes out in public ◇ verb act as a chaperone to

chaplain noun a member of the clergy accompanying an army, navy, etc

chapped adj of skin: cracked by cold or wet weather

chapter noun 1 a division of a book 2 a branch of a society or organization • **chapter of accidents** a series of accidents

char¹ verb (**charring, charred**) burn until black

char² verb (**charrring, charred**) do odd jobs of housework, cleaning, etc ◇ noun, informal a charwoman

charabanc /*sha*-ruh-bang/ noun, dated a bus used for day trips; a coach

character noun 1 the nature and qualities of someone or something 2 someone in a play, story or film 3 moral integrity 4 determination or perseverance 5 someone noted for eccentric behaviour

characteristic noun a typical and noticeable feature of someone or something ◇ adj typical • **characteristically** adv

characterize verb 1 be typical of 2 describe (as) • **characterization** noun

charade /shuh-*rahd*/ or /shuh-*rehd*/ noun 1 a ridiculous pretence 2 (**charades**) a game in which players have to guess a word from gestures representing its sound or meaning

charcoal noun wood burnt black, used for fuel or sketching

charge verb 1 accuse: *charged with murder* 2 ask (a price) 3 ask to do; give responsibility for 4 load (a gun) 5 attack in a rush ◇ noun 1 accusation for a crime 2 a price, a fee 3 an attack 4 the gunpowder in a shell or bullet 5 care, responsibility 6 someone looked after by another person • **charger** noun 1 a device for recharging batteries 2 a horse used in battle • **in charge** in command or control • **take charge of** take command of

chariot noun, hist a wheeled carriage used in battle • **charioteer** noun a chariot-driver

charisma /kuh-*riz*-muh/ noun impressive personal charm or authority

charismatic adj full of charisma • **charismatically** adv

charitable adj 1 willing to give; generous 2 of a charity: *charitable status* 3 kind in judging people; generous-minded • **charitably** adv

charity noun (plural **charities**) 1 donation of money to the poor etc 2 an organization that collects money and gives it to people in need 3 kindness

charlatan /*shah*-luh-tun/ noun someone who claims greater powers or abilities than they really have

charm noun 1 an impressively attractive personality 2 a small object worn hanging from a bracelet 3 something thought to have magical powers 4 a magic spell ◇ verb 1 please greatly; delight 2 put under a spell • **charming** adj

chart noun 1 a table or diagram giving particular information: *tempera-*

ture chart **2** a geographical map of the sea **3** a rough map ◇ *verb* make into a chart; plot

charter *noun* a written paper showing the official granting of rights, lands, *etc* ◇ *verb* hire (a boat, aeroplane, *etc*) ◇ *adj* hired for a special purpose: *charter flight* • **chartered** *adj* **1** qualified under the regulations of a professional body: *chartered surveyor* **2** hired for a purpose

charwoman *noun* a woman hired to do domestic cleaning

chary *adj* (**charier, chariest**) cautious • **charily** *adv* • **chariness** *noun*

chase *verb* **1** run after; pursue **2** hunt ◇ *noun* a pursuit, a hunt

chasm /kazm/ *noun* **1** a steep drop between high rocks *etc* **2** a wide difference; a gulf

chassis /shas-ee/ *noun* (*plural* **chassis**) **1** the frame, wheels and machinery of a motor vehicle **2** an aeroplane's landing carriage

chaste *adj* **1** never having had sex; virginal **2** pure in thought • **chastely** *adv* • **chastity** *noun*

chasten *verb* **1** make humble **2** scold • **chastened** *adj*

chastise *verb* **1** speak to severely; scold **2** punish, *esp* by beating • **chastisement** *noun*

chat *verb* (**chatting, chatted**) talk in an easy, friendly way ◇ *noun* a friendly conversation • **chat room** *noun* a place on the Internet where people can exchange messages • **chat show** *noun* a radio or TV programme in which personalities talk informally with their host

chateau /sha-toh/ *noun* (*plural* **chateaux**) a French castle or country house

chattels *plural noun* movable possessions • **goods and chattels** personal possessions

chatter *verb* **1** talk idly or rapidly; gossip **2** of teeth: rattle together because of cold • **chatterbox** *noun* someone who talks a great deal

chatty *adj* (**chattier, chattiest**) willing to talk; talkative • **chattily** *adv*

chauffeur /shoh-fuh/ *noun* someone employed to drive a motor-car

chauvinist /shoh-vin-ist/ *noun* a man who practises sexism towards women • **chauvinism** *noun* extreme nationalism or patriotism • **chauvinistic** *adj*

chav *noun, Brit slang* a feckless member of the working class

cheap *adj* **1** low in price; inexpensive **2** of poor quality or vulgar style **3** cruel and undeserved: *cheap jokes* • **cheapen** *verb* make cheap • **cheaply** *adv*

cheat *verb* **1** act dishonestly to gain an advantage **2** deceive ◇ *noun* **1** someone who cheats **2** a dishonest trick

check *verb* **1** see if (a total *etc*) is correct or accurate **2** see if (a machine *etc*) is in good condition or working properly **3** bring to a stop **4** hold back; restrain ◇ *noun* **1** a test of correctness or accuracy **2** a pattern of squares **3** a restraint **4** a sudden stop • **checked** *adj* patterned with squares • **check in** or **check out** record your arrival at or departure from (a hotel *etc*)

Do not confuse with: **cheque**

---

checkered *another spelling of* **chequered**

checkers *another spelling of* **chequers**

checkmate *noun, chess* a position from which the king cannot escape

checkout *noun* a place where payment is made in a supermarket

cheek *noun* **1** the side of the face below the eye **2** disrespectful behaviour; insolence **3** a buttock

cheeky *adj* (**cheekier**, **cheekiest**) showing a lack of respect; insolent • **cheekily** *adv* • **cheekiness** *noun*

cheep *verb* make a faint sound like a small bird ◇ *noun* the sound of a small bird

cheer *noun* a shout of approval, welcome or encouragement ◇ *verb* shout approval, welcome or encouragement • **cheerless** *adj* sad, gloomy • **cheer up** make or become less gloomy

cheerful *adj* in good spirits; happy • **cheerfully** *adv* • **cheerfulness** *noun*

cheerio *exclam* goodbye!

cheers *exclam* **1** good health! **2** *informal* thank you **3** *informal* goodbye

cheery *adj* (**cheerier**, **cheeriest**) lively and merry • **cheerily** *adv*

cheese *noun* a solid food made from milk • **cheesecake** *noun* a dessert with a biscuit base and a thick topping of flavoured cream cheese • **cheesecloth** *noun* loosely-woven cotton cloth • **cheeseparing** *adj* mean

cheesy *adj* (**cheesier**, **cheesiest**) **1** tasting of cheese **2** of a smile: broad **3** *informal* showing a lack of good taste; vulgar

cheetah *noun* a fast-running animal similar to a leopard

chef /shef/ *noun* a head cook in a restaurant

chemical *noun* a substance produced using the techniques of chemistry ◇ *adj* relating to the reactions between elements *etc*

chemist *noun* **1** someone who makes up and sells medicines; a pharmacist **2** someone who studies chemistry

chemistry *noun* the study of the elements and the ways they combine or react with each other

chemotherapy *noun* treatment for cancer that involves large doses of powerful drugs

chenille /shuh-*neel*/ *noun* a thick, velvety material or yarn

cheongsam /chong-*sam*/ *noun* a traditional Chinese woman's dress, tight-fitting with a high neck

cheque *or US* **check** *noun* a written order to a banker to pay money from a bank account to another person • **cheque book** *noun* a book containing cheques

---

Do not confuse with: **check**

---

chequered *or* **checkered** *adj* **1** marked like a chessboard **2** partly good, partly bad: *a chequered career*

chequers *or* **checkers** *plural noun* **1** a pattern of squares, *eg* on a chessboard **2** the game of draughts

cherish *verb* **1** protect and treat with fondness or kindness **2** keep in your mind or heart: *cherish a hope*

cheroot *noun* a small cigar

cherry *noun* (*plural* **cherries**) **1** a small bright-red fruit with a stone **2** the tree that produces this fruit

cherub *noun* (*plural* **cherubs** *or* **cherubim**) **1** an angel with a plump, childish face and body **2** a beautiful child

chervil *noun* a feathery herb related to the carrot

chess *noun* a game for two players in which pieces are moved in turn on a board marked in alternate black and white squares • **chessboard** *noun* • **chessman** *or* **chesspiece** *noun*

chest *noun* **1** the part of the body between the neck and the stomach **2** a large strong box • **chest of drawers** *noun* a piece of furniture fitted with a set of drawers

chesterfield *noun* a low-backed leather sofa

chestnut *noun* **1** a reddish-brown nut **2** the tree that produces this nut, the **horse chestnut** or **sweet chestnut 3** a reddish-brown horse **4** an old joke

cheviot noun a kind of sheep

chevron noun a V-shape, eg on a badge or road-sign

chew verb **1** break up (food) with the teeth before swallowing **2** reflect or ponder (on)

chez /sheh/ prep at the home of

chi /chee/ another spelling of **qi**

chiaroscuro /kyah-roh-skoo-roh/ noun dramatic contrast between light and dark in a painting etc

chic /sheek/ adj smart and fashionable ◊ noun fashionable elegance; style

chicanery /shi-keh-nuh-ree/ noun dishonest cleverness

chichi /shee-shee/ adj fashionable to the point of being self-conscious or affected

chick noun **1** a baby bird **2** slang a young woman

chicken noun **1** a young hen or cock, or meat from one **2** informal a coward ◊ adj, informal cowardly ● **chicken-hearted** adj cowardly ● **chicken out** avoid doing something out of fear

chickenfeed noun **1** food for poultry **2** something paltry or worthless, esp a ridiculously small amount of money

chickenpox noun an infectious disease that causes red, itchy spots

chickpea noun a plump light-brown edible seed of a plant of the pea family

chicory noun **1** a plant with sharp-tasting leaves eaten in salads **2** its root, roasted and ground to mix with coffee

chide verb scold

chief adj **1** most important; main **2** largest ◊ noun **1** a leader or ruler **2** the head of a department, organization, etc

chiefly adv for the most part; mainly

chieftain noun the head of a clan or tribe

chiffon /shif-on/ noun a thin flimsy material made of silk or nylon

chignon /shee-nyonh/ noun a knot or roll of hair on the back of the head

chihuahua /chi-wa-wa/ noun a breed of very small dog, originally from Mexico

chilblain noun a painful swelling on hands and feet, caused by cold weather

child noun (plural **children**) **1** a young human being **2** a son or daughter: is that your child? ● **childbirth** noun the act of giving birth to a baby ● **childcare** noun the task or job of looking after children ● **childhood** noun the time of being a child ● **childlike** adj innocent ● **childminder** noun someone paid to look after other people's children in his or her own home

childish adj **1** of or like a child **2** silly, immature ● **childishly** adv ● **childishness** noun

chill noun **1** coldness **2** an illness that causes fever and shivering **3** lack of warmth or enthusiasm ◊ adj cold ◊ verb **1** make cold **2** refrigerate

chilli noun **1** the hot-tasting pod of a kind of pepper, used in cooking to give a spicy flavour **2** a dish or sauce made with this

chilly adj (**chillier**, **chilliest**) unpleasantly cold

chime noun **1** the sound of bells ringing **2** (**chimes**) a set of bells, eg in a clock ◊ verb **1** ring **2** of a clock: strike

chimera /kai-mee-ruh/ noun a wildly unrealistic idea or plan ● **chimerical** adj wildly fanciful

chimney noun (plural **chimneys**) a passage allowing smoke or heated air to escape from a fire

• **chimneypot** noun a metal or earthenware pipe placed at the top of a chimney • **chimneystack** noun **1** a tall chimney, eg in a factory **2** a number of chimneys built up together • **chimneysweep** noun someone employed to clean chimneys

chimpanzee noun a type of African ape

chin noun the part of the face below the mouth

china noun **1** thin earthenware of great quality; porcelain **2** articles made of this

chinchilla noun a small S American animal with soft grey fur

chink noun **1** a narrow opening **2** the sound of light metallic objects, eg coins, hitting each other or a surface

chintz noun (plural **chintzes**) a cotton cloth with brightly coloured patterning

chip verb (**chipping**, **chipped**) break or cut small pieces (from or off) ◇ noun **1** a long thin piece of potato fried **2** a tiny piece of silicon with electrical circuits on it, used in computers and other electronic equipment **3** a small piece chipped off **4** a part damaged by chipping **5** US a potato or corn crisp • **chip and PIN** a system where the user of a credit or debit card types in their PIN on a device in a shop

chipmunk noun a kind of N American squirrel

chipolata noun a type of small sausage

chiropodist /ki-rop-uh-dist/ noun someone who treats minor disorders and diseases of the feet • **chiropody** noun

chiropractic /kai-ruh-prak-tik/ noun a treatment for muscular pain etc involving manipulation of the spinal column • **chiropractor** noun a therapist who uses chiropractic

chirp or **chirrup** verb of a bird: make a sharp, shrill sound

chirpy adj (**chirpier**, **chirpiest**) cheerful • **chirpily** adv • **chirpiness** noun

chisel noun a metal tool used to cut or hollow out wood, stone, etc ◇ verb (**chiselling**, **chiselled**) cut with a chisel

chit noun **1** a short note **2** a child: chit of a girl

chit-chat noun & verb gossip, talk

chivalry /shiv-ul-ri/ noun **1** kindness and politeness, esp on the part of men towards women **2** hist the standard of behaviour expected of knights in medieval times • **chivalrous** adj • **chivalrously** adv • **chivalrousness** noun

chive noun an onion-like herb used in cooking

chlorine noun a yellowish-green gas with a sharp smell, used as a bleach and disinfectant • **chlorinated** adj mixed with chlorine or a substance containing chlorine

chlorofluorocarbon noun a gas formerly used in refrigerators and as a propellant in aerosols, now generally avoided because it damages the ozone layer

chloroform noun a liquid whose vapour causes unconsciousness if inhaled

chock-a-block adj completely full or congested

chockfull adj completely full

chocolate noun **1** a sweet made from the seeds of the cacao tree **2** (also called: **cocoa**) a drink made from the seeds ◇ adj dark brown in colour • **chocolatey** adj tasting of chocolate

choice noun **1** the act of choosing or right to choose **2** something chosen ◇ adj of a high quality: choice vegetables

choir /kwai-uh/ noun **1** a group of

singers **2** a part of a church where a choir sits

Do not confuse with: **quire**

---

choke verb **1** stop or partly stop the breathing of **2** block or clog (a pipe etc) **3** have your breathing stopped or interrupted, eg by smoke ◊ noun a valve in a petrol engine that controls the inflow of air

cholera /kol-uh-ruh/ noun an infectious intestinal disease causing severe vomiting and diarrhoea

cholesterol noun a substance in body cells that carries fats through the blood

chomp verb, informal munch noisily

choose verb (**choosing**, **chose**, **chosen**) **1** select and take from two or several things: choose whichever book you like **2** decide (to) out of preference: we chose to leave before the film began

chop verb (**chopping**, **chopped**) **1** cut into small pieces **2** cut with a sudden blow ◊ noun **1** a chopping blow **2** a slice of meat containing a bone: mutton chop ● **chop and change** keep changing

chopper noun **1** a knife or axe for chopping **2** informal a helicopter

choppy adj (**choppier**, **choppiest**) of the sea: with a rough surface

chopsticks plural noun a pair of small sticks of wood, ivory, etc used instead of a knife and fork for eating food from SE Asia

choral adj sung by or written for a choir

chord noun **1** a musical sound made by playing several notes together **2** a straight line joining any two points on a curve

---

Do not confuse with: **cord**

---

chore noun **1** a dull, boring task **2** (**chores**) housework

choreography noun the arrangement of dance steps for a performance ● **choreographer** noun

chorister noun a member of a choir

chortle verb laugh quietly; chuckle

chorus noun (plural **choruses**) **1** a part of a song repeated after each verse **2** a band of singers and dancers in a musical show **3** a choir or choral group

chose past tense of **choose**

chosen past participle of **choose**

chow noun a Chinese breed of dog with a bushy coat and a blue-black tongue

chowder noun a thick soup containing cream

christen verb baptize and give a name to ● **christening** noun the ceremony of baptism

Christian noun a believer in Christianity ◊ adj of Christianity ● **Christian name** noun a first or personal name

Christianity noun the religion that follows the teachings of Jesus Christ

Christmas noun an annual Christian holiday or festival, in memory of the birth of Jesus Christ, held on 25 December ● **Christmas Eve** noun 24 December ● **Christmassy** adj suitable for Christmas ● **Christmas tree** noun an evergreen tree hung with lights, decorations and gifts at Christmas

chromatic adj **1** of colours **2** coloured **3** music of or written in a scale in which each note is separated from the next by a semitone

chrome noun metal with a shiny chromium plating

chromium noun a metal that does not rust

chromosome noun a part of a living cell that determines the characteristics of an individual

chronic adj **1** of a disease: lasting a long time **2** informal very bad • **chronically** adv

chronicle noun a record of events in order of time ◊ verb write down events in order • **chronicler** noun

chronological adj arranged in the order of the time of happening • **chronologically** adv

chronometer noun an instrument for measuring time

chrysalis noun an insect, esp a butterfly or moth, in its early stage of life, with no wings and encased in a soft cocoon

chrysanthemum noun a type of garden flower with a large bushy head

chubby adj (**chubbier**, **chubbiest**) fairly fat and round; plump • **chubbily** adv • **chubbiness** noun

chuck verb **1** throw, toss **2** pat gently under the chin • **chuck out** informal **1** get rid of as useless; throw away **2** force to leave; expel

chuckle noun a quiet laugh ◊ verb laugh quietly

chuffed adj, informal very pleased

chug verb (**chugging**, **chugged**) move slowly with a repeated mechanical throbbing noise

chum noun, informal a close friend • **chummy** adj very friendly

chump noun, informal a silly or foolish person; an idiot

chunk noun a thick piece

chunky adj (**chunkier**, **chunkiest**) large, thick or heavy

church noun (plural **churches**) **1** a building for public, esp Christian, worship **2** any group of people who meet together for worship • **churchyard** noun a burial ground next to a church

churlish adj bad-mannered, rude • **churlishly** adv • **churlishness** noun

churn noun a machine for making butter from milk ◊ verb **1** make (butter) in a churn **2** shake or stir about violently

chute /shoot/ noun **1** a sloping trough for sending water, parcels, etc to a lower level **2** a sloping structure for children to slide down, with steps for climbing back up

chutney noun (plural **chutneys**) a thick sauce made with vegetables or fruits and vinegar, eaten cold

chutzpah /xhuut-spah/ noun admirable confidence to do or say things that might offend; nerve

CIA abbrev Central Intelligence Agency, a US government department that protects government information and collects secret political and military information about other countries

cicada /si-kah-duh/ noun a chirping insect found in warm climates

cicely noun a plant related to chervil

CID abbrev Criminal Investigation Department, a branch of the UK police force

cider noun an alcoholic drink made from fermented apple juice

cigar noun a roll of tobacco leaves for smoking

cigarette noun a thin paper tube filled with shredded tobacco for smoking

C-in-C abbrev Commander-in-Chief

cinder noun a piece of burnt coal

cinema noun **1** a place where films are shown **2** films as an art form or industry

cinnamon noun a yellowish-brown spice obtained from the bark of a tropical tree

cipher noun **1** a secret system of writing; a code **2** the number zero **3**

someone of no importance

circa *prep* approximately, in dates: *circa 300 BC*

circadian /sur-*keh*-di-un/ *adj* relating to biological rhythms repeated every 24 hours

circle *noun* 1 a shape formed from an endless curved line 2 something in the form of a circle; a ring 3 a society or group of people 4 an upper tier of seats in a theatre *etc* ◇ *verb* 1 enclose in a circle 2 move round in a circle

circlet *noun* an ornamental headband

circuit *noun* 1 the path of an electric current 2 a connected group of places, events, *etc*: *the American tennis circuit* 3 a movement in a circle, *esp* one lap of a running track or race track

circuitous /sur-*kyoo*-it-us/ *adj* involving many detours or changes of direction; roundabout: *by a circuitous route* • **circuitously** *adv*

circular *adj* round, like a circle ◇ *noun* a letter sent round to a number of people • **circularize** *verb* send a circular to

circulate *verb* 1 move round 2 send to many people: *circulate a memo*

circulation *noun* 1 the movement of the blood round the body 2 the total sales of a newspaper or magazine 3 the act of circulating

circumcise *verb* cut off the end of the foreskin of, as part of a religious ceremony • **circumcision** *noun*

circumference *noun* 1 the outside line of a circle 2 the length of this line

circumnavigate *verb* sail round (the world) • **circumnavigator** *noun*

circumscribe *verb* 1 draw a line round 2 put limits on; restrict • **circumscription** *noun*

circumspect *adj* cautious • **circum-** **spection** *noun* caution

circumstance *noun* 1 a situation, action or event that affects someone 2 (**circumstances**) the state of someone's financial affairs

circumstantial *adj* of evidence: pointing to a conclusion without giving absolute proof

circumstantiate *verb* prove by giving details

circumvent *verb* 1 get round (a difficulty) 2 defeat by being cleverer; outwit • **circumvention** *noun*

circus *noun* (*plural* **circuses**) 1 a travelling company of acrobats, clowns, *etc* 2 a large sports arena in ancient times 3 a curving or circular street

cirrhosis /si-*roh*-sis/ *noun* a disease of the liver

cirrus *noun* thin fleecy cloud at high levels

CIS *abbrev* Commonwealth of Independent States, an alliance of most of the former Soviet Republics

cissy *or* **sissy** *noun, informal* someone who lacks courage, determination or strength

cistern *noun* a tank for storing water

citadel *noun* a fortress originally built to defend a city

citation *noun* 1 something quoted 2 a summons to appear in court 3 official recognition of an achievement or action

cite *verb* 1 quote as an example or as proof 2 summon to appear in court

---

Do not confuse with: **sight** and **site**

---

citizen *noun* someone who lives in a city or state, often someone regarded as officially belonging there • **citizenry** *noun* the inhabitants of a city or state • **citizenship** *noun* the rights or state of being a citizen

citric acid *noun* a sharp-tasting acid found in citrus fruits

citron *noun* a type of fruit similar to a lemon

citrus fruit *noun* one of a group of fruits including the orange, lemon and lime

city *noun* (*plural* **cities**) **1** a large town **2** a town with a cathedral • **the City** *Brit* the part of London regarded as the centre of business

civic *adj* **1** relating to a city, its citizens, or local public events **2** relating to or run by local government • **civics** *sing noun* the study of people's duties as citizens

civil *adj* **1** relating to a community **2** non-military, civilian **3** polite • **civil engineer** *noun* an engineer who plans bridges, roads, *etc* • **civil law** *noun* law concerned with citizens' rights, not criminal acts • **civil list** *noun* the expenses of the royal household • **civil marriage** *noun* a marriage that does not take place in church • **civil rights** *plural noun* the rights of a citizen • **civil service** *noun* the paid administrative officials of the country, excluding the armed forces • **civil war** *noun* war between citizens of the same country

civilian *noun* someone who is not in the armed forces ◇ *adj* non-military

civility *noun* politeness, good manners

civilization *noun* **1** life under a civilized system **2** a particular culture: *a prehistoric civilization* **3** making or becoming civilized

civilize *verb* bring (a people) under a regular system of laws, education, *etc* • **civilized** *adj* living under such a system; not savage

CJD *abbrev* Creutzfeld-Jakob disease, a fatal disease that attacks the brain

clad *adj*, *formal* clothed: *clad in leather from head to toe*

claim *verb* **1** demand as a right **2** state as a truth; assert (that) ◇ *noun* an act of claiming • **claimant** *noun* someone who makes a claim

clairvoyant *adj* **1** able to see into the future **2** able to contact the spirit world ◇ *noun* someone with clairvoyant powers • **clairvoyance** *noun*

clam *noun* a large shellfish with two shells hinged together

clamber *verb* climb awkwardly or with difficulty

clammy *adj* (**clammier**, **clammiest**) unpleasantly moist and sticky

clamour *noun* **1** an urgent public demand for something **2** a loud continuous noise ◇ *verb* **1** make an urgent public demand for something **2** make a loud noise • **clamorous** *adj* noisy

clamp *noun* a tool used to hold things together ◇ *verb* bind with a clamp • **clamp down on** suppress firmly

clan *noun* **1** a number of families with the same surname, traditionally under a single chieftain **2** an exclusive group; a clique • **clannish** *adj* loyal to each other, but showing little interest in others • **clansman, clanswoman** *noun* a member of a clan

clandestine *adj* done secretly • **clandestinely** *adv*

clang *verb* make a loud, deep ringing sound ◇ *noun* a loud, deep ring

clank *noun* a sound like that made by metal hitting metal ◇ *verb* make this sound

clap *verb* (**clapping**, **clapped**) **1** hit the hands together to show approval **2** strike noisily together **3** *informal* put suddenly; throw: *clap in jail* ◇ *noun* **1** the noise made by striking together two things, *esp* the hands **2** a burst of sound, *esp* thunder • **clapper** *noun* the tongue of a bell

claptrap *noun* meaningless or stupid words; nonsense

claret noun red wine from the Bordeaux region of France

clarify verb (**clarifies**, **clarifying**, **clarified**) 1 make clear and understandable 2 make (a liquid) clear and pure

clarinet noun a musical wind instrument, usually made of wood • **clarinettist** noun someone who plays the clarinet

clarion noun, old 1 a kind of trumpet 2 a shrill, rousing noise • **clarion call** noun a clear call to action

clarity noun clearness

clash noun (plural **clashes**) 1 a loud noise made by metal things hitting each other 2 a disagreement or fight 3 a sporting contest; a match or game ◇ verb 1 bang noisily together 2 disagree or fight 3 of events: be scheduled to take place at the same time 4 of two colours etc: not look well together

clasp noun 1 a hook or pin for fastening 2 a handshake 3 an embrace ◇ verb 1 hold closely; grasp 2 fasten

class noun (plural **classes**) 1 a rank or order of people or things 2 a group of schoolchildren or students taught together 3 a group of plants or animals with something in common 4 impressive elegance, quality or skill ◇ verb 1 place in a class 2 arrange in some order

classic noun 1 a great book or other work of art 2 something typical and influential of its kind 3 (**classics**) the study of ancient Greek and Latin literature ◇ adj 1 excellent 2 typical of its kind: a classic example 3 simple and elegant in style: a classic black dress

classical adj 1 of a classic or the classics 2 of music: with a serious, artistic object and played on the instruments of a traditional Western orchestra

classify verb (**classifies**, **classifying**, **classified**) 1 arrange in classes 2 put into a class or category • **classification** noun • **classified** adj of information: officially classed as secret, not to be made available publicly

classy adj (**classier**, **classiest**) elegant, stylish

clatter noun a noise of plates etc banged together

clause noun 1 a part of a sentence containing a finite verb 2 a part of a long legal document, eg a will or an act of parliament

claustrophobia noun an abnormal fear of enclosed spaces • **claustrophobic** adj

claw noun 1 an animal's or bird's foot with hooked nails 2 a hooked nail on one of these feet ◇ verb scratch or tear

clay noun soft, sticky earth, often used to make pottery, bricks, etc • **clayey** adj

claymore noun, hist a large sword used by Scottish Highlanders in battle

clean adj 1 free from dirt; pure 2 neat: a clean break 3 not obscene 4 showing no record of offences: a clean licence ◇ adv completely: got clean away ◇ verb make clean • **cleaner** noun 1 someone employed to clean a building etc 2 a substance that cleans • **cleanliness** noun • **cleanly** adv

cleanse /klenz/ verb make clean • **cleanser** noun a cream or liquid for cleaning the face • **cleansing** noun improvement of something by getting rid of undesirable elements of it

clear adj 1 bright 2 free from mist or cloud: clear sky 3 transparent 4 free from difficulty or obstructions 5 easy to see, hear or understand 6 after deductions and charges have been made: clear profit 7 with no stains or blemishes 8 without touching: clear of the rocks ◇ verb 1 make clear 2 empty 3 free from blame 4 leap over without touching **5** of the sky: become bright • **clearance** noun **1** distance between close objects **2** official permission **3** the process of removing • **clear-cut** adj distinct, obvious • **clearing** noun a treeless area in a wood or forest □ **clearly** adv • **clearness** noun • **clear out** or **clear off** go away

cleavage noun **1** the hollow between a woman's breasts **2** splitting **3** the way in which two things are split or divided

cleave verb (**cleaving, clove** or **cleft, cloven** or **cleft**) **1** divide, split **2** crack **3** follow (rules, principles, etc); stick (to)

cleaver noun a heavy knife for splitting meat carcases etc

clef noun a musical sign (♭ **treble clef** or ♯ **bass clef**) placed on a stave to fix the pitch of the notes

cleft noun an opening made by splitting; a crack ◊ past form of **cleave** • **cleft palate** noun an abnormal division in the roof of the mouth, present at birth

cleg noun a type of horsefly

clematis noun a flowering, climbing shrub

clement adj **1** of weather: mild **2** showing leniency or kindness; merciful • **clemency** noun readiness to forgive; mercy

clench verb press firmly together: clenching his teeth

clergy plural noun the ministers of the Christian church • **clergyman, clergywoman** noun a Christian minister

cleric noun a member of the clergy

clerical adj **1** relating to office work **2** relating to the clergy

clerk /klahk/ noun an office worker who writes letters, keeps accounts, etc ◊ verb act as clerk

clever adj **1** quick in learning and understanding **2** intelligent or skilful:

a clever answer • **cleverly** adv • **cleverness** noun

cliché /klee-sheh/ noun an idea, phrase, etc that has been used too much and now has little meaning

click noun a short sharp sound like a clock's tick ◊ verb **1** make this sound **2** comput press and release one of the buttons on a mouse

client noun **1** a customer of a shop etc **2** someone who goes to a lawyer etc for advice

clientele /klai-un-tel/ noun customers

cliff noun a very steep, rocky slope, esp by the sea

climate noun **1** the weather conditions of a particular area **2** general condition or situation: in the present cultural climate • **climatic** adj

climax noun (plural **climaxes**) **1** the point of greatest interest or excitement in a situation **2** the point of greatest sexual excitement; orgasm ◊ verb **1** reach the most interesting or exciting point **2** reach the point of greatest sexual excitement; have an orgasm

climb verb **1** go to the top of **2** go up using hands and feet **3** slope upward ◊ noun an act of climbing • **climber** noun **1** someone who climbs **2** a plant that climbs up walls

clinch verb **1** grasp tightly **2** settle (an argument, bargain, etc) ◊ noun (plural **clinches**) **1** boxing a position in which the boxers hold each other with their arms **2** a passionate embrace • **clincher** noun

cling verb (**clinging, clung**) stick or hang on (to) • **clingy** adj

clingfilm noun thin transparent plastic material used to wrap food

clinic noun a place or part of a hospital where a particular kind of treatment is given

clinical adj **1** of a clinic **2** based

on observation: *clinical medicine* **3** objective, cool and unemotional: *clinical approach* • **clinically** *adv*

clink *noun* a ringing sound of knocked glasses *etc* ◇ *verb*

clinker *noun* waste produced from smelting iron or burning coal

clip *verb* (**clipping, clipped**) **1** cut bits off the edges of **2** fasten with a clip ◇ *noun* **1** something clipped off **2** a short extract from a film or television programme **3** a small fastener **4** *informal* a sharp blow • **clipboard** *noun* **1** *comput* part of a computer's memory that holds data temporarily when it is transferred from one location to another **2** a board with a clip at the top, on which to rest and carry papers

clipper *noun* **1** a fast-sailing ship **2** (**clippers**) large scissors for clipping

clique /kleek/ *noun* a small group of people who help each other but keep others at a distance

clitoris *noun* a small sensitive organ at the front of a woman's external sex organs • **clitoral** *adj*

cloak *noun* **1** a loose outer garment **2** something that hides: *cloak of darkness* ◇ *verb* **1** cover with or as if with a cloak **2** hide • **cloakroom** *noun* a place where coats, hats, *etc* may be left for a time

cloche /klosh/ *noun* (*plural* **cloches**) a transparent frame for protecting plants

clock *noun* a machine for measuring time • **clockwise** *adj* turning or moving in the same direction as the hands of a clock • **clockwork** *adj* worked by machinery such as that of a clock • **clock in** *or* **clock out** record your time of arrival at, or departure from, work • **like clockwork** smoothly, without difficulties

clod *noun* **1** a thick lump of turf **2** a stupid man

clodhopper *noun* a stupid clumsy person • **clodhopping** *adj*

clog *noun* a shoe with a wooden sole ◇ *verb* (**clogging, clogged**) block (pipes *etc*)

cloisonné /klwa-zon-eh/ *noun* a form of enamelling with coloured areas divided by threads of metal

cloister *noun* **1** a roofed walkway round a courtyard inside a monastery, convent, school, *etc* **2** a monastery or convent • **cloistered** *adj* **1** shut up in a monastery *etc* **2** sheltered

clone *noun* a group of identical organisms reproduced by genetic engineering from a single parent cell ◇ *verb* produce a clone

clootie dumpling *noun* a Scottish steamed pudding made with suet and dried fruit

close[1] /klohs/ *adj* **1** near in time, place, *etc* **2** very dear: *a close friend* **3** decided by a small amount: *a close contest* **4** lacking fresh air; stuffy **5** ungenerous with money; mean **6** secretive ◇ *noun* **1** a narrow passage off a street **2** the gardens, walks, *etc* near a cathedral • **closely** *adv* • **closeness** *noun* • **close-up** *noun* a film or photograph taken very near the subject

close[2] /klohz/ *verb* **1** shut **2** finish ◇ *noun* the end • **closed-circuit television** *noun* a system of television cameras and monitors used for security purposes in a building or street

closet *noun*, *US* a cupboard ◇ *adj* done secretly: *a closet socialist* ◇ *verb* take into a room for a private conference • **closeted with** in private conference with

closure *noun* **1** the act of closing something, *esp* permanently **2** a point at which past unhappiness can be finally forgotten or accepted

clot *noun* **1** a lump that forms in blood, cream, *etc* **2** *informal* an idiot

◇ *verb* (**clotting, clotted**) form into clots

cloth *noun* 1 woven material of cotton, wool, silk, *etc* 2 a piece of this, used for cleaning, polishing, *etc*

clothe *verb* 1 put clothes on 2 provide with clothes 3 cover

clothes *plural noun* 1 things worn to cover the body, *eg* shirt, trousers, skirt 2 sheets and coverings for a bed; bedclothes • **clothing** *noun* clothes

cloud *noun* 1 a mass of tiny drops of water or ice floating in the sky 2 a mass of anything: *clouds of smoke* ◇ *verb* become dim or blurred • **cloudburst** *noun* a sudden heavy fall of rain • **clouded** *adj* • **cloudless** *adj*

cloudy *adj* (**cloudier, cloudiest**) 1 darkened with clouds 2 not clear or transparent

clout *noun, informal* 1 a blow 2 influence, power ◇ *verb* hit

clove[1] *noun* 1 a flower bud of the clove tree, used as a spice 2 a small section of a bulb of garlic

clove[2] *past tense of* **cleave**

cloven-hoofed *adj* having a divided hoof like an ox, sheep, *etc*

clover *noun* a field plant with leaves that usually have three parts • **in clover** in luxury

clown *noun* 1 a comedian with a painted face and comical clothes in a circus 2 a fool • **clowning** *noun* silly or comical behaviour • **clownish** *adj* awkward or ridiculous in behaviour or appearance

cloy *verb* of something sweet: become unpleasant when too much is taken • **cloying** *adj* • **cloyingly** *adv*

club *noun* 1 a group of people who meet for social events *etc* 2 the place where these people meet 3 a place where there is dancing to recorded pop music, and where alcohol is usually sold 4 a stick used to hit the ball in golf 5 (**clubs**) one of the four suits of playing cards 6 a heavy stick ◇ *verb* (**clubbing, clubbed**) beat with a club • **clubbing** *noun* the activity of going to clubs for dancing and drinking • **club together** put money into a joint fund for some purpose

cluck *noun* the sound made by a hen ◇ *verb* 1 make a hen's sound 2 make a disapproving sound with the tongue

clue *noun* a sign or piece of evidence that helps to solve a mystery • **not have a clue** not know at all

clump *noun* a cluster of trees or shrubs ◇ *verb* walk heavily

clumsy *adj* (**clumsier, clumsiest**) 1 awkward in movement or actions 2 tactless, thoughtless: *clumsy apology* • **clumsily** *adv* • **clumsiness** *noun*

clung *past form of* **cling**

clunky *adj* (**clunkier, clunkiest**) awkward or noisy in operation

cluster *noun* 1 a number of berries, flowers, *etc* growing together; a bunch 2 a crowd ◇ *verb* group together in clusters

clutch *verb* 1 hold firmly 2 seize, grasp ◇ *noun* (*plural* **clutches**) 1 a grasp 2 part of a vehicle engine used for changing gears, or the pedal or lever operating it

clutter *noun* 1 a muddled or disordered collection of things 2 disorder, confusion, untidiness ◇ *verb* (with **up**) fill or cover in an untidy, disordered way

cm *abbrev* centimetre

CND *abbrev* Campaign for Nuclear Disarmament

CO *abbrev* Commanding Officer

Co *abbrev* 1 Company 2 County

co- *prefix* joint, working with: *co-author/co-driver*

c/o *abbrev* care of

coach noun (plural **coaches**) 1 a bus for long-distance travel 2 a railway carriage 3 a trainer for sportsmen and sportswomen 4 a closed, four-wheeled horse carriage ◇ verb train or help to prepare for an examination, sports competition, etc

coagulate verb of a liquid: thicken, clot

coal noun a black mineral dug out of the earth and used for burning, making gas, etc • **coalfield** noun an area where there is coal to be mined • **coalmine** noun a mine from which coal is dug

coalesce /koh-uh-les/ verb come together and unite

coalition noun a joining together of different parts or groups

coarse adj 1 not fine in texture; rough, harsh 2 vulgar • **coarsely** adv • **coarsen** verb make coarse • **coarseness** noun

coast noun the border of land next to the sea ◇ verb 1 sail along or near a coast 2 move without the use of power on a bike, in a car, etc • **coastal** adj of or on the coast • **coastguard** noun an official who acts as a guard along the coast to help those in danger in boats etc • **coastline** noun the shape of the coast

coat noun 1 an outer garment with sleeves 2 an animal's covering of hair or wool 3 a layer of paint ◇ verb cover with a coating or layer • **coating** noun a covering • **coat of arms** noun the badge or crest of a family

coax verb persuade gently or with flattery

cob noun 1 a head of maize 2 a male swan

cobalt noun 1 a silvery metal 2 a blue colouring obtained from this

cobble noun a rounded stone used in paving roads (also called: **cobblestone**) ◇ verb 1 mend (shoes) 2 repair

roughly or hurriedly • **cobbler** noun someone who mends shoes • **cobble together** make or assemble haphazardly, using what is available

cobra noun a poisonous snake found in India and Africa

cobweb noun a spider's web

cocaine noun an illegal addictive drug in the form of a white powder

cochineal /koch-i-neel/ noun a scarlet dye, used to colour food, made from the dried bodies of certain insects

cock noun 1 the male of most kinds of bird, esp of poultry 2 slang the penis 3 a tap or valve for controlling the flow of liquid 4 a hammer-like part of a gun that fires the shot 5 a small heap of hay ◇ verb 1 tilt (the head) to one side 2 set (the ears) upright to listen 3 draw back the cock of a gun • **cockscomb** noun the comb or crest of a cock's head • **cocksure** adj quite sure, often without cause • **cock-up** noun, slang a mistake, or a disorganized situation that results from it

cockade noun a knot of ribbons worn on a hat

cockatoo noun a kind of parrot

cockatrice noun a mythological creature like a cock with a dragon's tail

cockerel noun a young cock

cocker spaniel noun a breed of small spaniel

cockle noun a type of shellfish • **cockleshell** noun the shell of a cockle • **cockles of the heart** someone's innermost feelings, esp of peace, sympathy or affection

cockney noun (plural **cockneys**) 1 someone born in the East End of London 2 the speech characteristic of this area

cockpit noun 1 the part of an aeroplane where the pilot sits 2 a pit where game cocks fight

cockroach noun (plural **cockroaches**) a type of large crawling insect

cocktail noun a mixed alcoholic drink

cocky adj (**cockier**, **cockiest**) irritatingly self-confident • **cockily** adv • **cockiness** noun

cocoa noun a drink made from the ground seeds of the cacao tree

coconut noun the large hard-shelled nut of a type of palm tree

cocoon noun a protective covering of silk spun by the larva of a butterfly, moth, etc

cod noun a large edible fish found in northern seas

coda noun a closing passage in a piece of music, book, etc

coddle verb 1 treat over-protectively; pamper 2 cook (an egg) gently over hot water

code noun 1 a way of signalling or sending secret messages, using letters etc agreed beforehand 2 a book or collection of laws, rules, etc

codger /koj-uh/ noun an old, eccentric man

codicil /kod-i-sil/ noun a note added to a will or treaty

codify verb (**codifies**, **codifying**, **codified**) arrange in an orderly way; classify

coed /koh-ed/ abbrev coeducational

coeducation noun the education of boys and girls together • **coeducational** adj

coeliac /see-li-ak/ adj suffering from an inability to digest wheat products

coerce verb force to do; compel • **coercion** noun • **coercive** adj using force

coexist verb exist at the same time or in the same place • **coexistence** noun • **coexistent** adj

C of E abbrev Church of England

coffee noun 1 a drink made from the roasted, ground beans of the coffee shrub 2 a pale brown colour

coffer noun a chest for holding money, gold, etc • **cofferdam** noun a watertight dam enclosing the foundations of a bridge

coffin noun a box in which a dead body is buried or cremated

cog noun a tooth on a wheel • **cogwheel** noun a toothed wheel

cogent adj of an argument: reasonable or believable • **cogency** noun • **cogently** adv

cogitate verb, formal think carefully • **cogitation** noun

cognac noun brandy from the region around the town of Cognac in southern France

cognizance noun, formal awareness, notice • **take cognizance of** take notice of, or take into consideration

cohabit verb live together as sexual partners without being married • **cohabitation** noun

cohere verb stick together

coherence noun connection between thoughts, ideas, etc

coherent adj 1 clear and logical in thought or speech 2 sticking together • **coherently** adv

cohesion noun the act of sticking together • **cohesive** adj

cohort noun 1 all the students on a course in a given year: the 2002 cohort 2 hist a tenth part of a Roman legion

coiffure /kwah-fur/ noun a style of hairdressing

coil verb wind in rings; twist ◇ noun 1 a wound arrangement of hair, rope, etc 2 a contraceptive device fitted in the uterus

coin noun a piece of stamped metal used as money ◇ verb 1 make up (a new word *etc*) **2** make metal into money

coinage *noun* **1** the system of coins used in a country **2** a newly-made word

coincide *verb* **1** (often with **with**) be the same as: *their interests coincide/ his story coincides with mine* **2** (often with **with**) happen at the same time as: *coincided with his departure*

coincidence *noun* the occurrence of two things simultaneously without planning • **coincidental** *adj* • **coincidentally** *adv*

coir /koy-uh/ *noun* the outside fibre of a coconut

coitus /koh-i-tus/ *noun, formal* sexual intercourse • **coitus interruptus** *noun* deliberate withdrawal of the penis before ejaculation during intercourse

coke *noun* **1** a type of fuel made by heating coal till the gas is driven out **2** *informal* cocaine

Col *abbrev* Colonel

colander *noun* a bowl with small holes in it for straining vegetables *etc*

cold *adj* **1** low in temperature **2** lower in temperature than is comfortable **3** unfriendly or disapproving ◇ *noun* **1** the state of being cold **2** an infectious viral disease causing shivering, running nose, *etc* • **cold-blooded** *adj* **1** of animals: having a body temperature that changes in response to external temperature **2** lacking in sympathy or humanity; cruel • **cold calling** *noun* the contacting of potential business contacts *etc* without appointment • **cold feet** *plural noun* lack of courage • **coldly** *adv* • **coldness** *noun* • **cold war** *noun* a power struggle between nations without open warfare

coleslaw *noun* a salad made from shredded cabbage, carrot and onion mixed with mayonnaise

colic *noun* a severe stomach pain

collaborate *verb* **1** work together

(with) **2** work with (an enemy) to betray your country • **collaboration** *noun* • **collaborator** *noun*

Do not confuse with: **corroborate**

collage /kol-ahzh/ *noun* a picture or design made of scraps of paper pasted on wood, card, *etc*

collagen *noun* a protein found in skin, bones, *etc*

collapse *verb* **1** of a structure: fall down or fall in **2** of a person: fall down because of illness or exhaustion **3** become unable to continue ◇ *noun* a falling down or caving in • **collapsible** *adj* of a chair *etc*: able to be folded up

collar *noun* part of a garment that fits round the neck ◇ *verb, informal* seize or arrest • **collarbone** *noun* either of two bones joining the breast bone and shoulder blade

collate *verb* **1** examine and compare **2** gather together and arrange in order: *collate the pages for the book*

collateral *noun* an additional security for repayment of a debt • **collateral damage** *noun* **1** unintentional damage or casualties resulting from a military attack **2** harm caused indirectly and unintentionally

collation *noun* **1** a light, often cold meal **2** a gathering together, *eg* of facts

colleague *noun* someone who works in the same company *etc* as yourself

collect *verb* **1** bring together **2** come together

collected *adj* **1** gathered together **2** calm, composed

collection *noun* **1** a number of objects gathered and kept together **2** the act of collecting **3** money gathered at a meeting, *eg* a church service

collective adj **1** acting together **2** involving several things or people: *collective decision* ◇ noun a business owned and managed by the workers

collector noun someone who collects a particular group of things: *stamp collector*

colleen noun, Irish a girl or young woman

college noun **1** an institution of further or higher education **2** one of the parts into which some large universities are divided • **collegiate** adj of a university: *divided into colleges*

collide verb come together with great force; clash

collie noun a breed of long-haired dog with a pointed nose

collier noun **1** someone who works in a coalmine **2** a ship that carries coal • **colliery** noun a coalmine

collision noun **1** a crash between two moving vehicles *etc* **2** a disagreement, a clash of interests *etc*

colloquial adj used in everyday speech but not in formal writing or speaking • **colloquialism** noun an example of colloquial speech • **colloquially** adv

collusion noun a secret agreement

cologne /kuh-*lohn*/ noun light perfume made with plant oils and alcohol

colon[1] noun a punctuation mark (:) used *eg* to introduce a list of examples

colon[2] noun a part of the bowel

colonel /*kur*-nul/ noun a senior army officer ranking above a major and below a general

colonial adj of colonies abroad • **colonialism** noun the policy of setting up colonies abroad

colonnade noun a row of columns or pillars

colony noun (*plural* **colonies**) **1** a country or territory ruled by a more powerful country **2** a group of people who settle in a colony overseas **3** a group of animals of the same type living together • **colonist** noun a settler • **colonize** verb set up a colony in

coloratura noun, music a passage sung with trills

colossal adj huge, enormous

colossus noun an enormous statue

colour or US **color** noun **1** a quality that an object shows in the light, *eg* redness, blueness, *etc* **2** a shade or tint **3** vividness, brightness **4** (**colours**) a flag or standard ◇ verb **1** put colour on **2** blush **3** influence: *coloured my attitude to life* • **colour-blind** adj unable to distinguish certain colours, *eg* red and green • **coloured** adj **1** having colour **2** offensive not white-skinned • **off colour** unwell

colourful adj **1** brightly coloured **2** of a description: vivid **3** with many interesting or exciting features • **colourfully** adv

colouring noun **1** shade or combination of colours **2** complexion

colourless adj **1** without colour **2** dull, bland

colt noun a young male horse

column noun **1** an upright stone or wooden pillar **2** something of a long or tall, narrow shape: *columns of smoke* **3** a vertical line of text on a page **4** a regular feature in a newspaper **5** an arrangement of troops *etc* one behind the other • **columnist** noun someone who writes a regular newspaper column

coma noun unconsciousness lasting a long time

comatose adj **1** in or of a coma **2** drowsy, sluggish

comb noun **1** a toothed instrument for separating or smoothing hair, wool, *etc* **2** the crest of certain birds **3**

a collection of cells for honey ◊ *verb* **1** arrange or smooth with a comb **2** search through thoroughly

combat *noun* a fight or struggle ◊ *verb* fight or struggle against ● **combatant** *noun* someone who is fighting ◊ *adj* fighting ● **combative** *adj* tending to quarrel or fight

combination *noun* **1** a set of things or people combined **2** a joining together of things or people **3** a series of letters or figures dialled to open a safe **4** (**combinations**) *old* underwear for the body and legs

combine *verb* **1** join or mix together **2** do (two or more things) at the same time: *combine domestic life with a challenging career* ◊ *noun* a number of traders *etc* who join together ● **combine harvester** *noun* a machine that both cuts and threshes crops

combustible *adj* liable to catch fire and burn ◊ *noun* anything that will burn ● **combustion** *noun* burning

come *verb* (**coming, came, come**) **1** move towards this place (*opposite of* **go**): *come here!* **2** draw near in time; approach: *Christmas is coming* **3** arrive: *we'll have tea when you come* **4** happen, occur: *the index comes at the end* **5** *slang* achieve a sexual orgasm ● **come about** happen ● **come across** *or* **come upon** meet or find accidentally ● **come by** obtain ● **come into** inherit ● **come of age** reach the age at which you become an adult for legal purposes ● **come off 1** be successful **2** happen ● **come round** *or* **come to** recover from a faint *etc* ● **come up** be mentioned ● **come upon** come across ● **come up with** think up or suggest ● **to come** in the future

comedian *noun* a performer who tells jokes, acts in comedy, *etc*

comedy *noun* (*plural* **comedies**) a light-hearted or amusing play (*contrasted with*: **tragedy**)

comely *adj* (**comelier, comeliest**) *dated* good-looking ● **comeliness** *noun*

comet *noun* a kind of moving star that has a tail of light

comfort *verb* help, soothe (someone in pain or distress) ◊ *noun* **1** the state of being physically relaxed and happy **2** something that brings this state: *home comforts* **3** a person or thing that makes someone stop being worried or sad

comfortable *adj* **1** physically relaxed and happy, with no unpleasant feelings **2** giving comfort ● **comfortably** *adv*

comfrey *noun* a plant with hairy leaves, used in herbal medicine

comic *adj* **1** of comedy **2** amusing, funny ◊ *noun* **1** a children's magazine with illustrated stories *etc* **2** a professional comedian ● **comical** *adj* funny, amusing ● **comically** *adv* ● **comic strip** *noun* a strip of small pictures outlining a story

comma *noun* a punctuation mark (,) indicating a pause in a sentence

command *verb* **1** give an order **2** be in charge of **3** look over or down on: *commanding a view* ◊ *noun* **1** an order **2** control: *in command of the situation*

commandant *noun* an officer in command of a place or of troops

commandeer *verb* seize (something) *esp* for the use of an army

commander *noun* **1** someone who commands **2** a naval officer next in rank below captain

commandment *noun* an order or command

commando *noun* (*plural* **commandoes**) a soldier in an army unit trained for special tasks

commemorate *verb* **1** bring to memory by means of a formal ceremony **2** serve as a memorial of • **commemoration** noun

commence verb begin • **commencement** noun

commend verb **1** praise **2** (with **to**) old give into the care of • **commendable** adj praiseworthy • **commendation** noun praise • **commendatory** adj praising

commensurate adj: **commensurate with** of a suitable size, quality or extent for; appropriate to

comment noun **1** a remark **2** a criticism ◊ verb remark (on)

commentary noun (plural **commentaries**) **1** a description of an event etc by someone who is watching it **2** a set of explanatory notes for a book etc

commentator noun **1** someone who gives a commentary on an event as it happens **2** someone who writes or broadcasts their opinions: political commentators

commerce noun the buying and selling of goods between people or nations; trade

commercial adj **1** of commerce **2** paid for by advertisements: commercial radio ◊ noun an advertisement on radio, TV, etc • **commercially** adv

commiserate verb sympathize (with) • **commiseration** noun pity

commissar noun, hist the head of a government department in the former Soviet Union

commissariat noun a department in the army etc that looks after the food supply

commission noun **1** a group of people appointed to investigate something **2** a fee for doing business on another's behalf **3** an order for a work of art **4** a document giving authority to an officer in the armed forces **5** the act of committing a crime, offence, etc ◊ verb employ to perform a task, esp to produce a work of art • **in** or

out of commission in or not in use

commissionaire noun a uniformed doorkeeper

commissioner noun **1** someone with high authority in a district **2** a member of a commission

commit verb (**committing, committed**) **1** make a promise to do: committed to finishing this book **2** do, perform: commit a crime **3** give or hand over; entrust

commitment noun **1** a promise **2** something that you have agreed to do at a particular time

committal noun the act of committing

committed adj strong in belief or support: a committed socialist

committee noun a number of people chosen from a larger body to attend to special business

commodious adj roomy, spacious

commodity noun (plural **commodities**) **1** an article to be bought or sold **2** (**commodities**) goods, produce

commodore noun an officer next above a captain in the navy

common adj **1** shared by all or many: common belief **2** seen or happening often: common occurrence **3** ordinary, normal **4** showing a lack of good taste; vulgar ◊ noun an area of land belonging to the people of a town, parish, etc • **common law** noun unwritten law based on custom • **Common Market** noun, dated the European Union • **common noun** noun a name for any one of a class of things (contrasted with: **proper noun**) • **common room** noun a room in a school or college in which students can relax • **common sense** noun practical good sense • **the House of Commons** the lower house of the British parliament

commoner noun an ordinary citizen who is not a member of the aristocracy or royalty

commonplace *adj* ordinary

commonwealth *noun* an association of self-governing states

commotion *noun* a disturbance among several people

communal *adj* to be shared by people; common • **communally** *adv*

commune *noun* a group of people living together, sharing work, *etc* ◊ *verb, formal* talk together

communicable *adj* able to be passed on to others: *communicable disease*

communicate *verb* 1 get in touch (with) 2 make known or pass on; tell 3 have a connecting door

communication *noun* 1 a means of conveying information 2 information conveyed 3 a message 4 a way of passing from place to place

communicative *adj* willing to give information, talkative • **communicatively** *adv*

communion *noun* 1 the act of sharing thoughts, feelings, *etc*; fellowship 2 (**Communion**) in the Christian Church, a service that commemorates the Last Supper

communiqué /kum-yoo-ni-keh/ *noun* an official announcement

communism *noun* a form of socialism where industry is controlled by the state • **communist** *adj* of communism ◊ *noun* someone who believes in communism

community *noun* (*plural* **communities**) 1 a group of people living in one place 2 the public in general 3 a racial, religious or ethnic group within society: *the Hindu community*

commute *verb* 1 travel regularly between two places, *eg* between home and work 2 change (a punishment) for one less severe

commuter *noun* someone who regularly travels some distance from their home to work

compact *adj* 1 fitted or packed closely together 2 of a quality newspaper: in a small format ◊ *noun* a bargain or agreement • **compact disc** *noun* a CD

companion *noun* someone who accompanies • **companionable** *adj* friendly • **companionship** *noun* friendship • **companionway** *noun* a staircase on a ship from deck to cabin

company *noun* (*plural* **companies**) 1 a business firm 2 the *usu* welcome presence of other people: *I'm glad of your company* 3 a part of a regiment 4 a ship's crew

comparative *adj* 1 judged by comparing with something else; relative: *comparative improvement* 2 near to being: *a comparative stranger* 3 *grammar* the degree of an adjective or adverb between positive and superlative, *eg* blacker, better, *more* courageous

compare *verb* 1 consider things together to see how similar or different they are 2 liken • **comparable** *adj* • **beyond compare** much better than all rivals

comparison *noun* an act of comparing

compartment *noun* a separate part or division, *eg* of a railway carriage • **compartmentalize** *verb* keep things separate and ordered in your mind

compass *noun* (*plural* **compasses**) 1 an instrument with a magnetized needle for showing direction 2 (**compasses**) an instrument with one fixed and one movable leg for drawing circles

compassion *noun* pity for another's suffering; mercy • **compassionate** *adj* pitying, merciful • **compassionately** *adv*

compatible *adj* 1 able to live with, agree with, *etc* 2 able to be connected to or used with (another piece of equipment) • **compatibility** *noun* • **compatibly** *adv*

compatriot *noun* a fellow countryman or countrywoman

compel *verb* (**compelling, compelled**) force to do something • **compelling** *adj* **1** so exciting that you give all your attention; gripping **2** of an argument: so obviously true or reasonable that you accept it immediately; persuasive

compensate *verb* make up for wrong or damage done, *esp* by giving money • **compensation** *noun* something given to make up for wrong or damage

compère *noun* someone who introduces acts as part of an entertainment ◇ *verb* act as compère

compete *verb* try to beat others in a race, contest, *etc*

competent *adj* **1** able to do things efficiently; capable **2** properly trained or qualified • **competence** *noun* • **competently** *adv*

competition *noun* **1** a contest between rivals **2** rivalry, *esp* between commercial companies

competitive *adj* **1** of sport: based on competitions **2** fond of competing with others • **competitively** *adv* • **competitiveness** *noun*

competitor *noun* a person, player or company that competes; a rival

compile *verb* make (a book *etc*) from information that has been collected • **compilation** *noun* • **compiler** *noun*

complacent *adj* so satisfied as to make no further effort to improve or take action • **complacence** *or* **complacency** *noun* • **complacently** *adv*

complain *verb* **1** express dissatisfaction about something **2** mention pain, disappointment, *etc* • **complainant** *noun* **1** someone who complains **2** the plaintiff in a law suit

complaint *noun* **1** a statement of dissatisfaction **2** an illness

complement *noun* **1** something that goes well with another **2** the number or quantity needed to fill something **3** the angle that must be added to a given angle to make up a right angle

---

Do not confuse with: **compliment**

---

complementary *adj* **1** going well together **2** making up a right angle

---

Do not confuse with: **complimentary**

---

complete *adj* **1** having nothing missing; whole **2** finished ◇ *verb* **1** finish **2** make whole • **completely** *adv* • **completeness** *noun* • **completion** *noun*

complex *adj* **1** made up of many parts **2** complicated, difficult ◇ *noun* (*plural* **complexes**) **1** a group of related buildings: *sports complex* **2** a set of repressed emotions and ideas that affect someone's behaviour **3** an unreasonable reaction or belief; an obsession: *has a complex about her height* • **complexity** *noun*

complexion *noun* **1** the colour or look of the skin of the face **2** appearance

compliance *noun* the act of agreeing with another's wishes

compliant *adj* agreeing, or being too willing to agree • **compliantly** *adv*

complicate *verb* make difficult by adding something • **complicated** *adj* difficult to understand or deal with because of the number of things involved

complication *noun* **1** a difficulty **2** a development in an illness that makes things worse

complicity *noun* (*plural* **complicities**) shared involvement in a crime or wrongdoing

compliment noun **1** an expression of praise or flattery **2** (**compliments**) good wishes ◇ verb praise, congratulate: *complimented me on my cooking*

Do not confuse with: **complement**

complimentary adj **1** flattering, praising **2** given free: *complimentary ticket*

Do not confuse with: **complementary**

comply verb (**complies, complying, complied**) agree to do something that someone else orders or wishes

component noun one of several parts, *eg* of a machine ◇ adj forming one of the parts of a whole

compose verb **1** create (a piece of music, a poem, *etc*) **2** put together or in order; arrange • **composed** adj quiet, calm

composer noun someone who writes music

composite adj made up of parts

composition noun **1** a created piece of writing or music **2** a mixture of things **3** the act of composing

compositor noun someone who puts together the types for printing

compos mentis adj sane, rational

compost noun a mixture of decayed plant matter used like soil or spread on soil

composure noun calmness, self-possession

compound adj **1** made up of a number of different parts **2** not simple ◇ noun **1** *chemistry* a substance formed from two or more elements **2** an enclosure round a building ◇ verb make (a problem) worse

comprehend verb **1** understand **2**

include • **comprehensible** adj able to be understood • **comprehensibly** adv • **comprehension** noun

comprehensive adj taking in or including much or all • **comprehensive school** noun a state-funded secondary school in which children of all abilities are taught together

compress verb **1** press together **2** force into a narrower or smaller space ◇ noun a pad used to create pressure on a part of the body or to reduce inflammation • **compression** noun

comprise verb **1** include, contain **2** consist of

compromise noun an agreement reached by both sides giving up something ◇ verb **1** make a compromise **2** put in a difficult or embarrassing position **3** risk losing or betraying: *refused to compromise his principles*

compulsion noun a force driving someone to do something

compulsive adj unable to stop yourself: *compulsive liar* • **compulsively** adv

Do not confuse: **compulsive** and **compulsory**

compulsory adj **1** requiring to be done **2** forced on someone • **compulsorily** adv

compunction noun regret

computation noun counting, calculation

compute verb count, calculate

computer noun an electronic machine that stores and sorts information of various kinds

comrade noun a companion, a friend • **comradeship** noun companionship

con verb (**conning, conned**) play a confidence trick on ◇ noun a trick, a deceit • **con man** noun someone who regularly cons people • **con trick** noun a confidence trick

concave adj hollow or curving inwards (contrasted with: **convex**)

concavity noun (plural **concavities**) a hollow

conceal verb 1 keep secret 2 keep covered or hidden • **concealment** noun

concede verb 1 accept defeat; give up 2 admit the truth of something: I concede that you may be right

conceit noun a too high opinion of yourself; vanity • **conceited** adj full of conceit; vain • **conceitedness** noun

conceive verb 1 form in the mind; think of; imagine 2 become pregnant • **conceivable** adj able to be imagined • **conceivably** adv

concentrate verb 1 direct all your attention or effort towards something 2 bring together in one place • **concentrated** adj made stronger or less dilute • **concentration** noun • **concentration camp** noun a prison camp with extremely harsh or cruel conditions

concentric adj of circles: placed one inside the other with the same centre point (contrasted with: **eccentric**)

concept noun 1 an idea 2 a new product or service

conception noun 1 the act of conceiving, esp of becoming pregnant 2 an idea

concern verb 1 have to do with 2 make uneasy; worry 3 interest, affect ◇ noun 1 anxiety 2 a cause of anxiety; a worry 3 a business • **concerning** prep about: concerning your application • **concern yourself with** be worried about

concert noun a musical performance • **in concert** together

Do not confuse with: **consort**

concerted adj planned or done together

concertina noun a type of musical wind instrument, with bellows and keys

concerto /kun-chur-toh/ noun (plural **concertos**) a long piece of classical music for a solo instrument with orchestral accompaniment

concession noun 1 something that you agree to in order end a dispute 2 a reduction in the price of something for children, the unemployed, senior citizens, etc 3 an official right to do something granted to someone

conch noun (plural **conches**) a large roundish sea shell

concierge /kon-si-airzh/ noun a warden in a residential building

conciliate verb win over (someone previously unfriendly or angry) • **conciliation** noun • **conciliatory** adj

concise adj using few words; brief • **concisely** adv • **conciseness** noun

conclude verb 1 end 2 reach a decision or judgement • **concluding** adj last, final

conclusion noun 1 end 2 final decision or judgement

conclusive adj providing certainty; deciding: conclusive proof • **conclusively** adv

concoct verb 1 mix together (a dish or drink) 2 make up; invent: concoct a story • **concoction** noun

concord noun agreement

concourse noun a large open space in a public building

concrete noun a mixture of sand, gravel and cement used in building ◇ adj 1 made of concrete 2 having solid physical reality, not abstract

concur verb (**concurring, concurred**) agree • **concurrence** noun

concurrent adj 1 happening together

2 agreeing • **concurrently** adv

concussion noun temporary harm done to the brain from a knock on the head

condemn verb **1** criticize severely **2** sentence to (a certain punishment) **3** declare (a building) unfit for use • **condemnation** noun

condensation noun **1** drops of liquid formed from vapour **2** the act of condensing

condense verb **1** of gas or vapour: turn into droplets of liquid **2** make smaller

condescend verb **1** act towards someone as if you are better than them **2** do, or agree to do, something that would normally be beneath you: she has condescended to reply • **condescending** adj • **condescendingly** adv • **condescension** noun

condiment noun a seasoning for food, esp salt or pepper

condition noun **1** the state in which anything is: in poor condition **2** something that must happen before some other thing happens **3** a point in a bargain, treaty, etc

conditional adj depending on certain things happening • **conditionally** adv

conditioning noun the influence of schooling, social customs, relationships with friends, etc on a person's behaviour or attitudes

condolence noun sharing in another's sorrow; sympathy

condom noun a contraceptive rubber sheath worn over the penis

condone verb allow (an offence) to go uncriticized or unpunished and so seem to accept it

conducive adj helping to make something exist or happen; favourable (to): conducive to peace

conduct verb **1** lead, guide **2** control,

be in charge of **3** direct (an orchestra) **4** transmit (electricity etc) **5** behave: conducted himself correctly ◇ noun behaviour • **conductance** noun the ability to conduct electricity etc • **conduction** noun transmission of heat, electricity, etc

conductor noun **1** someone who directs an orchestra **2** someone who collects fares on a bus etc **3** something that transmits heat, electricity, etc

conduit /kon-dyoo-it/ noun a channel or pipe carrying water, electric wires, etc

cone noun **1** a shape that is round at the bottom and comes to a point **2** the fruit of a pine or fir tree etc **3** a cone-shaped wafer filled with ice-cream

coney another spelling of **cony**

confectioner noun someone who makes or sells sweets, cakes, etc • **confectionery** noun **1** sweets, cakes, etc **2** the shop or business of a confectioner

confederacy noun (plural **confederacies**) **1** a league or alliance **2** (**Confederacy**) US hist the union of Southern states in the American Civil War

confederate adj **1** joined together by treaty **2** (**Confederate**) US hist supporting the Confederacy ◇ noun someone acting in an alliance with others

confederation noun a union or league

confer verb (**conferring, conferred**) **1** talk together **2** give, grant: confer a degree

conference noun a meeting for formal discussions

confess verb admit to doing wrong; own up • **confessed** adj admitted, not secret • **confession** noun an admission of wrongdoing

confetti plural noun small pieces of

coloured paper thrown at weddings and other celebrations

confidant /kon-fi-dant/ noun someone trusted with a secret

Do not confuse with: **confident**

---

confidante /kon-fi-dant/ noun a female confidant

confide verb: **confide in 1** tell secrets to **2** hand over to someone's care

confidence noun **1** belief in your own abilities; self-assurance **2** trust, belief **3** something told privately • **confidence trick** noun a trick to get money etc from someone by first gaining their trust

confident adj **1** believing in your own abilities; self-assured **2** certain of an outcome: confident that they would win • **confidently** adv

---

Do not confuse with: **confidant** and **confidante**

---

confidential adj **1** to be kept as a secret: confidential information **2** entrusted with secrets • **confidentially** adv

confiding adj trusting

configuration noun **1** the way things are arranged to make a pattern or system **2** comput the hardware that makes up a computer system

confine verb **1** keep within limits **2** imprison • **confines** plural noun limits

confinement noun **1** the state of being confined **2** imprisonment **3** dated the time of a woman's labour and childbirth

confirm verb **1** make sure **2** show to be true **3** admit into full membership of a church

confirmation noun **1** a making sure **2** proof **3** the ceremony by which

someone is made a full member of a church

confirmed adj settled in a habit, lifestyle, etc: a confirmed bachelor

confiscate verb take away, as a punishment • **confiscation** noun

conflagration noun a large, widespread fire

conflict noun **1** a struggle, a contest **2** fighting between armies; a battle **3** disagreement ◇ verb of statements etc: contradict each other • **conflicting** adj

confluence noun a place where rivers join

conform verb follow the example of most other people in behaviour, dress, etc • **conformation** noun

conformity noun (plural **conformities**) **1** the act of conforming **2** similarity

confound verb **1** puzzle, confuse **2** prove to be wrong

confront verb **1** face, meet: confronted the difficulty **2** bring face to face (with): confronted with the evidence • **confrontation** noun

confuse verb **1** make unable to understand; bewilder **2** put out of the proper order; mix up • **confusion** noun

confusing adj puzzling, bewildering • **confusingly** adv

congeal verb **1** become solid, esp by cooling **2** freeze

congenial adj agreeable, pleasant • **congenially** adv

congenital adj of a disease: present in someone from birth

conger /kong-guh/ noun a large eel that lives in the sea

congested adj **1** overcrowded **2** clogged **3** of part of the body: too full of blood • **congestion** noun

conglomeration noun a heap or collection

congratulate verb express joy to (someone) at their success • **congratulations** plural noun an expression of joy at someone's success • **congratulatory** adj

congregate verb come together in a crowd • **congregation** noun a gathering, esp of people in a church

congress noun (plural **congresses**) 1 a large meeting of people from different countries etc for discussion 2 (**Congress**) the parliament of the United States, consisting of the Senate and the House of Representatives

congruent adj of triangles: exactly matching

congruous adj suitable, appropriate • **congruity** noun • **congruously** adv

conical adj cone-shaped

conifer noun a cone-bearing tree • **coniferous** adj

conjecture noun a guess ◊ verb guess • **conjectural** adj

conjoined twins plural noun the formal or technical name for **Siamese twins**

conjugal adj of marriage

conjugate verb give the different grammatical forms of (a verb) • **conjugation** noun

conjunction noun 1 grammar a word that joins sentences or phrases, eg and and but 2 a union or combination • **in conjunction with** together with

conjunctivitis noun inflammation of the inside of the eyelid and surface of the eye

conjure verb perform tricks that seem magical • **conjuror** or **conjurer** noun someone who performs conjuring tricks

conker noun 1 a horse chestnut 2 (**conkers**) a game in which players try to hit and destroy each other's chestnut, held on the end of a string

connect verb 1 join or fasten together 2 link in the mind

connection noun 1 a physical link between things, eg pieces of electrical equipment 2 a link in the mind 3 a train, aeroplane, etc that takes you on the next part of a journey 4 an influential acquaintance or friend • **in connection with** concerning

connive verb 1 (with **at**) disregard (wrongdoing) and so seem to approve of it 2 (with **with**) make secret plans with (someone) to do something bad • **connivance** noun

connoisseur /kon-us-ur/ noun someone with an expert knowledge of a subject: wine connoisseur

connotation noun what is suggested by a word in addition to its simple meaning

connubial adj of marriage

conquer verb 1 take control of by force 2 overcome: conquered his fear of heights

conqueror noun a military leader who conquers

conquest noun 1 something won by force 2 an act of conquering

conquistador /kon-kee-stuh-daw/ noun, hist a soldier fighting for the Spanish crown in the New World

conscience noun an inner sense of what is right and wrong

conscientious adj working hard and carefully; diligent • **conscientiously** adv • **conscientiousness** noun

conscious adj 1 aware of yourself and your surroundings; awake 2 aware, knowing 3 deliberate, intentional: conscious decision • **consciously** adv • **consciousness** noun

conscript noun someone obliged by law to serve in the armed forces ◊ verb compel to serve in the armed forces • **conscription** noun

consecrate verb set apart for sacred

use • **consecration** noun

consecutive adj coming in order, one after the other

consensus noun an agreement of opinion

Do not confuse with: **census**

---

consent noun 1 agreement 2 permission ◇ verb agree (to) • **age of consent** the age at which someone is legally able to have sex

consequence noun 1 something that follows as a result 2 importance

consequent adj following as a result • **consequently** adv

consequential adj 1 following as a result 2 important • **consequentially** adv

conservation noun the maintaining of old buildings, the countryside, etc in an undamaged state • **conservationist** noun someone who encourages and practises conservation

conservative adj 1 resistant to change 2 moderate, not extreme: conservative estimate ◇ noun 1 someone of conservative views 2 (**Conservative**) a supporter of the Conservative Party • **Conservative Party** noun one of the main political parties of the UK

conservatory noun (plural **conservatories**) a room with large windows and a glass roof, for enjoying the sun or for growing plants

conserve verb keep from being wasted or lost; preserve

consider verb 1 think about carefully 2 think of as 3 pay attention to the wishes of

considerable adj fairly large; substantial • **considerably** adv

considerate adj taking others' wishes into account; thoughtful

consideration noun 1 serious thought 2 thoughtfulness for others 3 a small payment

considering prep taking into account: considering your age

consign /kun-sain/ verb put or send somewhere • **consignment** noun a load, eg of goods

consist verb be made up (of)

consistency noun (plural **consistencies**) 1 texture of a liquid or semi-liquid substance 2 the quality of always being the same

consistent adj 1 not changing; regular 2 of statements etc: not contradicting each other • **consistently** adv

consolation noun something that makes unpleasantness or disappointment easier to bear

console verb make more cheerful; cheer up ◇ noun a board with controls, switches, etc; a control panel

consolidate verb 1 make more secure or certain 2 unite • **consolidation** noun

consonant noun a letter of the alphabet that is not a vowel, eg b, c, d

consort noun 1 a husband or wife 2 a companion ◇ verb keep company (with)

Do not confuse with: **concert**

---

conspicuous adj easy to see or notice; clear • **conspicuously** adv • **conspicuousness** noun

conspiracy noun (plural **conspiracies**) a plot by a group of people • **conspirator** noun someone who takes part in a conspiracy

conspire verb plan or plot together

constable noun 1 a police officer of the lowest rank 2 hist a high officer of state

constabulary noun (plural **constabularies**) the police force

constant adj 1 never stopping 2 never changing 3 faithful • **constancy** noun • **constantly** adv always

constellation noun a group of stars

consternation noun worry and shock; dismay

constipation noun sluggish working of the bowels • **constipate** verb cause constipation in

constituency noun (plural **constituencies**) 1 a district that has a member of parliament 2 the voters in such a district

constituent noun 1 one of several parts that form something 2 a voter in a constituency ◊ adj making or forming

constitute verb 1 cause to exist; establish 2 be the elements that make up (something); form 3 be the equivalent of: this action constitutes a crime

constitution noun 1 the way in which something is made up 2 the natural condition of a body in terms of health etc: a weak constitution 3 a set of laws or rules governing a country or organization • **constitutional** adj of a constitution ◊ noun, dated a short walk for the sake of your health

constrain verb force to act in a certain way

constraint noun 1 compulsion, force 2 restraint, repression

constrict verb 1 press together tightly 2 surround and squeeze

construct verb build or make • **construction** noun 1 something built 2 the act of constructing 3 the arrangement of words in a sentence 4 meaning

constructive adj helping to improve: constructive criticism • **constructively** adv

consul noun 1 someone who looks after their country's affairs in a foreign country 2 hist a chief ruler in ancient Rome • **consular** adj

consulate noun 1 the official residence of a consul 2 the duties and authority of a consul

consult verb seek advice, information or opinions from • **consultation** noun • **consulting room** noun a room where a doctor sees patients

consultant noun 1 someone who gives professional or expert advice 2 the most senior grade of hospital doctor

consume verb 1 eat or drink up 2 use up 3 destroy or cause great harm to • **consumer** noun someone who buys goods

consummate /kon-suh-meht/ verb 1 complete 2 make (marriage) legally complete by having sex ◊ adj /kon-sum-ut/ very talented

consumption noun 1 the act of consuming 2 an amount consumed 3 old tuberculosis

cont or **contd** abbrev continued

contact noun 1 touch 2 communication 3 a person with whom you have dealings: business contact ◊ verb speak or write to • **contact lens** noun a plastic lens worn in contact with the eyeball instead of spectacles

contagious adj of disease: spreading from person to person, esp by touch

contain verb 1 hold or have inside 2 hold back: couldn't contain her anger

container noun a box, tin, jar, etc for holding anything

contaminate verb make impure or dirty • **contamination** noun

contd another spelling of **cont**

contemplate verb 1 look at or think about attentively 2 intend: contemplating suicide • **contemplation** noun

contemporary adj 1 belonging to the current period; modern 2 belonging to the period in question ◊ noun (plural **contemporaries**) 1 someone of roughly the same age as yourself **2** someone who lived at the same time as someone else

contempt *noun* complete lack of respect; scorn • **contempt of court** deliberate disobedience to and disrespect for the law and those who carry it out

contemptible *adj* deserving no respect at all

Do not confuse: **contemptible** and **contemptuous**

contemptuous *adj* expressing contempt; scornful

contend *verb* **1** struggle against **2** hold firmly to a belief; maintain (that)

content /kun-*tent*/ *adj* happy, satisfied ◇ *noun* happiness, satisfaction ◇ *verb* make happy; satisfy ◇ *noun* (**contents** /kon-*tents*/) the thing or things contained in something • **contented** *adj* happy, satisfied • **contentment** *noun* happiness, satisfaction

contention *noun* **1** an opinion strongly held **2** a quarrel or dispute

contentious *adj* causing people to have very different opinions • **contentiously** *adv*

contest *noun* **1** a competition **2** a fight ◇ *verb* **1** compete for **2** challenge the validity or fairness of • **contestant** *noun* a participant in a contest

context *noun* **1** the place in a book *etc* to which a certain part belongs **2** the background of an event, remark, *etc*

contiguous *adj* adjacent or touching • **contiguity** *noun* • **contiguously** *adv*

continent *noun* one of the five large divisions of the earth's land surface (Europe, Asia, Africa, Australia, America) • **continental** *adj* **1** of a continent **2** *Brit* European • **the Continent** *Brit* the mainland of Europe

contingency *noun* (*plural* **contingencies**) something that might happen

contingent *adj* depending (on) ◇ *noun* a group, *esp* of soldiers

continual *adj* happening again and again; very frequent or regular • **continually** *adv*

Do not confuse with: **continuous**

continuation *noun* **1** the act of continuing **2** a part that continues something; an extension

continue *verb* **1** keep on existing or happening **2** keep on doing something or going somewhere

continuity *noun* the state of having no gaps or breaks

continuous *adj* continuing without a gap or break • **continuously** *adv*

Do not confuse with: **continual**

contort *verb* twist or turn violently • **contortion** *noun* a violent twisting, *esp* of the body • **contortionist** *noun* someone who can twist their body into unusual positions

contour *noun* (often **contours**) outline, shape • **contour line** *noun* a line drawn on a map through points that are at the same height above sea level

contraband *noun* goods brought into a country illegally

contraception *noun* the prevention of conceiving children

contraceptive *noun* a device or drug used to prevent conception during sex ◇ *adj* used to prevent conception

contract *verb* **1** become or make smaller **2** start to suffer from (an illness) **3** promise in writing ◇ *noun* a written, legally binding agreement

contraction noun **1** a shortening **2** a shortened form of a word **3** a muscle spasm, eg during childbirth

contractor noun someone hired temporarily to do a specific job

contradict verb say the opposite of; deny • **contradiction** noun • **contradictory** adj

contralto noun (plural **contraltos**) the lowest singing voice in women

contraption noun a machine or device, esp of unusual design or questionable usefulness

contrapuntal see **counterpoint**

contrary[1] /kon-truh-ri/ adj opposite ◇ noun the opposite • **on the contrary** the opposite is true

contrary[2] /kun-treh-ri/ adj always doing or saying the opposite; perverse • **contrariness** noun

contrast verb **1** compare so as to show differences **2** show a marked difference from ◇ noun a difference between (two) things

contravene verb break (a law etc) • **contravention** noun

contretemps /konh-truh-tonh/ noun a minor disagreement or quarrel

contribute verb **1** give (money, help, etc) along with others **2** supply (articles etc) for a publication **3** help to cause: contributed to a nervous breakdown • **contribution** noun • **contributor** noun

contrite adj very sorry for having done wrong • **contrition** noun

contrive verb **1** plan **2** succeed in doing; manage: contrived to be out of the office • **contrivance** noun an act of contriving; an invention • **contrived** adj created or pretended for a particular circumstance, rather than occurring naturally or genuinely

control noun **1** authority to rule, manage, restrain, etc **2** (often **controls**) means by which a driver keeps a machine powered or guided ◇ verb (**controlling**, **controlled**) **1** exercise control over **2** have authority over • **controlled** adj • **controller** noun • **control tower** noun an airport building from which landing and take-off instructions are given

controversial adj likely to cause argument • **controversially** adv

controversy noun (plural **controversies**) a disagreement between people who have strongly held, opposing views

conundrum noun a difficult problem

conurbation noun a group of towns forming a single built-up area

convalesce verb recover health gradually after being ill • **convalescence** noun a gradual return to health and strength • **convalescent** noun someone convalescing from illness

convection noun the spreading of heat by the movement of heated air or water • **convector** noun a heater that works by convection

convene verb call or come together • **convener** noun **1** someone who calls a meeting **2** the chairman or chairwoman of a committee

convenience noun **1** the fact of being easy to arrange, deal with, etc; handiness **2** a means of giving ease or comfort **3** informal a public lavatory • **at your convenience** when it suits you best

convenient adj easy to arrange, deal with, etc • **conveniently** adv

convent noun a building where a community of nuns lives

convention noun **1** a way of behaving that has become usual; a custom **2** a large meeting; an assembly **3** a treaty or agreement • **conventional** adj **1** done by habit or custom **2** ordinary and rather unexciting • **conventionally** adv

converge *verb* come together • **convergence** *noun* • **convergent** *adj*

conversant *adj* (with **with**) having a good knowledge (of)

conversation *noun* informal talk • **conversational** *adj* **1** of conversation **2** talkative

converse[1] /kun-*vurs*/ *verb, formal* talk

converse[2] /kon-vurs/ *noun* the opposite ◇ *adj* opposite

convert *verb* **1** change (from one thing into another) **2** turn from one religion to another ◇ *noun* someone who has been converted to a different religion, way of thinking, *etc* • **conversion** *noun* • **convertible** *adj* able to be changed from one thing to another ◇ *noun* a car with a folding roof

convex *adj* curving outwards (contrasted with: **concave**) • **convexity** *noun*

convey *verb* **1** carry, transport **2** send **3** *law* hand over: *convey property* • **conveyance** *noun* **1** the act of conveying **2** a vehicle • **conveyancing** *noun* the act of transferring the ownership of property • **conveyor** or **conveyor belt** *noun* an endless moving mechanism for conveying articles, *esp* in a factory

convict *verb* declare or prove that someone is guilty ◇ *noun* someone found guilty of a crime and sent to prison • **conviction** *noun* **1** the passing of a guilty sentence on someone in court **2** a strong belief

convince *verb* make (someone) believe that something is true

convivial *adj* in which people behave in a friendly, welcoming way • **conviviality** *noun*

convocation *noun* a meeting, *esp* of bishops or heads of a university

convolvulus *noun* a twining plant with trumpet-shaped flowers

convoy *noun* **1** a number of merchant ships sailing together, protected by warships **2** a line of vehicles travelling together, with or without an armed guard ◇ *verb* go along with and protect

convulse *verb* cause to shake violently: *convulsed with laughter* • **convulsion** *noun* **1** a sudden stiffening or jerking of the muscles **2** a violent disturbance • **convulsive** *adj*

cony or **coney** *noun* (*plural* **conies** or **coneys**) **1** a rabbit **2** rabbit fur

coo *noun* a sound like that of a dove ◇ *verb* make this sound

cook *verb* **1** prepare (food) by heating **2** *informal* alter (accounts *etc*) dishonestly ◇ *noun* someone who cooks and prepares food • **cooker** *noun* **1** a kitchen appliance for cooking **2** an apple *etc* used in cooking, not for eating raw • **cookery** *noun* the art of cooking

cookie *noun, US* a biscuit

cool *adj* **1** slightly cold **2** not angry or upset; calm **3** showing no affection, enthusiasm or approval **4** *informal* acceptable or excellent **5** *informal* impressively fashionable or stylish ◇ *verb* make or grow cool; calm ◇ *exclam* that is agreed or that is acceptable; okay • **coolly** *adv* • **coolness** *noun*

coop *noun* a box or cage for hens *etc* ◇ *verb* shut (up) as in a coop • **cooper** *noun* someone who makes barrels

cooperate *verb* work or act together • **cooperation** *noun* **1** a working together **2** willingness to act together • **cooperative** *noun* a business or farm *etc* owned by the workers ◇ *adj* **1** willing to cooperate **2** jointly owned by workers, with profits shared • **cooperative society** or **co-op** *noun* a trading organization in which the profits are shared among members

co-opt *verb* choose (someone) to join a committee or other body

co-ordinate verb make things fit in or work smoothly together ◇ noun a pair or set of numbers identifying the position of a point on a graph or map • **co-ordination** noun

coot noun a water-bird with a white spot on its forehead

cop noun, Brit slang a police officer ◇ verb (**copping, copped**) catch, seize • **cop it** land in trouble • **cop out** avoid responsibility

cope verb struggle or deal successfully (with); manage

copier noun a machine that makes copies of documents, esp a photocopier

coping noun the top layer of stone in a wall • **coping stone** noun the top stone of a wall

copious adj plentiful • **copiously** adv

copper noun 1 a hard reddish-brown metal 2 a reddish-brown colour 3 a coin made from copper 4 a large container made of copper, for boiling water • **copperplate** noun a style of very fine and regular handwriting

copra noun the dried kernel of the coconut, yielding coconut oil

copse or **coppice** noun a wood of low-growing trees

copulate verb have sex

copy noun (plural **copies**) 1 an imitation 2 a print or reproduction of a picture etc 3 an individual example of a certain book etc ◇ verb 1 make a copy of 2 imitate • **copycat** noun someone who imitates someone else • **copyright** noun the right of one person or company to publish a book, perform a play, print music, etc ◇ adj of or protected by the law of copyright

coral noun a hard substance made from the skeletons of a tiny sea animal with a tube-shaped body • **coral reef** noun a rock-like mass of coral built up gradually on the sea bed

cord noun 1 thin rope or strong string 2 a thick strand of anything

---

Do not confuse with: **chord**

---

cordial adj affectionate and welcoming; friendly ◇ noun a refreshing soft drink • **cordiality** noun

cordite noun a kind of explosive

cordon noun a line of guards, police, etc keeping people back

cordon bleu /kaw-donh bluh/ adj of a cook or cooking: first-class, excellent

corduroy noun a ribbed cotton cloth resembling velvet

core noun the inner part of anything, esp fruit ◇ verb take the core out of (fruit)

corespondent noun a man or woman charged with having committed adultery with a wife or husband (the **respondent**)

Do not confuse with:
correspondent

---

corgi noun a breed of short-legged dog

coriander noun an Asian plant whose parsley-like leaves are used as a herb and whose seeds are ground as a spice

cork noun 1 the outer bark of a type of oak found in southern Europe etc 2 a stopper for a bottle etc made of cork ◇ verb plug or stop up with a cork • **corked** adj of wine: having an unwanted sour taste because a faulty cork has allowed air into the bottle • **corkscrew** noun a tool with a screw-like spike for taking out corks ◇ adj shaped like a corkscrew

corm noun the bulb-like underground

stem of certain plants

cormorant noun a large black or brown sea-bird with a curved bill

corn noun 1 maize 2 wheat or oats growing in a field 3 a small lump of hard skin, esp on a toe • **corncrake** noun a kind of bird with a harsh croaking cry • **corned beef** noun salted tinned beef • **cornflour** noun finely ground maize flour • **cornflower** noun a light blue wild flower common in wheat fields • **corny** adj, informal embarrassingly old-fashioned or sentimental

cornea noun the transparent covering of the eyeball

corner noun 1 the point where two walls, roads, etc meet 2 a small secluded place 3 informal a difficult situation ◇ verb force into a position from which there is no escape • **cornerstone** noun 1 the stone at the corner of a building's foundations 2 something upon which much depends

cornet noun 1 a musical instrument like a small trumpet 2 an ice-cream in a cone-shaped wafer

cornice noun an ornamental border round a ceiling

corolla noun the petals of a flower

corollary noun (plural **corollaries**) something that may be taken for granted when something else has been proved; a natural result

corona noun the Sun's outer atmosphere of hot luminous gases, visible during an eclipse

coronary noun (plural **coronaries**) 1 (short for **coronary thrombosis**) a blockage of one of the arteries supplying blood to the heart, which often causes a heart attack 2 informal a heart attack

coronation noun the crowning of a king or queen

coroner noun a government officer who holds inquiries into the causes of sudden or accidental deaths

coronet noun 1 a small crown 2 a hairband or decoration like a small crown

corporal[1] noun the rank next below sergeant in the British army

corporal[2] adj of the body • **corporal punishment** noun physical punishment by beating

corporate adj 1 provided for companies rather than for private individuals 2 of or forming a whole; united • **corporation** noun a body of people acting as one for administrative or business purposes

corps /kaw/ noun (plural **corps**) 1 a division of an army 2 an organized group

Do not confuse: **corps** and **corpse**

corpse noun a dead body

corpulent adj rather fat • **corpulence** noun

corpus noun (plural **corpora**) a collection of writing etc

corpuscle noun 1 a blood cell, red or white 2 a very small particle • **corpuscular** adj

corral noun, US a fenced enclosure for animals ◇ verb (**corralling**, **corralled**) enclose, pen

correct verb 1 remove errors from 2 put right 3 punish ◇ adj 1 having no errors 2 true • **correction** noun 1 the putting right of a mistake 2 punishment • **corrective** adj

correlation noun a direct connection between things • **correlate** verb

correspond verb 1 write letters to 2 be similar (to); match • **correspondence** noun 1 letters 2 likeness, similarity

correspondent noun 1 someone

who writes letters **2** someone who contributes reports to a newspaper *etc*

Do not confuse with:
corespondent

corridor *noun* a passageway

corroborate *verb* give evidence that strengthens evidence already given • **corroboration** *noun* • **corroborative** *adj*

Do not confuse with: **collaborate**

corrode *verb* **1** rust **2** destroy or get rid of gradually; erode • **corrosion** *noun* • **corrosive** *adj*

corrugated *adj* shaped into ridges: *corrugated iron*

corrupt *verb* **1** make evil or rotten **2** spoil the quality or purity of **3** bribe ◇ *adj* **1** morally bad; dishonest **2** spoiled • **corruptible** *adj* • **corruption** *noun*

corsair *noun, old* **1** a pirate **2** a pirate ship

corset *noun* a tight-fitting undergarment that gives a slimming effect

cortège /kaw-*tezh*/ *noun* a funeral procession

corvette *noun* a small fast warship, used against submarines

cosh *noun* (*plural* **coshes**) a short heavy stick used as a weapon ◇ *verb* hit with a cosh

cosmetic *noun* something designed to improve the appearance, *esp* of the face ◇ *adj* **1** applied as a cosmetic **2** done for appearances only; superficial

cosmic *adj* **1** of the universe or outer space **2** *informal* excellent

cosmonaut *noun, hist* an astronaut of the former USSR

cosmopolitan *adj* **1** including people from many countries **2** familiar with, or comfortable in, many different countries

cosmos *noun* the universe

cosset *verb* treat with too much kindness; pamper

cost *verb* (**costing, cost**) **1** be priced at **2** cause the loss of: *the war cost many lives* ◇ *noun* what must be spent or suffered in order to get something

costly *adj* **1** having a high price: expensive **2** resulting in major loss • **costliness** *noun*

costume *noun* **1** a set of clothes **2** clothes to wear in a play **3** fancy dress **4** a swimsuit • **costume jewellery** *noun* inexpensive jewellery

cosy *adj* (**cosier, cosiest**) warm and comfortable ◇ *noun* (*plural* **cosies**) a covering to keep a teapot warm

cot *noun* **1** a small high-sided bed for a very young child **2** *US* a camp bed • **cot death** *noun* the sudden unexplained death in sleep of an apparently healthy baby

coterie /*koh*-tuh-ri/ *noun* a small exclusive group of people; a clique

cottage *noun* a small house, *esp* in the countryside or a village • **cottage cheese** *noun* a soft, white cheese made from skimmed milk • **cottager** *noun* someone who lives in a cottage

cotton *noun* **1** a soft fluffy substance obtained from the seeds of the cotton plant **2** cloth made of cotton ◇ *adj* made of cotton • **cotton wool** *noun* cotton in a fluffy state, used for wiping or absorbing

couch *noun* (*plural* **couches**) a sofa ◇ *verb* express verbally: *couched in archaic language* • **couch grass** *noun* a kind of grass that is a troublesome weed • **couch potato** *noun* an inactive person who watches a lot of TV

cougar *noun, US* the puma

cough *noun* a noisy effort of the lungs to throw out air and unwanted matter from the throat ◇ *verb* make a cough

could *verb* 1 the form of the verb **can¹** used to express a condition: *he could afford it if he tried/I could understand a small mistake, but this is ridiculous* 2 past form of the verb **can¹**: *he asked if he could help*

coulis /koo-lee/ *noun* a thin sauce of puréed fruit

coulomb /koo-lom/ *noun* a unit of electric charge

council *noun* 1 the organization that runs most public affairs in a town or county, or the group of elected politicians that make its policies; a local authority 2 a group of people elected to run something or give advice on something • **councillor** *noun* a member of a council

---

Do not confuse with: **counsel**

---

counsel *noun* 1 advice 2 someone who gives legal advice; a lawyer ◇ *verb* (**counselling, counselled**) give advice to • **counselling** *noun* advice, *esp* given to someone in distress • **counsellor** *noun* someone who gives advice, *esp* to people in distress

---

Do not confuse with: **council**

---

count¹ *verb* 1 find the total number of; add up 2 say numbers in order (1, 2, 3, *etc*) 3 think, consider: *count yourself lucky!* ◇ *noun* 1 the act of counting 2 the number counted, *eg* of votes at an election 3 a charge made officially; an accusation 4 a point being considered • **countdown** *noun* a count backwards to zero from a certain number • **countless** *adj* too many to be counted; very many • **count on** rely on, depend on

count² *noun* a nobleman in certain countries

countenance *noun* 1 the face 2 the expression on someone's face ◇ *verb* consider giving permission for; allow

counter¹ *verb* answer or oppose (a move, act, *etc*) by another ◇ *adv* in the opposite direction ◇ *adj* opposed; opposite

counter² *noun* 1 a small plastic disc used in board games 2 a table across which payments are made in a shop

counter- *prefix* 1 against, opposing: *counter-argument* 2 opposite: *counter-clockwise*

counteract *verb* block or defeat (an action) by doing the opposite

counterattack *noun* an attack made in reply to an attack ◇ *verb* launch a counterattack

countercharge *noun* a charge against someone who has accused you ◇ *verb* make a countercharge against

counterfeit *adj* 1 not genuine or real; sham 2 made in imitation for criminal purposes: *counterfeit money* ◇ *verb* make a copy of

counterfoil *noun* a part of a cheque, postal order, *etc* kept by the payer or sender

countermand *verb* give an order that goes against (one already given)

counterpane *noun, dated* a top cover for a bed

counterpart *noun* someone or something that corresponds to or is very similar to another person or thing

counterpoint *noun* the combining of two or more melodies to make a piece of music • **contrapuntal** *adj* of or in counterpoint

counterpoise *noun* a weight that balances another weight

countersign *verb* sign your name

after someone else's signature to show that a document is genuine

counter-tenor *noun* the highest alto male voice

countess *noun* 1 a woman of the same rank as a count or earl 2 the wife or widow of a count or earl

countless *adj* too many to count

country *noun* (*plural* **countries**) 1 any of the political units into which the world is divided, with distinct borders; a nation 2 the land in which someone lives 3 an area that is not in a town or city; countryside 4 any area or stretch of land: *this is wolf country* ◇ *adj* belonging to the country • **countryman**, **countrywoman** *noun* someone belonging to a particular country • **countryside** *noun* the parts of a country other than towns and cities

county *noun* (*plural* **counties**) a division of a country

coup /koo/ *noun* 1 a sudden outstandingly successful move or act 2 a coup d'état

coup de grâce /koo duh *grahs*/ *noun* (*plural* **coups de grâce**) a merciful final blow

coup d'état /koo deh-*tah*/ *noun* (*plural* **coups d'état**) a sudden and violent overthrow of a government

couple *noun* 1 two things of a kind together; a pair 2 two people in a romantic relationship with each other ◇ *verb* join together • **couplet** *noun* two lines of rhyming verse • **coupling** *noun* a link for joining railway carriages *etc*

coupon *noun* a piece of paper that can be exchanged for goods or money

courage *noun* lack of fear; bravery

courageous *adj* brave, fearless • **courageously** *adv*

courgette *noun* a vegetable that is a

type of small marrow

courier *noun* 1 a person or company operating a private delivery service 2 someone who acts as guide for tourists

course *noun* 1 a path in which anything moves 2 a direction to be followed: *the ship held its course* 3 a series of classes, lectures, *etc* forming an educational unit 4 a part of a meal 5 a series of things done, taken, *etc*: *a course of antibiotics* 6 a track along which athletes, horses, *etc* run 7 line of action: *the best course to follow* 8 one of the rows of bricks in a wall ◇ *verb* 1 move quickly 2 hunt • **coursing** *noun* the hunting of hares with greyhounds • **in due course** after a while, in its proper time • **in the course of** during

court *noun* 1 a room or building where legal cases are heard or tried 2 an area marked out for playing tennis *etc* 3 an open space surrounded by buildings; a courtyard 4 the people who attend a monarch *etc* 5 a royal residence ◇ *verb* 1 try to gain the support or business of: *courting potential clients* 2 behave in a way that seems to invite: *courting disaster* 3 behave amorously towards with the aim of beginning a relationship; woo • **courtly** *adj* having fine manners • **courtship** *noun* the early stages of a romantic relationship • **courtyard** *noun* an open space surrounded by buildings

courtesy *noun* politeness • **courteous** *adj* polite; obliging • **courteously** *adv*

courtier *noun* a member of a royal court

court-martial *noun* (*plural* **courts-martial**) an internal court held to try those who break navy or army laws ◇ *verb* (**court-martialling**, **court-martialled**) try in a court-martial

couscous /*koos*-koos/ *noun* hard

wheat semolina, or a meal of this steamed and served with a spicy vegetable sauce, often with meat

cousin *noun* the son or daughter of an uncle or aunt

cove *noun* a small bay

coven *noun* a gathering or group of witches

covenant *noun* a solemn or binding agreement

cover *verb* 1 put or spread something on or over 2 hide 3 stretch over: *the hills were covered with heather/my diary covers three years* 4 include, deal with: *covering the news story* 5 be enough for: *five pounds should cover the cost* 6 travel over: *covering 3 kilometres a day* 7 point a weapon at: *had the gangster covered* ◊ *noun* 1 something that covers, hides or protects 2 a cover version • **coverage** *noun* 1 an area covered 2 the extent of news covered by a newspaper *etc* 3 the amount of protection given by an insurance policy • **coverlet** *noun* a bed cover • **cover-up** *noun* a deliberate concealment of unpleasant or potentially damaging truths, *esp* by people in authority • **cover version** *noun* a new recording of a song already recorded by another singer • **cover up** 1 cover completely 2 conceal deliberately

covert *adj* not done openly; clandestine ◊ *noun* a hiding place for animals or birds when hunted • **covertly** *adv*

covet *verb* desire eagerly, *esp* something belonging to another person • **covetous** *adj* • **covetously** *adv* • **covetousness** *noun*

covey *noun* (*plural* **coveys**) a flock of birds, *esp* partridges

cow *noun* 1 the female animal of any breed of cattle, used for giving milk 2 the female of an elephant, whale and some other large animals ◊ *verb* frighten into submission; subdue • **cowboy**, **cowgirl** *noun* a man or woman who

works with cattle on a ranch • **cowed** *adj* • **cowherd** *noun* someone who looks after cows • **cowshed** *noun* a shelter for cows

coward *noun* someone who has no courage and shows fear easily • **cowardice** *noun* lack of courage • **cowardly** *adj*

cower *verb* crouch down or shrink back through fear

cowl *noun* 1 a hood, *esp* that of a monk 2 a cover for a chimney

cowslip *noun* a small yellow wild flower

cox *noun* (*plural* **coxes**) the person who steers a racing crew

coxcomb *noun* 1 *hist* a headcovering notched like a cock's comb, worn by a jester 2 a vain or conceited person

coxswain /kok-sun/ *noun* 1 someone who steers a boat 2 an officer in charge of a boat and crew

coy *adj* modest or shy, *esp* affectedly so

coyote /kai-oh-ti/ *noun* (*plural* **coyote** *or* **coyotes**) a type of small North American wolf

coypu *noun* a large, beaverlike animal that lives in rivers and marshes in S America and Europe

CPU *abbrev* central processing unit

crab *noun* a sea creature with a shell and five pairs of legs, the first pair of which have large claws • **crab apple** *noun* a type of small, bitter apple • **crabbed** /krab-id/ *adj* bad-tempered • **crabwise** *adv* sideways like a crab

crack *verb* 1 (cause to) make a sharp, sudden sound 2 break partly, without falling to pieces 3 break into (a safe) 4 decipher (a code) 5 break open (a nut) 6 make (a joke) ◊ *noun* 1 a sharp sound 2 a split, a break 3 a narrow opening 4 *informal* a sharp, witty remark 5 *informal* a pure form of cocaine ◊ *adj* of excellent ability:

a *crack marksman* • **cracked** *adj* **1** split, damaged **2** mad, crazy • **crack up** become mentally unbalanced; collapse

cracker *noun* **1** a hollow paper tube containing a small gift, which breaks with a bang when the ends are pulled **2** a thin, crisp biscuit **3** *informal* something excellent: *a cracker of a story*

crackle *verb* make a continuous cracking noise

crackling *noun* **1** a cracking sound **2** the rind or outer skin of roast pork

cradle *noun* **1** a baby's bed, *esp* one that can be rocked **2** a frame under a ship that is being built

craft *noun* **1** a practical skill **2** a boat **3** slyness, cunning • **craftsman, craftswoman** or **craftworker** *noun* someone who does skilled work with their hands

crafty *adj* (**craftier, craftiest**) cunning, sly • **craftily** *adv* • **craftiness** *noun*

crag *noun* a rough steep rock

craggy *adj* (**craggier, craggiest**) **1** rocky **2** of a face: marked with deep lines

cram *verb* (**cramming, crammed**) **1** fill until full; stuff **2** learn facts for an examination in a short time

cramp *noun* **1** a painful stiffening of the muscles **2** (**cramps**) an acute stomach pain ◇ *verb* **1** confine in too small a space **2** hinder, restrict

cramped *adj* **1** without enough room **2** of handwriting: small and closely-written

crampon *noun* a metal plate with spikes, fixed to boots for climbing on ice or snow

cranberry *noun* (*plural* **cranberries**) a type of red, sour berry

crane *noun* **1** a large wading bird with long legs, neck and bill **2** a machine for lifting heavy weights ◇ *verb* stretch out (the neck) to see round or over something

cranium *noun* (*plural* **crania** or **craniums**) the skull

crank *noun* **1** a handle for turning an axle **2** a lever that converts a horizontal movement into a rotating one **3** an eccentric ◇ *verb* start (an engine) with a crank

cranky *adj* (**crankier, crankiest**) **1** odd, eccentric **2** cross, irritable

cranny *noun* (*plural* **crannies**) a small opening or crack

crap *noun, taboo slang* **1** faeces **2** something worthless; rubbish ◇ *adj* poor, low-quality

crape *another spelling of* **crêpe**

craps *sing noun* a gambling game in which a player rolls two dice

crapulent *adj* drinking alcohol to excess; drunken

crash *noun* (*plural* **crashes**) **1** a collision between vehicles that causes damage **2** a noise of heavy things breaking or banging together **3** the failure of a business ◇ *adj* short but intensive: *crash course in French* ◇ *verb* **1** be involved in a crash **2** of a business: fail **3** of a computer program: break down **4** *informal* (*also called* **gatecrash**) attend (a party) uninvited • **crash-helmet** *noun* a protective covering for the head worn by motorcyclists *etc* • **crash-land** *verb* land (an aircraft) in an emergency, causing some structural damage • **crash landing** *noun*

crass *adj* **1** showing an annoying lack of sensitivity or good taste; vulgar **2** stupid • **crassly** *adv* • **crassness** *noun*

crate *noun* a container for carrying goods, often made of wooden slats

crater *noun* **1** the bowl-shaped mouth of a volcano **2** a hole made by an explosion

cravat /kruh-vat/ noun a scarf worn in place of a tie

craven adj, old cowardly

crawfish noun same as **crayfish**

crawl verb 1 move on hands and knees 2 move slowly 3 be covered (with): crawling with wasps 4 behave in an overly obedient or helpful way for selfish motives; fawn ◇ noun 1 the act of crawling 2 a swimming stroke of kicking the feet and alternately rotating the arms • **crawler** noun, informal someone who behaves in an overly obedient or helpful way for selfish motives

crayfish or **crawfish** noun a shellfish similar to a small lobster

crayon noun a coloured pencil or stick of wax for drawing

craze noun a temporary fashion or enthusiasm

crazy adj (**crazier**, **craziest**) 1 very foolish or unreasonable; stupid 2 suffering from mental illness or disability; insane • **crazily** adv • **craziness** noun • **crazy paving** noun paving with stones of irregular shape

creak verb make a sharp, grating sound like a hinge in need of oiling

cream noun 1 the fatty substance that forms on milk 2 any thick liquid, esp a cosmetic or medicinal product: cleansing cream/shaving cream 3 the best part: cream of society ◇ verb 1 take the cream from 2 take away (the best part) • **creamy** adj full of or like cream

crease noun 1 a mark made by folding 2 cricket a line showing the position of a batsman and bowler ◇ verb 1 make creases in 2 become creased

create verb 1 bring into being; make 2 informal make a fuss • **creation** noun 1 the act of creating 2 something created • **creator** noun • **the Creator** God

creative adj having the ability to cre-

ate things; artistic • **creatively** adv • **creativity** noun

creature noun an animal or person

crèche /kresh/ noun a nursery for children

credentials plural noun 1 personal qualities and achievements that make someone suitable 2 documents carried as proof of identity, character, etc

credible adj able to be believed • **credibility** noun

Do not confuse with: **credulous**

---

credit noun 1 an arrangement to pay later for goods supplied now: buying on credit 2 recognition of good qualities, achievements, etc: give him credit for some common sense 3 a source of honour: a credit to the family 4 the side of an account on which payments received are entered 5 a sum of money in a bank account 6 belief, trust 7 (**credits**) the naming of people who have helped in a film etc ◇ verb 1 pay money into an account 2 believe 3 (with **with**) believe to have: I credited him with more sense • **credit card** noun a card allowing the holder to pay for purchased articles at a later date

creditable adj bringing honour or good reputation • **creditably** adv

creditor noun someone to whom money is owed

credulous adj believing too easily • **credulity** noun • **credulously** adv

---

Do not confuse with: **credible**

---

creed noun a belief, esp a religious one

creek noun 1 a small inlet or bay on the sea coast 2 a short river

creep verb (**creeping**, **crept**) 1 move

slowly and silently **2** move with the body close to the ground **3** shiver with fear or disgust: *makes your flesh creep* **4** of a plant: grow along the ground or up a wall ◇ *noun* **1** a move in a creeping way **2** *informal* an unpleasant person • **creep up on** approach silently from behind • **the creeps** *informal* a feeling of disgust or fear

creeper *noun* a plant that grows along the ground or up a wall

creepy *adj* (**creepier**, **creepiest**) unsettlingly sinister • **creepy-crawly** *noun, informal* a crawling insect

cremate *verb* burn (a dead body) • **cremation** *noun*

crematorium *noun* a place where dead bodies are burnt

crème fraîche /krem *fresh*/ *noun* very thick cream thickened with a culture of bacteria

crenellated *adj* of a building: with battlements

Creole /kree-ohl/ *noun* **1** (**creole**) a hybrid or pidgin language **2** a West Indian person of mixed European and Black African descent **3** *hist* a French or Spanish settler in Louisiana

creosote *noun* an oily liquid made from wood tar, used to keep wood from rotting

crêpe /krep/ or /krehp/ *noun* **1** a type of fine, crinkly material **2** /krep/ a thin pancake • **crêpe paper** *noun* paper with a crinkled appearance

crept *past form of* **creep**

crepuscular /kruh-*pus*-kyoo-luh/ *adj* **1** relating to twilight **2** dark, dim

crescendo *noun* (*plural* **crescendos**) **1** a musical passage of increasing loudness **2** a climax

crescent *noun* **1** a curved road or street **2** something in a curved shape ◇ *adj* shaped like the new or old moon; curved

cress *noun* a plant with small, slightly bitter-tasting leaves, used in salads

crest *noun* **1** a tuft on the head of a cock or other bird **2** the top of a hill, wave, *etc* **3** feathers on top of a helmet **4** a badge

crestfallen *adj* having lost hope or excitement; downhearted

cretin *noun, informal* an idiot

Creutzfeld-Jakob disease *see* CJD

crevasse /kruh-*vas*/ *noun* a deep split in snow or ice

Do not confuse: **crevasse** and **crevice**

---

crevice /krev-is/ *noun* a crack, a narrow opening

crew[1] *noun* **1** the people who operate a ship, aircraft, *etc* **2** a gang, a mob ◇ *verb* act as a member of a crew • **crew cut** *noun* an extremely short hairstyle

crew[2] *past form of* **crow**

crib *noun* **1** a child's bed **2** a container out of which farm animals eat; a manger **3** a ready-made translation of a school text *etc* ◇ *verb* (**cribbing**, **cribbed**) copy someone else's work

cribbage *noun* a type of card game in which the score is kept with a pegged board

crick *noun* a sharp pain, *esp* in the neck ◇ *verb* produce a crick in

cricket *noun* **1** a game played with bats, ball and wickets, between two sides of 11 players each **2** an insect similar to a grasshopper • **cricketer** *noun* someone who plays cricket

cried *past form of* **cry**

crime *noun* an act that is against the law

criminal *adj* **1** forbidden by law **2** morally very wrong ◇ *noun* someone guilty of a crime

crimson noun a deep red colour ◇ adj of this colour

cringe verb 1 shrink back in fear 2 behave in too humble a way

crinkle verb 1 wrinkle, crease 2 make a crackling sound • **crinkly** adj wrinkled

crinoline /krin-uh-lin/ noun a wide petticoat or skirt shaped by concentric hoops

cripple noun, dated offensive a disabled person ◇ verb 1 make less strong, less efficient, etc: their policies crippled the economy 2 make lame

crisis noun (plural **crises**) 1 a time of great danger or distress 2 a deciding moment

crisp adj 1 stiff and dry; brittle 2 cool and fresh: crisp air 3 firm and fresh: crisp lettuce ◇ noun a thin crisp piece of fried potato eaten cold • **crispness** noun • **crispy** adj

criss-cross adj having a pattern of crossing lines ◇ verb move across and back: railway lines criss-cross the landscape

criterion noun (plural **criteria**) a means or rule by which something can be judged; a standard

critic noun 1 someone who judges the merits or faults of a book, film, etc 2 someone who finds faults in a thing or person

critical adj 1 fault-finding 2 of criticism: critical commentary 3 having an important effect on an outcome: at the critical moment 4 very ill

criticism noun 1 a judgement or opinion on (something), esp one showing up faults 2 the act of criticizing

criticize verb 1 find fault with 2 give an opinion or judgement on

croak verb make a low, hoarse sound ◇ noun a low, hoarse sound • **croakily** adv • **croaky** adj

crochet /kroh-sheh/ noun a form of knitting done with one hooked needle ◇ verb work in crochet

crock noun 1 an earthenware pot or jar 2 a worthless, old and decrepit person or thing

crockery noun china or earthenware dishes

crocodile noun 1 a large reptile found in rivers in Asia, Africa, etc 2 a procession of children walking two by two • **crocodile tears** plural noun pretended tears

crocus noun (plural **crocuses**) a yellow, purple or white flower that grows from a bulb

croft noun a small farm with a cottage, esp in the Scottish Highlands • **crofter** noun someone who farms on a croft • **crofting** noun farming on a croft

croissant /kwa-sonh/ noun a curved roll of rich bread dough

crone noun an ugly old woman

crony noun (plural **cronies**) informal a close friend, esp one with undue influence

crook noun 1 a dishonest or criminal person 2 a shepherd's or bishop's stick curved at the end ◇ verb bend, or form into a hook

crooked /kruk-id/ adj 1 bent, hooked 2 dishonest, criminal • **crookedly** adv • **crookedness** noun

croon verb sing in a slow, sentimental style • **crooner** noun • **crooning** noun

crop noun 1 natural produce gathered for food from fields, trees or bushes 2 a part of a bird's stomach 3 a riding whip 4 a short haircut ◇ verb (**cropping, cropped**) 1 cut short 2 gather a crop (of wheat etc) • **come a cropper** 1 fail badly 2 have a bad fall • **crop up** happen unexpectedly

croquet /kroh-keh/ noun a game in

which players use long-handled mallets to drive wooden balls through hoops in the ground

croquette /kruh-*ket*/ noun a ball of potato *etc* coated in breadcrumbs

cross noun 1 a shape (+) or (×) formed of two lines intersecting in the middle 2 a crucifix, or the shape of one 3 a street monument marking the site of a market *etc* 4 the result of breeding an animal or plant with one of another kind: *a cross between a horse and a donkey* 5 something that has qualities, functions, *etc* of two other things: *a cross between a bedroom and living room* 6 a difficulty that must be endured ◇ verb 1 meet or intersect 2 go to the other side of (a room, road, etc) 3 lie or pass across: *where the road crosses the border* 4 breed (one kind) with (another) 5 go against the wishes of: *he didn't dare cross his father* ◇ adj bad-tempered, angry • **cross-country** adj of a race: across fields *etc*, not on roads • **cross-examine** verb question closely in court to test the accuracy of a statement *etc* • **cross-eyed** adj having a squint • **crossly** adv angrily • **crossness** noun bad temper, sulkiness • **cross-reference** noun a statement in a reference book directing the reader to further information in another section

crossbow noun a bow fixed horizontally on a wooden stand with a device for pulling back the bowstring

crossing noun 1 a place where a street, river, *etc* may be crossed 2 a journey over the sea

crossroads sing noun a place where roads cross each other

cross-section noun 1 a section made by cutting across something 2 a sample taken as representative of the whole: *a cross-section of voters*

crossword noun a puzzle in which letters are written into blank squares to form words

crotch noun (plural **crotches**) the area between the tops of the legs

crotchet noun a musical note (♩) equivalent to a quarter of a whole note or semibreve

crotchety adj bad-tempered

crouch verb 1 stand with the knees well bent 2 of an animal: lie close to the ground

croup[1] /kroop/ noun a children's disease causing difficulty in breathing and a harsh cough

croup[2] /kroop/ noun the hindquarters of a horse

croupier /kroo-pi-yeh/ noun someone who collects the money and pays the winners at gambling

croûton /kroo-ton/ noun a small piece of fried bread, sprinkled on soup *etc*

crow noun 1 any of a family of large birds, generally black 2 the cry of a cock 3 the happy sounds made by a baby ◇ verb (**crowing**, **crew** or **crowed**) 1 cry like a cock 2 boast 3 of a baby: make happy noises • **crow's-feet** plural noun fine wrinkles around the eye, produced by ageing • **crow's-nest** noun a sheltered and enclosed platform near the mast-head of a sailing ship, from which a lookout is kept • **as the crow flies** in a straight line

---

crew is used as the past form for the first sense only: *the cock crew*; otherwise the form is **crowed**: *crowed about his exam results*

---

crowbar noun a large iron bar used as a lever

crowd noun a number of people or things together ◇ verb 1 gather into a crowd 2 fill too full 3 keep too close to; impede

crown noun 1 a jewelled band worn on the head by monarchs on ceremonial occasions **2** the top of the head **3** the highest part of something **4** *Brit US, hist* a coin worth five shillings ◇ *verb* **1** put a crown on **2** make a monarch **3** *informal* hit on the head **4** finish happily: *crowned with success*

crucial *adj* extremely important; critical: *crucial question* • **crucially** *adv*

crucible *noun* a small container for melting metals *etc*

crucifix *noun* (*plural* **crucifixes**) a figure or picture of Christ fixed to the cross • **crucifixion** *noun* **1** the act of crucifying **2** death on the cross, *esp* that of Christ

crucify *verb* (**crucifies**, **crucifying**, **crucified**) put to death by fixing the hands and feet to a cross

cruddy *adj* (**cruddier**, **cruddiest**) *slang* dirty, worthless or despicable

crude *adj* **1** not purified or refined: *crude oil* **2** roughly made or done **3** using offensive or vulgar behaviour; rude • **crudely** *adv* • **crudity** *noun*

crudités /kroo-di-teh/ *plural noun* raw vegetables served as an appetizer

cruel *adj* (**crueller**, **cruellest**) **1** having no pity for others' suffering **2** causing pain or distress • **cruelly** *adv* • **cruelty** *noun*

cruet /kroo-it/ *noun* **1** a small jar for salt, pepper, mustard, *etc* **2** two or more such jars on a stand

cruise *verb* travel by car, ship, *etc* at a steady speed ◇ *noun* a journey by ship made for pleasure • **cruiser** *noun* a middle-sized warship

crumb *noun* a small bit of anything, *esp* bread

crumble *verb* **1** break into crumbs or small pieces **2** fall to pieces ◇ *noun* a baked dish of chopped fruit topped with crumbs • **crumbly** *adj*

crumpet *noun* a soft cake eaten warm with butter

crumple *verb* **1** crush into creases or wrinkles **2** become creased **3** collapse

crunch *verb* **1** chew hard so as to make a noise **2** crush ◇ *noun* **1** a noise of crunching **2** *informal* a testing moment

crusade *noun* **1** a long and energetic campaign to achieve a goal **2** *hist* a Christian expedition to regain the Holy Land from the Turks • **crusader** *noun* someone who goes on a crusade

crush *verb* **1** squeeze together **2** defeat convincingly or mercilessly **3** crease, crumple ◇ *noun* **1** a violent squeezing **2** a pressing crowd of people **3** a drink made by squeezing fruit

crushed *adj* **1** squeezed, squashed **2** completely defeated or discouraged

crust *noun* a hard outside layer, *eg* on bread, a pie, a planet

crustacean /krus-teh-shun/ *noun* one of a large group of animals with a hard shell, including crabs, lobsters, shrimps, *etc*

crusty *adj* (**crustier**, **crustiest**) **1** having a crust **2** easily made angry; irritable

crutch *noun* (*plural* **crutches**) **1** a stick held under the armpit or elbow, used for support in walking **2** a support, a prop

crux *noun* (*plural* **cruxes** *or* **cruces**) the most important or difficult part of a problem

cry *verb* (**cries**, **crying**, **cried**) **1** express emotion with tears; weep **2** make a loud sound in pain or sorrow **3** call loudly ◇ *noun* (*plural* **cries**) a loud call • **cry off** decide not to take part in something pre-arranged; cancel • **cry over spilt milk** be worried about a misfortune that is past

crying *adj* **1** weeping **2** calling loudly **3** requiring notice or attention: *a crying need*

cryogenics *noun* the branch of physics concerned with what happens at very low temperatures

crypt *noun* an underground room or chapel, *esp* one used for burial

cryptic *adj* difficult to understand; mysterious: *cryptic remark* • **cryptically** *adv*

cryptography *noun* the art of coding and reading codes • **cryptographer** *noun*

crystal *noun* 1 very clear glass often used for making drinking glasses *etc* 2 the regular shape taken by each small part of certain substances, *eg* salt or sugar

crystalline *adj* made up of crystals

crystallize *verb* 1 form into the shape of a crystal 2 of a plan, idea, *etc*: take shape • **crystallization** *noun*

cub *noun* 1 the young of certain animals, *eg* foxes 2 a Cub Scout • **Cub Scout** *noun* a junior Scout

cube *noun* 1 a solid shape with six equal square sides 2 the answer to a sum in which a number is multiplied by itself twice: *8 is the cube of 2*

cubic *adj* 1 of cubes 2 in the shape of a cube

cubicle *noun* a small room closed off in some way from a larger one

cubit *noun, hist* the distance from elbow to middle-finger tip, used as a measurement

cuckoo *noun* (*plural* **cuckoos**) a bird that visits Britain in summer and lays its eggs in the nests of other birds

cucumber *noun* a long green vegetable that grows on a creeping plant, used in salads

cud *noun* food regurgitated by certain animals, *eg* sheep and cows

cuddle *verb* put your arms round affectionately; hug ◇ *noun* an affectionate embrace; a hug

cudgel *noun* a heavy stick used as a weapon; a club ◇ *verb* (**cudgelling**, **cudgelled**) beat with a cudgel

cue¹ *noun* 1 a sign to tell an actor when to speak *etc* 2 a hint, an indication

cue² *noun* the stick used to hit a ball in snooker, pool and similar games

cuff *noun* 1 the end of a sleeve near the wrist 2 the turned-back hem of a trouser leg 3 a blow with the open hand ◇ *verb* hit with the open hand • **off the cuff** without planning or rehearsal

cufflinks *plural noun* a pair of ornamental pins used to fasten a shirt cuff without buttons

cuisine /kwi-zeen/ *noun* 1 a style of cooking: *Mexican cuisine* 2 the art of cookery

cul-de-sac /kul-duh-sak/ *noun* a street closed at one end

culinary *adj* of or used for cookery

cull *verb* 1 gather 2 choose from a group 3 pick out and kill (seals, deer, *etc*) for the good of the herd ◇ *noun* such a killing

culminate *verb* 1 reach the highest point 2 reach the final point; end (in): *culminated in divorce* • **culmination** *noun*

culottes *plural noun* a pair of women's loose shorts that looks like a skirt

culpable *adj* to blame; guilty

culprit *noun* 1 someone who is to blame for something 2 *English and US law* a prisoner accused but not yet tried

cult *noun* 1 a religious sect 2 a general strong enthusiasm for something: *the cult of physical fitness*

cultivate *verb* 1 grow (vegetables *etc*) 2 prepare (land) for growing crops 3 try to develop and improve: *cultivated my friendship* • **cultivated**

adj **1** farmed, ploughed **2** with a good all-round education; well-educated • **cultivation** *noun* • **cultivator** *noun*

culture *noun* **1** activities and events that involve the arts, *eg* the theatre, music festivals and visits to museums **2** educated tastes in the arts: *a woman of culture* **3** a type of civilization with its associated customs: *Mediterranean culture* **4** living cells grown in laboratory conditions **5** the cultivation of plants • **cultural** *adj* to do with culture • **cultured** *adj* well-educated in literature, art, *etc* • **culture shock** *noun* unease caused by being in a society or environment that is very different from your own

culvert *noun* an arched drain for carrying water under a road or railway

cum *prep* used for both of two stated purposes: *a newsagent-cum-grocer*

cumbersome *adj* awkward to handle

cumin *noun* a brown spice from the seeds of a Mediterranean plant, used in Middle-Eastern and Asian cooking

cummerbund *noun* a sash worn by a man around the waist as part of formal dress

cumulative *adj* increasing with additions: *cumulative effect* • **cumulatively** *adv*

cumulus *noun* a kind of cloud common in summer, made up of rounded heaps

cunnilingus *noun* oral stimulation of a woman's genitals

cunning *adj* **1** clever in a deceitful way; sly **2** skilful, clever ◇ *noun* **1** slyness **2** skill, knowledge

cup *noun* **1** a hollow container holding liquid for drinking **2** an ornamental container given as a prize in sports events, or the event itself ◇ *verb* (**cupping**, **cupped**) make (hands *etc*) into the shape of a cup • **cupful** *noun* (*plural* **cupfuls**) as much as fills a cup

• **cup tie** *noun* a game in a sports competition for which the prize is a cup

cupboard *noun* a shelved recess, or a box with drawers, used for storage

Cupid *noun* the Roman god of sexual love

cupidity *noun* greed

cupola /kyoo-puh-luh/ *noun* a curved ceiling or dome on the top of a building

cur *noun, old* **1** a dog of mixed breed; a mongrel **2** a cowardly or dishonourable person

curable *adj* able to be treated and cured

curate *noun* a junior member of the clergy in the Church of England, assisting a rector or vicar • **curate's egg** *noun* something that is good in some parts only

curative *adj* likely to cure

curator *noun* someone in charge of a museum, art gallery, *etc*

curb *verb* prevent from expanding or developing further; restrain ◇ *noun* a restraint

---

Do not confuse with: **kerb**

---

curd *noun* thickened or clotted milk

curdle *verb* of milk or cream: become sour and solid when no longer fresh • **curdle someone's blood** shock or terrify them

cure *noun* **1** something that brings about recovery from a disease **2** the ending of disease; healing ◇ *verb* **1** heal **2** get rid of (a bad habit *etc*) **3** preserve by drying, salting, *etc*

curfew *noun* an order forbidding people to be out of their houses after a certain hour

curio *noun* (*plural* **curios**) an article valued for its oddness or rarity

curiosity *noun* (*plural* **curiosities**) **1**

strong desire to find something out **2** something unusual; an oddity

curious adj **1** anxious to find things out **2** unusual, odd • **curiously** adv

curl verb **1** twist (hair) into small coils **2** of hair: grow naturally in small coils **3** of smoke: move in a spiral **4** form a curved shape **5** play the game of curling ◇ noun a small coil or roll, eg of hair

curler noun **1** something used to make curls **2** someone who plays the game of curling

curlew noun a wading bird with a very long thin bill and legs

curling noun a game played by throwing heavy, flat, rounded stones along a surface of ice

curly adj (**curlier**, **curliest**) having curls • **curliness** noun

curmudgeon noun a bad-tempered or miserly person

currant noun **1** a small black raisin **2** a berry of various kinds of soft fruit: redcurrant

---

Do not confuse: **currant** and **current**

---

currency noun (plural **currencies**) **1** the money used in a particular country **2** the state of being generally known: the story gained currency

current adj **1** belonging to the present time: the current year **2** generally known and talked about: that story is current ◇ noun a stream of water, air or electrical power moving in one direction • **current account** noun a bank account from which money may be withdrawn by cheque

curriculum noun (plural **curriculums** or **curricula**) the course of study at a university, school, etc • **curriculum vitae** noun a summary of a person's education and professional experience, given to a prospective

employer when applying for a job

curry[1] noun (plural **curries**) a dish containing a mixture of spices with a strong, peppery flavour ◇ verb (**curries**, **currying**, **curried**) make into a curry by adding spices • **curry powder** noun a selection of ground spices used in making curry

curry[2] verb rub down (a horse) • **curry favour** try hard to be someone's favourite

curse verb **1** use swear words **2** wish harm towards ◇ noun **1** a wish for someone to be harmed, often one appealing to God or a magic power **2** a great inconvenience or misfortune • **cursed** adj **1** under a curse **2** very much disliked; hateful

cursor noun a flashing device that appears on a VDU screen to show the position for entering data

cursory adj hurried • **cursorily** adv

curt adj impolitely short; abrupt • **curtly** adv • **curtness** noun

curtail verb make less or shorter; reduce • **curtailment** noun

curtain noun a piece of material hung to cover a window, stage, etc

curtsy or **curtsey** noun (plural **curtsies**) a bow made by bending the knees

curvature noun **1** a curving or bending **2** a curved piece **3** an abnormal curving of the spine

curve noun **1** a rounded line, like part of the edge of a circle **2** a bend: a curve in the road **3** a rounded line on a graph that represents data: a steep learning curve • **curvy** adj **1** curved in shape **2** having many curves **3** having a shapely figure

cushion noun **1** a casing stuffed with feathers, foam, etc, for resting on **2** a soft pad

cushy adj (**cushier**, **cushiest**) informal easy and comfortable: a cushy job

cusp noun 1 a point where two curves meet 2 a division between signs of the zodiac

custard noun a sweet sauce made from eggs, milk and sugar

custodian noun 1 a keeper 2 a caretaker, eg of a museum

custody noun 1 care, guardianship 2 imprisonment

custom noun 1 something done by habit 2 the fact that someone does something regularly or frequently; habit 3 the buying of goods at a shop 4 (**customs**) taxes on goods coming into a country 5 (**customs**) the government department that collects these • **custom-built** adj built to suit a particular purpose

customary adj usual

customer noun 1 someone who buys from a shop 2 informal a person: an awkward customer

cut verb (**cutting, cut**) 1 make a slit in, or divide, with a blade: cut a hole/cut a slice of bread 2 wound with a blade 3 trim with a blade etc: cut the grass/ my hair is needing cut 4 reduce in amount 5 shorten (a play, book, etc) by removing parts 6 divide (a pack of cards) in two 7 informal play truant from (school) ◇ noun 1 a slit made by cutting 2 a wound made with something sharp 3 a blow with a knife or other blade 4 the way something, esp hair, is cut 5 the shape and style of clothes 6 a piece of meat • **cut-and-dried** adj settled finally or beforehand • **cut glass** noun glass with ornamental patterns cut on the surface • **cut-price** adj sold at a price lower than usual • **cut-throat** noun a ruffian ◇ adj fiercely competitive: cut-throat business • **cut-up** adj distressed • **cut down** 1 take down by cutting 2 reduce • **cut down on** reduce the intake of • **cut in** interrupt • **cut off** 1 separate, isolate: cut off from the mainland 2 stop: cut off supplies • **cut out** 1 shape

(a dress etc) by cutting 2 informal stop doing 3 of an engine: fail

cute adj 1 endearingly pleasant to look at; pretty 2 clever

cuticle noun the skin at the bottom and edges of finger and toe nails

cutlass noun (plural **cutlasses**) a short broad sword

cutlery noun knives, forks, spoons, etc

cutlet noun a slice of meat with the bone attached

cutting noun 1 a piece cut from a newspaper 2 a trench cut in the earth or rock for a road etc 3 a shoot of a tree or plant ◇ adj wounding, hurtful: cutting remark • **cutting-edge** adj done using the very latest technology, styles, information, etc

cuttlefish noun a type of sea creature like a squid

cv abbrev curriculum vitae

cwt abbrev hundredweight

cyanide noun a kind of poison

cyber- /sai-buh/ prefix relating to computers or electronic media: cyberspace/cyber-selling

cyborg /sai-bawg/ noun a robot in human form; an android

cycle noun 1 a bicycle 2 a round of events following on from one another repeatedly: the cycle of the seasons 3 a series of poems, stories, etc written about a single person or event ◇ verb 1 ride a bicycle 2 move in a cycle; rotate

cyclist noun someone who rides a bicycle

cyclone noun 1 a whirling windstorm 2 a weather system with winds spiralling inwards towards an area of low pressure, bringing unsettled weather • **cyclonic** adj

cygnet /sig-nut/ noun a young swan

Do not confuse with: **signet**

cylinder *noun* **1** a tube-shaped object, *esp* hollow **2** in an engine, the tube inside which a piston moves up and down

cylindrical *adj* shaped like a cylinder

cymbals /*sim*-bulz/ *plural noun* brass, plate-like musical instruments, beaten together in pairs

cynic /*sin*-ik/ *noun* someone who believes the worst about people • **cynicism** *noun*

cynical *adj* **1** tending to believe the worst of people **2** motivated by self-interest, or by the belief that people will accept immoral behaviour, poor treatment, *etc* • **cynically** *adv*

Do not confuse with: **sceptical**

cypress *noun* a type of tall thin evergreen tree

cyst /sist/ *noun* a liquid-filled blister inside the body or just under the skin

cystitis *noun* inflammation of the bladder, often caused by infection

czar *another spelling of* **tsar**

czarina *another spelling of* **tsarina**

Dd

dab *verb* (**dabbing, dabbed**) touch gently with a pad *etc* to soak up moisture ◇ *noun* **1** the act of dabbing **2** a small lump of something soft **3** a small flatfish related to the flounder • **dab hand** *noun, informal* an expert

dabble *verb* **1** do in a half-serious way or as a hobby: *he dabbles in computers* **2** play in water with hands or feet • **dabbler** *noun*

da capo *music exclam* an instruction to return to the beginning of the piece

dace *noun* a type of small river fish

dachshund /daks-hoont/ *noun* a breed of dog with short legs and a long body

dad *or* **daddy** *noun, informal* father

dado /deh-doh/ *noun* (*plural* **dadoes** *or* **dados**) the lower part of an inside wall, decorated in a different way from the rest

daffodil *noun* a tall yellow flower that grows from a bulb

daft *adj* silly • **daftly** *adv* • **daftness** *noun*

dagger *noun* a short sword for stabbing

dahlia *noun* a garden plant with large flowers

Dáil /doyl/ *noun* the lower house of parliament in the Republic of Ireland

daily *adj & adv* every day ◇ *noun* (*plural* **dailies**) **1** a paper published every day **2** *dated* someone employed to clean a house regularly

dainty *adj* (**daintier, daintiest**) **1** small and neat **2** nice to eat ◇ *noun* (*plural*

dainties) *dated* a tasty morsel of food • **daintily** *adv* • **daintiness** *noun*

dairy *noun* (*plural* **dairies**) **1** a building for storing milk and making butter and cheese **2** a shop that sells milk, butter, cheese, *etc* • **dairy cattle** *noun* cows kept for their milk, not their meat • **dairy farm** *noun* a farm concerned with the production of milk, butter, *etc* • **dairymaid** *or* **dairyman** *noun* a woman or man working in a dairy • **dairy products** *plural noun* food made of milk, butter or cheese

dais /deh-is/ *noun* (*plural* **daises**) a platform for speakers at the front of a hall

daisy *noun* (*plural* **daisies**) a small common flower with white petals • **daisy chain** *noun* a string of daisies threaded through each other's stems • **daisywheel** *noun* a flat printing wheel in a typewriter or printer, with characters at the end of spokes

dalai lama *noun* the spiritual leader of Tibetan Buddhism

dale *noun* a valley

dally *verb* (**dallies, dallying, dallied**) **1** waste time idling or playing **2** move too slowly; dawdle • **dalliance** *noun* **1** a brief sexual relationship **2** idle or aimless behaviour

Dalmatian *noun* a breed of large spotted dog

dam *noun* **1** a wall built to keep back water **2** a lake created in this way ◇ *verb* (**damming, dammed**) **1** keep back by a dam **2** hold back, restrain (tears *etc*)

damage noun 1 harm, esp in the form of breakage 2 hurt or injury 3 (**damages**) money paid by one person to another to make up for injury, insults, etc ◇ verb spoil, make less effective or unusable

damask noun silk, linen or cotton cloth with designs in the weave

dame noun 1 a comic woman in a pantomime, played by a man in drag 2 (**Dame**) the title of a woman of the same rank as a knight

damn verb 1 condemn as wrong, bad, etc 2 sentence to unending punishment in hell ◇ exclam an expression of annoyance

damnable adj 1 deserving to be condemned 2 hateful • **damnably** adv

damnation noun 1 unending punishment in hell 2 condemnation

damning adj leading to conviction or ruin: damning evidence

damp noun 1 moist air 2 wetness, moistness ◇ verb 1 wet slightly 2 make less fierce or intense ◇ adj moist, slightly wet • **damper** noun • **dampness** noun

dampen verb 1 make or become damp; moisten 2 lessen (enthusiasm etc)

damsel noun, old a young unmarried woman

damson noun a type of small dark-red plum

dan noun a black-belt grade in martial arts

dance verb move in time to music ◇ noun 1 a sequence of steps in time to music 2 a social event with dancing • **dancer** noun

dandelion noun a common plant with a yellow flower

dandruff noun dead skin on the scalp that collects under the hair and falls off in flakes

dandy noun (plural **dandies**) old a man who pays great attention to his dress and looks

danger noun 1 potential harm: unaware of the danger 2 something potentially harmful: the canal is a danger to children

dangerous adj 1 likely to cause harm; unsafe 2 full of risks • **dangerously** adv

dangle verb hang loosely

dank adj unpleasantly damp or wet • **dankness** noun

dapper adj very smartly dressed

dappled adj marked with patches of colour or light and shade

dare verb 1 be brave or bold enough (to): I didn't dare tell him 2 challenge: dared him to cross the railway line • **daredevil** noun a rash person fond of taking risks ◇ adj rash, risky • **daring** adj bold, fearless ◇ noun boldness • **daringly** adv • **I dare say** I suppose: I dare say you're right

dark adj 1 without light 2 black or near to black 3 gloomy 4 evil: dark deeds • **dark** or **darkness** noun • **darken** verb make or become dark or darker • **dark-haired** adj having dark-brown or black hair • **dark horse** noun someone about whom little is known, esp someone who proves to have unexpected talents • **in the dark** knowing nothing about something

darling noun 1 a word showing affection 2 someone dearly loved; a favourite

darn verb mend (clothes) with crossing rows of stitches ◇ noun a patch mended in this way

dart noun a pointed weapon for throwing or shooting ◇ verb move quickly and suddenly

darts sing noun a game in which small darts are aimed at a board marked off in circles and numbered sections • **dartboard** noun the board used in playing darts

dash verb 1 rush with speed or violence 2 ruin (hopes) 3 throw or knock violently, esp so as to break ◇ noun (plural **dashes**) 1 a rush 2 a short line (-) that shows a break in a sentence etc 3 a small amount of a drink etc 4 a short race 5 stylishness or confidence • **dashing** adj smart and stylish

dashboard noun a control panel in front of a driver's seat

dastardly adj, formal cowardly

DAT or **Dat** abbrev digital audio tape

data plural noun (sing **datum**) 1 facts stored in a computer 2 available facts from which conclusions may be drawn

database noun, comput a collection of systematically stored files that are often connected with each other

date[1] noun 1 a statement of time in terms of the day, month and year, eg 23 December 1995 2 the time at which an event occurs 3 the period of time to which something belongs 4 an appointment, esp with a romantic partner ◇ verb 1 give a date to 2 belong to a certain time: dates from the 12th century 3 become old-fashioned: that dress will date quickly 4 meet socially for romantic reasons: they've been dating for months • **out of date** 1 old-fashioned 2 no longer valid • **up to date** 1 in fashion; modern 2 including or aware of the latest information

date[2] noun 1 a type of palm tree 2 its blackish, shiny fruit with a hard stone

datum sing of data

daub verb 1 smear 2 paint roughly

daughter noun a female child • **daughter-in-law** noun a son's wife

daunting adj intimidating or discouraging

dawdle verb move slowly • **dawdler** noun

dawn noun 1 the time of the morning when light appears 2 a beginning: dawn of a new era ◇ verb 1 become day 2 begin to appear • **dawn chorus** noun the singing of birds at dawn • **dawning** noun dawn • **dawn on** become suddenly clear to (someone)

day noun 1 the time of light, from sunrise to sunset 2 twenty-four hours, from one midnight to the next 3 the time or hours spent at work: a hard day at the office 4 (often **days**) a particular time or period: in the days of steam • **daylight** noun 1 the light of day; sunlight 2 a clear space between things • **day release** noun time off from work for training or education • **day in, day out** on and on, continuously • **the other day** recently: saw her just the other day

daydream noun an imagining of pleasant events while awake ◇ verb imagine in this way

Day-glo noun, trademark any of various luminously bright colours

daze verb 1 stun with a blow 2 confuse, bewilder

dazzle verb 1 shine on so as to prevent from seeing clearly 2 shine brilliantly 3 impress greatly

dB abbrev decibel(s)

DC abbrev 1 District of Columbia (US) 2 detective constable 3 direct current (compare with: **AC**) 4 music da capo

DDT abbrev dichlorodiphenyltrichloroethane, a highly toxic insecticide that is now banned in most countries

deacon noun 1 the lowest rank of clergy in the Church of England 2 a church official in other churches

dead adj 1 no longer living 2 with no activity or liveliness 3 with no physical feeling; numb 4 not working: the engine was dead 5 no longer in use: a dead language 6 complete, utter: dead silence 7 exact: dead centre ◇ adv 1 completely: dead certain 2 suddenly and completely: *stop dead* ◇ *noun* **1** people who have died: *speak well of the dead* **2** the time of greatest stillness *etc*: *the dead of night* • **dead-and-alive** *adj* having little liveliness or excitement; dull • **dead beat** *adj* having no strength left; exhausted • **dead end** *noun* **1** a road *etc* closed at one end **2** a job *etc* in which there is no prospect of promotion • **dead heat** *noun* a race in which two or more runners finish equal • **dead ringer** *noun, informal* someone who looks exactly like someone else

deaden *verb* lessen (pain *etc*)

deadline *noun* a date by which something must be done

deadlock *noun* a situation in which complete disagreement prevents any progress

deadly *adj* (**deadlier**, **deadliest**) **1** likely to cause death; fatal **2** very great: *deadly hush* ◇ *adv* intensely, extremely: *deadly serious* • **deadliness** *noun*

deadpan *adj* without expression on the face

deaf *adj* **1** unable to hear **2** refusing to listen • **deafness** *noun*

deafen *verb* **1** make deaf **2** be unpleasantly loud **3** make (walls *etc*) soundproof • **deafening** *adj*

deal *noun* **1** an agreement, *esp* in business **2** an amount or quantity: *a good deal of paper* **3** the dividing out of playing cards in a game **4** a kind of softwood ◇ *verb* (**dealing**, **dealt**) **1** trade (in) **2** have something to do (with), or do business (with) **3** give out • **dealer** *noun* **1** someone who deals out cards at a game **2** a trader **3** a stockbroker • **deal with** take action concerning; see to

dean *noun* **1** the chief religious officer in a cathedral church **2** the head of a faculty in a university

dear *adj* **1** high in price **2** highly val-

ued, or much loved ◇ *noun* **1** someone who is loved **2** someone who is lovable or charming ◇ *adv* at a high price • **dearly** *adv* • **dearness** *noun*

dearth /durth/ *noun* a scarcity or shortage

death *noun* **1** the state of being dead; the end of life **2** the end of something: *the death of steam railways* • **death blow** *noun* **1** a blow that causes death **2** an event that causes something to end • **death knell** *noun* **1** a bell announcing a death **2** something indicating the end of a scheme, hope, *etc* • **death mask** *noun* a plastercast taken of a dead person's face • **death rattle** *noun* a rattling in the throat sometimes heard before someone dies • **death toll** *noun* the number of people who have died as a result of something • **deathwatch beetle** *noun* an insect that makes a ticking noise and whose larva destroys wood • **death wish** *noun* a conscious or unconscious desire to die

deathly *adj* **1** very pale or ill-looking **2** deadly

debacle /di-*bah*-kul/ *noun* **1** an event that passes off disastrously **2** the collapse of something

debar *verb* (**debarring**, **debarred**) prevent from entering or from doing something

debase *verb* **1** lessen in value **2** make bad, disreputable, immoral, *etc* • **debased** *adj* • **debasement** *noun*

debatable *adj* liable to cause people to argue; arguable: *a debatable point* • **debatably** *adv*

debate *noun* **1** a discussion, *esp* a formal one before an audience **2** an argument ◇ *verb* engage in debate; discuss

debauchery *noun* behaviour regarded as immoral, *eg* excessive drunkenness or indulgence in casual sex • **debauched** *adj* involving debauchery

debilitate verb make physically weak • **debilitating** adj

debit noun 1 an amount taken from an account 2 an amount recorded as owing ◇ verb 1 withdraw from an account 2 mark down as owing • **debit card** noun a card used for making payments that are taken from an account at the time of buying

debonair adj of a man: charming and elegant

debrief verb gather information from a soldier, spy, etc after a mission • **debriefing** noun

debris /deb-ree/ noun 1 the remains of something broken, destroyed, etc 2 rubbish

debt /det/ noun 1 money that is owed 2 help or support that one person owes to another • **debtor** noun someone who owes a debt • **in debt** owing money • **in someone's debt** under an obligation to them

debunk verb show a claim, idea, etc to be false or unjustified

début /deh-byoo/ noun the first public appearance, eg of an actor ◇ adj first before the public: début concert

débutante noun a young woman making her first appearance at an upper-class party or social event

decade noun a period of ten years

decadence noun immoral behaviour or standards • **decadent** adj

decaff adj, informal decaffeinated ◇ noun, informal decaffeinated coffee

decaffeinated adj with the caffeine removed

decamp verb leave or run away

decant verb pour (wine etc) from a bottle into a decanter

decanter noun an ornamental bottle with a glass stopper, for serving wine, whisky, etc

decapitate verb cut the head from • **decapitation** noun

decathlon noun an athletics competition combining contests in ten separate disciplines

decay verb become bad, worse or rotten ◇ noun 1 the process of rotting or worsening 2 areas of rotted matter • **decayed** adj

decease noun, formal death

deceased adj, formal dead ◇ noun (**the deceased**) a dead person

deceit noun the act of deceiving

deceitful adj inclined to deceive; lying • **deceitfully** adv • **deceitfulness** noun

deceive verb tell lies to so as to mislead • **deceiver** noun

decelerate verb slow down • **deceleration** noun

December noun the twelfth month of the year

decent adj 1 respectable 2 fairly good but not excellent or outstanding; adequate: a decent performance 3 kind: decent of you to help • **decency** noun • **decently** adv

deception noun 1 the act of deceiving 2 something that deceives or is intended to deceive

deceptive adj misleading: appearances may be deceptive • **deceptively** adv

decibel noun a unit of loudness of sound

decide verb 1 make up your mind to do something: I've decided to take your advice 2 settle (an argument etc)

decided adj 1 clear: decided difference 2 with your mind made up: he was decided on the issue • **decidedly** adv definitely

deciduous adj of a tree: having leaves that fall in autumn

decimal adj 1 numbered by tens 2

of ten parts or the number 10 ◊ *noun* a decimal fraction • **decimal fraction** *noun* a fraction expressed in tenths, hundredths, thousandths, *etc*, separated by a decimal point • **decimal point** *noun* a dot used to separate units from decimal fractions, *eg* $0.1 = {}^1/_{10}$, $2.33 = {}^{233}/_{100}$

decimalize *verb* convert (figures or currency) to decimal form • **decimalization** *noun*

decimate *verb* make much smaller in numbers by destruction

decipher *verb* 1 translate (a code) into ordinary, understandable language 2 make out the meaning of: *can't decipher his handwriting*

decision *noun* 1 something that someone decides 2 firmness of opinion or intention: *acting with decision*

decisive *adj* 1 putting an end to a contest *etc*; final: *a decisive defeat* 2 showing firmness of opinion or intention: *a decisive manner* • **decisively** *adv*

deck *noun* 1 a platform forming the floor of a ship, bus, *etc* 2 a pack of playing cards 3 the turntable of a record player ◊ *verb* decorate, adorn • **deckchair** *noun* a collapsible chair of wood and canvas, for outdoor use • **clear the decks** get rid of old papers, work, *etc* before starting something fresh

declaim *verb* 1 make a speech in impressive, dramatic language 2 speak forcefully (against) • **declamation** *noun* • **declamatory** *adj*

declare *verb* 1 announce formally or publicly: *declare war* 2 say firmly 3 make officially known (goods or income on which tax is payable) 4 *cricket* end an innings before ten wickets have fallen • **declaration** *noun*

decline *verb* 1 say 'no' to; refuse: *I had to decline his offer* 2 become worse or weaker ◊ *noun* a gradual worsening or weakening

declivity *noun* (*plural* **declivities**) a downward slope

decode *verb* translate (a coded message) into ordinary, understandable language

decompose *verb* 1 rot, decay 2 separate into parts or elements • **decomposition** *noun*

décor /*deh*-kaw/ *noun* the decoration of, and arrangement of objects in, a room *etc*

decorate *verb* 1 make more attractive by adding ornaments *etc* 2 paint or paper the walls of (a room *etc*) 3 pin a badge or medal on (someone) as a mark of honour • **decoration** *noun* • **decorative** *adj* 1 ornamental 2 pretty • **decorator** *noun* someone who decorates houses, rooms, *etc*

decorous *adj* showing good manners

decorum *noun* polite behaviour

decoy *noun* something or someone intended to lead another into a trap ◊ *verb* lead into a trap

decrease *verb* make or become less in number, intensity, *etc* ◊ *noun* a lessening in number, intensity, *etc*

decree *noun* 1 a formal order or ruling 2 a judge's decision ◊ *verb* give an order or ruling

decrepit *adj* 1 weak and infirm because of old age 2 in ruins or disrepair • **decrepitude** *noun*

decry *verb* (**decries**, **decrying**, **decried**) express strong disapproval of

dedicate *verb* 1 devote yourself (to): *dedicated to his music* 2 inscribe or publish (a book *etc*) in tribute to someone or something: *I dedicate this book to my father* 3 set apart for a sacred purpose • **dedication** *noun*

deduce *verb* reach a conclusion based on available facts; conclude • **deduction** *noun*

Do not confuse: **deduce** and **deduct**

deduct *verb* take away (from); subtract • **deduction** *noun* a subtraction

deed *noun* **1** something done; an act **2** *law* a signed statement or agreement

deed poll *noun* a document by which someone legally changes their name

deem *verb, formal* have a particular opinion of; consider

deep *adj* **1** being or going far down **2** involved to a great extent: *deep in debt/deep in thought* **3** intense, strong: *a deep red colour/deep affection* **4** low in pitch **5** hard to understand: *a deeper meaning* ◇ *noun* (with **the**) the sea • **deepen** *verb* make deeper • **deep-freeze** *noun* a freezer for food • **deep-seated** *adj* of opinions, feelings, *etc*: strongly held or felt and not easily changed or dismissed; entrenched • **in deep water** in serious trouble

deer *noun* (*plural* **deer**) an animal with antlers in the male, such as the reindeer

deface *verb* spoil the appearance of; disfigure • **defacement** *noun*

de facto *adj* actual, but often not officially or legally recognized

defame *verb* try to harm the reputation of • **defamation** *noun* • **defamatory** *adj*

default *verb* fail to do something you ought to do, *eg* to pay a debt ◇ *noun, comput* the set option used by a computer unless it is deliberately changed by the operator • **defaulter** *noun* • **by default** because something else did not happen

defeat *verb* win a victory over; beat ◇ *noun* a win, a victory

defecate *verb* empty the bowels of

waste matter • **defecation** *noun*

defect /dee-fekt/ *noun* a lack of something needed for completeness or perfection; a flaw ◇ *verb* /di-fekt/ desert a country, political party, *etc* to join or go to another • **defection** *noun* **1** failure in duty **2** desertion

defective *adj* faulty; incomplete

Do not confuse with: **deficient**

defence or US **defense** *noun* **1** action taken to protect against or repel an attack **2** a means or method of protection **3** *law* the argument defending the accused person in a case (contrasted with: **prosecution**) **4** *law* the lawyer(s) putting forward this argument • **defenceless** *adj* without defence

defend *verb* **1** guard or protect against attack **2** *law* conduct the defence of • **defendant** *noun* **1** *law* the accused person in a law case **2** someone who resists attack • **defensible** *adj* **1** able to be defended **2** able to be justified

defensive *adj* **1** used for defence **2** expecting criticism and ready to justify your actions • **on the defensive** prepared to defend yourself against attack or criticism

defer *verb* (**deferring, deferred**) **1** put off to another time **2** give way (to): *he deferred to my wishes* • **deference** *noun* **1** willingness to consider the wishes *etc* of others **2** the act of giving way to another • **deferential** *adj* showing deference; respectful

defiance *noun* open disobedience or opposition • **defiant** *adj* • **defiantly** *adv*

defibrillator *noun* a machine that applies an electric current to stop irregular beating of the heart

deficiency *noun* (*plural* **deficiencies**) **1** the fact that something is lacking

2 an amount lacking

deficient adj lacking in what is needed

Do not confuse with: **defective**

---

deficit noun an amount by which a sum of money etc is too little

defile verb **1** make immoral or impure; corrupt **2** make dirty; soil • **defilement** noun

define verb **1** state the exact meaning of **2** fix the limits of **3** outline or show clearly

definite adj **1** certain, sure **2** having clear limits; fixed **3** exact • **definitely** adv • **definiteness** noun • **definite article** noun the name given to the word the

definition noun **1** an explanation of the exact meaning of a word or phrase **2** sharpness or clearness of outline

definitive adj **1** not able to be bettered: definitive biography **2** fixed, final • **definitively** adv

deflate verb **1** let the air out of (a tyre etc) **2** reduce in self-importance or self-confidence **3** reduce the level of activity in (an economy) • **deflation** noun • **deflationary** adj

deflect verb turn aside from an initial or intended course • **deflection** noun

deform verb **1** spoil the shape of **2** make ugly • **deformed** adj badly or abnormally formed • **deformity** noun **1** something abnormal in shape **2** the fact of being badly shaped

defraud verb **1** cheat **2** (with **of**) take by cheating or fraud

defray verb pay for (expenses)

defrost verb remove frost or ice (from); thaw

deft adj showing great skill with the hands • **deftly** adv • **deftness** noun

defunct adj no longer active or in use

defuse verb **1** remove the fuse from (a bomb) **2** make (a situation etc) less dangerous

---

Do not confuse with: **diffuse**

---

defy verb (**defies, defying, defied**) **1** resist or oppose openly **2** dare (someone) to do something; challenge **3** make impossible: its beauty defies description

degenerate adj having become immoral or very bad ◇ verb become bad or worse • **degeneration** noun

degrade verb **1** lower in grade or rank **2** bring disgrace on • **degradation** noun • **degrading** adj

degree noun **1** a step or stage in a process **2** rank or grade **3** amount, extent: a degree of certainty **4** a unit of temperature **5** a unit by which angles are measured, one 360th part of the circumference of a circle **6** a certificate given by a university, gained by examination or given as an honour

dehydrate verb **1** lose water from the body, esp to a dangerous degree **2** remove water from (food etc) • **dehydrated** adj • **dehydration** noun

deify /deh-i-fai/ verb (**deifies, deifying, deified**) worship as a god

deign /dehn/ verb behave as if doing a favour: she deigned to answer us

deity /deh-i-ti/ noun (plural **deities**) a god or goddess

déjà vu /deh-zhah voo/ noun the feeling of having experienced something before

dejected adj having lost hope, confidence or happiness; dispirited • **dejection** noun

delay verb **1** put off until a later time; postpone **2** cause to be late; hold up ◇ noun **1** a postponement **2** a hold-up

delectable adj very attractive or

delicious-looking • **delectably** adv

delectation noun delight, enjoyment

delegate verb give (a task) to someone else to do ◊ noun someone acting on behalf of another; a representative • **delegation** noun a group of delegates

delete verb take or cross out (eg a piece of writing) • **deletion** noun

deleterious /del-i-tee-ri-us/ adj, formal harmful

deli /del-i/ noun, informal a delicatessen

deliberate adj 1 intentional, not accidental 2 not hurried 3 slow in deciding ◊ verb think carefully or seriously (about) • **deliberately** adv

deliberation noun 1 careful thought 2 calmness, coolness 3 (**deliberations**) formal discussions

delicacy noun (plural **delicacies**) 1 something delicious to eat 2 the fact of being easily damaged or upset

delicate adj 1 not strong; frail 2 easily damaged 3 small and attractive; dainty: delicate features 4 easily upset 5 requiring skill or care: delicate operation

delicatessen noun a shop selling food cooked or prepared ready for eating

delicious adj 1 very pleasant to taste 2 giving pleasure • **deliciously** adv

delight verb 1 please greatly 2 take great pleasure (in) ◊ noun great pleasure • **delighted** adj • **delightful** adj very pleasing • **delightfully** adv

delinquent noun 1 someone guilty of an offence 2 someone who fails in their duty ◊ adj 1 guilty of an offence or misdeed 2 not carrying out your duties • **delinquency** noun

delirious adj 1 in a state of great mental confusion 2 wildly excited • **deliriously** adv

delirium noun 1 a delirious state,

esp caused by fever 2 wild excitement • **delirium tremens** noun a delirious disorder of the brain caused by excessive alcohol

deliver verb 1 carry to a person or place 2 give or make (eg a speech) 3 set free; rescue 4 assist at the birth of (a child) • **deliverance** noun

delivery noun (plural **deliveries**) 1 the act of taking something somewhere 2 the birth of a child 3 a style of speaking

delphinium noun a tall garden plant with blue flowers

delta noun the triangular stretch of land at the mouth of a river

delude verb deceive or mislead

deluge noun 1 a great flood of water 2 an overwhelming amount: deluge of work ◊ verb 1 flood, drench 2 overwhelm

delusion noun a false belief, esp as a symptom of mental illness • **delusory** adj

---

Do not confuse with: **allusion** and **illusion**

---

de luxe adj 1 very luxurious 2 with extra special features

delve verb 1 search through; rummage: delved in her bag for her keys 2 dig

demagogue /dem-uh-gog/ noun a leader who shamelessly appeals to voters' emotions

demand verb 1 ask for firmly: the opposition have demanded a public enquiry 2 insist: I demand that you listen 3 call for urgently: issues demanding attention ◊ noun 1 a forceful request 2 an urgent claim: many demands on his time 3 a need for certain goods etc

demean verb cause to lose dignity or respect; degrade

demeanour *noun* behaviour, conduct

demented *adj* insane

demesne /duh-*mehn*/ or /duh-*meen*/ *noun* a large area of privately owned land; an estate

demise *noun, formal* death or collapse

demo *abbrev* demonstration

demob *verb & noun, informal* **1** demobilize **2** demobilization

demobilize *verb* **1** break up an army after a war is over **2** free (a soldier) from army service ● **demobilization** *noun*

democracy *noun* (*plural* **democracies**) a system of government in which people elect political representatives

democrat *noun* **1** someone who believes in democracy **2** (**Democrat**) *US* a member of the American Democratic Party

democratic *adj* **1** of or governed by democracy **2** fair because everyone has a say: *a democratic decision* **3** (**Democratic**) *US* belonging to one of the two chief political parties in the USA ● **democratically** *adv*

démodé /deh-moh-*deh*/ *adj* no longer in fashion

demographic *adj* to do with population size and movement ● **demographically** *adv* ● **demography** *noun*

demolish *verb* **1** pull down (a building *etc*) **2** destroy completely ● **demolition** *noun*

demon *noun* an evil spirit ● **demonic** *adj*

demonstrate *verb* **1** show clearly; prove **2** show (a machine *etc*) in action **3** express an opinion by marching, showing placards, *etc* in public ● **demonstrable** *adj* able to be shown clearly ● **demonstrator** *noun*

demonstration *noun* **1** a showing, a display **2** a public expression of opinion by holding a procession, mass-meeting, *etc*

demonstrative *adj* **1** inclined to show feelings, *esp* affection, openly **2** pointing out; proving

demoralize *verb* take away the confidence of ● **demoralization** *noun* ● **demoralizing** *adj*

demote *verb* reduce to a lower rank or grade ● **demotion** *noun*

demur *verb* (**demurring, demurred**) say 'no'; object

demure *adj* appearing shy and modest ● **demurely** *adv*

den *noun* **1** the lair of a wild animal **2** a small private room for working *etc*

dendrochronology *noun* the dating of events by counting the rings in trees ● **dendrochronologist** *noun*

denial *noun* the act of denying ● **in denial** doggedly refusing to accept something

denier /*den*-i-uh/ *noun* a unit in which the thinness of stockings and tights is measured

denigrate *verb* attack the reputation of; defame

denim *noun* a hard-wearing cotton cloth used for jeans, overalls, *etc*

denizen *noun* a person who lives in or frequents a place

denomination *noun* **1** the value of a coin, stamp, *etc* **2** a branch of a religion **3** name, title ● **denominational** *adj*

denominator *noun* the lower number in a vulgar fraction by which the upper number is divided, *eg* the 3 in $^2/_3$

denote *verb* mean, signify

dénouement /deh-*noo*-monh/ *noun* the ending of a story where mysteries *etc* are explained

denounce *verb* **1** condemn or accuse publicly **2** inform against: *denounced*

him to the enemy • **denunciation**
noun

dense *adj* **1** closely packed together; thick **2** *informal* very stupid • **densely** *adv*

density *noun* (*plural* **densities**) **1** thickness **2** weight (of water) in proportion to volume **3** *comput* the extent to which data can be held on a floppy disk

dent *noun* a hollow made by a blow or pressure ◇ *verb* make a dent in

dental *adj* to do with teeth or dentistry

dentist *noun* a doctor who examines teeth and treats dental problems • **dentistry** *noun* the work of a dentist

dentures *plural noun* a set of false teeth

denude *verb* make bare; strip: *denuded of leaves* • **denudation** *noun*

denunciation *see* **denounce**

deny *verb* (**denies**, **denying**, **denied**) **1** declare to be untrue: *he denied that he did it* **2** refuse, forbid: *denied the right to appeal* • **deny yourself** do without things you want or need

deodorant *noun* a cosmetic that masks body odour

depart *verb* **1** go away; leave **2** stop following or sticking to: *departing from the plan* • **departure** *noun* **1** the act or time of leaving **2** a new activity or different course of action

department *noun* a self-contained section within a shop, university, government, *etc*

depend *verb* **1** (with **on**) rely **2** (with **on**) receive necessary financial support from **3** (with **on**) be controlled or decided by: *it all depends on the weather* • **dependable** *adj* to be trusted

dependant *noun* someone who is supported financially by another

Do not confuse: **dependant** and **dependent**

dependent *adj* relying or depending (on) • **dependence** *noun* the state of being dependent

depict *verb* **1** draw, paint, *etc* **2** describe

depilatory *adj* hair-removing: *depilatory cream* ◇ *noun* (*plural* **depilatories**) a hair-removing substance

deplete *verb* make much smaller in amount or number • **depletion** *noun*

deplore *verb* disapprove of strongly: *deplored his use of language* • **deplorable** *adj* extremely bad

deploy *verb* place in position ready for action

depopulate *verb* reduce greatly in population • **depopulated** *adj*

deport *verb* send (someone) out of a country • **deportation** *noun* • **deportment** *noun* **1** way of walking or holding the body **2** behaviour

depose *verb* remove from a high position, *esp* a monarch from a throne • **deposition** *noun*

deposit *verb* **1** leave or cause to settle in a place **2** put in for safe keeping, eg money in a bank ◇ *noun* **1** money paid in part payment of something **2** money put in a bank account **3** a solid that has settled at the bottom of a liquid **4** a layer of coal, iron, *etc* occurring naturally in rock • **deposit account** *noun* a bank account from which money must be withdrawn in person, not by cheque • **deposition** *noun* a written piece of evidence formally submitted to a court • **depository** *noun* a place where anything is deposited

depot /dep-oh/ *noun* **1** a storehouse **2** a building where railway engines, buses, *etc* are kept and repaired

deprave *verb* make morally bad

• **depraved** adj morally bad; wicked
• **depravity** noun

deprecate verb show disapproval of; condemn • **deprecation** noun

---

Do not confuse: **deprecate** and **depreciate**

---

depreciate verb 1 lessen the value of 2 fall in value • **depreciation** noun

depredations plural noun damage or plundering

depress verb 1 make gloomy or unhappy 2 press down 3 reduce the value or activity of • **depressing** adj

depression noun 1 a state of severe, often irrational sadness, pessimism or apathy 2 great sadness 3 a hollow 4 a low period in a country's economy, with unemployment, lack of trade, etc 5 a region of low atmospheric pressure

deprive verb: **deprive of** take away from • **deprivation** noun • **deprived** adj suffering from hardship; disadvantaged

Dept abbrev department

depth noun 1 deepness 2 a deep place 3 the deepest part: from the depth of her soul 4 the most intense period or state: the depth of winter/ depression 5 intensity, strength: depth of colour • **in depth** thoroughly, carefully • **out of your depth** involved in problems too difficult to understand or solve

deputation noun a group of people chosen and sent as representatives

deputy noun (plural **deputies**) 1 a second-in-command 2 a delegate, a representative • **deputize** verb take another's place, as substitute

derail verb cause to leave the rails • **derailment** noun

deranged verb mentally unstable; insane • **derangement** noun

derelict adj broken-down, abandoned ◇ noun a homeless person who lives on the streets; a tramp • **dereliction** noun neglect of what should be attended to: dereliction of duty

deride verb laugh at; mock • **derision** noun • **derisive** adj

de rigueur /duh ree-gur/ adj required by fashion or by the rules of politeness

derive verb 1 have as a source or origin 2 trace (a word) back to the beginning of its existence 3 receive, obtain: derive satisfaction • **derivation** noun • **derivative** adj not original ◇ noun 1 a word formed on the base of another word, eg fabulous from fable 2 (**derivatives**) stock market trading in futures and options

dermatitis noun inflammation of the skin

dermatology noun the study and treatment of skin diseases • **dermatologist** noun

derogatory adj 1 expressing dislike, disapproval or scorn; disparaging 2 harmful to someone's reputation, dignity, etc

derrick noun 1 a crane with a movable arm 2 a framework over an oil well that holds the drilling machinery

derring-do noun, old daring action

dervish noun a member of an austere Islamic sect known for their spinning dances

descant noun, music a tune played or sung above the main tune

descend verb 1 go or climb down 2 slope downwards 3 (with **from**) have as an ancestor: claims he's descended from Napoleon 4 go from a better to a worse state • **descendant** noun someone descended from another

descent noun 1 an act of descending 2 a downward slope

describe verb 1 give an account of in

words **2** draw the outline of; trace

description *noun* **1** the act of describing **2** an account in words **3** sort, kind: *people of all descriptions* • **descriptive** *adj*

descry *verb* (**descries**, **descrying**, **descried**) *formal* notice, see

desecrate *verb* **1** spoil (something sacred) **2** treat without respect • **desecration** *noun*

Do not confuse with: **desiccate**

---

desert[1] /di-*zurt*/ *verb* **1** run away from (the army) **2** leave, abandon: *deserted his wife/his courage deserted him* • **deserter** *noun* • **desertion** *noun*

desert[2] /*dez*-ut/ *noun* a stretch of barren country with very little water • **desert island** *noun* an uninhabited island in a tropical area

---

Do not confuse with: **dessert**

---

deserve *verb* have earned as a right; be worthy of: *you deserve a holiday* • **deservedly** *adv* justly • **deserving** *adj*

desiccate *verb* **1** preserve by drying: *desiccated coconut* **2** dry up

---

Do not confuse with: **desecrate**

---

design *verb* **1** decide on the shape, structure, *etc* of **2** *formal* plan or intend ◇ *noun* **1** the shape or structure of something **2** a painted picture, pattern, *etc* **3** *formal* an intention • **designer** *noun* someone who designs objects ◇ *adj* designed by a prominent fashion designer and *usu* displaying their logo prominently • **designing** *adj* crafty, cunning • **have designs on** plan to get for yourself

designate *verb* **1** appoint, select **2** name **3** point out; indicate ◇ *adj*

appointed to a post but not yet occupying it: *director designate* • **designation** *noun* a name, a title

desirable *adj* **1** which most people would like to have **2** sexually attractive • **desirability** *noun*

desire *verb* wish for greatly ◇ *noun* **1** a longing for **2** strong sexual feelings **3** a wish

desist *verb, formal* stop (doing something)

desk *noun* a table for writing, reading, *etc* • **desktop** *noun* **1** the writing or working surface of a desk **2** *comput* in a computer system, a window from which programs are opened, showing icons for available programs • **desktop publishing** *noun* the production of professional-looking leaflets, brochures, *etc* using personal computers

desolate *adj* **1** deeply unhappy **2** empty of people; deserted **3** in which very little grows; barren • **desolated** *adj* overcome by grief • **desolation** *noun* **1** deep sorrow **2** barren land **3** ruin

despair *noun* **1** lack of hope **2** a cause of despair: *she was the despair of her mother* ◇ *verb* give up hope • **despairing** *adj*

despatch *another spelling of* **dispatch**

desperado *noun* (*plural* **desperadoes** *or* **desperados**) a violent criminal

desperate *adj* **1** without hope, despairing **2** very bad; awful **3** reckless; violent • **desperately** *adv* • **desperation** *noun*

despicable *adj* offensively bad, wrong or unlikeable; contemptible

despise *verb* consider to be offensively bad, wrong or unlikeable; hate

despite *prep* in spite of: *we had a picnic despite the weather*

despoil *verb, formal* rob, plunder

despondent adj having lost all hope or optimism; downhearted • **despondency** noun

despot /des-pot/ noun a ruler with unlimited power used cruelly; a tyrant • **despotic** adj • **despotism** noun

dessert /di-zurt/ noun sweet food served at the end of a meal

---

Do not confuse with: **desert**

---

destination noun the place to which someone or something is going

destined adj 1 travelling towards; bound (for) 2 intended (for) by fate: destined to succeed

destiny noun (plural **destinies**) what is destined to happen; fate

destitute adj 1 in urgent need of food, shelter, etc; poverty-stricken 2 (with of) completely lacking in: destitute of wit • **destitution** noun

destroy verb 1 break or knock to pieces 2 put an end to 3 kill • **destroyer** noun 1 someone who destroys 2 a type of fast warship

destruction noun 1 the act of destroying or being destroyed 2 death • **destructible** adj able to be destroyed

destructive adj 1 doing great damage 2 of criticism: pointing out faults without suggesting any improvements • **destructively** adv • **destructiveness** noun

desultory /dez-ul-tri/ or /des-ul-tri/ adj 1 moving from one thing to another without a fixed plan; wandering 2 changing from subject to subject; rambling • **desultorily** adv • **desultoriness** noun

detach verb unfasten or separate • **detachable** adj able to be taken off: detachable lining • **detached** adj 1 standing apart, by itself: detached house 2 not personally or emotionally involved • **detachment** noun 1 the

state of being detached 2 a body or group (eg of troops on special service)

detail noun 1 a small part, fact, item, etc 2 small parts or features collectively: look at the detail 3 a small group of soldiers given a special assignment ◇ verb 1 describe fully, giving particulars 2 set to do a special job or task: detailed to wash the dishes • **detailed** adj with nothing left out • **in detail** giving attention to details

detain verb 1 hold back 2 make late 3 keep under guard

detect verb 1 discover 2 notice • **detection** noun

detective noun someone who tries to find criminals or watches suspects

détente /deh-tonht/ noun a lessening of hostility between nations

detention noun 1 imprisonment 2 a forced stay after school as punishment

deter verb (**deterring, deterred**) discourage or prevent through fear • **deterrent** noun something which deters

detergent noun a soapless substance used with water for washing dishes etc

deteriorate verb become worse: her health is deteriorating rapidly • **deterioration** noun

determine verb 1 decide (on) 2 fix, settle: determined his course of action • **determination** noun 1 firmness of intention and unwillingness to give in 2 the act of settling something • **determined** adj 1 decided on a purpose: determined to succeed 2 fixed, settled

deterrent see **deter**

detest verb dislike greatly; hate • **detestable** adj hateful • **detestation** noun hatred

dethrone verb remove from a throne

• **dethronement** *noun*

detonate *verb* (cause to) explode • **detonation** *noun* an explosion • **detonator** *noun* something that sets off an explosive

detour *noun* a longer, more indirect route than the usual or intended route

detox *verb, informal* remove harmful substances from (a person) ◇ *noun* the process of removing harmful substances from the body

detract *verb* take away (from); lessen • **detraction** *noun*

detriment *noun* harm, damage, disadvantage • **detrimental** *adj* causing harm or damage; disadvantageous

deuce *noun* 1 *tennis* a score of forty points each 2 a playing card with a value of two

devastate *verb* 1 cause great destruction in 2 overwhelm with grief *etc* • **devastation** *noun*

develop *verb* 1 (cause to) become bigger or more advanced 2 acquire gradually: *developed a taste for opera* 3 start to suffer from: *developing a cold* 4 of a story: unfold gradually 5 put new buildings on (land) 6 use chemicals to make (a photograph) appear • **developer** *noun* 1 a person or company that puts up new buildings 2 a chemical mixture used to make an image appear from a photograph • **developing** *adj* with a low level of economic development and relatively poor: *developing nations/ the developing world* • **development** *noun*

deviate *verb* move away from a normal or expected route, way of behaving or thinking, *etc* • **deviation** *noun*

device *noun* 1 a tool or instrument 2 a plan 3 a design on a coat of arms

Do not confuse with: **devise**

devil *noun* 1 an evil spirit 2 (**the Dev-**

il) Satan 3 a wicked person • **devilish** *adj* very wicked • **devil-may-care** *adj* not caring what happens • **devilment** *or* **devilry** *noun* mischief • **devil's advocate** *noun* someone who argues against something, *usu* for the sake of it

devious *adj* 1 using dishonest or sly methods to achieve selfish aims; sneaky 2 not direct or straightforward • **deviousness** *noun*

devise *verb* 1 think up or put together 2 plan, plot

Do not confuse with: **device**

devoid *adj* (with **of**) free from or lacking in: *devoid of curiosity*

devolution *noun* the delegation of certain legislative powers to regional or national assemblies • **devolutionist** *noun* a supporter of devolution

devolve *verb* 1 delegate (power) to a regional or national assembly 2 fall as a duty (on)

devote *verb* give up wholly (to) • **devoted** *adj* 1 loving and loyal 2 given up (to): *devoted to her work* • **devotee** *noun* a keen follower • **devotion** *noun* great love, loyalty or commitment

devour *verb* 1 eat up greedily 2 destroy

devout *adj* 1 earnest, sincere 2 religious • **devoutly** *adv* • **devoutness** *noun*

dew *noun* tiny drops of water that form from the air as it cools at night • **dewy** *adj* covered in dew; moist

dexterity *noun* skill, *esp* with the hands • **dexterous** *or* **dextrous** *adj*

DI *abbrev* donor insemination

diabetes *noun* a disease in which there is too much sugar in the blood • **diabetic** *adj* 1 suffering from diabetes 2 designed for people with diabetes ◇ *noun* someone with diabetes

diabolical *adj* **1** shockingly bad **2** very wicked • **diabolically** *adv*

diadem *noun* a kind of crown

diagnose *verb* identify (a cause of illness) after making an examination • **diagnosis** *noun* (*plural* **diagnoses**) • **diagnostic** *adj*

diagonal *adj* going from one corner to the opposite corner ◇ *noun* a line from one corner to the opposite corner • **diagonally** *adv*

diagram *noun* a drawing that explains something • **diagrammatic** *or* **diagrammatical** *adj* in the form of a diagram

dial *noun* **1** the face of a clock or watch **2** a device on which a measurement is displayed by means of a pointer ◇ *verb* (**dialling**, **dialled**) call (a number) on a telephone

dialect *noun* a way of speaking found only in a certain area or among a certain group of people

dialogue *noun* a talk between two or more people

diameter *noun* a line which dissects a circle, passing through its centre

diamond *noun* **1** a very hard, precious stone **2** a four-cornered shape (◊) **3** a playing card with red diamond symbols on it

diaper *noun, US* a baby's nappy

diaphragm /*dai*-uh-fram/ *noun* **1** a layer of muscle separating the lower part of the body from the chest **2** a thin dividing layer **3** a contraceptive device that fits over the cervix

diarrhoea /dai-uh-*ree*-uh/ *noun* frequent emptying of the bowels, with too much liquid in the faeces

diary *noun* (*plural* **diaries**) **1** a record of daily happenings, or a book in which they are recorded **2** a book in which appointments can be recorded

diaspora /dai-*as*-puh-ruh/ *noun* a widespread dispersion or migration of people

diatribe *noun* a long and angry attack in words

dice *or* **die** *noun* (*plural* **dice**) a small cube with numbered sides or faces, used in certain games ◇ *verb* (**dice**) cut (food) into small cubes

dichotomy /dai-*kot*-uh-mi/ *noun* a division into two contrasting groups or parts

dick *noun, taboo slang* **1** the penis **2** (*also* **dickhead**) an idiot, a fool

dictate *verb* **1** speak the text of (a letter *etc*) for someone else to write down **2** give firm commands ◇ *noun* an order, a command • **dictation** *noun*

dictator *noun* an all-powerful ruler who rules cruelly • **dictatorial** *adj* like a dictator; domineering

diction *noun* **1** clarity of speaking **2** choice of words

dictionary *noun* (*plural* **dictionaries**) **1** a book giving the words of a language in alphabetical order, together with their meanings **2** any alphabetically ordered reference book

did *past tense of* **do**

die¹ *verb* (**dying**, **died**) **1** lose life **2** wither • **diehard** *noun* an obstinate or determined person

die² *noun* **1** a stamp or punch for making raised designs on money *etc* **2** *sing form of* **dice**

dieresis /dai-uh-*ree*-sis/ *noun* a mark (¨) placed over a vowel to show it must be pronounced separately from the vowel immediately before it

diesel *noun* an internal-combustion engine in which heavy oil is ignited by heat generated by compression, or the heavy oil used as fuel for such an engine

diet¹ *noun* **1** food typically eaten: *a balanced diet* **2** a course of recommended foods, eg to lose weight: *on a diet* ◇ *verb* eat certain kinds of food only, *esp* to lose weight • **dietetic** *adj*

diet² *noun* **1** a council, an assembly **2** (**Diet**) the national legislature of Japan

differ *verb* **1** (with **from**) be unlike **2** disagree

difference *noun* **1** a point in which things differ **2** the amount by which one number is greater than another **3** a disagreement • **different** *adj* **1** unlike **2** separate • **differentiate** *verb* make a difference or distinction between

difficult *adj* **1** hard to do, understand or deal with **2** hard to please • **difficulty** *noun* **1** lack of easiness; hardness **2** anything difficult **3** anything that makes something difficult; a hindrance **4** (*plural*) troubles

diffident *adj* shy • **diffidence** *noun*

diffuse *verb* spread in all directions ◇ *adj* widely spread

Do not confuse with: **defuse**

dig *verb* (**digging**, **dug**) **1** turn up (earth) with a spade *etc* **2** make (a hole) by this means **3** poke or push (something) into (something) ◇ *noun* **1** a poke, a thrust **2** an archaeological excavation • **digger** *noun* a machine for digging

digest *verb* **1** break down (food) in the stomach into a form that the body can make use of **2** think over ◇ *noun* **1** a summing-up **2** a collection of written material • **digestible** *adj* able to be digested • **digestion** *noun* the act or power of digesting • **digestive** *adj* aiding digestion

digit *noun* **1** any of the numbers 0–9 **2** a finger or toe

digital *adj* **1** showing the time by means of a display of numbers, rather than with a pointer on a dial **2** storing and processing information in

the form of sequences of numbers that a computer or similar electronic device can read: *a digital camera* • **digital audio tape** *noun* a magnetic audio tape on which sound has been recorded digitally • **digital camera** *noun* a camera which stores images in digital form • **digital radio** *noun* radio broadcasting in which the sounds are transmitted in digital form • **digital television** *noun* television broadcasting in which the signal is transmitted in digital form and decoded by a special receiver

digitalis *noun* a family of plants, including the foxglove, from which a medicine used to treat heart disease is obtained

dignified *adj* serious in manner or appearance

dignitary *noun* (*plural* **dignitaries**) someone of high rank or office

dignity *noun* **1** manner showing a sense of your own worth or the seriousness of the occasion **2** high rank

digress *verb* wander from the point in speaking or writing • **digression** *noun*

dike¹ or **dyke** *noun* **1** a wall or embankment **2** a ditch

dike² or **dyke** *noun*, *informal* a lesbian

dilapidated *adj* falling to pieces; in disrepair

dilate *verb* make or become larger or wider • **dilatation** or **dilation** *noun*

dilatory *adj* slow to take action

dildo *noun* (*plural* **dildos**) an artificial penis used for sexual stimulation

dilemma *noun* a situation offering a difficult choice between two options

dilettante /dil-it-*an*-ti/ *noun* someone with a slight but not serious interest in several subjects

diligent *adj* hard-working; industrious • **diligence** *noun* • **diligently** *adv*

dilly-dally verb (**dilly-dallies**, **dilly-dallying**, **dilly-dallied**) move or act too slowly

dilute verb lessen the strength of (a liquid etc), esp by adding water ◇ adj • **diluted** adj • **dilution** noun

dim adj (**dimmer**, **dimmest**) 1 not bright or clear 2 not understanding clearly, stupid ◇ verb (**dimming**, **dimmed**) make or become dim • **dimly** adv • **dimness** noun

dime noun a tenth of a US or Canadian dollar, ten cents

dimension noun 1 a measurement of length, width or thickness 2 (**dimensions**) size, measurements

diminish verb make or grow less • **diminution** noun a lessening • **diminutive** adj very small ◇ noun a word formed from a noun to mean a small one of the same type, eg duckling or booklet

diminuendo noun (plural **diminuendos**) a fading or falling sound

dimple noun a small hollow, esp on the cheek or chin

dim sum noun a selection of Chinese foods, usu including steamed dumplings, served as an appetizer

din noun a loud noise ◇ verb (**dinning**, **dinned**) put (into) someone's mind by constant repetition

dine verb eat dinner

dinghy noun (plural **dinghies**) a small rowing boat

dingy adj (**dingier**, **dingiest**) dull, faded or dirty-looking • **dinginess** noun

dinner noun 1 a main evening meal 2 a midday meal; lunch

dinosaur noun any of various types of extinct giant reptile

dint noun a hollow made by a blow; a dent • **by dint of** by means of

diocese /dai-uh-sis/ noun a bishop's district

Dip abbrev diploma

dip verb (**dipping**, **dipped**) 1 plunge into a liquid quickly 2 go or push down briefly 3 slope down 4 look briefly into (a book etc) ◇ noun 1 a liquid in which anything is dipped 2 a creamy sauce into which biscuits etc are dipped 3 a downward slope 4 a hollow 5 a short bathe or swim

DipEd abbrev Diploma in Education

diphtheria noun an infectious throat disease

diphthong noun two vowel-sounds pronounced as one syllable (as in the word out)

diploma noun a written statement conferring a degree, confirming a pass in an examination, etc

diplomacy noun 1 the business of making agreements, treaties, etc between countries 2 skill in making people agree; tact

diplomat noun someone engaged in diplomacy • **diplomatic** adj 1 of diplomacy 2 tactful

dire adj dreadful: in dire need

direct adj 1 straight, not roundabout 2 frank, outspoken ◇ verb 1 point or aim at 2 show the way 3 order, instruct 4 control, organize 5 control the making of a film, play, etc and give instruction to actors • **direct debit** noun payment of a bill etc in which the payee is given the right to withdraw money automatically from your bank account • **directly** adv • **directness** noun • **direct speech** noun speech reported in the speaker's exact words • **direct tax** noun a tax on income or property

direction noun 1 the place or point to which someone moves, looks, etc 2 an order 3 guidance 4 (**directions**) instructions on how to get somewhere 5 the act of directing 6 the work of a director on a film, play, etc

director noun 1 a manager of a business *etc* **2** the person who controls the making of a film, play, *etc* and gives instructions to actors

directory *noun* (*plural* **directories**) **1** a book of names and addresses *etc* **2** *comput* a named group of files on a computer disk

dirge *noun* a slow sad song, *esp* a funeral hymn

dirk *noun* a kind of dagger

dirt *noun* any unclean substance such as mud, dust, dung, *etc* • **dirt track** *noun* an earth track for motorcycle racing

dirty *adj* (**dirtier, dirtiest**) **1** not clean; soiled **2** obscene or lewd ◇ *verb* (**dirties, dirtying, dirtied**) soil with dirt • **dirtily** *adv* • **dirtiness** *noun*

disable *verb* **1** take away normal physical or mental ability **2** make (a machine) stop working • **disability** *noun* lack of normal physical or mental ability • **disabled** *adj* • **disablement** *noun*

disabuse *verb* set right about a wrong belief or opinion: *she soon disabused him of that idea*

disadvantage *noun* an unfavourable circumstance or feature; a drawback • **disadvantaged** *adj* suffering a disadvantage, *esp* poverty or homelessness • **disadvantageous** *adj* not advantageous

disaffected *adj* discontented, rebellious • **disaffection** *noun*

disagree *verb* **1** (often with **with**) hold different opinions (from) **2** quarrel **3** (with **with**) make (someone) feel ill • **disagreeable** *adj* unpleasant • **disagreement** *noun*

disallow *verb* not allow

disappear *verb* go out of sight; vanish • **disappearance** *noun*

disappoint *verb* **1** fail to come up to the hopes or expectations (of) **2** fail to fulfil • **disappointed** *adj*

• **disappointment** *noun*

disapprove *verb* have an unfavourable opinion (of) • **disapproval** *noun*

disarm *verb* **1** take (a weapon) away from **2** get rid of war weapons **3** make less angry by being pleasant or charming • **disarmament** *noun* the removal or disabling of war weapons • **disarming** *adj* gaining friendliness; pleasant or charming: *a disarming smile*

disarrange *verb* make untidy • **disarrangement** *noun*

disarray *noun* disorder

disaster *noun* **1** an extremely unfortunate happening, often causing great damage or loss **2** a total failure • **disastrous** *adj* • **disastrously** *adv*

disband *verb* break up; separate: *the gang disbanded* • **disbandment** *noun*

disbelieve *verb* not believe • **disbelief** *noun* • **disbeliever** *noun*

disburse *verb* pay out • **disbursement** *noun*

disc *noun* **1** a flat, round shape **2** a CD, DVD or record **3** a piece of cartilage between vertebrae • **disc brakes** *plural noun* vehicle brakes which use pads that are hydraulically forced against discs on the wheels • **disc jockey** *noun, dated* a DJ

discard *verb* throw away as useless

discern *verb* see, notice or realize • **discernible** *adj* noticeable: *discernible differences* • **discerning** *adj* quick at noticing; discriminating: *a discerning eye* • **discernment** *noun*

discharge *verb* **1** unload (cargo) **2** set free **3** send away; dismiss **4** fire (a gun) **5** perform (duties) **6** pay (a debt) **7** give off (*eg* smoke) **8** let out (pus) ◇ *noun* **1** dismissal **2** pus *etc* discharged from the body **3** performance (of duties) **4** payment

disciple *noun* **1** someone who believes in another's teaching **2** *hist* one of the followers of Christ

discipline noun 1 order kept by means of control 2 punishment 3 a subject of study or training 4 training in an orderly way of life ◇ verb 1 bring to order 2 punish • **disciplinarian** noun someone who insists on strict discipline • **disciplinary** adj

disclaim verb refuse to have anything to do with; deny • **disclaimer** noun a denial

disclose verb make known; reveal • **disclosure** noun 1 the act of disclosing 2 something disclosed

disco noun (plural **discos**) an event or place where recorded music is played for dancing

discography noun (plural **discographies**) a history or catalogue of musical recordings • **discographer** noun

discolour or US **discolor** verb spoil the colour of; stain • **discoloration** noun

discombobulate verb, informal confuse greatly

discomfit verb 1 cause to feel uneasy or embarrassed; disconcert 2 thwart, defeat • **discomfiture** noun

discomfort noun lack of physical comfort or mental ease

discommode verb inconvenience

disconcert verb make anxious or upset

disconnect verb break the connection between; separate • **disconnected** adj 1 no longer connected; separated 2 of thoughts etc: not following logically, rambling

disconsolate adj sad, disappointed

discontent noun dissatisfaction • **discontented** adj dissatisfied, cross • **discontentment** noun

discontinue verb (cause to) stop

discord noun 1 disagreement, quarrelling 2 music a jarring of notes • **discordant** adj

discotheque noun, dated a disco

discount noun a small sum taken off the price of something: 10% discount ◇ verb 1 not consider; dismiss: completely discounted my ideas 2 allow for exaggeration in (eg a story)

discourage verb 1 take away the confidence, hope, etc of 2 try to prevent by showing dislike or disapproval: discouraged his advances • **discouragement** noun • **discouraging** adj giving little hope or encouragement

discourse noun 1 a speech or lecture 2 an essay 3 a conversation ◇ verb talk, esp at some length

discourteous adj not polite; rude • **discourteously** adv • **discourtesy** noun

discover verb 1 find out 2 find by chance, esp for the first time • **discoverer** noun • **discovery** noun 1 the act of finding or finding out 2 something discovered

discredit verb 1 refuse to believe 2 cause to doubt 3 bring disgrace on ◇ noun 1 disgrace 2 disbelief • **discreditable** adj disgraceful

discreet adj wisely cautious or tactful • **discreetly** adv • **discretion** noun

Do not confuse with: **discrete**

discrepancy noun (plural **discrepancies**) a difference or disagreement between two things: some discrepancy in the figures

discrete adj separate, distinct

Do not confuse with: **discreet**

discretion see discreet

discriminate verb 1 make or see differences (between); distinguish 2 unfairly treat people differently because of their gender, race, etc

- **discriminating** *adj* showing good judgement • **discrimination** *noun* 1 ability to discriminate 2 unfair treatment on grounds of gender, race, *etc*

discus *noun* a heavy disc thrown in an athletic competition

discuss *verb* talk about • **discussion** *noun*

disdain *verb* 1 look down on; scorn 2 be too proud to do; be above ◇ *noun* scorn • **disdainful** *adj*

disease *noun* illness • **diseased** *adj*

disembark *verb* go ashore • **disembarkation** *noun*

disembodied *adj* separated from the body, or seeming not to come from a person

disenfranchise *verb* take away the right to vote from

disengage *verb* cause to stop being connected; separate • **disengaged** *adj*

disentangle *verb* free from entanglement; unravel

disfavour or *US* **disfavor** *noun* dislike, disapproval

disfigure *verb* spoil the beauty or appearance of • **disfigurement** *noun*

disgorge *verb* cause to flow out

disgrace *noun* the state of being out of favour; shame ◇ *verb* bring shame on • **disgraceful** *adj* 1 shamefully bad 2 *informal* very bad • **disgracefully** *adv*

disgruntled *adj* dissatisfied or discontented; fed up

disguise *verb* 1 change the appearance of 2 hide (feelings *etc*) ◇ *noun* 1 a disguised state 2 a costume *etc* that disguises

disgust *noun* 1 strong dislike; loathing 2 indignation ◇ *verb* 1 cause loathing in; revolt 2 make indignant • **disgusting** *adj* sickening; causing disgust

dish *noun* (*plural* **dishes**) 1 a plate or bowl for food 2 food prepared for eating; a meal or course 3 a saucer-shaped aerial for receiving information from a satellite ◇ *verb* 1 serve (food) 2 deal (out); distribute

dishearten *verb* take away courage or hope from • **disheartened** *adj* • **disheartening** *adj*

dishevelled *adj* with messy hair and clothes

dishonest *adj* not honest • **dishonesty** *noun*

dishonour *noun* disgrace, shame ◇ *verb* cause shame to • **dishonourable** *adj* disgraceful

disillusion *verb* take away a false belief from • **disillusioned** *adj* • **disillusionment** *noun*

disinclined *adj* unwilling

disinfect *verb* destroy disease-causing germs in • **disinfectant** *noun* a substance that kills germs

disinherit *verb* take away the rights of (an heir) • **disinheritance** *noun* • **disinherited** *adj*

disintegrate *verb* fall to pieces; break down • **disintegration** *noun*

disinterested *adj* not influenced by personal feelings; unbiased

---

Do not confuse with:
uninterested

---

disjointed *adj* of speech *etc*: having parts that do not fit together well

disk *noun* a storage medium for computer data, either a computer's internal storage medium (**hard disk**) or an external medium onto which data can be copied (**floppy disk**) • **disk drive** *noun, comput* part of a computer that records data onto and retrieves data from disks • **diskette** *noun, dated* a floppy disk

dislike *verb* not like or approve of ◇ *noun* disapproval

dislocate verb **1** put (a bone) out of joint **2** disturb or disrupt • **dislocation** noun

dislodge verb **1** knock out of place accidentally **2** force to leave a place of rest, hiding or defence

disloyal adj not loyal; unfaithful • **disloyalty** noun

dismal adj **1** expressing or feeling sadness or sorrow; gloomy **2** of poor quality

dismantle verb **1** take to pieces **2** remove fittings, furniture, etc from

dismay verb cause to feel sad or without hope ◇ noun

dismember verb **1** cut the limbs from **2** tear to pieces

dismiss verb **1** refuse to consider or accept **2** remove (someone) from a job; sack **3** send away **4** close (a law case) • **dismissal** noun

dismount verb come down off a horse, bicycle, etc

disobey verb fail or refuse to do what is commanded • **disobedience** noun • **disobedient** adj refusing or failing to obey

disobliging adj not willing to carry out the wishes of others

disorder noun **1** lack of order; confusion **2** a disease ◇ verb throw out of order • **disorderly** adj **1** out of order **2** behaving in an offensively noisy and rough manner

disorientate verb make (someone) lose their sense of where they are

disown verb refuse or cease to recognize as your own

disparage verb speak of as being of little worth or importance; belittle • **disparagement** noun • **disparaging** adj

disparity noun (plural **disparities**) great difference; inequality

dispassionate adj **1** favouring no one; unbiased **2** calm, cool • **dispassionately** adv

dispatch or **despatch** verb **1** send off (a letter etc) **2** administer a fatal blow to; finish off **3** do or deal with quickly ◇ noun (plural **dispatches** or **despatches**) **1** the act of sending off **2** a report to a newspaper **3** speed in doing something **4** killing **5** (**dispatches**) official papers (esp military or diplomatic) • **dispatch box** noun **1** a case for official papers **2** the box beside which members of parliament stand to make speeches in the House of Commons • **dispatch rider** noun a courier who delivers military dispatches by motorcycle

dispel verb (**dispelling**, **dispelled**) make (thoughts or feelings) go away

dispense verb **1** give out **2** prepare (medicines) for giving out • **dispensable** adj able to be done without • **dispensary** noun a place where medicines are given out • **dispensation** noun special permission to break a rule etc • **dispenser** noun • **dispense with** do without or get rid of

disperse verb **1** scatter; spread **2** (cause to) vanish • **dispersal** or **dispersion** noun a scattering

dispirited adj sad or discouraged

displace verb **1** put out of the usual place **2** make disordered; disarrange **3** put (someone) out of a job or position • **displaced person** noun someone forced to leave his or her own country because of war, political reasons, etc • **displacement** noun

display verb set out for show ◇ noun **1** a show or exhibition **2** a screen or other means of displaying information

displease verb cause to feel annoyed or disapproving • **displeasure** noun annoyance or disapproval

dispose verb **1** get rid (of): they disposed of the body **2** make willing or likely **3** arrange, settle • **disposable**

adj intended to be thrown away • **disposal** *noun* • **disposed** *adj* willing, inclined • **at your disposal** available for your use

disposition *noun* **1** nature, personality **2** arrangement **3** *law* the handing over of property *etc* to another

dispossess *verb* take away from; deprive (of)

disproportionate *adj* too big or too little

disprove *verb* prove to be false

dispute *verb* argue about ◇ *noun* an argument • **disputable** *adj* not certain, able to be argued about • **disputation** *noun* an argument

disqualify *verb* (**disqualifies, disqualifying, disqualified**) **1** put out of a competition for breaking rules **2** take away a qualification or right from • **disqualification** *noun*

disquiet *noun* uneasiness, anxiety

disregard *verb* pay no attention to; ignore ◇ *noun* neglect

disrepair *noun* the state of needing to be repaired or refurbished

disrepute *noun* bad reputation • **disreputable** *adj* having a bad reputation or an appearance that is not respectable

disrespect *noun* lack of politeness; rudeness • **disrespectful** *adj*

disrobe *verb, formal* get undressed

disrupt *verb* **1** break up **2** throw (a meeting *etc*) into disorder • **disruption** *noun* • **disruptive** *adj* causing disorder

dissatisfy *verb* (**dissatisfies, dissatisfying, dissatisfied**) bring no satisfaction to; displease • **dissatisfaction** *noun* • **dissatisfied** *adj*

dissect *verb* **1** cut into parts for examination **2** analyse the detail of; scrutinize • **dissection** *noun*

dissemble *verb* disguise true inten-

tions or character • **dissembler** *noun*

disseminate *verb* spread (information *etc*) • **dissemination** *noun*

dissension *noun* disagreement, quarrelling

dissent *verb* **1** have a different opinion **2** refuse to agree ◇ *noun* disagreement • **dissenter** *noun* **1** someone who disagrees **2** a member of a church that has broken away from the officially established church

dissertation *noun* a long piece of writing on an academic subject

disservice *noun* harm or unfair treatment

dissident *noun* someone who disagrees, *esp* with a political regime

dissimilar *adj* not the same • **dissimilarity** *noun*

dissipate *verb* **1** (cause to) disappear **2** waste, squander • **dissipated** *adj* indulging in pleasures; dissolute • **dissipation** *noun*

dissociate *verb* separate • **dissociate yourself from** refuse to be associated with

dissolute *adj* having loose morals; debauched

dissolve *verb* **1** melt **2** break up **3** put an end to • **dissoluble** *adj* able to be dissolved • **dissolution** *noun*

dissonance *noun* **1** discord, *esp* used deliberately for musical effect **2** disagreement • **dissonant** *adj*

dissuade *verb* persuade not to do something • **dissuasion** *noun*

distaff *noun* a stick used to hold flax or wool being spun • **distaff side** *noun* the female side or line of descent (*contrasted with*: **spear side**)

distance *noun* **1** the space between things **2** a far-off place or point: *in the distance* **3** coldness of manner

distant *adj* **1** far off or far apart in place or time: *distant era/land* **2** not close in relationship: *distant cousin* **3** cold in manner • **distantly** *adv*

distaste *noun* dislike • **distasteful** *adj* disagreeable, unpleasant

distemper *noun* **1** a viral disease of dogs, foxes, *etc* **2** a kind of paint used chiefly for walls ◇ *verb* paint with distemper

distend *verb* stretch outwards; swell • **distension** *noun*

distil *verb* (**distilling, distilled**) **1** purify (liquid) by heating to a vapour and cooling, or produce alcoholic spirit in this way **2** extract the spirit or essence from **3** (cause to) fall in drops • **distillation** *noun* • **distiller** *noun* • **distillery** *noun* a place where whisky, brandy, *etc* is distilled

distinct *adj* **1** easily seen or noticed; clear: *a distinct improvement* **2** different: *the two languages are quite distinct* • **distinction** *noun* **1** a difference **2** outstanding worth or merit

---

Do not confuse: **distinct** and **distinctive**

---

distinctive *adj* different, special • **distinctively** *adv* • **distinctiveness** *noun*

distinguish *verb* **1** recognize a difference (between) **2** mark off as different **3** notice or recognize **4** give distinction to • **distinguished** *adj* **1** famous and well-respected **2** dignified

distort *verb* **1** twist out of shape **2** turn or twist (a statement *etc*) from its true meaning **3** make (a sound) unclear and harsh • **distortion** *noun*

distract *verb* **1** divert the attention of **2** entertain or amuse **3** make mad • **distracted** *adj* mad with pain, grief, *etc* • **distraction** *noun* **1** something that diverts your attention **2** anxiety, confusion **3** amusement **4** madness

distraught *adj* extremely agitated or anxious

distress *noun* **1** great pain, trouble, sorrow **2** a cause of suffering ◇ *verb* cause great pain or sorrow to • **distressed** *adj* • **distressing** *adj*

distribute *verb* **1** give or send out to several or many people **2** spread out widely • **distribution** *noun*

district *noun* a region of a country or town

distrust *noun* lack of trust; suspicion ◇ *verb* have no trust in • **distrustful** *adj*

disturb *verb* **1** interrupt **2** confuse, worry, upset • **disturbance** *noun* • **disturbing** *adj*

disuse *noun* the state of being no longer used • **disused** *adj* no longer used

ditch *noun* (*plural* **ditches**) a long narrow hollow trench dug in the ground, *esp* to carry water

dither *verb* **1** be undecided; hesitate **2** act in a nervous, uncertain manner ◇ *noun* a state of indecision

ditsy (**ditsier, ditsiest**) *adj, US informal* scatterbrained

ditto *noun* (often written as **do**) the same as already written or said • **ditto marks** *plural noun* a character (") written below a word in a text, meaning it is to be understood as repeated

ditty *noun* (*plural* **ditties**) a simple, short song

diuretic *adj* increasing the flow of urine ◇ *noun* a medicine with this effect

diva *noun* a leading female opera singer; a prima donna

divan *noun* **1** a bed with no headboard or footboard **2** a long, low couch without a back

dive *verb* (**diving, dived** or *US* **dove**) **1** plunge headfirst into water **2** swoop through the air **3** go down steeply and quickly ◇ *noun* an act of diving • **dive-bomb** *verb* bomb from an aircraft in a steep downward dive • **dive-bomber** *noun* • **diver** *noun* **1** someone who works under water using special breathing equipment **2** a type of diving bird

diverge *verb* **1** separate and go in different directions **2** be different • **divergence** *noun* • **divergent** *adj*

diverse *adj* different, various

diversify *verb* (**diversifies, diversifying, diversified**) make or become different or varied

diversion *noun* **1** an alteration to a traffic route **2** an amusement

diversity *noun* difference; variety

divert *verb* **1** change the direction of movement or flow of **2** entertain, amuse • **diverting** *adj* entertaining, amusing

divertimento *noun* (*plural* **divertimenti**) a light piece of chamber music

divest *verb* strip or deprive of: *divested him of his authority*

divide *verb* **1** separate into parts **2** share (among) **3** (cause to) go into separate groups **4** *maths* find out how many times one number contains another • **dividers** *plural noun* measuring compasses

dividend *noun* **1** a share of profits from a business **2** an amount to be divided (*compare with*: **divisor**)

divine *adj* **1** of a god; holy **2** *informal* extremely pleasant, beautiful, *etc*; wonderful ◇ *verb* **1** guess **2** foretell, predict • **divination** *noun* the art of foretelling • **diviner** *noun* someone who claims special powers in finding hidden water or metals • **divining rod** *noun* a forked stick used by diviners to guide them to hidden water *etc*

divinity *noun* (*plural* **divinities**) **1** a god **2** the nature of a god **3** religious studies

division *noun* **1** the act of dividing **2** the process of finding out how many times a large number contains a smaller number **3** a section, *esp* of an army **4** separation **5** disagreement • **divisible** *adj* able to be divided • **divisibility** *noun* • **divisional** *adj* of a division • **divisor** *noun* the number by which another number (the **dividend**) is divided

divorce *noun* **1** the legal ending of a marriage **2** a complete separation ◇ *verb* **1** end a marriage with **2** separate (from)

divot *noun* a piece of turf thrown up, *esp* in golf

divulge *verb* make (a secret *etc*) known; let out

Diwali *or* **Dewali** /di-*vah*-li/ *noun* the Hindu and Sikh festival of lamps, celebrated in October or November

Dixie *noun, US informal* the Southern states of the USA • **dixieland** *noun* an early style of jazz music from New Orleans

DIY *abbrev* do-it-yourself

dizzy *adj* (**dizzier, dizziest**) **1** feeling a spinning sensation in the head and likely to fall; giddy **2** causing giddiness: *from a dizzy height* • **dizziness** *noun*

DJ *abbrev* someone who plays recorded music for people to listen or dance to

djellabah /ji-*lah*-buh/ *noun* a Middle-Eastern hooded cloak with wide sleeves

djinni /jeen-i/ *or* /jin-i/ *noun* a spirit in Islamic folklore

DLitt *abbrev* Doctor of Letters or Doctor of Literature

DMus *abbrev* Doctor of Music

DNA *abbrev* deoxyribonucleic acid, a compound in living cells that carries genetic instructions for passing on hereditary characteristics

do verb (**does**, **doing**, **did**, **done**) **1** carry out, perform (a job etc) **2** perform an action on, eg clean (dishes), arrange (hair) etc **3** slang swindle **4** act: do as you please **5** get on: I hear she's doing very well/how are you doing? **6** be enough: a pound will do **7** used to avoid repeating a verb: I seldom see him now, and when I do, he ignores me **8** used with a more important verb, (1) in questions: do you see what I mean?, (2) in sentences with **not**: I do not know; and (3) for emphasis: I do hope she'll be there ◇ noun (plural **dos**) informal a social event; a party • **doer** noun • **do-gooder** noun someone who tries to help others in a self-righteous way • **doings** plural noun actions • **done** adj finished • **do away with** put an end to; abolish • **do down** informal speak of disparagingly; belittle • **do in** informal **1** make exhausted; wear out **2** murder • **done to death** too often repeated • **do or die** a desperate final attempt at something whatever the consequences • **do out of** swindle out of • **do someone proud** see **proud** • **do up 1** fasten **2** renovate

do abbrev ditto

docile adj easy to control or manage; tame • **docilely** adv • **docility** noun

dock noun **1** (often **docks**) a deepened part of a harbour where ships go for loading, repair, etc **2** the box in a law court where the accused person stands **3** a weed with large leaves ◇ verb **1** put in or enter a dock **2** clip or cut short **3** of a spacecraft: join onto another craft in space • **docker** noun someone who works in the docks • **dockyard** noun a naval harbour with docks, stores, etc

docket noun a label listing the contents of something

doctor noun **1** someone trained in and licensed to practise medicine **2** someone with the highest university degree in any subject ◇ verb alter for a dishonest purpose

doctrinaire adj inflexible or obstinate in beliefs; dogmatic

doctrine noun a firmly held political or religious belief • **doctrinal** adj

docudrama noun a film based on real events and characters

document noun a written statement giving proof, information, etc

documentary noun (plural **documentaries**) a film giving information about real people or events ◇ adj **1** of or in documents: documentary evidence **2** of a documentary

docusoap noun a television series that shows events in the lives of ordinary people, not actors

dodder verb move in a trembling way, esp as a result of old age

doddery adj shaky or slow because of old age

doddle noun, informal an easy task

dodge verb avoid by a sudden or clever movement ◇ noun, informal a trick • **dodgy** adj, informal unreliable or dishonest

dodo noun (plural **dodoes** or **dodos**) a type of large extinct bird

doe noun the female of certain animals, eg a deer, rabbit or hare

doer and **does** see do

doff noun take off (a hat) in greeting

dog noun **1** a four-footed animal often kept as a pet **2** an animal of the dog family which includes wolves, foxes, etc ◇ adj of an animal: male ◇ verb (**dogging**, **dogged**) **1** be annoyingly present; plague: dogged by ill health **2** follow and watch constantly • **dog-collar** noun **1** a collar for dogs **2** a clerical collar • **dog-eared** adj of a page: turned down at the corner • **dog-eat-dog** adj viciously competitive • **dogfight** noun a fight between aeroplanes at close quarters • **dogfish** noun a kind of small shark • **dogleg**

noun a sharp bend • **dog rose** noun the wild rose • **dogsbody** noun, informal someone who is given unpleasant or dreary tasks to do • **dog's breakfast** or **dog's dinner** noun, informal a complete mess • **dogtag** noun **1** a dog's identity disc **2** an identity disc worn by soldiers etc • **dog-tired** adj completely worn out • **dog-watch** noun the period of lookout from 4 to 6pm or 6 to 8pm on a ship • **a dog's life** a life of misery • **dog in the manger** someone who stands in the way of a plan or proposal • **go to the dogs** be ruined • **the Dogstar** Sirius

dogged /dog-id/ adj determined, stubborn: dogged refusal • **doggedly** adv • **doggedness** noun

doggerel noun badly-written poetry

doggy noun (plural **doggies**) informal a child's word for a dog • **doggy bag** noun a bag used to take away left-over food from a restaurant meal • **doggy paddle** noun a simple style of swimming

dogma noun an opinion, esp religious, accepted or fixed by an authority • **dogmatic** adj stubbornly forcing your opinions on others • **dogmatically** adv

doily or **doyley** noun (plural **doilies** or **doyleys**) a perforated paper napkin put underneath cakes etc

Dolby noun, trademark a system for reducing background noise, used in recording music or soundtracks

doldrums plural noun low spirits: in the doldrums

dole noun, informal unemployment benefit ◇ verb deal (out) in small amounts

doleful adj sad or without hope; mournful • **dolefully** adv • **dolefulness** noun

doll noun a toy in the shape of a small human being

dollar noun the main unit of curren-

cy in several countries, eg the USA, Canada, Australia and New Zealand

dollop noun a small shapeless mass

dolmen noun an ancient tomb in the shape of a stone table

dolphin noun a sea animal like a small whale with a snout

dolt noun a stupid person • **doltish** adj

domain noun **1** a kingdom **2** a country estate **3** an area of interest or knowledge **4** comput a website address, or the part of an email address that comes after the @ symbol

dome noun **1** the shape of a half sphere or ball **2** the roof of a building etc in this shape • **domed** adj

domestic adj **1** of the home **2** of relationships between people who live together **3** of an animal: tame, domesticated **4** of your own country, not foreign: domestic products ◇ noun, dated a live-in maid etc • **domesticated** adj **1** of an animal: used for farming or kept as a pet **2** fond of doing housework, cooking, etc • **domesticity** noun home life • **domestic science** noun, old cookery, needlework, etc, taught as a subject

domicile noun the country or house in which someone lives permanently

dominant adj most powerful or important; main or ruling • **dominance** noun

dominate verb **1** have command or influence over **2** be most strong or most noticeable: the castle dominates the skyline **3** tower above; overlook • **domination** noun

domineering adj trying to control others; overbearing

dominion noun **1** rule, authority **2** an area with one ruler or government

domino noun (plural **dominoes**) **1** a tile-like piece used in the game of dominoes 2 *hist* a long silk cloak worn at masked balls • **dominoes** *sing noun* a game played on a table with tile-like pieces marked with dots, each side of which must match a piece placed next to it

don *noun* a college or university lecturer ◇ *verb* (**donning, donned**) put on (a coat *etc*)

donation *noun* a gift of money or goods • **donate** *verb* present (a gift)

done *past participle of* do

donkey *noun* (*plural* **donkeys**) (*also called* **ass**) a type of animal with long ears, related to the horse

donor *noun* 1 a giver of a gift 2 someone who agrees to let their blood or body organs be used for transplant operations

don't *short for* do not

doodle *verb* scribble aimlessly ◇ *noun* a meaningless scribble

doom *noun* 1 inescapable death or other unpleasant fate 2 failure, ruin • **doomed** *adj* 1 bound to fail or be destroyed 2 destined, condemned

door *noun* 1 a hinged barrier that closes the entrance to a room or building 2 the entrance itself • **doorstep** *noun* the step in front of the door of a house • **doorway** *noun* the space filled by a door; the entrance

dope *noun, informal* 1 drugs; a drug 2 an idiot ◇ *verb* add a drug to

dork *noun, informal* a stupid, useless person

dormant *adj* in an inactive state: *a dormant volcano*

dormer *or* **dormer window** *noun* a small window jutting out from a sloping roof

dormitory *noun* (*plural* **dormitories**) a room with beds for several people

dormouse *noun* (*plural* **dormice**) a small animal that hibernates

dorsal *adj* of the back: *dorsal fin*

DOS /dos/ *abbrev, comput* disk operating system

dose *noun* 1 a quantity of medicine to be taken at one time 2 a bout of something unpleasant: *dose of flu* ◇ *verb* give medicine to

doss *verb, informal* lie down to sleep somewhere temporary • **dosshouse** *noun, informal* a cheap lodging-house

dossier /dos-i-eh/ *noun* a set of papers containing information about someone or subject

dot *noun* a small, round mark ◇ *verb* (**dotting, dotted**) 1 mark with a dot 2 scatter • **dotcom** *adj* of a business: trading through the Internet • **on the dot** exactly on time

dotage *noun* the foolishness and childishness of old age

dote *verb*: **dote on** be foolishly fond of

double *verb* 1 multiply by two 2 fold ◇ *noun* 1 twice as much: *he ate double the amount* 2 someone so like another as to be mistaken for them ◇ *adj* 1 containing twice as much: *a double dose* 2 made up of two of the same sort 3 folded over • **double agent** *noun* a spy paid by each of two rival countries, but loyal to only one of them • **double bass** *noun* a type of large stringed musical instrument • **double-breasted** *adj* of a coat: with one half of the front overlapping the other • **double-cross** *verb* cheat • **double-dealer** *noun* a deceitful, cheating person • **double-dealing** *noun* • **double-decker** *noun* a bus with two floors • **double Dutch** *noun* incomprehensible talk, gibberish • **double glazing** *noun* windows made from sealed units of two sheets of glass with a vacuum between them, designed to keep in heat or keep out noise • **double-take** *noun* a second look at something surprising or confusing • **doublethink** *noun* the holding of two contradictory opinions or ideas • **double time** noun payment for overtime work etc at twice the usual rate • **doubly** adv • **at the double** very quickly • **double back** go back the way you have come • **double up** 1 writhe in pain 2 share accommodation (with)

double entendre /doo-bul onh-tonh-druh/ noun a word or phrase with two meanings, one of them usually sexual

doublet noun, hist a man's close-fitting jacket

doubloon noun, hist an old Spanish gold coin

doubt verb 1 be unsure or undecided about 2 think unlikely: I doubt that we'll be able to go ◇ noun a lack of certainty or trust; suspicion • **doubtful** adj • **doubtless** adv • **no doubt** probably

douche /doosh/ noun an instrument that injects water into the body for cleansing

dough noun 1 a soft elastic mixture of flour and water baked to make bread, cakes, etc 2 informal money

doughnut noun a ring-shaped cake fried in fat

doughty /dow-ti/ adj (**doughtier**, **doughtiest**) strong; brave

dour /doo-uh/ adj stern and humourless

dove[1] noun a pigeon • **dovecote** noun a pigeon house

dove[2] US past form of **dive**

dovetail verb 1 of two parts: fit exactly one into the other 2 of two events: coincide neatly

dowdy adj (**dowdier**, **dowdiest**) dressed in dull or badly worn clothes

down[1] adv 1 towards or in a lower position: fell down/sitting down 2 to a smaller size: grind down 3 to a later generation: handed down from moth-

er to daughter 4 on the spot, in cash: £10 down ◇ prep 1 towards or in the lower part of: rolled back down the hill 2 along: strolling down the road ◇ adj going downwards: the down escalator • **down-at-heel** adj rather shabby • **downcast** adj sad • **downfall** noun ruin, defeat • **downhearted** adj discouraged • **download** verb transfer data from one computer to another, esp via the Internet • **downpour** noun a heavy fall of rain • **downright** adj absolutely: downright wrong • **downscale** verb reduce (a company etc) in size in order to improve efficiency • **downsize** verb reduce the number of people in a workforce, esp by redundancies • **downstairs** adj on a lower floor of a building ◇ adv to a lower floor • **downstream** adv further down a river, in the direction of its flow • **downtrodden** adj kept in a lowly, inferior position • **downwards** adv moving or leading down • **go down with** or **be down with** become or be ill with

down[2] noun light, soft feathers • **downy** adj soft, feathery

downs plural noun low, grassy hills

dowry noun (plural **dowries**) money and property given by a woman or her family to her husband on their marriage

doyley another spelling of **doily**

doz abbrev dozen

doze verb sleep lightly ◇ noun a light, short sleep

dozen adj twelve

DPhil abbrev Doctor of Philosophy

Dr abbrev doctor

drab adj of a dull colour or appearance • **drabness** noun

draft noun 1 a first version of something written or drawn 2 a group of people selected for a special purpose 3 US conscription into the army 4 an order for payment of money 5 US *spelling of* **draught** ◇ *verb* **1** make a rough plan or first version **2** select for a purpose **3** *US* conscript

---

Do not confuse with: **draught**

---

draftsman, **draftswoman** *US* spellings of **draughtsman**, **draughts-woman**

drag *verb* (**dragging**, **dragged**) **1** pull roughly **2** move slowly and heavily **3** trail along the ground **4** search (a river-bed *etc*) with a net or hook ◇ *noun*, *informal* **1** a dreary task **2** a tedious person **3** clothes for one sex worn by the other • **drag your feet** *or* **drag your heels** be slow to do something

dragon *noun* **1** an imaginary fire-breathing, winged reptile **2** a fierce, intimidating woman

dragonfly *noun* (**dragonflies**) a winged insect with a long body and double wings

dragoon *verb* force or bully (into)

drain *verb* **1** clear (land) of water by trenches or pipes **2** use up completely **3** drink the contents of (a glass *etc*) ◇ *noun* a channel or pipe used to carry off water *etc* • **drainage** *noun* the drawing-off of water by rivers, pipes, *etc* • **drained** *adj* **1** emptied of liquid **2** sapped of strength

drake *noun* a male duck

drama *noun* **1** a play for acting in the theatre **2** exciting or tense action • **dramatist** *noun* a playwright

dramatic *adj* **1** exciting, thrilling **2** sudden and striking: *a dramatic increase* **3** relating to plays • **dramatically** *adv*

dramatis personae /dram-uh-tis pur-*soh*-nai/ *plural noun* the characters in a play

dramatize *verb* **1** turn into a play for the theatre **2** make vivid or sensational • **dramatization** *noun*

drank *past tense of* **drink**

drape *verb* arrange (cloth) to hang gracefully ◇ *noun* (**drapes**) *US* curtains • **draper** *noun* a dealer in cloth • **drapery** *noun* **1** cloth goods **2** a draper's shop

drastic *adj* severe, extreme • **drastically** *adv*

draught /draft/ *noun* **1** a current of air **2** (**draughts**) a game for two, played by moving pieces on a squared board **3** the act of drawing or pulling **4** an amount drunk in one go; a gulp **5** the depth of water that a ship needs to float • **draughty** *adj* full of air currents, chilly

---

Do not confuse with: **draft**

---

draughtsman, **draughtswoman** *noun* **1** someone employed to draw plans **2** someone skilled in drawing

draw *verb* (**drawing**, **drew**, **drawn**) **1** make a picture with pencil, crayons, *etc* **2** score equal points in a game **3** pull after or along **4** attract: *drew a large crowd* **5** obtain money from a fund: *drawing a pension* **6** require (a depth) for floating: *this ship draws 20 feet* **7** approach, come: *night is drawing near* ◇ *noun* **1** an equal score **2** a lottery • **draw a blank** get no result • **draw a conclusion** form an opinion from evidence heard • **drawn and quartered** *hist* cut in pieces after being hanged • **draw on 1** use as a resource: *drawing on experience* **2** approach: *night was drawing on* • **draw out 1** lengthen **2** persuade (someone) to talk and be relaxed • **draw the line at** refuse to allow or accept • **draw up 1** come to a stop **2** move closer **3** plan, write out (a contract *etc*)

drawback *noun* a disadvantage

drawbridge *noun* a bridge at the entrance to a castle which can be drawn up or let down

drawer *noun* **1** a sliding box fitting

into a chest, table, *etc* **2** someone who draws

drawing *noun* a picture made by pencil, crayon, *etc* • **drawing pin** *noun* a pin with a large flat head for fastening paper on a board *etc* • **drawing room** *noun, dated* a sitting-room

drawl *verb* speak in a slow, lazy manner ◊ *noun* a drawling voice

drawn *past participle of* **draw**

dread *noun* great fear ◊ *adj* terrifying ◊ *verb* be greatly afraid of or worried about • **dreaded** *adj*

dreadful *adj* **1** causing great suffering or harm; terrible **2** *informal* very bad • **dreadfully** *adv*

dreadlocks *noun* hair woven into thick, twisted strands

dreadnought *noun, hist* a kind of battleship

dream *noun* **1** a series of images and sounds occurring in the mind during sleep **2** something imagined, not real **3** something very beautiful **4** a hope or ambition: *her dream was to go to Mexico* ◊ *verb* (**dreaming, dreamt** *or* **dreamed**) have a dream • **dream ticket** *noun* an ideal combination of candidates for election • **dream up** invent

dreamy *adj* (**dreamier, dreamiest**) **1** only half awake; sleepy **2** vague, dim **3** *informal* beautiful • **dreamily** *adv*

dreary *adj* (**drearier, dreariest**) not interesting, attractive or exciting in any way; dull • **drearily** *adv* • **dreariness** *noun*

dredge *verb* **1** drag a net or bucket along a riverbed or seabed to bring up fish, mud, *etc* **2** sprinkle with (sugar or flour) ◊ *noun* an instrument for dredging a river *etc* • **dredger** *noun* **1** a ship that digs a channel by lifting mud from the bottom **2** a perforated jar for sprinkling sugar or flour

dregs *plural noun* **1** sediment on the bottom of a liquid: *dregs of wine* **2** last remnants **3** a worthless or useless part

dreich /dreexh/ *adj, Scot* of weather; unpleasantly dull and wet

drench *verb* soak

dress *verb* **1** put on clothes **2** treat and bandage (wounds) **3** smooth and shape (stone) ◊ *noun* (*plural* **dresses**) **1** a one-piece woman's garment combining skirt and top **2** a style of clothing: *formal dress* ◊ *adj* of clothes: for formal use • **dress coat** *noun* a black tailcoat • **dressing gown** *noun* a loose, light coat worn indoors over pyjamas *etc* • **dress rehearsal** *noun* the final rehearsal of a play, in which the actors wear their costumes • **dressy** *adj* worn for formal occasions; smart

dresser *noun* a kitchen sideboard for dishes

dressing *noun* **1** a seasoned sauce poured over salads *etc* **2** a bandage

drew *past tense of* **draw**

drey *noun* (*plural* **dreys**) a squirrel's nest

dribble *verb* **1** let saliva run down the chin **2** (cause to) fall in small drops **3** *football* move the ball forward by short kicks

dried *see* **dry**

drift *verb* **1** go with the tide or current **2** be driven into heaps by the wind **3** wander about **4** live aimlessly ◊ *noun* **1** snow, sand, *etc* driven by the wind **2** the direction in which something is driven **3** the general meaning of someone's words • **drifter** *noun* someone who lives a roaming, aimless life • **driftwood** *noun* wood driven onto the seashore by winds or tides

drill *noun* **1** a tool for making holes in wood *etc* **2** military exercise **3** a row of seeds or plants ◊ *verb* **1** make a hole in with a drill **2** exercise (soldiers) **3** sow (seeds) in rows

drink *verb* (**drinking, drank, drunk**) **1** swallow (a liquid) **2** take alcoholic drink, *esp* excessively ◇ *noun* **1** liquid to be drunk **2** alcoholic liquids ● **drink in** listen to eagerly ● **drink to** drink a toast to ● **drink up** finish a drink

drip *verb* (**dripping, dripped**) **1** fall in drops **2** let (water *etc*) fall in drops ◇ *noun* **1** a drop **2** a continual dropping, *eg* of water **3** a device for adding liquid slowly to a vein *etc* ● **drip-dry** *verb* dry (a garment) by hanging it up to dry without wringing it first ● **dripping** *noun* fat from roasting meat

drive *verb* (**driving, drove, driven**) **1** control or guide (a car *etc*) **2** go in a vehicle: *driving to work* **3** force or urge along **4** hit (a ball, nail, *etc*) hard ◇ *noun* **1** a journey in a car **2** a private road to a house **3** an avenue or road **4** energy, enthusiasm **5** a campaign: *a drive to save the local school* **6** a games tournament: *whist drive* **7** a powerful stroke with a club or bat ● **drive-in** *noun, US* a cinema where the audience watches the screen while staying in their cars ● **driver** *noun* **1** someone who drives a car *etc* **2** a wooden-headed golf club **3** *comput* software that manages a device such as a printer that is connected to a computer ● **drive at** suggest or imply

drivel *noun, informal* nonsense ◇ *verb* (**drivelling, drivelled**) talk nonsense

driven *past participle of* **drive**

drizzle *noun* light rain ◇ *verb* rain lightly ● **drizzly** *adj*

droll *adj* **1** funny, amusing **2** odd

dromedary *noun* (*plural* **dromedaries**) an Arabian camel with one hump

drone *verb* **1** make a low humming sound **2** speak in a dull boring voice ◇ *noun* **1** a low humming sound **2** a dull boring voice **3** the low-sounding pipe of a set of bagpipes **4** a male bee **5** a lazy, idle person

drool *verb* **1** produce saliva **2** antici-

pate or admire something in an obvious way

droop *verb* **1** hang down: *your hem is drooping* **2** grow weak or discouraged

drop *noun* **1** a small round or pear-shaped blob of liquid **2** a small quantity: *a drop of whisky* **3** a fall from a height: *a drop of six feet* **4** a small flavoured sweet: *pear drop* ◇ *verb* (**dropping, dropped**) **1** fall suddenly **2** let fall **3** fall in drops **4** set down from a vehicle: *drop me at the corner* **5** give up (a friend, habit, *etc*); abandon ● **droplet** *noun* a tiny drop ● **droppings** *plural noun* animal or bird dung ● **drop off** fall asleep ● **drop out 1** withdraw from a class **2** withdraw from ordinary life or society

dross *noun* **1** scum produced by melting metal **2** waste material or impurities **3** anything worthless

drought /drowt/ *noun* a period of time when no rain falls

drove *noun* **1** a number of moving cattle or other animals **2** (**droves**) a great number of people ◇ *past tense* of **drive** ● **drover** *noun* someone who drives cattle

drown *verb* **1** die by suffocating in water **2** kill (someone) in this way **3** flood or soak completely **4** block out (a sound) with a louder one

drowsy *adj* (**drowsier, drowsiest**) sleepy ● **drowsily** *adv* ● **drowsiness** *noun*

drub *verb* (**drubbing, drubbed**) beat, thrash ● **drubbing** *noun* a thrashing

drudge *verb* do very humble or boring work ◇ *noun* someone who does such work ● **drudgery** *noun* hard, uninteresting work

drug *noun* **1** a substance used in medicine to treat illness, kill pain, *etc* **2** a stimulant or narcotic substance taken habitually for its effects ◇ *verb* (**drugging, drugged**) **1** administer or add drugs to **2** cause to lose consciousness by drugs ● **druggist** noun a chemist ● **drugstore** noun, US a shop selling newspapers, soft drinks, etc as well as medicines

druid noun a pre-Christian Celtic priest

drum noun **1** a musical instrument of skin etc stretched on a round frame and beaten with sticks **2** a cylindrical container: oil drum/biscuit drum ◇ verb (**drumming**, **drummed**) **1** beat a drum **2** tap continuously with the fingers ● **drummer** noun

drumstick noun **1** a stick for beating a drum **2** the lower part of the leg of a cooked chicken

drunk adj showing the effects (giddiness, unsteadiness, etc) of drinking too much alcohol ◇ noun someone who is drunk, or habitually drunk ◇ past participle of **drink** ● **drunkard** noun a drunk

drunken adj **1** habitually drunk **2** caused by too much alcohol: drunken stupor **3** involving much alcohol: drunken orgy ● **drunkenly** adv ● **drunkenness** noun

dry adj (**drier**, **driest**) **1** not moist or wet **2** thirsty **3** uninteresting: makes very dry reading **4** expressed in a quietly sarcastic way: dry humour **5** of wine: not sweet ◇ verb (**dries**, **drying**, **dried**) make or become dry ● **dry-clean** verb clean (clothes etc) with chemicals, not with water ● **dryly** or **drily** adv ● **dryness** noun ● **dry rot** noun a disease causing wood to become dry and crumbly ● **dry-stone** noun a stone wall built without mortar

dryad /drai-ad/ noun a mythological wood nymph

DSO abbrev Distinguished Service Order

DTP abbrev desktop publishing

dual adj made up of two; double

● **dual carriageway** noun a road divided by a central barrier or boundary, with each side used by traffic moving in one direction ● **dual-purpose** adj able to be used for more than one purpose

---

Do not confuse with: **duel**

---

dub verb (**dubbing**, **dubbed**) **1** name or nickname **2** add sound effects to a film **3** give (a film) a new soundtrack in a different language

dubbin or **dubbing** noun a grease for softening or waterproofing leather

dubious adj **1** doubtful, uncertain **2** probably dishonest: dubious dealings ● **dubiety** noun

ducat /duk-ut/ noun, hist an old European gold coin

duchess noun (plural **duchesses**) **1** a woman of the same rank as a duke **2** the wife or widow of a duke

duchy noun (plural **duchies**) the land owned by a duke or duchess

duck noun **1** a web-footed water bird with a broad flat beak **2** cricket a score of no runs ◇ verb **1** lower the head quickly as if to avoid a blow **2** push (someone's head) under water ● **duckling** noun a baby duck ● **duck out (of)** avoid responsibility (for) ● **lame duck** an inefficient, useless person or organization

duck-billed platypus see platypus

duct noun **1** a pipe for carrying liquids, electric cables, etc **2** a tube in the body that carries liquids secreted by glands

ductile adj **1** of metals: easily stretched to make wire **2** easily persuaded

dud adj, informal useless or broken

dudgeon noun: **in high dudgeon** very indignant

duds *plural noun, informal* clothes

due *adj* 1 needing to be paid; owed: *the rent is due next week* 2 expected to arrive *etc*: *they're due here at six* 3 proper, appropriate: *due care ◇ adv* directly: *due south ◇ noun* 1 something you have a right to: *give him his due* 2 (**dues**) the amount of money charged for belonging to a club *etc* • **due to** brought about by or caused by

duel *noun, hist* a formalized fight between two people armed with pistols or swords *◇ verb* (**duelling, duelled**) fight in a duel • **duellist** *noun* someone who fights in a duel

---

Do not confuse with: **dual**

---

duet /dyoo-*et*/ *noun* a piece of music for two singers or players

duff *adj, informal* useless or broken

duffel bag *noun* a cylindrical canvas bag tied with a drawstring

duffel coat *noun* a heavy woollen coat fastened with toggles

duffer *noun, informal* a stupid or incompetent person

dug *past form of* **dig**

dugout *noun* 1 *sport* a bench beside a pitch for team managers, trainers and substitute players 2 a boat made by hollowing out the trunk of a tree 3 a rough shelter dug out of earth

duke *noun* a nobleman next in rank below a prince • **dukedom** *noun* the title, rank or lands of a duke

dulcet *adj, formal* sounding pleasant; melodious

dull *adj* 1 not lively or interesting 2 slow to understand or learn 3 of weather: cloudy, not bright or clear 4 not bright in colour 5 of sounds: not clear or ringing 6 blunt, not sharp *◇ verb* make dull • **dullness** *noun* • **dully** *adv*

dulse *noun* a type of edible seaweed

duly *adv* at the proper or expected time; as expected: *he duly arrived*

dumb *adj* 1 without the power of speech 2 silent 3 *informal* stupid • **dumbly** *adv* in silence

dumbfound *verb* astonish

dummy *noun* (*plural* **dummies**) 1 a model used for displaying clothes *etc* 2 a mock-up of something used for testing or display 3 an artificial teat used to comfort a baby 4 *slang* a stupid person • **dummy run** *noun* a try-out; a practice

dump *verb* 1 unload and leave (rubbish *etc*) 2 throw down heavily *◇ noun* a place for leaving rubbish • **(down) in the dumps** depressed

dumpling *noun* a cooked ball of dough

dumpy *adj* (**dumpier, dumpiest**) short and thick or fat

dun *adj* of a greyish-brown colour *◇ verb* (**dunning, dunned**) demand payment

dunce *noun* a stupid or slow-learning person

dune *noun* a low hill of sand

dung *noun* animal excrement

dungarees *plural noun* trousers with a bib

dungeon *noun* a dark underground prison

duodenum *noun* the first part of the small intestine

dupe *noun* someone easily cheated *◇ verb* deceive or trick

duplicate *noun* an exact copy *◇ adj* exactly the same *◇ verb* make a copy or copies of • **duplication** *noun*

duplicity *noun* deceitful behaviour; double-dealing • **duplicitous** *adj* • **duplicitously** *adv* • **duplicitousness** *noun*

durable *adj* lasting a long time without

wearing out or breaking; hardwearing • **durability** noun

duration noun the time a thing lasts

duress /dyoo-*res*/ noun force or threats used to make someone do something

during prep **1** throughout all or part of: *we lived here during the war* **2** at a particular point within: *she died during the night*

dusk noun partial dark; twilight

dusky adj (**duskier**, **duskiest**) dark or shadowy • **duskiness** noun

dust noun **1** fine grains or specks of earth, sand, *etc* **2** fine powder ◇ verb **1** clean the dust off: *dusted the table* **2** sprinkle lightly with powder • **dustbin** noun a container for household rubbish • **dust bowl** noun an area with little rain in which the wind raises storms of dust • **duster** noun a cloth for removing dust • **dust jacket** noun a paper cover on a book • **dustman** noun someone employed to collect household rubbish • **dusty** adj covered with dust

dutiable adj of goods: liable for tax

dutiful adj obedient • **dutifully** adv

duty noun (*plural* **duties**) **1** something a person ought to do **2** an action required to be done **3** a tax **4** (**duties**) the various tasks involved in a job • **duty-free** adj not taxed

duvet /*doo*-veh/ noun a quilt stuffed with feathers or synthetic material, used instead of blankets

DVD abbrev digital versatile disc, a CD on which large amounts of audio-visual information can be stored

dwarf noun (*plural* **dwarfs** or **dwarves**) **1** offensive a person affect-ed by dwarfism **2** a variety of plant or animal that is smaller than the standard size ◇ verb make to appear small by comparison ◇ adj not growing to full or usual height: *a dwarf cherry-tree* • **dwarfism** noun a medical condition that causes the arms and legs to be much shorter than normal

dwell verb **1** live in a place; inhabit **2** (with **on**) think habitually about something: *dwelling on the past*

dwindle verb become smaller, less, *etc* gradually

dye verb give a colour to (fabric *etc*) ◇ noun a powder or liquid used for colouring

dying present participle of **die**[1]

dyke another spelling of **dike**

dynamic adj full of energy and new ideas • **dynamically** adv

dynamics sing noun the scientific study of movement and force

dynamite noun a type of powerful explosive

dynamo noun (*plural* **dynamos**) a machine for turning the energy produced by movement into electricity

dynasty /*din*-us-ti/ noun (*plural* **dynasties**) a succession of monarchs, leaders, *etc* of the same family • **dynastic** adj

dysentery /*dis*-un-tri/ noun an infectious disease causing fever, pain and diarrhoea

dyslexia noun a mental disorder that causes difficulty in reading and writing • **dyslexic** noun & adj

dyspepsia noun indigestion • **dyspeptic** adj

Ee

E *abbrev* **1** east; eastern **2** the drug Ecstasy

each *adj* of two or more things: every one taken individually: *there is a postbox on each side of the road/she was late on each occasion* ◇ *pronoun* every one individually: *each of them won a prize* • **each other** used when an action takes place between two (or, loosely, between more than two) people: *we don't see each other very often*

eager *adj* anxious to do or get (something); keen • **eagerly** *adv* • **eagerness** *noun*

eagle *noun* a kind of large bird of prey • **eaglet** *noun* a young eagle

ear *noun* **1** the part of the body through which you hear sounds **2** a head (of corn *etc*) • **eardrum** *noun* the membrane in the middle of the ear • **earlobe** *noun* the soft flesh forming the lower part of the ear • **earmark** *verb* mark or set aside for a special purpose • **earphones** *plural noun* a pair of tiny speakers fitting in or against the ear for listening to a radio *etc* • **ear-piercing** *adj* very loud or shrill • **earplugs** *plural noun* a pair of plugs placed in the ears to block off outside noise • **earshot** *noun* the distance at which a sound can be heard

earl *noun* a member of the British aristocracy ranking between a marquis and a viscount • **earldom** *noun* the lands or title of an earl

early *adj* (**earlier, earliest**) **1** in good time **2** at or near the beginning: *in an earlier chapter* **3** sooner than expected: *you're early!* ◇ *adv* • **earliness** *noun* • **early bird** *noun* **1** an early riser **2** someone who gains an advantage by acting more quickly than rivals

earn *verb* **1** receive (money) for work **2** deserve • **earnings** *plural noun* pay received for work done

earnest *adj* serious or sincere ◇ *noun* seriousness • **earnestly** *adv* • **earnestness** *noun* • **in earnest** meaning what you say or do

earth *noun* **1** the third planet from the sun, our world **2** the surface of our world **3** soil **4** the hole of a fox, badger, *etc* **5** an electrical connection with the ground ◇ *verb* connect electrically with the ground • **earthen** *adj* made of earth or clay • **earthenware** *noun* dishes made of clay; pottery • **earthly** *adj* of the earth as opposed to heaven • **earthquake** *noun* a shaking of the earth's crust • **earthshattering** *adj* of great importance • **earth tremor** *noun* a slight earthquake • **earthwork** *noun* an artificial bank of earth built as a defence • **earthworm** *noun* the common worm

earthy *adj* (**earthier, earthiest**) **1** like soil **2** covered in soil **3** involving rather crude language or themes; vulgar • **earthily** *adv* • **earthiness** *noun*

earwig *noun* a type of insect with pincers at its tail

ease *noun* **1** freedom from difficulty: *finished the race with ease* **2** freedom from pain, worry or embarrassment **3** rest from work ◇ *verb* **1** make or become less severe, tight, difficult, *etc* **2** move carefully and gradually: *ease the stone into position* • **at ease** comfortable, relaxed • **stand at ease**

stand with your legs apart and arms behind your back

easel *noun* a stand for an artist's canvas while painting *etc*

east *noun* the direction from which the sun rises, one of the four main points of the compass ◇ *adj* **1** in or to the east **2** of the wind: from the east ◇ *adv* in or towards the east • **easterly** *adj* **1** of the wind: coming from or facing the east **2** in or towards the east • **eastern** *adj* of the east • **eastward** or **eastwards** *adj & adv* towards the east

Easter *noun* **1** the Christian celebration of Christ's rising from the dead **2** the weekend when this is celebrated each year, sometime in spring

easy *adj* (**easier**, **easiest**) **1** not hard to do **2** free from pain, worry or discomfort • **easily** *adv* • **easiness** *noun*

eat *verb* (**eating**, **ate**, **eaten**) **1** chew and swallow (food) **2** destroy or corrode gradually • **eatable** *adj* fit to eat; edible

eaves *plural noun* the edge of a roof overhanging the walls • **eavesdrop** *verb* listen secretly to a private conversation • **eavesdropper** *noun*

ebb *noun* **1** the flowing away of the tide after high tide **2** a lessening or worsening ◇ *verb* **1** flow away **2** grow less or worse

ebony *noun* a type of black, hard wood ◇ *adj* **1** made of ebony **2** black

ebullient *adj* lively and enthusiastic • **ebullience** *noun* • **ebulliently** *adv*

eccentric *adj* **1** having an amusingly or endearingly strange way of behaving; odd **2** of circles: not having the same centre (*contrasted with*: **concentric**) • **eccentricity** *noun* oddness of manner or conduct

ecclesiastical *adj* of the church or clergy

ECG *abbrev* electrocardiogram or electrocardiograph

echelon /esh-uh-lon/ *noun* **1** a level or rank in a hierarchy **2** a formation of soldiers, planes, *etc*

echidna /ik-*id*-nuh/ *noun* a spiny, toothless Australian animal with a long snout

echo *noun* (*plural* **echoes**) **1** the repetition of a sound by its striking a surface and coming back **2** something that evokes a memory: *echoes of the past* ◇ *verb* **1** send back sound **2** repeat (a thing said) **3** imitate

éclair /i-*klair*/ *noun* an oblong sweet pastry filled with cream

eclampsia *noun* a toxic condition that can occur in the final months of pregnancy

éclat /eh-*klah*/ *noun* an impressive effect

eclectic *adj* covering a broad range of types or sources; wide-ranging: *eclectic tastes*

eclipse *noun* **1** the covering of the whole or part of the sun or moon, *eg* when the moon comes between the sun and the earth **2** loss of position or prestige ◇ *verb* **1** throw into the shade **2** cause (someone's achievement) to seem unimportant by comparison

eco- *prefix* relating to the environment: *ecofriendly/eco-summit*

ecology *noun* the study of plants, animals, *etc* in relation to their natural surroundings • **ecological** *adj* • **ecologically** *adv* • **ecologist** *noun*

e-commerce *noun* buying and selling goods on the Internet

economic *adj* **1** concerning the economy **2** making a profit • **economical** *adj* not wasting money or resources; thrifty • **economics** *sing noun* the study of how economies are run • **economist** *noun* someone who studies or is an expert on economics

economy *noun* (*plural* **economies**) **1** the management of a country's finances **2** the careful use of something, *esp* money • **economize** *verb* be careful in spending or using

ecstasy *noun* (*plural* **ecstasies**) 1 very great joy or pleasure 2 (**Ecstasy**) a hallucinogenic drug • **ecstatic** *adj* • **ecstatically** *adv*

ECT *abbrev* electro-convulsive therapy

ectoplasm *noun* a substance believed by spiritualists to surround mediums when they are in a trance

ecumenical *adj* concerned with the unity of the whole Christian church

eczema /ek-si-muh/ *noun* a skin disease causing red swollen patches on the skin • **eczematic** *adj*

Edam *noun* a mild Dutch cheese with a red outer skin

eddy *noun* (*plural* **eddies**) a circling current of water or air running against the main stream ◇ *verb* (**eddies**, **eddying**, **eddied**) flow in circles

edelweiss /eh-dul-vais/ *noun* an Alpine plant with white flowers

edge *noun* 1 the border of anything, farthest from the middle 2 the cutting side of a blade 3 sharpness: *put an edge on my appetite* 4 advantage: *Brazil had the edge at half-time* ◇ *verb* 1 put a border on 2 move little by little: *edging forward* • **edgeways** *adv* sideways • **edging** *noun* a border or fringe • **edgy** *adj* 1 unable to relax, irritable 2 strange and threatening in a stylish, exciting way • **on edge** nervous, edgy • **set someone's teeth on edge** grate on their nerves

edible *adj* fit to be eaten

edict *noun* an order or command

edifice *noun* a large building

edify *verb* (**edifies**, **edifying**, **edified**) improve the mind or morals of; enlighten • **edification** *noun*

edit *verb* prepare (a text, film, *etc*) for publication or broadcasting by deciding which parts to remove or change

edition *noun* 1 the form in which a book *etc* is published after being edited 2 the copies of a book, newspaper, *etc* printed at one time 3 a special issue of a newspaper, *eg* for a local area

editor *noun* 1 someone who edits a book, film, *etc* 2 the chief journalist of a newspaper or section of a newspaper: *the sports editor* • **editorial** *adj* of editing ◇ *noun* a newspaper column written by the chief editor

educate *verb* teach (people), *esp* in a school or college • **education** *noun* • **educational** *adj* of education • **educated guess** *noun* a guess based on some knowledge of the subject involved

EEG *abbrev* electroencephalogram or electroencephalograph

eel *noun* a long, ribbon-shaped fish

eerie *adj* strange and disturbing or frightening

efface *verb* rub out • **efface yourself** keep from being noticed

effect *noun* 1 the result of an action 2 strength, power: *the pills had little effect* 3 an impression produced: *the effect of the sunset* 4 general meaning 5 use, operation: *that law is not yet in effect* 6 (**effects**) goods, property ◇ *verb* bring about • **effective** *adj* 1 producing the desired effect or a pleasing effect 2 actual • **effectual** *adj* able to do what is required • **effectually** *adv*

Do not confuse with: **affect**

effeminate *adj* of a man: having qualities considered more typical of a woman

effervesce *verb* 1 froth up 2 be very lively, excited, *etc* • **effervescence** *noun* • **effervescent** *adj*

effete *adj* lacking strength or energy; weak

efficacious *adj, formal* effective • **efficacy** *noun*

efficient *adj* able to do things well; capable • **efficiency** *noun* • **efficiently** *noun*

effigy *noun* (*plural* **effigies**) a likeness of a person carved in stone, wood, *etc*

effluent *noun* **1** liquid industrial waste; sewage **2** a stream flowing from another stream or lake

effort *noun* **1** hard work or physical exertion **2** an attempt using a lot of strength or ability

effrontery *noun* shameless rudeness; impudence

effulgent *adj* shining brightly; radiant

effusive *adj* expressing enthusiasm, happiness or approval in an excited way; gushing • **effusively** *adv*

EFL *abbrev* English as a foreign language

eg *abbrev* for example (from Latin *exempli gratia*)

egg *noun* **1** an oval shell containing the embryo of a bird, insect or reptile **2** (*also called* **ovum**) a human reproductive cell **3** a hen's egg used for eating • **egg on** urge, encourage

eggplant *noun, US* an aubergine

ego *noun* **1** the conscious self **2** excessive personal pride; egotism

egotism *noun* **1** excessive personal pride **2** the habit of considering only your own interests; selfishness • **egotist** *noun* • **egotistic** *adj*

egregious *adj, formal* shockingly wrong, unfair or bad; outrageous

egress *noun, formal* a way out

egret *noun* a type of white heron

eider *or* **eider-duck** *noun* a northern sea duck • **eiderdown** *noun* **1** soft feathers from the eider **2** a feather quilt

eight *noun* the number 8 ◊ *adj* 8 in number • **eighth** *adj* the last of a series of eight ◊ *noun* one of eight equal parts

eighteen *noun* the number 18 ◊ *adj* 18 in number • **eighteenth** *adj* the last of a series of eighteen ◊ *noun* one of eighteen equal parts

eighty *noun* the number 80 ◊ *adj* 80 in number • **eightieth** *adj* the last of a series of eighty ◊ *noun* one of eighty equal parts

eisteddfod /ai-*stet*-fut/ *noun* a competitive performing arts festival in Wales

either *adj & pronoun* **1** one or other of two: *either bus will go there/either of the dates would suit me* **2** each of two; both: *there is a crossing on either side of the road* ◊ *conj* used with **or** to show alternatives: *either he goes or I do* ◊ *adv* any more than another: *that won't work either*

ejaculate *verb* **1** emit semen from the penis **2** shout out; cry • **ejaculation** *noun*

eject *verb* **1** cause to be thrown out **2** force to leave a house, job, *etc* • **ejection** *noun*

eke *verb*: **eke out** make last longer by adding to: *eked out the stew with more vegetables*

elaborate *adj* highly detailed or decorated ◊ *verb* **1** work out in detail: *you must elaborate your escape plan* **2** (*often with* **on**) explain fully • **elaboration** *noun*

élan /eh-*lan*/ *noun* impressive confidence or style

eland *noun* a type of African deer

elapse *verb* of time: pass

elastic *adj* able to stretch and spring back again, springy ◊ *noun* a springy cloth or ribbon consisting of cotton *etc* fibres interwoven with rubber • **elasticity** *noun*

elated *adj* very pleased • **elation** *noun*

elbow *noun* the joint where the arm bends ◇ *verb* push with the elbow; jostle • **elbow grease** *noun* 1 vigorous rubbing 2 hard work; effort • **elbow room** *noun* room to move freely

elder[1] *adj* older ◇ *noun* 1 an older member of a community, tribe, *etc* 2 a member of a ruling committee in a Presbyterian church • **elderly** *adj* nearing old age • **eldest** *adj* oldest

elder[2] *noun* a type of tree with purple-black berries • **elderberry** *noun* a berry from the elder tree

El Dorado *noun* an imaginary land of great wealth

elect *verb* 1 choose by voting 2 choose (to) ◇ *adj* 1 chosen 2 chosen for a post but not yet in it: *president elect* • **electorate** *noun* all those people who have the right to vote

election *noun* the choosing by vote of people to sit in parliament *etc* • **electioneer** *verb* campaign for votes in an election

electricity *noun* a form of energy used to give light, heat and power • **electric** *or* **electrical** *adj* produced or worked by electricity • **electrician** *noun* someone skilled in working with electricity • **electrify** *verb* 1 supply with electricity 2 excite greatly

electrocardiograph *noun* a machine that shows the beating of the heart as a diagram on a screen or a tracing on paper • **electrocardiogram** *noun* a tracing produced by an electrocardiograph

electroconvulsive therapy *noun* treatment of mental disorders that involves passing an electric current through the brain

electrocute *verb* kill by an electric current • **electrocution** *noun*

electrode *noun* a conductor through which an electric current enters or leaves a battery *etc*

electromagnetism *noun* 1 magnetic forces produced by electricity 2 the relation between electric and magnetic forces • **electromagnetic** *adj* 1 relating to electromagnetism 2 having both electrical and magnetic properties

electron *noun* a very light particle within an atom, having the smallest possible charge of electricity

electronic *adj* of or using very small electrical currents and circuits • **electronics** *sing noun* a branch of physics dealing with very small electrical currents and circuits

elegant *adj* 1 well-dressed, graceful and dignified 2 of clothes *etc*: well-made and tasteful • **elegance** *noun* • **elegantly** *adv*

elegy *noun* (*plural* **elegies**) a poem written on someone's death

element *noun* 1 a part of anything 2 a substance that cannot be split chemically into simpler substances, *eg* oxygen, iron, *etc* 3 a heating wire carrying the current in an electric heater 4 circumstances that suit someone best: *she is in her element when singing* 5 (**elements**) first steps in learning; basics 6 (**elements**) the powers of nature; the weather • **elemental** *adj* of the elements • **elementary** *adj* 1 at the first stage 2 simple

elephant *noun* a very large animal with a thick skin, a trunk and two ivory tusks • **elephantine** *adj* big and clumsy

elevate *verb* 1 raise to a higher position or rank 2 improve (the mind) 3 cheer (someone) up • **elevation** *noun* 1 the act of raising up 2 rising ground 3 height 4 a drawing of a building as seen from the side 5 an angle measuring height: *the sun's elevation* • **elevator** *noun, US* a lift in a building

eleven *noun* the number 11 ◇ *adj* 11 in number ◇ *noun* a team of eleven players, eg for cricket • **elevenses** plural noun a snack of coffee, biscuits, etc taken around mid-morning • **eleventh** adj the last of a series of eleven ◊ noun one of eleven equal parts

elf noun (plural **elves**) a tiny, mischievous supernatural creature • **elfin**, **elfish** or **elvish** adj like an elf

elicit verb **1** draw out (information etc) **2** cause people to express: the sight elicited gasps from the audience

Do not confuse with: **illicit**

eligible adj **1** fit or worthy to be chosen **2** having a right to receive something • **eligibility** noun

eliminate verb **1** get rid of **2** exclude, omit • **elimination** noun

élite or **elite** /eh-leet/ noun a part of a group selected as, or believed to be, the best

elixir /i-liks-uh/ noun a liquid believed to give eternal life, or to be able to turn iron etc into gold

elk noun a very large deer found in N Europe and Asia, related to the moose

ellipse noun (plural **ellipses**) an oval shape • **ellipsis** noun **1** the omission of a word or words in a text **2** marks (...) indicating missing words in a text • **elliptic** or **elliptical** adj **1** oval **2** having part of the words or meaning left out

elm noun a tree with a rough bark and leaves with saw-like edges

elocution noun **1** the art of what is thought to be correct speech **2** style of speaking

elongate verb stretch out lengthwise; make longer • **elongation** noun

elope verb run away from home to get married • **elopement** noun

eloquent adj **1** good at expressing thoughts in clear language **2** persuasive • **eloquence** noun

else adv otherwise: come inside or else you will catch cold ◊ adj other than the person or thing mentioned: someone else has taken her place • **elsewhere** adv in or to another place

elucidate verb make (something) easier to understand

elude verb **1** escape by a trick **2** be too difficult to remember or understand

Do not confuse with: **allude**

elusive adj hard to catch or achieve

Do not confuse with: **allusive** and **illusive**

elver noun a young eel

elves and **elvish** see elf

Elysium noun paradise

emaciated adj unpleasantly or unhealthily thin

email noun **1** a system for sending messages and computer files from one computer to another via the Internet **2** a message sent by email ◊ verb send an email to

emanate verb come out from; flow out • **emanation** noun

emancipate verb set free, eg from slavery or repressive social conditions • **emancipation** noun

emasculate verb **1** deprive of power or strength; weaken **2** castrate

embalm verb preserve (a dead body) from decay by treating it with spices or drugs

embankment noun a bank of earth or stone built to keep back water, or to carry a railway over low-lying places

embargo noun (plural **embargoes**) an official order forbidding something, *esp* trade with another country

embark *verb* **1** (with **on**) start (a new career *etc*) **2** go on board ship • **embarkation** *noun*

embarrass *verb* cause to feel uncomfortable and self-conscious • **embarrassing** *adj* • **embarrassment** *noun*

embassy *noun* (*plural* **embassies**) the offices and staff of an ambassador in a foreign country

embellish *verb* **1** add details to (a story *etc*) **2** decorate • **embellishment** *noun*

ember *noun* a piece of wood or coal glowing in a fire

embezzle *verb* use dishonestly for yourself (money entrusted to you) • **embezzlement** *noun*

emblazon *verb* **1** display in an obvious way **2** decorate with a bright design or coat of arms

emblem *noun* **1** an image that represents something: *the dove is the emblem of peace/the leek is the emblem of Wales* **2** a badge

embody *verb* (**embodies, embodying, embodied**) **1** give form to; represent: *embodying the spirit of the age* **2** include • **embodiment** *noun*

embolden *verb* **1** make brave **2** print in bold type

embolism *noun* an obstructing clot in a blood vessel

emboss *verb* make a pattern in leather, metal, *etc* that stands out from a flat surface • **embossed** *adj*

embrace *verb* **1** throw your arms round in affection **2** include **3** adopt eagerly ◊ *noun* an affectionate hug

embrocation *noun* ointment for rubbing on the body, *eg* to relieve stiffness

embroider *verb* **1** decorate with designs in needlework **2** add false details to (a story) • **embroiderer** *noun* • **embroidery** *noun*

embroil *verb* **1** get (someone) into a quarrel or difficult situation **2** throw into confusion

embryo *noun* (*plural* **embryos**) **1** a young animal or plant in its earliest stage of development, after the egg or seed has been fertilized **2** the beginning of anything • **embryonic** *adj* in an early stage of development

emend *verb* remove faults or errors from • **emendation** *noun*

Do not confuse with: **amend**

---

emerald *noun* a bright green precious stone

emerge *verb* **1** come out **2** become known or clear • **emergence** *noun* • **emergent** *adj* **1** newly formed or newly independent: *emergent nation* **2** arising

emergency *noun* (*plural* **emergencies**) an unexpected event requiring urgent action

emery *noun* a very hard mineral used for smoothing and polishing

emetic *adj* causing vomiting ◊ *noun* an emetic medicine

emigrate *verb* leave your country to settle in another • **emigrant** *noun* someone who emigrates • **emigration** *noun*

Do not confuse with: **immigrate**

émigré /e-mi-greh/ *noun* someone who emigrates for political reasons

eminent *adj* famous and well-respected • **eminence** *noun* **1** distinction, fame **2** a title of honour **3** a hill • **eminently** *adv* very, obviously: *eminently suitable*

Do not confuse with: **imminent**

---

emissary *noun* (*plural* **emissaries**)

someone sent on private, often secret, business

emit *verb* (**emitting, emitted**) send or give out (light, sound, *etc*) • **emission** *noun*

Emmy *noun* an annual award given by the American Academy of Television Arts and Sciences

emollient *adj* softening and smoothing ◇ *noun* an emollient substance

emolument *noun, formal* wages, salary

emoticon *noun* a combination of characters used *esp* in emails to express an emotional reaction, *eg* :-) means happiness or laughter

emotion *noun* a feeling that disturbs or excites the mind, *eg* fear, love, hatred • **emotional** *adj* **1** moving the feelings **2** of a person: having feelings easily excited • **emotionally** *adv* • **emotive** *adj* causing emotion rather than thought

empathy *noun* the ability to share another person's feelings *etc* • **empathize** *verb* have empathy

emperor *noun* the ruler of an empire

emphasis *noun* **1** greater attention or importance: *the emphasis is on playing, not winning* **2** stress placed on a word or words in speaking • **emphasize** *verb* put emphasis on • **emphatic** *adj* spoken strongly: *an emphatic 'no'* • **emphatically** *adv*

emphysema /em-fis-ee-muh/ *noun* a lung disease causing breathing difficulties

empire *noun* **1** a group of nations *etc* under the same ruling power **2** a large business organization including several companies

empirical *adj* based on experiment and experience, not on theory alone • **empirically** *adv* • **empiricism** *noun* • **empiricist** *noun*

employ *verb* **1** give work to **2** use **3** occupy the time of ◇ *noun* employment • **employee** *noun* someone who works for an employer • **employer** *noun* someone who gives work to another • **employment** *noun* work or an occupation

emporium *noun* (*plural* **emporia** or **emporiums**) a large shop or market

empower *verb* **1** give authorization to **2** give self-confidence to

empress *noun* the female ruler of an empire

empty *adj* (**emptier, emptiest**) **1** containing nothing or no one **2** unlikely to result in anything: *empty threats* ◇ *verb* (**empties, emptying, emptied**) make or become empty ◇ *noun* (*plural* **empties**) an empty bottle *etc* • **emptiness** *noun* • **empty-handed** *adj* bringing or taking away nothing • **empty-headed** *adj* unable to think or act sensibly; foolish

EMU *abbrev* European Monetary Union

emu *noun* an Australian bird that cannot fly

emulate *verb* try to do as well as, or better than • **emulation** *noun*

emulsion *noun* **1** a milky liquid, *esp* that made by mixing oil and water **2** water-based paint for walls

enable *verb* make it possible for; allow: *the money enabled him to retire*

enact *verb* **1** act out or perform **2** make a law

enamel *noun* **1** a glassy coating fired onto metal **2** paint with a glossy finish **3** the smooth white coating of the teeth ◇ *verb* (**enamelling, enamelled**) coat or paint with enamel • **enamelling** *noun*

enamoured *adj*: **enamoured of** fond of

encampment *noun* a military camp

encapsulate verb capture the essence of, or describe briefly and accurately

encephalitis noun inflammation of the brain

enchant verb 1 be very pleasing or attractive to; delight 2 put a spell on • **enchanter, enchantress** noun • **enchantment** noun

enchilada /en-chi-lah-duh/ noun a Mexican tortilla stuffed and cooked in a chilli sauce

enclave noun an area enclosed within foreign territory

enclose verb 1 put inside an envelope with a letter etc 2 put a wall, fence, etc around • **enclosure** noun 1 an area enclosed by a wall, fence, etc 2 the act of enclosing

encode verb, comput convert data into a form a computer can accept

encomium noun a speech full of praise; a eulogy

encompass verb include

encore /ong-kaw/ noun 1 an extra performance of a song etc in reply to audience applause 2 a call for an encore

encounter verb 1 meet by chance 2 come up against (a difficulty, enemy, etc) ◇ noun a meeting, match, fight, etc

encourage verb 1 give hope or confidence to 2 urge (to do) • **encouragement** noun • **encouraging** adj

encroach verb go beyond your rights or land and interfere with someone else's • **encroachment** noun

encrypt verb put information into a coded form • **encryption** noun

encumber verb give (someone) an unwelcome responsibility to deal with, heavy load to carry, etc • **encumbrance** noun an unwelcome responsibility, heavy load, etc

encyclopedia or **encyclopaedia** noun a reference book containing information on many subjects, or on a particular subject • **encyclopedic** or **encyclopaedic** adj giving complete information

end noun 1 the last point or part 2 the farthest point of the length of something: at the end of the road 3 a result aimed at 4 a small piece left over 5 death ◇ verb bring or come to an end • **ending** noun the last part • **on end** 1 standing on one end 2 in a series, without a stop: he has been working for days on end

endanger verb put in danger or at risk

endear verb make well-liked or loved • **endearing** adj appealing • **endearment** noun

endeavour verb try hard (to) ◇ noun a determined attempt

endemic adj of a disease: found regularly in a certain area

endive /en-div/ noun a plant with curly leaves eaten as a salad

endocrine /en-duh-krin/ noun of a gland: secreting hormones etc into the blood

endorse verb 1 give your support to (something said or written) 2 sign the back of (a cheque) to confirm receiving money for it 3 indicate on (a driving licence) that the owner has committed a motoring offence • **endorsement** noun

endow verb 1 give a talent, quality, etc to: nature endowed her with a good brain 2 give money for the buying and upkeep of: he endowed a bed in the hospital • **endowment** noun

endure verb put up with patiently and with strength or determination; bear or tolerate • **endurable** adj bearable • **endurance** noun the power of enduring

enema noun the injection of fluid into the rectum to clean out the bowels

enemy noun (plural **enemies**) 1 someone hostile to another; a foe 2 someone armed to fight against another 3 someone who is against something: an enemy of socialism

energy noun (plural **energies**) 1 strength to act; vigour 2 a form of power, eg electricity, heat, etc • **energetic** adj active, lively • **energetically** adv

enervate verb deprive of energy or strength; weaken

enfant terrible /onh-fonh te-reebl/ noun someone who behaves outrageously or unconventionally

enfold verb enclose or embrace

enforce verb cause (a law etc) to be carried out • **enforcement** noun

enfranchise verb 1 give the right to vote to 2 set free

engage verb 1 begin to employ (workers etc) 2 book in advance 3 take or keep hold of (someone's attention etc) 4 be busy with, be occupied (in) 5 of machine parts: fit together 6 begin fighting • **engaged** adj 1 bound by a promise of marriage 2 busy with something 3 of a telephone: in use • **engagement** noun 1 a promise of marriage 2 an appointment to meet 3 a fight: naval engagement • **engaging** adj pleasant, charming

engine noun 1 a machine that converts heat or other energy into motion 2 the part of a train that pulls the coaches; a locomotive

engineer noun 1 someone who works with, or designs, engines or machines 2 someone who designs or makes bridges, roads, etc ◊ verb bring about by clever planning • **engineering** noun the science of designing machines, building roads, bridges, etc

engrave verb 1 draw on (glass, metal, etc) with a special tool 2 make a deep impression on: engraved on his memory • **engraving** noun a print made from a cut-out drawing in metal or wood

engross verb take up the whole interest or attention of

engulf verb swallow up wholly

enhance verb make better or more attractive; improve

enigma noun something or someone difficult to understand; a mystery • **enigmatic** adj

enjoy verb 1 take pleasure in: enjoyed the party 2 have or experience (something beneficial): enjoying good health • **enjoyable** adj • **enjoyment** noun • **enjoy yourself** have a pleasant time

enlarge verb 1 make larger 2 (with on) say much or more about something • **enlargement** noun 1 an increase in size 2 a larger photograph made from a smaller one

enlighten verb give more knowledge or information to • **enlightenment** noun

enlist verb 1 join an army etc 2 obtain the support and help of

enliven verb make more active or cheerful

en masse /onh mas/ adv all together, as a large group

enmesh verb cause to be involved in something awkward or complicated; entangle

enmity noun hostility

ennui /on-wee/ noun, formal boredom, esp an overpowering boredom with life

enormity noun 1 the fact of being enormous; hugeness 2 extreme badness; outrageousness

enormous adj very large • **enormously** adv

enough adj & pronoun (in) the number or amount wanted or needed:

I have enough coins/do you want more bread or do you have enough? ◇ *adv* as much as is wanted or necessary: *she's been there often enough to know the way*

enquire, **enquiry** *etc see* **inquire**

enrage *verb* make angry

enrol or **enroll** *verb* (**enrolling**, **enrolled**) officially enter your name on a register of members, students, *etc* ● **enrolment** *noun*

en route /onh *root*/ *adv* on the way

ensconce *verb*: **ensconce yourself** settle yourself comfortably

ensemble /onh-*som*-bul/ *noun* **1** the parts of a thing taken together **2** an outfit of clothes **3** a group of musicians

enshrine *verb* **1** officially record (a principle, right, *etc*) as existing and therefore protect from being disregarded **2** treat as sacred; cherish

ensign /*en*-sun/ *noun* **1** the flag of a nation, regiment, *etc* **2** *hist* a young officer who carried the flag

enslave *verb* make a slave of

ensue *verb* **1** happen as a result **2** come after in time; follow

en suite /on *sweet*/ *noun & adj* (a bedroom) with its own bathroom

ensure *verb* make sure

Do not confuse with: **insure**

---

entail *verb* **1** bring as a result; involve: *the job entailed extra work* **2** make legal arrangements with regard to (land) such that the heir to it cannot sell any part of it

entangle *verb* **1** make tangled or complicated **2** involve (in difficulties) ● **entanglement** *noun*

entente /onh-*tont*/ *noun* a treaty

enter *verb* **1** go or come in or into **2** put (a name *etc*) onto a list **3** take part in, or register to take part **4** key (information) into a computer or other system

enterprise *noun* **1** an undertaking, *esp* if risky or difficult **2** boldness in trying new things **3** a business concern ● **enterprising** *adj*

entertain *verb* **1** amuse **2** receive as a guest **3** give a party **4** consider (*eg* a suggestion) **5** hold in the mind: *entertain a belief* ● **entertainer** *noun* someone who entertains professionally ● **entertaining** *adj* amusing ● **entertainment** *noun* a theatrical show

enthral *verb* (**enthralling**, **enthralled**) give great delight to

enthuse *verb* be enthusiastic (about)

enthusiasm *noun* great interest and eagerness ● **enthusiast** *noun* ● **enthusiastic** *adj* greatly interested and eager ● **enthusiastically** *adv*

entice *verb* attract with promises, rewards, *etc* ● **enticement** *noun* a bribe or an attractive promise ● **enticing** *adj*

entire *adj* whole, complete ● **entirely** *adv* ● **entirety** *noun*

entitle *verb* **1** give a name to (a book *etc*) **2** give (someone) a right to

entity *noun* (*plural* **entities**) something that physically exists, as opposed to something abstract

entomology *noun* the study of insects ● **entomologist** *noun*

entourage /onh-too-*rahzh*/ *noun* people who travel with or follow someone

entrails *plural noun* internal organs

entrance¹ /*en*-truns/ *noun* **1** a place for entering, *eg* a door **2** the act of coming in **3** the right to enter ● **entrant** *noun* someone who goes in for a race, competition, *etc*

entrance² /in-*trans*/ *verb* **1** delight, charm **2** put into a trance ● **entrancing** *adj*

entreat verb ask earnestly • **entreaty** noun

entrecote /onh-truh-koht/ noun a steak cut from between two ribs

entrée /on-treh/ noun 1 Brit a dish served between the starter and the main course of a large formal meal 2 US a main course

entrenched adj of opinions etc: firmly established and unlikely to be changed or given up

entre nous /onh-truh noo/ adv, formal between ourselves

entrepreneur /onh-truh-pruh-nur/ noun someone who starts new business ventures • **entrepreneurial** adj

entropy noun lack of organization or order

entrust verb place in someone else's care

entry noun (plural **entries**) 1 a place for entering; a doorway 2 a name or item in a record book 3 the right to enter or the act of entering

E-number noun an identification code for food additives, eg E102 for tartrazine

enumerate verb 1 count 2 mention individually • **enumeration** noun

enunciate verb 1 pronounce distinctly 2 state formally • **enunciation** noun

envelop verb 1 cover by wrapping 2 surround entirely: enveloped in mist

envelope noun a wrapping or cover, esp for a letter

environment noun 1 the combination of physical conditions that affect an animal or plant; natural surroundings 2 the situation in which you find yourself • **environmental** adj • **environmentalist** noun someone concerned about the harmful effects of human activity on the natural environment

environs /in-vai-runz/ plural noun surrounding area; neighbourhood

envisage /in-viz-ij/ verb 1 picture in the mind; visualize 2 consider, contemplate

envoy noun a messenger, esp one sent to deal with a foreign government

envy noun greedy desire to have someone else's property, qualities, etc ◇ verb (**envies**, **envying**, **envied**) feel envy for • **enviable** adj highly desirable • **envious** adj feeling envy • **enviously** adv

enzyme noun a type of protein that speeds up chemical changes in a living thing

eon another spelling of **aeon**

epaulet or **epaulette** noun a decoration on the shoulder of a uniform

ephemeral adj very short-lived; fleeting • **ephemerality** noun

epic noun a long poem, story, film, etc about heroic deeds ◇ adj 1 of an epic; heroic 2 on an impressively large scale

epicene adj common to both sexes

epicentre or US **epicenter** noun the centre of an earthquake

epicure noun someone who likes fine foods; a gourmet • **epicurean** adj

epidemic noun a widespread outbreak of a disease etc

epidermis noun the top covering of the skin • **epidermal** or **epidermic** adj

epidural noun (short for **epidural anaesthetic**) the injection of anaesthetic into the spine to ease pain in the lower half of the body, esp during childbirth

epiglottis noun a piece of skin at the back of the tongue that closes the windpipe during swallowing

epigram noun a short, witty saying • **epigrammatic** adj

epilepsy noun an illness causing attacks of unconsciousness and convulsions • **epileptic** adj **1** suffering from epilepsy **2** of epilepsy: an epileptic fit ◇ noun someone suffering from epilepsy

epilogue or US **epilog** noun **1** the very end part of a book, programme, etc **2** a speech at the end of a play

epiphany noun **1** a Christian festival celebrated on 6 January **2** a sudden revelation or insight

episcopal adj of or ruled by bishops • **episcopalian** adj belonging to a church ruled by bishops • **episcopacy** noun

episode noun **1** one of several parts of a story etc **2** an interesting event • **episodic** adj happening at irregular intervals, or consisting of separate periods or events

epistle noun a formal letter, esp one from an apostle of Christ in the Bible • **epistolary** adj written in the form of letters

epitaph noun words on a gravestone about a dead person

epithet noun a word used to describe someone; an adjective

epitome /i-pit-uh-mi/ noun a perfect example or representative of something: the epitome of good taste • **epitomize** verb be the epitome of something

EPNS abbrev electroplated nickel silver

epoch noun an extended period of time, often marked by a series of important events • **epoch-making** adj marking an important point in history

eponymous adj having the name that is in the title: the novel's eponymous hero

epoxy resin noun a type of synthetic adhesive

EPROM /ee-prom/ abbrev, comput erasable programmable read-only memory, a type of memory in computers

Epsom salts plural noun a medicine that helps clear out the bowels

equable adj **1** of calm temper **2** of climate: neither very hot nor very cold • **equably** adv

equal adj **1** of the same size, value, quantity, etc **2** evenly balanced **3** (with **to**) capable enough to do; fit for: not equal to the job ◇ noun someone of the same rank, cleverness, etc as another ◇ verb (**equalling, equalled**) **1** be or make equal to **2** be the same as • **equality** noun • **equalize** verb make equal • **equalizer** noun a goal etc that levels the score in a game • **equally** adv

equanimity noun evenness of temper; calmness

equate verb **1** regard or treat as the same **2** describe as being equal • **equation** noun a statement, esp in mathematics, that two things are equal

equator noun an imaginary line around the earth, halfway between the North and South Poles • **equatorial** adj on or near the equator

equerry /ek-wuh-ri/ noun (plural **equerries**) a royal attendant

equestrian adj **1** of horse-riding **2** on horseback ◇ noun a horse-rider

equi- prefix equal • **equidistant** adj equally distant • **equilateral** adj of a triangle: with all sides equal (compare with: **isosceles**)

equilibrium noun **1** equal balance between weights, forces, etc **2** a balanced state of mind or feelings

equine adj of or like a horse

equinox noun either of the times (about 21 March and 23 September) when the sun crosses the equator, making night and day equal in length • **equinoctial** adj

equip verb (**equipping, equipped**) supply with everything needed for a task • **equipment** noun a set of tools etc needed for a task; an outfit

equipoise noun, formal balance

equitable adj fair, just • **equitably** adv

equity noun 1 the amount by which the value of a property is greater than the mortgage on it 2 an ordinary share in a company 3 fairness in dealing with people 4 (**Equity**) the trade union for the British acting profession • **negative equity** see **negative**

equivalent adj equal in value, power, meaning, etc ◇ noun something that is the equal of another

equivocal adj 1 not giving a clear opinion or statement; cagey 2 having more than one meaning; ambiguous • **equivocally** adv

equivocate verb use ambiguous words in order to avoid giving a clear opinion or statement • **equivocation** noun

era noun a period in history: the Jacobean era/the era of steam

eradicate verb get rid of completely • **eradication** noun

erase verb 1 rub out 2 remove • **eraser** noun an object that erases writing; a rubber • **erasure** noun

ere prep & conj, old before: ere long

erect verb 1 build 2 set upright ◇ adj standing straight up • **erection** noun 1 an erect penis 2 something built or put up 3 the act of erecting

erg noun a unit of energy

ergo /ur-goh/ adv, formal therefore

ergonomic /ur-guh-nom-ik/ adj of a workplace, machine, etc: adapted or designed to suit human needs and comfort, esp so as to minimize physical discomfort • **ergonomically** adv • **ergonomics** sing noun

ermine noun 1 a stoat 2 its white fur

erode verb 1 destroy or be destroyed gradually 2 take away (rights etc), or be taken away, gradually • **erosion** noun

erogenous adj sensitive to sexual stimulation

erotic adj of or arousing sexual desire • **erotica** plural noun erotic art or literature • **eroticism** noun • **eroticize** verb make erotic

err verb 1 make a mistake 2 commit a sin

errand noun a short journey to carry a message, buy something, etc

errant adj 1 doing wrong 2 wandering in search of adventure: knight errant

erratic adj 1 not following a fixed course; irregular 2 not steady or reliable in behaviour • **erratically** adv

erratum /e-rah-tum/ noun (plural **errata**) an error in a book

erroneous adj wrong • **erroneously** adv

error noun 1 a mistake 2 wrongdoing

ersatz adj 1 not genuine or authentic; fake 2 badly made; shoddy

erstwhile adj former

erudite adj well-educated or well-read; learned • **erudition** noun

erupt verb break out or through • **eruption** noun 1 an outburst from a volcano 2 a rash or spot on the skin

escalate verb increase dramatically in amount, intensity, etc • **escalation** noun • **escalator** noun a moving staircase

escalope noun a slice of meat beaten to make it thinner before cooking

escape verb 1 get away safe or free 2 of gas etc: leak 3 slip from memory: his name escapes me ◇ noun the act of escaping • **escapade** noun an adventure • **escapement** noun a device that controls the movement of a watch or clock • **escapism** noun **1** books, films, etc that serve as an enjoyable escape from the harsh realities of life, rather than deal with intellectually or emotionally challenging themes **2** the tendency to escape from reality by daydreaming etc • **escapist** noun & adj

escarpment noun a steep side of a hill or rock

eschew verb, formal avoid

escort noun someone who accompanies others for protection, courtesy, etc ◇ verb act as escort to

escritoire noun a writing desk

escutcheon noun a shield with a coat of arms

Eskimo noun (plural **Eskimos**) dated offensive a member of the Inuit people

esoteric adj understood by a small number of people

ESP abbrev extrasensory perception

esparto noun a strong grass grown in Spain and N Africa, used for making paper and ropes

especially adv **1** more than others or more than in other cases; particularly: she likes meat, especially pork **2** to a great degree: be especially careful

---

Do not confuse: **especially** and **specially**

Esperanto noun an international language created in the 19th century

espionage noun spying, esp by one country to find out the secrets of another

esplanade noun a wide walkway along a seafront

espouse verb give a lot of support to (a cause)

espresso noun strong coffee made by forcing steam through ground coffee

esprit de corps /es-pree duh kaw/ noun loyalty to, or among, a group

espy /es-pai/ verb, old see or notice

Esq abbrev or **Esquire** noun a courtesy title equivalent to Mr, written after a man's name: Robert Brown, Esq

essay noun **1** a piece of writing on a particular subject **2** formal an attempt ◇ verb, formal try • **essayist** noun a writer of essays

essence noun **1** the most important part or quality of something **2** a concentrated extract from a plant etc: vanilla essence

essential adj absolutely necessary ◇ noun an absolute requirement • **essentially** adv **1** basically **2** necessarily

establish verb **1** set up (a business etc); found **2** show to be true; prove (that) **3** settle in position • **established** adj **1** firmly set up **2** accepted, recognized **3** of a church: officially recognized as national • **establishment** noun the premises of a business • **the Establishment** the people holding influential positions in a community

estate noun **1** a large piece of private land **2** land built on with houses, factories, etc: housing estate/industrial estate **3** someone's total possessions, esp as transferred or divided up in a will **4** an estate car • **estate agent** noun someone who sells and leases property for clients • **estate car** noun a car with a relatively large inside luggage compartment and a rear door • **the fourth estate** the press or the media

esteem verb think highly of; value ◇ noun high value or opinion • **esteemed** adj

estimate verb judge roughly the size, amount or value of something ◇ noun a rough judgement of size *etc* • **estimation** *noun* opinion, judgement

estranged *adj* no longer in a friendly relationship or no longer living together; separated • **estrangement** *noun*

estuary *noun* (*plural* **estuaries**) the wide lower part of a river where it meets the sea and where it is influenced by tides

et al *abbrev* and others (from Latin *et alii, aliae* or *alia*)

etc *or* **&c** *abbrev* and other things of the same sort (from Latin *et cetera*)

etch *verb* draw on metal or glass by eating out the lines with acid • **etching** *noun* a picture printed from an etched metal plate

eternal *adj* 1 lasting for ever 2 seemingly endless • **eternally** *adv* • **eternity** *noun* 1 time without end 2 the time or state after death

ether *noun* a colourless liquid used as an anaesthetic or solvent

ethereal *adj* having a delicate quality that seems to belong to the world of spirits or fairies • **ethereally** *adv* • **ethereality** *noun*

ethical *adj* involving or conforming to standards of morally good behaviour • **ethically** *adv* • **ethics** *sing noun* the branch of philosophy that deals with moral issues and notions of right and wrong

ethnic *adj* 1 of race or culture: *ethnic differences* 2 of non-Western or non-White culture: *ethnic jewellery* • **ethnically** *adv* • **ethnicity** *noun*

ethnocentric *adj* believing in the superiority of your own culture or racial group • **ethnocentrism** *noun*

ethnology *noun* the study of human cultures and civilizations • **ethnological** *adj* • **ethnologist** *noun*

ethos *noun* the character or attitudes of a group, community, *etc*

etiolate *verb* 1 of a plant: grow pale through lack of light 2 make feeble • **etiolated** *adj*

etiquette *noun* rules about correct social behaviour

etymology *noun* (*plural* **etymologies**) 1 the history of a particular word 2 the study of the history of words • **etymological** *adj* • **etymologist** *noun*

EU *abbrev* European Union

eucalyptus *noun* (*plural* **eucalyptuses** *or* **eucalypti**) a large Australian evergreen tree whose leaves produce a pungent oil

eucharist *noun* 1 the Christian sacrament that commemorates Christ's Last Supper and the promises made during it 2 bread and wine taken during this sacrament

eugenics *sing noun* the science of trying to improve a race or stock by selective breeding *etc* • **eugenicist** *noun & adj*

eulogy *noun* (*plural* **eulogies**) a speech, poem, *etc* written in praise of someone • **eulogize** *verb* praise greatly

eunuch /yoo-nuk/ *noun* a castrated man

euphemism *noun* a word or phrase used to refer to an unpleasant subject in a way that avoids upsetting or offending people, *eg* 'passed on' for 'died' • **euphemistic** *adj*

euphonious *adj, formal* having a pleasant sound; harmonious • **euphonium** *noun* a brass musical instrument with a low tone • **euphony** *noun*

euphoria *noun* a feeling of great happiness; joy • **euphoric** *adj*

eurhythmics *sing noun* the art of graceful movement of the body, *esp* to music

euro *noun* (**euros** *or* **euro**) the basic monetary unit for most countries in the European Union, equal to 100 cents

Euro- prefix of Europe or the European Union: Euro-budget/Eurocrat • **Eurosceptic** noun & adj, Brit (someone) opposed to strengthening the powers of the European Union

euthanasia noun the killing of someone painlessly, esp to end suffering

evacuate verb (cause to) leave a place because of danger • **evacuation** noun • **evacuee** noun someone who has been evacuated from danger

evade verb avoid or escape esp by cleverness or trickery • **evasion** noun • **evasive** adj with the purpose of evading something, eg a question or a blow: an evasive answer/move

evaluate verb find or state the value of

evanescent adj passing away quickly

evangelical adj 1 spreading Christian teaching 2 strongly advocating some cause • **evangelist** noun • **evangelistic** adj

evaporate verb 1 change into vapour 2 vanish • **evaporation** noun

evasion see evade

eve noun 1 the evening or day before a festival: New Year's Eve 2 the time just before an event: the eve of the revolution

even adj 1 level, smooth 2 of a number: able to be divided by 2 without a remainder (contrasted with: odd) ◇ adv 1 used to emphasize another word: even harder than before/even a child would understand 2 perhaps and which is stronger: he looked sad, depressed even ◇ verb make even or smooth • **even-handed** adv without bias or favouritism; fair • **evenly** adv • **evenness** noun • **even out** become equal • **get even** with get revenge on

evening noun the last part of the day and early part of the night

evensong noun an evening service in the Anglican church

event noun 1 an important happening 2 an item in a programme of performances, sports contests, etc • **eventful** adj exciting

eventual adj 1 final 2 happening as a result • **eventuality** noun a possible happening • **eventually** adv at last; finally

ever adv 1 at any time; at all: I won't ever see her again 2 that has existed or been done: the best ever • **evergreen** noun a tree or shrub with green leaves all the year round • **everlasting** adj lasting for ever; eternal • **evermore** adv, old forever

every adj each of several things without exception ◇ adv at stated intervals: trees planted every six feet • **everybody** or **everyone** pronoun each person without exception • **everyday** adj 1 daily 2 of the commonly seen or experienced type; usual • **everything** pronoun all things • **everywhere** adv in every place • **every other** one out of every two; alternate

evict verb force (someone) out of their house, esp by law • **eviction** noun

evidence noun 1 information given in a law case 2 a clear sign; proof

evident adj easily seen or understood • **evidently** adv

evil adj showing a clear desire to do harm; morally bad ◇ noun wickedness • **evilly** adv

evince verb, formal show, display: they evinced no surprise

eviscerate verb tear out the bowels of; gut

evoke verb cause to be felt or remembered: evoking memories of their childhood • **evocative** adj evoking vivid memories or creating a strong atmosphere

evolution noun 1 gradual development 2 the belief that the higher forms of life have gradually developed out of the lower forms • **evolutionary** adj

evolve verb 1 develop gradually 2 work out (a plan etc)

ewe noun a female sheep

ewer noun a large jug with a wide spout

ex noun, informal a former husband, wife or lover

ex- prefix 1 no longer; former: ex-husband/ex-president 2 outside, not in: ex-directory number

exacerbate verb make worse or more severe

Do not confuse with: **exasperate**

exact adj 1 accurate, precise 2 punctual ◇ verb force someone to pay, give, etc: exacting revenge • **exactly** adv • **exactness** noun accuracy, correctness

exacting adj 1 asking too much 2 demanding a lot of effort or strength; tiring

exaggerate verb cause to seem larger, more impressive, more severe, etc than is really the case • **exaggeration** noun

exalted adj high in rank or position • **exaltation** noun praise, esp of a religious nature

exam noun an examination

examination noun 1 a formal test of knowledge or skill: driving examination 2 a close inspection or inquiry 3 formal questioning

examine verb 1 look at or look into closely in order to find information 2 look over (someone's body) for signs of illness 3 put questions to (pupils etc) to test knowledge 4 question (a witness) in court • **examiner** noun

example noun something taken as a representative of its kind: an example of early French glass • **make an example of** punish in order to deter others from breaking rules

exasperate verb make very angry • **exasperation** noun

Do not confuse with: **exacerbate**

excavate verb 1 dig, dig up or dig out 2 uncover by digging • **excavation** noun 1 an area where digging is being done 2 a hollow made by digging • **excavator** noun a machine used for excavating

exceed verb be greater than or do more than

exceedingly adv very

excel verb (**excelling, excelled**) 1 do very well 2 be better than others

excellence noun the fact of being excellent; very high quality

Excellency noun (plural **Excellencies**) a title of ambassadors

excellent adj unusually or extremely good

except prep not including; apart from ◇ conj with the exception (that) ◇ verb not include or take into account; leave out • **excepting** prep not including • **except for** not including

exception noun 1 something left out 2 something unlike the rest: an exception to the rule • **take exception to** be offended by

exceptional adj much better than the rest; outstanding • **exceptionally** adv very, extremely

excerpt /ek-surpt/ noun a part chosen from a whole work: excerpt from a play

Do not confuse with: **exert**

excess noun 1 a going beyond what is usual or proper 2 the amount by which one thing is greater than another or greater than is needed 3 (**excesses**) very bad behaviour ◇ adj beyond the amount allowed or needed

Do not confuse with: **access**

excessive *adj* too much, too great, *etc* • **excessively** *adv*

exchange *verb* give (one thing) and get another in return ◇ *noun* **1** the act of exchanging **2** exchanging money of one country for that of another **3** the difference between the value of money in different places: *rate of exchange* **4** a central office or building: *telephone exchange* **5** a place where business shares are bought and sold

exchequer *noun* a government office concerned with a country's finances • **Chancellor of the Exchequer** *see* **chancellor**

excise[1] *verb* cut off or out • **excision** *noun*

excise[2] *noun* tax on goods *etc* made and sold within a country and on certain licences *etc*

excite *verb* **1** cause to feel a pleasant anticipation or tension **2** cause to want to take action • **excitable** *adj* easily excited • **excitement** *noun* • **exciting** *adj*

exclaim *verb* cry or shout out

exclamation *noun* a sudden shout • **exclamation mark** *noun* a punctuation mark (!) used for emphasis, to indicate surprise, *etc*

exclamatory *adj* shouting out

exclude *verb* **1** prevent from taking part or sharing **2** not include or consider **3** shut out • **exclusion** *noun*

exclusive *adj* **1** only open to certain people, *usu* rich or influential people; select: *an exclusive club* **2** not obtainable elsewhere: *exclusive offer* • **exclusive of** not including

excommunicate *verb* expel from membership of a church • **excommunication** *noun*

excoriate *verb* **1** criticize strongly **2** strip the skin from

excrement *noun* the solid waste released from the bowel through the anus

excrescence *noun* an unwelcome growth, *eg* a wart

excrete *verb* release (waste matter) from the body • **excreta** *plural noun* discharged bodily waste

excruciating *adj* **1** of pain *etc*: very severe **2** painfully bad: *an excruciating performance*

exculpate *verb* declare to be not guilty or not to blame; vindicate • **exculpation** *noun* • **exculpatory** *adj*

excursion *noun* an outing for pleasure, *eg* a day trip

excuse *verb* **1** forgive, pardon **2** set free from a duty or task; let off ◇ *noun* an explanation for having done something wrong • **excusable** *adj* pardonable

ex-directory *adj* not in the telephone directory

execrable *adj, formal* very bad

execrate *verb, formal* express hatred or very strong disapproval of

execute *verb* **1** put to death legally **2** perform: *execute a dance step* **3** carry out: *execute commands*

execution *noun* **1** killing by order of the law **2** a doing or performing • **executioner** *noun* someone with the job of putting condemned prisoners to death

executive *adj* **1** having power to act or carry out laws **2** for the use of managers or senior staff: *the executive dining room* ◇ *noun* **1** the part of a government with such power **2** a business manager

executor *noun* someone who sees that the requests stated in a will are carried out

exegesis /eks-uh-jee-sis/ *noun* a

critical discussion of a literary text

exemplary adj **1** good and worth following as an example: exemplary conduct **2** acting as a warning: exemplary punishment

exemplify verb (**exemplifies, exemplifying, exemplified**) **1** be an example of **2** demonstrate by example

exempt adj officially allowed to ignore something unwelcome that others are obliged to do, give, etc ◇ verb allow (someone) to ignore something unwelcome that others are obliged to do, give, etc • **exemption** noun

exercise noun **1** a task for practice **2** a physical routine for training muscles etc ◇ verb **1** give exercise to **2** use: exercise great care

---

Do not confuse with: **exorcize**

---

exert verb bring into action; use: exerting great influence • **exert yourself** make a great esp physical effort

---

Do not confuse with: **excerpt**

---

exertion noun or **exertions** plural noun effort or hard work, esp physical

exeunt /eks-i-unt/ verb leave the stage (a direction printed in a script)

exhale verb breathe out • **exhalation** noun

exhaust verb **1** tire out **2** use up completely: we've exhausted our supplies **3** say all that can be said about (a subject etc) ◇ noun a device for expelling waste fumes from fuel engines • **exhausted** adj **1** tired out **2** emptied; used up • **exhaustion** noun • **exhaustive** adj extremely thorough: exhaustive research • **exhaustively** adv

exhibit verb **1** put on public display; show **2** formal show (a quality) in behaviour ◇ noun something on dis-

play in a gallery etc • **exhibitor** noun

exhibition noun a public show in a gallery etc

exhibitionism noun a tendency to try to attract people's attention • **exhibitionist** noun

exhilarate verb make excitedly happy or lively • **exhilarating** adj • **exhilaration** noun

exhort verb, formal urge (to do) • **exhortation** noun

exhume verb dig up (a buried body) • **exhumation** noun

exigency noun (plural **exigencies**) formal an urgent need or demand

exigent adj, formal demanding immediate attention; urgent

exiguous adj, formal existing only in very small amounts; meagre

exile noun **1** someone who lives outside their own country, by choice or unwillingly **2** a period of living in a foreign country ◇ verb drive (someone) away from their own country; banish

exist verb **1** have life or appear in the world; be **2** live in poor circumstances • **existence** noun • **existent** adj

exit noun **1** a way out **2** the act of going out: a hasty exit

exodus noun a going away of many people (esp those leaving a country for ever)

exonerate verb declare not to be to blame; vindicate • **exoneration** noun

exorbitant adj going beyond what is usual or reasonable: exorbitant price • **exorbitance** noun

exorcize verb **1** drive out (an evil spirit) **2** free from possession by an evil spirit • **exorcism** noun the act of driving away evil spirits • **exorcist** noun

---

Do not confuse with: **exercise**

---

exotic adj 1 coming from a foreign country 2 interestingly colourful or strange

expand verb 1 grow wider or bigger 2 open out

expanse noun a wide stretch of land etc

expansion noun a growing, stretching or spreading

expansive adj 1 spreading out 2 saying a lot or giving a lot of information • **expansively** adv

expat noun, informal an expatriate

expatiate verb, formal talk a great deal (about something)

expatriate adj living outside your native country ◇ noun someone living abroad

expect verb 1 think of as likely to happen or arrive soon: what did you expect her to say? 2 think, assume: I expect he's too busy • **expectancy** noun • **expectant** adj 1 hopeful, expecting 2 waiting to become: an expectant mother • **expectation** noun • **expecting** adj, informal pregnant

expedient adj done for speed or convenience rather than fairness or truth ◇ noun something done to get round a difficulty • **expedience** or **expediency** noun

expedite verb cause to happen quickly or more quickly; hasten

expedition noun 1 a journey with a purpose, often for exploration 2 a group of people making such a journey • **expeditionary** adj of or forming an expedition

expeditious adj, formal fast • **expeditiously** adv

expel verb (**expelling**, **expelled**) 1 send away in disgrace, eg from a school 2 drive or force out • **expulsion** noun

expend verb use or spend (money, energy, resources, etc) • **expenditure** noun an amount spent or used up, esp money

expense noun 1 cost 2 a cause of spending: the house was a continual expense 3 (**expenses**) money spent in carrying out a job etc

expensive adj costing a lot of money • **expensively** adv

experience noun 1 an event in which you are involved: a horrific experience 2 knowledge gained from events, practice, etc ◇ verb go through; undergo • **experienced** adj skilled, knowledgeable

experiment noun a trial carried out to test (an idea, machine, chemical substance, etc) ◇ verb carry out experiments • **experimental** adj • **experimentally** adv

expert noun someone who is highly skilled or knowledgeable ◇ adj highly skilful or knowledgeable (in a particular subject) • **expertise** /ek-spuh-teez/ noun skill

expiate verb make up for (a crime etc) • **expiation** noun

expire verb 1 come to an end or become invalid: your visa has expired 2 die • **expiry** noun the end or finish

explain verb 1 make clear the meaning or significance of 2 give reasons for: please explain your behaviour

explanation noun 1 a statement which makes clear something difficult or puzzling 2 a reason given for something

explanatory adj intended to make something clear

expletive noun an exclamation, esp a swear word

explicable adj able to be explained • **explicably** adv

explicit adj plainly stated or shown; clear • **explicitly** adv • **explicitness** noun

explode verb 1 blow up like a bomb with loud noise 2 prove to be completely wrong or unfounded: *that explodes your theory*

exploit noun a daring deed; a feat ◇ verb 1 make use of selfishly 2 make good use of (resources *etc*) • **exploitation** noun

explore verb make a journey of discovery • **exploration** noun • **explorer** noun

explosion noun a sudden violent burst or blow-up

explosive adj 1 liable to explode 2 hot-tempered ◇ noun a substance or device that will explode • **explosively** adv

exponent noun someone who shows skill in a particular art or craft: *an exponent of karate* • **exponential** adj

export verb 1 sell goods *etc* in a foreign country 2 *comput* send data from one computer, system, program, *etc* to another ◇ noun 1 an act of exporting 2 something exported • **exportation** noun

expose verb 1 make (a hidden crime *etc*) widely known; uncover 2 lay open to the sun or wind 3 allow light to reach and act on (a film) • **exposition** noun 1 a public display 2 a statement explaining a writer's meaning • **exposure** noun

exposé /eks-poh-zeh/ noun a report *etc* exposing a scandal or crime

expostulate verb, formal protest • **expostulation** noun

exposure see expose

expound verb explain fully

express verb 1 put into words 2 show by action 3 press or squeeze out ◇ adj 1 clearly stated: *express instructions* 2 sent in haste: *express messenger* ◇ noun a fast train, bus, *etc*

expression noun 1 the look on someone's face: *expression of horror* 2 a word or phrase: *idiomatic expression* 3 the act of showing meaning or emotion through language, art, *etc* 4 a show of emotion in an artistic performance *etc* 5 pressing or squeezing out

expressive adj expressing meaning or feeling clearly • **expressively** adv

expropriate verb take (property *etc*) away from its owner

expulsion see expel

expunge verb cross out or cancel out

expurgate verb remove offensive material from (a book *etc*), censor

exquisite adj 1 extremely beautiful 2 excellent 3 very great, utter: *exquisite pleasure*

extempore /iks-*tem*-puh-reh/ & adj without being planned or prepared in advance; impromptu • **extemporize** verb make up on the spot; improvise

extend verb 1 make longer; stretch 2 hold out: *extended a hand* 3 last as long as: *my holiday extends into next week*

extension noun 1 a part added to a building 2 an additional amount of time on a schedule *etc* 3 a telephone connected with a main one

extensive adj 1 covering a large space 2 happening in many places 3 covering many subjects, areas, *etc*: *extensive changes* • **extensively** adv

extent noun 1 degree: *to a great extent* 2 the space something covers

extenuate verb 1 lessen 2 make to seem less bad: *extenuating circumstances* • **extenuation** noun

exterior adj on the outside; outer: *exterior wall* ◇ noun the outside of a building *etc*

exterminate verb kill off completely (a race, a type of animal, *etc*); wipe out • **extermination** noun

external adj 1 on the outside; outer 2 not central: external considerations

extinct adj 1 no longer active: extinct volcano 2 no longer found alive: the dodo is now extinct • **extinction** noun making or becoming extinct

extinguish verb 1 put out (a fire etc) 2 put an end to • **extinguisher** noun a spray containing chemicals for putting out fires

extirpate verb destroy completely; exterminate

Do not confuse with: **extricate** and **extrapolate**

---

extol verb (**extolling, extolled**) praise greatly

extort verb take by force or threats • **extortion** noun • **extortionate** adj of a price: unreasonably high

extra adj more than is usual or necessary; additional ◇ adv more than is average; unusually: extra large ◇ noun 1 something extra 2 someone employed to be one of a crowd in a film

extra- prefix outside or beyond: extramarital/extraordinary

extract verb 1 draw or pull out, esp by force: extract a tooth 2 remove selected parts of a book etc 3 draw out by pressure or chemical action ◇ noun 1 an excerpt from a book etc 2 a substance obtained by extraction: vanilla extract • **extraction** noun 1 the act of extracting 2 someone's descent or lineage: of Irish extraction

extracurricular adj done outside school or college hours

extradite verb hand over (someone wanted for trial) to the police of another country • **extradition** noun

extramarital adj happening outside a marriage: extramarital affair

extramural adj 1 of a university department: teaching courses other than the regular degree courses 2 taking place outside a university, or involving activities that are not part of a university course

extraneous adj having nothing to do with the subject: extraneous information • **extraneously** adv

extraordinary adj 1 unusual or surprising 2 not part of the regular routine: an extraordinary meeting 3 specially employed: ambassador extraordinary • **extraordinarily** adv

extrapolate verb draw conclusions based on known facts; infer

---

Do not confuse with: **extirpate** and **extricate**

---

extrasensory perception noun the ability to know things, esp what will happen in the future or what someone is thinking, without using any of the five senses

extraterrestrial adj from outside the earth ◇ noun a being from another planet

extravagant adj 1 spending money too freely; wasteful 2 too great; overblown: extravagant praise • **extravagance** noun • **extravagantly** adv

extravaganza noun an extravagant creation or production

extravert another spelling of **extrovert**

extreme adj 1 very great: extreme sadness 2 far from the ordinary or usual 3 far from the centre ◇ noun an extreme point or degree • **extremely** adv

extremist noun someone whose political ideas or actions are considered to be unreasonably extreme • **extremism** noun

extremity noun (plural **extremities**) 1 a part or place furthest from the centre **2** great distress or pain **3** (**extremities**) the hands and feet

extricate *verb* free from (difficulties *etc*)

Do not confuse with: **extirpate** and **extrapolate**

---

extrovert *noun* an outgoing, sociable person

extrude *verb* force (a substance) out, *esp* through a mould in order to shape it

exuberant *adj* in very high spirits • **exuberance** *noun* • **exuberantly** *adv*

exude *verb* give off in large amounts: *exuding sweat/exuded happiness*

exult *verb* be very glad; rejoice: *exulting in their victory* • **exultant** *adj* • **exultation** *noun*

eye *noun* **1** the part of the body with which you see **2** the ability to notice: *an eye for detail* **3** sight **4** something the shape of an eye, *eg* the hole in a needle ◇ *verb* (**eyeing, eyed**) look at with interest: *eyeing the last slice of cake* • **eyeball** *noun* the round part of the eye; the eye itself (the part between the eyelids) • **eyebrow** *noun* the hairy ridge above the eye • **eyelash** *noun* one of the hairs on the edge of the eyelid • **eyelet** *noun* a small hole for a lace *etc* • **eyelid** *noun* the skin covering of the eye • **eye-opener** *noun* something that makes you realize something shocking or unexpected • **eyesight** *noun* the ability to see • **eyesore** *noun* anything that is ugly, *esp* a building • **eyewitness** *noun* someone who sees a thing done (*eg* a crime committed)

eyrie *or* **eyry** /ee-ri/ *or* /ai-ri/ *noun* the nest of an eagle or other bird of prey

Ff

F *abbrev* degree(s) Fahrenheit

FA *abbrev, Brit* Football Association

fable *noun* a story about animals *etc*, including a lesson or moral

fabric *noun* **1** cloth **2** the walls, floor and roof of a building

fabricate *verb* make up (lies) • **fabrication** *noun*

fabulous *adj* **1** *informal* very good; excellent **2** existing only in stories; mythological • **fabulously** *adv* • **fabulousness** *noun*

façade /fuh-*sahd*/ *noun* **1** the front of a building **2** a deceptive appearance or way of behaving; a mask

face *noun* **1** the front part of the head **2** the front of anything **3** appearance ◇ *verb* **1** turn or stand in the direction of **2** stand opposite to **3** put an additional surface on • **face pack** *noun* a cosmetic paste applied to the face and left to dry • **face powder** *noun* cosmetic powder for the face • **face up to** deal with or accept boldly: *facing up to responsibilities*

facet *noun* **1** an aspect or characteristic **2** one side of a many-sided object, *eg* a cut gem

facetious *adj* not meant seriously; joking • **facetiously** *adv* • **facetiousness** *noun*

facial *adj* of the face • **facially** *adv*

facile /*fas*-ail/ *adj* showing a lack of serious thought; superficial, glib • **facilely** *adv*

facilitate *verb* **1** make easy **2** help to make possible • **facilitator** *noun*

facility *noun* **1** (**facilities**) buildings, equipment, *etc* provided for a purpose: *sports facilities* **2** *formal* ease **3** *formal* skill, ability

facsimile *noun* an exact copy

fact *noun* **1** something known or believed to be true **2** reality **3** *law* a deed • **in fact** actually, really

faction *noun* a separate group within a larger group: *rival factions*

factious *adj, formal* causing trouble • **factiously** *adv* • **factiousness** *noun*

factitious *adj* produced artificially • **factitiously** *adv* • **factitiousness** *noun*

factoid *noun* an unproved statement accepted as a fact

factor *noun* **1** something affecting a situation or course of events **2** a number that exactly divides into another (*eg* 3 is a factor of 6) **3** someone who works for another person, *esp* the manager of a country estate in Scotland • **factorize** *verb* find factors of

factory *noun* (*plural* **factories**) a workshop producing goods in large quantities

factotum *noun* someone employed to do all kinds of work

factual *adj* consisting of facts; real, not fictional: *factual account*

faculty *noun* (*plural* **faculties**) **1** power of the mind, *eg* reason **2** a natural power of the body, *eg* hearing **3** ability, aptitude **4** a department of study in a university: *Faculty of Arts*

fad *noun* **1** a temporary liking or fashion **2** an odd like or dislike • **faddy** *adj* having odd likes or dislikes

fade verb 1 (cause to) lose colour or strength 2 disappear gradually, eg from sight or hearing

faeces /fee-seez/ plural noun solid waste from the body; excrement

faff verb, informal behave in an annoyingly hesitant or unconfident way; dither: don't faff about

fag noun 1 informal a cigarette 2 informal a young schoolboy forced to do jobs for an older one in a public school 3 US slang, derog a male homosexual 4 dated tiring work • **fag end** noun, informal 1 a cigarette butt 2 the very end; tail end • **fagged out** dated informal tired out; exhausted

faggot or US **fagot** noun 1 a bundle of sticks 2 a ball of chopped meat 3 US slang, derog a male homosexual

Fahrenheit noun a temperature scale on which water freezes at 32° and boils at 212° ◇ adj measured on this scale: 70° Fahrenheit

fail verb 1 be unsuccessful, or declare (a student's work etc) to be unsuccessful 2 stop working normally; break down 3 lose strength 4 be lacking or insufficient 5 be disappointing to • **fail-safe** adj made to correct automatically, or be safe, if a fault occurs • **without fail** with complete regularity and certainty

failing noun a fault or weakness

failure noun 1 the act of failing 2 someone or something that fails

fain adv, old willingly: I would fain go with you

faint adj 1 lacking in strength, brightness, etc 2 about to lose consciousness: feel faint ◇ verb 1 become faint 2 fall down unconscious ◇ noun a loss of consciousness • **faintly** adv dimly, not clearly • **faintness** noun

Do not confuse with: **feint**

fair¹ adj 1 showing reasonable judgement or expectations and not biased; just: fair assessment 2 of a light colour: fair hair 3 of weather: clear and dry 4 good enough but not excellent; average 5 old beautiful • **fair-haired** adj having light-coloured hair; blond • **fairly** adv • **fairness** noun • **fair-weather friend** noun someone who is a friend only when things are going well

fair² noun 1 a travelling collection of merry-go-rounds, stalls, etc 2 an exhibition of goods from different producers etc: craft fair 3 a large market held at fixed times

fairground noun the location of the amusements and attractions of a fair

fairway noun 1 the mown part on a golf course, between the tee and the green 2 the deep-water part of a river

fairy noun (plural **fairies**) a small imaginary creature, human in shape, with magical powers • **fairy light** noun a small coloured light for decorating Christmas trees etc • **fairy story** or **fairy tale** noun 1 a traditional story of fairies, giants, etc 2 informal a lie

fait accompli /fet uh-kom-plee/ noun (plural **faits accomplis**) something already done and therefore impossible to prevent or challenge

faith noun 1 trust 2 belief in a religion or creed 3 loyalty to a promise: kept faith with them • **faithless** adj

faithful adj 1 keeping your promises; trustworthy 2 never having sex with someone who is not your husband, wife or regular partner during your relationship: always faithful to my wife 3 true, accurate: faithful account of events 4 believing in a particular religion or creed • **faithfully** adv • **faithfulness** noun

fake adj not genuine; forged or imitation ◇ noun 1 someone who is not what they pretend to be 2 a forgery ◇ verb make an imitation or forgery of

fakir /feh-ki-uh/ noun an Islamic or Hindu holy man

falcon noun a smallish, long-winged bird of prey

falconry noun the training of falcons for hunting • **falconer** noun

fall verb (**falling, fell, fallen**) 1 drop down to or towards the ground 2 become less 3 happen, occur: *Christmas falls on a Monday this year* 4 of a fortress *etc*: be captured 5 die in battle ◇ noun 1 a dropping down to or towards the ground 2 something that falls: *a fall of snow* 3 a lowering in value *etc* 4 an accident involving falling 5 ruin, downfall, surrender: *the fall of Rome* 6 (**falls**) a waterfall 7 *US* autumn • **fall guy** noun a scapegoat • **fallout** noun 1 radioactive dust resulting from the explosion of an atomic bomb *etc* 2 trouble or controversy that results from something: *the political fallout from this decision* • **fall flat** fail to have the intended effect • **fall for** 1 begin to be in love with 2 naively believe (something obviously untrue) • **fall in love** begin to be in love • **fall out with** quarrel with • **fall through** of a plan: fail, come to nothing

fallacy noun (*plural* **fallacies**) something believed to be true but really false • **fallacious** adj

fallible adj liable to make a mistake or to be wrong • **fallibility** noun

fallopian tubes plural noun two tubes along which egg cells pass from a woman's ovaries to her uterus

fallow¹ adj of land: left unsown for a time after being ploughed

fallow² adj of a yellowish-brown colour • **fallow deer** noun a type of yellowish-brown deer

false adj 1 untrue 2 not real, fake 3 not natural: *false teeth* • **falsehood** noun a lie • **falseness** or **falsity** noun the quality of being false • **falsies** plural noun, slang artificial breasts made of padding

falsetto noun a singing voice forced higher than its natural range

falsify verb (**falsifies, falsifying, falsified**) make false, *esp* alter for a dishonest purpose: *falsified his tax forms*

falter verb stumble or hesitate

fame noun the quality of being well-known; renown • **famed** adj famous

familiar adj 1 well-known 2 seen, known, *etc* before 3 well-acquainted (with) 4 friendly in a way that shows a lack of respect; cheeky • **familiarity** noun • **familiarize** verb make quite accustomed or acquainted (with)

family noun (*plural* **families**) 1 a couple and their children 2 the children alone 3 a group of people related to one another 4 a group of animals, languages, *etc* with common characteristics

famine noun a great shortage of food or water

famished adj very hungry

famous adj extremely well-known • **famously** adv, informal very well: *get along famously*

fan¹ noun 1 a device or appliance for making a rush of air 2 a small hand-held device for cooling the face ◇ verb (**fanning, fanned**) 1 cause a rush of air with a fan 2 increase the strength of: *fanning her anger* • **fanlight** noun a window above a door, usually semi-circular • **fan out** spread out in the shape of a fan

fan² noun an admirer or devoted follower: *a fan of traditional music*

fanatic noun someone who is wildly or excessively enthusiastic about something • **fanatic** or **fanatical** adj wildly or excessively enthusiastic • **fanatically** adv

fancy adj not plain; elaborate ◇ verb (**fancies, fancying, fancied**) 1 have a sudden wish for 2 *informal* consider to be sexually attractive 3 *old* think without being sure ◇ noun (*plural*

fancies) 1 a sudden liking or desire: *he had a fancy for ice-cream* **2** imagination **3** something imagined • **fancier** *noun* someone whose hobby is to keep prize animals, birds, *etc* • **fanciful** *adj* **1** inclined to have fancies **2** not real; imaginary • **fancifully** *adv* • **fancy dress** *noun* an elaborate costume worn *eg* for a party, often representing a famous character

fandango *noun* (*plural* **fandangos**) a Spanish dance for two with castanets

fanfare *noun* a loud flourish from a trumpet or bugle

fang *noun* **1** a long tooth of a wild animal **2** the poison-tooth of a snake

fanny *noun* (**fannies**) *slang* **1** *Brit, taboo* the vagina **2** *US* the buttocks

fantasize *verb* daydream

fantastic *adj* **1** *informal* excellent: *a fantastic party* **2** *informal* very great: *a fantastic amount* **3** very unusual; weird: *fantastic creatures*

fantasy *noun* (*plural* **fantasies**) **1** an imaginary scene, story, *etc* **2** an idea not based on reality

fanzine *noun, informal* **1** a magazine for a particular group of fans **2** a small-circulation magazine

FAO *abbrev* for the attention of

FAQ *abbrev* frequently asked question

far *adv* **1** at or to a long way: *far off* **2** very much: *far better* ◇ *adj* (**farther, farthest**) **1** a long way off; distant: *a far country* **2** more distant: *the far side* • **far-fetched** *adj* very unlikely: *a far-fetched story* • **far-flung** *adj* a great distance away; distant • **far-sighted** *adj* foreseeing what is likely to happen and preparing for it (*see also* **further**)

farce *noun* **1** a play full of comic misunderstandings or complexities **2** a ridiculous situation • **farcical** *adj* absurd, ridiculous

fare *noun* **1** the price of a journey **2** a paying passenger in a taxi *etc* **3** *formal* food ◇ *verb* get on (either well or badly): *they fared well in the competition* • **farewell** *exclam & noun* goodbye

farm *noun* **1** an area of land for growing crops, breeding and feeding animals *etc* **2** a place where certain animals, fish, *etc* are reared: *a salmon farm* ◇ *verb* work on a farm • **farmer** *noun* the owner or tenant of a farm • **farmhouse** *noun* the house attached to a farm • **farmstead** *noun* a farm and farmhouse • **farmyard** *noun* the yard surrounded by farm buildings • **farm out** give (paid work) to others outside your organization

farrago *noun* (*plural* **farragoes**) a confused mixture

farrow *noun* a litter of baby pigs ◇ *verb* give birth to a litter of pigs

fart *noun, taboo slang* **1** an outburst of wind from the anus **2** a despised person ◇ *verb* expel wind from the anus

farther and **farthest** *see* **far**

farthing *noun, hist* an old coin worth $\frac{1}{4}$ of an old penny

fascia /feh-shi-uh/ *noun* **1** a board with a sign on it, above a shop *etc* **2** a vehicle's dashboard

fascinate *verb* **1** hold the interest or attention of irresistibly **2** hypnotize • **fascinating** *adj* • **fascination** *noun*

fascism /fash-izm/ *noun* a form of authoritarian government characterized by extreme nationalism and suppression of individual freedom • **fascist** *noun* **1** a supporter of fascism **2** a right-wing extremist

fashion *noun* **1** the style in which something is made, *esp* clothes **2** a way of behaving or dressing which is popular for a time **3** a manner, a way: *acting in a strange fashion* ◇ *verb* make, form or shape • **fashionable** *adj* made or done in the latest style

• **after a fashion** to some extent, or in a way • **in fashion** fashionable

fast adj **1** quick-moving **2** of a clock: showing a time that is later than the correct time **3** of dyed colour: not likely to wash out ◇ adv **1** quickly **2** firmly: *stand fast* **3** soundly, completely: *fast asleep* ◇ verb go without food voluntarily, *eg* for religious reasons or as a protest ◇ noun abstinence from food • **fast food** noun ready-prepared or takeaway food • **fastness** noun • **fast-track** adj of a career: liable for quick promotion • **in the fast lane** having an exciting but stressful lifestyle

fasten verb make firm by tying, nailing, *etc*; fix

fastidious adj fussy about details and therefore difficult to please • **fastidiously** adv • **fastidiousness** noun

fat noun an oily substance made by the bodies of animals and by plants ◇ adj **1** having a lot of fat on the body; plump **2** thick, wide • **fatten** verb make or become fat • **fatty** adj containing a lot of fat

fatal adj causing death or disaster • **fatality** noun a death, *esp* caused by accident or disaster

fate noun **1** what the future holds; fortune, luck **2** death: *met his fate bravely* • **fated** adj doomed • **fateful** adj with important, *usu* unpleasant consequences; crucial, significant

father noun **1** a male parent **2** a priest **3** the creator or inventor of something: *Poe is the father of crime fiction* ◇ verb be the father of • **father-in-law** noun the father of someone's husband or wife • **fatherland** noun someone's native country

fathom noun a measure of depth of water (6 feet, 1.83 metres) ◇ verb finally understand the meaning of; get to the bottom of

fatigue /fuh-*teeg*/ noun **1** great tiredness **2** weakness or strain caused by

use: *metal fatigue* ◇ verb tire out

fatuous adj very foolish • **fatuously** adv • **fatuousness** noun

fatwa noun an official order issued by an Islamic authority

faucet noun, *US* a tap

fault noun **1** responsibility for something bad or wrong: *not my fault* **2** a mistake **3** a problem that causes something not to work properly • **faultless** adj perfect • **faultlessly** adv • **faulty** adj **1** not working properly **2** having a fault or faults

faun noun a mythological creature with a man's head and torso and a goat's legs and tail

fauna noun the animals of a district or country as a whole

faux /foh/ adj imitation: *faux leather*

faux pas /foh pah/ noun (*plural* **faux pas**) an embarrassing mistake; a blunder

favour noun **1** a kind action **2** approval or goodwill **3** a small gift ◇ verb **1** show preference for **2** be an advantage to: *the darkness favoured our escape* • **in favour of 1** in support of **2** for the benefit of

favourable adj **1** showing approval **2** making something easier to achieve; advantageous • **favourably** adv

favourite adj best liked ◇ noun **1** a liked or best-loved person or thing **2** a competitor, horse, *etc* expected to win a race • **favouritism** noun unfairly showing favour towards one person *etc* more than another

fawn[1] noun **1** a young deer **2** a light yellowish-brown colour ◇ adj of this colour

fawn[2] verb show too much devotion or obedience in order to win approval

fax noun **1** a machine that scans a document electronically and transfers the information by a telephone line to a receiving machine that produces a corresponding copy **2** a document copied and sent in this way ◇ *verb* **1** send by fax **2** send a fax message to

FBI *abbrev, US* Federal Bureau of Investigation, a department of the US government that deals with serious crimes

FE *abbrev* Further Education

fear *noun* an unpleasant feeling caused by the awareness of danger • **fearful** *adj* **1** timid, afraid **2** causing great harm or suffering; terrible **3** *informal* very bad: *a fearful headache* • **fearfully** *adv* • **fearless** *adj* brave, daring • **fearlessly** *adv* • **fearsome** *adj* causing fear; frightening

feasible *adj* able to be done; realistic or practical • **feasibility** *noun* • **feasibly** *adv*

feast *noun* **1** a very large meal **2** a festival day commemorating some event ◇ *verb* eat or hold a feast

feat *noun* a deed requiring some effort

feather *noun* one of the growths that form the outer covering of a bird • **feathery** *adj* **1** covered in feathers **2** like a feather

feature *noun* **1** an identifying mark or characteristic **2** (**features**) the various parts of someone's face, *eg* eyes, nose, *etc* **3** a special article in a newspaper *etc* **4** a special attraction **5** the main film in a cinema programme ◇ *verb* **1** have as a feature **2** take part (in) **3** be prominent in

February *noun* the second month of the year

fecund *adj, formal* fertile • **fecundity** *noun*

fed *past form of* **feed**

federal *adj* **1** consisting of separate states joined by treaty and governed centrally on some matters **2** relating to the whole of the United States, not a single state • **federated** *adj* joined after an agreement is made • **federa-**

tion *noun* a group of states *etc* joined together for a common purpose

fee *noun* a price paid for work done, or for a special service

feeble *adj* weak • **feebleness** *noun* • **feebly** *adv*

feed *verb* (**feeding, fed**) **1** give food to **2** eat food **3** supply with necessary materials ◇ *noun* food for animals: *cattle feed* • **feedback** *noun* **1** information on how well you are doing something or what people think of something **2** an unwanted loud signal from a speaker produced when some of the sound already amplified is picked up by the amplifier and amplified further • **fed up** tired, bored and disgusted

feel *verb* (**feeling, felt**) **1** explore by touch **2** be physically aware of: *he felt no pain* **3** believe, consider **4** think (yourself) to be: *I feel ill* **5** be sorry (for): *we felt for her in her grief* ◇ *noun* an act of touching • **feelgood** *adj* causing a feeling of comfort or security: *feelgood movie* • **feel like** have an inclination to have or do; want: *do you feel like going out tonight?*

feeler *noun* one of two thread-like parts on an insect's head for sensing danger *etc*

feeling *noun* **1** (**feelings**) what someone feels inside; emotions **2** emotion: *spoken with great feeling* **3** an impression or belief: *I've a feeling I've seen him before* **4** sense of touch **5** affection

feet *plural of* **foot**

feign /fehn/ *verb* pretend to feel or be: *feigning illness*

feint *noun* **1** a pretence **2** a move designed to make an opponent move the wrong way ◇ *verb* make a deceptive move

Do not confuse with: **faint**

feisty adj (**feistier, feistiest**) informal **1** showing a lot of character and determination; spirited **2** irritable, touchy

felafel /fuh-laf-ul/ noun a fried ball of chickpeas and spices

felicity noun, formal happiness • **felicitations** plural noun good wishes, congratulations • **felicitous** adj **1** lucky **2** very suitable

feline adj **1** of or relating to cats **2** like a cat

fell[1] past tense of **fall**

fell[2] noun a barren hill

fell[3] verb cut down (a tree)

fell[4] adj, old cruel, ruthless

fellatio /fuh-leh-shi-oh/ noun oral sexual stimulation of the penis

fellow noun **1** a man or boy **2** a member of an academic society, college, etc **3** an equal **4** one of a pair • **fellowship** noun **1** comradeship, friendship **2** an award to a university graduate

felon noun someone who commits a serious crime • **felony** noun a serious crime

felt[1] noun a type of rough cloth made of rolled and pressed wool

felt[2] past form of **feel**

female adj of the sex that produces children ◇ noun a person or animal of this sex

feminine adj **1** of or relating to women **2** characteristic of women • **femininity** noun

feminism noun a social and cultural movement aiming to win equal rights for women • **feminist** noun a supporter of feminism ◇ adj relating to this movement: feminist literature

femme fatale /fam fuh-tahl/ noun an irresistibly attractive woman who brings disaster on men

femoral adj relating to the thigh or thigh bone

femur noun the thigh bone

fen noun low marshy land, often covered with water

fence noun **1** a barrier of wooden posts, metal rails, etc enclosing an area **2** slang someone who receives stolen goods ◇ verb **1** enclose with a fence **2** fight with swords **3** give evasive answers when questioned • **fencing** noun **1** material for fences **2** the sport of fighting with swords, using blunted weapons

fend verb: **fend for yourself** look after and provide for yourself

fender noun **1** a low guard round a fireplace to keep in coal etc **2** a piece of matting over a ship's side acting as a buffer against the quay **3** US the bumper of a car

feng shui /fung shweh/ noun a Chinese philosophy in which the positioning of objects creates good or bad luck and health

fennel noun a plant whose strongly-smelling root, leaves and seeds are used in cooking

ferment verb **1** change by fermentation **2** stir up (trouble etc) ◇ noun

---

Do not confuse with: **foment**

---

fermentation noun **1** a reaction caused by bringing certain substances together, eg by adding yeast to dough in bread-making **2** great excitement or agitation

fern noun a plant with no flowers and feather-like leaves

ferocious adj fierce, savage • **ferociously** adv • **ferocity** noun

ferret noun a small weasel-like animal used to chase rabbits out of their warrens ◇ verb search busily and persistently

Ferris wheel noun a giant upright fairground wheel with seats hanging from its rim

ferrule noun a metal tip on a walking stick or umbrella

ferry noun (plural **ferries**) **1** a boat that carries passengers and vehicles across a channel **2** a crossing place for boats ◇ verb (**ferries**, **ferrying**, **ferried**) transport in a vehicle

fertile adj **1** able to produce children or young **2** on which plants grow well **3** full of ideas; creative ● **fertility** noun

fertilize verb **1** make (soil etc) fertile **2** cause (an egg or seed) to begin the process of reproduction ● **fertilization** noun ● **fertilizer** noun manure or chemicals used to make soil more fertile

fervent adj eagerly enthusiastic; zealous ● **fervently** adv

fervour noun eager enthusiasm; zeal

fest noun or **-fest** suffix a gathering or festival around some subject: news-fest/trade fest

fester verb of a wound: produce pus because of infection

festival noun **1** a season of musical, theatrical or other performances **2** a day of esp religious celebration

festive adj **1** in a happy, celebrating mood **2** of a feast ● **festivity** noun a celebration

festoon verb decorate with chains of ribbons, flowers, etc

feta noun a crumbly white cheese made from ewes' milk

fetch verb **1** go and get **2** bring in (a price): fetched £100 at auction

fete or **fête** noun a public event with stalls, competitions, etc to raise money ◇ verb entertain or praise lavishly

fetid adj having a rotten smell; stinking

fetish noun (plural **fetishes**) **1** an object of (esp sexual) obsession **2** a sacred object believed to carry super-

natural power ● **fetishist** noun ● **fetishistic** adj

fetlock noun the part of a horse's leg just above the foot

fetters plural noun, formal chains for imprisonment

fettle noun: **in fine fettle** in good health or condition

fettuccine /fet-uh-chee-ni/ noun pasta shaped in flat, wide strips

feu /fyoo/ noun, Scot a right to use land, a house, etc indefinitely in return for an annual payment

feud noun a private, drawn-out war between families, clans, etc

feudal adj, hist of a social system under which tenants were bound to give certain services to the overlord in return for their tenancies ● **feudalism** noun ● **feudalist** adj

fever noun an above-normal body temperature and quickened pulse ● **fevered** adj **1** having a fever **2** very excited ● **feverish** adj **1** having a slight fever **2** excited **3** too fast or frantic: feverish pace

few adj not many: only a few tickets left ● **a good few** or **quite a few** a considerable number; several

fey /feh/ adj **1** behaving in a strange way that seems affected; whimsical **2** clairvoyant

fez noun (plural **fezzes**) a brimless flowerpot-shaped hat worn by some Muslim men

ff abbrev following pages, lines, etc

fiancé /fee-onh-seh/ noun the man a woman is engaged to marry

fiancée /fee-onh-seh/ noun the woman a man is engaged to marry

fiasco noun (plural **fiascos**) a complete failure

fib verb (**fibbing**, **fibbed**) lie about something unimportant ◇ noun an unimportant lie

fibre noun 1 a thread or string 2 the essence or material of something: the fibre of her being 3 roughage in foods • **fibreboard** noun strong board made from compressed wood chips or other fibres • **fibrous** adj thread-like; stringy

fibreglass noun a lightweight material made of very fine threads of glass, used for building boats etc

fibre-optic adj of a cable: made of glass or plastic filaments that transmit light signals

fibula noun the thinner, outer bone in the lower leg (compare with: **tibia**)

fickle adj tending to change unpredictably and unhelpfully

fiction noun 1 stories about imaginary characters and events 2 a lie

fictional adj created for, or existing only in, a story; imagined: fictional character

---

Do not confuse: **fictional** and **fictitious**

---

fictitious adj 1 not real; imaginary 2 untrue

fiddle noun, informal 1 a cheat or swindle 2 a violin 3 a tricky or delicate operation ◇ verb 1 handle aimlessly; play (with) 2 interfere or tamper (with) 3 informal falsify (accounts etc) with the intention of cheating 4 play the violin • **fiddly** adj needing delicate or careful handling

fidelity noun 1 faithfulness 2 truth, accuracy

fidget verb move about restlessly

field noun 1 a piece of enclosed ground for pasture, crops, sports, etc 2 an area of land containing a natural resource: goldfield/coalfield 3 a branch of interest or knowledge 4 those taking part in a race ◇ verb, cricket catch the ball and return it • **field day** noun a day of unusual

activity or success • **field glasses** plural noun binoculars • **field gun** noun a light, mobile cannon • **field marshal** noun the highest ranking army officer

fiend noun 1 an evil spirit 2 a wicked person 3 an extreme enthusiast: a crossword fiend • **fiendish** adj

fierce adj 1 very angry-looking and seeming likely to attack; hostile 2 intense, strong: fierce competition • **fiercely** adv • **fierceness** noun

fiery (**fierier**, **fieriest**) adj 1 like fire 2 quick-tempered; volatile

fiesta noun a festival or carnival

FIFA /fee-fuh/ abbrev (in French) Fédération Internationale de Football Association, the International Football Federation

fife noun a small flute

fifteen noun the number 15 ◇ adj 15 in number • **fifteenth** adj the last of a series of fifteen ◇ noun one of fifteen equal parts

fifth adj the last of a series of five ◇ noun one of five equal parts

fifty noun the number 50 ◇ adj 50 in number • **fiftieth** adj the last of a series of fifty ◇ noun one of fifty equal parts

fig noun 1 a soft roundish fruit with thin, dark skin and red pulp containing many seeds 2 the tree on which it grows

fight verb (**fighting**, **fought**) 1 struggle with fists, weapons, etc 2 quarrel 3 go to war with ◇ noun a quarrel, struggle or battle • **fighter** noun 1 someone who fights 2 a fast military aircraft armed with guns

figment noun an idea or belief that exists in the mind only and is not based on reality

figurative adj of a word: used not in its ordinary meaning but to show likenesses, eg 'she was a tiger' for 'she was as ferocious as a tiger'; metaphorical

figure 201 **filth**

(*contrasted with*: **literal**) • **figurative-ly** *adv*

figure *noun* **1** outward form or shape **2** a number **3** a geometrical shape **4** an unidentified person: *a shadowy figure approached* **5** a diagram or drawing on a page **6** a set of movements in skating *etc* ◇ *verb* be included in; feature: *he figures in the story* • **figured** *adj* marked with a design: *figured silk* • **figurehead** *noun* a leader who has little real power • **figurine** *noun* a small carved or moulded figure • **figure out** work out; understand

filament *noun* a slender thread, *eg* of wire in a light bulb

filch *verb*, *informal* steal

file *noun* **1** a loose-leaf folder designed to hold papers **2** an amount of computer data held under a single name **3** a steel tool with a roughened surface for smoothing wood, metal, *etc* **4** a line of soldiers *etc* walking one behind another ◇ *verb* **1** put (papers *etc*) in a file **2** rub with a file **3** walk in a file • **file extension** *noun*, *comput* the 2- or 3-letter suffix that follows a full stop at the end of a computer file name

filet mignon /fee-leh mee-*nyonh*/ *noun* a small boneless cut of beef

filial *adj* of or typical of a son or daughter

filibuster *noun* a long speech given in parliament to delay the passing of a law

filigree *noun* very fine gold or silver work in lace or metal

fill *verb* **1** put (something) into until there is no room for more: *fill the bucket with water* **2** become full: *her eyes filled with tears* **3** satisfy or fulfil (a requirement *etc*) **4** occupy: *fill a post* **5** appoint someone to (a job *etc*): *have you filled the vacancy?* **6** put something in a hole to stop it up ◇ *noun* as much as is needed to fill: *we ate our fill* • **filler** *noun* **1** a material used to fill up holes in wood, plaster, *etc* **2** a substance added to increase bulk • **filling station** *noun*, *dated* a petrol station • **fill in 1** fill (a hole) **2** complete (a form *etc*) **3** do another person's job while they are absent: *I'm filling in for Anne* • **fill up** fill completely

fillet *noun* a piece of meat or fish with bones removed ◇ *verb* remove the bones from

filling *noun* **1** something used to fill a hole or gap **2** food inside a pie, sandwich, *etc* ◇ *adj* of food: satisfying

fillip *noun* an encouragement

filly *noun* (*plural* **fillies**) a young female horse

film *noun* **1** a series of images that present a story or information, recorded on Celluloid, videotape, *etc* and shown in a cinema or on television **2** a chemically-coated strip of Celluloid on which photographs are taken **3** a thin skin or coating ◇ *verb* **1** record images of on Celluloid **2** develop a thin coating: *his eyes filmed over* • **film star** *noun* a famous actor or actress in films

filo /fee-loh/ *noun* Middle-Eastern pastry in the form of paper-thin sheets

Filofax *noun*, *trademark* a diary-like organizer for keeping records of appointments *etc*

filter *noun* **1** a strainer for removing solid material from liquids **2** a green arrow on a traffic light signalling one lane of traffic to move while the main stream is held up ◇ *verb* **1** strain through a filter **2** move or arrive gradually: *the news filtered through* **3** of cars *etc*: join gradually a stream of traffic **4** of a lane of traffic: move in the direction shown by a filter

filth *noun* **1** very unpleasant dirt **2** anything morally obscene or physically disgusting • **filthily** *adv* • **filthiness** *noun* • **filthy** *adj* **1** very dirty **2** obscene, lewd

fin noun a flexible projecting part of a fish's body used for balance and swimming

final adj 1 last 2 not to be challenged or changed: the judge's decision is final ◇ noun the last contest in a competition: World Cup final • **finality** noun the quality of being final and decisive • **finalize** verb put (eg plans) in a final or finished form • **finally** adv

finale /fi-nah-leh/ noun the last part of anything (eg a concert)

finance noun 1 money affairs 2 the study or management of these 3 (**finances**) the money someone has to spend ◇ verb supply with sums of money • **financial** adj • **financially** adv • **financier** noun someone who manages (public) money

finch noun (plural **finches**) a small bird with a thick beak

find verb (**finding, found**) 1 come upon accidentally or after searching: I found an earring in the street 2 discover 3 judge to be: finds it hard to live on her pension ◇ noun something found, esp something of interest or value • **find out** discover, detect

fine¹ adj 1 made up of very small pieces, drops, etc: fine rain 2 not coarse: fine linen 3 thin, delicate: a fine membrane 4 of very good quality: fine wines 5 well, healthy: feeling fine 6 bright, not rainy: a fine day 7 beautiful or handsome: a fine woman 8 slight: a fine distinction • **fine arts** plural noun painting, sculpture, music and architecture • **finery** noun elaborate clothes and accessories

fine² noun money to be paid as a punishment ◇ verb order to pay (money) as punishment

fines herbes /feenz erb/ plural noun a mixture of herbs as a garnish

finesse /fi-nes/ noun cleverness and subtlety in handling situations etc

finger noun one of the five branch-ing parts of the hand ◇ verb touch with the fingers • **fingering** noun 1 the positioning of the fingers in playing a musical instrument 2 the showing of this by numbers • **fingerprint** noun the mark made by the tip of a finger, used by the police as a means of identification

finish verb 1 complete the making of, eating of, etc 2 stop: when do you finish work today? ◇ noun 1 the end (eg of a race) 2 the last coat of paint, polish, etc that produces the surface texture • **finished** adj 1 ended, complete 2 of a person: ruined, not likely to achieve further success etc

finite adj having an end or limit

fiord or **fjord** /fee-awd/ noun a long narrow inlet between steep hills, esp in Norway

fir noun a kind of cone-bearing tree

fire noun 1 a mass of burning material, objects, etc 2 a heating device: electric fire 3 the heat and light given off by something burning 4 eagerness, keenness ◇ verb 1 set on fire 2 make eager: fired by his enthusiasm 3 make (a gun) explode; shoot • **fire alarm** noun a device to sound a bell etc as a warning of fire • **firearm** noun a gun, eg a pistol • **fire brigade** noun a company of firefighters • **firedamp** noun a dangerous gas found in coal mines • **fire engine** noun a vehicle carrying firefighters and their equipment • **fire escape** noun a means of escape from a building in case of fire • **firefighter** noun a trained person whose job is putting out fires • **firefly** noun a type of insect which glows in the dark • **fireguard** noun a framework of iron placed in front of a fireplace for safety • **fireman, firewoman** noun a firefighter • **fireplace** noun a recess in a room below a chimney for a fire • **firewall** noun 1 a wall installed in a building to prevent fires from spreading 2 comput a piece of software that protects a network against unauthorized users • **firewood** noun wood for burning on a fire • **fireworks** plural noun 1 squibs, rockets, etc sent up at night for show 2 informal angry behaviour

firkin noun, old a small barrel

firm adj 1 not easily moved, shaken or pressed out of shape 2 with your mind made up ◇ noun a business company • **firmly** adv • **firmness** noun

firmament noun, formal the sky

first adj & adv before all others in place, time or rank ◇ adj before doing anything else ◇ noun 1 a first occurrence of something 2 a first-class honours degree • **first aid** noun treatment of a wounded or sick person before the doctor's arrival • **firstborn** noun the eldest child • **first-class** adj of the highest standard, best kind, etc • **first-hand** adj direct from the person involved • **first name** noun a person's name that is not their surname • **first-rate** adj first-class

firth noun a river estuary in Scotland

fiscal adj 1 relating to government finances 2 of financial matters generally

fish noun (plural **fish** or **fishes**) an animal that lives in water and breathes through gills ◇ verb 1 try to catch fish with rod, nets, etc 2 search (for): fishing for a handkerchief in her bag 3 try to obtain: fish for compliments • **fisherman** noun a man who fishes, esp for a living • **fishmonger** noun someone who sells fish for food • **fishy** adj 1 like a fish 2 arousing suspicion; dubious

fission noun splitting (see also **nuclear fission**)

fissure noun a crack

fist noun a tightly-shut hand • **fisticuffs** plural noun, old a fight with the fists

fit adj 1 having a strong healthy body through physical exercise 2 suited to a purpose; proper ◇ noun a sudden attack or spasm of laughter, illness, etc ◇ verb (**fitting**, **fitted**) 1 be of the right size or shape 2 be suitable • **fitful** adj coming, or doing something, in bursts or spasms • **fitfully** adv • **fitness** noun • **fitting** adj suitable ◇ noun something fixed or fitted in a room, house, etc • **fittingly** adv

five noun the number 5 ◇ adj 5 in number

fix verb 1 make firm; fasten 2 mend, repair • **fixed** adj settled; set in position • **fixedly** adv steadily, intently: staring fixedly

fixture noun 1 a piece of furniture etc fixed in position 2 an arranged sports match or race

fizz verb make a hissing sound ◇ noun a hissing sound • **fizzy** adj of a drink: forming bubbles on the surface

fizzle or **fizzle out** verb coming to nothing; fail

fjord another spelling of **fiord**

flabbergasted adj very surprised

flabby adj (**flabbier**, **flabbiest**) lacking firmness or tautness and suggesting weakness; limp • **flabbily** adv • **flabbiness** noun

flaccid /fla-sid/ adj 1 hanging loosely 2 limp, not firm

flag noun 1 a piece of cloth with a design representing a country, organization, etc, flown from a pole or waved by hand 2 a flat paving-stone ◇ verb (**flagging**, **flagged**) become tired or weak

flagellate verb, formal beat with a whip • **flagellation** noun whipping

flageolet¹ /flazh-uh-leh/ noun a variety of kidney bean

flageolet² /flazh-uh-leh/ noun a small high-pitched flute

flagon noun a large container for liquid

flagrant adj 1 clear or obvious 2

shamelessly bad or wicked • **flagrancy** *noun* • **flagrantly** *adv*

flail *verb* wave or swing in the air ◊ *noun, old* a tool for threshing corn

flair *noun* talent, skill: *a flair for languages*

flak *noun* **1** anti-aircraft fire **2** strong criticism

flake *noun* **1** a thin slice or chip of anything **2** a very small piece of snow *etc* ◊ *verb* form into flakes • **flaky** *adj* **1** forming flakes; crumbly: *flaky pastry* **2** *US informal* eccentric • **flake off** break off in flakes

flambé /*flom*-beh/ or **flambéed** *adj, cookery* cooked or served in flaming alcohol

flamboyant *adj* **1** impressively lively and eye-catching **2** too showy or colourful; gaudy

flame *noun* **1** the bright leaping light of a fire **2** *comput slang* a rude or abusive email ◊ *verb* **1** burn brightly **2** *comput slang* send an abusive email to • **flaming** *adj* **1** burning **2** red **3** violent: *a flaming temper*

flamingo *noun* (*plural* **flamingoes**) a long-legged wading bird of pink or bright-red colour

flammable *adj* easily set on fire

flan *noun* a flat, open tart

flange *noun* a raised edge on the rim of a wheel

flank *noun* a side, *eg* the side of an animal's body or of a formation of soldiers ◊ *verb* be or move at the side of

flannel *noun* **1** loosely woven woollen fabric **2** a small towel or face cloth **3** pleasant or flattering talk designed to charm or persuade

flannelette *noun* cotton fabric imitating flannel

flannels *plural noun* men's casual trousers made of thin fabric

flap *noun* **1** anything broad and loose-hanging: *tent flap* **2** the sound of a wing *etc* moving through air **3** *informal* a panic: *getting in a flap over nothing* ◊ *verb* (**flapping**, **flapped**) **1** hang down loosely **2** move with a flapping noise **3** *informal* get into a panic

flapjack *noun* **1** *Brit* a biscuit made with rolled oats, butter and sugar **2** *US* a pancake

flapper *noun, hist* a stylish confident young woman of the 1920s

flare *verb* **1** blaze up **2** widen towards the end or bottom ◊ *noun* **1** a bright light, *esp* one used at night as a signal, to show the position of a boat in distress *etc* **2** a widened end or bottom edge

flash *noun* (*plural* **flashes**) **1** a quick burst of light **2** a moment, an instant **3** a distinctive mark on a uniform **4** a bright electric light that illuminates a thing being photographed ◊ *verb* **1** shine out suddenly **2** pass quickly • **flashback** *noun* a scene depicting earlier, often remembered events • **flashlight** *noun, US* an electric torch • **in a flash** very quickly or suddenly

flasher *noun, slang* someone who exposes their genitals in public

flashy (**flashier**, **flashiest**) *adj* ostentatiously smart or impressive; showy

flask *noun* **1** an insulated bottle or vacuum flask **2** a small flat bottle **3** a narrow-necked bottle

flat *adj* **1** level: *a flat surface* **2** of a drink: no longer fizzy **3** leaving no doubt; downright: *a flat denial* **4** below the right musical pitch **5** of a tyre: punctured **6** dull, uninteresting ◊ *adv* stretched out: *lying flat on her back* ◊ *noun* **1** an apartment on one storey of a building **2** *music* a sign (♭) that lowers a note by a semitone **3** a punctured tyre • **flatfish** *noun* a sea fish with a flat body, *eg* a sole • **flatly** *adv* • **flatness** *noun* • **flat race** *noun* a horse race without jumps • **flat rate**

noun a rate which is the same in all cases • **flattish** *adj* almost, but not quite, flat • **flat out** as fast as possible or with as much effort as possible

flatten *verb* make or become flat

flatter *verb* praise insincerely • **flattery** *noun*

flatulence *noun* wind in the stomach • **flatulent** *adj*

flaunt /flawnt/ *verb* display in an obvious way: *flaunted his wealth*

Do not confuse with: **flout**

---

flautist /flawt-ist/ *noun* a flute player

flavour *noun* 1 taste: *lemon flavour* 2 quality or atmosphere: *an exotic flavour* ◇ *verb* give a taste to • **flavouring** *noun* an ingredient used to give a particular taste: *chocolate flavouring*

flaw *noun* a fault or imperfection • **flawless** *adj* with no faults or blemishes • **flawlessly** *adv*

flax *noun* a plant whose fibres are woven into linen cloth • **flaxen** *adj* 1 made of or looking like flax 2 of hair: fair

flay *verb* strip the skin off

flea *noun* a small, wingless, blood-sucking insect with great jumping power

fleck *noun* a spot or small patch • **flecked** *adj* marked with spots or patches

fled *past form of* **flee**

fledgling *noun* a young bird with fully-grown feathers

flee *verb* (**fleeing, fled**) run away from danger *etc*

fleece *noun* 1 a sheep's coat of wool 2 thick, warm, soft cotton or polyester fabric, or a warm sweater made of this ◇ *verb* 1 clip wool from 2 *informal* rob by cheating • **fleecy** *adj* soft and fluffy like wool

fleet *noun* 1 a number of ships 2 a number of cars or taxis ◇ *adj* moving with quick easy movements; nimble • **fleeting** *adj* passing quickly: *fleeting glimpse* • **fleetness** *noun* swiftness

flesh *noun* 1 the soft tissue that covers the bones of humans and animals 2 meat 3 the body 4 the soft edible part of fruit • **fleshy** *adj* fat, plump • **flesh and blood** 1 relations, family 2 human, mortal

fleur-de-lis *or* **fleur-de-lys** /flur-duh-*lee*/ *noun* a stylized heraldic design of a lily with three petals

flew *past tense of* **fly**

flex *verb* bend (a joint) or tighten (a muscle) ◇ *noun* a length of covered wire attached to electrical devices • **flexitime** *noun* a system in which an agreed number of hours' work is done at times chosen by the worker

flexible *adj* 1 easily bent 2 willing or able to adapt to new or different conditions • **flexibility** *noun* • **flexibly** *adv*

flick *verb* 1 strike lightly with a quick movement 2 remove (dust *etc*) with a movement of this kind ◇ *noun* a quick, sharp movement: *a flick of the wrist* • **flick knife** *noun* a knife with a blade that springs out of the handle at the press of a button

flicker *verb* 1 flutter 2 burn unsteadily ◇ *noun* a fluttering or unsteady burning

flier *noun* 1 a leaflet distributed as an advertisement 2 a pilot 3 *informal* a risky activity or business venture

flight *noun* 1 the act of flying 2 a journey by plane 3 the act of fleeing or escaping 4 a flock (of birds) 5 a number (of steps) • **flighty** *adj* tending to change opinions, decisions or allegiances unexpectedly; fickle • **flight attendant** *noun* a member of the staff of a passenger aircraft whose job is to look after passengers

flimsy adj (**flimsier, flimsiest**) **1** thin and easily torn or broken **2** weak: a flimsy excuse

flinch verb move or shrink back in fear, pain, etc

fling verb (**flinging, flung**) throw ◇ noun **1** a throw **2** a casual attempt **3** a brief romantic affair **4** a period of time devoted to pleasure

flint noun a kind of hard stone ◇ adj made of flint • **flintlock** noun, hist a gun fired by sparks from a flint

flip verb (**flipping, flipped**) **1** toss lightly, esp by pushing or flicking an edge **2** informal suddenly become very angry: she'll flip when she sees this mess ◇ noun a light toss or stroke • **flip side** noun **1** the reverse side of a record etc **2** the converse of anything

flippant adj showing a lack of seriousness • **flippancy** noun • **flippantly** adv

flipper noun **1** a limb of a seal, walrus, etc **2** a webbed rubber shoe worn by divers

flirt verb **1** behave towards in a romantic or sexual way without any serious intentions **2** (with **with**) take a brief casual interest (in) ◇ noun someone who flirts • **flirtation** noun • **flirtatious** adj fond of flirting

flit verb (**flitting, flitted**) **1** move quickly and lightly from place to place **2** move house

float verb **1** keep on the surface of a liquid without sinking **2** suggest for consideration: float an idea **3** offer for sale shares in (a company) ◇ noun **1** a cork etc on a fishing line **2** a van delivering milk etc **3** a platform on wheels, used in processions **4** a sum of money set aside for giving change

flock[1] noun **1** a number of animals or birds together **2** a large number of people **3** the congregation of a church ◇ verb (with **together**) gather or move in a crowd

flock[2] noun **1** a shred or tuft of wool **2** wool or cotton waste

floe /floh/ noun a sheet of floating ice

flog verb (**flogging, flogged**) **1** beat with a whip **2** slang sell • **flogging** noun

flood noun **1** a great flow, esp of water **2** a great quantity: a flood of letters **3** the rise or flow of the tide ◇ verb **1** (cause to) overflow **2** cover or fill with water • **floodlight** verb (**floodlighting, floodlit**) illuminate with floodlighting ◇ noun a light used to floodlight • **floodlighting** noun strong artificial lighting to illuminate a stadium, stage, etc

floor noun **1** the base level of a room, on which people walk **2** a storey of a building: a third-floor flat ◇ verb **1** make a floor in (a room) **2** informal knock flat **3** informal puzzle: floored by the question

floozie noun, dated informal a sexually promiscuous woman

flop verb (**flopping, flopped**) **1** sway or swing about loosely **2** fall or sit down suddenly and heavily **3** move about clumsily **4** fail badly ◇ noun **1** an act of flopping **2** a complete failure • **floppy** adj soft and flexible, esp to an unwanted extent • **floppy disk** noun, comput a storage medium for computer data, in the form of a thin flexible disk inside a rigid plastic case

flora noun the plants of a district or country as a whole

floral adj of, or in the form of, flowers

florid adj **1** with a flushed or ruddy complexion **2** too ornate

florist noun a seller or grower of flowers • **floristry** noun

floss noun **1** thin, often waxed thread for passing between the teeth to clean them **2** fine silk thread ◇ verb clean (teeth) with dental floss

flotilla *noun* a fleet of small ships

flotsam *noun* floating objects washed from a ship or wreck

flounce[1] *verb* walk away suddenly and impatiently, *eg* in anger

flounce[2] *noun* a gathered decorative strip sewn onto the hem of a dress

flounder[1] *verb* 1 struggle to move your legs and arms in water, mud, *etc* 2 have difficulty speaking or thinking clearly, or in acting efficiently

Do not confuse with: **founder**

flounder[2] *noun* a small flatfish

flour *noun* 1 finely ground wheat 2 any grain crushed to powder: *rice flour*

flourish *verb* 1 be successful, *esp* financially 2 grow well; thrive 3 be healthy 4 wave as a show or threat; brandish ◇ *noun* (*plural* **flourishes**) 1 fancy strokes in writing 2 a sweeping movement with the hand, sword, *etc* 3 showy splendour 4 an ornamental passage in music

floury *adj* (**flourier**, **flouriest**) 1 covered with flour 2 with a crumbly or powdery texture

Do not confuse with: **flowery**

flout *verb* disobey or defy openly: *flouted the speed limit*

Do not confuse with: **flaunt**

flow *verb* 1 run in a stream, like water 2 move or come out in an unbroken run 3 of the tide: rise ◇ *noun* a smooth or unbroken run: *flow of ideas*

flower *noun* 1 the part of a plant or tree from which fruit or seeds grow 2 the best of anything ◇ *verb* 1 of plants *etc*: produce a flower 2 be at your best; flourish ● **flowering** *noun*

flowery *adj* 1 full of or decorated with flowers 2 using fine-sounding, fancy language: *flowery prose style*

Do not confuse with: **floury**

flown *past participle of* **fly**

fl oz *abbrev* fluid ounce(s)

flu *noun* an infectious illness with fever, headache and muscle pains

fluctuate *verb* 1 vary in number, price, *etc* 2 be always changing ● **fluctuation** *noun*

flue *noun* a passage for air and smoke in a stove or chimney

fluent *adj* finding words easily in speaking or writing without any awkward pauses ● **fluency** *noun*

fluff *noun* soft, downy material ◇ *verb* make a mistake, *esp* in speaking (lines) ● **fluffy** *adj*

fluid *noun* a substance whose particles can move about freely, *ie* a liquid or gas ◇ *adj* 1 flowing 2 not settled or fixed: *my plans for the weekend are fluid*

fluke[1] *noun* an accidental or unplanned success

fluke[2] *noun* a small worm which harms sheep

fluke[3] *noun* the part of an anchor which holds fast in sand

flume *noun* a water chute

flummox *verb* confuse totally; bewilder

flung *past form of* **fling**

flunk *verb, slang* fail

flunky *noun* (*plural* **flunkies**) 1 a servant 2 a servile person

fluorescent light *noun* a type of bright electric light

fluoride *noun* a chemical added to water or toothpaste to prevent tooth decay ● **fluoridize** *or* **fluoridate** *verb* add fluoride to

flurry noun (plural **flurries**) **1** a sudden commotion or burst of activity **2** a sudden gust of wind or fall of wind-blown snow ◊ verb (**flurries**, **flurrying**, **flurried**) excite

flush noun (plural **flushes**) **1** a reddening of the face **2** freshness, glow ◊ verb **1** become red in the face **2** clean by a rush of water ◊ adj **1** (with **with**) having the surface level with the surface around **2** informal well supplied with money

fluster noun excitement caused by hurry ◊ verb harass or confuse

flute noun **1** a high-pitched musical wind instrument **2** a tall narrow wine glass ● **fluted** adj decorated with grooves

flutter verb move (eyelids, wings, etc) back and forth quickly ◊ noun **1** a quick beating of pulse etc **2** a state of nervous excitement: in a flutter

flux noun an ever-changing flow: in a state of flux

fly noun (plural **flies**) **1** a small winged insect **2** a fish-hook made to look like a fly to catch fish **3** a flap of material with buttons or a zip at the front of trousers ◊ verb (**flies**, **flying**, **flew**, **flown**) **1** move through the air on wings or in an aeroplane **2** run away ● **flying saucer** noun a disc-shaped object believed to be an alien spacecraft ● **flying squad** noun a group of police officers organized for fast action or movement ● **flyover** noun a road built on pillars to cross over another ● **flysheet** noun the outer covering of a tent ● **flywheel** noun a heavy wheel that enables a machine to run at a steady speed

flyer another spelling of **flier**

FM abbrev frequency modulation (compare with: **AM**)

foal noun a young horse ◊ verb give birth to a foal

foam noun **1** a mass of small bubbles on liquids **2** a lightweight cellular material used for packaging, insulation, etc ◊ verb produce foam ● **foam rubber** noun sponge-like form of rubber for stuffing chairs, mattresses, etc

fob[1] noun **1** a small watch pocket **2** an ornamental chain hanging from such a pocket

fob[2] verb: **fob off** force to accept (something worthless): I won't be fobbed off with a silly excuse

focaccia /fuh-kach-uh/ noun a flat round Italian bread topped with olive oil and herbs

focal adj central, pivotal: focal point

fo'c'sle another spelling of **forecastle**

focus noun (plural **focuses** or **foci**) **1** the point at which rays of light meet **2** the subject, person, object, etc to which attention is directed **3** the degree to which objects viewed through a lens can be seen clearly ◊ verb (**focuses**, **focusing**, **focused**) **1** get the right length of ray of light for a clear picture **2** direct (one's attention etc) to one point

fodder noun dried food, eg hay or oats, for farm animals

foe noun, formal an enemy

foetal /fee-tul/ adj relating to a foetus ● **foetal alcohol syndrome** noun a range of birth defects caused by an excessive alcohol intake during pregnancy

foetus /fee-tus/ noun a young human being or animal in the womb or egg

fog noun thick mist ◊ verb **1** cover in fog **2** cause to be confused or obscured ● **foggy** adj ● **foghorn** noun a horn used as a warning to or by ships in fog

fogy or **fogey** noun (plural **fogies** or **fogeys**) someone with old-fashioned views

foie gras /fwah grah/ noun rich

expensive pâté made from fattened goose liver

foil noun 1 metal in the form of paper-thin sheets 2 a dull person against which someone else seems brighter 3 a blunt sword with a button at the end, used in fencing practice ◇ verb defeat, disappoint

foist verb 1 palm off (something undesirable) on someone 2 pass off as genuine

fold verb lift one side and lay it on top of another ◇ noun 1 a side laid on top of another 2 an enclosure for sheep etc 3 of a business etc: to fail and close down permanently • **folder** noun a cover to hold papers

foliage noun leaves

folio noun (plural **folios**) 1 a leaf (two pages back to back) of a book 2 a page number 3 a sheet of paper folded once

folk noun 1 people 2 a nation or race 3 (**folks**) family or relations • **folkie** noun, informal a folk music fan • **folk music** noun traditional music of a particular culture • **folk song** noun a traditional song of the kind passed on orally

folklore noun the study of the customs, beliefs, stories, etc of a people • **folklorist** noun someone who studies or collects folklore

follicle noun the pit surrounding a root of hair

follow verb 1 go or come after 2 happen as a result 3 act according to: follow your instincts 4 understand: I don't follow you 5 work at (a trade)

follower noun 1 someone who follows 2 a supporter or disciple: a follower of United

following noun supporters: the team has a large following ◇ adj next in time: we left the following day ◇ prep after, as a result of: following the fire, the house collapsed

folly noun (plural **follies**) 1 foolishness 2 a purposeless building

foment verb provoke or stir up (a rebellion etc)

Do not confuse with: **ferment**

fond adj loving or affectionate; tender • **fondly** adv • **fondness** noun • **fond of** having a liking for

fondant noun a soft sweet or paste made of flavouring, sugar and water

fondle verb cuddle or stroke in a loving or sexual way; caress

fondue noun a dish of hot cheese or oil etc into which pieces of food are dipped before being eaten

font noun 1 a basin holding water for baptism 2 an excellent source: a font of knowledge 3 the style of printed letters and numbers

food noun substances that people and animals eat to stay alive • **foodie** noun, informal someone who takes great interest in food • **food processor** noun an electrical appliance for chopping, blending, etc food • **foodstuff** noun something used for food

fool noun 1 a silly person 2 hist a court jester 3 a dessert made of fruit, sugar and whipped cream ◇ verb behave in a silly or joking way • **fool about** behave in a playful or silly manner

foolhardy adj taking foolish risks; rash

foolish adj not sensible in thought or behaviour; silly • **foolery** or **foolishness** noun foolish behaviour • **foolishly** adv

foolproof adj unable to go wrong

foolscap noun paper for writing or printing, 17 × 13in (43 × 34cm)

foot noun (plural **feet**) 1 the part of the leg below the ankle 2 the lower part of anything 3 a measurement of twelve inches, 30cm ◇ verb pay (a bill *etc*) ● **football** *noun* **1** a game played by two teams of 11 on a field with a round ball; soccer **2** *US* a game played with an oval ball that can be handled or kicked; American football **3** a ball used in football ● **footer** *noun* text that appears at the bottom of each page of a document ● **foothill** *noun* a smaller hill at the foot of a mountain ● **foothold** *noun* **1** a place to put the foot in climbing **2** a firm position from which to begin something ● **footing** *noun* **1** the stability of the position of your feet: *lost my footing* **2** the state of a friendship or other relationship: *on a friendly footing* ● **footlight** *noun* a light at the front of a stage, which shines on the actors ● **footloose** *adj* with no responsibilities or romantic attachments ● **footnote** *noun* a note at the bottom of a page ● **footpath** *noun* a path or track for walkers ● **footplate** *noun* a driver's platform on a steam railway engine ● **footprint** *noun* a mark left by a foot ● **footsore** *adj* tired out from too much walking ● **footstep** *noun* the sound of someone's foot when walking ● **footstool** *noun* a low stool for supporting the feet when sitting ● **footwear** *noun* shoes *etc* ● **foot the bill** pay up ● **my foot!** an exclamation of disbelief ● **not put a foot wrong** do everything correctly or appropriately

Footsie *another (informal)* name for FTSE

footsie *noun, informal* the rubbing of a foot against someone's leg *etc* in sexual play

fop *noun, old* a man who is vain about his dress ● **foppish** *adj*

for *prep* **1** sent to or to be given to: *there is a letter for you* **2** towards: *headed for home* **3** during (an amount of time): *waited for three hours* **4** on behalf of: *acting for my client* **5** because of: *for no good reason* **6** at the price of: *£5 for a ticket* **7** in order to obtain: *only doing it for the money*

forage *noun* food for horses and cattle ◇ *verb* search for food, fuel, *etc*

foray *noun* **1** a sudden raid **2** a brief journey

forbade *past tense of* **forbid**

forbearing *adj* patient and self-controlled ● **forbearance** *noun* patience and self-control

forbid *verb* (**forbidding**, **forbade**, **forbidden**) order not to ● **forbidden** *adj* ● **forbidding** *adj* rather frightening

force *noun* **1** strength, power or violence **2** the police or a similar body **3** a group of workers, soldiers, *etc* **4** (**forces**) members of the army, navy and air force ◇ *verb* **1** make, compel: *forced him to go* **2** get by violence: *force an entry* **3** break open and inflict: *force her opinions on us* **5** make vegetables *etc* grow more quickly ● **forced** *adj* done unwillingly or unnaturally: *a forced laugh* ● **forceful** *adj* acting with power ● **forcefully** *adv* ● **forcible** *adj* done by force ● **forcibly** *adv*

forceps *noun* surgical pincers for holding or lifting

ford *noun* a shallow crossing-place in a river ◇ *verb* cross (water) on foot

fore *noun*: **to the fore** into a position of prominence or importance

forearm[1] *noun* the part of the arm between elbow and wrist

forearm[2] *verb* prepare beforehand

foreboding *noun* a feeling of coming danger or evil

forecast *verb* tell about beforehand; predict ◇ *noun* a prediction

forecastle or **fo'c'sle** (both /fohk-sul/) *noun* **1** a raised deck at the front of a ship **2** the part of a ship under the deck, containing the crew's quarters

foreclose *verb* **1** order the repayment of (a mortgage) earlier than the due date because of a failure to keep up payments **2** prevent from doing or having; preclude

forefather *noun, formal* an ancestor

forefinger *noun* the finger next to the thumb

forefront *noun* the very front

foregone *adj*: **a foregone conclusion** a result that can be guessed rightly in advance (*see also* **forgo**)

foreground *noun* the part of a view or picture nearest the person looking at it

forehead *noun* the part of the face above the eyebrows

foreign *adj* **1** belonging to another country **2** not familiar **3** not belonging naturally in a place *etc*: *a foreign body in an eye* • **foreigner** *noun* **1** someone from another country **2** somebody unfamiliar

foreleg *noun* an animal's front leg

forelock *noun* the lock of hair next to the forehead

foreman *noun* (*plural* **foremen**) **1** an overseer of a group of workers **2** the leader of a jury

foremast *noun* a ship's mast nearest the bow

foremost *adj* the most famous or important

forensic *adj* relating to courts of law or criminal investigation: *forensic medicine*

forerunner *noun* an earlier example or sign of what is to follow: *the forerunner of cinema*

foresee *verb* (**foreseeing**, **foresaw**, **foreseen**) see or know beforehand

foreshore *noun* the part of the shore between high and low tidemarks

foresight *noun* ability to see what will happen later

foreskin *noun* a fold of skin covering the end of the penis

forest *noun* **1** a large piece of land covered with trees **2** a dense arrangement of objects • **forester** *noun* a worker in a forest • **forestry** *noun* the science of forest-growing

forestall *verb* upset someone's plan by acting earlier than they expect

foretaste *noun* a sample of what is to come

foretell *verb* (**foretelling**, **foretold**) tell in advance; prophesy

forethought *noun* thought or care for the future

foretold *past form of* **foretell**

forewarn *verb* warn beforehand • **forewarning** *noun*

forewent *past tense of* **forgo**

forewoman *noun* **1** a woman overseer **2** a head woman in a shop or factory

foreword *noun* a piece of writing at the beginning of a book

---

Do not confuse with: **forward**

---

forfeit *verb* lose (a right) as a result of doing something: *forfeit the right to appeal* ◊ *noun* something given in compensation or punishment for an action, *eg* a fine • **forfeiture** *noun* the loss of something as a punishment

forge *noun* **1** a blacksmith's workshop **2** a furnace in which metal is heated ◊ *verb* (**forging**, **forged**) **1** hammer (metal) into shape **2** imitate for criminal purposes **3** move steadily on: *forged ahead with the plan* • **forger** *noun*

forgery *noun* (*plural* **forgeries**) **1** something imitated for criminal purposes **2** the act of criminal forging

forget *verb* (**forgetting**, **forgot**, **forgotten**) lose or put away from the memory • **forgetful** *adj* likely to forget • **forgetfully** *adv* • **forgetfulness** *noun*

forgive *verb* (**forgiving**, **forgave**, **forgiven**) **1** be no longer angry with **2** overlook (a fault, debt, *etc*) • **forgive-**

ness noun pardon • **forgiving** adj

forgo verb (**forgoes**, **forgoing**, **forewent** or **forwent**, **foregone** or **forgone**) choose not to do or have; do without

forgot and **forgotten** see **forget**

fork noun 1 a pronged tool for piercing and lifting things 2 the point where a road, tree, etc divides into two branches ◇ verb divide into two branches etc • **fork-lift truck** noun a power-driven truck with steel prongs that can lift and carry heavy packages

forlorn adj looking touchingly sad; pitiful • **forlorn hope** noun a wish that seems to have no chance of being granted

form noun 1 shape or appearance 2 kind, type 3 a paper with printed questions and space for answers 4 a school class 5 a long seat 6 the nest of a hare ◇ verb 1 give shape to 2 make up

formal adj 1 done according to custom or convention 2 of manner: stiffly polite or businesslike • **formal dress** noun clothes required to be worn on formal social occasions, eg balls and banquets • **formality** noun 1 something that must be done but has little meaning: the nomination was only a formality 2 cold correctness of manner • **formally** adv

format noun 1 the size, shape, etc of a printed book 2 the design or arrangement of an event, eg a television programme 3 comput the description of the way data is arranged on a disk ◇ verb (**formatting**, **formatted**) 1 arrange into a specific format 2 comput arrange data for use on a disk 3 comput prepare (a disk) for use by dividing it into sectors

formation noun 1 arrangement, eg of aeroplanes in flight 2 the act of forming

former adj 1 of an earlier time 2 of the first-mentioned of two (contrasted with: **latter**) • **formerly** adv in earlier times; previously

formic adj relating to ants • **formic acid** noun an acid found in ants

formidable adj 1 impressive and rather frightening 2 difficult to overcome

formula noun (plural **formulae** or **formulas**) 1 a set of rules to be followed 2 a structure, method, etc that is often used, esp successfully 3 an arrangement of signs or letters used in chemistry, arithmetic, etc to express an idea briefly, eg H_2O = water • **formulate** verb 1 set down clearly: formulate the rules 2 make into a formula

fornicate verb, formal have sex outside marriage • **fornication** noun • **fornicator** noun

forsake verb (**forsaking**, **forsook**, **forsaken**) desert or abandon • **forsaken** adj deserted and rather depressing

forswear verb, formal give up

fort noun a place of defence against an enemy

forte /faw-teh/ noun someone's particular talent or speciality

forth adv forward, onward • **forthcoming** adj 1 happening soon 2 willing to share knowledge; friendly and open • **forthright** adj outspoken, straightforward • **forthwith** adv immediately

fortieth adj the last of a series of forty ◇ noun one of forty equal parts

fortifications plural noun walls etc built to strengthen a position

fortify verb (**fortifies**, **fortifying**, **fortified**) strengthen against attack

fortitude noun courage in facing danger or bearing pain

fortnight noun two weeks • **fortnightly** adj & adv once a fortnight

fortress noun (plural **fortresses**) a fortified place

fortuitous adj happening by chance and usu welcome • **fortuitously** adv • **fortuitousness** noun

fortunate adj lucky • **fortunately** adv

fortune noun 1 luck, good or bad 2 a large sum of money

forty noun the number 40 ◇ adj 40 in number

forum noun 1 a place, publication, event, etc that offers the chance for discussion 2 a meeting to discuss a particular subject 3 hist a marketplace in ancient Rome

forward adj 1 advancing: a forward movement 2 near or at the front 3 too quick to speak or act; pert 4 of fruit: ripe earlier than usual ◇ verb 1 send on (letters) 2 help towards success: forwarded his plans • **forward** or **forwards** adv onward, towards the front

---

Do not confuse with: **foreword**

---

forwent past tense of **forgo**

fossil noun the hardened remains of the shape of a plant or animal found in rock • **fossilize** verb change into a fossil

foster verb 1 bring up (a child who is not your own) 2 help or encourage • **foster child** noun a child fostered by a family • **foster parent** noun someone who fosters a child

fought past form of **fight**

foul adj 1 very dirty 2 smelling or tasting bad 3 stormy: foul weather/in a foul temper ◇ verb 1 become entangled 2 dirty 3 play unfairly ◇ noun a breaking of the rules of a game • **foul play** noun a criminal act

found[1] verb 1 establish, set up 2 shape by pouring melted metal into a mould • **foundation** noun 1 the underground structure on which a building rests 2 a sum of money left or set aside for a special purpose 3 the idea, fact, etc that is the basis of an argument, point of view, etc 4 an organization etc supported in this way 5 a cream applied to the skin before putting on make-up • **founder** noun someone who founds • **foundry** noun a workshop where metal founding is done

found[2] past form of **find**[1]

founder[1] verb 1 of a ship: sink 2 of a horse: stumble and go lame

---

Do not confuse with: **flounder**

---

founder[2] see **found**[1]

foundling noun a child abandoned by its parents

fountain noun 1 a rising jet of water 2 the pipe or structure from which it comes 3 the beginning of anything

four noun the number 4 ◇ adj 4 in number • **fourth** adj the last of a series of four ◇ noun 1 one of four equal parts 2 music an interval of four notes

fourteen noun the number 14 ◇ adj 14 in number • **fourteenth** adj the last of a series of fourteen ◇ noun one of fourteen equal parts

fowl noun a bird, esp a domestic cock or hen

fox noun (plural **foxes**) a wild animal related to the dog, with reddish-brown fur and a long bushy tail ◇ verb 1 trick by cleverness 2 puzzle, baffle • **foxhound** noun a breed of dog trained to chase foxes • **fox terrier** noun a breed of dog trained to drive foxes from their earths

foxglove noun a tall wild flower

foxtrot noun a ballroom dance made up of walking steps and turns

foxy adj (**foxier**, **foxiest**) 1 cunning 2 informal sexually attractive

foyer /foy-eh/ noun an entrance hall to a theatre, hotel, etc

FP abbrev Former Pupil(s)

fps abbrev frames (of photographic film) per second

fracas /frak-ah/ noun 1 a noisy quarrel 2 noisy commotion; uproar

fraction noun 1 a part, not a whole number, eg $1/4$ or $4/5$ 2 a small part

fractious adj irritated or quarrelsome

fracture noun a break in something hard, esp in a bone of the body

fragile adj easily broken • **fragility** noun

fragment noun a part broken off or a small part remaining ◊ verb break into pieces • **fragmentary** adj broken • **fragmentation** noun

fragrant adj sweet-smelling • **fragrance** noun sweet scent • **fragrantly** adv

frail adj 1 physically weak 2 easily tempted to behave immorally • **frailty** noun weakness

frame noun 1 a structure that surrounds or encloses something 2 build of human body 3 a single picture in a cinema film, strip cartoon, etc 4 state (of mind) ◊ verb 1 put a frame round 2 express or put together: how did you frame the answer? 3 slang make (someone) appear to be guilty of a crime • **framework** noun the outline or skeleton of something

franchise noun 1 the right to vote in a general election 2 a right to sell the goods of a particular company ◊ verb give a business franchise to

Franco- prefix of France; French: Francophile

frangipani noun perfume from red jasmine flowers

frank adj expressing opinions openly; candid ◊ verb mark a letter by machine to show that postage has been paid • **frankly** adv • **frankness** noun

frankfurter noun a smooth-skinned smoked sausage

frankincense noun a sweet-smelling resin used as incense

frantic adj wildly excited or anxious • **frantically** adv

fraternal adj of or typical of a brother • **fraternally** adv

fraternity noun (plural **fraternities**) 1 a group of men; a brotherhood 2 a North American male college society (compare with: **sorority**)

fraternize verb make friends with or spend time with

fratricide noun 1 the murder of a brother 2 someone who murders their brother

fraud noun 1 deliberate deception with the aim of gaining a benefit 2 a fake or impostor • **fraudulence** or **fraudulency** noun • **fraudulent** adj • **fraudulently** adv

fraught adj 1 anxious, tense 2 (with **with**) filled

fray verb wear away ◊ noun 1 a fight or brawl 2 a scene of lively action

freak noun 1 an unusual event 2 an odd or eccentric person 3 informal a keen fan: film freak

freckle noun a small brown spot on the skin

free adj 1 costing nothing 2 not imprisoned, shut in or contained; at liberty 3 generous 4 frank, open ◊ verb 1 make or set free 2 (with **from** or **of**) get rid (of) • **freebase** noun, slang refined cocaine • **freehand** adj of drawing: done without the help of rulers, tracing, etc • **freehold** adj of an estate: belonging to the holder or their heirs for all time • **freelance** or **freelancer** noun someone working independently (such as a writer who is not employed by any one newspaper)

• **freeloader** *noun, informal* someone who lives lazily on the hospitality of others; a sponger • **Freemason** *noun* a member of a men's society sworn to secrecy • **free radical** *noun* an atom containing an unpaired electron, some types of which can cause cancer if they enter the body • **free-range** *adj* **1** of poultry: allowed to move about freely and feed out of doors **2** of eggs: laid by poultry of this kind • **free speech** *noun* the right to express opinions of any kind • **freestyle** *adj* of swimming, skating, *etc*: in which any style may be used • **freeware** *noun* computer software that can legally be copied and distributed, but not resold for profit

-free *suffix* not containing or involving: *additive-free/cruelty-free*

freebie *noun, informal* a free event, performance, promotional gift, *etc*

freedom *noun* the fact of being free to go anywhere, say anything, *etc*; liberty

freeze *verb* (**freezing**, **froze**, **frozen**) **1** turn into ice **2** make (food) very cold in order to preserve **3** go stiff with cold, fear, *etc* **4** fix (prices or wages) at a certain level • **freezing point** *noun* the point at which liquid becomes a solid (of water, 0°C)

freezer *noun* a type of cabinet in which food is made, or kept, frozen

freight *noun* **1** goods carried by a vehicle; cargo **2** a charge for carrying a load • **freighter** *noun* a ship or aircraft that carries cargo • **freight train** *noun* a goods train

French *adj* of France or in a style originating in France • **French horn** *noun* a brass musical instrument consisting of a long looped tube with a very wide end • **French letter** *noun, Brit dated slang* a condom • **French polish** *noun* a kind of varnish for furniture • **French toast** *noun* bread dipped in egg and fried • **French window** *noun* a long window also used as a door • **take French leave** go or stay away without permission

frenetic *adj* wildly energetic or busy; frantic • **frenetically** *adv*

frenzy *noun* **1** a fit of madness **2** wild excitement • **frenzied** *adj* mad • **frenziedly** *adv*

frequent *adj* happening often ◇ *verb* visit often • **frequency** *noun* **1** the rate at which something happens **2** the number per second of vibrations, waves, *etc*

fresco *noun* (*plural* **frescoes** *or* **frescos**) a picture painted on a wall while the plaster is still damp

fresh *adj* **1** new, unused: *fresh sheet of paper* **2** newly made or picked; not preserved: *fresh fruit* **3** cool, refreshing: *fresh breeze* **4** not tired **5** cheeky, impertinent ◇ *adv* newly: *fresh-laid eggs* • **freshen** *verb* **1** make fresh **2** of wind *etc*: become stronger • **freshly** *adv* • **freshness** *noun* • **freshwater** *adj* of inland rivers, lakes, *etc*, not of the sea

fresher *or* **freshman** *noun* a first-year university student

fret[1] *verb* (**fretting**, **fretted**) worry or show discontent • **fretful** *adj* • **fretfully** *adv*

fret[2] *noun* one of the ridges on the neck of a guitar

fretsaw *noun* a narrow-bladed, fine-toothed saw for fretwork

fretwork *noun* decorative cut-out work in wood

Freudian /froyd-i-un/ *adj* revealing unexpressed or unconscious thoughts or desires • **Freudian slip** *noun* a mistake in speaking that reveals what you were really thinking but did not want to say

friar *noun* a member of one of the Roman Catholic brotherhoods, *esp* someone who has vowed to live in poverty • **friary** *noun* a friars' house

friction noun 1 rubbing of two things together 2 the force that prevents rough surfaces from moving smoothly over each other 3 the wear caused by rubbing 4 quarrelling or bad feeling

Friday noun the sixth day of the week

fridge noun, informal refrigerator

fried see fry[1]

friend noun 1 someone who likes and knows another person well 2 a sympathizer or helper

friendly adj (friendlier, friendliest) 1 kind 2 (with with) on good terms ◊ noun (plural friendlies) a sports match that is not part of a competition • friendliness noun

-friendly suffix 1 not harmful towards: dolphin-friendly 2 compatible with or easy to use for: child-friendly

friendship noun the state of being friends; mutual affection

fries see fry[1]

frieze noun 1 a part of a wall below the ceiling, often ornamented with designs 2 a picture on a long strip of paper etc, often displayed on a wall

frig verb (frigging, frigged) slang 1 masturbate 2 have sexual intercourse with • frigging adj used as a general term of annoyance or disgust

frigate noun a small warship

fright noun sudden fear: gave me a fright/took fright and ran away • frighten verb make afraid • frightening adj • frighteningly adv

frightful adj 1 causing terror 2 informal very bad • frightfully adv

frigid adj 1 sexually unresponsive 2 cold in manner 3 frozen, cold • frigidity noun • frigidly adv

frill noun 1 an ornamental edging 2 an unnecessary ornament

fringe noun 1 a border of loose threads 2 hair cut to hang over the forehead 3 a border of soft material, paper, etc ◊ verb edge round

Frisbee noun, trademark a plastic plate-like object skimmed through the air as a game

frisk verb 1 skip about playfully 2 informal search someone closely for concealed weapons etc • friskily adv • friskiness noun • frisky adj

frisson /free-sonh/ noun a shiver of fear or excitement; a thrill

fritter noun a piece of fried batter containing fruit etc

fritter away verb waste, squander

frivolity noun (plural frivolities) lack of seriousness

frivolous adj playful, not serious • frivolously adv

frizzy adj (frizzier, frizziest) of hair: massed in small curls

fro adv: to and fro forwards and backwards

frock noun 1 a woman's or girl's dress 2 a monk's wide-sleeved garment • frock coat noun a man's long coat

frog noun a small greenish jumping animal living on land and in water • frogman noun, informal an underwater diver with flippers and breathing apparatus • frogmarch verb seize (someone) from behind and push them forward while holding their arms tight behind their back

frolic verb (frolics, frolicking, frolicked) play light-heartedly ◊ noun a merry, light-hearted playing • frolicsome adj

from prep 1 used before the place, person, etc that is the starting point of an action etc: sailing from England to France/the office is closed from Friday to Monday/a present from my dad/translated from French/hanging from a nail 2 used to show separation: warn them to keep away from there

fromage frais /from-ahzh fre/ noun

a low-fat cheese with the consistency of whipped cream

frond noun a leaf-like growth, esp a branch of a fern or palm

front noun 1 the part of anything nearest the person who sees it 2 the part that faces the direction in which something moves 3 the fighting line in a war ◊ adj at or in the front ● **frontage** noun the front part of a building ● **in front of** at the head of or before

frontier noun 1 a boundary between countries 2 a limit: crossing the frontier of scientific knowledge

frontispiece noun a picture at the very beginning of a book

frost noun 1 frozen dew 2 the coldness of weather needed to form ice ◊ verb 1 cover with frost 2 US ice (a cake) ● **frostbite** noun damage to body tissues caused by very low temperatures ● **frosted** adj ● **frosting** noun, US icing on a cake etc ● **frosty** adj cold, unwelcoming: gave me a frosty look

froth noun foam on liquids ◊ verb throw up foam ● **frothy** adj

frown verb wrinkle the brows in deep thought, disapproval, etc ◊ noun 1 a wrinkling of the brows 2 a disapproving look ● **frown on** disapprove of

frowzy adj rough and tangled

froze and **frozen** see freeze

frugal adj 1 careful in spending; thrifty 2 not at all generous or plentiful; small: a frugal meal ● **frugality** noun ● **frugally** adv

fruit noun 1 a fleshy edible part of a plant that contains the seeds and generally has a sweet or bitter but not savoury flavour 2 formal the part of any plant containing the seed, including parts commonly referred to as vegetables 3 result: all their hard work bore fruit ● **fruitarian** noun someone who eats only fruit ● **fruiterer** noun someone who sells fruit ● **fruitful** adj

1 producing a lot of fruit 2 producing good results: a fruitful meeting ● **fruitless** adj useless, done in vain ● **fruit machine** noun a gambling machine into which coins are put

fruition noun a good and fully developed state

frump noun a plain, badly or unfashionably dressed woman ● **frumpish** adj

frustrate verb 1 cause to feel impatiently annoyed at not achieving or acquiring something 2 prevent from being done or fulfilled: frustrated his wishes ● **frustrated** adj ● **frustration** noun

fry[1] verb (**fries, frying, fried**) cook in hot fat ◊ noun (**fries**) pieces of fried potato; chips ● **fried** adj cooked in hot fat

fry[2] noun a young fish ● **small fry** unimportant people or things

ft abbrev foot, feet

ftp abbrev, comput file transfer protocol, by which large files and programs are accessed from a remote computer

FTSE abbrev the Financial Times Stock Exchange 100-Share Index, recording share prices of the 100 top UK companies

fuchsia /fyoo-shuh/ noun a plant with long hanging flowers

fuck verb, taboo slang have sexual intercourse (with) ◊ noun 1 an act of sexual intercourse 2 a sexual partner 3 something of little or no value ● **fucker** noun a general term of abuse ● **fuck about** or **around** play around, act foolishly ● **fuck all** nothing ● **fuck off** go away ● **fuck up** spoil by doing badly; mess up

fuddle verb confuse, muddle

fuddy-duddy noun (plural **fuddy-duddies**) a boringly conservative or unadventurous person

fudge¹ *noun* a soft, sugary sweet

fudge² *verb* **1** avoid giving a direct answer or clear opinion **2** cover up mistakes or problems relating to ◇ *noun* **1** a vague answer or opinion **2** a cover-up

fuel *noun* a substance such as coal, gas or petrol used to keep a fire or engine going

fugitive *noun* someone who is running away from the police *etc*: *a fugitive from justice* ◇ *adj* running away; on the run

fugue /fyoog/ *noun* a piece of music with several interwoven tunes

fulcrum *noun* (*plural* **fulcrums** or **fulcra**) the point on which a lever turns or a balanced object rests

fulfil *verb* (**fulfilling, fulfilled**) carry out (a task, promise, *etc*) • **fulfilment** *noun*

full *adj* **1** holding as much as can be held **2** plump or fleshy: *full face/lips* **3** complete: *a full day's work* ◇ *adv* (used with *adjs*) fully: *full-grown* • **full moon** *noun* the moon when it appears at its largest • **fullness** *noun* • **full stop** *noun* a punctuation mark (.) placed at the end of a sentence • **fully** *adv* • **full of** *adj* having a great deal or plenty of

fullback *noun* a defensive player in team games such as football

fulmar *noun* a large white sea bird

fulminate *verb, formal* **1** speak angrily or passionately against something **2** flash like lightning • **fulmination** *noun*

fulsome *adj, formal* overdone: *fulsome praise*

fumble *verb* **1** use the hands awkwardly **2** drop (a thrown ball *etc*)

fume *verb* **1** give off smoke or vapour **2** be in a silent rage

fumes *plural noun* smoke or vapour

fumigate *verb* kill germs by means of strong fumes • **fumigation** *noun*

fun *noun* a good time; enjoyment: *are you having fun?* • **funfair** *noun* an amusement park • **make fun of** make others laugh at; ridicule or tease

function *noun* **1** a special purpose or task of a machine, person, part of the body, *etc* **2** an arranged public gathering ◇ *verb* **1** work, operate: *the engine isn't functioning properly* **2** carry out usual duties: *I can't function at this time in the morning* • **functionary** *noun* an official

fund *noun* **1** a sum of money to be used for a special purpose: *charity fund* **2** a store or supply

fundamental *adj* **1** dealing with the most basic or essential elements: *fundamental principles/fundamental to her happiness* **2** of great or far-reaching importance ◇ *noun* **1** (**fundamentals**) the first stages **2** a necessary part • **fundamentalism** *noun* the beliefs or actions of someone who follows religious or political principles very strictly, *usu* to an extent that seems excessive to most people • **fundamentalist** *noun & adj*

funeral *noun* the ceremony of burial or cremation • **funereal** *adj* mournful

fungus *noun* (*plural* **fungi** /fung-gee/) **1** a soft, spongy plant growth, *eg* a mushroom **2** disease-growth on animals and plants

funicular railway *noun* a railway with carriages pulled uphill by a cable

funk *noun, dated informal* fear, panic

funky *adj* (**funkier, funkiest**) *informal* **1** fashionable, trendy **2** odd, eccentric **3** of music: with a strong, rhythmical, uplifting or stirring beat

funnel *noun* **1** a cone ending in a tube, for pouring liquids into bottles **2** a tube or passage for escape of smoke, air, *etc* ◇ *verb* (**funnelling, funnelled**) pass through a funnel; channel

funny *adj* (**funnier, funniest**) **1** amusing

2 odd • **funnily** adv • **funny bone** noun part of the elbow that gives a prickly feeling when knocked

fur noun **1** the short fine hair of certain animals **2** their skins covered with fur **3** a coating on the tongue, on the inside of kettles, etc ◇ verb (**furring**, **furred**) line or cover with fur • **furrier** noun someone who trades in or works with furs

furbish verb rub until bright; burnish

furious adj extremely angry • **furiously** adv

furlong noun one-eighth of a mile (220 yards, 201.17 metres)

furnace noun a very hot oven for melting iron ore, making steam for heating, etc

furnish verb **1** provide furniture and fittings for (a room, house, etc) **2** supply: furnished with enough food for a week • **furnishings** plural noun fittings and furniture

furniture noun movable articles in a house, eg tables, chairs

furore /fyoo-raw-reh/ noun uproar; excitement

furrow noun **1** a groove made by a plough **2** a deep groove **3** a deep wrinkle ◇ verb **1** cut deep grooves in **2** wrinkle: furrowed brow

furry adj (**furrier**, **furriest**) covered with fur

further adv & adj **1** to a greater distance or degree: can't walk any further/no further delay **2** in addition: nothing further to say/take further steps to solve the problem ◇ verb help the progress of • **furthermore** adv in addition to what has been said • **furthest** adv to the greatest distance or degree

furtive adj stealthy, sly: furtive glance • **furtively** adv

fury noun violent anger

furze another name for **gorse**

fuse verb (**fusing**, **fused**) **1** melt **2** join together **3** put a fuse in (a plug etc) **4** of a circuit etc: stop working because of the melting of a fuse ◇ noun **1** easily-melted wire put in an electric circuit for safety **2** any device for causing an explosion to take place automatically

fuselage /fyoo-zuh-lahzh/ noun the body of an aeroplane

fusion noun **1** melting **2** a merging: a fusion of musical traditions (see also **nuclear fusion**)

fuss noun **1** unnecessary activity, excitement or attention, often about something unimportant: making a fuss about nothing **2** strong complaint ◇ verb **1** be unnecessarily concerned about details **2** worry too much

fussy adj (**fussier**, **fussiest**) **1** too concerned about details **2** clearly favouring one thing over another: either will do; I'm not fussy **3** over-elaborate: a fussy design • **fussily** adv • **fussiness** noun

fusty adj (**fustier**, **fustiest**) mouldy or stale-smelling

futile adj having no effect; useless • **futility** noun uselessness

futon /foo-ton/ noun a sofa bed with a low frame and detachable mattress

future adj happening later in time ◇ noun **1** the time to come: foretell the future **2** the part of your life still to come: planning for their future **3** grammar the tense of verbs used for talking about future time

fuzz noun **1** fine, light hair or feathers **2** Brit slang the police • **fuzzy** adj **1** covered with fuzz; fluffy **2** tightly curled: fuzzy hairdo

Gg

g *abbrev* gram

gabble *verb* talk fast; chatter ◇ *noun* fast talk

gaberdine *noun* **1** a closely woven woollen fabric **2** a heavy overcoat

gable *noun* the triangular area of wall at the end of a building with a ridged roof

gadabout *noun, dated informal* someone who loves going out or travelling

gadfly *noun* (*plural* **gadflies**) a fly that bites cattle

gadget *noun* a small simple machine or tool

Gaelic /gal-ik/ *noun* **1** an ancient Celtic language spoken by some people in the Scottish Highlands **2** an ancient Celtic language spoken in some parts of Ireland ◇ *adj* written or spoken in Gaelic

gaff *noun* **1** a large hook used for landing large fish such as salmon **2** a pole used for raising the top of a sail • **blow the gaff** *informal* let out a secret

gaffe *noun* a socially embarrassing remark or action

gag *verb* (**gagging, gagged**) **1** silence by stuffing something in the mouth **2** prevent from speaking openly or telling the truth ◇ *noun* **1** a piece of cloth *etc* put in or over someone's mouth to silence them **2** *informal* a joke

gaggle *noun* a flock of geese

gaiety and **gaily** *see* **gay**

gain *verb* **1** win or earn **2** reach (a place) **3** get closer, *esp* in a race: gaining on the leader **4** of a clock: go ahead of the correct time **5** take on (*eg* weight) ◇ *noun* **1** something gained **2** profit

gainsay *verb, formal* deny

gait *noun* way of walking

Do not confuse with: **gate**

---

gaiter *noun* a covering that fits over the top of a shoe and reaches up over the ankle or to the knee

gala *noun* **1** a public festival **2** a sports meeting: swimming gala

galaxy *noun* (*plural* **galaxies**) **1** a system of stars **2** an impressive gathering • **the Galaxy** the Milky Way

gale *noun* a strong wind

gall /gawl/ *noun* **1** a bitter liquid produced by the liver and stored in the **gall bladder**; bile **2** bitterness of feeling **3** a growth on trees and plants caused by infestation with insects ◇ *verb* annoy or make bitter • **galling** *adj* annoying or frustrating

gallant *adj* **1** brave, noble **2** of a man: polite or attentive towards women ◇ *noun* a gallant man • **gallantry** *noun*

galleon *noun, hist* a large Spanish sailing ship

gallery *noun* (*plural* **galleries**) **1** a room or building for displaying works of art **2** the top floor of seats in a theatre **3** a long passage

galley *noun* (*plural* **galleys**) **1** *hist* a long, low-built ship driven by oars **2** a ship's kitchen • **galley slave** *noun,* *hist* a prisoner condemned to row in a galley

gallivant *verb, informal* travel or go out for pleasure

gallon *noun* a measure for liquids (8 pints, 3.636 litres)

gallop *verb* **1** of a horse: move at the fastest running pace **2** move or develop very fast ◇ *noun* a fast pace, or a ride at a fast pace

gallows *sing noun* a wooden framework on which criminals were hanged

gallus /gal-us/ *adj, Scot* full of spirit or character; bold

galore *adv* in plenty: *whisky galore*

galosh or **golosh** *noun* (*plural* **galoshes** or **goloshes**) a rubber shoe worn over ordinary shoes in wet weather

galvanic *adj* produced by the action of acids or other chemicals on metal • **galvanism** *noun* • **galvanometer** *noun* an instrument for measuring electric currents

galvanize *verb* **1** provoke into taking action **2** coat (iron *etc*) with zinc using chemicals and electricity **3** stimulate by electricity

gambit *noun* **1** *chess* a first move involving sacrificing a piece to make the player's position stronger **2** an opening move in a transaction, or an opening remark in a conversation

gamble *verb* **1** play games for money **2** risk money on the result of a game, race, *etc* **3** take a wild chance ◇ *noun* **1** a bet on a result **2** a risk

gambol *verb* (**gambolling**, **gambolled**) leap playfully

game *noun* **1** a contest played according to rules **2** (**games**) an athletics competition **3** wild animals and birds hunted for sport ◇ *adj* **1** full of confidence and courage; plucky **2** *old* of a limb: lame • **gamekeeper** *noun*

someone who looks after game birds, animals, fish, *etc* • **gaming** *noun & adj* gambling • **big game** large animals that are hunted, *eg* lions

gammon *noun* salted and smoked meat from the leg of a pig

gamut *noun* **1** the whole range or extent of anything **2** the range of notes of an individual voice or musical instrument

gander *noun* a male goose

gang *noun* **1** a group of people who meet regularly **2** a team of criminals **3** a number of labourers

gangrene *noun* the rotting of some part of the body • **gangrenous** *adj*

gangsta *noun* **1** a style of rap music with violent lyrics **2** a singer of this kind of music

gangster *noun* a member of a gang of criminals

gangway *noun* **1** a passage between rows of seats **2** a movable bridge leading from a quay to a ship

gannet *noun* a large white sea bird

gantry *noun* (*plural* **gantries**) a platform or structure for supporting a travelling crane *etc*

gaol *another spelling of* **jail**

gaoler *another spelling of* **jailer**

gap *noun* **1** an opening or space between things **2** a difference or disparity: *the generation gap* • **gap year** a year spent by a student between school and university doing non-academic activities

gape *verb* **1** open the mouth wide (as in surprise) **2** be wide open

garage *noun* **1** a building for storing a car (or cars) **2** a business that carries out car repairs, sells cars, sells petrol, *etc*

garam masala /ga-rum muh-*sah*-luh/ *noun* a mixture of ground spices used in Asian cookery

garb noun, formal dress ◇ verb clothe

garbage noun **1** things thrown away; rubbish **2** stupid things said or written; nonsense

garble verb mix up; muddle: garbled account of events

Garda noun **1** the police force of the Republic of Ireland **2** a police officer in the Garda

garden noun a piece of ground on which flowers or vegetables are grown ◇ verb work in a garden • **gardener** noun someone who looks after a garden • **garden party** noun a large tea party held outdoors

gardenia noun a tropical plant producing large, waxy white flowers

gargantuan adj extremely large; huge

gargle verb rinse the throat with a liquid, without swallowing

gargoyle noun a grotesque carving of a human or animal head, jutting out from a roof

garish adj tastelessly over-bright: a garish book cover • **garishness** noun

garland noun flowers or leaves tied or woven into a circle

garlic noun an onion-like plant with a strong smell and taste, used in cooking

garment noun an article of clothing

garner verb, formal collect and store; gather

garnet noun a semi-precious stone, usually red in colour

garnish verb decorate (a dish of food) ◇ noun (plural **garnishes**) a decoration on food • **garnishing** noun

garret noun an attic room

garrison noun a body of troops guarding a town or other position, or the building they occupy

garrotte verb strangle by tightening a wire, cord, etc round the neck

garrulous adj fond of talking • **garrulity** or **garrulousness** noun

garter noun a wide elastic band worn round the thigh to keep a stocking up

gas noun (plural **gases**) **1** a substance that, like air, has no fixed shape and expands to fill the available space **2** any such natural or manufactured substance used as a fuel **3** US petrol ◇ verb (**gases, gassing, gassed**) poison with gas • **gaseous** adj • **gas mask** noun a covering for the face to prevent breathing in poisonous gas • **gasometer** noun a huge tank for storing gas • **gasworks** noun a factory where gas is made

gash noun (plural **gashes**) a deep, open cut ◇ verb cut deeply into

gasket noun a paper disc or other padding placed between the two sides of a joined tube, pipe, etc to make the joint airtight or gas-tight

gasoline noun, US petrol

gasp noun the sound made by a sudden intake of breath prompted by surprise, pain, etc ◇ verb **1** make a gasp **2** breathe with difficulty **3** say breathlessly **4** informal want badly: gasping for a cup of tea

gastric adj relating to the stomach: gastric ulcer

gate noun **1** a door across an opening in a wall, fence, etc **2** the number of people at a football match **3** the total entrance money paid by those at a football match

---

Do not confuse with: **gait**

---

gateau /gat-oh/ noun (plural **gateaus** or **gateaux**) a rich cake, usually layered and filled with cream

gatecrash verb go to (a party) uninvited • **gatecrasher** noun

gateway noun **1** an opening containing a gate **2** an entrance **3** *comput* a connection between networks

gather *verb* **1** bring together, or meet, in one place **2** pick (flowers *etc*) **3** increase in: *gather speed* **4** come to the conclusion (that); learn: *I gather you don't want to go* • **gathering** *noun* a crowd

gauche /gohsh/ *adj* awkward and clumsy in people's company

gaucho /gow-choh/ *noun* (*plural* **gauchos**) a cowboy of the South American plains, noted for horse-riding

gaudy *adj* (**gaudier, gaudiest**) vulgarly bright in colour; showy • **gaudily** *adv* • **gaudiness** *noun*

gauge /gehj/ *verb* **1** measure **2** make a guess about; estimate ◇ *noun* **1** a measuring device **2** size from side to side; width or thickness • **broad gauge** or **narrow gauge** a distance between the rails on a railway that is greater or less than the standard distance (4ft 8in, 1.435 metre)

gaunt *adj* unhealthily thin or thin-faced; haggard

gauntlet¹ *noun* **1** a long glove with a guard for the wrist, used by motorcyclists *etc* **2** *hist* an iron glove worn with armour • **take up the gauntlet** accept a challenge • **throw down the gauntlet** offer a challenge

gauntlet² *noun*: **run the gauntlet** expose yourself to criticism, hostility, *etc*

gauze *noun* thin cloth that can be seen through

gavel *noun* a small hammer used by a judge or auctioneer

gavotte /guh-*vot*/ *noun* a lively type of dance

gawky *adj* (**gawkier, gawkiest**) physically awkward

gawp *verb* stare in an overly curious or interested way

gay *adj* **1** homosexual **2** full of fun;

merry **3** brightly coloured ◇ *noun* a homosexual person, *esp* a man • **gaiety** *noun* • **gaily** *adv*

gaze *verb* look steadily ◇ *noun* a fixed look

gazebo /guh-zee-boh/ *noun* (*plural* **gazebos**) an open-sided wooden or canvas shelter in a garden

gazelle *noun* a small agile deer found in Africa and Asia

gazette *noun* a newspaper, *orig* one containing lists of government notices • **gazetteer** *noun* a geographical dictionary

gazpacho /gas-*pach*-oh/ *noun* a Spanish chilled soup of crushed garlic, tomatoes and peppers

gazump /guh-*zump*/ *verb, informal* raise the price of property after accepting a verbal offer from (someone), but before contracts are signed

gazunder /guh-zun-duh/ *verb, informal* lower an offer for property being sold by (someone) just before contracts are signed

GB *abbrev* **1** Great Britain **2** (**Gb**) gigabyte

GBH or **gbh** *abbrev* grievous bodily harm

GC *abbrev* George Cross

GCSE *abbrev* General Certificate of Secondary Education, an examination taken by pupils at age 16 in England and Wales

GDP *abbrev* gross domestic product

gear *noun* **1** clothing and equipment needed for a particular job, sport, *etc* **2** a connection by means of a set of toothed wheels between a car engine and the wheels ◇ *verb* (with **to**) adapt to or design for

geek *noun, informal* an eccentric or socially awkward person

geese *plural of* **goose**

geisha /geh-shuh/ *noun* a Japanese

girl trained to entertain men

gel /jel/ *noun* a jelly-like substance, *esp* one used for fixing the hair in place

gelatine *noun* a jelly-like substance made from animal bones and used in food

gelatinous *adj* jelly-like

geld *verb* castrate (an animal)

gelding *noun* a castrated horse

gem *noun* 1 a precious stone, *esp* when cut 2 something greatly valued

gendarme /zhonh-dahm/ *noun* a member of a French armed police force

gender *noun* 1 the fact of being either male or female; sex: *gender-specific diseases* 2 (in grammar, *esp* in languages other than English) any of three types of noun: masculine, feminine or neuter

gene *noun* the basic unit of heredity responsible for passing on specific characteristics from parents to offspring

genealogy *noun* (*plural* **genealogies**) 1 the history of families from generation to generation 2 a personal family history • **genealogical** *adj* • **genealogist** *noun* someone who studies or makes genealogies

general *adj* 1 not detailed; broad: *a general idea of the person's interests* 2 involving everyone: *a general election* 3 to do with several different things: *general knowledge* 4 of most people: *the general opinion* ◇ *noun* a high-ranking army officer • **generally** *adv* 1 in most cases, usually 2 by most people: *generally known* • **general practitioner** *noun* a doctor who treats most ordinary illnesses • **in general** generally

generalize *verb* make a broad general statement, meant to cover all individual cases • **generalization** *noun* a view, statement, *etc* that is too general

generate *verb* cause to exist; produce: *generate electricity/generate goodwill* • **generator** *noun* a machine for making electricity *etc*

generation *noun* 1 a single stage in family descent, or the time between the birth of a person and their children, reckoned at around 30 years 2 people born at about the same time: *the 90s generation* 3 creation, making

generic *adj* 1 applicable to any member of a group or class; general 2 of a product: sold under the name of the supermarket or other shop selling it, or under no name at all

generous *adj* giving plentifully; kind • **generosity** *noun* • **generously** *adv*

genesis *noun* beginning, origin

genetic *adj* 1 relating to genes 2 inherited through genes: *genetic disease* • **genetically** *adv* • **genetically modified** *adj* containing genes that have been technologically altered to produce certain characteristics that are not natural: *genetically modified soya beans* • **genetic engineering** *noun* changes made to the genes of an organism to produce characteristics that are not natural • **genetic fingerprinting** *noun* chemical analysis of DNA from samples of blood, hair, *etc* carried out to determine a person's identity, *esp* for the purposes of criminal investigation • **genetics** *sing noun* the study of genes

genial *adj* good-natured • **geniality** *noun* • **genially** *adv*

genie *noun* (*plural* **genii**) a guardian spirit

genitals *plural noun* the organs of sexual reproduction

genius *noun* (*plural* **geniuses**) 1 unusual cleverness 2 someone who is unusually clever

genocide *noun* the deliberate extermination of a race of people • **genocidal** *adj*

genome *noun* the full set of genes of a living thing: *the human genome*

genotype *noun* the full set of genes of an individual person or animal

genre /zhonh-ruh/ *noun* a particular type of literature, music, *etc*

gent *noun, informal* a man • **the gents** *informal* a men's public toilet

genteel *adj* well-mannered, *esp* in a way that seems insincere or excessive

gentile /jen-tail/ *noun* a person who is not Jewish

gentility *noun* **1** good manners, refinement, often in excess **2** aristocracy

gentle *adj* **1** mild-mannered, not cruel or violent **2** mild, not extreme: *gentle breeze* • **gentleness** *noun* • **gently** *adv*

gentleman *noun* (*plural* **gentlemen**) **1** a polite word for a man **2** a well-mannered or honourable man **3** an aristocratic man • **gentlemanly** *adj* behaving in a polite manner

gentrify *verb* (**gentrifies, gentrifying, gentrified**) change a residential area in ways that make it more middle-class

gentry *noun* wealthy, land-owning people who are not members of the aristocracy

genuine *adj* **1** real, not fake: *genuine antique* **2** honest and straightforward in dealings with people • **genuinely** *adv* • **genuineness** *noun*

genus *noun* (*plural* **genera**) (in the classification of plants and animals) a group that is larger than a species and smaller than a family

geography *noun* the study of the surface of the earth and its inhabitants • **geographer** *noun* someone who studies geography • **geographic** *or* **geographical** *adj*

geology *noun* the study of the earth's history as shown in its rocks and soils • **geological** *adj* • **geologist** *noun* someone who studies geology

geometric *or* **geometrical** *adj* of a shape or pattern: made up of angles and straight lines

geometry *noun* the branch of mathematics that deals with the study of lines, angles, and figures • **geometric** *or* **geometrical** *adj* **1** to do with geometry **2** of a pattern: using lines and simple shapes • **geometrician** *noun* someone who studies geometry

Geordie *noun, Brit informal* someone who was born or lives in Newcastle or, loosely, on Tyneside

geranium *noun* a plant with thick leaves and bright red or pink flowers

gerbil /jur-bil/ *noun* a small, rat-like desert animal, often kept as a pet

geriatric *adj* **1** for or dealing with old people **2** *informal* very old ◇ *noun* an old person

germ *noun* **1** a small living organism that can cause disease **2** the earliest or initial form of something, *eg* a fertilized egg **3** something from which anything grows: *germ of an idea* • **germicide** *noun* a germ-killing substance

germane *adj* very relevant or closely related • **germanely** *adv*

German shepherd *noun* a breed of large wolf-like dog; an alsatian

germinate *verb* begin to grow; sprout • **germination** *noun*

gerrymander *verb* dishonestly rearrange (voting districts *etc*) to suit a political purpose • **gerrymandering** *noun*

gerund *noun* a noun with the ending *-ing*, *eg* watch*ing*, wait*ing*

gesso /jes-oh/ noun (plural **gessoes**) 1 plaster of Paris 2 a plastered surface for painting on

gesticulate verb wave the hands and arms about in excitement etc • **gesticulation** noun • **gesticulatory** adj

gesture noun 1 a meaningful action with the hands, head, etc 2 an action expressing your feelings or intent: a gesture of good will

get verb (**getting**, **got** or US **getting**, **got**, **gotten**) 1 obtain: get a pay rise 2 fetch: I'll get more chairs 3 possess or carry: have you got the tickets? 4 cause to be done: get your hair cut 5 receive: get a letter/not getting a good picture on the TV 6 cause to be in some condition: get the car started/get your hair wet 7 arrive: what time did you get home? 8 catch or have (a disease): I think I've got flu 9 become: get rich • **get at** 1 reach 2 hint at: what are you getting at? 3 criticize continually: stop getting at me 4 slang try to influence by bribes or threats • **get away with** escape punishment for • **get on with** be on friendly terms with • **get over** recover from • **get up** 1 stand up 2 get out of bed

geyser /gee-zuh/ noun 1 a natural hot spring 2 a device that heats domestic water when the tap is turned on

ghastly adj (**ghastlier**, **ghastliest**) 1 very ill: feeling ghastly 2 horrible, ugly 3 unhealthily or frighteningly pale 4 very bad • **ghastliness** noun

ghee /gee/ noun clarified butter used in Asian cookery

gherkin noun a small pickled cucumber

ghetto noun (plural **ghettos**) a poor residential part of a city in which a certain group (esp of immigrants) lives

ghost noun the spirit of a dead person • **ghostly** adj like a ghost

ghoul /gool/ noun 1 an evil spirit which robs dead bodies 2 someone unnaturally interested in death and disaster • **ghoulish** adj

GHQ abbrev general headquarters

giant noun 1 an imaginary being like a human but enormous 2 a very tall or large person ◊ adj huge

giantess noun a female giant

gibber /jib-uh/ verb 1 speak nonsense 2 make meaningless noises; babble

gibberish noun words without meaning or sense; rubbish

gibbet noun, hist a gallows where criminals were executed, or hung up after execution

gibbon noun a large, tailless ape

gibe another spelling of **jibe**

giblets plural noun edible organs from the inside of a chicken etc

giddy adj (**giddier**, **giddiest**) 1 unsteady, dizzy 2 causing dizziness: from a giddy height • **giddily** adv • **giddiness** noun

gift noun 1 something freely given, eg a present 2 a natural talent: a gift for music 3 informal something easily done: the exam paper was a gift • **gifted** adj having special natural power or ability • **look a gift horse in the mouth** find fault with a gift

gigabyte noun, comput a measure of data storage equal to 1024 megabytes

gigantic adj of giant size; huge • **gigantically** adv

giggle verb laugh in a nervous or silly manner ◊ noun a nervous or silly laugh

gigolo /jig-uh-loh/ noun a male lover kept by a woman at her expense

gigot /jig-ut/ noun a leg of mutton or lamb

gild verb 1 cover with a thin coating of gold 2 make bright • **gild the lily** try to improve something already beautiful enough

---

Do not confuse with: **guild**

---

gill[1] /jil/ noun a measure ($\frac{1}{4}$ pint, 11.36 centilitres) for liquids

gill[2] /gil/ noun one of the openings on the side of a fish's head through which it breathes

gillie /gil-i/ noun an assistant and guide to someone fishing or shooting on a Scottish estate

gilt adj 1 covered with thin gold 2 gold in colour ◇ noun thin gold used for gilding • **gilt-edged** adj not risky, safe to invest in: gilt-edged stocks

---

Do not confuse with: **guilt**

---

gimcrack /jim-krak/ adj, dated derog cheap and badly-made

gimlet noun a small tool for boring holes by hand

gimmick noun something meant to attract attention

gin[1] noun an alcoholic drink made from grain, flavoured with juniper berries

gin[2] noun a trap or snare

ginger noun a spicy root used as a seasoning in food, or the powdered spice prepared from it ◇ adj 1 flavoured with ginger 2 reddish-brown in colour: ginger hair

gingerbread noun cake flavoured with ginger

gingerly adv very carefully and gently: opened the door gingerly

gingham /ging-um/ noun a striped or checked cotton cloth

gingival /jin-jai-vul/ adj relating to the gums

gingivitis /jin-ji-vai-tus/ noun inflammation of the gums

ginkgo /ging-koh/ noun (plural **ginkgoes**) a Chinese tree with fan-shaped leaves

ginseng /jin-seng/ noun a root grown in the Far East, believed to have restorative powers

Gipsy another spelling of **Gypsy**

giraffe noun an African animal with very long legs and neck

gird verb, formal bind round • **gird up your loins** prepare to deal with a difficult situation

girder noun a beam of iron, steel or wood used in building

girdle noun 1 a tight-fitting piece of underwear to slim the waist 2 old a belt for the waist

girl noun a female child or young woman • **girlfriend** noun a regular female companion, especially in a romantic relationship • **girlhood** noun the state or time of being a girl • **girlie** adj 1 girlish 2 pornographic: girlie magazines • **girlish** adj like a girl

giro /jai-roh/ noun (plural **giros**) 1 a system by which payment may be made through banks, post offices, etc 2 (also called **girocheque**) a form like a cheque by which such payment is made 3 informal social security paid by girocheque

girth noun 1 measurement round the middle 2 a strap tying a saddle on a horse

gismo or **gizmo** noun (plural **gismos** or **gizmos**), informal 1 a gadget 2 a thing of which you do not know or cannot remember the name

gist /jist/ noun the main points or ideas of a story, argument, etc: give me the gist of the story

give verb (**giving**, **gave**, **given**) 1 hand over freely or in exchange 2 utter (a shout or cry) 3 break, crack: the bridge gave under the weight of the train 4 produce: this lamp gives a good light • **giver** noun • **give away**

1 hand over (something) to someone without payment **2** betray • **give in** stop trying or resisting and admit defeat; yield • **give over** *informal* stop (doing something) • **give rise to** cause • **give up 1** hand over **2** stop trying or resisting and admit defeat; yield **3** stop, abandon (a habit *etc*) • **give way 1** let traffic crossing your path go before you **2** collapse **3** stop opposing or resisting; yield

glacé *adj* iced or sugared: *glacé cherries*

glacial *adj* **1** of ice or glaciers **2** icy, cold: *glacial expression*

glacier *noun* a slowly-moving river of ice in valleys between high mountains

glad *adj* **1** pleased: *I'm glad you were able to come* **2** giving pleasure: *glad tidings* • **glad eye** *noun* an ogle • **glad hand** *noun* a ready but insincere welcome • **gladly** *adv* • **gladness** *noun* • **glad rags** *plural noun* best clothes

gladden *verb* make glad

glade *noun* an open space in a wood

gladiator *noun, hist* in ancient Rome, a man trained to fight with other men or with animals for the amusement of spectators • **gladiatorial** *adj*

glaikit *adj, Scot* stupid or stupid-looking

glam *adj, slang* glamorous

glamour *noun* **1** physical attractiveness created by fashionable clothes, hairstyle, make-up, *etc* **2** impressive wealth and celebrity: *the glamour of a footballer's life* • **glamorous** *adj* • **glamorously** *adv*

glance *noun* a quick look ◇ *verb* take a quick look at • **glance off** hit and fly off sideways

gland *noun* a part of the body that takes substances from the blood and stores them for later use or elimination by the body • **glandular** *adj*

glare *noun* **1** an unpleasantly bright light **2** an angry or fierce look ◇ *verb* **1** shine with an unpleasantly bright light **2** look angrily

glaring *adj* **1** dazzling **2** very clear; obvious: *glaring mistake* • **glaringly** *adv*

glass *noun* (*plural* **glasses**) **1** a hard transparent substance used to make windows, bottles, *etc* **2** a drinking container made of glass **3** (**glasses**) lenses in a frame worn over the eyes to correct poor eyesight; spectacles **4** *old* a mirror ◇ *adj* made of glass • **glass ceiling** *noun* a barrier to promotion at work experienced by some women but not officially recognized • **glasshouse** *noun* a greenhouse

glassy *adj* (**glassier**, **glassiest**) of eyes: without expression • **glassily** *adv*

glaucoma /glaw-*koh*-muh/ *noun* an eye disease causing dimness in sight

glaze *verb* **1** cover with a thin coating of glass or other shiny stuff **2** ice (a cake *etc*) **3** put panes of glass in a window **4** of eyes: become glassy ◇ *noun* **1** a shiny surface, *esp* applied to pottery **2** sugar icing • **glazier** *noun* someone who sets glass in window-frames

gleam *verb* **1** glow **2** flash ◇ *noun* **1** a beam of light **2** brightness

glean *verb* **1** collect (information) bit by bit **2** *old* gather corn in handfuls after the reapers

glee *noun* **1** joy **2** a song in parts

gleeful *adj* merry • **gleefully** *adv*

glen *noun* in Scotland, a long narrow valley

glib *adj* **1** quickly said and showing little thought: *glib reply* **2** speaking fluently but insincerely and superficially • **glibly** *adv* • **glibness** *noun*

glide *verb* **1** move smoothly and easily **2** travel by glider ◇ *noun* the act of gliding

glider noun a lightweight aeroplane without an engine, towed into the sky by another aeroplane

glimmer noun 1 a faint light 2 a faint indication: *a glimmer of hope* ◇ verb burn or shine faintly

glimpse noun a brief view ◇ verb get a brief look at

glint verb sparkle, gleam ◇ noun a sparkle or gleam

glisten verb sparkle because wet or icy

glitch noun a sudden brief failure to function, *esp* in electronic equipment

glitter verb sparkle ◇ noun 1 sparkling 2 shiny granules used for decorating paper *etc* • **glittery** adj

glitzy adj (**glitzier**, **glitziest**) superficially attractive or glamorous • **glitz** noun

gloaming noun twilight, dusk

gloat verb look at or think about with malicious joy: *gloating over their rivals' defeat*

global adj 1 of or affecting the whole world: *global warming* 2 applying generally: *global increase in earnings* • **global village** noun the modern world of fast international travel and instant communication

globalize verb (**globalizing**, **globalized**) to spread commercial or cultural activities into all parts of the world • **globalization** noun

globe noun 1 the earth 2 a ball with a map of the world drawn on it 3 a ball, a sphere 4 a glass covering for a lamp

globule noun 1 a droplet 2 a small ball-shaped piece • **globular** adj ball-shaped

gloom noun 1 dullness or darkness 2 sadness or pessimism • **gloomily** adv • **gloomy** adj 1 sad, depressed 2 dimly lit

glorify verb (**glorifies**, **glorifying**, **glorified**) 1 make glorious 2 praise highly

glorious adj 1 splendid 2 deserving great praise 3 delightful • **gloriously** adv

glory noun (*plural* **glories**) 1 fame, honour 2 impressive appearance or display; splendour ◇ verb take great pleasure (in)

gloss noun 1 brightness on the surface 2 paint for wood or metal that gives a hard shiny finish ◇ verb 1 make bright 2 write an explanatory note about 3 (with **over**) try to hide (a fault *etc*) by treating it quickly or superficially • **glossy** adj shiny or highly polished

glossary noun (*plural* **glossaries**) a list of words with their meanings

glove noun 1 a covering for the hand with a separate part for each finger 2 a boxing glove

glow verb 1 burn without flame 2 give out a steady light 3 be flushed from heat, cold, *etc* 4 be radiant with emotion: *glow with pride* ◇ noun 1 a glowing state 2 great heat 3 bright light • **glowing** adj 1 giving out a steady light 2 flushed 3 radiant 4 full of praise: *glowing report* • **glow-worm** noun a kind of beetle that glows in the dark

glower /glow-uh/ verb stare (at) with an angry frown; scowl (at) • **glowering** adj 1 scowling 2 threatening

glucose noun a sugar found in fruits *etc*

glue noun a substance for sticking things together ◇ verb join with glue • **gluey** adj sticky

glum adj (**glummer**, **glummest**) sad, gloomy • **glumly** adv • **glumness** noun

glut noun an over-supply: *a glut of fish on the market* ◇ verb (**glutting**, **glutted**) 1 supply too much to (a market) 2 feed greedily till full

gluten *noun* a sticky protein found in wheat, oats and other cereals

glutinous *adj* sticky, gluey

glutton *noun* **1** someone who eats too much **2** someone who is eager for anything: *a glutton for punishment* ● **gluttonous** *adj* **1** fond of overeating **2** eating greedily ● **gluttony** *noun* greed in eating

glycerine *noun* a colourless, sticky, sweet-tasting liquid

GM *abbrev* genetically modified, or made with genetically modified crops: *GM crops/foods*

GMT *abbrev* Greenwich Mean Time

gnarled /narld/ *adj* knotty, twisted

gnash /nash/ *verb* grind (the teeth)

gnat /nat/ *noun* a small blood-sucking fly; a midge

gnaw /naw/ *verb* bite at with a scraping action

gnome /nohm/ *noun* a small imaginary human-like creature who lives underground, often guarding treasure

GNP *abbrev* gross national product

gnu /noo/ *noun* a type of African antelope

GNVQ *abbrev* General National Vocational Qualification, an examination in a vocational subject

go *verb* (**goes, going, went, gone**) **1** to move: *I want to go home/when are you going to Paris?* **2** leave: *time to go* **3** lead: *that road goes north* **4** become: *go mad* **5** work: *the car is going at last* **6** intend (to do): *I'm going to have a bath* **7** be removed or taken: *the best seats have all gone now* **8** be given, awarded, *etc*: *the first prize went to Janet* **9** fit into available space *etc*: *these clothes won't go in the drawer/five into three doesn't go* ◇ *noun* **1** the act or process of going **2** energy, spirit **3** *informal* an attempt, a try: *have a go* ● **go-ahead** *adj* eager to succeed ◇ *noun* permission to

act ● **go-between** *noun* someone who helps two people to communicate with each other ● **go kart** *noun* a small low-powered racing car ● **go-slow** *noun* a slowing of speed at work as a form of protest ● **from the word go** from the start ● **go about** deal with; tackle ● **go ahead** proceed (with) ● **go along with** agree with ● **go back on** fail to keep (a promise *etc*) ● **go for 1** aim to get **2** attack ● **go off 1** explode **2** become rotten **3** come to dislike ● **go on 1** continue **2** talk too much ● **go round** be enough for everyone: *will the trifle go round?* ● **go steady with** have a stable romantic relationship with; date ● **go the whole hog** do something thoroughly ● **go through 1** experience or suffer **2** be officially accepted or passed ● **go under** be ruined ● **go up 1** increase **2** ascend ● **go without** have to survive without having ● **on the go** very active

goad *verb* provoke into angry behaviour ◇ *noun* **1** provocation **2** a stick for driving cattle

goal *noun* **1** the upright posts between which the ball is to be driven in football and other games **2** a score in football and other games **3** anything aimed at or wished for: *my goal is to get to Z*

goat *noun* an animal of the sheep family with horns and a long-haired coat

goatee *noun* a pointed beard growing only on the front of the chin

gob *noun, slang* the mouth ● **gob-smacked** *adj, slang* shocked, astonished ● **gobstopper** *noun* a hard round sweet for sucking

gobble *verb* **1** eat quickly **2** make a noise like a turkey

goblet *noun, hist* **1** a large cup without handles **2** a drinking glass with a stem

goblin *noun* a mischievous, ugly spirit in folklore

god, **goddess** noun a supernatural being who is worshipped • **God** noun the creator and ruler of the world in the Christian, Jewish and Muslim religions • **godly** adj living a morally good life • **godspeed** exclam a wish for success or for a safe journey

godfather noun 1 a male godparent 2 the male head of a criminal organization, esp the Mafia

godmother noun a female godparent

godparent noun someone who agrees to see that a child is brought up according to the beliefs of the Christian Church

godsend noun a very welcome piece of unexpected good fortune

goggle-eyed adj with eyes staring in surprise or wonder

goggles plural noun spectacles for protecting the eyes from dust, sparks, etc

goitre /goy-tuh/ noun a swelling in the neck

gold noun 1 a precious yellow metal 2 a rich yellow colour ◇ adj 1 made of gold 2 golden in colour • **goldfield** noun a place where gold is found • **goldfinch** noun a small multicoloured bird with a broad beak • **gold leaf** noun gold beaten to a thin sheet • **goldsmith** noun a maker of gold articles

golden adj 1 of or like gold 2 very fine • **golden handshake** noun money given by a firm to a retiring senior employee • **golden rule** noun a guiding principle • **golden share** noun a large share in a company that prevents its being taken over • **golden wedding** noun a 50th anniversary of a wedding etc

goldfish noun a golden-yellow Chinese carp, often kept as a pet

golf noun a game in which a ball is struck with a club and aimed at a series of holes on a large open course • **golf club** noun 1 a club used in golf 2 a society of golf players 3 the place where they meet • **golfer** noun someone who plays golf

golosh another spelling of **galosh**

gondola noun 1 a canal boat used in Venice 2 a car suspended from an airship, cable railway, etc 3 a shelved display unit in a supermarket • **gondolier** noun a boatman who rows a gondola

gone past participle of **go**

gong noun 1 a metal plate which makes a booming sound when struck, used to summon people to meals etc 2 slang a medal

good adj (**better**, **best**) 1 having desired or positive qualities: a good butcher will bone it for you 2 virtuous: a good person 3 kind: she was good to me 4 pleasant, enjoyable: a good time 5 fairly large; substantial: a good income • **good-for-nothing** adj useless, lazy • **goodly** adj, old 1 large 2 ample, plentiful • **good morning**, **good day**, **good afternoon**, **good evening**, **good night** and **goodbye** exclam words used as greeting when meeting or leaving someone • **good name** noun good reputation • **good-natured** adj kind, cheerful • **goodness** noun 1 the quality of being generous or morally good 2 the nourishing quality of food • **goods** plural noun 1 personal belongings 2 things to be bought and sold • **goodwill** noun 1 kind wishes 2 a good reputation in business

goofy adj (**goofier**, **goofiest**) 1 of teeth: sticking out at the front; prominent 2 US silly

goose noun (plural **geese**) a web-footed bird larger than a duck • **goose bumps** or **goose pimples** plural noun small bumps on the skin caused by cold or fear • **goose step** noun a military march with knees locked

gooseberry noun (plural **gooseber-ries**) a sour-tasting, pale green berry

gopher noun 1 a burrowing rodent found in arid areas of N America 2 comput an early type of search engine

gore¹ noun a mass of blood ◇ verb run through with horns, tusks, etc: gored by an elephant

gore² noun a triangular-shaped piece of cloth in a garment etc

gorge noun 1 the throat 2 a narrow valley between hills ◇ verb (**gorging, gorged**) eat greedily till full: gorging himself on chocolate biscuits

gorgeous adj 1 extremely attractive or beautiful; lovely 2 showy, splendid 3 informal very enjoyable, tasty or otherwise pleasant

gorgon noun 1 a mythological monster whose glance turned people to stone 2 a very stern-looking person

gorgonzola noun a strongly flavoured Italian blue cheese

gorilla noun the largest kind of ape

Do not confuse with: **guerrilla**

---

gormless adj, Brit stupid, senseless

gorse noun a prickly bush with yellow flowers

gory adj (**gorier, goriest**) full of gore; bloody: a very gory film

goshawk noun a hawk with short wings

gosling noun a young goose

gospel noun 1 the teaching of Christ 2 informal the absolute truth

gossamer noun 1 fine spider-threads floating in the air or lying on bushes 2 a very thin material

gossip noun 1 talk, not necessarily true, about other people's personal affairs etc 2 someone who listens to and passes on gossip ◇ verb (**gossip-ing, gossiped**) 1 engage in gossip 2 chatter

got past form of **get**

gothic adj 1 of a style of architecture with pointed arches 2 of a style of literature dealing with eerie events or settings

gouache /goo-ash/ noun 1 paint containing water, gum and honey 2 painting done with this paint

Gouda /gow-duh/ noun a mild-flavoured round Dutch cheese

gouge /gowj/ noun a chisel with a hollow blade for cutting grooves ◇ verb (**gouging, gouged**) scoop (out)

goulash /goo-lash/ noun (plural **goulashes**) a stew of meat and vegetables, flavoured with paprika

gourd /gawd/ noun 1 a large fleshy fruit 2 the skin of a gourd used to carry water etc

gourmand /gaw-monh/ noun a glutton

gourmet /gaw-meh/ noun someone with a taste for good wines or food

gout noun a painful swelling of the smaller joints, especially of the big toe
• **gouty** adj suffering from gout

govern verb 1 rule, control 2 put into action the laws etc of a country

governess noun a woman who teaches young children at their home

government noun 1 a body of people, usu elected, with the power to control the affairs of and make the laws of a country 2 rule; control

governor noun 1 someone elected or appointed to the committee that governs the affairs of a school, hospital or other institution 2 the elected head of a US state

gown noun 1 a woman's formal dress 2 a loose robe worn by members of the clergy, lawyers, teachers, etc

goy noun (plural **goyim**) a Jewish

word for a person who is not Jewish; a Gentile

GP *abbrev* general practitioner

GPS *abbrev* global positioning satellite, a portable navigation device that uses satellite information to help sailors, walkers, *etc* precisely identify their location

grab *verb* (**grabbing**, **grabbed**) **1** seize or grasp suddenly: *grabbed me by the arm* **2** secure possession of quickly: *grab a seat* **3** get in a hurry: *grab a bite to eat* ◇ *noun* a sudden grasp or catch

grace *noun* **1** beauty of form or movement **2** a short prayer at a meal **3** the title of a duke or archbishop **4** favour, mercy: *by God's grace* • **graceful** *adj* elegant in movement or appearance • **gracefully** *adv* • **grace note** *noun*, *music* a short note played before the main note in a melody • **gracious** *adj* kind, polite • **graciously** *adv* • **graciousness** *noun* • **with good (or bad) grace** willingly (or unwillingly)

grade *noun* a step or placing according to quality or rank; class ◇ *verb* arrange in order, *eg* from easy to difficult • **gradation** *noun* arrangement in order of rank, difficulty, *etc* • **gradient** *noun* a slope on a road, railway, *etc* • **gradual** *adj* going or progressing slowly but steadily • **gradually** *adv* • **make the grade** do as well as is necessary

graduate *verb* **1** pass university examinations and receive a degree **2** divide into regular spaces ◇ *noun* someone who has received a degree • **graduation** *noun* the act of getting a degree from a university

graffiti *plural noun* words or drawings scratched or painted on a wall *etc*

graft *verb* **1** fix a shoot or twig of one plant onto another for growing **2** fix (skin) from one part of the body onto another part **3** transfer (an organ) from one person's body to another **4** work hard ◇ *noun* **1** living tissue (*eg* skin) which is grafted **2** a shoot grafted **3** hard work **4** profit gained by illegal or unfair means

Grail *noun* the plate or cup believed to have been used by Christ at the Last Supper

grain *noun* **1** a seed *eg* of wheat, oats **2** corn in general **3** a very small quantity **4** a very small measure of weight **5** the run of the lines of fibre in wood, leather, *etc* • **against the grain** against your natural feelings or instincts

gram *or* **gramme** *noun* the basic unit of weight in the metric system

grammar *noun* **1** the correct use of words in speaking or writing: *his grammar is very bad* **2** the rules applying to a particular language: *French grammar* • **grammarian** *noun* an expert on grammar • **grammar school** *noun* a kind of secondary school • **grammatical** *adj* relating to, or correct according to, the rules of grammar • **grammatically** *adv*

gramme *another spelling of* **gram**

Grammy *noun* an annual award given by the American National Academy of Recording Arts and Sciences

Gramophone *noun*, *trademark*, *old* a record-player

granary *noun* (*plural* **granaries**) a storehouse for grain

grand *adj* great, noble or fine ◇ *noun*, *slang* a sum of a thousand pounds • **grandchild**, **granddaughter** *and* **grandson** *noun* a child of a son or daughter • **grand duke** *noun* a duke of specially high rank • **grandfather** *noun* a father's or mother's father • **grand master** *noun* a chess player of the greatest ability • **grandmother** *noun* a father's or mother's mother • **grand opera** *noun* opera in which all the dialogue is sung • **grand piano** *noun* a piano with a large flat top • **grand prix** /gronh pree/ *noun* of a series of races for the world motor racing championship • **grandstand** *noun* rows of raised seats at a sports ground

grandee *noun* a man of high rank, *esp* in Spain or Portugal

grandeur /grand-yuh/ *noun* greatness

grandiloquent *adj* speaking in a high-sounding language

grandiose *adj* planned on a large scale

granite *noun* a hard rock of greyish or reddish colour

granny *noun* (*plural* **grannies**) *informal* a grandmother

grant *verb* 1 give, allow (something asked for) 2 admit as true ◇ *noun* money awarded for a special purpose • **granted** or **granting** *conj* (often with **that**) even if; assuming: *granted that you are right* • **take for granted** 1 assume that (something) will happen without checking 2 treat (someone) casually, without respect or kindness

granule *noun* a tiny grain or part • **granular** *adj* made up of grains • **granulated** *adj* broken into grains

grape *noun* the green or black smooth-skinned berry from which wine is made • **grapefruit** *noun* a sharp-tasting fruit like a large yellow orange • **grapeshot** *noun* shot that scatters when fired • **grapevine** *noun* 1 a plant on which grapes grow 2 *informal* the spreading of news, rumour

graph *noun* lines drawn on squared paper to show changes in quantity, *eg* in temperature, money spent

graphic *adj* 1 relating to writing, drawing or painting 2 describing things vividly 3 explicit: *graphic violence* ◇ *noun* a painting, print, illustration or diagram • **graphically** *adv* • **graphics** *sing noun* the art of drawing ◇ *plural noun* visual images, *esp* on a computer

graphite *noun* a form of carbon used in making pencils

grapple *verb*: **grapple with** 1 struggle with physically 2 try to deal with

grasp *verb* 1 clasp and grip with the fingers or arms 2 understand ◇ *noun* 1 a grip with the hand or arms 2 someone's power of understanding • **grasping** *adj* greedy, mean

grass *noun* (*plural* **grasses**) 1 the plant covering fields of pasture 2 a kind of plant with long narrow leaves, *eg* wheat, reeds, bamboo 3 *dated slang* marijuana • **grasshopper** *noun* a type of jumping insect • **grass snake** *noun* a type of green harmless snake • **grass widow** *noun*, *dated* a woman whose husband is temporarily away • **grass widower** *noun*, *dated* a man whose wife is temporarily away • **grassy** *adj* covered with grass

grate *noun* a framework of iron bars for holding a fire ◇ *verb* 1 rub down into small pieces 2 make a harsh, grinding sound 3 irritate • **grater** *noun* an instrument with a rough surface for rubbing cheese *etc* into small pieces • **grating** *noun* a frame of iron bars

grateful *adj* 1 feeling thankful 2 showing or giving thanks • **gratefully** *adv*

gratify *verb* (**gratifies**, **gratifying**, **gratified**) please or satisfy • **gratification** *noun* pleasure or satisfaction

gratis *adv* for nothing, without payment

gratitude *noun* thankfulness

gratuitous *adj* done or shown without good reason; uncalled-for: *gratuitous violence* • **gratuitously** *adv*

gratuity *noun* (*plural* **gratuities**) a money gift in return for a service; a tip

grave *noun* a pit in which a dead person is buried ◇ *adj* 1 severe or important: *grave error* 2 not cheerful; solemn • **gravely** *adv* • **graveness**

noun • **gravestone** *noun* a stone placed to mark a grave • **graveyard** *noun* a place where the dead are buried, a cemetery

gravel *noun* small stones or pebbles • **gravelly** *adj* 1 containing small stones 2 of a voice: rough and deep

graven *adj, old* carved: *graven images*

gravitate *verb* move towards as if strongly attracted (to) • **gravitation** *noun*

gravity *noun* 1 the force that attracts things towards earth and causes them to fall to the ground 2 severity or importance: *gravity of the situation* 3 seriousness or solemnity

gravy *noun* (*plural* **gravies**) a sauce made from juices of meat that is cooking • **gravy train** *noun* a situation producing large, easy profits

gray *US spelling of* **grey**

graze *verb* 1 feed on (growing grass) 2 scrape the skin of 3 touch lightly in passing ◇ *noun* 1 a scraping of the skin 2 a light touch • **grazing** *noun* grass land for animals to graze on

grease *noun* 1 thick animal fat 2 an oily substance ◇ *verb* smear with grease or apply grease to • **grease paint** *noun* theatrical make-up • **greasily** *adv* • **greasiness** *noun* • **greasy** *adj*

great *adj* 1 very large 2 very talented: *a great singer* 3 *informal* very good; excellent 4 very important, distinguished: *Alexander the Great* • **great-grandchild** *noun* the son or daughter of a grandson or granddaughter • **great-grandfather**, **great-grandmother** *noun* the father and mother of a grandfather or grandmother • **greatly** *adv* very much • **greatness** *noun*

grebe *noun* a freshwater diving bird

greed *noun* great and selfish desire for food, money, *etc*

greedy *adj* (**greedier**, **greediest**) full of greed • **greedily** *adv* • **greediness** *noun*

green *adj* 1 of the colour of growing grass *etc* 2 inexperienced, naive 3 concerned with care of the environment: *the party's green policies* ◇ *noun* 1 the colour of growing grass 2 a piece of ground covered with grass 3 a member of the Green Party, or an environmentalist generally 4 (**greens**) green vegetables for food • **green belt** *noun* open land surrounding a city • **greenery** *noun* green plants • **greenfly** *noun* the aphid • **greengage** *noun* a kind of plum, green but sweet • **greengrocer** *noun* someone who sells fresh vegetables • **greenhouse** *noun* a building with large glass panes in which plants are grown • **greenhouse effect** *noun* the warming up of the earth's surface due to excess carbon dioxide in the atmosphere • **Green Party** *noun* a political party concerned with conserving natural resources and decentralizing political and economic power • **have green fingers** be a skilful gardener • **the green light** permission to go ahead with a plan

greet *verb* 1 meet someone with kind words 2 say hello *etc* to 3 react to, respond to: *greeted the news with relief* • **greeting** *noun* 1 words of welcome or kindness 2 reaction, response

gregarious *adj* 1 liking the company of others; sociable 2 living in flocks and herds

gremlin *noun* an imaginary mischievous creature

grenade *noun* a small bomb thrown by hand

grew *past tense of* **grow**

grey *or US* **gray** *adj* 1 of a colour between black and white 2 relating to elderly people: *the grey economy* ◇ *noun* 1 grey colour 2 a grey horse

• **grey matter** *noun, informal* brains

greyhound *noun* a breed of fast-running dog

grid *noun* 1 a grating of bars, *esp* one covering the entrance to a drain 2 a network of lines, *eg* for helping to find a place on a map 3 a network of wires carrying electricity over a wide area
• **gridiron** *noun* 1 a frame of iron bars for cooking food over a fire 2 *US* a football field

grief *noun* 1 deep sorrow, *esp* after bereavement 2 *informal* trouble or bother • **come to grief** meet with misfortune

grievance *noun* a cause for complaining

grieve *verb* feel grief or sorrow

grievous *adj* 1 painful; serious 2 causing grief

griffin or **griffon** *noun* a mythological animal with the body and legs of a lion and the beak and wings of an eagle

grill *verb* 1 cook directly under heat (provided by an electric or gas cooker) 2 cook on a grid over a fire, *eg* a barbecue 3 question closely ◇ *noun* 1 the part of a cooker used for grilling 2 grilled food 3 a restaurant serving grilled food 4 a frame of bars for grilling food on

grille *noun* a metal grating over a door, window, *etc*

grim *adj* (**grimmer, grimmest**) 1 fierce-looking; stern 2 very unpleasant; terrible: *a grim sight* 3 unyielding; stubborn: *grim determination* • **grimly** *adv* • **grimness** *noun*

grimace *noun* a twisting of the face in fun or pain ◇ *verb* a twisted facial expression

grime *noun* dirt • **grimily** *adv* • **griminess** *noun* • **grimy** *adj*

grin *verb* (**grinning, grinned**) smile broadly ◇ *noun* a broad smile • **grin**

and bear it suffer something without complaining

grind *verb* (**grinding, ground**) 1 crush to powder 2 sharpen by rubbing 3 rub together: *grinding his teeth* ◇ *noun* hard or unpleasant work • **grinder** *noun* someone or something that grinds

grindstone *noun* a revolving stone for grinding or sharpening tools • **back to the grindstone** back to work • **keep your nose to the grindstone** work hard without stopping

grip *noun* 1 a firm hold on a surface that prevents slipping: *these shoes have a good grip* 2 a way of holding or grasping; control: *a loose grip* 3 a handle or part for holding 4 a large travelling bag ◇ *verb* (**gripping, gripped**) take a firm hold of • **gripping** *adj* holding all your attention; compelling

gripe *noun* 1 a sharp stomach pain 2 *informal* a complaint ◇ *verb* complain

grisly *adj* (**grislier, grisliest**) involving death or injury in a very unpleasant way; gruesome

───────────────

Do not confuse with: **grizzly**

───────────────

grist *noun* corn for grinding • **grist to the mill** something that brings profit or advantage

gristle *noun* a tough elastic substance in meat • **gristly** *adj*

grit *noun* 1 a mixture of rough sand and gravel, spread on icy surfaces 2 courage ◇ *verb* (**gritting, gritted**) 1 apply grit to (an icy surface): *has the road been gritted?* 2 clench: *grit your teeth* • **grittily** *adv* • **grittiness** *noun* • **gritty** *adj*

grits *plural noun, US* coarsely ground maize

grizzled *adj* grey or greying

grizzly *adj* grey in colour ◇ *noun*

(*plural* **grizzlies**) *informal* a grizzly bear • **grizzly bear** *noun* a type of large bear of N America

---

Do not confuse with: **grisly**

---

groan *verb* **1** moan in pain, disapproval, *etc* **2** be full or loaded: *a table groaning with food*

groats *plural noun* oat grains without the husks

grocer *noun* a dealer in certain kinds of food and household supplies • **groceries** *plural noun* food *etc* sold by grocers

groggy *adj* (**groggier**, **groggiest**) weak and light-headed after illness or blows

groin *noun* the part of the body where the inner thigh joins the torso

groom *noun* **1** a bridegroom **2** someone in charge of horses ◇ *verb* **1** look after (a horse) **2** make smart and tidy

groove *noun* a furrow, a long hollow ◇ *verb* cut a groove (in)

grope *verb* search (for) by feeling as if blind: *groping for his socks in the dark*

gross *adj* **1** very fat **2** great, obvious: *gross error* **3** of money: total, before any deductions for tax *etc*: *gross profit* **4** *US informal* disgusting, revolting ◇ *noun* **1** the whole taken together **2** twelve dozen • **grossly** *adv* • **grossness** *noun*

grotesque *adj* very unnatural or strange-looking

grotto *noun* (*plural* **grottoes** or **grottos**) a cave

grouch *verb* grumble or complain ◇ *noun* **1** a complaining person **2** a bad-tempered complaint • **grouchy** *adj*

ground¹ *noun* **1** the surface of the earth **2** (*also* **grounds**) a good reason: *ground for complaint* **3** (**grounds**) lands surrounding a large house *etc* **4** (**grounds**) dregs: *coffee grounds* ◇ *verb* **1** of a ship: strike the seabed and become stuck **2** prevent (aeroplanes) from flying • **grounded** *adj* **1** of aeroplanes: unable to fly **2** of a child: forced to stay in the house as a punishment • **ground floor** *noun* the storey of a building at street level • **groundhog** *noun, US* a marmot • **grounding** *noun* the first steps in learning something • **groundless** *adj* without reason • **groundnut** *noun, US* a peanut • **groundswell** *noun* **1** broad ocean waves **2** a growing general feeling or opinion • **groundwork** *noun* the first stages of a task

ground² *past form of* **grind**

groundsel *noun* a common wild plant with small yellow flowers

group *noun* a number of people or things together ◇ *verb* **1** form or gather into a group **2** classify

grouse¹ *noun* (*plural* **grouse**) a game bird hunted on moors and hills

grouse² *noun* (*plural* **grouses**) a grumble or complaint ◇ *verb* grumble or complain

grove *noun* a small group of trees

grovel *verb* (**grovelling**, **grovelled**) **1** crawl or lie on the ground **2** be overly humble

grow *verb* (**growing**, **grew**, **grown**) **1** become bigger or stronger: *the local population is growing* **2** become: *grow old* **3** cause (plants, trees, *etc*) to grow: *grow from seed* **4** cause to expand or increase: *grow the economy*

growl *verb* utter a deep sound like a dog ◇ *noun* a dog's deep sound

grown *past participle of* **grow**

growth *noun* **1** growing **2** increase: *growth in market shares* **3** something that grows **4** something abnormal that grows on or in the body

grub *noun* **1** a worm-like larva of an

insect **2** *informal* food ◊ *verb* (**grub-bing, grubbed**) dig

grubby *adj* (**grubbier, grubbiest**) dirty • **grubbily** *adv* • **grubbiness** *noun*

grudge *verb* **1** be unwilling to grant or allow: *I grudge him his success* **2** give unwillingly or reluctantly ◊ *noun* a feeling of resentment: *she bears a grudge against me*

gruel *noun* a thin mixture of oatmeal boiled in water • **gruelling** *adj* straining, exhausting

gruesome *adj* inspiring horror or disgust; horrible

gruff *adj* **1** rough in manner **2** of a voice: deep and harsh

grumble *verb* complain in a bad-tempered, discontented way ◊ *noun* a complaint

grumpy *adj* (**grumpier, grumpiest**) cross, bad-tempered • **grumpily** *adv* • **grumpiness** *noun*

grunge *noun* **1** *informal* grime, dirt **2** a style of music with loud, discordant guitar sounds • **grungy** *adj*

grunt *verb* make a sound like that of a pig ◊ *noun* a pig-like snort

guacamole /gwa-kuh-*moh*-leh/ *noun* a Mexican dish of mashed avocado, chillies and olive oil

guarantee *noun* **1** a promise to do something **2** a statement by the maker that something will work well **3** money that will be forfeited if a promise is broken ◊ *verb* give a guarantee

guarantor *noun* someone who promises to pay if another person fails to keep an agreement to pay

guard *verb* keep safe from danger or attack ◊ *noun* **1** a person or group whose duty it is to protect **2** a screen *etc* that protects from danger **3** someone in charge of a railway train or coach **4** *sport* a position of defence • **guarded** *adj* careful, not revealing

much: *guarded comments* • **guard-edly** *adv*

guardian *noun* **1** someone with the legal right to take care of an orphan **2** someone who protects or guards • **guardianship** *noun*

guava *noun* **1** a yellow pear-shaped fruit **2** the tree on which this fruit grows

gubbins *noun, informal* a number of things, *esp* items of equipment or possessions

gubernatorial *adj, US* relating to a state governor: *gubernatorial election*

guddle *noun, Scot* a messy place or confused situation

gudgeon *noun* a type of small freshwater fish

guerrilla *noun* a member of a small independent armed force using surprise tactics, *esp* against government or occupying troops ◊ *adj* of fighting: in which many small bands acting independently make sudden raids on an enemy

Do not confuse with: **gorilla**

guess *verb* **1** say without sure knowledge: *I can only guess the price* **2** *US* suppose: *I guess I'll go* ◊ *noun* (*plural* **guesses**) an estimate • **guesswork** *noun* guessing

guest *noun* a visitor received and entertained in another's house or in a hotel *etc*

guff *noun, informal* rubbish, nonsense

guffaw *verb* laugh loudly ◊ *noun* a loud laugh

GUI /goo-ee/ *abbrev, comput* graphic user interface, a system that represents programs and operations as icons that you click on to activate

guide *verb* **1** show the way to; direct

2 influence or advise ◇ *noun* **1** someone who shows tourists around **2** someone who leads travellers on a route unfamiliar to them **3** a guidebook **4** (**Guide**) a girl belonging to the Guides Association • **guidance** *noun* help or advice towards doing something • **Guide Association** *noun* an international organization, similar to the Scout Association, that teaches outdoor and life skills to girls and young women • **guidebook** *noun* a book with information for tourists about a place • **guided missile** *noun* an explosive rocket which after being fired can be guided to its target by radio waves • **guidelines** *plural noun* advice or instructions on how to do something

guild *noun* **1** an association for those working in a particular trade or profession **2** a society or social club

---

Do not confuse with: **gild**

---

guile *noun* the ability to deceive or trick people • **guileless** *adj* completely honest or sincere in dealings with people

guillemot /gil-i-mot/ *noun* a diving sea bird

guillotine /gil-uh-teen/ *noun* **1** *hist* an instrument with a falling blade used for executing by beheading **2** a machine with a blade for cutting paper **3** the limiting of discussion time in parliament by prearranging voting times ◇ *verb* **1** behead with the guillotine **2** cut (paper) with a guillotine **3** use a parliamentary guillotine on

guilt *noun* **1** a sense of shame **2** blame for wrongdoing, *eg* breaking the law • **guiltily** *adv* • **guilty** *adj*

Do not confuse with: **gilt**

---

guinea *noun* **1** *hist* a British gold coin **2** a sum of money equal to £1.05,

sometimes used in expressing prices, fees, *etc*

guinea fowl *noun* a bird resembling a pheasant, with spotted feathers

guinea pig *noun* **1** a rodent about the size of a rabbit **2** someone used as the subject of an experiment

guise *noun* appearance, dress, *esp* in disguise: *in the guise of a priest* • **guiser** *noun* a child who dresses up and goes round houses collecting money in return for performing • **guising** *noun*

guitar *noun* a stringed musical instrument with frets

gulag /goo-lag/ *noun, hist* a labour camp for political prisoners in the former Soviet Union

gulch *noun* (*plural* **gulches**) a narrow rocky valley

gulf *noun* **1** a large inlet of the sea **2** a vast difference or separation

gull *noun* a seagull

gullet *noun* a passage by which food goes down into the stomach

gullible *adj* easily tricked

gully *noun* (*plural* **gullies**) a channel worn by water

gulp *verb* swallow quickly and in large mouthfuls ◇ *noun* a sudden fast swallowing

gum *noun* **1** the firm flesh in which the teeth grow **2** sticky juice from some trees and plants **3** a flavoured gummy sweet for eating or chewing ◇ *verb* (**gumming**, **gummed**) stick with gum • **gummy** *adj* sticky

gumbo *noun* thick soup containing okra

gumption *noun* good sense

gumtree *noun*: **up a gumtree** in a mess

gun *noun* any weapon firing bullets or shells • **gunboat** *noun* a small warship with heavy guns • **gun carriage**

noun a wheeled support for a field-gun • **gun dog** *noun* a dog trained to fetch birds *etc* after they have been shot • **gunfire** *noun* the firing of guns • **gunmetal** *noun* a mixture of copper and tin • **gunpowder** *noun* an explosive in powder form • **gun-running** *noun* bringing guns into a country illegally • **stick to your guns** keep determinedly to your opinion

gung-ho *adj* boisterously or foolishly enthusiastic, *esp* to go to war

gunk *noun, informal* unpleasantly sticky or dirty material

gunwale or **gunnel** (both /gun-ul/) *noun* the upper edge of a boat's side

gurgle *verb* **1** of water: make a bubbling sound **2** make such a sound, *eg* in pleasure ◇ *noun*

guru *noun* **1** a Hindu spiritual teacher **2** a revered instructor or adviser; a mentor

gush *verb* **1** flow out in a strong stream **2** talk at length with exaggerated emotions: *gushing on about the wedding* ◇ *noun* (*plural* **gushes**) a strong or sudden flow: *gush of tears*

gusset *noun* a piece of material sewn into a seam to strengthen or widen part of a garment, *esp* at the crotch

gust *noun* a sudden blast of wind • **gusty** *adj* windy

gusto *noun* enthusiasm

gut *noun* **1** a narrow passage in the lower part of the body; the intestine **2** animal intestines used as strings for musical instruments **3** (**guts**) spirit, courage ◇ *verb* (**gutting**, **gutted**) **1** take out the inner, inedible parts of: *gut a fish* **2** destroy completely, *esp* by fire: *gutted the building*

gutta-percha *noun* a waterproof material similar to but less elastic than rubber

gutter *noun* **1** a water channel on a roof, at the edge of a roadside, *etc* **2** (**the gutter**) a state of extreme poverty or degraded living • **gutter press** *noun* that part of the press that specializes in sensational journalism • **guttersnipe** *noun, old* a poor child living in the streets

guttural *adj* harsh in sound, as if formed in the throat

guy¹ *noun* **1** *informal* a man **2** *informal* (**guys**) people in a group, whether male or female: *are you ready, guys?* **3** *Brit* an effigy of Guy Fawkes, traditionally burned on 5 November

guy² *noun* a steadying rope, *esp* supporting a tent

guzzle *verb* eat or drink greedily

gym *noun, informal* **1** a gymnasium **2** a school class involving physical exercises or sports; PE

gymkhana *noun* a meeting for competitions, *esp* in horse-riding

gymnasium *noun* (*plural* **gymnasiums** or **gymnasia**) a building or room equipped for physical exercises

gymnast *noun* someone who does gymnastics • **gymnastic** *adj* • **gymnastics** *plural noun* exercises to strengthen the body

gypsum *noun* a chalk-like mineral

Gypsy or **Gipsy** *noun* (*plural* **Gypsies** or **Gipsies**) a member of a travelling people; a Romany

gyrate *verb* whirl round • **gyration** *noun* • **gyratory** *adj*

Hh

haar noun a cold mist or fog, esp from the sea

habeas corpus noun a request to produce a prisoner in person and give the reasons for their detention

haberdashery noun materials such as thread and buttons for sewing, mending, etc • **haberdasher** noun someone who sells haberdashery

habit noun 1 something you are used to doing: nasty habits 2 someone's usual behaviour 3 the dress of a monk or nun • **make a habit of** do regularly or frequently

habitable adj fit to live in

habitat noun the natural home of an animal or plant

habitation noun, formal a dwelling place; a home

habitual adj usual • **habitually** adv

habituate verb make accustomed

habitué noun a frequent visitor or attender: a habitué of nightclubs

hacienda /has-i-en-duh/ noun a large house on a ranch in Spanish-speaking countries

hack verb 1 cut or chop up roughly 2 ride on horseback, esp along ordinary roads ◇ noun 1 a writer who does hard work for low pay 2 a riding horse kept for hire 3 a rough cut, a gash

hacker noun someone who gains unauthorized access to government or commercial computer systems

hackles plural noun 1 the feathers on the neck of a farmyard cock 2 the hair on a dog's neck • **make someone's hackles rise** make them angry

hackneyed adj used so often as to be no longer original: a hackneyed phrase

hacksaw noun a saw for cutting metal

haddock noun (plural **haddock** or **haddocks**) a medium-sized edible N Atlantic fish

Hades /hay-deez/ noun the ancient Greek underworld, home of the dead

hadj /haj/ noun a Muslim pilgrimage to Mecca

haemoglobin or US **hemoglobin** /heem-uh-gloh-bin/ noun the oxygen-carrying substance in red blood cells

haemophilia or US **hemophilia** /hee-muh-fil-i-uh/ noun a hereditary disease causing extreme bleeding when cut • **haemophiliac** noun someone suffering from haemophilia

haemorrhage or US **hemorrhage** /hem-uh-rij/ noun a large amount of bleeding

haemorrhoids /hem-uh-roydz/ plural noun painful swollen veins around the anus

haft noun a handle of a knife etc

hag noun 1 an ugly old woman 2 a witch

haggard adj gaunt and hollow-eyed from tiredness

haggis noun (plural **haggises**) a Scottish dish made from chopped sheep's offal, suet and oatmeal, traditionally cooked in a sheep's stomach

haggle *verb* argue determinedly over a price

hagiography *noun* a biography of a saint • **hagiographer** *noun* a saint's biographer • **hagiographic** *adj* 1 of a hagiography 2 *formal* highly praising

ha-ha *noun* a sunken fence

haiku /hai-koo/ *noun* a Japanese form of poem written in three lines of 5, 7 and 5 syllables

hail[1] *verb* 1 call to in order to attract the attention of 2 greet, welcome ◇ *noun* 1 a call from a distance 2 greeting, welcome • **hail-fellow-well-met** *adj* friendly and familiar on first meeting, *esp* overly so • **hail from** come from

hail[2] *noun* 1 frozen raindrops 2 a falling mass: *a hail of bullets* ◇ *verb* 1 shower with hail 2 descend in a mass • **hailstone** *noun* a piece of hail

hair *noun* a thread-like growth on the skin of an animal, or the whole mass of these on the head • **hairdresser** *noun* someone who cuts and styles hair • **hairdryer** *noun* an electrical device that blows hot air to dry hair • **hair-raising** *adj* terrifying • **hair's breadth** *noun* a very small distance • **hairspray** *noun* a fine spray to fix a hairstyle • **hairspring** *noun* a very fine spring in a watch *etc* • **split hairs** argue about unimportant details

hairy *adj* (**hairier, hairiest**) 1 covered with hair 2 risky, dangerous

hake *noun* an edible sea fish similar to a cod

halal /hal-al/ *noun* meat from animals that have been slaughtered according to Islamic law ◇ *adj* made with or dealing in meat from animals slaughtered in this way

halberd *noun, hist* a battleaxe fixed on a long pole

halcyon /hal-si-un/ *adj*: **halcyon days** a time of peace and happiness

hale *adj*: **hale and hearty** healthy

half *noun* (*plural* **halves**) one of two equal parts ◇ *adj* 1 being one of two equal parts: *a half bottle of wine* 2 not full or complete: *a half smile* ◇ *adv* partly, to some extent: *looked half-dead* • **half-baked** *adj* not properly thought out and rather silly • **half-board** *noun* a hotel charge for bed, breakfast and another meal • **half-breed** or **half-caste** *noun, derog offensive* someone with a father and mother of different races • **half-brother** or **half-sister** *noun* a brother or sister sharing only one parent • **half-crown** *noun, hist* a British coin before decimal currency, worth two shillings and sixpence ($12^1/_2$ pence) • **half-hearted** *adj* not eager • **half-life** *noun* the time in which the radioactivity of a substance falls to half its original value • **half-mast** *adv* of a flag: hoisted half-way up the mast to show that someone important has died • **halfpenny** /hehp-ni/ *noun, hist* a coin worth half of a penny • **half-time** *noun* an interval half-way through a sports game • **half-way** *adv & adj* at or to a point equally far from the beginning and the end • **half-wit** *noun* an idiot • **half-witted** *adj* stupid, idiotic • **at half-cock** not completely ready; unprepared

halibut *noun* a large edible flatfish

halitosis *noun* bad breath

hall *noun* 1 a passage at the entrance to a house 2 a large public room 3 a large country house

hallmark *noun* 1 a mark put on gold and silver articles to show quality 2 a characteristic sign: *the hallmark of a good editor*

hallo another spelling of **hello**

hallowed *adj, old* holy, sacred

Hallowe'en *noun* the evening of 31 October, traditionally a time when spirits are believed to be around and children dress up as witches and monsters

hallucination *noun* something seen that is not really there • **hallucinatory** *adj* causing hallucinations

hallucinogen *noun* a substance that causes hallucinations • **hallucinogenic** *adj*

halo *noun* (*plural* **haloes** *or* **halos**) **1** a circle of light surrounding the sun or moon **2** a circle of light depicted around the head of a saint *etc* as a sign of holiness

halogen *noun* one of a group of elements that includes chlorine and iodine ◊ *adj* using halogen to produce a bright light: *halogen headlights*

halt *verb* **1** come or bring to a stop **2** be lame; limp **3** be uncertain or hesitant ◊ *noun* **1** a stop; a standstill: *call a halt* **2** stopping place ◊ *adj* lame • **halting** *adj* uncertain or hesitant • **haltingly** *adv*

halter *noun* a rope tied round the head of a horse for leading it • **halterneck** *noun* a woman's sleeveless dress or top with a single strap around the neck

halva *noun* a Middle-Eastern dessert or sweet made from crushed sesame seeds

halve *verb* divide in two

halyard *noun* a rope for raising or lowering a sail or flag

ham¹ *noun* **1** meat from a salted and dried pig's thigh, or the thigh itself **2** the back of the human thigh • **ham-fisted** *adj* clumsy

ham² *noun, informal* **1** an actor who overacts **2** an amateur radio operator

hamburger *noun* a round cake of minced beef, cooked by frying or grilling; a burger

hamlet *noun* a small village

hammer *noun* **1** a tool with a heavy metal head for beating metal, driving nails, *etc* **2** a striking piece in a clock, piano, pistol, *etc* ◊ *verb* **1** drive or shape with a hammer **2** defeat overwhelmingly • **hammer and tongs** determinedly or violently

hammock *noun* a length of netting, canvas, *etc* hung up by the corners and used as a bed

hammy *adj* (**hammier**, **hammiest**) *informal* **1** overacted **2** badly done; inexpert • **hammily** *adv*

hamper¹ *verb* prevent from making progress or moving forward; impede

hamper² *noun* a large basket with a lid, *esp* one for food

hamster *noun* a small rodent with large cheek pouches, often kept as a pet

hamstring *noun* a tendon at the back of the knee • *verb* **1** make lame by cutting the hamstring **2** make ineffective or powerless

hand *noun* **1** the part of the human body at the end of the arm **2** a pointer, *eg* on a clock **3** help, aid: *can you give me a hand?* **4** side, direction: *left-hand side* **5** a group of playing-cards dealt to someone **6** a worker or labourer: *a farmhand* **7** a style of handwriting: *not in my wife's hand* **8** clapping, applause: *a big hand* **9** involvement: *I had a hand in organizing the event* **10** a measure (four inches, 10.16 centimetres) for the height of horses ◊ *verb* **1** pass (something) with the hand **2** (with **over**) give • **handbag** *noun* a small bag for personal belongings • **handbill** *noun* a small printed notice • **handbook** *noun* a small book giving information or directions • **handcart** *noun* a small cart transported by hand • **handcuffs** *plural noun* steel bands joined by a short chain, put round the wrists of prisoners • **handgun** *noun* a gun held and fired in one hand • **handhold** *noun* something that the hand can grip, *eg* in climbing • **hand-in-hand** *adj* **1** holding hands **2** in partnership • **hand-me-down** *noun* a second-hand piece of clothing, *esp* one that used to belong to another member of the family • **handout** noun a sheet or bundle of information given out at a lecture etc • **hand-picked** adj chosen carefully • **handshake** noun holding and shaking a person's hand in greeting or agreeing a deal • **hands-on** adj **1** involving yourself closely **2** involving practical experience • **hand-to-hand** adj of fighting: at close quarters • **hand-to-mouth** adj with barely enough to live on and nothing to spare • **handwriting** noun writing with pen or pencil • **at first hand** directly from the source • **at hand** nearby • **change hands** pass to another owner • **hand over fist** in large amounts and very quickly • **in hand 1** in your possession: cash in hand **2** being done or prepared • **out of hand 1** out of control **2** at once • **out of someone's hands** no longer their concern • **take in hand** take charge of • **try your hand at** have a go at; attempt • **wash your hands of** give up all responsibility for

handful noun (plural **handfuls**) **1** as much as can be held in one hand **2** a small amount **3** a demanding child, pet, etc

handicap noun **1** something that makes an action more difficult **2** a disadvantage, such as having to run a greater distance, given to the best competitors in a race **3** a race in which handicaps are given **4** dated a physical or mental disability ◇ verb **1** give a handicap to **2** burden, impede

handicapped adj **1** having or given a handicap **2** dated physically or mentally disabled

handicraft noun skilled work done by hand, not machine

handiwork noun **1** thing(s) made by hand **2** something done by a particular person etc: the handiwork of a sick mind

handkerchief noun a small cloth for wiping the nose etc

handle verb **1** touch, hold or use with the hand **2** manage to deal with ◇ noun **1** the part of anything meant to be held in the hand **2** a way of understanding something

handlebars plural noun a steering bar at the front of a bicycle with a handle at each end

handsome adj **1** good-looking **2** generous: a handsome gift

handy adj (**handier**, **handiest**) **1** useful or convenient to use **2** easily reached; nearby **3** clever with the hands • **handily** adv • **handiness** noun • **handyman** noun a man who does odd jobs

hang verb (**hanging**, **hung** or **hanged**) **1** fix or be fixed to a point off the ground **2** be suspended in the air **3** (with **down**) droop or fall downwards **4** attach (wallpaper) to a wall **5** (past form **hanged**) put a prisoner to death by putting a rope round their neck and letting them fall • **hangdog** adj guilty-looking • **hang gliding** noun an activity in which you fly by means of a large kite from which you hang in a harness • **hanging** noun an execution in which the prisoner is hanged • **hangman** noun an executioner who hangs people • **get the hang of** learn how to do or use • **hang about** or **hang around** loiter • **hang back** hesitate • **hang fire** delay • **hang on 1** depend on **2** wait, linger

hangar noun a shed for aeroplanes

Do not confuse: **hangar** and **hanger**

hanger noun a device on which a garment is hung • **hanger-on** noun (plural **hangers-on**) someone who stays near someone in the hope of gaining some advantage

hangnail noun a torn shred of skin beside a fingernail

hangover noun **1** uncomfortable

after-effects of being drunk **2** something remaining: *a hangover from the 60s* • **hungover** *adj* suffering from a hangover

hank *noun* a coil or loop of string, rope, wool, *etc*

hanker *verb* long for: *hankering after a chocolate biscuit*

hankie or **hanky** *noun* (*plural* **hankies**) *informal* a handkerchief

Hansard *noun* the printed record of debates in the British parliament

hansom cab *noun* a light two-wheeled horse-drawn cab with the driver's seat raised behind

Hanukkah /han-uh-kuh/ *noun* the Jewish festival of lights held in mid-December

haphazard *adj* done in a random, unplanned or unsystematic way • **haphazardly** *adv*

hapless *adj* unlucky

happen *verb* **1** take place **2** chance to do: *did you happen to see the news?* • **happening** *noun* an event

happy *adj* (**happier**, **happiest**) **1** feeling or showing pleasure or contentment **2** fortunate: *a happy coincidence* **3** willing: *happy to help* • **happily** *adv* • **happiness** *noun* • **happy-go-lucky** *adj* taking things as they come; easygoing

hara-kiri *noun* a Japanese form of ritual suicide in which the stomach is cut open with a sword

harangue *noun* a loud aggressive speech ◊ *verb* deliver a harangue

harass *verb* annoy persistently; pester • **harassment** *noun*

harbinger *noun* a sign of something to come: *harbinger of spring*

harbour *noun* **1** a place of shelter for ships **2** any place of safety ◊ *verb* **1** give shelter or refuge **2** store in the mind: *harbouring ill will*

hard *adj* **1** not easily broken or put out of shape; firm **2** not easy to do, understand, *etc*; difficult **3** not easy to please; demanding **4** not easy to bear; wearing **5** having no kind or gentle feelings; cruel **6** of water: containing many minerals and so not forming a good lather **7** of drugs: readily causing addiction; addictive ◊ *adv* strongly or violently • **hard copy** *noun* computer data that is printed on paper • **hardcore** *adj* of pornography *etc*: very explicit; graphic • **hard disk** *noun*, *comput* a hard-cased disk able to store large amounts of data, fixed into a base unit • **harden** *verb* make hard • **hard-headed** *adj* shrewd, realistic and not influenced by emotion • **hard-hearted** *adj* having no kind feelings • **hard labour** *noun* tiring work given to prisoners as part of their punishment • **hard luck** or **hard lines** *noun* bad luck • **hardly** *adv* **1** only just: *could hardly keep her eyes open* **2** barely: *hardly enough food for one person* • **hardness** *noun* the state of being hard • **hard-nosed** *adj* tough and unsentimental • **hardship** *noun* something difficult to bear • **hard shoulder** *noun* the surfaced strip on the outer edges of a motorway, used when stopping in an emergency • **hard up** *adj* short of money • **hardware** *noun* **1** *comput* the physical components of a computer, as distinct from the programs it runs (*contrasted with*: **software**) **2** ironmongery • **hardwood** *noun* the tough, close-grained wood of certain trees, including oak, ash, elm, *etc* • **hard and fast** strict, rigid • **hard of hearing** rather deaf

hardy *adj* (**hardier**, **hardiest**) strong, robust, tough • **hardiness** *noun*

hare *noun* a fast-running animal like a large rabbit • **harebell** *noun* a plant with blue, bell-shaped flowers • **harebrained** *adj* mad, foolish • **harelip** *noun* a split in the upper lip at birth

harem /hah-rum/ or /hah-reem/ *noun* **1** the women's rooms in an Islamic house **2** a set of wives and concubines

haricot /ha-ri-koh/ *noun* a type of bean

hark *exclam* listen! • **hark back to** recall or refer to (a previous time, remark, *etc*)

harlequin /hah-li-kwin/ *noun* a comic pantomime character wearing a multicoloured costume

harlot *noun, old* a prostitute

harm *noun* physical damage or injury, or psychological damage ◇ *verb* **1** damage or injure **2** do wrong to • **harmful** *adj* • **harmfully** *adv* • **harmless** *adj* • **harmlessly** *adv*

harmonica *noun* a mouth organ

harmonious *adj* **1** having a pleasant sound **2** with no disagreement; friendly • **harmoniously** *adv*

harmonium *noun* a musical wind instrument like a small organ

harmonize *verb* **1** bring into harmony **2** go well (with) **3** *music* add the different parts to a melody • **harmonization** *noun*

harmony *noun* (*plural* **harmonies**) **1** agreement of one part, colour or sound with another **2** agreement between people: *living in harmony* **3** *music* a part intended to agree in sound with the melody • **harmonic** *adj* relating to harmony ◇ *noun, music* a ringing sound produced by lightly touching a string being played

harness *noun* **1** an arrangement of straps *etc* attaching something to the body: *parachute harness* **2** the leather and other fittings for a working horse ◇ *verb* **1** use as a resource: *harnessing the power of the wind* **2** put a harness on a horse • **in harness** working, not on holiday or retired

harp *noun* a triangular stringed musical instrument played upright by plucking with the fingers ◇ *verb* play the harp • **harper** *or* **harpist** *noun* a

harp player • **harp on about** talk too much about

harpoon *noun* a spear tied to rope, used for killing whales ◇ *verb* strike with a harpoon

harpsichord *noun* an early musical instrument with keys, played like a piano

harpy *noun* (*plural* **harpies**) **1** a mythological creature with a woman's body, and the wings, feet and claws of a bird of prey **2** a cruel woman

harridan *noun* a bullying woman

harrier *noun* **1** a breed of small dog for hunting hares **2** a bird of prey **3** a cross-country runner

harrow *noun* a frame with iron spikes for breaking up lumps of earth ◇ *verb* **1** drag a harrow over **2** distress greatly

harrowing *adj* very distressing

harry *verb* (**harries**, **harrying**, **harried**) harass or worry

harsh *adj* rough, bitter or cruel • **harshly** *adv* • **harshness** *noun*

hart *noun* the stag or male deer, *esp* from the age of six years

hartebeest *or* **hartbeest** *noun* a type of S African antelope

harum-scarum *adj* wild and thoughtless; reckless

harvest *noun* **1** the time of the year when ripened crops are gathered in **2** the crops gathered at this time ◇ *verb* gather in (a crop) • **harvester** *noun* **1** a farm worker who helps with the harvest **2** (*also called* **combine harvester**) a large machine that cuts and threshes grain **3** a creature like a spider • **harvest home** *noun* a feast held after a harvest is gathered in

has *see* have

has-been *noun* someone no longer important or popular

hash *noun* a dish of chopped meat

etc • **make a hash of** spoil completely

hashish *noun* a strong form of cannabis

hasp *noun* a clasp, *eg* on a padlock

hassle *verb* cause problems for ◇ *noun* difficulty or trouble

hassock *noun* a thick cushion used as a footstool or for kneeling on

haste *noun* urgency • **hasten** *verb* 1 go or cause to go quickly; hurry 2 do eagerly and promptly • **hastily** *adv* • **make haste** hurry

hasty *adj* (**hastier, hastiest**) done without thinking; hurried

hat *noun* a covering for the head • **hatter** *noun* someone who makes or sells hats • **keep something under your hat** keep it secret

hatch *noun* (*plural* **hatches**) a door or cover over an opening in a floor, wall, *etc* ◇ *verb* 1 produce young from eggs 2 think up and set in motion (a plan *etc*) • **hatchback** *noun* a car with a sloping rear door that opens upwards • **hatchery** *noun* a place for hatching eggs (*esp* of fish) • **hatchway** *noun* an opening in a floor or ship's deck

hatchet *noun* a small axe • **hatchet-faced** *adj* with a thin face and sharp features • **hatchet job** *noun* 1 a severe critical attack on someone or their good reputation 2 a severe reduction • **bury the hatchet** put an end to a quarrel

hate *verb* dislike very much ◇ *noun* great dislike • **hateful** *adj* causing hatred • **hatred** *noun* extreme dislike

hat-trick *noun* 1 *cricket* the putting out of three batsmen by three balls in a row 2 *football* three goals scored by the same player 3 any action performed three times in a row

haughty *adj* (**haughtier, haughtiest**) looking on others with scorn; disdainful • **haughtily** *adv* • **haughtiness** *noun*

haul *verb* pull with force; drag ◇ *noun* 1 a strong pull 2 *informal* a difficult or tiring job: *a long haul* 3 an amount gathered at one time: *a haul of fish* 4 a rich find; booty • **haulage** *noun* 1 the carrying of goods 2 money charged for this • **haulier** *noun* a company that transports goods

haunch *noun* (*plural* **haunches**) 1 the fleshy part of the hip 2 a leg and loin of meat, *esp* venison

haunt *verb* 1 visit often 2 of a ghost: inhabit, linger in (a place) ◇ *noun* a place often visited • **haunted** *adj* inhabited by ghosts

haute couture /oht koo-tyawr/ *noun* high fashion, or the fashion industry

haute cuisine /oht kwi-zeen/ *noun* cooking of the highest standard

have *verb* (**has, having, had**) 1 used with another verb to show that an action is in the past and completed: *we have decided to move house* 2 own, possess: *do you have a cat?* 3 hold, contain: *the hotel has a swimming pool* 4 give birth to: *have a baby* 5 suffer from: *have a cold* 6 cause to be done: *have your hair cut* 7 put up with: *I won't have him being so rude* • **have done with** finish • **have it out** settle by argument

haven *noun* a place of safety or shelter

haver *verb, Scot* 1 speak nonsense 2 be slow or hesitant; dawdle

haversack *noun, dated* a rucksack

havoc *noun* great destruction, disorder or confusion

haw *noun* a berry of the hawthorn tree

hawk *noun* a bird of prey like a falcon ◇ *verb* 1 hunt birds with trained hawks 2 carry goods about for sale • **hawker** *noun* a door-to-door salesman

hawthorn *noun* a prickly tree with white flowers and small red berries

hay noun cut and dried grass, used as cattle food • **hay fever** noun an illness with effects like a bad cold, caused by pollen etc • **hayrick** or **haystack** noun hay built up into a large mound

haywire adj in a state of disorder

hazard noun 1 risk of harm or danger 2 an object or circumstance that presents a difficulty or danger 3 chance ◇ verb 1 risk 2 put forward (a guess) at the risk of being wrong • **hazardous** adj dangerous, risky

haze noun a thin mist • **hazily** adv • **haziness** noun • **hazy** adj 1 misty 2 not clearly expressed or understood; vague

hazel noun a nut-producing tree of the birch family ◇ adj light, greenish brown in colour • **hazelnut** noun a light brown nut produced by the hazel tree

H-bomb noun a hydrogen bomb

he pronoun a male person or animal already spoken about (used only as the subject of a verb): he ate a banana

head noun 1 the uppermost part of the body, containing the brain, skull, etc 2 someone's mind: can't get that tune out of my head 3 a person in charge; a chief ◇ verb 1 lead or be in charge of 2 go at the front of 3 go in the direction of: heading for home 4 hit (a ball) with the head 5 (with **off**) turn aside, deflect: head off an attack • **headache** noun 1 a pain in the head 2 a worrying problem • **headband** noun a band worn round the head • **headboard** noun a board across the top end of a bed • **headdress** noun a covering for the head • **header** noun 1 football a shot at goal striking the ball with the head 2 a piece of text that appears at the top of each page of a document • **headfirst** adv 1 with the head first: fall headfirst down the stairs 2 rashly, without thinking • **heading** noun the title of a book or chapter • **head-**

land noun a point of land running out into the sea, a cape • **headlight** noun a strong light on the front of a motor car etc • **headline** noun a line in large letters at the top of a newspaper page • **headlong** adj & adv headfirst • **headmaster, headmistress** or **headteacher** noun the principal teacher of a school • **head-on** adj & adv with the head or front first • **headphones** plural noun a listening device that fits over the ears • **headquarters** sing noun & plural noun 1 a place from which the chief officers of an army etc control their operations 2 the main office of a business etc • **headrest** noun a support for the head in a vehicle etc • **headscarf** noun a scarf worn over the head • **headstone** noun a gravestone • **headstrong** adj determined, stubborn • **headway** noun forward movement • **headwind** noun a wind blowing straight in your face • **heady** adj exciting • **head over heels** completely, thoroughly • **off your head** mad, crazy • **per head** per person

heal verb make or become healthy or sound; cure

health noun 1 someone's physical condition: how's your health? 2 good or natural physical condition: restored to health • **healthy** adj 1 in good health or condition 2 encouraging good health • **your health** (as a toast) a wish that someone may have good health

heap noun 1 a pile of things thrown one on top of another 2 a great many (of) ◇ verb throw in a pile

hear verb (**hearing, heard**) 1 receive (sounds) by the ear 2 listen to 3 be told; understand: I hear you want to speak to me • **hearing** noun 1 the act or power of listening 2 a court case • **hearsay** noun gossip or rumour • **hear! hear!** exclam shouted to show agreement with a speaker • **will not hear of** will not allow: he wouldn't hear of her going there alone

hearse noun a car for carrying a dead body to the grave etc

heart noun 1 the part of the body that pumps blood around the body 2 the inner or chief part of anything: the heart of the problem 3 courage: take heart 4 will, enthusiasm: his heart isn't in it 5 love, affection: with all my heart 6 a sign (♥) representing a heart, or often love 7 this sign used in one of the suits on playing cards • **heartache** noun sorrow, grief • **heartbeat** noun the pulsing of the heart • **heart-broken** adj very upset • **heartburn** noun a burning feeling in the chest after eating; indigestion • **hearten** verb encourage • **heart failure** noun the sudden stopping of the heart's beating • **heartfelt** adj felt deeply; sincere • **heartless** adj cruel • **heart-rending** adj very moving or upsetting • **heart-strings** plural noun inmost feelings of love • **heart throb** noun a sexually attractive person, with whom others fall in love • **heart-to-heart** noun a frank, intimate discussion

hearth noun a fireplace

hearty adj (heartier, heartiest) 1 strong, healthy 2 of a meal: large, satisfying 3 insincerely eager or cheerful • **heartily** adv

heat noun 1 high temperature 2 anger 3 a round in a competition, race, etc 4 the most intense part: the heat of battle ◇ verb make or become hot • **heat wave** noun a period of hot weather • **in heat** of a female animal: ready for mating in the breeding season

heath noun 1 barren, open country 2 heather

heathen noun someone who does not believe in an established religion, esp someone who worships idols ◇ adj of heathens; pagan

heather noun a plant with small purple or white flowers that grows on moorland ◇ adj of the colour of purple heather

heave verb 1 lift by force 2 throw 3 rise and fall 4 let out (esp a long sigh)

heaven noun 1 (often **the heavens**) the sky 2 the dwelling place of God; paradise 3 any place of great happiness • **heavenly** adj 1 living in heaven 2 informal delightful • **heavenly body** noun a star, planet or moon

heavy adj (heavier, heaviest) 1 of great weight 2 great in amount, force, etc: heavy rainfall 3 not easy to bear: a heavy responsibility 4 severe or intense: heavy fighting in the north 5 sleepy: eyes feeling heavy • **heavily** adv • **heaviness** noun • **heavy-handed** adj lacking finesse or tact; clumsy • **heavy metal** noun a very loud form of rock music in which electric guitars are dominant • **heavy-weight** noun 1 a fighter in the highest weight category in boxing, wrestling and other contact sports 2 someone very important or powerful

hebdomadal /heb-dom-uh-dul/ adj, formal weekly

heckle verb interrupt (a speaker) with abusive shouts or jeers • **heckler** noun someone who heckles

hectare noun 10,000 square metres

hectic adj involving a lot of rushed activity; feverish

hector verb bully

hedge noun a fence of bushes or shrubs ◇ verb 1 make a hedge 2 shut in with a hedge 3 avoid giving a straight answer • **hedgehog** noun a small animal with prickly spines on its back • **hedgerow** noun a row of bushes forming a hedge • **hedge your bets** keep open two or more possible courses of action

hedonism noun 1 selfish enjoyment, esp indulgence in pleasures that some people disapprove of, such as casual sex and excessive drinking of alcohol 2 the belief that pleasure is the most important aim in life • **hedonist** noun someone who lives a life of selfish enjoyment • **hedonistic** adj

heebie-jeebies plural noun **1** a fit of nerves **2** the creeps

heed verb pay attention to • **heedless** adj not thinking or caring about • **pay heed to** take notice of

heel noun the back part of the foot ◇ verb **1** hit (esp a ball) with the heel **2** put a heel on (a shoe) **3** of a ship: lean over • **take to your heels** or **show a clean pair of heels** run away

hefty adj (**heftier, heftiest**) **1** powerful, muscular **2** heavy

hegemony noun complete influence or power over others

Hegira /hi-jai-ruh/ noun the Muslim system of calculating dates, beginning from the year of Muhammad's escape from Mecca, in AD 622; the Islamic era

heifer /hef-uh/ noun a young cow

height noun **1** distance from bottom to top **2** the state of being high **3** the highest point **4** (often **heights**) a high place • **heighten** verb make higher

heinous /hee-nus/ adj extremely bad or cruel; wicked: heinous crime • **heinously** adv • **heinousness** noun

heir or **heiress** noun the legal inheritor of a title or property on the death of the owner • **heir-apparent** noun someone expected to receive a title or property when the present holder dies • **heirloom** noun something that has been handed down in a family from generation to generation

heist noun, slang an armed robbery

held past form of **hold**

helicopter noun a flying machine kept in the air by propellers rotating on a vertical axis

heliograph noun a signalling device with mirrors that uses the sun's rays to produce flashes of light

heliotrope noun **1** a plant with small, sweet-smelling, lilac-blue flowers **2** a light purple colour

helium noun a very light gas

helix noun a spiral shape like the thread of a screw

hell noun **1** a place where the spirits of sinners go after death **2** the dwelling place of the Devil **3** any place of great misery or pain • **hellish** adj • **hellishly** adv • **hellbent on** determined to

hello or **hallo** or **hullo** noun (plural **hellos** or **helloes** etc) a greeting used between people: I said hello to him/ Hello! How are you?

helm noun the wheel or handle by which a ship is steered • **helmsman** noun the person who steers

helmet noun an armoured or protective covering for the head

help verb **1** do something useful for; aid **2** give the means for doing something to **3** stop yourself from (doing): I can't help liking him ◇ noun **1** aid, assistance **2** someone who assists • **helpful** adj doing something useful • **helpfully** adv • **helping** noun a share, esp of food • **helpless** adj useless or powerless • **helplessly** adv • **helpline** noun a telephone service offering advice or information • **helpmate** noun, old a partner • **help yourself** take what you want

helter-skelter noun a spiral slide in a fairground etc ◇ adv in a great hurry or in confusion

hem noun the border of a garment folded over and stitched ◇ verb (**hemming, hemmed**) put or form a hem on • **hem in** surround or restrict

hemisphere noun **1** a half of a sphere or ball-shape **2** half of the earth: western hemisphere/southern hemisphere • **hemispherical** adj like half a ball in shape

hemlock noun a poisonous plant with spotted leaves

hemoglobin US spelling of **haemoglobin**

hemophilia US spelling of **haemophilia**

hemorrhage US spelling of **haemorrhage**

hemp noun a plant used for making ropes, bags, sails, etc and from which the drug cannabis is derived

hen noun **1** a female bird **2** a female domestic fowl • **henpecked** adj of a husband: dominated by his wife

hence adv **1** from this place or time: ten years hence **2** for this reason: hence, I am unable to go • **henceforth** or **henceforward** adv from now on

henchman noun a faithful supporter, esp one willing to do dishonest or immoral things

henna noun a reddish plant dye used for colouring the hair etc

hepatitis noun inflammation of the liver caused by one of several viruses

heptagon noun a flat shape with seven straight sides • **heptagonal** adj

her pronoun a female person already spoken about (used only as the object in a sentence): have you seen her? ◇ adj belonging to such a person: her house • **hers** pronoun something belonging to such a person: the idea was hers • **herself** pronoun **1** used reflexively: she washed herself **2** used for emphasis: she herself won't be there but her brother will

herald noun **1** something that is a sign of future things **2** hist someone who carries and reads important notices ◇ verb **1** be a sign of **2** announce loudly • **heraldic** adj of heraldry • **heraldry** noun the study of coats of arms, crests, etc

herb noun a plant whose leaves are used in cooking or in making medicines

herbaceous adj **1** of a plant: with soft, non-woody stems **2** of a flowerbed: filled with such plants

herbal adj of or using herbs: herbal remedy • **herbalism** noun the study and use of plants in medicine • **herbalist** noun

herbivore noun an animal that feeds on grass etc • **herbivorous** adj

Herculean adj requiring tremendous strength or effort: a Herculean task

herd noun **1** a group of animals of one kind **2** (**the herd**) the majority or people ◇ verb group together like a herd of animals

here adv at, in or to this place: he's here already/come here! • **hereabouts** adv in this area • **hereafter** adv after this • **hereby** adv by this means • **the hereafter** life after death

heredity noun the passing on of physical qualities from parents to children • **hereditary** adj passed on in this way

heresy /he-ruh-see/ noun (plural **heresies**) an opinion that goes against the official (esp religious) view • **heretic** noun someone who holds or teaches such an opinion • **heretical** adj

heritage noun **1** something passed on by or inherited from an earlier generation **2** the buildings, countryside and cultural traditions that define a people or nation

hermaphrodite /hur-maf-ruh-dait/ noun an animal that has the qualities of both male and female sexes

hermeneutic /hur-muh-nyoo-tik/ adj relating to interpretation, esp of Biblical texts

hermetically adv: **hermetically sealed** closed completely and airtight

hermit noun someone who lives alone, often for religious reasons • **hermitage** noun the dwelling of a hermit • **hermit crab** noun a kind of crab that lives in the abandoned shell of a shellfish

hernia *noun* the bursting out of part of an internal organ through a weak spot in surrounding body tissue

hero (*plural* **heroes**), **heroine** *noun* **1** someone much admired for their bravery **2** the main character in a story, film, *etc* • **heroic** *adj* **1** as brave as a hero **2** of heroes • **heroically** *adv* • **heroism** *noun* bravery

heroin *noun* a highly addictive drug derived from morphine

heron *noun* a large water bird with long legs and a long neck

herpes /hur-peez/ *noun* a name for various types of contagious skin disease

herring *noun* (*plural* **herring** or **herrings**) an edible silvery sea fish that moves in large shoals

hers, **herself** *see* **her**

hertz *noun* a unit of frequency for radio waves *etc*

hesitate *verb* **1** pause because of uncertainty **2** be unwilling (to do something): *I hesitate to ask* • **hesitancy** *noun* • **hesitant** *adj* • **hesitation** *noun*

hessian *noun* a type of coarse cloth

heterodox *noun* having an opinion other than the accepted one (*contrasted with*: **orthodox**) • **heterodoxy** *noun*

heterogeneous *adj* made up of many different kinds (*contrasted with*: **homogeneous**)

heterosexual *noun* someone who is sexually attracted to people of the opposite sex ◇ *adj* attracted to people of the opposite sex • **heterosexuality** *noun*

het up *adj, informal* angry or agitated

heuristic /hyoo-ris-tik/ *adj* encouraging the learner to find their own answers or to experiment

hew *verb* (**hewing**, **hewed**, **hewn** or

hewed) cut or shape with an axe *etc*

hex *noun* a spell to bring bad luck; a curse

hexagon *noun* a flat shape with six straight sides • **hexagonal** *adj*

heyday *noun* the time of greatest strength; the prime

HGV *abbrev* heavy goods vehicle (now **LGV**)

hi *exclam, informal* **1** hello **2** hey

hiatus /hai-eh-tus/ *noun* a gap or pause

hibernate *verb* of an animal: spend the winter in a dormant state • **hibernation** *noun* • **hibernator** *noun*

hibiscus *noun* a tropical tree with large colourful flowers

hiccup *noun* **1** an uncontrolled spasm of the diaphragm that causes a loud gasping sound like a burp **2** (**hiccups**) a fit of such gasping **3** a minor setback or difficulty ◇ *verb* make a hiccuping sound

hick *noun, derog* an unsophisticated person from the country; a bumpkin

hickory *noun* (*plural* **hickories**) a N American tree

hide[1] *verb* (**hiding**, **hid**, **hidden**) put or keep out of sight ◇ *noun* a concealed place from which to watch birds *etc* • **hidden** *adj* **1** put out of sight; concealed **2** unknown: *hidden meaning* • **hidebound** *adj* not open to new ideas

hide[2] *noun* the skin of an animal • **hiding** *noun* a beating

hideous *adj* **1** extremely unpleasant to look at **2** frighteningly unpleasant or disgusting; ghastly • **hideously** *adv* • **hideousness** *noun*

hie /hai/ *verb, old* hurry

hierarchy *noun* a number of people or things arranged in order of rank • **hierarchical** *adj*

hieratic *adj* of a priest or priests

hieroglyphics *plural noun* ancient Egyptian writing in which pictures are used as letters

hi-fi *adj, dated* to do with the high-quality reproduction of recorded sound

higgledy-piggledy *adv & adj* in a complete muddle

high *adj* 1 in a place far above 2 extending far upwards; tall 3 senior or important 4 great, large: *high hopes/high prices* 5 of sound: acute in pitch; shrill 6 extremely happy or excited; euphoric 7 under the influence of drugs or alcohol 8 of meat: beginning to go bad ◇ *adv* 1 far above in the air 2 in a senior or important position 3 to a great degree • **highball** *noun, US* an alcoholic drink and mixer (*eg* whisky and soda) with ice in a tall glass • **highbrow** *adj* intellectual (*contrasted with*: **lowbrow**) • **High Court** *noun* a supreme court • **Higher** *noun* an examination in Scottish secondary schools, usually taken at the end of the 5th year • **high-fidelity** *adj, dated* reproducing recorded sound very clearly • **high-five** *noun* a sign of greeting made by slapping together one another's raised palms • **high-flier** *noun* a highly ambitious person set to be very successful • **high-flown** *adj* using words that sound too grand or pompous • **high-handed** *adj* taking no account of others' wishes; overbearing • **high jinks** *plural noun* lively games or play • **highlander** *noun* someone who comes from a mountainous region, *esp* the Scottish Highlands • **highly** *adv* very: *highly delighted* • **highly-strung** *adj* easily excited or made nervous • **Highness** *noun* a title of a monarch • **highroad** *noun, dated* a main road • **high-spirited** *adj* naturally cheerful and lively; vivacious • **high tea** *noun* a cooked meal in the late afternoon • **high tide** *or* **high water** *noun* the time when the tide is farthest up the shore • **high treason** *noun* the crime of acting against the safety of your own country • **highway** *noun* the public road • **Highway Code** *noun* a set of official rules for road users in Britain • **highwayman** *noun, hist* a robber who attacked people on the public road • **for the high jump** expecting trouble or punishment • **on your high horse** behaving with exaggerated pride or superiority • **the highlands** a mountainous region, *esp* the north of Scotland • **the high seas** the open seas

highlight *noun* 1 the most enjoyable or memorable part: *highlights from the match/the highlight of the week* 2 a lighter patch in hair *etc* 3 a bright spot or area in a picture ◇ *verb* make the focus of attention; emphasize • **highlighter** *noun* a coloured felt-tip pen used to mark but not obscure lines of text

hijack *verb* steal (a car, aeroplane, *etc*) while it is moving, forcing the driver or pilot to take a new route ◇ *noun* the action of hijacking a vehicle *etc* • **hijacker** *noun*

hike *verb* travel on foot through countryside ◇ *noun* a country walk • **hiker** *noun*

hilarious *adj* extremely funny • **hilariously** *adv* • **hilarity** *noun*

hill *noun* a mound of high land, less high than a mountain • **hilly** *adj*

hillock *noun* a small hill

hilt *noun* the handle of a sword • **up to the hilt** to a great extent; thoroughly

him *pronoun* a male person already spoken about (used only as the object in a sentence): *I saw him yesterday/what did you say to him?* • **himself** *pronoun* 1 used reflexively: *he cut himself shaving* 2 used for emphasis: *he wrote it himself*

hind *noun* a female deer ◇ *adj* placed behind • **hindmost** *adj* farthest behind • **hindsight** *noun* wisdom or knowledge got only after something has happened

hinder *verb* prevent the progress of; obstruct • **hindrance** *noun* something that hinders

Hindu *noun* a member of an eastern religion that involves the worship of several gods and belief in reincarnation • **Hinduism** *noun*

hinge *noun* a joint on which a door, lid, *etc* turns ◇ *verb* **1** move on a hinge **2** depend (on): *everything hinges on the weather*

hint *noun* **1** a remark that suggests a meaning without stating it clearly: *I'll give you a hint* **2** a slight impression; a suggestion: *a hint of panic in her voice* ◇ *verb* suggest without stating clearly: *he hinted that he might be there*

hinterland *noun* an area lying inland from the coast

hip[1] *noun* the part of the side of the body just below the waist • **hip flask** *noun* a small pocket flask for alcohol

hip[2] *noun* the fruit of the wild rose

hip[3] *adj, dated informal* very fashionable; trendy

hippie *noun* a member of a youth movement emphasizing love and peace and rebelling against the more conservative elements of conventional society, *esp* in the 1960s

Hippocratic oath *noun* an oath taken by a doctor agreeing to observe a code of medical ethics

hippodrome *noun* **1** an arena for horse-racing **2** a large theatre

hippopotamus *noun* (*plural* **hippopotami** *or* **hippopotamuses**) a large African animal living in and near rivers

hire *verb* give or get the use of by paying money ◇ *noun* money paid for work done, or for the use of something belonging to another person • **hire-purchase** *noun* a way of buying an article by paying for it in instalments

hirsute *adj, formal* hairy

his *adj* belonging to him: *his book* ◇ *pronoun*: *that jacket is his*

Hispanic *adj* **1** descended from a Spanish or Spanish-speaking family **2** Spanish

hiss *verb* make a sound like a snake ◇ *noun* (*plural* **hisses**) such a sound, made to show anger or displeasure

histamine *noun* a chemical present in pollen *etc* that can cause an allergic reaction

histology *noun* the study of animal tissue • **histological** *adj* • **histologist** *noun*

history *noun* (*plural* **histories**) **1** the study of the past **2** a description of past events, society, *etc* • **historian** *noun* someone who studies or writes history • **historic** *adj* important in the development of events and likely to be remembered as such • **historical** *adj* **1** of history **2** true of something in the past

---

Do not confuse: **historic** and **historical**

---

histrionic *adj* relating to stage-acting or actors • **histrionics** *plural noun* an exaggerated show of strong feeling

hit *verb* (**hitting**, **hit**) **1** strike with a blow **2** occur suddenly to: *it finally hit me* ◇ *noun* **1** a blow or stroke **2** a shot that hits a target **3** a success **4** a successful song, recording, *etc* **5** *comput* a successful attempt to access a website or a particular item in a database **6** *slang* a murder by criminals **7** *slang* a dose of a drug • **hit-and-miss** *adj* sometimes successful and sometimes not • **hit-and-run** *adj* of a driver: driving away after causing injury without reporting the accident • **hitman** *noun, slang* someone employed to kill or attack others • **hit the ceiling** *or* **hit the roof** explode with anger • **hit the ground running** react, or begin working, immediately and efficiently • **hit the nail on the head** identify the important point, be exactly right • **hit upon** come upon; discover

hitch *verb* 1 fasten with a hook *etc* 2 lift with a jerk 3 hitchhike ◇ *noun* (*plural* **hitches**) 1 a jerk 2 an unexpected stop or delay 3 a type of knot

hitchhike *verb* travel by getting lifts in other people's vehicles • **hitchhiker** *noun*

hither *adv, old* to this place • **hitherto** *adv* up till now • **hither and thither** back and forwards

HIV *abbrev* human immunodeficiency virus, the virus that can cause AIDS • **HIV-positive** *adj* infected with HIV

hive *noun* 1 place where bees live 2 a busy place: *hive of industry*

hives /haivz/ *sing noun* nettle rash

HM *abbrev* Her or His Majesty

HMS *abbrev* 1 Her or His Majesty's Service 2 Her or His Majesty's Ship

hoard *noun* a hidden store of treasure, food, *etc* ◇ *verb* store up secretly

Do not confuse with: **horde**

hoarding *noun* a screen of boards displaying an advertisement or enclosing a building site

hoarse *adj* having a harsh voice, *eg* from a cold or cough

hoary *adj* (**hoarier**, **hoariest**) 1 white with age 2 very old • **hoar frost** *noun* white frost

hoax *noun* (*plural* **hoaxes**) a trick played to deceive someone ◇ *verb* play a hoax on

hob *noun* 1 the top of a cooker, with rings for heating *etc* 2 a small shelf next to a fireplace for keeping pans *etc* hot

hobble *verb* 1 walk with short unsteady steps 2 tie the legs of (a horse *etc*) loosely 3 prevent from making progress; hamper

hobby *noun* (*plural* **hobbies**) a favourite way of passing your spare time

hobby-horse *noun* 1 a toy wooden horse 2 a favourite subject of discussion

hobgoblin *noun* a mischievous fairy

hobnail *noun* a large nail used for horseshoes and in the soles of heavy boots

hobnob *verb* (**hobnobbing**, **hobnobbed**) be on friendly terms (with); socialize (with)

hobo *noun* (*plural* **hoboes**) *derog* a homeless person who lives on the street; a tramp

Hobson's choice *noun* the choice of having the thing that is offered or having nothing at all

hock¹ *noun* a joint on the hind leg of an animal, below the knee

hock² *noun* a white German wine

hock³ *verb, slang* pawn • **in hock** pawned

hockey *noun* an eleven-a-side ball-game played with clubs curved at one end

hocus-pocus *noun* deception or trickery

hod *noun* 1 a wooden trough on a pole, for carrying bricks and mortar 2 a container for coal

hodge-podge *same as* **hotchpotch**

hoe *noun* a tool used for weeding, loosening earth, *etc* ◇ *verb* use a hoe

hog *noun* a pig ◇ *verb, informal* (**hogging**, **hogged**) take or use selfishly • **hogwash** *noun* nonsense • **road hog** an inconsiderate driver who refuses to let others pass *etc*

Hogmanay /hog-muh-*neh*/ *noun* the name in Scotland for 31 December and the celebrations held that night

hoick *verb* pull sharply (up)

hoi polloi *plural noun* ordinary people, *esp* when regarded as lacking education or good taste; the masses

hoisin /hoy-sin/ *noun* a sweet, hot Chinese sauce made with soy beans and chilli

hoist *verb* lift up; raise ◇ *noun* a device for lifting things

hoity-toity *adj* behaving in a superior way; haughty

hokum /hoh-kum/ *noun, US* pretentious rubbish; claptrap

hold *verb* (**holding, held**) **1** keep in your possession or power; have **2** contain **3** occupy (a position *etc*) **4** put on; organize: *hold a meeting* **5** apply: *that rule doesn't hold any longer* **6** celebrate: *hold Christmas* **7** think or believe (that) ◇ *noun* **1** grip, grasp **2** influence: *a hold over the others* **3** a large space for carrying a ship's cargo • **holdall** *noun* a large carrying bag with a zip • **holder** *noun* **1** container **2** someone who holds (a position *etc*) • **holding** *noun* an amount of land, shares, *etc* held • **hold-up** *noun* an armed attempt at robbery • **hold forth** speak at length • **hold good** continue to be true • **hold out** refuse to give in • **hold over** keep till later • **hold up 1** prevent from making progress; hinder **2** offer as an example to be copied **3** attack and demand money from

hole *noun* **1** an opening in something solid **2** a pit or burrow **3** a dirty or miserable place • **in a hole** in a difficult situation

Holi *noun* a Hindu Spring festival

holiday *noun* **1** a period away from work for rest **2** a day when businesses *etc* are closed

holistic *adj* of medicine: treating the patient as a whole rather than the individual disease or symptoms • **holism** *noun*

hollow *adj* **1** having empty space inside, not solid **2** false or unreal: *hollow victory/hollow smile* ◇ *noun* **1** a sunken place **2** a dip in the land ◇ *verb* scoop (out)

holly *noun* (*plural* **hollies**) an evergreen shrub with scarlet berries and prickly leaves

hollyhock *noun* a very tall garden flower

Hollywood *noun* the American cinema industry, based in Hollywood, California

holocaust *noun* **1** (**the Holocaust**) the mass murder of Jewish people by the Nazis during World War II **2** any genocide **3** a great destruction by fire

hologram *noun* a 3-D image created by laser beams

holograph *noun* a document written entirely by one person

holster *noun* a case for a pistol

holt *noun* an otter's den

holy *adj* (**holier, holiest**) **1** of or like God **2** religious or righteous **3** for religious use; sacred • **holier-than-thou** *adj* showing an annoying pride in moral superiority over others • **holiness** *noun* • **holy of holies** *noun* an inner sanctum • **holy week** *noun* the week before Easter • **holy writ** *noun* the Bible

homage *noun* a show of respect that acknowledges a debt: *paying homage to the pioneers of cinema*

home *noun* **1** the place where someone lives **2** the house of someone's family **3** a centre or place of origin: *Nashville is the home of country music* **4** a place where children, the elderly, *etc* live and are looked after ◇ *adj* **1** of someone's house or family: *home comforts* **2** domestic, not foreign: *home affairs* ◇ *adv* **1** towards home **2** to the full length or extent:

drive the nail home • **home economics** *sing noun* the study of how to run a home • **homeless** *adj* having no home • **homely** *adj* **1** plain but pleasant **2** *US* plain, not attractive • **home-made** *adj* made at home • **home page** *noun* the first page of a website • **home rule** *noun* government of a country *etc* by its own parliament • **Home Secretary** *noun, Brit* the government minister who deals with domestic issues, *eg* law and order, and immigration • **homesick** *adj* longing to be at home • **homespun** *adj* simple and unaffected • **homestead** *noun* a farmhouse • **home truth** *noun* a frank statement of something true but unpleasant • **homewards** *adv* towards home • **homework** *noun* work for school *etc* done at home • **homing** *adj* of a pigeon: having the habit of making for home • **bring home to** make (someone) realize

homeopathy *or* **homoeopathy** *noun* the treatment of illness by small quantities of substances that produce symptoms similar to those of the illness • **homeopath** *noun* a practitioner of homeopathy • **homeopathic** *adj* of or using homeopathy

homicide *noun* **1** the killing of a human being **2** someone who kills a person • **homicidal** *adj*

homily *noun* (*plural* **homilies**) **1** a plain, practical sermon **2** a talk giving advice

homoeopathy *another spelling of* homeopathy

homoeostasis *noun* a tendency towards health or a stable condition • **homoeostatic** *adj*

homoerotic *adj* relating to homosexual desire • **homoeroticism** *noun*

homogeneous *adj* made up of parts of the same kind (*contrasted with*: heterogeneous) • **homogeneity** *noun*

homogenize *verb* **1** change something so that it is the same in all parts or aspects **2** treat (milk) so that the cream does not separate and rise to the surface • **homogenization** *noun*

homograph *noun* a word that has the same spelling as, but a different meaning to, another, *eg* the *bark* of a dog and the *bark* of a tree

homonym *noun* a homograph, *esp* one that belongs to a different word class from another, *eg* the public entertainment called a *fair* and the word *fair* meaning 'just'

homophone *noun* a word that is pronounced the same as another but has a different spelling to it, *eg* pair and *pear*

homo sapiens *noun* a human being

homosexual *noun* someone who is sexually attracted to people of the same sex ◇ *adj* sexually attracted to people of the same sex • **homosexuality** *noun*

Hon *abbrev* **1** Honourable **2** Honorary

hone *verb* **1** make (a good talent or skill) even better **2** sharpen (a knife *etc*)

honest *adj* not inclined to steal, cheat, *etc*; fair and truthful • **honestly** *adv* • **honesty** *noun*

honey *noun* **1** a sweet, thick fluid made by bees from the nectar of flowers **2** *informal* sweetheart, dear • **honey trap** *noun* a planned sexual seduction to trap someone into blackmail *etc*

honeycomb *noun* a network of wax cells in which bees store honey • **honeycombed** *adj* patterned with holes like honey cells

honeydew *noun* a sweet-tasting melon with a smooth rind

honeymoon *noun* a holiday spent immediately after marriage ◇ *verb* spend a honeymoon • **honeymooner** *noun*

honeysuckle *noun* a climbing shrub with sweet-smelling flowers

honk *noun* a noise like the cry of the wild goose or the sound of a vehicle horn ◇ *verb* make this sound

honky-tonk *noun* a jangly style of piano music

honorary *adj* **1** done to give honour **2** without payment • **honorarium** *noun* a fee for services not paid for by wages

honour *or US* **honor** *noun* **1** respect for truth, honesty, *etc* **2** fame, glory **3** reputation, good name **4** a title of respect, *esp* to a judge: *Your Honour* **5** a privilege **6** (**honours**) recognition given for exceptional achievements ◇ *verb* **1** give respect to **2** give high rank to **3** pay money when due: *honour a debt* • **honourable** *adj* worthy of honour • **honourably** *adv* • **do the honours** perform a ceremonial task

hood *noun* **1** a covering for the head **2** a protective cover for anything **3** *US* the bonnet of a car • **hoodie** *noun, informal* a hooded jacket or sweat-shirt

hoodwink *verb* deceive

hoof *noun* (*plural* **hoofs** *or* **hooves**) the horny part on the feet of certain animals (*eg* horses) • **on the hoof** *informal* on the move, while moving

hoo-ha *noun, informal* a noisy fuss

hook *noun* **1** a bent piece of metal *etc* for hanging things on **2** a piece of metal on the end of a line for catching fish ◇ *verb* hang or catch with a hook • **hooked** *adj* **1** curved, bent **2** caught by a hook **3** *slang* addicted or fascinated • **by hook or by crook** by one means or another, whatever the cost

hookah *or* **hooka** *noun* a tobacco pipe in which the smoke is drawn through water

hooker *noun, slang* a prostitute

hookey *noun*: **play hookey** *US* play truant

hooligan *noun* a wild, destructive or violent person • **hooliganism** *noun* wild, destructive or violent behaviour

hoop *noun* a thin ring of wood or metal

hoopoe /hoop-oo/ *noun* a medium-sized bird with a curved beak and a large crest, found in Africa, Asia and parts of Europe

hooray *another spelling of* **hurrah**

hoot *verb* **1** sound (a siren, car horn, *etc*) **2** of an owl: call, cry **3** laugh loudly ◇ *noun* **1** the sound made by a car horn, siren or owl **2** a shout of scorn or disgust **3** *informal* someone or something extremely funny • **hooter** *noun* **1** a siren or horn which makes a hooting sound **2** *slang* a large nose

Hoover *noun, trademark* a vacuum cleaner • **hoover** *verb* vacuum (a floor *etc*)

hop[1] *verb* (**hopping, hopped**) leap on one leg ◇ *noun* a short jump on one leg • **hopper** *noun* a funnel for shaking down corn to a grinding machine

hop[2] *noun* a climbing plant with bitter-tasting fruits used in brewing beer

hope *noun* **1** the state of expecting or wishing something good to happen **2** something desired ◇ *verb* expect or wish good to happen • **hopeful** *adj* ◇ *noun* a person who is trying to fulfil an ambition or competing to be successful • **hopefully** *adv* • **hopeless** *adj* **1** without hope **2** very bad • **hopelessly** *adv*

hopscotch *noun* a hopping game over lines drawn on the ground

horde *noun* a large crowd or group

Do not confuse with: **hoard**

---

horizon *noun* **1** the imaginary line formed where the earth meets the sky **2** the limit of someone's experience or knowledge • **horizontal** *adj* lying level or flat • **horizontally** adv

hormone noun a substance produced by certain glands of the body, which acts on a particular organ • **hormonal** adj

horn noun 1 a hard growth on the heads of certain animals, eg deer, sheep 2 something curved or sticking out like an animal's horn 3 part of a vehicle used to give a warning sound 4 a brass wind instrument, esp the French horn • **horned** adj having horns • **horny** adj 1 hard like horn 2 slang sexually aroused

hornbill noun any of various African and Asian birds with a horny growth on their bill

hornet noun a kind of large wasp • **stir up a hornet's nest** cause a commotion or violent reaction

hornpipe noun a lively sailor's dance

horoscope noun a prediction of someone's future based on the position of the stars at their birth

horrendous adj, informal very unpleasant; awful • **horrendously** adv

horrible adj 1 causing intense fear or disgust; horrific 2 very bad; awful • **horribly** adv

horrid adj causing hatred or disgust

horrific adj 1 causing intense fear; terrifying 2 very unpleasant; awful • **horrifically** adv

horrify verb (**horrifies**, **horrifying**, **horrified**) frighten or disgust greatly; shock: we were horrified by his behaviour • **horrifying** adj • **horrifyingly** adv

horror noun 1 intense fear; terror 2 something that causes fear 3 an unruly or demanding child

hors d'oeuvre /aw durv/ noun a savoury food served at the beginning of a meal; an appetizer

horse noun 1 a four-footed animal with hooves and a mane 2 a wooden frame for drying clothes on 3 a piece of gymnastic equipment for vaulting • **horse chestnut** noun a tree that produces a shiny, bitter-tasting nut called a conker • **horsefly** noun a large fly that bites • **horse laugh** noun a loud, harsh laugh • **horseplay** noun rough play • **horsepower** noun a unit of mechanical power for vehicle engines (short form: hp) • **horseradish** noun a plant with a sharp-tasting root that is used in sauces • **horseshoe** noun 1 a shoe for horses, made of a curved piece of iron 2 a horseshoe-shaped thing • **horsy** or **horsey** adj fond of horses • **from the horse's mouth** directly from the source, first-hand • **horses for courses** people will do best in situations that suit them individually

horticulture noun the study and art of gardening • **horticultural** adj • **horticulturist** noun

hosanna noun an exclamation of praise to God

hose noun 1 (plural **hoses**) a rubber tube for carrying water 2 (plural **hose**) old coverings for the legs or feet, eg stockings • **hosiery** noun stockings, tights and socks

hospice noun a home providing special nursing care for people with a terminal illness

hospitable adj showing kindness to guests or strangers • **hospitably** adv • **hospitality** noun

hospital noun a building for the treatment of ill and injured people

host¹, **hostess** noun 1 someone who welcomes and entertains guests 2 an innkeeper or hotel-keeper

host² noun a very large number

hostage noun someone held prisoner by an enemy to make sure that an agreement will be kept to

hostel noun a building providing simple affordable accommodation • **hostelry** noun, old an inn • **hostler** or **ostler** noun, hist a servant in charge of horses at an inn

hostile adj **1** showing dislike or opposition (to) **2** not friendly **3** of an enemy: hostile fire • **hostility** noun **1** unfriendliness or dislike **2** (**hostilities**) acts of warfare

hot adj (**hotter, hottest**) **1** very warm **2** spicy **3** passionate **4** slang popular or sought after **5** slang sexually attractive **6** slang stolen • **hot air** noun meaningless talk • **hotbed** noun a centre or breeding ground for anything: a hotbed of rebellion • **hot-blooded** adj full of anger or passion • **hot dog** noun a hot sausage in a roll • **hotfoot** adv in great haste • **hot-headed** adj inclined to act rashly without thinking • **hothouse** noun **1** a heated glasshouse for plants **2** an institution or environment that encourages people to develop their talents rapidly ◇ verb give (someone) intensive schooling or training, esp at an early age • **hotline** noun **1** a dedicated telephone line offering a public service, esp one answering inquiries relating to a major accident **2** a direct telephone line between heads of government • **hot potato** noun a touchy subject • **hot seat** noun a position of responsibility • **hot on someone's heels** following them closely • **hot under the collar** indignant, enraged • **in hot water** in trouble • **sell like hot cakes** sell very quickly

hotchpotch noun (plural **hotchpotches**) a confused mixture

hotel noun a building with several rooms for paying guests to stay in

hound noun a dog used in hunting ◇ verb hunt or pursue

hour noun **1** sixty minutes, the 24th part of a day **2** a time or occasion: the hour of reckoning • **hourglass** noun an instrument that measures the hours by the running of sand from one glass into another • **hourly** adj happening or done every hour ◇ adv every hour

houri /hoo-uh-ri/ noun a female spirit in the Islamic paradise

house noun **1** a building in which people live **2** a household **3** a business firm **4** one of several divisions of a large school, comprising pupils from several classes ◇ verb provide a house for; accommodate • **house arrest** noun confinement under guard in a private house, hospital, etc • **houseboat** noun a river barge with a cabin for living in • **housebreaker** noun someone who breaks into a house to steal • **housecoat** noun a dressing gown • **household** noun the people who live together in a house • **householder** noun someone who owns or pays the rent of a house • **housekeeper** noun someone employed to look after the running of a house • **house-proud** adj proud of keeping your house clean and tidy • **house-trained** adj of a pet: trained to urinate and defecate outdoors • **house-warming** noun a party held when someone moves into a new house • **housewife** noun a woman who looks after a house and her family • **housework** noun the work of keeping a house clean and tidy • **housing** noun **1** accommodation, eg houses, flats, etc **2** a casing for a machine etc • **a household name** or **a household word** someone or something which everyone is talking about • **like a house on fire** very successfully, extremely well • **on the house** given at no cost; complimentary

hovel noun a small squalid house or flat

hover verb **1** stay in the air in the same spot **2** stay nearby; linger **3** be undecided or uncertain

hovercraft noun a vehicle able to travel over land or sea, supported on a cushion of air

how adv 1 in what manner: *how are they getting there?* 2 to what extent: *how old are you?/how cold is it outside?* 3 to a great extent: *how young he seems/how well you play* 4 by what means: *how do you switch this on?* 5 in what condition: *how is she?* • **however** adv 1 no matter how 2 in spite of that

howdah noun a seat fixed on an elephant's back

howitzer noun a short cannon that fires shells over relatively short distances

howl verb 1 make a long, loud sound like that of a dog or wolf 2 yell in pain or anger 3 laugh loudly ◊ noun a howling sound • **howler** noun, informal a ridiculous and embarrassing mistake

hoyden noun, old a tomboy • **hoydenish** adj

HP or **hp** abbrev 1 hire-purchase 2 horsepower

HQ abbrev headquarters

hr abbrev hour

HRH abbrev Her or His Royal Highness

HRT abbrev hormone replacement therapy

HTML abbrev hypertext mark-up language, the language used to create documents on the World Wide Web

hub noun 1 the centre part of a wheel through which the axle passes 2 a thriving centre of anything: *the hub of the entertainment industry*

hubbub noun a confused sound of many voices

hubby noun (**hubbies**) informal a husband

hubris noun arrogance or over-confidence, *esp* when likely to result in disaster

huddle verb crowd together ◊ noun a close group

hue noun colour or shade

hue and cry noun a loud public protest; an uproar

huff noun a fit of bad temper and sulking • **huffily** adv • **huffiness** noun • **huffy** adj inclined to sulk

hug verb (**hugging, hugged**) 1 hold tightly with the arms 2 keep close to: *hugging the kerb* ◊ noun a tight embrace

huge adj extremely big • **hugeness** noun

hugger-mugger adj done in secret; hush-hush

hula-hoop noun a light hoop for spinning round the waist

hulk noun 1 something very big and sometimes clumsy 2 an old ship unfit for use • **hulking** adj very big and sometimes clumsy

hull noun the body or framework of a ship

hullabaloo noun a noisy disturbance or protest

hullo another spelling of **hello**

hum verb (**humming, hummed**) 1 make a buzzing sound like that of bees 2 sing with the lips shut 3 of a place: be noisily busy ◊ noun 1 the noise of bees 2 any buzzing, droning sound • **hummingbird** noun a small brightly-coloured bird that beats its wings rapidly, making a humming noise

human adj 1 relating to people as opposed to animals or gods 2 having natural qualities, feelings, *etc* ◊ noun a man, woman or child • **humanism** noun a set of ideas about or interest in ethics and mankind, not including religious belief • **humanist** noun • **humanitarian** adj concerned with improving people's lives • **humanity** noun 1 men and women in general 2 kindness, gentleness

humane adj showing kindness or

mercy • **humanely** adv

humble adj 1 modest 2 not of high rank; ordinary or lowly ◇ verb 1 cause to feel unimportant 2 cause to feel ashamed of personal comfort, good fortune, etc • **humbling** adj • **eat humble pie** admit a mistake openly

humbug noun 1 foolish words; nonsense 2 a kind of hard minty sweet

humdinger noun, informal someone or something exceptional

humdrum adj not at all interesting or exciting; dull

humerus noun the bone of the upper arm

humid adj of air etc: unpleasantly moist; damp • **humidifier** noun a device that controls the amount of humidity in the air • **humidity** noun

humiliate noun cause to feel foolish or ashamed; ridicule • **humiliating** adj • **humiliation** noun

humility noun humble state of mind; modesty

hummus noun a paste made from ground chickpeas and olive oil

humongous or **humungous** adj, informal extremely large; enormous

humorous adj funny, amusing • **humorously** adv

humour or US **humor** noun 1 the ability to see things as amusing or ridiculous 2 the amusing aspect: failed to see the humour of the situation 3 state of mind; mood ◇ verb please or placate (someone) by doing as they wish • **humorist** noun a comedian or comic writer

hump noun 1 a lump or mound 2 a lump on the back • **humpback** noun 1 a back with a hump 2 someone with a hump on their back • **humpbacked** adj 1 with a hump on the back 2 of a bridge: rising and falling so as to form a hump shape

humungous another spelling of humongous

humus /hyoom-us/ noun the rich top layer of soil

hunch noun (plural **hunches**) a suspicion that something is untrue or is going to happen etc • **hunchback** noun humpback • **hunchbacked** adj humpbacked

hundred noun the number 100 ◇ adj 100 in number • **hundredth** adj the last of a hundred (things etc) ◇ noun one of a hundred equal parts • **hundredweight** noun 112 lb, 50.8kg (often written **cwt**)

hunger noun 1 a desire for food 2 a strong desire for anything ◇ verb 1 go without food 2 long (for) • **hunger strike** noun a refusal to eat as a protest • **hungrily** adv • **hungry** adj wanting or needing food

hunk noun, informal a muscular, sexually attractive man • **hunky** adj

hunker verb: **hunker down** squat

hunky-dory adj in a good situation; fine

hunt verb 1 chase animals or birds for food or sport 2 search (for) ◇ noun 1 a time spent chasing wild animals 2 a search • **huntsman, huntswoman** noun someone who hunts, esp foxes with hounds

hurdle noun 1 a light frame to be jumped over in a race 2 a difficulty that must be overcome

hurdy-gurdy noun (plural **hurdy-gurdies**) a barrel organ

hurl verb throw with force

hurly-burly noun noisy activity or protest; commotion

hurrah or **hurray** exclam a shout of joy, approval, etc

hurricane noun a violent storm of wind blowing at a speed of over 75 miles (120 kilometres) per hour • **hurricane lamp** noun a lamp specially made to stay lit in strong wind

hurry verb (**hurries, hurrying, hurried**) **1** act or move quickly **2** make (someone) act quickly ◇ noun eagerness to act quickly; haste • **hurried** adj done in a hurry • **hurriedly** adv

hurt verb **1** cause pain or distress to: my leg hurts **2** injure physically; wound: I've hurt my arm **3** damage or spoil ◇ noun **1** pain, distress **2** damage • **hurtful** adj causing pain, distress or damage • **hurtfully** adv

hurtle verb rush at great speed

husband noun a man to whom a woman is married ◇ verb spend or use (eg money, strength) carefully • **husbandry** noun **1** farming **2** management **3** care with money; thrift

hush exclam be quiet! ◇ noun, informal silence, quiet ◇ verb make quiet • **hush-hush** adj, informal top secret • **hush up** stop (a scandal etc) becoming public

husk noun the dry thin covering of certain fruits and seeds

husky¹ adj (**huskier, huskiest**) **1** of a voice: deep and rough **2** big and strong • **huskily** adv • **huskiness** noun

husky² noun (plural **huskies**) a Canadian sledge-dog

hussar /huh-zahr/ noun a light-armed horse soldier

hussy noun (plural **hussies**) **1** a promiscuous girl or woman **2** dated a disrespectful girl or woman

hustings plural noun political campaigning just before an election

hustle verb **1** push rudely **2** hurry

hut noun a small wooden building

hutch noun (plural **hutches**) a box in which pet rabbits are housed

hyacinth noun a sweet-smelling flower which grows from a bulb

hyaena another spelling of **hyena**

hybrid noun **1** an animal or plant bred from two different kinds, eg a mule, which is a hybrid from a horse and a donkey **2** a word formed of parts from different languages

hydra noun **1** a mythological many-headed snake that grew two heads for each one cut off **2** a sea creature that can divide and re-divide itself

hydrant noun a connection to which a hose can be attached to draw water off the main water supply

hydraulic adj **1** worked by the pressure of water or other fluid **2** carrying water

hydro noun (plural **hydros**) a hotel with a swimming pool and gymnasium etc

hydro- prefix involving water: hydro-dynamics

hydroelectricity noun electricity obtained from water power • **hydro-electric** adj

hydrofoil noun **1** a device on a boat that raises it out of the water as it accelerates **2** a boat with hydrofoils

hydrogen noun the lightest gas, which with oxygen makes up water • **hydrogen bomb** noun an extremely powerful bomb using hydrogen

hydrophobia noun **1** fear of water, a symptom of rabies **2** rabies itself • **hydrophobic** adj

hyena or **hyaena** noun a dog-like wild animal with a howl sounding like laughter

hygiene /hai-jeen/ noun the maintaining of cleanliness as a means to health • **hygienic** adj

hymen noun the thin membrane that partially closes the vagina of a virgin

hymn noun a religious song of praise • **hymnal** or **hymnary** noun a book of hymns

hype /haip/ informal noun **1** extravagant advertisement or publicity **2**

a hypodermic syringe ◇ *verb* **1** promote extravagantly **2** inject yourself with a drug • **hype up** hype

hyper- *prefix* to a greater extent than usual; excessive: *hypersensitive*

hyperbole /hai-*pur*-buh-li/ *noun* exaggeration • **hyperbolical** *adj*

hyperlink *noun, comput* a cross-reference link that the user can click on to access other relevant information from the same or another file

hypermarket *noun* a large supermarket

hypernym *noun* a general word whose meaning contains several specific words, *eg dance* is a hypernym of *waltz* and *reel* (*contrasted with*: **hyponym**)

hypertension *noun* high blood pressure

hypertext *noun, comput* electronic text containing cross-references that can be accessed by clicking with the mouse

hyphen *noun* a short stroke (-) used to link or separate parts of a word or phrase: *touch-and-go/re-election* • **hyphenate** *verb*

hypnosis *noun* **1** a sleep-like state in which suggestions are obeyed **2** hypnotism • **hypnotic** *adj* **1** of hypnosis or hypnotism **2** causing a sleep-like state • **hypnotically** *adv* • **hypnotism** *noun* the act of putting someone into hypnosis • **hypnotist** *noun* • **hypnotize** *verb* put someone into hypnosis

hypo- *prefix* below, under: *hypotension*

hypoallergenic *adj* specially formulated in order to reduce the risk of allergy

hypochondria *noun* over-anxiety

about your own health • **hypochondriac** *noun & adj*

hypocrite /*hip*-uh-krit/ *noun* someone who pretends to be something they are not, or to believe something they do not • **hypocrisy** *noun* • **hypocritical** *adj*

hypodermic *adj* used for injecting drugs just below the skin: *hypodermic syringe/hypodermic needle* ◇ *noun* a hypodermic syringe

hypoglycaemia *noun* an abnormally low amount of sugar in the blood • **hypoglycaemic** *adj*

hyponym *noun* one of a group of words whose meanings are included in a more general term, *eg guitar* and *piano* are hyponyms of *musical instrument* (*contrasted with*: **hypernym**)

hypotenuse *noun* the longest side of a right-angled triangle

hypothermia *noun* an abnormally low body temperature caused by exposure to cold

hypothesis /hai-*poth*-uh-sis/ *noun* (*plural* **hypotheses**) something taken as true for the sake of argument • **hypothetical** *adj* supposed • **hypothetically** *adv*

hyssop *noun* an aromatic plant used in perfumes and herbal medicine

hysterectomy *noun* (*plural* **hysterectomies**) surgical removal of the womb

hysteria *noun* **1** a nervous excitement causing uncontrollable laughter, crying, *etc* **2** a nervous illness • **hysterical** *adj* • **hysterically** *adv* • **hysterics** *plural noun* a fit of hysteria

Hz *abbrev* hertz

Ii

I *pronoun* the word used by a speaker or writer in mentioning themselves (as the subject of a verb): *you and I/I, myself*

IBA *abbrev* Independent Broadcasting Authority

ibex *noun* (*plural* **ibexes**) a wild mountain goat

ibid *adv* in the same book, article, *etc*

IBS *abbrev* irritable bowel syndrome

ice *noun* **1** frozen water **2** ice cream ◇ *verb* **1** cover with icing **2** freeze ● **ice age** *noun* an age when the earth was mostly covered with ice ● **iceberg** *noun* a huge mass of floating ice ● **icebox** *noun*, *US* refrigerator ● **icecap** *noun* a permanent covering of ice, as at the north and south poles ● **ice cream** *noun* a sweet creamy mixture, flavoured and frozen ● **ice floe** *noun* a piece of floating ice ● **ice hockey** *noun* hockey played with a rubber disc (called a **puck**) on an ice rink ● **ice skate** *noun* a skate for moving on ice ● **ice skating** *noun* ● **dry ice** solid carbon dioxide

ichthyology /ik-thi-*ol*-uh-ji/ *noun* the study of fishes ● **ichthyologist** *noun*

icicle *noun* a hanging, pointed piece of ice formed by the freezing of dropping water

icing *noun* powdered sugar, mixed with water or egg-white, spread on cakes or biscuits ● **icing on the cake** something added but not really necessary

icky *adj* (**ickier**, **ickiest**) *informal* disgusting, repulsive

icon *noun* **1** *comput* a small graphic image which is clicked to access a particular program **2** (*also* **ikon**) a painted or mosaic image of Christ or a saint

iconoclasm *noun* **1** the attacking of long-established beliefs **2** the act of breaking images ● **iconoclast** *noun* ● **iconoclastic** *adj*

iconography *noun* the way in which ideas or beliefs are represented in pictures

icy *adj* (**icier**, **iciest**) **1** covered with ice **2** very cold **3** very unfriendly or disapproving; hostile ● **icily** *adv* ● **iciness** *noun*

ID *abbrev* identification ◇ *noun*, *US* a means of identification, *eg* a driving licence

I'd *short for* I would, I should or I had: *I'd sooner go than stay*

id *noun* the unconscious part of the personality, the source of instincts and dreams

idea *noun* **1** a thought or notion **2** a plan

ideal *adj* **1** perfect **2** existing in the imagination only (*contrasted with*: **real**) ◇ *noun* **1** the highest and best **2** a standard of perfection ● **idealism** *noun* ● **idealist** *noun* someone who thinks that perfection can be reached ● **idealistic** *adj* ● **idealization** *noun* ● **idealize** *verb* think of as perfect ● **ideally** *adv* in ideal circumstances: *ideally all children should have a place in nursery school*

identical *adj* the same in all details ● **identically** *adv*

identify verb (**identifies**, **identifying**, **identified**) say who or what someone or something is: he identified the man as his attacker ● **identifiable** adj able to be identified, recognizable ● **identification** noun ● **identify with 1** feel close to or involved with **2** think of as the same; equate: identifying money with happiness

identikit picture noun a rough picture of a wanted person that police put together from descriptions

identity noun (plural **identities**) **1** who or what someone or something is **2** the state of being the same

ideogram noun a written character that represents an idea rather than a sound

ideology noun (plural **ideologies**) a set of ideas, often political or philosophical ● **ideological** adj ● **ideologically** adv

idiocy see idiot

idiolect noun the language spoken by an individual person, including their vocabulary, pronunciation, etc

idiom noun a common expression whose meaning cannot be guessed from the individual words, eg 'I'm feeling under the weather' ● **idiomatic** adj **1** using words in a way that sounds natural, like a native speaker's language: not an idiomatic translation **2** involving idioms: an idiomatic expression ● **idiomatically** adv

idiosyncrasy noun (plural **idiosyncrasies**) a personal oddness of behaviour ● **idiosyncratic** adj ● **idiosyncratically** adv

idiot noun a stupid or foolish person ● **idiocy** noun stupidity or foolishness ● **idiotic** adj ● **idiotically** adv

idle adj **1** not working or being used **2** lazy **3** meaningless: idle chatter ◇ verb **1** spend time in doing nothing **2** of an engine: run without doing

any work ● **idleness** noun ● **idler** noun ● **idly** adv

idol noun **1** someone much admired **2** an image worshipped as a god ● **idolater** noun ● **idolatrous** adj ● **idolatry** noun ● **idolize** verb admire or love greatly

idyll noun **1** a poem on a pastoral theme **2** a time or place of pleasure and contentment

idyllic adj very happy and content; blissful ● **idyllically** adv

ie abbrev that is, that means (from Latin id est)

if conj **1** on condition that, or supposing that: If you go, I'll go **2** whether: do you know if she'll be there?

iffy adj, informal **1** dubious, uncertain **2** not in good health or good working order: engine sounds a bit iffy

igloo noun a rounded Inuit snow hut

igneous adj **1** of rock: formed when lava or magma cools and solidifies **2** relating to fire

ignite verb **1** set on fire **2** catch fire

ignition noun **1** the part of a vehicle engine that makes it start working **2** the act of setting on fire or catching fire

ignoble adj **1** dishonourable **2** of a low social class; lowly

ignominy /ig-nuh-min-i/ noun disgrace or dishonour ● **ignominious** adj ● **ignominiously** adv

ignoramus /ig-nuh-reh-mus/ noun a stupid person

ignorant adj **1** knowing very little **2** informal behaving rudely ● **ignorance** noun ● **ignorant of** unaware of

ignore verb take no notice of

iguana /i-gwah-nuh/ noun a type of tree lizard

ikebana /eek-i-bah-nuh/ noun the Japanese art of flower arranging

ikon another spelling of **icon**

ilk noun type or kind

I'll short for I shall, I will

ill adj 1 physically unwell; sick 2 evil, bad 3 unlucky ◇ adv badly ◇ noun 1 evil 2 (**ills**) misfortunes or troubles • **ill-at-ease** adj uncomfortable • **ill-gotten** adj got in a dishonest or unethical way • **ill-humoured** or **ill-natured** adj bad-tempered • **ill-starred** adj unlucky • **ill-treat** or **ill-use** verb treat badly • **ill-will** or **ill-feeling** noun dislike or resentment

illegal adj against the law • **illegality** noun

illegible adj impossible to read • **illegibility** noun • **illegibly** adv

illegitimate adj born of parents not married to each other

illicit adj not allowed according to social customs or laws; forbidden • **illicitly** adv

---

Do not confuse with: **elicit**

---

illiterate adj not able to read or write • **illiteracy** noun

illness noun disease, sickness

illogical adj not showing sound reasoning • **illogicality** noun • **illogically** adv

illuminate verb 1 light up 2 make more clear • **illuminated** adj of a manuscript: decorated with ornamental lettering • **illumination** noun 1 the act of illuminating 2 (**illuminations**) a decorative display of lights

illusion noun 1 something that deceives the mind or eye 2 a mistaken belief • **illusory** adj

---

Do not confuse with: **allusion** and **delusion**

---

illusory or **illusive** adj not real

Do not confuse with: **allusive** and **elusive**

---

illustrate verb 1 draw pictures for (a book etc) 2 show by example; explain • **illustration** noun 1 a picture in a book etc 2 an example that illustrates • **illustrative** adj • **illustrator** noun someone who illustrates books etc

illustrious adj famous, distinguished

I'm short for I am

image noun 1 a picture of some kind, eg a painting or the picture on a television screen 2 a striking likeness: she is the image of her mother 3 something pictured in the mind 4 public reputation

imagery noun words that suggest images, used to make a piece of writing more vivid

imaginary adj existing only in the imagination, not real

Do not confuse with: **imaginative**

---

imagination noun the power of forming pictures in the mind of things not present or experienced

imaginative adj 1 having a lively imagination 2 done with imagination: an imaginative piece of writing • **imaginatively** adv

---

Do not confuse with: **imaginary**

---

imagine verb 1 form a picture in the mind, esp of something that does not exist 2 think, suppose

imago /i-meh-goh/ noun a pupa

imam noun 1 the priest who leads the prayers in a mosque 2 (**Imam**) an Islamic leader

imbecile noun a stupid person • **imbecility** noun stupidity

imbibe *verb, formal* drink (in)

imbroglio /im-*broh*-lyoh/ *noun* (*plural* **imbroglios**) a confused situation; a tangle

imbue *verb* fill or affect (with): *imbued her staff with enthusiasm*

IMF *abbrev* International Monetary Fund, an organization that helps keep world economies stable

imitate *verb* do or be the same as; copy • **imitation** *noun* a copy ◇ *adj* made to look like: *imitation leather* • **imitator** *noun*

immaculate *adj* completely clean and very neat; spotless • **immaculately** *adv*

immaterial *adj* of little importance

immature *adj* not mature • **immaturely** *adv* • **immaturity** *noun*

immediate *adj* 1 happening straight away: *immediate reaction* 2 close: *immediate family* 3 direct: *my immediate successor* • **immediacy** *noun* • **immediately** *adv* without delay

immemorial *adj* going further back in time than can be remembered • **immemorially** *adv*

immense *adj* very large • **immensely** *adv* • **immensity** *noun*

immerse *verb* plunge into liquid • **immersion** *noun* • **immersion heater** *noun* an electric water-heater inside a hot-water tank • **immerse yourself in** give your whole attention to

immigrate *verb* come into a country and settle there • **immigrant** *noun* someone who immigrates • **immigration** *noun*

Do not confuse with: **emigrate**

---

imminent *adj* about to happen: *imminent danger* • **imminently** *adv*

Do not confuse with: **eminent**

---

immiscible *adj, formal* not able to be mixed, as *eg* water and oil

immobile *adj* 1 not moving 2 not easily moved • **immobility** *noun* • **immobilize** *verb* put out of action

immoderate *adj* going beyond reasonable limits; extreme • **immoderately** *adv* • **immoderation** *noun*

immolate *verb* sacrifice • **immolation** *noun*

immoral *adj* 1 morally wrong; unscrupulous 2 sexually improper • **immorality** *noun* • **immorally** *adv*

Do not confuse with: **amoral**

---

immortal *adj* 1 living for ever 2 famous for ever • **immortality** *noun* unending life or fame • **immortalize** *verb* make immortal or famous for ever

immovable *adj* not able to be moved or changed • **immovably** *adv*

immune *adj* 1 not likely to catch a particular disease: *immune to measles* 2 not able to be affected by: *she is immune to his charm* • **immune system** *noun* the natural defensive system of an organism that identifies and neutralizes harmful matter within itself • **immunity** *noun* • **immunize** *verb* make someone immune to (a disease), *esp* by inoculation • **immunodeficiency** *noun* weakened ability to produce antibodies • **immunosuppressant** *noun* a drug that prevents the body producing antibodies and so rejecting a transplanted organ *etc*

immunology *noun* the study of the human immune system • **immunological** *adj* • **immunologist** *noun*

imp *noun* 1 a small malignant spirit 2 a mischievous child • **impish** *adj*

impact *noun* 1 the blow of one thing striking another; a collision 2 strong effect: *made an impact on the audience* ◇ *verb* press firmly together

• **impact on** effect strongly

impair *verb* damage, weaken • **impairment** *noun*

impala *noun* a large African antelope

impale *verb* pierce through with something pointed

impart *verb* tell (information, news, *etc*) to others

impartial *adj* not favouring one side over another; unbiased • **impartiality** *noun* • **impartially** *adv*

impassable *adj* of a road: not able to be driven through

impasse /anh-pas/ *noun* a situation with no obvious prospect of progress or escape

impassioned *adj* showing great enthusiasm or other strong emotion

impassive *adj* showing or feeling no emotion at all • **impassively** *adv*

impatient *adj* **1** restlessly eager **2** irritable, short-tempered • **impatience** *noun* • **impatiently** *adv*

impeach *verb* accuse publicly of, or charge with, misconduct • **impeachment** *noun*

impeccable *adj* faultless, perfect • **impeccably** *adv*

impecunious *adj*, *formal* having little or no money; poor

impede *verb* obstruct the progress or movement of; hinder • **impediment** *noun* **1** a hindrance **2** a speech defect, *eg* a stutter or stammer

impel *verb* (**impelling**, **impelled**) **1** urge **2** drive or push on

impending *adj* about to happen: *an impending storm*

impenetrable *adj* **1** not allowing light *etc* through **2** impossible to understand; incomprehensible

impenitent *adj* not sorry for wrongdoing; unrepentant

imperative *adj* **1** necessary, urgent **2** *grammar* expressing command, *eg look!* or *read this* • **imperatively** *adv*

imperceptible *adj* so small as not to be noticed • **imperceptibly** *adv*

imperfect *adj* having a fault or flaw, not perfect • **imperfection** *noun* a fault or a flaw • **imperfectly** *adv*

imperial *adj* **1** of an emperor or empire **2** commanding, superior • **imperialism** *noun* the policy of annexing the territory of, and ruling, other nations and people • **imperialist** *adj*

imperil *verb* (**imperilling**, **imperilled**) put in danger

imperious *adj* having an air of authority, haughty • **imperiously** *adv*

impermanence *noun* lack of permanence; transitoriness • **impermanent** *adj* • **impermanently** *adv*

impermeable *adj* not able to be passed through: *impermeable by water*

impersonal *adj* **1** not influenced by personal feelings **2** not connected with any person • **impersonally** *adv*

impersonate *verb* dress up as, or act the part of, someone • **impersonation** *noun* • **impersonator** *noun* someone who impersonates others

impertinent *adj* **1** not polite or not showing respect; cheeky **2** not pertinent; irrelevant • **impertinence** *noun* • **impertinently** *adv*

imperturbable *adj* not easily worried or upset; calm • **imperturbably** *adv*

impervious *adj*: **impervious to** not able to be affected by: *impervious to suggestions*

impetigo /im-puh-*tai*-goh/ *noun* a kind of skin disease

impetuous *adj* tending to rush into action; rash • **impetuosity** *noun* • **impetuously** *adv*

impetus *noun* **1** the feeling that you should do something; motivation **2** the force that causes an object to move; momentum

impiety *noun* lack of respect for holy things • **impious** *adj* • **impiously** *adv*

impinge *verb* (with **on** or **upon**) **1** have a negative effect on; interfere (with) **2** come into contact with

impious *see* **impiety**

implacable *adj* not able to be soothed or calmed • **implacably** *adv*

implant *verb* fix in firmly, *esp* in the mind ◇ *noun* an artificial organ, graft, *etc* inserted into the body

implement *noun* a tool ◇ *verb* carry out or fulfil (*eg* a promise) • **implementation** *noun*

implicate *verb* show or suggest the involvement of: *the statement implicates you in the crime* • **implication** *noun* something meant though not actually said

implicit *adj* **1** meant though not actually said; understood **2** unquestioning: *implicit obedience* • **implicitly** *adv*

implode *verb* collapse inwards suddenly • **implosion** *noun*

implore *verb* ask for urgently or earnestly; beg

imply *verb* (**implies**, **implying**, **implied**) suggest: *her silence implies disapproval*

Do not confuse with: **infer**

impolite *adj* not polite; rude • **impolitely** *adv* • **impoliteness** *noun*

imponderable *noun* & *adj* (something) unable to be judged or evaluated

import *verb* bring in (goods) from abroad for sale ◇ *noun* **1** the act of importing **2** goods imported **3** *formal* meaning, significance • **importation**

noun • **importer** *noun*

important *adj* having a great effect, influence or significance; special • **importance** *noun* • **importantly** *adv*

importune *verb*, *formal* keep asking for something • **importunate** *adj* repeatedly asking • **importunity** *noun*

impose *verb* **1** force to accept, adopt, pay, *etc* **2** take advantage of or inconvenience • **imposing** *adj* impressive, commanding attention • **imposition** *noun* a burden or inconvenience

impossible *adj* **1** not able to be done or not able to happen **2** extremely difficult to deal with; intolerable • **impossibility** *noun* • **impossibly** *adv*

impostor *noun* someone who pretends to be someone else in order to deceive • **imposture** *noun* deceiving in this way

impotent *adj* **1** without power or effectiveness **2** of a male: unable to achieve or maintain an erection • **impotence** *noun* • **impotently** *adv*

impound *verb* seize possession of (something) by law

impoverish *verb* **1** make financially poor **2** lessen in quality: *an impoverished culture* • **impoverishment** *noun*

impracticable *adj* not able to be done • **impracticability** *noun*

Do not confuse: **impracticable** and **impractical**

impractical *adj* lacking common sense • **impracticality** *noun*

imprecation *noun* a curse

imprecise *adj* not precise; vague • **imprecisely** *adv*

impregnable *adj* too well-protected to be taken by attack

impregnate *verb* **1** saturate: *impregnated with perfume* **2** make pregnant

impresario noun (plural **impresarios**) the organizer of an entertainment

impress verb 1 arouse the interest or admiration of 2 mark by pressing upon 3 fix deeply in the mind

impression noun 1 someone's thoughts or feelings about something: my impression is that it's likely to rain 2 a deep or strong effect: the film left a lasting impression on me 3 a mark made by pressing 4 a quantity of copies of a book printed at one time • **impressionable** adj easily influenced or affected • **impressionably** adv • **impressionism** noun an artistic or literary style aiming to reproduce personal impressions of things or events • **impressionist** noun 1 a follower of impressionism 2 an entertainer who impersonates people • **impressive** adj having a strong effect on the mind • **impressively** adv

imprimatur noun a licence to print or publish

imprint verb 1 stamp or press on a surface 2 fix in the mind ◇ noun 1 the printer's or publisher's name etc on a book 2 a common title for a series of related books from one publisher

imprison verb shut up in, or as if in, a prison • **imprisonment** noun

improbable adj not likely to happen • **improbability** noun

impromptu adj & adv without preparation or rehearsal

improper adj 1 not suitable; wrong 2 indecent • **improper fraction** noun a fraction greater than 1 eg $^5/_4$ or $^{11}/_8$ • **impropriety** noun something improper, esp something that breaks social rules

improve verb make or become better • **improvement** noun

improvident adj not thinking sensibly or carefully, esp about future circumstances • **improvidence** noun • **improvidently** adv

improvise verb 1 put together from available materials: we improvised a stretcher 2 create (a tune, script, etc) spontaneously: the actors had to improvise their lines • **improvisation** noun

impudent adj showing a lack of respect; cheeky • **impudence** noun • **impudently** adv

impugn verb attack in words; criticize

impulse noun 1 a sudden urge resulting in sudden action 2 a sudden force or push • **impulsive** adj acting on impulse, without taking time to consider • **impulsively** adv • **impulsiveness** noun

impunity noun freedom from punishment, blame, injury or loss

impure adj 1 having the purity spoiled by being mixed with other substances; adulterated 2 sexually immoral; obscene 3 unclean from a religious point of view • **impurity** noun

impute verb think of as being caused, done, etc by someone: imputing the blame to others • **imputation** noun suggestion of fault; blame

in prep 1 showing position in space or time: sitting in the garden/born in the 60s 2 showing state, manner, medium, form, etc: in part/in cold blood/in code/standing in a circle ◇ adv 1 towards the inside, not out 2 in power 3 informal in fashion ◇ adj 1 that is in, inside or for coming in: the in door 2 informal fashionable ◇ abbrev inch(es) • **be in for 1** be trying to get (a prize etc) 2 be about to receive (trouble, punishment)

in- prefix 1 into, on, towards: inshore 2 not: inaccurate

inability noun (plural **inabilities**) lack of power, means, etc (to do something)

in absentia /in ab-sen-shuh/ adv in

the absence of (someone receiving a degree *etc*)

inaccessible *adj* 1 not able to be easily reached or obtained 2 impossible to understand

inaccurate *adj* 1 not correct 2 not exact • **inaccuracy** *noun*

inactive *adj* 1 doing little physical activity 2 not working, operating or functioning • **inaction** *noun* lack of action • **inactivity** *noun* idleness or rest

inadequate *adj* 1 not enough, or not good enough 2 unable to cope with a situation

inadmissible *adj* not allowable: *inadmissible evidence*

inadvertent *adj* unintentional

inadvisable *adj* not advisable; unwise

inalienable *adj* not able to be taken away or transferred: *inalienable rights*

inalterable *adj* not able to be altered

inane *adj* silly, foolish • **inanity** *noun* an empty, meaningless remark

inanimate *adj* without life

inapplicable *adj* not applicable

inapposite *adj* not suitable or relevant

inappropriate *adj* not suitable

inapt *adj* unsuitable • **inaptitude** *or* **inaptness** *noun* unfitness, awkwardness

---

Do not confuse with: **inept**

---

inarticulate *adj* 1 unable to express yourself clearly 2 said indistinctly

inasmuch as *conj* because, since

inattentive *adj* not paying attention • **inattention** *noun*

inaudible *adj* not loud enough to be heard

inaugurate *verb* mark the beginning of (eg a presidency) with a ceremony • **inaugural** *adj* • **inauguration** *noun*

inauspicious *adj* unlikely to end in success; unlucky

inauthentic *adj* not authentic; false

inborn *adj* innate, natural: *inborn talent*

in-box *noun, comput* a file for storing incoming electronic mail

inbred *adj* 1 inborn 2 resulting from inbreeding • **inbreeding** *noun* repeated mating within the same family

inc *abbrev* 1 incorporated 2 inclusive 3 including

Inca *noun* a member of a civilization that flourished in Peru before the 16th century • **Incan** *adj*

incalculable *adj* not able to be counted or estimated

incandescent *adj* 1 white-hot 2 extremely angry; furious

incantation *noun* a spell

incapable *adj* 1 unable (to do what is needed or expected) 2 helpless (through drink *etc*)

incapacitate *verb* 1 take away power, strength or rights 2 make disabled • **incapacity** *noun* 1 inability 2 disability

incarcerate *verb* imprison • **incarceration** *noun*

incarnate *adj* having human form • **incarnation** *noun* appearance in the form of a human body

incendiary *adj* meant for setting buildings *etc* on fire: *an incendiary bomb*

incense *verb* make angry ◇ *noun* a mixture of resins and spices burned to give off fumes, *esp* in religious ceremonies

incentive *noun* something that encourages someone to do something

inception noun beginning

incessant adj going on without pause; ceaseless • **incessantly** adv

incest noun illegal sexual intercourse between close relatives • **incestuous** adj 1 involving incest 2 done within a closely-knit group

inch noun (plural **inches**) one twelfth of a foot (about 2.5 centimetres) ◇ verb move very gradually

inchoate /in-koh-eht/ adj in the early stages of development; rudimentary

incidence noun 1 the frequency of something occurring 2 a falling of a ray of light etc

incident noun a happening

incidental adj 1 happening in connection with something: an incidental expense 2 casual • **incidentally** adv by the way

incinerate verb burn to ashes • **incineration** noun • **incinerator** noun an apparatus for burning rubbish etc

incipient adj beginning to exist: an incipient dislike

incise verb cut into; engrave

incision noun 1 a deliberate cut 2 the act of cutting into something

incisive adj speaking or acting in a clear, firm way; sharp

incisor noun a front tooth

incite verb provoke into taking action; urge on • **incitement** noun

incivility noun (plural **incivilities**) impoliteness

inclement adj of weather: stormy • **inclemency** noun

incline verb 1 lean, slope (towards) 2 bend, bow 3 tend to have (a particular opinion) ◇ noun a slope • **inclination** noun 1 liking or tendency 2 a slope or angle • **inclined** adj

include verb involve or consider along with others; count in • **inclusion** noun • **inclusive** adj including

everything mentioned: from Tuesday to Thursday inclusive is 3 days

incognito /in-kog-nee-toh/ adj & adv with identity concealed; disguised ◇ noun (plural **incognitos**) a disguise

incoherent adj 1 speaking in an unconnected, rambling way 2 unconnected, rambling • **incoherence** noun

incombustible adj not able to be burned by fire

income noun personal earnings

incoming adj approaching, next

incommode verb, formal cause trouble for; inconvenience

incommunicado adj & adv without means of communicating with others

incomparable adj without equal

incompatible adj 1 of statements: contradicting each other 2 of people: not suited, bound to disagree • **incompatibility** noun

incompetent adj not good enough at doing a job • **incompetence** noun • **incompetently** adv

incomplete adj not finished

incomprehensible adj not able to be understood; puzzling • **incomprehensibly** adv • **incomprehension** noun

inconceivable adj not able to be imagined or believed

inconclusive adj not leading to a definite decision or conclusion • **inconclusiveness** noun

incongruous adj 1 not matching well 2 out of place; unsuitable • **incongruity** noun

inconsequential adj unimportant • **inconsequence** noun • **inconsequentially** or **inconsequently** adv

inconsiderable adj slight or unimportant

inconsiderate adj not thinking of others

inconsistent *adj* not consistent; contradictory

inconsolable *adj* too upset to be comforted

inconspicuous *adj* not noticeable

inconstant *adj* often changing • **inconstancy** *noun*

incontinent *adj* **1** unable to control the bladder or bowels **2** uncontrolled, unrestrained • **incontinence** *noun*

incontrovertible *adj* too convincing to be doubted or disproved

inconvenient *adj* causing awkwardness or difficulty • **inconvenience** *noun & verb* (cause) trouble or difficulty (to)

incorporate *verb* **1** contain as parts of a whole: *the new building incorporates a theatre, cinema and restaurant* **2** take account of; include: *the new text incorporates the author's changes* • **incorporated** *adj* (short form **inc**) formed into a company or society

incorrect *adj* wrong

incorrigible *adj* too bad to be put right or reformed

incorruptible *adj* **1** not able to be bribed or otherwise corrupted **2** not likely to decay

increase *verb* make or become greater or more numerous; grow ◊ *noun* **1** growth **2** the amount added by growth • **increasingly** *adv* more and more

incredible *adj* impossible to believe • **incredibility** *noun* • **incredibly** *adv*

Do not confuse: **incredible** and **incredulous**

---

incredulous *adj* not believing what is said • **incredulity** *noun* • **incredulously** *adv*

increment *noun* one of a series of small increases, *esp* in a salary

incriminate *verb* show that (someone) has taken part in a crime

incubator *noun* **1** a large heated box for hatching eggs **2** a hospital crib for rearing premature babies • **incubate** *verb* brood, hatch • **incubation period** the time that it takes for a disease to develop from infection to the first symptoms

incubus *noun* an evil spirit in the shape of a man believed to have sex with women in their sleep (*compare with*: **succubus**)

inculcate *verb* impress something on (the mind) by constant repetition

incumbent *adj* resting on (someone) as a duty: *it is incumbent upon me to warn you* ◊ *noun* someone who has an official position at the moment

incur *verb* (**incurring, incurred**) bring (blame, debt, *etc*) upon yourself

incurable *adj* unable to be cured

incurious *adj* not curious; uninterested

incursion *noun* an invasion or raid

indebted *adj* having cause to be grateful: *we are indebted to you for your kindness* • **indebtedness** *noun*

indecent *adj* offending against normal or usual standards of (*esp* sexual) behaviour • **indecency** *noun* • **indecent assault** *noun* an assault involving indecent behaviour but not rape

indecipherable *adj* **1** illegible **2** incomprehensible

indecision *noun* slowness in making up your mind; hesitation • **indecisive** *adj* **1** not coming to a definite result **2** unable to make up your mind

indecorous *adj*, *formal* breaking social rules or customs; unseemly • **indecorousness** *or* **indecorum** *noun*

indeed *adv* **1** in fact: *she is indeed a splendid cook* **2** (used for emphasis) really: *did he indeed?* ◊ *exclam* expressing surprise

indefatigable *adj* untiring

indefensible *adj* **1** too bad to justify or excuse; inexcusable **2** unable to be defended

indefinable *adj* not able to be stated or described clearly

indefinite *adj* **1** not fixed; uncertain **2** without definite limits • **indefinite article** *noun* the name given to the adjectives *a* and *an* • **indefinitely** *adv* for an indefinite period of time

indehiscent /in-di-*his*-unt/ *adj* of fruit: not opening when mature

indelible *adj* unable to be rubbed out or removed

indelicate *adj* likely to embarrass or offend someone; impolite • **indelicacy** *noun*

indemnify *verb* (**indemnifies, indemnifying, indemnified**) **1** compensate for loss **2** exempt (from)

indemnity *noun* **1** security from damage or loss **2** compensation for loss

indent *verb* **1** begin a new paragraph by going in from the margin **2** (with **for**) apply for (stores, equipment, *etc*) • **indentation** *noun* **1** a hollow or dent **2** an inward curve in an outline, coastline, *etc*

indenture *noun* a written agreement ◇ *verb* bind by a written agreement

independent *adj* **1** free to think or act for yourself **2** not relying on someone else for support, guidance, *etc* **3** of a country: self-governing • **independence** *noun*

indescribable *adj* not able to be described

indestructible *adj* not able to be destroyed

indetectable *adj* not able to be detected

indeterminate *adj* not fixed; indefinite

index *noun* (*plural* **indexes**) **1** an alphabetical list giving the page number of subjects mentioned in a book **2** an indication **3** (*plural* **indices**) *maths* an upper number that shows how many times a number is multiplied by itself (*eg* 4^3 means $4 \times 4 \times 4$) **4** a numerical scale showing changes in the cost of living, wages, *etc* • **index-linked** *adj* of pensions *etc*: directly related to the cost-of-living index

Indian *adj* **1** of India or in a style originating in India **2** *old* belonging to the native people of America • **Indian corn** *noun* maize • **Indian ink** *noun* a very black ink used by artists • **Indian summer** *noun* a period of summer warmth in autumn

indicate *verb* **1** be a sign of **2** point out • **indication** *noun* a sign • **indicative** *adj* being a sign of: *indicative of his attitude* • **indicator** *noun* **1** something that is a sign of something else **2** a flashing light on either side of a vehicle for signalling to other drivers

indices *plural of* **index** (sense 3)

indict /in-*dait*/ *verb* accuse formally of a crime • **indictment** *noun*

indie *noun, informal* an independent record, film or television company

indifferent *adj* **1** neither very good nor very bad; average **2** (with **to**) showing no interest in • **indifference** *noun*

indigenous *adj* native to a country or area

indigent *adj* very poor; impoverished • **indigence** *noun*

indigestion *noun* discomfort or pain experienced in digesting food • **indigestible** *adj* difficult to digest

indignant *adj* angry, *esp* because of wrong done to yourself or others • **indignation** *noun* • **indignity** *noun* **1** loss of dignity **2** insult

indigo *noun* a purplish-blue colour ◇ *adj* purplish-blue

indirect adj 1 not straight or direct 2 not affecting or affected directly • **indirect speech** noun speech reported not in the speaker's actual words, eg they said that they'd leave this morning (contrasted with: **direct speech**) • **indirect tax** noun a tax on particular goods, paid by the customer in the form of a higher price

indiscreet adj 1 giving away too much information 2 not cautious enough; rash • **indiscretion** noun a rash or unwise remark or act

indiscriminate adj making no distinction between one person (or thing) and another: indiscriminate buying/indiscriminate killing

indispensable adj that you cannot do without; essential

indisposed adj unwell • **indisposition** noun

indisputable adj not able to be denied

indistinct adj not clear

indistinguishable adj 1 difficult to make out 2 too alike to tell apart

individual adj 1 relating to or designed for a single person or thing 2 distinctive, unusual ◇ noun a single person or thing • **individualist** noun someone with a distinctive style • **individualistic** adj • **individuality** noun 1 separate existence 2 the quality of standing out from others

indivisible adj not able to be divided

indoctrinate verb teach to accept a certain set of ideas and reject all others

indolent adj lazy • **indolence** noun

indomitable adj having a very strong, determined character

indoor adj done etc inside a building • **indoors** adv in or into a building etc

indubitable adj not to be doubted

induce verb 1 persuade 2 cause to be experienced; bring on • **inducement** noun something that encourages or persuades: money is an inducement to work

induct verb install (someone) formally in a new position, new school, etc

induction noun 1 the formal installation of someone in a new position, new school, etc 2 the production of electricity in something by placing it near an electric source 3 the drawing of conclusions from particular cases • **inductive** adj

indulge verb 1 be inclined to give in to the wishes of; spoil: she indulges that child too much 2 not resist or restrain: indulging his sweet tooth • **indulgence** noun 1 the act of indulging someone's wishes 2 a pardon for a sin • **indulgent** adj tending to give in to others' wishes

industrious adj hard-working

industry noun (plural **industries**) 1 a branch of trade or manufacture: the clothing industry 2 steady attention paid to work • **industrial** adj • **industrial action** noun strikes or periods of work to rule • **industrialist** noun someone involved in organizing an industry

inebriated adj drunk

inedible adj not eatable, esp because too disgusting or rotten

ineffable adj not able to be put into words; indescribable

ineffective adj having no effect; useless

ineffectual adj achieving nothing

inefficient adj 1 not efficient 2 wasting time, energy, etc • **inefficiency** noun

inelegant adj not elegant or graceful • **inelegance** noun

ineligible adj not suitable to be chosen

ineluctable *adj, formal* unavoidable

inept *adj* clumsy or clumsily done • **ineptitude** *noun*

Do not confuse with: **inapt**

---

inequality *noun* (*plural* **inequalities**) **1** lack of equality; unfairness **2** unevenness

inert *adj* **1** not moving or able to move **2** not wanting to move or take action **3** not lively **4** chemically inactive • **inertia** *noun* • **inertness** *noun*

inescapable *adj* unable to be avoided

inessential *adj* not essential; unnecessary

inestimable *adj* too good or great to be measured or fully appreciated

inevitable *adj* not able to be avoided; inescapable • **inevitability** *noun*

inexact *adj* not exact; approximate

inexcusable *adj* too bad to excused; unforgivable

inexhaustible *adj* not likely to be used up; very plentiful

inexorable *adj* unable to be changed or avoided

inexpensive *adj* cheap in price

inexperience *noun* lack of (skilled) knowledge or experience • **inexperienced** *adj*

inexpert *adj* unskilled or amateurish

inexplicable *adj* not able to be explained

inexplicit *adj* not clear

inexpressible *adj* not able to be described in words

in extremis *adv* if the situation becomes desperate

inextricable *adj* not able to be disentangled or regarded as separate • **inextricably** *adv*

infallible *adj* **1** never making an error **2** certain to produce the desired result: *infallible cure* • **infallibility** *noun*

infamous *adj* having a very bad reputation; notorious • **infamy** *noun* public disgrace or bad reputation; notoriety

infant *noun* a baby • **infancy** *noun* **1** early childhood; babyhood **2** the beginning of anything: *when psychiatry was in its infancy* • **infanticide** *noun* **1** the murder of a child **2** a person who murders a child • **infantile** *adj* **1** childish **2** of babies

infantry *noun* foot-soldiers

infatuated *adj* filled with foolish love • **infatuation** *noun*

infect *verb* **1** fill with disease-causing germs **2** pass on disease to **3** cause (eg enthusiasm) to be spread • **infection** *noun* **1** a disease that can be spread to others **2** something that spreads widely and affects many people • **infectious** *adj* likely to spread from person to person

infelicitous *adj, formal* unfortunate or inappropriate: *an infelicitous remark*

infer *verb* (**inferring, inferred**) reach a conclusion from facts or reasoning • **inference** *noun*

Do not confuse with: **imply**

---

inferior *adj* **1** lower in any way **2** not of best quality ◇ *noun* someone lower in rank *etc* • **inferiority** *noun* • **inferiority complex** *noun* a constant feeling that you are less good in some way than others

infernal *adj* **1** of hell **2** *informal* used for expressing general dislike or annoyance; damned • **inferno** *noun* **1** hell **2** (*plural* **infernos**) a raging fire

infertile *adj* **1** of soil: not producing much **2** not able to have children or young • **infertility** *noun*

infest verb swarm over: infested with lice • **infestation** noun

infidel adj someone who does not believe in a particular religion (esp Christianity) • **infidelity** noun unfaithfulness or disloyalty

infighting noun rivalry or quarrelling between members of the same group

infiltrate verb enter (an organization etc) secretly to spy or cause damage • **infiltration** noun

infinite adj without end or limit • **infinitesimal** adj very small • **infinitive** noun, grammar the base form of a verb, used with to, eg in 'I hate to lose' • **infinity** noun space or time without end

infirm adj weak or ill • **infirmary** noun a hospital • **infirmity** noun 1 a physical weakness 2 a character flaw

in flagrante delicto /in fluh-gran-teh di-lik-toh/ adv in the act of doing something bad; red-handed

inflame verb 1 make hot or red 2 arouse anger, violence or passion in • **inflamed** adj

inflammable adj 1 easily set on fire 2 easily excited • **inflammation** noun swelling in a part of the body, with pain, redness and a feeling of heat

inflammatory adj arousing passion, esp anger

inflate verb 1 blow up (a balloon, tyre, etc) 2 puff up (with pride); exaggerate: an inflated sense of her own importance 3 increase to a great extent • **inflation** noun 1 the act of inflating 2 an economic situation in which prices and wages keep forcing each other to increase

inflect verb 1 change the tone of (your voice) 2 vary the endings of (a verb) to show tense, number, etc • **inflection** noun • **inflectional** adj

inflexible adj 1 unwilling or unable to change plans, opinions, etc; unbending 2 stiff and unable to be bent; rigid • **inflexibility** noun

inflict verb impose (something unpleasant) on someone • **infliction** noun

in-flight adj happening or used during an air flight: in-flight movie

inflorescence noun a blossoming of flowers on a plant

inflow noun a flowing in; influx

influence noun the power to affect other persons or things, or the fact of affecting them ◇ verb have power over • **influential** adj

influenza noun, formal flu

influx noun 1 a flowing in 2 the arrival of large numbers of people or things

info noun, informal information

inform verb 1 give knowledge to 2 (with on) tell (on); betray • **informant** noun someone who informs • **informer** noun someone who gives information to the police or authorities

informal adj relaxed, casual or friendly, or for use in such circumstances • **informality** noun

information noun knowledge or news • **information technology** noun the use of computers and other electronic devices to store, process and transmit information • **informative** adj giving information

infra- prefix below, beneath: infra-human

infraction noun a breach of rules or laws; a violation

infra-red adj of rays of heat: with wavelengths longer than visible light

infrastructure noun 1 the systems that are needed to allow a country to function properly, including such things as transport networks, a health system and an education system 2 the basic structure of a system or organization; framework

infrequent adj happening seldom; rare • **infrequently** adv

infringe verb break (a rule or law) • **infringement** noun

infuriate verb make extremely angry; enrage • **infuriating** adj

infuse verb 1 pour on or over 2 fill the mind (with a desire etc) • **infusion** noun 1 the act of infusing 2 a tea formed by steeping a herb etc in water

ingenious adj 1 skilful in inventing 2 cleverly thought out • **ingenuity** noun cleverness; quickness of ideas

---

Do not confuse with: **ingenuous**

---

ingénue /anh-zheh-noo/ noun a naive young girl

ingenuous adj so honest and innocent as to be incapable of deceiving people; artless • **ingenuousness** noun

---

Do not confuse with: **ingenious**

---

inglenook noun a fireside corner

inglorious adj bringing shame or dishonour

ingot noun a block of metal (esp gold or silver) cast in a mould

ingrained adj deeply fixed or established: ingrained laziness

ingratiate verb work your way into someone's favour by flattery etc • **ingratiating** adj

ingratitude noun lack of gratitude or thankfulness

ingredient noun one of the things of which a mixture is made

ingrown adj of a nail: growing into the flesh

inhabit verb live in • **inhabitant** noun someone who lives permanently in a place

inhale verb breathe in • **inhalant** noun a medicine that is inhaled as a spray • **inhalation** noun the act of inhaling • **inhaler** noun a device for breathing in medicine, steam, etc

inhere verb, formal be an essential part

inherent adj existing as a natural part or characteristic; innate

inherit verb 1 receive property etc as an heir 2 get (a characteristic) from your parents etc: she inherits her sense of humour from her father • **inheritance** noun something received by will when a relative dies • **inheritor** noun an heir

inhibit verb prevent from developing or progressing, or from expressing something openly; hold back • **inhibited** adj unable to let yourself go • **inhibition** noun a holding back of natural impulses etc, restraint

inhospitable adj unwelcoming or unfriendly

inhuman adj not human, esp not showing normal human kindness • **inhumanity** noun

inhumane adj cruel

inimical adj opposing or preventing

inimitable adj impossible to imitate

iniquity noun (plural **iniquities**) 1 something very unfair or morally very bad 2 the quality of being morally bad; wickedness • **iniquitous** adj very unfair or morally very bad

initial adj of or at a beginning: initial difficulties ◇ noun the letter beginning a word, esp someone's name ◇ verb (**initialling**, **initialled**) sign with the initials of your name

initiate verb 1 begin, start: initiate the reforms 2 give first lessons to 3 admit formally to a society etc • **initiation** noun • **initiative** noun 1 the opportunity or right to take the first step 2 readiness to take action or take a lead

inject *verb* **1** force (a liquid) into the veins or muscles with a syringe **2** put (*eg* enthusiasm) into • **injection** *noun*

in-joke *noun* a joke only understood by a particular group

injudicious *adj, formal* unwise

injunction *noun* an official order or command

injure *verb* cause harm or damage to • **injured** *adj* **1** physically hurt **2** offended • **injury** *noun* **1** physical harm or damage **2** a wrong done to someone

injustice *noun* **1** unfairness **2** a wrong done to someone

ink *noun* a coloured liquid used in writing, printing, *etc* ◇ *verb* mark with ink • **inky** *adj* **1** of or covered in ink **2** very dark

inkling *noun* a hint or slight sign

inlaid *past form of* inlay

inland *adj* **1** not beside the sea **2** happening inside a country ◇ *adv* towards the inner part of a country • **Inland Revenue** *noun* the government department that collects taxes

in-law *noun* a relative by marriage

inlay *noun* decoration made by fitting pieces of different shapes and colours into a background ◇ *verb* (**inlaying**, **inlaid**) fit into a background as decoration • **inlaid** *adj*

inlet *noun* a small bay

in loco parentis *adv* having a position of responsibility for a child's safety while the parent or guardian is not there, as, for example, a teacher has

inmate *noun* a resident or occupant (*esp* of an institution): *the inmates of the prison*

inmost *adj* the farthest in

inn *noun* a small country hotel • **innkeeper** *noun* someone who keeps an inn

innards *plural noun* **1** internal parts **2** entrails

innate *adj* existing as a natural characteristic; inborn

inner *adj* **1** on the inside **2** of feelings *etc*: hidden • **inner city** *noun* a densely populated central area of a city with bad housing and social deprivation • **innermost** *adj* **1** farthest in **2** most secret or private

innings *sing noun* **1** a team's turn for batting in cricket **2** a turn at something

innocent *adj* **1** not guilty or not to blame; blameless **2** harmless • **innocence** *noun*

innocuous *adj* not harmful

innovation *noun* something new

innuendo *noun* (*plural* **innuendoes**) an indirect reference; a hint

innumerable *adj* too many to be counted

innumerate *adj* not understanding arithmetic or mathematics • **innumeracy** *noun*

inoculate *verb* inject (someone) with a mild form of a disease to prevent them later catching it • **inoculation** *noun*

inoffensive *adj* giving no offence; harmless

inoperative *adj* not active or working

inopportune *adj* happening at a bad or inconvenient time

inordinate *adj* going beyond the limit; unreasonably great

inorganic *adj* not of animal or vegetable origin

in-patient *noun* a patient who stays in a hospital during their treatment (*contrasted with*: **out-patient**)

input *noun* **1** opinions or suggestions contributed to a discussion **2** data fed into a computer (*contrasted with*: **out-**

put) **3** an amount (of energy, labour, etc) put into something

inquest noun a legal inquiry into a case of sudden death

inquire or **enquire** verb ask • **inquirer** or **enquirer** noun • **inquiring** or **enquiring** adj questioning, curious • **inquiry** or **enquiry** noun **1** a question **2** a search for information or an official investigation

inquisition noun a careful questioning or investigation • **inquisitor** noun an official investigator

inquisitive adj **1** very curious **2** fond of prying; nosy • **inquisitively** adv • **inquisitiveness** noun

inroad noun a raid • **make inroads into** use up large amounts of: the holiday made inroads into their savings

insane adj not sane; mad • **insanity** noun

insanitary adj encouraging the spread of disease

insatiable adj not able to be satisfied: insatiable appetite • **insatiably** adv

inscribe verb write or engrave (eg a name) on a book, monument, etc • **inscription** noun the writing on a book, monument, etc

inscrutable adj difficult to understand or interpret; mysterious

insect noun a small six-legged creature with wings and a body divided into sections • **insecticide** noun powder or liquid for killing insects • **insectivorous** adj feeding on insects

insecure adj **1** lacking confidence in your abilities, your position in life, etc **2** not safe or firm • **insecurity** noun

inseminate verb **1** make pregnant, esp artificially **2** formal introduce (attitudes, ideas, etc) • **insemination** noun

insensate adj unable to feel things physically

insensible adj **1** not aware; unconscious **2** not having feeling

insensitive adj **1** (with to) not feeling: insensitive to cold **2** unsympathetic (to): insensitive to her grief **3** not careful to avoid offending others • **insensitivity** noun

inseparable adj not able to be separated or kept apart • **inseparably** adv

insert verb put in or among ◇ noun **1** a separate leaflet or pullout section in a magazine etc **2** a special feature added to a television programme etc • **insertion** noun

in-service adj happening as part of someone's work: in-service training

inset noun **1** a small picture, map, etc in a corner of a larger one **2** an insert

inshore adj carried on near the shore ◇ adv to or near the shore

inside noun **1** the side, space or part within **2** indoors ◇ adj **1** being on or in the inside **2** indoor **3** coming from or done by someone within an organization: inside information ◇ adv to, in or on the inside ◇ prep to the inside of; within

insidious adj **1** developing gradually and largely unnoticed but causing great harm **2** attractive but harmful

insight noun ability to consider a matter and understand it clearly

insignia plural noun signs or badges showing that someone holds an office, award, etc

insignificant adj of little importance • **insignificance** noun • **insignificantly** adv

insincere adj not truly meaning what you say • **insincerity** noun

insinuate verb **1** hint (at something unpleasant) **2** put in gradually and secretly **3** work yourself into (someone's favour etc) • **insinuation** noun a sly hint

insipid adj 1 lacking character, interest or liveliness; dull 2 lacking flavour; tasteless

insist verb 1 urge something strongly: insist on punctuality 2 refuse to change decisions, intentions or opinions: he insists on walking there 3 go on saying (that): she insists that she saw a UFO

insistent adj 1 refusing to change decisions, intentions or opinions 2 compelling attention • **insistence** noun • **insistently** adv

in situ adv in its normal or final position; in place

insolent adj showing a lack of respect; cheeky • **insolence** noun

insoluble adj 1 not able to be dissolved 2 of a problem: not able to be solved

insolvent adj not able to pay your debts ◇ noun a person who is not able to pay their debts • **insolvency** noun

insomnia noun sleeplessness • **insomniac** noun someone who suffers from insomnia

insouciant adj, formal not worrying or caring; unconcerned • **insouciance** noun

inspect verb 1 look carefully at or into in order to judge; examine 2 look over (troops etc) ceremonially • **inspection** noun careful examination • **inspector** noun 1 an official who inspects 2 a police officer below a superintendent and above a sergeant in rank

inspiration noun 1 something or someone that influences or encourages others 2 a brilliant idea 3 formal breathing in • **inspirational** adj inspiring

inspire verb 1 be the source of creative ideas 2 encourage 3 formal breathe in • **inspired** adj 1 seeming to be aided by higher powers 2 brilliantly good

inst abbrev this month: 10th inst

instability noun lack of steadiness or stability (esp in the personality)

install or **instal** verb (installs or instals, installing, installed) 1 place in position, ready for use: has the electricity been installed? 2 introduce formally to a new job etc • **installation** noun

instalment noun 1 a part of a sum of money paid at fixed times until the whole amount is paid 2 one part of a serial story

instance noun an example or particular case ◇ verb mention as an example • **at the instance of** at the request of

instant adj 1 immediate or urgent 2 able to be prepared almost immediately: instant coffee ◇ noun 1 a very short time; a moment 2 point or moment of time: I need it this instant • **instantaneous** adj done or happening very quickly • **instantly** adv immediately

instead adv in place of someone or something: you can go instead • **instead of** in place of

instep noun the arching, upper part of the foot

instigate verb encourage people to do (esp something bad) • **instigation** noun

instil or **instill** verb (instils or instills, instilling, instilled) put (esp ideas into the mind) firmly but gradually

instinct noun a natural feeling or knowledge that someone has without thinking and without being taught • **instinctive** adj due to instinct

institute noun a society, organization, etc or the building it uses ◇ verb set up; establish • **institution** noun 1 an organization, building, etc established for a particular purpose (esp care or education) 2 an established custom • **institutional** adj

instruct verb 1 teach 2 direct or command • **instruction** noun 1 (**instructions**) guidance on how something is to be done or used 2 a command 3 teaching • **instructive** adj containing or giving information or knowledge • **instructor** noun

instrument noun 1 something used for a particular purpose; a tool 2 a device for producing musical sounds, eg a piano or a flute • **instrumental** adj 1 helpful in bringing something about 2 written for or played by musical instruments, without voice accompaniment • **instrumentalist** noun someone who plays on a musical instrument

insubordinate adj refusing to obey orders or show proper respect; rebellious • **insubordination** noun

insufferable adj not able to be endured

insufficient adj not enough • **insufficiency** noun

insular adj 1 narrow-minded or prejudiced 2 of an island or islands • **insularity** noun

insulate verb 1 cover with a material that will not let through electrical currents, heat, frost, etc 2 make separate from others; isolate • **insulation** noun

insulin noun a substance used in the treatment of diabetes

insult verb treat with scorn or rudeness ◇ noun a rude or scornful remark • **insulting** adj scornful, rude

insuperable adj that cannot be overcome

insure verb arrange for payment of a sum of money on (something) if it should be lost, damaged, stolen, etc • **insurance** noun

---

Do not confuse with: **ensure**

---

insurgent adj rising up in rebellion ◇ noun a rebel • **insurgency** noun

insurmountable adj of a difficulty or problem: not able to be got over

insurrection noun a rising up in rebellion

intact adj whole or unbroken

intaglio /in-*tahl*-yoh/ noun 1 sculpture carved into a background, not raised from the surface (contrasted with: **relief**) 2 a gemstone with a hollowed-out design (contrasted with: **cameo**)

intake noun 1 an amount of people or things taken in: *this year's intake of students* 2 the part of an engine or system where something, eg fuel or air, enters

intangible adj 1 not able to be felt by touch 2 difficult to define or describe; not clear

integer /in-ti-juh/ noun a whole number, not a fraction • **integral** adj 1 of or essential to a whole: *an integral part of the machine* 2 made up of parts forming a whole

integrate verb 1 fit parts together to form a whole 2 enable (racial groups) to mix freely and live on equal terms • **integration** noun

integrity noun 1 honesty 2 wholeness or completeness

integument noun an external layer; a covering

intellect noun the thinking power of the mind • **intellectual** adj showing or requiring intellect ◇ noun someone with academic interests

intelligent adj quick at understanding and learning; clever • **intelligence** noun 1 mental ability 2 information sent; news • **intelligible** adj able to be understood

intelligentsia noun the intellectuals within a particular society

intemperate adj 1 going beyond reasonable limits; uncontrolled 2 tending to drink too much alcohol

• **intemperance** noun

intend verb mean or plan to (do something)

intense adj 1 very great 2 tending to have strong feelings; emotional • **intensely** adv • **intensity** noun strength, eg of feeling, colour, etc

intensify verb (**intensifies**, **intensifying**, **intensified**) make more concentrated; increase

intensive adj using or requiring large amounts of resources • **intensive care** noun a unit in a hospital where a patient's condition is carefully monitored

intent noun purpose ◇ adj 1 using all your concentration; attentive 2 determined (on) • **intention** noun 1 what someone means to do; an aim 2 meaning • **intentional** adj done on purpose • **intentionally** adv

inter verb (**interring**, **interred**) bury • **interment** noun

inter- prefix between, among, together: intermingle/interplanetary

interact verb have an effect on one another • **interactive** adj allowing two-way communication, esp between a computer and its user

intercede verb 1 act as peacemaker between two people, nations, etc 2 take action on someone's behalf • **intercession** noun • **intercessor** noun

intercept verb 1 stop or seize on the way 2 partially block out (a view, the light, etc); cut off

interchange verb 1 put each in the place of the other 2 alternate ◇ noun 1 the act of interchanging 2 a junction of two or more major roads on separate levels • **interchangeable** adj able to be used one for the other

intercom noun a telephone system within a building, aeroplane, etc

intercourse noun 1 communication 2 dealings between people etc 3 sexual intercourse

interdict noun an order forbidding something

interest noun 1 special attention or curiosity 2 someone's personal concern or field of study 3 advantage or benefit 4 a sum paid for the loan of money ◇ verb catch or hold the attention of • **interested** adj having or taking an interest • **interest group** noun a group that puts pressure on politicians to achieve a political aim • **interesting** adj holding the attention

interface noun, comput a connection between two parts of the same system

interfere verb 1 (with **in**) take part in what is not your business; meddle 2 (with **with**) get in the way of; hinder: interfering with her work • **interference** noun 1 the act of interfering 2 the spoiling of radio or television reception by another station or disturbance from traffic etc

interim noun time between; the meantime ◇ adj temporary

interior adj 1 inner 2 inside a building 3 inland ◇ noun 1 the inside of anything 2 the inland part of a country

interject verb 1 make a sudden remark in a conversation 2 exclaim • **interjection** noun a word or phrase of exclamation, eg Ah! and Oh dear!

interleave verb insert pages etc between existing ones

interlock verb 1 lock or clasp together 2 fit into each other

interlocution noun, formal dialogue, conversation • **interlocutor** noun the person to whom you are speaking

interloper noun someone unwanted or disliked who joins a group, takes up a position or enters a place; an intruder

interlude *noun* **1** an interval **2** a short piece of music played between the parts of a play, film, *etc*

intermarry *verb* (**intermarries, intermarrying, intermarried**) **1** marry with members of another race *etc* **2** marry with members of the same group, race, *etc* ● **intermarriage** *noun*

intermediary *noun* (*plural* **intermediaries**) someone who acts between two people in trying to settle a quarrel

intermediate *adj* in the middle of a range of sizes, levels of quality, *etc*; middle

interment *see* inter

Do not confuse with: **internment**

intermezzo /in-tuh-*met*-zoh/ *noun* (*plural* **intermezzos**), *music* a short movement separating sections of a symphony

interminable *adj* boringly long; never-ending

intermission *noun* an interval or pause

intermittent *adj* stopping every now and then and starting again

intern *verb* keep (someone from an enemy country) prisoner during a war ● **internee** *noun* someone who is confined in this way ● **internment** *noun*

Do not confuse with: **interment**

internal *adj* **1** of the inner part, *esp* of the body **2** within a country, organization, *etc*; inside: *internal affairs*

international *adj* **1** happening between nations **2** concerning more than one nation **3** worldwide ◇ *noun* a sports match between teams of two countries

internecine *adj* causing deaths on both sides: *internecine feud*

Internet *noun* an international computer network linking users through telephone or broadband lines

interplanetary *adj* between planets

interplay *noun* the action of one thing on another

interpose *verb* **1** place or come between **2** make (a remark *etc*) which interrupts someone

interpret *verb* **1** explain the meaning of something **2** translate **3** bring out the meaning of (music, a part in a play, *etc*) in performance **4** understand the meaning of something to be ● **interpretation** *noun* ● **interpreter** *noun* someone who translates the words of a speaker into another language, as they are spoken

interregnum /in-tuh-*reg*-num/ *noun* the time between the end of one reign and the beginning of the next

interrogate *verb* examine by asking questions ● **interrogation** *noun* ● **interrogative** *noun* a word used in asking a question, *eg* who? and where? ◇ *adj* questioning ● **interrogator** *noun*

interrupt *verb* **1** stop (someone) while they are saying or doing something **2** stop doing (something) **3** get in the way of (a view *etc*); block ● **interruption** *noun*

intersect *verb* of lines: meet and cross ● **intersection** *noun* **1** the point where two lines cross **2** a crossroads

intersperse *verb* scatter here and there in ● **interspersion** *noun*

interstice /in-*tur*-stis/ *noun* a small gap between things; a chink

intertwine *verb* twine or twist together

interval *noun* **1** a short pause between parts of a performance *etc* **2** a time or space between two things

intervene *verb* **1** come or be

between, or in the way **2** join in a fight or quarrel in order to stop it • **intervention** noun

interview noun a formal meeting of one person with others to apply for a job, give information to the media, etc ◇ verb **1** ask questions etc of in an interview **2** conduct an interview

intestate adj without having made a will: he died intestate

intestine noun one of the various sections of the tube from the stomach to the anus that takes solid waste out of the body • **intestinal** adj

intimacy noun (plural **intimacies**) **1** close friendship **2** familiarity **3** sexual intercourse

intimate adj **1** knowing a lot about; familiar (with) **2** of friends: very close **3** private, personal: intimate details **4** having a sexual relationship (with) ◇ noun a close friend ◇ verb **1** hint **2** announce • **intimately** adv • **intimation** noun **1** a hint **2** announcement

intimidate verb **1** frighten or threaten into doing something **2** cause to feel frightened or overawed • **intimidating** adj • **intimidation** noun

into prep **1** to the inside: into the room **2** towards: into the millennium **3** to a different state: a tadpole changes into a frog **4** maths expressing the idea of division: 2 into 4 goes twice **5** informal very interested in: she's really into martial arts

intolerable adj too bad, painful, etc to put up with

intolerant adj not willing to put up with (people of different ideas, religion, etc) • **intolerance** noun

intone verb say in a serious or singing voice • **intonation** noun the rise and fall of the voice

intoxicate verb **1** make drunk **2** make very happy, enthusiastic or excited • **intoxicant** noun a strong drink • **intoxication** noun drunkenness

intra- prefix within: intra-uterine

intractable adj **1** refusing to obey or be controlled; stubborn **2** of a problem: difficult to solve • **intractability** noun

intranet noun a computer network that can be accessed only by a limited set of authorized users eg within a particular institution

intransigent adj refusing to change opinions and come to an agreement • **intransigence** noun

intransitive adj, grammar of a verb: not needing an object, eg to go, to fall

intravenous adj put directly into a vein: intravenous drip

in-tray noun an office tray for letters and work still to be dealt with (contrasted with: out-tray)

intrepid adj without fear; brave • **intrepidity** noun

intricate adj having many details or aspects; complicated • **intricacy** noun

intrigue noun **1** a secret plot **2** a secret love affair ◇ verb **1** secretly plot to do something; scheme **2** rouse the curiosity of; fascinate • **intriguing** adj

intrinsic adj belonging to something as part of its nature

introduce verb **1** bring in or put in **2** make (someone) known to another person • **introduction** noun **1** the introducing of someone or thing **2** a section at the beginning of a book etc briefly explaining its contents • **introductory** adj coming at the beginning

introspective adj tending to examine your own thoughts and feelings; inward-looking • **introspection** noun

introvert noun someone who is uncommunicative and withdrawn

intrude verb put yourself into a situation or go into a place uninvited

• **intruder** *noun* someone who breaks in or intrudes • **intrusion** *noun* • **intrusive** *adj*

intuition *noun* **1** ability to understand something without thinking it out **2** an instinctive feeling or belief

Inuit *noun* **1** a member of the people of the Arctic regions of Greenland, Canada and N Alaska, formerly known as Eskimos **2** their language

Inuktitut *noun* the Inuit language spoken in the Canadian Arctic

inundate *verb* **1** overwhelm: *inundated with work* **2** flood • **inundation** *noun*

inure *verb* make accustomed (to): *inured to pain*

invade *verb* **1** enter (a country etc) as an enemy to take possession **2** interfere with (someone's rights, privacy, etc) • **invader** *noun* • **invasion** *noun*

invalid[1] /in-*val*-id/ *adj* **1** not legally effective **2** not based on good judgement or reasoning • **invalidate** *verb* make invalid • **invalidity** *noun*

invalid[2] /in-vuh-lid/ *noun* someone who is ill or disabled ◇ *verb* **1** make an invalid of **2** (with **out**) discharge from the army as an invalid

invaluable *adj* extremely useful or essential

invariable *adj* unchanging • **invariably** *adv* always or usually

invasion *see* **invade**

invective *noun* abusive words

inveigle *verb* trick or persuade someone into doing something • **inveiglement** *noun*

invent *verb* **1** make or think up for the first time **2** make up (a story, an excuse) • **invention** *noun* something invented • **inventive** *adj* good at inventing; resourceful • **inventor** *noun*

inventory /in-vun-tri/ *noun* (*plural* **inventories**) a detailed list of contents

invert *verb* **1** turn upside down **2** reverse the order of • **inverse** *adj* opposite, reverse ◇ *noun* the opposite • **inversely** *adv* • **inversion** *noun* **1** a turning upside-down **2** a reversal • **inverted commas** *plural noun* commas written or printed upside down (' ' or " ") to show where direct speech begins and ends

invertebrate *adj* of an animal: not having a backbone ◇ *noun* an animal with no backbone, *eg* a worm or insect

invest *verb* **1** put money in a firm, property, *etc* to make a profit **2** give a particular quality to **3** *old* besiege • **investiture** *noun* a ceremony held before someone takes on an important position • **investment** *noun* **1** money invested **2** something in which money is invested **3** *old* a siege • **investor** *noun* someone who invests

investigate *verb* search into with care • **investigation** *noun* a careful search • **investigator** *noun*

inveterate *adj* **1** firmly fixed in a habit: *an inveterate gambler* **2** of a feeling *etc*: deep-rooted • **inveteracy** *noun*

invidious *adj* likely to cause bad feeling or envy

invigilate *verb* supervise (an examination *etc*) • **invigilator** *noun*

invigorate *verb* cause to feel healthy and full of energy • **invigorating** *adj*

invincible *adj* not able to be defeated or overcome • **invincibility** *noun*

inviolable *adj* not to be disregarded, harmed or broken • **inviolability** *noun* • **inviolate** *adj* not harmed

invisible *adj* not able to be seen • **invisibility** *noun*

invite *verb* **1** ask (someone) to do something, *esp* to come for a meal *etc* **2** seem to ask for: *inviting punishment* • **invitation** *noun* a request to do something • **inviting** *adj* tempting, attractive

in vitro *adj* of fertilization: carried out in a test tube, in a laboratory

invocation *see* invoke

invoice *noun* a document sent with goods with details of money owed for them ◇ *verb* send such a document to

invoke *verb* 1 call upon in prayer 2 ask for (eg help) • **invocation** *noun*

involuntary *adj* not done intentionally or willingly • **involuntarily** *adv*

involve *verb* 1 take part (in) or be concerned (in): *involved in publishing/ involved in the scandal* 2 have as a consequence; require: *the job involves a lot of driving* • **involved** *adj* complicated • **involvement** *noun*

invulnerable *adj* not able to be hurt or harmed • **invulnerability** *noun*

inward *adj* 1 placed within something 2 situated in the mind or soul ◇ *adv* (also **inwards**) towards the inside • **inwardly** *adv* 1 within 2 in your heart; privately

in-your-face *adj, slang* demanding attention in a forthright or aggressive way

IOC *abbrev* International Olympic Committee

iodine *noun* a liquid chemical used to kill germs

ion *noun* an electrically-charged atom or group of atoms • **ionizer** *noun* a device that sends out negative ions to improve the quality of the air

iota *noun* a little bit; a jot

IOU *abbrev* I owe you: a note given as a receipt for money borrowed

iPod *noun, trademark* a portable digital music player

ipso facto *adv* by that fact; thereby

IQ *abbrev* intelligence quotient, a measure of someone's performance in a standard test of intelligence

IRA *abbrev* Irish Republican Army, a paramilitary organization with the aim of uniting Northern Ireland and the Republic of Ireland

irascible *adj* easily made angry; bad-tempered • **irascibility** *noun*

irate *adj* angry

ire *noun, formal* anger

iridescent *adj* 1 shimmering with changing colours 2 coloured like a rainbow • **iridescence** *noun*

iridology *noun* diagnosis of illness by examining the irises of someone's eyes • **iridologist** *noun*

iris *noun* (*plural* **irises**) 1 the coloured part of the eye around the pupil 2 a lily-like flower which grows from a bulb

irk *verb* annoy (someone) • **irksome** *adj* annoying

iron *noun* 1 a common metal, widely used to make tools *etc* 2 an appliance for pressing clothes 3 an iron instrument: *a branding iron* 4 a golf club with a metal (originally iron) head 5 (**irons**) a prisoner's chains ◇ *adj* 1 made of iron 2 stern, resolute: *iron will* 3 of a rule: not to be broken ◇ *verb* 1 press (clothes) with an iron 2 (with **out**) smooth out (difficulties) • **the Iron Age** human culture at the stage of using iron for tools *etc* • **the Iron Curtain** *hist* the border separating the West from the countries of the former Soviet bloc

ironmonger *noun* a shopkeeper selling household tools, gardening equipment, *etc* • **ironmongery** *noun* goods sold by an ironmonger

irony *noun* (*plural* **ironies**) 1 a form of humour in which someone says the opposite of what is obviously true 2 an absurd contradiction or paradox: *the irony of it was that she would have given him the money if he hadn't stolen it* • **ironic** *or* **ironical** *adj* • **ironically** *adv*

irrational *adj* against logic or

common sense • **irrationality** *noun*

irregular *adj* **1** not happening at regular intervals **2** not smooth, even or straight **3** against the rules • **irregularity** *noun*

irrelevant *adj* not having to do with what is being spoken about • **irrelevancy** *noun*

irreparable *adj* not able to be repaired or made better

irreplaceable *adj* too good or rare to be replaced

irrepressible *adj* not restrainable or controllable

irreproachable *adj* not able to be criticized or blamed

irresistible *adj* too attractive or charming to be resisted

irresolute *adj* not able to make up your mind or keep to a decision

irrespective *adj* taking no account of: *irrespective of the weather*

irresponsible *adj* having no sense of responsibility; thoughtless

irreverent *adj* having no respect, *eg* for holy things • **irreverence** *noun*

irrevocable *adj* not to be changed

irrigate *verb* supply (land) with water by canals *etc* • **irrigation** *noun*

irritate *verb* **1** annoy **2** cause discomfort to (the skin, eyes, *etc*) • **irritable** *adj* easily annoyed • **irritable bowel syndrome** *noun* a condition with recurring but irregular symptoms of diarrhoea, constipation and abdominal pain • **irritation** *noun*

ISA *abbrev* Individual Savings Account

ISBN *abbrev* International Standard Book Number, an identification number given to a published book

Islam *noun* **1** the Muslim religion, founded by the prophet Mohammed **2** the Muslim world • **Islamic** *adj*

island *noun* **1** an area of land surrounded by water **2** an isolated place; a haven • **islander** *noun* an inhabitant of an island • **traffic island** a platform in the middle of a road for pedestrians to stand on while waiting to cross

isle *noun, formal* an island

-ism *suffix* **1** indicating a system, set of beliefs, *etc*: *socialism/Catholicism* **2** indicating prejudice against a particular group: *racism/sexism*

ISO *abbrev* International Standards Organization

isobar *noun* a line on a weather map connecting places where atmospheric pressure is the same

isolate *verb* **1** place or keep separate from other people or things **2** consider (something) by itself: *isolate the problem* • **isolation** *noun*

isomer *noun* a chemical substance with the same molecular weight as another, but with its atoms in a different arrangement • **isomeric** *adj*

isosceles *adj* of a triangle: having two sides equal (*compare with*: **equilateral**)

isotherm *noun* a line on a weather map connecting places that have the same temperature

isotope *noun* an atom with the same atomic number as, but different mass number from, another

ISP *abbrev* Internet service provider, a company that provides individuals with access to the Internet

issue *verb* **1** publish or make available to buy or have **2** give out (orders *etc*) **3** go or come out ◇ *noun* **1** a matter that is being discussed or a problem that is being dealt with **2** one number in a series of magazines *etc* **3** the copies of a book published at one time **4** (**issues**) emotional or psychological problems, *esp* difficulty in accepting facts or circumstances: *still has issues with her parents* **5** *formal* a flowing out **6** *formal* children: *he died* *without issue* • **take issue with** disagree with

isthmus /is-mus/ *noun* (*plural* **isthmuses**) a narrow neck of land connecting two larger portions

IT *abbrev* information technology

it *pronoun* **1** the thing spoken of: *I meant to bring the book, but I left it at home* **2** used in sentences with no definite subject: *it snowed today/it is too late now* **3** used in phrases as a kind of object: *go it alone/brave it out*

italics *plural noun* a kind of printed type that *slopes to the right* • **italicize** *verb* print in italics

itch *noun* **1** an irritating feeling in the skin, made better by scratching **2** a strong desire ◇ *verb* **1** have an itch **2** be impatient (to do) or long (to): *itching to open his presents* • **itchy** *adj*

item *noun* a separate article or detail in a list • **itemize** *verb* list item by item; detail

itinerant *adj* travelling from place to place ◇ *noun* someone who travels around, *esp* a homeless person or a pedlar

itinerary *noun* (*plural* **itineraries**) a route or plan of a journey

its *adj* belonging to it: *keep the hat in its box*

Do not confuse: **its** and **it's**

it's *short for* it is

itself *pronoun* **1** used reflexively: *the cat licked itself* **2** used for emphasis or contrast: *after I've read the introduction, I'll begin the book itself*

ITV *abbrev* Independent Television, the main commercial television network in the UK

IU *or* **IUD** *abbrev* intra-uterine (contraceptive) device, a contraceptive device that fits inside the neck of the womb

IV *abbrev* intravenous, *esp* an intravenous drip

IVF *abbrev* in vitro fertilization, the fertilization of an embryo in a test tube before replacing it in the womb

ivory *noun* (*plural* **ivories**) the hard white substance that forms the tusks of the elephant, walrus, *etc*

ivy *noun* (*plural* **ivies**) a creeping evergreen plant

Jj

jab verb (**jabbing, jabbed**) poke or stab ◇ noun **1** a poke or stab **2** informal an injection

jabber verb talk rapidly and indistinctly

jacinth /jas-inth/ noun **1** a type of precious stone **2** a reddish-orange colour

jack noun **1** a device with a lever for raising heavy weights **2** (also called **knave**) the playing card between ten and queen • **jackboots** plural noun large boots reaching above the knee • **jack-in-the-box** noun a doll fixed to a spring inside a box that leaps out when the lid is opened • **jackknife** noun **1** a large folding knife **2** a dive forming a sharp angle and then straightening ◇ verb of a vehicle and its trailer: swing together to form a sharp angle • **jack up 1** raise with a jack **2** raise (prices etc) steeply

jackal noun a dog-like wild animal

jackass noun **1** a male ass **2** informal an idiot • **laughing jackass** the kookaburra

jackdaw noun a type of small crow

jacket noun **1** a short coat **2** a loose paper cover for a book • **jacket potato** noun a baked potato

jackpot noun a fund of prize money that increases until someone wins it

Jacobean noun, hist relating to the period of James VI of Scotland, I of England (1603–25)

Jacobite noun, hist a supporter of James VII of Scotland, II of England and his descendants

Jacuzzi /juh-koo-zi/ noun, trademark a bath fitted with a device that agitates the water

jade noun a hard green mineral substance used for ornaments

jaded adj tired or bored

jagged adj rough-edged; uneven

jaguar noun a S American animal like a leopard

jail noun a prison • **jailbird** noun a convict or ex-convict • **jailer** noun someone in charge of a jail or prisoners

Jain /jain/ noun a member of an ascetic Indian religion similar to Buddhism • **Jainism** noun

jalapeño /ha-luh-pehn-yoh/ noun a hot Mexican chilli pepper

jalopy /juh-lop-ee/ noun an old car, aeroplane or other vehicle

jam noun **1** a soft food consisting of fruit boiled with sugar **2** a situation or blockage in which people or things are squeezed into too small a space; a crush **3** informal a difficult situation ◇ verb (**jamming, jammed**) **1** press or squeeze tight **2** crowd full **3** stick and so be unable to move: the back wheel has jammed **4** cause interference with another radio station's broadcast **5** music play with other musicians in an improvised style • **jam-packed** adj packed tightly; congested • **jam session** noun an informal gathering to play improvised music

jamb noun the side post of a door

jamboree noun **1** a large, lively gathering **2** a rally of Scouts

JANET /jan-ut/ abbrev Joint Academic Network, a computer network linking universities in the UK

jangle verb **1** make a harsh ringing noise **2** irritate

janitor noun **1** a caretaker **2** a doorkeeper

January noun the first month of the year

jape noun, informal a practical joke or other trick

japonica noun a Japanese flowering plant

jar noun a glass or earthenware bottle with a wide mouth ◊ verb (**jarring**, **jarred**) **1** have a harsh, startling effect **2** not match or go well with • **jarring** adj harsh, startling

jargon noun **1** special words used within a particular trade, profession, etc **2** derog impressive-sounding but meaningless words

jasmine noun a shrub with white or yellow sweet-smelling flowers

jaundice noun a disease that causes the skin and eyes to turn yellow • **jaundiced** adj **1** having jaundice **2** disillusioned because of many bad experiences; cynical

jaunt noun a short journey for pleasure

jaunty adj (**jauntier**, **jauntiest**) cheerful or lively • **jauntily** adv

javelin noun a long spear for throwing, or the athletics event in which it is thrown

jaw noun **1** the lower part of the face, including the mouth and chin **2** (**jaws**) an animal's mouth • **jawbone** noun the upper or lower bone of the jaw

jay noun a blue and red bird of the crow family

jaywalking noun walking carelessly among traffic • **jaywalker** noun

jazz noun a style of music with a strong rhythm, syncopation, improvisation, etc, based on African-American folk music • **jazzy** adj colourful or flamboyant • **jazz up** make more lively or colourful

jealous adj **1** wanting to have what someone else has; envious **2** guarding closely possessions, relationships, etc and angrily suspicious of potential rivals • **jealousy** noun

jeans plural noun casual denim trousers

Jeep noun, trademark a small army motor vehicle

jeer verb make fun of; scoff (at) ◊ noun a scoffing remark

Jehovah noun the Hebrew God of the Old Testament

jejune /juh-joon/ adj, formal naive, inexperienced

jelly noun (plural **jellies**) **1** a soft wobbly food consisting of fruit juice boiled with sugar and gelatine **2** a trembling state

jellyfish noun a small sea animal with thin tentacles and a round translucent jelly-like body

jemmy noun (plural **jemmies**) a burglar's iron tool

jeopardy /jep-uh-di/ noun danger • **jeopardize** verb put in danger or at risk

jerboa noun a small rat-like desert animal with very long hindlegs

jerk verb pull suddenly and sharply ◊ noun a sudden sharp move • **jerkily** adv • **jerky** adj moving or coming in jerks

jerkin noun a type of short coat

jeroboam /je-ruh-boh-um/ noun a bottle of wine equivalent to 6 standard bottles, or to 4 bottles of champagne

jerry-built adj, dated hastily and badly built

jersey noun (plural **jerseys**) a sweater

jest noun a joke ◇ verb joke

jester noun, hist a comic entertainer employed to amuse a royal court etc

jet noun 1 a jet plane 2 a spout of flame, air or liquid 3 a hard black mineral, used for ornaments and jewellery • **jet-black** adj very black • **jet lag** noun tiredness caused by the body's inability to cope with being in a new time zone • **jet plane** noun an aeroplane driven by jet propulsion • **jet propulsion** noun high-speed forward motion produced by sucking in air or liquid and forcing it out from behind • **jet set** noun, dated rich people who enjoy frequent expensive holidays • **jetstream** noun 1 the exhaust of a jet engine 2 a band of high-speed winds far above the earth

jetsam noun goods thrown overboard and washed ashore

jettison verb 1 throw overboard 2 abandon

jetty noun (plural **jetties**) a small pier

Jew noun someone who is of the race or religion of the ancient Israelites • **Jewish** adj of the Jews • **Jew's harp** noun a small harp-shaped musical instrument played between the teeth

jewel noun 1 a precious stone 2 someone or something highly valued • **jewelled** or US **jeweled** adj decorated with jewels • **jeweller** or US **jeweler** noun someone who makes or sells articles made of precious jewels and metals • **jewellery** or US **jewelry** noun articles made or sold by a jeweller

Jezebel noun a sexually immoral or scheming woman

jib noun 1 a three-cornered sail in front of a ship's foremast 2 the jutting-out arm of a crane • **jib at** (**jibbing**, **jibbed**) refuse to do; object

jibe or **gibe** verb make comments intended to annoy or ridicule someone; jeer ◇ noun a jeer

jiffy noun, informal a moment: I'll be there in a jiffy

Jiffy bag noun, trademark a padded envelope for posting

jig noun a lively dance or tune ◇ verb (**jigging**, **jigged**) jump about

jiggery-pokery noun, informal trickery or deceit

jiggle verb jump or cause to jump or jerk about

jigsaw or **jigsaw puzzle** noun a puzzle consisting of many different shaped pieces that fit together to form a picture

jihad /jee-had/ noun an Islamic holy war

jilt verb end a relationship with (a lover)

jingle noun 1 a clinking sound like that of coins 2 a simple rhyme

jingoism noun aggressive patriotism, usu accompanied by great dislike of other nations and peoples • **jingoistic** adj

jinx noun someone or something thought to bring bad luck

jitterbug noun an energetic dance to rock music, popular in the 1940s

jitters plural noun: **have the jitters** be very nervous

jittery adj very nervous, or shaking with nerves

jive noun a style of fast dancing to jazz music, popular in the 1950s

job noun 1 someone's daily work 2 any piece of work • **jobbing** adj doing odd jobs of work for payment: jobbing gardener • **job centre** noun a government office where information about available jobs is shown • **job lot** noun a collection of odds and ends • **Jobseeker's Allowance** noun, Brit a social-security allowance paid to the unemployed • **jobshare** noun the division of one job between two people, each working part-time

jock noun, slang **1** derog offensive a Scotsman or Scotswoman **2** US an athletic college student

jockey noun (plural **jockeys**) someone who rides a horse in a race ◇ verb push your way into a good position

jockstrap noun a genital support for men while playing sports

jocose adj, formal humorous • **jocosity** noun

jocular adj involving joking, or said in a joking way • **jocularity** noun • **jocularly** adv

jodhpurs /jod-puz/ plural noun riding breeches that fit tightly from knee to ankle

joey noun (plural **joeys**) Aust informal a young kangaroo

jog verb (**jogging**, **jogged**) **1** run at a gentle pace **2** push slightly; nudge ◇ noun • **jogger** noun someone who runs gently to keep fit • **jogging** noun • **jog someone's memory** make someone remember something

joggle verb shake slightly

joie de vivre /jwa duh veevr/ noun enthusiasm for life; spirit

join verb **1** put or come together **2** connect or fasten **3** become a member of **4** come and meet or be with ◇ noun the place where two or more things join • **joiner** noun someone who makes wooden fittings and the wooden parts of buildings • **joint** noun **1** the place where two or more things join **2** the place where two bones are joined, eg an elbow or knee **3** meat containing a bone ◇ adj **1** united **2** shared among more than one person, group, etc • **jointly** adv together • **join battle** begin fighting in battle

joist noun the beam to which the boards of a floor or the laths of a ceiling are nailed

jojoba /hoh-hoh-buh/ noun a desert shrub with edible seeds whose oil is used in cosmetics

joke noun something said or done to cause laughter ◇ verb make a joke; tease • **joker** noun **1** someone who jokes **2** an extra playing card in a pack, with a picture of a jester on it

jolly adj (**jollier**, **jolliest**) very cheerful or enjoyable • **jollification** noun noisy festivity or celebration • **jolliness** or **jollity** noun merriment

jolt verb **1** shake suddenly **2** go forward with sudden jerks ◇ noun a sudden jerk

joss stick noun a stick of gum that gives off a sweet smell when burned

jostle verb push or knock against

jot noun a very small part ◇ verb (**jotting**, **jotted**) write down hurriedly or briefly • **jotter** noun a book for taking notes or writing schoolwork

joule /jool/ noun a unit of energy

journal noun **1** a personal account of each day's events; a diary **2** a magazine dealing with a specialized, usu academic, subject • **journalism** noun the business of recording daily events for the media • **journalist** noun • **journalistic** adj

journey noun (plural **journeys**) a distance travelled ◇ verb travel • **journeyman** noun someone whose apprenticeship is finished

journo noun (plural **journos**), informal a journalist

joust noun, hist the armed contest between two knights on horseback at a tournament ◇ verb fight on horseback at a tournament

jovial adj cheerful, good-humoured • **joviality** noun

jowl noun the lower part of the jaw or cheek, esp when hanging

joy noun gladness • **joyful** or **joyous** adj full of joy • **joyless** adj dismal

• **joyriding** *noun* reckless driving for fun in a stolen car • **joystick** *noun* the controlling lever of an aircraft or a similar lever used for playing a computer game

JP *abbrev* Justice of the Peace

Jr *abbrev* Junior: *John Brown Jr*

jubilant *adj* showing or expressing great happiness at success; triumphant • **jubilation** *noun*

jubilee *noun* celebrations arranged for the anniversary of a wedding, coronation, *etc*

Judaism *noun* the Jewish religion or way of life • **Judaic** *adj*

Judas *noun* a traitor

judder *noun* a strong vibration or jerky movement

judge *verb* 1 form an opinion about 2 decide the winners in a competition *etc* 3 make a decision on (a law case) after hearing all the evidence ◇ *noun* 1 an official who hears cases in the law-courts and decides on them according to the country's or state's laws 2 someone skilled in evaluating anything: *a good judge of character* • **judgement** *or* **judgment** *noun* 1 a decision in a law case 2 an opinion 3 good sense in forming opinions • **judgemental** *adj* too eager to pass moral judgements or to criticize

judicial *adj* of a judge or court of justice • **judicially** *adv*

judiciary *noun* the judges of a country or state

judicious *adj* wise • **judiciously** *adv*

judo *noun* a Japanese form of wrestling for self-defence

jug *noun* a dish for liquids with a handle and a shaped lip for pouring

juggernaut *noun* a large articulated lorry

juggle *verb* 1 toss a number of things (balls, clubs, *etc*) into the air and catch them in order 2 have to deal with several different things at once 3 present (statistics) in a deceitful way • **juggler** *noun*

jugular vein *noun* the large vein at the side of the neck

juice *noun* the liquid in vegetables, fruits, *etc* • **juicy** *adj* 1 full of juice 2 sensational or scandalous

jujitsu *noun* a Japanese martial art similar to judo

jujube /joo-joob/ *noun* a spiny shrub with a dark red fruit

jukebox *noun* a coin-operated machine that plays selected recorded songs automatically

julep *noun, US* a sweet cocktail made with alcohol, sugar and mint

juliennes *plural noun* vegetables cut into very thin strips for cooking

July *noun* the seventh month of the year

Juma *noun* the Islamic Sabbath, held on Friday

jumble *verb* put into a disordered state; muddle ◇ *noun* a confused mixture • **jumble sale** *noun* a sale of odds and ends, cast-off clothing, *etc*

jumbo *noun* (*plural* **jumbos**) a child's name for an elephant ◇ *adj* very large • **jumbo jet** *noun* a large jet aircraft

jump *verb* 1 spring off the ground with the feet; leap 2 make a sudden startled movement ◇ *noun* 1 a leap 2 a sudden start • **jumpily** *adv* • **jumpsuit** *noun* a one-piece garment combining trousers and top • **jumpy** *adj* easily startled

jumper *noun* a woollen garment with sleeves, covering the upper body; a sweater

junction *noun* a place or point of joining, *esp* of roads or railway lines

juncture *noun, formal* point in time: *it's too early to decide at this juncture*

June *noun* the sixth month of the year

jungle *noun* a dense growth of trees and plants in tropical areas

junior *adj* 1 younger 2 in a lower class or rank ◇ *noun* someone younger: *he is my junior*

juniper *noun* an evergreen shrub with prickly leaves and berries that are used to give gin its flavour

junk[1] *noun* worthless articles; rubbish • **junk bond** *noun* a bond offering a high yield but low security • **junk food** *noun* convenience food with little nutritional value • **junkie** or **junky** *noun, derog* a drug addict • **junk mail** *noun* unsolicited mail, *esp* advertising material

junk[2] *noun* a Chinese flat-bottomed sailing ship, high in the bow and stern

junket *noun* 1 a paid trip made on official business, *esp* one on which pleasure competes well with business 2 a dish made of curdled milk sweetened and flavoured • **junketing** *noun, dated* celebrations; merriment

junta /*huun*-tuh/ *noun* a government formed following a successful coup d'état

jurisdiction *noun* 1 a legal authority or power 2 the district over which a judge, court, *etc* has power

jurisprudence *noun* the study or knowledge of law

jury *noun* (*plural* **juries**) 1 a group of people selected to reach a decision on whether an accused prisoner is guilty or not 2 a group of judges for a competition *etc* • **juror**, **juryman** or **jurywoman** *noun* someone who serves on a jury

just *adj* 1 fair in judgement; unbiased 2 correct ◇ *adv* 1 exactly: *just right* 2 not long since: *only just arrived* 3 merely, only: *just enough food* 4 really: *just beautiful* • **justly** *adv*

justice *noun* 1 fairness in making judgements 2 what is right or rightly deserved 3 a judge • **Justice of the Peace** (*short form* **JP**) a citizen who acts as a judge for certain matters

justifiable *adj* able to be justified or defended • **justifiably** *adv*

justify *verb* (**justifies**, **justifying**, **justified**) 1 prove or show to be right or desirable 2 *printing* make (text) form an even margin down the page • **justification** *noun* good reason

jut *verb* (**jutting**, **jutted**) stand or stick out

jute *noun* coarse fibre from the bark of an Asian plant, used for making sacking, canvas, *etc*

juvenile *adj* 1 of or for young people 2 childish ◇ *noun* a young person

juxtapose *verb* place or consider side by side • **juxtaposition** *noun*

Kk

K *noun, informal* a thousand pounds

k *abbrev* kilo-; one thousand

kabaddi /kuh-*bah*-di/ *noun* an Asian game resembling tag, played barefoot by teams of seven

kabuki /kuh-*boo*-ki/ *noun* a stylized form of Japanese theatre

kaftan *another spelling of* **caftan**

kaiser /*kai*-zuh/ *noun, hist* a German emperor

kalanchoe /kul-an-*koh*-ee/ *noun* a plant with flower clusters on long stems

kale *noun* a type of cabbage with open curled leaves

kaleidoscope *noun* a tube held to the eye and turned so that loose, coloured shapes reflected in two mirrors change patterns • **kaleidoscopic** *adj* 1 with changing colours 2 changing quickly • **kaleidoscopically** *adv*

kamikaze /ka-mi-*kah*-zi/ *noun, hist* a Japanese pilot trained to make a suicidal attack ◇ *adj* suicidal or self-destructive

kangaroo *noun* a large Australian animal with long hindlegs and great jumping power, the female carrying its young in a pouch on the front of her body

kaolin *noun* China clay

kapok /*keh*-pok/ *noun* light waterproof fibre fluff from the seeds of a tropical tree, used for padding

kaput /kuh-*puut*/ *adj, slang* broken, not working

karaoke /ka-ri-*oh*-ki/ *noun* an entertainment of singing well-known songs against pre-recorded backing music

karate /kuh-*rah*-ti/ *noun* a Japanese martial art using blows and kicks

karma *noun* in Buddhist belief, someone's destiny as determined by their actions in a previous life

kayak /*kai*-yak/ *noun* 1 a lightweight canoe for one person, manoeuvred with a single paddle 2 an Inuit sealskin canoe

KB *or* **Kb** *abbrev, comput* kilobyte

kcal *abbrev* kilocalorie

kebab *noun* small pieces of meat or vegetables cooked on a skewer

kedgeree *noun* a dish made with rice, fish and hard-boiled eggs

keek *verb, Scot* take a quick look; peek

keel *noun* the piece of a ship's frame that lies lengthways along the bottom • **keelhaul** *verb, hist* punish (a sailor) by hauling under the keel of a ship with ropes • **keelson** *noun* a ship's inner keel • **keel over** 1 fall over 2 of a ship: tip over sideways

keen¹ *adj* 1 eager, enthusiastic 2 bitingly cold 3 very sharp • **keenly** *adv* • **keenness** *noun*

keen² *verb* wail in grief; lament • **keening** *noun*

keep *verb* (**keeping, kept**) 1 not give or throw away 2 take care of, *esp* by providing financial support for; look after 3 fulfil (a promise) 4 remain in a position or state 5 (*also with* **on**) continue (doing something): *keep taking the tablets* 6 of food: stay in good condition **7** celebrate: *keep Christmas* **8** have in stock ◇ *noun* **1** food, board **2** a castle stronghold • **keeper** *noun* someone who looks after something: *zookeeper* • **keeping** *noun* care, charge • **keepsake** *noun* a gift in memory of an occasion *etc* • **in keeping with 1** suited to **2** following (rules, customs, *etc*) • **keep out 1** exclude **2** stay outside • **keep up** go on with; continue • **keep up with** go as fast *etc* as

keg *noun* a small cask or barrel

kelp *noun* a type of large brown seaweed

kelpie *noun* a Celtic water-sprite in the shape of a horse

kelvin *noun* a measure of temperature

ken *noun* the extent of someone's knowledge or understanding: *beyond the ken of the average person* ◇ *verb, Scot* know

kendo *noun* a Japanese martial art using bamboo sticks

kennel *noun* **1** a hut for a dog **2** (**kennels**) a place where dogs can be looked after

kept *past form of* **keep**

keratin *noun* the substance from which horns and nails are made

kerb *noun* the edge of something, *esp* a pavement • **kerb crawling** *noun* driving a car slowly in order to pick up prostitutes

---

Do not confuse with: **curb**

---

kerchief *noun* a square of cloth used as a headscarf

kerfuffle *noun* a commotion or fuss

kernel *noun* **1** a soft substance in the shell of a nut, or inside the stone of a fruit **2** the important part of anything

kerosine *noun* paraffin oil

kestrel *noun* a type of small falcon that hovers

ketch *noun* (*plural* **ketches**) a two-masted sailing ship

ketchup *noun* a flavouring sauce made from tomatoes *etc*

kettle *noun* a pot with a spout for heating liquids

kettledrum *noun* a drum made of a metal bowl covered with stretched skin *etc*

key *noun* **1** a device that is turned in a corresponding hole to lock or unlock, tighten, tune, *etc* **2** a lever pressed on a piano *etc* to produce a note **3** a button on a computer keyboard or typewriter that is pressed to type letters **4** the main note of a piece of music **5** something that explains a mystery or deciphers a code **6** a book containing answers to exercises ◇ *verb* type on a computer keyboard or typewriter ◇ *adj* important, essential • **keyboard** *noun* **1** the keys of a typewriter or computer **2** an electronic musical instrument with keys arranged as on a piano *etc* **3** the keys of a piano or organ arranged along a flat board • **keyed-up** *adj* excited • **keyhole** *noun* the hole in which a key of a door is placed • **keynote** *noun* **1** the main note of a piece of music **2** the main point about anything • **keypad** *noun* a device with buttons that can be pushed to operate a device, *eg* a telephone • **keystone** *noun* the stone at the highest point of an arch holding the rest in position

kg *abbrev* kilogram(s)

KGB *abbrev, hist* Committee of State Security (in Russian, *Komitet Gosudarstvennoi Bezopasnosti*), the secret police force of the former Soviet Union

khaki *adj* greenish-brown in colour ◇ *noun* **1** greenish-brown **2** cloth of this colour used for military uniforms

kibbutz /ki-*buutz*/ *noun* (*plural*

kibbutzim) a farming settlement in Israel in which all people share the work

kibosh /kai-bosh/ verb, informal ruin or destroy

kick verb 1 hit or strike out with the foot 2 of a gun: spring back violently when fired ◇ noun 1 a blow with the foot 2 the springing-back of a gun when fired • **kickoff** noun the start (of a football game) • **for kicks** informal for fun

kid noun 1 informal a child 2 a young goat 3 the skin of a young goat ◇ adj made of kid leather • **kids' stuff** informal something very easy or tame • **with kid gloves** very carefully or tactfully

kidnap verb (**kidnapping, kidnapped**) carry (someone) off by force, often demanding money in exchange • **kidnapper** noun • **kidnapping** noun

kidney noun (plural **kidneys**) either of a pair of organs in the lower back that filter waste from the blood and produce urine • **kidney bean** noun a bean with a curved shape like a kidney

kilim /ki-leem/ noun a Middle-Eastern woven rug

kill verb 1 put to death 2 put an end to 3 cause a lot of pain or distress to ◇ noun 1 the act of killing 2 the animals killed by a hunter • **killer** noun • **be in at the kill** be there at the most exciting moment

kiln noun a large oven or furnace for baking pottery, bricks, etc or for drying grain, hops, etc

kilobyte noun, comput a measure of storage capacity equal to 1000 bytes

kilocalorie noun a measure of energy equal to 1000 calories

kilogram or **kilogramme** noun a measure of weight equal to 1000 grams (about 2 lb)

kilohertz noun a unit of frequency of sound and radio waves equal to

1000 cycles per second

kilometre noun a measure of length equal to 1000 metres (about $\frac{5}{8}$ of a mile)

kilowatt noun a measure of electrical power equal to 1000 watts

kilt noun a pleated tartan skirt reaching to the knee, part of traditional Scottish dress

kilter noun: **out of kilter** out of sequence or off balance

kimono /ki-moh-noh/ noun (plural **kimonos**) a loose Japanese robe, fastened with a sash

kin noun members of the same family, relations • **kith and kin** see kith • **next of kin** your nearest relative

kind noun 1 a sort or type 2 goods, not money: paid in kind ◇ adj having good feelings towards others; generous, gentle • **kind-hearted** adj kind • **kindliness** noun • **kindly** adv in a kind way ◇ adj kind, warm-hearted • **kindness** noun

kindergarten noun a nursery school

kindle verb 1 stir up (feelings) 2 light a fire 3 catch fire

kindling noun material for starting a fire

kindred adj of the same sort; related: a kindred spirit ◇ noun relatives, relations

kinesiology /ki-nee-zi-ol-uh-ji/ noun the study of human movement and posture

kinetic adj of or expressing motion: kinetic energy

king noun 1 the inherited male ruler of a nation 2 a playing card with a picture of a king 3 the most important chess piece • **kingdom** noun 1 the area ruled by a king 2 any of the three major divisions of natural objects, ie animal, vegetable or mineral • **kingly** adj like a king; royal • **kingpin** noun the most important person in an organization

kingcup *noun* marsh marigold

kingfisher *noun* a type of small fish-eating bird with brightly coloured feathers

kink *noun* **1** a bend or curl in a rope, hair, *etc* **2** a peculiarity of the mind

kinky *adj* (**kinkier, kinkiest**) **1** twisted, contorted **2** *informal* sexually unusual or perverted

kinsfolk *plural noun, dated* relations, relatives

kinsman, kinswoman *noun, dated* a close relation

kiosk *noun* **1** a small stall for the sale of papers, sweets, *etc* **2** a public telephone box

kip *noun, slang* **1** a short sleep **2** a bed ◇ *verb* sleep

kipper *noun* a smoked and dried herring

kir /kee-uh/ *noun* a drink of white wine mixed with blackcurrant syrup or liqueur

kirk *noun, Scot* a church

kirsch /kee-uhsh/ *noun* a liqueur made from cherries

kismet *noun* destiny, fate

kiss *verb* **1** touch lovingly with the lips **2** touch gently ◇ *noun* (*plural* **kisses**) • **kiss of life** *noun* a mouth-to-mouth method of restoring breathing

kit *noun* the equipment or clothing necessary for a particular job

kitchen *noun* a room where food is cooked • **kitchenette** *noun* a small kitchen • **kitchen garden** *noun* a vegetable garden

kite *noun* **1** a light frame covered with paper or light cloth, for flying in the air **2** a kind of hawk

kith *noun*: **kith and kin** friends and relatives

kitsch *noun* vulgarly tasteless art *etc*

kitten *noun* a young cat • **kittenish** *adj* behaving like a kitten; playful • **have kittens** *informal* make a great fuss

kittiwake *noun* a type of gull

kitty¹ *noun* (*plural* **kitties**) a sum of money set aside for a purpose

kitty² *noun* (*plural* **kitties**), *informal* a kitten

kiwi *noun* **1** a fast-running almost wingless bird of New Zealand **2** a kiwi fruit **3** *informal* a person from New Zealand • **kiwi fruit** *noun* an edible fruit with a thin hairy skin and bright green flesh

kleptomania *noun* an uncontrollable desire to steal • **kleptomaniac** *noun & adj*

klondyker *noun* a factory ship processing fish for sale in a foreign country

km *abbrev* kilometre(s)

knack /nak/ *noun* a special clever ability

knackered /nak-ud/ *adj, informal* **1** extremely tired; exhausted **2** damaged beyond repair

knapsack /nap-sak/ *noun, dated* a rucksack

knave /nehv/ *noun* **1** a cheating rogue **2** in playing cards, the jack • **knavery** *noun* dishonesty • **knavish** *adj* cheating or wicked

knead /need/ *verb* **1** work (dough *etc*) by pressing with the fingers **2** massage

knee /nee/ *noun* the joint at the bend of the leg • **kneecap** *noun* the flat round bone on the front of the knee joint • **kneecapping** *noun* a form of torture or punishment in which the victim is shot or otherwise injured in the kneecap

kneel /neel/ *verb* (**kneeling, knelt**) go down on one or both knees

knell /nel/ noun **1** the tolling of a bell for a death or funeral **2** a warning of a sad end or failure

knickerbockers /nik-uh-bok-uz/ plural noun loose breeches tucked in at the knee

knickers /nik-uz/ plural noun women's or girls' underpants

knick-knack /nik-nak/ noun a small, ornamental article

knife /naif/ noun (plural **knives**) a tool for cutting ◊ verb stab • **at knife point** under threat of injury with a knife

knight /nait/ noun **1** hist an aristocrat trained to use arms **2** an aristocratic rank for a man, with the title Sir, that is not inherited by a son **3** a piece used in chess ◊ verb raise to the rank of knight • **knight errant** noun, hist a knight who travelled in search of adventures • **knighthood** noun the rank of a knight • **knightly** adj **1** of knights **2** gallant and courageous

knit /nit/ verb (**knitting, knitted**) **1** form a garment from yarn or thread by means of thin pointed rods **2** join closely • **knitting** noun work done by knitting • **knitting needles** plural noun a pair of thin pointed rods used in knitting

knob /nob/ noun **1** a small rounded projection or mass **2** a round doorhandle

knock /nok/ verb **1** tap on a door to have it opened **2** strike, hit **3** drive or be driven against ◊ noun **1** a tap on a door **2** a sudden stroke or hit • **knocker** noun a hinged weight on a door for knocking with • **knock-kneed** adj having knees that touch in walking • **knock back** informal eat or drink greedily • **knock down 1** demolish **2** informal reduce in price • **knock off** informal **1** stop work for the day **2** copy illegally • **knock out 1** hit (someone) hard enough to make them unconscious **2** force (someone) out of a competition by defeating

them • **knock up 1** put together hastily **2** slang make pregnant

knoll /nohl/ noun a small rounded hill

knot /not/ noun **1** a hard lump, eg one made by tying string, or found in wood at the join between trunk and branch **2** a tangle **3** a small gathering of people **4** a measure of speed for ships (about 1.85 kilometre per hour) ◊ verb (**knotting, knotted**) tie in a knot

knotted adj full of knots • **get knotted!** exclam, informal expressing anger or defiance towards someone

knotty adj (**knottier, knottiest**) **1** having knots **2** difficult, complicated: a knotty problem

know /noh/ verb (**knowing, knew, known**) **1** be aware or sure of **2** recognize • **knowing** adj showing a secret awareness of something • **knowingly** adv intentionally

knowledge /nol-ij/ noun **1** things that are known **2** information

knowledgeable /nol-ij-uh-bul/ adj showing or having knowledge • **knowledgeably** adv

knuckle /nuk-ul/ noun a joint of the fingers • **knuckleduster** noun a metal covering worn on the knuckles as a weapon • **knucklehead** noun, informal an idiot • **knuckle under** give in; yield

koala /ko-ah-luh/ noun an Australian tree-climbing animal resembling a small bear

kofta noun an Indian dish of balls of minced, spiced meat

kohlrabi /kohl-rah-bi/ noun a type of cabbage with a turnip-shaped stem

kookaburra /kook-uh-buh-ruh/ noun a large kingfisher of Australia and New Guinea with a chuckling cry

kooky adj (**kookier, kookiest**) informal eccentric

kopeck *noun* a Russian coin, equal to a hundredth of a rouble

Koran /kuh-*rahn*/ *noun* the sacred book of Islam

kosher *adj* 1 pure and clean according to Jewish law 2 acceptable or honest

kowtow to *verb* treat with too much respect

kraal *noun* a South African village

krill *noun* a small shrimp-like creature eaten by whales *etc*

krypton *noun* an inert gas present in the air, used in fluorescent lighting

Kt *abbrev* Knight

kudos /*kyoo*-dos/ *noun* respect that you get because of your status or achievements; prestige

kulfi *noun* Indian ice-cream made with boiled, reduced milk

kumquat /*kum*-kwot/ *noun* a small Chinese orange with a sweet rind

kung fu /kung *foo*/ *noun* a Chinese form of self-defence

kw *abbrev* kilowatt(s)

kyrie /*kee*-ri-yeh/ *noun* 1 a prayer in the Roman Catholic mass following the opening anthem 2 a musical setting for this

Ll

l *abbrev* litre

lab *noun, informal* a laboratory

label *noun* a small written note fixed onto something listing its contents, price, *etc* ◇ *verb* (**labelling, labelled**) **1** fix a label to **2** call something by a certain name

labial *adj* of the lips

laboratory *noun* (*plural* **laboratories**) a room with equipment for scientific research

labour *or US* **labor** *noun* **1** hard work **2** workers on a job **3** the process of childbirth ◇ *verb* **1** work hard to move slowly or with difficulty **2** emphasize (a point) too greatly • **laborious** *adj* requiring hard work; tiring • **laboured** *adj* showing signs of effort, and often therefore seeming unnatural • **labourer** *noun* someone who does heavy unskilled work • **Labour Party** *noun* one of the main political parties of the UK

labrador *noun* a large black or fawn-coloured dog, often used for retrieving game

laburnum *noun* a tree with large clusters of yellow flowers and poisonous seeds

labyrinth *noun* a maze

lace *noun* **1** a cord for fastening shoes *etc* **2** decorative fabric made with fine thread ◇ *verb* **1** fasten with a lace **2** add alcohol to (a drink)

lacerate *verb* **1** make tears in; rip **2** wound • **laceration** *noun*

lachrymal *adj* of tears

lack *verb* **1** be needed but not present **2** be without (something needed) ◇ *noun* the absence of something needed

lackadaisical *adj* showing a lack of effort or enthusiasm; half-hearted • **lackadaisically** *adv*

lackey *noun* (*plural* **lackeys**) **1** a servant **2** someone who acts like a slave

lacklustre *or US* **lackluster** *adj* not at all interesting or lively; dull

laconic *adj* using few words to express meaning • **laconically** *adv*

lacquer *noun* a varnish for wood or metal ◇ *verb* put lacquer on

lacrosse *noun* a twelve-a-side ball-game played with sticks that have a shallow net at the end

lactate *verb* produce or secrete milk

lactic *adj* of milk • **lactic acid** *noun* a substance produced in muscles after physical exertion

lactose *noun* a type of sugar found in milk

lacuna *noun* (*plural* **lacunae**) *formal* a gap or space

lad *noun* a boy • **the lads** a man's male friends

ladder *noun* **1** a set of rungs or steps between two supports, for climbing up or down **2** a run from a broken stitch in a stocking *etc*

laddish *adj* typical of young men, *esp* in being loud, vulgar or aggressive • **laddishness** *noun* laddish behaviour

laden *adj* carrying a heavy load; loaded

ladette *noun, informal* a young woman who often behaves in a noisy drunken way

lading *noun* cargo

ladle *noun* a large spoon for lifting out liquid ◇ *verb* lift with a ladle

lady *noun* (*plural* **ladies**) **1** a refined or elegant woman **2** a polite word for a woman **3** a title for the wife of a knight, lord or baronet, or a daughter of a member of the aristocracy **4** (**ladies**) a public lavatory for women • **Her Ladyship** the title used in addressing a titled lady

ladybird *noun* a small beetle, usually red with black spots

lag *verb* (**lagging, lagged**) **1** move or progress slowly and fall behind **2** cover (a boiler or pipes) with a warm covering ◇ *noun* a delay • **lagging** *noun* material for covering pipes *etc*

lager *noun* a light beer • **lager lout** *noun* a drunken and aggressive or violent young man

laggard *noun, dated* someone who lags behind ◇ *adj* lagging behind

lagoon *noun* a shallow stretch of water separated from the sea by low sandbanks, rocks, *etc*

laid *past form of* **lay**[1]

lain *past participle of* **lie**[2]

lair *noun* the den of a wild animal

Do not confuse with: **layer**
---

laird *noun* in Scotland, a landowner

laissez-faire /les-ay-*fair*/ *noun* a general principle of not interfering

laity *see* **lay**[2]

lake *noun* a large stretch of water surrounded by land

Lallans *noun* the Scots language, *esp* as used in literature

lama *noun* a Buddhist priest of Tibet

lamb *noun* **1** a young sheep **2** the meat of this animal **3** a gentle person

lambast /lam-*bast*/ *noun* criticize or reprimand severely

lame *adj* **1** unable to walk because of injuries to the foot or leg **2** not good enough: *a lame excuse* ◇ *verb* make lame • **lame duck** *noun* an inefficient or weak person or organization • **lamely** *adv* • **lameness** *noun*

lamé /*lah*-meh/ *noun* a fabric interwoven with metallic thread

lament *verb* **1** feel or express grief for; mourn **2** regret ◇ *noun* **1** a show of grief **2** a mournful poem or piece of music • **lamentation** *noun*

lamentable *adj* **1** pitiful **2** very bad • **lamentably** *adv*

laminated *adj* made by putting layers together: *laminated glass*

Lammas *noun* 1 August, an old feast day celebrating the beginning of the harvest

lamp *noun* a device that gives out light, containing an electric bulb, candle, *etc* • **lamppost** *noun* a pillar supporting a street lamp

lampoon *noun* a piece of ridicule or satire directed at someone ◇ *verb* ridicule or satirize

lamprey *noun* (*plural* **lampreys**) a type of fish like an eel

LAN /lan/ *abbrev, comput* local area network, a network connecting all the computers in a large building or area

lance *noun* a long shaft of wood with a pointed head ◇ *verb* cut open (a boil *etc*) with a knife • **lance corporal** *noun* a soldier with rank just below a corporal

lancer *noun* a light cavalry soldier

lancet *noun* a sharp surgical instrument

land *noun* **1** the solid portion of the earth's surface **2** ground **3** soil **4** an area known for a particular quality *etc: a land of great beauty* ◇ *verb* **1** arrive on land or on shore **2** set (an aircraft, ship, *etc*) on land or on shore • **landed** *adj* owning large areas of land: *landed gentry* • **landfall** *noun* **1** an approach to land after a voyage **2** the land approached • **landfill** *noun* a site where rubbish is buried under the ground • **landlocked** *adj* surrounded by land, *esp* having no coastline • **landlubber** *noun, old* someone who works on land and knows little about the sea • **landmark** *noun* **1** an object on land that serves as a guide **2** an important event • **landmine** *noun* a bomb laid on or near the surface of the ground that explodes when someone passes over it

landau /*lan*-dow/ *noun, hist* a horse-drawn carriage with a removable top

landing *noun* **1** a coming ashore or to ground **2** a place for getting on shore **3** the level part of a staircase between the flights of steps

landlord, **landlady** *noun* **1** the owner of land or accommodation for rent **2** the owner or manager of a pub

landscape *noun* **1** an area of land being viewed; a scene **2** a painting, photograph, *etc* of inland scenery • **landscape gardening** *noun* gardening for picturesque effect

landslide *noun* a mass of land that slips down from the side of a hill • **landslide victory** *noun* a win in an election in which a great mass of votes goes to one side

lane *noun* **1** a narrow street or passage **2** a subdivision of a wide road for a single line of traffic **3** a part of the sea or air to which ships or aircraft must keep

language *noun* **1** human speech **2** the speech of a particular people or nation

languid *adj* lacking energy or liveliness

languish *verb* **1** be in a difficult or unpleasant situation **2** lose energy or strength **3** long (for) • **languishing** *adj*

languor *noun* a languid state; listlessness

laniard *another spelling of* **lanyard**

lank *adj* **1** of hair: straight and limp **2** tall and thin

lanky *adj* (**lankier**, **lankiest**) tall and thin

lanolin *noun* a fat extracted from sheep's wool

lantern *noun* a case for holding or carrying a light • **lantern-jawed** *adj* with a long thin face and hollow cheeks

lanyard *or* **laniard** *noun* **1** a short rope used for fastening things on a ship **2** a cord for hanging a whistle *etc* round the neck

lap *verb* (**lapping**, **lapped**) **1** lick up with the tongue **2** wash or flow against **3** (with **up**) accept (praise *etc*) greedily **4** get a lap ahead of other competitors in a race ◇ *noun* **1** the front part, from waist to knees, of someone seated **2** one round of a racetrack or competition course • **lapdog** *noun* a small pet dog • **laptop** *noun* a compact portable computer combining screen, keyboard and processor in one unit

laparoscope *noun* a long optical tube used for examining internal organs without cutting • **laparoscopy** *noun* surgical examination with a laparoscope

lapel *noun* the part of a coat joined to the collar and folded back on the chest

lapidary *noun* (*plural* **lapidaries**) someone who cuts, polishes and shapes gems and stones ◇ *adj* engraved on stone

lapis lazuli /*lap*-is *laz*-yoo-li/ *noun* a deep-blue stone containing several minerals

lapsang souchong /*lap*-sang

soo-shong/ _noun_ a Chinese tea with a smoky flavour

lapse _verb_ **1** fall into bad habits **2** be no longer valid ◇ _noun_ **1** a mistake or failure **2** a period of time passing

lapwing _noun_ a medium-sized European crested bird; a peewit

larceny _noun_ stealing, theft

larch _noun_ (_plural_ **larches**) a cone-bearing deciduous tree

lard _noun_ the melted fat of a pig ◇ _verb_ **1** put strips of bacon in meat before cooking **2** apply thickly; smear

larder _noun_ **1** a room or place where food is kept **2** stock of food

large _adj_ great in size, amount, _etc_ • **largely** _adv_ to a great extent; mainly • **largeness** _noun_ • **at large 1** at liberty, free **2** in general: _the public at large_

largesse /lah-_zhes_/ _noun_ generosity, _esp_ in giving money

largo _adj & adv, music_ (to be played) slowly

lariat /_la_-ri-ut/ _noun_ **1** a rope for fastening horses while they are grazing **2** a lasso

lark _noun_ **1** a general name for several kinds of singing bird **2** a piece of fun or mischief ◇ _verb_ behave mischievously or boisterously; fool about

larkspur _noun_ a tall plant with blue, white or pink spurred flowers, a kind of delphinium

larva _noun_ (_plural_ **larvae**) an insect in its first stage after coming out of the egg; a grub

laryngitis _noun_ inflammation of the larynx

larynx _noun_ (_plural_ **larynxes** or **larynges**) the upper part of the windpipe containing the cords that produce the voice

lasagne /luh-_zan_-yuh/ _plural noun_ flat sheets of pasta ◇ _sing noun_ (or **lasagna**) a baked dish made with this

lascar _noun, old_ an East Indian sailor

lascivious /luh-_siv_-i-us/ _adj_ showing an unpleasant sexual interest; lewd • **lasciviously** _adv_ • **lasciviousness** _noun_

laser _noun_ **1** a very narrow powerful beam of light **2** an instrument that concentrates light into such a beam • **laser printer** _noun_ a computer printer that uses a laser to apply a pigment to the paper

lash _noun_ (_plural_ **lashes**) **1** a thong or cord of a whip **2** a stroke with a whip **3** an eyelash ◇ _verb_ **1** strike with a whip **2** fasten tightly with a rope _etc_ **3** attack with bitter words • **lash out 1** kick or swing out without thinking **2** speak angrily **3** spend extravagantly

lass _noun_ (_plural_ **lasses**) _informal_ a girl

lassitude _noun_ lack of energy; weariness

lasso /la-_soo_/ _noun_ (_plural_ **lassoes** or **lassos**) a long rope with a loop that tightens when the rope is pulled, used for catching wild horses _etc_ ◇ _verb_ (**lassoes**, **lassoing**, **lassoed**) catch with a lasso

last _adj_ **1** coming after all the others: _last person to arrive_ **2** the final one remaining: _last ticket_ **3** most recent: _my last employer_ ◇ _verb_ **1** continue to exist or happen **2** remain in good condition **3** be enough for (someone): _this food will last us a week_ ◇ _noun_ a foot-shaped tool on which shoes are made or repaired • **lastly** _adv_ finally • **last-minute** _adj_ done at the very last possible time, immediately before something else is due to happen • **at last** in the end • **on your last legs** completely worn out and about to collapse • **the last rites** religious ceremonies performed for a dying person • **the last straw** the last in a series of unpleasant events, which makes a situation unbearable • **the last word 1** the final comment or decision about something **2** the most modern or advanced thing of its kind • **to the last** to the end

latch noun (plural **latches**) **1** a wooden or metal catch used to fasten a door **2** a light lock for a door ◇ verb fasten with a latch • **latchkey** noun a key to raise the latch of a door • **latchkey child** noun a child who regularly returns home to an empty house

late adj & adv **1** coming after the expected time: his train was late **2** far on in time: it's getting late **3** recently dead: the late author **4** recently, but no longer, holding an office or position: the late chairman **5** recent: our late disagreement • **lately** adv recently • **lateness** noun • **of late** recently

latent adj existing but not yet developed, used or expressed: latent ability/ latent hostility

lateral adj of, at, to or from the side • **lateral thinking** noun thinking that seeks new ways of looking at a problem and does not merely proceed in logical stages

latex noun the milky juice of plants, esp of the rubber tree, a rubber-like substance produced from it

lath /lahth/ noun a thin narrow strip of wood

Do not confuse: **lath** and **lathe**

---

lathe /lehdh/ noun a machine for turning and shaping articles of wood, metal, etc

lather noun **1** a foam or froth, eg from soap and water **2** informal a state of agitation ◇ verb cover with lather

Latin noun the language of ancient Rome

latitude noun **1** the distance, measured in degrees, of a place north or south of the equator (compare with: longitude) **2** freedom of action or choice: the new job allows him far more latitude than his previous one

latrine noun a toilet in a camp, barracks, etc

latte /la-teh/ noun a cup of strong coffee mixed with steamed milk

latter adj **1** the last of two things mentioned (contrasted with: **former**): between working and sleeping, I prefer the latter **2** recent • **latter-day** adj of recent times • **latterly** adv recently

lattice noun **1** a network of crossed strips **2** a window constructed this way

laud verb, formal praise • **laudatory** adj expressing praise

laudable adj worthy of being praised; admirable • **laudably** adv

laudanum /lawd-uh-num/ noun a morphine solution used in the past as a pain-killing and recreational drug

laugh verb make sounds with the voice in showing amusement, scorn, etc ◇ noun **1** the sound of laughing **2** informal an amusing incident or person • **laughable** adj comical or ridiculous • **laughably** adv • **laughing stock** noun an object of scornful laughter

laughter noun the act or noise of laughing

launch verb **1** put (a product) on the market with publicity **2** slide a boat or ship into water, esp on its first voyage **3** fire off (a rocket etc) **4** start off on a course **5** throw, hurl ◇ noun (plural **launches**) **1** the act of launching **2** a large motor boat

launder verb **1** wash and iron clothes etc **2** put (illegally obtained money) into an honest business in order to hide its origins

launderette noun a shop where customers may wash clothes etc in washing machines

laundry noun (plural **laundries**) **1**

a place where clothes are washed **2** clothes to be washed

laureate /lo-ri-ut/ adj honoured for artistic or intellectual distinction: poet laureate

laurel noun **1** the bay tree, from which ceremonial wreaths were made **2** (**laurels**) honours or victories gained • **rest on your laurels** be content with past successes and not try for any more

lava noun molten rock thrown out by a volcano, which becomes solid as it cools

lavatory noun (plural **lavatories**) a toilet

lavender noun **1** a sweet-smelling plant with small pale purple flowers **2** a pale-purple colour

lavish adj very generous ◇ verb spend or give very freely

law noun **1** the official rules that apply in a country or state **2** one such rule **3** a scientific rule stating the conditions under which certain things always happen • **law-abiding** adj obeying the law • **law court** noun a place where people accused of crimes are tried • **lawful** adj allowed by law • **lawfully** adv • **lawless** adj paying no attention to, and not observing, the laws • **lawsuit** noun a quarrel or dispute to be settled by a court of law

lawn noun **1** an area of smooth grass eg as part of a garden **2** a kind of fine linen • **lawnmower** noun a machine for cutting grass • **lawn tennis** noun tennis played on a grass court

lawyer noun someone whose work it is to give advice in matters of law

lax adj **1** not strict enough **2** showing a lack of care; negligent • **laxity** or **laxness** noun

laxative noun a medicine that loosens the bowels

lay¹ verb (**laying**, **laid**) **1** place or set down **2** put (eg a burden, duty) on (someone) **3** set in order; arrange **4** of a hen: produce eggs **5** bet money; wager **6** cause to leave or subside: lay a ghost • **laid-back** adj, informal relaxed, easy-going • **laid-up** adj ill in bed • **layabout** noun a lazy idle person • **layby** noun a parking area at the side of a road • **lay about** beat all over • **lay down 1** assert: laying down the law **2** store (eg wine) • **lay off 1** dismiss (workers) temporarily **2** informal stop: lay off arguing • **lay up** store for future use • **lay waste** ruin or destroy

Do not confuse with: **lie**

lay² adj **1** not of the clergy **2** without special training in a particular subject • **laity** noun ordinary people, not members of the clergy • **layman**, **laywoman** noun someone without special training in a subject

lay³ noun, old a short poem or song

layer noun a thickness forming a covering or level • **layered** adj having a number of distinct layers: layered cake

Do not confuse with: **lair**

layette /leh-et/ noun a complete outfit for a baby

lay figure noun a jointed model of a human figure used by artists

laze verb be lazy; idle

lazy adj (**lazier**, **laziest**) not inclined to work or make an effort; idle • **lazily** adv • **laziness** noun • **lazybones** sing noun, informal an idler

lb abbrev pound(s) (in weight)

lbw abbrev, cricket leg before wicket

LCD abbrev liquid crystal display

lea noun, old a meadow

leach verb seep slowly through or out of something

Do not confuse with: **leech**

lead¹ /leed/ verb (**leading**, **led**) 1 show the way by going first 2 direct or guide 3 be the most important or influential member of 4 persuade 5 live (a busy, quiet, etc life) 6 of a road: go (to a place) ◇ noun 1 the first or front place 2 guidance or direction 3 a leash for a dog etc • **leading question** noun a question asked in such a way as to suggest the desired answer

lead² /led/ noun 1 a soft bluish-grey metal 2 the part of a pencil that writes, really made of graphite 3 a weight used for sounding depths at sea etc • **lead-free** adj of petrol: unleaded

leaden adj 1 made of lead 2 dull grey in colour 3 heavy or slow 4 lacking vitality or interest; dull

leader noun 1 someone who leads or goes first; a chief 2 a column in a newspaper expressing the editor's opinions • **leadership** noun 1 the position of leader 2 the ability to lead

leaf noun (plural **leaves**) 1 a part of a plant growing from the side of a stem 2 a page of a book 3 a hinged flap on a table etc • **leafy** adj • **turn over a new leaf** begin again and do better

leaflet noun a small printed sheet

league noun 1 an association of clubs for games 2 a union of people, nations, etc established for the benefit of each other 3 old a measure of distance, approximately 3 miles (about 4.8 kilometres) • **in league with** allied with

leak noun 1 a hole through which gas, liquid, etc escapes 2 an escape of gas, liquid, etc 3 a release of secret information ◇ verb 1 of a substance: escape through a hole 2 give (secret information) to the media etc • **leakage** noun a leaking

lean verb (**leaning**, **leant**) 1 slope over to one side 2 rest (against) 3 rely (on) ◇ adj 1 thin 2 producing or containing very little; scanty 3 of meat: not fat • **lean-burn** adj of an engine: able to run on a reduced amount of fuel • **leaning** noun a liking for, or interest in, something • **lean-to** noun a shed etc built against another building or wall

leap verb (**leaping**, **leapt**) 1 move with jumps 2 jump (over) ◇ noun a jump • **leapfrog** noun a game in which one player leaps over another's bent back • **leap year** noun a year that has 366 days (February having 29), occurring every fourth year

learn verb (**learning**, **learnt** or **learned**) 1 get to know (something) 2 gain skill • **learned** /lur-nid/ adj having or showing great knowledge • **learner** noun • **learning** noun knowledge

lease noun 1 an agreement giving the use of a house etc on payment of rent 2 the period of this agreement ◇ verb let or rent • **lease-back** noun an arrangement in which the buyer of a property leases it back to the seller • **leasehold** noun property or land held by lease

leash noun (plural **leashes**) a strap or rope by which a dog etc is held; a lead ◇ verb put (a dog etc) on a leash

least adj the smallest amount of anything: he had the least money ◇ adv (often with **the**) the smallest or lowest degree: I like her least • **at least** at any rate; anyway • **not in the least** not at all

leather noun the skin of an animal, prepared by tanning for use ◇ verb beat physically; thrash • **leathering** noun a thrashing • **leathery** adj with a rough surface or coarse, grainy texture

leave verb (**leaving**, **left**) 1 go away; depart 2 allow to remain 3 abandon 4 hand down to someone in a will 5 give over to someone's responsibility, care, etc: leave the choice to her

◇ *noun* **1** permission to do something (*eg* to be absent) **2** a holiday • **leavings** *plural noun* things left over • **take your leave of 1** part from **2** say goodbye to

leaven /lev-un/ *noun* yeast • **leavened** *adj* raised with yeast

lecher *noun* a man who shows an unpleasant or unwanted sexual desire • **lecherous** *adj* showing an unpleasant or unwanted sexual desire • **lechery** *noun*

lectern *noun* a stand on which a speaker can rest notes, a book, *etc* to be read from

lecture *noun* **1** a discussion of a certain subject, written or read to an audience **2** a scolding ◇ *verb* **1** deliver a lecture **2** scold • **lecturer** *noun* someone who lectures, *esp* a university teacher

LED *abbrev* light-emitting diode

led *past form of* **lead¹**

ledge *noun* **1** a shelf or projecting rim: *window-ledge* **2** an underwater ridge

ledger *noun* the accounts book of an office or shop

lee *noun* the side away from the wind, the sheltered side • **leeward** *adj & adv* in the direction towards which the wind blows • **leeway** *noun* **1** freedom to decide or move; latitude **2** lost time, ground, *etc*: *a lot of leeway to make up* **3** a ship's drift off course

leech *noun* (*plural* **leeches**) a kind of blood-sucking worm

---

Do not confuse with: **leach**

---

leek *noun* a long green and white vegetable of the onion family

leer *noun* a sly, sidelong or lustful look ◇ *verb* look sideways or lustfully (at)

leery *adj*: **leery of** wary of

lees *plural noun* dregs that settle at the bottom of liquid, *esp* wine

left¹ *adj* on or of the side of the body that in most people has the less skilful hand (*contrasted with*: **right**) ◇ *adv* on or towards the left side ◇ *noun* **1** the left side **2** a political grouping with left-wing ideas *etc* • **left-field** *adj, informal* odd, eccentric • **left-handed** *adj* **1** using the left hand rather than the right **2** awkward • **left-wing** *adj* of or holding socialist or radical political views, ideas, *etc*

left² *past form of* **leave**

leg *noun* **1** one of the limbs by which humans and animals walk **2** a long slender support for a table *etc* **3** one stage in a journey, contest, *etc* • **leggings** *plural noun* outer coverings for the lower legs • **leggy** *adj* having long legs • **legless** *adj, informal* drunk • **legroom** *noun* room to move the legs

legacy *noun* (*plural* **legacies**) **1** something that is left by will **2** something left behind by the previous occupant of a house, job, *etc* • **legatee** *noun* someone to whom a legacy is left

legal *adj* **1** allowed by law; lawful **2** of law • **legality** *noun* the state of being legal • **legalize** *verb* make lawful

legalism *noun* the practice of following laws or rules strictly • **legalist** *noun* • **legalistic** *adj* sticking rigidly to the law or rules

legate *noun* an ambassador, *esp* from the Pope

legation *noun* an official body of people acting on behalf of their government abroad

legato /li-gah-toh/ *adj & adv, music* (to be played) smoothly

legend *noun* **1** a traditional story handed down; a myth **2** a caption **3** a famous person whom people admire • **legendary** *adj* **1** of legend; famous **2** not to be believed

legerdemain /lej-uh-duh-*mehn*/

noun conjuring by quickness of the hand

leggings, **leggy** *see* leg

legible *adj* able to be read easily • **legibility** *noun*

legion *noun* **1** *hist* a body of from three to six thousand Roman soldiers **2** a great many • **legionary** *noun, hist* a soldier of a legion

legionnaire's disease *noun* a serious disease similar to pneumonia caused by a bacterium

legislate *verb* make laws • **legislation** *noun* • **legislative** *adj* lawmaking • **legislator** *noun* someone who makes laws • **legislature** *noun* the part of the government that has the powers of making laws

legitimate *adj* **1** lawful **2** reasonable or fair **3** of a child: born of parents married to each other • **legitimacy** *noun*

legume /leh-*goom*/ *noun* a plant of the pea or bean family

leisure *noun* time free from work; spare time • **leisure centre** *noun* a set of buildings where sports facilities of various kinds are provided for the public • **leisured** *adj* not occupied with business • **leisurely** *adj* unhurried: *leisurely pace*

leitmotiv /*lait*-moh-teef/ *noun* **1** a musical theme in an opera associated with a particular character *etc* **2** a recurring theme in literature *etc*

lemming *noun* **1** a small rat-like animal of the arctic regions, reputed to follow others of its kind over sea-cliffs *etc* when migrating **2** someone who follows others unquestioningly

lemon *noun* **1** an oval fruit with pale yellow rind and sour juice **2** the tree on which this fruit grows

lemonade *noun* a soft drink flavoured with lemons

lemur /*lee*-muh/ *noun* an animal

related to the monkey but with a pointed nose

lend *verb* (**lending**, **lent**) **1** give use of (something) for a time **2** give (a quality) to someone or something: *his presence lent an air of respectability to the occasion* • **lend itself to** be suitable for or adapt easily to

length *noun* **1** extent from end to end in space or time **2** the quality of being long **3** a great extent **4** a piece of something cut from a longer piece • **lengthen** *verb* make or grow longer • **lengthways** *or* **lengthwise** *adv* in the direction of the length • **lengthy** *adj* **1** long **2** tiresomely long • **at length 1** in detail **2** at last

lenient *adj* punishing only lightly; merciful • **lenience** *or* **leniency** *noun*

lenitive *adj, formal* soothing or making something seem less serious

lens *noun* (*plural* **lenses**) **1** a piece of glass curved on one or both sides, used in spectacles, cameras, *etc* **2** the part of the eye that focuses light on the retina

Lent *noun* in the Christian church, a period of fasting before Easter, lasting forty days

lent *past form of* lend

lentil *noun* the seed of a pod-bearing plant, used in soups *etc*

leonine *adj* like a lion

leopard /*lep*-ud/ *noun* an animal of the cat family with a spotted skin • **leopardess** *noun* a female leopard

leotard *noun* a tight-fitting garment worn for dancing, gymnastics, *etc*

leper *noun* **1** someone with leprosy **2** an outcast • **leprosy** *noun* a contagious skin disease causing thickening or numbness in the skin

lepidopterology *noun* the study of butterflies and moths • **lepidopterist** *noun*

leprechaun /*lep*-ruh-kawn/ *noun* a

creature like a small person in Irish folklore

lesbian noun a female homosexual ◇ adj of a woman: homosexual

lese-majesty /lehz-*maj*-us-ti/ noun an offence against the state; treason

lesion noun a wound

less adj 1 not as much: *take less time* 2 smaller: *think of a number less than 40* ◇ adv not as much, or to a smaller extent: *he goes less often than he should* ◇ noun a smaller amount: *he has less than I have* ◇ prep minus: *5 less 2 equals 3* • **lessen** verb make smaller • **lesser** adj smaller

lessee /les-*ee*/ noun someone with a lease for a property, business, *etc*

lesson noun 1 something that is learned or taught 2 a part of the Bible read in church 3 a period of teaching

lest conj for fear that; in case

let verb (**letting, let**) 1 allow 2 grant use of (*eg* a house, shop, farm) in return for payment; lease • **let down** fail to do as expected; disappoint • **let off** not punish; excuse • **let up** become less

lethal adj causing death

lethargy /*leth*-uh-ji/ noun a lack of energy or interest; sleepiness • **lethargic** adj

LETS /lets/ abbrev local exchange trading system, a type of barter system

letter noun 1 a mark expressing a sound 2 a written message 3 *formal* (**letters**) learning: *a woman of letters* • **lettering** noun the way in which letters are formed • **to the letter** according to the exact meaning of the words: *following instructions to the letter*

lettuce noun a green plant whose leaves are used in a salad

leucocyte /*loo*-kuh-sait/ noun a white blood corpuscle

leukaemia /loo-*kee*-mi-uh/ noun a cancerous disease of the white blood cells in the body

levee noun, *US* a river embankment

level adj 1 flat, even or smooth 2 horizontal ◇ verb (**levelling, levelled**) 1 make flat, smooth or horizontal 2 make equal 3 aim (a gun *etc*) 4 pull down (a building *etc*) ◇ noun 1 a height, position, *etc* in comparison with some standard: *water level* 2 an instrument for showing whether a surface is level: *spirit level* 3 personal rank or degree of understanding: *a bit above my level* 4 a flat, smooth surface • **level crossing** noun a place where a road crosses a railway track • **level-headed** adj having good sense • **level playing-field** noun a position of equality from which to compete fairly

lever noun 1 a handle for operating a machine 2 a bar of metal, wood, *etc* used to raise or shift something heavy 3 a method of gaining advantage • **leverage** noun 1 the use of a lever 2 power, influence

leveret noun a young hare

leviathan /li-*vai*-uh-thun/ noun 1 anything huge or powerful 2 a huge mythological sea monster

levitation noun the illusion of raising a heavy object in the air without support • **levitate** verb float in the air

levity noun lack of seriousness; frivolity

levy verb (**levies, levying, levied**) collect by order (*eg* a tax, army conscripts) ◇ noun (*plural* **levies**) money, troops, *etc* collected by order

lewd adj taking delight in indecent thoughts or acts • **lewdness** noun

lexical adj of words

lexicographer noun someone who compiles or edits a dictionary • **lexicography** noun

lexicon noun 1 a dictionary 2 a glossary of terms

LGV *abbrev* large goods vehicle

liable *adj* **1** legally responsible (for) **2** likely or apt (to do something or happen) **3** (with **to**) likely to suffer from: *liable to colds* • **liability** *noun* **1** legal responsibility **2** a disadvantage **3** a debt

liaise /lee-ehz/ *verb* communicate or be in contact (with), *esp* in order to cooperate on something

liaison /lee-eh-zon/ *noun* **1** contact or communication **2** a sexual affair

liana *noun* a climbing tropical plant

liar *see* **lie¹**

lib *noun, informal* liberation: *women's lib*

libation *noun, informal* alcoholic drink

Lib Dem *abbrev* Liberal Democrat

libel *noun* something written that damages another's reputation ◇ *verb* (**libelling, libelled**) write a libel about • **libellous** *adj* • **libellously** *adv*

liberal *adj* **1** giving or providing a lot; generous **2** tolerant of different opinions and lifestyles; open-minded • **Liberal** *noun* a member of the former Liberal Party • **Liberal Democrats** *plural noun* one of the main political parties of the UK • **liberality** *noun*

liberate *verb* set free • **liberation** *noun*

libertine *noun, old* someone who lives an immoral life

liberty *noun* (*plural* **liberties**) **1** freedom, *esp* of speech or action **2** (**liberties**) rights, privileges • **take liberties** behave rudely or impertinently

libido *noun* sexual drive • **libidinous** *adj*

library *noun* (*plural* **libraries**) **1** a collection of books, records, *etc* **2** a building or room housing these • **librarian** *noun* the keeper of a library

libretto *noun* (*plural* **libretti** or **librettos**) the words of an opera or musical

lice *plural of* **louse**

licence *noun* **1** a form giving permission to do something, *eg* to keep a television set, drive a car, *etc* **2** freedom of action

---

Do not confuse: **licence** and **license**

---

license *verb* give a licence to (someone) or for (something) • **licensee** *noun* someone to whom a licence is given

licentious *adj* behaving immorally • **licentiousness** *noun*

lichen /*lai*-kun/ *noun* a large group of moss-like plants that grow on rocks *etc*

licit *adj, formal* legal or allowable

lick *verb* **1** pass the tongue over **2** of flames: reach up ◇ *noun* **1** the act of licking **2** a tiny amount • **lick into shape** make vigorous improvements on

licorice *another spelling of* **liquorice**

lid *noun* **1** a cover for a box, pot, *etc* **2** the cover of the eye

lido /*lee*-doh/ *noun* **1** an open-air swimming pool **2** a bathing beach

lie¹ *noun* a false statement meant to deceive ◇ *verb* (**lies, lying, lied**) tell a lie • **liar** *noun* someone who tells lies

lie² *verb* (**lies, lying, lay, lain**) **1** rest in a flat position **2** be or remain in a state or position ◇ *noun* the position or situation in which something lies • **lie in wait** keep hidden in order to surprise someone • **lie low** keep quiet or hidden • **the lie of the land** the present state of affairs

---

Do not confuse with: **lay**

liege /leezh/ *noun* **1** a lord or superior **2** a loyal subject

lieu /loo/ *noun*: **in lieu of** instead of

Lieut *abbrev* Lieutenant

lieutenant /lef-*ten*-unt/ *noun* **1** an army officer next below captain **2** in the navy, an officer below a lieutenant-commander **3** a rank below a higher officer: *lieutenant-colonel*

life *noun* (*plural* **lives**) **1** the period between birth and death: *a long life* **2** the state of being alive: *signs of life* **3** lively or interesting qualities: *no life in the city* **4** way of living: *a hectic life* **5** the story of someone's life: *the life of Nelson* **6** living things: *animal life* • **lifebelt** *noun* a ring filled with air for keeping someone afloat • **lifeboat** *noun* a boat for rescuing people in difficulties at sea • **lifeblood** *noun* a source of necessary strength or life • **lifebuoy** *noun* a float to support someone awaiting rescue at sea • **life cycle** *noun* the various stages through which a living thing passes • **life drawing** *noun* drawing from a live human model • **life jacket** *noun* a buoyant jacket for keeping someone afloat in water • **lifeless** *adj* **1** dead **2** not lively; spiritless • **lifelike** *adj* like a living person • **lifeline** *noun* a vital means of communication • **lifelong** *adj* lasting the length of a life • **life-size** *adj* full size, as in life • **lifespan** *noun* the length of someone's life • **lifestyle** *noun* the way in which someone lives • **life-support machine** *noun* a device for keeping a human being alive during severe illness, space travel, *etc* • **lifetime** *noun* the period during which someone is alive

lift *verb* **1** take and put in a higher position; raise **2** *informal* steal **3** of fog: disappear, disperse ◇ *noun* **1** a moving platform carrying goods or people between floors in a large building **2** a ride in someone's car *etc* **3** a boost to the spirits or confidence

• **lift-off** *noun* the take-off of a rocket, spacecraft, *etc*

ligament *noun* a tough substance that connects the bones of the body

ligature *noun* **1** something used to tie or bind **2** a printed character formed from two or more letters, *eg* æ

light¹ *noun* **1** the brightness given by the sun, moon, lamps, *etc* that makes things visible **2** a source of light, *eg* a lamp **3** a flame on a cigarette lighter ◇ *adj* **1** bright **2** of a colour: pale **3** illuminated by light ◇ *verb* (**lighting**, **lit** *or* **lighted**) **1** illuminate with light **2** set fire to • **lighten** *verb* **1** make or become brighter **2** of lightning: to flash • **lightening** *noun* a making or becoming lighter or brighter • **lighter** *noun* a device that produces a flame • **lighthouse** *noun* a tower-like building with a flashing light to warn or guide ships • **lighting** *noun* a type or system of lights • **lightship** *noun* a ship anchored in a fixed position to serve as a lighthouse • **light year** *noun* the distance light travels in a year (6 billion miles) • **bring to light** cause to become known; reveal • **come to light** be revealed or discovered • **in the light of** taking into consideration (information *etc*)

light² *adj* **1** not heavy **2** easy to bear or do **3** easy to digest **4** moving easily and gracefully; nimble **5** lively **6** not serious or solemn; cheerful **7** not intellectually or emotionally challenging: *light music* **8** of rain *etc*: little in quantity • **lighten** *verb* make less heavy • **lighter** *noun* a large open boat used for unloading and loading ships • **light-fingered** *adj* inclined to steal • **light-headed** *adj* dizzy • **light-hearted** *adj* cheerful • **lightly** *adv* • **lightweight** *noun* **1** a fighter in a low or the lowest weight category in boxing, wrestling and other contact sports **2** someone with little importance or authority

light³ *verb* (**lighting**, **lit** *or* **lighted**)

old (with **on**) **1** land (on) after flying or being blown; settle **2** come upon by chance

lightning *noun* an electric flash in the clouds • **lightning conductor** *noun* a metal rod on a building *etc* that conducts electricity down to earth

---

Do not confuse with: **lightening**

---

ligneous *adj* woody; wooden

lignite *noun* a soft brown type of coal

like¹ *adj* the same as or similar to ◊ *prep* **1** in the same way as: *he sings like an angel* **2** such as: *animals like cats and dogs* ◊ *noun* something or someone that is the equal of another: *you won't see her like again* • **likelihood** *noun* probability • **likely** *adj* **1** probable **2** liable (to do something) ◊ *adv* probably • **liken** *verb* think of as similar; compare • **likeness** *noun* **1** similarity, resemblance **2** a portrait, photograph, *etc* of someone • **likewise** *adv* **1** in the same way **2** also

like² *verb* **1** enjoy (something) or think (something) is good or nice **2** be fond of (someone) • **likeable** *or* **likable** *adj* of pleasant character and easy to like • **liking** *noun* **1** fondness **2** satisfaction: *to my liking*

lilac *noun* a small tree with hanging clusters of pale purple or white flowers ◊ *adj* of pale purple colour

lilliputian /lil-i-*pyoo*-shun/ *adj* extremely small; minuscule

lilt *noun* a pleasant rising and falling rhythm ◊ *verb* have this rhythm

lily *noun* (*plural* **lilies**) a tall plant grown from a bulb with large white or coloured flowers • **lily-of-the-valley** *noun* a plant with small white bell-shaped flowers

limb *noun* **1** a leg or arm **2** a branch of a tree

limber *adj* bending or stretching easily; supple • **limber up** exercise so as to become supple

limbo¹ *noun* the land bordering Hell, reserved for those unbaptized before death • **in limbo** forgotten, neglected

limbo² *noun* a W Indian dance in which the dancer passes under a low bar

lime *noun* **1** (*also called* **quicklime**) a white substance used in making cement **2** a tree related to the lemon **3** its greenish-yellow fruit **4** another name for the linden tree • **limelight** *noun* public attention

limerick *noun* a type of humorous rhymed poetry in five-line verses

limit *noun* **1** the farthest point or place **2** a boundary **3** largest (or smallest) extent, degree, *etc* **4** restriction ◊ *verb* set or keep to a limit • **limitation** *noun* **1** something that limits **2** a weak point or flaw • **limited company** *noun* a company that is owned by shareholders who have liability for debts only according to the extent of their share

limo *noun, informal* a limousine

limousine *noun* a large luxurious car

limp *adj* **1** not stiff; floppy **2** weak ◊ *verb* **1** walk lamely **2** of a damaged ship *etc*: move with difficulty ◊ *noun* **1** the act of limping **2** a limping walk

limpet *noun* **1** a small cone-shaped shellfish that clings to rocks **2** someone who is difficult to get rid of

limpid *adj* of water *etc*: clear, transparent

linchpin *noun* **1** a pin-shaped rod used to keep a wheel on an axle **2** someone or something that is essential to a business, plan, *etc*

linctus *noun* a syrupy medicine for sore throats *etc*

linden *noun* a large tree with

heart-shaped leaves; a lime tree

line noun **1** a row of people, printed words, etc **2** a cord, rope, etc **3** a long thin stroke or mark **4** a wrinkle **5** a railway **6** a telephone connection **7** a short letter **8** a family from generation to generation **9** course, direction **10** a company or service of ships or aircraft **11** a particular interest, activity, etc: not really my line **12** (**lines**) army trenches **13** (**lines**) a written school punishment exercise ◇ verb **1** (often with **up**) place in a row or alongside of **2** form lines along (a street) **3** mark out with lines **4** cover on the inside: line a dress • **lineage** /lin-i-ij/ noun descent, traced back to your ancestors • **lineal** /lin-i-ul/ adj directly descended through the father, grandfather, etc • **lineament** /lin-i-uh-munt/ noun a feature, esp of the face • **linear** /lin-i-uh/ adj **1** made of lines **2** in one dimension (length, breadth or height) only • **liner** noun a ship or aeroplane working on a regular service • **linesman, lineswoman** noun an umpire at a boundary line • **lining** noun a covering on the inside

linen noun **1** lightweight cloth made of flax **2** articles made of linen: table linen

ling[1] noun a long slender fish like the cod

ling[2] noun heather

linger verb **1** stay for a long time or for longer than expected **2** be slow or reluctant to leave; loiter

lingerie /lanh-zhuh-ree/ plural noun women's underwear

lingo noun (plural **lingoes**) a language or dialect

lingua franca noun a language used amongst people from different nations etc so that they can communicate

linguini /ling-gween-i/ plural noun pasta in long thin flat strands

linguist noun **1** someone skilled in languages **2** someone who studies language • **linguistic** adj • **linguistics** sing noun the scientific study of languages and of language in general

liniment noun an oil or ointment rubbed into the skin to cure stiffness in the muscles, joints, etc

link noun **1** a ring of a chain **2** a single part of a series **3** anything connecting two things ◇ verb **1** join closely **2** be connected **3** connect physically; join • **linkage** noun

links plural noun **1** a stretch of flat or slightly hilly ground near the seashore **2** a golf course by the sea

linnet noun a small songbird of the finch family

lino noun, informal linoleum • **linocut** noun a design for printing cut into a block of linoleum

linoleum noun a type of smooth, hard-wearing covering for floors

linseed noun flax seed • **linseed oil** noun oil from flax seed

lint noun **1** a soft woolly material for putting over wounds **2** fine pieces of fluff

lintel noun a beam or long stone forming the top of a doorway or window

lion noun a powerful animal of the cat family, the male of which has a shaggy mane • **lioness** noun a female lion • **lionize** verb treat as a celebrity • **the lion's share** the largest share

lip noun **1** either of the two fleshy flaps in front of the teeth that form the rim of the mouth **2** the edge of a container etc • **lip reading** noun reading what someone says from the movement of their lips • **lip service** noun saying one thing but believing another: paying lip service to the rules • **lipstick** noun a cosmetic stick for colouring the lips

liposuction noun a surgical operation to remove unwanted body fat

liquefy verb (**liquefies, liquefying, liquefied**) make or become liquid • **liquefaction** noun

liqueur /lik-yaw/ noun a strong sweet alcoholic drink

Do not confuse with: **liquor**

---

liquid noun a flowing, water-like substance ◊ adj 1 flowing 2 looking like water 3 soft and clear

liquidate verb 1 wind up the affairs of (a bankrupt business company); close down 2 slang kill, murder • **liquidation** noun • **liquidator** noun • **liquidize** verb 1 make liquid 2 make into a purée • **liquidizer** noun a machine for liquidizing

liquor /lik-uh/ noun an alcoholic drink, esp a spirit (eg whisky)

Do not confuse with: **liqueur**

---

liquorice or **licorice** noun 1 a plant of the pea family with a sweet-tasting root 2 a black, sticky sweet flavoured with this root

lisp verb 1 say th for s or z because of being unable to pronounce these letters correctly 2 speak imperfectly, like a child ◊ noun a speech disorder of this kind

lissome adj moving gracefully and with ease; nimble

list¹ noun a series of names, numbers, prices, etc written down one after the other ◊ verb write (something) down in this way • **listed building** noun one protected from being knocked down because it is of architectural or historical interest

list² verb of a ship: lean over to one side ◊ noun a slope to one side

listen verb 1 give your attention to in order to hear 2 pay attention to; heed: never listen to my advice • **listener** noun

listeria noun a bacterium found in certain foods which can damage the nervous system if not killed during cooking • **listeriosis** noun a brain disease caused by eating food contaminated with listeria bacteria

listless adj without energy or interest; weary • **listlessness** noun

lists plural noun, hist the ground enclosed for a battle between knights on horseback

lit past form of **light¹** and **light³**

litany noun (plural **litanies**) 1 a set form of prayer 2 a long list or catalogue

liter US spelling of **litre**

literal adj following the exact or most obvious meaning • **literally** adv exactly as stated: he was literally blinded by the flash

literary adj 1 relating to books, authors, etc 2 knowledgeable about books • **literacy** noun ability to read and write • **literate** adj able to read and write

literature noun 1 the books etc that are written in any language 2 anything in written form, eg brochures or catalogues

lithe adj bending the body easily; supple

lithium noun a metallic element whose salts are used in treating some mental illnesses

lithograph noun a picture made from a drawing done on stone or metal • **lithographer** noun • **lithography** noun printing done by this method

litigation noun a law case

litigious /lit-ij-us/ adj fond of taking your grievances to court

litmus paper noun treated paper that changes colour when dipped in an acid or alkaline solution • **litmus test** noun something that indicates underlying attitudes *etc*

litre *noun* a metric measure of liquids (1.76 pint)

litter *noun* **1** an untidy mess of paper, rubbish, *etc* **2** a heap of straw used as bedding for animals **3** a number of animals born at one birth **4** *hist* a bed for carrying the sick and injured ◊ *verb* **1** scatter rubbish carelessly about **2** produce a litter of young

little *adj* small in quantity or size ◊ *pronoun* (**a little**) a small amount, distance, *etc*: *have a little more/move a little to the right* ◊ *adv* **1** not much: *was little impressed* **2** not at all: *little does she know*

liturgy *noun* (*plural* **liturgies**) the form of service of a church ● **liturgical** *adj*

live¹ /liv/ *verb* **1** be alive: *live for ever* **2** have your home; dwell: *lives in Edinburgh* **3** pass your life: *lived a hectic life* **4** survive: *live to tell the tale* **5** to be lifelike or vivid: *the painting lives on the canvas* ● **livelihood** *noun* someone's means of living, *eg* their daily work ● **live and let live** allow others to live as they please ● **live down** live until (an embarrassment *etc*) is forgotten by others ● **live on 1** keep yourself alive by eating or drinking (something) **2** be supported by (earnings, investments, *etc*) ● **live up to** be as good as expected

live² /laiv/ *adj* **1** having life; not dead **2** full of energy **3** of a television broadcast *etc*: seen as the event takes place, not recorded **4** charged with electricity and apt to give an electric shock ● **liven** *verb* make lively ● **livestock** *noun* farm animals ● **liveware** *noun, comput, informal* the people operating a system, as opposed to the hardware and equipment ● **livewire** *noun* a very lively, energetic person

livelong *adj, old* whole: *the livelong day*

lively *adj* (**livelier, liveliest**) **1** full of energy and enthusiasm **2** full of busy activity **3** in which people express strong opinions ● **liveliness** *noun*

liver *noun* a large gland in the body that carries out several important functions including purifying the blood

livery *noun* (*plural* **liveries**) **1** the colours and designs painted on a vehicle, *esp* when they represent an organization **2** the uniform of a manservant *etc* ● **livery stable** *noun* a stable where horses are kept for hire

livid *adj* **1** very angry **2** of a bluish lead-like colour

living *adj* **1** having life **2** currently in existence or use **3** of a likeness: exact ◊ *noun* means of living, *esp* paid employment ● **living room** *noun* a room in a house for relaxing in; a sitting room ● **living wage** *noun* a wage on which it is possible to live comfortably ● **living will** *noun* a document stating that a person would prefer to be allowed to die rather than be kept alive on a life-support machine

lizard *noun* a four-footed reptile

llama *noun* a S American animal of the camel family without a hump

lo *exclam, old* look

loach *noun* (*plural* **loaches**) a type of small river fish

load *verb* **1** put on what is to be carried **2** put the ammunition in (a gun) **3** put a film in (a camera) **4** weight for some purpose: *loaded dice* ◊ *noun* **1** as much as can be carried at once **2** cargo **3** a heavy weight or task **4** the power carried by an electric circuit ● **loaded question** *noun* a question meant to trap someone into making a damaging admission ● **loadline** *noun* a line along a ship's side to mark the waterline when fully loaded

loaf *noun* (*plural* **loaves**) a shaped mass of bread ◊ *verb* pass time idly or lazily ● **loafer** *noun* **1** an idler **2** (**loafers**) casual shoes

loam noun rich soil • **loamy** adj

loan noun something lent, esp a sum of money ◊ verb lend

loath or **loth** /lohth/ adj unwilling (to)

Do not confuse: **loath** and **loathe**

---

loathe verb /lohdh/ dislike greatly • **loathing** noun great hate or disgust • **loathsome** adj causing loathing or disgust; horrible

loaves plural of **loaf**

lob noun 1 tennis a ball high overhead dropping near the back of the court 2 cricket a slow, high ball bowled underhand ◊ verb (**lobbing, lobbed**) 1 send such a ball 2 informal throw (something)

lobby noun (plural **lobbies**) 1 a small entrance hall 2 a passage off which rooms open 3 a group of people who try to influence the government or other authority ◊ verb (**lobbies, lobbying, lobbied**) 1 try to influence (public officials) 2 conduct a campaign to influence public officials

lobe noun 1 the hanging-down part of an ear 2 a division of the brain, lungs, etc

lobelia noun a garden plant with clusters of very small flowers of various colours

lobotomy noun a surgical operation on the front lobes of the brain carried out in cases of schizophrenia etc • **lobotomize** verb 1 perform a lobotomy on 2 make bland or spiritless

lobster noun a kind of shellfish with large claws, used for food • **lobster pot** noun a basket in which lobsters are caught

local adj of or confined to a certain place ◊ noun, informal 1 the pub nearest someone's home 2 (**locals**) the people living in a particular place or area • **local colour** noun 1 details in a story that make it more interesting and realistic 2 activities, sights and other experiences you have in a place you are visiting that make you feel you are really experiencing life in it • **locale** noun scene, location • **local government** noun administration of the local affairs of a district etc by elected inhabitants • **locality** noun a particular place and the area round about • **localize** verb confine to one area • **locate** verb 1 find 2 set in a particular place: a house located in the Highlands • **location** noun 1 the place where something is; situation 2 the act of locating • **on location** of filming etc: in natural surroundings, not in a studio

loch noun 1 in Scotland, a lake 2 in Scotland, an inlet of the sea

lock noun 1 a fastening for doors etc needing a key to open it 2 a part of a canal for raising or lowering boats 3 a section of hair 4 (**locks**) hair 5 a tight hold ◊ verb 1 fasten with a lock 2 become fastened 3 (with **up**) shut in with a lock • **locker** noun a small lockable cupboard in a large building, for individual use • **locker room** noun a room for changing clothes and storing personal belongings • **locket** noun a little ornamental case hung round the neck • **lockjaw** noun a form of tetanus that stiffens the jaw muscles • **lockout** noun the locking out of workers by their employer during wage disputes • **locksmith** noun a person who makes, repairs and fits locks • **lockup** noun a lockable garage • **lock, stock and barrel** completely

locomotion noun movement from place to place • **locomotive** noun a railway engine ◊ adj of or capable of locomotion

locum noun (plural **locums**) a doctor, dentist, etc taking another's place for a time

locus noun (plural **loci**) a point in space

locust *noun* a large insect of the grasshopper family that destroys growing plants

lode *noun* a vein containing metallic ore • **lodestar** *noun* the Pole star • **lodestone** *noun* **1** a form of the mineral magnetite with magnetic properties **2** a magnet

lodge *noun* **1** a small house, often at the entrance to a larger building **2** a beaver's dwelling **3** a house occupied during the shooting or hunting season **4** a branch of a society ◇ *verb* **1** live in rented rooms **2** become fixed (in) **3** make (a complaint, appeal, *etc*) officially **4** put in a safe place • **lodger** *noun* someone who stays in rented rooms • **lodging** *noun* **1** a place to stay, sleep, *etc* **2** (**lodgings**) a room or rooms rented in someone else's house

loess /loh-is/ *noun* a loamy deposit found in river valleys

loft *noun* **1** a room just under a roof **2** a gallery in a hall, church, *etc*

lofty *adj* (**loftier, loftiest**) **1** high up **2** noble: *lofty ambitions* **3** too proud; haughty: *a lofty attitude* • **loftily** *adv* • **loftiness** *noun*

log *noun* **1** a thick, rough piece of wood, part of a felled tree **2** a device for measuring a ship's speed **3** a logbook ◇ *verb* (**logging, logged**) write down (events) in a logbook • **logjam** *noun* **1** a piling up of floating logs **2** congestion that brings traffic *etc* to a standstill • **log on** *or* **log off** start or finish using a computer by entering a password

loganberry *noun* a kind of fruit like a large raspberry

logbook *noun* **1** an official record of a ship's or aeroplane's progress **2** the registration documents of a motor vehicle **3** a record of progress, attendance, *etc*

loggerhead *noun*: **at loggerheads** quarrelling

loggia /lohj-i-uh/ *noun* (*plural* **loggie** *or* **loggias**) a covered walkway behind a row of pillars in a classical building

logic *noun* **1** the study of reasoning correctly **2** correctness of reasoning • **logical** *adj* according to the rules of logic or sound reasoning • **logically** *adv*

logo *noun* (*plural* **logos**) a symbol of a business firm *etc* consisting of a simple picture or lettering

loin *noun* **1** the back of an animal cut for food **2** (**loins**) the area around the genitals, or the genitals themselves **3** (**loins**) the part of the body between the bottom rib and the pelvis • **loincloth** *noun* a piece of cloth worn round the hips, *esp* in India and south-east Asia

loiter *verb* **1** stand around **2** move slowly

loll *verb* **1** lie lazily about **2** of the tongue: hang down or out

lollipop *noun* a large boiled sweet on a stick • **lollipop man, lollipop woman**, *noun, Brit* someone employed to stop cars to allow schoolchildren to cross the street, who carries a pole with a disc at the top

lollop *verb* **1** bound clumsily **2** lie around idly; lounge

lolly *noun, informal* (*plural* **lollies**) **1** a lollipop **2** money

lone *adj* **1** not accompanied by others; by itself **2** without a partner or spouse; single: *lone parents*

lonely *adj* (**lonelier, loneliest**) **1** not accompanied by others **2** lacking or needing companionship; alone **3** of a place: having few people • **loneliness** *noun* • **lonesome** *adj* **1** not accompanied by others **2** feeling lonely

long *adj* **1** measuring a lot from end to end **2** measuring a certain amount: *cut a strip 2cm long/the film is 3 hours long* **3** far-reaching: *a long memory* **4** seeming to pass slowly: *it's been* *a long day* ◇ *adv* **1** for a great time: *thought long and hard* **2** through the whole time: *all day long* ◇ *verb* wish very much (for): *longing to see him again* • **longbow** *noun* a large bow bent by the hand in shooting • **longhand** *noun* writing in full (*contrasted with:* **shorthand**) • **longing** *noun* a strong desire • **long johns** *plural noun* men's underwear reaching from the waist to the ankles • **long jump** *noun* an athletics event in which competitors take a running start and try to jump as far as possible into a sand pit • **long-range** *adj* **1** able to reach a great distance **2** looking a long way into the future • **longship** *noun, hist* a Viking sailing ship • **long-sighted** *adj* able to see things at a distance but not those close at hand • **long-standing** *adj* begun a long time ago and having lasted all that time • **long-suffering** *adj* having a lot of troubles to put up with, often without complaining • **long-term** *adj* **1** extending over a long time **2** taking the future, not just the present, into account • **long-wave** *adj* of radio: using wavelengths over 1000 metres (*compare with:* **short-wave**) • **long-winded** *adj* using too many words • **before long** soon • **in the long run** in the end • **so long** *informal* goodbye

longevity /lon-*jev*-i-ti/ *noun* great length of life

longitude *noun* the distance, measured in degrees, of a place east or west of the Greenwich meridian (*compare with:* **latitude**)

loo *noun, informal* a toilet

loofah *noun* the fibrous fruit of a tropical plant, used as a rough sponge

look *verb* **1** turn the eyes towards so as to see **2** appear, seem: *you look tired/it looks as if I can go after all* **3** face: *his room looks south* ◇ *noun* **1** the act of looking: *have a look at this* **2** the expression on someone's face: *a blank look* **3** appearance: *didn't like the look of the food* **4** (**looks**)

personal appearance • **lookalike** *noun* someone who looks physically like another • **looker** *noun, informal* someone attractive or good-looking • **look-in** *noun* a chance to do something • **looking glass** *noun, old* a mirror • **lookout** *noun* **1** (someone who keeps) a careful watch **2** a high place for watching from **3** concern, responsibility • **look alive** *dated informal* get ready for action • **look down on** think of as being inferior • **look for** search for • **look forward to** anticipate with pleasure • **look into** investigate • **look on** **1** stand by and watch **2** think of (as): *he looks on her as his mother* • **look out!** be careful! • **look over** examine briefly • **look sharp** *dated informal* hurry up

loom *noun* a machine for weaving cloth ◇ *verb* appear indistinctly, often threateningly

loony *noun* (*plural* **loonies**) *informal* an insane person; a lunatic ◇ *adj* insane

loop *noun* **1** a doubled-over part in a piece of string *etc* **2** a U-shaped bend • **loophole** *noun* **1** a way of evading a duty, responsibility, *etc* without technically breaking a rule or law **2** a narrow slit in a wall • **in the loop** *or* **out of the loop** belonging, or not belonging, to the group of people who are informed about something • **loop the loop** fly (an aircraft) upwards, back and down as if going round a circle

loose *adj* **1** not tight; slack **2** not tied; free **3** not closely packed together; dispersed **4** not exact; vague **5** done rather unskilfully or carelessly; casual ◇ *verb* **1** make loose; slacken **2** untie • **loose-leaf** *adj* having a cover that allows pages to be inserted or removed • **loosely** *adv* • **loosen** *verb* make loose or looser • **break loose** escape • **on the loose** free

---

Do not confuse with: **lose**

loot *noun* goods stolen or plundered ◇ *verb* plunder, ransack

lop *verb* (**lopping, lopped**) cut off the top or ends of ● **lop-eared** *adj* of an animal: having ears hanging down ● **lopsided** *adj* leaning to one side, not symmetrical

lope *verb* run with a long stride

loquacious *adj, formal* talkative ● **loquaciousness** *or* **loquacity** *noun*

lord *noun* 1 a title for a male member of the aristocracy, bishop, judge, *etc* 2 *hist* the owner of a country estate 3 *old* a master, a ruler 4 (**Lord**: with **the**) a title that Christians give to God or Christ ● **lordly** *adj* 1 relating to a lord 2 noble, proud ● **lordship** *noun* 1 used in addressing a lord: *his lordship* 2 power, rule ● **drunk as a lord** extremely drunk ● **lord it over someone** act in a domineering manner towards them ● **the House of Lords** the upper house of the British parliament ● **the Lord's day** a way that some Christians refer to Sunday

lore *noun* knowledge, beliefs, *etc* handed down

lorgnette /lawn-yet/ *noun* eyeglasses with a handle that you hold up to your eye, rather than wear on your face

lorry *noun* (*plural* **lorries**) a motor vehicle for carrying heavy loads; a truck

lose *verb* (**losing, lost**) 1 leave (something) where it cannot be found: *I've lost my keys* 2 no longer have: *he's losing his hair* 3 have (something) taken away from: *she lost her job* 4 waste (time) 5 miss (a chance *etc*) 6 not win (a game) ● **loser** *noun* 1 someone who loses a game 2 someone unlikely to succeed at anything

Do not confuse with: **loose**

loss *noun* (*plural* **losses**) 1 the act

of losing 2 something that is lost 3 waste, harm, destruction ● **at a loss** uncertain what to do or say

lost *adj* 1 not able to be found 2 no longer possessed 3 not won 4 ruined ● **lost in** with your attention completely taken up by; engrossed in: *lost in thought*

lot *noun* 1 a large number or quantity 2 someone's fortune or fate 3 a separate portion ● **draw lots** decide who is to do something by drawing names out of a hat *etc*

loth *another spelling of* **loath**

lotion *noun* a liquid for treating or cleaning the skin or hair

lottery *noun* (*plural* **lotteries**) an event in which money or prizes are won through drawing lots

lotto *noun* a game like bingo

lotus *noun* (*plural* **lotuses**) 1 a kind of water lily 2 a mythical tree whose fruit caused forgetfulness

louche /loosh/ *adj* probably not honest or morally right; shady

loud *adj* 1 making a great sound; noisy 2 far too bright or bold; showy ● **loud** *or* **loudly** *adv* ● **loudhailer** *noun* a megaphone with microphone and amplifier ● **loudmouth** *noun, informal* someone who talks offensively and too much ● **loudness** *noun* ● **loudspeaker** *noun* a device for converting electrical signals into sound

lounge *verb* 1 lie back in a relaxed way 2 move about lazily ◇ *noun* a room for relaxing in, in a house, airport, hotel, *etc* ● **lounge lizard** *noun* a man who spends a lot of time at parties, in pubs, *etc* ● **lounger** *noun* a lazy person ● **lounge suit** *noun* a man's suit for everyday (but not casual) wear

lour *see* **lower²**

louse *noun* (*plural* **lice**) a small blood-sucking insect sometimes found on the bodies of animals and people

lousy adj (**lousier, lousiest**) 1 informal of poor quality; inferior 2 swarming with lice

lout noun a bad-mannered or loudly aggressive man

louvre or US **louver** /loo-vuh/ noun a slat set at an angle • **louvre door** noun a slatted door allowing air and light to pass through • **louvre window** noun 1 a window covered with sloping slats 2 a window with narrow panes that can be set open at an angle

love verb 1 have very strong romantic feelings for (someone) 2 like very much ◇ noun 1 a great liking or affection, or a thing greatly liked 2 a loved person 3 tennis a score of zero • **lovable** adj worthy of love • **love affair** noun a relationship between people in love but not married • **lovebite** noun a mark on the skin ostensibly caused by biting during lovemaking • **love child** noun an illegitimate child • **lovemaking** noun 1 sexual play and intercourse 2 courtship • **lovesick** adj full of feelings of love, often for someone who does not return the feelings • **loving** adj full of love • **lovingly** adv • **in love (with)** 1 feeling love and desire (for) 2 having a great liking (for): in love with his own voice • **make love to** 1 have sex with 2 make romantic advances to; court

lovely adj (**lovelier, loveliest**) beautiful; delightful • **loveliness** noun

lover noun 1 someone with whom a person has a love affair 2 someone whom a person loves 3 an admirer or enthusiast: an art lover

low adj 1 not lying or reaching far up; not high 2 of a voice: not loud 3 cheap: low air-fare 4 feeling sad or depressed 5 of a humble social status 6 showing a desire to be hurtful; nasty ◇ adv 1 in or to a low position 2 not loudly 3 cheaply ◇ verb make the noise of cattle; moo • **lowbrow** adj appealing to the tastes of ordinary or uneducated people; (contrasted with: **highbrow**) • **lowdown** noun, informal information • **low-key** adj not elaborate or attention-seeking • **lowland** noun flattish country, without high hills • **lowness** noun • **keep a low profile** not make your presence known

lower[1] /loh-uh/ adj less high ◇ verb 1 make less high: lower the price 2 let or come down: lower the blinds • **lowercase** adj of a letter: not capital, eg a not A (contrasted with: **upper-case**)

lower[2] or **lour** /low-uh/ verb 1 of the sky: become dark and cloudy 2 frown • **lowering** adj

lowly adj (**lowlier, lowliest**) low in rank, esp social rank; humble • **lowliness** noun

loyal adj always showing support and affection, or a sense of duty; faithful • **loyalist** noun someone loyal to their sovereign or country • **loyally** adv • **loyalty** noun

lozenge noun 1 a diamond-shaped figure 2 a small sweet for sucking

LP noun a long-playing record, a twelve-inch plastic disc on which music is recorded

LSD abbrev 1 lysergic acid diethylamide, a hallucinogenic drug 2 dated pounds, shillings and pence (British coinage before decimalization)

Lt abbrev Lieutenant

Ltd abbrev limited company

lubricate verb 1 apply oil etc to (something) to overcome friction and make movement easier 2 informal ply with alcohol • **lubricant** noun something that lubricates; an oil • **lubrication** noun • **lubricator** noun

lucerne noun another name for alfalfa, a type of plant used for feeding cattle

lucid adj 1 thinking clearly or expressing your thoughts clearly; not confused 2 easily understood • **lucidity** noun • **lucidly** adv

Lucifer *noun* the Devil

luck *noun* **1** fortune, either good or bad: *as luck would have it* **2** good fortune: *have any luck?* • **luckless** *adj* unfortunate

lucky *adj* (**luckier, luckiest**) **1** having good luck; fortunate **2** bringing good luck: *lucky charm* • **luckily** *adv*

lucrative *adj* bringing in a lot of money; profitable

lucre /loo-kuh/ *noun, formal* money

Luddite *noun* someone who knows very little about modern technology or is opposed to it

ludicrous *adj* ridiculous • **ludicrously** *adv*

ludo *noun* a game played with counters on a board

lug[1] *verb* (**lugging, lugged**) pull or drag with effort • **lugger** *noun* a small sailing vessel

lug[2] *noun, informal* the ear

luggage *noun* suitcases and other travelling baggage

lugubrious *adj* sad and gloomy; mournful • **lugubriously** *adv* • **lugubriousness** *noun*

lugworm *noun* a large worm found on the seashore, used for fishing bait

lukewarm *adj* **1** neither hot nor cold enough **2** not very keen; unenthusiastic

lull *verb* soothe or calm ◇ *noun* a period of calm

lullaby *noun* (*plural* **lullabies**) a song to lull children to sleep

lumbago *noun* a pain in the lower part of the back

lumbar *adj* of or in the lower part of the back

lumber *noun* **1** sawn-up timber **2** discarded old furniture *etc* ◇ *verb* move about clumsily

lumberjack *noun* someone who fells, saws and shifts trees

luminary *noun* (*plural* **luminaries**) **1** an inspiring and well-respected teacher or leader **2** *formal* the sun, moon, *etc* as a source of light

luminescent *adj* giving out light • **luminescence** *noun*

luminous *adj* **1** giving light **2** shining; clear • **luminosity** *noun* • **luminously** *adv*

lump *noun* **1** a small, solid mass of indefinite shape **2** a swelling **3** the whole taken together: *considered in a lump* **4** a heavy or dull person ◇ *verb* **1** form into lumps **2** treat as being alike: *lumped all of us together* • **lumpectomy** *noun* surgery to remove a lump in the breast • **lumpish** *adj* heavy or dull • **lump sum** *noun* an amount of money given all at once • **lumpy** *adj* full of lumps

lumpen proletariat *noun* the poorest social class; the underclass

lunacy *noun* **1** extreme foolishness **2** insanity

lunar *adj* of the moon: *lunar eclipse*

lunatic *noun* someone who is insane ◇ *adj* insane

lunch *noun* (*plural* **lunches**) a midday meal ◇ *verb* eat lunch

luncheon *noun, formal* lunch

lung *noun* either of the two bag-like organs that fill with and expel air in the course of breathing

lunge *noun* a sudden thrust or push ◇ *verb* thrust or plunge forward suddenly

lupin *noun* a tall plant with flowers on long spikes

lurch *verb* roll or pitch suddenly to one side; stagger ◇ *noun* a pitch to one side • **leave in the lurch** leave in a difficult position without help

lure *verb* attract towards or away; entice ◇ *noun* something that entices

Lurex *noun, trademark* a shiny clothing fabric made from plastic-coated aluminium thread

lurid *adj* **1** unpleasant and shocking: *lurid details* **2** unpleasantly bright or bold; garish: *lurid book cover* **3** of a complexion: unhealthily pale; ghostly

lurk *verb* **1** move or act secretly and slyly **2** keep out of sight; be hidden ● **lurker** *noun* ● **lurking** *adj* vague, hidden

luscious *adj* **1** deliciously sweet and juicy **2** voluptuously attractive: *luscious lips*

lush *adj* of grass *etc*: thick and plentiful ◇ *noun, slang* a person who frequently drinks too much alcohol; a drunk

lust *noun* **1** a strong sexual desire **2** a greedy desire for power, riches, *etc* ◇ *verb* have a strong desire (for) ● **lustful** *adj* ● **lustfully** *adv*

lustre or US **luster** *noun* glossy brightness; shine ● **lustrous** *adj* bright, shining

lusty *adj* (**lustier, lustiest**) strong and healthy ● **lustily** *adv* ● **lustiness** *noun*

lute *noun* a stringed musical instrument with a pear-shaped, round-backed body and fretted neck ● **lutenist** *noun* a lute player

lutein *noun* the yellow pigment in egg-yolks

luxuriant *adj* **1** growing thickly and healthy-looking **2** richly decorated

Do not confuse with: **luxurious**

luxuriate *verb* **1** be luxuriant **2** take delight (in)

luxurious *adj* extremely comfortable ● **luxuriously** *adv* ● **luxuriousness** *noun*

Do not confuse with: **luxuriant**

luxury *noun* (*plural* **luxuries**) **1** extremely comfortable and expensive surroundings or lifestyle **2** something very pleasant or expensive but not necessary: *having a car is a luxury*

lychee /*lai*-chee/ *noun* a small Chinese fruit with rough skin and translucent flesh

Lycra *noun, trademark* a lightweight synthetic elastic fabric

lying *see* **lie**

lymph *noun* a colourless fluid in the body ● **lymph gland** *noun* one of the glands carrying lymph

lynch *verb* condemn and put to death without legal trial

lynx *noun* (*plural* **lynxes**) a wild animal of the cat family

lyre *noun* an ancient stringed musical instrument, played like a harp

lyric *noun* **1** a short poem, often expressing the poet's feelings **2** (**lyrics**) the words of a song ◇ *adj* of a lyric

lyrical *adj* **1** lyric **2** song-like **3** full of enthusiastic praise ● **lyrically** *adv*

Mm

M *abbrev* the Roman numeral for a thousand (from Latin *mille*)

m *abbrev* **1** metre(s) **2** mile(s) **3** married **4** male **5** masculine

MA *abbrev* Master of Arts

macabre *adj* dealing unpleasantly with death; gruesome

macadamia *noun* an edible nut from an Australian evergreen tree

macadamize *verb* surface (a road) with small broken stones

macaroni *noun* pasta shaped into short hollow tubes

macaroon *noun* a sweet cake or biscuit made with ground almonds and sugar

macaw *noun* a long-tailed brightly-coloured parrot

Mace *noun, trademark* a stinging liquid for spraying into the eyes of an attacker, sometimes used by the police in crowd control

mace[1] *noun* a heavy staff with an ornamental head, carried as a sign of office

mace[2] *noun* a spice made from the covering of a nutmeg

machete /muh-*shet*-i/ *noun* a heavy knife used to cut through foliage *etc*

Machiavellian *adj* cleverly and ruthlessly deceiving people in order to secretly achieve selfish aims

machinations *plural noun* a crafty, *usu* sinister scheme; a plot

machine *noun* **1** a device that contains a working arrangement of wheels, levers, *etc* **2** an efficient organization,

esp a political one **3** *informal* a bicycle or motorcycle ◇ *verb* sew *etc* with a machine • **machine code** *noun* a system of symbols that can be understood by a computer • **machine gun** *noun* an automatic rapid-firing gun • **machinist** *noun* a machine maker or operator

machinery *noun* **1** machines in general **2** the working parts of a machine **3** organization: *machinery of local government*

machismo /muh-*chiz*-moh/ or /muh-*kiz*-moh/ *noun* overt or aggressive masculinity

Mach number /mak/ *noun* the ratio of the speed of an aircraft to the velocity of sound (*eg* Mach 5 = 5 times the speed of sound)

macho /*mach*-oh/ *adj* overtly or aggressively masculine

mackerel *noun* an edible sea fish with wavy markings

mackintosh *noun* (*plural* **mackintoshes**) *dated* a waterproof overcoat

macramé /muh-*krah*-meh/ *noun* ornamental knotted threading

macro *noun, comput* a single instruction that prompts a computer to carry out a series of short instructions embedded in it

macrobiotic *adj* of diet: consisting of organic food, especially raw vegetables

mad *adj* **1** having an unbalanced mind; insane **2** wildly foolish **3** furious with anger • **mad cow disease** *noun* BSE • **madhouse** *noun* **1** a place of confusion and noise **2** *hist* a hospital for people with mental illnesses; an asylum • **madman, madwoman** noun someone who is mad • **madness** noun • **like mad** very quickly or energetically

madam noun a polite form of address to a woman

madcap adj foolishly rash: madcap scheme ◇ noun a rash, hot-headed person

madden verb make angry or mad • **maddening** adj extremely annoying

made past form of **make**

madeira noun 1 a kind of fortified white wine 2 a plain rich sponge cake

madly adv 1 insanely 2 extremely: madly in love

Madonna noun the Virgin Mary as depicted in art

madrigal noun a part-song for several voices

maelstrom /mehl-strum/ noun 1 a whirlpool 2 any place of great confusion

maestro /mai-stroh/ noun (plural **maestros**) someone highly skilled in an art, especially music

magazine noun 1 a periodical publication containing articles, stories and pictures 2 a storage place for military equipment 3 a place for extra cartridges in a rifle

magenta noun a reddish-purple colour ◇ adj of this colour

maggot noun a small worm-like creature that is the larva of a bluebottle etc • **maggoty** adj full of maggots

Maghreb /mag-reb/ noun the countries of NW Africa as a group, sometimes including Libya

Magi see magus

magic noun 1 the supposed use of supernatural forces to influence things in ways that cannot be explained or

are remarkable 2 conjuring tricks ◇ adj 1 using magic 2 used in magic 3 magical • **black magic** magic performed for an evil purpose; witchcraft

magical adj 1 of or produced by magic 2 very wonderful or mysterious • **magically** adv

magician noun someone who performs conjuring tricks

magisterial adj 1 having an air of authority 2 of magistrates • **magisterially** adv

magistrate noun a judge in a minor court in England and Wales

magma noun molten rock when it is below the earth's surface

magnanimous noun behaving in a generous and polite way, esp towards an opponent • **magnanimity** noun • **magnanimously** adv

magnate /mag-neht/ noun someone with great power or wealth

Do not confuse with: **magnet**

---

magnesia noun a white powder formed from magnesium

magnesium noun a white metal that burns with an intense white light

magnet noun 1 a piece of iron, steel, etc that has the power to attract other pieces of metal 2 someone or something that attracts strongly

---

Do not confuse with: **magnate**

---

magnetic adj 1 having the powers of a magnet 2 strongly attractive: magnetic personality • **magnetic north** noun the direction in which the magnetized needle of a compass points • **magnetic tape** noun tape on which sound, pictures, computer material, etc can be recorded

magnetism noun 1 the attractive

power of a magnet **2** great charm or attraction

magnetize verb **1** make magnetic **2** attract (someone) greatly

magneto noun (plural **magnetos**) a device producing electric sparks, eg for lighting the fuel in an engine

magnificent adj **1** very impressive in appearance or action **2** extremely good; excellent • **magnificence** noun • **magnificently** adv

magnify verb (**magnifies, magnifying, magnified**) **1** cause to appear larger by using special lenses **2** exaggerate • **magnification** noun

magniloquent adj, formal of speech: excessively grand; pompous • **magniloquence** noun

magnitude noun size or importance, esp when great

magnolia noun **1** a tree that produces large white or purplish sweet-scented flowers **2** a pale creamy or pinkish white colour

magnum noun a bottle of wine or champagne equal to two ordinary bottles

magnum opus noun a great work; a masterpiece

magpie noun a black-and-white bird of the crow family, known for its habit of collecting objects

magus noun (plural **magi**) an ancient Persian priest or astrologer • **the Magi** the three wise men who brought gifts to the infant Christ

Magyar noun the Hungarian language

Maharajah noun an important Indian prince, especially the ruler of a state

Maharani noun a Maharajah's wife

maharishi noun a Hindu religious teacher or leader

Mahdi noun the Islamic messiah

mah-jong /mah-jong/ noun a Chinese table game played with small painted bricks

mahogany noun **1** a tropical American hardwood tree **2** its hard reddish-brown wood, often used for furniture

maid noun **1** a woman who cleans rooms in a hotel **2** old an unmarried woman

maiden noun, old **1** a young unmarried woman **2** a woman who is a virgin ◇ adj **1** first, initial: maiden speech/maiden voyage **2** unmarried: maiden aunt • **maiden name** noun the surname of a married woman before she took her husband's name when she was married • **maiden over** noun, cricket an over in which no runs are made

mail[1] noun **1** letters, parcels, etc carried by post **2** email ◇ verb post • **mailbox** noun a section of a computer file where messages for a particular user are stored • **mail order** noun an order for goods to be sent by post • **mailshot** noun unsolicited advertising material sent by post

mail[2] noun body armour of steel rings or plates

maim verb cause serious injury to, esp by destroying or cutting off a limb

main adj most important; chief ◇ noun **1** (**the mains**) the network of pipe or wires that supply gas, water or electricity **2** a large pipe that supplies gas or water **3** old the ocean • **mainframe** noun a large powerful computer used by large organizations • **mainland** noun a large piece of land off whose coast smaller islands lie • **mainline** verb, slang inject drugs intravenously • **mainly** adv on most occasions or in most respects; chiefly • **mainsail** noun the principal sail of a ship or boat • **mainspring** noun **1** the spring that makes the wheels move in a watch or clock **2** the main cause of any action: *mainspring of the revolution* • **mainstay** noun the main support • **in the main** for the most part

mainstream adj done by, or considered normal by, most people in society: *not one of the mainstream religions* ◇ noun (**the mainstream**) the styles, ways of behaving, *etc* adopted by most people in society

maintain verb 1 keep (something) as it is 2 continue to keep (something) in good working order 3 support (a family *etc*) 4 continue to state (an opinion) firmly in the face of opposition

maintenance noun 1 work done to keep something in good order; upkeep 2 means of support, *esp* money for food, clothing, *etc*

maize noun a cereal crop grown in N and S America

Maj abbrev Major

majesty noun (*plural* **majesties**) 1 a title used in addressing a king or queen: *Your Majesty* 2 greatness of rank or manner • **majestic** adj stately, regal

majolica noun pottery with bright bold designs and thick glaze

major adj great in size, importance, *etc* (contrasted with: **minor**) ◇ noun a senior army officer

majority noun (*plural* **majorities**) 1 the greater number or quantity 2 the difference in amount between the greater and the lesser number 3 the age when someone becomes legally an adult (18 in the UK)

make verb (**making, made**) 1 construct, create or manufacture 2 cause to be: *he makes me mad at times* 3 bring about: *make trouble* 4 amount to: *2 and 2 make 4* 5 earn: *she made £300 last week* 6 force: *I made him do it* 7 undergo (a journey *etc*) 8 prepare (a meal *etc*): *I'll make some tea* ◇ noun 1 kind, shape, form 2 brand • **makeover** noun a complete change

in style of dress, appearance, *etc* • **maker** noun • **makeshift** adj used for a time, for want of something better • **make-up** noun cosmetics • **make believe** pretend • **make do** manage with what is available • **make good 1** be successful 2 carry out (a promise) 3 make up for (a loss) • **make light of** treat as unimportant • **make much of** treat as important, often unnecessarily • **make nothing of 1** be unable to understand, do, *etc* 2 make light of • **make off** run away • **make out 1** see in the distance or indistinctly 2 claim or state 3 write out (a cheque, bill, *etc*) • **make up 1** form a whole: *eleven players make up the side* 2 invent (a false story) 3 put make-up on the face 4 be friendly again after a quarrel • **make up for** give or do something in return for damage done • **on the make** informal 1 looking for personal gain 2 looking for a sexual partner

malachite noun a green mineral used as a gemstone

maladjusted adj psychologically unable to deal with everyday situations or relationships

maladministration noun bad management, especially of public affairs

maladroit adj, formal 1 clumsy, awkward 2 dealing with something in an insensitive way; tactless

malady noun (*plural* **maladies**) old illness

malaise noun a feeling or general air of depression or despondency

malapropism noun the use of a wrong word that sounds similar to the one intended, *eg contemptuous* for *contemporary*

malaria noun a fever caused by the bite of a particular mosquito • **malarial** adj

male adj of the sex that is able to father children or young; masculine ◇ noun a member of this sex

malediction *noun, formal* a curse or cursing • **maledictory** *adj*

malefactor *noun, old* someone who does something bad or criminal; an evildoer

malevolent *adj* wishing to harm others; spiteful • **malevolence** *noun* • **malevolently** *adv*

malformation *noun* faulty or wrong shape

malfunction *verb* fail to work or operate properly ◊ *noun* failure to operate

malice *noun* a desire to harm; ill will

malicious *adj* intending harm; spiteful • **maliciously** *adv* • **maliciousness** *noun*

malign /muh-*lain*/ *verb* say bad things about

malignant *adj* **1** of a disease: likely to cause death (*contrasted with*: **benign**) **2** wishing someone harm; nasty • **malignantly** *adv*

malinger *verb* pretend to be ill to avoid work *etc* • **malingerer** *noun*

mall /mol/ *noun* a shopping centre

mallard *noun* the male of the common wild duck

malleable *adj* **1** of metal: able to be beaten out by hammering **2** of people: easy to influence • **malleability** *noun*

mallet *noun* a heavy wooden hammer

malnutrition *noun* lack of sufficient or proper food; undernourishment

malodorous *adj, formal* having a bad smell

malpractice *noun* behaviour that breaks the rules of a profession; misconduct

malt *noun* **1** barley or other grain soaked then dried for use in making beer or whisky **2** a malt whisky • **malt whisky** *noun* whisky made entirely from a mash that contains only malted barley, no other cereal grains

maltreat *verb* treat roughly or unkindly • **maltreatment** *noun*

mama or **mamma** *noun, informal* mother

mamba *noun* a large deadly African snake, black or green in colour

mammal *noun* a member of the class of animals of which the female parent feeds the young with her own milk • **mammalian** *adj*

mammary *adj* of a female breast or breasts: *mammary gland*

mammogram *noun* an X-ray taken of a woman's breast to detect early signs of cancer

mammon *noun, formal* money considered as the root of evil

mammoth *noun* a prehistoric animal like a very large elephant ◊ *adj* extremely large; enormous: *mammoth savings*

man *noun* (*plural* **men**) **1** a grown-up human male **2** the human race **3** *informal* a husband **4** a piece in chess or draughts ◊ *verb* (**manning, manned**) supply with workers or crew; staff: *man the boats* • **manful** *adj* courageous • **manfully** *adv* • **manhandle** *verb* handle roughly • **manhole** *noun* a hole (into a drain, sewer, *etc*) large enough to let a man through • **manhood** *noun* the state of being a man • **mankind** *noun* the human race • **mannish** *adj* of a woman: behaving or looking like a man • **man-of-war** *noun, old* a warship • **manpower** *noun* the number of people available for work; staff • **the man in the street** the ordinary person • **to a man** *dated* every single one

manacle *noun, formal* a handcuff ◊ *verb* put handcuffs on

manage *verb* **1** have control or charge of **2** deal with a situation successfully; cope: *can't manage on his* *own* **3** succeed: *managed to finish on time*

manageable *adj* easily managed or controlled • **manageably** *adv*

management *noun* **1** those in charge of a business *etc* **2** the art of managing a business *etc*

manager *noun* someone in charge of a business *etc*

manageress *noun, dated* a woman manager

mañana /man-yah-na/ *noun* sometime in the future

Mancunian *noun* someone born or living in Manchester

mandarin *noun* **1** a small orange-like citrus fruit **2** a high-ranking civil servant or other official **3** *hist* a senior Chinese official

mandate *noun* **1** power to act on someone else's behalf **2** a command

mandatory *adj* compulsory • **mandatorily** *adv*

mandible *noun* the jaw or lower jawbone

mandolin *or* **mandoline** *noun* a round-backed stringed instrument similar to a lute

mandrake *noun* a poisonous plant of the potato family with a forked root

mandrill *noun* a large baboon from W Africa with a red and blue muzzle

mane *noun* **1** long hair on the head and neck of a horse or male lion **2** a long or thick head of hair

maneuver *US spelling of* **manoeuvre**

manga *noun* a Japanese adult comic book

manganese *noun* a hard brittle metal of a greyish-white colour

mange /mehnj/ *noun* a skin disease of dogs, cats, *etc*

mangel-wurzel *noun* a kind of beetroot used as cattle food

manger *noun* a box or trough holding dry food for horses and cattle

mangetout /monhzh-too/ *noun* a thin pea with an edible pod

mangle *noun* a machine for squeezing water out of clothes or for smoothing them ◊ *verb* **1** squeeze (clothes) through a mangle **2** crush, tear or otherwise damage badly

mango *noun* (*plural* **mangoes**) **1** the fruit of a tropical Indian tree, with juicy orange flesh **2** the tree that produces mangoes

mangrove *noun* a tree that grows in swamps in hot countries

mangy *adj* (**mangier**, **mangiest**) **1** shabby, squalid **2** of an animal: suffering from mange

mania *noun* **1** a form of mental illness in which the sufferer is over-active, over-excited and unreasonably happy **2** extreme fondness or enthusiasm: *a mania for stamp-collecting*

maniac *noun* **1** a mad person **2** a very rash or over-enthusiastic person

manic *adj* **1** suffering from mania **2** very energetic or excited • **manically** *adv*

manicure *noun* **1** the care of hands and nails **2** professional treatment for the hands and nails ◊ *verb* perform a manicure on • **manicurist** *noun* someone who performs manicures

manifest *adj* easily seen or understood ◊ *verb* show plainly • **manifestation** *noun* • **manifestly** *adv* obviously or clearly

manifesto *noun* (*plural* **manifestoes** *or* **manifestos**) a public announcement of intentions, *eg* by a political party

manifold *adj* many and various

manila *noun* strong brown paper used for stationery *etc*

manioc *noun* tapioca

manipulate *verb* handle so as to turn to your own advantage • **manipulation** *noun*

manky *adj* (**mankier, mankiest**) *slang* dirty • **mankiness** *noun*

manly *adj* (**manlier, manliest**) displaying qualities considered admirable in a man, *esp* physical strength or bravery • **manliness** *noun*

manna *noun* an unexpected or delicious treat

mannequin /man-i-kin/ *noun* 1 someone who models clothes; a fashion model 2 a display dummy

manner *noun* 1 the way in which something is done 2 the way in which someone behaves 3 (**manners**) polite behaviour towards others • **mannerism** *noun* an odd individual gesture or way of behaving • **mannerly** *adj* polite • **all manner of** all kinds of

manoeuvre *or US* **maneuver** /muh-noo-vuh/ *noun* 1 a movement that must be done carefully and with skill 2 a battle-training exercise for troops, ships or aircraft 3 a clever handling of affairs, *esp* for selfish reasons ◊ *verb* 1 perform a manoeuvre 2 handle cleverly; manipulate

manor *noun* 1 a large house, usually attached to a country estate 2 *hist* the land belonging to a lord or squire • **manorial** *adj*

manqué /monh-keh/ *adj* unfulfilled in a particular ambition: *poet manqué*

mansard roof *noun* a roof with a divided slope that is steeper in the lower part

manse *noun* the house of a minister in certain Christian churches, *eg* the Church of Scotland

mansion *noun* a large house

manslaughter *noun* the crime of killing someone without deliberate intent

mantelpiece *noun* a shelf over a fireplace

mantis *noun* an insect of the cockroach family, with large spiny forelegs (*also called*: **praying mantis**)

mantle *noun* 1 a covering: *mantle of snow* 2 a thin, transparent shade around the flame of a gas or paraffin lamp 3 a cloak or loose outer garment

mantra *noun* a word or phrase chanted or repeated inwardly in meditation

manual *adj* 1 of the hand or hands 2 worked by hand 3 working with the hands: *manual worker* ◊ *noun* a handbook giving instructions on how to use something: *a car manual* • **manually** *adv*

manufacture *verb* make (articles or materials) in large quantities, *usu* by machine ◊ *noun* 1 the process of manufacturing 2 a manufactured article • **manufacturer** *noun*

manure *noun* a substance, especially animal dung, spread on soil to make it more fertile ◊ *verb* spread manure on

manuscript *noun* 1 the prepared material for a book *etc* before it is printed 2 a book or paper written by hand

Manx cat *noun* a tailless breed of cat

many *adj* a large number of: *many people were present* ◊ *pronoun* a large number of people or things: *many survived* • **many a** a large number of: *many a voice was raised*

Maori /mow-ri/ *adj* belonging or relating to the aboriginal Polynesian people of New Zealand ◊ *noun* a member of this race

map *noun* a flat drawing of all or part of the earth's surface, showing geographical features ◊ *verb* (**mapping, mapped**) 1 make a map of 2 (**map out**) plan or decide beforehand

maple noun **1** a tree related to the sycamore, one variety of which produces sugar **2** its hard light-coloured wood used for furniture etc

maquette /ma-ket/ noun an artist's scaled-down model of a piece of sculpture etc

mar verb (**marring, marred**) spoil

maracas plural noun a pair of filled gourds shaken as a percussion instrument

maraschino /ma-ruh-shee-noh/ noun a liqueur distilled from cherries

marathon noun a long-distance foot-race, usually covering 26 miles 385 yards

maraud verb wander around attacking people and destroying things • **marauder** noun • **marauding** adj

marble noun **1** limestone that takes a high polish, used for sculpture, decorating buildings, etc **2** a small glass ball used in a children's game

marcasite noun crystals formed from iron and used in jewellery

March noun the third month of the year

march¹ verb **1** (cause) to walk in time with regular step **2** go on steadily ◇ noun (plural **marches**) **1** a marching movement **2** a piece of music for marching to **3** the distance covered by marching **4** a steady progression of events: the march of time

march² noun a boundary or border

marchioness /mah-shuh-nes/ noun (plural **marchionesses**) a woman marquess

Mardi Gras /mah-di grah/ noun a carnival held on Shrove Tuesday in certain countries

mare noun a female horse

margarine noun an edible spread similar to butter, made mainly of vegetable fats

margarita noun a cocktail made with tequila and lime juice

margin noun **1** an edge or border **2** the blank edge on the page of a book **3** additional space or room; allowance: margin for error

marginal adj **1** of little effect or importance: marginal improvement **2** of a political constituency: without a clear majority for any one candidate or party **3** of or in a margin ◇ noun a marginal political constituency • **marginalize** verb make less important or central • **marginally** adv

marguerite /mah-guh-reet/ noun a kind of large daisy

mariachi noun one of a band of musicians playing traditional Mexican dance music

marigold noun a small plant with a yellow flower

marijuana /ma-ri-wah-nuh/ noun a drug made from the plant hemp

marimba noun an African instrument like a xylophone, often used in jazz music

marina noun a place with moorings for yachts, dinghies, etc

marinade noun a mixture of oil, wine, herbs, spices, etc in which food is steeped for flavour • **marinade** or **marinate** verb soak in a marinade

marine adj of the sea ◇ noun a soldier serving on board a ship

mariner /ma-rin-uh/ noun, old a sailor

marionette noun a puppet moved by strings

marital adj of marriage • **maritally** adv

maritime adj **1** of the sea or ships **2** lying near the sea

marjoram noun a sweet-smelling herb used in cooking

mark noun **1** a sign that can be seen

2 a patch of dirt that spoils something; a stain **3** a target aimed at **4** a point used to assess the merit of a piece of schoolwork *etc* **5** the starting-line in a race: *on your marks!* ◇ *verb* **1** make a mark on; stain **2** award marks to (a piece of schoolwork *etc*) **3** stay close to (an opponent in football *etc*) **4** pay attention to **5** (**mark off**) separate, distinguish • **marked** *adj* easily noticed: *marked improvement* • **markedly** *adv* noticeably • **marker** *noun* **1** someone who marks the score at games **2** a pen with a thick point, for writing on boards *etc* **3** a counter *etc* used to mark a score • **marksman, markswoman** *noun* someone who shoots well • **mark time 1** move the feet up and down, as if marching, but without going forward **2** keep things going without progressing • **up to the mark** coming up to the required standard

market *noun* **1** a public place for buying and selling **2** (a country, place, *etc* where there is) a need or demand (for certain types of goods) ◇ *verb* put on sale • **market forces** *plural noun* the effect of competition on the price and availability of goods • **market garden** *noun* a garden in which fruit and vegetables are grown to be sold • **marketing** *noun* the act or practice of advertising and selling • **marketplace** *noun* **1** an area in a town *etc* where a market is held **2** the commercial world of buying and selling • **on the market** for sale

marlin *noun* a large ocean fish related to the swordfish

marlinspike *noun* a spike for separating the strands of a rope *etc*

marmalade *noun* a jam made from citrus fruit, *esp* oranges

Marmite *noun, trademark* a savoury spread made from yeast and vegetable extracts

marmoset *noun* a type of small monkey found in America

marmot *noun* a burrowing animal of the squirrel family (*also called*: **woodchuck** or **groundhog**)

maroon¹ *noun* **1** a brownish-red colour **2** a firework used as a distress signal ◇ *adj* brownish-red

maroon² *verb* **1** abandon on an island *etc* without means of escape **2** leave in a helpless or uncomfortable position

marquee /mah-kee/ *noun* a large tent used for large gatherings, *eg* a wedding reception or circus

marquess or **marquis** /mah-kwis/ *noun* (*plural* **marquesses** or **marquises**) a nobleman below a duke in rank

marquetry /mahk-i-tri/ *noun* the inlaying of wood with small pieces of different-coloured wood, ivory, *etc*

marriage *noun* **1** the ceremony by which two people become husband and wife; a wedding **2** the state of being married, or the relationship between people who are married to each other **3** a joining together: *marriage of minds* • **marriageable** *adj* suitable or old enough for marriage

marrow *noun* **1** the soft substance in the hollow part of bones **2** a long thick-skinned vegetable

marry *verb* (**marries, marrying, married**) join, or be joined, together in marriage

marsh *noun* (*plural* **marshes**) a piece of low-lying wet ground • **marsh gas** *noun* methane • **marsh marigold** *noun* a marsh plant with yellow flowers (*also called*: **kingcup**)

marshal *noun* **1** a high-ranking officer in the army or air force **2** someone in charge of crowd control at large outdoor public events **3** *US* a law-court official **4** *US* the head of a police force ◇ *verb* (**marshalling, marshalled**) **1** arrange (troops, facts, arguments, *etc*) in order **2** show the way; lead

Guide to effective writing

Contents

Global English

British	US	South African	Australian
alcohol	liquor	dop	grog
barbeque	barbecue	braai	barbie
bumpkin	hayseed	gomgat	bushie
chap	cove	ou	bloke
cinema	movie theater	bioscope	cinema
clobber	whale	donner	job
cool box	cooler	cooler box	esky
crisps	chips	skyfies	chips
Englishman	limey	Khaki	pom
flip-flops	flip-flops	slip-slops	thongs
get lost!	vamoose!	voetsak!	choof off!
great	swell	lekker	bonzer
mate	dude	boet	cobber
off-licence	liquor store	bottle store	bottle shop
pickup truck	pickup	bakkie	ute
plastered	loaded	gesuip	full as a boot
plimsolls	sneakers	tackies	sandshoes
sweets	candy	lekkers	lollies
trainers	sneakers	tackies	joggers
tramp	hobo	bergie	dero
trousers	pants	pants	strides

Commonly misspelt words

abbreviation	acoustics	advertisement
aberration	acquaint	amateur
abysmal	acquiesce	ancillary
accelerate	acquire	anoint
accessory	acquit	anonymous
accidently	acrylic	Antarctic
accommodate	address	appalling
accommodation	adjourn	apparent
according	admissible	Arctic
achieve	adolescent	argument
achievement	advantageous	asphalt

assassinate	commemorate	ecstasy
assimilate	commiserate	Edinburgh
Australia	commissionaire	efficient
authoritative	commitment	eighth
autumn	committed	eliminate
bankruptcy	committee	embarrass
beautiful	communicate	embarrassment
because	concede	equipment
beginner	conceit	especially
beginning	conceive	exaggerate
believe	conscience	exceed
beneficial	conscientious	excellent
benefit	conscious	excite
besiege	consensus	exhilarate
billionaire	convenient	existence
bosses	corollary	exorbitant
Brittany	corroborate	experience
broccoli	credibility	exuberant
brought	curriculum	facilities
Buddha	deceive	faculties
buoyant	definite	faithfully
bureaucracy	definitely	fascinate
business	desiccated	fatigue
caffeine	desperate	February
calendar	detach	fierce
career	development	fiery
Caribbean	diaphragm	fluorescent
category	difference	foreign
ceiling	different	foreigner
cemetery	difficult	forfeit
census	diphtheria	forty
changeable	diphthong	four
chaos	disappear	fourth
chief	disappoint	friend
colleague	disappointment	gauge
collectible	discipline	grammar
colonel	discuss	granddaughter
colossal	dramatically	grateful
column	drunkenness	guarantee

guard
harass
harassed
harassment
healthy
height
heinous
hierarchy
honorary
humorist
humorous
hygiene
hypocrisy
idiosyncrasy
ignorance
illegible
illustrate
immediate
immediately
immigrant
impeccable
inconceivable
incur
indefinitely
independence
independent
indispensable
innocent
innocuous
inoculate
inoculation
inseparable
instead
intelligence
intercede
interpret
interrupt
itinerary
it's (it is)

its (of it)
jeopardize (or
  jeopardise)
jodhpurs
knowledge
laborious
legacy
leisure
liaise
liaison
library
lieutenant
loose
lose
maintenance
manageable
martyr
medicine
Mediterranean
memento
millennium
millionaire
miniature
miscellaneous
mischief
mischievous
Mississippi
misspell
mnemonic
mortgage
necessarily
necessary
niece
nineties
noticeable
nowadays
obscene
occasion
occasionally

occur
occurred
occurrence
occurring
officer
official
omission
omit
omitted
opportunity
orchestra
oscillate
parallel
paraphernalia
parliament
pastime
peccadillo
people
perceive
perennial
permanent
perseverance
personnel
pharaoh
Philippines
pizza
playwright
pneumatic
pneumonia
Portuguese
possess
possession
practitioner
precede
preceding
predecessor
preferred
preparation
privilege

proceed
procession
professional
pronunciation
psychiatry
publicly
punctuate
pursue
Pyrenees
query
questionnaire
queue
receipt
receive
recommend
reconnaissance
referred
reign
relevant
relief
relieve
religion
remembrance
reminiscent
rendezvous
repertoire
repetition
reservoir
resistant
resources
responsibility

responsible
restaurant
resuscitate
rhyme
rhythm
ridiculous
rigorous
sacrilege
sacrilegious
satellite
scene
schedule
schizophrenia
scissors
secretary
seize
separate
sergeant
sheriff
siege
sincerely
sixth
succeed
success
successful
suddenness
sufficient
supersede
system
tariff
technician

temperature
temporarily
temporary
therefore
thief
threshold
throughout
tomorrow
truly
twelfth
twentieth
tyranny
unnecessary
until
unwieldy
vaccination
vacillate
vacuum
variegated
veterinary
vigorous
weather
Wednesday
weight
weird
whether
wholly
withhold
women
yacht

Memory prompts for spelling

There are some words that many people find difficult to spell. Here is a list of some commonly misspelt words, with a tip to help remember each one. Sometimes the word is split up to show another word inside, and for many others there are mnemonics – rhymes or other phrases to keep in mind for the words that trouble you the most.

accidentally	He accident**ally** shot an **ally**.
accommodation	Good a**cc**o**mm**odation has **c**omfortable **c**hairs and **m**odern **m**achines.
achieve	Achieve follows the rule: **i** before **e**, except after **c**.
address	Letters are **d**irectly **d**elivered, **s**afe and **s**ound.
argument	Chew **gum** over an ar**gum**ent.
assassination	Words within the word: **ass-ass**-i-**nation**
beautiful	**B**ig **e**lephants **a**re **u**sually **beau**tiful.
believe	I be**lie**ved a **lie**.
broccoli	**Broccoli** may **c**ause **c**ramp **o**r **l**ight **i**ndigestion.
business	Work **busi**ly at your **busi**ness.
calendar	A cal**end**ar shows the **end** of the ye**ar**.
ceiling	The **cei**ling **c**overs **e**verything **i**nside.
cemetery	Word within the word: ce-**meter**-y
changeable	Words within the word: **change-able**
chaos	**C**yclones, **h**urricanes **a**nd **o**ther **s**torms.
column	At the end of a colum**n** is an **n**.
committee	**M**any **m**eetings **t**ake **t**ime – **e**veryone's **e**xhausted.
conscience	Word within the word: con-**science**
definitely	Word within the word: de-**finite**-ly
deliberate	It was a de**liberate** attempt to **liberate** the captives.
desperate	In des**per**ate **per**il
disappear	Remember – a single **s** and a pair of **p**'s.
disappoint	Remember – a single **s** and a pair of **p**'s.
embarrass	I went **r**eally **r**ed and smiled **s**hyly.
exaggerate	A bra**gger** will always ex**agger**ate.

6

excellent	Word within the word: ex-**cell**-ent
fierce	**F**ighting **i**s **e**specially **fie**rce.
forty	**For**ty **for**gets the **u**.
friend	Share your **fri**es with your **frie**nd.
gauge	To **gauge** is to **g**et **a u**seful **g**eneral **e**stimate.
guarantee	**G**et **u**p **a**nd **rant** about the **guarant**ee.
guard	The **gu**ard has a **gu**n.
guilty	You [**u**] and **I** are **gui**lty.
height	**E**veryone **i**s **g**uessing **h**ow **t**all.
hygiene	**Y**ou **g**et **i**ll unless you follow the rules of h**ygi**ene.
independent	Word within the word: indepen-**dent**
indispensable	Only the most **able** people are indispens**able**.
innocent	**In no cent**ury have more **innocent** people died.
innocuous	**Innocu**ous ingredients are found **in no cu**rry.
interrupt	It's **r**eally **r**ude to inte**rr**upt.
jodhpurs	Remember the hidden **h** for **h**orse.
leisure	It's our **lei**sure time, so **l**et's **e**njoy **i**t.
liaise	You need two eyes [two **i**'s] to l**ia**ise properly.
lieutenant	The **lieu**tenant will **lie u**tterly.
maintenance	The **main ten**t is where the d**ance** is held.
manageable	Words within the word: **manage-able**
millennium	A mi**ll**e**nn**ium is a **l**ot **l**onger than **n**inety-**n**ine years.
mischief	**C**ausing **h**avoc **i**s **e**xcellent **f**un.
misspell	Don't **miss** an **s** out of mi**ss**pell.
mortgage	We took a **mort**gage on the **mort**ar.
necessary	One **c**ollar and two **s**leeves are ne**cess**ary on a shirt.
niece	Niece follows the rule: **i** before **e**, except after **c**.
noticeable	Words within the word: **not-ice-able**
obscene	He will cut any **scene** he considers ob**scene**.

occasion	It's an o**cc**a**s**ion to seize [two **c**'s] an **s**.
occurrence	**C**rimson **c**ats and **r**ed **r**abbits are rare o**ccurr**ences.
parallel	Word within the word: par-**all**-el
parliament	**Liam** is a Member of Par**liam**ent.
permanent	The **man** **ent**ered the country as a per**manent** resident.
pharaoh	**P**yramids **h**ouse **a**ncient **r**elics **a**nd **o**ther **h**istorical items.
pneumonia	**P**eople **n**ever **e**xpect **u**s to get **pneu**monia.
possession	I'm in po**sses**sion of four **s**'s.
privilege	Word within the word: privi-**leg**-e
proceed	Pro**c**eed **c**arefully, **e**xamining **e**very **d**etail.
pronunciation	Word within the word: pro-**nun**-ci-a-tion
questionnaire	There are **no** **n**ew questions in this questio**nn**aire.
queue	There are two **u**gly **e**lves in the q**ueue**.
receipt	A rece**ip**t for the money **I** **p**aid **t**hem.
receive	Receive follows the rule: **i** before **e**, except after **c**.
recommend	I re**comm**end **c**ooked **m**arsh**m**allows.
reign	**R**ulers **e**verywhere **ign**ore their subjects.
relief	Relief follows the rule: **i** before **e**, except after **c**.
repetition	A parrot is a **pet** that loves repe**t**ition.
reservoir	The **reserv**oir provides a **reserv**e of water.
rhyme	**R**emember **h**ow **y**ou **rhy**me.
rhythm	**R**hythm **h**elps **y**ou **t**o **h**ear **m**usic.
satellite	**Tell** me what a sa**tell**ite is.
scissors	**S**he **c**ut **i**t **s**nipping **s**wiftly.
secretary	Can your **secret**ary keep a **secret**?
seize	To **sei**ze is to **s**natch **e**agerly **i**n.
separate	The se**para**te strings of a **para**chute.
siege	**S**tuck **i**nside, **e**veryone **g**ot **e**xcited.
sincerely	Words within the word: **since-rely**
succeed	Two **c**'s and two **e**'s will help you su**cce**ed.
supersede	**Se**mi-**de**tached houses super**sede** all others.

8

temperature	Don't lose your **temper** at high **temper**atures.
valuable	**U**nusual **a**ntiques are val**ua**ble.
Wednesday	Word breakdown: Wed-nes-day
weight	We **w**eigh **e**verything **i**n **g**rams **h**ere **t**oday.
weird	It's w**ei**rd that it's spelt **ei**.
wholly	Was the **holly** w**holly** destroyed?
yacht	**Y**es, **a**ll **c**raft **h**ave **t**riangular **s**ails.

Guide to writing better English

Introduction

Everyone studies English at school, but when people try to put this learning into practice later in life, it often seems they are not properly equipped to communicate effectively. Knowledge and practical ability are missing.

This section is designed to address some gaps and weaknesses. It will help equip you with the tools and skills you need to be able to write different types of documents – and to write them clearly and effectively. But, perhaps most important of all, it aims to give you confidence in your writing and in your knowledge of the written word, so you can produce documents of a higher quality.

How to use this section

This section is broken down into four separate but complementary units to help you improve your writing.

- **Planning and drafting**: how to get over those first hurdles before you even put finger to keyboard and then filling in the substance around your plan and revising your work.
- **Sentences and paragraphs**: how these basic building blocks of writing work; how to make them clear and effective.
- **Effective writing style**: choosing the best word; cutting out unnecessary words; making sure your writing says what you mean it to say.

9

- **Good punctuation**: from apostrophes to commas to quotation marks, and all points in between.

By the end, you will be better equipped to produce clear, more effective English.

Planning and drafting

There are two distinct aspects to creating a piece of writing. Firstly, you need to plan it: research it, gather your thoughts and decide how the piece will be structured. Secondly, you need to write it: go through a first draft and then rework it or shorten it until it meets the brief, checking that it has no mistakes.

When you are writing an extended piece of work – for example a essay or report – it needs to have a clear and coherent structure, which means it needs to be well thought out from the start. By the time you have thought about your objectives and completed any research, you should have a clear idea of what you are setting out to do. You now need to draw up a plan of how to do it.

Your plan needs to have a clear structure, allowing you to introduce information and ideas in a logical order. There are many possible approaches. However, most plans should start with three clearly identifiable parts:

- an introduction, in which you state what you are intending to do and why you are doing it
- a main body containing information, arguments and evidence
- a conclusion, in which you summarize what you have previously said, and state clearly any conclusions or recommendations

Converting research notes into a plan
Within this general structure, you need to arrange the things you want to say in your document. This can be done in a few stages:
- Write down all of the arguments or points you have

assembled during the course of your research. At this stage, all you need is a brief note of each point.

* Collect these arguments into groups under a series of general headings.
* Now fit the general headings together into the most logical order. If there are arguments for and against something, group all of the arguments for it together, then group all of the arguments against it together. Do not go backwards and forwards between the two.
* Make sure the order you have come up with fulfils your original goals. If there are any obvious gaps in the order, you may need to go back and do more research to fill these in.

It is a good idea to start with a simple outline and move on to something more complex, fleshing out the bones only once you have built the skeleton. Do not be afraid to cross things about and move them around as you develop your plan – that is what this stage is all about.

Lateral thinking

If you find it difficult to organize your thoughts, put aside the approach mentioned above, and see instead whether any more 'lateral' ways of organizing your material emerge from the material itself. Here are some possible techniques:

* Write a key word or underlying idea in the middle of a large sheet of paper, then write related words and ideas all over the sheet, drawing lines from the centre to related items, as well as between related items, to form a web or network of connected ideas.
* Use question words such *who*, *why*, *where*, *when*, *what* and *how* to generate possible ideas for approaches to the topic. Imagine the questions your readers would ask you if they had the opportunity to speak to you in person.
* Write single words or ideas on index cards and lay them out on the floor, arranging related items into groups or piles.

Once you have decided what the key ideas or points are, assess their relative importance, and decide in what order you want to deal with them. There may be several different ways of arranging your material. What is important is that your plan covers all of the material and that it provides a clear structure for what you have to say.

Having established a basic plan, you may wish to expand this into a more detailed plan, or you may wish to move on to your first draft of the document.

Traditionally, at this early stage writers used pen and paper to create a plan, adding notes and crossing things out as they went. However, computers now make it easy to put down many ideas, and then reorder them by dragging blocks of text around the screen to build up a structure. Whichever method you use, do not be afraid to change your mind – it is better to make alterations to your plan early rather than later when things are more settled.

Drafting – getting started

Once you have come up with a plan that meets your aims, you are ready to start writing. It is a good idea to get through this stage as quickly as possible, so make a start without assuming that the first thing you write will necessarily still be there in your final version. The important thing is to get started – it is far easier to make changes once you have something to work with, rather than wasting time staring anxiously at an empty screen and wondering what to do. In short, just do it!

Drafting – filling out the plan

Once you start to write, you should find that the preparation work you have done pays off, and the writing begins to flow more easily.

Keep in mind the following points as you write:

- Follow your plan. Build on the work that went into producing your plan, and the plan will help you organize your ideas.
- Do not think you have to complete a paragraph before moving on. If you get stuck, go on to the next paragraph and come back later. You will then be able to look at it with fresh eyes and perhaps see what needs to be changed. If you are really stuck, delete the whole paragraph and start again.
- It is likely that new ideas and insights will occur to you as

you write. If new ideas present themselves, do not be afraid to 'go with the flow' and change what you are doing to take account of them – provided that they can be accommodated within your plan.

- Try to deal proportionately with the various different points and arguments. Don't spend a long period on a single point and then skirt around other points that are more important.
- Think about the people who will be reading the document and try to make life easy for them. If people are going to use the document to retrieve information, think about making it easy to scan by using headings, lists and tables. If people are going to read it as a continuous piece, make sure that it is divided and up into manageable paragraphs and that there is a coherent and logical structure.
- If you make a statement or express an opinion, back this up with evidence in the form of facts and figures or quotations. However, use facts and figures selectively and appropriately. Don't overwhelm your readers with them.

General revising

Once you have finished a single complete version of your document, you have the opportunity to change and improve it. It is usually more helpful to produce something that is complete but imperfect and then revise that, rather than wasting time trying to produce something perfect first time.

Check that all the points in your plan have been covered in a logical order, and that everything you have included is in fact necessary to your argument.

Check also that you have dealt with each issue clearly, and that you move smoothly from one point to the next. If you have not done this, add extra material to explain, introduce or summarize where necessary, as this will make your work more polished.

Once you are satisfied with the overall structure and content, you can concentrate on getting the introduction and the conclusion right. You may find that what you originally said in your introduction is no longer valid because you have made changes during the writing process. Now is the time to get it right.

Checking the details

If you are happy that your document is well-organized and coherent as a whole, you can turn your attention to the details: check the 'seven Cs', making sure your writing is:

- **Correct**: There should be no errors in facts, spelling, grammar or punctuation.
- **Consistent**: Things should be expressed in the same way each time you refer to them, and you should follow the same style and the same layout throughout.
- **Clear**: The language should be easy to read, the information be easy to understand, and text be attractively laid out, with plenty of space and enough headings to help your readers – but not so many that they interrupt the flow of the document.
- **Complete**: All of the relevant material should be included, including explanations of unfamiliar terms and abbreviations, any background information, and acknowledgment of your sources.
- **Concise**: The information should be presented in the simplest and most direct way possible.
- **Courteous**: The tone should be polite, and there should be no words which will offend or alienate.
- **Careful**: Nothing should be capable of misconstruction, nothing should be overstated, and everything should be justified.

Shortening

Sometimes you have to work to a specified word count, or you have to shorten your previous work for another use.

The first thing to look for are unnecessary words. Delete any words that could be omitted without changing the meaning of the sentence:

✗   *Often the practical aspect is considered the crucial element.*
✓   *Often the practical aspect is crucial.*

Sentences and paragraphs

Before you can expect to produce good and clear English, you need to get the basics right. So the place to start is with the building blocks of writing: sentences and paragraphs. Once you understand what they are, how they work and how best to structure them, you can then move on to producing documents which communicate effectively.

What is a sentence?

A definition that might be familiar to you is that it is 'something which starts with a capital letter and ends with a full stop'. However, this can be misleading; the following phrases follow these criteria but they are not sentences: *No parking. Gentlemen's outfitters.*

A sentence is something more: it is a grammatical construction which can stand alone without feeling incomplete. It is built according to the agreed rules of grammar, and it is the largest unit to which the rules of grammar apply.

The shortest sentence has a subject and a finite verb (a verb that describes a complete action):
Peter cried. Peter is the subject; *cried* is the verb. Most simple sentences have a subject, a verb and an object: *John trimmed the hedge. John* is the subject; *trimmed* is the verb; *the hedge* is the object.

A sentence is not to be confused with a fragment, which needs something else to complete it, as in this example: *Rising and falling as they went.* This needs something more to make it a full sentence: *Rising and falling as they went, the horses slowly swam across the river.*

Many sentences have two parts: a 'main clause' and a 'secondary clause'. The main clause can stand by itself as a complete sentence; the secondary clause cannot:

✓   *The horses slowly swam across the river.*

✗   *Rising and falling as they went.*

Another way of looking at this is to think of the two separate clauses as a control unit and a support unit. Look at this

15

clause: *The shop sells furniture.* This is a control unit and a complete sentence. Now consider this clause: *Especially hand-crafted chairs.* This is a support unit and not a complete sentence.

But see what happens when we put the two together: *The shop sells furniture, especially hand-crafted chairs.* Now we have a control unit plus a support unit and so the support unit can stand as part of a complete sentence.

Support units can be used at different places in a sentence, either before, after, or in the middle of a control unit. Placing a support unit first sets the scene for the sentence, as in these examples: *To tell you the truth, I couldn't care less. His argument in tatters, Peter walked out of the room.*

By splitting the control unit and placing the support unit in the middle, you can give more information to the reader. You should generally put this type of support unit between two commas, brackets or dashes: *The old mansion, our company's HQ since 1988, was on fire. The car park (which can take 150 cars) is in danger of flooding.*

Placing the support unit at the end of the control unit gives it more impact and a stronger feeling of adding extra information: *Telnet's workers get free lunches, sometimes twice a week. Jon went home, although he didn't want to.*

Sentence length

Short, concise sentences communicate your point more clearly than sentences which ramble on and on. As a guide, sentences should be no more than 15 to 20 words long. However, while short sentences have a sense of vigour and urgency and keep your readers on their toes, a succession of short sentences soon becomes repetitive and boring. So variety is the answer: keep most sentences short, but also include the occasional longer sentence to add variety and improve the flow.

Keeping sentences short

There are several techniques you can use to make a long, flabby sentence shorter and more punchy. It may be that you can split it into separate sentences. Look at this example: *The technology is called the Advanced Dispensing System (ADS) and provides high levels of security for dispensing drugs, while also enabling clinicians to remotely monitor and, if required, remotely control drug usage in real time.*

This sentence contains 35 words. The meaning would be far clearer if cut it were split into two, by making the first clause into a separate sentence and adding a subject for the verb at the beginning of the new second sentence to make it stand by itself: *The technology is called the Advanced Dispensing System (ADS).* **It** *provides high levels of security for dispensing drugs, while also enabling clinicians to remotely monitor and, if required, remotely control drug usage in real time.*

Another way of keeping sentences short and snappy is to cut out unnecessary words. Look at this example: *An example of financial advisory services at Jumbo Bank is the provision of these services to low-income households*. The sentence could be rewritten using eleven words rather than eighteen: *For example, Jumbo Bank provides financial advisory services to low-income households.*

Joining sentences together

While clear English is often achieved through using short sentences, excessive use of short sentences sometimes make your writing seem unsophisticated and weak. It is sometimes better to join two short sentences together to make one, more sophisticated, unit.

Look at the following simple sentences:
The lorry drove away.
The delegates laughed at their mistakes.
The trainer wasn't happy.
The observer felt uncomfortable

You can join simple sentences together using words such as *and*, *but*, *whereas* and *although*. (These 'joining words' are called conjunctions.)

In these examples, simple sentences have been joined together using conjunctions to make longer ones:

*The delegates laughed at their mistakes **but** the trainer wasn't happy.*
*The delegates laughed at their mistakes **although** the observer felt uncomfortable.*

A key point to remember is that it is not enough to use just a comma to join complete sentences together:

✗   *The cat sat on the desk, the dog ran down the road.*
✗   *The delegates laughed at their mistakes, the trainer wasn't happy.*

Active and passive sentences

In an active sentence the subject carries out the action described by the verb. An active sentence usually follows the pattern of subject + verb + object: *Peter opened his diary.* In this example *Peter* is the subject; *opened* is the verb; *his diary* is the object.

In a passive sentence the subject has something done to it. A passive sentence usually follows the pattern of subject + passive verb + agent: *The diary was opened by Peter.* In this example *The diary* is the subject; *was opened* is the verb; *Peter* is the agent.

Active sentences are far more punchy and tend to be shorter. It is good practice to use active sentences rather than passive. It will make your writing clearer and more succinct. However, there are some occasions when using the passive can help communicate what you are trying to say more effectively: the passive can be used as a more tactful way of writing, taking the full impact away from something you do not want to stress or draw attention to: *Journal entry errors were made in the books.*

By using the active (*Our accountant made journal entry errors in the books*) all the blame goes on a named person – but perhaps this is not what you want to stress. By using the passive, the person remains anonymous and the focus of the sentence is on simply admitting there were errors.

Paragraphs

A paragraph is a logical collection of sentences. Unlike sentences, paragraphs are not governed by rules of grammar: they are simply there as a visual aid to lead the reader through the text by splitting it into manageable chunks.

In some written communications – in particular, essays and other academic materials – paragraphs tend to be as long as is needed to argue a particular point. In business English, however, it is best to keep paragraphs short and snappy.

When deciding how long a paragraph should be, consider your likely readers and their attention span. There is nothing more off-putting than having long wedges of text without any breaks. So keep in mind the following guidelines:

- Aim for a minimum of two and a maximum of six sentences in a paragraph.
- Avoid one-sentence paragraphs, as they feel disjointed and weak. If a one-sentence paragraph comprises one long sentence, you may need to split that sentence into two or more sentences to make a more effective paragraph.
- Look at sentences for their sense: is there a logical break where a paragraph might end and a new one start?
- Is the paragraph so long that it will put the readers off? If so, can it be split up and a linking word or an introductory phrase added to restart the flow after the break?

Effective paragraph structure

Now that we have established what a paragraph is, let's look at some ways of making paragraphs work effectively. One simple way of making a paragraph work is to make the main point first and then support it with argument or fact. Look at this example:

Our range of partitions offers clear advantages over other, similar systems. It is particularly suited to swimming-pool changing rooms. Every element is water-resistant and will not degrade in a wet environment.

It makes a statement in the first sentence, gives a supporting example in the second and backs up this example with fact in the third.

A paragraph will also work well if you can link its component sentences and relate them to the main point you are is making. One good way of doing this is to number the different supporting points which supplement the main argument of the paragraph:

> Our range of partitions offers clear advantages over other, similar systems. **Firstly**, it is particularly suited to swimming-pool changing rooms: every element is water-resistant and will not degrade in a wet environment. **Secondly**, it is vandal-resistant and can withstand hammer and knife attack. And, **finally**, it is available in a range of colours and finishes to suit even the most adventurous design scheme.

An alternative way of making the sentences flow together more smoothly is to use conjunctions to link the sentences:

> Our range of partitions offers clear advantages over other, similar systems. It is particularly suited to swimming-pool changing rooms: every element is water-resistant and will not degrade in a wet environment. **In addition,** it is vandal-resistant and can withstand hammer and knife attack. It is **also** available in a range of colours and finishes to suit even the most adventurous design scheme.

Finally, adding a comment or a summary as the final sentence finishes a paragraph with a flourish and gives it impact, as in the following example:

> Our range of partitions offers clear advantages over other, similar systems. Firstly, it is particularly suited to swimming-pool changing rooms: every element is water-resistant and will not degrade in a wet environment. Secondly, it is vandal-resistant and can withstand hammer and knife attack. And, finally, it is available in a range of colours and finishes to suit even the most adventurous design scheme. **In short, it combines style, strength and long-term use.**

Effective writing style

Good written communication depends on the words and phrases you use. Clarity and impact are significantly improved by taking care with your vocabulary. In addition, by cutting out nonsense and pomposity, you can win your readers over more successfully. This section looks at different ways of making your writing clearer and more effective.

The best word for the job

Choosing the right word makes your writing more powerful, and helps you communicate more clearly. Always think about the specific words you choose. Don't make the mistake of using a longer word just because you think it will help you to appear clever and sophisticated: in fact, it may simply alienate the reader.

Look at this list of pairs of words. Each pair have the same meaning, but the words in the first column are more complicated, while those in the second column are simpler. There is a time and place for both, but if in doubt use the simple word:

accomplish	do	facilitate	help
additional	more	finalize	finish
advantageous	helpful	impacted	affected
anticipate	expect	implement	carry out
apparent	clear	modify	change
benefit	help	perform	do
capability	ability	permit	let
component	part	possess	own
concerning	about	proceed	start
contains	has	provide	give
demonstrate	show	purchase	buy
desire	want	require	need
determine	decide	reside	live
employ	use	submit	hand over
establish	prove	transmit	send
evident	clear	utilize	use
fabricate	make	verify	confirm

Jargon

Jargon refers to words or expressions used by particular groups of people or professions. The crucial point to consider is whether the reader will understand the jargon you might be tempted to use.

If you are writing for people who work in the same business as you, then jargon can be extremely useful: your readers will understand it and you can communicate effectively. But if your readers won't understand it – or if you are in any doubt whether they will – then do not use jargon terms. If you are writing for a mixed audience, then use technical terms with care. It may be a good idea to provide definitions of technical terms in a glossary.

Every business has its own jargon. For example, it is perfectly acceptable within the railway industry to talk about a *clockface timetable*. For people within the industry, this is a very neat way of expressing a well-established concept (it means that trains are always at the same minutes before or after the hour). To anyone outside the business, however, the term is meaningless and would need a full explanation.

Slang, buzzwords and clichés

While there may sometimes be a place for jargon in business, there are some types of language you should always try to avoid:

- **Slang** originates from groups of people who are outside the mainstream of society or see themselves as different in some way. Occasionally slang words become accepted as standard, but mostly they stay outside the vocabulary suitable for standard English.
- **Buzzwords** are words which are used to falsely impress. They often borrow from jargon: many of them have been imported from the IT industry. Examples include *ballpark figure* and *blue-sky thinking*.
- **Clichés** are hackneyed phrases or expressions which are mostly superfluous and meaningless. Phrases such as *at the end of the day* and *when all is said and done* have no place in clear English.

Here are some examples of jargon, slang, buzzwords and clichés that you should try to avoid. In many cases they can replaced with a simple alternative:

all things considered	in short
at this moment in time	now
backlash	reaction, counterattack
ballpark figure	estimate
blend together	blend
blue-sky thinking	original thinking
clamp down	tighten up on
crackdown	attack
crunch	crisis
cutting edge	very advanced
downsize	reduce in size
drill down	look at in more detail
fact of the matter	the main point
fighting for his life	critically ill or injured
helicopter view	an overview
in respect of	about
in terms of	for
last but not least	last
link together	link
move the goalposts	change the requirements
put on the back burner	postpone
reinventing the wheel	unnecessary repetition of work
quantum leap	significant step
restructuring	making redundancies
singing from the same hymn sheet	in agreement
skill set	skills
state of the art	latest
thinking outside the box	lateral thinking
water under the bridge	in the past

The following words can usually be left out altogether without affecting the meaning:

actually	in point of fact
as a matter of fact	to all intents and purposes
at the end of the day	to be fair
basically	when all's said and done
in actual fact	

Put the action into the verb

A common source of redundancy in language is the use of a noun to do the work of a verb. This is called 'nominalization'. Look at these examples: *The proposal was given as a submission to the management team. We believe she took the decision to go.* The phrases *given as a submission* and *took the decision* in fact mean *submitted* and *decided* respectively. In each case, the writer has made a noun do the work of a verb. By making a verb do its proper job – which is to describe the action – we can make the sentences shorter and clearer: *The proposal was submitted to the management team. We believe she decided to go.*

This device of putting the action into a noun instead of a verb is often used because it seems to have more weight and dignity. It doesn't: it simply uses several words when one will do.

Here are some more examples of 'nominalization'. In each case it would be neater to use a simple verb:

to make an agreement	to agree
to give consideration to	to consider
to carry out evaluations	to evaluate
to give an indication of	to indicate
to make reductions	to reduce
to make recommendations	to recommend
to find a solution to	to solve
to have a tendency to	to tend to

Ambiguity and lack of clarity

The whole point of communication is that the person at the other end receives a clear picture of what you have in your mind. Careless and sloppy writing can lead to ambiguity (where the reader might take a different message from the one you want to send) or lack of clarity (where the reader isn't clear what is going on at all). To avoid this, it is a good idea to read your work back to make sure it really says what you mean it to say.

Look at the following example: *A piano is being sold by a lady with carved legs.*

Undoubtedly the lady doesn't really have carved legs, but that is what the sentence seems to be saying. There are several clearer ways of getting the meaning across: *A piano with carved legs is being sold by a lady. A piano, which has carved legs, is being sold by a lady. A lady is selling a carved-leg piano.*

Follow these tips to help you avoid ambiguity in your writing:

- Be aware of the potential for ambiguity to creep in to your writing: read it and think if it is really saying what you want it to say.
- Use simple and clear sentence structures.
- If your meaning isn't clear, then add in details to improve clarity.
- Don't assume your reader will understand: if in doubt, change it.
- Show your writing to someone else: they may have a different way of interpreting what you have written.

Good punctuation

Using the right punctuation makes what you are trying to say clear – and increases the chance of your reader understanding your writing the first time they read it. This section is designed to give you an overview of how to use different punctuation marks correctly.

Apostrophes

To illustrate how important an apostrophe can be in communicating what you really mean, look at these words: *ill, shell, well, hell, were.*

It's perfectly clear what these words mean. But if you add an apostrophe, the meaning changes completely: *I'll* (*I will*), *she'll* (*she will*), *we'll* (*we will*), *he'll* (*he will*), *we're* (*we are*).

Now look at these two phrases:
> *the bands on stage*
> *the band's on stage*

In the first example, without the apostrophe, *bands* is a plural and refers to more than one band being on the stage at that time. In the second example, *band's* is a contraction of *band is* and refers to one band.

These examples all demonstrate that an apostrophe is not an optional extra: it is needed to make your writing communicate exactly what you want to say.

Uses of the apostrophe
The apostrophe has two uses:

- to mark the omission of something
- to show that something is a possessive

Firstly, an apostrophe can be used to replace something that has been removed (one letter or several letters). Whatever remains is moved together around the apostrophe. So *it is* becomes *it's* and *who will* becomes *who'll*: *It's time to go home. Who'll chair the meeting?*

If you remove some numbers when writing a year or decade, you add an apostrophe: *the summer of '09. We experienced major growth throughout the '90s.*

Secondly, an apostrophe is also used to show that something belongs to someone or something:
the lady's handbag   (*the handbag belonging to the lady*)
the boy's books   (*the books belonging to the boy*)

Note that the idea of possession is present in many phrases that indicate a period of time, such as:
one week's holiday   (*a holiday of one week*)
two years' experience   (*the experience gained over two years*)

Positioning the apostrophe
When an apostrophe shows possession, the best way to check if you have it in the right place is to turn the sentence around. If you turn *the boy's books* around into *the books belonging to the boy*, you will then identify that you are talking about the singular noun *boy*. The apostrophe should always go after the name of the thing you are talking about:
the man's diary   (*the diary belonging to the man*)
IBM's staff   (*the staff at IBM*)
the team's proposal   (*the proposal by the team*)

When the word with the apostrophe is a plural, the apostrophe should still go after the name of the thing you are talking about. Again, you can check that you have got it right by turning the sentence around: *the boys' books* (*the books belonging to the boys*).

By turning the sentence around, you can identify that you are talking about the plural noun *boys*, so this time the apostrophe needs to go after the *s*.

Remember that not all plural nouns end in *s*. With plurals such as *children* and *geese*, the apostrophe comes before the *s*:

the children's department   (*the department for children*)
the geese's eggs   (*the eggs of the geese*)

Common misuses of the apostrophe

People who are not clear about the correct use the apostrophe sometimes put them in places where they don't belong, and this can get in the way of the meaning. There are many words that end in *s* that do not need an apostrophe.

Do not use an apostrophe for a verb that ends in *s*:

✓   *The window lets the light in.*
✗   *The window let's the light in.*

Do not use an apostrophe for the simple plural form of a noun:

✓   *We sell pizzas.*
✗   *We sell pizza's.*

There is sometimes a temptation to do this with the plural forms of abbreviations and dates:

✓   *a superb range of CDs*
✗   *a superb range of CD's*
✓   *the 1990s*
✗   *the 1990's*

Plural forms of words that consist of a single letter are an exception. It is a good idea to use an apostrophe here simply to avoid confusion:

There are two o's and two s's in looses.

Mind your p's and q's.

Another class of words that causes difficulty are the words such as *yours*, *hers* and *ours*, which are called 'possessive pronouns'. These words – as their name suggests – already indicate possession, so they do not need an apostrophe:

I returned the book, which was hers.
Ours is a generation which knows how to enjoy life.
Whose desk needs cleaning?

The possessive pronoun that causes most difficulty for writers is *its*. It is worth making a special effort to remember that the only time you write *it's* is when it means 'it is' or 'it has':

✓   *It's been a long time since I saw you.*
✗   *The company has lost it's way recently.*
✓   *The company has lost its way recently.*

Inverted commas or quotation marks

Inverted commas are used to show the beginning and end of direct speech or excerpts from other material. They come in pairs:

Rob Thornton said, 'Our new factory will provide significant employment for the village.'

Inverted commas may be written as single or double marks – there is no hard-and-fast rule to follow. The key is to choose one style and apply it consistently.

For clarity, never use the same style of inverted commas when you have one quotation within another: use single for the main quote and double for the secondary, or vice versa:

'When she screamed out "Help!", I started to get worried,' said Mike.
"When she screamed out 'Help!', I started to get worried," said Mike.

Quotation marks should enclose the exact words of the speaker. If words identifying the speaker appear in the middle, close the quotation marks and then reopen them:

'Our new factory will provide significant employment for the village,' commented Rob Thornton, 'and will for many years to come.'

The rule for placing a punctuation mark at the end of quoted speech is that, if the punctuation applies to the quote itself, it goes inside the quotation mark:

He remarked, 'I'm going to be only ten minutes late.'

But if the punctuation does not apply to the quote, but rather to the whole sentence, it goes after the final quotation mark:

He remarked that he would be 'only ten minutes late'.

Although quotation marks come in pairs, there is one special case: if a quote continues into another paragraph, you do not put in closing marks until the end of the complete quote. You do, however, use a quotation mark at the beginning of each new paragraph:

'Our new factory,' said Rob Thornton, 'will be opening in September. We are confident that this will provide significant opportunities for the village.

'In addition, we are creating 50 new jobs in our Cardiff offices. These will bring the total staff of the company up to 460.'

Commas

Commas are used to break up a sentence and create a pause, in a number of different ways.

A comma separates the different elements in a simple list:

The following items are needed: pencil, ruler, rubber, paper, highlighter and stapler.

Notice that in this example there is no comma before the word *and*. But a comma here can be useful if you want to separate the final item more clearly. Compare these two examples:

The telephone operators yawned, stretched, grimaced, coughed and squirmed with boredom.

The telephone operators yawned, stretch, grimaced, coughed, and squirmed with boredom.

In the first example, everything was caused by boredom; the final comma in the second example changes the meaning, so that only the squirming was caused by boredom.

A comma can also be used to clarify meaning. Compare the following sentences:

Below, the keyboard was broken.
Below the keyboard was broken.

In the first instance, the keyboard itself was broken; in the second, something else which is underneath the keyboard is broken.

A comma can also be used to separate extra information in a sentence. A pair of commas is used to separate information which isn't absolutely essential to the sense of the sentence. These are called 'bracketing commas', and do the same work as brackets or dashes:

The leader, who lived in a private apartment, needed regular meetings to be kept informed.
The building, which included private meeting rooms and sports facilities, was available for general use.

In both cases, the whole phrase inside the commas could be removed and the sentence would still make sense:

The leader needed regular meetings to be kept informed.
The building was available for general use.

If the information is essential to the meaning, however, then it is not separated from the rest of the sentence by commas. Consider the difference between these two sentences:

Staff who regularly go on holiday will miss out on certain benefits.
Staff, who regularly go on holiday, will miss out on certain benefits.

In the first example, only those members of staff who regularly go on holiday will miss out on benefits. The whole phrase *Staff who regularly go on holiday* is the subject of the sentence and cannot be interrupted by a comma. But in the second example, all the staff will miss out on certain benefits, and all of them regularly go on holiday. *Staff* is the subject of the sentence, while *who regularly go on holiday* is a subordinate (supporting) unit and needs to be separated from the main part of the sentence by two commas.

If the extra information comes at the beginning or the end of a sentence, a single comma is enough to separate it from the main part of the sentence:

> *They went to the board room, which was on the top floor.*
> *If you don't meet the deadline, you will miss the*
> *opportunity.*

In the first sentence, *They went to the board room* is the main part of the sentence (the control unit); *which was on the top floor* adds extra information and could not stand alone. In the second sentence, *You will miss the opportunity* is the main part of the sentence (control unit); *If you don't meet the deadline* adds extra information and could not stand alone.

A comma can be used to mark the beginning or end of speech or a quotation in the middle of a sentence:

> *John said, 'I'll be there at eight.'*
> *'I'll be there at eight,' said John.*

Common misuses of the comma

A comma must *never* appear between a subject and its verb:

✗   *John, knew he would never succeed.*
✓   *John knew he would never succeed.*
✗   *London, is the capital of England.*
✓   *London is the capital of England.*

If commas are used in pairs to bracket extra information, then the sentence should work if the extra information is removed:

✗   *She said that most, if not all of, the staff were leaving.*

f you take out the information within the commas, you are left with an incomplete fragment:

✗   *She said that most the staff were leaving.*

So the second comma needs to be placed more carefully:

✓   *She said that most, if not all, of the staff were leaving.*

Now, if you take out the information within the commas, you are left with a complete sentence:

✓   *She said that most of the staff were leaving.*

It is important not to leave out the second comma when you

want to separate supplementary information in the middle of a sentence:

✘   *The product, which was selling well would now be manufactured in India.*

✓   *The product, which was selling well, would now be manufactured in India.*

Colons

Colons are used to introduce things.

A common use of colons is in a two-part sentence when the second part expands on or explains a completed statement. This second part could either stand alone as a separate sentence or be a subordinate (supporting) clause:

> *Sally didn't attend the meeting: she had to fly to Glasgow.*
> *Mark shivered: a combination of nerves and the cold.*

A colon can also introduce a list, as in the following example:

> *The following areas are closed: cafeteria, library, terrace and garden.*

The most common use of colons in business English is to introduce quotations, for example in press releases:

> *Gemma Green, Marketing Director, is delighted with the results: 'We were convinced it would be successful and this has proved our point.'*

Semicolons

Whereas colons always introduce things, semicolons always connect things of equal importance. The two cannot be used interchangeably. Semicolons can join together short sentences which, if they ran separately, might sound rather disjointed and staccato:

> *Jones sat on one side. Smith sat on the other. The document was on the table between them.*

Using semicolons, the story flows and the tension mounts:

Jones sat on one side; Smith sat on the other; the document was on the table between them.

Changing the final semicolon to a full stop creates a dramatic change: *Jones sat on one side; Smith sat on the other. The document was on the table between them.*

Here is another example of how using semicolons can make a difference:

> *The hotel nestles in a hollow; all around are grazing sheep and cattle; trees in the distance mark out the boundaries.*

Using semicolons here makes the description flow and create a unified picture. Using short sentences and full stops would give it a more punchy but disjointed feel:

> *The hotel nestles in a hollow. All around are grazing sheep and cattle. Trees in the distance mark out the boundaries.*

By using one full stop and one semicolon, we can shift the focus firmly to the hotel and its location:

> *The hotel nestles in a hollow. All around are grazing sheep and cattle; trees in the distance mark out the boundaries.*

Another use of the semicolon is to bring together two statements which, when joined, create a balance:

> *The racket is short and light to use; the ball is white and easy to see.*
> *Some called him a genius; others claimed he was a fraud.*

Finally, if a list contains elements which have internal punctuation, these can be separated more clearly by using a semicolon:

> *The following elements are needed: a screen, with an anti-glare cover; a keyboard, mouse and mouse mat; a colour printer, with or without paper; and speakers.*

If commas were used to separate the elements, the list would be very confusing.

Exclamation marks

Perhaps the last word on exclamation marks was written by H W Fowler, who observed that using them excessively is 'a certain indication of an unpractised writer or of one who wants to add a spurious dash of sensation to something unsensational'.

In short, exclamation marks should be used with caution.

Brackets

Brackets are used to separate words from the rest of a sentence. This is usually either to provide extra information or to show options, as in these examples:

Look out for the best restaurants (like the Café Royal, which has a great reputation).

The report showed quite clearly (page 200, line 6) that it was true.

In both these cases, the words in the brackets could be dropped and would leave a perfectly complete sentence. They simply add more information and colour.

Brackets can be useful as they allow you to accommodate a range of possibilities without having to tailor your writing to each specific case:

Your letter(s) will be returned.

Your child (children) should arrive at 10am.

Square brackets may be used if you need an additional set of brackets within brackets:

The report presented evidence about the disaster (and its aftermath [reported below]).

Square brackets can also be used to add in information which is needed to make the sense clear:

Business to business is not in our plans [for new business] but we never say never.

Dashes

A dash can create dramatic effect. It creates more of a pause than using a comma:

Everyone expected a pay rise – but not as much as 50 per cent.

It seemed the best product for us – after they'd reduced the price.

A pair of dashes can be used to separate extra information within a sentence. A pair of dashes does the same work as a pair of brackets or commas:

He got together his things – pencil, ruler, rubber, pen and ink – and started the exam.

Note that the dash should not be used to do the work of a colon:

✗　*The place was devastated – trees uprooted; windows broken; tiles on the ground.*

✓　*The place was devastated: trees uprooted; windows broken; tiles on the ground.*

Hyphens

Some words that are created by combining two shorter words are always hyphenated. Here are some examples:

close-knit	closed-circuit	co-op	co-worker
cross-country	do-it-yourself	flip-flop	front-end
know-all			

Hyphens are also used to join words together to remove ambiguity from written English. Take this example:

> *man-eating dog seen in park*
> *man eating dog seen in park*

With the hyphen, it is clear that the dog is prone to eating humans; without the hyphen, it is clear that the man is prone to eating dogs. So, if two words jointly describe another word and would cause confusion if left separate, then use a hyphen:

> *highest-quality service*
> *a red-haired girl*
> *a two-year sentence*
> *a low-key approach*

marshmallow noun 1 a spongy jellylike sweet made from sugar and egg-whites etc 2 a marsh plant with pink flowers, similar to the hollyhock

marshy adj (**marshier**, **marshiest**) wet underfoot; boggy

marsupial noun an animal that carries its young in a pouch, eg the kangaroo

martello tower noun a round coastal fort

marten noun an animal related to the weasel

martial adj 1 of war or battle 2 warlike • **martial art** noun any combative sport or method of self-defence of SE Asian origin • **martial law** noun the government of a country by its army

Martian noun a potential or imaginary being from the planet Mars

martin noun a bird of the swallow family

martinet noun someone who keeps strict order; a disciplinarian

martini noun (plural **martinis**) a cocktail made with gin or vodka and vermouth

Martinmas noun 11 November, the feast of St Martin

martyr /mah-tuh/ noun someone who suffers death or hardship for their beliefs ◇ verb execute or make suffer for beliefs • **martyrdom** noun the death or suffering of a martyr

marvel noun something astonishing or wonderful ◇ verb (**marvelling**, **marvelled**) feel amazement (at)

marvellous adj 1 astonishing, extraordinary 2 informal very good; excellent • **marvellously** adv

Marxist noun a follower of the communist theories of Karl Marx • **Marxism** noun

marzipan noun a mixture of ground almonds, sugar, etc used in cake-making and confectionery

mascara noun a cosmetic paint used to colour the eyelashes

mascarpone /mas-kuh-poh-ni/ noun a soft Italian cream cheese

mascot noun a person, animal or thing believed to bring good luck

masculine adj 1 of the male sex 2 showing qualities such as physical strength or bravery considered admirable in a man; manly • **masculinity** noun

mash verb beat or crush into a pulp ◇ noun 1 mashed potato 2 a mixture of bran, meal, etc, used as animal food 3 a mixture of malted barley or other cereal and water from which beer or alcoholic spirit is made

mask noun 1 a cover for the face for disguise or protection 2 a pretence or disguise ◇ verb 1 hide or disguise (something) 2 cover the face with a mask

masochism /mas-uh-kizm/ noun an unnatural pleasure taken in being dominated or treated cruelly • **masochist** noun someone who takes such pleasure • **masochistic** adj

mason noun 1 someone who carves stone 2 a Freemason • **masonic** adj

masonry noun the stone or brick parts of buildings

masque /mahsk/ noun an old type of theatre performance with actors wearing masks

masquerade /mahs-kuh-rehd/ noun 1 pretence 2 a dance at which masks are worn ◇ verb pretend to be someone else: masquerading as a journalist

mass noun (plural **masses**) 1 a lump or quantity gathered together 2 a large quantity 3 the main part or body 4 a measure of the quantity of matter in an object 5 (**Mass**) (in some Christian churches) the celebration of Christ's last supper with his disciples 6 (**Mass**) music for a Mass ◇ adj 1 of or consisting of large numbers or quantities **2** of a mass ◇ *verb* form into a mass • **mass media** *noun* television, radio and newspapers; the media • **mass production** *noun* production in large quantities of articles all exactly the same • **the masses** people of the lowest social class; working-class people

massacre *noun* the merciless killing of a large number of people ◇ *verb* kill (a large number) in a cruel way

massage /ma-sahzh/ *noun* the rubbing of parts of the body to remove pain or tension ◇ *verb* perform massage on

masseur *noun* someone who performs massage

masseuse *noun* a female masseur

massif /ma-seef/ *noun* a central mountain mass

massive *adj* **1** very big and bulky **2** very large • **massively** *adv*

mast *noun* a long upright pole holding up the sails *etc* in a ship, or holding an aerial, flag, *etc*

mastectomy *noun* the surgical removal of a woman's breast

master *noun* **1** the male owner of a dog *etc* **2** a male teacher **3** someone who is very skilled in something; an expert **4** a degree awarded by universities: *Master of Arts* **5** the commander of a merchant ship ◇ *adj* main and controlling: *master switch* ◇ *verb* **1** become able to use or use properly: *I've finally mastered this computer program* **2** overcome, defeat • **masterful** *adj* strong-willed • **master key** *noun* a key made to open a number of different locks • **masterly** *adj* showing the skill of an expert or master • **mastermind** *verb* work out the details of (a scheme *etc*) ◇ *noun* a person who masterminds (a scheme *etc*) • **master of ceremonies** *noun* someone who directs the form and order of events at a public occasion; a compère • **masterpiece** *noun* the best example of

someone's work, *esp* a very fine picture, book, piece of music, *etc* • **masterstroke** *noun* a clever act or move

mastery *noun* **1** great skill (in) **2** control (of)

mastic *noun* a waterproof putty-like substance used in the building trade as a sealant or filler

masticate *verb, formal* chew • **mastication** *noun*

mastiff *noun* a breed of large, powerful dog

mastitis *noun* inflammation of a breast or udder

mastodon *noun* an extinct animal similar to an elephant

masturbate *verb* stimulate the sexual organs to a state of orgasm • **masturbation** *noun* • **masturbator** *noun*

mat *noun* **1** a piece of material (coarse plaited plant fibre, carpet, *etc*) for wiping shoes on, covering the floor, *etc* **2** a piece of material, wood, *etc* put below dishes at table ◇ *adj* another spelling of **matt** • **matted** *adj* thickly tangled • **matting** *noun* material from which mats are made

matador *noun* the person who kills the bull in bullfights

match[1] *noun* (*plural* **matches**) **1** a contest or game **2** a person or thing that goes well with another **3** a thing that is similar to another **4** an equal **5** someone suitable for marriage ◇ *verb* **1** be of the same make, size, colour, *etc* **2** set (two things, teams, *etc*) against each other **3** hold your own with; equal • **matchless** *adj* far better than all others • **matchmaker** *noun* someone who tries to arrange marriages or partnerships

match[2] *noun* (*plural* **matches**) a small stick of wood tipped with a substance that catches fire when rubbed against an abrasive surface • **matchbox** *noun* a box for holding matches • **matchstick** *noun* a single match • **match-**

wood *noun* wood broken into small pieces

mate *noun* **1** a friend **2** an assistant worker: *plumber's mate* **3** a husband or wife **4** the sexual partner of an animal, bird, *etc* **5** a merchant ship's officer, next in rank to the captain ◇ *verb* come together, or bring (animals) together, to breed

material *noun* **1** something out of which anything is, or may be, made **2** cloth, fabric ◇ *adj* **1** able to be seen and felt; solid or physical **2** concerned with physical comfort, money, *etc*, rather than spiritual matters: *a material outlook on life* **3** important or significant: *material difference* • **materially** *adv* to a significant extent; greatly

materialism *noun* **1** a tendency to attach too much importance to material things (eg physical comfort, money) **2** the belief that only things we can see or feel really exist or are important • **materialist** *noun* • **materialistic** *adj*

materialize *verb* **1** happen **2** appear in bodily form

maternal *adj* **1** of a mother **2** like a mother; motherly **3** related through your mother: *maternal grandmother* • **maternally** *adv*

maternity *noun* the state of being a mother; motherhood ◇ *adj* of or for a woman having or about to have a baby: *maternity clothes*

math *noun, US informal* mathematics

mathematics *sing noun* the study of measurements, numbers and quantities and their relationships • **mathematical** *adj* **1** of or done by mathematics **2** very exact • **mathematician** *noun* an expert in mathematics

maths *noun, informal* mathematics

matinée /mat-i-neh/ *noun* an afternoon performance in a theatre or cinema • **matinée coat** *noun* a baby's short jacket

matins *plural noun* the morning service in certain churches

matriarch /meh-tri-ark/ *noun* a woman who is the head of a family or community • **matriarchal** *adj*

matrices *plural of* **matrix**

matricide *noun* **1** the killing of your own mother **2** someone who kills their own mother

matriculate *verb* admit, or be admitted, to a university • **matriculation** *noun*

matrilineal *adj* of family descent: progressing through the female line • **matrilineally** *adv*

matrimony *noun, formal* marriage • **matrimonial** *adj* relating to marriage • **matrimonially** *adv*

matrix *noun* (*plural* **matrices**) **1** a mass of rock in which gems *etc* are found **2** a rectangular table of data **3** a mould in which metals *etc* are shaped

matron *noun* **1** a senior nurse in charge of a hospital **2** *old* a woman in charge of housekeeping or nursing in a school, hostel, *etc* **3** *old* a married woman • **matronly** *adj* **1** of a woman: dignified **2** rather plump

matt *or* **mat** *adj* having a dull surface; not shiny or glossy

matter *noun* **1** a subject written or spoken about **2** (**matters**) affairs, business **3** trouble, difficulty: *what is the matter?* **4** anything that takes up space, can be seen, felt, *etc*; material, substance **5** *formal* importance: *of no great matter* **6** pus ◇ *verb* be of importance: *it doesn't matter* • **matter-of-fact** *adj* not emotional or excited; calm • **a matter of course** something that is to be expected • **a matter of opinion** a subject on which different opinions are held • **as a matter of fact** in fact

mattock noun a tool like a pickaxe for breaking up soil

mattress noun (plural **mattresses**) a thick layer of padding covered in cloth, usually as part of a bed

mature adj **1** fully grown or developed **2** having the calm good sense associated with adults **3** having a fully developed flavour; ripe ◇ verb **1** (cause to) become mature **2** of an insurance policy etc: be due to be paid out • **maturely** adv • **maturity** noun ripeness

matzo noun (plural **matzos** or **matzoth**) a wafer or cracker eaten during Passover

maudlin adj sad and sentimental

maul verb hurt badly by rough or savage treatment

Maundy Thursday noun the day before Good Friday in the Christian calendar

mausoleum noun a large or elaborate tomb

mauve adj of a purple colour

maverick noun someone who refuses to conform; a determined individualist

mavis noun the song thrush

maw noun **1** an animal's jaws or gullet **2** a wide or gaping cavity

mawkish adj sentimental in a way that seems weak or silly • **mawkishly** adv

maxi- prefix very large or long: maxiskirt

maxim noun a general truth or rule about behaviour etc

maximum adj greatest, most ◇ noun (plural **maxima**) **1** the greatest number or quantity **2** the highest point or degree

May noun the fifth month of the year

may verb (**may**, **might**) **1** used with another verb to express permission or possibility: you may watch the film/I thought I might find him there **2** used to express a wish: may your wishes come true

maybe adv perhaps

Mayday noun the first day of May

mayday noun an international distress signal

mayfly noun (**mayflies**) a short-lived insect that appears in May

mayhem noun widespread chaos or confusion

mayo /meh-oh/ noun, informal mayonnaise

mayonnaise /meh-uh-nehz/ noun a cold thick sauce made of eggs, oil and vinegar or lemon juice

mayor noun the chief elected public official of a city or town • **mayoress** noun a mayor's wife

---

Note: mayor is used for a woman mayor, never mayoress

---

maypole noun a decorated pole traditionally danced around on Mayday

maze noun **1** a series of winding paths in a park etc, planned to make exit difficult and designed as an amusement **2** something complicated and confusing: maze of regulations

mazurka noun a lively Polish dance or dance music

Mb abbrev megabyte(s)

MBE abbrev Member of the Order of the British Empire

MC abbrev **1** Master of Ceremonies **2** Military Cross

MCC abbrev Marylebone Cricket Club

MCP abbrev male chauvinist pig

MD abbrev **1** Doctor of Medicine (from Latin Medicinae Doctor) **2** Managing Director

MDF *abbrev* medium density fibre-board, a strong board used in furniture and house-building

MDMA *abbrev* methylene-dioxy-methamphetamine, the drug Ecstasy

ME *abbrev* myalgic encephalomyelitis, a condition of chronic fatigue and muscle pain following a viral infection

me *pronoun* the word used by a speaker or writer in mentioning themselves: *she kissed me/give it to me*

mea culpa /*meh*-uh *kuul*-puh/ *exclam* it is my fault

mead *noun* an alcoholic drink made with honey

meadow *noun* a field of grass

meadowsweet *noun* a wild flower with sweet-smelling cream-coloured flowers

meagre *or US* **meager** *adj* **1** scanty, not enough **2** *old* poor in quality **3** *old* thin • **meagreness** *noun*

meal[1] *noun* the food taken at one time, *eg* breakfast or dinner

meal[2] *noun* grain ground to a coarse powder

mealy-mouthed *adj* avoiding speaking in a frank or direct way

mean[1] *verb* (**meaning, meant**) **1** intend to express; indicate: *what do you mean?/when I say no, I mean no* **2** intend: *how do you mean to do that?* • **meaning** *noun* **1** what is intended to be expressed or conveyed **2** purpose or intention • **meaningful** *adj* **1** full of significance; expressive **2** having an effect; significant • **meaningfully** *adv* • **meaningless** *adj* • **mean well** have good intentions

mean[2] *adj* **1** ungenerous with money **2** unkind **3** poor or of low social status; lowly • **meanly** *adv* • **meanness** *noun*

mean[3] *adj* **1** midway between two other points, quantities, *etc*; middle **2** average ◇ *noun* • **meanwhile** *adv* in the time between two happenings • **in the meantime** meanwhile

meander /mi-*an*-duh/ *verb* **1** of a river: flow in a winding course **2** wander about slowly and aimlessly

means *plural noun* **1** the way something is done or brought about **2** money, property, *etc*: *a woman of means* • **by all means 1** of course **2** in every way possible • **by no means** certainly not

measles *noun* an infectious disease causing red spots

measly *adj* (**measlier, measliest**) *informal* ungenerously small

measure *noun* **1** size or amount **2** an instrument or container for finding the size or amount **3** (**measures**) a plan of action: *measures to prevent crime* **4** musical time **5** a law brought before parliament to be considered ◇ *verb* **1** find out the size, quantity, *etc* by using some form of measure **2** be of a certain length, amount, *etc* **3** indicate the measurement of **4** mark (off) or weigh (out) in portions • **measured** *adj* steady and unhurried • **measurement** *noun* **1** the size, amount, *etc* found by measuring **2** the act of measuring • **for good measure** as a bonus

meat *noun* animal flesh used as food

meaty *adj* (**meatier, meatiest**) **1** full of meat **2** full of interest or usefulness

Mecca *noun* **1** Saudi Arabian city that is a place of pilgrimage for Muslims **2** any place that attracts large numbers of visitors

mechanic *noun* a skilled worker with tools or machines

mechanical *adj* **1** worked by machinery **2** of machinery: *mechanical engineering* **3** done without thinking • **mechanically** *adv*

mechanics *noun* **1** *sing* the study and art of constructing machinery **2**

plural the actual details of how something works: *the mechanics of the plan are beyond me*

mechanism *noun* **1** a piece of machinery **2** the way a piece of machinery works **3** an action that produces a particular result

mechanize *verb* **1** equip (a factory *etc*) with machinery **2** supply (troops) with armoured vehicles • **mechanization** *noun*

Med *noun, informal* the Mediterranean Sea or the region around it

medal *noun* a metal disc stamped with a design, inscription, *etc*, made to commemorate an event or given as a prize • **medallion** *noun* a large medal or piece of jewellery like one • **medallist** *noun* someone who has gained a medal

meddle *verb* **1** concern yourself with things that are not your business **2** interfere or tamper (with) • **meddler** *noun* • **meddlesome** *adj* fond of meddling

media *noun*: **the media** television, radio and newspapers as a form of communication

mediaeval *another spelling of* **medieval**

median *noun* **1** a straight line from an angle of a triangle to the centre of the opposite side **2** the middle value or point of a series ◇ *adj* mid, middle

mediate *verb* settle a dispute (between) • **mediation** *noun* • **mediator** *noun* someone who tries to settle a dispute between people

medic *noun, informal* a doctor or medical student

medical *adj* of doctors or their work ◇ *noun* a physical examination carried out by a doctor

medicate *verb* give medicine to • **medicated** *adj* including medicine or disinfectant

medication *noun* **1** medical treatment **2** a medicine

medicinal *adj* **1** used as a medicine **2** used in medicine • **medicinally** *adv*

medicine *noun* **1** something given to a sick person to make them better **2** the science of the treatment of illness • **medicine man** *noun* a tribal healer or shaman

medieval *or* **mediaeval** *adj* of or in the Middle Ages

mediocre *adj* not very good, ordinary • **mediocrity** *noun*

meditate *verb* **1** contemplate religious or spiritual matters **2** think deeply and in quietness **3** think carefully about something • **meditative** *adj* thoughtful • **meditatively** *adv*

meditation *noun* **1** contemplation on a religious or spiritual theme **2** deep, quiet thought

medium *noun* (*plural* **media** *or* **mediums**) **1** a means or substance through which an effect is produced **2** (*plural* **mediums**) someone through whom spirits (of dead people) are said to speak ◇ *adj* middle or average in size, quality, *etc* • **the media** *see* **media**

medley *noun* (*plural* **medleys**) **1** a mixture **2** a piece of music put together from a number of other pieces

meek *adj* gentle, uncomplaining and submissive • **meekly** *adv* • **meekness** *noun*

meerkat *noun* a S African animal related to the mongoose

meerschaum /mee-uh-shum/ *noun* **1** a fine white clay used to make tobacco pipes **2** a pipe made of this

meet *verb* (**meeting**, **met**) **1** come together in order to spend time with; join **2** make the acquaintance of **3** have to deal with **4** be suitable for, satisfy: *able to meet the demand* **5** pay (costs *etc*) fully ◇ *noun* a gathering for a sports event ◇ *adj, old* proper, suitable • **meeting** *noun* a gathering of people for a particular purpose

mega adj, slang **1** huge **2** very good; excellent

mega- prefix great, huge: Hollywood megastars

megabyte noun, comput approximately one million bytes

megahertz noun a unit of frequency of sound and radio waves equal to one million cycles per second

megalith noun a huge stone erected in prehistoric times

megalomania noun **1** an obsessive desire for power **2** an exaggerated idea of your own importance or abilities • **megalomaniac** noun someone suffering from megalomania

megaphone noun a portable cone-shaped device with microphone and amplifier to increase sound

megaton adj of a bomb: having an explosive force equal to a million tons of TNT

melancholy adj sad or depressed ◇ noun lowness of spirits; sadness • **melancholic** adj

mélange /meh-lonzh/ noun a mixture, a medley

melanin noun the dark pigment in human skin or hair

melanoma noun a skin tumour that usually develops from a mole

melba toast noun thin curled slices of toasted bread

meld verb merge or blend

mêlée /mel-ay/ noun a confused brawl involving large numbers of people

mellifluous adj sweet-sounding • **mellifluously** adv • **mellifluousness** noun

mellow adj **1** having become more relaxed with age **2** of light, colour, etc: soft, not harsh **3** of food: having developed a full flavour with age ◇ verb make or become mellow • **mellowness** noun

melodeon noun a type of accordion

melodious adj pleasant sounding; tuneful • **melodiously** adv • **melodiousness** noun

melodrama noun a film or play with a sensational or exaggerated plot

melodramatic adj exaggerated, sensational, over-dramatic • **melodramatically** adv

melody noun (plural **melodies**) **1** a tune **2** pleasant music • **melodic** adj of melody • **melodically** adv

melon noun a large round fruit with soft juicy flesh

melt verb **1** make or become liquid, eg by heating **2** disappear gradually: the crowd melted away **3** soften in feeling: his heart melted at the sight • **meltdown** noun the process in which the radioactive fuel in a nuclear reactor overheats and melts through the insulation into the environment

member noun **1** someone who belongs to a club or organization **2** a limb or organ of the body • **Member of Parliament** noun (shortened to **MP**) someone elected to the House of Commons • **membership** noun **1** the membership of a club etc **2** the state of being a member

membrane noun a thin skin or covering, especially as part of a human or animal body, plant, etc

memento noun (plural **mementos**) something by which an event is remembered • **memento mori** noun an object used as a reminder of human mortality

memo noun (plural **memos**) short for memorandum

memoirs plural noun a personal account of someone's life; an autobiography • **memoirist** noun a writer of memoirs

memorable *adj* worth remembering or easily remembered • **memorably** *adv*

memorandum *noun* (*plural* **memoranda**) **1** a brief note sent to colleagues in an office *etc* **2** a written statement of something under discussion **3** a note that acts as a reminder

memorial *noun* a monument commemorating an historical event or people ◇ *adj* commemorating an event or person

memorize *verb* learn by heart

memory *noun* (*plural* **memories**) **1** the power to remember **2** the mind's store of remembered things **3** something remembered **4** *comput* that part of a computer into which programs are loaded for using **5** what is remembered about someone • **in memory of** in remembrance of or as a memorial of

menace *noun* **1** potential harm or danger **2** someone persistently threatening or annoying ◇ *verb* be a danger to; threaten

menacing *adj* looking evil or threatening

ménage /meh-*nazh*/ *noun* a household

menagerie /muh-*naj*-uh-ree/ *noun* **1** a collection of wild animals **2** a place where these are kept

mend *verb* **1** repair **2** make or become better ◇ *noun* a repaired part • **on the mend** getting better; recovering

mendacious *adj, formal* not true; lying • **mendaciously** *adv* • **mendacity** *noun*

mendicant *noun* a beggar ◇ *adj* begging

menhir /*men*-hi-uh/ *noun* a prehistoric standing stone

menial *adj* of work: unskilled, unchallenging

meningitis *noun* an illness caused by inflammation of the covering of the brain

menopause *noun* the ending of menstruation in middle age

menorah *noun* a candelabrum used in Jewish ceremonies

menses *plural noun* the discharge of blood *etc* during menstruation

menstruation *noun* the monthly discharge of blood from a woman's womb • **menstrual** *adj* of menstruation • **menstruate** *verb* undergo menstruation

mensuration *noun, formal* measurement of length, height, *etc*

mental *adj* **1** of the mind **2** done, made, happening, *etc* in the mind: *mental arithmetic* **3** of illness: affecting the mind • **mentally** *adv* • **mental hospital** *noun* a hospital for people suffering from mental illness

mentality *noun* (*plural* **mentalities**) **1** type of mind or way of thinking **2** mental power

menthol *noun* a sharp-smelling substance obtained from peppermint oil

mention *verb* **1** speak of briefly **2** remark (that) ◇ *noun* an act of mentioning; a remark

mentor *noun* someone who gives advice as a tutor or supervisor

menu *noun* (*plural* **menus**) **1** (a card with) a list of dishes to be served at a meal **2** *comput* a list of options

MEP *abbrev* Member of the European Parliament

mercantile *adj* of buying and selling; trading

Mercator's projection *noun* a map of the globe in the form of a rectangle evenly marked with lines of latitude and longitude

mercenary *adj* **1** influenced above all by the desire for money **2** working for money ◇ *noun* (*plural* **mercenaries**) a soldier paid by a foreign country to fight in its army

mercerized *adj* of thread *etc*: treated with caustic soda to increase its strength and absorbency

merchandise *noun* goods to be bought and sold • **merchandiser** *noun*

merchant *noun* someone who carries on a business in the buying and selling of goods; a trader ◇ *adj* of trade • **merchant bank** *noun* a bank that provides financial services to companies and other organizations • **merchantman** *noun, old* a trading ship • **merchant navy** *noun* ships and crews employed in trading

merciful *adj* willing to forgive or be lenient • **mercifully** *adv*

merciless *adj* showing no mercy; cruel • **mercilessly** *adv*

mercury *noun* an element that is a heavy, silvery liquid metal • **mercurial** *adj* lively, active or changeable

mercy *noun* (*plural* **mercies**) 1 lenience or forgiveness towards an enemy *etc*; pity 2 something very fortunate or welcome • **at someone's mercy** in their power

mere *adj* nothing more than: *mere nonsense*

merely *adv* only, simply

meretricious *adj, formal* superficially attractive; flashy

Do not confuse with: **meritorious**

---

merge *verb* 1 combine or join together 2 come together gradually; blend

merger *noun* a joining together, *eg* of business companies

meridian *noun* 1 an imaginary line around the globe passing through the north and south poles 2 the highest point of the sun's path 3 *Chinese med* a main energy channel in the body

meringue /muh-*rang*/ *noun* a baked

cake or shell made of sugar and egg-white

merino *noun* (*plural* **merinos**) 1 a sheep with very fine soft wool 2 its wool, or a soft fabric made from it

merit *noun* 1 positive worth or value 2 a valuable or commendable quality ◇ *verb* deserve

meritorious *adj, formal* deserving honour or reward

Do not confuse with: **meretricious**

---

mermaid *noun* an imaginary sea creature with a woman's upper body and a fish's tail

merry *adj* (**merrier**, **merriest**) 1 cheerful and lively 2 slightly drunk • **merrily** *adv* • **merriment** *noun*

merry-go-round *noun, Brit* a fairground roundabout with wooden horses *etc* for riding on

mesh *noun* (*plural* **meshes**) 1 network, netting 2 the opening between the threads of a net ◇ *verb* 1 of gears *etc*: interconnect, engage 2 combine or work well together

mesmeric *adj* 1 commanding complete attention; fascinating 2 hypnotic • **mesmerically** *adv*

mesmerize *verb* 1 hold the attention of completely; fascinate 2 hypnotize

mesolithic *adj* referring to the period between paleolithic and neolithic

meson /*mee*-zon/ *noun, physics* a particle with a mass between that of a proton and an electron

mess *noun* (*plural* **messes**) 1 an untidy or disgusting sight 2 disorder, confusion 3 the place where members of the armed forces eat their meals together • **mess up** make untidy, dirty or muddled • **mess with** *US informal* interfere with

message *noun* 1 a piece of news or

information sent from one person to another **2** an idea communicated by a work of art

messenger *noun* someone who carries a message

messiah *noun* a saviour or deliverer

Messrs *plural of* **Mr**

messy *adj* (**messier, messiest**) **1** untidy or disordered **2** dirty • **messily** *adv* • **messiness** *noun*

met *past tense of* **meet**

metabolic *adj* of metabolism • **metabolically** *adv*

metabolism *noun* **1** the combined chemical changes in the cells of a living organism that provide energy for living processes and activity **2** the conversion of nourishment into energy

metal *noun* any of a group of substances (*eg* gold, silver, iron, *etc*) able to conduct heat and electricity

---

Do not confuse with: **mettle**

---

metallic *adj* **1** made of metal **2** shining like metal: *metallic thread*

metallurgy *noun* the study of metals • **metallurgic** *or* **metallurgical** *adj* • **metallurgist** *noun*

metamorphose *verb* change completely in appearance or character

metamorphosis *noun* (*plural* **metamorphoses**) **1** a change in form, appearance, character, *etc*; a transformation **2** a physical change that occurs during the growth of some creatures, *eg* from a tadpole into a frog

metaphor *noun* a way of describing something by suggesting that it is, or has the qualities of, something else, as in *the camel is the ship of the desert*

metaphorical *adj* using a metaphor or metaphors • **metaphorically** *adv*

metaphysics *noun* **1** the study of being and knowledge **2** any abstract writing or thinking • **metaphysical** *adj* • **metaphysician** *noun*

meteor *noun* a small piece of matter moving rapidly through space, becoming bright as it enters the earth's atmosphere

meteoric *adj* **1** extremely rapid: *meteoric rise to fame* **2** of a meteor

meteorite *noun* a meteor that falls to the earth as a piece of rock

meteorologist *noun* someone who studies or forecasts the weather

meteorology *noun* the study of weather and climate • **meteorological** *adj*

mete out *verb, formal* deal out (punishment *etc*)

meter[1] *noun* an instrument for measuring the amount of gas, electricity, *etc* used ◇ *verb* measure with a meter

meter[2] *US spelling of* **metre**

Do not confuse with: **metre**

---

meth *noun, informal* methamphetamine

methadone *noun* a synthetic drug similar to morphine, used to treat addiction

methamphetamine *noun* a synthetic drug derived from amphetamine

methane *noun* a colourless gas produced by rotting vegetable matter

methanol *noun* a colourless liquid used as a solvent and antifreeze

method *noun* **1** a planned or regular way of doing something **2** orderly arrangement • **methodology** *noun* methods used and the principles that lie behind them

methodical *adj* done or acting

according to some plan; systematic • **methodically** *adv*

meths *noun, informal* methylated spirits

methyl *noun* a poisonous alcohol found in nature

methylated spirits *plural noun* an alcohol with added violet dye, used as a solvent or fuel

meticulous *adj* careful and accurate about small details • **meticulously** *adv* • **meticulousness** *noun*

métier */meh-ti-eh/ noun, formal* occupation or profession

metonym *noun* the use of the name of part of a thing to stand for the whole, *eg the ring* for *boxing* • **metonymy** *noun*

metre *or US* **meter** *noun* **1** the main unit of length in the metric system (about 1.1 yards) **2** the arrangement of syllables or stresses in poetry, or of musical notes, in a regular rhythm

---

Do not confuse with: **meter¹**

---

metric *adj* **1** of the metric system **2** metrical • **metric system** *noun* the system of weights and measures based on tens (1 metre = 10 decimetres = 100 centimetres *etc*)

metrical *adj* of poetry: written in a regular rhythm of syllables or stresses

metrication *noun* the change to a metric system of measurement

metronome *noun* an instrument that keeps a regular beat, used for music practice

metropolis *noun (plural* **metropolises***)* a large city, usually the capital city of a country • **metropolitan** *adj* situated in, or to do with, a large city

mettle *noun, formal* courage • **on your mettle** out to do your best

---

Do not confuse with: **metal**

---

mew *noun* a whining cry made by a cat *etc* ◇ *verb* cry in this way

mews *noun* buildings (originally stables) built around a yard or in a lane

mezzanine *noun* **1** a low storey between two main storeys **2** *US* a balcony in a theatre

mezzo */met-soh/ noun (plural* **mezzos***) informal* a mezzo-soprano

mezzo-soprano *noun (plural* **mezzo-sopranos***)* **1** a woman with a singing voice between alto and soprano **2** a singing voice between alto and soprano

mg *abbrev* milligram(s)

MHz *abbrev* megahertz

MI5 *abbrev* a British government counter-espionage agency

MI6 *abbrev* a British espionage and intelligence agency

miaow *noun* the sound made by a cat ◇ *verb* make the sound of a cat

miasma */mai-az-muh/ noun* an unhealthy or depressing atmosphere

mica */mai-kuh/ noun* a mineral that glitters and divides easily into thin transparent layers

mice *plural of* **mouse**

Michaelmas */mik-ul-mus/ noun* the festival of St Michael, 29 September

mickey *noun:* **take the mickey** *informal* make fun of someone; tease

micro *noun, dated informal (plural* **micros***)* a microcomputer

micro- *prefix* very small: *microelectronics*

microbe *noun* a minute living organism, *esp* a disease-causing bacterium

microchip *noun* a tiny piece of silicon with a complex electronic circuit printed on it

microcomputer *noun, dated* a

small desktop computer; a PC

microcosm *noun* a version on a small scale: *a microcosm of society*

microfiche /mai-kruh-feesh/ *noun* a sheet of microfilm designed to be stored in a file

microfilm *noun* narrow photographic film on which books, newspapers, *etc* are recorded in miniaturized form ◇ *verb* record on microfilm

microphone *noun* an instrument that picks up sound waves for broadcasting, recording or amplifying

microprocessor *noun* a computer processor consisting of one or more microchips

microscope *noun* a scientific instrument that magnifies very small objects placed under its lens

microscopic *adj* 1 so small as to be visible only under a microscope 2 extremely small; minuscule ● **microscopically** *adv*

microsecond *noun* a millionth of a second

microsurgery *noun* delicate surgery carried out under a microscope ● **microsurgeon** *noun* a surgeon who performs microsurgery

microwave *noun* 1 a microwave oven 2 a very short radio wave ● **microwave oven** *noun* an oven that cooks food by passing microwaves through it

mid- *prefix* placed or occurring in the middle: *mid-morning*

midday *noun* noon

midden *noun* a rubbish or dung heap

middle *noun* the point or part of anything equally distant from its ends or edges; the centre ◇ *adj* 1 occurring in the middle or centre 2 coming between extreme positions *etc*: *trying to find a middle way* ● **middle-aged** *adj* between youth and old age

● **middle class** *noun* the class of people between the working and upper classes ● **middle-of-the-road** *adj* blandly average or unadventurous ● **in the middle of** in the midst of doing, busy doing ● **the Middle Ages** the period of European history roughly between AD 500 and AD 1500

middling *adj* 1 of middle size or quality 2 neither good nor bad; mediocre

midge *noun* a small biting insect

midget *noun* an abnormally small person or thing ◇ *adj* very small

midnight *noun* twelve o'clock at night ◇ *adj* occurring at midnight

midriff *noun* the middle of the body, just below the ribs

midst *noun* the middle ● **in our midst** among us

midsummer *noun* the time around 21 June, the summer solstice and longest day in the year

midway *adv* half-way

midwife *noun* (*plural* **midwives**) a nurse trained to assist women during childbirth ● **midwifery** /mid-*wif*-uh-ri/ *noun* the practice or occupation of being a midwife

midwinter *noun* the time around 21 December, the winter solstice and shortest day in the year

mien /meen/ *noun*, *formal* appearance

might¹ *past tense of* **may**

might² *noun* power or strength

mighty *adj* (**mightier**, **mightiest**) very great or powerful ◇ *adv*, *US informal* very ● **mightily** *adv* ● **mightiness** *noun*

migraine /mee-grehn/ *noun* a severe form of headache

migrant *noun* 1 someone migrating, or recently migrated, from another country 2 a bird that migrates annually

migrate *verb* 1 change your home to another area or country 2 of birds: fly to a warmer region for the winter • **migration** *noun*

migratory *adj* 1 migrating 2 wandering

mike *noun, informal* a microphone

milch cow *noun* 1 a cow kept for milk production 2 a ready source of money

mild *adj* 1 not harsh or severe; gentle 2 of taste: not sharp or bitter 3 of weather: not cold • **mildly** *adv* • **mildness** *noun*

mildew *noun* a whitish mark on plants, fabric, *etc* caused by fungus • **mildewed** *adj*

mile *noun* a measure of length (1.61 kilometres or 1760 yards) • **mileage** *noun* 1 distance in miles 2 travel expenses counted by the mile • **milestone** *noun* 1 a stone beside the road showing the number of miles to a certain place 2 something that marks an important event

milieu /meel-yur/ *noun* surroundings

militant *adj* favouring or taking part in forceful action ◇ *noun* someone who is militant

military *adj* of soldiers or warfare ◇ *noun* (**the military**) the army

militate *verb* 1 fight or work (against) 2 act to your disadvantage

---

Do not confuse with: **mitigate**

---

militia *noun* a group of fighters, not regular soldiers, trained for emergencies

milk *noun* 1 a white liquid produced by female animals as food for their young 2 this liquid, *esp* from cows, used as a drink for people ◇ *verb* 1 draw milk from 2 take (money *etc*) from • **milk float** *noun* a lightweight vehicle that makes deliveries of milk to homes • **milkmaid** *noun, old* a woman who milks cows • **milkman** *noun* a man who sells or delivers milk • **milk tooth** *noun* a tooth from the first set of teeth in humans and mammals • **milky** *adj* 1 of the colour or consistency of milk 2 white • **the Milky Way** a bright band of stars seen in the night sky

mill *noun* 1 a machine for grinding or crushing grain, coffee, *etc* 2 a building where grain is ground 3 a factory ◇ *verb* 1 grind (grain) 2 cut grooves round the edge of (a coin) 3 move round and round in a crowd • **miller** *noun* someone who grinds grain • **millrace** *noun* the stream of water that turns a millwheel • **millstone** *noun* 1 one of two heavy stones used to grind grain 2 something felt as a burden or hindrance • **mill wheel** *noun* a waterwheel that drives the machinery of a mill

millennium *noun* (*plural* **millennia**) a period of a thousand years

millet *noun* a type of grain used for food

milli- *prefix* thousand, or a thousandth part of: *millisecond*

milligram *noun* a thousandth of a gram

millilitre *noun* a thousandth of a litre

millimetre *noun* a thousandth of a metre

milliner *noun* someone who makes and sells women's hats • **millinery** *noun* the goods sold by a milliner

million *noun* a thousand thousands (1,000,000) ◇ *adj* one million in number • **millionth** *adj* the last of a million (things *etc*) ◇ *noun* one of a million equal parts

millionaire *noun* someone who has a million pounds (or dollars) or more

millipede *noun* a small crawling insect with a long body and many pairs of legs

millisecond *noun* a thousandth of a second

mime *noun* **1** a theatrical art using body movements and facial expressions in place of speech **2** a play performed through mime **3** an actor who performs mime ◇ *verb* **1** mouth the words of a recorded song to give the illusion of singing **2** perform a mime **3** express through mime

mimic *verb* (**mimics, mimicking, mimicked**) imitate, especially in a mocking way ◇ *noun* someone who mimics • **mimicry** *noun*

mimosa *noun* a tree producing bunches of yellow scented flowers

min *abbrev* **1** minimum **2** minute (of time)

minaret *noun* a tall tower on a mosque, from which Muslims are called to prayer

mince *verb* **1** shred (meat) into small pieces **2** walk in a prim or effeminate way with short steps ◇ *noun* meat shredded by a machine • **mince pie** *noun* a pie filled with mincemeat • **mincer** *noun* a machine for mincing food • **not mince words/matters** not try to soften an unpleasant fact or statement

mincemeat *noun* a chopped-up mixture of dried fruit, suet and spices • **make mincemeat of** defeat or beat severely

mind *noun* **1** the power of thinking and understanding, or the place where it takes place **2** intention: *I've a good mind to tell him so* ◇ *verb* **1** look after: *mind the children* **2** watch out for: *mind the step* **3** take exception; object: *do you mind if I open the window?* • **change your mind** change your opinion or intention • **in two minds** undecided • **make up your mind** decide • **mindful of** paying attention to • **out of your mind** mad or foolish • **presence of mind** ability to act calmly and sensibly • **speak your mind** speak frankly

minder *noun* **1** someone who looks after a child **2** a bodyguard

mindless *adj* foolish or pointless • **mindlessly** *adv*

mine[1] *pronoun* a thing or things belonging to me: *that drink is mine*

mine[2] *noun* **1** an underground pit or system of tunnels from which metals, coal, *etc* are dug **2** a heavy charge of explosive material ◇ *verb* **1** dig or work a mine **2** lay explosive mines in • **minefield** *noun* an area covered with explosive mines • **miner** *noun* someone who works in a mine • **minesweeper** or **minelayer** *noun* a ship that removes or places explosive mines

mineral *noun* a natural substance mined from the earth, *eg* coal, metals, gems, *etc* ◇ *adj* of or containing minerals • **mineral water** *noun* **1** water containing small amounts of minerals **2** *informal* carbonated water

mineralogy *noun* the study of minerals • **mineralogist** *noun*

minestrone *noun* a thick Italian vegetable soup containing rice or pasta

mingle *verb* **1** mix **2** move around speaking to various people at a party *etc*; circulate

mingy /min-ji/ *adj* (**mingier, mingiest**) *informal* ungenerous or ungenerously small; mean

mini- *prefix* smaller than average; compact: *minibus/minicab*

miniature *adj* made on a small scale ◇ *noun* **1** a small-scale painting **2** a small bottle of spirits

minibus *noun* (*plural* **minibuses**) a type of small bus

minidish *noun* a small satellite dish used to receive digital television

minidisk *noun* a very small storage medium for digital information, with the appearance of a miniature floppy disk

minim *noun, music* a note (♩) equal to two crotchets, or half a semibreve, in length

minimal *adj* very little, the lowest possible

minimize *verb* 1 cause to seem small or unimportant 2 make as small as possible

minimum *noun* (*plural* **minima**) the smallest possible or acceptable quantity ◇ *adj* the least possible

minion *noun* a slave-like follower

miniscule *another spelling of* **minuscule**

The **miniscule** spelling is not yet standard

---

minister *noun* 1 the head of a government department: *minister of trade* 2 a member of the clergy; a vicar or priest ◇ *verb* (**minister to**) supply the needs of • **ministerial** *adj* of a minister

ministry *noun* (*plural* **ministries**) 1 a government department or its headquarters 2 the work of a member of the clergy

mink *noun* a small weasel-like animal or its highly-valued fur

minnow *noun* a type of very small river or pond fish

minor *adj* 1 of less importance, size, etc 2 relatively small or unimportant (*contrasted with*: **major**) ◇ *noun* someone not yet legally of age (*ie* in the UK, under 18) • **minority** *noun* 1 the smaller number or part 2 the state of being a minor

Minotaur *noun* a mythological creature with a bull's head, living in the Cretan labyrinth

minster *noun* a large church or cathedral

minstrel *noun, hist* a medieval travelling musician

mint¹ *noun* a plant with strong-smelling leaves, used as flavouring

mint² *noun* 1 a place where coins are made 2 *informal* a large sum of money: *cost a mint* ◇ *verb* make coins • **minted** *adj, slang* very rich; loaded • **in mint condition** in perfect condition

minuet *noun* 1 a kind of slow, graceful dance 2 the music for this

minus *prep* 1 used to show subtraction, represented by the sign (–): *five minus two equals three or 5−2=3* 2 *informal* without: *I'm minus my car today* ◇ *adj* of a quantity: less than zero

minuscule *adj* extremely small; minute

minute¹ /min-it/ *noun* 1 a sixtieth part of an hour 2 in measuring an angle, the sixtieth part of a degree 3 a very short time 4 (**minutes**) notes taken of what is said at a meeting

minute² /main-yoot/ *adj* 1 very small 2 very exact

minutiae /mai-nyoo-shi-ai/ *plural noun* minute or exact details

minx *noun* (*plural* **minxes**) a cheeky young girl

miracle *noun* 1 a wonderful act beyond normal human powers 2 a fortunate happening with no natural cause or explanation • **miraculous** *adj* • **miraculously** *adv*

mirage /mi-rahzh/ *noun* something imagined but not really there, *eg* an oasis seen by travellers in the desert

mire *noun* deep mud • **miry** *adj*

mirror *noun* a backed piece of glass which shows the image of someone looking into it ◇ *verb* 1 reflect like a mirror 2 copy exactly

mirth *noun* merriment or laughter • **mirthful** *adj* • **mirthless** *adj*

mis- *prefix* wrong(ly), bad(ly): *mispronounce/misapply*

misadventure *noun* an unlucky happening

misandry *noun* hatred of men

misanthropist *noun* someone who hates or distrusts people in general • **misanthropic** *adj* • **misanthropy** *noun*

misappropriate *verb* put to a wrong use, *eg* use (someone else's money) for yourself

misbehave *verb* behave badly • **misbehaviour** *noun*

misc *abbrev* miscellaneous

miscarriage *noun* **1** the accidental loss of a foetus during pregnancy **2** a going wrong; failure: *miscarriage of justice*

miscarry *verb* (**miscarries, miscarrying, miscarried**) **1** have a miscarriage in pregnancy **2** go wrong or astray **3** be unsuccessful

miscegenation /mis-e-jun-*eh*-shun/ *noun* intermarriage or interbreeding between different races

miscellaneous *adj* made up of several kinds; assorted • **miscellaneously** *adv*

miscellany *noun* (*plural* **miscellanies**) a mixture or collection of things, *eg* pieces of writing

mischance *noun, formal* an unlucky accident

mischief *noun* **1** naughtiness **2** *old* harm or damage • **mischievous** *adj* tending or likely to cause trouble • **mischievously** *adv*

misconceive *verb* misunderstand • **misconception** *noun* a wrong idea; a misunderstanding

misconduct *noun* bad or immoral behaviour

misconstrue *verb* misunderstand • **misconstruction** *noun*

miscreant /*mis*-kri-unt/ *noun* someone who does something bad or illegal

misdeed *noun* a bad deed; a crime

misdemeanour *noun* a minor offence

miser *noun* someone who hoards money and spends very little • **miserly** *adj* very ungenerous with money; mean

misery *noun* (*plural* **miseries**) **1** great unhappiness, pain, poverty, *etc* **2** *informal* an habitually unhappy person • **miserable** *adj* **1** very unhappy **2** involving great poverty or hardship

misfire *verb* **1** of a gun: fail to go off **2** of a plan: go wrong

misfit *noun* **1** someone who cannot fit in happily in society *etc* **2** something that fits badly

misfortune *noun* **1** bad luck **2** an unlucky accident

misgiving *noun* fear or doubt, *eg* about the result of an action

misguided *adj* showing, or acting from, bad judgement or wrong beliefs • **misguidedly** *adv*

mishandle *verb* handle carelessly or roughly

mishap *noun* an unlucky accident

mishmash *noun* a confused or jumbled assortment; a hotchpotch

misinform *verb* inform wrongly

misinterpret *verb* interpret wrongly

misjudge *verb* judge unfairly or wrongly

mislay *verb* (**mislaying, mislaid**) put (something) aside and forget where it is; lose

mislead *verb* (**misleading, misled**) give a false idea (to); deceive • **misleading** *adj*

mismatch *noun* an unsuitable match

misnomer noun a wrong or unsuitable name

miso /mee-soh/ noun fermented soy bean paste

misogynist /mis-oj-i-nist/ noun a man who hates women • **misogyny** noun

misplace verb put in the wrong place; mislay

misprint noun a mistake in printing

misquote verb make a mistake in repeating something written or said

misrepresent verb give a wrong idea of (someone's words, actions, etc)

Miss noun (plural **Misses**) 1 a form of address used before the surname of an unmarried woman 2 (**miss**) a young woman or girl

miss verb 1 fail to hit, see, hear, understand, etc 2 discover the loss or absence of 3 feel the lack of: missing old friends ◇ noun (plural **misses**) 1 the act of missing 2 a failure to hit a target 3 a loss • **missing** adj lost • **miss out** 1 leave out 2 be left out of something worthwhile or advantageous

missal noun the Mass book of the Roman Catholic Church

misshapen adj badly or abnormally shaped

missile noun 1 a type of flying bomb, either self-propelled or launched and allowed to fall 2 an object that is thrown or fired, esp as a weapon

mission noun 1 a task that someone is sent to do 2 a group of representatives sent to another country 3 a group sent to spread a religion 4 the headquarters of such groups 5 someone's chosen task or purpose: his only mission is to make money • **mission statement** noun a declaration made by an organization outlining its aims, ethos, etc

missionary noun (plural **mission-** aries) someone sent abroad etc to spread a religion

missive noun, formal something sent, eg a letter

misspell verb (**misspelling, misspelled** or **misspelt**) spell wrongly • **misspelling** noun

misspent adj spent unwisely; wasted: misspent youth

mist noun a cloud of moisture in the air • **misty** adj • **mist up** or **mist over** cover or become covered with mist

mistake noun a wrong action or statement; an error ◇ verb (**mistaking, mistook, mistaken**) 1 make an error about 2 wrongly believe (one thing or person) to be another • **mistaken** adj making an error, unwise: mistaken belief • **mistakenly** adv

mister full form of **Mr**

mistletoe noun a plant with white berries, used as a Christmas decoration

mistreat verb treat badly; abuse

mistress noun (plural **mistresses**) 1 a female owner of a dog etc 2 a woman who is the lover though not the legal wife of a man 3 a woman skilled in something 4 old a female teacher 5 full form of **Mrs**

mistrust noun a lack of trust or confidence in ◇ verb have no trust or confidence in

misunderstand verb (**misunderstanding, misunderstood**) take a wrong meaning from what is said or done • **misunderstanding** noun 1 a mistake about a meaning 2 a slight disagreement

misuse noun bad or wrong use ◇ verb 1 use wrongly 2 treat badly

mite noun 1 something very small, eg a tiny child 2 a very small spider-like animal 3 hist a very small coin

mitigate verb make (punishment, pain, etc) less great or severe

• **mitigating circumstances** *plural noun* facts or events that make someone's bad actions seem less bad or more understandable • **mitigation** *noun*

Do not confuse with: **militate**

---

mitre *noun* **1** the pointed headdress worn by archbishops and bishops **2** a slanting joint between two pieces of wood

mitt *or* **mitten** *noun* a glove without separate divisions for the four fingers

mix *verb* **1** put two or more things together so they make a single thing or substance; blend **2** (**mix up**) put in the wrong order or a different order **3** associate with other people ◇ *noun* a mixture or blending

mixed *adj* **1** consisting of different kinds **2** for both sexes: *mixed doubles* **3** jumbled together • **mixed blessing** *noun* something good that happens that also has bad aspects • **mixed-up** *adj* **1** confused, bewildered **2** with emotional problems that make ordinary life or relationships difficult; maladjusted

mixer *noun* **1** a machine that mixes food **2** a soft drink added to alcohol **3** someone who mixes socially

mixture *noun* **1** a number of things mixed together **2** a medicine

mizzenmast *noun* the mast nearest the stern of a ship

ml *abbrev* millilitre(s)

MLitt *abbrev* Master of Letters or Literature (from Latin *Magister Litterarum*)

mm *abbrev* millimetre(s)

mnemonic /ni-mon-ik/ *noun* a rhyme *etc* that helps you to remember something

MO *abbrev* medical officer

moan *noun* a low sound of grief or pain ◇ *verb* make this sound

moat *noun* a deep trench round a castle *etc*, often filled with water

mob *noun* a noisy crowd ◇ *verb* (**mobbing, mobbed**) crowd round, or attack, in disorder

mobie *or* **mobey** *noun, slang* a mobile phone

mobile *adj* **1** able to move or be moved easily **2** set up inside a vehicle that travels around: *a mobile library* **3** not relying on fixed cables *etc*; portable **4** *informal* having a car for your personal use ◇ *noun* **1** a decoration or toy hung so that it moves slightly in the air **2** *informal* a mobile phone • **mobile phone** *noun* a portable phone that operates by means of a radio system • **mobility** *noun*

mobilize *verb* gather (troops *etc*) together ready for active service • **mobilization** *noun*

Möbius strip /muh-bi-us/ *noun, maths* a one-sided surface made by twisting and joining together the ends of a rectangular strip

moccasin *noun* a soft leather shoe of the type originally worn by Native Americans

mocha /mok-uh/ *noun* **1** a fine coffee **2** coffee and chocolate mixed together **3** a deep brown colour

mock *verb* cause to appear foolish; ridicule ◇ *adj* false, pretended or imitation: *a mock battle* • **mockery** *noun* **1** the act of mocking **2** a ridiculously inadequate imitation

MOD *abbrev* Ministry of Defence

Mod *noun* an annual festival of Gaelic music and literature

modal verb *noun, grammar* a verb that modifies the sense of a main verb, *eg* can, may, must, *etc*

mode *noun* **1** a way of behaving or doing something **2** any of several settings of a machine that make it perform different functions

model noun 1 any of several types or designs of a thing 2 a small-scale copy of something: model railway 3 a living person who poses for an artist 4 someone employed to wear and display new clothes ◇ adj 1 acting as a model 2 of an excellent kind worthy of being copied; perfect: model behaviour ◇ verb (**modelling**, **modelled**) 1 make a model of 2 shape according to a particular pattern 3 wear and display (clothes)

modem noun a device that transmits information from a computer along telephone or broadband cables

moderate verb make or become less great or severe ◇ adj 1 keeping within reason; not extreme 2 of average quality, ability, etc • **moderately** adv • **moderation** noun 1 a lessening or calming down 2 the practice of not going to extremes

modern adj belonging to the present or to recent times; not old or old-fashioned • **modernity** noun • **modernize** verb bring up to date

modest adj 1 not exaggerating achievements; not boastful 2 not very large: modest salary 3 of clothes; not revealing much bare flesh; decent • **modesty** noun

modicum noun (plural **modicums**) formal a small quantity or amount: a modicum of kindness

modify verb (**modifies**, **modifying**, **modified**) 1 make a change in: modified my design 2 make less extreme: modified his demands • **modification** noun

modish adj fashionable • **modishly** adv • **modishness** noun

modular adj of or composed of separate units

modulate verb 1 vary or soften in tone or pitch 2 music change key • **modulation** noun

module noun 1 a course forming a unit in an educational scheme 2 a separate, self-contained section of a spacecraft 3 architecture a standard unit of size

modus operandi noun a method of working

modus vivendi noun a way of life or living

mogul noun 1 a powerful businessman or businesswoman; a magnate 2 a mound of hard snow forming an obstacle on a ski-slope

mohair noun 1 the long silky hair of an Angora goat 2 fabric made from this

Mohammed noun the prophet who was the founder of Islam

moist adj very slightly wet; damp • **moisten** verb make slightly wet; dampen

moisture noun water or other liquid in tiny drops in the atmosphere or on a surface

moisturize verb add moisture to • **moisturizer** noun a cosmetic cream that restores moisture to the skin

molar noun a back tooth used for grinding food

molasses sing noun a thick dark syrup left when sugar is refined

mole¹ noun 1 a small burrowing animal with tiny eyes and soft fur 2 a spy who successfully infiltrates a rival organization • **molehill** noun a small heap of earth thrown up by a burrowing mole

mole² noun a small dark spot on the skin, often raised

molecule noun the smallest part of a substance that has the same qualities as the substance itself • **molecular** adj

molest verb 1 injure or abuse sexually 2 old annoy or torment • **molester** noun

moll noun a gangster's girlfriend

mollify *verb* (**mollifies**, **mollifying**, **mollified**) cause to become less angry or hostile

mollusc *noun* one of a group of boneless animals, usually with hard shells, *eg* shellfish and snails

mollycoddle *verb* treat with too much care or protection; pamper

molten *adj* of metal *etc*: melted and therefore in liquid form

moment *noun* **1** a very short space of time; an instant **2** *formal* importance

momentary *adj* lasting only for a moment • **momentarily** *adv*

momentous *adj* of great importance

momentum *noun* (*plural* **momenta**) the force of a moving body

monarch *noun* a king, queen, emperor or empress • **monarchist** *noun* someone who believes in government by a monarch

monarchy *noun* (*plural* **monarchies**) **1** government by a monarch **2** an area governed by a monarch

monastery *noun* (*plural* **monasteries**) a building housing a community of monks • **monastic** *adj* of or like monasteries or monks • **monasticism** *noun* the way of life in a monastery

Monday *noun* the second day of the week

monetarism *noun* an economic policy based on control of a country's money supply • **monetarist** *noun & adj*

monetary *adj* of money or coinage

money *noun* **1** coins and banknotes used for payment **2** wealth • **moneyed** *or* **monied** *adj* wealthy

mongoose *noun* (*plural* **mongooses**) a small weasel-like animal that kills snakes

mongrel *noun* an animal of mixed breed

moniker *or* **monicker** *noun* a nickname

monitor *noun* **1** a computer screen **2** an instrument used to check the operation of a system or apparatus **3** a screen in a television studio showing the picture being transmitted **4** a school pupil given certain responsibilities ◇ *verb* keep a check on

monk *noun* a member of a male religious community living secluded in a monastery

monkey *noun* (*plural* **monkeys**) **1** a long-tailed mammal that walks on four legs **2** a mischievous child • **monkey nut** *noun* a peanut • **monkey puzzle** *noun* a pine tree with prickly spines along its branches • **monkey wrench** *noun* an adjustable spanner • **monkey about** fool about

monkfish *noun* a sea fish with a very wide mouth, used as food

mono *adj* short for **monophonic** ◇ *noun*, *informal* **1** monophonic sound reproduction **2** a monophonic ringtone on a mobile phone

mono- *prefix* one, single: *monolingual*

monochrome *adj* **1** black and white **2** in one colour

monocle *noun* a single lens worn to correct sight in one eye

monogamy *noun* marriage to one husband or wife at a time • **monogamous** *adj*

monogram *noun* two or more letters, usually initials, made into a single design

monolith *noun* **1** an upright block of stone, *esp* one erected in prehistoric times **2** a large powerful organization considered as a single uniform entity, not a diverse collection of individuals • **monolithic** *adj* frustratingly or boringly uniform

monologue *noun* a long speech by one person

monophonic *adjective* reproducing sound on one channel only

monoplane *noun* an aeroplane with a single pair of wings

monopolize *verb* **1** take up the whole of: *monopolizing the conversation* **2** have exclusive rights to

monopoly *noun* (*plural* **monopolies**) **1** an exclusive right to make or sell something **2** complete unshared possession, control, *etc*

monorail *noun* a railway on which the trains run along a single rail

monosyllable *noun* a word of one syllable ● **monosyllabic** *adj* using very few words, *esp* so few as to appear rude or hostile

monotone *noun* a single, unchanging tone

monotonous *adj* **1** unchanging and dull **2** in a single tone ● **monotonously** *adv*

monotony *noun* boring lack of variety

monsoon *noun* **1** a wind that blows in the Indian Ocean **2** the rainy season caused by the south-west monsoon in summer

mons pubis *noun* the soft mound of tissue above the human genitals

monster *noun* **1** a huge terrifying creature **2** something of unusual size or appearance **3** an evil person ◇ *adj, informal* huge

monstrosity *noun* (*plural* **monstrosities**) **1** something unnatural or outrageous **2** something very ugly

monstrous *adj* **1** huge and *usu* ugly **2** outrageous or extremely cruel

montage /mon-*tazh*/ *noun* **1** a picture made up of bits of other pictures **2** in a film: a sequence of short clips, *esp* one that condenses events taking place over a long period

month *noun* a twelfth part of a year, approximately four weeks

monthly *adj & adv* happening once a month ◇ *noun* (*plural* **monthlies**) a magazine *etc* published once a month

monument *noun* a building, pillar, tomb, *etc* built in memory of someone or an event

monumental *adj* **1** extremely large; enormous **2** of monuments or in the form of a monument ● **monumentally** *adv*

moo *noun* the sound made by a cow

mooch *verb* **1** get things by asking; cadge **2** wander about aimlessly

mood *noun* the state of a person's feelings or temper

moody *adj* (**moodier**, **moodiest**) **1** often changing in mood **2** bad-tempered ● **moodily** *adv* ● **moodiness** *noun*

mooli *noun* a long white root vegetable from E Africa

moon *noun* the heavenly body that travels round the earth once each month and reflects light from the sun ◇ *verb* **1** show your naked bottom in public as a joke **2** *dated* spend time daydreaming, *esp* about someone you love ● **moonbeam** *noun* a beam of light from the moon ● **moonlight** *noun* the light of the moon ◇ *verb* work secretly and often illegally at a second job ● **moonshine** *noun* **1** the shining of the moon **2** foolish ideas or talk; rubbish ● **moonstone** *noun* a precious stone with a pearly shine

moor *noun* a large stretch of open ground, often covered with heather ◇ *verb* tie up or anchor (a ship *etc*) ● **moorhen** *noun* a water bird that is a female coot ● **moorings** *plural noun* **1** the place where a ship is moored **2** the anchor, rope, *etc* holding it ● **moorland** *noun* a stretch of moor

moose *noun* (*plural* **moose**) a large deer-like animal found in N America

moot point *noun* an issue about

which people have very different opinions

mop noun 1 a pad of sponge or a bunch of short pieces of coarse yarn etc on a handle for washing or cleaning 2 a thick head of hair ◇ verb (**mopping**, **mopped**) 1 clean with a mop 2 clean or wipe: mopped his brow • **mop up** clean up

mope verb be unhappy and gloomy

moped noun a lightweight motorcycle that is pedalled to start the engine

moquette noun fabric with a velvety pile and canvas backing, used for upholstery

moraine noun a line of rocks and gravel left by a glacier

moral adj 1 relating to standards of behaviour and character 2 of correct or acceptable behaviour or character ◇ noun 1 (**morals**) principles and standards of (esp sexual) behaviour 2 the lesson of a story • **morality** noun moral standards • **moralize** verb 1 speak about morals in a critical or lecturing way 2 draw a lesson from a story or event • **moral support** noun encouragement without active help • **moral victory** noun a failure that can really be seen as a success

morale /muh-rahl/ noun spirit and confidence

morass /muh-ras/ noun (plural **morasses**) 1 a bewildering mass of something: a morass of regulations 2 a marsh or bog

moratorium noun (plural **moratoria**) an official suspension or temporary ban

morbid adj 1 too concerned with gloomy, unpleasant things 2 diseased or otherwise unhealthy • **morbidity** noun • **morbidly** adv

mordant adj sharply sarcastic or critical ◇ noun a substance used to fix dye or make paint stick to a surface

more adj a greater number or amount

of: more money ◇ adv to a greater extent: more beautiful/more than I can say ◇ noun 1 a greater proportion or amount 2 a further or additional number: more where this came from

moreish adj, informal of food etc: enjoyable, making you want more

morel /muh-rel/ noun a mushroom with a honeycombed cap

morello /muh-rel-oh/ noun a sour-tasting cherry

moreover adv, formal besides

mores /maw-rehz/ plural noun customs that reflect the values of a particular society

morganatic adj of a marriage: in which the woman has no claim to the title or property of her husband

morgue /mawg/ noun a place where dead bodies are laid, awaiting identification etc

moribund adj 1 dying 2 lacking strength or liveliness

morn noun, formal morning

morning noun the part of the day before noon ◇ adj of or in the morning • **morning-after pill** noun a contraceptive pill that can be taken two or three days after sex • **morning star** noun Venus when it rises before the sun

morocco noun a fine goatskin leather first brought from Morocco

moron noun a very stupid person; an idiot • **moronic** adj

morose adj silently gloomy or bad-tempered • **morosely** adv

morphine noun a pain-killing drug

morphology noun the study of the forms of words • **morphological** adj • **morphologist** noun

morris dance noun a traditional English country dance in which male dancers carry sticks and wear bells

morrow noun, old: **the morrow** the

day after the day in question

morse noun a signalling code of signals made up of dots and dashes

morsel noun a small piece, eg of food

mortal adj **1** liable to die **2** causing death; deadly: mortal injury ◇ noun a human being • **mortally** adv fatally: mortally wounded

mortality noun (plural **mortalities**) **1** the state of being mortal **2** death **3** frequency of death; death-rate: infant mortality

mortar noun **1** a mixture of lime, sand and water, used for fixing stones etc **2** a short wide gun that fires shells over short distances **3** a heavy bowl for crushing and grinding substances with a pestle

mortarboard noun a university or college cap with a square flat top

mortgage noun a sum of money lent for the purpose of buying, or one of several regular repayments of the sum ◇ verb offer (buildings etc) as security for money borrowed

mortice another spelling of **mortise**

mortician noun, US an undertaker

mortify verb (**mortifies**, **mortifying**, **mortified**) **1** cause to feel ashamed or humble **2** of a part of the flesh: die • **mortification** noun

mortise or **mortice** noun a hole in a piece of wood that receives the shaped end (**tenon**) of another piece • **mortise lock** or **mortice lock** noun a lock whose mechanism is sunk into the edge of a door

mortuary noun (plural **mortuaries**) a place where dead bodies are kept before burial or cremation

mosaic noun a picture or design made up of many small pieces of coloured glass, stone, etc

Moses basket noun a portable cot for babies

Moslem another spelling of **Muslim**

mosque noun an Islamic place of worship

mosquito noun (plural **mosquitoes** or **mosquitos**) a biting or blood-sucking insect, often carrying disease

moss noun (plural **mosses**) a very small flowerless plant, found in moist places • **mossy** adj covered with moss

most adj the greatest number or amount of: most children attend school regularly ◇ adv **1** very: most grateful **2** to the greatest extent: the most ill of the family ◇ noun the greatest number or amount: he got most • **mostly** adv in most cases; mainly • **at most** not more than • **for the most part** mostly

MOT noun a compulsory annual check of the roadworthiness of vehicles over a certain age

mote noun a particle of dust; a speck

motel noun a hotel built to accommodate travelling motorists and their vehicles

motet noun a piece of church music for several voices

moth noun **1** a flying insect similar to a butterfly but seen mostly at night **2** the cloth-eating grub of the clothes-moth • **moth-eaten** adj **1** full of holes made by moths **2** in a worn condition; tatty

mothball noun a small ball of chemical used to protect clothes from moths ◇ verb (also **put in mothballs**) postpone or put aside for later use etc

mother noun **1** a female parent **2** the female head of a convent ◇ verb **1** treat (someone) with great or excessive care **2** be the mother of • **motherboard** noun, comput a printed circuit board that holds a computer's principal components and into which other boards can be slotted • **motherhood** noun the state of being a mother • **mother-in-law** *noun* the mother of your husband or wife • **mother-in-law's tongue** *noun* a houseplant with thick spiky leaves • **motherland** *noun* the country of your birth • **motherly** *adj* of or like a mother • **mother-of-pearl** *noun* a hard shiny substance that forms inside certain shells • **mother tongue** *noun* a native language

motif *noun* (*plural* **motifs**) **1** a single shape or symbol in a complex pattern **2** a distinctive feature or idea in a piece of music, a play, *etc*

Do not confuse with: **motive**

---

motion *noun* **1** the act or state of moving **2** a single movement **3** a suggestion put before a meeting for discussion ◇ *verb* **1** make a signal by a movement or gesture **2** direct (someone) in this way: *the policeman motioned us forward* • **motionless** *adj* not moving

motive *noun* the cause of someone's actions; a reason • **motivate** *verb* cause (someone) to act in a certain way • **motivation** *noun*

Do not confuse with: **motif**

---

motley *adj* made up of different kinds or colours

motocross *noun* the sport of motorcycle racing across rough terrain

motor *noun* **1** an engine that creates motion **2** *slang* a car ◇ *verb* **1** *slang* travel very fast **2** *dated* travel by car • **motorcade** *noun* a procession of cars carrying a head of state *etc* • **motorist** *noun* someone who drives a car • **motorize** *verb* supply with an engine

motorbike or **motorcycle** *noun* a two-wheeled vehicle with a petrol-driven engine • **motorcyclist** *noun*

motorway *noun* a major road with two or more lanes on each carriageway, for fast traffic

mottled *adj* marked with spots or blotches

motto *noun* (*plural* **mottoes**) a phrase that acts as a guiding principle or rule

mould[1] *noun* a shape into which a liquid is poured to take on that shape when it cools or sets: *jelly mould* ◇ *verb* **1** form in a mould **2** control the development of

mould[2] *noun* **1** a fluffy growth on stale food *etc* **2** soil containing rotted leaves *etc* • **mouldy** *adj* affected by mould; stale

moulder *verb* crumble away to dust

moulding *noun* a decorated border of moulded plaster round a ceiling *etc*

moult *verb* of an animal: shed feathers or fur

mound *noun* **1** a small hill **2** a pile

mount *verb* **1** go up; ascend **2** climb on to (a horse, bicycle, *etc*) **3** fix (a picture *etc*) on to a backing or support **4** fix (a gemstone) in a casing **5** organize (*eg* an exhibition or a search) ◇ *noun* **1** a support or backing for display **2** a horse, bicycle, *etc* to ride on **3** *old* a mountain • **The Mounties** *informal* the Canadian mounted police

mountain *noun* **1** a large hill **2** a large quantity • **mountain ash** *noun* the rowan tree • **mountain bike** *noun* a bicycle with a sturdy frame, chunky tyres and often with a suspension system, designed for use on rough terrain • **mountaineer** *noun* someone who climbs mountains

mountainous *adj* **1** having many mountains **2** huge

mountebank *noun*, *dated* someone who deceives or swindles others; a charlatan

mourn *verb* **1** grieve for (someone

dead) **2** be sorrowful • **mourner** noun • **mournful** adj sad

mourning noun **1** the showing of grief **2** the period during which someone grieves **3** dark-coloured clothes traditionally worn by mourners

mouse noun (plural **mice**) **1** a small gnawing animal found in houses and fields **2** a timid and rather uninteresting person **3** comput a device moved by hand that causes corresponding cursor movements on a screen • **mouse mat** noun, comput a non-slip rubberized mat for operating a mouse on

moussaka /moo-sah-kuh/ noun a Greek dish of minced lamb and aubergines topped with a cheese sauce

mousse /moos/ noun a frothy set dish including eggs, cream, etc, either sweet or savoury

moustache or US **mustache** noun a line of unshaved hair above a man's upper lip

mousy adj (**mousier, mousiest**) **1** of a light-brown colour **2** timid and rather uninteresting

mouth noun **1** the opening in the head through which an animal or person eats and makes sounds **2** the point of a river where it flows into the sea **3** any opening or entrance ◇ verb make the shape of (words) with your lips but without sounding them • **mouthful** noun (plural **mouthfuls**) as much as fills the mouth • **mouth organ** noun a small wind instrument moved across the lips

mouthpiece noun **1** the part of a musical instrument, tobacco-pipe, etc held in the mouth **2** someone who speaks for others

move verb **1** (cause to) change place or position **2** change your house **3** affect the feelings of, esp cause to feel tearful **4** rouse into action **5** propose or suggest formally ◇ noun **1** a thing that someone does; an action **2** a

change of house **3** a shifting of pieces in a game of chess etc • **movable** adj able to be moved, changed, etc

movement noun **1** the act or manner of moving **2** a change of position **3** a division of a long piece of classical music **4** a group of people united in a common aim: the peace movement **5** an organized attempt to achieve an aim: the movement to reform the divorce laws

movie noun a cinema film • **the movies** the cinema

moving adj **1** in motion **2** causing emotion, esp tearfulness • **movingly** adv

mow verb (**mowing, mowed, mown**) **1** cut (grass, hay, etc) with a scythe or machine (**mow down**) destroy in great numbers • **mower** noun a machine for mowing

mozzarella /mot-suh-rel-uh/ noun a soft, white Italian curd cheese

MP abbrev **1** Member of Parliament **2** Military Police

mpg abbrev miles per gallon

mph abbrev miles per hour

MPhil abbrev Master of Philosophy

MP3 abbrev, comput MPEG-1 Layer 3, a compressed file format that allows fast downloading of audio data from the Internet

Mr noun (short for **mister**) the form of address used before a man's surname

Mrs noun (short for **mistress**) the form of address used before a married woman's surname

MRSA abbrev methicillin-resistant Staphylococcus aureus, a bacterium resistant to most antibiotics

MS abbrev **1** multiple sclerosis **2** manuscript

Ms noun a form of address used before the surname of a married or unmarried woman

MSc *abbrev* Master of Science

MSG *abbrev* monosodium glutamate, a food additive widely used in Chinese cooking

much *adv* to or by a great extent: *much faster/hasn't improved much* ◊ *pronoun* **1** a great amount: *much still to be done* **2** something important: *made much of it* ◊ *adj* a great amount of: *the subject of much discussion* • **much the same** nearly the same

mucilage *noun* a sticky or gluey substance

muck *noun* dung, dirt or filth • **muckraking** *noun* looking for scandals to expose

mucous *adj* like or covered by mucus

Do not confuse: **mucous** and **mucus**

---

mucus *noun* slimy fluid secreted by the nose and other membranes as lubrication and protection against disease

mud *noun* wet, soft earth • **mudguard** *noun* a shield or guard over wheels to catch mud splashes

muddle *verb* **1** make confused **2** mix up **3** make a mess of ◊ *noun* **1** a mess **2** a state of confusion

muddy *adj* (**muddier, muddiest**) **1** covered with mud **2** unclear or confused

muesli /myooz-li/ *noun* a mixture of grains, nuts and fruit eaten with milk as a breakfast food

muezzin /moo-ez-in/ *noun* an Islamic priest who calls out the hour of prayer from a mosque

muff¹ *noun* a tube of warm fabric to cover and keep the hands warm

muff² *verb* fail in an opportunity, *eg* to catch a ball

muffin *noun* **1** a round, flat breadlike cake toasted and eaten hot with butter **2** *US* a small sweet cake

muffle *verb* **1** deaden (a sound) **2** wrap up for warmth *etc*

muffler *noun* **1** a scarf **2** *US* a silencer for a car

mufti *noun* clothes worn by soldiers *etc* when off duty

mug¹ *noun* **1** a large cup that has no accompanying saucer **2** *informal* a stupid person **3** *informal* the face

mug² *verb* (**mugging, mugged**) attack and rob (someone) in the street • **mugger** *noun*

mug³ *verb*: **mug up** *informal* study hard in preparation for a test; swot up

muggy *adj* (**muggier, muggiest**) of weather: unpleasantly warm, damp and airless • **mugginess** *noun*

mugwump *noun, US* **1** a big chief, a boss **2** a political independent or maverick

mulatto *noun* (*plural* **mulattoes**) *old* a person of mixed race

mulberry *noun* (*plural* **mulberries**) **1** a tree on whose leaves silkworms are fed **2** its purple berry

mulch *noun* loose straw *etc* laid down to protect plant roots ◊ *verb* cover with mulch

mule¹ *noun* an animal bred from a horse and an ass

mule² *noun* a backless slipper

mulish *adj* stubborn

mullah *noun* an Islamic teacher

mulled *adj* of wine *etc*: mixed with spices and served warm

mullet *noun* a small edible sea fish

mulligatawny *noun* an East Indian curried soup

mullion *noun* an upright division in a window

mull over *verb* think carefully about in order to reach a decision; ponder over

multi- *prefix* many: *multipurpose tools*

multicoloured *adj* many-coloured

multicultural *adj* consisting of people of different racial and religious cultures • **multiculturalism** *noun*

multifarious *adj* of many kinds

multimedia *adj* of a computer: able to run various sound and visual applications

multimillionaire *noun* someone who has property worth several million pounds (or dollars)

multinational *noun* a very large company that trades in several different countries

multiple *adj* **1** affecting many parts: *multiple injuries* **2** involving many things of the same sort, *eg* vehicles: *a multiple crash* ◇ *noun* a number or quantity that contains another an exact number of times • **multiple sclerosis** *noun* a progressive nerve disease resulting in paralysis (shortened to **MS**)

multiplex *noun* a cinema with several screens showing different films

multiply *verb* (**multiplies, multiplying, multiplied**) **1** increase **2** increase a number by adding it to itself a certain number of times: *2 multiplied by 3 is 6* • **multiplication** *noun* the act of multiplying • **multiplier** *noun* the number by which another is to be multiplied • **a multiplicity of** a great number of

multitasking *noun, comput* the action of running several processes simultaneously

multitude *noun* a great number; a crowd • **multitudinous** *adj, formal* very many

mum¹ *noun, informal* mother

mum² *adj* silent

mumble *verb* speak in a low voice and unclearly

mummy¹ *noun* (*plural* **mummies**) *informal* mother

mummy² *noun* (*plural* **mummies**) a dead body preserved by wrapping in bandages and treating with wax, spices, *etc* • **mummify** *verb* (**mummifies, mummifying, mummified**) make into a mummy

mumps *sing noun* an infectious disease affecting glands at the side of the neck, causing swelling

munch *verb* chew noisily • **the munchies** *informal* a craving for food, induced by drugs or alcohol

mundane *adj* boringly ordinary or unexceptional; everyday

municipal *adj* of or owned by a city or town • **municipality** *noun* an area covered by local government; a town or city

munificent *adj, formal* very generous • **munificence** *noun*

munitions *plural noun* weapons and ammunition used in war

Munro *noun* (*plural* **Munros**) a British or Irish mountain over 3000 feet high • **Munro-bagger** *noun* someone who aims to climb every Munro

mural *adj* of or on a wall ◇ *noun* a painting or design on a wall

murder *verb* kill someone unlawfully and on purpose ◇ *noun* the act of murdering • **murderer** *noun* someone who commits murder • **murderous** *adj* capable or guilty of murder; wicked

murky *adj* (**murkier, murkiest**) frighteningly or depressingly dark; gloomy • **murkiness** *noun*

murmur *noun* **1** a low continuous sound **2** a hushed way of speaking ◇ *verb* **1** make a murmur **2** make complaints in an irritated way; grumble

Murphy's law noun the law that if something can go wrong, it will

muscat noun a musky variety of grape, used to make wine

muscle noun 1 fleshy tissue that contracts and stretches to cause body movements 2 an area of this in the body 3 physical strength or power

muscular adj 1 of muscles 2 with well-developed muscles • **muscular dystrophy** noun a hereditary disease in which the muscles gradually deteriorate

Muse noun one of the nine goddesses of poetry, music, dancing, etc in classical mythology

muse verb think (over) in a quiet, leisurely way

museum noun (plural **museums**) a building for housing and displaying objects of artistic, scientific or historic interest

mush noun 1 any soft, pulpy substance 2 an overly sentimental film, song, etc

mushroom noun an edible fungus, usually umbrella-shaped ◇ verb grow very quickly: buildings mushroomed all over town

mushy adj (**mushier**, **mushiest**) 1 soft and pulpy 2 overly sentimental • **mushiness** noun

music noun 1 sounds produced by instruments, with or without voices 2 the art of arranging and combining such sounds 3 symbols representing such sounds, or sheets or books containing these 4 a sweet or pleasant sound

musical adj 1 of music 2 sounding sweet or pleasant 3 having a talent for music ◇ noun a play with singing • **musically** adv

musician noun 1 someone who plays a musical instrument 2 a specialist in music

musicology noun the study of music • **musicologist** noun

musk noun a strong perfume obtained from the male musk deer or artificially • **musk deer** noun a small hornless deer found in Central Asia • **muskrat** noun a musquash • **musky** adj

musket noun an early kind of rifle loaded through the barrel • **musketeer** noun a soldier armed with a musket

Muslim or **Moslem** noun a follower of the Islamic religion ◇ adj Islamic

muslin noun a fine, soft cotton cloth

musquash noun (plural **musquashes**) a large N American water rat

mussel noun an edible shellfish with two separate halves to its shell

must verb 1 used with another verb to express necessity: I must finish this today 2 expressing compulsion: you must do as you're told 3 expressing certainty or probability: that must be the right answer ◇ noun something that must be done; a necessity

mustache US spelling of **moustache**

mustang noun a N American wild horse

mustard noun 1 a plant with sharp-tasting seeds 2 a hot yellow paste made from its seeds

muster verb gather up or together (eg troops, courage) • **pass muster** be accepted as satisfactory

musty adj (**mustier**, **mustiest**) smelling old and stale • **mustiness** noun

mutable adj changeable

mute adj 1 not able to speak 2 saying nothing; silent 3 of a letter in a word: not pronounced ◇ noun, dated a mute person

muted adj 1 of a sound: made quieter, hushed 2 of a colour: not bright

mutilate verb 1 inflict great physical

injury on; maim **2** damage greatly • **mutilation** *noun*

mutiny *verb* (**mutinies**, **mutinying**, **mutinied**) **1** use force to take over from people in power **2** refuse to obey the commands of military officers ◇ *noun* (*plural* **mutinies**) refusal to obey commands; rebellion • **mutineer** *noun* someone who takes part in a mutiny • **mutinous** *adj* refusing to obey orders; rebellious

mutt *noun*, *informal* a dog, *esp* a mongrel

mutter *verb* speak in a low voice, *esp* complainingly; mumble

mutton *noun* meat from a mature sheep

mutual *adj* **1** given by each to the other(s): *mutual help* **2** shared by two or more: *mutual friend* • **mutually** *adv*

Muzak *noun*, *trademark* recorded music played in shops *etc*

muzzle *noun* **1** an animal's nose and mouth **2** a fastening placed over an animal's mouth to prevent it biting **3** the open end of a gun ◇ *verb* **1** put a muzzle on (a dog *etc*) **2** prevent from speaking freely

muzzy *adj* (**muzzier**, **muzziest**) not able to think clearly; confused • **muzziness** *noun*

my *adj* belonging to me: *this is my book*

mycology *noun* the study of fungi • **mycologist** *noun*

mynah *noun* a black bird of SE Asia that can be trained to imitate human speech

myopia *noun* short-sightedness • **myopic** *adj* **1** short-sighted **2** failing to think further ahead than the immediate future

myriad /*mi*-ri-ad/ *noun* a very great number ◇ *adj* very many, countless

myrrh /mur/ *noun* a bitter-tasting resin used in medicines, perfumes, *etc*

myrtle *noun* a type of evergreen shrub with dark blue berries

myself *pronoun* **1** used reflexively: *I can see myself in the mirror* **2** used for emphasis: *I wrote this myself*

mysterious *adj* difficult to understand or explain; puzzling • **mysteriously** *adv* • **mysteriousness** *noun*

mystery *noun* (*plural* **mysteries**) **1** something that cannot be or has not been explained; something puzzling **2** a deep secret

mystic *noun* someone whose life is devoted to trying to achieve direct knowledge of God and religious truths and who meditates for long periods of time • **mystical** *adj* having a secret or sacred meaning beyond ordinary human understanding

mystify *verb* (**mystifies**, **mystifying**, **mystified**) **1** be beyond the understanding of; puzzle **2** cause to be confused

mystique /mis-*teek*/ *noun* an atmosphere of mystery about someone or something

myth *noun* **1** a story about gods, heroes, *etc* of ancient times; a fable **2** something imagined or untrue • **mythical** *adj* **1** of a myth **2** invented or imagined, not real or true

mythology *noun* **1** the study of myths **2** a collection of myths • **mythological** *adj* of myth or mythology • **mythologist** *noun*

myxomatosis *noun* a contagious disease of rabbits

Nn

N *abbrev* **1** north **2** northern

naan *another spelling of* **nan**

nab *verb* (**nabbing**, **nabbed**) *informal* **1** snatch, seize **2** arrest

nabob /neh-bob/ *noun, hist* a local governor in India

nacre *noun* /neh-kuh/ mother-of-pearl

nadir *noun* the lowest point of anything, *eg* despair

naevus *or US* **nevus** /nee-vus/ *noun* (*plural* **naevi** *or US* **nevi**) a birthmark

naff *adj, slang* inferior, crass, tasteless

nag¹ *verb* (**nagging**, **nagged**) **1** find fault with and scold constantly **2** to cause (someone) anxiety or pain ◇ *noun* someone who persistently nags

nag² *noun, derog* an old, worn-out horse

nail *noun* **1** a hard covering protecting the tips of the fingers and toes **2** a thin pointed piece of metal for fastening wood *etc* ◇ *verb* **1** fasten with nails **2** *informal* catch, trap

naive *or* **naïve** /nah-eev/ *adj* **1** inexperienced and too trusting **2** simple and unsophisticated ● **naivety** *or* **naïveté** *noun*

naked *adj* **1** without clothes **2** having no covering **3** blatant: *naked lie* ● **nakedly** *adv* ● **nakedness** *noun*

namby-pamby *adj* oversentimental and feeble

name *noun* **1** a word by which a person, place or thing is known **2** fame, reputation: *making a name for himself* **3** an offensive description: *don't call people names* **4** authority: *I arrest you in the name of the king* ◇ *verb* **1** give a name to **2** speak of by name, mention **3** appoint ● **nameless** *adj* without a name, not named ● **namely** *adv* that is to say ● **nameplate** *noun* a small panel having on it the name of a person, house, *etc* ● **namesake** *noun* someone with the same name as another

nan *or* **naan** *noun* a flat round Indian or Pakistani bread

nanny *noun* (*plural* **nannies**) a children's nurse

nanny-goat *noun* a female goat

nano- *prefix* **1** a thousand millionth: *nanosecond* **2** microscopic in size: *nanotechnology*

nap *noun* **1** a short sleep **2** a woolly or fluffy surface on cloth **3** a card game similar to whist ◇ *verb* (**napping**, **napped**) take a short sleep ● **caught napping** taken unawares

napalm *noun* /neh-pahm/ inflammable petroleum jelly, used to make bombs

nape *noun* the back of the neck

naphtha *noun* a highly flammable, clear liquid, obtained from coal and other substances

napkin *noun* a small piece of cloth or paper for wiping the lips and hands, protecting clothing, *etc* at meals

nappy *noun* (*plural* **nappies**) a piece of cloth, or thick pad, put between a baby's legs to absorb urine and faeces

narcissism *noun* excessive admiration for oneself or one's appearance • **narcissistic** *adj*

narcissus *noun* (*plural* **narcissi** or **narcissuses**) a plant like a daffodil with a white, star-shaped flower

narcotic *noun* a type of drug that brings on sleep or stops pain

nark *noun* a persistent complainer • **narky** *adj* irritable, complaining

narrate *verb* tell a story • **narration** *noun* the telling of a story • **narrative** *noun* a story ◇ *adj* telling a story • **narrator** *noun*

narrow *adj* 1 of small extent from side to side, not wide: *a narrow road* 2 with little to spare: *a narrow escape* 3 restricted, limited: *narrow interests* 4 intolerant or prejudiced: *narrow views* ◇ *verb* make or become narrow • **narrowly** *adv* closely; barely • **narrow-minded** *adj* unwilling to accept or tolerate new ideas • **narrows** *plural noun* a narrow sea passage, a strait

narwal or **narwhal** *noun* a kind of whale with a large tusk

NASA *abbrev, US* National Aeronautics and Space Administration

nasal *adj* 1 of the nose 2 sounded through the nose

nascent *adj* beginning to develop, in an early stage • **nascency** *noun*

nasturtium *noun* a climbing plant with brightly-coloured flowers

nasty (**nastier, nastiest**) *adj* 1 very disagreeable or unpleasant 2 of a problem *etc*: difficult to deal with • **nastily** *adv* • **nastiness** *noun*

natal *adj* of birth

nation *noun* the people living in the same country, or under the same government

national *adj* of or belonging to a nation ◇ *noun* someone belonging to a nation: *a British national* • **national**

anthem *noun* a nation's official song or hymn • **national insurance** *noun* a system of state insurance to which employers and employees contribute • **nationally** *adv*

nationalism *noun* 1 patriotism 2 the desire to bring the people of a nation together under their own government: *Scottish nationalism* • **nationalist** *noun & adj* • **nationalistic** *adj*

nationality *noun* (*plural* **nationalities**) membership of a particular nation

nationalize *verb* place (industries *etc*) under the control of the government • **nationalization** *noun*

native *adj* 1 of the place of one's birth or upbringing: *my native land* 2 of a particular country: *native to Australia* 3 possessed naturally, inborn: *native intelligence* ◇ *noun* 1 someone born in a certain place: *a native of Scotland* 2 an inhabitant of a country from earliest times before the discovery by explorers, settlers, *etc*

Nativity *noun* (**the Nativity**) the birth of Christ

NATO *abbrev* North Atlantic Treaty Organization

natty *adj* (**nattier, nattiest**) *informal* trim, tidy, smart • **nattily** *adv*

natural *adj* 1 of nature 2 produced by nature, not artificial 3 of a quality *etc*: present at birth, not learned afterwards 4 unpretentious, simple 5 of a result *etc*: expected, normal ◇ *noun* 1 someone with a natural ability 2 *music* a note which is neither a sharp nor a flat, shown by the sign (♮) • **natural gas** *noun* gas suitable for burning as fuel, found in the earth or under the sea • **natural history** *noun* the study of animals and plants • **naturalist** *noun* someone who studies animal and plant life • **naturalize** *verb* give the rights of a citizen to (someone born in another country) • **naturally** *adv* 1 by nature, as a natural characteristic: *swimming came naturally to her* **2** using natural methods: *natural childbirth* **3** of course: *naturally, I was angry* • **natural resources** *plural noun* the natural wealth of a country in its forests, minerals, water, *etc* • **natural selection** *noun* evolution by survival of the fittest, who pass their characteristics onto the next generation

nature *noun* **1** the things which make up the physical world, *eg* animals, trees, rivers, mountains, *etc* **2** the qualities which characterize someone or something: *a kindly nature* • **-natured** *adj* (added to another word) having a certain temper or personality: *good-natured*

naturism *noun* the belief in nudity practised openly • **naturist** *noun*

naturopathy *noun* treatment of disease through a combination of herbs, diet, exercise, *etc*

naught *noun* nothing: *plans came to naught*

Do not confuse with: **nought**

---

naughty *adj* (**naughtier, naughtiest**) misbehaving • **naughtily** *adv* • **naughtiness** *noun*

nausea *noun* a feeling of sickness • **nauseate** *verb* make sick, fill with disgust • **nauseated** *adj* sickened, disgusted • **nauseating** *adj* sickening, disgusting • **nauseous** *adj* **1** feeling sick **2** sickening, disgusting

nautical *adj* of sailing, ships or sailors • **nautical mile** *noun* 1.85km (6080ft)

nautilus *noun* (*plural* **nautiluses** or **nautili**) a small sea creature related to the octopus

naval *see* **navy**

nave *noun* the middle or main part of a church

navel *noun* the small hollow in the centre of the front of the belly

navigate *verb* **1** steer or pilot a ship, aircraft, *etc* on its course **2** sail on, over or through • **navigable** *adj* able to be used by ships • **navigation** *noun* the art of navigating • **navigator** *noun* someone who steers or sails a ship *etc*

navvy *noun* (*plural* **navvies**) a labourer working on roads *etc*

navy *noun* (*plural* **navies**) **1** a nation's warships **2** the men and women serving on these • **naval** *adj* of the navy • **navy blue** *noun & adj* very dark blue

nay *adv, old* no

Nazi /*nah*-tsi/ *noun, hist* a member of the German National Socialist Party, a fascist party ruling Germany in 1933–45 • **Nazism** *noun*

NB *or* **nb** *abbrev* note well (from Latin *nota bene*)

NCO *abbrev* non-commissioned officer

NE *abbrev* north-east; north-eastern

neap tide *noun* a type of tide where there is least variation between low and high water

near *adj* **1** not far away in place or time **2** closer of two: *the near bank of the river* **3** closely related: *a near relative* **4** barely avoiding or almost reaching (something): *a near disaster* ◇ *adv* (also **near to**) close to: *came near to hitting him* ◇ *prep* **1** a short distance from: *near the town centre* **2** close to: *near tears* ◇ *verb* approach • **nearby** *adj & adv* to or at a short distance: *a nearby shelter/do you live nearby?* • **nearly** *adv* almost: *nearly four o'clock* • **nearside** *adj* of the side of a vehicle: furthest from the centre of the road (*contrasted with*: **offside**) • **near-sighted** *adj* short-sighted

neat *adj* **1** trim, tidy **2** skilfully done **3** of an alcoholic drink: not diluted with water *etc* • **neaten** *verb*

neb *noun, Scot* a nose

nebula noun (plural **nebulae**) a shining cloud-like appearance in the night sky, produced by very distant stars or by a mass of gas and dust

nebulous adj hazy, vague

necessary adj not able to be done without ◇ noun (plural **necessaries**) something that cannot be done without, such as food, clothing, etc • **necessarily** adv • **necessitate** verb make necessary; force • **necessity** noun 1 something necessary 2 great need; want, poverty

neck noun 1 the part between the head and body 2 a narrow passage or area: neck of a bottle/neck of land • **necktie** noun, US a man's tie • **neck and neck** running side by side, staying exactly equal

necklace noun a string of beads or precious stones etc worn round the neck

necromancer noun someone who works with black magic • **necromancy** noun

necropolis noun (plural **necropolises**) a cemetery

nectar noun 1 the sweet liquid collected from flowers by bees to make honey 2 the drink of the ancient Greek gods 3 a delicious drink

nectarine noun a kind of peach with a smooth skin

née /neh/ adj born (in stating a woman's surname before her marriage): Mrs Janet Brown, née Phillips

need verb 1 be without, be in want of: many people need food 2 require: you need strength for this job ◇ noun 1 necessity, needfulness 2 difficulty, want, poverty • **needful** adj necessary • **needless** adj unnecessary • **needlessly** adv • **needy** adj poor

needle noun 1 a small, sharp piece of steel used in sewing, with a small hole (**eye**) at the top for thread 2 a long thin piece of metal, wood, etc used eg in knitting 3 a thin hollowed-out piece of steel attached to a hypodermic syringe etc 4 the moving pointer in a compass 5 the long, sharp-pointed leaf of a pine, fir, etc 6 a stylus on a record-player • **needlework** noun sewing and embroidery

neep noun, Scot a turnip

ne'er adj, formal never • **ne'er-do-well** noun a lazy, worthless person

nefarious adj very wicked; villainous, shady

negate verb 1 prove the opposite 2 refuse to accept, reject (a proposal etc)

negative adj 1 meaning or saying 'no', as an answer (contrasted with: **positive**) 2 of a person, attitude, etc: pessimistic ◇ noun 1 a word or statement by which something is denied 2 the photographic film, from which prints are made, in which light objects appear dark and dark objects appear light • **negative equity** noun the value of a property falling below that of the mortgage held on it

neglect verb 1 treat carelessly 2 fail to give proper attention to 3 fail to do ◇ noun lack of care and attention • **neglectful** adj

negligée /neg-li-zheh/ noun a women's loose dressing-gown made of thin material

negligent adj careless • **negligence** noun • **negligently** adv

---

Do not confuse: **negligent** and **negligible**

---

negligible adj not worth thinking about, very small: a negligible amount

negotiate verb 1 discuss a subject (with) in order to reach agreement 2 arrange (a treaty, payment, etc) 3 get past (an obstacle or difficulty) • **negotiable** adj able to be negotiated

• **negotiation** *noun* • **negotiator** *noun*

Negro *noun* (*plural* **Negroes**) *offensive* a Black African, or Black person of African descent • **negroid** *adj* Black, dark-skinned

neigh *verb* cry like a horse ◇ *noun* a horse's cry

neighbour *or US* **neighbor** *noun* someone who lives near another • **neighbourhood** *noun* surrounding district or area: *in the neighbourhood of Paris/a poor neighbourhood* • **neighbouring** *adj* near or next in position • **neighbourly** *adj* friendly and helpful • **in the neighbourhood of** approximately, nearly

neither *adj & pronoun* not either: *neither bus goes that way/neither can afford it* ◇ *conj* (sometimes with **nor**) used to show alternatives in the negative: *neither Bill or David knew the answer/she is neither eating nor sleeping*

nematode *noun* a long thin parasitic worm

nemesis *noun* fate, punishment that is bound to follow wrongdoing

neo- *prefix* new

neolithic *adj* relating to the later Stone Age

neologism *noun* a new word or expression • **neologistic** *adj*

neonatal *adj* of newly-born babies

neon lighting *noun* a form of lighting containing neon and giving a red glow, used *eg* for advertising signs

neophyte *noun* **1** a new convert **2** a novice, a beginner

nephew *noun* the son of a brother or sister, or of a brother-in-law or sister-in-law

nepotism *noun* favouritism towards one's relations, *esp* when making official appointments • **nepotistic** *adj*

nerd *noun* a socially inept, irritating person • **nerdish** *adj*

nerve *noun* **1** one of the fibres which carry feeling from all parts of the body to the brain **2** courage, coolness **3** *informal* impudence, cheek ◇ *verb* strengthen the nerve or will of • **nervy** *adj* excitable, jumpy

nervous *adj* **1** of the nerves **2** easily excited or frightened; timid • **nervously** *adv* • **nervousness** *noun* • **nervous system** *noun* the brain, spinal cord and nerves of an animal or human being

nest *noun* **1** a structure in which birds (and some animals and insects) live and rear their young **2** a shelter, a den ◇ *verb* build a nest and live in it • **nestling** *noun* a young newly hatched bird

nestle /nes-ul/ *verb* **1** lie close together as in a nest **2** settle comfortably

Net *noun* (**the Net**) the Internet

net *noun* **1** a loose arrangement of crossed and knotted cord, string or thread, used for catching fish, wearing over the hair, *etc* **2** fine meshed material, used to make curtains, petticoats, *etc* ◇ *adj* (also **nett**) **1** of profit *etc*: remaining after expenses and taxes have been paid **2** of weight: not including packaging ◇ *verb* (**netting**, **netted**) **1** catch or cover with a net **2** put (a ball) into a net **3** make by way of profit • **netball** *noun* a team game in which a ball is thrown into a high net • **netting** *noun* fabric of netted string, wire, *etc* • **network** *noun* **1** an arrangement of lines crossing one another **2** a widespread organization **3** a system of linked computers, radio stations, *etc*

nether *adj* lower • **nethermost** *adj* lowest

nett *see* **net**

nettle *noun* a plant covered with hairs which sting sharply ◇ *verb* make angry, provoke • **nettlerash** *noun* a skin rash, like that caused by a sting from a nettle

neur- or **neuro-** prefix of the nerves: neuromuscular

neuralgia noun a pain in the nerves, esp in those of the head and face

neurosis noun (plural **neuroses**) a type of mental illness in which the patient suffers from extreme anxiety • **neurotic** adj 1 suffering from neurosis 2 loosely obsessive or hypersensitive ◇ noun someone suffering from neurosis • **neurotically** adv

neuter adj 1 grammar neither masculine nor feminine 2 of an animal: neither male nor female 3 of an animal: infertile, sterile ◇ verb sterilize (an animal)

neutral adj 1 taking no side in a quarrel or war 2 of a colour: not strong or definite ◇ noun 1 someone or a nation that takes no side in a war etc 2 the gear position used when a vehicle is remaining still • **neutrality** noun • **neutralize** verb 1 make neutral 2 make useless or harmless

neutrino noun (plural **neutrinos**) an uncharged particle with zero mass when at rest

neutron noun one of the uncharged particles which, together with protons, make up the nucleus of an atom • **neutron bomb** noun a nuclear bomb that kills people by intense radiation but leaves buildings intact

never adv 1 not ever; at no time 2 under no circumstances • **nevertheless** adv in spite of that: I hate football, but I'll come nevertheless

nevus US spelling of **naevus**

new adj 1 recent; not seen or known before 2 not used or worn; fresh • **newbie** noun someone new to a scene, esp the Internet • **newcomer** noun someone lately arrived • **newfangled** adj objectionably modern • **newly** adv • **newness** noun

news sing noun 1 report of a recent event 2 new information • **newsagent**

noun a shopkeeper who sells newspapers • **newsgroup** noun, comput a special-interest group of Internet users • **newspaper** noun a set of folded sheets of paper containing news, printed daily or weekly

newt noun a small lizard-like animal, living on land and in water

next adj nearest, closest in place, time, etc: the next page ◇ adv in the nearest place or at the nearest time: she won and I came next/do that sum next

nexus noun a bond, a connection

NHS abbrev National Health Service

nib noun a pen point

nibble verb take little bites (of) ◇ noun a little bite

nicad adj of a battery: having electrodes of nickel and cadmium

NICAM or **Nicam** noun near-instantaneous companded audio multiplexing, a system for transmitting digital sound with standard TV signals

nice adj 1 agreeable, pleasant 2 careful, precise, exact: a nice distinction • **nicely** adv pleasantly; very well

nicety noun (plural **niceties**) a small fine detail • **to a nicety** with great exactness

niche /neesh/ noun 1 a hollow in a wall for a statue, vase, etc 2 a suitable place in life: she hasn't yet found her niche 3 a gap in a market for a type of product

nick noun 1 a little cut, a notch 2 slang prison, jail ◇ verb 1 cut notches in 2 slang steal 3 slang arrest

nickel noun 1 a greyish-white metal used for mixing with other metals and for plating 2 US a 5-cent coin

nickname noun an informal name used instead of someone's real name, eg for fun or as an insult

nicotine noun a poisonous

substance contained in tobacco

niece *noun* the daughter of a brother or sister, or of a brother-in-law or sister-in-law

niff *noun, slang* a bad smell

nifty *adj* (**niftier, niftiest**) *slang* **1** speedy, agile **2** fine, smart, neat

niggardly *adj* mean, stingy

nigger *noun, offensive* a Black man or woman

niggle *verb* irritate, rankle ◇ *noun* **1** an irritation **2** a minor criticism • **niggling** *adj* **1** of a worry or fear: small but always present **2** unimportant, trivial, fussy

nigh *adj, old* near

night *noun* **1** the period of darkness between sunset and sunrise **2** darkness ◇ *adj* **1** of or for night **2** happening, active, *etc* at night • **nightdress** or **nightgown** *noun* a garment worn in bed • **nightfall** *noun* the beginning of night • **nightly** *adj & adv* **1** by night **2** every night • **night-watchman** *noun* someone who looks after a building during the night

nightingale *noun* a small bird, the male of which sings beautifully, chiefly at night

nightmare *noun* a frightening dream

nightshade *noun* a family of plants some of which have poisonous berries, *eg* deadly nightshade

nihilism *noun* belief in nothing, extreme scepticism • **nihilist** *noun* • **nihilistic** *adj*

nil *noun* nothing

nimble *adj* quick and neat, agile • **nimbleness** *noun* • **nimbly** *adv*

nimbus *noun* a rain cloud

NIMBY *abbrev* not in my back yard, *ie* not wanting something to take place in your neighbourhood

nine *noun* the number 9 ◇ *adj* 9 in number

ninepins *noun* a game in which nine bottle-shaped objects are set up and knocked down by a ball

nineteen *noun* the number 19 ◇ *adj* 19 in number • **nineteenth** *adj* the last of a series of nineteen ◇ *noun* one of nineteen equal parts

ninety *noun* the number 90 ◇ *adj* 90 in number • **ninetieth** *adj* the last of a series of ninety ◇ *noun* one of ninety equal parts

ninja *noun, hist* an assassin in feudal Japan, trained in martial arts

ninny *noun* (*plural* **ninnies**) a fool

ninth *adj* the last of a series of nine ◇ *noun* one of nine equal parts

nip *verb* (**nipping, nipped**) **1** pinch, squeeze tightly **2** be stingingly painful **3** bite, cut (off) **4** check the growth of, damage (plants *etc*) **5** *informal* go nimbly or quickly ◇ *noun* **1** a pinch **2** a sharp coldness in the weather: *a nip in the air* **3** a small amount: *nip of whisky* • **nip and tuck** *informal* cosmetic surgery

nipper *noun, informal* **1** a child, a youngster **2** (**nippers**) pincers, pliers

nipple *noun* the pointed part of the breast from which a baby sucks milk

nippy *adj* (**nippier, nippiest**) *informal* **1** speedy, nimble **2** frosty, very cold

Nirvana *noun* **1** the state to which a Buddhist or Hindu aspires **2** (**nirvana**) a blissful state

nit *noun* the egg of a louse or other small insect

nitrate *noun* a substance formed from nitric acid, often used as a soil fertilizer

nitric acid *noun* a strong acid containing nitrogen

nitrogen *noun* a gas forming nearly four-fifths of ordinary air • **nitroglycerine** *noun* a powerful kind of explosive

nitty-gritty *noun, informal* the

essential part of any matter, situation or activity

nitwit *noun* a very stupid person

No or **no** *abbrev* number

no *adj* 1 not any: *they have no money* 2 not a: *he is no cheat* ◇ *adv* not at all: *the patient is no better* ◇ *exclam* expressing a negative: *are you feeling better today? No* ◇ *noun* (*plural* **noes** or **nos**) 1 a refusal 2 a vote against • **no-ball** *noun, cricket* a bowled ball disallowed by the rules • **nobody** *pronoun* not any person ◇ *noun* someone of no importance: *just a nobody* • **no one** or **no-one** *pronoun* not any person, nobody • **no-show** *noun* someone expected who does not arrive • **no-win** *adj* of a situation: in which you are bound to lose or fail • **no dice** no answer, no success • **no doubt** surely • **no go** not possible, futile • **no joke** not something to laugh about or dismiss • **no way** *informal* under no circumstances

nobble *verb, slang* 1 drug or interfere with (a horse) to stop it winning a race 2 get hold of 3 persuade, coerce 4 seize, arrest

Nobel prize *noun* an annual international prize awarded for achievements in arts, science, politics, *etc*

noble *adj* 1 honourable 2 of aristocratic birth ◇ *noun* an aristocrat • **nobility** *noun* 1 the aristocracy 2 goodness of mind or character • **nobleman, noblewoman** *nouns* • **nobly** *adv*

nobody see **no**

nocturnal *adj* happening or active at night • **nocturnally** *adv*

nocturne *noun* a piece of music intended to have the dreamy atmosphere of night-time

nod *verb* (**nodding, nodded**) 1 bend the head forward quickly, often as a sign of agreement 2 let the head drop in weariness ◇ *noun* an action of nodding • **nodding acquaintance**

with a slight knowledge of • **nod off** fall asleep

noddle *noun, slang* 1 the head 2 intelligence

node *noun* 1 the swollen part of a branch or twig where a leaf-stalk joins it 2 a swelling

nodule *noun* a small rounded lump

Noël *noun* Christmas

noise *noun* a sound, often one which is loud or harsh ◇ *verb, old* spread (a rumour *etc*) • **noiseless** *adj* • **noisy** *adj* making a loud sound

nomad *noun* 1 one of a group of people without a fixed home who wander with their animals in search of pasture 2 someone who wanders from place to place • **nomadic** *adj*

no-man's-land *noun* land owned by no one, *esp* that lying between two opposing armies

nom de plume *noun* (*plural* **noms de plume**) a pen-name

nomenclature *noun* 1 a system of naming 2 names

nominal *adj* 1 in name only 2 very small compared to actual value: *a nominal fee for his services*

nominate *verb* propose (someone) for a post or for election; appoint • **nomination** *noun* • **nominee** *noun* someone whose name is put forward for a post

non- *prefix* not (used with many words to change their meaning to the opposite): *non-violence/non-smoking*

nonagenarian *noun* someone from ninety to ninety-nine years old

nonce *noun*: **for the nonce** for the moment, in the meantime

nonchalant *adj* not easily roused or upset, cool • **nonchalance** *noun* • **nonchalantly** *adv*

non-commissioned *adj* belonging to the lower ranks of army officers

non-committal *adj* unwilling to express, or not expressing, an opinion

nonconformist *noun* someone who does not agree with those in authority, *esp* in church matters ◊ *adj* not agreeing with authority

nondescript *adj* not easily described, lacking anything noticeable or interesting

none *adv* not at all: *none the worse* ◊ *pronoun* not one, not any

nonentity *noun* (*plural* **nonentities**) someone of no importance

non-existent *adj* not existing, not real

nonplussed *adj* taken aback, confused

nonsense *noun* 1 words that have no sense or meaning 2 foolishness • **nonsensical** *adj* • **nonsensically** *adv*

non sequitur *noun* a remark unconnected with what has gone before

non-stop *adj* going on without a break or pause

noodle *noun* a long thin strip of pasta, often made with egg

nook *noun* 1 a corner 2 a small recess • **every nook and cranny** *informal* everywhere

nooky *noun, slang* sexual intercourse

noon *noun* twelve o'clock midday

no one *see* **no**

noose *noun* a loop in a rope *etc* that tightens when pulled

nor *conj* used (often with **neither**) to show alternatives in the negative: *neither James nor I can speak French*

Nordic *adj* 1 relating to Finland or Scandinavia 2 of skiing: involving cross-country and jumping events

norm *noun* a pattern or standard to judge other things from

normal *adj* ordinary, usual according to a standard • **normality** *noun* • **normally** *adv*

north *noun* the direction to the left of someone facing the rising sun, one of the four main points of the compass ◊ *adj* 1 of or in the north 2 of the wind: from the north ◊ *adv* in or towards the north • **north-east** *noun* the point of the compass midway between north and east • **northerly** *adj* 1 of the wind: coming from or facing the north 2 in or towards the north • **northern** *adj* of the north • **north pole** *see* **pole** • **northward** or **northwards** *adj & adv* towards the north • **north-west** *noun* the point of the compass midway between north and west

nose *noun* 1 the part of the face by which people and animals smell and breathe 2 a jutting-out part, *eg* the front of an aeroplane ◊ *verb* 1 move forward cautiously 2 smell, or examine with the nose 3 track or detect 4 touch or rub with the nose • **nosedive** *noun* a headfirst dive ◊ *verb* dive headfirst • **nosegay** *noun, dated* a bunch of flowers • **nosey** or **nosy** *adj* inquisitive, fond of prying

nostalgia *noun* a longing for past times • **nostalgic** *adj* • **nostalgically** *adv*

nostril *noun* either of the two openings of the nose

not *adv* expressing a negative, refusal or denial: *I am not going/give it to me, not to him/I did not break the window*

notable *adj* worth taking notice of; important, remarkable ◊ *noun* an important person • **notability** *noun* a well-known person • **notably** *adv* 1 in a notable or noticeable way 2 particularly

notary *noun* (*plural* **notaries**) an official who sees that written documents are drawn up in a way required by law

notation noun **1** the showing of numbers, musical sounds, etc by signs: sol-fa notation **2** a set of such signs

notch noun (plural **notches**) a small V-shaped cut ◇ verb make a notch • **notched** adj

note noun **1** a sign or piece of writing to draw someone's attention **2** (**notes**) details for a speech, from a talk, etc set down in a short form **3** a short explanation **4** a short letter **5** a piece of paper used as money: £5 note **6** a single sound or the sign standing for it in music **7** a key on a piano etc ◇ verb **1** make a note of **2** notice • **notebook** noun **1** a small book for taking notes **2** a small laptop computer • **noted** adj well-known • **notepaper** noun writing paper • **noteworthy** adj notable, remarkable • **of note** well-known, distinguished • **take note of** notice particularly

nothing noun **1** no thing, not anything **2** nought, zero **3** something of no importance ◇ adv not at all: he's nothing like his father • **nothingness** noun **1** non-existence **2** space, emptiness

notice noun **1** a public announcement **2** attention: the colour attracted my notice **3** a warning given before leaving, or before dismissing someone from, a job ◇ verb see, observe, take note of • **noticeable** adj easily noticed, standing out • **noticeboard** noun a board on which notices are displayed

notify verb (**notifies, notifying, notified**) **1** inform **2** give notice of • **notifiable** adj that must be reported: a notifiable disease • **notification** noun

notion noun **1** an idea **2** a vague belief or opinion

notorious adj well known because of badness: a notorious criminal • **notoriety** noun

notwithstanding prep in spite of: notwithstanding his poverty, he refused all help

nougat /noo-gah/ or /nug-ut/ noun a sticky kind of sweet containing nuts etc

nought noun the figure 0, zero

Do not confuse with: **naught**

---

noun noun, grammar the word used as the name of someone or something, eg John and tickets in the sentence John bought the tickets

nourish verb **1** feed **2** encourage the growth of • **nourishing** adj giving the body what is necessary for health and growth • **nourishment** noun **1** food **2** an act of nourishing

nous /nows/ noun common sense

nouveau riche /noo-voh reesh/ noun someone who has recently acquired wealth but not good taste

nova noun (plural **novae** or **novas**) a star that suddenly increases in brightness for a period

novel /nov-ul/ adj new and strange ◇ noun a book telling a long story • **novelist** noun a writer of novels

novelty noun (plural **novelties**) **1** something new and strange **2** newness **3** a small, cheap souvenir or toy

November noun the eleventh month of the year

novice noun a beginner

now adv **1** at the present time: I can see him now **2** immediately before the present time: I thought of her just now **3** in the present circumstances: I can't go now because my mother is ill ◇ conj (often with **that**) because, since: you can't go out now that it's raining • **nowadays** adv in present times, these days • **now and then** or **now and again** sometimes, from time to time

nowhere adv not in, or to, any place

noxious adj harmful: noxious fumes

Do not confuse with: **obnoxious**

---

nozzle noun a spout fitted to the end of a pipe, tube, etc

NSPCC abbrev National Society for the Prevention of Cruelty to Children

nuance noun a slight difference in meaning or colour etc

nub noun a small lump, a knob

nubile adj of a woman: sexually attractive

nuclear adj 1 of a nucleus, esp that of an atom 2 produced by the splitting of the nuclei of atoms • **nuclear energy** noun energy released or absorbed during reactions taking place in atomic nuclei • **nuclear family** noun the family unit made up of the mother and father with their children • **nuclear fission** noun the splitting of atomic nuclei • **nuclear fusion** noun the creation of a new nucleus by merging two lighter ones, with release of energy • **nuclear reactor** noun apparatus for producing nuclear energy • **nuclear waste** noun radioactive waste material • **nuclear weapon** noun a bomb, missile, etc using nuclear energy

nucleus noun (plural **nuclei**) 1 the central part of an atom 2 the central part round which something collects or from which it grows: the nucleus of my book collection 3 the part of a plant or animal cell that controls its development

nude adj without clothes, naked ◇ noun 1 an unclothed human figure 2 a painting or statue of such a figure • **nudism** noun • **nudist** noun someone who advocates going without clothes in public • **nudity** noun the state of being nude • **in the nude** naked

nudge noun a gentle push, eg with the elbow or shoulder ◇ verb

nugatory adj insignificant, trifling

nugget noun a lump, esp of gold

nuisance noun someone or something annoying or troublesome

nuke noun, slang a nuclear weapon ◇ verb, slang attack with a nuclear weapon

null adj: **null and void** having no legal force

nullify verb (**nullifies, nullifying, nullified**) 1 make useless or of no effect 2 declare to be null and void

numb adj having lost the power to feel or move ◇ verb make numb

number noun 1 a word or figure showing how many, or showing a position in a series 2 a collection of people or things 3 a single issue of a newspaper or magazine 4 a popular song or piece of music ◇ verb 1 count 2 give numbers to 3 amount to in number • **numberless** adj more than can be counted

numeral noun a figure (eg 1, 2, etc) used to express a number • **numerator** noun the number above the line in vulgar fractions, eg 2 in $^2/_3$ • **numerical** adj of, in, using or consisting of numbers • **numerous** adj many

numerate adj having some understanding of mathematics and science

numerology noun prediction of future events by studying numbers • **numerologist** noun

numinous adj producing spiritual or deeply religious feelings

numismatics sing noun the study of coins • **numismatist** noun someone who collects and studies coins

numskull noun a stupid person

nun noun a member of a female religious group living in a convent • **nunnery** noun a house where a group of nuns live

nuncio /nun-shi-oh/ noun (plural

nuncios) **1** an ambassador from the Pope **2** a messenger

nuptial *adj* of marriage • **nuptials** *plural noun* a wedding ceremony

nurse *noun* someone who looks after sick or injured people, or small children ◇ *verb* **1** look after sick people *etc* **2** give (a baby) milk from the breast **3** hold or look after with care: *he nurses his tomato plants* **4** encourage (feelings) in yourself: *nursing her wrath* • **nursing home** *noun* a small private hospital

nursery *noun* (*plural* **nurseries**) **1** a room for young children **2** a place where young plants are reared **3** a nursery school • **nursery school** *noun* a school for very young children

nurture *verb* bring up, rear; nourish ◇ *noun* care, upbringing; food, nourishment

nut *noun* **1** a fruit with a hard shell which contains a kernel **2** a small metal block with a hole in it for screwing on the end of a bolt • **nutcrackers** *plural noun* an instrument for cracking nuts open • **nuthatch** *noun* (*plural* **nuthatches**) a small bird living on nuts and insects • **nutty** *adj* **1** containing, or having the flavour of, nuts **2** *informal* mad, insane • **in a nutshell** expressed very briefly

nutmeg *noun* a hard aromatic seed used as a spice in cooking

nutrient *noun* a substance which provides nourishment

nutrition *noun* nourishment; food • **nutritious** *adj* valuable as food, nourishing

nuzzle *verb* **1** press, rub or caress with the nose **2** lie close to, snuggle, nestle

NVQ *abbrev, Brit* National Vocational Qualification

NW *abbrev* north-west; north-western

NY *abbrev* New York (city or state)

nylon *noun* **1** a synthetic material made from chemicals **2** (**nylons**) stockings made of nylon

nymph *noun* **1** a mythological female river or tree spirit **2** an insect not yet fully developed

nymphomania *noun* excessively strong sexual desire in women • **nymphomaniac** *noun* someone suffering from nymphomania

NZ *abbrev* New Zealand

Oo

O! or **Oh!** exclam expressing surprise, admiration, pain, etc

oaf noun (plural **oafs**) a stupid or clumsy person

oak noun **1** a tree that produces acorns as fruit **2** its hard wood • **oak** or **oaken** adj made of oak • **oak apple** noun a growth on the leaves and twigs of oaks, caused by insects

OAP abbrev, dated Old Age Pensioner, an elderly person or a person of pensionable age

oar noun a pole for rowing, with a flat blade on the end ◊ verb row • **oarsman**, **oarswoman** noun someone who rows • **put your oar in** interfere

oasis noun (plural **oases**) **1** a place in a desert where water is found and trees etc grow **2** a place or period that brings welcome relief from noise, worry, hard work, etc

oast noun a large oven to dry hops • **oasthouse** noun a building containing this

oat noun a cereal plant or its grain (**oats**), used as food

oatcake noun a thin flat savoury biscuit made of oatmeal

oath noun (plural **oaths**) **1** a solemn promise to speak the truth, keep your word, be loyal, etc **2** a swear word

oatmeal noun meal made by grinding down oat grains

obbligato noun (plural **obbligatos**) music an instrumental accompaniment

obdurate adj unreasonably refusing to change an opinion or decision; stubborn • **obdurately** adv

OBE abbrev (Officer of the) Order of the British Empire

obedience, **obedient** see obey

obeisance /oh-beh-suns/ noun, formal a bow or curtsy showing respect

obelisk noun a tall four-sided pillar with a pointed top

obese adj very fat, esp unhealthily so • **obesity** noun

obey verb do what you are told to do: obey the instructions • **obedience** noun **1** the act of obeying **2** willingness to obey • **obedient** adj • **obediently** adv

obfuscate verb, formal make unclear; obscure

obituary noun (plural **obituaries**) a notice in a newspaper of someone's death, sometimes with a brief biography

object noun **1** something that can be seen or felt **2** an aim or purpose: our main object is not to make money **3** grammar the word in a sentence which stands for the person or thing that is affected by the action of the verb, eg me in the sentence he hit me ◊ verb (often with **to**) feel or show disapproval (of) • **objection** noun **1** the act of objecting **2** a reason for objecting • **objectionable** adj nasty • **objective** adj not influenced by personal interests; impartial ◊ noun aim, purpose, goal

objet d'art /ob-zheh dah/ noun (plural **objets d'art** /ob-zheh dah/) an article with artistic value

oblige verb 1 force (someone) to do something; compel: we were obliged to go home 2 formal do a favour for: oblige me by shutting the door • **obligation** noun 1 a promise or duty by which someone is bound: under an obligation to help 2 a debt of gratitude for a favour received • **obligatory** adj 1 compulsory 2 required as a duty • **obliged** adj owing or feeling gratitude • **obliging** adj ready to help others

oblique /uh-bleek/ adj 1 slanting 2 not direct or straightforward; indirect: an oblique reference • **obliquely** adv • **obliqueness** noun

obliterate verb 1 blot out (writing etc); efface 2 destroy completely • **obliteration** noun

oblivion noun 1 unconsciousness 2 the state of being forgotten • **oblivious** adj 1 unaware (of) or not paying attention (to) 2 forgetful

oblong noun a flat shape with four straight sides that is longer than it is wide or tall; a rectangle ◇ adj of the shape of an oblong

obnoxious adj causing great dislike or disgust; offensive • **obnoxiously** adv

---

Do not confuse with: **noxious**

---

oboe noun (plural **oboes**) a high-pitched woodwind instrument • **oboist** noun someone who plays the oboe

obscene adj 1 sexually indecent; lewd 2 disgusting • **obscenity** noun

obscure adj 1 unknown, not famous: an obscure poet 2 dark 3 not clear or easily understood ◇ verb 1 darken 2 make less clear • **obscurity** noun

obsequies /ob-suh-kwiz/ plural noun funeral rites

obsequious /ob-see-kwi-us/ adj trying to win favour by flattery,

willingness to agree, etc • **obsequiousness** noun

observe verb 1 notice 2 watch with attention 3 remark (that) 4 obey (a law etc) 5 keep alive by regular use; preserve: observe a tradition • **observance** noun the act of keeping (a law, tradition, etc) • **observant** adj good at noticing • **observation** noun 1 the act of seeing and noting; attention 2 a remark • **observatory** noun a place for making observations of the stars • **observer** noun someone sent to listen to, but not take part in, a discussion etc

obsess verb 1 fill the mind completely 2 informal think or worry to an unreasonable degree • **obsession** noun 1 a feeling or idea that someone cannot stop thinking about 2 the state of being obsessed • **obsessive** adj 1 forming an obsession 2 having or likely to have an obsession

obsidian noun a glassy black volcanic rock

obsolescent adj going out of date or out of use • **obsolescence** noun

---

Do not confuse: **obsolete** and **obsolescent**

---

obsolete adj gone out of use

obstacle noun something that prevents progress or movement; a hindrance • **obstacle race** noun a race in which obstacles have to be passed, climbed, etc

obstetrics sing noun the branch of medicine that deals with the treatment of women before, during and after childbirth • **obstetric** or **obstetrical** adj of obstetrics • **obstetrician** noun a doctor trained in obstetrics

obstinate adj unreasonably refusing to change an opinion or decision; stubborn • **obstinacy** noun stubbornness

obstreperous adj tending to behave in a loud and unreasonable way

obstruct verb prevent from passing, flowing or making progress • **obstruction** noun 1 a hindrance 2 something that blocks a passage; a blockage

obtain verb 1 get possession or use of; gain 2 formal be in use or valid: that rule still obtains • **obtainable** adj able to be got

obtrusive adj 1 too noticeable 2 tending to thrust yourself forward; pushy • **obtrusiveness** noun

obtuse adj 1 of an angle: greater than a right angle (contrasted with: **acute**) 2 slow to understand, or pretending not to understand in order to infuriate others • **obtuseness** noun

obverse noun the side of a coin showing the head or main design

obviate verb prevent or remove (a need, difficulty, etc)

obvious adj easily seen or understood; evident • **obviously** adv

ocarina noun a simple musical instrument like a short fat flute

occasion noun 1 a particular time: on that occasion 2 a special event: a great occasion 3 a cause or reason 4 opportunity ◇ verb cause

occasional adj happening or used now and then • **occasionally** adv

Occident noun, formal the West • **occidental** adj

occlude verb 1 block up or shut out 2 of the teeth: bite or come together • **occlusion** noun

occult adj 1 supernatural 2 secret or mysterious ◇ noun supernatural forces or happenings

occupy verb (**occupies, occupying, occupied**) 1 live in or have possession of 2 keep busy 3 take up (space, time, etc) 4 be in possession of (a foreign country etc) after invading • **occupancy** noun the act, fact or period of occupying • **occupant** noun • **occupation** noun 1 the state of occupying a place 2 someone's trade or job 3 possession of something • **occupier** noun someone who has possession of a house etc

occur verb (**occurring, occurred**) 1 happen 2 be found; exist 3 (with **to**) come into the mind of: that never occurred to me • **occurrence** noun 1 something that happens; an event 2 the act or fact of occurring

ocean noun 1 the stretch of salt water surrounding the land of the earth; sea 2 one of five main divisions of this, ie the Atlantic, Pacific, Indian, Arctic or Antarctic

ocelot /os-uh-lot/ noun a wild American cat like a small leopard

oche /ok-i/ noun the line behind which a darts player must stand to throw

ochre /oh-kuh/ noun a fine pale-yellow or red clay, used for colouring

o'clock adv used after a number from one to twelve to indicate the number of hours after midday or midnight: three o'clock

octagon noun a flat shape with eight straight sides • **octagonal** adj having eight sides

octane noun a colourless liquid found in petroleum and used in petrol

octave noun, music a range of eight notes, eg from one C to the C next above or below it

octavo noun (plural **octavos**) a size of book page produced by folding a standard sheet three times to give eight leaves or 16 pages

octet noun a group of eight lines of poetry, eight singers, etc

October noun the tenth month of the year

octogenarian noun someone from eighty to eighty-nine years old

octopus noun (plural **octopuses**) a deep-sea creature with eight arms that have suckers

ocular adj of the eye

oculist noun someone who specializes in diseases and defects of the eye

OD /oh-dee/ noun, slang an overdose of drugs ◇ verb (**OD's**, **OD'ing**, **OD'd**) take an overdose

odd adj 1 of a number: leaving a remainder of one when divided by two, eg the numbers 3, 17, 31 (contrasted with: even) 2 unusual, strange 3 not one of a matching pair or group: an odd glove/odd screw 4 (**odds**) chances or probability: the odds are that they will win 5 (**odds**) difference: it makes no odds • **oddity** noun 1 a strange person or thing 2 queerness, strangeness • **odd jobs** plural noun jobs of different kinds, not part of regular employment • **oddments** plural noun scraps • **at odds** 1 quarrelling 2 not matching each other • **odds and ends** objects, scraps, etc of different kinds

ode noun a poem in which a person or thing is addressed directly: ode to autumn

odious adj, formal extremely unpleasant or offensive; hateful • **odiously** adv • **odium** noun deep dislike; hatred

odour noun smell, either pleasant or unpleasant • **odourless** adj without smell

odyssey /od-uh-si/ noun a long, adventurous journey

oedema /ee-dee-muh/ or US **edema** /i-dee-muh/ noun an accumulation of fluid in body tissue, causing swelling

oesophagus /ee-sof-uh-gus/ or US **esophagus** /i-sof-uh-gus/ noun the tube connecting the mouth to the stomach; the throat

oestrogen /ees-truh-jun/ or US **estrogen** /es-truh-jun/ noun a female sex hormone that regulates the menstrual cycle, prepares the body for pregnancy, etc • **oestrogenic** adj

oestrus /ees-trus/ or US **estrus** /es-trus/ noun the period during which a female mammal is ready for conceiving; heat

oeuvre /urv-ruh/ noun, formal the complete works of an artist, writer, etc

of prep 1 belonging to or associated with: the people of Glasgow 2 from in distance or time: within two miles of his home 3 from among: one of my pupils 4 made from: a house of bricks 5 indicating an amount, measurement, etc: a gallon of petrol 6 on the subject of; concerning: talk of old friends 7 containing or comprising: a class of twenty children/a cup of coffee 8 indicating a cause: die of hunger 9 indicating removal or taking away: robbed her of her jewels 10 indicating a connection between an action and its object: the joining of the pieces 11 indicating character, qualities, etc: a man of good taste/it was good of you to come 12 US (in telling the time) before: ten of eight

off adv 1 away from a place, or from a particular state, position, etc: he walked off rudely/your work has gone off/switch the light off 2 entirely, completely: finish off your work ◇ adj 1 cancelled: the holiday is off 2 no longer fresh enough to eat or drink; bad: the meat is off 3 not working or not on: the control is in the off position 4 not quite pure in colour: off-white ◇ prep 1 away from: fell off the table 2 taken away: 10% off the usual price 3 below the normal standard: off his game • **badly off** poor • **be off** leave quickly • **off and on** occasionally • **off the cuff** see **cuff** • **off the wall** see **wall** • **well off** rich

offal noun 1 the parts of an animal

unfit for use as food **2** certain internal organs of an animal (heart, liver, *etc*) that are eaten

off-beam *adj* inaccurate or misguided

offbeat *adj* unconventional or eccentric

off-chance *noun* a slight chance • **on the off-chance** just in case

off-colour *adj* feeling slightly ill

offcut *noun* a piece of wood, fabric, *etc* remaining from a larger piece

offence or US **offense** *noun* **1** annoyance, anger or hurt feelings, or a cause of them **2** a wrongdoing or crime • **take offence at** be annoyed, angry or upset at

offend *verb* **1** cause to feel annoyed, angry or upset **2** do wrong or commit a crime • **offender** *noun*

offensive *adj* **1** insulting or disgusting **2** used for attack or assault: *an offensive weapon* ◇ *noun* **1** the position of someone who attacks **2** an attack

offer *verb* **1** put forward (a gift, suggestion, *etc*) for acceptance or refusal **2** give (a choice, chance, *etc*) **3** say that you are willing to do something ◇ *noun* **1** an act of offering **2** a bid of money **3** something proposed • **offering** *noun* **1** a gift **2** a collection of money in church

offhand *adj* **1** said or done without thinking or preparation **2** unfriendly or impolite ◇ *adv* without preparation; impromptu

office *noun* **1** a place where business of a non-manual kind is carried on **2** the people working in such a place **3** a position of authority, *esp* in the government **4** *formal* a duty or job **5** *formal* (**offices**) helpful things done for someone • **officer** *noun* **1** someone who carries out a public duty **2** someone holding a commission in the armed forces **3** a member of a police force

official *adj* **1** done or given out by people in power: *official announcement/ official action* **2** forming part of the tasks of a job: *official duties* ◇ *noun* someone who holds an office in the service of the government, a local authority, *etc* • **officially** *adv* **1** as an official; formally **2** as announced or said in public (though not necessarily truthfully): *officially she's ill, but she's actually on holiday*

Do not confuse with: **officious**

---

officiate *verb* perform a duty or service, *esp* as a clergyman at a wedding *etc*

officious *adj* fond of interfering, *esp* in a pompous way • **officiously** *adv* • **officiousness** *noun*

Do not confuse with: **official**

---

offie *noun*, *slang* an off-licence

offing *noun*: **in the offing** expected to happen soon; forthcoming

off-licence *noun* a shop selling alcohol that must not be drunk on the premises

off-limits *adj* not to be entered, touched, used, *etc*

off-line *adj*, *comput* **1** of a piece of computer equipment: not connected to a computer **2** of a computer: not connected to the Internet or another network

offload *verb* **1** unload **2** get rid of (something) by passing it onto someone else

offpeak *adj* not at the time of highest use, demand or charge

off-putting *adj* causing aversion

offset *verb* make up for: *the cost of the project was partly offset by a government grant*

offshoot *noun* **1** a shoot growing

out of a plant's main stem **2** a small business, project, *etc* created out of a larger one: *an offshoot of an international firm*

offshore *adj & adv* **1** in or on the sea close to the coast **2** abroad, in or to a country where people pay less tax: *offshore investments* **3** from the shore: *offshore winds*

offside *adj & adv, informal* **1** illegally ahead of the ball, *eg* in football, in a position between the ball and the opponent's goal **2** of the side of a vehicle: nearest to the centre of the road (*contrasted with*: **nearside**)

offspring *noun* **1** someone's child or children **2** the young of animals *etc*

OFT *abbrev* Office of Fair Trading

oft *adv, formal* often

often *adv* many times

ogle *verb* eye (someone) impudently in order to show admiration

ogre *noun* **1** a mythological man-eating giant **2** someone extremely frightening or threatening

Oh! *another spelling of* **O!**

ohm *noun* a unit of electrical resistance ● **ohmage** *noun* electrical resistance measured in ohms

OHMS *abbrev* On Her (or His) Majesty's Service

oil *noun* **1** a greasy liquid obtained from plants (*eg* olive oil), from animals (*eg* whale oil), and from minerals (*eg* petroleum) **2** (**oils**) oil colours for painting ◇ *verb* smear with oil, put oil on or in ● **oil colour** *noun* paint made by mixing a colouring substance with oil ● **oilfield** *noun* an area where mineral oil is found ● **oil painting** *noun* a picture painted in oil colours ● **oil rig** *noun* a structure set up for drilling an oil well ● **oilskin** *noun* **1** cloth made waterproof with oil **2** a heavy coat made of this ● **oil well** *noun* a hole drilled into the earth's surface or into the sea bed to extract petroleum

● **oily** *adj* **1** of or like oil **2** insincerely friendly or flattering

oink *noun* the noise of a pig ◇ *verb* make this noise

ointment *noun* a greasy substance rubbed on the skin to soothe, heal, *etc*

OK *or* **okay** *exclam, adj & adv* used for showing agreement, approval or understanding; all right ● **okay** *verb* (**okays**, **okaying**, **okayed**) give approval of or permission for

okapi /oh-*kah*-pi/ *noun* a Central African animal related to the giraffe

okra *noun* a tropical plant with edible pods

old *adj* **1** advanced in age; elderly **2** having a certain age: *ten years old* **3** having existed a long time or been done, bought, *etc* a long time ago: *an old joke/my old coat* **4** earlier than the present one; former: *our old teacher* **5** worn-out through frequent use: *old trousers* **6** no longer useful or generally disliked: *who'd buy this old thing?* ● **old age** *noun* the later part of life ● **old-fashioned** *adj* in a style common in the past ● **old guard** *noun* the conservative element in an organization *etc* ● **old hand** *noun* someone with long experience in a job *etc* ● **old maid** *noun* **1** *derog* a spinster **2** a game played by passing and matching playing cards ● **old-timer** *noun* **1** *derog* an old person **2** someone with experience; a veteran ● **of old** long ago

oleander /oh-li-*an*-duh/ *noun* an evergreen shrub with spiky leaves and red or white flowers

olfactory *adj* of or used for smelling: *olfactory glands*

oligarchy /*ol*-i-gah-ki/ *noun* government by a small exclusive group ● **oligarch** *noun* a member of an oligarchy ● **oligarchic** *or* **oligarchical** *adj*

olive *noun* **1** a small oval fruit with

a hard stone, pressed to produce a cooking oil **2** the Mediterranean tree on which this fruit grows ◊ *adj* of a yellowish-green colour • **olive branch** *noun* a sign of a wish for peace

ombudsman *noun* (*plural* **ombudsmen**) an official appointed to look into complaints against the government

omega *noun* the last letter of the Greek alphabet

omelette *or* **omelet** *noun* beaten eggs fried in a single layer in a pan

omen *noun* a sign of future events

ominous *adj* suggesting future trouble

omit *verb* (**omitting**, **omitted**) **1** leave out **2** fail to do • **omission** *noun* **1** something omitted **2** the act of omitting

omnibus *noun* (*plural* **omnibuses**) *old* a bus ◊ *adj* **1** widely comprehensive **2** having miscellaneous contents • **omnibus edition** *noun* a radio or TV programme made up of material from preceding editions of the series

omnipotent /om-*nip*-uh-tunt/ *adj* having absolute, unlimited power: *an omnipotent ruler* • **omnipotence** *noun*

omnipresent *adj* being present everywhere at the same time • **omnipresence** *noun*

omniscient *adj* knowing everything • **omniscience** *noun*

omnivorous *adj* feeding on all kinds of food • **omnivorousness** *noun*

on *prep* **1** touching or fixed to the outer or upper side: *on the table* **2** supported by: *standing on one foot* **3** about: *a book on Scottish history* **4** receiving, taking, *etc*: *suspended on half-pay/on antibiotics* **5** occurring in the course of a specified time: *on the following day* **6** with: *do you have your cheque book on you?* **7** next to or near: *a city on the Rhine* **8** indicating membership of: *on the committee* **9** in the

process or state of: *on sale/on show* **10** by means of: *can you play that on the piano?* **11** followed by: *disaster on disaster* ◊ *adv* **1** so as to be touching or fixed to the outer or upper side: *put your coat on* **2** onwards, further: *they carried on towards home* **3** at a further point: *later on* ◊ *adj* **1** working or in use: *the television is on* **2** arranged: *do you have anything on this afternoon?* • **from now on** after this time; henceforth • **on and off** occasionally or intermittently • **you're on!** I agree, accept the challenge, *etc*

once *adv* **1** at an earlier time in the past: *people once lived in caves* **2** for one time only: *I've been to Paris once in the last two years* ◊ *noun* one time only: *do it just this once* ◊ *conj* when: *once you've finished, you can go* • **all at once** suddenly • **at once 1** immediately: *come here at once!* **2** (sometimes with **all**) at the same time; together: *trying to do several things all at once* • **once and for all** for the last time • **once upon a time** at some time in the past

oncology *noun* the study of tumours • **oncological** *adj* • **oncologist** *noun* a doctor who specializes in tumours

oncoming *adj* approaching from the front: *oncoming traffic*

one *noun* **1** the number 1 **2** a particular person or thing: *she's the one I want to meet* ◊ *pronoun* **1** a single person or thing: *one of my cats* **2** in formal or pompous English used instead of **you**, meaning anyone: *one must do what one can* ◊ *adj* **1** a single: *we had only one reply* **2** the same: *we are all of one mind* **3** an unnamed (*time etc*): *one day soon* • **oneself** *pronoun* **1** used reflexively: *wash oneself* **2** used for emphasis: *one usually has to finish the job oneself* • **one-sided** *adj* with one person, side, *etc* having a great advantage over the other • **one-to-one** *adj* in which attention *etc* is devoted solely to a single person, not shared among several: *one-to-one nursing* • **one-way** *adj* meant for traffic moving in one direction only • **one another** used when an action takes place between two or more people: *they looked at one another*

onerous *adj* difficult to do or put up with: *onerous task*

ongoing *adj* continuing: *ongoing talks*

onion *noun* a bulb vegetable with a strong taste and smell • **oniony** *adj* tasting of onions • **know your onions** *informal* know your subject or job well

on-line *adj* **1** of a piece of computer equipment: connected to a computer **2** of a computer: connected to the Internet or another network

onlooker *noun* someone who watches an event but does not take part in it

only *adv* **1** not more than: *only two weeks left* **2** and no others; solely: *only you are invited* **3** no longer ago than: *I saw her only yesterday* **4** indicating an unavoidable result: *he'll only be offended if you ask* **5** (with **too**) extremely: *only too pleased to help* ◇ *adj* single, solitary: *an only child* ◇ *conj, informal* except that; but: *I'd like to go, only I have to work*

ono *abbrev* or nearest offer

onomatopoeia /on-uh-mat-uh-*pee*-uh/ *noun* the forming of a word that sounds like the thing it refers to, eg moo, swish • **onomatopoeic** *adj*

onrush *noun* a rush forward

onset *noun* **1** beginning **2** a fierce attack

onslaught *noun* a fierce attack

onto *prep* to a place or position on

ontology *noun* the study of pure being or essence • **ontologic** or **ontological** *adj* • **ontologist** *noun*

onus *noun* a burden or responsibility

onward *adj* going forward in place or time • **onward** or **onwards** *adv*

onyx *noun* a precious stone with layers of different colours

oodles *plural noun, informal* lots (of); many

ooze *verb* **1** flow gently or slowly **2** overflow with (a quality); exude: *she oozes elegance* ◇ *noun* **1** soft mud **2** a gentle flow

op *abbrev* **1** opus **2** optical: *op art*

opacity see **opaque**

opal *noun* a bluish-white precious stone with flecks of various colours

opalescent *noun* milky and iridescent • **opalescence** *noun*

opaque /oh-*pehk*/ *adj* not able to be seen through • **opacity** *noun*

op cit *adv* in the book *etc* cited

OPEC *abbrev* Organization of the Petroleum-Exporting Countries

open *adj* **1** allowing people or things to come in and out; not closed **2** not enclosed or fenced **3** showing the inside or inner part; uncovered **4** not blocked **5** free for all to enter **6** speaking honestly or frankly **7** of land: without many trees ◇ *verb* **1** make open **2** begin • **open air** *noun* any place not indoors or underground • **open-air** *adj* happening outside • **open book** *noun* something that can be easily seen or understood • **open-cast** *adj* of a mine: excavating in the open, above ground • **open-ended** *adj* without definite limits • **opener** *noun* **1** something that opens: *tin opener* **2** an initial comment or action that gets something started • **open-heart** *adj* of surgery: performed on a heart that has been temporarily stopped, with blood being circulated by a heart-lung machine • **opening** *noun* **1** a hole or gap **2** an opportunity **3** a vacant job • **openly** *adv* without trying to hide or conceal anything • **open-minded** *adj* ready to consider or accept new ideas • **open-plan** *adj* of an office: with desks *etc* in the same room, not divided by walls or partitions • **open verdict** *noun* a coroner's official decision that the cause of someone's death is not known • **in the open 1** in the open air **2** widely known, not secret • **open to** likely or willing to receive: *open to attack/open to suggestions* • **with open arms** warmly or enthusiastically

opera[1] *noun* a play in which the characters sing accompanied by an orchestra • **operatic** *adj*

opera[2] *plural of* **opus**

operate *verb* **1** function or work **2** control (a machine *etc*) **3** perform a surgical operation **4** be in force or use • **operating** *adj* of or for an operation on someone's body • **operating system** *noun, comput* software that manages all other programs on a computer and any hardware devices linked to it

operation *noun* **1** the cutting of a part of the human body to examine or treat disease; surgery **2** action or use: *a rule not in operation here* **3** method or way of working **4** (**operations**) movements of armies, troops

operative *adj* **1** in action or use; working **2** of a rule *etc*: in force ◇ *noun, formal* a worker

operator *noun* **1** someone who works a machine **2** someone who connects telephone calls in a telephone exchange

operetta *noun* a play with music and singing and a fairly light-hearted theme

ophthalmic /of-*thal*-mik/ *adj* relating to the eye: *an ophthalmic surgeon* • **ophthalmologist** *noun* a doctor who specializes in eye diseases and injuries

opiate *noun* **1** a drug containing opium, used to make someone sleep **2** anything that calms or dulls the mind or feelings

opine *verb, formal* give as an opinion

opinion *noun* **1** what someone thinks or believes **2** a professional judgement or point of view: *he wanted another opinion on his son's case* **3** judgement of the value of someone or something: *I have a low opinion of her* • **opinionated** *adj* expressing strong opinions in an annoyingly firm or loud way

opium *noun* a drug made from the dried juice of a type of poppy

opossum *noun* a small American animal that carries its young in a pouch

opponent *noun* someone who opposes; an enemy, a rival

opportune *adj* coming at the right time or a convenient time; timely

opportunist *noun* someone who takes advantage of available opportunities, and is usually willing to disregard principles • **opportunism** *noun* • **opportunistic** *adj*

opportunity *noun* (*plural* **opportunities**) a chance (to do something)

oppose *verb* **1** disapprove of and try to prevent the success or progress of **2** compete against

opposite *adj* **1** across from; facing: *the opposite corner* **2** lying on the other side (of): *the opposite bank* **3** as different as possible: *she holds the opposite opinion* ◇ *prep* **1** across from: *he lives opposite the post office* **2** acting a role in a play, opera, *etc* in relation to another: *she played Ophelia opposite his Hamlet* ◇ *noun* something as different as possible (from something else): *black is the opposite of white* • **opposite number** *noun* a person who does the same job, has the same position, *etc* as another but in a different place, situation or organization

opposition *noun* **1** attempts to prevent the success or progress of something, motivated by disapproval; resistance **2** people who resist **3** the political party that is against the governing party

oppress verb **1** govern harshly like a tyrant **2** treat cruelly **3** worry greatly; distress • **oppression** noun • **oppressive** adj **1** governing harshly **2** of weather: unpleasantly warm and airless; close • **oppressively** adv

opprobrium noun, formal **1** public disgrace or severe public criticism **2** something that brings public disgrace or criticism • **opprobrious** adj expressing severe criticism

opt verb **1** (with **for**) choose **2** decide (to do) • **opt out** decide not to (do something)

optic or **optical** adj relating to the eyes or sight • **optical illusion** noun an impression that something seen is different from what it is • **optics** sing noun the science of light

optician noun someone who makes and sells spectacles

optimal adj optimum

optimism noun the habit of taking a bright, hopeful view of things (contrasted with: **pessimism**) • **optimist** noun someone who tends to take a positive view of things • **optimistic** adj

optimum adj best possible: optimum conditions

option noun **1** something chosen, or something available to choose **2** the right or power to choose; choice • **optional** adj left to choice, not compulsory

opulent adj expensive and luxurious • **opulence** noun riches

opus noun (plural **opera**) an artistic work, esp a piece of classical music

or conj **1** used (often with **either**) to show alternatives: would you prefer tea or coffee? **2** because if not: you'd better go or you'll miss your bus

oracle noun **1** someone thought to be very wise or knowledgeable **2** hist a sacred place where a god answered questions • **oracular** adj

oral adj **1** spoken, not written: oral literature **2** relating to the mouth ◇ noun an oral examination or test • **orally** adv by mouth

---

Do not confuse with: **aural**

---

orange noun a round juicy citrus fruit with a thick reddish-yellow skin

orang-utan noun a large ape with long reddish hair

oration noun a formal public speech • **orator** noun a public speaker • **oratory** noun the art of speaking well in public

oratorio noun (plural **oratorios**) a religious story set to music, performed by soloists, choir and often orchestra

orb noun anything in the shape of a ball; a sphere

orbit noun **1** the path of a planet round a sun, or of a satellite round a planet **2** range or area of influence: within his orbit ◇ verb move in an orbit

Orcadian adj of or from Orkney ◇ noun someone born or living in Orkney

orchard noun a large garden of fruit trees

orchestra noun a group of musicians playing together under a conductor • **orchestral** adj • **orchestrate** verb **1** arrange (a piece of music) for an orchestra **2** organize so as to produce the best effect

orchid noun a plant with unusually shaped, often brightly coloured, flowers

ordain verb **1** declare something to be law **2** receive (a member of the clergy) into the Church • **ordinance** noun a command; a law • **ordination** noun

ordeal noun **1** a very unpleasant experience **2** a hard trial or test

order noun **1** an instruction to take action, made by someone in authority **2** a request made to a supplier or manufacturer **3** a tidy or efficient state **4** a number of things arranged according to a system **5** an accepted way of doing things **6** peaceful conditions: *law and order* **7** a position in a hierarchy; a rank **8** a society or brotherhood, eg of monks ◇ verb **1** give an instruction to; command **2** put in an order for (something) to a supplier or manufacturer: *I've ordered another copy of the book* **3** arrange according to a system • **in order 1** correct according to what is regularly done **2** in a tidy arrangement • **in order to** for the purpose of: *in order to live you must eat* • **out of order 1** not working **2** not correct or acceptable according to rules or expectations **3** not in a tidy arrangement

orderly adj **1** in proper order **2** well-behaved ◇ noun (plural **orderlies**) **1** a hospital attendant who does routine jobs **2** a soldier who carries the orders and messages of an officer

ordinal adj of or in an order • **ordinal number** noun a number that shows order in a series, eg first, second, third (contrasted with: **cardinal number**)

ordinance see **ordain**

ordinary adj **1** of the common kind; usual **2** not particularly good; unexceptional • **ordinarily** adv • **ordinariness** noun • **out of the ordinary** unusual

ordination see **ordain**

Ordnance Survey noun a government office that produces official detailed maps

ordure noun, formal excrement

ore noun a mineral from which a metal is obtained: *iron ore*

oregano /o-ri-*gah*-noh/ or US /o-reg-uh-noh/ noun a Mediterranean herb used in cooking

organ noun **1** an internal part of the body, eg the liver **2** a large musical wind instrument with a keyboard **3** a means of spreading information or propaganda, eg a newspaper: *an organ of conservatism* • **organism** noun any living thing • **organist** noun someone who plays the organ

organdie noun a fine thin stiff muslin

organic adj **1** of food or food products: grown or produced without the use of artificial fertilizers etc **2** of living things **3** developing in a way that seems natural **4** of or produced by the bodily organs • **organically** adv

organize verb **1** give an orderly structure to; arrange **2** make the necessary preparations for (eg an event) or take the necessary action to obtain (eg tickets) • **organization** noun **1** a group of people working together for a purpose **2** the act of organizing

orgasm noun the climax of sexual excitement ◇ verb experience an orgasm • **orgasmic** adj

orgy noun (plural **orgies**) **1** a party in which a group of people indulge in casual sex **2** any party that involves excessive drinking and riotous behaviour **3** any act of frenzied indulgence: *a shopping orgy* • **orgiastic** adj

oriel noun a small room with a bay window built out from a wall

Orient noun, old the countries of the East • **oriental** adj from the countries of the East

orientate verb **1** find your position and sense of direction **2** arrange to face a particular direction • **orientation** noun

orienteering noun the sport of

finding your way across country with the help of map and compass

orifice noun, formal an opening, esp in the body

origami /o-ri-gah-mi/ noun the Japanese art of folding paper

origin noun 1 the starting point 2 the place from which someone or something comes 3 cause

original adj 1 first ever done or produced 2 not thought of before and not copied from someone else 3 in the first form, from which copies or translations are made ◇ noun 1 the earliest version 2 a model from which other things are made • **originality** noun • **originally** adv

originate verb 1 bring or come into being 2 produce

orison /o-ri-zun/ noun, formal a prayer

ormolu /aw-muh-loo/ noun gilded bronze or other metal, used for ornamentation

ornament noun something added to give or enhance beauty ◇ verb serve as a decoration on or in; adorn • **ornamental** adj used for ornament; decorative • **ornamentation** noun

ornate adj richly decorated • **ornately** adv

ornery adj, US informal easily annoyed or made angry; cantankerous

ornithologist noun someone who studies or is an expert on birds • **ornithological** adj • **ornithology** noun

orotund /o-ruh-tund/ adj of a voice: deep and impressive-sounding

orphan noun a child who has lost one or usu both parents • **orphanage** noun a home for orphans

orthodox adj following the established religious, political or social customs or views; conventional (con-

trasted with: **heterodox**) • **orthodoxy** noun

orthography noun an established system of spelling • **orthographic** or **orthographical** adj

orthopaedics or US **orthopedics** sing noun the branch of medicine that deals with bone diseases and injuries • **orthopaedic** adj

Oscar noun, trademark an annual award given by the American Academy of Motion Picture Arts and Sciences

oscillate verb 1 swing to and fro like the pendulum of a clock 2 keep changing your mind • **oscillation** noun

osier /ohz-i-uh/ noun 1 a type of willow tree whose twigs are used for weaving baskets etc 2 a twig from this tree

osmosis noun 1 the natural movement of a liquid through a membrane from a place where it is less concentrated to a place where it is more concentrated 2 gradual absorption or assimilation

osprey noun (plural **ospreys**) a large eagle that eats fish

ostensible adj of a reason etc: apparent, but not always real or true

ostentatious adj intended to catch the eye; showy • **ostentation** noun

osteopath noun someone who treats injuries to bones, muscles, etc by manipulating the patient's body, not by drugs or surgery • **osteopathy** noun

osteoporosis noun a disease that makes bones porous and brittle, caused by lack of calcium

ostler another spelling of **hostler**

ostracize verb exclude (someone) from the company of a group of people • **ostracism** noun

ostrich noun (plural **ostriches**) a

very large African bird with black and white feathers that cannot fly but runs very fast ● **ostrich-like** adj avoiding facing up to difficulties (after the ostrich's supposed habit of burying its head in the sand when chased)

other adj **1** the second of two: *where is the other sock?* **2** not previously mentioned; remaining: *these are for the other children* **3** different or additional: *there must be some other reason* **4** (with **every**) second: *every other day* **5** recently past: *the other day* ◇ pronoun **1** the second of two **2** those not previously mentioned: *the others arrived the next day* **3** the previous one: *one after the other* ● **otherwise** conj or else, if not ◇ adv **1** in other respects **2** in a different way ◇ adj different: *the truth is otherwise* ● **other than** except: *no hope other than to retreat* ● **someone or other** or **something or other** someone or something not named or specified: *there's always someone or other here*

otiose /oh-ti-ohs/ adj serving no useful purpose; redundant

otter noun an animal that lives on fish and lives partly in water and partly on land, with a long body, smooth fur and sharp teeth

Ottoman adj, hist relating to the Turkish empire from the 14th to the 19th centuries

ottoman noun (plural **ottomans**) a low, cushioned seat without a back

ouch! exclam expressing pain

ought verb **1** used with other verbs to indicate duty or need: *we ought to set an example/I ought to practise more* **2** to indicate what can be reasonably expected: *the weather ought to be fine*

ounce noun a unit of weight, one-sixteenth of a pound, 28.35 grammes

our adj belonging to us: *our house* ● **ours** pronoun something belonging to us: *the green car is ours* ● **our-**

selves pronoun **1** used reflexively: *we exhausted ourselves swimming* **2** used for emphasis: *we ourselves don't like it, but other people may*

oust verb **1** force out of a position of authority: *the president was ousted* **2** force out of a position of authority and take the place of: *she ousted him as leader of the party*

out adv **1** into or towards the open air: *go out for a walk* **2** from a place inside: *take out a handkerchief* **3** not inside: *out of prison* **4** far from here: *out in the Far East* **5** not at home, not in the office, *etc*: *she's out at the moment* **6** aloud: *shouted out* **7** published or available to buy: *is the book out yet?* **8** inaccurate by a particular amount: *the total was five pounds out* **9** dismissed from a game of cricket, baseball, *etc* **10** informal on strike **11** no longer in power or office **12** to or at an end: *hear me out* **13** no longer hidden: *the secret is out* **14** finished, having won at cards *etc* **15** determined: *out to win* **16** openly admitting to being homosexual ● **out-and-out** adj used for emphasizing negative qualities; thorough: *an out-and-out liar* ● **outer** adj nearer the edge, surface, *etc*, or further away ● **outermost** adj nearest the edge or furthest away ● **outing** noun an excursion

outback noun the wild interior parts of Australia

outbid verb (**outbidding**, **outbid**) offer a higher price than (somebody else)

outboard adj on the outside of a ship or boat: *an outboard motor*

outbreak noun a sudden and violent beginning, *eg* of war or disease

outbuilding noun a building that is separate from the main buildings

outburst noun a bursting out, *esp* of angry feelings

outcast noun someone driven away from friends and home

outcome noun a result

outcrop noun the part of a rock formation that can be seen at the surface of the ground

outcry noun (plural **outcries**) a widespread show of anger, disapproval, etc

outdo verb (**outdoes, outdoing, outdid, outdone**) do better than

outdoor adj of or in the open air • **outdoors** adv 1 outside the house 2 in or into the open air

outfit noun 1 a set of clothes worn together, often for a special occasion etc 2 informal a group of people • **outfitter** noun a seller of outfits, esp men's clothes

outgoings plural noun money spent or being spent

outgrow verb (**outgrowing, outgrew, outgrown**) get too big or old for (clothes, toys, etc)

outhouse noun a shed

outlandish adj looking or sounding very strange

outlaw noun a criminal, esp someone on the run from the law ◇ verb 1 forbid formally or officially; ban 2 place beyond the protection of the law

outlay noun money paid out

outlet noun 1 a passage to the outside, eg for a water-pipe 2 a means of expressing or getting rid of (a feeling, energy, etc) 3 a market for goods

outline noun 1 the outer line of a figure in a drawing etc 2 a sketch showing only the main lines 3 a rough sketch 4 a brief description ◇ verb 1 draw an outline of 2 give a brief description of the main features of

outlive verb live longer than

outlook noun 1 what is thought likely to happen: the weather outlook 2 a view from a window etc

outlying adj far from the centre; distant

outnumber verb be greater in number than: their team outnumbered ours

out-of-date or **out of date** adj no longer valid or current: this voucher is out of date/an out-of-date ticket

out-patient noun a patient who does not stay in a hospital while receiving treatment (contrasted with: **in-patient**)

outpost noun 1 a military station in front of or far from the main army 2 a remote place

output noun 1 the goods produced by a machine, factory, etc, or the amount of work done by a person 2 data produced by a computer program (contrasted with: **input**)

outrage noun 1 something done that shocks people or causes offence 2 an act of great violence ◇ verb 1 insult or shock 2 hurt by violence; injure • **outrageous** adj 1 greatly offensive to accepted standards of morality or decency 2 extravagant

outré /oo-treh/ adj beyond what is normal; extravagant

outright adv completely ◇ adj complete, thorough

outset noun start, beginning

outside noun the outer surface or place: the outside of the box ◇ adj 1 in, on or of the outer surface or place: the outside seat 2 relating to leisure rather than your full-time job: outside interests 3 slight: an outside chance of winning ◇ adv in or into the open air: let's eat outside ◇ prep beyond the range or limits of: go outside the building/locked outside working hours • **outsider** noun 1 someone not included in a particular social group 2 a runner etc whom no one expects to win • **at the outside** at the most: ten miles at the outside

outsize *adj* of a very large size

outskirts *plural noun* the outer borders of a city *etc*

outsource *verb* buy (parts, services, *etc*) from another company, rather than manufacturing or providing them yourself • **outsourcing** *noun*

outspoken *adj* forceful and frank in speech

outstanding *adj* **1** excellent **2** of a debt: unpaid

outstretched *adj* reaching out

out-tray *noun* an office tray for letters and work already dealt with (*contrasted with*: **in-tray**)

outvote *verb* defeat by a greater number of votes

outward *adj* **1** towards or on the outside **2** of a journey: away from home, not towards it • **outwardly** *or* **outwards** *adv* on the outside; externally

outweigh *verb* be more important than: *the advantages outweigh the disadvantages*

outwit *verb* (**outwitting, outwitted**) defeat by cunning

outwith *prep, Scot* outside of

ouzo /oo-zoh/ *noun* a Greek aniseed-flavoured liqueur

ova *plural of* **ovum**

oval *adj* having the shape of an egg ◇ *noun* an egg shape

ovary *noun* (*plural* **ovaries**) one of two organs in the female body in which eggs are formed

ovation *noun* an outburst of applause

oven *noun* a closed compartment for baking

over *prep* **1** higher than; above: *the number is over the door/she won over £200/we've lived here for over thirty years* **2** across: *going over the bridge* **3** on the other side of: *the house over* the road **4** on top of: *threw his coat over the body* **5** here and there on: *paper scattered over the carpet* **6** on the subject of; about: *they quarrelled over money* **7** by means of: *over the telephone* **8** during, throughout: *over the years* **9** while doing, having, *etc*: *fell asleep over his dinner* ◇ *adv* **1** in the space above: *two planes flew over* **2** across a distance: *he walked over and spoke* **3** downwards: *did you fall over?* **4** above in number *etc*: *aged four and over* **5** as a remainder: *three left over* **6** from beginning to end; through: *read the passage over* ◇ *adj* finished: *the sale is over* ◇ *noun, cricket* a series of six balls bowled from one end of the wicket • **overly** *adv* excessively • **over again** once more

over- *prefix* to too great an extent: *overcook/over-excited*

overall *noun* **1** a garment worn over ordinary clothes to protect them against dirt **2** hard-wearing trousers with a bib, worn as work clothes ◇ *adj* **1** from one end to the other: *overall length* **2** including everything: *overall cost* • **over all** altogether

overawe *verb* frighten or astonish into silence

overbalance *verb* lose your balance and fall

overbearing *adj* wanting to control other people's behaviour; domineering

overboard *adv* out of a ship into the water: *fell overboard*

overcast *adj* of the sky: cloudy

overcharge *verb* **1** charge too great a price **2** fill or load too heavily

overcoat *noun* a long heavy coat

overcome *verb* get the better of; defeat ◇ *adj* helpless from exhaustion, emotion, *etc*

overdo *verb* **1** put too much effort into **2** exaggerate: *they rather over-*

did the sympathy **3** cook (food) for too long

overdose *noun* too great an amount of medicine taken ◇ *verb* take too much medicine

overdraw *verb* draw more money from the bank than you have in your account • **overdraft** *noun* the amount of money overdrawn from a bank

overdue *adj* **1** arriving later than the stated time: *the train is overdue* **2** of a bill *etc*: still unpaid although the time for payment has passed

overflow *verb* **1** flow or spill over: *the river overflowed its banks/the crowd overflowed into the next room* **2** be so full as to flow over: *the bath is overflowing* ◇ *noun* **1** a running-over of liquid **2** a pipe or channel for getting rid of excess water *etc*

overgrown *adj* **1** covered with wild plant growth **2** grown too large

overhang *verb* jut out over

overhaul *verb* examine carefully and carry out repairs ◇ *noun* a thorough examination and repair

overhead *adv* directly above: *the aeroplane flew overhead* ◇ *adj* placed high above the ground: *overhead cables* ◇ *noun* (**overheads**) the general expenses of a business *etc*

overhear *verb* hear what you were not meant to hear

overjoyed *adj* extremely pleased or happy

overland *adv & adj* on or by land, not sea

overlap *verb* **1** extend over and partly cover (each other or something else): *the two pieces of cloth overlapped* **2** cover a part of the same area or subject as another; partly coincide ◇ *noun* the amount by which something overlaps

overleaf *adj* on the other side of a leaf of a book

overload *verb* **1** load or fill too much **2** put too great an electric current through

overlook *verb* **1** look down on from a higher point, giving a view of: *the house overlooked the village* **2** fail to notice; miss **3** decide not to punish; forgive

overlord *noun, hist* a lord with power over other lords

overmuch *adv* too much

overnight *adv* **1** during the night: *staying overnight with a friend* **2** in a very short time: *he changed completely overnight* ◇ *adj* **1** for the night: *an overnight bag* **2** got or made in a very short time: *an overnight success*

overpass *noun* a road going over another road, railway, canal, *etc*

overpower *verb* **1** defeat through greater strength **2** cause to feel helpless; overwhelm • **overpowering** *adj* **1** unable to be resisted **2** very strong; overwhelming: *overpowering smell*

overrate *verb* value more highly than is deserved: *his new film is overrated*

overreach *verb*: **overreach yourself** try to do or get more than you can and so fail

override *verb* **1** take manual control of (something normally automatic) **2** ignore: *overriding the teacher's authority* • **overriding** *adj* more important that all others; dominant

overrule *verb* go against or cancel (an earlier judgement or request)

overrun *verb* **1** grow or spread over: *overrun with weeds* **2** take possession of (a country)

overseas *adj & adv* in or to another country over the sea; abroad

oversee *verb* watch over; supervise • **overseer** *noun*

overshadow *verb* lessen the importance of by doing or being better than

oversight noun **1** something left out or forgotten by mistake **2** failure to notice

overstep verb go further than (a set limit, rules, etc)

overt adj not hidden or secret; open

overtake verb catch up with and pass

overthrow verb defeat and force out of power

overtime noun **1** time spent working beyond the agreed normal hours **2** payment for this, usually at a higher rate

overtone noun an additional meaning or association, not directly stated

overture noun **1** a proposal intended to open discussions: overtures of peace **2** a piece of music played as an introduction to an opera

overweening adj **1** extremely conceited; arrogant **2** of pride: excessive

overwhelm verb **1** cause to feel helpless or unable to cope: overwhelmed with grief **2** defeat completely **3** load with too great an amount • **overwhelming** adj

overwork verb work more than is good for you • **overworked** adj

overwrought adj excessively nervous or excited; agitated

oviparous adj (of animals) producing eggs that hatch outside the mother's body

ovoid adj egg-shaped

ovulate verb produce eggs from the ovary that are ready to be fertilized • **ovulation** noun

ovum noun (plural **ova**) the egg from which the young of animals and people develop

owe verb **1** be in debt to: I owe Peter three pounds **2** have (someone or something) to thank for: he owes his success to his family • **owing to** because of

owl noun a bird of prey that comes out at night • **owlet** noun a young owl

own verb **1** have as a possession **2** formal confess to be true; admit ◇ adj belonging to the person mentioned: is this all your own work? • **own goal** noun a goal scored by mistake against your own side • **hold your own** keep your place or position in the face of a challenge • **on your own 1** by your own efforts **2** alone

owner noun someone who possesses anything • **ownership** noun possession

ox noun (plural **oxen**) a male cow, usually castrated, used for drawing loads etc

Oxbridge noun Oxford and Cambridge Universities ◇ adj of or typical of Oxbridge

oxide noun a compound of oxygen and another element

oxidize verb **1** combine with oxygen **2** become rusty

oxygen noun a gas with no taste, colour or smell, forming part of the air and of water • **oxygenate** verb

oyster noun an edible shellfish certain types of which produce pearls in their shell • **oystercatcher** noun a small black and white wading bird that eats limpets and mussels

Oz noun, informal Australia

oz abbrev ounce(s)

ozone noun a form of oxygen • **ozone-friendly** adj free from chemicals that damage the ozone layer • **ozone layer** noun a layer of the upper atmosphere that protects the earth from the sun's ultraviolet rays

Pp

p *abbrev* **1** page **2** pence

PA *abbrev* **1** public address (system) **2** personal assistant

pa *abbrev* per annum

pace *noun* **1** a step **2** rate of walking, working, progressing, *etc*; speed ◇ *verb* **1** measure by steps **2** walk backwards and forwards impatiently or angrily • **pacemaker** *noun* **1** someone who sets the pace in a race **2** a device used to correct weak or irregular heart rhythms

pachyderm /pak-i-durm/ *noun* a thick-skinned animal such as an elephant

pacify *verb* (**pacifies, pacifying, pacified**) **1** make less angry or hostile; calm **2** make peaceful • **pacifist** *noun* someone who is against war and works for peace

pack *noun* **1** a number of things wrapped together as a unit; a bundle **2** a set of playing cards **3** a group of animals, *esp* dogs or wolves ◇ *verb* **1** place (clothes *etc*) in a case or bag for a journey **2** press or crowd together closely • **pack animal** *noun* an animal that carries loads on its back • **pack ice** *noun* a mass of large pieces of floating ice driven together by wind, currents, *etc* • **pack in** cram in tightly

package *noun* **1** a bundle, a parcel **2** a number of things provided as a single item **3** a package holiday ◇ *verb* **1** put into a container **2** wrap • **package holiday** or **package tour** *noun* a holiday or tour arranged by an organizer with all travel and accommodation included in the price

packet *noun* **1** a small parcel **2** a container made of paper, cardboard, *etc*

packing *noun* **1** the act of putting things in cases or bags for a journey **2** material for wrapping goods to pack **3** something used to fill an empty space • **packing case** *noun* a wooden box for transporting goods • **send packing** send (someone) away forcefully

pact *noun* **1** an agreement **2** a treaty or contract

pad *noun* **1** a soft cushion-like object to prevent jarring or rubbing *etc* **2** a bundle of sheets of paper fixed together **3** a soft fleshy underpart on an animal's paw **4** a rocket-launching platform ◇ *verb* (**padding, padded**) **1** stuff or protect with a soft material **2** (often with **out**) fill up with unnecessary material **3** walk making a dull, soft noise • **padding** *noun* **1** stuffing material **2** words included in a speech, book, *etc* just to fill space or time

paddle *verb* **1** move forward by the use of paddles; row **2** wade in shallow water ◇ *noun* a short oar with a broad blade • **paddle steamer** *noun* a steamboat driven by two large wheels made up of paddles

paddock *noun* a small closed-in field used for pasture

paddy or **paddy field** *noun* a muddy field in which rice is grown

padlock *noun* a removable lock with a hinged hook

paean /pee-un/ *noun* a song of triumph, praise or thanksgiving

paediatrics or *US* **pediatrics**

/peed-i-at-riks/ *sing noun* the treatment of children's diseases • **paediatrician** *or US* **pediatrician** *noun*

paedophile *or US* **pedophile** /peed-uh-fail/ *noun* someone who has sexual desire for children

paella /pai-el-uh/ *or* /pa-eh-ya/ *noun* a Spanish rice dish of fish or chicken, vegetables and saffron

pagan *adj* 1 of a religion in which many gods are worshipped, *esp* a religion that existed before Christianity 2 *derog* not believing in any religion; heathen ◇ *noun* a pagan person • **paganism** *noun*

page *noun* 1 one side of a blank, written or printed sheet of paper 2 a boy who carries the train of the bride's dress in a marriage service 3 a boy servant ◇ *verb* send a message to the pager of (someone), *esp* in order to summon them • **pager** *noun* a small portable electronic communication device that makes a sound or displays a message to show that the carrier is wanted somewhere

pageant *noun* 1 an elaborate parade or display 2 a show or procession made up of scenes from history • **pageantry** *noun* elaborate show or display

paginate *verb, comput* number the pages of a document automatically • **pagination** *noun*

pagoda *noun* an Eastern temple, *esp* in China or India, or a building in the style of one

paid *past form of* **pay**

pail *noun* an open container of tin, zinc, plastic, *etc* for carrying liquids; a bucket

pain *noun* 1 the feeling of being physically or emotionally hurt 2 threat of punishment: *under pain of death* 3 (**pains**) care: *takes great pains with his work* ◇ *verb* cause suffering to; distress • **pained** *adj* showing pain or

distress • **painful** *adj* 1 causing pain 2 annoying, or annoyingly slow • **painfully** *adv* • **painkiller** *noun* a medicine taken to lessen pain • **painless** *adj* • **painlessly** *adv* • **painstaking** *adj* done with great care • **painstakingly** *adv*

paint *verb* 1 apply liquid colour to, *esp* with a brush 2 make a picture of using liquid colours 3 describe in words ◇ *noun* a liquid substance used for colouring and applied with a brush, a spray, *etc* • **painter** *noun* 1 someone whose trade is painting 2 an artist who creates pictures using paint 3 a rope used to fasten a boat • **painting** *noun* 1 the act or art of creating pictures with paint 2 a painted picture

pair *noun* 1 two of the same kind 2 a set of two ◇ *verb* 1 join to form a pair 2 go in twos 3 mate

pajamas *US spelling of* **pyjamas**

pakora *noun* an Indian dish of balls of chopped vegetables coated in batter and fried

pal *noun, informal* a friend

palace *noun* the large impressive house of a king, queen, archbishop or aristocrat

palaeography /pehl-i-og-ruh-fi/ *noun* the study of historical styles of handwriting • **palaeographer** *noun* • **palaeographic** *or* **palaeographical** *adj*

palaeolithic *or* **paleolithic** /pehl-i-uh-lith-ik/ *adj* relating to the early Stone Age when people used stone tools

palaeontology /pehl-i-un-tol-uh-ji/ *noun* the study of fossils • **palaeontological** *adj* • **palaeontologist** *noun*

palatable *adj* 1 pleasant to the taste 2 acceptable or pleasing: *the truth is often not palatable*

palate *noun* 1 the roof of the mouth 2 taste

Do not confuse with: **palette** and **pallet**

palatial /puh-*leh*-shul/ *adj* like a palace; magnificent

palaver /puh-*lah*-vuh/ *noun* an unnecessary fuss

pale[1] *noun* a wooden stake used in making a fence • **paling** *noun* a row of wooden stakes forming a fence

pale[2] *adj* **1** light or whitish in colour **2** not bright ◇ *verb* make or turn pale

palette *noun* **1** a board or plate on which an artist mixes paints **2** a range of colours used for something or used by a particular artist

Do not confuse with: **pallet** and **palate**

palfrey *noun, old* a horse for riding, not one used in battle

palimpsest *noun* a manuscript written, or drawing made, on top of an earlier work that has been erased

palindrome *noun* a word or phrase that reads the same backwards as forwards, *eg* level

paling *see* **pale**[1]

palisade *noun* a fence of pointed wooden stakes

pall /pawl/ *noun* **1** the cloth over a coffin at a funeral **2** a dark covering or cloud: *a pall of smoke* ◇ *verb* become dull or uninteresting • **pallbearer** *noun* one of the people carrying or walking beside the coffin at a funeral

pallet *noun* **1** a straw bed or mattress **2** a platform that can be lifted by a fork-lift truck for stacking goods

Do not confuse with: **palette** and **palate**

palliative *adj* making something less severe or harsh ◇ *noun* something that lessens pain, *eg* a drug

pallid *adj* pale

pallor *noun* paleness

palm *noun* **1** a tall tree with broad fan-shaped leaves that grows in hot countries **2** the inner surface of the hand between the wrist and the start of the fingers • **palmist** *noun* someone who claims to tell fortunes by the lines and markings of the hand • **palmistry** *noun* the telling of fortunes in this way • **palmtop** *noun* a computer small enough to be held in the hand • **palm off** give with the intention of getting rid of: *that shopkeeper palmed off a foreign coin on me*

palpable *adj* **1** able to be touched or felt **2** easily noticed; obvious

palpate *verb* examine by touch • **palpation** *noun*

palpitate *verb* of the heart: beat rapidly; throb • **palpitations** *plural noun* uncomfortable rapid beating of the heart

palsy *noun* a loss of power and feeling in the muscles • **palsied** *adj*

paltry *adj* (**paltier, paltriest**) of a ridiculously or insultingly low amount or value

pampas *plural noun* the vast treeless plains of S America

pamper *verb* spoil (a child *etc*) by giving too much attention to

pamphlet *noun* a small thin book; a booklet • **pamphleteer** *noun* a writer of political pamphlets

pan *noun* **1** a pot used in cooking; a saucepan **2** the bowl of a toilet **3** a shallow dent in the ground ◇ *verb* (**panning, panned**) move a television or film camera sideways in a pivoting way • **panhandle** *verb, US* beg on the streets • **pan out** turn out (well or badly)

pan- *prefix* all, whole: *pan-European*

panacea /pan-uh-*see*-uh/ *noun* a cure for all things

panache /puh-*nash*/ *noun* impressive stylishness

pancake *noun* a thin cake of flour, eggs, sugar and milk, fried in a pan

pancreas *noun* a gland lying behind the stomach that carries out digestive and hormonal functions

panda *noun* 1 a large black-and-white bear-like animal found in Tibet *etc* 2 a raccoon-like animal found in the Himalayas • **panda car** *noun*, *Brit dated informal* a police patrol car

pandemic *adj* of a disease *etc*: occurring over a wide area and affecting a large number of people ◇ *noun* a pandemic disease

pandemonium *noun* a state of confusion and uproar

pander *noun*, *old* a pimp • **pander to** indulge the wishes or whims of

Pandora's box *noun* something that causes unexpected havoc

p and p *or* **p & p** *abbrev* postage and packing

pane *noun* a sheet of glass

panegyric /pan-i-*ji*-rik/ *noun* a speech or piece of writing praising someone or something greatly

panel *noun* 1 a flat rectangular piece forming a section of something 2 a group of people chosen to judge a contest, take part in a television quiz, *etc* 3 a board with controls and instruments on it, *eg* in an aircraft • **panelled** *adj*

pang *noun* a sudden sharp pain or strong feeling; a twinge

panic *noun* 1 a sudden and great fright 2 fear that spreads from person to person ◇ *verb* (**panics**, **panicking**, **panicked**) 1 cause to feel panic 2 act wildly through fear

panini *plural noun* grilled sandwiches

pannier *noun* 1 a bag or basket attached to a bicycle *etc*, for carrying things 2 a basket slung on a horse's back

panoply *noun* (*plural* **panoplies**) 1 the ceremonial dress, equipment, *etc* associated with a particular event: *the panoply of a military funeral* 2 *hist* a full suit of armour

panorama *noun* a wide view of a landscape, scene, *etc*

pansy *noun* (*plural* **pansies**) 1 a flower like the violet but larger 2 *dated informal offensive* an effeminate or homosexual man

pant *verb* 1 gasp for breath 2 say breathlessly 3 wish eagerly (for)

pantechnicon *noun*, *dated* a large van for transporting furniture

pantheism *noun* 1 the belief that all things in the physical universe are part of God 2 belief in many gods • **pantheist** *noun* a believer in pantheism • **pantheistic** *or* **pantheistical** *adj*

pantheon *noun* 1 all the gods of a particular people or religion 2 all the famous or outstanding people associated with a particular activity

panther *noun* 1 a large leopard 2 *US* a puma

pantomime *noun* a comic Christmas play with songs, based on a popular fairy tale

pantry *noun* (*plural* **pantries**) a room for storing food

pants *plural noun* 1 underpants 2 women's short-legged knickers 3 *US* trousers ◇ *adj*, *informal* of poor quality • **panties** *plural noun* women's or girls' knickers with short legs • **pantyhose** *plural noun*, *US* tights

pap *noun* 1 semi-liquid food for babies or sick people 2 worthless reading matter or entertainment

papa *noun* a child's name for **father**

papacy *noun* the position or power of the Pope • **papal** *adj*

paparazzo /pap-uh-*rat*-soh/ *noun* (*plural* **paparazzi**) a press photographer who hounds celebrities

papaya *noun* a green-skinned edible fruit from S America (*also called*: **pawpaw**)

paper *noun* 1 a material in the form of thin stiff sheets made from wood pulp, used for writing or wrapping 2 a single sheet of this 3 a newspaper 4 an essay on a learned subject 5 a set of examination questions 6 (**papers**) documents proving someone's identity, nationality, *etc* ◇ *verb* put wallpaper on • **paperback** *noun* a book bound in a flexible paper cover • **paperchase** *noun* a game in which one runner leaves a trail of paper so that others may track them • **paper tiger** *noun* someone who appears to be powerful but really is not • **paper trail** *noun* a set of documents that allow someone to trace a series of events • **paperweight** *noun* a heavy glass, metal, *etc* object used to keep a pile of papers in place

papier-mâché /pap-yeh-*ma*-sheh/ *noun* a substance consisting of paper pulp and some sticky liquid or glue, shaped into models, bowls, *etc*

papoose *noun*, *old* a Native American baby

paprika *noun* a type of ground red pepper

papyrus /puh-*pai*-rus/ *noun* (*plural* **papyri** *or* **papyruses**) a reed used by the ancient Egyptians *etc* to make paper

par *noun* 1 an accepted standard, value, *etc* 2 *golf* the number of strokes allowed for each hole if the play is perfect • **below par** 1 not up to standard 2 not feeling very well • **on a par with** equal to or comparable with

parable *noun* a story (*eg* in the Bible) that teaches a moral lesson

parabola /puh-*rab*-uh-luh/ *noun* 1 a curve, *esp* the curving course followed by an object thrown in the air 2 the intersection of a cone with a plane parallel to its side

paracetamol *noun* a pain-relieving drug

parachute *noun* an umbrella-shaped device made of light material and rope that supports someone or something dropping slowly to the ground from an aeroplane ◇ *verb* drop or arrive by parachute • **parachutist** *noun* someone dropped by parachute from an aeroplane

parade *noun* 1 a procession of people, vehicles, *etc* in celebration of some event 2 an orderly arrangement of troops for inspection or exercise ◇ *verb* 1 march in a procession 2 display in an obvious way 3 arrange (troops) in order

paradigm /*pa*-ruh-daim/ *noun* an example showing a certain pattern

paradise *noun* 1 heaven 2 a place or state of great happiness

paradox *noun* (*plural* **paradoxes**) a statement or situation containing elements that seem to contradict each other but are both true or real • **paradoxical** *adj* • **paradoxically** *adv*

paraffin *noun* a type of oil that burns and is used as a fuel (for heaters, lamps, *etc*)

paragliding *noun* the sport of gliding using a large kite-like canopy from which you hang in a seated position

paragon *noun* a model of perfection or excellence: *a paragon of good manners*

paragraph *noun* 1 a division of a piece of writing shown by beginning the first sentence on a new line 2 a short item in a newspaper

parakeet noun a type of small parrot

parallel adj 1 of lines: going in the same direction and never meeting, always remaining the same distance apart 2 similar or alike in some way: parallel cases ◇ noun 1 a parallel line 2 something comparable in some way with something else 3 a line marking latitude, drawn east and west across a map or round a globe at a set distance from the equator • **parallel port** noun a socket or plug for connecting a device such as a printer to a computer

parallelogram noun a flat four-sided figure the opposite sides of which are parallel and equal in length

paralyse or US **paralyze** verb 1 cause to lose sensation and the power of movement in a part of the body 2 make helpless or ineffective 3 bring to a halt • **paralysis** noun loss of sensation and the power of movement in part of the body • **paralytic** adj 1 suffering from paralysis 2 informal helplessly drunk ◇ noun a paralysed person

paramedic noun a member of an ambulance crew trained to give temporary emergency treatment • **paramedical** adj

parameter noun a boundary or limit

Do not confuse with: **perimeter**

paramilitary adj 1 organized like an army and carrying out terrorist activities 2 acting as reinforcements for a regular military force ◇ noun (plural **paramilitaries**) a member of a paramilitary force

paramount adj 1 very greatest: of paramount importance 2 above all others in rank or power

paramour noun, old a lover

paranoia noun 1 a form of mental disorder characterized by delusions of grandeur, persecution, etc 2 intense, irrational fear or suspicion

paranormal adj beyond what is normal in nature; supernatural

parapet noun a low wall on a bridge or balcony to prevent people falling over the side

paraphernalia /pa-ruh-fuh-nehl-i-uh/ plural noun belongings or equipment

paraphrase verb express (a piece of writing) in other words ◇ noun an expression in different words

paraplegia noun paralysis of the lower part of the body and legs • **paraplegic** adj affected by paraplegia ◇ noun someone who suffers from paraplegia

parasite noun an animal, plant or person living on another without being any use in return • **parasitic** adj

parasol noun a light umbrella used as a sunshade

paratroops plural noun soldiers carried by air to be dropped by parachute into enemy country • **paratrooper** noun

parboil verb boil (food) slightly

parcel noun a wrapped and tied package to be sent by post ◇ verb (**parcelling, parcelled**) 1 (with out) divide into portions 2 (with up) wrap up as a package • **part and parcel** an absolutely necessary part

parched adj 1 hot and very dry 2 thirsty • **parch** verb

parchment noun 1 the dried skin of a goat or sheep used for writing on 2 paper resembling this

pardon verb 1 forgive 2 free from punishment 3 allow to go unpunished ◇ noun 1 forgiveness 2 the act of pardoning • **pardonable** adj able to be forgiven

pare verb 1 peel or cut off the edge or outer surface of 2 make smaller gradually • **parings** plural noun small pieces cut away or peeled off

parent noun a father or mother • **parentage** noun descent from parents or ancestors • **parental** adj 1 of parents 2 with the manner or attitude of, or acting in the role of, a parent

parenthesis noun (plural **parentheses**) 1 a word or group of words in a sentence forming an explanation or comment, often separated by brackets or dashes, eg he and his wife (so he said) were separated 2 (**parentheses**) brackets • **parenthetical** adj

par excellence /pah ek-suh-lonhs/ adj superior to all others of the kind

pariah /puh-rai-uh/ noun someone greatly disliked and avoided or excluded; an outcast

parish noun (plural **parishes**) a district with its own church and minister or priest • **parishioner** noun a member of a parish

parity noun equality in status or level

park noun 1 a public area with grass and trees 2 an enclosed piece of land surrounding a country house ◇ verb stop and leave (a car etc) in a place for a time

parka noun a type of thick jacket with a hood

Parkinson's disease noun a disease causing trembling in the limbs and rigid muscles

parley verb (**parleys, parleying, parleyed**) hold a conference, esp with an enemy ◇ noun (plural **parleys**) a meeting between enemies to settle terms of peace etc

parliament noun 1 the main lawmaking council of a nation 2 Brit the House of Commons and the House of Lords • **parliamentary** adj

parlour noun, dated a sitting room

in a house • **parlourmaid** noun, dated a female domestic servant who brings food and serves people

Parma ham noun an Italian smoked ham

Parmesan noun a hard Italian cheese, often grated over dishes

parochial adj 1 interested only in local affairs; narrow-minded 2 relating to a parish • **parochially** adv

parody noun (plural **parodies**) an amusing imitation of someone's writing style, subject matter, etc ◇ verb (**parodies, parodying, parodied**) make a parody of

parole noun the release of a prisoner before the end of a sentence on condition that they will have to return if they break the law ◇ verb release on parole

paroxysm noun a fit of pain, rage, laughter, etc • **paroxysmal** adj

parquet /pah-keh/ noun a floor covering of wooden blocks arranged in a pattern

parr noun a young salmon before it leaves a river for the sea

parricide noun 1 the murder of a parent or close relative 2 someone who commits such a crime

parrot noun a tropical bird with a hooked bill and often brightly coloured feathers

parry verb (**parries, parrying, parried**) 1 deflect (a blow) 2 avoid giving a direct answer to (a question)

parse verb name the parts of speech of (words in a sentence) and say how the words are connected with each other

Parsee or **Parsi** noun a member of an Indian religious sect descended from the Persian Zoroastrians

parsimony noun, formal great care in spending money or reluctance to spend money • **parsimonious** adj

parsley noun a bright green leafy herb, used in cookery

parsnip noun a yellowish carrot-shaped vegetable

parson noun a member of the clergy, esp one in charge of a parish • **parsonage** noun a parson's house • **parson's nose** noun the piece of flesh at the tail-end of a cooked chicken or other bird

part noun 1 a piece that, together with others, forms a whole; a component: the various parts of a car engine 2 a character taken by an actor in a play; a role 3 a role in an action or event: played a vital part in the campaign 4 a portion or share 5 music the notes to be played or sung by a particular instrument or voice 6 (**parts**) talents: a man of many parts ◇ verb 1 divide 2 leave each other and go different ways 3 put or keep apart • **part exchange** noun the purchase of new goods in which old goods are given as part payment • **partly** adv not wholly or completely • **part of speech** noun one of the grammatical groups into which words are divided, eg noun, verb, adjective, preposition • **part song** noun a song in which singers sing different parts in harmony • **in good part** without being hurt or without taking offence • **part with** give away (often something you would prefer to keep) • **take someone's part** support them in an argument etc

partake verb (**partaking, partook, partaken**): **partake of** 1 eat or drink some of something 2 take a part in

parthenogenesis noun reproduction from an unfertilized egg

partial adj 1 in part only, not total or complete: partial payment 2 having a liking for (someone or something): partial to cheese • **partiality** noun 1 the favouring of one thing more than another; bias 2 a particular liking (for something) • **partially** adv

participate verb 1 take part (in) 2 have a share in • **participant** noun someone who takes part in anything • **participation** noun • **participatory** adj

participle noun a form of a verb that can be used with other verbs to form tenses, eg 'he was eating' or 'she has arrived', used as an adjective, eg 'stolen jewels', or used as a noun, eg 'running makes me tired'

particle noun a very small piece: a particle of sand

particular adj 1 relating to a single definite person, thing, etc considered separately from others: I want this particular colour 2 special: take particular care of the china 3 difficult to please; fussy: particular about her food ◇ noun (**particulars**) the facts or details about someone or something

parting noun 1 the act of leaving each other, or the time when this is done 2 a line dividing hair on the head brushed in opposite directions

partisan adj giving strong support or loyalty to a particular cause, theory, etc, often without considering other points of view ◇ noun someone with partisan views

partition noun 1 the dividing of a country into separate territories 2 a wall between rooms, or a screen that serves to divide a room into sections ◇ verb 1 divide into parts 2 divide by making a wall etc

partner noun 1 someone who shares the ownership of a business etc with another or others 2 one of a pair of people working together in a game, in dancing, etc 3 a husband, wife or lover ◇ verb act as partner to • **partnership** noun

partridge noun a type of bird that is shot as game

parturition noun, formal childbirth

party noun (plural **parties**) 1 a gathering

of guests for a celebration: *birthday party/dinner party* **2** a group of people travelling together: *party of tourists* **3** a number of people with the same plans or ideas: *a political party* **4** someone involved in an action, court case or legal agreement • **party line** *noun* **1** a shared telephone line **2** policy laid down by the leaders of a political party

parvenu /*pah*-vuh-noo/ *noun* (*plural* **parvenus**) *derog* someone with newly acquired wealth or power

PASCAL *noun* a high-level computer programming language

paschal /*pask*-ul/ *adj* **1** relating to the Jewish festival of Passover **2** relating to Easter

pas de deux /pah duh *duh*/ *noun* a ballet sequence involving two dancers

pashmina *noun* a shawl made from the wool of Himalayan goats

paso doble /pa-suh *doh*-bleh/ *noun* a Spanish dance like a two-step

pass *verb* **1** go, move, travel, *etc*: *he passed out of sight over the hill* **2** give by hand: *pass the salt* **3** go by: *I saw the bus pass our house* **4** overtake: *the car passed me on the inside* **5** of parliament: put (a law) into force **6** be successful in an examination **7** be declared healthy or in good condition after an inspection **8** come to an end: *the feeling of dizziness soon passed* **9** hand on: *he passed the story on to his son* **10** spend (time): *passing a pleasant hour by the river* **11** make, utter (*eg* a remark) ◇ *noun* **1** a ticket or card allowing someone to go somewhere **2** success in an examination **3** a narrow passage over or through a range of mountains **4** a sexual advance • **passer-by** *noun* (*plural* **passers-by**) someone who happens to pass by when something happens • **passkey** *noun* a key that can open several locks • **pass off 1** present (a forgery

etc) as genuine **2** turn out (well or badly) • **pass on 1** go forward; proceed **2** hand on **3** die • **pass out** faint • **pass up** fail to take up (an opportunity)

passable *adj* **1** fairly good **2** of a river *etc*: able to be crossed • **passably** *adv*

passage *noun* **1** a corridor **2** a part of the text of a book **3** a journey in a ship **4** a way through **5** the act of passing: *passage of time* • **passageway** *noun* a corridor or passage

passé /*pas-eh*/ *adj* no longer current or fashionable

passenger *noun* a traveller, not a member of the crew, in a train, ship, aeroplane, *etc*

passing *adj* **1** going by: *a passing car* **2** not lasting long: *passing interest* **3** casual: *passing remark* ◇ *noun* **1** the act of someone or something that passes **2** a going away or a coming to an end **3** death

passion *noun* strong feeling, *esp* sexual feeling, love or anger • **passionate** *adj* **1** easily moved to passion **2** full of passion • **passionately** *adv* • **passion flower** *noun* a tropical climbing plant with flowers thought to resemble a crown of thorns • **passion fruit** *noun* the edible, oblong fruit of the passion flower • **the Passion** the sufferings and death of Christ

passive *adj* **1** making no resistance **2** acted upon, not acting • **passively** *adv* • **passiveness** or **passivity** *noun* • **passive smoking** *noun* the involuntary inhaling of smoke from tobacco smoked by others

Passover *noun* a Jewish festival celebrating the exodus of the Israelites from Egypt

passport *noun* an official card or booklet giving the holder's identity and giving the right to travel abroad

password *noun* **1** a word typed into a computer to allow access to restricted data **2** a secret word that allows those who know it to go past a guard and into a place

past noun **1** (**the past**) the time gone by **2** someone's previous life or career **3** grammar the past tense ◇ adj **1** of an earlier time: *past kindnesses* **2** recently ended: *the past year* **3** gone, finished: *the time for argument is past* ◇ prep **1** after: *it's past midday* **2** up to and beyond: *go past the traffic lights* ◇ adv by: *she walked past, looking at no one* • **past perfect** noun a tense used for describing an action that took place before the main past actions being described, formed, in English, using *had* and a past participle

pasta noun **1** a dough used in making spaghetti, macaroni, *etc* **2** the prepared shapes of this, *eg* spaghetti

paste noun **1** a gluey liquid for sticking paper *etc* together **2** any soft, kneadable mixture: *almond paste* **3** pastry dough **4** fine glass used to make imitation gems • **pasteboard** noun cardboard

pastel adj of a colour: soft, pale ◇ noun **1** a chalk-like crayon used for drawing **2** a drawing made with this

pasteurize verb heat food (*esp* milk) in order to kill harmful germs in it

pastiche /pas-*teesh*/ noun a humorous imitation; a parody

pastille noun a small sweet, sometimes sucked as a medicine

pastime noun a spare-time interest; a hobby

pastor noun a member of the clergy • **pastoral** adj **1** relating to or depicting country life **2** done for the purpose of giving emotional support or religious advice

pastrami /pus-*trah*-mi/ noun seasoned smoked beef cut into thin slices

pastry noun (*plural* **pastries**) **1** a mixture of flour and water baked and

used to make the bases and crusts of pies, tarts, *etc* **2** a small cake

pasture noun ground covered with grass on which cattle graze • **pasturage** noun grazing land

pasty[1] /*pehs*-ti/ adj (**pastier, pastiest**) **1** like paste **2** pale

pasty[2] /*pas*-ti/ noun (*plural* **pasties**) a pie containing meat and vegetables in a covering of pastry

pat noun **1** a light, quick blow or tap with the hand **2** a small lump of butter **3** a small pile of cattle dung ◇ verb (**patting, patted**) strike gently; tap • **off pat** memorized thoroughly, ready to be said when necessary

patch verb **1** mend (clothes) by putting in a new piece of material to cover a hole **2** (with **up**) mend, *esp* hastily or clumsily **3** (with **up**) settle (a quarrel) ◇ noun (*plural* **patches**) **1** a piece of material sewn on to mend a hole **2** a small piece of ground **3** comput a file that corrects a fault in a computer program • **patchwork** noun fabric formed of small patches or pieces of material sewn together

patchouli /puh-*choo*-li/ noun a perfume oil obtained from the dried branches of an Asian tree

patchy adj (**patchier, patchiest**) of mixed or inconsistent quality • **patchily** adv • **patchiness** noun

pate /peht/ noun, formal the head: *a bald pate*

pâté /*pat*-eh/ noun a paste made of finely minced meat, fish or vegetables, flavoured with herbs, spices, *etc*

patella noun the kneecap

patent noun an official written statement granting someone the sole right to make or sell something that they have invented ◇ adj **1** protected from copying by a patent **2** easily seen; obvious ◇ verb obtain a patent for (an invention) • **patent leather** noun leather with a very glossy surface

• **patently** adv clearly: patently obvious

paterfamilias /peh-tuh-fuh-mil-i-as/ noun the male head of a family or household

paternal adj 1 of a father 2 like a father; fatherly 3 on the father's side of the family: my paternal grandfather • **paternalism** noun • **paternalistic** adj • **paternally** adv

paternity noun the state or fact of being a father • **paternity leave** noun leave of absence from work for a father after the birth of a child

path noun 1 a way made by people or animals walking on it; a track 2 the route to be taken by a person or vehicle: in the lorry's path 3 a course of action • **pathway** noun a path

pathetic adj 1 causing pity 2 causing contempt, esp because ridiculously inadequate: a pathetic attempt • **pathetically** adv

pathology noun the study of diseases • **pathological** adj 1 relating to disease 2 informal compulsive, obsessive: pathological liar • **pathologist** noun 1 a doctor who makes post-mortem examinations 2 a doctor who studies the causes and effects of disease

pathos /peh-thos/ noun a quality that arouses pity: the pathos of the situation made me weep

patience noun 1 the ability or willingness to be patient 2 a card game played by one person (also called: **solitaire**)

patient adj suffering delay, discomfort, etc without complaint or anger ◇ noun someone under the care of a doctor etc • **patiently** adv

patina /pat-i-nuh/ noun a film that forms on the surface of exposed metals etc

patio noun (plural **patios**) a paved open yard attached to a house

patisserie /puh-tees-uh-ri/ noun a shop selling French pastries and cakes

patois /pat-wah/ noun a dialect of language spoken by the ordinary people of a certain area

patriarch /peh-tri-ahk/ noun 1 the male head of a family or tribe 2 the head of the Greek Orthodox Church • **patriarchal** adj • **patriarchy** noun

patrician adj aristocratic

patricide noun 1 the murder of your own father 2 someone who commits such a murder • **patricidal** adj

patrimony noun property handed down from a father or ancestors

patriot noun someone who loves and is loyal to their country • **patriotic** adj • **patriotically** adv • **patriotism** noun love of and loyalty to your country

patrol verb (**patrolling**, **patrolled**) keep guard or watch by moving regularly around an area etc ◇ noun 1 the act of keeping guard in this way 2 the people keeping watch 3 a small group of Scouts or Guides • **patrol car** noun a police car used to patrol an area

patron noun 1 someone who gives financial and other support to (an artist, a form of art, etc) 2 a customer of a shop • **patronage** noun the support given by a patron • **patronize** verb 1 treat (someone) as an inferior; look down on: don't patronize me 2 be a patron towards: patronize your local shops • **patron saint** noun a saint chosen as the protector of a country etc

patronymic /pat-ruh-nim-ik/ noun a name derived from a father or male ancestor

patter¹ verb of rain, footsteps, etc: make a quick tapping sound ◇ noun the sound of falling rain, of footsteps, etc

patter² noun 1 fast talk, esp a salesman's charming or persuasive talk 2 the jargon of a particular group

pattern noun 1 a coherent series of events or features 2 a model or guide for making something 3 a decorative design 4 a sample: *a book of tweed patterns* • **patterned** adj having a design, not self-coloured

patty noun (plural **patties**) a small flat cake of chopped meat etc

paucity noun, formal smallness of number or quantity

paunch noun (plural **paunches**) a fat stomach

pauper noun a very poor person

pause noun 1 a short stop during an activity or event 2 a break or hesitation in speaking or writing 3 music a symbol (⌢) showing the holding of a note or rest ◇ verb stop for a short time

pave verb lay (a street) with stone or concrete to form a level surface for walking on • **pave the way for** prepare or make the way easy for

pavement noun a paved path at the side of a road for pedestrians

pavilion noun 1 a building in a sports ground with facilities for changing clothes 2 a large ornamental building 3 a large tent

paw noun the foot of an animal ◇ verb 1 of an animal: scrape with one of the front feet 2 handle or touch (someone) roughly or rudely 3 strike out at (something) wildly with the hand: *paw the air*

pawn verb put (an article of some value) in someone's keeping in exchange for a sum of money which, when repaid, buys back the article ◇ noun 1 chess a small piece of the lowest rank 2 someone who lets themselves be used by another for some purpose • **pawnbroker** noun someone who lends money in exchange for pawned articles • **pawnshop** noun a pawnbroker's place of business • **in**

pawn having been pawned

pawpaw another word for **papaya**

pay verb (**paying, paid**) 1 give (money) in exchange for (goods etc): *I paid £30 for it* 2 suffer the punishment (for) 3 be advantageous or profitable: *it pays to be prepared* 4 give (eg attention) ◇ noun money given or received for work; wages • **payable** adj requiring to be paid • **pay-as-you-earn** adj of income tax: deducted from a salary before it is given to the worker • **payee** noun someone to whom money is paid • **payment** noun 1 the act of paying 2 money paid for goods etc • **payphone** noun a coin- or card-operated public telephone • **payroll** noun 1 a list of people entitled to receive pay 2 the money for paying wages • **pay off** 1 pay in full and discharge (workers) owing to lack of work 2 have good results: *his hard work paid off* • **pay out** 1 spend 2 give out (a length of rope etc)

PAYE abbrev pay-as-you-earn

PC abbrev 1 personal computer 2 police constable 3 political correctness, or politically correct

pc abbrev per cent

PCC abbrev Press Complaints Commission

PE abbrev physical education

pea noun 1 a vegetable that is the small round green seed of a climbing plant 2 the climbing plant itself • **peashooter** noun a small toy tube for blowing dried peas through as missiles

peace noun 1 quietness or calm 2 freedom from war or disturbance 3 a treaty bringing this about • **peaceable** adj of a quiet nature and fond of peace • **peaceful** adj quiet and calm • **peacefully** adv • **peace offering** noun something offered as an apology or gesture of reconciliation

peach noun (plural **peaches**) 1 a

juicy, velvet-skinned fruit with a large hard seed **2** the tree on which it grows **3** an orange-pink colour

peacock *noun* a large bird the male of which has brightly coloured, patterned tail feathers

peahen *noun* a female peacock

peak *noun* **1** the pointed top of a mountain or hill **2** the highest point **3** the brim of a cap that juts out at the front ◇ *verb* **1** rise to a peak **2** reach the highest point: *prices peaked in July and then fell steadily* ● **peaked** *adj* **1** pointed **2** of a cap: having a peak ● **peaky** *adj* looking pale and unhealthy

peal *noun* **1** a set of bells tuned to each other **2** the sequence of sounds rung on such bells **3** a succession of loud sounds: *peals of laughter* ◇ *verb* sound loudly

---

Do not confuse with: **peel**

---

peanut *noun* (*also called* **groundnut, monkey-nut**) a type of nut similar to a pea in shape ● **peanut butter** *noun* a paste of ground roasted peanuts, spread on bread *etc*

pear *noun* **1** a fruit that narrows towards the stem and bulges at the end **2** the tree on which it grows ● **go pear-shaped** *informal* go wrong

pearl *noun* **1** a gem formed in the shell of the oyster and several other shellfish **2** a valuable remark *etc*: *pearls of wisdom* ● **the pearly gates** the entrance to heaven

peasant *noun* **1** someone who works and lives on a farm, *esp* someone with a simple or poor life in a fairly poor country **2** *derog* an uneducated or uncultured person

pease pudding *noun* a dish of boiled, mashed peas

peat *noun* turf cut out of boggy places, dried and used as fuel

pebble *noun* a small, roundish stone ● **pebbledash** *noun* a coating for outside walls with small stones set into the mortar ● **pebbly** *adj* **1** full of pebbles **2** rough, knobbly

pecan *noun* **1** an oblong, thin-shelled nut common in N America **2** the tree on which this nut grows

peccadillo *noun* (*plural* **peccadilloes** *or* **peccadillos**) a minor piece of bad behaviour; a misdemeanour

peccary *noun* (*plural* **peccaries**) a S American animal like a pig

peck *verb* **1** strike (something) with the beak **2** pick (something) up with the beak **3** eat only a little of **4** kiss (someone) quickly and briefly ◇ *noun* **1** a sharp blow with the beak **2** a brief kiss ● **peckish** *adj* slightly hungry

pectin *noun* a carbohydrate occurring in fruit and used as a setting agent in jellies and jams

pectoral *adj* of the breast or chest: *pectoral muscles*

peculiar *adj* **1** rather strange; odd: *a very peculiar person* **2** belonging to one person or thing only: *a custom peculiar to England* ● **peculiarity** *noun* a particular feature that marks someone or something off as different from others in some way ● **peculiarly** *adv*

pecuniary *adj, formal* of money

pedagogical /ped-uh-*goj*-ik-ul/ *adj* to do with teaching or teachers

pedal *noun* **1** a lever worked by the foot on a bicycle, piano, harp, *etc* **2** a key worked by the foot on an organ ◇ *verb* (**pedalling, pedalled**) **1** work the pedals of **2** ride on a bicycle

pedant /*ped*-unt/ *noun* **1** someone overly fussy about minor details **2** someone who makes a great show of their knowledge ● **pedantic** /pid-*ant*-ik/ *adj* ● **pedantry** *noun* **1** fussiness about unimportant details **2** a display of knowledge

peddle *verb* travel from door to door selling goods

pederasty *noun* anal sexual intercourse between a man and a boy • **pederast** *noun* someone who practises pederasty

pedestal *noun* the foot or support of a pillar, statue, *etc*

pedestrian *noun* someone who goes or travels on foot ◇ *adj* 1 for people on foot 2 unexciting, dull: *a pedestrian account* • **pedestrian crossing** *noun* a place where pedestrians may cross the road when the traffic stops

pediatrics, **pediatrician** *US spellings of* **paediatrics**, **paediatrician**

pedicure *noun* a treatment for the feet which includes treating corns, cutting nails, *etc* • **pedicurist** *noun* someone who gives a pedicure

pedigree *noun* 1 the ancestry of a pure-bred animal 2 a list of someone's ancestors 3 a distinguished descent or ancestry ◇ *adj* of an animal: pure-bred, from a long line of ancestors of the same breed

pediment *noun* a triangular structure over the front of an ancient Greek building

pedlar *noun* someone who peddles; a hawker

pedometer *noun* an instrument for measuring the distance covered by a walker

pee *verb* (**pees**, **peeing**, **peed**) *informal* urinate ◇ *noun* 1 the act of urinating 2 urine

peek *verb* look briefly and often secretively; peep ◇ *noun* a brief, often secretive look

peel *verb* 1 strip off the outer covering or skin of (a fruit or vegetable): *peel an apple* 2 of skin, paint, *etc*: come off in small pieces 3 lose skin in small flakes, *eg* as a result of sunburn ◇ *noun* skin or rind

Do not confuse with: **peal**

peelie-wally *adj, Scot* unhealthily or unattractively pale

peep *verb* 1 look through a narrow opening, round a corner, *etc* 2 look slyly or quickly (at) 3 begin to appear: *the sun peeped out* 4 make a high, small sound ◇ *noun* 1 a quick, often secretive look 2 a high, small sound • **peeping Tom** *noun* someone who spies secretly on others; a voyeur

peer *verb* look at with half-closed eyes, as if with difficulty ◇ *noun* 1 someone's equal in rank, merit or age 2 a nobleman of the rank of baron upwards 3 a member of the House of Lords • **peerage** *noun* 1 a peer's title 2 the peers as a group • **peerless** *adj* better than all others

peeve *verb, informal* irritate • **peeved** *adj* annoyed

peevish *adj* bad-tempered

peewit *noun* the lapwing

peg *noun* 1 a pin or stake of wood, metal, *etc* 2 a hook fixed to a wall for hanging clothes *etc* ◇ *verb* (**pegging**, **pegged**) 1 fasten with a peg 2 fix (prices *etc*) at a certain level

peignoir /pehn-*wahr*/ *noun* a woman's light dressing-gown

pejorative *adj* showing disapproval, scorn, *etc*: *a pejorative remark* • **pejoratively** *adv*

Pekinese *or* **Pekingese** *noun* a breed of small dog with a long coat and flat face

pelagic *adj* living near the surface or middle layer of the sea

pelf *noun, old* money or wealth

pelican *noun* a large water bird with a pouched bill for storing fish

pelican crossing *noun* a street crossing where the lights are operated by pedestrians

pellagra *noun* a disease marked by shrivelled skin and paralysis, caused by the lack of certain vitamins

pellet *noun* 1 a small ball of shot *etc* fired from a gun 2 any substance in the form of a small hard solid mass

pell-mell *adv* in great confusion; headlong

pellucid *adj* able to be seen through clearly; transparent

Pelmanism *noun* a card-game in which cards are spread out face down and must be picked up in matching pairs

pelmet *noun* a strip or band hiding a curtain rail

pelota *noun* a Basque ball-game played against a marked wall with a basket-like racket strapped to the players' wrists

pelt *noun* the untreated skin of an animal ◇ *verb* 1 throw things at 2 run fast 3 of rain: fall heavily • **at full pelt** at top speed

pelvis *noun* the frame of bone that circles the body below the waist • **pelvic** *adv*

pemmican *noun* dried meat, pressed hard into cakes

pen¹ *noun* an instrument with a point or nib for writing in ink ◇ *verb* (**penning, penned**) write (*eg* a letter) • **pen friend** *noun* someone you have never seen, *usu* living abroad, with whom you exchange letters • **penknife** *noun* a pocket knife with folding blades • **pen name** *noun* a name adopted by a writer instead of their own name

pen² *noun* a small enclosure for sheep, cattle, *etc* ◇ *verb* (**penning, penned**) enclose in a pen

pen³ *noun* a female swan

penal *adj* of or as punishment • **penalize** *verb* 1 punish 2 put at a disadvantage • **penal servitude** *noun* imprisonment with hard labour as an added punishment

penalty *noun* (*plural* **penalties**) 1 punishment 2 a disadvantage given to a player or team that breaks a rule of a game

penance *noun* punishment willingly suffered by someone to make up for a wrong

pence *plural of* **penny**

penchant /*ponh-shonh*/ *noun* a liking for (something) or a tendency to want (something)

pencil *noun* an object for writing or drawing with, consisting of a thin cylinder of wood containing a length of graphite ◇ *verb* (**pencilling, pencilled**) draw, mark, *etc* with a pencil

pendant *noun* 1 an ornament hung from a necklace *etc* 2 a necklace with such an ornament

pendent *adj* hanging

pending *adj* awaiting a decision or attention: *this matter is pending* ◇ *prep* until the coming of: *pending confirmation*

pendulous *adj* hanging down; drooping

pendulum *noun* a swinging weight that drives the mechanism of a clock

penetrate *verb* 1 pierce or pass into or through 2 enter by force • **penetrating** *adj* 1 of a sound: piercing 2 keenly seeking information; probing: *penetrating question* • **penetration** *noun*

penguin *noun* a large sea bird of Antarctic regions, which cannot fly

penicillin *noun* a medicine that kills bacteria, obtained from mould

penile *adj* of the penis

peninsula *noun* a long narrow piece of land almost surrounded by water • **peninsular** *adj*

penis *noun* the part of the body of a male human or animal used in sexual intercourse and for urinating

penitent adj sorry for your sins ◇ noun a penitent person • **penitential** adj • **penitentiary** noun, US a prison

pennant noun a long flag coming to a point at the end

pennate adj, formal wing-shaped

penny noun 1 a coin worth $1/_{100}$ of £1 2 (plural **pence**) used to show an amount in pennies: the newspaper costs forty-two pence 3 (plural **pennies**) used for a number of coins: I need five pennies for the coffee machine • **penniless** adj having no money • **penny-farthing** noun a old type of bicycle with a large front wheel and small rear wheel • **penny-pinching** adj ungenerous with money; stingy

pension noun a sum of money paid regularly to a retired person, a widow, someone wounded in war, etc • **pensionable** adj having or giving the right to a pension: pensionable age • **pensioner** noun someone who receives a pension, esp someone who has reached the normal age of retirement • **pension off** dismiss or allow to retire with a pension

pensive adj thoughtful • **pensively** adv • **pensiveness** noun

pentagon noun a flat shape with five straight sides • **pentagonal** adj • **the Pentagon** the headquarters of the US armed forces in Washington, DC

pentathlon noun a five-event athletics contest • **pentathlete** noun an athlete who takes part in this event

pentatonic adj, music of a scale: consisting of five notes, ie a major scale omitting the fourth and seventh

Pentecost noun 1 a Jewish festival held fifty days after Passover 2 a Christian festival held seven weeks after Easter

penthouse noun a luxurious flat at the top of a building

pent-up adj 1 of emotions: not freely expressed 2 kept enclosed or locked up

penultimate adj last but one

penumbra noun a light shadow surrounding the main shadow of an eclipse

penury noun the state of being very poor; poverty • **penurious** adj impoverished, penniless

peon noun an agricultural labourer in S America

peony noun (plural **peonies**) a type of garden plant with large red, white or pink flowers

people plural noun 1 the men, women and children of a country or nation 2 persons generally ◇ verb 1 fill with people 2 make up the population of; inhabit • **people carrier** noun a type of vehicle with enough seats for a large family

pep noun, informal energy or spirit • **pep pill** noun a pill containing a stimulating drug • **pep talk** noun a talk meant to encourage or arouse enthusiasm • **pep up** fill with energy or liveliness; invigorate

pepper noun 1 a spicy powder used as a flavouring for food, obtained from the dried and crushed berries of a tropical shrub 2 the shrub on which the berries grow 3 a hot-tasting hollow fruit containing many seeds, eaten raw, cooked or pickled ◇ verb 1 sprinkle with pepper 2 (with **with**) throw at or hit: peppered with bullets • **pepper-and-salt** adj mixed black and white: pepper-and-salt hair • **peppercorn** noun the dried berry of the pepper plant • **pepper mill** noun a small device for grinding peppercorns over food • **peppery** adj 1 containing a lot of pepper 2 inclined to be hot-tempered

peppermint *noun* **1** a type of plant with a powerful taste and smell **2** a flavouring taken from this and used in sweets *etc*

pepperoni *noun* a spicy beef and pork sausage

peptic *adj* of the digestive system: *peptic ulcer*

per *prep* **1** in, out of: *five per cent (ie five out of every hundred)* **2** for each: *£2 per dozen* **3** in each: *six times per week* • **per annum** in each year • **per capita** *or* **per head** for each person • **per cent** in every hundred

peradventure *adv, old* by chance

perambulator *noun, old* a pram

perceive *verb* **1** become aware of through the senses **2** see **3** understand • **perceptible** *adj* able to be seen or understood • **perception** *noun* the ability to perceive; understanding • **perceptive** *adj* able or quick to perceive or understand • **perceptively** *adv*

percentage *noun* the rate per hundred

perch¹ *noun* (*plural* **perches**) **1** a rod or high place on which birds stand **2** a high seat or position ◇ *verb* of birds: stand in a high place

perch² *noun* (*plural* **perches**) a type of freshwater fish

perchance *adv, old* by chance; perhaps

percolate *verb* **1** of a liquid: drip or drain through small holes **2** cause (a liquid) to do this **3** of news *etc*: pass slowly down or through • **percolator** *noun* a device for percolating: *a coffee percolator*

percussion *noun* **1** musical instruments played by striking, *eg* drums, cymbals, *etc* **2** a striking of one object against another • **percussionist** *noun* a musician who plays percussion • **percussive** *adj* making a loud striking noise

perdition *noun* **1** utter loss or ruin **2** everlasting punishment

peregrinations *plural noun, formal* wanderings

peregrine *noun* a type of falcon

peremptory *adj* **1** urgent **2** of a command: to be obeyed at once **3** domineering, dictatorial

perennial *adj* **1** lasting through the year **2** everlasting, perpetual **3** of a plant: growing from year to year without replanting or sowing ◇ *noun* a perennial plant

perfect *adj* **1** with no faults or defects; flawless **2** finished in every detail; complete **3** exact: *a perfect circle* ◇ *verb* **1** make perfect **2** finish • **perfection** *noun* **1** the state of being perfect **2** the highest state or degree • **perfectionist** *noun* someone who is satisfied only by perfection

perfidious *adj, formal* treacherous, unfaithful • **perfidiousness** *noun* • **perfidy** *noun*

perforate *verb* make a hole or holes through • **perforated** *adj* pierced with holes

perforce *adv, old* necessarily or unavoidably

perform *verb* **1** do or carry out **2** act (a part) on the stage **3** provide entertainment for an audience **4** play (a piece of music) • **performance** *noun* **1** an entertainment in a theatre *etc* **2** the act of doing something **3** the power with which a machine, car, *etc* works • **performer** *noun* someone who acts or performs

perfume *noun* **1** a fragrant liquid put on the skin; scent **2** pleasant smell; fragrance ◇ *verb* **1** put scent on or in **2** give a sweet smell to • **perfumery** *noun* a shop where perfume is sold or a factory where perfume is made

perfunctory *adj* done carelessly or half-heartedly: *perfunctory inspection* • **perfunctorily** *adv*

perhaps adv it may be (that); possibly: perhaps she'll resign

peri- prefix around: pericardium

peril noun a great danger • **perilous** adj very dangerous • **perilously** adv • **at your peril** at the risk of being harmed or punished

perimeter noun 1 the outer edge of any area 2 the outside line enclosing a shape

---

Do not confuse with: **parameter**

---

perinatal adj relating to the period between the seventh month of pregnancy and the first week of the baby's life

perineum noun the part of the body between the genitals and the anus • **perineal** adj

period noun 1 a stretch of time 2 a stage in the earth's development or in history 3 a full stop after a sentence 4 a time of menstruation

periodic adj 1 happening at regular intervals, eg every month or year 2 happening every now and then: a periodic clearing out of rubbish

periodical noun a magazine that appears at regular intervals ◇ adj issued or done at regular intervals; periodic

peripatetic adj moving from place to place; travelling

peripheral adj 1 of or on a periphery; away from the centre 2 of little importance; marginal

periphery noun (plural **peripheries**) 1 the line surrounding something 2 an outer boundary or edge

periphrastic adj, formal using more words than are necessary; roundabout

periscope noun a tube with mirrors by which a viewer in a submarine etc is able to see objects on the surface

perish verb 1 be destroyed completely 2 die or decay • **perishable** adj liable to go bad or become worn quickly

peristyle noun a group of columns surrounding a building

peritoneum noun a membrane in the stomach and pelvis • **peritonitis** noun inflammation of the peritoneum

periwig noun, hist a wig

periwinkle noun 1 a small shellfish shaped like a small snail, eaten as food when boiled 2 a creeping evergreen plant with a small blue flower

perjure verb (with **yourself** etc) tell a lie when you have sworn to tell the truth, esp in a court of law • **perjurer** noun • **perjury** noun

perk¹ noun something of value allowed in addition to payment for work; a fringe benefit

perk² verb: **perk up** recover energy or spirits • **perkily** adv • **perkiness** noun • **perky** adj in good spirits; jaunty

perm noun a wave or curl put into the hair by a special process and usu lasting for some months ◇ verb give (hair) a perm

permaculture noun farming without using artificial fertilizers and with minimal weeding

permafrost noun permanently frozen subsoil

permanent adj not temporary; lasting • **permanence** or **permanency** noun • **permanently** adv • **permanent wave** noun a perm

permeate verb 1 pass into through small holes 2 fill or reach every part of • **permeable** adj

permit verb 1 agree to; allow 2 make possible ◇ noun a written order allowing someone to do something: a fishing permit • **permissible** adj allowable • **permission** noun freedom given to do something • **permissive** adj **1** allowing something to be done **2** lenient; tolerant • **permissiveness** noun

permutation noun the arrangement of numbers, letters, etc in a certain order

pernicious adj destructive • **perniciousness** noun

pernickety adj fussy about small details

peroration noun, formal **1** the closing part of a speech **2** a speech

peroxide noun the chemical hydrogen peroxide, used for bleaching hair etc • **peroxide blonde** noun, informal a woman whose hair has been bleached

perpendicular adj **1** standing upright; vertical **2** at right angles (to) ◇ noun a line at right angles to another

perpetrate verb commit (a sin, error, etc) • **perpetration** noun • **perpetrator** noun

Do not confuse with: **perpetuate**

perpetual adj continuing all the time or for a long time; everlasting • **perpetually** adv

perpetuate verb cause to last for ever or for a long time • **perpetuity** noun • **in perpetuity 1** for ever **2** for the length of someone's life

Do not confuse with: **perpetrate**

perplex verb **1** cause to be puzzled; bewilder **2** make more complicated • **perplexity** noun **1** a puzzled state of mind **2** something that puzzles

perquisite noun, formal a perk

per se /puh seh/ adv in itself; essentially

persecute verb **1** harass over a period of time **2** cause to suffer, esp because of religious beliefs

• **persecution** noun • **persecutor** noun

Do not confuse with: **prosecute**

persevere verb keep trying to do a thing in spite of difficulties • **perseverance** noun the act of persevering

persimmon noun a plum-like fruit from an African or American tree

persist verb **1** continue to have an idea or belief **2** continue to do something in spite of difficulties **3** survive after others have perished; last • **persistence** noun • **persistent** adj **1** refusing to be discouraged or swayed; obstinate **2** not dying out; lasting • **persistently** adv

person noun **1** a human being **2** someone's body: jewels hidden on his person **3** form, shape: trouble arrived in the person of Gordon • **personable** adj likeable • **personage** noun, formal a well-known person • **in person** personally, not represented by someone else

persona noun the outward part of the personality presented to others; social image

personal adj **1** of your own; private: personal belongings **2** of a remark: insulting or offensive to the person it is aimed at • **personal column** noun a newspaper column containing personal messages, advertisements, etc • **personal organizer** noun a small portable loose-leaf file containing a diary and an address book, maps, indexes, etc • **personal stereo** noun a small portable music player with earphones

Do not confuse with: **personnel**

personality noun (plural **personalities**) **1** all of a person's characteristics as seen by others **2** a well-known person

personally adv **1** speaking from

your own point of view **2** by your own action, not using an agent or representative: *he thanked me personally*

persona non grata *noun* someone disliked or out of favour

personify *verb* (**personifies, personifying, personified**) **1** be a perfect example of **2** talk about (things, ideas, *etc*) as if they were living persons • **personification** *noun*

personnel *noun* the people employed in a firm *etc*

Do not confuse with: **personal**

---

perspective *noun* **1** a point of view **2** the giving of a sense of depth, distance, *etc* in a painting like that in real life • **in perspective 1** of an object in a painting *etc*: of a size in relation to other things that it would have in real life **2** of an event: in its true degree of importance when considered in relation to other events: *keep things in perspective*

Perspex *noun, trademark* a transparent plastic that looks like glass

perspicacious *adj* of clear or sharp understanding • **perspicacity** *noun* keenness of understanding

perspicuity *noun* clearness in expressing thoughts • **perspicuous** *adj*

perspire *verb* sweat • **perspiration** *noun* sweat

persuade *verb* cause (someone) to do or think something by arguing with them or advising them • **persuasion** *noun* **1** the act of persuading **2** a firm belief, *esp* a religious belief • **persuasive** *adj* having the power to convince • **persuasiveness** *noun*

pert *adj* **1** attractively small or firm: *a pert nose* **2** very confident or cheeky, *esp* in an attractive way: *a pert young woman*

pertain *verb, formal* (with **to**) have to do with: *duties pertaining to the job*

pertinacious *adj* holding strongly to an idea; obstinate • **pertinacity** *noun*

pertinent *adj* connected with the subject spoken about; relevant

perturb *verb* make very anxious or uneasy • **perturbation** *noun* great worry; anxiety

peruse *verb* read with care • **perusal** *noun*

pervade *verb* spread through: *silence pervaded the room*

perverse *adj* obstinate in holding to the wrong point of view; unreasonable • **perverseness** *or* **perversity** *noun* stubbornness

pervert *verb* **1** turn away from what is normal or right: *pervert the course of justice* **2** cause to behave in a criminal or evil way; corrupt ◊ *noun* someone who commits unnatural or perverted acts • **perversion** *noun* **1** the act of perverting **2** an unnatural or perverted act

pessary *noun* (**pessaries**) a cotton plug containing medicine *etc* inserted into the vagina

pessimism *noun* the habit of thinking that things will always turn out badly (*contrasted with:* **optimism**) • **pessimist** *noun* someone who tends to think in this way • **pessimistic** *adj* • **pessimistically** *adv*

pest *noun* **1** a troublesome person or thing **2** a creature that is harmful or destructive, *eg* a mosquito • **pesticide** *noun* any substance that kills animal pests • **pestilence** *noun* a deadly disease that spreads • **pestilent** *or* **pestilential** *adj* **1** very unhealthy **2** troublesome

pester *verb* annoy continually

pestle *noun* a tool for crushing things to powder

pesto *noun* a sauce made with ground pine nuts, basil, olive oil and Parmesan cheese

pet noun 1 a tame animal kept in the home for companionship 2 a favourite 3 a fit of sulking ◇ adj 1 kept as a pet 2 favourite 3 main: my pet hate ◇ verb (**petting, petted**) fondle • **pet name** noun a name used to express affection or love • **pettish** adj sulky

petal noun one of the leaf-like parts of a flower

petard noun: **hoist with your own petard** caught in a trap of your own making

peter verb: **peter out** fade or dwindle away to nothing

petite adj small and neat in appearance

petit fours /puh-tee faw/ plural noun small fancy cakes or biscuits

petition noun a request or note of protest signed by many people and sent to a government or authority ◇ verb send a petition to • **petitioner** noun

petrel noun a small, long-winged seabird

petrify verb (**petrifies, petrifying, petrified**) 1 turn (someone) stiff with fear 2 turn into stone • **petrifaction** noun

petrol noun petroleum when refined as fuel for use in vehicles

petroleum noun oil in its raw, unrefined form, extracted from natural wells below the earth's surface

petticoat noun an underskirt worn by women

pettifogging noun arguing over trivialities or details

petty adj (**pettier, pettiest**) of little importance; trivial • **pettiness** noun • **petty cash** noun money paid or received in small sums • **petty officer** noun a rank of officer in the navy equal to a non-commissioned officer in the army

petulant adj 1 tending to sulk at the slightest thing 2 unreasonably impatient • **petulance** noun

petunia noun a flowering plant with trumpet-shaped flowers

pew noun a seat or bench in a church

pewter noun a mixture of tin and lead

PG abbrev parental guidance, a certificate awarded to a film denoting possible unsuitability for young children

pH noun a measure of the alkalinity or acidity of a solution

phagocyte /feh-guh-sait/ noun a white blood corpuscle that surrounds and destroys bacteria

phalanx noun (plural **phalanxes**) 1 a group of supporters 2 a company of foot soldiers in an oblong-shaped formation

phallus noun a representation of a penis • **phallic** adj

phantasm noun a vision or an illusion

phantasmagoria noun a dreamlike series of visions or hallucinations

phantom noun a ghost

Pharaoh noun, hist a ruler of ancient Egypt

pharmaceutical adj relating to the making up of medicines and drugs

pharmacology noun the scientific study of drugs and their effects • **pharmacological** adj • **pharmacologist** noun

pharmacopoeia /fah-muh-kuh-pee-uh/ noun a list of drugs with directions for their preparation

pharmacy noun (plural **pharmacies**) 1 a chemist's shop 2 the art of preparing medicines • **pharmacist** noun someone who prepares and sells medicines

pharynx noun (plural **pharnyges** or **pharynxes**) the back part of the throat behind the tonsils • **pharyngitis** *noun* inflammation of the pharynx

phase *noun* **1** one in a series of changes in the shape or appearance of something, *eg* the moon **2** a stage in the development of something, *eg* a war or a scheme

PhD *abbrev* Doctor of Philosophy, a higher university degree

pheasant *noun* a bird with brightly coloured feathers that is shot as game

phenobarbitone *noun* a sedative and hypnotic drug

phenol *noun* an acid used as a powerful disinfectant

phenomenon *noun* (*plural* **phenomena**) **1** an event, *esp* in nature, that is observed by the senses: *the phenomenon of lightning* **2** something remarkable or very unusual; a wonder • **phenomenal** *adj* very unusual or impressive; remarkable • **phenomenally** *adv* extremely: *phenomenally successful*

pheromone *noun* a chemical secreted by the body that attracts or influences other people or animals

phew *exclam* used to express relief

phial /*fai*-ul/ *noun* a small glass bottle

philanderer *noun* a man who has casual sexual relationships with women; a womanizer • **philander** *verb*

philanthropy *noun* the giving of money for the benefit of others, *esp* for public projects • **philanthropic** *adj* • **philanthropist** *noun* someone who does good to others

philately *noun* the study and collecting of stamps • **philatelist** *noun*

philharmonic *adj* (in names of orchestras *etc*) music-loving

philistine *noun* someone ignorant of, or hostile to, culture and the arts

philology *noun* the study of words and their history • **philologist** *noun*

philosopher *noun* someone who studies philosophy • **philosophical** *adj* **1** of philosophy **2** tending to see problems in context and not to be upset by them

philosophy *noun* (*plural* **philosophies**) **1** the study of the nature of the universe and of human behaviour **2** someone's personal view of life

philtre /*fil*-tuh/ *noun, formal* a love potion

phlegm /flem/ *noun* **1** thick slimy matter brought up from the throat by coughing **2** coolness of temper; calmness • **phlegmatic** *adj* not easily upset or angered

phlox /floks/ *noun* a garden plant with flat white or purplish flowers

phobia *noun* an intense, often irrational fear or dislike

phoenix /*fee*-niks/ *noun* a mythological bird believed to burn itself and to rise again from its ashes

phone *noun* a telephone • **phonecard** *noun* a card that can be used to pay for calls in certain public telephones

phoneme *noun* the smallest meaningful unit of sound in any language

phonetic *adj* **1** relating to the sounds of language **2** of a word: spelt according to sound, *eg flem* for 'phlegm' • **phonetics** *sing noun* **1** the study of the sounds of language **2** a system of writing according to sound

phoney *or* **phony** *adj* (**phonier**, **phoniest**) *informal* not genuine or sincere; fake

phonology *noun* **1** the study of speech sounds **2** any particular system of speech sounds • **phonological** *adj* • **phonologically** *adv* • **phonologist** *noun*

phosphorus *noun* a wax-like poisonous substance that gives out light in the dark • **phosphate** *noun* a soil fertilizer that contains phosphorus

photo 415 **piccolo**

• **phosphorescence** noun faint glow of light in the dark • **phosphorescent** adj

photo noun (plural **photos**) informal a photograph

photocopy noun (plural **photocopies**) a copy of a document made using a photocopier ◇ verb make a photocopy of • **photocopier** noun a device that photographs and develops images of a document on paper

Photofit noun, trademark a method of making identification pictures by combining photographs of individual features

photogenic adj looking good or attractive in photographs

photography noun the art of taking pictures with a camera • **photograph** noun a picture taken with a camera ◇ verb take a picture with a camera • **photographer** noun • **photographic** adj

photosensitive adj affected or operated by light

Photostat noun, trademark 1 a special camera for making photographic copies of documents, pages of books, etc 2 a photographic copy so made

photosynthesis noun the conversion of light into complex compounds by plants

phrase noun 1 a small group of words expressing a single idea, eg 'after dinner', 'on the water' 2 a short saying or expression 3 music a short group of bars forming a distinct unit ◇ verb express in words: he could have phrased it more tactfully • **phraseology** noun someone's personal choice of words and phrases

phrenology noun the study of the surface of the skull as a sign of personality etc • **phrenologist** noun

phylactery noun (plural **phylacteries**) a small box containing a piece of Scripture worn on the wrist or forehead by Orthodox Jews

phylum /fai-lum/ noun (plural **phyla**) a main division of the animal or vegetable kingdoms, subdivided into classes

physical adj 1 relating to the body: physical strength/physical exercises 2 relating to things that can be seen or felt • **physically** adv

physician noun a doctor specializing in medical rather than surgical treatment

physics sing noun the science that includes the study of heat, light, sound, electricity, magnetism, etc • **physicist** noun someone who specializes in physics

physiognomy /fiz-i-on-uh-mi/ noun the features or expression of the face

physiology noun the study of the way in which living bodies work, including blood circulation, food digestion, etc • **physiological** adj • **physiologist** noun

physiotherapy noun the treatment of disease by bodily exercise, massage, etc rather than by drugs • **physiotherapist** noun

physique noun 1 the build of someone's body 2 bodily strength

PI abbrev private investigator

piano noun (plural **pianos**) a large musical instrument played by striking keys • **pianist** noun someone who plays the piano

piazza /pee-at-suh/ noun a marketplace or town square surrounded by buildings

pibroch /pee-broxh/ noun music for bagpipes, which is free in rhythm, consisting of a theme and variations

picador noun a bullfighter armed with a lance and mounted on a horse

piccalilli noun a vegetable pickle

piccolo noun (plural **piccolos**) a small high-pitched flute

pick verb 1 choose 2 pluck or gather (flowers, fruit, etc) 3 nibble (at) 4 remove food, mucus, etc from (teeth, the nose, etc) 5 open (a lock) with a tool other than a key ◇ noun 1 choice: take your pick 2 the best or best part 3 a pickaxe 4 an instrument for picking, eg a toothpick • **pick a quarrel** start a quarrel deliberately • **pick on 1** single out for criticism or bullying 2 nag at • **pick up 1** lift up 2 learn (a language, habit, etc) casually 3 give (someone) a lift in a car 4 find or get by chance 5 improve or gain strength

pickaxe noun a heavy tool for breaking ground, pointed at one end or both ends

picket noun 1 a number of workers on strike who prevent others from going into work 2 a pointed stake 3 a small sentry-post or guard ◇ verb 1 of striking workers: protest at a place of work and try to dissuade others from working 2 fasten (a horse etc) to a stake

pickle noun 1 chopped vegetables preserved in vinegar and spices, eaten cold 2 informal an awkward, unpleasant situation ◇ verb preserve with vinegar and spices

pickpocket noun someone who robs people's pockets or handbags

picky adj (**pickier**, **pickiest**) fussy • **pickiness** noun

picnic noun a meal eaten out-of-doors, often during an outing etc ◇ verb (**picnics**, **picnicking**, **picnicked**) have a picnic • **no picnic** informal an unpleasant task or situation

pictorial adj 1 consisting of pictures 2 containing pictures

picture noun 1 a painting or drawing 2 a portrait 3 a photograph 4 a film 5 (**pictures**) the cinema 6 a vivid description ◇ verb 1 make a picture of 2 see in the mind; imagine

picturesque adj such as would make a good or striking picture; pretty, colourful

piddling adj trifling, minor

pidgin noun a language made up of two others in a distorted form

---

Do not confuse with: **pigeon**

---

pie noun meat, fruit or other food baked in a casing or covering of pastry • **pie-eyed** adj, dated informal drunk

piebald adj white and black in patches

piece noun 1 a part or portion of anything 2 a single article or example: a piece of paper 3 an artistic work: a piece of popular music 4 a coin 5 an object that you move in chess, draughts, etc ◇ verb put (together)

pièce de résistance /pyes duh reh-zi-stonhs/ noun the best item or work

piecemeal adv by pieces or little by little

piecework noun work paid according to how much is done, not to the time spent on it

pied adj with two or more colours in patches

pied-à-terre /pyeh-da-tair/ noun a second home in a city

pier noun 1 a platform built from the shore into the sea as a landing place for ships 2 a pillar supporting an arch, bridge, etc

pierce verb 1 make a hole through 2 force a way into • **piercing** adj shrill and loud; sharp

pierrot /pee-uh-roh/ noun a comic entertainer with a white face and loose white clothes

pietà /pye-ta/ noun a painting etc of the Virgin Mary with the dead Christ

piety see **pious**

piffle noun nonsense

pig noun 1 a farm animal from whose

flesh ham and bacon are made **2** an oblong moulded piece of metal • **piggery** noun or **pigsty** noun a place where pigs are kept • **piggyback** noun a ride on someone's back with your arms round their neck • **piggybank** noun a child's container for savings in the form of a toy pig with a slit along its back • **pigheaded** adj stubborn • **piglet** noun a young pig • **pigskin** noun leather made from a pig's skin • **pigtail** noun hair formed into a plait

pigeon noun a bird of the dove family • **pigeonhole** noun a small division in a case or desk for papers etc ◇ verb put into a category, esp an unfairly narrow or general category

pigment noun **1** paint or other substance used for colouring **2** a substance in animals and plants that gives colour to the skin etc • **pigmentation** noun colouring of skin etc

pigmy another spelling of **pygmy**

pike noun **1** a large fierce freshwater fish **2** a weapon like a spear with a long shaft and a sharp head

Pilates /pi-lah-teez/ noun a type of exercise system

pilau /pee-low/ noun an Indian dish of rice, meat and spices

pilchard noun a small sea fish like a herring, often tinned

pile noun **1** a number of things lying one on top of another, a heap **2** a great quantity **3** a large building **4** a large stake or pillar driven into the earth as a foundation for a building, bridge, etc **5** the thick, soft surface on carpets and on cloth such as velvet ◇ verb (often with **up**) make or form a pile or heap

pilfer verb steal small things • **pilfering** noun

pilgrim noun a traveller to a holy place • **pilgrimage** noun a journey to a holy place

pill noun **1** a tablet of medicine **2** (often with **the**) a contraceptive in the form of a small tablet taken by mouth

pillage verb seize goods and money, esp as loot in war ◇ noun the act of plundering in this way

pillar noun **1** an upright support for roofs, arches, etc **2** an upright post or column built as a monument **3** someone or something that gives support: a pillar of the community • **pillarbox** noun, dated an upright public box for posting letters; a postbox

pillion noun **1** a seat for a passenger on a motorcycle **2** old a light saddle for a passenger on horseback, behind the main saddle

pillory verb (**pillories**, **pillorying**, **pilloried**) mock or criticize fiercely in public ◇ noun (plural **pillories**) hist a wooden frame fitted over the head and hands of wrongdoers as a punishment

pillow noun a soft cushion for the head ◇ verb rest or support on a pillow • **pillowcase** or **pillowslip** noun a cover for a pillow

pilot noun **1** someone who flies an aeroplane **2** someone who steers a ship in or out of a harbour **3** a first or single episode of a proposed television or radio series broadcast to test audience response **4** a guide, a leader ◇ verb **1** broadcast as a pilot **2** steer or guide • **pilot light** noun **1** a small gas flame from which larger jets are lit **2** an electric light showing that a current is switched on • **pilot scheme** noun a scheme introduced on a small scale to act as a guide to a full-scale one

pimento noun (plural **pimentos**) a mild type of red pepper

pimp noun a man who manages prostitutes and takes money from them

pimpernel noun a plant of the primrose family, with small pink or scarlet flowers

pimple *noun* a small round infected swelling on the skin • **pimpled** or **pimply** *adj* having pimples

PIN /pin/ *abbrev* personal identification number, a number that you key into a machine to withdraw or transfer money

pin *noun* 1 a short pointed piece of metal with a head, used for fastening fabric, fastening paper to walls, *etc* 2 a wooden or metal peg 3 a skittle ◇ *verb* (**pinning**, **pinned**) 1 fasten with a pin 2 hold fast, pressed against something: *the bloodhound pinned him to the ground*

piña colada /pee-nuh kuh-*lah*-duh/ *noun* a drink of rum, pineapple juice and coconut

pinafore *noun* 1 an apron to protect the front of a dress 2 a sleeveless dress worn over a jersey, blouse, *etc*

pinball *noun* a game played on a slot-machine in which a ball runs down a sloping board between obstacles

pince-nez /panhs-*neh*/ *noun* a pair of eyeglasses with a spring for gripping the nose

pincers *plural noun* 1 a tool like pliers but with sharp points for gripping, pulling out nails, *etc* 2 the large front claws of a crab or lobster

pinch *verb* 1 squeeze (*esp* flesh) between the thumb and forefinger, nip 2 grip tightly, *esp* hurt by tightness 3 *informal* steal ◇ *noun* (*plural* **pinches**) 1 a squeeze 2 a small amount (*eg* of salt) • **pinched** *adj* of a face: looking cold, pale or thin • **at a pinch** if really necessary or urgent • **feel the pinch** suffer from lack of money

pinchbeck *adj* in poor imitation

pine *noun* 1 an evergreen tree with needle-like leaves that produces cones 2 the soft wood of such a tree, used for furniture *etc* ◇ *verb* 1 long (for something) 2 lose strength, energy or health

pineal gland *noun* a gland in the brain that releases a hormone at night which causes sleepiness

pineapple *noun* a large tropical fruit shaped like a pine cone

ping *noun* a whistling sound such as that of a bullet ◇ *verb* make a whistling sound • **Ping-Pong** *noun, trademark* table tennis

pinion *noun* a small toothed wheel ◇ *verb* 1 hold (someone) fast by binding or holding their arms 2 cut or fasten the wings of (a bird)

pink *noun* 1 a pale red colour 2 a sweet-scented garden flower like a carnation 3 a healthy or good state: *feeling in the pink* ◇ *verb* 1 of an engine: make a faint clinking noise 2 cut (cloth *etc*) with pinking scissors • **pinking scissors** or **pinking shears** *plural noun* scissors with blades that give cloth a zigzag edge

pinkie *noun, informal* the little finger

pinnacle *noun* 1 a slender spire or turret 2 a high pointed rock or mountain 3 the highest point

pinnie *noun, informal* an apron or overall

pinochle /*peen*-uk-ul/ *noun* a card game played with two packs with the lowest cards removed

pint *noun* a liquid measure equal to just over $\frac{1}{2}$ litre

Pinyin *noun* a system for transcribing Chinese using Roman characters

pioneer *noun* 1 an explorer 2 an inventor, or an early exponent of something: *pioneers of the cinema* ◇ *verb* act as a pioneer

pious *adj* respectful in religious matters • **piety** *noun*

pip *noun* 1 a seed of a fruit 2 a spot or symbol on dice or cards 3 a star on an army officer's tunic 4 a short bleep as part of a time signal *etc* on the radio

pipe noun 1 a tube for carrying water, gas, etc 2 a tube with a bowl at the end, for smoking tobacco 3 (**pipes**) a musical instrument made of several small pipes joined together 4 (**pipes**) bagpipes ◇ verb 1 convey (eg water) by pipe 2 play (notes, a tune) on a pipe or pipes 3 whistle or chirp 4 speak in a shrill high voice • **pipe clay** noun a fine white clay used to whiten leather and used in making clay pipes • **piped music** noun continuous background music played throughout a building • **pipeline** noun a long line of pipes, eg to carry oil from an oilfield • **piper** noun someone who plays a pipe, esp the bagpipes • **in the pipeline** in preparation and soon to be done or soon to become available • **pipe down** stop talking • **pipe up** say something after being silent

pipette noun a small glass tube used in laboratories

piping noun 1 a length of tubing 2 a system of pipes 3 a narrow ornamental cord for trimming clothes 4 a strip of decorative icing round a cake ◇ adj high-pitched, esp unpleasantly so; shrill • **piping hot** adj very hot

pippin noun a kind of apple

pipsqueak noun, informal an insignificant, or very small, person

piquant /pee-konh/ adj 1 sharp-tasting or spicy 2 arousing interest

pique /peek/ noun anger caused by wounded pride or resentment ◇ verb 1 make angry 2 arouse (curiosity)

piranha noun a S American river fish that eats flesh

pirate noun 1 someone who robs ships at sea 2 someone who illegally copies or publishes material without permission from the copyright-holder ◇ verb illegally copy or publish (copyright material) without permission from the copyright-holder • **piracy** noun • **piratical** adj

pirouette noun a rapid whirling on the toes in dancing ◇ verb twirl in a pirouette

piss verb, slang urinate ◇ noun, slang 1 urine 2 an act of urinating • **pissed** adj, slang 1 extremely drunk 2 US annoyed • **piss about** or **piss around** slang behave foolishly or lazily • **pissed off** slang annoyed • **piss off** slang go away

pistachio noun (plural **pistachios**) a greenish nut often used as a flavouring

piste /peest/ noun a ski trail

pistil noun the seed-bearing part of a flower

pistol noun a small gun held in the hand

piston noun a round piece of metal that moves up and down inside a cylinder, eg in an engine • **piston rod** noun the rod to which a piston is fitted

pit noun 1 a hole in the ground 2 a place from which coal and other minerals are dug 3 the ground floor of a theatre behind the stalls 4 (often **pits**) a place beside the racecourse for repairing and refuelling racing cars etc 5 informal an armpit 6 (**the pits**) slang an awful or intolerable situation or place ◇ verb (**pitting**, **pitted**) set one thing or person against another: pitting my wits against his • **pitted** adj marked with small holes

pitch noun (plural **pitches**) 1 the field for certain sports 2 an attempt at selling or persuading: sales pitch 3 the height or depth of a note 4 a thick dark substance obtained by boiling down tar 5 a throw 6 a peak, an extreme point: reach fever pitch 7 cricket the ground between wickets 8 the spot reserved for a street seller or street-entertainer 9 the slope of a roof etc ◇ verb 1 fix a tent etc in the ground 2 throw, esp suddenly and violently 3 fall heavily; lurch: pitch forward 4 set the level or key of a tune

• **pitchblende** noun a black mineral made up of uranium oxides • **pitch-dark** adj very dark • **pitched battle** noun a battle on chosen ground between sides arranged in position beforehand • **pitchfork** noun a fork for lifting and throwing hay

pitcher noun a kind of large jug

piteous see pity

pitfall noun a possible danger

pith noun 1 the soft substance in the centre of plant stems 2 the white substance under the rind of an orange, lemon, etc 3 the important part of anything • **pithy** adj 1 full of meaning, to the point: a pithy saying 2 full of pith

pitiable see pity

piton /pee-ton/ noun an iron peg for attaching a rope to in mountaineering

pitta noun a flat oval E Mediterranean bread

pittance noun a very small wage or allowance

pituitary gland noun a gland in the brain affecting growth

pity noun (plural **pities**) 1 feeling for the sufferings of others; sympathy 2 a cause of grief 3 a regrettable fact ◇ verb (**pities**, **pitying**, **pitied**) feel sorry for • **piteous** or **pitiable** adj deserving pity; wretched • **pitiful** adj evoking pity

pivot noun 1 the pin or centre on which anything turns 2 something or someone greatly depended on ◇ verb 1 turn on a pivot 2 depend (on) • **pivotal** adj

pixel noun, comput the smallest element in a screen display

pixy or **pixie** noun (plural **pixies**) a kind of fairy

pizza noun a flat piece of dough spread with tomato, cheese, etc and baked

pizzazz noun flamboyant style; panache

pizzicato /pit-si-kah-toh/ adv played by plucking the strings rather than by using the bow

placard noun a printed notice fixed to a wall or carried on a protest march

placate verb make less angry; calm

place noun 1 any area, building, or other physical location 2 a particular spot 3 an open space in a town: market place 4 a seat in a theatre, on a train, at a table, etc 5 a position in a race 6 a position on a course, in a job, etc 7 rank ◇ verb 1 put in a particular place, esp carefully 2 find a place for 3 give (an order for goods etc) 4 remember who someone is: I can't place him at all • **placed** adj 1 having a place 2 among the first three in a competition • **in place** 1 in the proper position 2 suitable • **in place of** instead of • **out of place** 1 not in the proper position 2 unsuitable

placebo /pluh-see-boh/ noun (plural **placebos**) an inactive medicine given to humour a patient, or used in drug trials

placenta /pluh-sen-tuh/ noun a part of the womb that connects an unborn mammal to its mother, shed at birth

placid adj calm, not easily disturbed • **placidity** noun

plagiarize verb steal or borrow from the writings or ideas of someone else without permission • **plagiarism** noun • **plagiarist** noun

plague noun 1 a fatal infectious disease carried by rat fleas 2 a great and troublesome quantity: a plague of flies ◇ verb pester or cause trouble for (someone) continually

plaice noun a type of edible flatfish

plaid noun a long piece of cloth, esp tartan, worn over the shoulder

plain adj 1 simple or ordinary

2 without ornament or decoration **3** easy to see or understand; clear **4** not physically attractive **5** flat or level ◇ *noun* a level stretch of land • **plain-clothes** *adj* of a police detective: wearing ordinary clothes, not uniform • **plain-spoken** *adj* speaking your thoughts frankly

plaintiff *noun* someone who takes action against another in the law courts

plaintive *adj* sad, sorrowful

plait /plat/ *noun* **1** a length of hair arranged by intertwining three or more separate pieces **2** a set of threads *etc* intertwined in this way ◇ *verb* form into a plait

plan *noun* **1** a scheme or arrangement to do something **2** a diagram of a building, town, *etc* as if seen from above ◇ *verb* (**planning**, **planned**) **1** make a sketch or plan of **2** decide or arrange to do (something)

plane[1] *noun* an aeroplane

plane[2] *noun* **1** a level surface **2** a carpentry tool for smoothing wood **3** a standard (of achievement *etc*) ◇ *adj* flat or level ◇ *verb* **1** smooth with a plane **2** glide over water *etc*

plane[3] *noun* a type of tree with broad leaves

planet *noun* any of the bodies, *eg* the earth or Venus, that move round the sun or round another fixed star • **planetary** *adj*

planetarium *noun* (*plural* **planetariums**) a building with a domed ceiling on which dots of light representing planets and stars are projected to represent the night sky to an audience

plangent *adj* resonant and rather mournful

plank *noun* a long flat piece of timber

plankton *noun* tiny living creatures floating in seas, lakes, *etc*

plant *noun* **1** a living growth from the ground, with a stem, root and leaves **2** a factory **3** machinery ◇ *verb* **1** put (something) into the ground so that it will grow **2** put (an idea) into the mind **3** put in position: *plant a bomb* **4** set down firmly: *plant your feet on the floor* **5** *informal* place (something) as false evidence

plantain *noun* a coarse green-skinned tropical fruit like a banana

plantation *noun* **1** an area planted with trees **2** an estate for growing cotton, sugar, rubber, tobacco, *etc* • **planter** *noun* the owner of a plantation

plaque *noun* **1** a decorative plate of metal, china, *etc* for fixing to a wall **2** a film of saliva and bacteria that forms on the teeth

plasma *noun* the liquid part of blood and certain other fluids • **plasma screen** *noun* a high-quality screen for computers and televisions

plaster *noun* **1** a mixture of lime, water and sand that sets hard, for covering walls *etc* **2** (*also called* **plaster of Paris**) a fine mixture containing gypsum, used for moulding, making casts for broken limbs, *etc* **3** a small dressing that can be stuck over a wound ◇ *adj* made of plaster ◇ *verb* **1** apply plaster to **2** cover too thickly (with) • **plastered** *adj*, *slang* drunk • **plasterer** *noun* someone who plasters walls

plastic *noun* a chemically manufactured substance that can be moulded when soft, formed into fibres, *etc* ◇ *adj* **1** made of plastic **2** easily moulded or shaped • **plastic bullet** *noun* a cylinder of PVC fired from a gun, used by police in crowd control • **plastic explosive** *noun* mouldable explosive material • **plasticity** *noun* the quality of being easily moulded • **plastic surgery** *noun* an operation to repair or replace damaged areas of skin, or to improve the appearance of a facial or bodily feature

Plasticine noun, trademark a soft clay-like substance used for modelling

plate noun 1 a shallow dish for holding food 2 a flat piece of metal, glass, china, etc 3 gold and silver articles 4 a sheet of metal used in printing 5 a book illustration 6 the part of false teeth that fits to the mouth ◇ verb cover with a coating of metal • **plate glass** noun glass in thick sheets, used for shop windows, mirrors, etc • **plating** noun a thin covering of metal

plateau noun (plural **plateaus** or **plateaux**) 1 a broad level stretch of high land 2 a steady, unchanging state: prices have now reached a plateau

platelet noun a tiny blood particle that plays a part in clotting

platform noun 1 a raised level surface for passengers at a railway station 2 a raised floor for speakers, entertainers, etc

platinum noun a heavy and very valuable steel-grey metal

platitude noun a dull, ordinary remark made as if it were important

platonic adj of a relationship: not sexual

platoon noun a section of a company of soldiers

platter noun a large flat plate

platypus noun (plural **platypuses**) (also called **duck-billed platypus**) a small water animal of Australia that has webbed feet and lays eggs

plaudits plural noun praise

plausible adj 1 seeming to be truthful or honest 2 seeming probable or reasonable • **plausibility** noun

play verb 1 take part in a game 2 have fun 3 act (on a stage etc) 4 perform on (a musical instrument) 5 carry out (a trick) 6 trifle or fiddle (with): don't play with your food 7 gamble 8 move over lightly: the firelight played on his face ◇ noun 1 amusement, recreation 2 gambling 3 a story for acting; a drama 4 freedom of movement 5 a way of behaving: foul play • **playboy** noun an irresponsible rich man only interested in pleasure • **player** noun 1 someone who plays a game, musical instrument, etc: a lute player 2 dated an actor • **playground** noun an open area for playing at school, in a park, etc • **playgroup** noun a group of young children who play together supervised by adults • **playing card** noun one of a pack of cards used in playing card games • **playmate** noun a friend with whom you play • **play-off** noun 1 a game to decide a tie 2 a game between the winners of other competitions • **playschool** noun a nursery school or playgroup • **plaything** noun a toy • **playwright** noun a writer of plays • **play at** treat in a lighthearted, not serious way: he only plays at being a business man • **play off** set (one person) against another to gain some advantage or amusement for yourself • **play on** make use of (someone's feelings) to turn to your own advantage • **play on words** a pun • **play the game** act fairly and honestly

playful adj 1 wanting to play: a playful kitten 2 fond of joking • **playfully** adv • **playfulness** noun

PLC abbrev public limited company

plea noun 1 an excuse 2 an accused person's answer to a charge in a law court 3 an urgent request • **plea bargaining** noun the arranging of lenient terms for an accused person willing to plead guilty before their trial begins

plead verb 1 state your case in a law court 2 (with **with**) beg earnestly 3 give as an excuse • **plead guilty** or **not guilty** admit or deny guilt in a law court

pleasant adj giving pleasure; agreeable or enjoyable • **pleasantness** noun • **pleasantry** noun a good-humoured joke • **pleasurable** adj giving pleasure; pleasant

please verb 1 give pleasure or delight to 2 satisfy 3 like or want (to do): do as you please ◇ exclam added for politeness to a command or request: please keep off the grass • **if you please** please

pleasure noun 1 enjoyment 2 something that you would like to have or do; desire: what is your pleasure? • **at your pleasure** when or if you please

pleat noun a fold in cloth that has been pressed or stitched down ◇ verb put pleats in • **pleated** adj

pleb noun, informal someone who has no taste or culture; a boor

plebeian adj 1 of the ordinary or common people 2 lacking culture or taste; vulgar

plebiscite noun a vote by everyone in an area on a special issue

plectrum noun a small piece of horn, metal, etc used for plucking the strings of a guitar

pledge noun 1 something handed over as security for a loan 2 a solemn promise ◇ verb 1 promise solemnly: pledged himself to carry out the plan 2 give as security for a loan; pawn 3 drink to the health of; toast

plenary adj involving all members or people attending, not just one separate group

plenty noun 1 a full supply, as much as is needed 2 a large number or quantity (of) • **plenteous** or **plentiful** adj available in large amounts; abundant

plethora noun too large a quantity of anything: a plethora of politicians

pleurisy noun an illness in which the covering of the lungs becomes inflamed

pliable adj 1 easily bent or folded 2 easily persuaded • **pliant** adj pliable

plié /plee-eh/ noun a ballet movement with the knees bent and body upright

pliers plural noun a tool used for gripping, bending and cutting wire, etc

plight noun a bad state or situation ◇ verb, old promise solemnly; pledge

plimsoll noun a light rubber-soled canvas shoe for sports • **Plimsoll line** noun a ship's loadline

plink noun a short, high-pitched sound

plinth noun 1 the square slab at the foot of a column 2 the base or pedestal of a statue, vase, etc

PLO abbrev Palestine Liberation Organization

plod verb (**plodding, plodded**) 1 walk or travel slowly, steadily and tiredly 2 work on steadily • **plodder** noun a dull but hard-working person

plonk noun, informal cheap wine

plop noun the sound made by a small object falling into water ◇ verb (**plopping, plopped**) make this sound

plot noun 1 a small piece of ground 2 a plan for an illegal or malicious action 3 the story of a play, novel, etc ◇ verb (**plotting, plotted**) 1 plan secretly 2 make a chart or graph of 3 mark (points) on a chart or graph • **plotter** noun

plough noun a farm tool for turning up the soil ◇ verb 1 turn up the ground in furrows 2 work (through) slowly: ploughing through the ironing • **ploughman** noun a farm worker who operates a plough • **ploughman's lunch** noun a cold dish of bread, cheese and pickle • **ploughshare** noun the blade of a plough • **the Plough** a group of seven stars forming a shape like an old-fashioned plough

plover noun any of several kinds of bird that nest on the ground in open country

ploy *noun* something done in order to bring about a secret aim; a stratagem

pluck *verb* **1** pull out or off **2** pick (flowers, fruit, *etc*) **3** strip off the feathers of (a bird) before cooking ◇ *noun* courage or spirit • **plucky** *adj* brave or determined • **pluck up courage** prepare yourself to face a danger or difficulty

plug *noun* **1** an object fitted into a hole to stop it up, *esp* into a basin to prevent water from draining away **2** a fitting on an appliance put into a socket to connect with an electric current **3** *informal* a brief promotional mention of something ◇ *verb* (**plugging**, **plugged**) **1** stop up with a plug **2** *informal* mention by way of promoting or advertising

plum *noun* **1** a soft fruit, often dark red or purple, with a stone in the centre **2** the tree that produces this fruit ◇ *adj* very good, very profitable, *etc*: *a plum job* • **plum cake** or **plum pudding** *noun* a rich cake or pudding containing dried fruit

plumage *see* **plume**

plumb *noun* a lead weight hung on a string (**plumb line**), used to test if a wall has been built straight up ◇ *adj* & *adv* perfectly vertical ◇ *verb* test the depth of (the sea *etc*)

plumber *noun* someone who fits and mends water, gas and sewage pipes • **plumbing** *noun* **1** the work of a plumber **2** the drainage and water systems of a building *etc*

plume *noun* **1** a feather, *esp* an ornamental one **2** something looking like a feather: *a plume of smoke* • **plumage** *noun* the feathers of a bird

plummet *verb* **1** fall fast from a very high place; plunge **2** fall quickly and suddenly to a much lower level ◇ *noun* a weight of lead hung on a line, used for taking depths at sea

plump *adj* pleasantly fat or rounded ◇ *verb* **1** beat or shake (cushions *etc*)

back into shape **2** sit or sink down heavily **3** (with **for**) choose

plunder *verb* carry off goods by force; loot ◇ *noun* goods seized by force

plunge *verb* **1** dive (into water *etc*) **2** rush or lurch forward **3** thrust suddenly (into): *he plunged the knife into its neck* ◇ *noun* a thrust; a dive

pluperfect *noun, grammar* a tense used for describing an action that took place before the main past actions being described, formed, in English, using *had* and a past participle; the past perfect

plural *noun, grammar* the form that shows more than one, *eg mice* is the plural of *mouse* ◇ *adj* more than one • **plurality** *noun*

plus *prep* used to show addition and represented by the sign (+): *five plus two equals seven* ◇ *adj* of a quantity more than zero ◇ *adv, informal* and a bit more: *she earns £20,000 plus*

plus fours *plural noun* baggy trousers reaching to just below the knees

plush *adj* luxurious ◇ *noun* cloth with a soft velvety surface on one side

plutocrat *noun* someone who is powerful because of their wealth • **plutocratic** *adj*

ply *verb* (**plies**, **plying**, **plied**) **1** work at steadily **2** make regular journeys: *the ferry plies between Oban and Mull* **3** use (a tool) energetically **4** keep supplying (someone) with (food, questions to answer, *etc*) • **plywood** *noun* a board made up of thin sheets of wood glued together • **two-, three-,** *etc* **ply** having two, three, *etc* layers or strands

PM *abbrev* prime minister

pm *abbrev* after noon (from Latin *post meridiem*)

PMS *abbrev* premenstrual syndrome

PMT *abbrev* premenstrual tension

pneumatic /nyoo-*mat*-ik/ *adj* 1 filled with air 2 worked by air: *pneumatic drill*

pneumonia /nyoo-*moh*-ni-uh/ *noun* a disease in which the lungs become inflamed

PO *abbrev* post office

poach *verb* 1 cook gently in boiling water or stock 2 catch fish or hunt game illegally • **poacher** *noun* someone who hunts or fishes illegally

pocket *noun* 1 a small pouch or bag, *esp* as part of a garment 2 a personal supply of money: *well beyond my pocket* 3 a small isolated area: *a pocket of unemployment* ◇ *verb* 1 put in a pocket 2 steal • **pocketbook** *noun*, *US* a wallet • **pocket money** *noun* an allowance of money for personal spending • **in** *or* **out of pocket** having gained or lost money on a deal *etc*

pockmark *noun* a scar or small hole in the skin left by disease

pod *noun* a long seed-case of the pea, bean, *etc*

podcast *noun* a sound broadcast released on the Internet that can be downloaded and played at the listener's convenience

podgy *adj* (**podgier**, **podgiest**) short and fat

podium *noun* a low pedestal or small platform, *esp* for a medal-winner or speaker to stand on

poem *noun* a piece of imaginative writing set out in lines that often have a regular rhythm or rhyme

poesy *noun*, *old* poetry

poet *noun* someone who writes poetry • **poetaster** /*poh*-it-as-tuh/ *noun* a writer of bad poetry

poetic *adj* of or like poetry • **poetically** *adv* • **poetic justice** *noun* a fitting reward or punishment • **poetic licence** *noun* a departure from truth, logic, *etc* for the sake of effect

poetry *noun* 1 the art of writing poems 2 poems

po-faced *adj* ridiculously solemn; humourless

pogo stick *noun* a child's stick with a spring in it for jumping up and down

pogrom *noun* an organized massacre of a group of people

poignant /*poyn*-yunt/ *adj* causing strong feelings of sadness or sympathy; moving • **poignancy** *noun*

poinsettia *noun* a plant, originally from Mexico, with large scarlet or white petal-like leaves

point *noun* 1 a sharp end of anything 2 a dot: *decimal point* 3 a full stop in punctuation 4 an exact place or spot 5 an exact moment of time 6 the main issue in a discussion, an argument, *etc* 7 the meaning of a joke 8 a mark in a competition 9 a purpose or advantage: *there is no point in going* 10 a movable rail used to direct a railway engine from one line to another 11 an electrical wall socket 12 a headland: *Lizard Point* 13 a mark of character: *he has many good points* ◇ *verb* 1 direct or aim 2 indicate with a gesture: *pointing to the building* 3 make pointed: *point your toes* 4 fill (wall joints) with mortar • **point-blank** *adj* 1 of a shot: fired from very close range 2 of a question: direct • **pointed** *adj* 1 having a point; sharp 2 of a remark: obviously aimed at someone • **pointer** *noun* 1 a rod for pointing 2 a type of dog used to show where game has fallen • **pointless** *adj* having no meaning or purpose

poise *noun* 1 a state of balance 2 dignity and self-confidence ◇ *verb* 1 keep something balanced or steady 2 hover in the air • **poised** *adj* 1 in a state of readiness; prepared: *poised for action* 2 well balanced

poison *noun* 1 a substance that, when taken into the body, kills or harms 2 anything harmful ◇ *verb* 1 kill or harm with poison **2** add poison to **3** make bitter or bad: *poisoned her mind* • **poison ivy** *noun* a N American plant the juice of which causes a skin rash • **poisonous** *adj* **1** harmful because of containing poison **2** causing evil • **poison-pen letter** *noun* a malicious anonymous letter • **poison pill** *noun, informal* a merger of companies organized in order to prevent a threatened takeover bid

poke *verb* **1** push (*eg* a finger or stick) into something **2** search about inquisitively ◇ *noun* **1** a nudge or prod **2** a prying search • **poker** *noun* **1** a rod for stirring up a fire **2** a card game in which players bet on their chance of winning • **poky** *adj* cramped and shabby

polar and **polarity** *see* **pole**

polarize *verb* **1** split into opposing sides **2** give polarity to

Polaroid *noun, trademark* **1** a camera that develops individual pictures in a few seconds **2** (**Polaroids**) sunglasses **3** a plastic through which light is seen less brightly

polder *noun* land below sea-level reclaimed for use

pole *noun* **1** a long rod or post **2** the north or south end of the earth's axis (the **north pole** or **south pole**) **3** either of the opposing points of a magnet or electric battery • **polar** *adj* of the regions round the north or south poles • **polarity** *noun* the state of having two opposite poles • **pole star** *noun* the star most directly above the north pole • **pole vault** *noun* a sport in which an athlete jumps over a very high bar with the aid of a very long flexible pole

polecat *noun* **1** a large kind of weasel **2** *US* a skunk

polemic *or* **polemical** *adj* expressing strong, often controversial views • **polemicist** *noun* someone who writes polemic material

police *noun* the body of men and women whose work it is to see that laws are obeyed *etc* ◇ *verb* keep law and order in (a place) by use of police • **policeman**, **policewoman** *noun* • **police station** *noun* the headquarters of the police in a district

policy *noun* (*plural* **policies**) **1** an agreed course of action **2** a written agreement with an insurance company

polio *noun* poliomyelitis

poliomyelitis *noun* a disease of the spinal cord, causing weakness or paralysis of the muscles

polish *verb* **1** make smooth and shiny by rubbing **2** make minor changes to improve (a piece of writing *etc*) **3** make more polite ◇ *noun* **1** a substance used for polishing **2** a gloss on a surface **3** fine manners, style, *etc*

polite *adj* having or showing good manners; courteous • **politely** *adv* • **politeness** *noun*

politic *adj* showing wisdom and good judgement

political *adj* of government, politicians or politics • **political correctness** *noun* the use of words or expressions that are regarded as acceptable because they avoid offence, *esp* to groups of people who have been discriminated against in the past • **politically** *adv* • **politically correct** *adj* using language that avoids causing offence • **politician** *noun* someone involved in politics, *esp* a member of a parliament or other legislative body • **politicize** *verb* make aware of political issues • **politicking** *noun* activities with a political aim, *esp* shameless vote-seeking • **politico** *noun* (*plural* **politicos** *or* **politicoes**) *informal* a politician • **politics** *sing noun* the business or study of government

polka *noun* a lively dance or the music for it

poll *noun* **1** a counting of voters at

an election **2** total number of votes **3** (*also called* **opinion poll**) a test of public opinion by questioning ◇ *verb* **1** receive (votes): *they polled 5000 votes* **2** cut or clip off (hair, branches, *etc*) ● **polling station** *noun* a place where voting is done ● **poll tax** *noun, Brit* the community charge, a former local tax under which all individuals in a community were taxed at the same rate

pollard *noun* a tree with its top cut off to allow new growth ◇ *verb* cut the top off (a tree)

pollen *noun* the fertilizing powder of flowers ● **pollinate** *verb* fertilize with pollen ● **pollination** *noun*

pollute *verb* **1** make dirty or impure **2** make (the environment) harmful to life ● **pollutant** *noun* a substance that pollutes ● **pollution** *noun* **1** substances that pollute **2** the act of polluting something, *esp* the natural environment

polo *noun* a game like hockey played on horseback ● **polo neck** *noun* **1** a close-fitting collar with a part turned over at the top **2** a jumper with a collar like this

polonaise *noun* a slow Polish dance

poltergeist *noun* a kind of ghost believed to move furniture and throw objects around a room

poly *noun* **1** polythene **2** a polyphonic ringtone on a mobile phone

poly- *prefix* many: *polysyllabic*

polyanthus *noun* a garden plant with small flowers like pansies

polyester *noun* a synthetic material often used in clothing

polygamy *noun* the fact of having more than one wife or husband at the same time ● **polygamist** *noun* ● **polygamous** *adj*

polyglot *adj* speaking, or written in, many languages ◇ *noun* someone fluent in many languages

polygon *noun* a flat shape with several straight sides ● **polygonal** *adj*

polygraph *noun* an instrument that measures pulse rate *etc*, used as a lie-detector

polymath *noun* someone with knowledge of a wide range of subjects

polymer *noun* a chemical compound with large molecules

polymorphous *noun* occurring in several different forms

polyp *noun* **1** a small sea animal with arms or tentacles **2** a kind of tumour

polyphony *noun* musical composition in parts, each with a separate melody ● **polyphonic** *adj* consisting of a complex sequence of musical notes

polystyrene *noun* a lightweight synthetic material used as a packing material and for making disposable items

polysyllable *noun* a word of three or more syllables ● **polysyllabic** *adj*

polytechnic *noun, dated* a college that teaches technical and vocational subjects

polythene *noun* a type of plastic that can be moulded when hot

polyunsaturated *adj* of a fat or oil: containing no cholesterol

polyurethane *noun* a resin used to produce foam materials

pomegranate *noun* a fruit with a thick skin, many seeds and pulpy edible flesh

pommel *noun* **1** the knob on the hilt of a sword **2** the high part of a saddle

pomp *noun* solemn and splendid ceremony

pompous *adj* inappropriately grand or ridiculously self-important; pretentious ● **pomposity** *noun*

poncho *noun* (*plural* **ponchos**) a S American cloak made of a blanket with a hole for the head, or a woman's fashion garment made in this style

pond noun a small lake or pool

ponder verb think over; consider • **ponderous** adj **1** awkwardly heavy **2** clumsy

poniard /pon-yud/ noun a kind of small dagger

pontiff noun **1** a Roman Catholic bishop **2** the Pope • **pontifical** adj **1** of a pontiff **2** pompous in speech • **pontificate** verb speak in a pompous or lecturing manner

pontoon[1] noun a flat-bottomed boat used to support a temporary bridge (a **pontoon bridge**)

pontoon[2] noun a card-game in which players try to collect 21 points

pony noun (plural **ponies**) a small horse • **pony trekking** noun riding cross-country in small parties

poodle noun a breed of dog with curly hair often clipped in a fancy way

pool noun **1** a small area of still water **2** a deep part of a river **3** a joint fund or stock (of money, vehicles, typists, etc) **4** the money played for in a gambling game ◇ verb put (money etc) into a joint fund • **football pools** organized betting on football match results

poop noun **1** a ship's stern **2** a high deck in the stern

poor adj **1** having little money or property **2** not good: this work is poor **3** lacking (in): poor in sports facilities **4** deserving pity: poor Tom has broken his leg • **poorly** adj in bad health; ill • **the poor** people who live difficult lives because of lack of money

pop noun **1** a sharp high-pitched noise, eg that made by a cork coming out of a bottle **2** a fizzy soft drink **3** popular music from the 1950s onwards ◇ verb (**popping**, **popped**) **1** make a popping noise **2** move quickly, dash: pop in/pop along the road

◇ adj of music: in any of various popular styles developed after the 1950s

popadom another spelling of **poppadom**

popcorn noun a kind of maize that bursts open when heated

pope noun the bishop of Rome, head of the Roman Catholic Church

popinjay noun, old someone who is conceited about their clothes

poplar noun a tall, narrow quick-growing tree

poplin noun strong cotton cloth

poppadom or **poppadum** or **popadom** noun a thin circle of dough fried in oil until crisp, typically eaten with Indian food

poppy noun (plural **poppies**) **1** a tall wild flower with delicate red petals, or a garden variety with much larger flowers of varying colour **2** a real or imitation small poppy worn in remembrance of the dead of the two world wars

populace noun the people of a country or area

popular adj **1** of the people: popular vote **2** liked by most people **3** widely held or believed: popular belief • **popularity** noun the state of being generally liked • **popularize** verb make popular or widely known • **popularly** adv

population noun the number of people living in a place • **populate** verb fill (an area) with people

populist adj appealing to the mass of people, esp at the expense of serious thought or artistic merit • **populism** noun

populous adj full of people

porcelain noun a kind of fine china

porch noun (plural **porches**) a covered entrance to a building

porcine adj of or like a pig

porcupine *noun* a very large rodent covered with long sharp quills

pore *noun* **1** a tiny hole **2** the hole of a sweat gland in the skin

pore over *verb* study closely or eagerly

Do not confuse with: **pour**

---

pork *noun* the flesh of a pig, prepared for eating

porn *noun, informal* pornography

pornography *noun* literature, photographs and films that contain sexually explicit material that is of little artistic merit and is often offensive • **pornographic** *adj*

porous *adj* **1** having pores **2** allowing fluid to pass through • **porosity** *noun*

porpoise *noun* a blunt-nosed sea animal of the dolphin family

porridge *noun* a food made from oatmeal boiled in water or milk

port *noun* **1** a harbour **2** a town with a harbour **3** the left side of a ship as you face the front **4** a dark-red fortified wine **5** a socket or plug for connecting a hardware device to a computer

portable *adj* able to be lifted and carried ◇ *noun* a portable device • **portability** *noun*

portal *noun* **1** a grand entrance or doorway **2** *comput* a website that brings together information relating to a specific subject

portcullis *noun* (*plural* **portcullises**) a grating that is let down quickly to close a gateway

portend *verb* give warning of (something bad); foretell

portent *noun* a sign that something bad is going to happen • **portentous** *adj* **1** indicating that something bad is going to happen **2** solemn or pompous • **portentousness** *noun*

porter *noun* **1** someone employed to carry luggage, push hospital trolleys, *etc* **2** a doorkeeper **3** a kind of dark brown beer

portfolio *noun* (*plural* **portfolios**) **1** a set of paintings, photographs, *etc* kept or shown as evidence of artistic talent **2** a case for carrying papers, drawings, *etc* **3** the job of a government minister

porthole *noun* a small round window in a ship's side

portico *noun* (*plural* **porticoes** or **porticos**) a row of columns in front of a building forming a porch or covered walk

portion *noun* **1** a part **2** a share or helping ◇ *verb* divide into parts

portly *adj* (**portlier**, **portliest**) rather fat and *usu* dignified-looking

portmanteau /pawt-*man*-toh/ *noun* a large leather travelling case hinged so that it opens into two halves

portrait *noun* **1** a drawing, painting, or photograph of a person **2** a description of a person, place, *etc*

portray *verb* (**portraying**, **portrayed**) **1** make a painting or drawing of **2** describe in words **3** act the part of • **portrayal** *noun*

Portuguese man-of-war *noun* a stinging jellyfish

pose *noun* **1** a position of the body: *a relaxed pose* **2** behaviour put on to impress others; a pretence ◇ *verb* **1** position yourself for a photograph *etc* **2** (with **as**) pretend or claim to be what you are not: *posing as an expert* **3** put forward (a problem, question, *etc*) • **poser** *noun* **1** someone who poses to impress others **2** a difficult question • **poseur** *noun* a poser

posh *adj, informal* **1** upper-class, or of upper-class people **2** expensive and of the best quality

posit *verb* assume as true for the sake of argument; postulate

position noun 1 the place where something is; location 2 manner of standing, sitting, etc; posture: in a crouching position 3 a rank or job: a high position in a bank ◇ verb put in a particular place

positive adj 1 meaning or saying 'yes': a positive answer (contrasted with: **negative**) 2 not able to be doubted: positive proof 3 certain, convinced: I am positive that she did it 4 definite: a positive improvement 5 greater than zero 6 grammar of an adjective or adverb: of the first degree of comparison, eg big, not bigger or biggest

positron noun a particle with a positive electrical charge

posse /pos-i/ noun 1 hist a group of mounted law enforcers assisting a sheriff in the American West 2 informal any group of people

possess verb 1 own or have 2 take hold of your mind: anger possessed her ● **possessed** adj 1 in the power of an evil spirit 2 obsessed 3 self-possessed; calm ● **possession** noun 1 something owned or carried with you 2 the state of possessing or of being possessed ● **possessive** adj 1 grammar of an adjective: showing possession, as do the adjectives my, mine, your, their, etc 2 over-protective and jealous in attitude ● **possessor** noun an owner

posset noun a drink of milk curdled with wine or vinegar, formerly used as a remedy for colds

possible adj 1 able to happen or to be done 2 not unlikely ● **possibility** noun something that may happen or that may be done ● **possibly** adv perhaps

possum noun: **play possum** pretend to be asleep or dead

post noun 1 an upright pole or stake 2 the service that delivers letters and parcels, or letters and par-

cels that have been delivered 3 a job: teaching post 4 a place of duty: the soldier remained at his post 5 a settlement or camp: military post/ trading post ◇ verb 1 put (a letter) in a postbox for collection 2 send or station somewhere: posted abroad 3 put up (a notice etc) ● **postage** noun money paid for sending a letter or parcel by post ● **postage stamp** noun a small printed label on a letter or parcel showing that postage has been paid ● **postal** adj of or by post ● **postal order** noun a document bought at a post office which can be exchanged for a stated amount of money ● **postbox** noun a box with an opening in which to post letters etc ● **postcard** noun a card for sending a message by post ● **postcode** noun a short series of letters and numbers, used for sorting mail by machine ● **poster** noun 1 a large notice or placard 2 a large printed picture ● **post-free** adv without charge for postage ● **posthaste** adv, dated with great speed ● **postie** noun, dated informal a postman or postwoman ● **postman, postwoman** noun someone who delivers letters ● **postmark** noun a date stamp put on a letter at a post office ● **postmaster, postmistress** noun an official in charge of a post office ● **post office** noun an office for receiving and sending off letters by post etc

post- prefix after: post-war/post-tax

postdate verb mark (a cheque) with a future date so that it cannot be cashed immediately

posterior adj situated behind or at the back of ◇ noun the buttocks

posterity noun 1 all future generations 2 someone's descendants

postern noun a back door or gate to a castle etc

postgraduate adj of study etc: following on from a first university degree ◇ noun someone continuing to study after a first degree

posthumous adj 1 of a book: published after the author's death 2 of a medal: awarded after the death of the recipient

postilion or **postillion** noun, old a carriage driver who rides on one of the horses

postmortem noun an examination of a dead body carried out to find out the cause of death

postpone verb put off to a future time; delay • **postponement** noun

postscript noun a remark added at the end of a letter, after the sender's name

postulant noun someone applying to enter a religious order

postulate verb assume or take for granted (that)

posture noun 1 the manner in which someone holds themselves in standing or walking 2 a position of the body; a pose

postwar adj relating to the time after a war

posy noun (plural **posies**) a small bunch of flowers

pot noun 1 a deep container used for cooking food 2 a container in which a plant is grown 3 (**pots**) informal a great deal: pots of money 4 slang marijuana ◇ verb (**potting**, **potted**) 1 plant in a pot 2 make articles of baked clay • **pot belly** noun a protruding stomach • **potboiler** noun a book with a sensational plot, written to sell • **pothole** noun 1 a deep cave 2 a hole worn in a road surface • **potholer** noun someone who explores caves • **pot plant** noun a household plant kept in a pot • **pot shot** noun a casual or random shot • **potted** adj 1 of meat: pressed and preserved in a jar 2 condensed and simplified: potted history • **take pot-luck** take whatever is available or offered

potash noun potassium carbonate, obtained from the ashes of wood, esp when used as a garden fertilizer

potassium noun a type of silvery-white metal

potato noun (plural **potatoes**) 1 a very common round vegetable that is the fleshy root of an orig American plant 2 the plant of which it is the root • **couch potato** see **couch**

poteen /po-cheen/ noun Irish whiskey illegally distilled

potent adj powerful, strong or impressive • **potency** noun

potentate noun a powerful ruler

potential adj that may develop or happen; possible ◇ noun the possibility of further development • **potentiality** noun a possibility

potion noun a drink containing medicine or poison

potpourri /poh-paw-ree/ noun 1 a scented mixture of dried petals used to give a room a pleasant fragrance 2 a mixture or medley

potter noun someone who makes articles of baked clay ◇ verb do small odd jobs

pottery noun 1 articles made of baked clay 2 (plural **potteries**) a place where such things are made 3 the art of making them

potty[1] adj (**pottier**, **pottiest**) informal 1 eccentric or mad 2 obsessively enthusiastic or fond

potty[2] noun (plural **potties**) informal a container for a small child to use as a toilet

pouch noun (plural **pouches**) 1 a pocket or small bag 2 a bag-like fold on the front of a kangaroo, for carrying its young

pouffe /poof/ noun a low, stuffed seat without back or arms

poultice noun a wet dressing spread on a bandage and put on inflamed skin to soothe it ◇ *verb* put a poultice on

poultry *noun* farmyard birds, eg hens, ducks, geese, turkeys, kept for their meat and eggs • **poulterer** *noun* someone who sells poultry and game

pounce *verb* **1** (with **on**) jump (on) in attack **2** (with **on**) take advantage of eagerly ◇ *noun* a sudden jumping attack

pound *noun* **1** the standard unit of money in Britain, shown by the sign (£), equal to 100 new pence **2** a measure of weight, written lb, equal to 16 ounces (about $\frac{1}{2}$ kilogram) **3** an enclosure for animals ◇ *verb* **1** beat into powder **2** beat heavily **3** walk or run with heavy steps

pour *verb* **1** flow in a stream: *the blood poured out* **2** cause to flow into a container: *pour the tea* **3** rain heavily

---

Do not confuse with: **pore**

---

pout *verb* push out the lips, either sulkily to show displeasure, or sexily ◇ *noun* a sulky or sexy pushing out of the lips

poverty *noun* **1** the state of being poor **2** lack: *poverty of ideas*

POW *abbrev* prisoner of war

powder *noun* **1** a substance made up of very fine particles **2** face powder **3** gunpowder ◇ *verb* **1** sprinkle or dab with powder **2** grind down to powder • **powdered** *adj* **1** in fine particles **2** covered with powder • **powdery** *adj* **1** covered with powder **2** like powder: *powdery snow*

power *noun* **1** strength or force **2** ability to do things **3** authority or legal right **4** a strong nation **5** someone in authority **6** the force used for driving machines: *electric power/steam power* **7** *maths* the product obtained by multiplying a number by itself a

given number of times (eg $2 \times 2 \times 2$ or 2^3 is the third power of 2) ◇ *verb* provide the energy to work or drive (eg a machine) • **power cut** *noun* a break in the supply of electricity to an area • **power-driven** or **powered** *adj* worked by electricity, not by hand • **powerful** *adj* • **powerless** *adj* without power or ability • **power station** *noun* a building where electricity is produced

pow-wow *noun* **1** *hist* a Native American gathering for debate **2** *informal* any conference or discussion

pp *abbrev* pages

PR *abbrev* **1** proportional representation **2** public relations

practicable *adj* able to be used or done • **practicability** *noun*

Do not confuse: **practicable** and **practical**

---

practical *adj* **1** preferring action to thought, or good at physical tasks **2** likely to be effective or useful **3** learned by practice, rather than from books: *practical knowledge* • **practical joke** *noun* a joke consisting of action, not words • **practically** *adv* **1** in a practical way **2** in effect, in reality **3** almost: *practically empty*

practice *noun* **1** repeated performance done to improve skill: *piano practice/in practice for the race* **2** the business of a doctor, lawyer, *etc* **3** the actual doing of something: *I always intend to get up early but in practice I stay in bed* **4** habit: *it is my practice to get up early*

Do not confuse: **practice** and **practise**

---

practise or US **practice** *verb* **1** perform or exercise repeatedly to improve a skill: *he practises judo nightly* **2** make a habit of: *practise* *self-control* **3** follow (a profession): *practise dentistry* • **practitioner** *noun* someone engaged in a profession: *a medical practitioner*

pragmatic *adj* relating to fact or to real situations, rather than to ideas or theories; practical • **pragmatism** *noun* • **pragmatist** *noun*

prairie *noun* a stretch of level grassland in N America

praise *verb* **1** speak highly of **2** glorify (God) by singing hymns *etc* ◇ *noun* expressions of approval • **praiseworthy** *adj* deserving to be praised

praline *noun* a sweet consisting of nuts and caramelized sugar

pram *noun* a small wheeled carriage for a baby, pushed by hand

prance *verb* **1** walk in a strutting way; swagger **2** dance about **3** of a horse: spring from the hind legs

prank *noun* a trick played for mischief

prat *noun, informal* an idiot

prate *verb* talk foolishly

prattle *verb* talk or chatter meaninglessly ◇ *noun* meaningless talk

prawn *noun* a type of shellfish like a large shrimp

pray *verb* **1** speak to God or a deity in prayer **2** ask earnestly; beg • **praying mantis** *see* **mantis**

Do not confuse with: **prey**

prayer *noun* **1** a request, or thanks, given to God or a deity **2** an earnest request for something

pre- *prefix* before: *prewar*

preach *verb* **1** give a sermon **2** speak in favour of; advise: *preach caution* • **preacher** *noun* a religious teacher

preamble *noun* something said as an introduction

prearrange *verb* arrange beforehand

precarious *adj* uncertain, unstable or dangerous

precaution *noun* care taken beforehand to avoid an accident *etc* • **precautionary** *adj*

precede *verb* go before in time, rank or importance • **precedence** *noun* the right to go before; priority • **preceding** *adj* going before; previous

Do not confuse with: **proceed**

precedent *noun* a past action that serves as an example or rule for the future

precentor *noun* someone who leads the singing in a church or the prayers in a synagogue

precept *noun* a guiding rule; a commandment

precinct *noun* **1** an area enclosed by the boundary walls of a building **2** (**precincts**) the area closely surrounding any place **3** *US* an administrative district • **shopping precinct** a shopping area that is closed to traffic

precious *adj* **1** highly valued or valuable **2** over-fussy or precise

precipice *noun* a steep cliff

precipitate *verb* **1** hasten (death, illness, *etc*) **2** force into (hasty action *etc*) **3** throw headfirst ◇ *adj* **1** hasty, rash **2** headlong ◇ *noun* sediment at the bottom of a liquid • **precipitation** *noun* **1** rainfall **2** great hurry

precipitous *adj* very steep • **precipitousness** *noun*

précis /preh-see/ *noun* (*plural* **précis**) a summary of a piece of writing

precise *adj* **1** exact or accurate **2** definite • **precisely** *adv* • **precision** *noun* exactness or accuracy

preclude *verb* make impossible; prevent • **preclusion** *noun* • **preclusive** *adj*

precocious adj of a child: unusually talented or mature • **precocity** noun

precognitive adj knowing beforehand; foretelling • **precognition** noun

preconceive verb form (ideas etc) before having actual knowledge or experience • **preconception** noun an idea formed without actual knowledge

precondition noun a condition that must be met before something can happen

precursor noun something that is an earlier form: the precursor of jazz

predate verb happen before in time

predator noun a bird or animal that kills others for food • **predatory** adj 1 of a predator 2 using other people for your own advantage

predecease verb die before (someone)

predecessor noun the previous holder of a job or office

predestine verb decide that (something) will certainly happen in the future

predetermine verb decide that (something) will certainly happen in the future

predicament noun an unfortunate or difficult situation

predicate noun, grammar the whole of the part of a sentence that is not the subject and that says something about the subject, eg has green eyes in the sentence Anne has green eyes

predict verb say that (something) will happen; forecast • **predictable** adj able to be foretold • **prediction** noun an act of predicting or something predicted

predilection noun a liking for something; a preference

predispose verb 1 make (someone) in favour of something beforehand: we were predisposed to believe her 2

make liable (to): predisposed to colds • **predisposition** noun

predominate verb 1 be the strongest or most numerous 2 have control (over) • **predominance** noun • **predominant** adj 1 ruling 2 most noticeable or outstanding • **predominantly** adv

pre-eminent adj better than all others; outstanding • **pre-eminence** noun • **pre-eminently** adv

pre-empt verb block or stop by making a first move • **pre-emptive** adj

preen verb 1 of a bird: arrange its feathers 2 smarten your appearance in a conceited way • **preen yourself** show obvious pride in your achievements

prefabricated adj built of parts made beforehand, ready to be fitted together

preface noun an introduction to a book etc ◇ verb precede or introduce (with)

prefect noun 1 the head of an administrative district in France etc 2 a senior pupil in some schools with certain powers • **prefecture** noun an area controlled by a prefect

prefer verb (**preferring, preferred**) 1 like better: I prefer tea to coffee 2 put forward (a claim or request) • **preferable** adj more desirable • **preference** noun 1 greater liking 2 something preferred: what is your preference? • **preferential** adj giving preference • **preferment** noun promotion

prefix noun (plural **prefixes**) a syllable or word at the beginning of a word which adds to its meaning, eg dis-, un-, re-, in dislike, unhappy, regain

pregnant adj 1 carrying a foetus in the womb 2 full of meaning: pregnant pause • **pregnancy** noun the state of being pregnant

prehensile adj able to grasp or hold: prehensile tail

prehistoric adj relating to the time before history was written down • **prehistory** noun

prejudge verb decide (something) before hearing the facts of a case

prejudice noun 1 an unfair feeling for or against anything 2 an opinion formed without careful thought 3 harm or injury ◇ verb 1 fill with prejudice 2 do harm to; damage: his late arrival prejudiced his chances of success • **prejudiced** adj showing prejudice • **prejudicial** adj damaging or harmful

prelate noun a bishop or archbishop • **prelacy** noun the office of a prelate

preliminary adj going before something and often acting as preparation for it: preliminary investigation ◇ noun (plural **preliminaries**) something that goes before

prelude noun 1 a piece of music played as an introduction to the main piece 2 a preceding event: a prelude to a brilliant career

premarital adj before marriage

premature adj coming, born, etc before the right, proper or expected time

premeditate verb think out beforehand; plan: premeditated murder • **premeditation** noun

premenstrual adj experienced just before menstruation

premier adj most important or best; leading ◇ noun a prime minister

Do not confuse: **premier** and **première**

première noun a first performance of a play or first showing of a film

premise or **premiss** noun (plural **premises** or **premisses**) something assumed or stated from which a conclusion is drawn

premises plural noun a building and its grounds

premium noun (plural **premiums**) 1 a payment on an insurance policy 2 a reward • **at a premium** very desirable and therefore difficult to obtain

premonition noun a feeling that something, usu something bad, is going to happen; a forewarning

prenatal adj before birth, or before giving birth

prenuptial adj before marriage

preoccupy verb (**preoccupies, preoccupying, preoccupied**) completely occupy the attention or thoughts of; engross • **preoccupation** noun • **preoccupied** adj deep in thought

preordain verb decide beforehand

prep noun, informal preparation • **prep school** noun a preparatory school

prepaid past form of **prepay**

preparatory adj 1 acting as an introduction or first step 2 (with **to**) coming (before) and acting as preparation (for) • **preparatory school** noun a private school educating children of primary-school age

prepare verb 1 make or get ready 2 train or equip • **preparation** noun 1 an act of preparing 2 study for a lesson 3 something prepared for use, eg a medicine • **prepared** adj 1 ready 2 willing

prepay verb (**prepaying, prepaid**) pay beforehand • **prepayment** noun

preponderance noun greater amount or number: a preponderance of young people in the audience

preposition noun, grammar a word placed before a noun or pronoun to show its relation to another word, eg 'through the door', 'in the town', 'written by me'

Do not confuse with: **proposition**

prepossessing adj making a good impression

preposterous adj very foolish; absurd

prequel noun a book or film that deals with events happening before those covered in an existing work

pre-Raphaelite noun one of a group of 19th-century British artists who painted in a style seen as a return to the period before the early-16th-century painter Raphael

prerequisite noun something that is necessary before another thing can happen

prerogative noun a right enjoyed by someone because of their rank or position

presage verb be a sign of (usu something bad)

presbyter noun a minister or elder in a Presbyterian church

Presbyterian adj 1 of a church: managed by ministers and elders together 2 belonging to such a church ◇ noun a member of a Presbyterian church

presbytery noun (plural **presbyteries**) 1 a body of presbyters who manage the affairs of a church 2 the house of a Roman Catholic priest

prescient adj knowing or seeming to know what will happen in the future • **prescience** noun

prescribe verb 1 lay down as a rule 2 order the use of (a medicine) • **prescriptive** adj laying down rules

Do not confuse with: **proscribe**

prescription noun 1 a doctor's written instructions for preparing and taking a medicine 2 something prescribed

Do not confuse with: **proscription**

presence noun 1 the state of being present (contrasted with: **absence**) 2 the effect someone's being present has on people around them, esp when it commands attention • **in your presence** while you are present • **presence of mind** calmness and ability to act sensibly in an emergency, difficulty, etc

present¹ adj 1 here, in this place 2 happening or existing now: present rates of pay/the present situation ◇ noun 1 the time now 2 grammar the tense describing events happening now, eg 'we are on holiday' • **presently** adv soon

present² noun a gift ◇ verb 1 hand over (a gift) formally 2 propose or offer 3 introduce (someone) to another person • **present yourself** 1 introduce yourself 2 go to a place

presentation noun 1 the giving of a present, award, etc 2 something presented 3 a formal talk or demonstration 4 a showing of a play etc

presentiment noun a feeling that something bad is about to happen; a foreboding

preservative noun a substance added to food to prevent it from going bad

preserve verb 1 keep in existence, maintain 2 treat (food) so that it will not go bad 3 keep safe from harm: the Lord preserve us ◇ noun 1 jam 2 a place where game animals, birds, etc are protected; a reserve • **preservation** noun

preside verb be in charge at a meeting etc

president noun 1 the leading member of a society, club, etc 2 the head of a republic • **presidency** noun the position or office of a president

press verb 1 push on, against, or

down **2** urge to take action **3** iron (clothes *etc*) ◇ *noun* **1** (**the press**) newspapers as a news medium **2** a printing machine **3** a crowd • **pressing** *adj* requiring immediate action; urgent

pressgang *noun, hist* a group of men employed to carry off people by force into the army or navy ◇ *verb* **1** force (someone) to do something: *pressganged into joining the committee* **2** *hist* carry off in a pressgang

pressure *noun* **1** force acting on or against a surface **2** strong persuasion or compulsion **3** worries or anxieties; stress **4** urgency • **pressure cooker** *noun* a pan in which food is cooked quickly by steam under pressure • **pressure group** *noun* a group of people who try to influence the authorities on a particular issue • **pressurize** *verb* **1** force (someone) to do something **2** fit (an aeroplane *etc*) with a device that maintains normal air pressure

prestidigitation *noun, formal* magic tricks • **prestidigitator** *noun* a conjurer

prestige *noun* good reputation or important influence owing to rank, success, *etc* • **prestigious** *adj* having or giving prestige

presume *verb* **1** suppose to be true based on available facts but without proof **2** (with **on**) take advantage of (someone's kindness *etc*) • **presumably** *adv* probably, based on available facts • **presumption** *noun* **1** a belief based on available facts **2** impertinent behaviour • **presumptuous** *adj* unsuitably bold • **presumptuousness** *noun*

presuppose *verb* take for granted

pretend *verb* **1** make believe; fantasize **2** make a false claim: *pretending to be ill* • **pretence** *noun* **1** the act of pretending **2** a false claim • **pretender** *noun* someone who lays claim to something (*esp* to the crown)

pretension *noun* **1** pretentious behaviour **2** a claim, whether true or not

pretentious *adj* deliberately seeking to impress others or make others feel inferior • **pretentiousness** *noun*

preternatural *adj* beyond what is natural; extraordinary or abnormal

pretext *noun* an excuse

pretty *adj* (**prettier, prettiest**) pleasing or attractive to see, listen to, *etc* ◇ *adv* to a fairly large degree; quite: *pretty good* • **prettiness** *noun*

pretzel *noun* a crisp salted biscuit, twisted in shape

prevail *verb* **1** be more dominant or successful; win through **2** (with **against** or **over**) gain control over **3** (with **on**) persuade: *she prevailed on me to stay* **4** be most usual or common • **prevailing** *adj* **1** most common or dominant: *the prevailing mood* **2** controlling • **prevalence** *noun* • **prevalent** *adj* common, widespread

prevaricate *verb* avoid speaking honestly or directly • **prevarication** *noun* • **prevaricator** *noun*

prevent *verb* stop (something) from happening or stop (someone) from doing something • **prevention** *noun* • **preventive** *or* **preventative** *adj* helping to prevent illness or something bad

preview *noun* a chance to view a performance, exhibition, *etc* before its official opening

previous *adj* going before in time; former • **previously** *adv*

prey *noun* **1** an animal killed by others for food **2** a victim ◇ *verb* (with **on**) **1** seize and eat: *preying on smaller birds* **2** harass or victimize

Do not confuse with: **pray**

price noun 1 the money for which something is bought or sold; the cost 2 something that must be given up in order to gain something: *the price of fame* • **priceless** adj 1 very valuable 2 informal very funny

prick verb 1 pierce slightly 2 give a sharp pain to 3 stick up (the ears) ◇ noun 1 a pricking feeling on the skin 2 slang the penis 3 slang an idiot

prickle noun a sharp point on a plant or animal ◇ verb 1 be prickly 2 feel prickly • **prickly** adj 1 full of prickles 2 stinging, pricking

pride noun 1 too great an opinion of yourself 2 pleasure in having done something well 3 dignity 4 a group of lions • **pride yourself on** feel or show pride in

priest noun 1 a member of the clergy in the Roman Catholic and Anglican churches 2 an official in a non-Christian religion • **priestess** noun a female, non-Christian priest • **priesthood** noun 1 priests collectively 2 the position of a priest

prig noun a smug, self-righteous person • **priggish** adj • **priggishly** adv

prim adj 1 disapproving of anything remotely sexual or unsavoury; prudish 2 unnecessarily formal or polite; stiff

prima ballerina noun the leading female dancer of a ballet company

prima donna noun 1 a leading female opera singer 2 a woman who is over-sensitive and temperamental

primaeval another spelling of **primeval**

prima facie /prai-muh *feh-shi*/ adj of evidence: enough to bring a case to court

primal adj 1 relating to the beginnings of life 2 basic or fundamental

primary adj 1 first 2 most important, chief • **primary colours** plural noun colours from which all others can be

made, eg red, blue and yellow • **primary school** noun a school for the early stages of education

primate noun 1 a member of the highest order of mammals, which includes humans, monkeys and apes 2 an archbishop

prime adj 1 first in time or importance 2 of the best quality; excellent ◇ noun the time of greatest health and strength: *the prime of life* ◇ verb 1 prepare the surface of for painting: *prime a canvas* 2 supply with detailed information: *she was well primed before the meeting* • **prime minister** noun the head of a government • **primer** noun 1 a simple introductory book on a subject 2 a substance for preparing a surface for painting

primeval or **primaeval** adj 1 relating to the beginning of the world 2 primitive, instinctive

primitive adj 1 belonging to very early times or very early stages of development 2 old-fashioned 3 not skilfully made; rough

primogeniture noun 1 the fact of being born first 2 the rights of a first-born child

primrose noun a pale-yellow spring flower common in woods and hedges

Primus stove noun, trademark a portable oil-fuelled cooking stove

prince noun 1 the son of a king or queen 2 a ruler of certain states • **princely** adj splendid or impressive: *a princely reward*

princess noun (plural **princesses**) the daughter of a king or queen

principal adj most important; chief ◇ noun 1 the head of a school or university 2 a leading part in a play etc 3 money in a bank on which interest is paid • **principality** noun a state ruled by a prince • **principally** adv on most occasions or in most respects; chiefly

Do not confuse: **principal** and **principle**

principle noun 1 (**principles**) someone's personal rules of behaviour, sense of right and wrong, etc 2 a general truth or law 3 the theory on which the working of a machine is based

print verb 1 mark letters on paper with type 2 write in capital letters 3 publish in printed form 4 stamp patterns on (cloth etc) 5 make a finished photograph ◇ noun 1 a mark made by pressure: footprint 2 printed lettering 3 a photograph made from a negative 4 a printed reproduction of a painting etc 5 cloth printed with a design • **printout** noun the printed information produced by a computer • **in print** of a book: published and available to buy • **out of print** of a book: no longer published and not available to buy new

printer noun 1 a machine that makes a printed version of data from a computer 2 someone who prints books, newspapers, etc

prior[1] adj 1 earlier 2 previous (to)

prior[2] noun the head of a priory • **prioress** noun the female head of a priory • **priory** noun a building where a community of monks or nuns live

priority noun (plural **priorities**) 1 the right to be first or to be considered first: ambulances must have priority in traffic 2 something that must be done first: our priority is to get him into hospital 3 first position

prise verb force open or off with a lever: prised off the lid

prism noun a glass tube with triangular ends that splits white light into its different constituent colours

prison noun 1 a building for holding criminals 2 a place where someone is confined against their will • **prisoner** noun someone held under arrest

or locked up • **prisoner of war** noun someone captured by the enemy forces during war

pristine adj in the original unspoilt state

privacy noun freedom from being seen by others

private adj 1 relating to an individual, not to the general public; personal 2 not open to the public 3 not generally known; secret 4 tending not to reveal personal details ◇ noun the lowest rank of ordinary soldier • **private eye** noun, informal a detective • **privately** adv • **private parts** plural noun the external sexual organs

privation noun 1 the fact of not having basic needs or comforts; hardship 2 the act of taking something away; loss

privatize verb transfer from state to private ownership

privet noun a type of shrub used for hedges

privilege noun a right available to one person or to only a few people • **privileged** adj having privileges

privy adj: privy to knowing about (something secret or private) ◇ noun (**privies**) dated a toilet • **privy council** noun an appointed group of advisers to a king or queen

prize noun 1 something won in a competition 2 a reward 3 something captured 4 something highly valued ◇ adj very fine, worthy of a prize ◇ verb value highly • **prize fight** noun, dated a boxing match fought for money

pro noun, informal a professional

pro- prefix in favour of, backing: pro-devolution • **pros and cons** the arguments for and against anything

probable adj 1 likely to happen 2 likely to be true • **probability** noun 1 likelihood 2 something likely to happen • **probably** adv very likely

probation noun 1 a trial period in a new job etc 2 a system of releasing prisoners on condition that they commit no more offences and report regularly to the authorities • **probationer** noun someone who is training to be a member of a profession

probe noun 1 a long, thin instrument used to examine a wound 2 a thorough investigation 3 a spacecraft designed for exploring deep space ◇ verb 1 examine very carefully 2 investigate thoroughly to find out information

probity noun goodness of character

problem noun 1 a matter that is difficult to deal with 2 a question to be solved • **problematic** or **problematical** adj difficult to deal with or resolve

proboscis noun (plural **proboscises**) 1 an animal's nose, esp an elephant's trunk 2 an insect's mouth

procedure noun 1 an accepted or official method of doing something 2 a course of action

proceed verb 1 go on with; continue 2 begin (to do something) 3 take legal action (against) • **proceeds** plural noun profit made from a sale etc

---

Do not confuse with: **precede**

---

proceeding noun 1 (**proceedings**) the things said in a meeting, or a record of these 2 a court case 3 a step forward

process noun (plural **processes**) 1 a series of operations carried out in doing something, eg manufacturing goods 2 a series of events producing change or development 3 a court case • **processor** noun a machine or person that processes something • **in the process of** in the course of

procession noun a line of people or vehicles moving forward in order

proclaim verb announce publicly or declare openly • **proclamation** noun an official announcement made to the public

procrastinate verb put something off till a later time; delay • **procrastination** noun

procreate verb reproduce • **procreation** noun

procurator fiscal noun (plural **procurators fiscal**) the senior law officer of a district in Scotland

procure verb obtain or bring about

prod verb (**prodding, prodded**) 1 poke 2 urge on

prodigal adj spending money recklessly; wasteful • **prodigality** noun

prodigy noun (plural **prodigies**) 1 someone astonishingly clever: child prodigy 2 a wonder • **prodigious** adj 1 astonishing 2 enormous

produce verb 1 bring into being 2 bring about; cause 3 do the job of producer of (a film or play) 4 make or manufacture ◇ noun food grown or produced on a farm or in a garden • **producer** noun someone who makes the practical and financial arrangements for a film to be made or a play to be staged and may also have some artistic input, together with the director

product noun 1 something produced 2 a result 3 maths the number that results from the multiplication of two or more numbers • **production** noun • **productive** adj 1 producing useful results 2 yielding a lot, eg of crops • **productivity** noun the rate of work done

Prof abbrev Professor

profane adj 1 not sacred 2 treating holy things without respect • **profanity** noun 1 swearing 2 lack of respect for sacred things

profess verb 1 declare (a belief etc) openly 2 pretend or claim: he *professes to be an expert on Scott* • **professed** *adj* **1** declared **2** pretended

profession *noun* **1** an occupation requiring special training, *eg* that of a doctor, lawyer, teacher, *etc* **2** an open declaration

professional *adj* **1** of a profession **2** earning a living from a game or an art (*contrasted with*: **amateur**) **3** skilful, competent or principled ◇ *noun* **1** someone who works in a profession **2** someone who earns money from a game or art • **professionalism** *noun* • **professionally** *adv*

professor *noun* **1** a teacher of the highest rank in a university **2** *US* a university teacher • **professorship** *noun*

proffer *verb* offer

proficiency *noun* skill • **proficient** *adj* skilled

profile *noun* **1** an outline **2** a side view of a face, head, *etc* **3** a short description of someone's life, achievements, *etc* • **profiling** *noun* outlining the characteristics of someone or something: *DNA profiling*

profit *noun* **1** money got by selling an article for a higher price than was paid for it **2** gain or benefit ◇ *verb* gain or benefit (from) • **profitable** *adj* bringing profit or gain

profiteer *noun* someone who makes large profits unfairly ◇ *verb* make large profits

profligate *adj* **1** living an immoral life **2** very extravagant ◇ *noun* a profligate person • **profligacy** *noun*

pro forma *noun* an official standard form with blanks to be filled in

profound *adj* **1** showing great knowledge or understanding: *a profound comment* **2** deeply felt **3** very deep • **profundity** *noun*

profuse *adj* given in large quantities; abundant • **profusion** *noun*

progenitor *noun, formal* an ancestor • **progeny** *noun* children

progesterone *noun* a female sex hormone that maintains pregnancy

prognosis *noun* (*plural* **prognoses**) a prediction of the course of a disease

prognosticate *verb* foretell • **prognostication** *noun*

program *noun* a set of instructions telling a computer to carry out certain actions ◇ *verb* (**programs**, **programming**, **programmed**) **1** prepare instructions to be carried out by a computer **2** give instructions to

programme or *US* **program** *noun* **1** a television or radio broadcast **2** a booklet with details of an entertainment, ceremony, *etc* **3** a scheme, a plan

progress *noun* **1** forward movement towards a destination **2** improvement towards an aim ◇ *verb* **1** go forward **2** improve • **progression** *noun* • **progressive** *adj* **1** going forward **2** in favour of change or reform

prohibit *verb* **1** forbid **2** prevent • **prohibition** *noun* the forbidding by law of making and selling alcoholic drinks • **prohibitive** *adj* **1** prohibiting **2** of a price: far too expensive

project *noun* **1** a plan or scheme **2** a task **3** a piece of study or research ◇ *verb* **1** throw out or up **2** jut out **3** cast (an image, a light, *etc*) onto a surface **4** plan, propose • **projectile** *noun* something fired or thrown; a missile • **projection** *noun* **1** an act of projecting (*eg* light or a film) **2** something that sticks out • **projectionist** *noun* someone who operates a film projector • **projector** *noun* a machine for projecting cinema pictures on a screen

prolapse *noun* a body organ, *esp* a womb, that falls out of place

prole *noun, derog informal* a proletarian

proletariat *noun* the ordinary

working people • **proletarian** noun a member of the proletariat, esp when regarded as uneducated or uncultured

proliferate verb grow or increase rapidly • **prolific** adj producing a lot

prolix adj, formal using too many words; tiresomely long • **prolixity** noun

prologue noun a preface or introduction to a play etc

prolong verb make longer

prom noun, informal 1 a promenade 2 a promenade concert

promenade noun 1 a level roadway or walk, esp by the seaside 2 a relaxed walk; a stroll ◇ verb walk for pleasure • **promenade concert** noun a concert at which a large part of the audience stands instead of being seated

prominent adj 1 easily seen or noticed 2 famous or distinguished • **prominence** noun

promiscuous adj 1 having many sexual relationships 2 old containing things of different types; miscellaneous • **promiscuity** noun

promise verb 1 give your word (to do or not do something) 2 show signs for the future: the weather promises to improve ◇ noun 1 a statement of something promised 2 a sign of something to come 3 a sign of future success or talent: his painting shows great promise • **promising** adj showing signs of being successful or talented

promontory noun (plural **promontories**) a headland that juts out into the sea

promote verb 1 raise to a higher rank 2 encourage 3 encourage the sales of; advertise • **promotion** noun • **promotional** adj

prompt adj 1 quick or immediate 2 punctual ◇ verb 1 cause to take action 2 supply words to an actor who has forgotten their lines • **prompter** noun • **promptly** adv • **promptness** noun

promulgate verb make widely known • **promulgation** noun

prone adj 1 inclined (to): prone to laziness 2 lying face downward

prong noun the spike of a fork • **pronged** adj having prongs

pronoun noun a word used instead of a noun, eg I, you, who

pronounce verb 1 speak (words, sounds) 2 announce (eg an opinion); declare • **pronounced** adj noticeable, marked • **pronouncement** noun a statement or announcement • **pronunciation** noun the way a word is said

pronto adv, informal quickly

proof noun 1 evidence that makes something clear beyond doubt 2 the standard strength of whisky etc 3 a copy of a printed sheet for correction before publication ◇ adj able to keep out or withstand: proof against attack/waterproof • **proofread** verb read printed page proofs of a text • **proofreader** noun

prop noun 1 a support 2 a piece of furniture or other equipment used on stage by actors in a play; a stage property 3 informal a propeller ◇ verb (**propping**, **propped**) hold up or support

propaganda noun 1 the spreading of ideas to influence public opinion 2 material used for this, eg posters, leaflets • **propagandist** noun someone who spreads propaganda

propagate verb 1 spread 2 produce seedlings or young plants • **propagator** noun

propane noun a gas used as fuel

propel verb (**propelling**, **propelled**) drive forward • **propellant** noun 1 an explosive for firing a rocket 2 the gas in an aerosol spray • **propeller** noun a shaft with revolving blades that drives forward a ship, aircraft, etc • **propulsion** noun an act of driving forward

propensity noun (plural **propensities**) a natural inclination: a propensity for bumping into things

proper adj 1 right, correct: the proper way to do it 2 full, thorough: a proper search 3 well-behaved or rather prim • **properly** adv 1 in the right way 2 thoroughly • **proper noun** grammar a name for a particular person, place or thing, eg Shakespeare, the Parthenon (contrasted with: **common noun**)

property noun (plural **properties**) 1 land or buildings owned 2 a quality

prophecy noun (plural **prophecies**) 1 the activity of foretelling the future 2 something prophesied

Do not confuse: **prophecy** and **prophesy**

prophesy verb (**prophesies**, **prophesying**, **prophesied**) foretell the future; predict

prophet noun 1 someone who claims to foretell events 2 someone who tells what they believe to be the will of God

prophylactic noun 1 something that helps to prevent disease 2 a condom

propinquity noun, formal nearness

propitiate verb calm the anger of • **propitious** adj favourable: propitious circumstances

proponent noun someone in favour of a thing; an advocate

proportion noun 1 a part of a total amount: a large proportion of income is taxed 2 relation in size, number, etc compared with something else: the proportion of girls to boys is small • **proportional** or **proportionate** adj in proportion • **proportional representation** noun a voting system in which parties are represented in a parliament in proportion to the number of votes cast for them, not the number of parliamentary seats they win • **in** or **out of proportion** appropriate or inappropriate in size or degree when compared with other things

propose verb 1 put forward for consideration; suggest 2 intend 3 make an offer of marriage (to) • **proposal** noun 1 anything proposed 2 an offer of marriage 3 an act of proposing

proposition noun 1 something proposed; a suggestion 2 a statement 3 a situation that must be dealt with: a tough proposition

Do not confuse with: **preposition**

propound verb put forward for consideration

proprietor noun an owner, esp of a hotel

propriety noun (plural **proprieties**) 1 behaviour that follows social rules; good manners or decency 2 suitability

propulsion see propel

pro rata adv in proportion

prorogue verb, formal discontinue meetings of (a parliament etc) for a period • **prorogation** noun

prosaic adj not interesting; dull • **prosaically** adv

proscenium /proh-see-ni-um/ noun the front part of a stage

prosciutto /pruh-shoo-toh/ noun cured, uncooked Italian ham

proscribe verb say that (something) must not be done; prohibit • **proscription** noun • **proscriptive** adj

Do not confuse with: **prescribe**

prose noun 1 writing that is not poetry 2 ordinary written or spoken language

prosecute verb 1 bring a court action against 2 formal carry on

(studies, an investigation, *etc*)

Do not confuse with: **persecute**

---

prosecution *noun* **1** *law* the people bringing the case in a trial (*contrasted with*: **defence**) **2** an act of prosecuting

proselyte *noun, formal* a convert • **proselytize** *verb* make converts

prosody *noun* study of the rhythms and construction of poetry

prospect *noun* **1** a future outlook or expectation: *the prospect of a free weekend/a job with good prospects* **2** a view or scene ◇ *verb* search for gold or other minerals • **prospective** *adj* likely to be or likely to happen: *a prospective candidate/the prospective election* • **prospector** *noun* someone who prospects for gold or other minerals

prospectus *noun* (*plural* **prospectuses**) a booklet giving information about a school, organization, *etc*

prosper *verb* do well; succeed • **prosperity** *noun* success, *esp* bringing wealth • **prosperous** *adj* wealthy or successful

prostate *noun* a gland in a man's bladder that releases a fluid used in semen

---

Do not confuse with: **prostrate**

---

prosthesis /pros-*thee*-sis/ *noun* (*plural* **prostheses**) an artificial replacement part for the body • **prosthetics** *sing noun* the study and use of artificial body parts

prostitute *noun* someone who offers sexual intercourse for payment • **prostitution** *noun*

prostrate *adj* **1** lying flat face downwards **2** worn out; exhausted ◇ *verb* **1** lie on the ground as a sign of respect: *prostrated themselves before*

the emperor **2** tire out completely; exhaust • **prostrated** *adj* worn out by grief, tiredness, *etc* • **prostration** *noun*

Do not confuse with: **prostate**

---

protagonist *noun* a main character in a play *etc*

protean *adj* changing shape often and easily

protect *verb* keep safe from danger, harm or damage • **protective** *adj* giving protection or intended to protect • **protector** *noun* someone who protects • **protectorate** *noun* a country that is partly governed and defended by another country

protection *noun* **1** the act of protecting **2** safety, shelter • **protectionism** *noun* the protection of domestic industries against foreign competition by taxing imports • **protectionist** *noun & adj*

protégé, protégée /*proh*-tuh-zheh/ *noun* a person who is taught or helped in their career by someone important or powerful

protein *noun* a substance present in milk, eggs, meat, *etc* which is a necessary part of a human or animal diet

pro tem *adj & adv* to be used in the meantime; temporary

protest *verb* **1** object strongly **2** declare forcefully or solemnly: *protesting his innocence* ◇ *noun* a strong objection • **protestation** *noun* **1** a protest **2** a solemn declaration • **protester** *or* **protestor** *noun*

Protestant *noun* a member of one of the Christian churches that broke away from the Roman Catholic Church at the time of the Reformation ◇ *adj* of or belonging to such a church

protocol *noun* correct procedure

proton *noun* a particle with a

positive electrical charge, forming part of the nucleus of an atom (*compare with*: **electron**)

protoplasm *noun* a semi-liquid substance that is the main material of all living cells

prototype *noun* the original model from which something is copied

protozoan *noun* a tiny creature made up of a single cell

protracted *adj* lasting a long time, *esp* boringly or irritatingly long • **protractor** *noun* an instrument for drawing and measuring angles on paper

protrude *verb* stick out or thrust forward • **protrusion** *noun*

protuberance *noun* a swelling or bulge • **protuberant** *adj*

proud *adj* 1 thinking too highly of yourself; conceited 2 feeling pleased at an achievement *etc* 3 dignified and self-respecting: *too proud to accept the money*

prove *verb* 1 show to be true or correct 2 turn out (to be): *his prediction proved correct* 3 try out; test

provenance *noun* where something came from or who produced it; origin

provender *noun*, *formal* food, *esp* for horses and cattle

proverb *noun* a well-known wise saying, *eg* 'nothing ventured, nothing gained' • **proverbial** *adj* well-known or widely spoken of

provide *verb* supply • **providing that** on condition that

providence *noun* 1 foresight; thrift 2 (**Providence**) God • **provident** *adj* thinking of or saving for the future • **providential** *adj* coming as if by divine help; fortunate

province *noun* 1 a division of a country 2 the extent of someone's duties or knowledge 3 (**provinces**) all parts of a country outside the capital • **provin-**

cial *adj* 1 of a province or provinces 2 narrow-minded

provision *noun* 1 an agreed arrangement 2 a guiding rule 3 a condition 4 (**provisions**) a supply of food • **provisional** *adj* used for the time being; temporary

proviso *noun* (*plural* **provisos**) a condition laid down beforehand

provoke *verb* 1 result in 2 cause to become angry or take action: *don't let him provoke you* • **provocation** *noun* • **provocative** *adj* 1 likely or tending to make people angry 2 likely to arouse sexual interest • **provoking** *adj* annoying

provost *noun* the chief magistrate of a burgh in Scotland

prow *noun* the front part of a ship

prowess *noun* skill, ability

prowl *verb* go about stealthily

proximity *noun* nearness

proxy *noun* (*plural* **proxies**) someone who acts or votes on behalf of another

prude *noun* someone who is overly shocked by remotely vulgar or sexual subjects • **prudery** *noun* • **prudish** *adj*

prudent *adj* wise and cautious • **prudence** *noun* • **prudently** *adv*

prune¹ *verb* 1 trim (a tree) by cutting off unneeded twigs 2 shorten or reduce

prune² *noun* a dried plum

prurient *adj* too concerned with sexual matters • **prurience** *noun*

pry *verb* (**pries**, **prying**, **pried**) look closely into things that are not your business • **prying** *adj*

PS *abbrev* postscript

psalm *noun* a sacred song • **psalmist** *noun* a writer of psalms

psalter *noun* a book of psalms

p's and q's *plural noun* correct social manners

psephologist *noun* someone who studies elections and voting trends

pseudo /soo-doh/ *or* **pseud** /sood/ *adj, informal* false, fake, pretended: *His Spanish accent is pseudo* • **pseud** *noun, informal* a fraud

pseudo- /soo-doh/ *prefix* false or falsely: *pseudoscientific*

pseudonym *noun* a false name used by an author

psoriasis *noun* a skin disease causing red scaly patches

psychedelic *adj* **1** bright and multi-coloured **2** of drugs: increasing perception of sound and colour and inducing hallucinations

psychiatry *noun* the treatment of mental illness • **psychiatric** *adj* • **psychiatrist** *noun* someone who treats mental illness

psychic /sai-kik/ *or* **psychical** *adj* **1** relating to the mind **2** able to read other people's minds, or tell the future

psycho- /sai-koh/ *prefix* relating to the mind or to mental disorders: *psychotherapy*

psychoanalysis *noun* a method of treating mental illness by discussing with the patient its possible causes in their past • **psychoanalyse** *verb* treat by psychoanalysis • **psychoanalyst** *noun*

psychology *noun* the science that studies the human mind • **psychological** *adj* of psychology or the mind • **psychologist** *noun*

psychosis *noun* (*plural* **psychoses**) a mental illness that causes a loss of contact with reality • **psychotic** *adj*

psychosomatic *adj* of an illness: having a psychological cause

psychotherapy *noun* treatment of mental illness by psychoanalysis *etc* • **psychotherapist** *noun*

PT *abbrev* physical training

pt *abbrev* **1** part **2** pint

PTA *abbrev* parent teacher association

ptarmigan /tah-mi-gun/ *noun* a mountain-dwelling bird of the grouse family that turns white in winter

Pte *abbrev* Private (military)

pterodactyl /te-ruh-dak-til/ *noun* an extinct flying reptile

PTO *abbrev* please turn over

pub *noun* a building where alcoholic drinks can be bought and drunk

puberty *noun* the time during youth when the body becomes sexually mature

pubic *adj* of the lowest part of the abdomen, above the genitals: *pubic hair*

public *adj* **1** relating to or shared by the people of a community or nation in general: *public opinion/public library* **2** generally or widely known: *a public figure* ◇ *noun* (**the public**) people in general • **public address system** *noun* a system of microphones, amplifiers and loudspeakers used to enable an audience to hear voices, music, *etc* • **publican** *noun* the owner or manager of a pub • **publication** *noun* **1** the act of making news *etc* public **2** the act of publishing a book, newspaper, *etc* **3** a published book, magazine, *etc* • **public house** *noun, formal* a pub • **publicist** *noun* an advertising agent • **publicity** *noun* advertising, or the fact of being brought to public attention • **publicize** *verb* bring to public attention; advertise • **public relations** *sing noun* **1** the relations between a business *etc* and the public **2** a department of a business *etc* dealing with this • **in public** in front of or among other people

publish *verb* **1** prepare and put out (a book *etc*) for sale **2** make generally known • **publisher** *noun* a person or company who publishes books

puce *adj* of a brownish-purple colour

pucker *verb* wrinkle ◇ *noun* a wrinkle or fold

pudding *noun* 1 the sweet course of a meal; dessert 2 a sweet dish made with eggs, flour, milk, *etc* 3 a type of sausage: *mealy pudding*

puddle *noun* a small, often muddy pool

pudendum *noun* (*plural* **pudenda**) the female external sex organs

puerile /pyoo-uh-rail/ *adj* childish or silly • **puerility** *noun*

puff *verb* 1 blow out in small gusts 2 breathe heavily, *eg* after running 3 swell (up or out) ◇ *noun* 1 a short, sudden gust of wind, breath, *etc* 2 a powder puff • **puffball** *noun* a ball-shaped mushroom containing a powdery mass of spores • **puff pastry** *noun* a light, flaky kind of pastry • **puffy** *adj* 1 swollen or flabby 2 breathing heavily

puffin *noun* a smallish black-and-white seabird with a short, thick beak

pug *noun* a breed of small dog with a snub nose

pugilist *noun, formal* a boxer • **pugilism** *noun* boxing

pugnacious *adj* fond of fighting or quarrelling • **pugnacity** *noun*

puke *noun & verb, slang* vomit

pukka *adj, informal* 1 of very good quality; excellent 2 genuine, not fake

pulchritude *noun, formal* beauty

pull *adj* 1 move or try to move (something) towards yourself by force 2 stretch, strain: *pull a muscle* 3 tear: *pull to pieces* ◇ *noun* 1 the act of pulling 2 a pulling force, *eg* of a magnet 3 a handle for pulling 4 *informal* influence, *esp* the power to attract • **pullout** *noun* a section that can be detached from a magazine *etc* • **pull**

through get safely to the end of a difficult or dangerous experience • **pull up** stop in a vehicle • **pull yourself together** regain self-control or self-possession

pullet *noun* a young hen

pulley *noun* (*plural* **pulleys**) a grooved wheel fitted with a cord and set in a block, used for lifting weights *etc*

Pullman *noun, dated* luxurious or superior seating on a train, in a cinema, *etc*

pullover *noun* a knitted garment for the top half of the body; a jersey

pulmonary *adj* relating to the lungs

pulp *noun* 1 the soft fleshy part of a fruit 2 a soft mass of wood *etc* that is made into paper 3 any soft mass ◇ *verb* reduce to pulp • **pulpy** *adj*

pulpit *noun* an enclosed platform in a church from which the minister or priest preaches a sermon

pulsar *noun* a distant source of regular radio signals in space, possibly a star

pulsate *verb* beat, throb

pulse *noun* 1 the beating or throbbing of the heart and blood vessels as blood flows through them 2 any strong, rhythmically intermittent sound or light ◇ *verb* throb, pulsate

pulses *plural noun* beans, peas, lentils and other edible seeds

pulverize *verb* make or crush into powder

puma *noun* an American wild animal like a large cat

pumice *or* **pumice stone** *noun* a piece of light solidified lava used for smoothing skin and for rubbing away stains

pummel *verb* (**pummelling, pummelled**) beat with the fists

pump *noun* 1 a machine used for making water rise to the surface 2 a machine for drawing out or forcing in air, gas, *etc*: *bicycle pump* **3** a kind of thin- or soft-soled shoe for dancing, gymnastics, *etc* ◇ *verb* **1** raise or force with a pump **2** *informal* draw out information from by clever questioning

pumpernickel *noun* a coarse dark rye-bread

pumpkin *noun* a very large rounded orange or yellow fruit with stringy edible flesh

pun *noun* a play on words that sound similar but have different meanings, *eg* 'two *pears* make a *pair*' ◇ *verb* (**punning**, **punned**) make a pun

punch[1] *verb* **1** hit with the fist **2** make a hole in with a tool: *punch a ticket* ◇ *noun* (*plural* **punches**) **1** a blow with the fist **2** a tool for punching holes • **punch-drunk** *adj* dizzy from being hit • **punchline** *noun* the words that give the main point to a joke • **punchy** *adj* having a powerful effect; striking

punch[2] *noun* a drink made of spirits or wine, water, sugar and fruit • **punchbowl** *noun* a bowl for mixing punch

punctilious *adj* paying attention to details, *esp* in behaviour; fastidious

punctual *adj* **1** on time, not late **2** strict in keeping the time of appointments • **punctuality** *noun*

punctuate *verb* **1** divide up sentences using commas, full stops, *etc* **2** interrupt at intervals: *the silence was punctuated by occasional coughing* • **punctuation** *noun* the use of punctuation marks • **punctuation marks** *plural noun* the symbols used in punctuating sentences, *eg* full stop, comma, colon and question mark

puncture *noun* **1** an act of pricking or piercing **2** a small hole made with a sharp point **3** a hole in a tyre

pundit *noun* an expert

pungent *adj* **1** sharp-tasting or sharp-smelling **2** of a remark: strongly sarcastic

punish *verb* **1** make (someone) suffer for a fault or crime **2** inflict suffering on **3** treat roughly or harshly • **punishable** *adj* likely to bring punishment • **punishment** *noun* pain or constraints inflicted for a fault or crime • **punitive** *adj* inflicting punishment or suffering

punk *noun* **1** a loud, often discordant style of pop music that largely promoted anti-establishment values, popular in the mid 1970s and early 1980s **2** a style of dress adopted by followers of punk, characterized by tight ripped clothes adorned with zips, chains and pins and spiky colourful hairstyles **3** *US* a worthless or stupid person

punnet *noun* a small container for holding fruit

punt *noun* a flat-bottomed boat with square ends ◇ *verb* **1** move (a punt) by pushing a pole against the bottom of a river **2** kick (a ball) with the end of the toes

punter *noun* **1** someone who gambles **2** a customer or client **3** an ordinary person

puny *adj* (**punier**, **puniest**) little and weak • **puniness** *noun*

pup *noun* **1** a young dog (also **puppy**) **2** the young of certain other animals, *eg* a seal • **puppy fat** *noun* temporary fat in childhood or adolescence • **puppy love** *noun* immature love when very young

pupa *noun* (*plural* **pupae**) the stage in the growth of an insect in which it changes from a larva to its mature form, *eg* from a caterpillar into a butterfly • **pupate** *verb* become a pupa

pupil *noun* **1** someone who is being taught by a teacher **2** the round opening in the middle of the eye through which light passes

puppet *noun* **1** a doll that is moved by strings or wires; a marionette **2** a doll that fits over the hand and is moved by the fingers **3** someone who acts exactly as they are told to

puppy *see* **pup**

purchase *verb* buy ◇ *noun* **1** something that is bought **2** the act of buying **3** the power to lift by using a lever *etc* **4** firm grip or hold • **purchaser** *noun* someone who buys

purdah *noun, hist* the seclusion of Hindu or Islamic women from strangers, behind a screen or under a veil

pure *adj* **1** not mixed with other substances: *pure gold* **2** utter, absolute, nothing but: *pure nonsense* **3** free from faults or sin, innocent **4** completely clean; spotless **5** free from dust, dirt, *etc* • **purely** *adv* **1** wholly, entirely: *purely on merit* **2** merely, only: *purely for the sake of appearance* • **purist** *noun* someone who insists on correctness • **purity** *noun* the state of being pure

purée /*pyaw-reh*/ *noun* food made into a pulp by being put through a sieve or liquidizing machine ◇ *verb* make into a purée

purgative *noun* a medicine that clears waste matter out of the body ◇ *adj*

purgatory *noun* **1** in the Roman Catholic Church, a place where souls are made pure before entering heaven **2** a state of suffering for a time

purge *verb* **1** make clean; purify **2** clear (something) of anything unwanted: *purged the party of her enemies*

purify *verb* (**purifies, purifying, purified**) make pure • **purification** *noun*

puritan *noun* **1** someone of strict, often narrow-minded morals **2** (**Puritan**) *hist* one of a group believing in strict simplicity in worship and daily life • **puritanical** *adj* • **puritanism** *noun*

purity *see* **pure**

purl *verb* knit in stitches made with the wool in front of the work

purlieus /*pur-lyooz*/ *plural noun, formal* **1** the places in which someone usually spends their time **2** outskirts or borders

purloin *verb, formal* steal

purple *noun* a dark colour formed by the mixture of blue and red

purport *verb* **1** claim or pretend: *he purports to be a film expert* **2** have as a meaning ◇ *noun* meaning

purpose *noun* **1** aim, intention **2** use, function (of a tool *etc*) ◇ *verb, formal* intend • **purposeful** *adj* having an aim • **purposefully** *adv* determinedly • **purposely** *adv* intentionally • **on purpose** intentionally • **to the purpose** to the point

---

Do not confuse: **purposefully** and **purposely**

---

purr *noun* the low, murmuring sound made by a cat when pleased ◇ *verb* of a cat: make this sound

purse *noun* **1** a small bag for carrying money **2** *US* a handbag ◇ *verb* close (the lips) tightly • **purser** *noun* the officer who looks after a ship's money • **purse strings** *plural noun* the control of a source of money

pursue *verb* **1** follow after (in order to overtake or capture); chase **2** be engaged in (studies, an enquiry, *etc*); do **3** follow (a route, path, *etc*) • **pursuer** *noun* someone who pursues • **pursuit** *noun* **1** the act of pursuing **2** an occupation or hobby

purulent *adj* full of pus or like pus

purvey *verb* supply (food *etc*) as a business • **purveyor** *noun*

pus *noun* a thick yellowish liquid produced from infected wounds

push *verb* **1** press hard against **2** thrust

(something) away with force; shove **3** force or urge to do something **4** make a big effort ◊ noun **1** a thrust **2** effort **3** *informal* energy and determination • **pushchair** noun a folding chair on wheels for a young child to ride in • **pushy** adj aggressively assertive

pusillanimous adj, formal cowardly • **pusillanimity** noun

pussy noun (plural **pussies**) informal a cat or kitten • **pussyfoot** verb act timidly or non-committally • **pussy willow** noun an American willow tree with silky catkins

pustule noun a small pimple containing pus

put verb (**putting, put**) **1** place or lay in a particular position; set: put the book on the table **2** bring to a certain position or state: put the light on/put it out of your mind **3** express: put the question more clearly • **put-up job** noun, informal a dishonest scheme • **put about 1** spread (news) **2** change course at sea • **put by** set aside or save up • **put down** defeat • **put in for** make a claim for; apply for • **put off 1** delay **2** make (someone) change their plan or intention • **put out 1** extinguish (a fire, light, etc) **2** inconvenience or annoy • **put up 1** build **2** suggest (a plan, candidate, etc) **3** let (someone) stay in your house etc **4** stay as a guest in someone's house • **put up with** bear patiently; tolerate

putative adj accepted as being • **putatively** adv

putrefy verb (**putrefies, putrefying, putrefied**) go bad; rot • **putrefaction** noun • **putrescence** noun the state of going bad • **putrescent** adj going bad • **putrid** adj rotting

putt verb hit (a golf ball) towards the hole from a position on the green

• **putter** noun a golf club used for this

putty noun a cement made from ground chalk, used in putting glass in windows etc

puzzle verb **1** present with a difficult problem or situation etc **2** be difficult (for someone) to understand: her moods puzzled him **3** (with **out**) consider long and carefully in order to solve (a problem) ◊ noun **1** a toy or riddle to test knowledge or skill: crossword puzzle/jigsaw puzzle **2** a difficulty that needs a lot of thought

PVC abbrev polyvinyl chloride

pygmy or **pigmy** (plural **pygmies** or **pigmies**) noun one of a race of very small human beings

pyjamas or US **pajamas** plural noun a sleeping suit consisting of trousers or shorts and a jacket

pylon noun **1** a high steel tower supporting electric power cables **2** a guiding mark at an airfield

pyramid noun **1** a solid shape with flat sides that come to a point at the top **2** hist a building of this shape used as a tomb in ancient Egypt

pyre noun a pile of wood on which a dead body is burned

Pyrex noun, trademark a type of heat-resistant glassware for cooking

pyromaniac noun someone who gets pleasure from starting fires • **pyromania** noun

pyrotechnics plural noun a display of fireworks

Pyrrhic victory noun a victory gained at very great cost

python noun a large non-poisonous snake that crushes its victims

Qq

QC abbrev Queen's Counsel

QED abbrev for quod erat demonstrandum, which was to be demonstrated (from Latin)

qi /chee/ noun in Chinese medicine, the life-force in each person

qt¹ abbrev quart

qt² noun: on the qt informal on the quiet; secretly

qua adv, formal in the capacity of, or thought of as

quack noun 1 the cry of a duck 2 someone who falsely claims to have medical knowledge or training ◇ verb make the noise of a duck

quad noun 1 a quadruplet 2 a quadrangle

quadrangle noun 1 a figure with four equal sides and angles 2 a four-sided courtyard surrounded by buildings in a school, college, etc • quadrangular adj

quadrant noun 1 one quarter of the circumference or area of a circle 2 an instrument used in astronomy, navigation, etc for measuring heights

quadraphonic adj of recorded sound: relayed through a minimum of four speakers

quadratic adj involving the square, but no higher power, of an unknown quantity or variable: a quadratic equation

quadrennial adj happening every four years

quadri- prefix four

quadrilateral noun a four-sided

shape or area ◇ adj four-sided

quadrille noun a dance for four couples arranged to form a square

quadriplegia noun paralysis of both arms and both legs • quadriplegic noun someone suffering from quadriplegia

quadruped noun a four-footed animal

quadruple adj 1 four times as much or as many 2 made up of four parts ◇ verb make or become four times greater: the price has quadrupled • quadruplet noun one of four children born to the same mother at one birth

quaff verb drink up eagerly

quagmire noun wet, boggy ground

quaich /kwehxh/ noun, Scot a shallow ornamental cup with two handles

quail noun a type of small bird like a partridge ◇ verb shrink back in fear

quaint adj pleasantly odd, esp because of being old-fashioned

quake verb (quaking, quaked) shake, tremble with fear ◇ noun, informal an earthquake

Quaker noun a member of a religious group opposed to violence and war, founded in the 17th century

qualify verb (qualifies, qualifying, qualified) 1 be suitable for a job or position 2 pass a test 3 lessen the force of (a statement) by adding or changing words • qualification noun 1 a skill that makes someone suitable for a job 2 a qualifying statement

• **qualified** adj having the necessary qualifications for a job

quality noun (plural **qualities**) **1** degree of worth: cloth of poor quality **2** an outstanding feature: kindness is a quality admired by all • **qualitative** adj relating to quality rather than quantity

qualm noun doubt about whether something is morally right

quandary noun (plural **quandaries**) **1** a state of uncertainty **2** a situation in which it is difficult to decide what to do

quango noun (plural **quangos**) an official body, funded and appointed by government, that supervises some national activity

quantify verb (**quantifies**, **quantifying**, **quantified**) state the quantity of • **quantifiable** adj • **quantification** noun

quantity noun (plural **quantities**) **1** amount: a large quantity of paper **2** a symbol that represents an amount: x is the unknown quantity • **quantitative** adj relating to quantity, not quality

quantum noun **1** an amount or quantity **2** physics the smallest unit of any form of physical energy • **quantum leap** noun a huge, dramatic change

quarantine noun the isolation of people or animals who might be carrying an infectious disease ◇ verb put in quarantine

quark noun, physics a particle that is the smallest unit of matter

quarrel noun an angry disagreement or argument ◇ verb (**quarrelling**, **quarrelled**) **1** disagree violently or argue angrily (with) **2** find fault (with) • **quarrelsome** adj inclined to quarrel

quarry verb (plural **quarries**) **1** a pit from which stone is taken for building **2** a hunted animal **3** someone or something eagerly looked for ◇ verb (**quarries**, **quarrying**, **quarried**) dig (stone etc) from a quarry

quart noun a measure of liquids, 1.136 litre (2 pints)

quarter noun **1** one of four equal parts of something **2** a district **3** a fourth part of a year; three months **4** direction: no help came from any quarter **5** mercy shown to an enemy: no quarter was given by either side **6** (**quarters**) lodgings, accommodation ◇ verb **1** divide into four equal parts **2** accommodate • **quarterdeck** noun the upper deck of a ship between the stern and the mast nearest it • **quarter-final** noun a match in a competition immediately before a semifinal • **quartermaster** noun an officer who looks after soldiers' accommodation and supplies

quarterly adj happening every three months ◇ adv every three months ◇ noun (plural **quarterlies**) a magazine published every three months

quartet noun **1** a group of four musicians or singers **2** a piece of music written for such a group

quarto noun (plural **quartos**) a size of book page in which a standard sheet is folded to give four leaves or eight pages

quartz noun a hard substance often in crystal form, found in rocks

quasar noun a star-like object (not really a star) that gives out light and radio waves

quash verb **1** put down (eg a rebellion) **2** cancel (eg a judge's decision)

quasi- prefix to some extent, but not completely: quasi-historical

quatrain noun a poetic stanza of four lines

quaver verb **1** shake or tremble **2** speak in a shaking voice ◇ noun **1** a trembling of the voice **2** music a note (♪) equal to half a crotchet in length

quay /kee/ noun a solid landing place

for loading and unloading boats

queasy adj (**queasier, queasiest**) 1 feeling nauseous 2 easily shocked or disgusted • **queasiness** noun

queen noun 1 a female monarch 2 the wife of a king 3 the most powerful piece in chess 4 a high value playing card with a picture of a queen 5 an egg-laying female bee, ant or wasp • **queen bee** noun 1 an egg-laying female bee 2 a woman who is or likes to be the centre of attention • **queenly** adj of or like a queen • **queen mother** noun the mother of the reigning king or queen, who was once herself queen

Queensberry rules plural noun standards of proper behaviour in a boxing match

queer adj 1 odd, strange 2 informal (sometimes derog) homosexual ◇ noun, informal (sometimes derog) a homosexual man

quell verb 1 crush (a rebellion etc) 2 remove (fears, suspicions, etc)

quench verb 1 drink and so satisfy (thirst) 2 put out (eg a fire)

quenelle /kuh-nel/ noun a poached dumpling of chicken, fish, etc

querulous /kwe-ruh-lus/ adj complaining

query noun (plural **queries**) 1 a question 2 a question mark (?) ◇ verb (**queries, querying, queried**) question (eg a statement)

quest noun a search

question noun 1 something requiring an answer, eg 'where do you live?' 2 a subject, matter, etc: the energy question/a question of ability 3 a matter for dispute or doubt: there's no question of him leaving ◇ verb 1 ask questions of (someone) 2 express doubt about • **questionable** adj doubtful • **question mark** noun a symbol (?) put after a question in writing • **questionnaire** noun a written list of questions to be answered by several people to provide information for a survey • **out of the question** not even to be considered; unthinkable

queue noun a line of people waiting, eg for a bus ◇ verb stand in, or form, a queue

quibble verb avoid an important part of an argument by quarrelling over details ◇ noun a petty argument or complaint

quiche /keesh/ noun an open pastry case filled with a mixture of beaten eggs, cheese and other foods and baked

quick adj 1 done or happening in a short time 2 acting without delay; fast-moving: a quick brain ◇ noun 1 a tender area of skin under the nails 2 old (**the quick**) people who are alive; the living ◇ adv, informal quickly • **quicken** verb become or make faster • **quicklime** noun lime that has not been mixed with water • **quickly** adv without delay; rapidly • **quicksand** noun a sandy bog that sucks in anyone who stands on it • **quicksilver** noun, old mercury • **quickstep** noun a ballroom dance like a fast foxtrot • **quick-tempered** adj easily made angry

quid noun, slang a pound (£1)

quiddity noun (plural **quiddities**) 1 the essence or nature of something 2 formal a quibble

quid pro quo noun 1 a returned favour 2 a retaliation

quiescent /kwai-es-unt/ adj, formal not active • **quiescence** noun

quiet adj 1 making little or no noise 2 calm: a quiet life ◇ noun 1 the state of being quiet 2 lack of noise; peace ◇ verb make or become quiet • **quieten** verb make or become quiet • **quietly** adv • **quietness** noun

---

Do not confuse with: **quite**

quiff *noun* a tuft of hair brushed up and back from the forehead

quill *noun* **1** a large feather of a goose or other bird, made into a pen **2** one of the sharp spines of a porcupine

quilt *noun* a thick bedcover filled with down, feathers, *etc* • **quilted** *adj* made of two layers of material with padding between them

quin *noun* a quintuplet

quince *noun* a pear-like fruit with a sharp taste, used to make jam *etc*

quinine *noun* a bitter drug taken from the bark of a S American tree, used to treat malaria

quinoa /kee-*noh*-uh/ *noun* a S American plant whose seeds are cooked like rice

quinquennial *adj* **1** happening once every five years **2** lasting five years

quinsy *noun* acute tonsillitis with pus forming round the tonsils

quintessential *adj* of the most typical or classic kind • **quintessence** *noun* • **quintessentially** *adv*

quintet *noun* **1** a group of five musicians or singers **2** a piece of music written for such a group

quintuplet *noun* one of five children born to a mother at the same time

quip *noun* a witty remark or reply ◇ *verb* (**quipping, quipped**) make a witty remark

quire *noun* a set of 24 sheets of paper

Do not confuse with: **choir**

quirk *noun* **1** an odd feature of someone's behaviour **2** a sudden happening or change, *usu* unpleasant: *quirk of fate*

quirky *adj* (**quirkier, quirkiest**) **1** rather odd or eccentric **2** full of sudden changes • **quirkily** *adv* • **quirkiness** *noun*

quisling *noun* someone who collaborates with an enemy

quit *verb* (**quitting, quit** *or* **quitted**) **1** stop doing: *I'm going to quit smoking* **2** *informal* resign from (a job) • **be quits** be even with each other

quite *adv* **1** to a great degree; entirely: *quite empty* **2** to some degree; fairly: *quite good*

Do not confuse with: **quiet**

quiver[1] *verb* tremble or shake ◇ *noun* a trembling or shaking movement

quiver[2] *noun* a carrying case for arrows

quixotic *adj* having admirable but foolish and unrealistic aims • **quixotically** *adv*

quiz *verb* (**quizzes, quizzing, quizzed**) question ◇ *noun* (*plural* **quizzes**) a competition to test knowledge • **quizzical** *adj* of a look: as if asking a question, *esp* mockingly

quoits *sing noun* a game in which heavy flat rings (**quoits**) are thrown onto small posts

quorum /*kwaw*-rum/ *noun* the least number of people who must be present at a meeting before any business can be done • **quorate** *adj* of a meeting: attended by a quorum

quota *noun* a part or share to be given or received by each member of a group

quotation *noun* **1** the words that someone says or writes, repeated elsewhere **2** the act of repeating something said or written **3** a price stated for proposed work • **quotation marks** *plural noun* marks used in writing to show that someone's words are being repeated exactly, *eg* 'he said, "I'm going out" '

quote *verb* **1** repeat the words of (someone) exactly as said or written **2** state (a price for something)

quoth *verb, old* said

quotidian *adj, formal* daily

quotient *noun, maths* the result obtained by dividing one number by another, *eg* 4 is the quotient when 12 is divided by 3

qv *abbrev* which see (from Latin *quod vide*), used for referring a reader to another particular book or passage

qwerty *noun* (*plural* **qwertys**) a standard arrangement of keys on a typewriter keyboard, with the top line of letters beginning Q,W,E,R,T,Y

Rr

R *abbrev* King or Queen (from Latin *rex* or *regina*)

RA *abbrev* Royal Academy

rabbi *noun* (*plural* **rabbis**) a Jewish priest or teacher of the law • **rabbinical** *adj*

rabbit *noun* a small, burrowing, long-eared animal

rabble *noun* a disorderly, noisy crowd

rabid *adj* **1** of a dog: suffering from rabies **2** violently enthusiastic or extreme: *a rabid nationalist*

rabies *noun* (*also called*: **hydrophobia**) a disease transmitted by the bite of an infected animal, causing fear of water and madness

raccoon *or* **racoon** *noun* a small furry animal of N America

race¹ *noun* **1** a group of people with the same ancestors and physical characteristics **2** descent: *of noble race*

race² *noun* a competition to find the fastest person, animal, vehicle, *etc* ◇ *verb* **1** run fast **2** take part in a race • **racecourse** *or* **racetrack** *noun* a course over which races are run • **racehorse** *noun* a horse bred and used for racing • **racy** *adj* of a story: full of action, and often involving sexual exploits

raceme /ras-eem/ *noun* a plant stalk with flowers growing along it

racial *adj* of or according to race • **racism** *or* **racialism** *noun* **1** prejudice on the grounds of race **2** the belief that some races of people are superior to others • **racist** *or* **racial-**
ist *noun* someone who dislikes or discriminates against people of other races ◇ *adj* involving racism

rack *noun* **1** a framework for holding letters, plates, coats, *etc* **2** *hist* an instrument for torturing victims by stretching their joints **3** a bar with teeth which fits into and moves a toothed wheel • **rack and ruin** a state of neglect and decay • **rack your brains** think hard about something

racket¹ *or* **racquet** *noun* **1** a bat made up of a strong frame strung with gut or nylon for playing tennis, badminton, *etc* **2** (**rackets**) a form of tennis played against a wall

racket² *noun* **1** a loud unpleasant noise; a din **2** *informal* a dishonest way of making a profit • **racketeer** *noun* someone who makes money dishonestly

raconteur *noun* someone who tells stories in an entertaining way

racoon *another spelling of* **raccoon**

racquet *another spelling of* **racket¹**

RADA /rah-duh/ *abbrev* Royal Academy of Dramatic Art

radar *noun* a method of detecting solid objects using radio waves that bounce back off the object and form a picture of it on a screen

radiant *adj* **1** sending out rays of light, heat, *etc* **2** showing joy and happiness: *a radiant smile* • **radiance** *noun* brightness, splendour

radiate *verb* **1** send out rays of light, heat, *etc* **2** spread or send out from a centre

radiation noun **1** the giving off of rays of light, heat, etc or of radioactive rays **2** radioactivity

radiator noun **1** a device, esp a series of connected hot-water pipes, that sends out heat **2** the part of a vehicle that cools the engine

radical adj **1** thorough: a radical change **2** basic, deep-seated: radical differences **3** advocating dramatic political changes: the radical wing of the party ◇ noun someone who has radical political views

radicchio /ruh-dee-ki-oh/ noun a purple-leaved variety of chicory

radio noun (plural **radios**) a device for sending and receiving signals by means of electromagnetic waves ◇ verb (**radios, radioing, radioed**) send a message to (someone) by radio

radioactive adj giving off rays of energy that are potentially dangerous but that can be harnessed for use in medicine • **radioactivity** noun the potentially harmful energy given off by some substances, eg uranium, as their nuclei disintegrate spontaneously

radiography noun photography of the interior of the body by X-rays • **radiographer** noun

radiology noun **1** the study of radioactive substances and radiation **2** the branch of medicine involving the use of X-rays and radium • **radiologist** noun

radiotherapy noun the treatment of certain diseases by X-rays or radioactive substances • **radiotherapist** noun

radish noun (plural **radishes**) a plant with a sharp-tasting root, eaten raw in salads

radium noun a radioactive metal used in radiotherapy

radius noun (plural **radii**) **1** a straight line from the centre to the circumference of a circle **2** an area within a certain distance from a central point

RAF abbrev Royal Air Force

raffia noun strips of fibre from the leaves of a palm tree, used in weaving mats etc

raffish adj stylish and expressing self-confidence

raffle noun a way of raising money by selling numbered tickets, one or more of which wins a prize ◇ verb give as a prize in a raffle

raft noun a number of logs etc fastened together and used as a boat

rafter noun one of the sloping beams supporting a roof

rag noun **1** a torn or worn piece of cloth **2** (**rags**) worn-out, shabby clothes ◇ adj made of rags: a rag doll ◇ verb (**ragging, ragged**) play tricks on; tease • **ragbag** noun a random or confused collection • **rag doll** noun a floppy doll made of scrap material • **ragged** adj **1** dressed in torn, shabby clothes **2** torn and tattered • **rag-rolling** noun a technique of decorating by rolling a folded cloth over a freshly painted surface • **the rag trade** the fashion or clothes industry

ragamuffin noun a ragged, dirty child

rage noun great anger; fury ◇ verb **1** be violently angry **2** of a storm, battle, etc: be violent • **all the rage** very fashionable or popular

ragga noun a style of rap music

raglan noun a cardigan or coat with the sleeves in one piece with the shoulders

ragout /ra-goo/ noun a highly seasoned meat-and-vegetable stew

ragtime noun a style of jazz music with highly syncopated melody

ragwort noun a large coarse weed with a yellow flower

raid noun 1 a short, sudden attack 2 an unexpected visit by the police to catch a criminal, recover stolen goods, etc ◇ verb make a raid on • **raider** noun

rail noun 1 a bar of metal used in fences 2 (**rails**) strips of steel that form the track on which trains run 3 the railway: I came here by rail ◇ verb (with **against** or **at**) speak angrily or bitterly • **railing** noun a fence or barrier of rails • **railway** or US **railroad** noun a track laid with steel rails on which trains run

raiment noun, old clothing

rain noun 1 water falling from the clouds in drops 2 a great number of things falling ◇ verb pour or fall in drops: It's raining today • **rainbow** noun 1 the brilliant coloured bow or arch sometimes seen in the sky opposite the sun when rain is falling 2 a member of the most junior branch of the Guides • **raincheck** noun, US an arrangement to keep an appointment etc at a later, postponed date • **raincoat** noun a waterproof coat • **rainfall** noun the amount of rain that falls in a certain time • **rainforest** noun a tropical forest with very heavy rainfall • **rainy** adj 1 during which a lot of rain falls; wet: a rainy day 2 full of rain: rainy skies

raise verb 1 lift up: raise the flag 2 make higher or greater: raise the price 3 bring up (a subject) for consideration 4 bring up (a child, family, etc) 5 breed or grow (eg pigs, crops) 6 collect, get together (a sum of money)

Do not confuse with: **raze**

raisin noun a dried grape

raison d'être /reh-zonh de-truh/ noun reason for existing

Raj /rahzh/ noun, hist the time of British rule in India, 1858–1947

rajah /rah-jah/ noun, hist an Indian prince

rake¹ noun a tool like a large comb with a long handle, for smoothing earth, gathering hay, etc ◇ verb 1 draw a rake over 2 scrape (together) 3 aim gunfire at (eg a ship) from one end to the other

rake² noun, old a man who lives an immoral life • **rakish** adj at a slanting, jaunty angle

rally verb (**rallies**, **rallying**, **rallied**) 1 gather again: rally troops 2 come together for a joint action or effort: the club's supporters rallied to save it 3 recover from an illness ◇ noun (plural **rallies**) 1 a large gathering 2 a political mass meeting 3 an improvement in health after an illness 4 tennis a long series of shots before a point is won or lost 5 a motor race over a course that includes ordinary roads and off-road sections • **rallying** noun long-distance motor-racing over public roads and off-road areas

RAM /ram/ abbrev, comput random access memory

ram noun 1 a male sheep 2 something heavy, esp as part of a machine, for ramming ◇ verb (**ramming**, **rammed**) 1 press or push down hard 2 of a ship, car, etc: run into and cause damage to • **ram-raid** noun a raid by smashing into a shop window with a stolen car

Ramadan noun 1 the ninth month of the Islamic calendar, a period of fasting by day 2 the fast itself

ramble verb 1 walk about for pleasure, esp in the countryside 2 speak in an aimless or confused way ◇ noun a country walk taken for pleasure • **rambler** noun 1 someone who rambles 2 a climbing rose or other plant

rambunctious adj boisterous and exuberant

ramekin /ram-i-kin/ noun 1 a small baking dish for a single portion of food **2** a baked mixture of cheese and eggs

ramification *noun* **1** a consequence, usually indirect and one of several **2** a branch or part of a subject, plot, *etc*

ramp *noun* a sloping surface (*eg* of a road) • **ramping** *noun* the pushing up of prices (*esp* of shares) illegally or dishonestly

rampage *verb* rush about angrily or violently • **on the rampage** rampaging

rampant *adj* **1** widespread and uncontrolled **2** *heraldry* standing on the left hind leg: *lion rampant*

rampart *noun* a mound or wall built as a defence

ramrod *noun* **1** a rod for pushing the charge down a gun barrel **2** someone strict or inflexible in their views

ramshackle *adj* badly made and falling to pieces

ran *past tense of* **run**

ranch *noun* (*plural* **ranches**) a large farm in N America for rearing cattle or horses

rancid *adj* of butter: smelling or tasting stale

rancour *noun* long-lasting bitterness or hatred • **rancorous** *adj*

rand *noun* the standard unit of S African money

R and B *abbrev* rhythm and blues

R and D *abbrev* research and development

random *adj* done without any aim or plan; chance: *a random sample* • **random access memory** *noun* a computer memory into which programs are loaded • **at random** without any plan or purpose

randy (**randier**, **randiest**) *adj* full of sexual desire; lustful

rang *past tense of* **ring**

range *noun* **1** extent, number: *a wide range of goods* **2** a line or row: *a range of mountains* **3** the distance which an object can be thrown, or across which a sound can be heard **4** the distance between the top and bottom notes of a singing voice or musical instrument **5** a piece of ground with targets for shooting or archery practice **6** a large kitchen stove with a flat top ◊ *verb* **1** set in a row or in order **2** wander (over) **3** stretch, extend • **ranger** *noun* a keeper who looks after a forest or park • **Ranger Guide** *noun* an older member of the Guide movement

rank *noun* **1** a row or line (*eg* of soldiers) **2** class, order: *the upper ranks of society/the rank of captain* **3** (**ranks**) private soldiers, not officers ◊ *verb* **1** place in order of importance, merit, *etc* **2** have a place in an order: *apes rank above dogs in intelligence* ◊ *adj* **1** having a strong, unpleasant taste or smell **2** absolute: *rank nonsense* **3** of a plant: growing too plentifully • **rank and file 1** soldiers of the rank of private **2** ordinary people, the majority

rankle *verb* cause lasting annoyance, bitterness, *etc*

ransack *verb* search (a place) thoroughly and destructively

ransom *noun* the price paid for the freeing of a captive ◊ *verb* pay money to free (a captive)

rant *verb* talk foolishly and angrily for a long time

rap[1] *noun* **1** a sharp blow or knock **2** *slang* a criminal charge ◊ *verb* (**rapping**, **rapped**) **1** (often with **on**) strike with a quick, sharp blow **2** (with **out**) speak sharply

rap[2] *noun* **1** a style of popular music with a strong beat and lyrics spoken or chanted **2** *informal* an informal talk or discussion

rapacious *adj* eager to seize as much as possible; greedy

rape[1] *verb* have sexual intercourse

with (someone) against their will, usually by force ◇ *noun* the act of raping • **rapist** *noun* someone who commits rape

rape² *noun* a type of plant like the turnip whose seeds give oil

rapid *adj* quick, fast: *a rapid rise to fame* • **rapidity** *noun* swiftness • **rapidly** *adv* • **rapids** *plural noun* a part in a river where the current flows swiftly

rapier *noun* a type of light sword with a narrow blade

rapport /ra-*pawr*/ *noun* a good relationship based on mutual understanding

rapprochement /ruh-*prosh*-monh/ *noun* a renewal of contact or friendly relations after a period of estrangement or hostility

rapt *adj* having the mind fully occupied; engrossed: *rapt attention*

rapture *noun* great delight • **rapturous** *adj*

rare *adj* **1** seldom found; uncommon **2** of meat: lightly cooked

---

Do not confuse with: **unique**

---

rarefy or **rarify** *verb* (**rarefies** or **rarifies**, **rarefying** or **rarifying**, **rarefied** or **rarified**) make thin or less dense

raring *adj*: **raring to go** very keen to go, start, *etc*

rarity *noun* (*plural* **rarities**) **1** something uncommon **2** uncommonness

rascal *noun* a naughty person

rash *adj* acting, or done, without thought ◇ *noun* abnormal redness or outbreak of spots on the skin • **rashness** *noun* the state of being rash

rasher *noun* a thin slice of bacon or ham

rasp *noun* **1** a coarse file **2** a rough, grating sound ◇ *verb* **1** rub with a file

2 make a rough, grating noise **3** say in a rough voice • **rasping** *adj* of a sound: rough and unpleasant

raspberry *noun* (*plural* **raspberries**) **1** a type of red berry similar to a blackberry **2** the bush on which this fruit grows

rat *noun* a rodent similar to but much larger than a mouse ◇ *verb* (**ratting**, **ratted**) hunt or kill rats • **rat race** *noun* ordinary working life regarded as an endless round of futile activity or an empty struggle to succeed • **ratty** *adj* irritable • **rat on** inform against

ratatouille /rat-uh-*twee*/ or /rat-uh-*too*-i/ *noun* a Mediterranean vegetable stew

ratchet *noun* a toothed wheel, *eg* in a watch

rate *noun* **1** the frequency with which something happens or is done: *a high rate of road accidents* **2** speed: *speak at a tremendous rate* **3** level of cost, price, *etc*: *paid at a higher rate* **4** (**rates**) the sum of money to be paid by the owner of a shop *etc* to pay for local public services ◇ *verb* **1** value: *I don't rate his work very highly* **2** work out the value of for taxation *etc* • **rateable value** *noun* a value of a shop *etc* used to work out the rates to be paid on it

rather *adv* **1** to some degree; fairly: *It's rather cold today* **2** more willingly: *I'd rather talk about it now than later* **3** more correctly speaking: *He agreed, or rather he didn't say no*

ratify *verb* (**ratifies**, **ratifying**, **ratified**) approve officially and formally: *ratified the treaty* • **ratification** *noun*

rating *noun* a sailor below the rank of an officer

ratio *noun* (*plural* **ratios**) the proportion of one thing to another: *a ratio of two parts flour to one of sugar*

ration *noun* **1** a measured amount of food given out at intervals **2** an allowance ◇ *verb* **1** deal out (eg food) in measured amounts **2** allow only a certain amount to (someone)

rational *adj* **1** able to reason **2** based on reason; sensible or logical: *rational arguments* • **rationality** *noun* • **rationally** *adv*

rationale /rash-uh-*nahl*/ *noun* the underlying principle or reasoning on which something is based

rationalize *verb* think up a good reason for (an action or feeling) so as not to feel guilty about it • **rationalization** *noun*

rattle *verb* **1** make short, sharp, repeated sounds: *the coins rattled in the tin* **2** fluster or irritate (someone) ◇ *noun* **1** a sharp noise quickly repeated **2** a baby's toy that makes such a sound when shaken • **rattler** *noun* a rattlesnake • **rattle off** go through (a list of names *etc*) quickly

rattlesnake *noun* a poisonous snake with bony rings on its tail that rattle when it moves

ratty *see* rat

raucous *adj* hoarse, harsh: *a raucous voice*

raunchy *adj* (**raunchier**, **raunchiest**) sexually suggestive; lewd

ravage *verb* cause destruction or damage to; plunder ◇ *plural noun* damaging effects: *the ravages of time*

rave *verb* **1** talk wildly, as if mad **2** *informal* talk very enthusiastically (about) ◇ *noun* a large party held in a warehouse *etc* with electronic music • **raver** *noun* someone who has a lively or wild social life • **raving** *adj* mad, crazy

raven *noun* a large black bird that is the largest of the crow family ◇ *adj* of hair: black and glossy

ravenous *adj* very hungry

ravine *noun* a deep, narrow valley between hills

ravioli *plural noun* little pasta cases with savoury fillings

ravish *verb* **1** plunder **2** rape **3** delight • **ravishing** *adj* extremely beautiful or attractive

raw *adj* **1** not cooked **2** still in its natural state before being prepared or refined: *raw cotton/raw text* **3** of weather: cold **4** sore • **a raw deal** unjust treatment

ray *noun* **1** a line of light, heat, *etc* **2** a small degree or amount: *a ray of hope* **3** one of several lines going outwards from a centre **4** a kind of flat-bodied fish

rayon *noun* a type of artificial silk

raze *verb* knock flat (a town, house, *etc*); destroy

Do not confuse with: **raise**

---

razor *noun* a sharp-edged instrument for shaving • **razorbill** *noun* a type of seabird • **razorfish** *noun* a type of long narrow shellfish

razzmatazz *noun* glamorous or extravagant display

RC *abbrev* Roman Catholic

re *prep* on the subject of; about

re- *prefix* **1** again, once more: *recreate* **2** back: *reclaim*

reach *verb* **1** arrive at: *reach the summit/your message never reached me* **2** stretch out (a hand) so as to touch: *I couldn't reach the top shelf* **3** extend ◇ *noun* **1** a distance that can be travelled easily: *within reach of home* **2** the distance someone can stretch their arm **3** a straight part of a stream or river between bends

react *verb* **1** act or behave in response to something **2** undergo a chemical change: *metals react with sulphuric acid* • **reaction** *noun* **1** behaviour or feelings in response to something **2** a chemical change **3** a movement against a situation or belief: *a reaction against Victorian morality* ● **reactionary** *adj* favouring a return to old ways, laws, *etc* ◊ *noun* someone who holds reactionary views

read *verb* (**reading**, **read**) **1** look at and understand, or say aloud, written or printed words **2** study a subject in a university or college: *reading law* **3** *comput* process (data) ● **readable** *adj* quite interesting ● **read-only memory** *noun, comput* a part of a computer's memory that can only be read, not written to ● **read-out** *noun* data, or a display of it, produced by a piece of measuring equipment

reader *noun* **1** someone who reads books *etc* **2** someone who reads manuscripts for a publisher **3** a senior university lecturer **4** a reading book for children

ready *adj* (**readier**, **readiest**) **1** prepared: *packed and ready to go* **2** willing: *always ready to help* **3** quick: *too ready to find fault* **4** available for use: *your coat is ready for collection* ● **readily** *adv* easily or willingly ● **readiness** *noun* ● **ready-made** *adj* prepared in advance and ready to use

real *adj* **1** actually existing, not imagined (*contrasted with*: **ideal**) **2** not imitation; genuine: *real leather* **3** sincere: *a real love of music* ● **realism** *noun* the showing or viewing of things as they really are ● **realist** *noun* someone who claims to see life as it really is ● **reality** *noun* that which is real and not imaginary; truth ● **really** *adv* **1** in fact **2** very: *really dark hair* ● **the real McCoy** the genuine article, not a poor imitation

realistic *adj* **1** lifelike **2** viewing things as they really are ● **realistically** *adv*

realize *verb* **1** come to understand; know: *I never realized you could sing* **2** make real; accomplish: *realize an ambition* **3** get (money) for: *realized £16,000 on the sale of the*

house ● **realization** *noun*

realm *noun* **1** an area of activity or interest **2** a kingdom or country

realpolitik /reh-*al*-po-li-teek/ *noun* politics based on practical realities, not idealism

realty *noun* real estate ● **realtor** *noun* an estate agent

ream *noun* **1** a measure for paper equal to 500 sheets or, more strictly, 20 quires or 480 sheets **2** (**reams**) a large quantity, *esp* of paper: *she wrote reams in her English exam*

reap *verb* **1** cut and gather (corn *etc*) **2** gain: *reap the benefits of hard work* ● **reaper** *noun* **1** someone who reaps **2** a machine for reaping

rear *noun* **1** the back part of anything **2** the last part of an army or fleet **3** the buttocks ◊ *verb* **1** bring up (children) **2** breed (animals) **3** of an animal: stand on its hindlegs ● **rear admiral** *noun* an officer who commands the rear division of the fleet ● **rearguard** *noun* troops that protect the rear of an army ● **bring up the rear** come or be last in a series

reason *noun* **1** cause or excuse: *what is the reason for this noise?* **2** purpose: *what is your reason for visiting America?* **3** the power of the mind to form opinions, judge right and truth, *etc* **4** common sense ◊ *verb* **1** think out (opinions *etc*) **2** (with **with**) try to persuade (someone) by arguing ● **reasonable** *adj* **1** sensible **2** fair

reassure *verb* take away the doubts or fears of ● **reassurance** *noun* ● **reassuring** *adj*

rebarbative *adj* repellent

rebate *noun* a part of a payment or tax that is given back to the payer

rebel *noun* someone who opposes or fights against those in power ◊ *verb* (**rebelling**, **rebelled**) fight against or oppose those in power ● **rebellion** *noun* **1** an open or armed fight against those in power **2** a refusal to obey • **rebellious** adj • **rebelliousness** noun

reboot verb restart (a computer) using its start-up programs

rebound verb bounce back: the ball rebounded off the wall ◇ noun **1** the act of rebounding **2** a reaction following an emotional situation or crisis

rebuff noun a blunt refusal or rejection ◇ verb reject bluntly

rebuke verb speak to angrily for doing something wrong; scold ◇ noun a scolding

rebut verb (**rebutting, rebutted**) deny (what has been said) • **rebuttal** noun

recalcitrant adj stubbornly disobedient • **recalcitrance** noun

recall verb **1** call back: recalled to headquarters **2** remember ◇ noun **1** a signal or message to return **2** the act of recalling or remembering

recant verb **1** take back what you have said **2** reject your beliefs publicly • **recantation** noun

recap verb (**recapping, recapped**) go over again quickly the main points of (eg a discussion)

recapture verb capture (what has escaped or been lost)

recast verb (**recasting, recast**) shape in a new form

recede verb **1** go back **2** become more distant **3** slope backwards • **receding** adj **1** going or sloping backwards **2** becoming more distant

receipt noun **1** a written note saying that money has been received **2** the act of receiving (esp money or goods)

receive verb **1** have something given or brought to you: receive a gift/ receive a letter **2** meet and welcome: receiving visitors **3** take (goods), knowing them to be stolen

receiver noun **1** the part of a telephone through which words are heard and into which they are spoken **2** an apparatus through which television or radio broadcasts are received **3** someone who receives stolen goods

recent adj happening, done or made only a short time ago • **recently** adv

receptacle noun an object designed to receive or hold things

reception noun **1** a welcome: a warm reception **2** a large celebration at which guests are welcomed **3** the quality of radio or television signals • **receptionist** noun someone employed in an office or hotel to answer the telephone etc

receptive adj quick to take in or accept ideas etc • **receptivity** noun

recess noun (plural **recesses**) **1** part of a room set back from the rest; an alcove **2** the time during which parliament or the law courts do not work **3** remote parts: in the recesses of my memory

recession noun **1** a long period of slow economic activity with high unemployment **2** the act of moving back • **recessive** adj

recherché /ruh-shur-sheh/ adj rare or unusual

recidivism noun the habit of relapsing into crime or bad behaviour • **recidivist** noun & adj

recipe noun instructions on how to prepare or cook a certain kind of food

recipient noun someone who receives something

reciprocal adj both given and received: reciprocal affection

reciprocate verb feel or do the same in return: his dislike of me is reciprocated

recite verb repeat aloud from memory • **recital** noun **1** the act of reciting **2** a short performance of classical music **3** the facts of a story told one after the other • **recitation** *noun* a poem *etc* recited

reckless *adj* done without considering consequences or dangers; rash • **recklessly** *adv* • **recklessness** *noun*

reckon *verb* 1 consider or believe 2 count • **reckoning** *noun* 1 the settling of debts, grievances, *etc* 2 payment for sins 3 estimation or calculation 4 a sum

reclaim *verb* 1 claim back 2 drain (land once waterlogged) and use it for something 3 make (waste land) fit for use • **reclamation** *noun*

recline *verb* lean or lie on your back or side • **reclining** *adj*

recluse *noun* someone who lives alone and avoids other people • **reclusive** *adj*

recognize *verb* 1 know from a previous meeting *etc* 2 acknowledge the existence of: *everyone recognized his talent* 3 show appreciation of: *they recognized his courage by giving him a medal* • **recognition** *noun* act of recognizing • **recognizable** *adj*

recoil *verb* 1 shrink back in horror or fear 2 of a gun: jump back after a shot is fired ◇ *noun* a shrinking back

recollect *verb* remember • **recollection** *noun* 1 the act or power of remembering 2 something remembered; a memory

recommend *verb* 1 advise: *I recommend that you take a long holiday* 2 speak highly of • **recommendation** *noun* 1 the act of recommending 2 a point in favour of someone or something

recompense *verb* pay money to or reward (a person) to make up for loss, inconvenience, *etc* ◇ *noun* payment in compensation

reconcile *verb* 1 bring together in friendship after a quarrel 2 show that two statements, facts, *etc* do not contradict each other 3 (with **to**) cause to

accept something patiently: *I became reconciled to her absence* • **reconciliation** *noun*

recondite *adj, formal* known or understood by very few people

reconnaissance /ri-*kon*-i-suns/ *noun* a survey to obtain information, *esp* before a battle

reconnoitre /rek-uh-*noy*-tuh/ *verb* make a reconnaissance of

reconstitute *verb* 1 put back into its original form: *reconstitute the milk* 2 form in a different way

record *verb* 1 write down for future reference 2 put (music, speech, *etc*) on tape or disc so that it can be listened to later 3 show in writing (eg a vote) 4 show or register: *the thermometer recorded 30°C yesterday* ◇ *noun* 1 a written report of facts 2 the best known performance: *John holds the school record for the mile* 3 a round, flat piece of plastic on which sounds are recorded for playing on a record player • **record player** *noun* a machine for playing records • **break** or **beat the record** do better than any previous performance • **off the record** of a remark *etc*: not to be made public

recorder *noun* 1 a machine for recording sounds or images on tape *etc* 2 a type of simple musical wind instrument 3 a judge in certain courts

recording *noun* 1 a piece of recorded music, speech, *etc* 2 the act of recording

recount *verb* 1 count again 2 tell (the story of) ◇ *noun* a second count, *esp* of votes in an election

recoup *verb* recover (expenses, losses, *etc*)

Do not confuse with: **recuperate**

---

recourse *noun*: **have recourse to**

make use of in an emergency

recover *verb* **1** get possession of again **2** become well again after an illness • **recoverable** *adj* able to be recovered

re-cover *verb* cover again

recovery *noun* (*plural* **recoveries**) **1** a return to good health after illness or injury **2** the regaining of something lost *etc*

recreant *noun, old* a coward

recreate *verb* create again (something lost or past)

recreation *noun* enjoyable activities done in your spare time

recriminate *verb* accuse your accuser in return • **recriminations** *plural noun* accusations made by someone who is themselves accused • **recriminatory** *adj*

recruit *noun* a newly-enlisted soldier, member, *etc* ◇ *verb* enlist (someone) in an army, political party, *etc* • **recruitment** *noun*

rectangle *noun* a four-sided shape with all its angles right angles and its opposite sides equal in length; an oblong or square • **rectangular** *adj*

rectify *verb* (**rectifies**, **rectifying**, **rectified**) put right • **rectifiable** *adj*

rectilineal *or* **rectilinear** *adj* in a straight line or lines

rectitude *noun, formal* honesty or politeness

recto *noun* the right-hand page of an open book (*compare with*: **verso**)

rector *noun* **1** a member of the Anglican clergy in charge of a parish **2** the headmaster of some Scottish secondary schools **3** a Scottish university official elected by the students • **rectory** *noun* the house of an Anglican rector

rectum *noun* the lower part of the alimentary canal, ending at the anus

recumbent *adj, formal* lying down

recuperate *verb* recover strength or health • **recuperation** *noun*

Do not confuse with: **recoup**

---

recur *verb* (**recurring**, **recurred**) happen again • **recurrence** *noun* • **recurrent** *adj* happening every so often

recycle *verb* **1** treat (used material) by some process in order to make it usable again **2** use again or for a different purpose

red *adj* of the colour of blood ◇ *noun* this colour • **redbreast** *noun* the robin • **red deer** *noun* a type of reddish-brown deer • **redden** *verb* make or grow red • **red-handed** *adv* in the act of doing wrong: *caught red-handed* • **red herring** *noun* something mentioned to lead a discussion away from the main subject; a false clue • **red-hot** *adj* having reached a degree of heat at which metals glow red • **Red Indian** *noun, dated offensive* a Native American person • **red-letter day** *noun* a day that is especially important or happy for some reason • **red light** *noun* **1** a danger signal **2** a signal to stop • **redness** *noun* • **redskin** *noun, dated offensive* a Native American person • **red tape** *noun* unnecessary and troublesome rules or procedures • **redwood** *noun* a North American tree that grows to a great height • **see red** suddenly become very angry

redeem *verb* **1** make amends for (faults or unpleasantness) **2** save from sin or condemnation **3** buy back (*eg* articles from a pawnbroker) • **redeeming** *adj* making up for other faults: *a redeeming feature* • **redemption** *noun* • **the Redeemer** *noun* a name some Christians use for Jesus Christ

redeploy *verb* move (*eg* soldiers, workers) to a different place where they will be more useful

redolent *adj* **1** making you think (of):

redolent of earlier times **2** smelling (of) **3** *old* sweet-smelling

redouble *verb* make twice as great: *redouble your efforts*

redoubtable *adj* not easily defeated or discouraged; bold

redress *noun* something done or given to make up for a loss or wrong; compensation ◇ *verb* make up for (a wrong *etc*)

reduce *verb* **1** make smaller **2** lessen **3** force by circumstances to do a particular unpleasant thing: *reduced to begging in the streets* **4** bring to a lower rank or state **5** change into other terms: *reduce pounds to pence* • **reducible** *adj* • **reduction** *noun*

redundant *adj* **1** of a worker: no longer needed because of the lack of a suitable job and therefore dismissed **2** more than is needed • **redundancy** *noun*

reduplicate *verb* double or repeat

reed *noun* **1** a tall stiff grass growing in moist or marshy places **2** a part, originally made of reed, of certain wind instruments that vibrates when the instrument is played • **reedy** *adj* **1** high-pitched and lacking in power: *a reedy voice* **2** full of reeds **3** like a reed

reef *noun* a chain of rocks lying at or near the surface of the sea • **reef knot** *noun* a very secure knot that consists of intertwining loops

reefer *noun* **1** a short coat of a style formerly worn by sailors **2** *slang* a marijuana cigarette

reek *noun* **1** a strong unpleasant smell **2** *old* smoke ◇ *verb* **1** have a strong unpleasant smell **2** *old* send out smoke

reel *noun* **1** a cylinder of plastic, metal or wood on which thread, film, fishing lines, *etc* may be wound **2** a length of cinema film **3** a lively Scottish or Irish dance ◇ *verb* **1** wind on a

reel **2** (with **in**) pull in (a fish on a line) **3** stagger • **reel off** repeat or recite quickly, without pausing

reeve *noun, hist* a bailiff or chief magistrate

ref *abbrev* reference ◇ *noun* a referee

refectory *noun* (*plural* **refectories**) a communal dining hall for monks, students, *etc*

refer *verb* (**referring, referred**) **1** (with **to**) mention **2** turn (to) for information **3** apply or relate (to) **4** direct (to) for information, consideration, *etc*: *I refer you to the managing director*

referee *noun* **1** a judge in a sports match **2** someone willing to provide information about someone's character, work record, *etc* **3** someone to whom a matter is taken for settlement

reference *noun* **1** the act of referring **2** a mention **3** a note about a person's character, work, *etc* • **reference book** *noun* a book to be consulted for information, *eg* an encyclopedia • **reference library** *noun* a library of books to be looked at for information but not taken away

referendum *noun* (*plural* **referenda** *or* **referendums**) a vote by the people of a country on some important matter

refine *verb* **1** purify for use **2** make better or more exact • **refined** *adj* **1** purified **2** polite, well-mannered and elegant • **refinement** *noun* **1** good manners and good taste **2** an improvement • **refinery** *noun* a place where a substance, *eg* sugar or oil, is refined for use

refit *verb* (**refitting, refitted**) repair damages (*esp* to a ship)

reflation *noun* an increase in the amount of currency, economic activity, *etc* after deflation

reflect *verb* **1** throw back (light or

heat): *reflecting the sun's heat* **2** give an image of: *reflected in the mirror* **3** (with **on**) create a bad or good impression of in turn: *her behaviour reflects well on her mother* **4** (with **on**) think over something carefully • **reflection** *noun* **1** an image reflected in a mirror **2** the act of throwing back light or heat **3** a bad or good impression created in turn • **reflective** *adj* thoughtful • **reflector** *noun* something (*eg* a piece of shiny metal) which throws back light

reflex *noun* (*plural* **reflexes**) an action that is automatic, not intended, *eg* jerking the leg when the kneecap is struck ◊ *adj* done as a reflex; unthinking

reflexive *adj, grammar* showing that the object (**reflexive pronoun**) of the verb (**reflexive verb**) is the same as its subject, *eg* in 'he cut himself', *himself* is a *reflexive pronoun* and *cut* a *reflexive verb*

reflexology *noun* a way of treating illness or stress by massaging particular areas on the soles of the feet • **reflexologist** *noun* a practitioner of reflexology

reform *verb* **1** make changes or corrections to **2** give up bad habits ◊ *noun* changes, or a change, made in order to improve something • **reformer** *noun* someone who wishes to bring about changes or improvements

re-form *verb* form again (*eg* a society)

reformation *noun* a change for the better • **the Reformation** the religious movement in the Christian Church in the 16th century from which the Protestant Church arose

refract *verb* change the direction of (a ray of light) • **refraction** *noun*

refractory *adj* not easily controlled; unruly

refrain *verb* keep yourself back (from doing something): *please refrain from smoking* ◊ *noun* a chorus coming at the end of each verse of a song

refresh *verb* give new strength, energy or life to • **refresher course** *noun* a course of study intended to keep up or increase existing knowledge of a subject • **refreshing** *adj* **1** bringing back strength, energy or life **2** cooling • **refreshments** *plural noun* food and drink • **refresh your memory** go over facts again so that they are clear in your mind

refrigerator *noun* a storage machine that keeps food cold and so prevents it from going bad • **refrigerate** *verb* • **refrigeration** *noun*

refuel *verb* (**refuelling**, **refuelled**) supply with, or take in, fresh fuel

refuge *noun* a place of safety (from attack, danger, *etc*) • **refugee** *noun* someone who seeks protection from persecution in another country

refulgent *adj, formal* giving off very bright light; beaming

refund *verb* pay back ◊ *noun* a payment returned, *eg* for unsatisfactory goods

refurbish *verb* renovate and decorate

refuse[1] /ri-fyooz/ *verb* **1** say that you will not do something: *he refused to leave the room* **2** not give (*eg* permission); withhold • **refusal** *noun* • **refusenik** *noun* someone who refuses to comply with a political regime

refuse[2] /ref-yoos/ *noun* things that are thrown aside as worthless; rubbish

refute *verb* prove wrong (something that has been said or written) • **refutation** *noun*

regain *verb* **1** win back again **2** get back to: *regain the shore*

regal *adj* royal • **regalia** *plural noun* symbols of royalty, *eg* a crown and sceptre

regale /ri-*gehl*/ *verb* entertain lavishly

regard *verb* **1** look upon; consider: *I regard you as a nuisance* **2** look at carefully **3** pay attention to ◇ *noun* **1** concern **2** affection **3** respect **4** (**regards**) good wishes • **regarding** *prep* to do with; concerning: *a reply regarding his application* • **regardless of** paying no care or attention to • **with regard to** *or* **in regard to** concerning

regatta *noun* a meeting for yacht or boat races

regency *see* **regent**

regenerate *verb* make new and good again, *esp* improve a run-down area • **regeneration** *noun*

regent *noun* someone who governs in place of a king or queen • **regency** *noun* **1** rule by a regent **2** the period of a regent's rule **3** *Brit & US, hist* the period during which George IV was regent, 1715–23

reggae *noun* a strongly rhythmic type of rock music, originally from the West Indies

regicide *noun* **1** the killing of a monarch **2** someone who kills a monarch

régime *or* **regime** *noun* method or system of government or administration

regimen *noun* diet and habits to be followed for good health

regiment *noun* a large group of soldiers consisting of several companies, commanded by a colonel ◇ *verb* organize or control too strictly • **regimental** *adj* of a regiment • **regimentation** *noun* too strict control

region *noun* **1** a large area of land, *esp* one of several main areas into which a country is divided **2** an area of anything: *in the chest region* • **regional** *adj* • **in the region of** somewhere near: *in the region of £10*

register *noun* **1** a written list (eg of attendances at school, of those eligible to vote, *etc*) **2** the distance between the highest and lowest notes of a voice or instrument **3** how formal or informal a word or expression is ◇ *verb* **1** write down in a register **2** record or cast (a vote *etc*) **3** show or record: *a thermometer registers temperature* • **registered letter** *noun* a letter insured against loss by the post office • **registrar** *noun* a public official who keeps a register of births, deaths and marriages • **registry** *noun* an office where a register is kept • **registry office** *noun* an office where records of births, marriages and deaths are kept and where civil marriages may be performed

regius *adj* of a university professor: holding a chair created by the crown

regress *verb* go back to an earlier and *usu* less desirable state

regret *verb* (**regretting, regretted**) **1** be sorry about: *I regret any inconvenience you have suffered* **2** be sorry (to have to say something): *we regret to inform you* ◇ *noun* sorrow for anything • **regretful** *adj* • **regretfully** *adv* • **regrettable** *adj* to be regretted; unwelcome • **regrettably** *adv*

regular *adj* **1** done according to rule or habit; usual **2** arranged in order; even: *regular teeth* **3** happening at certain fixed times **4** having normal bowel movements ◇ *noun* a soldier of the regular army • **regularity** *noun* • **regularly** *adv* • **regular army** *noun* the part of the army that is kept always in training, even in times of peace

regulate *verb* **1** control by rules **2** adjust to a certain level or rate • **regulation** *noun* a rule or order • **regulator** *noun* someone or something that regulates

regurgitate *verb* bring back into the mouth after swallowing • **regurgitation** *noun*

rehabilitate *verb* **1** give back rights,

powers or health to **2** train or accustom (*esp* a criminal released from prison) to live a normal life • **rehabilitation** *noun*

rehash *verb* express in different words or present in a different way

rehearsal *noun* **1** a private practice of a play, concert, *etc* before performance in public **2** a practice for a future event or action • **rehearse** *verb* **1** practise beforehand **2** recount (facts, events, *etc*) in order

Reich /raixh/ *noun, hist* a period of German empire

reign *noun* **1** the rule of a monarch **2** the time during which a king or queen rules ◇ *verb* **1** rule as monarch **2** prevail: *silence reigned at last*

reimburse *verb* pay (someone) an amount to cover expenses • **reimbursement** *noun*

rein *noun* **1** one of two straps attached to a bridle for guiding a horse **2** (**reins**) a simple device for controlling a child when walking ◇ *verb* control with reins

reincarnation *noun* the rebirth of the soul in another body after death

reindeer *noun* (*plural* **reindeer**) a type of deer found in far northern regions

reinforce *verb* **1** add a material that provides extra strength or resilience to **2** add troops, workers, *etc* to give extra power or efficiency to • **reinforcement** *noun* **1** the act of reinforcing **2** something that strengthens **3** (**reinforcements**) additional troops

reinstate *verb* put back in a former job or position • **reinstatement** *noun*

reiterate *verb* repeat several times • **reiteration** *noun*

reject *verb* **1** cast aside as unwanted **2** refuse to take: *she rejected his offer of help* **3** turn down (eg an application, request) ◇ *noun* something discarded or refused • **rejection** *noun*

rejig *verb* (**rejigging**, **rejigged**) rearrange or reorganize

rejoice *verb* feel or show joy • **rejoicing** *noun*

rejoinder *noun* an answer to a reply

rejuvenate *verb* make young again • **rejuvenation** *noun*

relapse *verb* fall back into ill health or bad habits ◇ *noun* a falling back into ill health or bad habits

relate *verb* **1** show a connection between (two or more things) **2** tell (a story) • **related** *adj* **1** (often with **to**) of the same family (as): *I'm related to him/we are not related* **2** connected

relation *noun* **1** someone who is of the same family, either by birth or marriage **2** a connection between two or more things • **relationship** *noun* connection

relative *noun* someone who is of the same family *etc* ◇ *adj* comparative: *relative merits* • **relatively** *adv* more or less: *relatively hot* • **relativity** *noun*

relax *verb* **1** become or make less tense **2** slacken (eg your grip or control) **3** make (laws or rules) less severe • **relaxation** *noun* **1** a slackening **2** rest from work; leisure

relay *verb* (**relaying**, **relayed**) receive and pass on (eg a message, a television programme) ◇ *noun* **1** the sending out of a radio or television broadcast received from another station **2** a fresh set of people to replace others in a job *etc* **3** a relay race • **relay race** *noun* a race in which members of each team take over from each other, each running a set distance • **in relays** in groups that take over from one another in series

release *verb* **1** let go of **2** allow to leave prison or captivity **3** allow (news *etc*) to be made public ◇ *noun* a setting free

relegate *verb* 1 put down (to a lower position, group, *etc*) 2 leave (a task *etc*) to someone else • **relegation** *verb*

relent *verb* agree to something originally dismissed • **relentless** *adj* 1 without pity 2 refusing to be turned from a purpose • **relentlessly** *adv*

relevant *adj* having to do with what is being spoken about • **relevance** *noun*

reliable, **reliance** *see* **rely**

relic *noun* 1 something left over from a past time 2 the remains of a holy person, or an ancient object associated with them, preserved as a sacred object

relief *noun* 1 a lessening of pain or anxiety 2 release from a post or duty 3 people taking over someone's duty *etc* 4 help given to those in need: *famine relief* 5 the act of freeing (a town *etc*) from a siege 6 a way of carving or moulding in which the design stands out from its background

relieve *verb* 1 lessen (pain or anxiety) 2 take over a duty from (someone else) 3 come to the help of (a town *etc* under attack)

religion *noun* belief in, or worship of, a god • **religious** *adj*

relinquish *verb* give up; abandon: *relinquish control*

reliquary /rel-i-kwuh-ri/ *noun* a container for religious relics

relish *verb* 1 enjoy 2 like the taste of ◊ *noun* (*plural* **relishes**) 1 enjoyment 2 flavour 3 a thick spicy sauce eaten cold as an accompaniment

relocate *verb* move to another position, place, house, *etc*

reluctant *adj* unwilling • **reluctance** *noun*

rely *verb* (**relies**, **relying**, **relied**) 1 have full trust in 2 depend on or need • **reliability** *noun* the tendency of

a machine, vehicle, *etc* to run well without breaking down • **reliable** *adj* able to be trusted or counted on • **reliance** *noun* trust or dependence • **reliant** *adj*

REM *abbrev* rapid-eye movement, the movement of the eyes behind the eyelids during dreaming

remain *verb* 1 stay in a place 2 be left: *only two tins of soup remained* 3 be still the same: *the problem remains unsolved* • **remainder** *noun* 1 something that is left behind after removal of the rest 2 *maths* the number left after subtraction or division • **remains** *plural noun* 1 things that are left 2 a dead body

remake *noun* a second making of a film *etc* ◊ *verb* make again, often in a different way

remand *verb* put (someone) back in prison until more evidence is found • **on remand** having been remanded

remark *noun* something said ◊ *verb* 1 say 2 comment (on) 3 *formal* notice • **remarkable** *adj* particularly good, noticeable or unusual • **remarkably** *adv*

remedial *adj* 1 acting as a remedy 2 relating to the teaching of children with learning difficulties • **remedially** *adv*

remedy *noun* (*plural* **remedies**) a cure for an illness, solution to a problem, *etc* ◊ *verb* 1 cure 2 put right

remember *verb* 1 keep in mind 2 recall after having forgotten 3 send your best wishes (to): *remember me to your mother* 4 give a present to: *he remembered her in his will* • **remembrance** *noun* 1 the act of remembering 2 memory 3 something given to remind someone of a person or event; a keepsake 4 (**remembrances**) a friendly greeting

remind *verb* 1 bring (something) back to a person's mind: *remind me to post that letter* 2 cause (someone) to think about (someone or something) by resemblance: *she reminds me of her sister* • **reminder** *noun* something that reminds

reminiscence *noun* 1 something remembered from the past 2 (**reminiscences**) memories, *esp* told or written • **reminisce** *verb* think and talk about things remembered from the past • **reminiscent** *adj* 1 reminding (of): *reminiscent of Paris* 2 in a mood to remember and think about past events *etc*

remiss *adj* showing a lack of thought or care

remission *noun* 1 a shortening of a prison sentence 2 a lessening of a disease or illness

remit *noun* someone's area of authority or responsibility ◇ *verb* (**remitting, remitted**) 1 pardon (a crime *etc*) 2 wipe out, cancel (a debt *etc*) 3 lessen, become less intense 4 send (money) 5 hand over (eg a prisoner to a higher court) • **remittance** *noun*

remnant *noun* a small piece or amount left over

remonstrate *verb* protest (about) • **remonstrance** *noun*

remorse *noun* regret about something done in the past • **remorseful** *adj* • **remorseless** *adj* having no remorse; callous

remote *adj* 1 far away in time or place 2 isolated, far from other people 3 slight: *a remote chance* ◇ *noun* a remote control • **remote control** *noun* a small portable device that operates a piece of electrical equipment from a distance • **remote-control** *adj* operated by means of a remote control

removal *noun* the act of removing something, *esp* of moving furniture to a new home

remove *verb* 1 take (something) from its place 2 dismiss from a job 3 take off (clothes *etc*) 4 get rid of: *remove a*

stain ◇ *noun* a stage away (from): *one remove from anarchy* • **removed** *adj* 1 distant (from) 2 of cousins: separated by a generation: *first cousin once removed*

remunerate *verb* pay (someone) for something done • **remuneration** *noun* pay or salary • **remunerative** *adj* profitable

renaissance *noun* 1 a period of cultural revival and growth 2 a rebirth of something

renal *adj* of the kidneys

rend *verb* (**rending, rent**) tear (apart) or divide violently

render *verb* 1 cause to be: *his words rendered me speechless* 2 translate into another language 3 perform (music *etc*) 4 give (eg thanks) • **rendering** *noun* 1 a translation 2 a performance

rendezvous /ron-deh-voo/ *noun* (*plural* **rendezvous**) 1 an arranged meeting 2 a meeting place fixed beforehand

rendition *noun* a particular person's performance or interpretation of a song, piece of music, *etc*

renegade *noun* someone who deserts their own side, religion or beliefs

renew *verb* 1 make valid for a further period (eg a driving licence) 2 begin again: *renew your efforts* 3 replace: *renew the water in the tank* • **renewal** *noun*

rennet *noun* a substance used in curdling milk for making cheeses *etc*

renounce *verb* give up publicly or formally • **renunciation** *noun*

renovate *verb* make (something) like new again; mend • **renovation** *noun*

renown *noun* fame • **renowned** *adj* famous

rent¹ *noun* payment made for the use of property or land ◇ *verb* (also with

out) pay or receive rent for (a house etc) • **rental** noun money paid as rent • **rent boy** noun a young male homosexual prostitute

rent² noun a tear or split ◇ verb past form of **rend**

renunciation see **renounce**

reorganize verb put in a different order • **reorganization** noun

rep noun 1 a representative: sales rep 2 repertory theatre

repair verb 1 mend 2 make up for (a wrong) 3 old move: repair to the drawing room ◇ noun 1 a mend 2 mending: in need of repair 3 state or condition: in bad repair • **reparation** noun compensation for a wrong

repartee noun 1 an exchange of witty remarks 2 skill in witty conversation

repast noun, old a meal

repatriate verb send (someone) back to their own country • **repatriation** noun

repay verb (**repaying**, **repaid**) 1 pay back 2 give or do something in return: he repaid her kindness with a gift • **repayment** noun

repeal verb do away with (esp a law) ◇ noun a cancellation of a law etc

repeat verb 1 say or do over again 2 say from memory 3 pass on (someone's words) ◇ noun a programme broadcast for a second time • **repeatedly** adv again and again • **repeater** noun a gun that fires several shots • **repetition** noun • **repetitive** adj repeating something to a boring degree

repel verb (**repelling**, **repelled**) 1 drive back or away 2 disgust • **repellent** adj disgusting ◇ noun something that repels: insect repellent

repent verb 1 be sorry for your actions 2 (with **of**) regret • **repentance** noun • **repentant** adj repenting

repercussion noun an indirect or resultant effect of something that has happened

repertoire noun the range of works performed by a musician, theatre company, etc

repertory noun (plural **repertories**) repertoire • **repertory theatre** noun a theatre with a permanent company which performs a series of plays

repetition, **repetitive** see **repeat**

repine verb, formal be unhappy or discontented

replace verb 1 put (something) back where it was 2 put in place of another

replenish verb refill (a stock, supply)

replete adj full, esp having eaten enough

replica noun an exact copy or small-scale model of something

reply verb (**replies**, **replying**, **replied**) speak or act in answer to something ◇ noun (plural **replies**) an answer

report verb 1 give information about events for a newspaper or news broadcast 2 pass on news 3 give a description of (an event) 4 make a formal complaint against ◇ noun 1 a news article 2 a statement of facts or an assessment of quality 3 an account or description 4 a rumour 5 a written description of a school pupil's work 6 a loud noise • **reporter** noun a news journalist

repose noun, formal sleep or rest ◇ verb 1 rest 2 place (eg trust in a person)

repository noun (plural **repositories**) a storage place for safekeeping

repossess verb take back (goods, property), esp because of non-payment

reprehensible adj deserving blame or severe criticism • **reprehension** noun

represent verb 1 speak or act on behalf of others: *representing the tenants' association* 2 stand for or be a symbol of: *each letter represents a sound* 3 show or depict • **representation** noun 1 an image 2 a strong claim or appeal

representative adj 1 typical, characteristic: *a representative specimen* 2 standing or acting for others ◇ noun 1 someone who acts or speaks on behalf of others 2 a travelling salesman for a company

repress verb 1 use force to limit the freedoms of 2 keep (eg feelings) under control • **repression** noun • **repressive** adj

reprieve verb 1 pardon (a criminal) 2 relieve from trouble or difficulty ◇ noun 1 a pardon 2 temporary escape from something unpleasant

reprimand verb scold severely; censure ◇ noun a censure

reprint verb print more copies of (a book etc) ◇ noun another printing of a book

reprisal noun something bad done in return; retaliation

reproach verb scold or blame ◇ noun 1 blame or discredit 2 a cause of blame or censure • **reproachful** adj

reprobate noun someone of immoral habits ◇ adj immoral

reproduce verb 1 produce a copy of 2 produce (children or young) • **reproduction** noun

reproof noun criticism for a fault or mistake • **reprove** verb scold or blame • **reproving** adj

reptile noun a cold-blooded scaly animal such as a snake or crocodile • **reptilian** adj

republic noun a form of government in which power is in the hands of elected representatives with a president at its head • **Republican** adj

belonging to the more conservative of the two main political parties in the United States

repudiate verb refuse to acknowledge or accept: *repudiate a suggestion* • **repudiation** noun

repugnant adj causing disgust or distaste; hateful • **repugnance** noun

repulse verb 1 drive back 2 reject or snub 3 cause to feel disgusted • **repulsion** noun disgust

repulsive adj causing disgust; loathsome • **repulsiveness** noun

reputation noun 1 opinion held by people in general of a particular person or thing 2 good name • **reputable** adj having a good reputation • **repute** noun reputation • **reputed** adj 1 considered (to be something): *reputed to be dangerous* 2 supposed: *the reputed author of the book* • **reputedly** adv in the opinion of most people

request verb ask for ◇ noun 1 an occasion when someone asks for something 2 something asked for

requiem /rek-wi-um/ noun a hymn or mass sung for the dead

require verb 1 need 2 demand or order • **requirement** noun 1 something needed 2 a demand

requisite adj required, necessary ◇ noun something needed or necessary • **requisition** noun a formal request for supplies, eg for a school or army ◇ verb take for official use

requite verb 1 give back in return 2 avenge (one action) by another • **requital** noun payment in return

rerun noun a repeated television programme ◇ verb run again

rescind verb do away with (*esp* a law)

rescue verb 1 save from danger 2 free from capture ◇ noun an act of saving someone or something from danger or capture

research noun (plural **researches**) close and careful scientific or academic study to try to find out new facts: cancer research ◊ verb study carefully • **researcher** noun someone who does research

resemble verb look like or be like: he doesn't resemble his sister • **resemblance** noun likeness

resent verb feel annoyed or insulted by • **resentful** adj • **resentment** noun annoyance

reservation noun 1 the act of reserving something for future use; booking 2 an exception or condition: she agreed to the plan, but with certain reservations 3 doubt, objection: I had reservations about his appointment 4 an area of land set aside by treaty for Native American people in the United States and Canada

reserve verb 1 have kept for you (eg a seat, a table); book 2 set aside for future use ◊ noun 1 something reserved 2 (**reserves**) troops outside the regular army kept ready to help those already fighting 3 a piece of land set apart for some reason: nature reserve 4 reluctance to speak or act openly; shyness • **reserved** adj 1 kept back for a particular person or purpose; booked or assigned 2 reluctant to speak openly; shy • **reservist** noun a member of a military reserve

reservoir /rez-uh-vwah/ noun an artificial lake where water is kept in store

reshuffle verb rearrange ministerial posts within (a government cabinet) ◊ noun a rearrangement of a cabinet

reside verb 1 live (in) 2 of authority etc: be placed (in) • **residence** noun 1 the building where someone lives 2 living, or time of living, in a place

resident noun someone who lives in a particular place: a resident of Dublin ◊ adj 1 living in (a place) 2 living in a place of work: resident caretaker

• **residential** adj 1 of an area: containing houses rather than shops, offices, etc 2 providing accommodation: a residential course

residue noun an amount left over or a substance left behind • **residual** adj

resign verb give up (a job, position, etc) • **resigned** adj accepting something unpleasant and unavoidable without complaining • **resignedly** adv • **resign yourself to** accept (a situation) patiently and calmly

resignation noun 1 the act of resigning 2 a letter to say you are resigning 3 patient, calm acceptance of a situation

resilient adj 1 able to recover easily from misfortune, hurt, etc 2 of an object: readily recovering its original shape after being bent, twisted, etc • **resilience** noun

resin noun a sticky substance produced by certain plants, eg firs and pines • **resinous** adj

resist verb 1 struggle against; oppose 2 stop yourself from (doing something)

resistance noun 1 the act of resisting 2 an organized opposition, esp to an occupying force 3 ability to turn a passing electrical current into heat • **resistant** adj

resit verb sit (an examination) again ◊ noun a retaking of an examination

resolute adj with your mind made up; determined • **resolutely** adv

resolution noun 1 determination of mind or purpose 2 a firm decision (to do something) 3 a proposal put before a meeting 4 a decision expressed by a public meeting

resolve verb 1 decide firmly (to do something) 2 solve (a difficulty) 3 break up into parts ◊ noun a firm purpose

resonate verb 1 echo 2 have an effect on the feelings or circumstances of very many people • **resonance** *noun* a deep, echoing tone • **resonant** *adj* echoing, resounding

resort *noun* a popular holiday destination ◇ *verb* **1** turn (to) in a difficulty: *resorting to bribery* **2** begin to use • **in the last resort** when all else fails

resound *verb* **1** sound loudly **2** echo • **resounding** *adj* **1** echoing **2** thorough: *a resounding victory*

resources *plural noun* **1** the natural sources of wealth in a country *etc* **2** money or other property **3** an ability to handle situations skilfully and cleverly • **resourceful** *adj* good at finding ways out of difficulties

respect *verb* **1** feel a high regard for **2** treat with consideration: *respect his wishes* ◇ *noun* **1** high regard; esteem **2** consideration **3** a particular detail or characteristic: *alike in some respects* **4** (**respects**) good wishes • **respectful** *adj* showing respect • **respective** *adj* belonging to each (person or thing mentioned) separately: *my brother and his friends went to their respective homes* (eg each went to their own home) • **respectively** *adv* in the order given: *James, Andrew and Ian were first, second and third respectively* • **in respect of** concerning • **with respect to** with reference to

respectable *adj* **1** worthy of respect **2** having a good reputation **3** fairly good: *a respectable score* • **respectability** *noun*

respire *verb* breathe • **respiration** *noun* breathing • **respirator** *noun* **1** a mask worn over the mouth and nose to purify the air taken in **2** a device to help people breathe when they are too ill to do so naturally

respite *noun* a pause or rest: *no respite from work*

resplendent *adj* very bright or splendid in appearance

respond *verb* **1** answer **2** react in response to: *I waved but he didn't*

respond 3 show a positive reaction to: *responding to treatment* • **respondent** *see* **corespondent**

response *noun* **1** a reply **2** an action, feeling, *etc* in answer to another

responsible *adj* **1** (sometimes with **for**) being the cause of: *responsible for this mess* **2** liable to be blamed (for): *responsible for the conduct of his staff* **3** involving making important decisions *etc*: *a responsible post* **4** trustworthy • **responsibility** *noun*

responsive *adj* quick to react or reacting in a positive or pleasant way • **responsiveness** *noun*

rest *noun* **1** a break from work **2** a period of sleeping or relaxing **3** *music* a pause in playing or singing for a given number of beats **4** a support or prop: *book rest* **5** what is left; the remainder **6** the others, those not mentioned: *I went home but the rest went to the cinema* ◇ *verb* **1** stop working for a time **2** sleep or relax **3** lean or place on a support **4** depend (on), be based on: *the case rests on your evidence* **5** stop, develop no further: *I can't let the matter rest* further • **restful** *adj* **1** relaxing **2** relaxed • **restive** *adj* restless • **restless** *adj* **1** unable to keep still **2** nervous or impatient • **rest with** be the responsibility of: *the choice rests with you*

restaurant *noun* a place where meals may be bought and eaten • **restaurateur** *noun* the owner or manager of a restaurant

restitution *noun* **1** the return of what has been lost or taken away **2** compensation for harm or injury done

restive *see* **rest**

restore *verb* **1** put or give back **2** repair (a building, a painting, *etc*) so that it looks as it used to **3** cure (a person) • **restoration** *noun* • **restorative** *adj* giving strength or health

restrain *verb* **1** hold back (from) **2** keep under control • **restraint** *noun* **1**

the act of restraining **2** self-control **3** a tie or bond used to restrain

restrict *verb* **1** keep within certain bounds; limit: *restricted space for parking* **2** make available only to certain people: *restricted area* • **restriction** *noun* • **restrictive** *adj* restricting

result *noun* **1** a consequence of something already done or said **2** a score in a game **3** the answer to a sum ◇ *verb* **1** (with *from*) be the result or effect of **2** (with *in*) have as a result: *result in a draw* • **resultant** *adj* happening as a result

resume *verb* **1** begin again after an interruption: *resume a discussion* **2** take again: *he resumed his seat* • **resumption** *noun*

résumé /reh-zoo-meh/ *noun* **1** a summary **2** *US* a curriculum vitae

resurgent *adj* becoming prominent, powerful or successful again • **resurgence** *noun*

resurrection *noun* **1** a rising from the dead **2** (**Resurrection**) the rising of Christ from the dead **3** the act of bringing something back into use • **resurrect** *verb* bring back to life or into use

resuscitate *verb* bring back to consciousness; revive • **resuscitation** *noun*

retail *verb* **1** sell goods to someone who is going to use them, not to another seller **2** *old* tell (eg a story) fully and in detail ◇ *noun* the sale of goods to the actual user • **retailer** *noun* a shopkeeper

retain *verb* **1** keep possession of **2** keep (something) in mind **3** hold back or in place **4** reserve (someone's services) by paying a fee in advance • **retainer** *noun* **1** a fee for services paid in advance **2** *old* a servant to a rich family

retake *verb* take or capture again

◇ *noun* the filming of part of a film again

retaliate *verb* do something bad to someone in return for something they have done; hit back • **retaliation** *noun*

retard *verb, formal* **1** keep from making progress; hinder **2** make slow or late • **retardation** *noun* • **retarded** *adj, dated* having learning difficulties

retch *verb* make the actions and sound of vomiting, without actually vomiting

retd *abbrev* retired

retention *noun* **1** the act of holding in or keeping **2** the act of retaining the services of (eg a lawyer) • **retentive** *adj* able to hold or retain well: *retentive memory*

reticent *adj* unwilling to speak openly and freely; reserved • **reticence** *noun*

retina *noun* (*plural* **retinas** or **retinae**) the part of the back of the eye that receives the image of what is seen

retinue *noun* the people travelling with or assisting someone important

retire *verb* **1** give up work permanently, usually because of age **2** go to bed **3** move back; retreat • **retiral** *noun* retirement • **retired** *adj* **1** having given up work **2** out-of-the-way; quiet • **retirement** *noun* **1** the act of retiring from work **2** someone's life after they have given up work • **retiring** *adj* avoiding being noticed; shy

retort *verb* make a quick and witty reply ◇ *noun* **1** a quick, witty reply **2** a glass bottle with a long curving neck, used in laboratories

retouch *verb* improve or repair with artwork

retrace *verb* go over again: *retrace your steps*

retract *verb* **1** take back (something

said or given) **2** draw back or in: *the cat retracted its claws* • **retractable** *adj* able to be retracted • **retraction** *noun*

retread *noun* a remoulded tyre

retreat *verb* **1** move back; withdraw **2** go away ◊ *noun* **1** a movement backwards in the face of an advance by an enemy **2** a withdrawal **3** a quiet, peaceful place

retrench *verb* begin to spend less; cut back • **retrenchment** *noun*

retrial *noun* a new hearing of a law case

retribution *noun* punishment

retrieve *verb* **1** get back (something lost); recover **2** search for and fetch • **retriever** *noun* a breed of dog trained to find and fetch shot birds

retro *adj* made or done in a style from the past

retroflex *adj* bent backwards

retrograde *adj* **1** going from a better to a worse stage **2** going backward

retrospect *noun*: **in retrospect** considering or looking back on the past

retrospective *adj* **1** looking back on past events **2** of a law: applying to the past as well as the present and the future ◊ *noun* an exhibition of films, art, *etc* that features works from all stages of someone's career

retroussé /ruh-*troos*-eh/ *adj* of a nose: turned up

retsina *noun* a Greek wine flavoured with resin

return *verb* **1** go or come back **2** give, send, pay, *etc* back **3** elect to parliament ◊ *noun* **1** the act of returning **2** a profit: *return on your investment* **3** a statement of income for calculating income tax • **return match** *noun* a second match played between the same team or players • **return ticket** *noun* a ticket that covers a journey both to and from a place • **by return** sent by the first post back

reunion *noun* a meeting of people who have not seen each other for some time • **reunite** *verb* join after having been separated

Rev or **Revd** *abbrev* Reverend

rev *noun* a revolution of an engine ◊ *verb* (**revving**, **revved**) (often with **up**) increase the speed of (an engine)

revamp *verb* renew the appearance of; renovate

reveal *verb* **1** make known **2** show

reveille /ri-*val*-i/ *noun* an early-morning bugle call designed to waken soldiers, scouts, *etc*

revel *verb* (**revelling**, **revelled**) **1** take great delight (in) **2** celebrate ◊ *noun* (**revels**) festivities • **reveller** *noun* • **revelry** *noun*

revelation *noun* **1** the act of revealing something **2** something interesting or unexpected that is made known

revenge *noun* **1** harm done to someone in return for harm they themselves have committed **2** the desire to do such harm ◊ *verb* **1** inflict punishment in return for harm done: *revenging his father's murder* **2** (with **yourself**) take revenge: *he revenged himself on his enemies*

revenue *noun* **1** money received as payment **2** a country's total income

reverberate *verb* **1** echo and re-echo; resound **2** have an important effect that lasts for a long time • **reverberation** *noun*

revere *verb* look upon with great respect • **reverence** *noun* great respect • **reverent** or **reverential** *adj* showing respect

reverend *adj* **1** worthy of respect **2** (**Reverend**) a title given to a member of the clergy (*short form*: **Rev** or **Revd**)

Do not confuse: **reverend** and **reverent**

reverie noun a daydream

reverse verb 1 move backwards 2 turn upside down or the other way round 3 undo (a decision, policy, etc) ◊ noun 1 the opposite (of) 2 the other side (of a coin etc) 3 a defeat • **reversal** noun the act of reversing or being reversed • **reversible** adj of clothes: able to be worn with either side out

revert verb 1 go back to an earlier topic or state 2 be returned to a previous owner • **reversion** noun

review verb 1 give an opinion or criticism of (an artistic work) 2 consider again: review the facts 3 inspect (eg troops) ◊ noun 1 a critical opinion of a book etc 2 a magazine consisting of reviews 3 a second look in order to consider again; a reconsideration 4 an inspection of troops etc • **reviewer** noun someone who reviews books, films, etc; a critic

Do not confuse with: **revue**

revile verb say harsh things about

revise verb 1 correct faults in and make improvements in 2 study notes etc in preparation for an examination 3 change (eg an opinion) • **revision** noun 1 the act of revising 2 a revised version of a book etc

revive verb bring or come back to life, use or popularity • **revival** noun 1 a return to life, use, etc 2 a fresh show of interest: a religious revival • **revivalist** noun someone who helps to create a religious revival

revivify verb (**revivifies, revivifying, revivified**) put new life or energy into

revoke verb 1 cancel (a decision etc) 2 fail to follow suit in a card-game • **revocation** noun

revolt verb 1 rise up (against); rebel 2 cause to feel disgust ◊ noun a rebellion • **revolting** adj causing disgust

revolution noun 1 a general uprising against those in power 2 a complete change in ideas, ways of doing things, etc 3 a full turn round a centre 4 the act of turning round a centre • **revolutionize** verb bring about a complete change in

revolutionary adj 1 bringing about great changes 2 relating to a revolution ◊ noun (plural **revolutionaries**) someone who is involved in, or is in favour of, revolution

revolve verb roll or turn round • **revolver** noun a pistol with a cylindrical chamber for bullets that revolves to reload when the pistol is fired

revue noun a light-hearted theatre show with short topical plays or sketches

Do not confuse with: **review**

revulsion noun 1 disgust 2 a sudden change of feeling

reward noun 1 something given in return for work done or for good behaviour etc 2 a sum of money offered for helping to find a criminal, lost property, etc ◊ verb 1 give a reward to 2 give a reward for (a service) • **rewarding** adj giving pleasure or satisfaction

rewind verb wind back (eg a videotape) to an earlier point

rewrite verb write again and in a different form • **rewritable** adj

RGN abbrev Registered General Nurse

Rh abbrev rhesus

rhapsody noun (plural **rhapsodies**) music or poetry that expresses strong feeling • **rhapsodize** verb talk or write enthusiastically (about) • **go into rhapsodies over** show wild enthusiasm for

rhesus factor noun a substance normally present in human blood • **rhesus-negative** adj not having this substance in the blood • **rhesus-positive** adj having this substance

rhetoric noun 1 the art of good speaking or writing 2 language that is too showy, consisting of unnecessarily long or difficult words, etc • **rhetorical** adj • **rhetorical question** noun a question asked for its effect, not because an answer is expected

rheumatism noun a disease which causes stiffness and pain in the joints • **rheumatic** adj

rhinestone noun an artificial diamond

rhino noun (plural **rhinos**) a rhinoceros

rhinoceros noun (plural **rhinoceroses**) a large, thick-skinned animal with one or two horns on its nose

rhinoplasty noun plastic surgery on the nose

rhizome /rai-zohm/ noun an underground plant stem producing roots and shoots

rhododendron noun a flowering shrub with thick evergreen leaves and large flowers

rhomboid noun a parallelogram

rhombus noun (plural **rhombi** or **rhombuses**) a geometrical shape with four equal straight sides and angles that are not right angles; a diamond

rhubarb noun a plant with long red-skinned stalks that are edible when cooked

rhyme noun 1 a similarity in sounds between words or their endings, eg humble and crumble, or convention and prevention 2 a word that sounds like another 3 a short poem ◇ verb (sometimes with **with**) sound like: harp rhymes with carp

rhythm noun 1 a regular repeated pattern of sounds or beats in music or poetry 2 a regularly repeated pattern of movements • **rhythm and blues** noun a type of music combining the styles of rock-and-roll and the blues • **rhythmic** or **rhythmical** adj • **rhythm method** noun a method of contraception by abstaining from intercourse when a woman is most fertile

rial another spelling of **riyal**

rib noun 1 any of the bones that curve round and forward from the backbone, enclosing the heart and lungs 2 a spar of wood in the framework of a boat, curving up from the keel 3 a ridged knitting pattern • **ribbed** adj arranged in ridges and furrows

ribald adj of language: humorous in a rather vulgar way

ribbon noun a narrow strip of silk or other material, used for decoration, tying hair, etc

riboflavin noun a vitamin found in milk, liver and some other foods

rice noun the seeds of a plant, grown for food in well-watered ground in tropical countries • **rice cake** noun a light cake made with puffed rice grains • **rice paper** noun thin edible paper often put under baking to prevent it sticking

rich adj 1 having a lot of money or valuables; wealthy 2 valuable: a rich reward 3 (with **in**) having a lot of: rich in natural resources 4 of food: containing a lot of fat 5 of material: heavily decorated or textured; lavish 6 of a colour: deep in tone • **riches** plural noun wealth • **richly** adv • **richness** noun

Richter scale /rixh-tuh/ noun a scale for measuring the intensity of earthquakes

rickets sing noun a children's disease caused by lack of calcium, with softening and bending of the bones • **rickety** adj 1 unsteady and likely to collapse: *a rickety table* **2** suffering from rickets

rickshaw *noun* a two-wheeled carriage pulled by a man, used as transport in some S Asian countries

ricochet /rik-uh-sheh/ *verb* (**ricocheting**, **ricocheted** or **ricochetted**) of a bullet: rebound at an angle from a surface

ricotta *noun* a soft Italian sheep's-milk cheese

rictus *noun* an unnatural gaping of the mouth, *eg* in horror

rid *verb* (**ridding**, **rid**) make free from; clear of: *rid the city of rats* • **get rid of** free yourself of • **good riddance to** I am happy to have got rid of

riddle *noun* **1** a puzzle in the form of a question that describes something in a misleading way **2** something difficult to understand **3** a tray with holes for separating large objects from smaller ones

ride *verb* (**riding**, **rode**, **ridden**) **1** travel on a horse or bicycle, or in a vehicle **2** travel on and control (a horse) **3** of a ship: float at anchor ◇ *noun* **1** a journey on horseback, bicycle, *etc* **2** a path through a wood, for riding horses • **rider** *noun* **1** someone who rides **2** something added to what has already been said • **ride up** of a skirt *etc*: work itself up out of position

ridge *noun* **1** a long crest on high ground **2** a raised part between furrows

ridicule *verb* laugh at; mock ◇ *noun* mockery • **ridiculous** *adj* deserving to be laughed at; very silly

rife *adj* very common: *disease was rife in the country*

riff-raff *noun* worthless or undesirable people

rifle[1] *noun* a gun fired from the shoulder

rifle[2] *verb* **1** search through and rob **2** steal

rift *noun* **1** a crack **2** a disagreement between friends • **rift valley** *noun* a long valley formed by the fall of part of the earth's crust

rig *verb* (**rigging**, **rigged**) **1** (with **out**) clothe, dress **2** equip **3** fix (an election result) illegally or dishonestly • **rigging** *noun* ship's spars, ropes, *etc* • **rig up 1** fit (a ship) with sails and ropes **2** make or build hastily

right *adj* **1** on or belonging to the side of the body which in most people has the more skilful hand (*contrasted with*: **left**) **2** correct or true **3** fair or morally good **4** straight ◇ *adv* **1** to or on the right side **2** correctly **3** straight **4** all the way: *right along the pier and back* ◇ *noun* **1** something you are entitled to: *a right to a fair trial* **2** the right-hand side, direction, *etc* **3** the conservative side in politics **4** something good which ought to be done ◇ *verb* mend, set in order • **right angle** *noun* an angle of 90°, like one of those in a square • **rightful** *adj* by right; proper: *the rightful owner* • **right-handed** *adj* using the right hand more easily than the left • **Right Honourable** *adj* used before the names of cabinet ministers in the British government • **right-of-way** *noun* a road or path over private land along which people may go as a right • **right-wing** *adj* of conservative views in politics • **by right** because you have the right • **in your own right** not because of anyone else; independently

righteous *adj* living a virtuous life; morally good • **righteousness** *noun*

rigid *adj* **1** not easily bent; stiff **2** strict • **rigidity** *noun*

rigmarole *noun* **1** a long, annoyingly complicated procedure **2** a long, rambling speech

rigor mortis *noun* stiffening of the body after death

rigour noun 1 strictness or harshness 2 strict accuracy • **rigorous** adj 1 strictly accurate 2 very strict

rile verb cause to become angry or annoyed

rill noun, formal a small stream

rim noun an edge or border, eg the top edge of a cup

rime noun thick white frost

rind noun a thick firm covering, eg fruit peel, bacon skin or the outer covering of cheese

ring noun 1 a small hoop worn on the finger, on the ear, etc 2 a hollow circle 3 an enclosed space for boxing, circus performances, etc 4 the sound of a bell being struck 5 a small group of people formed for business or criminal purposes: a drug ring ◇ verb (**ringing**, **rang** or **ringed**, **rung** or **ringed**) 1 (past **rang**) make the sound of a bell 2 strike (a bell etc) 3 call by telephone 4 (past **ringed**) go all the way round; circle round 5 mark (a bird etc) by putting on a ring • **ringleader** noun someone who takes the lead in mischief etc • **ringlet** noun a long curl of hair • **ringmaster** noun someone who is in charge of the performance in a circus ring • **ring road** noun a road that circles a town etc avoiding the centre • **ringtone** noun a sound or tune made by a mobile phone when ringing • **ringworm** noun a skin disease causing circular red patches

rink noun a sheet of ice, often artificial, for skating or curling

rinse verb 1 wash lightly to remove soap etc 2 clean (a cup, your mouth, etc) by swilling with water ◇ noun 1 the act of rinsing 2 liquid colour for the hair

riot noun 1 a noisy disturbance by a crowd 2 a striking display: a riot of colour 3 a hilarious event ◇ verb take part in a riot • **riotous** adj noisy and uncontrolled

RIP abbrev may he or she rest in peace

rip verb (**ripping**, **ripped**) 1 tear apart or off 2 come apart ◇ noun a tear • **rip-off** noun, slang a cheat or swindle • **ripstop** adj of fabric: woven so as to prevent tearing • **let rip** express yourself fully, without restraint

ripe adj 1 of fruit etc: ready to be picked or eaten 2 fully developed; mature • **ripen** verb make or become ripe • **ripeness** noun

riposte noun a quick return or reply

ripple noun 1 a little wave or movement on the surface of water 2 a soft sound etc that rises and falls quickly and gently: a ripple of laughter

RISC abbrev reduced instruction set computer, a computer with a very fast processor

rise verb (**rising**, **rose**, **risen**) 1 move to a higher level, amount, etc 2 get up from bed 3 stand up 4 move upwards 5 of a river: have its source (in): the Rhone rises in the Alps 6 rebel (against) ◇ noun 1 an increase in level, amount, etc 2 a slope upwards • **rising** noun 1 an act of rising 2 a rebellion • **give rise to** cause

risible adj laughable

risk noun a chance of loss or injury; a danger ◇ verb 1 take the chance of: risk death 2 take the chance of losing: risk one's health • **risky** adj possibly resulting in loss or injury

risotto noun (plural **risottos**) a dish made with rice

risqué /ris-keh/ adj slightly lewd or suggestive

rissole noun a fried cake or ball of minced meat, fish, etc

rite noun a solemn ceremony, esp a religious one

ritual noun a traditional way of carrying out religious worship etc ◇ adj relating to a rite or ceremony

- **ritualistic** *adj* done in a set, unchanging way

rival *noun* someone who tries to equal or beat another ◇ *verb* (**rivalling**, **rivalled**) **1** be as good as **2** try to equal • **rivalry** *noun*

riven *adj, old* split

river *noun* a large stream of water flowing across land

rivet *noun* a bolt for fastening plates of metal together ◇ *verb* **1** fasten with a rivet **2** fix firmly (someone's attention *etc*): *riveted to the spot*

riviera *noun* a warm coastal area

rivulet *noun* a small stream

riyal or **rial** *noun* the main unit of currency in Saudi Arabia and the Yemen

RN *abbrev* Royal Navy

RNIB *abbrev* Royal National Institute for the Blind

RNLI *abbrev* Royal National Lifeboat Institution

roach *noun* (*plural* **roaches**) a type of freshwater fish

road *noun* **1** a hard, level surface for vehicles and people **2** a way of getting to somewhere; a route **3** (**roads**) a place where ships may lie at anchor (*also called*: **roadstead**) • **roadhog** *noun* a reckless or selfish driver • **roadie** *noun* a member of the crew who transport, set up and dismantle equipment for rock, jazz, *etc* musicians • **road movie** *noun* a film showing the travels of a character or characters • **roadway** *noun* the part of a road used by cars *etc* • **roadworthy** *adj* of a vehicle: fit to be used on the road

roam *verb* wander about

roan *noun* a horse with a dark-brown coat spotted with grey or white

roar *verb* **1** make a loud, deep sound **2** laugh loudly **3** say (something) loudly ◇ *noun* a loud, deep sound or laugh

roast *verb* cook or be cooked in an oven or over a fire ◇ *adj* roasted: *roast beef* ◇ *noun* **1** meat roasted **2** meat for roasting

rob *verb* (**robbing**, **robbed**) steal from • **robber** *noun* • **robbery** *noun* the act of stealing

robe *noun* **1** a long loose garment **2** *US* a dressing-gown **3** (**robes**) the official dress of a judge *etc* ◇ *verb, formal* dress

robin *noun* a small bird with a red breast

robot *noun* **1** a mechanical man or woman **2** a machine that can do the work of a person • **robotic** *adj*

robust *adj* **1** fit and healthy **2** strongly built; solid **3** of an argument, evidence, *etc*: difficult to argue against or dismiss; convincing • **robustness** *noun*

rock *noun* **1** a large lump of stone **2** a hard sweet made in sticks **3** music with a heavy beat and simple melody (*also called*: **rock music**) ◇ *verb* sway backwards and forwards or from side to side • **rock-and-roll** or **rock'n'roll** *noun* a simpler, earlier form of rock music • **rock cake** *noun* a small rough-textured cake • **rocker** *noun* a curved support on which a chair, cradle, *etc* rocks • **rockery** *noun* a collection of stones amongst which small plants are grown • **rocking-chair** or **rocking-horse** *noun* a chair or a toy horse that rocks backwards and forwards on rockers • **rocky** *adj* **1** full of rocks **2** inclined to rock; unsteady **3** *informal* full of difficulties or changing fortunes

rocket *noun* **1** a tube containing inflammable materials, used for launching a spacecraft, signalling and as a firework **2** a spacecraft ◇ *verb* move upwards rapidly: *prices are rocketing*

rococo /ruh-*koh*-koh/ *adj* extravagantly ornamented, grotesque

rod noun 1 a long thin stick 2 a stick with a line on it, for fishing 3 hist a measure of distance, about 5 metres

rode past tense of **ride**

rodent noun any of various animals with large teeth, eg a rat or a beaver

rodeo noun (plural **rodeos**) 1 a show of riding by cowboys 2 a round-up of cattle for marking

roe noun 1 the eggs of fishes 2 (also **roe deer**) a small kind of deer 3 a female red deer • **roebuck** noun the male roe deer

roentgen /ruhnt-yun/ noun a unit for measuring X-rays

rogue noun a dishonest or mischievous person; a rascal • **roguery** noun dishonesty or mischief • **roguish** adj

roister verb, old enjoy yourself noisily • **roisterer** noun

rôle noun a part played by an actor

roll verb 1 move along by turning over like a wheel 2 of a ship: rock from side to side 3 of thunder etc: rumble 4 wrap round and round: roll up a carpet 5 flatten with a roller: roll the lawn ◇ noun 1 a sheet of paper, length of cloth, etc rolled into a cylinder 2 a very small loaf of bread, for one person 3 a rocking movement 4 a list of names 5 a long, rumbling sound • **roll-call** noun the calling of names from a list • **roller** noun 1 a cylindrical tool for flattening 2 a tube over which hair is rolled and styled 3 a small solid wheel 4 a long heavy wave on the sea • **Rollerblades** plural noun, trademark rollerskates with the wheels in a single line • **roller-skates** plural noun skates with wheels at each corner of the shoe • **rolling pin** noun a roller for flattening dough • **rolling stock** noun the stock of engines, carriages, etc that run on a railway

rollicking adj noisy and full of fun

rollmop noun a rolled fillet of herring, pickled in vinegar

ROM abbrev, comput read-only memory

Roman adj of Rome or in a style originating in Rome or its ancient empire • **Roman Catholic** adj belonging to the Church whose head is the Pope • **Roman numeral** noun a capital letter used to represent a number, eg V for 5

romance noun 1 a love affair 2 a love story 3 the atmosphere or behaviour associated with love 4 a story about heroic events not likely to happen in real life ◇ verb write or tell imaginative stories • **romantic** adj 1 of romance, or inspiring romance 2 full of feeling and imagination 3 relating to love • **romanticism** noun

Romanesque adj of architecture: in a style between Roman and Gothic

Romany noun 1 (plural **Romanies**) a gypsy 2 the gypsy language

romp verb 1 play in a lively way 2 move quickly and easily ◇ noun 1 a lively game 2 a light-hearted story, film, etc with a lot of action • **rompers** plural noun a short suit for a baby

rondel noun a poem written in stanzas of thirteen or fourteen lines

rondo noun (plural **rondos**) a musical composition with a recurring section

rood noun, old 1 a measure of area equal to a quarter of an acre 2 a cross carrying an image of Christ

roof noun (plural **roofs**) 1 the top covering of a building, car, etc 2 the upper part of the mouth ◇ verb cover with a roof

rook noun 1 a kind of crow 2 chess the castle • **rookery** noun 1 a nesting place of rooks 2 a breeding place of penguins or seals • **rookie** noun, informal a new recruit

room noun 1 an inside compartment in a house 2 space: room for everybody 3 (**rooms**) lodgings • **roomy** adj having plenty of space

roost noun a perch on which a bird rests at night ◇ verb sit or sleep on a roost • **rooster** noun a farmyard cock

root noun **1** the underground part of a plant **2** the base of anything, eg a tooth **3** a cause or source **4** a word from which other words have developed ◇ verb **1** form roots and begin to grow **2** be fixed **3** of an animal: turn up ground in a search for food **4** to search (about) • **root-and-branch** adj & adv thorough(ly) or complete(ly) • **rooted** adj firmly planted • **root out** or **root up 1** tear up by the roots **2** get rid of completely • **take root 1** form roots and grow firmly **2** become firmly fixed

rope noun **1** a thick cord made by twisting strands together **2** anything resembling a thick cord ◇ verb **1** fasten or catch with a rope **2** enclose or mark off with a rope • **ropy** adj **1** like ropes; stringy **2** informal slightly ill; unwell **3** informal of a fairly low standard

rorqual /raw-kwul/ noun a type of whale with a fin on its back

Rorschach test /raw-shaxh/ noun a psychological test in which someone must interpret the shapes made by ink-blots

rosary noun (plural **rosaries**) **1** a set of prayers **2** a string of beads used in saying prayers **3** a rose garden

rose¹ past tense of **rise**

rose² noun **1** a type of flower, often scented, growing on a usu prickly bush **2** a deep pink colour • **rosehip** noun the fruit of the rose • **rosewood** noun a dark Brazilian or Indian wood that smells of roses when cut • **rosy** adj **1** attractively red or pink **2** (of the future etc) bright, hopeful

rosé /roh-zay/ noun a pink-coloured wine produced by removing red grape-skins during fermentation

rosemary noun an evergreen sweet-smelling shrub, used as a cooking herb

rosette noun a badge shaped like a rose, made of ribbons

roster noun a list showing a repeated order of duties etc

rostrum noun (plural **rostrums** or **rostra**) a platform for public speaking

rot verb (**rotting, rotted**) go bad; decay ◇ noun **1** decay **2** informal nonsense • **rotten** adj **1** decayed **2** worthless or disgraceful • **rotter** noun, dated informal a very bad, worthless person

rota noun a list of duties etc to be repeated in a set order

rotary adj turning round like a wheel

rotate verb **1** turn round like a wheel **2** go through a repeating series of changes • **rotation** noun

Rotavator noun, trademark a machine for tilling soil

rote noun: **by rote** off by heart; automatically

rotisserie noun a spit for roasting meat

rotor noun a turning part of a motor, dynamo, etc

rotten, rotter see **rot**

Rottweiler /rot-vail-uh/ noun a large powerful German dog with a smooth coat

rotund adj rather fat; plump • **rotundity** noun

rouble or **ruble** noun a standard unit of Russian coinage

roué /roo-eh/ noun, dated a debauched man; a rake

rouge /roozh/ noun a powder or cream used to add colour to the cheeks

rough adj **1** not smooth **2** coarse or harsh **3** noisy and boisterous **4** not exact: a rough guess **5** stormy ◇ noun

1 a hooligan or bully **2** strips of long grass at the sides of the fairways on a golf course • **roughage** noun bran or fibre in food • **roughcast** noun plaster mixed with fine gravel, used for coating outside walls • **roughen** verb make rough • **rough and ready** not fine or carefully made, but effective • **rough out** sketch or shape roughly

roulade /roo-lahd/ noun a meat or vegetable dish shaped into a long roll

roulette noun a gambling game played with a ball that is placed on a spinning wheel with numbered compartments

round adj **1** shaped like a circle **2** plump **3** even, exact: a round dozen ◇ adv & prep **1** on all sides (of); around: look round the room **2** in a circle (about): the earth moves round the sun **3** from one (person, place, etc) to another: the news went round ◇ noun **1** a circle or something like it in shape **2** each stage of a contest **3** a series of calls or deliveries **4** a usual route: a postman's round **5** a burst of firing, cheering, etc **6** a single bullet or shell **7** a song in which the singers take up the tune in turn ◇ verb **1** make or become round **2** of a ship: go round (eg a headland) • **rounders** sing noun a ball game played with a bat in which players run around a series of stations • **Roundhead** noun a supporter of Parliament during the English Civil War • **roundly** adv boldly or plainly • **round trip** noun, US a journey to a place and back • **round on** make a sudden attack on • **round up** gather or drive together

roundabout noun **1** a road junction where traffic moves in a circle **2** a revolving machine for children to ride on in a park etc ◇ adj not straight or direct: a roundabout route

roundel noun a round painting, glass panel, etc

rouse verb **1** awaken **2** stir up, excite • **rousing** adj stirring, exciting

rout /rowt/ noun a complete defeat ◇ verb defeat utterly

route /root/ noun the course to be followed; a way of getting to somewhere ◇ verb fix the route of • **router** noun a device in a computer or communications network that finds the most efficient route to send messages

routine noun a fixed, unchanging order of doing things ◇ adj regular, usual: routine enquiries

roux /roo/ noun (plural **roux**) a paste of flour and water used to thicken sauces etc

rove verb wander or roam • **rover** noun **1** someone who never settles in a place for long before moving on; a wanderer **2** hist a pirate

row[1] /roh/ noun **1** a line of people or things **2** a trip in a rowing boat ◇ verb drive (a boat) by oars • **rower** noun someone who rows • **rowing boat** noun a boat rowed by oars

row[2] /row/ noun **1** a noisy quarrel **2** a noise **3** informal a scolding

rowan noun (also called: **mountain ash**) a tree with clusters of bright red berries

rowdy adj (**rowdier, rowdiest**) noisy, disorderly • **rowdyism** noun

rowlock /rol-uk/ noun a place to rest an oar on the side of a rowing boat

royal adj **1** relating to a king or queen **2** splendid, magnificent: royal welcome • **royal blue** noun & adj a deep, bright blue • **royal icing** noun stiff cake icing made with egg-white • **royalist** noun someone who is in favour of the system of monarchy, as opposed to a republican • **royal jelly** noun a jelly secreted by worker bees to feed developing larvae • **royalty** noun **1** the state of being royal **2** royal people as a whole **3** a sum paid to the author of a book for each copy sold

RP abbrev Received Pronunciation, the accepted accent of standard English

rpm *abbrev* revolutions per minute

rps *abbrev* revolutions per second

RSA *abbrev* 1 Royal Society of Arts 2 Royal Scottish Academy

RSAMD *abbrev* Royal Scottish Academy of Music and Drama

RSI *abbrev* repetitive strain injury, painful swelling of the tendons of the hand or lower arm caused by prolonged manual work

RSPB *abbrev* Royal Society for the Protection of Birds

RSPCA *abbrev* Royal Society for the Prevention of Cruelty to Animals

RSVP *abbrev* please reply (from French *répondez, s'il vous plaît*)

Rt Hon *abbrev* Right Honourable

Rt Rev *abbrev* Right Reverend

rub *verb* (**rubbing, rubbed**) 1 move one thing against the surface of another 2 clean or polish (something) 3 (with **out** or **away**) remove (a mark) ◇ *noun* 1 the act of rubbing 2 a wipe ● **rub in** 1 work into (a surface) by rubbing 2 keep reminding someone of (something unpleasant)

rubber *noun* 1 a tough elastic substance made from plant juices 2 a piece of rubber used for erasing pencil marks 3 an odd number (three or five) of games in cards, cricket, *etc* ● **rubber bullet** *noun* a hard rubber pellet fired by police in riot control ● **rubberneck** *verb, informal* stare insensitively or stupidly ◇ *noun* someone who rubbernecks ● **rubber stamp** *noun* an instrument with rubber figures or letters for stamping dates *etc* on paper ● **rubber-stamp** *verb* authorize or approve, often automatically without assessing

rubbish *noun* 1 unwanted or leftover things thrown away; waste 2 nonsense

rubble *noun* small rough stones, bricks, *etc* left from a building

rubella *noun* German measles

Rubicon *noun*: **cross the Rubicon** take a decisive step

rubicund *adj* red or rosy-faced

ruble *another spelling of* **rouble**

rubric *noun* 1 a heading 2 a guiding rule

ruby *noun* (*plural* **rubies**) a type of red precious stone

ruche /roosh/ *noun* a frill

ruck *noun* a wrinkle or crease

rucksack *noun* a bag carried on the back by walkers, climbers, *etc*

ruckus *noun* (*plural* **ruckuses**) *US* a noisy disturbance or protest; an uproar

ructions *plural noun* a noisy disturbance

rudder *noun* a device fixed to the stern of a boat, or tail of an aeroplane, for steering

ruddy *adj* (**ruddier, ruddiest**) 1 red 2 of the face: rosy, in good health

rude *adj* 1 showing bad manners; impolite 2 coarse or vulgar; lewd 3 roughly made; crude: *a rude shelter* 4 startling and sudden: *a rude awakening* ● **rudely** *adv* ● **rudeness** *noun*

rudiments *plural noun* the first simple rules or facts of anything ● **rudimentary** *adj* in an early stage of development

rue *verb* be sorry for or about; regret ◇ *noun* a shrub with bitter-tasting leaves ● **rueful** *adj* sorrowful or regretful

ruff *noun* 1 *hist* a pleated frill worn round the neck 2 a band of feathers round a bird's neck

ruffian *noun* a violent or brutal person

ruffle *verb* 1 shake or push (eg hair, a bird's feathers) out of its neat state 2 annoy or offend

rug noun 1 a floor mat 2 a blanket

rugby noun a team sport in which an oval ball can be thrown or kicked

rugged adj 1 having a rough, uneven appearance 2 strong, robust 3 of a man: attractive in a way that suggests physical strength and outdoor living

ruin noun 1 complete loss of money etc 2 a downfall 3 (**ruins**) broken-down remains of buildings ◇ verb 1 destroy 2 spoil completely: ruin your chances 3 make very poor • **ruination** noun • **ruined** adj in ruins; destroyed • **ruinous** adj 1 ruined 2 likely to cause ruin

rule noun 1 government: under military rule 2 a regulation: school rules 3 what usually happens 4 a guiding principle 5 a measuring ruler ◇ verb 1 be in power; govern 2 decide (that) 3 draw (a line) 4 mark with lines • **ruler** noun 1 someone who rules 2 a marked tool for measuring length and drawing straight lines • **ruling** adj 1 governing 2 most important ◇ noun a decision that must be obeyed or accepted • **as a rule** usually • **rule out** choose not to consider; leave out

rum[1] noun an alcoholic spirit made from sugar-cane

rum[2] adj (**rummer**, **rummest**) dated informal rather strange; odd

rumba noun an Afro-Cuban dance in a square pattern

rumble verb make a low rolling noise like that of thunder etc ◇ noun a low rolling noise

rumbustious noun boisterous • **rumbustiousness** noun

ruminant noun an animal, such as a cow, that chews the cud • **ruminate** verb 1 chew the cud 2 be deep in thought • **rumination** noun deep thought

rummage verb search messily (in or through) ◇ noun a messy search

rummy noun a card game played with hands of seven cards

rumour noun 1 general talk 2 a story passed from person to person which may not be true ◇ verb 1 spread a rumour of 2 tell widely

rump noun 1 the hind part of an animal 2 the meat from this part

rumple verb 1 make untidy 2 crease

rumpus noun (plural **rumpuses**) a noisy protest or angry reaction; uproar

rumpy-pumpy noun, slang sexual intercourse

run verb (**running**, **ran**, **run**) 1 move fast on foot; hurry 2 race 3 travel: the train runs every day 4 of water: flow 5 of a machine: work 6 spread (rapidly): this colour is running 7 continue in time or space; extend: the programme runs for two hours/the railway line runs along the coast 8 operate (machinery etc) 9 organize or conduct (a business etc) ◇ noun 1 a trip 2 a spell of running 3 a continuous period: a run of good luck 4 a ladder in a stocking etc 5 free use of: the run of the house 6 a single score in cricket 7 an enclosure for animals • **runaway** noun a person, animal or vehicle that runs away • **run-down** adj in poor health or condition • **run-of-the-mill** adj ordinary • **runway** noun a path for aircraft to take off from or land on • **run a risk** take a chance of loss, failure, etc • **run down** 1 knock (someone) down 2 speak ill of • **run into** 1 collide with 2 meet accidentally • **run out of** become short of • **run over** knock down or pass over with a car

rune noun a letter of an early alphabet used in ancient writings • **runic** adj written in runes

rung[1] noun a step of a ladder

rung[2] past participle of **ring**

runnel noun a small stream

runner noun 1 someone who runs

2 a messenger **3** a rooting stem of a plant **4** a blade of a skate or sledge • **runner-up** noun (plural **runners-up**) someone who comes second in a race or competition • **do a runner** slang leave without paying a bill

running noun **1** the act of moving fast **2** management or control ◇ adj **1** for use in running **2** carried on continuously: running commentary **3** giving out fluid: running sore ◇ adv one after another: three days running • **in** or **out of the running** having or not having a chance of success

runrig noun, Scot a system of dividing land into strips for leasing to tenants

runt noun **1** the smallest animal in a litter **2** an undersized, weak person

rupee noun the standard currency of India, Pakistan and Sri Lanka

rupture noun **1** a breaking, eg of a friendship **2** a tear in a part of the body ◇ verb break or burst

rural adj of the countryside (contrasted with: **urban**)

ruse noun a cunning plan or trick

rush¹ verb **1** move quickly; hurry **2** make (someone) hurry **3** take (an enemy etc) by a sudden attack ◇ noun **1** a hurry **2** a quick, forward movement • **rush hour** noun the period at the beginning or end of the working day when roads, trains, etc are busy because people are travelling to or from work

rush² noun (plural **rushes**) a tall grass-like plant growing near water

rusk noun a hard dry biscuit like toast

russet adj reddish-brown ◇ noun a type of apple of russet colour

rust noun a reddish-brown coating on metal, caused by air and moisture ◇ verb form rust • **rustproof** adj resistant to rust

rustic adj **1** relating to the countryside **2** roughly made **3** simple and unsophisticated ◇ noun someone who lives in the country • **rusticate** verb live in the countryside • **rusticity** noun **1** country living **2** simplicity

rustle verb **1** of fabric, leaves, etc: make a soft, whispering sound **2** steal (cattle) **3** informal (with **up**) prepare quickly: rustle up a meal ◇ noun a soft, whispering sound • **rustler** noun someone who steals cattle

rusty adj (**rustier**, **rustiest**) **1** covered with rust **2** informal showing lack of practice: my French is rusty

rut noun a deep track made by a wheel etc • **rutted** adj full of ruts • **in a rut** having a dull, routine way of life

rutabaga /roo-tuh-beh-guh/ noun, US a yellow turnip; a swede

ruthless adj having or showing no pity; cruel • **ruthlessness** noun

RV abbrev, US recreational vehicle, eg a camper van

rye noun a kind of grain • **ryebread** noun bread made with flour from this grain • **rye grass** noun a grass grown for feeding cattle

Ss

s *abbrev* second(s)

Sabbath *noun* the day of the week regularly set aside for religious services and rest (among Muslims, Friday; Jews, Saturday; and Christians, Sunday)

sabbatical *noun* a period of paid leave from work, *esp* for an academic

sable *noun* a small weasel-like animal with dark brown or blackish fur ◇ *adj* black or dark brown in colour

sabotage *noun* deliberate destruction of machinery, an organization, *etc* by enemies or dissatisfied workers ◇ *verb* destroy or damage deliberately • **saboteur** *noun* someone who carries out sabotage

sabre *noun, hist* a curved sword used by cavalry • **sabre-rattling** *noun* an obvious display of force designed to frighten an enemy

sac *noun* a bag-like part of a plant or animal body that contains liquid

saccharin *noun* a very sweet substance used as a sugar substitute

saccharine *adj* overly sentimental or insincerely pleasant

sacerdotal *noun* of a priest; priestly

sachet /sa-sheh/ *noun* **1** a small sealed packet containing powder or liquid, *eg* shampoo **2** a small bag to hold handkerchiefs *etc*

sack¹ *noun* **1** a large bag of coarse cloth for holding flour *etc* **2** (**the sack**) *informal* dismissal from your job ◇ *verb, informal* dismiss from a job • **sackcloth** *noun* **1** coarse cloth for making sacks **2** a garment made of this worn as a sign of repentance • **sacking** *noun* sackcloth • **get the sack** *informal* be dismissed from your job

sack² *noun* the plundering of a captured town ◇ *verb* plunder

sackbut *noun* an early wind instrument with a slide like a trombone

sacral *adj* of the sacrum

Do not confuse with: **sacred**

---

sacrament *noun* a religious ceremony, *eg* baptism or communion • **sacramental** *adj*

sacred *adj* **1** holy **2** dedicated to some purpose or person: *sacred to her memory* **3** religious: *sacred music*

Do not confuse with: **sacral**

---

sacrifice *noun* **1** the giving up of something for the benefit of another person, or to gain something more important **2** something given up for this purpose **3** the offering of an animal killed for this purpose to a god **4** an animal *etc* offered to a god ◇ *verb* **1** give up (something) for someone or something else **2** offer (an animal *etc*) as a sacrifice to a god

sacrificial *adj* of or for sacrifice • **sacrificially** *adv*

sacrilege *noun* the use of something holy in a blasphemous way • **sacrilegious** *adj* • **sacrilegiously** *adv*

sacristy *noun* (*plural* **sacristies**) a

room for keeping sacred utensils *etc* in a church

sacrosanct *adj* **1** very sacred **2** not to be harmed or touched

sacrum /seh-krum/ *noun* a triangular bone forming part of the human pelvis

SAD *abbrev* seasonal affective disorder, a form of depression caused by lack of sunlight in winter

sad *adj* **1** feeling a lack of happiness; unhappy **2** showing sorrow **3** causing sorrow: *sad story* **4** *informal* worthy of pity, contempt or ridicule • **sadness** *noun*

sadden *verb* make or become sad

saddle *noun* **1** a seat for a rider on the back of a horse or bicycle **2** a cut or joint of meat from the back of an animal ◇ *verb* put a saddle on (an animal) • **saddlebag** *noun* a bag attached to a horse saddle • **saddler** *noun* a maker of saddles and harnesses • **saddle with** burden with: *saddled with debts*

saddo /sad-oh/ *noun, slang* (*plural* **saddoes**) someone with an inadequate personality or lifestyle

sadhu /sa-doo/ *noun* (*plural* **sadhus**) a Hindu who lives a very simple life for religious reasons

sadism /seh-dizm/ *noun* taking pleasure in being cruel to others • **sadist** *noun* • **sadistic** *adj*

SAE *or* **sae** *abbrev* stamped addressed envelope

safari *noun* an expedition for observing or hunting wild animals • **safari park** *noun* an enclosed area where wild animals are kept outdoors and on view to visitors

safe *adj* **1** unharmed **2** free from harm or danger **3** reliable or trustworthy ◇ *noun* **1** a lockable box for keeping money and valuables **2** a storage place for meat *etc*

safeguard *noun* anything that gives protection or security ◇ *verb* protect • **safety** *noun* freedom from harm or danger ◇ *adj* giving protection or safety: *safety harness* • **safety belt** *noun* a seatbelt • **safety pin** *noun* a curved pin in the shape of a clasp, with a guard covering its point • **safe and sound** unharmed

safflower *noun* an Indian thistle-like plant whose dried leaves produce a red dye

saffron *noun* a type of crocus from which is obtained a yellow food dye and flavouring agent

sag *verb* (**sagging**, **sagged**) droop or sink in the middle

saga *noun* **1** an ancient story about heroes *etc* **2** a novel or series of novels about several generations of a family **3** a long detailed story

sagacious *adj, formal* very wise, quick at understanding • **sagaciously** *adv* • **sagacity** *noun*

sage *noun* **1** a type of herb with grey-green leaves which are used for flavouring **2** a wise man ◇ *adj* wise • **sagebrush** *noun* a desert shrub of N America • **sagely** *adv*

sago *noun* a white starchy substance obtained from a palm-tree, often used in puddings

said *adj* mentioned before: *the said shopkeeper* ◇ *verb* past form of **say**

sail *noun* **1** a sheet of canvas spread out to catch the wind and drive forward a ship or boat **2** a journey in a ship or boat **3** an arm of a windmill ◇ *verb* **1** travel in a ship or boat (with or without sails) **2** navigate or steer a ship or boat **3** begin a sea voyage **4** glide along easily • **sailboard** *noun* a surfboard fitted with a mast and sail, for windsurfing • **set sail** set out on a sea voyage

sailor *noun* **1** someone who sails **2** a member of a ship's crew

saint noun 1 a very good or holy person 2 a title conferred after death on a holy person by the Roman Catholic Church (short form: **St**) • **sainted** or **saintly** adj very holy or very good

Saint Bernard or **St Bernard** noun a breed of very large dog famous for its use in mountain rescues

sake[1] noun 1 benefit or advantage: for my sake 2 cause or purpose: for the sake of making money

sake[2] /sa-ki/ noun a Japanese alcoholic drink made from fermented rice

salaam /suh-lahm/ noun a low bow with the right palm on the forehead, a form of Eastern greeting ◇ verb perform this greeting

salacious adj containing a lot of sexual detail • **salaciously** adv • **salaciousness** noun

salad noun a dish of raw vegetables, eg lettuce, cucumber, etc • **salad cream** or **salad dressing** noun sauce for putting on salad • **salad days** plural noun early days; youth

salamander noun a kind of small lizard-like animal

salami noun a type of highly seasoned sausage

salary noun (plural **salaries**) fixed wages regularly paid for work

salchow /sal-koh/ noun, ice-skating a jump in which a skater takes off from one foot, spins, and lands on the other foot

sale noun 1 the exchange of anything for money 2 a selling of goods at reduced prices 3 an auction • **saleroom** noun an auction room • **salesman**, **saleswoman** noun someone who sells or shows goods to customers

salient adj 1 most important or prominent; main: salient points of the speech 2 pointing outwards: salient angle

saline adj containing salt; salty: a saline solution

saliva noun the liquid that forms in the mouth to help digestion; spittle • **salivary** adj of or producing saliva • **salivate** verb 1 produce saliva 2 anticipate or admire something with enthusiasm

sallow[1] adj of complexion: pale and yellowish

sallow[2] noun a type of willow tree

sally noun (plural **sallies**) 1 a sudden rush forward 2 a short trip; an excursion 3 a witty remark or retort ◇ verb (**sallies**, **sallying**, **sallied**) rush out suddenly • **sally forth** set off purposefully

salmon noun a large fish with yellowish-pink flesh

salmonella noun a bacterium that causes food poisoning

salon noun 1 a shop in which hairdressing etc is done 2 a large room for receiving important guests 3 a gathering of such people

saloon noun 1 a passengers' dining-room in a ship 2 a car that is not an estate or a convertible 3 a bar serving alcoholic drinks, esp such a bar in a pub that has a smarter, quieter area known as the **lounge**

salopettes plural noun quilted trousers held up by shoulder-straps, worn for skiing

salsa noun 1 a type of Latin American dance music 2 a spicy sauce made from tomatoes, chillies, etc

salsify noun a plant with an edible root that tastes of oysters

salt noun 1 a substance used for seasoning, either mined from the earth or obtained from sea water 2 a substance formed from a metal and an acid 3 old informal a sailor ◇ adj 1 containing salt: salt water 2 tasting of salt 3 preserved in salt: salt herring ◇ verb 1 sprinkle with salt 2 preserve with salt • **salt cellar** *noun* a small container for salt • **salt-pan** *noun* a dried-up hollow near the sea where salt can be found

saltire /sol-tai-uh/ *noun* the flag of Scotland, a white cross on a blue background

saltpetre or US **saltpeter** /sawlt-pee-tuh/ *noun, old* potassium nitrate

salty *adj* (**saltier, saltiest**) **1** tasting of salt **2** containing a lot of sexual detail; racy

salubrious *adj* **1** health-giving **2** pleasant and respectable

salutary *adj* **1** beneficial, useful: *salutary lesson* **2** giving health or safety

salute *verb* **1** *military* raise the hand to the forehead to show respect to **2** honour someone by a firing of guns *etc* **3** greet with words, an embrace, *etc* ◊ *noun* an act or way of saluting • **salutation** *noun* an act of greeting

salvage *noun* **1** goods saved from destruction or waste **2** the act of saving the cargo of a sinking ship, goods from a fire, *etc* **3** payment made for this act ◊ *verb* save from loss or ruin

salvation *noun* **1** an act, means or cause of saving: *the arrival of the police was his salvation* **2** the saving of humanity from sin

salve *noun* an ointment for healing or soothing ◊ *verb* soothe (pride, conscience, *etc*)

salver *noun* a small tray, often of silver

salvo *noun* (*plural* **salvos**) a great burst of gunfire, clapping, *etc*

Samaritans *plural noun* an organization that provides a telephone helpline for people in distress

samba *noun* **1** a lively Brazilian dance or a ballroom dance developed from it **2** music for this dance

same *adj* **1** exactly alike; identical: *we both had the same feeling* **2** not

different; unchanged: *he still looks the same* **3** mentioned before: *the same person came again* ◊ *pronoun* the thing just mentioned • **sameness** *noun* lack of change or variety • **all the same** or **just the same** in spite of that • **at the same time** nevertheless

samizdat *noun* in the former Soviet Union, literature forbidden by the state, or the production of such literature

samosa *noun* a fried Indian pastry with a spicy filling

samovar *noun* a Russian tea-urn

sampan *noun* a kind of small boat used in SE Asian countries

sample *noun* a small part given to show what the whole is like ◊ *verb* **1** test a sample of: *sample a cake* **2** mix a short extract from one recording into another • **sampler** *noun* **1** someone who samples **2** a piece of needlework *etc* showing skill in different techniques

samurai *noun, hist* a member of the military caste in feudal Japan

sanatorium *noun, dated* **1** a hospital, *esp* for people suffering from respiratory diseases **2** a sickroom in a school *etc*

sanctify *verb* (**sanctifies, sanctifying, sanctified**) make holy or sacred • **sanctification** *noun*

sanctimonious *adj* pretending to be, or irritatingly proud of being, morally better than others; self-righteous

sanction *noun* **1** permission or approval **2** a penalty for breaking a law or rule **3** (**sanctions**) measures applied to force another country *etc* to stop a course of action

sanctity *noun* holiness

sanctuary *noun* (*plural* **sanctuaries**) **1** a sacred place **2** the most sacred part of a temple or church **3** a place of safety from arrest or violence **4** a protected reserve for birds or animals

sanctum noun: **inner sanctum** a very sacred or private room etc

sand noun **1** a mass of tiny particles of crushed rocks etc **2** (**sands**) a stretch of sand on the seashore ◊ verb **1** smooth or polish with sandpaper **2** add sand to • **sandbag** noun a bag filled with sand, used as a protective barrier • **sand dune** noun a ridge of sand blown up by the wind • **sand martin** noun a small bird which nests in sandy banks • **sandpaper** noun paper with a layer of sand glued to it for smoothing and polishing • **sandpiper** noun a type of wading bird • **sandpit** noun a shallow pit full of sand for playing in • **sandshoe** noun a light shoe with a rubber sole • **sandstone** noun a soft rock made of layers of sand pressed together

sandal noun a shoe with straps to hold the sole onto the foot

sandalwood noun a fragrant E Indian wood

sandwich noun (plural **sandwiches**) two slices of bread, or a split roll, stuffed with a filling ◊ verb fit between two other objects, events, etc

sandy adj (**sandier**, **sandiest**) **1** covered with sand **2** like sand **3** of hair: yellowish-red in colour

sane adj **1** of sound mind, not mad **2** sensible • **sanely** adv • **sanity** noun

sang past tense of **sing**

sangfroid /sonh-frwah/ noun calmness in difficult situations; composure

sanguinary adj bloodthirsty or bloody

Do not confuse: **sanguinary** and **sanguine**

---

sanguine adj **1** hopeful or cheerful **2** of a complexion: ruddy

sanitary adj **1** promoting good health, esp by having good drainage and sewage disposal **2** free from dirt, infection, etc • **sanitary towel** noun a pad of absorbent material worn to soak up menstrual blood

sanitation noun arrangements for protecting health, esp drainage and sewage disposal

sanity noun **1** soundness of mind; good mental health **2** good sense or judgement

sank past tense of **sink**

sanserif /san-se-rif/ noun a printing type without serifs

Sanskrit noun the ancient literary language of India

sap noun **1** the juice in plants, trees, etc **2** informal a weakling or fool ◊ verb (**sapping**, **sapped**) weaken (someone's strength etc)

sapling noun a young tree

saponaceous adj soapy or soap-like

sapphire noun a precious stone of a deep blue colour

sappy adj (**sappier**, **sappiest**) informal foolishly weak or sentimental

Saracen noun, hist an Islamic opponent of the medieval Christian Crusaders

sarcasm noun **1** a hurtful remark made in scorn **2** the use of such remarks

sarcastic adj **1** containing sarcasm **2** often using sarcasm; scornful • **sarcastically** adv

sarcoma noun a tumour

sarcophagus noun a stone coffin

sardine noun a young pilchard, often tinned in oil • **like sardines** crowded closely together

sardonic adj mocking, scornful

sari noun a long cloth wrapped round the waist and brought over the shoulder, traditionally worn by Indian women

sarnie noun, informal a sandwich

sarong noun a skirt traditionally worn by Malay men and women

SARS abbrev Severe Acute Respiratory Syndrome, a contagious lung infection

sarsaparilla /sars-puh-*ril*-uh/ noun 1 a tropical American plant whose root is used in medicine 2 a soft drink flavoured with its root

sarsen noun a large eroded block of sandstone

sartorial adj relating to dress or clothes: sartorial elegance

SAS abbrev Special Air Service, a regiment of the British Army trained to carry out secret missions behind enemy lines

sash¹ noun (plural **sashes**) a decorative band worn round the waist or over the shoulder

sash² noun (plural **sashes**) a sliding frame for window panes

sashimi noun a Japanese dish of thin slices of raw fish

sassafras /sas-uh-fras/ noun a N American laurel tree whose bark is used as a stimulant

Sassenach /sas-uh-naxh/ noun, Scot, derog an English person

sat past form of **sit**

Satan noun the Devil • **Satanic** adj of Satan; devilish • **satanism** noun devil worship • **satanist** noun

satchel noun a leather bag for carrying schoolbooks, typically worn on the back

sate verb, formal satisfy fully • **sated** adj

satellite noun 1 a communication device that orbits the earth and transmits information from one part of the world to another 2 a moon orbiting a larger planet 3 a state controlled by a more powerful neighbour • **satellite**

television noun the broadcasting of television programmes via satellite

satiate /seh-shi-eht/ verb satisfy fully • **satiety** noun

satin noun a closely woven silk with a glossy surface • **satinwood** noun a smooth kind of wood

satire noun 1 a piece of writing etc that makes fun of particular people or events 2 ridicule, scorn • **satirical** adj • **satirist** noun a writer of satire • **satirize** verb

satisfaction noun 1 a feeling of pleasure or comfort 2 something that satisfies 3 compensation for damage etc

satisfactory adj fulfilling the necessary requirements; good enough • **satisfactorily** adv

satisfy verb (**satisfies, satisfying, satisfied**) 1 give enough (of something) to 2 do enough or be good enough to please 3 give enough to lessen or quieten: satisfied her curiosity 4 convince: satisfied that he was innocent 5 fulfil: satisfy all our requirements

SATs abbrev, Brit standard assessment tasks

satsuma noun a small seedless orange

saturate verb 1 soak or immerse in water 2 cover or fill completely (with): saturated with information • **saturation** noun

Saturday noun the seventh day of the week

saturnine adj gloomy, sullen

satyr /sat-uh/ noun a mythological creature, half man, half goat, living in the woods

sauce noun 1 a thick liquid cooked or served with food 2 informal disrespectful behaviour; cheek

saucepan noun a deep-sided cooking pan with a long handle

saucer noun a small, shallow dish

for placing under a cup

saucy adj (**saucier**, **sauciest**) impudent, cheeky

sauerkraut /sow-uh-krowt/ noun a dish of finely-cut cabbage pickled in salted water

sauna noun a room filled with dry steam to induce sweating

saunter verb stroll about without hurrying ◇ noun a leisurely stroll

sausage noun minced meat seasoned and stuffed into an edible tube

sauté /soh-teh/ verb fry quickly in a small amount of oil or butter

savage adj 1 wild, untamed 2 fierce and cruel 3 uncivilized 4 very angry ◇ noun 1 an uncivilized person 2 someone fierce or cruel ◇ verb attack very fiercely • **savagely** adv • **savagery** noun

savanna or **savannah** noun a grassy, treeless plain in Africa

save verb 1 bring out of danger; rescue 2 protect from harm, damage or loss 3 keep from spending or using: saving money/saves time 4 put money aside for the future ◇ prep except (for): all the CDs were broken save this one • **saving grace** noun a good quality that makes up for faults • **savings** plural noun money put aside for the future • **save up** put money aside for future use

saviour noun 1 someone who saves others from harm or evil 2 (**Saviour**) a name some Christians use for Jesus Christ

savoir-faire /sav-wah fair/ noun knowledge of what to do, esp in social situations

savour verb 1 taste or experience with enjoyment 2 taste or smell of 3 have a trace or suggestion (of): his reaction savours of jealousy ◇ noun 1 characteristic taste or flavour 2 an interesting quality

savoury adj 1 having a pleasant taste or smell 2 salt or sharp in flavour; not sweet ◇ noun (plural **savouries**) a savoury dish or snack

savoy noun a dark-green winter cabbage with crinkly leaves

savvy adj, slang wise, shrewd ◇ verb understand

saw[1] noun 1 a tool with a toothed edge for cutting wood etc 2 old a wise saying ◇ verb (**sawing**, **sawed**, **sawn**) cut with a saw

saw[2] past tense of **see**

sawdust noun a dust of fine fragments of wood, the product of sawing

sawmill noun a mill where wood is sawn up

sax noun, informal a saxophone

saxifrage noun a type of rock plant

Saxon noun, hist one of a Germanic people who invaded Britain in the 5th century

saxophone noun a wind instrument with a curved metal tube and keys for the fingers • **saxophonist** noun a player of the saxophone

say verb (**saying**, **said**) 1 speak, utter: why don't you say 'Yes'? 2 express in words; state: they said they knew him ◇ noun 1 the right to speak: no say in the matter 2 the opportunity to speak: I've had my say • **I say!** dated 1 an exclamation expressing surprise or protest 2 a phrase used to try to attract attention • **that is to say** in other words

saying noun 1 something often said 2 a proverb

scab noun 1 a crust formed over a sore 2 any of several diseases of animals or plants 3 informal, derog a person who works when colleagues are on strike; a blackleg

scabbard noun the sheath in which the blade of a sword is kept

scabby adj (**scabbier**, **scabbiest**) 1 covered in scabs 2 informal disgusting, revolting

scabies noun an itchy skin disease

scabious noun a plant of the teasel family

scabrous adj 1 rough and flaky 2 rather vulgar or indecent; rude

scaffold noun a platform on which people are put to death

scaffolding noun a framework of poles and platforms used by people doing repairs on a building etc

scald verb 1 burn with hot liquid or steam 2 heat (milk etc) just short of boiling point ◇ noun a burn caused by hot liquid or steam

scale noun 1 a set of regularly spaced marks for measurement on a thermometer etc 2 a series or system of increasing values: salary scale 3 music a group of notes going up or down in order 4 the measurements of a map compared with the actual size of the area shown: drawn to the scale 1:50,000 5 the size of a business etc: manufacture on a small scale 6 a small thin flake on the skin of a fish or snake 7 (**scales**) a weighing machine ◇ verb 1 climb up 2 remove scales from 3 remove in thin layers • **scaly** adj having a body covered in scales

scallion noun a spring onion

scallop /skol-up/ noun a shellfish with a pair of hinged fan-shaped shells • **scalloped** adj of an edge: cut into curves or notches

scallywag noun, informal a mischievous person; a rascal

scalp noun 1 the outer covering of the skull 2 the skin and hair on top of the head ◇ verb cut the scalp from

scalpel noun a small, thin-bladed knife used in surgery

scam noun, US informal a trick

designed to get money unfairly; a swindle

scamp noun a rascal

scamper verb 1 run about playfully 2 run off in haste

scampi plural noun large prawns cooked for eating

scan verb (**scanning**, **scanned**) 1 pass an X-ray, ultrasonic wave, etc over 2 informal read quickly, skim over 3 comput input into a computer by means of a scanner 4 examine carefully 5 count the beats in a line of poetry 6 of poetry: have the correct number of beats ◇ noun an act of scanning • **scanner** noun a machine that scans, esp a machine that converts a visual image into data that can be input into a computer • **scansion** noun scanning of poetry

scandal noun 1 something disgraceful or shocking 2 talk or gossip about people's (supposed) misdeeds • **scandalize** verb shock, horrify • **scandalmonger** noun someone who spreads gossip or scandal

scandalous adj 1 shameful, disgraceful 2 containing scandal • **scandalously** adv

scant adj hardly enough: pay scant attention

scanty adj (**scantier**, **scantiest**) little or not enough in amount: scanty clothing • **scantily** adv

scapegoat noun someone who bears the blame for the wrongdoing of others

scapula noun the shoulder blade

scar noun 1 the mark left by a wound or sore 2 any disfiguring mark or blemish ◇ verb (**scarring**, **scarred**) mark with a scar

scarab noun a beetle regarded as sacred by the ancient Egyptians

scarce adj 1 not plentiful or not enough 2 seldom found; rare • **make**

yourself scarce go away; leave

scarcely adv 1 only just; barely: could scarcely hear 2 surely not: you can scarcely expect me to eat that

scarcity noun (plural **scarcities**) the fact of being available only in very small amounts or not at all

scare verb 1 cause to be afraid; frighten 2 cause to jump in fright; startle ◇ noun a sudden fright or alarm

scarecrow noun a figure set up to scare birds away from crops

scarey another spelling of **scary**

scarf noun (plural **scarves** or **scarfs**) a strip of material worn round the neck, shoulders or head

scarlatina noun a mild form of scarlet fever

scarlet noun a bright red colour ◇ adj bright red • **scarlet fever** noun an infectious illness causing a rash

scarper verb, slang run away

SCART plug noun, electronics a plug with 21 pins, used to connect parts of a video or audio system

scary or **scarey** adj, informal frightening

scat exclam, informal go away!

scathing adj scornfully or hurtfully critical: scathing remark

scatological adj full of references to faeces or defecation: scatological humour

scatter verb 1 throw loosely about; sprinkle 2 spread widely 3 flee in all directions • **scatterbrain** noun someone who frequently forgets things • **scattered** adj thrown or spread about widely • **scattering** noun a small amount thinly spread or scattered

scatty adj (**scattier**, **scattiest**) informal scatterbrained

scavenger noun an animal that feeds on dead flesh

SCE abbrev Scottish Certificate of Education

scenario /suh-nah-ri-oh/ noun 1 a situation that may arise 2 a scene-by-scene outline of a play, film, etc 3 an outline of a plan or project

---

Do not confuse with: **scene**

---

scene noun 1 the place where something happens: scene of the accident 2 a landscape 3 a division of a play or opera 4 an area of activity: the music scene 5 a show of bad temper: don't create a scene

scenery noun 1 the painted background on a theatre stage 2 the general appearance of a stretch of country

scenic adj 1 providing a pleasant view; picturesque 2 of scenery

scent noun 1 perfume 2 an odour 3 the trail of smell used to track an animal etc ◇ verb 1 give a pleasant smell to: roses scented the air 2 discover by the smell 3 have a suspicion of; sense: scent danger

sceptic /skep-tik/ noun someone who doubts what they are told • **sceptical** adj unwilling to believe; doubtful • **sceptically** adv • **scepticism** noun

---

Do not confuse with: **septic**

Do not confuse: **sceptical** and **cynical**

---

sceptre /sep-tuh/ noun an ornamental rod carried by a monarch on ceremonial occasions

schadenfreude /shah-dun-froy-duh/ noun pleasure taken in the misfortunes of others

schedule /shed-yool/ or /sked-yool/ noun 1 the time set for doing something: I'm two weeks behind schedule

2 a written statement of details **3** a form for filling in information ◇ *verb* **1** form into a schedule **2** plan, arrange

schema /skee-muh/ *noun, formal* a scheme or plan

schematic *adj* according to a plan • **schematically** *adv*

scheme /skeem/ *noun* **1** a plan or systematic arrangement **2** a dishonest or crafty plan ◇ *verb* make schemes; plot • **scheming** *adj* crafty, cunning

scherzo /skurt-soh/ *noun* (*plural* **scherzos**), *music* a fast, lively movement in a symphony or other long piece of classical music

schism /skizm/ or /sizm/ *noun* a breaking away from the main group

schist /shist/ *noun* a type of rock that splits easily into layers

schizo /skit-soh/ *noun* (*plural* **schizos**) & *adj, slang* (a) schizophrenic

schizophrenia /skit-soh-*free*-ni-uh/ *noun* a mental illness involving a complete change in personality and behaviour • **schizophrenic** *noun* & *adj* (someone) suffering from schizophrenia

schlock *noun, informal* tacky or shoddy goods • **schlocky** *adj*

schmaltz *noun, informal* sentimentality • **schmaltzy** *adj*

schmuck *noun, informal* an idiot

schnapps *noun* a strong dry alcoholic spirit of German or Dutch origin

schnitzel *noun* a veal cutlet

scholar *noun* **1** someone of great learning **2** someone who has been awarded a scholarship **3** a pupil or student • **scholarship** *noun* **1** learning **2** a sum of money given to help a clever student to carry on further studies • **scholastic** *adj* of schools or scholars

scholarly *adj* showing or having knowledge, high intelligence and love

of accuracy • **scholarliness** *noun*

school *noun* **1** a place for teaching, *esp* children **2** a group of artists, writers, *etc* who share the same ideas **3** a large number of fish, whales, *etc* ◇ *verb* **1** educate in a school **2** train by practice • **schoolchild** *noun* (*plural* **schoolchildren**) a **schoolboy** or **schoolgirl** who attends a school • **schooling** *noun* **1** education in a school **2** training • **schoolmate** *noun* someone taught at the same school as yourself • **schoolmaster**, **schoolmistress** *noun* a teacher at a school

schooner *noun* **1** a two-masted sailing ship **2** a large sherry glass **3** *US & Aust* a large beer glass

schwa /shwah/ *noun* an unstressed vowel sound

sciatic /sai-*at*-ik/ *adj* relating to the hip

sciatica /sai-*at*-ik-uh/ *noun* severe pain in the upper part of the leg

science *noun* **1** knowledge obtained by observation and experiment **2** a branch of this knowledge, *eg* chemistry, physics, biology, *etc* **3** these sciences considered together • **science fiction** *noun* stories dealing with future life on earth, space travel, other planets, *etc*

scientific *adj* **1** of science **2** done according to the methods of science • **scientifically** *adv*

scientist *noun* someone who studies one or more branches of science

sci fi *abbrev* science fiction

scimitar *noun* a sword with a short curved blade

scintillate *verb* **1** sparkle **2** show brilliant wit *etc*

scion /sai-un/ *noun* **1** a young member of a family **2** a descendant **3** a cutting for grafting on another plant

scissors *plural noun* a cutting instrument with two hinged blades

sclerosis *noun* hardening, *esp* of the arteries

scoff[1] *verb* express scorn

scoff[2] *verb, informal* eat greedily

scold *verb* blame or rebuke with angry words ◇ *noun* a bad-tempered person • **scolding** *noun*

scone *noun* a small plain cake made with flour and water

scoop *noun* 1 a hollow instrument used for lifting loose material, water, *etc* 2 an exclusive news story ◇ *verb* lift or dig out with a scoop

scooter *noun* 1 a two-wheeled toy vehicle pushed along by foot 2 a low-powered motorcycle

scope *noun* 1 opportunity or room to do something: *scope for improvement* 2 extent, range: *outside the scope of this dictionary*

scorch *verb* 1 burn slightly; singe 2 dry up with heat

scorching *adj* 1 very hot 2 harsh, severe: *scorching criticism*

score *noun* 1 the total number of points gained in a game 2 a reason, account: *don't worry on that score* 3 a written piece of music showing separate parts for voices and instruments 4 (**scores**) a great many: *scores of people* 5 a set of twenty 6 a line or notch cut into something 7 an account, a debt: *settle old scores* ◇ *verb* 1 gain (points) 2 keep a note of points gained in a game 3 mark with lines or notches • **score out** cross out

scorn *verb* 1 look down on; despise 2 refuse (help *etc*) because of pride ◇ *noun* the feeling of despising something or someone • **scornful** *adj* full of scorn • **scornfully** *adv*

scorpion *noun* a spider-like creature with a poisonous sting in its tail

Scotch *noun, informal* whisky • **Scotch egg** *noun* a hard-boiled egg covered in sausage-meat and bread-crumbs • **Scotch tape** *noun, trademark* adhesive tape • **Scotch terrier** *noun* a breed of small rough-coated dog

scotch *verb* reveal to be untrue or dismiss as untrue

scot-free *adj* unhurt or unpunished

scoundrel *noun, dated* a dishonest or unprincipled man

scour *verb* 1 clean by hard rubbing; scrub 2 search thoroughly

scourge *noun* 1 a cause of great suffering 2 a whip ◇ *verb* 1 whip, lash 2 cause to suffer; afflict

Scouse *noun, Brit* a native or inhabitant of Liverpool

scout *noun* 1 a guide or spy sent ahead to bring back information 2 (**Scout**) a member of the Scout Association

scowl *verb* wrinkle the brows in displeasure or anger ◇ *noun* a frown

Scrabble *noun, trademark* a word-building game

scrabble *verb* scratch or grope about

scraggy *adj* (**scraggier**, **scraggiest**) 1 long and thin 2 uneven and untidy-looking

scram *exclam* go away!

scramble *verb* 1 struggle to seize something before others 2 climb or move using both hands and feet 3 mix or toss together: *scrambled eggs* 4 jumble up (a message) to make it unintelligible without decoding ◇ *noun* 1 a rush and struggle to get something 2 a motorcycle race over rough ground

scrap *noun* 1 a small piece; a fragment 2 a picture for pasting in a scrapbook 3 *informal* a fight 4 parts of a car *etc* no longer required: *sold as scrap* 5 (**scraps**) small pieces left over; odds and ends ◇ *verb* (**scrapping**, **scrapped**) 1 abandon as useless 2 *informal* fight or quarrel • **scrapbook** *noun* a blank book in which to stick pictures *etc* • **scrap metal** *noun* metal for melting and re-using

scrape *verb* 1 rub and mark with something sharp 2 drag or rub against or across a surface with a harsh grating sound 3 (with **up** or **together**) collect (money *etc*) with difficulty ◇ *noun* 1 a mark or sound made by scraping 2 *informal* a difficult situation • **scrape through** only just avoid failure

scrapheap *noun* a heap of old metal and other discarded items • **on the scrapheap** no longer needed

scrapie *noun* a disease of sheep

scrappy *adj* (**scrappier, scrappiest**) 1 made up of odd scraps, not well put together 2 done without skill or elegance • **scrappily** *adv*

scratch *verb* 1 draw a sharp point across the surface of 2 mark by doing this 3 tear or dig with claws, nails, *etc* 4 rub with the nails to relieve or stop itching 5 withdraw from a competition ◇ *noun* (*plural* **scratches**) 1 a mark or sound made by scratching 2 a slight wound ◇ *adj* 1 *golf* too good to be allowed a handicap 2 of a team: made up of players hastily got together • **come up to scratch** be satisfactory • **start from scratch** start from nothing, right at the beginning

scrawl *verb* write or draw untidily or hastily ◇ *noun* 1 untidy, hasty or bad writing 2 something scrawled

scrawny *adj* (**scrawnier, scrawniest**) unhealthily or unattractively thin; skinny

scream *verb* utter a shrill, piercing cry as in pain, fear, *etc*; shriek ◇ *noun* a shrill cry

scree *noun* loose stones covering a steep mountain side

screech *verb* utter a harsh, shrill and sudden cry ◇ *noun* a harsh shrill cry

screed *noun* a long boring speech or letter

screen *noun* 1 the surface on which cinema films are projected 2 the surface on which a television picture, or computer data, appears 3 a flat covered framework that shelters something from view or protects it from heat, cold, *etc* 4 something that shelters from wind, danger, difficulties, *etc* ◇ *verb* 1 shelter, hide 2 make a film of 3 show on a screen 4 sift, sieve 5 sort out (the good from the bad) by testing 6 conduct examinations on someone to test for disease • **screen saver** *noun* a moving image displayed on the screen when a computer is not in use • **screen off** hide behind, or separate by, a screen

screw *noun* 1 a nail with a slotted head and a winding groove or ridge (called the **thread**) on its surface 2 a kind of propeller with spiral blades, used in ships and aircraft 3 a turn or twist of a screw *etc* ◇ *verb* 1 fasten or tighten with a screw 2 fix (*eg* a stopper) in place with a twisting movement 3 twist, turn round (your head *etc*) 4 crumple or pucker • **screwdriver** *noun* a tool for turning screws

scribble *verb* 1 write carelessly 2 make untidy or meaningless marks with a pencil *etc* ◇ *noun* 1 careless writing 2 meaningless marks; a doodle

scribe *noun, hist* 1 a clerk who copied out manuscripts 2 a Jewish teacher of law

scrimp *verb* be sparing or stingy with money: *scrimping and saving for a holiday*

scrimshaw *noun* decorative engraving on shells or bone, traditionally done by sailors

script *noun* 1 the text of a play, talk, *etc* 2 handwriting like print

scripture *noun* 1 the sacred writings

of a religion **2** (**Scripture**) the Christian Bible

scrofula noun a disease of the lymph nodes in the neck

scroll noun **1** a piece of paper rolled up **2** an ornament shaped like this • **scroll up** or **down** comput move text on a screen in order to see more of the same document

scrotum noun the bag of skin enclosing the testicles

scrounge verb, slang get by shamelessly asking or begging ◊ noun an attempt to scrounge: on the scrounge • **scrounger** noun

scrub verb (**scrubbing, scrubbed**) rub hard in order to clean ◊ noun countryside covered with low bushes

scruff noun the back of the neck • **scruffy** adj untidy

scrum or **scrummage** noun, rugby a restarting of play in which the forwards of the opposing sides bunch together

scrumptious adj, informal delicious

scrunch verb crumple

scruple noun doubt over what is right or wrong that keeps someone from doing something ◊ verb hesitate because of a scruple • **scrupulous** adj careful over the smallest details

scrutiny noun (plural **scrutinies**) careful examination • **scrutinize** verb examine very closely

SCSI /skuz-ee/ abbrev, comput small computer systems interface, a method of connecting a PC to peripheral devices

scuba noun breathing apparatus used by divers

scud verb (**scudding, scudded**) move or sweep along quickly: scudding waves

scuff verb scrape or scratch lightly

scuffle noun a confused fight

scull noun a short oar ◊ verb move (a boat) with a pair of these or with one oar worked at the back of the boat

scullery noun (plural **sculleries**) a room for rough kitchen work

sculptor, sculptress noun an artist who carves or models figures in wood, stone, clay, etc • **sculpture** noun **1** the art of the sculptor or sculptress **2** a piece of their work

scum noun **1** foam that rises to the surface of liquids **2** worthless or despised people: the scum of the earth

scunner noun, Scot a nuisance

scupper noun a hole in the side of a ship to drain water from the deck ◊ verb put an end to; ruin: scupper his chances

scurf noun small flakes of dead skin (esp on the scalp)

scurrilous adj insulting or abusive: a scurrilous attack

scurry verb (**scurries, scurrying, scurried**) hurry along; scamper

scurvy noun a type of disease caused by a lack of fresh fruit and vegetables

scuttle noun **1** a fireside container for coal **2** an opening with a lid in a ship's deck or side ◊ verb **1** make a hole in (a ship) in order to sink it **2** hurry along; scamper

scuzzy adj (**scuzzier, scuzziest**) slang very dirty or disreputable

scythe /saidh/ noun a hand tool for cutting crops or grass, consisting of large curved blade on a long handle ◊ verb cut with a scythe

SE abbrev south-east or south-eastern

sea noun **1** the mass of salt water covering most of the earth's surface **2** a great stretch of water of less size than an ocean **3** a great expanse or number: a sea of faces • **sea anemone** noun a type of small plant-like animal found on rocks at the seashore • **seabird** noun any marine bird • **seaboard**

noun land along the edge of the sea
• **sea dog** *noun* an old sailor or a pirate
• **seafarer** *noun, old* a traveller by sea; a sailor • **seafaring** *adj* • **seafront** *noun* a promenade with its buildings facing the sea • **seagoing** *adj* of a ship: sailing on the ocean • **seagull** *noun* a type of web-footed sea bird • **seahorse** *noun* a type of small fish with a horse-like head and neck • **sea level** *noun* the level of the surface of the sea • **sea lion** *noun* a large kind of seal the male of which has a mane • **seaman** *noun* (*plural* **seamen**) a sailor, *esp* a member of a ship's crew who is not an officer • **seamanship** *noun* the art of steering and looking after ships at sea • **seaplane** *noun* an aeroplane that can take off from and land on the water • **seascape** *noun* a picture of a scene at sea • **seashore** *noun* the land next to the sea • **seasick** *adj* made ill by the rocking movement of a ship • **seaside** *noun* the land beside the sea • **sea trout** *noun* a type of large trout living in the sea but spawning in rivers • **sea urchin** *noun* a type of small sea creature with a spiny shell • **seaward** *adj & adv* towards the sea • **seaweed** *noun* any of many kinds of plants growing in the sea • **seaworthy** *adj* of a ship *etc*: in a good enough condition to go to sea • **at sea 1** on the sea **2** completely puzzled

seal¹ *noun* a furry sea animal living partly on land

seal² *noun* **1** a piece of wax with a design pressed into it, attached to a document to show that it is legal or official **2** a piece of wax used to keep a parcel closed **3** anything that closes tightly **4** a piece of sticky paper with a picture on it: *a Christmas seal* ◇ *verb* **1** close up completely **2** mark or fasten with a seal **3** make (legally) binding and definite: *seal a bargain* • **sealant** *noun* any material used for sealing a gap • **sealing wax** *noun* a hard kind of wax for sealing letters, documents, *etc*

seam *noun* **1** the line formed by the sewing together of two pieces of cloth **2** a line or layer of metal, coal, *etc* in the earth • **seamstress** *noun* a woman who sews for a living • **the seamy side** the more unpleasant side (*eg* of life)

séance /*seh*-ohns/ *noun* a meeting of people to receive messages from the spirits of the dead

sear *verb* **1** scorch or burn **2** hurt severely • **searing** *adj* extremely hot

search *verb* **1** look over in order to find something **2** (with **for**) look for; seek ◇ *noun* (*plural* **searches**) **1** an act of searching **2** an attempt to find • **search engine** *noun* a computer program that looks for information the user wants to find on the Internet • **searching** *adj* examining closely and carefully: *searching question* • **searchlight** *noun* a strong beam of light used for picking out objects at night • **search warrant** *noun* permission given to the police to search a house *etc* for stolen goods *etc*

season *noun* **1** one of the four divisions of the year (spring, summer, autumn, winter) **2** the proper, usual or legal time for an activity ◇ *verb* **1** add (salt *etc*) to improve the flavour of (food) **2** dry (wood) till it is ready for use • **seasonable** *adj* **1** happening at the proper time **2** of weather: suitable for the season • **seasonal** *adj* **1** of the seasons or a season **2** of work *etc*: taking place in one particular season only • **seasoned** *adj* **1** of food: flavoured **2** of wood: ready to be used **3** trained, experienced: *a seasoned traveller* • **seasoning** *noun* something (*eg* salt, pepper) added to food to give it more taste • **season ticket** *noun* a ticket that can be used repeatedly for a certain period of time

---

Do not confuse: **seasonable** and **seasonal**

---

seat *noun* **1** a piece of furniture for

sitting on **2** the part of a chair on which you sit **3** a place in parliament, on a council, *etc* **4** the centre of some activity: *the seat of government* **5** the buttocks **6** a mansion ◇ *verb* **1** put in a particular seat **2** have seats for (a certain number): *the room seats forty* • **seatbelt** *noun* a belt fixed to a seat in a car *etc* to prevent a passenger from being thrown out of the seat in the event of an accident

sebaceous *adj* secreting sebum

sebum *noun* an oily substance secreted by the skin and hair

sec[1] *abbrev* **1** second **2** secretary

sec[2] *noun, informal* a short while; a second: *hang on a sec*

secateurs *plural noun* a tool like scissors for trimming bushes *etc*

secede *verb* break away from a group, society, *etc* • **secession** *noun*

seclude *verb* keep (yourself) apart from people's notice or company • **seclusion** *noun*

second *adj* **1** next after the first in time, place, *etc* **2** other, alternate: *every second week* **3** another of the same kind as: *they thought him a second Mozart* ◇ *noun* **1** the 60th part of a minute of time, or of a degree (in measuring angles) **2** a short while; a moment: *wait a second* **3** someone or something that is second **4** an article not quite perfectly made: *these gloves are seconds* **5** an attendant to someone who boxes or fights a duel ◇ *verb* **1** support or back up **2** /si-*kond*/ transfer temporarily to a special job • **secondary** *adj* second in position or importance • **secondary school** *noun* a school for pupils between 11 and 18 • **second-best** *adj* next to the best, not the best • **second-hand** *adj* **1** having been used by someone else; not new: *second-hand clothes* **2** of a shop: dealing in second-hand goods • **secondly** *adv* in the second place • **second nature** *noun* a firmly fixed habit:

organizing people is second nature to Margaret • **second-rate** *adj* not of the best quality; inferior

secret *adj* **1** hidden from, or not known by, others **2** secretive ◇ *noun* a fact, plan, *etc* that is not told or known • **secrecy** *noun* the state of being secret; mystery • **secretive** *adj* inclined to hide or conceal your feelings, activities, *etc* • **secret service** *noun* a government department dealing with spying

secretary *noun* (*plural* **secretaries**) **1** someone employed to write letters, keep records, *etc* in an office **2** someone elected to deal with the written business of a club *etc* • **secretarial** *adj* of a secretary or their work • **Secretary of State** *noun* **1** a government minister in charge of an administrative department **2** *US* the person in charge of foreign affairs

secrete *verb* **1** of a part of the body: store up and give out (a fluid) **2** conceal in a secret place; hide • **secretion** *noun*

sect *noun* a group of people who hold views, *esp* in religious matters, regarded as unorthodox or controversial • **sectarian** *adj* **1** showing hostility to people outside one's own group **2** loyal to a sect **3** narrow-minded

section *noun* **1** a part or division: *a section of the community* **2** a thin slice of a specimen for examination under a microscope **3** the view of the inside of anything when it is cut right through or across: *a section of a plant*

sector *noun* **1** a part, section or area **2** a three-sided part of a circle whose sides are two radii and a part of the circumference

secular *adj* **1** of worldly, not spiritual or religious things **2** of music *etc*: not sacred or religious

secure *adj* **1** free from danger or fear; safe **2** firmly fixed or fastened: *the* *lock is secure* **3** confident: *secure in the knowledge that she had no rivals* ◇ *verb* **1** make safe, firm or established: *secure your position* **2** seize, get hold of: *secure the diamonds* **3** fasten: *secure the lock*

security *noun* **1** safety **2** (**securities**) property or goods which a lender may keep until the loan is paid back

secy *abbrev* secretary

sedan *noun* **1** an enclosed chair for one person, carried on two poles by two bearers (*also called:* **sedan chair**) **2** *US* a saloon car

sedate *adj* calm, serious and dignified ● **sedateness** *noun*

sedative *noun* a medicine with a calming, soothing effect ◇ *adj* calming, soothing ● **sedation** *noun* the use of sedatives to calm a patient

sedentary *adj* of a job *etc*: involving a lot of sitting

sedge *noun* a type of coarse grass growing in swamps and rivers

sediment *noun* the grains or solid parts that settle at the bottom of a liquid

sedition *noun* the stirring up of rebellion against the government ● **seditious** *adj* encouraging rebellion; rebellious

seduce *verb* **1** tempt (someone) away from right or moral behaviour **2** persuade (someone) to have sexual intercourse **3** attract ● **seducer** *noun* ● **seduction** *noun* ● **seductive** *adj* attractive or tempting

sedulous *adj* working very hard; diligent

see *verb* (**seeing**, **saw**, **seen**) **1** have the power of sight **2** notice by means of the eye: *he can see us coming* **3** form a picture of in the mind **4** understand: *I see what you mean* **5** find out: *I'll see what is happening* **6** make sure: *see that he finishes his homework* **7** accompany: *I'll see you home*

8 meet: *I'll see you at the usual time* ◇ *noun* the district over which a bishop or archbishop has authority ● **seeing that** because ● **see through 1** take part in to the end **2** not be deceived by (a person, trick, *etc*) ● **see to** attend to the preparation of: *see to a meal*

seed *noun* **1** the part of a tree, plant, *etc* from which a new plant may grow **2** a seed-like part of a grain or a nut **3** the beginning from which anything grows: *the seeds of rebellion* **4** a seeded player in a tournament **5** *old* children or descendants ◇ *verb* **1** of a plant: produce seed **2** sow **3** remove the seeds from (*eg* a fruit) **4** arrange (good players) in a tournament so that they do not compete against each other till the later rounds ● **go to seed** *or* **run to seed 1** of a plant: develop seeds **2** of a person, area, *etc*: deteriorate

seedling *noun* a very young plant in its early stages of growth

seedy *adj* (**seedier**, **seediest**) **1** dirty or disreputable; shabby **2** rather unwell; sickly **3** full of seeds

seek *verb* (**seeking**, **sought**) **1** look or search for **2** try (to do something): *seek to establish proof* **3** try to get (advice *etc*) ● **sought after** in great demand; popular

seem *verb* **1** appear to be: *he seems kind* **2** appear: *she seems to like it* ● **seeming** *adj* apparent but not actual or real: *a seeming success* ● **seemly** *adj* **1** following social rules about decency **2** suitable

seen *past participle of* **see**

seep *verb* flow slowly through a small opening, leak

seer *noun* a prophet

seersucker *noun* a lightweight ribbed cotton fabric

seesaw *noun* **1** a plank balanced across a stand so that one end of it goes up when the other goes down **2**

an up-and-down movement like that of a seesaw ◇ *verb* **1** go up and down on a seesaw **2** move with a seesaw-like movement

seethe *verb* **1** boil **2** be very angry • **seething** *adj*

segment *noun* **1** a part cut off **2** a part of a circle cut off by a straight line

segregate *verb* separate (someone or a group) from others • **segregation** *noun*

seine *noun* a large type of fishing net

seismic /saiz-mik/ *adj* of earthquakes • **seismograph** *noun* an instrument that records earthquake shocks and measures their force

seize *verb* **1** take suddenly by force **2** overcome: *seized with fury* **3** (with **up**) of machinery: become stuck, break down • **seizure** *noun* **1** sudden capture **2** a sudden attack of illness, rage, *etc*

seldom *adv* not often; rarely: *you seldom see an owl during the day*

select *verb* pick out from several according to your preference; choose ◇ *adj* **1** of very good quality **2** allowing only certain people in; exclusive • **selection** *noun* **1** the act of choosing **2** things chosen **3** a number of things from which to choose • **selective** *adj* **1** selecting carefully **2** of weedkiller: harmless to garden plants • **selector** *noun* someone who chooses (*eg* members for a national team)

self *noun* (*plural* **selves**) **1** someone's own person **2** someone's personality; character • **self-assured** *adj* trusting in your own ability; confident • **self-centred** *adj* concerned only with things that affect you personally • **self-confident** *adj* believing in your own abilities • **self-conscious** *adj* too aware of your faults and concerned about how others perceive you and therefore embarrassed in the company of others • **self-contained**

adj **1** of a house: complete in itself, not sharing any part with other houses **2** of a person: self-reliant • **self-control** *noun* control over yourself, your feelings, *etc* • **self-defence** *noun* the defence of your own person, property, *etc* • **self-denial** *noun* the act of doing without something that you want or need • **self-effacing** *adj* keeping yourself from being noticed; modest • **self-esteem** *noun* respect for yourself; conceit • **self-evident** *adj* clear enough to need no proof • **self-expression** *noun* expressing your own personality in your activities • **self-important** *adj* having a mistakenly high sense of your importance • **self-indulgent** *adj* too ready to satisfy your own inclinations and desires • **self-interest** *noun* a selfish desire to consider only your own interests or advantage • **selfless** *adj* thinking of others before yourself; unselfish • **self-made** *adj* owing your success *etc* to your own efforts: *a self-made man* • **self-portrait** *noun* an artist's portrait of himself or herself • **self-possessed** *adj* calm and confident in mind or manner • **self-raising flour** *noun* flour already containing an ingredient to make it rise • **self-reliant** *adj* trusting in your own abilities *etc* • **self-respect** *noun* respect for yourself and concern for your own character and reputation • **self-righteous** *adj* thinking highly of your own goodness and virtue • **self-sacrifice** *noun* the act of giving up your own life, possessions, *etc* in order to do good to others • **selfsame** *adj* the very same • **self-satisfied** *adj* too satisfied with yourself; smug • **self-service** *adj* of a restaurant: where customers help or serve themselves • **self-sufficient** *adj* needing no help or support from anyone else • **self-willed** *adj* determined to have your own way; obstinate

selfish *adj* caring only for your own pleasure or advantage • **selfishly** *adv* • **selfishness** *noun*

sell verb (**selling**, **sold**) **1** give or hand over for money **2** have or keep for sale: *he sells newspapers* **3** be sold for; cost: *this book sells for £20* • **seller** noun someone who sells

Sellotape noun, trademark transparent adhesive tape used for sticking pieces of paper together

selvage noun the firm edge of a piece of cloth, that does not fray

semantic adj relating to the meaning of words

semaphore noun a form of signalling using the arms to form different positions for each letter

semblance noun an outward, often false, appearance: *a semblance of listening*

semen noun the liquid that carries sperm

semester noun, US either one of two terms into which the academic year is divided at some universities

semi- prefix **1** half **2** informal partly • **semiconductor** noun a material that can both allow and prevent an electrical current from passing • **semi-detached** adj of a house: joined to another house on one side but not on the other • **semifinal** noun the stage or match of a contest immediately before the final • **semi-precious** adj of a stone: having some value, but not considered a gem

semibreve noun, music a note (o) that is equal to four crotchets in length

semicircle noun half of a circle

semicolon noun the punctuation mark (;)

seminal adj very influential in a particular activity or area of study

seminar noun a class at university or college in which students discuss a particular subject with the teacher

seminary noun (plural **seminaries**) a training college for priests

semiotics plural noun the study of signs and symbols • **semiotician** noun someone who studies semiotics

Semitic adj Jewish

semitone noun, music half a tone

semolina noun the hard particles of wheat sifted from flour, used for puddings etc

Semtex noun, trademark a material used to make explosives

senate noun **1** the upper house of parliament in the USA, Australia, etc **2** the governing council of some universities **3** hist the law-making body in ancient Rome • **senator** noun a member of a senate

send verb (**sending**, **sent**) **1** have (something) carried or delivered to a place **2** make (someone) go • **sender** noun • **send-off** noun a friendly farewell for someone going on a journey etc • **send for** order to be brought

senile adj **1** of old age **2** showing the mental feebleness that sometimes comes with old age • **senility** noun

senior adj **1** higher in rank **2** older in age ◇ noun **1** someone in a senior position **2** a senior citizen • **senior citizen** noun someone who has reached retirement age • **seniority** noun the fact of being senior • **senior moment** noun, informal a moment of forgetfulness or silly behaviour ascribed to ageing

senna noun the dried leaves of certain plants, used as a laxative

sensation noun **1** a feeling through any of the five senses **2** a vague effect: *a floating sensation* **3** a state of excitement: *causing a sensation* • **sensational** adj causing great excitement, horror, etc, and often deliberately designed to

sense noun **1** one of the five powers by which humans feel or notice (hearing, taste, sight, smell, touch) **2** a feeling: *a sense of loss* **3** an ability to understand or appreciate: *a sense of humour* **4** (**senses**) right mind, common sense: *take leave of his senses* **5** ability to act in a reasonable way: *he had the sense not to argue* **6** ability to be understood: *your sentence does not make sense* **7** meaning: *to what sense of this word are your referring?* ◇ *verb* feel, realize: *sense disapproval* • **senseless** *adj* **1** foolish **2** stunned, unconscious • **sensor** *noun* a device that detects and measures physical changes • **sensory** *adj* of the senses

sensible *adj* **1** wise or reasonable in the circumstances **2** able to be felt or noticed **3** (with **of**) aware of • **sensibility** *noun* **1** ability to feel **2** the fact that someone has strong or delicate feelings about something

sensitive *adj* **1** feeling something strongly or painfully **2** strongly affected by light, movements, *etc* • **sensitivity** *noun* • **sensitize** *verb* make sensitive (*esp* to light)

sensual *adj* **1** of the senses rather than the mind **2** to do with physical, *esp* sexual, pleasure • **sensuality** *noun* • **sensually** *adv*

Do not confuse: **sensual** and **sensuous**

---

sensuous *adj* **1** pleasing to the senses **2** easily affected through the senses • **sensuosity** *noun* • **sensuously** *adv*

sent *past form of* **send**

sentence *noun* **1** a number of words that together make a complete statement **2** a judgement announced by a judge or court ◇ *verb* condemn to a particular punishment

sentient *adj* thinking, reasoning

sentiment *noun* **1** a thought expressed in words **2** a show of feeling or emotion, often excessive • **sentimental** *adj* having or showing too much feeling or emotion • **sentimen-**

tality *noun*

sentinel *noun* a soldier on guard

sentry *noun* (*plural* **sentries**) a soldier posted to guard an entry

sepal *noun* one of the green leaves beneath the petals of a flower

separate *verb* **1** set or keep apart **2** divide into parts **3** disconnect **4** go different ways **5** live apart by choice ◇ *adj* **1** placed, kept, *etc* apart **2** divided **3** not connected **4** different • **separation** *noun* a dividing or putting apart • **separatism** *noun* • **separatist** *noun* someone who withdraws from or urges separation from an established church, state, *etc*

Sephardic *adj* relating to the Jewish people of Spain, Portugal or N Africa

sepia *noun* a reddish-brown colour

sept *noun* a division of a clan

sept- *prefix* seven: *septuplet*

September *noun* the ninth month of the year

septet *noun* a group of seven musicians or singers

septic *adj* of a wound: full of germs that are poisoning the blood • **septicaemia** *noun* blood-poisoning • **septic tank** *noun* a tank in which sewage is partially purified

---

Do not confuse with: **sceptic**

---

septuagenarian *noun* someone from seventy to seventy-nine years old

sepulchre *noun* a tomb • **sepulchral** *adj* **1** dismal, gloomy **2** of a voice: deep, hollow in tone **3** of tombs

sequel *noun* **1** a story that is a continuation of an earlier story **2** *old* a result of something that happens; a consequence

sequence *noun* **1** the order of events in time **2** a number of things following in order; a connected series

sequestered *adj* of a place: lonely, quiet

sequestrate *verb* keep apart; isolate

sequin *noun* a small round sparkling ornament sewn on a dress *etc*

sequoia /si-*kwoy*-uh/ *noun* a giant N American redwood tree

seraglio /si-*rah*-lyo/ *noun* (*plural* **seraglios**) a harem

seraph *noun* (*plural* **seraphs** or **seraphim**) an angel of the highest rank • **seraphic** *adj* like an angel

sere *adj, formal* dry, withered

serenade *noun* music played or sung in the open air at night, *esp* under a woman's window ◇ *verb* sing or play a serenade (to)

serendipity *noun* the state of making a lucky find • **serendipitous** *adj*

serene *adj* 1 calm 2 happy, peaceful and unworried • **serenity** *noun* calmness, peacefulness

serf *noun, hist* a slave bought and sold with the land on which he worked • **serfdom** *noun* slavery

serge *noun* a strong type of cloth

sergeant *noun* 1 an army rank above corporal 2 a rank in the police force above constable • **sergeant-major** *noun* an army rank above sergeant

series *noun* (*plural* **series**) 1 a number of things following each other in order 2 a set of things of the same kind: *a series of books on art* • **serial** *noun* a story that is published, broadcast or televised in instalments • **serial port** *noun* a type of socket for connecting a device such as a mouse to a computer

serif *noun* a short line or stroke on the end of a printed letter

serious *adj* 1 showing thought about important matters; solemn: *serious*

expression on her face 2 not joking, in earnest: *serious remark* 3 needing careful thought; important: *a serious matter* 4 having dangerous results: *serious accident* • **seriously** *adv* • **seriousness** *noun*

sermon *noun* a talk given by a minister or priest during a church service

serpent *noun, old* a snake • **serpentine** *adj* full of twists or curves; winding

serrated *adj* having notches or teeth like a saw

serried *adj* crowded together: *serried ranks*

serum *noun* 1 a clear watery fluid in blood that helps fight disease 2 a fluid injected into the body to help fight disease

servant *noun* 1 someone paid to work for another, *esp* in helping to run a house 2 a government employee: *civil servant/public servant*

serve *verb* 1 give out food, goods, *etc* 2 attend or wait upon at table 3 be able to be used (as): *the cave will serve as a shelter* 4 be suitable for: *serve a purpose* 5 carry out duties as a member of the armed forces 6 undergo (a sentence in prison *etc*) 7 *tennis* start play by throwing up the ball and hitting it with the racket 8 work for and obey • **serve someone right** be deserved by them

server *noun* a computer that stores and manages data from other smaller computers on a network

service *noun* 1 something provided for the needs of people: *bus service/services for tourists* 2 the duty required of a servant or other employee 3 a performance of (public) worship 4 use: *bring the new machine into service* 5 time spent in the armed forces 6 (**services**) the armed forces 7 (**services**) public supply of water, gas, electricity, *etc* 8 a set of dishes: *dinner service* ◇ *verb* keep (a car, machine, *etc*) in good working order by regular repairs • **serviceable** *adj* lasting or staying good for a long time: *serviceable clothes* • **active service** a soldier's service in battle • **at your service** ready to help or be of use

serviette *noun* a table napkin

servile *adj* obeying too easily or eagerly: *a servile attitude to his employer* • **servility** *noun* • **servitude** *noun* the state of being under strict control; slavery

sesame /ses-uh-mi/ *noun* a SE Asian plant whose seeds produce an edible oil

sesquicentenary *or* **sesquicentennial** *noun* a hundred and fiftieth anniversary

session *noun* **1** a period of time spent on a particular activity **2** a meeting of a court, council, *etc* **3** the period of the year when classes are held in a school *etc*

sestet *noun* a group of six musicians *etc*

set *verb* (**setting**, **set**) **1** adjust (a clock, machine, *etc*) so that it is ready to work or perform some function **2** place or put **3** fix in the proper place (*eg* broken bones) **4** arrange (a table for a meal, jewels in a necklace, *etc*) **5** fix (a date, a price, *etc*) **6** fix hair (in waves or curls) **7** give (a task *etc*): *set him three problems* **8** put in a certain state or condition: *set free* **9** (with **off**, **out** or **forth**) start (on a journey *etc*) **10** of a jelly *etc*: become firm or solid **11** compose music for: *he set the poem to music* **12** of the sun: go out of sight below the horizon ◊ *adj* **1** fixed or arranged beforehand; ready: *all set* **2** fixed, stiff: *a set expression on his face* ◊ *noun* **1** a number of things of a similar kind, or used together: *set of carving tools* **2** an apparatus: *a television set* **3** scenery made ready for a play *etc* **4** a group of people **5** pose, position: *the set of his head* **6** a

series of six or more games in tennis **7** a fixing of hair in waves or curls **8** a badger's burrow (*also called*: **sett**) **9** a street paving-block (*also called*: **sett**) • **setback** *noun* a problem that causes a temporary obstacle to progress or success • **set square** *noun* a triangular drawing instrument, with one right angle • **setting** *noun* **1** an arrangement **2** a background: *against a setting of hills and lochs* • **set about 1** begin (doing something) **2** attack • **set in** begin: *winter has set in* • **set on** attack

sett *another spelling of* set (*noun* senses 8 and 9)

settee *noun* a sofa

setter *noun* a dog trained to point out game in hunting

settle *verb* **1** place in a final, firm or comfortable position **2** come to rest **3** agree over (a matter): *settle the price* **4** (sometimes with **down**) become calm or quiet **5** (sometimes with **down**) make your home in a place **6** pay (a bill) **7** fix, decide (on) **8** bring (a quarrel *etc*) to an end **9** sink to the bottom ◊ *noun* a long high-backed bench • **settlement** *noun* **1** the act of settling **2** a decision or agreement **3** payment for a bill **4** money given to a woman on her marriage **5** a number of people who have come to live in a country • **settler** *noun* someone who goes to live in a new country

seven *noun* the number 7 ◊ *adj* 7 in number

seventeen *noun* the number 17 ◊ *adj* 17 in number • **seventeenth** *adj* the last of a series of seventeen ◊ *noun* one of seventeen equal parts

seventh *adj* the last of a series of seven ◊ *noun* one of seven equal parts

seventy *noun* the number 70 ◊ *adj* 70 in number • **seventieth** *adj* the last of a series of seventy ◊ *noun* one of seventy equal parts

sever *verb* **1** cut off **2** separate • **sev-**

erance *noun*

several *adj* **1** more than one or two, but not many **2** various **3** different: *going their several ways* ◇ *pronoun* more than one or two people, things, *etc*, but not a great many

severe *adj* **1** serious: *a severe illness* **2** harsh, strict **3** very plain and simple, not fancy • **severity** *noun*

sew *verb* (**sewing, sewed, sewn**) **1** join together with a needle and thread **2** make or mend in this way • **sewer** *noun*

sewer *noun* an underground drain for carrying off water and waste matter • **sewage** *noun* water and waste matter • **sewerage** *noun* a network of sewers

sex *noun* **1** sexual intercourse or sexual behaviour **2** either of the two classes (male or female) into which animals are divided according to the part they play in producing children or young • **sexy** *adj* sexually attractive

sex- *prefix* six

sexagenarian *noun* someone from sixty to sixty-nine years old

sexism *noun* discrimination against someone on the grounds of their sex • **sexist** *noun & adj*

sexology *noun* the study of human sexual behaviour • **sexologist** *noun*

sextant *noun* an instrument used for calculating distances by means of measuring angles *eg* the distance between two stars

sextet *noun* a group of six musicians or singers

sexton *noun* someone who has various responsibilities in a church, *eg* bellringing, grave-digging, *etc*

sexual *adj* **1** relating to sexual intercourse or other pleasurable behaviour of a physically intimate nature **2** of sex or gender • **sexuality** *noun* • **sexually**

adv • **sexual intercourse** *noun* physical union between a man and a woman involving the insertion of the penis into the vagina

SF *abbrev* science fiction

SFX *abbrev* special effects

sgraffito /zgruh-fee-toh/ *noun* decorative artwork in which layers are scraped away to reveal different colours

shabby *adj* (**shabbier, shabbiest**) **1** worn-looking **2** poorly dressed **3** of behaviour: mean, unfair • **shabbily** *adv*

shack *noun* a roughly-built hut

shackle *verb* **1** fasten with a chain **2** prevent from acting freely; hinder • **shackles** *plural noun* chains fastening a prisoner's legs or arms

shade *noun* **1** slight darkness caused by cutting off some light **2** a place not in full sunlight **3** a screen from the heat or light **4** the deepness or a variation of a colour **5** the dark parts in a picture **6** a very small amount or difference: *a shade larger* **7** (**shades**) *informal* sunglasses **8** *old* a ghost ◇ *verb* **1** shelter from the sun or light **2** make parts of a picture darker **3** change gradually, *eg* from one colour into another • **shading** *noun* the marking of the darker places in a picture

shadow *noun* **1** shade caused by some object coming in the way of a light **2** the dark shape of that object on the ground **3** a dark part in a picture **4** a very small amount: *a shadow of doubt* ◇ *verb* **1** put in the shade; darken **2** follow someone about secretly and watch them closely • **shadow cabinet** *noun* leading members of the opposition in parliament • **shadowy** *adj*

shady *adj* (**shadier, shadiest**) **1** sheltered from light or heat **2** *informal* dishonest, underhand: *a shady character*

shaft noun **1** anything long and straight **2** the rod on which the head of an axe, arrow, etc is fixed **3** a revolving rod that turns a machine or engine **4** the pole of a cart to which the horses are tied **5** the deep, narrow passageway leading to a mine **6** a deep vertical hole for a lift **7** a ray (of light)

shag verb (**shagging**, **shagged**) slang **1** have sexual intercourse **2** have sexual intercourse with ◇ noun an act of sexual intercourse

shaggy adj (**shaggier**, **shaggiest**) rough, hairy or woolly

shagpile adj of a carpet: having a thick pile

shah noun a title formerly given to the king or ruler of various Middle Eastern countries

shake verb (**shaking**, **shook**, **shaken**) **1** move backwards and forwards or up and down with quick, jerky movements **2** make or be made unsteady **3** shock, disturb: his parting words shook me ◇ noun **1** the act of shaking or trembling **2** a shock **3** a drink mixed by shaking or stirring quickly: milk shake

shaky adj (**shakier**, **shakiest**) unsteady; trembling ● **shakily** adv

shale noun a kind of rock from which oil can be obtained

shall verb **1** used to form future tenses of other verbs when the subject is I or we: I shall tell you later **2** used for emphasis, or to express a promise, when the subject is you, he, she, it or they: you shall go if I say you must/ you shall go if you want to (see also **should**)

shallot /shuh-lot/ noun a kind of onion

shallow adj **1** not deep **2** not capable of thinking or feeling deeply ◇ noun (often **shallows**) a place where the water is not deep

shalom exclam peace be with you, a Jewish greeting

sham noun something that is not what it appears to be, a pretence ◇ adj false, imitation, pretended: a sham fight ◇ verb (**shamming**, **shammed**) pretend, feign: shamming sleep

shaman /sheh-mun/ noun a tribal healer or medicine man

shamble verb walk in a shuffling or awkward manner ● **shambles** plural noun, informal a confused or disordered situation; a mess

shambolic adj, slang chaotic

shame noun **1** an uncomfortable feeling caused by realization of guilt or failure **2** disgrace or dishonour **3** informal a pity: it's a shame that you can't go ◇ verb **1** cause to feel shame **2** (with **into**) cause (someone to do something) by making them ashamed: they shamed him into paying his share ● **shamefaced** adj showing shame or embarrassment ● **shameful** adj disgraceful ● **shameless** adj feeling or showing no shame ● **put to shame** cause to feel ashamed

shammy another spelling of **chamois**

shampoo noun **1** a soapy liquid used for cleaning the hair **2** a similar liquid used for cleaning carpets or upholstery **3** an act of washing something with shampoo ◇ verb wash with shampoo

shamrock noun a plant like clover with leaves divided in three

shandy noun (plural **shandies**) a drink of beer and lemonade

shanghai verb **1** trick into doing something unpleasant **2** force to go to sea as a sailor

Shangri-la noun an imaginary paradise

shank noun **1** the part of the leg between the knee and the foot **2** a long straight part (of a tool etc)

shank's pony *noun, dated informal* transport in the form of your own feet; walking

shan't *short for* shall not

shanty *noun* (*plural* **shanties**) **1** a roughly-made hut **2** a sailors' song • **shantytown** *noun* an area of makeshift, squalid housing

shape *noun* **1** the form or outline of anything **2** a mould for a jelly *etc* **3** a jelly *etc* turned out of a mould **4** condition: *in good shape* ◇ *verb* **1** make into a certain form **2** model, mould **3** (often with **up**) develop (in a particular way): *our plans are shaping up well* • **shapeless** *adj* having no shape or regular form • **shapely** *adj* having an attractive shape

shard *noun* a sharp fragment of glass, pottery, *etc*

share *noun* **1** one part of something that is divided among several people **2** one of the parts into which the money of a business firm is divided ◇ *verb* **1** divide out among a number of people **2** allow others to use (your possessions *etc*) **3** have or use in common with someone else: *we share a liking for music* • **shareholder** *noun* someone who owns shares in a business company • **shareware** *noun* computer software that is made available for a small fee

shark *noun* **1** a large, very fierce, flesh-eating fish **2** *informal* a swindler

sharp *adj* **1** having a thin edge or fine point that can cut or pierce **2** hurting, stinging, biting: *sharp wind/ sharp words* **3** alert, quick-witted **4** severe, inclined to scold **5** *music* of a note: raised half a tone in pitch **6** of a voice: shrill **7** of an outline: clear ◇ *adv* punctually: *come at ten o'clock sharp* ◇ *noun, music* a sign (♯) showing that a note is to be raised half a tone • **sharpen** *verb* make or grow sharp • **sharpener** *noun* an instrument for sharpening: *pencil sharp-*

ener • **sharper** *noun* a cheat, *esp* at cards • **sharp practice** *noun* cheating • **sharp-sighted** *adj* having keen sight • **sharp-witted** *adj* alert, intelligent • **look sharp** hurry

shatter *verb* **1** break in pieces **2** upset, ruin (hopes, health, *etc*)

shave *verb* **1** cut away hair with a razor **2** scrape away the surface of (wood *etc*) **3** touch lightly, or just avoid touching, in passing ◇ *noun* **1** the act of shaving **2** a narrow escape: *a close shave* • **shaven** *adj* shaved • **shavings** *plural noun* very thin slices of wood *etc*

shawl *noun* a loose covering for the shoulders

she *pronoun* a woman, girl or female animal already spoken about (used only as the subject of a verb): *when the girl saw us, she waved*

sheaf *noun* (*plural* **sheaves**) a bundle (*eg* of corn, papers) tied together

shear *verb* (**shearing**, **sheared**, **shorn**) **1** clip, cut (*esp* wool from a sheep) **2** cut through or cut off • **shears** *plural noun* large scissors

---

Do not confuse with: **sheer**

---

sheath *noun* **1** a case for a sword or dagger **2** a long close-fitting covering **3** *dated* a condom • **sheathe** *verb* put into a sheath

shebang *noun, informal*: **the whole shebang** everything

shed *noun* **1** a building for storage or shelter: *coalshed/bicycle shed* **2** an outhouse ◇ *verb* **1** throw or cast off (leaves, a skin, clothing) **2** pour out (tears, blood) **3** give out (light *etc*)

sheen *noun* reflected brightness; gloss

sheep *noun* **1** an animal whose flesh is used as food and whose fleece is used for wool **2** a very meek person who lacks confidence • **sheep dip** *noun* a liquid for disinfecting sheep • **sheepdog** noun a dog trained to look after sheep • **sheepish** adj embarrassed or shamefaced • **sheepshank** noun a knot used for shortening a rope • **sheepskin** noun 1 the skin of a sheep 2 a kind of leather made from this

sheer adj 1 very steep: sheer drop from the cliff 2 pure, not mixed: sheer delight/sheer nonsense 3 of cloth: very thin or fine ◇ adv straight up and down, very steeply ◇ verb turn aside from a straight line; swerve

---

Do not confuse with: **shear**

---

sheet noun 1 a large piece of linen, cotton, nylon, etc for a bed 2 a large thin piece of metal, glass, ice, etc 3 a piece of paper 4 a sail 5 the rope fastened to the lower corner of a sail • **sheet anchor** noun a large anchor for use in emergencies • **sheeting** noun any material from which sheets are made • **sheet lightning** noun lightning that appears in great sheets or flashes

sheikh /shehk/ noun an Arab chief

shekel /shek-ul/ noun, hist an ancient Jewish weight and coin

shelf noun (plural **shelves**) 1 a board fixed on a wall, for putting things on 2 a flat layer of rock; a ledge 3 a bank of sand

shell noun 1 a hard outer covering (of a shellfish, egg, nut, etc) 2 a husk or pod (eg of peas) 3 a metal case filled with explosive fired from a gun 4 a framework, eg of a building not yet completed or burnt out: only the shell of the warehouse was left ◇ verb 1 take the shell from (a nut, egg, etc) 2 fire shells at

shellac noun a type of resin once used to make gramophone records

shellfish noun a water creature covered with a shell, eg an oyster, limpet or mussel

shelter noun 1 a building that acts as a protection from harm, rain, wind, etc 2 the state of being protected from any of these ◇ verb 1 give protection to 2 put in a place of shelter or protection 3 go to, or stay in, a place of shelter • **take shelter** go to a place of shelter

shelve verb 1 put up shelves in 2 put aside (a problem etc) for later consideration 3 of land: slope gently

shenanigans plural noun, informal silly, underhand or mischievous behaviour

shepherd, **shepherdess** noun someone who looks after sheep ◇ verb (**shepherd**) guide or lead into a place • **shepherd's pie** noun a dish of minced meat covered with mashed potatoes

sherbet noun 1 a fizzy drink 2 powder for making this

sheriff noun 1 the senior representative of a monarch in a county, whose duties include keeping the peace 2 in Scotland, the chief judge of a county 3 US the chief law-enforcement officer of a county

sherry noun a strong kind of wine, often drunk before a meal

shiatsu /shee-at-soo/ noun a Japanese therapy that treats illness by applying pressure to certain points of the body

shibboleth /shib-uh-leth/ noun a word or attribute that identifies members of a group

shied past form of **shy**

shield noun 1 a broad piece of metal carried by a soldier etc as a defence against weapons 2 a shield-shaped trophy won in a competition 3 a shield-shaped plaque bearing a coat-of-arms 4 anything that protects from harm ◇ verb protect, defend, shelter

shift verb 1 change the position of; move: shift the furniture/trying to *shift the blame* **2** change position or direction: *the wind shifted* **3** get rid of ◇ *noun* **1** a change of position; a move **2** a change: *shift of emphasis* **3** a group of workers on duty at the same time: *day shift/night shift* **4** a specified period of work or duty **5** a loose-fitting lightweight dress • **shiftless** *adj* having no set plan or purpose; lazy • **shifty** *adj* not to be trusted, looking dishonest • **shift for yourself** manage to get on by your own efforts

shiitake /shee-i-*ta*-ki/ *noun* a dark brown Japanese mushroom

Shiite /shee-ait/ *noun* a follower of a branch of Islam practised mainly in Iran ◇ *adj* following this branch of Islam

shilling *noun, Brit hist* a silver-coloured coin in use before decimalization, worth 1/20 of £1 (now the 5 pence piece)

shillyshally *verb* (**shillyshallies, shillyshallying, shillyshallied**) hesitate in making up your mind; waver

shimmer *verb* shine with a quivering or unsteady light ◇ *noun* a quivering light

shin *noun* the front part of the leg below the knee • **shin up** climb

shindig *noun, informal* a party or celebration

shindy *noun* (*plural* **shindies**), *informal* a noise or uproar

shine *verb* (**shining, shone**) **1** give out or reflect light **2** be bright **3** polish (shoes *etc*) **4** be very good at: *he shines at arithmetic* ◇ *noun* **1** brightness **2** an act of polishing • **shining** *adj* **1** very bright and clear **2** admired, distinguished: *a shining example*

shingle *noun* coarse gravel of rounded stones on the shores of rivers or of the sea • **shingles** *sing noun* an infectious disease causing a painful rash

shinty *noun* a Scottish ball-game resembling hockey

shiny *adj* (**shinier, shiniest**) having a bright or polished surface; glossy • **shinily** *adv* • **shininess** *noun*

ship *noun* a large vessel for journeys across water ◇ *verb* (**shipping, shipped**) **1** take onto a ship **2** send by ship **3** go by ship • **shipmate** *noun* a fellow sailor • **shipment** *noun* **1** an act of putting on board ship **2** a load of goods sent by ship • **shipping** *noun* • **shipshape** *adj* in good order; neat and trim • **shipwreck** *noun* **1** the sinking or destruction of a ship (*esp* by accident) **2** a wrecked ship **3** ruin • **shipwrecked** *adj* involved in a shipwreck • **shipwright** *noun* someone who is employed to build or repair ships • **shipyard** *noun* the yard in which ships are built or repaired

shire *noun* a county

shirk *verb* avoid or evade (doing your duty *etc*) • **shirker** *noun*

shirt *noun* **1** a garment worn by men on the upper part of the body, having a collar, sleeves and buttons down the front **2** a similar garment for a woman

shish kebab *noun* pieces of meat and vegetables grilled on a skewer

shit *noun, taboo slang* **1** excrement, faeces **2** an unpleasant or despicable person ◇ *verb* (**shitting, shitted** or **shat**) empty the bowels ◇ *exclam* expressing anger, annoyance, displeasure, *etc* • **shitty** *adj* very unpleasant; disagreeable

shiver *verb* **1** tremble with cold or fear **2** break into small pieces; shatter ◇ *noun* **1** the act of shivering **2** a small broken piece: *shivers of glass*

shoal *noun* **1** a group of fishes moving and feeding together **2** a shallow place, *esp* a sandbank

shock *noun* **1** a sudden forceful blow **2** a feeling of fright, horror, dismay, *etc* **3** a state of weakness or illness following such feelings **4** the effect on the body of an electric current passing through it **5** an earthquake **6** a bushy mass (of hair) ◇ *verb* **1** give a shock to **2** upset or horrify • **shock absorber** *noun* a device in an aircraft, car, *etc* for lessening the impact or force of bumps • **shocking** *adj* causing horror, outrage or dismay

shod *adj* wearing shoes ◇ *verb* past form of **shoe**

shoddy *adj* (**shoddier, shoddiest**) of poor material or quality: *shoddy goods*

shoe *noun* **1** a stiff outer covering for the foot that does not reach above the ankle **2** a rim of iron nailed to the hoof of a horse ◇ *verb* (**shoeing, shod**) put shoes on (a horse) • **shoehorn** *noun* a curved piece of horn, metal, *etc* for making a shoe slip easily over your heel • **shoelace** *noun* a cord or string used for fastening a shoe • **shoemaker** *noun* someone who makes and mends shoes • **on a shoestring** with very little money

shone past form of **shine**

shoo *exclam* used to scare away birds, animals, *etc* ◇ *verb* (**shooing, shooed**) drive or scare away

shoogle *verb, Scot* shake

shook see **shake**

shoot *verb* (**shooting, shot**) **1** send a bullet from a gun, or an arrow from a bow **2** hit or kill with an arrow, bullet, *etc* **3** let fly swiftly and with force **4** move very swiftly or suddenly **5** kick for a goal **6** score (a goal) **7** of a plant: grow new buds **8** photograph, film **9** slide (a bolt) ◇ *noun* **1** a new sprout on a plant **2** an expedition to shoot game **3** land where game is shot • **shooting brake** *noun, old* an estate car • **shooting star** *noun* a meteor

shop *noun* **1** a place where goods are sold **2** a workshop ◇ *verb* (**shopping, shopped**) **1** visit shops and buy goods **2** *slang* betray (someone) to the police • **shopfitter** *noun* a person whose job is to install the counters, shelves, *etc*

in a shop • **shopfitting** *noun* • **shopkeeper** *noun* someone who owns and keeps a shop • **shoplifter** *noun* someone who steals goods from a shop • **shopper** *noun* someone who shops; a customer • **shop steward** *noun* a worker elected by the other workers as their representative • **talk shop** *informal* talk about work when off duty

shore *noun* the land bordering on a sea or lake ◇ *verb* prop (up); support: *shoring up an unprofitable organization*

shorn *past participle of* **shear**

short *adj* **1** not long: *short skirt* **2** not tall **3** not lasting long; brief: *short talk* **4** less than it should be **5** rude, sharp, abrupt **6** of pastry: crisp and crumbling easily ◇ *adv* **1** suddenly, abruptly: *stop short* **2** not as far as intended: *the shot fell short* ◇ *noun* **1** a short film **2** a short-circuit **3** (**shorts**) short trousers ◇ *verb* short-circuit • **shortage** *noun* a lack • **shortbread** *noun* a thick biscuit made of butter and flour *etc* • **shortcoming** *noun* a fault or defect • **short cut** *noun* a short way of going somewhere or doing something • **shorten** *verb* make less in length • **shorthand** *noun* a method of swift writing using strokes and dots to show sounds (*contrasted with:* **longhand**) • **short-handed** *adj* having fewer workers than usual • **short list** *noun* a list of candidates selected from the total number of applicants or contestants • **shortlived** *adj* living or lasting only a short time • **shortly** *adv* **1** soon **2** curtly, abruptly **3** briefly • **short-sighted** *adj* **1** seeing clearly only things that are near **2** taking no account of what may happen in the future • **short-tempered** *adj* easily made angry • **short-term** *adj* intended to last only a short time • **shortwave** *adj* of radio: using wavelengths between 10 and 100 metres (*compare with:* **long-wave**) • **give short shrift** waste little time or consideration on

• **in short** in a few words • **short of**
1 not having enough: *short of money*
2 not as much or as far as; less than:
*5 miles short of Inverness/£5 short of
the price* **3** without going as far as: *he
didn't know how to get the money,
short of stealing it*

short-circuit *noun* the missing out
of a major part of an intended electric
circuit, sometimes causing blowing of
fuses ◇ *verb* **1** of an electrical appliance: have a short-circuit **2** bypass (a
difficulty *etc*)

shot *noun* **1** something that is fired **2**
small lead bullets used in cartridges **3**
a single act of shooting **4** the sound of
a gun being fired **5** a marksman **6** a
turn in a game **7** an attempt at doing
something, guessing, *etc* **8** a photograph **9** a scene in a motion picture
◇ *adj* **1** of silk: showing changing
colours **2** streaked or mixed with (a
colour *etc*) ◇ *verb past form of* **shoot**
• **shotgun** *noun* a long-barrelled gun
that fires shot • **a shot in the dark** a
guess

should *verb* **1** the form of the verb
shall used to express a condition:
I should go if I had time **2** used to
mean 'ought to': *you should know
that already*

shoulder *noun* **1** the part of the
body between the neck and upper
arm **2** the upper part of an animal's
foreleg **3** a hump or ridge: *the shoulder of the hill* ◇ *verb* **1** carry on the
shoulders **2** bear the full weight of (a
burden *etc*) **3** push with the shoulder
• **shoulder blade** *noun* the broad flat
bone of the shoulder

shout *noun* **1** a loud cry or call **2** a
loud burst (of laughter *etc*) ◇ *verb*
make a loud cry

shove *verb* push roughly ◇ *noun* a
rough push

shovel *noun* a spade-like tool used
for lifting coal, gravel, *etc* ◇ *verb* lift
or move with a shovel

show *verb* (**showing**, **showed**,
shown) **1** allow, or cause, to be seen:
show me your new dress **2** be able
to be seen: *your underskirt is showing* **3** exhibit or display (an art collection *etc*) **4** point out (the way *etc*)
5 direct, guide: *show her to a seat* **6**
make clear; demonstrate: *that shows
that I was right* ◇ *noun* **1** a performance or entertainment **2** a display or
exhibition • **show business** *noun* the
branch of the theatre concerned with
variety entertainments • **showroom**
noun a room where goods are laid
out for people to see • **showy** *adj* **1**
making an impressive display **2** bright
or fancy in a rather vulgar way • **show
off 1** show or display (something) **2**
try to impress others with your talents
etc • **show up 1** cause to stand out
clearly **2** make obvious; expose

shower *noun* **1** a short fall of rain
2 a bath in which water is sprayed
from above **3** the apparatus that
sprays water for this **4** a large quantity: *a shower of questions* **5** *US* a
party at which gifts are given, *eg* to
someone about to be married or who
has just had a baby ◇ *verb* **1** pour
(something) down on **2** bathe under
a shower • **showerproof** *adj* of material, a coat, *etc*: able to withstand
light rain • **showery** *adj* raining from
time to time

shown *past participle of* **show**

shrank *past tense of* **shrink**

shrapnel *noun* **1** a shell containing
bullets *etc* that scatter on explosion **2**
splinters of metal, a bomb, *etc*

shred *noun* **1** a long, narrow piece,
cut or torn off **2** a scrap, a very small
amount: *not a shred of evidence*
◇ *verb* (**shredding**, **shredded**) cut or
tear into shreds

shrew *noun* **1** a small mouse-like
type of animal with a long nose **2**
a quarrelsome or scolding woman
• **shrewish** *adj* quarrelsome or bad-
tempered

shrewd *adj* clever or cunning

shriek *verb* make a shrill scream or laugh ◇ *noun* a shrill scream or laugh

shrift *noun*: **give someone short shrift** dismiss them quickly

shrike *noun* a bird that preys on smaller birds

shrill *adj* of a sound or voice: high in tone; piercing • **shrilly** *adv*

shrimp *noun* **1** a small, long-tailed edible shellfish **2** *informal derog* a small person

shrine *noun* a holy or sacred place

shrink *verb* (**shrinking, shrank, shrunk**) **1** make or become smaller **2** draw back in fear and disgust (from) ◇ *noun, informal usu derog* a psychiatrist • **shrinkage** *noun* the amount by which something grows smaller • **shrinkwrap** *noun* clear plastic film for wrapping, heated so that it shrinks to fit tightly ◇ *verb* wrap with this type of film • **shrunken** *adj* shrunk

shrive *verb* (**shriving, shrove, shriven**) *old* **1** hear a confession **2** confess

shrivel *verb* (**shrivelling, shrivelled**) dry up and wrinkle or wither

shroud *noun* **1** a cloth covering a dead body **2** something that covers: *a shroud of mist* **3** (**shrouds**) the ropes from the mast to a ship's sides ◇ *verb* cover

Shrove Tuesday *noun* the day before Ash Wednesday

shrub *noun* a small bush or plant • **shrubbery** *noun* a place where shrubs grow

shrug *verb* (**shrugging, shrugged**) show doubt, lack of interest, *etc* by drawing up the shoulders ◇ *noun* a movement of the shoulders to show lack of interest • **shrug off** treat as being unimportant; dismiss

shrunk, shrunken *see* shrink

shtetl /shtet-ul/ *noun, hist* a Jewish community in E Europe

shtook *noun, slang* trouble, bother

shtoom *adj, slang* quiet, silent: *keeping shtoom*

shudder *verb* tremble from fear, cold or disgust ◇ *noun* a trembling

shuffle *verb* **1** mix, rearrange (*eg* playing-cards) **2** move by dragging or sliding the feet along the ground without lifting them **3** move (the feet) in this way ◇ *noun* **1** a rearranging **2** a dragging movement of the feet

shun *verb* (**shunning, shunned**) keep away from; avoid

shunt *verb* move (railway trains, engines, *etc*) onto a side track ◇ *noun* a minor collision in which one vehicle goes into the back of another

shut *verb* (**shutting, shut**) **1** move (a door, window, lid, *etc*) so that it covers an opening **2** close, lock (a building *etc*) **3** become closed: *the door shut with a bang* **4** confine in a building *etc*: *shut the dog in his kennel* • **shutter** *noun* **1** a cover for a window **2** a cover that closes over a camera lens as it takes a picture • **shut down** close (a factory *etc*) • **shut up 1** close completely **2** *informal* stop speaking or making other noise

shuttle *noun* **1** the part of a weaving loom which carries the cross thread from side to side **2** a transport service that makes regular short trips between two places • **shuttlecock** *noun* a rounded cork stuck with feathers, used in the game of badminton

shy *adj* (**shyer, shyest**) **1** lacking confidence in the presence of others **2** not wanting to attract attention **3** of a wild animal: easily frightened, timid ◇ *verb* (**shies, shying, shied**) **1** jump or turn suddenly aside in fear **2** throw, toss ◇ *noun* a try, an attempt • **shyly** *adv* • **shyness** *noun* • **fight shy of** keep away from; avoid

shyster *noun, slang* a swindler

SI *abbrev, French* Système International (d'Unités), the metric unit system

Siamese adj • **Siamese cat** a fawn-coloured domestic cat • **Siamese twins** plural noun twins joined by their flesh at birth (formal name **conjoined twins**)

sibilant adj of a sound: hissing

sibling noun a brother or sister

sibyl noun a prophetess, esp of ancient Rome or Greece

sic adv in this way, written in brackets after a word to show that it is quoted correctly, even though it may look wrong

sick adj 1 wanting to vomit 2 vomiting 3 not physically well; ill 4 (with **of**) tired of • **sick bed** or **sickroom** noun a bed or room for people to rest in when ill • **sicken** verb make or become sick • **sickening** adj 1 causing sickness 2 disgusting, revolting • **sick leave** noun time off work for illness • **sickly** adj 1 unhealthy 2 feeble • **sickness** noun

sickle noun a hooked knife for cutting or reaping grain, hay, etc • **sickle-cell anaemia** noun a hereditary disease in which the red blood cells are distorted in a sickle shape

side noun 1 an edge, border or boundary line 2 a surface that is not the top, bottom, front or back 3 either surface of a piece of paper, cloth, etc 4 the right or left part of the body 5 a division, a part: the north side of the town 6 an aspect or point of view: all sides of the problem 7 a slope (of a hill) 8 a team or party that is opposing another ◇ adj 1 on or towards the side: side door 2 additional but less important: side issue ◇ verb (with **with**) support (one person, group, etc against another) • **sideboard** noun a piece of furniture in a dining-room for holding dishes etc • **sidecar** noun a small car for a passenger, attached to a motorcycle • **side effect** noun an additional (often bad) effect, eg of a drug • **sideline** noun an extra bit of business outside regular work • **sidelong** adj & adv from or to the side: sidelong glance • **sideshow** noun a less important show that is part of a larger one • **sidestep** verb avoid by stepping to one side • **sidetrack** verb turn (someone) away from what they were going to do or say • **sidewalk** noun, US a pavement • **sideways** adv 1 with the side foremost 2 towards the side • **siding** noun a short line of rails on which trucks are shunted off the main line • **take sides** choose to support a party, person, etc against another

sidereal /sai-dee-ri-ul/ adj relating to the stars

sidle verb 1 go or move sideways 2 move stealthily; sneak

SIDS abbrev sudden infant death syndrome, the sudden unexplained death of a very young child in sleep; cot death

siege /seej/ noun 1 an attempt to capture a town etc by keeping it surrounded by an armed force 2 a constant attempt to gain control • **lay siege to** besiege

siemens unit noun a unit of electrical conductance

sienna noun a reddish-brown or yellowish-brown pigment used in paints

sierra noun a range of mountains with jagged peaks

siesta noun a short sleep or rest taken in the afternoon

sieve /siv/ noun a container with a mesh used to separate liquids from solids, or fine pieces from coarse pieces etc ◇ verb put through a sieve

sift verb 1 separate by passing through a sieve 2 consider and examine closely: sifting all the evidence

sigh noun a long, deep-sounding breath showing tiredness, longing or regret ◇ verb give out a sigh

sight noun 1 the act or power of

seeing **2** an occasion when you see something; a glimpse: *catch sight of her* **3** (often **sights**) something worth seeing: *the sights of London* **4** something or someone unusual, ridiculous, shocking, *etc*: *she's quite a sight in that hat* **5** a guide on a gun for taking aim ◇ *verb* **1** get a view of; see suddenly **2** look at through the sight of a gun ● **sight reading** *noun* playing or singing from music that has not been seen previously ● **sightseeing** *noun* visiting the main buildings, monuments, *etc* of a place

---

Do not confuse with: **site** and **cite**

---

sign *noun* **1** a mark with a special meaning; a symbol **2** a gesture (eg a nod, wave of the hand) to show your meaning **3** an advertisement or notice giving information **4** something that shows what is happening or is going to happen: *signs of irritation/a sign of good weather* ◇ *verb* **1** write your name on (a document, cheque, *etc*) **2** make a sign or gesture to **3** show (your meaning) by a sign or gesture ● **signboard** *noun* a board with a notice ● **signpost** *noun* a post with a sign, *esp* one showing direction and distances to certain places ● **sign on** enter your name on a list for work, the army, *etc*

signal *noun* **1** a gesture, light or sound giving a command, warning, *etc*: *air-raid signal* **2** something used for this purpose: *railway signals* **3** the wave of sound received or sent out by a radio *etc* set ◇ *verb* (**signalling**, **signalled**) **1** make signals (to) **2** send (information) by signal ◇ *adj* remarkable: *a signal success* ● **signalman** *noun* someone who works railway signals, or who sends signals

signature *noun* **1** a signed name **2** an act of signing **3** *music* the flats or sharps at the beginning of a piece

of music that show its key, or figures showing its timing ● **signatory** *noun* someone who has signed an agreement *etc* ● **signature tune** *noun* a tune used to identify a particular radio or television series *etc* played at the beginning or end of the programme

signet *noun* a small seal, usually bearing someone's initials ● **signet ring** *noun* a ring imprinted with a signet

---

Do not confuse with: **cygnet**

---

signify *verb* (**signifies**, **signifying**, **signified**) **1** be a sign of; mean **2** make known by a gesture; show: *signifying disapproval* **3** have meaning or importance ● **significance** *noun* **1** meaning **2** importance ● **significant** *adj* meaning much; important: *no significant change* ● **significantly** *adv*

Sikh *noun* a member of an eastern religion that broke away from Hinduism in the 16th century ● **Sikhism** *noun*

silage *noun* green fodder preserved in a silo

silence *noun* **1** absence of sound or speech **2** a time of quietness ◇ *verb* cause to be silent ● **silencer** *noun* a device on a car engine, gun, *etc* for making noise less ● **silent** *adj* **1** free from noise **2** not speaking ● **silently** *adv*

silhouette *noun* **1** an outline drawing of someone, often in profile, filled in with black **2** a dark outline seen against the light

silica *noun* a white or colourless substance of which flint, sandstone, quartz, *etc* are mostly made up

silicon *noun* a chemical element that acts as a semiconductor ● **silicon chip** *noun* a tiny piece of silicon with electrical circuits on it, used in computers and other electronic equipment

silk noun **1** very fine soft fibres spun by silkworms **2** thread or cloth made from this ◊ adj **1** made of silk **2** soft, smooth • **silken** adj **1** made of silk **2** smooth like silk • **silkworm** noun the caterpillar of certain moths which spins silk • **silky** adj like silk

silkie noun a mythological creature, half a human and half a seal

sill noun a ledge of wood, stone, etc below a window or a door

silly adj (**sillier**, **silliest**) not sensible; foolish

silo noun (plural **silos**) **1** a tower for storing grain etc **2** a pit or air-tight chamber for holding silage **3** an underground chamber built to contain a guided missile

silt noun sand or mud left behind by flowing water • **silt up** become blocked by mud

silver noun **1** a white precious metal able to take on a high polish **2** money made of silver or of a metal alloy resembling it **3** objects (esp cutlery) made of, or plated with, silver ◊ adj made of, or looking like, silver ◊ verb **1** cover with silver **2** become like silver • **silverfish** noun a wingless, silvery insect, sometimes found in houses • **silver foil** or **silver leaf** noun silver beaten to paper-thinness, used for decoration • **silversmith** noun someone who makes or sells articles of silver • **silver wedding** noun a 25th anniversary of a wedding • **silvery** adj **1** like silver **2** of sound: ringing and musical

SIM card noun a removable electronic card inside a mobile phone that stores information about the subscriber

simian adj ape-like

similar adj alike in some respects • **similarity** noun • **similarly** adv **1** in the same, or a similar, way **2** likewise, also

simile /sim-i-lee/ noun an expression using 'like' or 'as', in which one thing is likened to another that is well-known for a particular quality (eg 'as black as night', 'to swim like a fish')

simmer verb cook gently just below or at boiling-point

simnel cake noun a fruit cake covered with marzipan, traditionally eaten at Easter

simper verb **1** smile in a silly manner **2** say with a simper ◊ noun a silly smile • **simpering** adj

simple adj **1** not difficult or complicated; easy **2** not fancy; plain: simple hairstyle **3** ordinary: simple, everyday objects **4** of humble rank: a simple peasant **5** nothing but; mere: the simple truth **6** too trusting and easily cheated **7** old having learning difficulties • **simpleton** noun, old derog a person with learning difficulties • **simplicity** noun the state of being simple

simplify verb (**simplifies**, **simplifying**, **simplified**) make simpler • **simplification** noun **1** an act of making something simpler **2** a simple form of anything

simply adv **1** in a simple manner **2** merely: I do it simply for the money **3** absolutely: simply beautiful

simulacrum /sim-yoo-leh-krum/ noun (plural **simulacra**) formal a resemblance or image

simulate verb **1** pretend to have or feel; feign: she simulated illness **2** have the appearance of; look like • **simulated** adj **1** pretended **2** having the appearance of: simulated leather • **simulation** noun

simulcast noun a simultaneous television and radio broadcast of the same event

simultaneous adj happening, or done, at the same time • **simultaneously** adv

sin noun **1** a wicked act, esp one

that breaks religious laws **2** wrongdoing **3** *informal* a shame, pity ◇ *verb* (**sinning, sinned**) commit a sin or do wrong • **sinful** *adj* wicked • **sinner** *noun* • **original sin** the supposed sinful nature of all human beings since the time of Adam's sin

since *adv* **1** (often with **ever**) from that time onwards: *I have avoided him ever since* **2** at a later time: *we have since become friends* **3** ago: *long since* **4** from the time of: *since his arrival* ◇ *conj* **1** after the time when: *I have been at home since I returned from Italy* **2** because: *since you are going, I will go too*

sincere *adj* **1** meaning what you say or do; true: *a sincere friend* **2** truly felt: *a sincere desire* • **sincerely** *adv* • **sincerity** *noun*

sinecure *noun* a job for which someone receives money but has little or no work to do

sine qua non /si-neh kwah *non*/ *noun* an indispensable condition

sinew *noun* **1** a tough cord that joins a muscle to a bone **2** (**sinews**) equipment and resources necessary for something: *sinews of war* • **sinewy** *adj* slim and muscular

sing *verb* (**singing, sang, sung**) **1** make musical sounds with your voice **2** utter (words, a song, *etc*) by doing this • **singer** *noun* • **sing-song** *noun* **1** a gathering of people singing informally together **2** an up-and-down tone of voice ◇ *adj* in an up-and-down voice

singe *verb* burn slightly on the surface; scorch ◇ *noun* a surface burn

single *adj* **1** one only **2** not double **3** not married **4** for one person: *a single bed* **5** between two people: *single combat* **6** for one direction of a journey only: *a single ticket* • **single-handed** *adj* working *etc* by yourself • **single-minded** *adj* having one aim only • **singleness** *noun* the state of being single • **single parent** *noun* a parent who brings up a child without a partner • **singly** *adv* one by one, separately • **single out** treat differently in some way

singlet *noun, dated* a vest

singular *adj* **1** *grammar* showing that there is only one person or thing **2** exceptional: *singular success* **3** unusual, strange: *a singular sight* • **singularly** *adv* strangely, exceptionally: *singularly ugly*

sinister *adj* suggesting evil

sink *verb* (**sinking, sank, sunk**) **1** go down below the surface of the water *etc* **2** go down or become less: *my hopes sank* **3** become much more ill or weak **4** let yourself fall (into): *sink into a chair* **5** make by digging (a well *etc*) **6** push (your teeth *etc*) deep into (something) **7** invest (money *etc*) into a business ◇ *noun* a basin in a kitchen, bathroom, *etc*, with a water supply connected to it and a drain for carrying off dirty water *etc* • **sinker** *noun* a weight fixed to a fishing line *etc*

Sino- *prefix* relating to China or the Chinese: *Sino-Tibetan*

sinuous *adj* bending in and out; winding • **sinuosity** *noun*

sinus *noun* (*plural* **sinuses**) an air cavity in the head connected with the nose • **sinusitis** *noun* inflammation of (one of) the sinuses

sip *verb* (**sipping, sipped**) drink in very small quantities ◇ *noun* a taste of a drink; a swallow

siphon *or* **syphon** *noun* **1** a bent tube for drawing off liquids from one container into another **2** a glass bottle for soda water *etc* containing such a tube ◇ *verb* **1** draw (off) through a siphon **2** (with **off**) take (part of something) away gradually: *he siphoned off some of the club's funds*

sir *noun* **1** a polite form of address

used to a man **2** (**Sir**) the title of a knight or baronet

sire noun **1** a male parent, esp of a horse **2** hist a title used in speaking to a king ◇ verb of an animal: be the male parent of

siren noun **1** an instrument that gives out a loud hooting noise as a warning **2** a mythical sea nymph whose singing enchanted sailors and tempted them into danger **3** an attractive but dangerous woman

sirloin noun the upper part of the loin of beef

sirocco noun a hot dry wind blowing from N Africa to the Mediterranean coast

sirrah noun, old sir

sisal noun a fibre from a W Indian plant, used for making ropes

sissy another spelling of **cissy**

sister noun **1** a female person born of the same parents as yourself **2** a senior nurse, often in charge of a hospital ward **3** a nun ◇ adj **1** closely related **2** of similar design or structure • **sisterhood** noun **1** the state of being a sister **2** a religious community of women • **sister-in-law** noun **1** the sister of your husband or wife **2** the wife of your brother or of your brother-in-law • **sisterly** adj like a sister

sit verb (**sitting**, **sat**) **1** rest on the buttocks; be seated **2** of a bird: perch **3** rest on eggs in order to hatch them **4** be an official member: sit in parliament/sit on a committee **5** of a court etc: meet officially **6** pose (for a photographer, painter, etc) **7** take (an examination etc) • **sit-in** noun an occupation of a building etc by protesters • **sitter** noun **1** someone who poses for a portrait etc **2** a babysitter **3** a bird sitting on eggs • **sit tight** stay in one place, or be unwilling to move from it • **sit up 1** sit with your back straight **2** stay up instead of going to bed

sitcom noun a television comedy series with a running theme

site noun **1** a place where a building, town, etc is or is to be placed **2** comput a website ◇ verb select a place for (a building etc)

Do not confuse with: **sight** and **cite**

---

sitting noun **1** the state or time of sitting **2** a time during which one of several groups has its turn to eat in a dining room ◇ adj **1** seated **2** for sitting in or on **3** in office: sitting member of parliament **4** in possession: sitting tenant • **sitting room** noun a room in a house for relaxing in; a living room

situated adj placed

situation noun **1** the place where anything stands **2** a job **3** a state of affairs; circumstances: in an awkward situation

sitz bath noun a therapeutic hip-bath in hot water

six noun the number 6 ◇ adj 6 in number • **six-pack** noun **1** a package of six cans of beer etc sold together **2** informal a set of well-developed stomach muscles • **sixth** adj the last of a series of six ◇ noun one of six equal parts • **at sixes and sevens** in confusion

sixpence noun, old a silver-coloured coin worth $\frac{1}{40}$ of £1

sixteen noun the number 16 ◇ adj 16 in number • **sixteenth** adj the last of a series of sixteen ◇ noun one of sixteen equal parts

sixty noun the number 60 ◇ adj 60 in number • **sixtieth** adj the last of a series of sixty ◇ noun one of sixty equal parts

size noun **1** space taken up by anything **2** measurements, dimensions **3** largeness **4** a class into which shoes and clothes are grouped according to size: *she takes a size 4 in shoes* **5** a weak kind of glue • **sizeable** *or* **sizable** *adj* fairly large • **size up** form an opinion of (a person, situation, *etc*)

sizzle *verb* **1** make a hissing sound **2** fry

ska *noun* a style of Jamaican music similar to reggae

skate *noun* **1** a steel blade attached to a boot for gliding on ice **2** a roller-skate **3** a type of large flatfish ◇ *verb* move on skates • **skateboard** *noun* a narrow board on four rollerskate wheels • **skateboarding** *noun* the sport of going on a skateboard

skean-dhu /skee-un-*doo*/ *noun* a decorative dagger worn with Highland dress

skedaddle *verb, informal* run off in a hurry

skein /skeen/ *noun* a coil of thread or yarn, loosely tied in a knot

skeleton *noun* **1** the bony framework of an animal or person, without the flesh **2** any framework or outline ◇ *adj* of staff *etc*: reduced to a very small or minimum number • **skeletal** *adj* of or like a skeleton • **skeleton key** *noun* a key from which the inner part has been cut away so that it can open many different locks

skerry *noun* a reef of rock

sketch *noun* (*plural* **sketches**) **1** a rough plan or drawing **2** a short or rough account **3** a short play, dramatic scene, *etc* ◇ *verb* **1** draw roughly **2** give the main points of **3** draw in pencil or ink • **sketchy** *adj* **1** roughly done **2** not thorough; incomplete: *my knowledge of geography is rather sketchy*

skew *adj & adv* not properly straight or level; slanting ◇ *verb* **1** put at a slant or send along a slanting course **2** change (something) slightly in a way that makes it not quite accurate

skewer *noun* a long pin of wood or metal for holding meat together while roasting *etc* ◇ *verb* fix with a skewer or with something sharp

ski *noun* (*plural* **skis**) one of a pair of long narrow strips of wood or metal that are attached to boots for gliding over snow ◇ *verb* (**skiing, skied**) move or travel on skis

skid *noun* **1** a slide sideways: *the car went into a skid* **2** a wedge put under a wheel to stop it on a steep place **3** (**skids**) logs *etc* on which things can be moved by sliding ◇ *verb* **1** of a wheel: slide along without turning **2** slip sideways • **on the skids** on the way down • **put the skids under** hurry along

skiff *noun* a small light boat

skill *noun* cleverness at doing a thing, either from practice or as a natural gift • **skilful** *adj* having or showing skill • **skilfully** *adv* • **skilled** *adj* **1** having skill, *esp* through training **2** of a job: requiring skill

skillet *noun* a small metal pan with a long handle, for frying food

skim *verb* (**skimming, skimmed**) **1** remove cream, scum, *etc* from the surface of (something) **2** move lightly and quickly over (a surface) **3** read quickly, missing parts • **skimmed milk** *noun* milk from which all the cream has been skimmed

skimp *verb* **1** give (someone) hardly enough **2** do (a job) imperfectly **3** spend too little money (on): *skimping on clothes* • **skimpy** *adj* **1** of clothes: very short or tight **2** too small

skin *noun* **1** the natural outer covering of an animal or person **2** a thin outer layer on a fruit **3** a thin film that forms on a liquid ◇ *verb* (**skinning, skinned**) strip the skin from • **skin-deep** *adj* on the surface; superficial • **skin diver** *noun* a diver who wears simple equipment (originally someone who dived naked for pearls) • **skinflint** *noun* a very mean person

• **skinny** adj very thin • **by the skin of your teeth** very narrowly

skint adj, Brit informal with very little money; broke

skip verb (**skipping**, **skipped**) 1 go along with a rhythmic step and hop 2 jump over a turning rope 3 leap, esp lightly or joyfully 4 leave out (parts of a book, a meal, etc) ◇ noun 1 an act of skipping 2 a large metal container for transporting refuse 3 the captain of a team, eg at bowls • **skipping rope** noun a rope used in skipping

skipper noun the captain of a ship, aeroplane or team ◇ verb act as captain for (a ship, team, etc)

skirl noun a shrill sound, esp that made by bagpipes

skirmish noun (plural **skirmishes**) 1 a fight between small groups of soldiers 2 a short sharp contest or disagreement ◇ verb fight briefly or informally

skirt noun 1 a garment, worn by women, that hangs from the waist 2 the lower part of a dress 3 (**skirts**) the outer edge or border ◇ verb pass along, or lie along, the edge of • **skirting** or **skirting board** noun the narrow board next to the floor round the walls of a room

skit noun a satirical sketch, play or piece of writing

skitter verb 1 skim over a surface 2 move quickly and lightly

skittish adj 1 having a playful or frivolous character 2 easily frightened or startled; jumpy

skittle noun 1 a bottle-shaped object used as a target in bowling 2 (**skittles**) a game in which skittles are knocked over by a ball

skive verb, informal (often with **off**) avoid doing a task or duty • **skiver** noun a shirker

skivvy noun (plural **skivvies**) informal derog a domestic servant, esp a cleaner

skua noun a type of large seagull

skulduggery or US **skullduggery** noun dishonest or underhand behaviour

skulk verb 1 stay hidden 2 move stealthily away; sneak

skull noun 1 the bony case that encloses the brain 2 the head • **skull and crossbones** noun the sign on a pirate's flag • **skullcap** noun a cap that fits closely to the head

skunk noun 1 a small American animal that defends itself by giving off a bad smell 2 a contemptible person

sky noun (plural **skies**) the space above our heads; the upper atmosphere • **sky diving** noun jumping with a parachute as a sport • **skylark** noun the common lark which sings while hovering far overhead • **skylarking** noun mischievous behaviour • **skylight** noun a window in a roof or ceiling • **skyline** noun the horizon • **skyscraper** noun a high building of very many storeys

slab noun a thick flat slice or piece of anything: stone slab/cut a slab of cake

slack adj 1 not firmly stretched 2 not firmly in position 3 not strict 4 lazy and careless 5 not busy: slack holiday season ◇ noun 1 the loose part of a rope 2 a mixture of small pieces of coal and coal-dust 3 (**slacks**) loose, casual trousers ◇ verb 1 do less work than you should; be lazy 2 slacken • **slacken** verb 1 make or become looser 2 make or become less active, less busy or less fast etc

slag noun waste left from metal-smelting ◇ verb (**slagging**, **slagged**) slang criticize fiercely or make fun of cruelly

slain past participle of **slay**

slake verb 1 quench or satisfy (thirst, longing, etc) 2 put out (fire) 3 mix (lime) with water

slalom /slah-lum/ noun **1** a downhill, zigzag ski run among posts or trees **2** an obstacle race in canoes

slam verb (**slamming**, **slammed**) **1** shut (a door, lid, etc) with a loud noise **2** put down with a loud noise ◇ noun **1** the act of slamming **2** (also **grand slam**) a winning of every trick in cards or every contest in a competition etc

slander noun an untrue statement (in England, a spoken one) aimed at harming someone's reputation ◇ verb speak slander against (someone) • **slanderous** adj

slang noun **1** popular words and phrases that are used in informal, everyday speech or writing **2** the special language of a particular group: Cockney slang ◇ verb speak abusively to or about • **slanging match** noun a heated argument in which insults are traded

slant verb **1** slope **2** lie or move diagonally or in a sloping position **3** give or present (facts or information) in a distorted way that suits your own purpose ◇ noun **1** a slope **2** a diagonal direction **3** a point of view

slap noun a blow with the palm of the hand or anything flat ◇ verb (**slapping**, **slapped**) give a slap to • **slapdash** adj hasty and careless • **slapstick** adj involving boisterous physical comedy ◇ noun comedy in this style

slash verb **1** make long cuts in **2** strike at violently ◇ noun (plural **slashes**) **1** a long cut **2** a sweeping blow

slat noun a thin strip of wood, metal or other material • **slatted** adj having slats

slate noun an easily split blue-grey rock, used for roofing and in the past for writing on ◇ adj **1** made of slate **2** slate-coloured ◇ verb **1** cover with slate **2** say or write harsh things to or about: the play was slated

slattern noun, dated derog **1** a dirty and untidy-looking woman **2** a woman who has many casual sexual relationships; a slut

slaughter noun **1** the killing of animals, esp for food **2** cruel killing of great numbers of people ◇ verb **1** kill (an animal) for food **2** kill brutally • **slaughterhouse** noun a place where animals are killed in order to be sold for food

slave noun, hist **1** a person who is owned by someone and forced to work for them **2** someone who serves another devotedly **3** someone who works very hard **4** someone who is addicted to something: a slave to fashion ◇ verb work as or like a slave • **slavery** noun **1** the state of being a slave **2** the system of owning slaves • **slavish** adj thinking or acting exactly according to rules or instructions

slaver noun saliva running from the mouth ◇ verb let saliva run out of the mouth

Slavic adj relating to a group of E European people or their languages, including Russian, Polish, Czech and Bulgarian

slay verb (**slaying**, **slew**, **slain**) formal kill

sleazy adj (**sleazier**, **sleaziest**) **1** considered to operate low moral standards; disreputable **2** dirty and neglected-looking; squalid • **sleaze** or **sleaziness** noun

sled or **sledge** noun a vehicle made for sliding over snow ◇ verb ride on a sledge • **sledgehammer** noun a large, heavy hammer

sleek adj **1** smooth, glossy **2** of an animal: well-fed and well-cared for **3** elegant and well-groomed

sleep verb (**sleeping**, **slept**) rest with your eyes closed in a state of natural unconsciousness • **sleeper** noun **1** someone who sleeps **2** a beam of wood or metal supporting railway lines **3** a sleeping car or sleeping berth on a railway train • **sleeping bag** noun a large warm bag for sleeping in, used by campers *etc* • **sleeping car** *noun* a railway coach with beds or berths • **sleepwalker** *noun* someone who walks *etc* while asleep • **go to sleep 1** pass into the state of being asleep **2** of a limb: become numb • **put to sleep 1** cause to go to sleep **2** put (an animal) to death painlessly, *eg* by an injection of a drug • **sleep with** *informal* have sexual intercourse with

sleepless *adj* during which you have no sleep • **sleeplessly** *adv* • **sleeplessness** *noun*

sleepy *adj* (**sleepier**, **sleepiest**) **1** wanting to sleep; drowsy **2** looking as if needing sleep **3** in which there is very little activity or excitement: *sleepy town* • **sleepily** *adv* • **sleepiness** *noun*

sleet *noun* rain mixed with snow or hail

sleeve *noun* **1** the part of a garment that covers the arm **2** a cover for a record **3** a cover for an arm-like piece of machinery • **sleeveless** *adj* without sleeves

sleigh /sleh/ *noun* a large horse-drawn sledge

sleight-of-hand /slait-uv-*hand*/ *noun* skill and quickness of hand movement in performing card tricks *etc*

slender *adj* **1** thin, narrow **2** attractively slim **3** small in amount: *by a slender margin*

sleuth /slooth/ *noun* someone who tracks down criminals; a detective

slew[1] *verb* (**slewing**, **slewed**) swing round

slew[2] *past tense of* **slay**

slice *noun* **1** a thin, broad piece of something: *slice of toast* **2** a broad-bladed utensil for serving fish *etc* ◇ *verb* **1** cut into slices **2** cut through **3** cut (off from *etc*) **4** *golf* hit (a ball) in such a way that it curves away to the

direction you are facing

slick *adj* **1** clever, often too much so **2** smooth ◇ *noun* a thin layer of spilt oil

slide *verb* (**sliding**, **slid**) **1** move smoothly over a surface **2** slip **3** pass quietly or secretly ◇ *noun* **1** an act of sliding **2** a smooth, slippery slope or track **3** a child's toy for sliding down; a chute **4** a groove or rail on which a thing slides **5** a fastening for the hair **6** a picture for showing on a screen **7** a piece of glass on which to place objects to be examined under a microscope • **slide rule** *noun* an instrument used for calculating, made up of one ruler sliding against another • **sliding scale** *noun* a scale of wages, charges, *etc* which can be changed according to outside conditions

slight *adj* **1** of little amount or importance: *slight breeze/slight quarrel* **2** small or slender ◇ *verb* insult by ignoring ◇ *noun* an insult or offence

slim *adj* **1** attractively thin; slender **2** small, slight: *slim chance* ◇ *verb* (**slimming**, **slimmed**) **1** make slender **2** use means (such as eating less) to become slender

slime *noun* sticky, half-liquid material, *esp* thin, slippery mud • **slimy** *adj* **1** covered with slime **2** oily or greasy

sling *noun* **1** a bandage hanging from the neck or shoulders to support an injured arm **2** a strap with a string attached to each end, for flinging stones **3** a net of ropes *etc* for hoisting and carrying heavy objects ◇ *verb* (**slinging**, **slung**) **1** *informal* throw **2** throw with a sling **3** move or swing by means of a sling

slink *verb* (**slinking**, **slunk**) sneak away, move stealthily

slip *verb* (**slipping**, **slipped**) **1** slide accidentally and lose footing or balance: *slip on the ice* **2** fall out of place or out of your control: *the plate slipped from my grasp* **3** move quickly and easily **4** move quietly, quickly and secretly **5** escape from: *slip your mind* ◇ *noun* **1** the act of slipping **2** a minor mistake **3** a strip or narrow piece of anything (*eg* paper) **4** a slim, slight person: *a slip of a girl* **5** a thin undergarment worn under a dress, an underskirt **6** a cover for a pillow **7** *cricket* a fielding position next to the wicketkeeper **8** a slipway • **slip-knot** *noun* a knot made with a loop so that it can slip • **slipped disc** *noun* displacement of one of the discs between the vertebrae causing severe back pain • **slipper** *noun* a loose indoor shoe • **slippery** *adj* **1** causing skidding or slipping **2** not trustworthy • **slip road** *noun* a road by which vehicles join or leave a motorway • **slipshod** *adj* untidy and careless • **slipstream** *noun* the stream of air driven back by an aircraft propeller *etc* • **slip-up** *noun* a mistake • **slipway** *noun* a smooth slope on which a ship is built • **slip up** make a mistake

slit *verb* (**slitting, slit**) **1** make a long narrow cut in **2** cut into strips ◇ *noun* a long narrow cut or opening

slither *verb* **1** slide or slip about (*eg* on mud) **2** move with a gliding motion • **slithery** *adj* slippery

sliver *noun* a thin strip or slice

slob *noun* a lazy and untidy person

slobber *verb* let saliva dribble from the mouth; slaver

sloe *noun* a small black fruit, often used to flavour gin

slog *verb* (**slogging, slogged**) work or walk on steadily, *esp* with difficulty ◇ *noun* **1** a difficult spell of work **2** a long tiring walk

slogan *noun* an easily remembered and frequently repeated phrase, used in advertising *etc*

sloop *noun* a one-masted sailing ship

slop *verb* (**slopping, slopped**) **1** flow over; spill **2** splash ◇ *noun* **1** spilt liquid **2** (**slops**) dirty water **3** (**slops**) thin, tasteless food • **sloppy** *adj* **1** careless and untidy in a silly way **3** wet and muddy

slope *noun* **1** a position or direction that is neither level nor upright; a slant **2** a surface with one end higher than the other, *eg* a hillside ◇ *verb* be in a slanting, sloping position

slosh *verb* **1** splash noisily or roughly **2** *informal* hit

slot *noun* **1** a small, narrow opening, *eg* to insert coins **2** a position in a schedule *etc* ◇ *verb* (**slotting, slotted**) **1** make a slot in **2** (sometimes with **into**) find a position or place for • **slot machine** *noun* a vending machine worked by putting a coin in a slot

sloth *noun* **1** laziness **2** a slow-moving S American animal that lives in trees • **slothful** *adj* lazy

slouch *noun* a hunched-up body position ◇ *verb* walk with shoulders rounded and head hanging • **no slouch** a skilful or competent person

slough[1] /slow/ *noun* a bog or marsh

slough[2] /sluf/ *noun* the cast-off skin of a snake ◇ *verb* **1** cast off (*eg* a skin) **2** get rid of (*eg* worries) **3** of skin: come (off)

slovenly *adj* untidy, careless or dirty

slow *adj* **1** not fast **2** not hasty or hurrying **3** of a clock: behind in time **4** not quick in learning ◇ *verb* (often with **down**) make or become slower • **slowcoach** *noun* someone who moves, works, *etc* slowly • **slowly** *adv* • **slow-motion** *adj* **1** slower than normal movement **2** of a film: slower than actual motion • **slowness** *noun* • **slow-worm** *noun* a snake-like, legless lizard

sludge *noun* soft, slimy mud

slug *noun* **1** a snail-like animal with no shell **2** a small piece of metal used as a bullet **3** a heavy blow • **sluggard** *noun* someone who has slow and lazy habits • **sluggish** adj moving slowly • **sluggishly** adv

sluice noun **1** a sliding gate for controlling a flow of water in an artificial channel (also called: **sluicegate**) **2** the stream that flows through this ◇ verb clean out with a strong flow of water

slum noun **1** an overcrowded part of a town where the houses are dirty and unhealthy **2** a house in a slum

slumber verb, formal sleep ◇ noun sleep

slump verb **1** fall or sink suddenly and heavily **2** lose value suddenly ◇ noun a sudden fall in values, prices, etc

slung past form of **sling**

slunk past form of **slink**

slur verb (**slurring**, **slurred**) **1** pronounce indistinctly **2** speak or write about in a very negative way ◇ noun **1** a blot or stain (on someone's reputation) **2** a criticism or insult

slurp verb drink noisily ◇ noun a noisy gulp

slurry noun **1** thin, liquid cement **2** liquid waste

slush noun **1** watery mud **2** melting snow **3** something foolishly sentimental **4** silly sentimentality • **slushy** adj **1** covered with slush or like slush **2** sentimental in a silly way

slut noun **1** derog a woman who has many casual sexual relationships **2** dated a dirty, untidy woman • **sluttish** adj

sly adj **1** cunning **2** deceitful • **slyly** adv • **slyness** noun • **on the sly** secretly, surreptitiously

smack verb **1** hit hard with the open hand; slap **2** have a trace or suggestion (of): this smacks of treason ◇ noun **1** an act of smacking **2** the sound made by smacking **3** a noisy kiss **4** a flavour **5** a trace **6** a small fishing vessel ◇ adv with sudden violence: run smack into the door

small adj **1** not big or great; little **2** not important; minor: a small matter **3** not having a large or successful business: a small businessman **4** of a voice: soft ◇ noun the most slender or narrow part: the small of the back ◇ adv into small pieces: cut up small • **small arms** plural noun weapons that can be carried easily by one person • **small beer** noun something trivial or unimportant • **small hours** plural noun the hours just after midnight • **smallminded** adj having narrow opinions or attitudes; petty • **smallpox** noun a serious infectious illness causing a rash of large pimples (**pocks**) • **small talk** noun polite conversation about nothing very important

smarmy adj (**smarmier**, **smarmiest**) charming in a very insincere way

smart adj **1** clever and quick in thought or action; intelligent **2** well-dressed **3** brisk **4** sharp, stinging ◇ noun a sharp, stinging pain ◇ verb **1** feel a sharp, stinging pain **2** feel annoyed, resentful, etc after being insulted • **smart card** noun a plastic card that can store and transmit information • **smarten** verb (also **smarten up**) to make or become smarter

smash verb **1** break into pieces; shatter **2** strike with force: smash a ball with a racket **3** crash (into etc): the car smashed into the wall ◇ noun (plural **smashes**) **1** an act of smashing **2** a collision of vehicles; a crash **3** the ruin of a business etc • **smashed** adj, slang drunk

smattering noun a very slight knowledge of a subject

smear verb **1** spread (something sticky or oily) **2** smudge with (something sticky etc) **3** become smeared **4** say or write very negative or insulting things about ◇ noun a smudge of something sticky • **smear campaign** noun a deliberate attempt to ruin a reputation • **smear test** noun the taking of a sample of cells from a woman's cervix for examination

smell noun **1** the sense or power of being aware of things through your nose **2** an act of using this sense **3** something sensed through the nose; a scent ◇ verb (**smelling, smelt** or **smelled**) **1** notice by the sense of smell: *I smell gas* **2** use your sense of smell on: *smell this fish* **3** give off a particular smell: *this room smells lovely* **4** give off an unpleasant smell: *your feet smell* • **smelling salts** plural noun strong-smelling chemicals in a bottle, used to revive fainting people • **smelly** adj having a bad smell • **smell out** find out by prying or inquiring closely

smelt[1] verb **1** melt (ore) in order to separate the metal from other material **2** past form of **smell**

smelt[2] noun a fish related to the salmon

smile verb **1** show pleasure by drawing up the corners of the lips **2** (sometimes with **on**) be favourable to: *fortune smiled on him* ◇ noun an act of smiling • **smiley** noun a stylized representation of a smiling face, eg the emoticon :-)

smirch verb make dirty; stain ◇ noun a stain

smirk verb smile in a self-satisfied or foolish manner ◇ noun a self-satisfied or foolish smile

smite verb (**smiting, smote, smitten**) old hit hard • **smitten with** strongly attracted by

smith noun a worker in metals; a blacksmith • **smithy** noun the workshop of a smith

smithereens plural noun fragments

smitten see smite

smock noun a loose shirt-like garment, sometimes worn over other clothes as a protection

smog noun thick, smoky fog

smoke noun **1** the cloud-like gases and particles of soot given off by anything burning **2** an act of smoking (a cigarette etc) ◇ verb **1** give off smoke **2** inhale and exhale tobacco smoke from a cigarette, pipe, etc **3** cure or preserve (ham, fish, etc) by applying smoke **4** darken (eg glass) by applying smoke • **smokeless** adj **1** burning without smoke **2** where the emission of smoke is prohibited: *a smokeless zone* • **smoker** noun **1** someone who smokes tobacco **2** a railway compartment in which smoking is allowed • **smokescreen** noun anything (orig smoke) meant to confuse or mislead • **smoky** adj **1** full of smoke **2** tasting of smoke

smolt noun a young salmon

smooch verb, informal kiss and cuddle; pet

smooth adj **1** not rough **2** having an even surface **3** without lumps: *a smooth sauce* **4** hairless **5** without breaks, stops or jolts: *smooth journey* **6** too agreeable in manner ◇ verb **1** make smooth **2** calm, soothe **3** free from difficulty

smorgasbord noun a selection of Swedish savoury foods eaten as a starter or appetiser

smote past tense of smite

smother verb **1** kill by keeping air from, eg by covering over the nose and mouth **2** die by this means **3** conceal or repress (feelings etc) **4** put an end to (a rebellion etc)

smoulder verb **1** burn slowly without bursting into flame **2** exist in a hidden state **3** show otherwise hidden emotion, eg anger, hate: *her eyes smouldered with hate*

smudge noun a smear ◇ verb make dirty with spots or smears

smug adj too obviously pleased with yourself

smuggle verb **1** take (goods) into, or

out of, a country without paying the required taxes **2** send or take secretly • **smuggler** *noun* someone who smuggles goods

smut *noun* **1** a spot of dirt or soot **2** vulgar or indecent talk *etc* • **smutty** *adj* **1** indecent or vulgar **2** very dirty; grimy

snack *noun* a light, hasty meal

snaffle *verb, slang* steal

snag *noun* a difficulty, an obstacle ◇ *verb* (**snagging, snagged**) catch or tear on something sharp

snail *noun* **1** a soft-bodied, small, crawling animal with a shell **2** someone who is very slow • **snail mail** *noun, informal* the ordinary postal service, as distinct from electronic mail

snake *noun* **1** a legless reptile with a long body that moves along the ground with a winding movement **2** anything snake-like in form or movement **3** a deceitful or treacherous person

snap *verb* (**snapping, snapped**) **1** make a sudden bite **2** (with **up**) eat up, or grab, eagerly **3** break or shut suddenly with a sharp noise **4** cause (the fingers) to make a sharp noise **5** speak sharply **6** take a photograph of ◇ *noun* **1** the noise made by snapping **2** a sudden spell (*eg* of cold weather) **3** a card game in which players try to spot matching cards **4** a photograph • **snapdragon** *noun* a garden plant whose flower, when pinched, opens and shuts like a mouth • **snapshot** *noun* a quickly taken photograph

snappy *adj* (**snappier, snappiest**) inclined to speak sharply; irritable • **snappily** *adv*

snare *noun* **1** a noose or loop that draws tight when pulled, for catching an animal **2** a trap **3** a hidden danger or temptation ◇ *verb* catch in or with a snare

snarl *verb* **1** growl, showing the teeth **2** speak in a furious, spiteful tone **3** become tangled ◇ *noun* **1** a growl, a furious noise **2** a tangle, a knot **3** a muddled or confused state

snatch *verb* **1** seize or grab suddenly **2** take quickly when you have time: *snatch an hour's sleep* ◇ *noun* (*plural* **snatches**) **1** an attempt to seize **2** a small piece or quantity: *a snatch of music*

snazzy *adj* (**snazzier, snazziest**) *informal* smart and stylish

sneak *verb* **1** creep or move in a stealthy, secretive way **2** tell on others ◇ *noun* **1** someone who tells tales **2** a deceitful, underhand person

sneaky *adj* (**sneakier, sneakiest**) done or acting in a dishonest or unfair way; underhand • **sneakily** *adv*

sneer *verb* show contempt by a scornful expression, words, *etc* ◇ *noun* a scornful expression or remark

sneeze *verb* make a sudden, unintentional and violent blowing noise through the nose and mouth ◇ *noun* an involuntary blow through the nose

snicker *verb* **1** snigger **2** of a horse: neigh

snide *adj* expressing dislike or criticism maliciously: *snide remark*

sniff *verb* **1** draw in air through the nose with a slight noise, *eg* when having a cold, or showing disapproval **2** smell (a scent *etc*) **3** (with **at**) treat with scorn or suspicion ◇ *noun* a quick drawing in of air through the nose

sniffle *noun* a light sniff; a snuffle ◇ *verb* sniff lightly

snifter *noun* **1** *informal* a short drink **2** a bulbous glass for drinking brandy *etc*

snigger *verb* laugh in a quiet, sly manner ◇ *noun* a quiet, sly laugh

snip *verb* (**snipping, snipped**) cut off

sharply, *esp* with a single cut ◇ *noun* **1** a cut with scissors **2** a small piece snipped off **3** *informal* a bargain: *a snip at the price*

snipe *noun* a bird with a long straight beak, found in marshy places ◇ *verb* **1** (with **at**) shoot at from a place of hiding **2** (with **at**) attack with critical remarks ● **sniper** *noun* someone who shoots at a single person from cover

snippet *noun* a little piece, *esp* of information or gossip

snitch *noun, informal* an informer; a tell-tale ◇ *verb* inform (on)

snivel *verb* (**snivelling, snivelled**) **1** have a running nose, *eg* because of a cold **2** whine or complain tearfully ◇ *noun* **1** a running nose **2** a whine

snob *noun* someone who looks down on people who are less educated or in a lower social class ● **snobbery** *noun* ● **snobbish** *adj* ● **snobbishness** *noun*

snog *verb* (**snogging, snogged**) *slang* kiss and cuddle; pet

snood *noun* a hood

snooker *noun* a game like billiards in which coloured balls are potted in order

snoop *verb* spy or pry in a sneaking secretive way ◇ *noun* someone who pries

snooty *adj* (**snootier, snootiest**) having a superior or condescending attitude; haughty

snooze *verb* sleep lightly; doze ◇ *noun* a light sleep

snore *verb* make a snorting noise in your sleep while breathing ◇ *noun* a snorting sound made in sleep

snorkel *noun* **1** a tube with one end above the water worn in the mouth to enable an underwater swimmer to breathe **2** a similar device for bringing air into a submarine

snort *verb* **1** force air noisily through the nostrils **2** make such a noise to express disapproval, anger, laughter, *etc* ◇ *noun* a loud noise made through the nostrils

snot *noun* mucus of the nose ● **snotty** *adj* supercilious

snout *noun* the projecting nose and mouth of an animal, *eg* of a pig

snow *noun* frozen water vapour that falls in light white flakes ◇ *verb* fall down in, or like, flakes of snow ● **snow blindness** *noun* dimness of sight caused by the brightness of light reflected from the snow ● **snowboard** *noun* a single board used like a ski on snow ● **snowdrift** *noun* a bank of snow blown together by the wind ● **snowdrop** *noun* a small white flower growing from a bulb in early spring ● **snowflake** *noun* a flake of snow ● **snowline** *noun* the height up a mountain above which there is always snow ● **snowman** *noun* a figure shaped like a human being, made of snow ● **snowplough** *noun* a large vehicle for clearing snow from roads *etc* ● **snowshoe** *noun* a long broad frame with a mesh, one of a pair for walking on top of snow ● **snowy** *adj* **1** covered with snow **2** perfectly white **3** pure, *esp* morally so ● **snowed under** overwhelmed

snowball *noun* a ball made of snow pressed hard together ◇ *verb* **1** throw snowballs **2** grow increasingly quickly: *unemployment has snowballed*

SNP *abbrev* Scottish National Party

snub *verb* (**snubbing, snubbed**) treat scornfully or insultingly, *esp* by ignoring ◇ *noun* an act of snubbing ◇ *adj* of a nose: short and turned up at the end

snuff *verb* put out or trim the wick of (a candle) ◇ *noun* powdered tobacco for drawing up into the nose ● **snuffbox** *noun* a box for holding snuff ● **snuff movie** *noun* an illegal film showing torture and the deliberate killing of those acting in it

snuffle *verb* make a sniffing noise through the nose, *eg* because of a cold ◇ *noun* a sniffling through the nose

snug *adj* **1** lying close and warm **2** cosy and comfortable **3** closely fitting • **snuggle** *verb* **1** curl up comfortably **2** draw close to for warmth, affection, *etc*

so *adv* **1** as shown, *eg* by a hand gesture: *so high* **2** to such an extent, to a great extent: *so heavy/you look so happy* **3** in this or that way: *point your toes so* **4** correct: *is that so?* **5** (used in contradicting) indeed: *It's not true. It is so* ◇ *conj* therefore: *you don't need it, so don't buy it* • **so-and-so** *noun, informal* **1** this or that person or thing **2** used instead of a stronger insult: *she's a real so-and-so, saying that to you!* • **so-called** *adj* called by such a name, often mistakenly: *a so-called expert* • **so-so** *adj* not particularly good • **so as to** in order to • **so far** up to this or that point • **so forth** more of the same sort of thing: *pots, pans and so forth* • **so much for** that is the end of: *so much for that idea!* • **so that** with the purpose or result that • **so what?** what difference does it make? does it matter?

soak *verb* **1** let stand in a liquid until wet through **2** drench (with) **3** (with **up**) suck up; absorb • **soaking** *adj* wet through ◇ *noun* an instance of becoming very wet or making something very wet; a, drenching • **soaking wet** *adj* thoroughly wet; drenched

soap *noun* **1** a mixture containing oils or fats and other substances, used in washing **2** *informal* a soap opera • *verb* use soap on • **soapbox** *noun* **1** a small box for holding soap **2** a makeshift platform for standing on when speaking to a crowd out of doors • **soap opera** *noun* a television series about a group of characters and their daily lives • **soapsuds** *plural noun* soapy water worked into a froth

• **soapy** *adj* **1** like soap **2** full of soap

soar *verb* **1** fly high into the air **2** of prices, levels, *etc*: rise high and quickly

sob *verb* (**sobbing, sobbed**) weep noisily ◇ *noun* a noisy weeping • **sob story** *noun* a story told to arouse sympathy

sober *adj* **1** not drunk **2** of a rather serious character; staid **3** not elaborate; plain ◇ *verb* (sometimes with **up**) make or become sober • **soberly** *adv* • **soberness** or **sobriety** *noun* the state of being sober

sobriquet /so-bri-keh/ *noun* a nickname

Soc *abbrev* Society

soccer *noun* football

sociable *adj* fond of the company of others; friendly • **sociability** or **sociableness** *noun*

social *adj* **1** relating to society or to a community: *social history* **2** living in communities: *social insects* **3** of companionship: *social gathering* **4** of rank or level in society: *social class* • **socialite** *noun* someone who mixes with people of high social status • **socialize** *verb* to meet with people informally • **social security** *noun* the system, paid for by taxes, of providing insurance against old age, illness, unemployment, *etc* • **social work** *noun* work that deals with the care of the people in a community, *esp* of the poor or underprivileged • **social worker** *noun*

socialism *noun* the belief that a country's wealth should belong to the people as a whole, not to private owners • **socialist** *noun & adj*

society *noun* **1** humanity considered as a whole **2** a community of people **3** a social club; an association **4** the class of people who are wealthy, fashionable, *etc* **5** company or companionship: *I enjoy his society*

sociology noun the study of human society • **sociological** adj • **sociologist** noun

sociopath noun a person with a personality disorder that causes very antisocial behaviour

sock noun a short stocking

socket noun a hollow into which something is fitted: an electric socket

sod¹ noun a piece of earth with grass growing on it; a turf

sod² noun, Brit slang an obnoxious person • **Sod's law** noun the law that the most inconvenient thing is the most likely to happen • **sod off** go away

soda noun 1 the name of several substances formed from sodium 2 soda water • **soda water** noun water through which gas has been passed, making it fizzy • **baking soda** sodium bicarbonate, a powder used as a raising agent in baking

sodden adj soaked through and through

sodium noun a metallic element from which many substances are formed, including common salt

sodomy noun anal intercourse • **sodomite** noun

sofa noun a kind of long upholstered seat with back and arms • **sofa bed** noun a sofa incorporating a fold-away bed

soft adj 1 easily put out of shape when pressed 2 not hard or firm 3 not loud 4 of a colour: not bright or glaring 5 not strict enough 6 lacking strength, courage or determination 7 lacking common sense 8 of a drink: not alcoholic 9 of water: containing little calcium etc ◊ adv gently or quietly • **soften** verb make or grow soft • **soft-hearted** adj kind and generous • **software** noun, comput programs etc as opposed to the machines (contrasted with: **hardware**) • **softwood** noun the wood of a cone-bearing tree (eg fir, larch)

soggy adj (**soggier**, **soggiest**) 1 soaked 2 soft and wet

soi-disant /swa-deez-onh/ adj as is claimed to be; would-be

soil noun 1 the upper layer of the earth in which plants grow 2 loose earth; dirt ◊ verb make dirty

soirée /swah-reh/ noun an evening get-together

sojourn /so-jurn/ noun a short stay ◊ verb stay for a time

solace noun something that makes pain or sorrow easier to bear; comfort ◊ verb comfort

solar adj 1 relating to the sun 2 influenced by the sun 3 powered by energy from the sun's rays • **solar system** noun the sun with the planets (including the earth) going round it

sold past form of **sell**

solder noun melted metal used for joining metal surfaces ◊ verb join (with solder) • **soldering iron** noun an electric tool for soldering joints

soldier noun someone in military service, esp someone who is not an officer

sole¹ noun 1 the underside of the foot 2 the underside of a shoe etc ◊ verb put a sole on (a shoe etc)

sole² adj 1 only: the sole survivor 2 belonging to one person or group only: the sole right • **solely** adv only, alone

sole³ noun a small type of flat fish

solecism noun 1 grammar a mistake in speech or writing 2 a breach of good manners • **solecistic** or **solecistical** adj

solemn adj 1 serious, earnest 2 of an occasion: celebrated with special ceremonies • **solemnity** noun • **solemnize** verb carry out (a wedding etc) with religious ceremonies

sol-fa noun, music a system of syllables (do, ray, me, etc) to be sung to the notes of a scale

solicit verb 1 ask earnestly for: solicit advice 2 ask (someone for something) 3 offer yourself as a prostitute • **solicitude** noun care or anxiety about someone or something

solicitor noun a lawyer who advises people about legal matters

solicitous adj 1 considerate or careful, esp in looking after someone 2 anxious • **solicitously** adv

solid adj 1 fixed in shape, not in the form of gas or liquid 2 in three dimensions, with length, breadth and height 3 not hollow 4 firm, strongly made 5 made or formed completely of one substance: solid silver 6 reliable, sound: solid business 7 informal without a break: three solid hours' work ◇ noun 1 a substance that is solid 2 a shape that has three dimensions • **solidarity** noun unity of interests etc • **solidity** noun the state of being solid

solidify verb (**solidifies, solidifying, solidified**) make or become firm or solid

solidus noun a slanting stroke; a slash (/)

soliloquy /suh-*lil*-uh-kwi/ noun (plural **soliloquies**) a speech made by an actor etc to themselves • **soliloquize** verb speak to yourself, esp on the stage

solipsism /*sol*-ip-sizm/ noun the belief that nothing is knowable except the self • **solipsistic** adj

solitaire noun a card-game for one player (also called: **patience**)

solitary adj 1 lone, alone 2 single: not a solitary crumb remained

solitude noun the state of being alone; lack of company

solo noun (plural **solos**) a musical piece for one singer or player ◇ adj performed by one person alone: solo flight • **soloist** noun someone who plays or sings a solo

solstice noun the time of longest daylight (**summer solstice** about 21 June in N hemisphere) or longest darkness (**winter solstice** about 21 December in N hemisphere)

soluble adj 1 able to be dissolved or made liquid 2 of a problem etc: able to be solved • **solubility** noun

solution noun 1 a liquid with something dissolved in it 2 the act of solving a problem etc 3 an answer to a problem, puzzle, etc

solve verb 1 clear up or explain (a mystery) 2 discover the answer or solution to

solvency noun the state of being able to pay all debts • **solvent** adj able to pay all debts ◇ noun anything that dissolves another substance

somatic adj relating to sleep

sombre /*som*-buh/ adj gloomy, dark, dismal

sombrero noun (plural **sombreros**) a broad-brimmed Mexican hat

some adj 1 several 2 a few: some oranges, but not many 3 a little: some bread, but not much 4 certain: some people are rich ◇ pronoun 1 a number or part out of a quantity: please try some 2 certain people: some won't be happy • **somehow** adv in some way or other • **sometime** adv at a time not known or stated definitely • **sometimes** adv at times, now and then • **somewhat** adv rather: somewhat boring • **somewhere** adv in some place

somebody or **someone** noun 1 an unknown or unnamed person: somebody I'd never seen before 2 an important person: he really is somebody now

somersault noun a forward or backward roll in which the heels go over the head ◇ *verb* perform a somersault

something *pronoun* **1** a thing not known or not stated **2** a thing of importance **3** a slight amount; a degree: *he has something of his father's looks*

somnambulist *noun* a sleepwalker

somnolence *noun* sleepiness • **somnolent** *adj* sleepy or causing sleepiness

son *noun* a male child • **son-in-law** *noun* a daughter's husband

sonata /suh-*nah*-tuh/ *noun* a piece of classical music with three or more movements, usually for one instrument

son et lumière /son eh loom-*yair*/ *noun* a display of lights and sound effects, often describing a historical event

song *noun* **1** a piece of music to be sung **2** singing • **songbird** *noun* a bird with a complex and tuneful call • **songster, songstress** *nouns, old* a singer • **for a song** (bought, sold, *etc*) very cheaply

sonic *adj* of sound waves • **sonic boom** *noun* an explosive sound that can be heard when an aircraft reaches then exceeds the speed of sound

sonnet *noun* a type of poem in fourteen lines

sonorous *adj* impressively loud and deep or clear • **sonority** *noun*

soon *adv* **1** in a short time from now or from the time mentioned: *he will come soon* **2** early: *too soon to tell* **3** (with **as**) as readily, as willingly: *I would as soon stand as sit* • **sooner** *adv* more willingly; rather: *I would sooner stand than sit* • **sooner or later** at some time in the future

soot *noun* the black powder left by smoke • **sooty** *adj* like, or covered with, soot

soothe *verb* **1** calm or comfort (a

person, feelings, *etc*) **2** help or ease (a pain *etc*) • **soothing** *adj*

soothsayer *noun* someone who predicts the future

sop *noun* **1** something done or given to pacify someone **2** bread dipped in soup *etc* ◇ *verb* soak (up) • **sopping** *adj* wet through

sophism *noun* a convincing but false argument or explanation intended to deceive • **sophist** *noun* • **sophistic** *adj*

sophisticated *adj* **1** of a person: living an elegant, cultured life **2** highly developed, complicated or elaborate

sophomore *noun, US* a second-year college student

soporific *adj* causing sleep ◇ *noun* something that causes sleep

soppy *adj* (**soppier, soppiest**) sentimental in a silly way

soprano *noun* (*plural* **sopranos**) **1** a woman's or boy's singing voice of the highest pitch **2** a singer with this voice

sorbet *noun* a dessert of fruit-flavoured, smoothly crushed ice

sorcerer, sorceress *noun* someone who works magic spells; a witch or wizard • **sorcery** *noun* magic, witchcraft

sordid *adj* **1** disgusting because morally bad or wrong **2** revoltingly dirty; filthy

sore *adj* painful ◇ *noun* a painful, inflamed spot on the skin • **sorely** *adv* very greatly: *sorely in need* • **soreness** *noun*

sorghum /*saw*-gum/ *noun* a grass similar to sugar cane

sorority *noun* (*plural* **sororities**) a society of female students (*compare with*: **fraternity**)

sorrel *noun* a type of plant with sour-tasting leaves

sorrow *noun* sadness caused by a loss, disappointment, *etc* ◊ *verb* be sad • **sorrowful** *adj*

sorry *adj* (**sorrier, sorriest**) **1** feeling regret for something you have done: *I'm sorry I mentioned it* **2** feeling sympathy or pity (for): *sorry for you* **3** miserable: *in a sorry state*

sort *noun* a kind of (person or thing): *the sort of sweets I like* ◊ *verb* separate things, putting each in its place: *sort letters* • **a sort of** used of something that is like something else, but not exactly: *he wore a sort of crown* • **of a sort** *or* **of sorts** of a kind, usually not very good: *a party of sorts* • **out of sorts** not feeling very well

sortie *noun* **1** a single flight by a military aircraft **2** a sudden attack made by the defenders of a place on those who are trying to capture it

SOS *noun* **1** a code signal calling for help **2** any call for help

sot *noun, dated* a drunkard • **sottish** *adj* stupid with drink

sotto voce /sot-oh vo-cheh/ *adv* in a low voice, so as not to be overheard

soufflé /soo-fleh/ *noun* a light sweet or savoury dish made of baked whisked egg

sough /sow/ *verb* of the wind: make a sighing sound

sought *past form of* **seek**

soul *noun* **1** the part of someone that is not the body; the spirit **2** a person: *a dear old soul* **3** someone who is a perfect example (of): *the soul of kindness* • **soulful** *adj* full of feeling • **soulless** *adj* **1** having no emotional sensitivity **2** lacking interest or atmosphere

sound *noun* **1** anything that can be heard; a noise **2** a distance from which something may be heard: *within the sound of Bow Bells* **3** a narrow stretch of water ◊ *verb* **1** strike you as being: *that sounds awful* **2** (with **like**) resemble in sound: *that sounds like Henry's voice* **3** make a noise with: *sound a horn* **4** examine by listening carefully to: *sound a patient's chest* **5** measure (the depths of water) **6** (with **out**) try to find out someone's opinions: *I'll sound him out tomorrow* ◊ *adj* **1** healthy, strong **2** of sleep: deep **3** thorough: *a sound beating* **4** reliable: *sound opinions* • **soundproof** *adj* built or made so that sound cannot pass in or out ◊ *verb* make soundproof • **soundtrack** *noun* **1** the music or songs from a film **2** the strip on a film where the speech and music are recorded

soup *noun* a liquid food made by heating meat or vegetables in water or stock

soupçon /soop-sonh/ *noun* the slightest amount; a hint

sour *adj* **1** having an acid or bitter taste, often as a stage in going bad: *sour milk* **2** bad-tempered ◊ *verb* make sour

source *noun* **1** the place where something has its beginning or is found **2** a spring, *esp* one from which a river flows

souse *verb* soak (*eg* herrings) in salted water

south *noun* the direction to the right of someone facing the rising sun, one of the four main points of the compass ◊ *adj* **1** of or in the south **2** of the wind: from the south ◊ *adv* in or towards the south • **south-east** *noun* the point of the compass midway between south and east ◊ *adj* in the south-east or south-west • **southerly** *adj* **1** of the wind: coming from or facing the south **2** in or towards the south • **southern** *adj* of the south • **south pole** *see* **pole** • **southward** *or* **southwards** *adj & adv* towards the south • **south-west** *noun* the point of the compass midway between south and west • **sou'wester** *noun* a kind of wide-brimmed waterproof hat sometimes worn by fishermen

souvenir *noun* something bought or given as a reminder of a person, place or occasion

sovereign *noun* **1** a king or queen **2** *hist* a British gold coin worth £1 ◇ *adj* **1** having its own government: *sovereign state* **2** supreme, highest: *sovereign lord* • **sovereignty** *noun* independent political power, or a state with such power

sow[1] /sow/ *noun* a female pig

sow[2] /soh/ *verb* (**sowing, sowed, sown** *or* **sowed**) **1** scatter (seeds) so that they may grow **2** cover (an area) with seeds • **sower** *noun*

soya bean *or* **soy bean** *noun* a kind of bean, rich in protein, used as an ingredient in many foods

soy sauce *noun* a sauce made from soya beans, used in Chinese cooking

spa *noun* a place where people go to drink or bathe in the water from a natural spring

space *noun* **1** an empty place; a gap **2** the distance between objects **3** the empty region in which all stars, planets, *etc* are situated **4** an uncovered part on a sheet of paper **5** length of time: *in the space of a day* ◇ *verb* put things apart from each other, leaving room between them • **spacecraft** *noun* a vehicle for travelling in space • **spaceman, spacewoman** *noun*, *dated* a traveller in space; an astronaut • **spaceship** *noun* a manned spacecraft

spacious *adj* having plenty of room • **spaciousness** *noun*

spade *noun* **1** a tool with a long handle and a broad blade for digging in the earth **2** one of the four suits of playing cards • **call a spade a spade** say plainly and clearly what you mean

spaghetti *noun* pasta in the form of long strands

spake *verb*, *old* spoke

spam *noun* electronic junk mail ◇ *verb* send out unsolicited electronic messages *esp* advertising

span *noun* **1** the full time anything lasts **2** an arch of a bridge **3** an old measure of length that is distance between the tips of the little finger and the thumb when the hand is spread out (about 23 centimetres, 9 inches) ◇ *verb* (**spanning, spanned**) stretch across: *the bridge spans the river*

spangle *noun* a thin sparkling piece of metal used as an ornament ◇ *verb* sprinkle with spangles *etc*

spaniel *noun* a breed of dog with large, hanging ears

spank *verb* strike with the flat of the hand, *esp* as a punishment ◇ *noun* a slap with the hand, *esp* on the buttocks • **spanking** *noun* a beating with the hand, *esp* as a punishment ◇ *adj*, *dated* fast: *a spanking pace*

spanner *noun* a tool for gripping and turning nuts, bolts, *etc*

spar *noun* a long piece of wood or metal used as a ship's mast ◇ *verb* (**sparring, sparred**) **1** fight for practice, *esp* in boxing **2** have a lively argument

spare *adj* **1** kept for use when needed: *spare tyre* **2** with a lean body: *spare but strong* ◇ *verb* **1** do without: *I can't spare you today* **2** afford, set aside: *I can't spare the time to do it* **3** avoid causing (trouble *etc*) to **4** treat with mercy ◇ *noun* another of the same kind (eg a tyre, part of a machine) kept for emergencies • **sparing** *adj* careful, economical • **to spare** over and above what is needed

spark *noun* **1** a small red-hot part thrown off from something burning **2** a trace: *a spark of humanity* **3** a lively person ◇ *verb* make sparks • **spark-plug** *or* **sparking plug** *noun* a device in a car engine that produces a spark to ignite the gases that drive the pistons and keep the engine running

sparkle noun 1 a little spark 2 brightness or liveliness ◇ verb 1 shine in a glittering way 2 be lively or witty 3 bubble • **sparkling** adj 1 glittering 2 of a drink: bubbling, fizzy 3 witty

sparrow noun a type of small dull-coloured bird • **sparrowhawk** noun a type of short-winged hawk

sparse adj 1 not much or not enough 2 thinly scattered

spartan adj of conditions etc: hard, without luxury

spasm noun 1 a sudden involuntary jerk of the muscles 2 a strong, short burst (eg of anger, work) • **spasmodic** adj 1 occurring in spasms 2 coming now and again, not regularly • **spasmodically** adv

spastic adj suffering from brain damage that has resulted in extreme muscle spasm and paralysis

spat past form of **spit**

spate noun 1 a sudden rush: a spate of new books 2 flood: the river is in spate

spatial adj of or relating to space • **spatially** adv

spats plural noun short gaiters reaching just above the ankle

spatter verb splash (eg with mud)

spatula /spach-uh-luh/ noun a kitchen tool with a broad blunt blade, used for lifting food

spawn noun a mass of eggs of fish, frogs, etc ◇ verb 1 of fish etc: lay eggs 2 cause, produce

spay verb remove the ovaries of (a female animal)

speak verb (**speaking, spoke, spoken**) 1 say words; talk 2 hold a conversation (with) 3 make a speech 4 be able to talk (a certain language) • **speak your mind** give your opinion openly • **speak up** 1 speak more loudly or clearly 2 give your opinion openly

spear noun 1 a long weapon with an iron or steel point, made for throwing or jabbing 2 a long pointed shoot or leaf (esp of grass) ◇ verb pierce with a spear • **spear side** noun the male side or line of descent (contrasted with: **distaff side**)

special adj 1 not ordinary; exceptional: special occasion/special friend 2 put on for a particular purpose: special train 3 belonging to one person or thing and not to others: special skills/a special tool for drilling holes in tiles • **specialist** noun someone who studies one branch of a subject or field: heart specialist • **speciality** noun something for which a person, place, etc is well-known • **specialization** noun • **specialize** verb work in, or study, a particular job, subject, etc • **specialized** adj of knowledge: obtained by specializing • **specially** adv for a special purpose: made this cake specially for you • **specialty** noun a branch of work in which someone specializes

Do not confuse: **specially** and **especially**

species noun (plural **species**) 1 a group of plants or animals that are alike in most ways, divided into varieties or breeds 2 a kind (of anything) • **specie** /spee-shi/ noun gold and silver coins

specific adj giving all the details clearly; particular, exactly stated: a specific purpose • **specifically** adv • **specification** noun 1 the act of specifying 2 a full description of details (eg in a plan or contract)

specify verb (**specifies, specifying, specified**) 1 set down or say clearly (what is wanted) 2 make particular mention of

specimen noun something used as a sample of a group or kind of anything, esp for study or for putting in a collection

specious /spee-shus/ adj looking or seeming good but really not so good

speck noun 1 a small spot 2 a tiny piece (eg of dust) • **speckle** noun a spot on a different-coloured background • **speckled** adj dotted with speckles

spectacle noun 1 a striking or wonderful sight 2 (**spectacles**) glasses that someone wears to improve eyesight

spectacular adj making a great show or display; impressive • **spectacularly** adv

spectator noun someone who watches (an event eg a football match)

spectre noun a ghost • **spectral** adj ghostly

spectrum noun (plural **spectra** or **spectrums**) 1 the band of colours as seen in a rainbow, sometimes formed when light passes through water or glass 2 the range or extent of anything

speculate verb 1 guess 2 wonder (about) 3 buy goods, shares, etc in order to sell them again at a profit • **speculation** noun • **speculative** adj speculating • **speculator** noun

speculum noun an instrument inserted in a woman's vagina to help a doctor view her cervix etc

sped past form of **speed**

speech noun 1 the power of making sounds that have meaning for other people 2 a way of speaking: his speech is always clear 3 (plural **speeches**) a (formal) talk given to an audience • **speech day** noun the day at the end of a school year when speeches are made and prizes given out • **speechless** adj so surprised, shocked, etc that you cannot speak

speed noun 1 quickness of, or rate of, movement or action 2 slang amphetamine ◇ verb (**speeding**, **sped** or **speeded**) 1 (past **sped**) (cause to) move along quickly; hurry 2 (past **speeded**) drive very fast in a vehicle, esp faster than is allowed by law • **speed camera** or **speedcam** noun a camera beside a road designed to identify speeding drivers • **speeding** noun driving at an illegally high speed • **speed limit** noun the greatest speed permitted on a particular road • **speedometer** noun an instrument in a vehicle that shows how fast you are travelling • **speedway** noun the sport of riding round a dirt track on a lightweight motorcycle • **speedy** adj going quickly

speedwell noun a type of small plant with blue flowers

speleologist noun someone who studies or explores caves • **speleology** noun

spell noun 1 words which, when spoken, are supposed to have magic power 2 magic or other powerful influence 3 a (short) space of time 4 a turn (at work, rest, play, etc) ◇ verb (**spelling**, **spelt** or **spelled**) 1 give or write correctly the letters that make up a word 2 be a sign of; signify: this defeat spells disaster for us all • **spellbound** adj extremely impressed by something or giving all your attention to it; captivated • **spelling** noun 1 the ability to spell words 2 the study of spelling words correctly • **spell out** say (something) very frankly or clearly

spelt see **spell**

spelunking noun exploring in caves as a hobby

spend verb (**spending**, **spent**) 1 use (money) for buying 2 use (energy etc) 3 pass (time): I spent a week there 4 use up energy or force: the storm spent itself and the sun shone • **spendthrift** noun someone who spends money freely and carelessly • **spent** adj having lost force or power; exhausted: a spent bullet

sperm *noun* **1** the male sex-cell that fertilizes the female egg **2** the liquid that carries these cells; semen • **spermatozoon** *noun* (plural **spermatozoa**) a male sex cell contained in sperm • **sperm bank** *noun* a store of semen for use in artificial insemination • **spermicide** *noun* a substance that kills spermatozoa • **sperm whale** *noun* a kind of whale from the head of which a waxy substance called **spermaceti** is obtained

spew *verb* vomit

sphagnum *noun* a kind of moss

sphere *noun* **1** a ball or similar perfectly round object **2** a position or level in society: *he moves in the highest spheres* **3** range (of influence or action) • **spherical** *adj* having the shape of a sphere

sphincter *noun* a ringlike muscle that narrows an opening, *esp* such a muscle at the anus

Sphinx *noun* **1** a mythological monster with the head of a woman and the body of a lioness **2** the large stone model of the Sphinx in Egypt **3** (**sphinx**) someone whose real thoughts you cannot guess

spice *noun* **1** any substance used for flavouring, *eg* pepper, nutmeg **2** anything that adds liveliness or interest ◇ *verb* flavour with spice

spick-and-span *adj* neat, clean and tidy

spicy *adj* (**spicier**, **spiciest**) **1** full of spices **2** lively and sometimes slightly indecent: *a spicy tale* • **spiciness** *noun*

spider *noun* an insect-like creature with eight legs that spins a web • **spidery** *adj* **1** like a spider **2** of handwriting: having fine, sprawling strokes

spiel /speel/ or /shpeel/ *noun, informal* a long or often repeated story or speech

spigot *noun* **1** a peg for sealing a hole **2** *US* a tap

spike *noun* **1** a pointed piece of wood, metal, *etc* **2** a type of large nail **3** an ear of corn **4** a head of flowers **5** a potentially damaging surge of current in an electric circuit ◇ *verb* **1** pierce with a spike **2** make useless **3** *informal* add an alcoholic drink *esp* to a soft drink • **spiked** *adj* having spikes (*esp* of shoes for running) • **spiky** *adj* having spikes or a sharp point

spill *verb* (**spilling**, **spilt** or **spilled**) run out or overflow, or allow liquid to run out or overflow ◇ *noun* **1** a fall **2** a thin strip of wood or twisted paper for lighting a candle, a pipe, *etc* • **spillage** *noun* an act of spilling, or what is spilt • **spill the beans** *informal* give away a secret, *esp* unintentionally

spin *verb* (**spinning**, **spun**) **1** draw out (cotton, wood, silk, *etc*) and twist into threads **2** (cause to) whirl round quickly **3** travel quickly, *esp* on wheels **4** produce a fine thread as a spider does ◇ *noun* **1** a whirling motion **2** a ride (*esp* on wheels) • **spin doctor** *noun* someone employed by a public figure to speak to the media *etc* on their behalf • **spin drier** *noun* a machine for taking water out of clothes by whirling them round • **spinner** *noun* • **spinneret** *noun* in a spider *etc*, the organ for producing thread • **spinning wheel** *noun* a machine for spinning thread, consisting of a wheel that drives spindles • **spin a yarn** tell a long story • **spin out** make to last a long or longer time

spina bifida /spai-nuh *bif*-id-uh/ *noun* a birth defect that leaves part of the spinal cord exposed and *usu* causes a degree of paralysis

spinach *noun* a type of plant whose leaves are eaten as vegetables

spinal *see* **spine**

spindle *noun* **1** the pin from which the thread is twisted in spinning wool or cotton **2** a pin on which anything turns round (*eg* that in the centre of the turntable of a record-player)

• **spindly** *adj* long and thin

spindrift *noun* the spray blown from the tops of waves

spine *noun* **1** the line of linked bones running down the back in animals and humans; the backbone **2** a ridge **3** a stiff, pointed spike on the body of an animal, *eg* a porcupine **4** a thorn • **spinal cord** *noun* a cord of nerve cells in the spine • **spineless** *adj* **1** having no spine; invertebrate **2** having no courage or determination; weak

spinet *noun* a kind of small harpsichord

spinnaker *noun* a light triangular sail

spinney *noun* (*plural* **spinneys**) a small clump of trees

spinster *noun, dated* a mature woman who is not married

spiny *adj* (**spinier, spiniest**) **1** covered with spines **2** troublesome

spiral *adj* **1** coiled round like a spring **2** winding round and round, getting further and further away from the centre ◇ *noun* **1** anything with a spiral shape **2** a spiral movement **3** an increase that gets ever more rapid ◇ *verb* (**spiralling, spiralled**) **1** move in a spiral **2** increase ever more rapidly

spire *noun* a tall, sharp-pointed tower (*esp* on the roof of a church)

spirit *noun* **1** the soul **2** a being without a body; a ghost: *an evil spirit* **3** liveliness or boldness: *he acted with spirit* **4** a feeling or attitude: *a spirit of kindness* **5** the intended meaning: *the spirit of the laws* **6** a distilled alcoholic drink, *eg* whisky **7** any distilled liquid, *eg* white spirit **8** (**spirits**) strong alcoholic drinks in general (*eg* whisky) **9** (**spirits**) state of mind, mood: *in high spirits* ◇ *verb* (*esp* with **away**) remove quickly and often in a secret or underhand way • **spirited** *adj* lively • **spiritual** *adj* having to do with the soul or with ghosts ◇ *noun* an emotional religious song of a kind originally developed by African American slaves • **spiritualism** *noun* the belief that living people can communicate with the souls of dead people • **spiritualist** *noun* someone who holds this belief

spit *noun* **1** the liquid that forms in a person's mouth **2** a metal bar on which meat is roasted **3** a long piece of land running into the sea ◇ *verb* (**spitting, spat** *or* **spitted**) **1** (*past form* **spat**) throw liquid out from the mouth **2** (*past form* **spat**) rain slightly **3** (*past form* **spitted**) pierce with something sharp • **spitting image** *noun* an exact likeness • **spittoon** *noun* a kind of dish into which you may spit

spite *noun* the wish to hurt someone, *esp* their feelings ◇ *verb* annoy out of spite • **spiteful** *adj* • **in spite of 1** taking no notice of: *he left in spite of his father's command* **2** although something has happened or is a fact: *the ground was dry in spite of all the rain*

spittle *noun* spit

splash *verb* **1** spatter with water, mud, *etc* **2** move or fall with a splash or splashes ◇ *noun* (*plural* **splashes**) **1** the sound made by, or the scattering of liquid caused by, something hitting water *etc* **2** a mark made by splashing (*eg* on your clothes) **3** a bright patch: *a splash of colour* • **make a splash** attract a lot of attention

splay *verb* turn out at an angle • **splay-footed** *adj* with flat feet turned outward

spleen *noun* **1** a spongy blood-filled organ inside the body, near the stomach **2** bad temper

splendid *adj* **1** magnificent, brilliant **2** *informal* excellent • **splendidly** *adv* • **splendour** *noun*

splenetic *adj, formal* irritable

splice *verb* **1** join (two ends of a rope) by twining the threads together **2** join (two pieces of film) in editing ◇ *noun* a joint made in this way

splint *noun* a rigid support tied to a broken limb to keep it in a fixed position

splinter *noun* a sharp, thin, broken piece of wood, glass, *etc* ◇ *verb* split into splinters • **splinter group** *noun* a group that breaks away from a larger one

split *verb* 1 cut or break lengthways 2 crack, break 3 divide into pieces or groups *etc* ◇ *noun* a crack, a break • **splitting** *adj* of a headache: severe, intense • **a split second** a fraction of a second • **split your sides** laugh heartily • **the splits** the feat of going down on the floor with one leg stretched forward and the other back

splutter *verb* 1 make spitting noises 2 speak hastily and unclearly

spoil *verb* 1 make useless, valueless or not enjoyable; ruin 2 give in to the wishes of (a child *etc*) and so ruin its character 3 of food: become bad or useless 4 (*past form* **spoiled**) rob, plunder ◇ *noun* (often **spoils**) things taken by force; plunder • **spoilsport** *noun* someone who refuses to join in other people's fun • **spoiling for** eager for (*esp* a fight)

spoke¹ *past tense of* **speak**

spoke² *noun* one of the ribs or bars from the centre to the rim of a wheel

spoken *past participle of* **speak**

spokesman, **spokeswoman** *noun* someone who speaks on behalf of others

spoliation *noun, formal* plundering

sponge *noun* 1 the soft elastic skeleton of a sea animal that can soak up water and is used for washing 2 an artificial object like this used for washing 3 the sea animal itself 4 a light cake or pudding ◇ *verb* 1 wipe with a sponge 2 *informal* live off money *etc* given by others • **sponger**

noun, informal someone who lives at others' expense • **spongy** *adj* soft like a sponge • **throw in the sponge** give up a fight or struggle

sponsor *noun* 1 a business firm that gives funding in return for an opportunity to advertise its name or products 2 someone who takes responsibility for introducing something; a promoter 3 someone who promises to pay a sum of money if another person completes a set task, *eg* a walk, swim, *etc* ◇ *verb* act as a sponsor to • **sponsorship** *noun* money given by a business sponsor

spontaneous *adj* 1 not planned beforehand 2 natural, not forced • **spontaneity** *noun*

spoof *noun* a satirical imitation

spook *noun* a ghost • **spooky** *adj* frightening

spool *noun* a reel for thread, film, *etc*

spoon *noun* a piece of metal *etc* with a hollow bowl at one end, used for lifting food to the mouth ◇ *verb* lift with a spoon • **spoonfeed** *verb* 1 feed (a baby *etc*) with a spoon 2 teach in a way that does not encourage independent thought

spoonerism *noun* a mistake in speaking in which the first sounds of words change position, as in *every crook and nanny* for *every nook and cranny*

spoor *noun* the footmarks or trail left by an animal

sporadic *adj* happening here and there or now and again • **sporadically** *adv*

spore *noun* the seed of certain plants (*eg* ferns, fungi)

sporran *noun* a small pouch worn hanging in front of a kilt

sport *noun* 1 games such as football, tennis, skiing, *etc* in general 2 any one game of this type 3 a good-natured, obliging person ◇ *verb* 1 wear: *sporting* a pink tie **2** dated have fun; play • **sporting** adj **1** fond of sport **2** believing in fair play; good-natured • **sporting chance** noun a reasonably good chance • **sports car** noun a small, fast car with only two seats • **sportsman, sportswoman** noun **1** someone who plays sports **2** someone who shows fair play in sports • **sportsmanlike** adj

spot noun **1** a small mark or stain, eg of mud or paint **2** a round mark that is part of a pattern on material etc **3** a pimple **4** a place ◇ verb **1** catch sight of **2** mark with spots • **spotless** adj very clean • **spotlight** noun a bright light that is shone on an actor on the stage ◇ verb (**spotlighting, spotlighted**) **1** show up clearly **2** draw attention to • **spotted** or **spotty** adj covered with spots • **in a spot** in trouble • **on the spot 1** at the scene of some event **2** right away; immediately **3** in an embarrassing or difficult position

spouse noun a husband or wife

spout noun **1** the part of a kettle, teapot, etc through which liquid is poured out **2** a strong jet of liquid ◇ verb pour or spurt out

sprain noun a painful twisting, eg of an ankle ◇ verb twist painfully

sprang past tense of **spring**

sprat noun a small fish similar to a herring

sprawl verb **1** sit, lie or fall with the limbs spread out widely **2** of a town etc: spread out in an untidy, irregular way

spray noun **1** a fine mist of liquid like that made by a waterfall **2** a device with many small holes for producing spray **3** a liquid for spraying **4** a small bouquet of flowers ◇ verb cover with a mist or fine jets of liquid

spread verb (**spreading, spread**) **1** put widely or thinly over an area: spread the butter on the bread **2** cover: spread the bread with jam **3** open out (eg your arms, a map) **4** scatter or distribute over a wide area, length of time, etc ◇ noun **1** the extent or range (of something) **2** a food which is spread on bread: sandwich spread **3** informal a large meal laid out on a table • **spread-eagled** adj with limbs spread out • **spreadsheet** noun a computer program with which data can be viewed on screen and manipulated

spree noun a spell of carefree or careless activity: a spending spree

sprig noun a small twig or shoot

sprightly adj (**sprightlier, sprightliest**) lively, brisk • **sprightliness** noun

spring verb (**springing, sprang, sprung**) **1** jump, leap **2** move swiftly **3** (with **back**) return suddenly to an earlier position when released **4** set off (a trap etc) **5** reveal unexpectedly: he sprang the news on me **6** come from: his bravery springs from his love of adventure ◇ noun **1** a coil of wire used for its elastic properties **2** the season of the year following winter, when plants begin to grow again **3** a small stream flowing out from the ground **4** the ability to stretch and spring back **5** a leap • **springboard** noun a springy board from which swimmers may dive • **springbok** noun a type of deer found in S Africa • **spring cleaning** noun a thorough cleaning of a house, esp in the spring • **springy** adj able to spring back into its former position etc; elastic • **spring a leak** begin to leak • **spring up** appear suddenly

sprinkle verb scatter or cover in small drops or pieces • **sprinkler** noun something that sprinkles water • **sprinkling** noun a few

sprint verb run at full speed ◇ noun a short running race • **sprinter** noun

sprite noun **1** a supernatural spirit **2** comput an icon that can be moved about a screen

sprocket noun one of a set of teeth on the rim of a wheel

sprog noun, informal a child

sprout verb 1 begin to grow 2 put out new shoots ◇ noun 1 a young bud 2 (**sprouts**) Brussels sprouts

spruce adj neat, smart ◇ noun a kind of fir-tree

sprung past participle of **spring**

spry adj light on the feet; nimble

spud noun, informal a potato

spume noun froth, foam

spun past form of **spin**

spunk noun 1 a determined or brave attitude; pluck 2 slang ejaculated semen

spur noun 1 a sharp point worn by a horse-rider on the heel and used to urge on a horse 2 a claw-like point at the back of a bird's leg 3 anything that urges someone on 4 a small line of mountains running off from a larger range ◇ verb (**spurring**, **spurred**) 1 urge on 2 use spurs on (a horse) • **on the spur of the moment** without thinking beforehand

spurious adj not useful, reasonable or genuine, although appearing to be • **spuriousness** noun

spurn verb reject with scorn

spurt verb pour out in a sudden stream ◇ noun 1 a sudden stream pouring or squirting out 2 a sudden increase of effort: put a spurt on

sputter verb make a noise as of spitting and throw out moisture in drops

sputum noun mucus and spittle from the nose, throat, etc

spy noun (plural **spies**) someone who secretly collects (and reports) information about another person, country, firm, etc ◇ verb (**spies**, **spying**, **spied**) 1 (with **on**) watch secretly 2 catch sight of; spot • **spyglass** noun a small telescope

sq abbrev square

squabble verb quarrel noisily ◇ noun a noisy quarrel

squad noun 1 a group of soldiers, workmen, etc doing a particular job 2 a group of people • **squaddie** noun, informal a private in the army

squadron noun a number of military aircraft forming a unit • **squadron leader** noun an air force officer ranking below a wing commander

squalid adj 1 very dirty; filthy 2 contemptible

squall noun 1 a sudden violent storm 2 a squeal or scream • **squally** adj stormy

squalor noun dirty or squalid living conditions

squander verb waste (money, goods, strength, etc) • **squanderer** noun

square noun 1 a flat shape with four equal sides and four right angles, of this shape: □ 2 an open space enclosed by buildings in a town 3 the answer when a number is multiplied by itself, eg the square of 3 is 9 ◇ adj 1 shaped like a square 2 equal in scores in a game 3 of two or more people: not owing one another anything 4 straight or level ◇ verb 1 make straight or level 2 multiply a number by itself 3 be consistent (with): that doesn't square with what you said earlier 4 (with **up**) settle (a debt) ◇ adv 1 in a straight or level position 2 directly or exactly: hit square on the nose • **square foot**, **square metre**, etc noun an area equal to that of a square each side of which is one foot, metre, etc long • **square meal** noun a satisfying meal • **square root** noun the number which, multiplied by itself, gives a certain other number (eg 3 is the square root of 9) • **a square deal** fair treatment

squash verb 1 crush flat or to a pulp 2 put down, defeat (rebellion etc) ◇ noun 1 a game with rackets and a rubber ball played in a walled court 2 concentrated fruit syrup, or a juice made by diluting it **3** a crowded state

squat verb (**squatting**, **squatted**) **1** sit down on the heels **2** settle without permission in property that you do not pay rent for ◇ adj short and thick • **squatter** noun someone who squats in a building, on land, etc

squaw noun, derog a Native American woman or wife

squawk verb give a harsh cry ◇ noun a harsh cry

squeak verb give a short, high-pitched sound ◇ noun a high-pitched noise • **squeaky** adj

squeal verb **1** give a loud, shrill cry **2** informal inform on • **squealer** noun

squeamish adj **1** easily sickened or shocked **2** feeling sick

squeegee noun a sponge for washing windows etc

squeeze verb **1** hold tightly or press firmly **2** force out (liquid or juice from) by pressing **3** force a way: squeeze through the hole in the wall ◇ noun **1** a squeezing or pressing **2** a few drops got by squeezing: a squeeze of lemon juice **3** a crowd of people crushed together

squelch noun a sound made by contact with a watery or sticky substance ◇ verb make this sound

squib noun a type of small firework • **damp squib** something that is much less impressive or exciting than people expect it to be

squid noun a sea animal with tentacles, related to the cuttlefish

squiggle noun a curly or wavy mark • **squiggly** adj curly

squillions plural noun, informal a great many; millions

squint verb **1** screw up the eyes in looking at something **2** have the eyes looking in different directions ◇ noun **1** a fault in eyesight that causes squinting **2** informal a quick look; a glance

squire noun, hist **1** a country landowner **2** a knight's servant

squirm verb wriggle or twist the body, esp in pain or embarrassment

squirrel noun a small gnawing animal, either reddish-brown or grey, with a bushy tail

squirt verb shoot out a narrow jet of liquid ◇ noun a narrow jet of liquid

Sr abbrev senior

SS abbrev steamship

St abbrev **1** saint **2** street

st abbrev stone (in weight)

stab verb (**stabbing**, **stabbed**) **1** wound or pierce with a pointed weapon **2** poke (at) ◇ noun **1** the act of stabbing **2** a wound made by stabbing **3** a sharp pain • **have a stab at** make an attempt at

stable noun **1** a building for keeping horses **2** a number of animals or people managed by someone ◇ verb put or keep (horses) in a stable ◇ adj firm, steady • **stability** noun steadiness • **stabilize** verb make steady

staccato adj of sounds: sharp and separate, like the sound of tapping ◇ adj & adv, music (with each note) sounded separately and clearly

stack noun a large pile ◇ verb put in a pile

stadium noun (plural **stadiums** or **stadia**) a large sports ground or racecourse with seats for spectators

staff noun **1** workers employed in a business, school, etc **2** a stick or pole carried in the hand **3** music a stave ◇ verb supply (a school etc) with staff

stag noun a male deer • **stag party** noun a party for men only, held before one of them gets married

stage noun **1** a platform for performing or acting on **2** (with **the**) the acting profession **3** a step in development: the first stage of the plan

4 a part of a journey ◇ *verb* **1** prepare and put on a performance of (a play *etc*) **2** arrange (an event, *eg* an exhibition) • **stagecoach** *noun, hist* a coach running every day with passengers • **stage fright** *noun* an actor's fear when acting in public *esp* for the first time • **stage whisper** *noun* a loud whisper • **staging** *noun* **1** scaffolding **2** putting on the stage • **on the stage** in the theatre

stagger *verb* **1** walk unsteadily; totter **2** astonish **3** arrange (things) so that they do not begin or end together • **staggered** *adj* • **staggering** *adj* astonishing

stagnant *adj* of water: not flowing and therefore not fresh or pure • **stagnate** *verb* **1** remain for a long time in the same situation and so become bored, inactive, *etc* **2** of water: remain still and so become impure • **stagnation** *noun*

staid *adj* having a boringly serious attitude

stain *verb* **1** give a different colour to (wood *etc*) **2** mark or make dirty by accident ◇ *noun* **1** a liquid that dyes or colours something **2** a mark that is not easily removed **3** something shameful in someone's character or reputation • **stained glass** *noun* coloured glass cut into shapes and joined into panes with lead • **stainless steel** *noun* a mixture of steel and chromium that does not rust

stair *noun* **1** one or all of a number of steps one after the other **2** (**stairs**) a series or flight of steps • **staircase** *noun* a stretch of stairs with rails on one or both sides

stake *noun* **1** a strong stick pointed at one end **2** money put down as a bet **3** *hist* a post to which people were tied to be burned ◇ *verb* **1** risk **2** bet (money) **3** mark the limits or boundaries (of a field *etc*) with stakes • **at stake 1** able to be won or lost **2** in great danger: *his life is at stake* • **have**

a stake in be concerned in, because you have something to gain or lose • **stake a claim** establish ownership or right (to something)

stalactite *noun* a spike of limestone hanging from the roof of a cave, formed by the dripping of water containing lime

stalagmite *noun* a spike of limestone, like a stalactite, rising from the floor of a cave

stale *adj* **1** of food: no longer fresh **2** no longer interesting because heard, done, *etc* too often before **3** not able to do your best (because of overworking, boredom, *etc*)

stalemate *noun* **1** *chess* a position in which a player cannot move without putting their king in danger, which ends the game **2** a position in an argument in which neither side can win

stalk *noun* the stem of a plant or of a leaf or flower ◇ *verb* **1** follow or watch (someone) persistently, either threateningly or because of an obsession **2** walk quickly and angrily • **stalker** *noun*

stall *noun* **1** a table on which things are laid out for sale **2** a simple shop or counter, *eg* at a market **3** a seat in a church (*esp* for choir or clergy) **4** (**stalls**) theatre seats on the ground floor ◇ *verb* **1** of a car engine: come to a halt without the driver intending it to do so **2** of an aircraft: lose flying speed and so fall out of control **3** *informal* avoid action or decision for the time being

stallion *noun* a male horse, *esp* one kept for breeding purposes

stalwart *noun* a long-standing and committed supporter

stamen *noun* one of the thread-like spikes in the middle of a flower that carry the pollen

stamina *noun* the strength to keep going

stammer verb **1** have difficulty in saying the first letter of words in speaking **2** stumble over words ◇ noun a speech difficulty of this kind

stamp verb **1** bring the foot down firmly on the ground **2** stick a postage stamp on **3** mark with a design cut into a mould and inked **4** fix or mark deeply: *forever stamped in my memory* ◇ noun **1** a label showing that postage has been paid; a postage stamp **2** a design made by stamping **3** a mould made for stamping • **stamping ground** noun someone's favourite or usual place to be • **stamp out 1** put out (a fire) by stamping **2** put an end to; suppress

stampede noun **1** a wild rush of frightened animals **2** a sudden, wild rush of people ◇ verb rush wildly

stance noun **1** a way of standing **2** an opinion

stanch or **staunch** verb stop (esp blood) from flowing

stanchion noun an upright iron bar used as a support

stand verb (**standing, stood**) **1** be on your feet, not lying or sitting down **2** rise to your feet **3** of an object: be or cause to be in a particular place: *it stood by the door/stood the case in the corner* **4** tolerate: *I cannot stand this heat* **5** remain: *this law still stands* **6** be a candidate (for): *he stood for parliament* **7** be short (for): *PO stands for Post Office* **8** treat (someone) to: *stand you tea* ◇ noun **1** something on which anything is placed **2** an object made to hold, or for hanging, things: *a hat-stand* **3** lines of raised seats from which people may watch games *etc* **4** an effort made to support, defend, resist, *etc*: *a stand against violence* **5** *US* a witness box in a law court • **stand-alone** noun & adj, *comput* (of) a system, device, *etc* that can operate unconnected to any other • **standby** noun **1** readiness to act **2** someone or something that is ready

to act or help • **standing** noun social position or reputation ◇ adj **1** on your feet **2** placed on end **3** not moving **4** lasting, permanent: *a standing joke* • **standoffish** adj unfriendly • **standpoint** noun the position from which you look at something (*eg* a question, problem); point of view • **standstill** noun a complete stop • **stand by** be ready or available to be used or help in an emergency *etc* • **stand down** withdraw (from a contest) or resign (from a job) • **stand fast** refuse to give in • **stand in for** take another's place, job, *etc* for a time • **stand out** be noticeable • **stand to reason** be likely or reasonable • **stand up for** defend strongly • **stand up to** face or oppose bravely

standard noun **1** a level against which things may be judged **2** a level of excellence aimed at: *artistic standards* **3** a large flag *etc* on a pole ◇ adj **1** normal, usual: *a standard charge* **2** ordinary, without extras: *the standard model* • **standard bearer** noun the leader of a movement or cause • **standardization** noun • **standardize** verb make all of one kind or size • **standard lamp** noun a kind of tall lamp that stands on the floor of a room *etc* • **standard of living** noun a level of material comfort considered necessary by a particular group of society *etc*

stank *past tense of* **stink**

stanza noun a verse of a poem

staple noun **1** a U-shaped iron nail **2** a piece of wire driven through sheets of paper to fasten them together **3** the main item in a country's production, a person's diet, *etc* ◇ verb fasten with a staple ◇ adj main

star noun **1** any of the bodies in the sky appearing as points of light **2** the fixed bodies which are really distant suns, not the planets **3** an object, shape or figure with a number of pointed rays (often five) **4** a leading actor or actress or other well-known performer ◇ *adj* for or of a star (in a film *etc*) ◇ *verb* (**starring, starred**) **1** act the main part (in a play or film) **2** of a play *etc*: have as its star • **stardom** *noun* the state of being a leading performer • **starfish** *noun* a type of small sea creature with five points or arms • **the Stars and Stripes** the flag of the United States of America

starboard *noun* the right side of a ship, as you look towards the bow (or front) ◇ *adj*

starch *noun* (*plural* **starches**) **1** a white carbohydrate found in flour, potatoes, bread, biscuits, *etc* **2** a form of this used for stiffening clothes • **starchy** *adj* **1** of food: containing starch **2** stiff and unfriendly

stare *verb* look with a fixed gaze ◇ *noun* a fixed gaze

stark *adj* **1** barren or bare **2** harsh, severe **3** sheer: *stark idiocy* ◇ *adv* completely: *stark naked*

starling *noun* a common bird with dark, glossy feathers

starry *adj* (**starrier, starriest**) full of stars or shining like stars

start *verb* **1** begin (an action): *he started to walk home* **2** get (a machine *etc*) working: *he started the car* **3** jump or jerk (*eg* in surprise) ◇ *noun* **1** the act of starting (*eg* on a task, journey) **2** a sudden movement of the body **3** a sudden shock: *you gave me a start* **4** in a race *etc*, the advantage of beginning before, or farther forward than, others, or the amount of this: *a start of five metres* • **starter** *noun* **1** someone or something that starts an action, race, *etc* **2** the first course of a meal

startle *verb* give a shock or fright to • **startled** *adj* • **startling** *adj*

starve *verb* **1** die for want of food **2** suffer greatly from hunger **3** deprive of something needed or wanted badly: *starved of company here* • **starvation** *noun*

stash *verb, informal* store in a hidden place ◇ *noun* a hidden supply of something, *esp* illegal drugs

state *noun* **1** the condition (of something): *the bad state of the roads* **2** the people of a country under a government **3** *US* an area and its people with its own laws forming part of the whole country **4** a government and its officials **5** great show; pomp: *the king drove by in state* ◇ *adj* **1** of the government **2** national and ceremonial: *state occasions* **3** *US* of a certain state of America: *the state capital of Texas is Austin* ◇ *verb* say or write, *esp* clearly and fully • **stateliness** *noun* • **stately** *adj* noble-looking; dignified • **statement** *noun* something that is said or written • **state-of-the-art** *adj* most up-to-date • **stateroom** *noun* a large cabin in a ship • **stateside** *adj & adv, informal* of or in the United States • **statesman** *noun* someone skilled in government • **statesmanlike** *adj*

static *adj* not moving ◇ *noun* **1** atmospheric disturbances that cause poor reception of radio or television programmes **2** electricity on the surface of objects that will not conduct it, *eg* hair, nylons, *etc* (*also called*: **static electricity**)

station *noun* **1** a building with a ticket office, waiting rooms, *etc* where trains, buses or coaches stop to pick up or set down passengers **2** a place that is the centre for work of some kind: *fire station/police station* **3** rank, position: *lowly station* ◇ *verb* **1** assign to a position or place **2** take up a position: *stationed himself by the door*

stationary *adj* standing still, not moving

Do not confuse: **stationary** and **stationery**

stationery *noun* writing paper, envelopes, pens, *etc* • **stationer** *noun* someone who sells these

statistics 1 *plural noun* figures and facts set out in order: *statistics of road accidents for last year* 2 *sing noun* the study of these: *statistics is not an easy subject* • **statistical** *adj* • **statistician** *noun* someone who produces or studies statistics

statue *noun* a likeness of someone or an animal, carved in stone, metal, *etc* • **statuesque** *adj* like a statue in dignity *etc* • **statuette** *noun* a small statue

stature *noun* 1 height 2 importance or reputation

status *noun* rank or reputation in relation to others • **status quo** *noun* the state of affairs now existing, or existing before a certain time or event • **status symbol** *noun* a possession that is thought to show the high status of the owner, *eg* a powerful car

statute *noun* a written law of a country • **statutory** *adj* according to law

staunch *adj* loyal ◇ *verb see* **stanch**

stave *noun* 1 a set of spaced lines on which music is written 2 one of the strips making the side of a barrel ◇ *verb* (**staving**, **stove** *or* **staved**) 1 (with **in**) crush in 2 (with **off**) keep from happening

stay *verb* 1 continue to be: *stayed calm/stay here while I go for help* 2 live (for a time): *staying in a hotel* 3 *old* stop ◇ *noun* 1 time spent in a place 2 a rope running from the side of a ship to the mast 3 (**stays**) *old* corsets • **stay put** remain in the same place

St Bernard *see* **Saint Bernard**

STD *abbrev* sexually transmitted disease

stead *noun* place: *she went in my stead* • **stand you in good stead** turn out to be helpful to you: *his German stood him in good stead*

steadfast *adj* 1 firmly fixed 2 faithful, loyal • **steadfastly** *adv* • **steadfastness** *noun*

Steadicam *noun, trademark* a cinema camera with counterbalances to produce a smooth picture while being moved

steading *noun* farm buildings

steady *adj* (**steadier**, **steadiest**) 1 not moving or changing 2 not easily upset or put off 3 even, regular, unchanging: *moving at a steady pace* ◇ *verb* (**steadies**, **steadying**, **steadied**) make or become steady • **steadily** *adv* • **steadiness** *noun*

steak *noun* a thick slice of meat or fish for cooking

steal *verb* (**stealing**, **stole**, **stolen**) 1 take (something not belonging to you) without permission 2 move quietly 3 take quickly or secretly: *stole a look at him*

stealth *noun* secret or quiet movements or actions ◇ *adj* of a military aircraft *etc*: made of materials that make it difficult or impossible to detect by radar or similar means • **stealthily** *adv* • **stealthy** *adj*

steam *noun* 1 vapour from hot liquid, *esp* from boiling water 2 power produced by steam: *in the days of steam* ◇ *verb* 1 give off steam 2 cook by steam 3 open or loosen by putting into steam: *steam open the envelope* • **steamboat** *noun* a steamer • **steam engine** *noun* an engine, *esp* a railway engine, worked by steam • **steamer** *noun* a ship driven by steam • **steamroller** *noun* a steam-driven engine with large and very heavy wheels, used for flattening the surfaces of roads • **steamship** *noun* a steamer • **steam up** of glass: become covered with condensed steam in the form of small drops of water

steamy *adj* (**steamier**, **steamiest**) 1 full of steam: *steamy atmosphere* 2 *informal* full of sexual passion; erotic

steed *noun, old* a horse

steel *noun* 1 a very hard mixture of iron and carbon 2 a bar of steel for sharpening knife blades • **steely**

adj hard, cold, strong, *etc* like steel
• **of steel** hard, strong: *a grip of steel*
• **steel yourself** get up courage

steep *adj* 1 of a slope: rising nearly straight up 2 *informal* of a price: very high ◇ *verb* 1 soak in a liquid 2 fill with knowledge of: *steeped in French literature*

steeple *noun* a tower of a church *etc* rising to a point; a spire • **steeplechase** *noun* 1 a race run across open country, over hedges, *etc* 2 a race over a course or track on which obstacles have been built • **steeplejack** *noun* someone who climbs steeples or other high buildings to make repairs

steer *verb* 1 control the course of (a car, ship, discussion, *etc*) 2 follow (a course) ◇ *noun* a young ox raised for its beef • **steerage** *noun, old* the part of a ship set aside for the passengers who pay the lowest fares • **steering** *noun* the parts of a ship, car, *etc* which have to do with controlling its course • **steering wheel** *noun* the wheel in a road vehicle used by the driver to steer it • **steer clear of** keep away from

stellar *adj* 1 of the stars 2 containing many very well-known performers; star-studded

stem *noun* 1 the part of a plant from which the leaves and flowers grow 2 the thin support of a wineglass ◇ *verb* (**stemming, stemmed**) 1 stop, halt: *stem the bleeding* 2 start, spring (from): *hate stems from envy*

stench *noun* a strong unpleasant smell

stencil *noun* 1 a sheet of metal, cardboard, *etc* with a pattern cut out 2 the drawing or design made by rubbing ink or brushing paint *etc* over a cut-out pattern ◇ *verb* (**stencilling, stencilled**) make a design or copy with a stencil

stenographer *noun, US* a shorthand typist • **stenography** *noun, US* shorthand

stentorian *adj, formal* 1 of the voice: loud 2 loud-voiced

Do not confuse with: **stertorous**

step *noun* 1 a movement of the leg in walking, running, *etc* 2 the distance covered by this 3 a particular movement of the feet, as in dancing: 4 the sound made by the foot in walking *etc*: *heard a step outside* 5 a riser on a stair, or a rung on a ladder 6 one of a series of moves in a plan, career, *etc*: *take the first step* 7 a way of walking: *springy step* 8 (**steps**) a flight of stairs 9 (**steps**) a stepladder ◇ *verb* (**stepping, stepped**) 1 take a step 2 walk, move: *step this way, please* • **stepladder** *noun* a ladder with a support on which it rests • **stepping stone** *noun* 1 a stone rising above water or mud, used to cross on 2 anything that helps you to advance • **in step** 1 of two or more people walking: with the same foot going forward at the same time 2 acting *etc* in agreement (with) • **out of step** not in step (with) • **step up** increase (*eg* production) • **take steps** begin to do something for a certain purpose

step- *prefix* related as the result of a second marriage: *stepdaugther/stepfather*

steppe *noun* a dry, grassy treeless plain in SE Europe and Asia

stereo *adj,* short for **stereophonic** ◇ *noun* (*plural* **stereos**) *dated* audio equipment consisting of a record player and/or tape recorder with amplifier and loudspeakers

stereo- *prefix* in three dimensions

stereophonic *adj* of sound: giving a lifelike effect, with different instruments, voices, *etc* coming from two speakers

stereotype *noun* 1 a fixed metal plate for printing, with letters *etc* moulded onto its surface 2 something fixed and unchanging **3** a characteristic type of person • **stereotyped** or **stereotypical** adj fixed, not changing: stereotyped ideas

sterile adj **1** unable to have children or reproduce **2** producing no ideas etc: sterile imagination **3** free from germs • **sterility** noun the state of being sterile

sterilize verb **1** make free from germs, by boiling etc **2** make unable to have children or reproduce • **sterilization** noun

sterling noun British money when used in international trading: one pound sterling ◇ adj **1** of silver: of a certain standard of purity **2** worthy, good: sterling qualities

stern¹ adj **1** looking or sounding angry or displeased **2** severe, strict, harsh: stern prison sentence • **sternly** adv • **sternness** noun the state or quality of being stern

stern² noun the back part of a ship

steroid noun **1** any of a number of substances produced by the body to regulate its functions **2** a medicine or drug containing steroids, esp one used illegally by athletes to enhance performance (see also **anabolic steroids**)

stertorous adj making a snoring noise

Do not confuse with: **stentorian**

---

stethoscope noun an instrument used by a doctor to listen to a patient's heartbeat or breath sounds

Stetson noun, trademark a soft wide-brimmed hat worn traditionally by cowboys

stevedore /steev-uh-daw/ noun someone employed to load and unload ships

stew verb cook by boiling slowly ◇ noun **1** a dish of stewed food, often containing meat and vegetables **2** informal a state of worry; a flap

steward noun **1** dated a flight attendant on an aircraft **2** someone who shows people to their seats at a meeting etc **3** an official at a race meeting etc **4** someone who manages an estate or farm for someone else

stewardess noun, dated a female flight attendant

stick noun **1** a long thin piece of wood, esp a branch or twig from a tree **2** a piece of wood shaped for a special purpose: hockey-stick/drumstick **3** a long piece (eg of rhubarb) ◇ verb (**sticking, stuck**) **1** push or thrust (something): stick the knife in your belt **2** fix with glue etc: I'll stick the pieces back together **3** be or become caught, fixed or held back: stuck in the ditch **4** (with **to**) keep to (eg a decision) • **sticker** noun a label, poster, etc that can be fixed onto a surface • **sticking plaster** noun a kind of tape with a sticky surface, used to protect slight cuts etc • **stick-in-the-mud** noun someone who is against new ideas, change, etc • **stick up for** speak or fight in defence of

stickleback noun a type of small river-fish with prickles on its back

stickler noun someone who attaches great importance to a particular (often small) matter: stickler for punctuality

sticky adj (**stickier, stickiest**) **1** clinging closely like glue, treacle, etc **2** covered with something sticky **3** difficult: a sticky problem • **stickiness** noun

stiff adj **1** not easily bent or moved **2** of a mixture, dough, etc: thick, not easily stirred **3** cold and distant in manner **4** hard, difficult: stiff examination **5** severe: stiff penalty **6** strong: stiff drink • **stiffly** adv • **stiff-necked** adj proud, obstinate

stiffen verb make or become stiff

stifle verb **1** suffocate **2** put out

(flames) **3** keep back (tears, a yawn, etc) • **stifling** adj very hot and stuffy

stigma noun **1** (plural **stigmata**) a mark of disgrace **2** (plural **stigmas**) in a flower, the top of the pistil • **stigmatize** verb cause to feel ashamed and socially inferior: stigmatized for life

stile noun a step or set of steps for climbing over a wall or fence

stiletto noun (plural **stilettos**) **1** a high, very thin heel, or a woman's shoe with such a heel **2** a dagger with a narrow blade

still adj **1** not moving **2** calm, without wind **3** of drinks: not fizzy ◇ verb make calm or quiet ◇ adv **1** up to the present time or the time spoken of: it was still there **2** even so; nevertheless: it's difficult but we must still try **3** even: still more people ◇ noun an apparatus for distilling spirits, eg whisky • **stillborn** adj of a child: dead at birth • **still life** noun a picture of something that is not living, eg a bowl of fruit • **stillness** noun the state of being still • **stillroom** noun a pantry or room where drinks, food, etc are kept

stilted adj awkward in a way that suggests embarrassment or insincerity

stilts plural noun **1** long poles with footrests on which someone may walk clear of the ground **2** tall poles supporting a structure above ground or water

stimulant noun something that makes you feel more active or lively

stimulate verb **1** make more active or lively **2** encourage **3** excite • **stimulation** noun

stimulus noun (plural **stimuli**) **1** something that provokes a reaction in a living thing **2** something that causes someone to make a greater effort

sting noun **1** the part of some animals and plants, eg the wasp and the nettle, that can prick the skin and cause pain or irritation **2** the act of piercing with a sting **3** the wound, swelling or pain caused by a sting ◇ verb (**stinging, stung**) **1** pierce with a sting or cause pain like that of a sting **2** be painful; smart: made his eyes sting **3** hurt the feelings of: stung by his words

stingy /stin-ji/ adj not generous, esp with money; mean • **stinginess** noun

stink noun a bad smell ◇ verb (**stinking, stank** or **stunk, stunk**) give out a bad smell

stint noun **1** a fixed amount of work: my daily stint **2** limit: praise without stint ◇ verb allow (someone) very little: don't stint on the ice cream

stipend /stai-pend/ noun pay, salary, esp of a parish minister • **stipendiary** adj

stipple verb paint or mark with tiny dots from a brush

stipulate verb state as a condition of doing something • **stipulation** noun something stipulated; a condition

stir verb (**stirring, stirred**) **1** move (liquid) in a circular motion, esp with a spoon, often in order to mix it **2** move slightly: he stirred in his sleep **3** arouse (a person, a feeling, etc) ◇ noun disturbance or fuss • **stirring** adj exciting • **stir up** cause (eg trouble)

stirrup noun a metal loop hung from a horse's saddle as a support for the rider's foot

stitch noun (plural **stitches**) **1** the loop made in thread, wool, etc by a needle in sewing or knitting **2** a sharp, sudden pain in your side ◇ verb put stitches in; sew

stoat noun a type of small fierce animal similar to a weasel, sometimes called an ermine when in its white winter fur

stock noun **1** the supply of goods held in a shop, warehouse, etc **2** the capital of a business company divided into shares **3** liquid (used for soup) obtained by boiling meat, bones, *etc* **4** the animals of a farm (*also called*: **livestock**) **5** a type of scented garden flower **6** family, race: *of ancient stock* **7** the handle of a whip, rifle, *etc* **8** (**stocks**) *hist* a wooden frame, with holes for the ankles and wrists, in which criminals *etc* were fastened as a punishment **9** (**stocks**) the wooden framework on which a ship is supported when being built ◊ *verb* **1** keep a supply of (for sale) **2** supply (a farm with animals *etc*) ◊ *adj* **1** known by everyone: *a stock joke* **2** usually stocked (by a shop *etc*) • **stock-still** *adj* perfectly still • **stocktaking** *noun* a regular check of the goods in a shop or warehouse • **take stock of** form an opinion or estimation about (a situation *etc*)

stockade *noun* a fence of strong posts set up round an area or building for defence

stockbroker *noun* someone who buys and sell shares in business companies on behalf of others • **stock exchange** *noun* **1** a place where stocks and shares are bought and sold **2** an association of people who do this • **stock-in-trade** *noun* **1** the necessary equipment *etc* for a particular trade *etc* **2** someone's usual ways of speaking, acting, *etc*: *sarcasm is part of his stock-in-trade* • **stock market** *noun* the stock exchange; dealings in stocks and shares

stocking *noun* a close-fitting covering in a knitted fabric for the leg and foot

stockpile *noun* a reserve supply ◊ *verb* build up a store of

stocky *adj* (**stockier**, **stockiest**) with a short broad body • **stockiness** *noun*

stodgy *adj* (**stodgier**, **stodgiest**) **1** of food: heavy, not easily digested **2** of a person, book, *etc*: dull • **stodginess** *noun*

stoic *noun* someone who bears pain or hardship bravely and quietly • **stoical** *adj* • **stoicism** *noun* the bearing of pain *etc* patiently

stoke *verb* put coal, wood, or other fuel on (a fire) • **stoker** *noun* someone who looks after a furnace

stole[1] *noun* a length of silk, linen or fur worn over the shoulders

stole[2], **stolen** *see* **steal**

stolid *adj* not at all lively, excited or emotional • **stolidity** *noun* • **stolidly** *adv*

stomach *noun* **1** the bag-like part of the body into which food passes when swallowed **2** desire or courage (for something): *no stomach for a fight* ◊ *verb* put up with; tolerate: *can't stomach her rudeness*

stomp *verb* stamp the feet noisily

stone *noun* **1** the material of which rocks are made **2** a (small) loose piece of this **3** a piece of this shaped for a certain purpose: *tombstone* **4** a precious stone, *eg* a diamond **5** the hard shell around the seed of some fruits, *eg* peach, cherry **6** a measure of weight equal to 14 pounds or 6.35 kilograms **7** a piece of hard material that forms in the kidney, bladder, *etc*, causing pain ◊ *verb* **1** throw stones at **2** take the stones out of fruit ◊ *adj* made of stone • **stone-cold** *adj* very cold • **stone-dead** *adj* completely dead • **stoneware** *noun* a kind of pottery made out of coarse clay • **stonework** *noun* something that is built of stone, *esp* the stone parts of a building • **the Stone Age** human culture before the use of metal

stony *adj* (**stonier**, **stoniest**) **1** like stone **2** covered with stones **3** hard, cold in manner: *stony look* • **a stone's throw** a very short distance • **leave no stone unturned** do everything possible

stood *past form of* **stand**

stooge noun an assistant, esp a comedian's straight man

stookie noun, Scot a plaster cast for a broken limb

stool noun 1 a seat without a back 2 a mass of faeces • **stool pigeon** noun, slang a police informer

stoop verb 1 bend the body forward and downward 2 be low or wicked enough to do a certain thing: I wouldn't stoop to stealing ◇ noun 1 the act of stooping 2 a forward bend of the body

stop verb (**stopping, stopped**) 1 bring to a halt: stop the car 2 prevent from doing: stop him from working 3 put an end to: stop this nonsense 4 come to an end: the rain has stopped 5 (with **up**) block (a hole etc) ◇ noun 1 the state of being stopped 2 a place where something stops 3 a full stop 4 a knob on an organ that brings certain pipes into use • **stopcock** noun a tap for controlling the flow of liquid through a pipe • **stopgap** noun something that is used in an emergency until something better is found • **stoppage** noun a halt, esp in work in a factory • **stopper** noun something that stops up an opening, esp in the neck of a bottle or jar • **stop press** noun a space in a newspaper for news put in at the last minute • **stopwatch** noun a watch that can be stopped and started, used in timing races

store noun 1 a supply from which things are taken when needed 2 a place where goods are kept 3 a shop 4 a collected amount or number ◇ verb put aside for future use • **storage** noun 1 the act of storing 2 the state of being stored: our furniture is in storage • **storehouse** or **storeroom** noun a building or room where goods are stored • **in store** awaiting: trouble in store • **set (great) store by** value highly

storey noun (plural **storeys**) all that part of a building on the same floor

Do not confuse with: **story**

stork noun a wading bird with a long bill, neck and legs

storm noun 1 a sudden burst of bad, windy weather 2 a violent outbreak, eg of anger ◇ verb 1 be in a fury 2 rain, blow, etc violently 3 attack (a stronghold etc) violently • **a storm in a teacup** a great fuss over nothing • **go down a storm** be popular or well received

stormy adj (**stormier, stormiest**) 1 affected by storms or high winds 2 of a person, situation, etc: violent, passionate, unpredictable

story noun (plural **stories**) an account of events, real or imaginary • **storied** adj, dated mentioned in stories; famous • **storyboard** noun a series of drawings forming an outline for shooting a scene in a film

Do not confuse with: **storey**

stout adj 1 having a broad or rather fat body; stocky 2 brave: stout resistance 3 strong: stout walking-stick ◇ noun a strong, dark-coloured beer • **stout-hearted** adj, dated having a brave heart • **stoutness** noun

stove[1] noun an apparatus using coal, gas or electricity etc, used for heating, cooking, etc

stove[2] past form of **stave**

stow verb put away neatly and safely • **stowaway** noun someone who hides in a ship in order to travel without permission or without paying a fare

straddle verb 1 sit or stand with one leg on each side of (eg a chair or horse) 2 extend over from one side to the other

straggle verb 1 wander from the line of a march etc 2 lag behind 3 grow or spread beyond the intended limits:

his long beard straggled over his chest
• **straggler** *noun* someone who straggles • **straggly** *adj* spread out untidily

straight *adj* **1** not bent or curved: *a straight line* **2** direct and honest; frank: *a straight answer* **3** in the proper position or order: *your tie isn't straight* **4** of a hanging picture *etc*: placed level with ceiling or floor **5** without anything added: *a straight vodka* **6** expressionless: *he kept a straight face* **7** not comic: *a straight actor* **8** *informal* conventional, and perhaps rather boring, in tastes **9** *slang* heterosexual ◇ *adv* **1** by the shortest way; directly: *straight across the desert* **2** with no delays or diversions: *I came straight here after work* **3** fairly, frankly: *he's not playing straight with you* ◇ *noun* (with **the**) the straight part of a racecourse *etc* • **straighten** *verb* make straight • **straight fight** *noun* a contest between two people only • **straightforward** *adj* **1** without any difficulties **2** frank • **straightness** *noun* the state of being straight • **straight away** immediately

Do not confuse with: **strait**

strain *verb* **1** hurt (a muscle or other part of the body) by overworking or misusing it **2** work or use to the fullest: *he strained his ears to hear the whisper* **3** make a great effort: *he strained to reach the rope* **4** stretch too far, to the point of breaking (a person's patience *etc*) **5** separate liquid from a mixture of liquids and solids by passing it through a sieve ◇ *noun* **1** an injury to a muscle *etc* caused by straining it **2** the emotional effect of too much work, worry, *etc*: *suffering from strain* **3** too great a demand: *a strain on my patience* **4** a kind, breed: *a strain of fowls* **5** (**strains**) music heard at a distance: *the strains of a violin* **6** manner: *they grumbled on in the same strain for hours* • **strained** *adj* **1** done with effort, not naturally:

a strained conversation **2** unfriendly: *strained relations* • **strainer** *noun* a sieve

strait *noun* **1** a narrow strip of sea **2** (**straits**) difficulties, hardships: *dire straits* • **straitened** *adj* poor • **straitjacket** *noun* a jacket with long sleeves tied behind to prevent a violent or mentally ill person from using their arms • **straitlaced** *adj* strict in attitude and behaviour

Do not confuse with: **straight**

strand *noun* **1** a length of something soft and fine, *eg* hair or thread **2** *old* the shore of a sea or lake

stranded *adj* **1** of a ship: run aground on the shore **2** left helpless without money or friends

strange *adj* **1** unusual, odd: *a strange look on his face* **2** not known, seen, heard, *etc* before; unfamiliar: *the method was strange to me* **3** not accustomed (to) **4** foreign: *a strange country* • **strangely** *adv* • **strangeness** *noun*

stranger *noun* **1** someone who is unknown to you **2** a visitor • **a stranger to** someone who is quite unfamiliar with: *a stranger to hard work*

strangle *verb* **1** kill by gripping or squeezing the throat tightly **2** prevent oneself from giving (*eg* a scream, a sigh) **3** stop the growth of • **stranglehold** *noun* a tight control over something that prevents it from escaping or developing

strangulate *verb* press so as to stop the flow of blood or air; constrict • **strangulation** *noun*

strap *noun* a narrow strip of leather, cloth, *etc* used to hold things in place or together *etc* ◇ *verb* (**strapping**, **strapped**) **1** bind or fasten with a strap *etc* **2** beat with a strap • **straphanger** *noun*, *informal* a standing passenger in a train *etc* • **strapping** *adj* tall and strong: *strapping young man*

stratagem *noun* a plan for deceiving or outwitting an enemy

strategic *adj* **1** giving an advantage: *a strategic position* **2** done for a practical reason: *a strategic retreat* **3** of weapons: designed for a long-range attack • **strategically** *adv*

strategy *noun* (*plural* **strategies**) the art of guiding, forming or carrying out a plan • **strategist** *noun* someone who plans military operations

strathspey *noun* a Scottish dance tune that is slower than a reel

stratify *verb* (**stratifies**, **stratifying**, **stratified**) form layers or levels • **stratification** *noun*

stratosphere *noun* the layer of the earth's atmosphere between 10 and 60 kilometres above the earth • **stratospheric** *adj*

stratum *noun* (*plural* **strata**) **1** a layer of rock or soil **2** a level of society

stratus *noun* low, spread-out clouds

straw *noun* **1** stalks of wheat or similar crops, used as bedding for farm animals **2** a paper or plastic tube for sucking up a drink

strawberry *noun* a small juicy red fruit with pips on its surface, or the low creeping plant which bears it • **strawberry blonde** *noun* a woman with reddish blond hair

stray *verb* **1** wander **2** lose your way, become separated (from companions *etc*) ◇ *adj* **1** wandering, lost **2** happening *etc* here and there: *a stray example* ◇ *noun* a wandering animal that is lost or has been abandoned

streak *noun* **1** a strip that is different in colour from its surroundings **2** a smear of dirt, polish, *etc* **3** a trace of some quality in one's character: *a streak of selfishness* **4** a flash (eg of lightning) ◇ *verb* **1** mark with streaks **2** *informal* move very fast • **streaked** *adj* • **streaker** *noun*, *informal* some-

one who runs naked in public

streaky *adj* (**streakier**, **streakiest**) marked with streaks • **streakiness** *noun* • **streaky bacon** *noun* bacon with streaks of fat and lean

stream *noun* **1** a flow (of water, air, light, *etc*) **2** a small river; a brook **3** any steady flow of people or things: *a stream of traffic* ◇ *verb* flow or pour out • **streamer** *noun* **1** a long strip of paper used for decorating rooms **2** a narrow flag blowing in the wind • **streamline** *verb* **1** shape (a vehicle *etc*) so that it cuts through air or water as easily as possible **2** make more efficient: *we've streamlined our methods of paying*

street *noun* a road lined with houses *etc* • **street cred** *noun* the approval of people with knowledge of current urban tastes in fashion, music, *etc* • **streetwalker** *noun* a prostitute • **streets ahead of** much better than • **up someone's street** ideally suited to someone's interests or abilities

strength *noun* **1** the state of being strong **2** an available number or force (of soldiers, volunteers, *etc*) • **strengthen** *verb* make or become stronger • **on the strength of** judging by, or on the basis of

strenuous *adj* making or needing great effort: *the plans met strenuous resistance/squash is a strenuous game* • **strenuousness** *noun*

strep throat *noun*, *US informal* a severe throat infection

stress *noun* (*plural* **stresses**) **1** nervous strain: *the stress of modern life* **2** emphasis, importance **3** extra weight laid on a part of a word (as in *but*ter) **4** physical force exerted on something ◇ *verb* put stress, pressure, emphasis or strain on • **stressful** *adj*

stretch *verb* **1** draw out to greater length, or too far, or from one point to another: *don't stretch that elastic too far/stretch a rope from post to post* **2**

be able to be drawn out to a greater length or width: *that material stretches* **3** exert, or cause to exert: *the work stretched him to the full* **4** hold (out) **5** make (*eg* words, the law) appear to mean more than it does ◇ *noun* (*plural* **stretches**) **1** the act of stretching the body **2** the ability to stretch **3** a length in distance or time: *a stretch of bad road* • **stretcher** *noun* a light folding bed with handles for carrying the sick or wounded • **stretch limo** *noun* a luxurious extra-long limousine • **at a stretch** continuously: *working three hours at a stretch* • **at full stretch** at the limit, using all resources

strew *verb* (**strewing, strewn** *or* **strewed**) **1** scatter: *papers strewn over the floor* **2** cover (with): *the floor was strewn with papers*

striated *adj* streaked

stricken *adj* **1** deeply affected emotionally, *eg* by grief **2** badly wounded or injured

strict *adj* **1** insisting on exact obedience to rules **2** exact: *the strict meaning of a word* **3** allowing no exception: *strict orders* • **strictly** *adv* • **strictness** *noun* • **stricture** *noun* criticism or blame

stride *verb* (**striding, strode, stridden**) **1** walk with long steps **2** take a long step **3** walk over, along, *etc* ◇ *noun* **1** a long step **2** the distance covered by a step **3** a step forward • **take in your stride** manage to do easily

strident *adj* of a sound: loud and harsh • **stridency** *noun*

strife *noun* quarrelling or fighting

strike *verb* (**striking, struck**) **1** hit with force **2** attack: *the enemy struck at dawn* **3** light (a match) **4** make (a musical note) sound **5** of a clock: sound (*eg* at ten o'clock with ten chimes) **6** (often with **off** or **out**) cross out, cancel **7** hit or discover suddenly: *strike oil* **8** take a course: *he struck out across the fields* **9** stop working

(in support of a claim for more pay *etc*) **10** give (someone) the impression of being: *did he strike you as lazy?* **11** affect, impress: *I am struck by her beauty* **12** make (an agreement *etc*) • **striking** *adj* **1** noticeable: *a striking resemblance* **2** impressive • **strike camp** take down tents • **strike home 1** of a blow: hit the point aimed at **2** of a remark: have the intended effect • **strike up 1** begin to play or sing (a tune) **2** begin (a friendship, conversation, *etc*)

string *noun* **1** a long narrow cord for binding or tying, made of threads twisted together **2** a piece of wire or gut producing a note on a musical instrument **3** (**strings**) the stringed instruments in an orchestra **4** a line of objects threaded together: *string of pearls* **5** a number of things coming one after another: *string of abuse* ◇ *verb* (**stringing, strung**) **1** put on a string **2** stretch out in a line • **stringed** *adj* having strings • **string along** give false expectations to; deceive • **string up** hang

stringent *adj* strictly enforced: *stringent rules* • **stringency** *noun* strictness

stringy *adj* (**stringier, stringiest**) **1** like string **2** of meat: tough and fibrous

strip *noun* a long narrow piece (*eg* of paper) ◇ *verb* (**stripping, stripped**) **1** remove (*eg* leaves, fruit) from **2** remove your clothes, or the clothes from (someone else) **3** deprive: *stripped of his disguise* **4** make bare or empty: *strip the bed* • **strip cartoon** *noun* a line of drawings that tell a story • **strip search** *noun* a body search of someone who had been asked to strip • **striptease** *noun* an act in which a performer removes clothes artistically, *usu* to music

stripe *noun* **1** a band of colour different from the background on which it lies **2** a blow with a whip or rod ◇ *verb* make stripes on • **stripy** *adj* patterned with stripes

stripling *noun, old* a young man

strive *verb* (**striving, strove, striven**) **1** try hard **2** *old* fight

strobe *noun* a light that produces a flickering beam

strode *past tense of* **stride**

stroganoff *noun* a rich beef stew in a cream sauce

stroke *noun* **1** a blow (*eg* with a sword, whip) **2** something unexpected: *a stroke of good luck* **3** one movement (of a pen, an oar) **4** one chime of a clock **5** one complete movement of the arms and legs in swimming **6** a particular style of swimming: *breast stroke* **7** a way of striking the ball (*eg* in tennis, cricket) **8** a sudden interruption in blood flow to the brain, causing paralysis ◇ *verb* rub gently, *esp* as a sign of affection • **at a stroke** in a single action or effort

stroll *verb* walk slowly in a leisurely way ◇ *noun* a leisurely walk; an amble

strong *adj* **1** not easily worn away: *strong cloth* **2** not easily defeated *etc* **3** powerful: *strong wind* **4** with great physical strength **5** commanding respect or obedience **6** of a smell, colour, *etc*: very noticeable **7** of a feeling: intense: *strong dislike* **8** in number: *a workforce 500 strong* • **strong-box** *noun* a box for storing valuable objects or money • **stronghold** *noun* a place built to withstand attack; a fortress • **strongly** *adv* • **strong point** *noun* something in which a person excels • **strongroom** *noun* a room for storing valuable objects or money

strop *noun* **1** a strip of leather on which a razor is sharpened **2** *informal* a fit of bad-tempered disobedience ◇ *verb* (**stropping, stropped**) sharpen a razor

stroppy *adj* (**stroppier, stroppiest**) *informal* disobedient in a bad-tempered way

strove *past tense of* **strive**

struck *past form of* **strike**

structure *noun* **1** something built, or its basic shape or framework **2** the way the parts of anything are arranged: *the structure of the story* • **structural** *adj* • **structurally** *adv*

strudel *noun* a thin pastry filled with fruit and spices

struggle *verb* **1** try hard (to do something) **2** twist and fight to escape **3** fight (with or against someone) **4** move with difficulty: *struggling through the mud* ◇ *noun* **1** a great effort **2** a fight

strum *verb* (**strumming, strummed**) play (a guitar *etc*) with a brushing movement of the fingers

strung *past form of* **string** • **highly strung** easily excited or agitated

strut *verb* (**strutting, strutted**) walk in a self-important way ◇ *noun* **1** a self-important way of walking **2** a bar that supports something

strychnine /strik-neen/ *noun* a bitter poisonous drug

stub *noun* a small stump, *eg* of a pencil or cigarette, left over ◇ *verb* (**stubbing, stubbed**) **1** put out (*eg* a cigarette) by pressing it **2** knock (your toe) painfully against something

stubble *noun* **1** the short ends of the stalks of corn left after it is cut **2** a short growth of beard

stubborn *adj* **1** unwilling to give way; obstinate **2** of resistance *etc*: strong, determined **3** difficult to manage or deal with • **stubbornly** *adv* • **stubbornness** *noun*

stubby *adj* (**stubbier, stubbiest**) short and thick: *stubby fingers*

stucco *noun* (*plural* **stuccos**) **1** a kind of plaster used for covering walls, moulding ornaments, *etc* **2** artistic work done in stucco

stuck *past form of* **stick**

stud *noun* **1** a button with two heads

for fastening a collar **2** a decorative knob on a surface **3** a collection of horses kept for breeding, or one of these ◇ *verb* **1** cover or fit with studs **2** sprinkle thickly (with): *the meadow is studded with flowers*

student *noun* someone who studies, *esp* at college, university, *etc*

studio *noun* (*plural* **studios**) **1** the workshop of an artist or photographer **2** a building or place in which cinema films are made **3** a room from which television or radio programmes are broadcast

studious *adj* **1** studying carefully and a lot **2** careful: *his studious avoidance of quarrels* • **studiously** *adv* • **studiousness** *noun*

study *verb* (**studies, studying, studied**) **1** gain knowledge of (a subject) by reading, experiment, *etc* **2** look carefully at **3** consider carefully (*eg* a problem) ◇ *noun* (*plural* **studies**) **1** the gaining of knowledge of a subject: *the study of art* **2** a room where someone reads and writes **3** a work of art done as an exercise, or to try out ideas for a later work **4** a piece of music which is meant to develop the skill of the player • **studied** *adj* **1** not natural; insincere: *a studied smile* **2** done on purpose; intentional: *a studied insult*

stuff *noun* **1** substance or material of any kind: *what is that stuff all over the wall?* **2** the material of which anything is made **3** cloth, fabric ◇ *verb* **1** pack full **2** fill the skin of (a dead animal) to preserve it **3** fill (a prepared bird) with stuffing before cooking • **stuffed shirt** *noun* an unadventurous or conservative person • **get stuffed** *slang* go away

stuffing *noun* **1** feathers, scraps of material, *etc* used to stuff a cushion, chair, *etc* **2** breadcrumbs, onions, *etc* packed inside a fowl or other meat and cooked with it

stuffy *adj* (**stuffier, stuffiest**) **1** unpleasantly full of stale air **2** *informal* with conservative and old-fashioned ideas • **stuffily** *adv* • **stuffiness** *noun*

stultify *verb* (**stultifies, stultifying, stultified**) be so boring as to dull the mind

stumble *verb* **1** trip in walking **2** walk unsteadily **3** make mistakes or hesitate in speaking **4** (with **on**) find by chance ◇ *noun* the act of stumbling • **stumbling block** *noun* a difficulty in the way of a plan or of progress

stump *noun* **1** the part of a tree, leg, tooth, *etc* left after the main part has been cut away **2** *cricket* one of the three wooden stakes that make up a wicket ◇ *verb* **1** *cricket* put out (a batsman) by touching the stumps with the ball **2** puzzle completely **3** walk stiffly or heavily • **stumpy** *adj* short and thick • **stump up** *informal* pay up

stun *verb* (**stunning, stunned**) **1** knock senseless by a blow *etc* **2** surprise or shock very greatly: *stunned by the news*

stung *past form of* **sting**

stunk *past form of* **stink**

stunt *noun* **1** a daring trick **2** something done to attract attention: *a publicity stunt* ◇ *verb* stop the growth of • **stunted** *adj* small and badly shaped

stupefy *verb* (**stupefies, stupefying, stupefied**) **1** astonish **2** make unconscious • **stupefaction** *noun*

stupendous *adj* extremely good, great or impressive; wonderful

stupid *adj* **1** foolish: *a stupid thing to do* **2** slow at learning **3** stupefied (*eg* from lack of sleep) • **stupidity** *noun* • **stupidly** *noun*

stupor *noun* the state of being only partly conscious

sturdy *adj* (**sturdier, sturdiest**) strong-looking or strongly built • **sturdily** *adv* • **sturdiness** *noun*

sturgeon noun a large fish from which caviar is taken

stutter verb speak in a halting, jerky way; stammer ◇ noun a stammer

sty[1] noun (plural **sties**) an inflamed swelling on the eyelid

sty[2] noun (plural **sties**) an enclosure for pigs

Stygian adj extremely gloomy or unpleasant; hellish

style noun 1 manner of acting, writing, speaking, etc 2 fashion: in the style of the late 19th century 3 an air of elegance 4 the middle part of the pistil of a flower ◇ verb give a name to; call: styling himself 'Lord John' • **stylish** adj done in an impressive style • **stylized** adj in a bold style that is clearly not meant to be natural • **in style** with no expense or effort spared

stylus noun (plural **styluses**) a needle for a record player

stymie /stai-mi/ verb, Scot prevent from developing, progressing or taking place; impede

suave /swahv/ adj polite and charming in an insincere way; smooth

sub- prefix 1 under, below: submarine 2 less than: a sub-four-minute time 3 lower in rank or importance: sublieutenant

subaltern noun an officer in the army under the rank of captain

subconscious noun the contents of the mind of which someone is not themselves aware ◇ adj of the subconscious, not conscious or aware: a subconscious desire for fame

subcontract verb give a contract for (work forming part of a larger contract) to another company

subculture noun an identifiable group within a larger culture

subcutaneous adj beneath the skin

subdivide verb divide into smaller

parts • **subdivision** noun a part made by subdividing

subdue verb 1 make quieter, less enthusiastic or less optimistic: he seemed subdued after the fight 2 conquer (an enemy etc) 3 keep under control (eg a desire) 4 make less bright (eg a colour, a light)

subedit verb edit (text) at a secondary or later stage

subject noun 1 something or someone spoken about, studied, etc 2 grammar the word in a sentence or clause which stands for the person or thing doing the action of the verb (eg cat is the subject in 'the cat drank the milk') 3 someone under the power of another: the king's subjects 4 a member of a nation with a monarchy: a British subject ◇ adj 1 (with to) depending on: subject to your approval 2 (with to) liable to suffer from (eg colds) 3 under the power of another: a subject nation ◇ verb (often with to) force to submit (to) • **subjection** noun the act of subjecting or the state of being subjected

subjective adj based on personal feelings, thoughts, etc; not impartial • **subjectivity** noun

subjoin verb, formal add at the end

sub judice /sub joo-dis-eh/ adj being the subject of a current court case and therefore not to be discussed publicly

subjugate verb bring under your power; make obedient

subjunctive adj, grammar of a verb: in a form that indicates possibility, contingency, etc ◇ noun a subjunctive form of a verb

sublet verb let out (rented property) to another person, eg while the original tenant is away

sublieutenant noun an officer in the navy below the rank of lieutenant

sublime adj very noble, great or grand • **sublimity** noun

subliminal adj working below the level of consciousness: subliminal messages • **subliminally** adv

submachine gun noun a light machine gun fired from the hip or shoulder

submarine noun a type of ship that can travel under water ◇ adj under the surface of the sea

submerge verb cover with water • **submergence** or **submersion** noun • **submersible** noun a boat that can operate under water

submit verb (**submitting, submitted**) **1** give in; yield **2** offer for someone to select or make a judgement about • **submission** noun **1** an idea, statement, etc offered for consideration **2** readiness to do as others say; meekness **3** the act of submitting • **submissive** adj tending to do as others say; meek • **submissively** adv

subordinate adj (often with **to**) lower in rank or importance (than) ◇ noun someone who is subordinate ◇ verb (with **to**) consider as of less importance than • **subordination** noun

suborn verb persuade (someone) to do something illegal, esp by bribery

subpoena /suh-pee-nuh/ noun an order for someone to appear in court ◇ verb order to appear in court

subscribe verb **1** promise to take and pay for a number of issues of a magazine etc **2** (with **to**) agree with (an idea, statement, etc) **3** make a contribution (esp of money) towards a charity • **subscription** noun

subsequent adj coming after in time

subservient adj always willing to do as others say • **subservience** noun

subside verb **1** get less and less **2** sink into the ground • **subsidence** noun the sinking of a building into the ground

subsidiary adj **1** of secondary importance **2** of a company: controlled by another company **3** acting as a help

subsidy noun (plural **subsidies**) money paid by a government etc to help an industry • **subsidize** verb give money as a help

subsist verb **1** exist **2** (with **on**) live on (a kind of food etc) • **subsistence** noun **1** existence **2** means or necessities for survival

subsoil noun the layer of the earth just below the surface soil

substance noun **1** a material that can be seen and felt: glue is a sticky substance **2** general meaning (of a talk, essay, etc) **3** thickness, solidity **4** wealth, property: a woman of substance

substantial adj **1** solid, strong **2** large: a substantial building **3** able to be seen and felt **4** in the main, but not in detail: substantial agreement • **substantially** adv for the most part: substantially the same

substantiate verb give proof of, or evidence for

substantive noun, grammar a noun

substitute verb (with **for**) put in place of or instead of ◇ noun someone or something used instead of another • **substitution** noun

substratum noun (plural **substrata**) **1** a layer lying underneath **2** a foundation

subsume verb include in something larger

subterfuge noun a cunning trick to get out of a difficulty etc

subterranean adj found under the ground

subtitle noun **1** a second additional title of a book etc **2** a translation of the dialogue of a foreign-language film, appearing at the bottom of the screen

subtle *adj* **1** difficult to describe or explain: *a subtle difference* **2** cunning: *by a subtle means* • **subtlety** *noun* • **subtly** *adv*

subtotal *noun* a total of one set of figures within a larger group

subtract *verb* take (one number, quantity, *etc*) from another • **subtraction** *noun*

suburb *noun* a residential area on the outskirts of a town • **suburban** *adj* of suburbs • **suburbia** *noun* the suburbs

subversive *adj* likely to overthrow (government, discipline, *etc*)

subway *noun* **1** an underground crossing for pedestrians *etc* **2** an underground railway

succeed *verb* **1** (with **in**) manage to do what you have been trying to do **2** get on well **3** come after in time or in a series **4** (often with **to**) follow in order (to the throne *etc*)

success *noun* (*plural* **successes**) **1** the achievement of something you have been trying to do **2** someone who succeeds **3** something that turns out well • **successful** *adj* **1** having achieved what was aimed at **2** having achieved wealth or social status **3** turning out as planned • **succession** *noun* **1** the act of following after **2** the right of becoming the next holder (of a throne *etc*) **3** a number of things coming one after the other: *a succession of failures* • **successive** *adj* following one after the other • **successor** *noun* someone who has a job, position or role after another • **in succession** one after another

succinct *adj* expressed in a few words; brief: *a succinct reply*

succour *verb* help in time of distress ◇ *noun* help

succubus *noun* an evil spirit in the shape of a woman believed to have sexual intercourse with men in their sleep (*compare with*: **incubus**)

succulent *adj* **1** juicy **2** of a plant: having thick juicy leaves or stems

succumb *verb* give in (to): *succumbed to temptation*

such *adj* **1** of a kind previously mentioned: *such things are difficult to find* **2** similar: *doctors, nurses and such people* **3** so great: *his excitement was such that he shouted out loud* **4** used for emphasis: *it's such a disappointment!* ◇ *pronoun* thing, people, *etc* of a kind already mentioned: *such as these are not to be trusted* • **such-and-such** *adj & pronoun* any given (person or thing): *such-and-such a book* • **as such** by itself • **such as** of the same kind as

suck *verb* **1** draw into the mouth **2** hold in the mouth and lick hard (*eg* a sweet) **3** (often with **up** or **in**) draw in, absorb **4** *US slang* be contemptibly bad: *that movie really sucks* ◇ *noun* **1** a sucking action **2** the act of sucking

sucker *noun* **1** a side shoot rising from the root of a plant **2** a part of an animal's body by which it sticks to objects **3** a pad (of rubber *etc*) that can stick to a surface **4** *informal* someone easily fooled

suckle *verb* of a woman or female animal: give milk from the breast or teat • **suckling** *noun* a baby or young animal that still sucks its mother's milk

sucrose *noun* a sugar found in sugar beet

suction *noun* **1** the act of sucking **2** the process of reducing the air pressure, and so producing a vacuum, on the surface or between surfaces

sudden *adj* happening all at once without being expected: *a sudden attack* • **suddenly** *adv* • **suddenness** *noun*

Sudoku *noun* a type of puzzle in

which numbers must be entered into a square grid

suds *plural noun* frothy, soapy water

sue *verb* start a law case against

suede /swehd/ *noun* a kind of leather with a soft, dull surface

suet /*soo*-it/ *noun* a kind of hard animal fat

suffer *verb* **1** feel pain or punishment **2** put up with; tolerate **3** go through, undergo (a change *etc*) **4** *old* allow • **suffering** *noun* • **on sufferance** allowed or tolerated but not really wanted

suffice *verb* be enough, or good enough

sufficient *adj* enough • **sufficiently** *adv*

suffix *noun* (*plural* **suffixes**) a small part added to the end of a word to make another word, such as *-ness* to *good* to make *goodness*, or *-ly* to *quick* to make *quickly*

suffocate *verb* **1** kill by preventing the breathing of **2** die from lack of air **3** feel unable to breathe freely: *suffocating in this heat* • **suffocation** *noun*

suffrage *noun* the right to vote: *women's suffrage*

suffuse *verb* spread over • **suffusion** *noun*

sugar *noun* a sweet substance obtained mostly from sugar cane and sugar beet ◊ *verb* mix or sprinkle with sugar • **sugar beet** *noun* a vegetable whose root yields sugar • **sugar cane** *noun* a tall grass from whose juice sugar is obtained • **sugar daddy** *noun* an older man who lavishes money on a younger woman in exchange for companionship and, often, sex • **sugary** *adj* **1** tasting of sugar **2** too sweet

suggest *verb* **1** put forward for consideration; propose **2** put into the mind; hint • **suggestible** *adj* easily influenced by suggestions • **suggestion** *noun* **1** an idea put forward **2** a slight trace: *a suggestion of anger in her voice* **3** an act of suggesting

suggestive *adj* **1** suggesting something sexually improper: *suggestive remarks* **2** (with **of**) giving the idea of: *suggestive of mental illness*

suicide *noun* **1** the taking of your own life **2** someone who kills themselves • **suicidal** *adj* **1** of or considering suicide **2** likely to cause your death or ruin: *suicidal action*

sui generis /*soo*-i jen-uh-ris/ *adj* of its own kind; unique

suit *noun* **1** a set of clothes to be worn together **2** a case in a law court **3** one of the four divisions (spades, hearts, diamonds, clubs) of playing cards **4** *old* a request for permission to court a woman ◊ *verb* **1** be convenient or suitable for: *the climate suits me* **2** look well on: *that dress suits you* **3** (with **to**) make suitable for: *suited his words to the occasion* • **suitability** *noun* • **suitable** *adj* **1** fitting the purpose **2** just what is wanted; convenient • **suitcase** *noun* a travelling case for carrying clothes *etc* • **suitor** *noun, dated* a man who tries to gain the love of a woman • **follow suit** do what someone else has done

suite *noun* **1** a self-contained set of rooms in a larger building **2** a set of matching furniture

sulk *verb* keep silent because of being displeased • **sulky** *adj* • **the sulks** a fit of sulking

sullen *adj* angry and silent; sulky • **sullenness** *noun*

sully *verb* (**sullies**, **sullying**, **sullied**) make less good; spoil

sulphur *noun* a yellow substance found in the ground that gives off a choking smell when burnt, used in matches, gunpowder, *etc* • **sulphuric acid** *noun* a powerful acid widely used in industry

sultan noun 1 hist the head of the Turkish Ottoman empire 2 an Islamic ruler

sultana noun 1 a light-coloured raisin 2 a sultan's wife

sultry adj 1 of weather: very hot and close 2 of a woman: having a sexually suggestive appearance

sum noun 1 the amount made by two or more things added together 2 a quantity of money 3 a problem in arithmetic 4 the general meaning (of something that is said or written) • **summing-up** noun • **sum total** noun 1 the sum of several smaller sums 2 the main point or total effect of something • **sum up** give the main points of (a discussion, evidence in a trial, etc)

summary noun (plural **summaries**) a shortened form (of a story, statement, etc) giving only the main points ◊ adj 1 short, brief 2 done without wasting time or words • **summarily** adv • **summarize** verb state the main points of

summer noun the warmest season of the year, following spring ◊ adj relating to summer • **summerhouse** noun a small house in a garden for sitting in

summit noun 1 the highest point of a hill etc 2 a conference between heads of governments

summon verb 1 order (someone) to come to you, appear in a court of law, etc 2 (with **up**) gather up (courage, strength, etc) • **summons** noun (plural **summonses**) an order to appear in court

sumo noun a Japanese form of wrestling

sump noun 1 part of a vehicle engine that contains the oil 2 a small drainage pit

sumptuous adj extremely luxurious

sun noun 1 the round body in the sky that gives light and heat to the earth 2 sunshine or sunny weather ◊ verb (**sunning, sunned**) (with **yourself**) lie in the sunshine, sunbathe • **sunbathe** verb lie or sit in the sun to acquire a suntan • **sunbeam** noun a ray of light from the sun • **sunburn** noun a burning or redness caused by overexposure to the sun • **sunburned** or **sunburnt** adj affected by sunburn • **sundial** noun an instrument for telling the time from the shadow of a rod on its surface cast by the sun • **sunflower** noun a large yellow flower with petals like rays of the sun • **sunglasses** plural noun spectacles with tinted lenses that shield the eyes from sunlight • **sunlight** noun the light from the sun • **sunlit** adj lighted up by the sun • **sunny** adj 1 full of sunshine 2 cheerful: sunny nature • **sunrise** noun the rising of the sun in the morning • **sunset** noun the setting of the sun in the evening • **sunshine** noun 1 bright sunlight 2 cheerfulness • **sunstroke** noun a serious illness caused by over-exposure to very hot sunshine • **suntan** noun a browning of the skin caused by exposure to the sun

sundae noun a sweet dish of ice-cream served with fruit, syrup, etc

Sunday noun the day between Saturday and Monday, considered to be the first day of the week

sundry adj of various kinds: sundry articles for sale • **sundries** plural noun odds and ends

sung past participle of **sing**

sunk adj 1 on a lower level than the surroundings; sunken 2 informal in a situation in which success or survival is impossible; done for • **sunken** adj 1 that has been sunk 2 of cheeks etc: hollow

Sunni noun a follower of the most widely practised branch of Islam ◊ adj of or following this branch of Islam

sup verb (**supping, supped**) eat or drink in small mouthfuls

super adj, informal extremely good

super- *prefix* very good, powerful, fast, *etc*: *superbikes/supernova/super-market*

superannuate *verb* make (someone) retire from their job because of old age • **superannuation** *noun* a pension given to someone retired

superb *adj* excellent: *a superb view*

superbug *noun* a bacterium that is very resistant to drugs

supercilious *adj* looking down on others; haughty • **superciliousness** *noun*

superficial *adj* **1** of a wound: affecting the surface of the skin only, not deep **2** not thorough or detailed: *superficial interest* **3** apparent at first glance, not actual: *superficial likeness* **4** of a person: not capable of deep thoughts or feelings • **superficiality** *noun* • **superficially** *adv*

Do not confuse: **superficial** and **superfluous**

---

superfluous *adj* beyond what is enough or necessary • **superfluity** *noun*

superhuman *adj* **1** divine, godly **2** greater than would be expected of an ordinary person: *superhuman effort*

superimpose *verb* lay or place (one thing on another)

superintend *verb* be in charge or control; manage • **superintendent** *noun* **1** a police officer above a chief inspector **2** someone who is in charge of an institution, building, *etc*

superior *adj* **1** higher in place or rank **2** better or greater than others: *superior forces/superior goods* **3** having an air of being better than others ◇ *noun* someone better than, or higher in rank than, others • **superiority** *noun*

superlative *adj* **1** better than, or going beyond, all others: *superlative*

skill **2** *grammar* an adjective or adverb of the highest degree of comparison, *eg* kindest, worst, most boringly

supermarket *noun* a large self-service store selling food and household goods

supernatural *adj* thought or claimed to be caused by forces that are not natural • **supernaturally** *adv*

supernova *noun* an exploding star surrounded by a bright cloud of gas

supernumerary *adj* above the usual or required number; surplus ◇ *noun* (*plural* **supernumeraries**) something beyond the required number; an extra

supersede *verb* **1** take the place of: *he superseded his brother as head-master* **2** replace (something with something else)

supersonic *adj* faster than the speed of sound: *supersonic flight*

superstition *noun* **1** belief in magic and in things that cannot be explained by reason **2** an example of such belief, *eg* not walking under ladders • **superstitious** *adj* having superstitions

supervene *verb* come after or in addition

supervise *verb* be in charge of work and see that it is properly done • **supervision** *noun* the act of supervising; control, inspection • **supervisor** *noun*

supine *adj* **1** lying on the back **2** not showing any interest or energy

supper *noun* a meal taken in the evening

supplant *verb* take the place of somebody or something: *the baby supplanted the dog in her affections*

supple *adj* **1** bending the body easily; flexible **2** of an object: bending easily without breaking • **suppleness** *noun* • **supply** *adv*

supplement *noun* **1** something

added to supply a need or lack **2** a special section added to the main part of a newspaper or magazine ◇ *verb* make or be an addition to: *a second job to supplement his income* • **supplementary** *adj* added to supply a need; additional

suppliant *adj* asking earnestly and humbly

supplicate *verb* ask earnestly; beg • **supplicant** *noun* • **supplication** *noun* a humble, earnest request

supply *verb* (**supplies, supplying, supplied**) **1** provide (what is wanted or needed) **2** provide (someone with something) ◇ *noun* (*plural* **supplies**) **1** something supplied **2** a stock or store **3** (**supplies**) a stock of essentials, *eg* food, equipment, money, *etc* ◇ *adj* of a teacher: filling another's place or position for a time

support *verb* **1** take part of the weight of and hold up **2** help or encourage **3** supply with a means of living: *support a family* **4** *formal* put up with: *I can't support lies* ◇ *noun* **1** an act of supporting **2** something that supports • **supporter** *noun* someone who supports (*esp* a football club)

suppose *verb* **1** assume for the sake of argument: *suppose that we have £100 to spend* **2** believe to be probable: *I suppose you know* **3** used to give a polite order: *suppose you leave now* • **supposed** *adj* believed (often mistakenly) to be so: *her supposed generosity* • **supposedly** *adv* according to what is supposed • **supposing** *conj* in the event that: *supposing it rains* • **supposition** *noun* **1** something supposed **2** the act of supposing • **be supposed to** be required or expected to (do)

suppository *noun* (*plural* **suppositories**) a medicated plug inserted into the rectum or vagina

suppress *verb* **1** keep from being expressed or communicated **2** put an end to (a rebellion *etc*) • **suppression** *noun* the act of suppressing

suppurate *verb* of a wound: be full of, or discharge, pus

supra- *prefix* above: *supramolecular*

supreme *adj* **1** most powerful: *supreme ruler* **2** very great: *supreme courage* • **supremacist** *noun* someone who believes in the supremacy of their own race *etc*: *white supremacist* • **supremacy** *noun* highest power or authority • **supremo** *noun* (*plural* **supremos**) *informal* a boss or leader

surcharge *noun* an extra charge or tax

sure *adj* **1** having no doubt: *I'm sure that I can come* **2** certain (to do, happen, *etc*): *he is sure to be there* **3** reliable, dependable: *a sure method* • **sure-footed** *adj* unlikely to slip or stumble • **be sure** see to it that: *be sure that he does it* • **make sure** act so that, or check that, something is sure • **sure of yourself** confident • **to be sure 1** certainly! **2** undoubtedly: *to be sure, you are correct*

surely *adv* **1** without doubt **2** expressing a little doubt: *surely you won't tell him?* **3** without hesitation, mistake, *etc*

surety *noun* (*plural* **sureties**) **1** someone who promises that another person will do something, *esp* appear in court **2** a pledge or guarantee

surf *noun* the foam made by the breaking of waves ◇ *verb* **1** ride on a surfboard **2** browse randomly through the Internet • **surfboard** *noun* a long narrow board on which someone can ride over surf • **surfer** *noun* someone who surfs • **surfing** *noun* the sport of riding on a surfboard

surface *noun* the outside or top part of anything, *eg* of the earth or of a road ◇ *verb* **1** come up to the surface of water **2** become known, apparent or present **3** put a (smooth) surface on ◇ *adj* **1** on the surface **2** travelling on the surface of land or water: *surface mail*

surfeit *noun* too much of anything

surge *verb* 1 move (forward) like waves 2 rise suddenly or excessively ◇ *noun* 1 a sudden rise or increase (of pain *etc*) 2 the swelling of a large wave 3 a swelling or rising movement like this

surgeon *noun* a doctor who performs operations in which someone's body is cut open to examine or remove a diseased part • **surgery** *noun* 1 treatment of diseases *etc* by operation 2 a doctor's or dentist's consulting room • **surgical** *adj* • **surgically** *adv*

surly (**surlier**, **surliest**) *adj* unfriendly and impolite; gruff • **surliness** *noun*

surmise *verb* conclude from information available; presume ◇ *noun* a supposition

surmount *verb* 1 overcome (a difficulty *etc*) 2 climb over or get over • **surmountable** *adj*

surname *noun* a person's last name or family name

surpass *verb* be more or better than: *his work surpassed my expectations*

surplice *noun* a loose white gown worn by members of the clergy

Do not confuse: **surplice** and **surplus**

surplus *noun* the amount left over after what is needed has been used up ◇ *adj* left over

surprise *noun* 1 the feeling caused by an unexpected happening 2 an unexpected happening ◇ *verb* 1 cause someone to feel surprise 2 come upon (someone) suddenly and without warning • **take by surprise** come upon, or capture, without warning

surreal *adj* dreamlike, using images from the subconscious • **surrealism**

noun the use of surreal images in art • **surrealist** *noun & adj*

surrender *verb* 1 stop fighting or resisting and admit defeat: *surrender to the enemy* 2 *formal* hand over ◇ *noun* an act of surrender, *esp* in a war

surreptitious *adj* done in a secret or underhand way

surrogate *noun* a substitute • **surrogacy** *noun*

surround *verb* 1 be all round (someone or something) 2 put things all round (someone or something) ◇ *noun* a border • **surroundings** *plural noun* 1 the area round a place 2 the people and places with which you have to deal in daily life

surtax *noun* an extra tax *esp* on income

surtitles *plural noun* a translation of an opera libretto projected on a screen above the audience

surveillance *noun* a close watch or constant guard

survey *verb* (**surveys**, **surveying**, **surveyed**) 1 look over 2 inspect or examine 3 make careful measurements of (a piece of land *etc*) ◇ *noun* (*plural* **surveys**) 1 a detailed examination or inspection, *esp* of people's opinions 2 a piece of writing giving results of this 3 a general view 4 a careful measuring of land *etc* 5 a map made with the measurements obtained • **surveyor** *noun* someone who makes surveys of land, buildings, *etc*

survive *verb* 1 remain alive, continue to exist (after an event *etc*) 2 live longer than: *he survived his wife* • **survival** *noun* 1 the state of surviving 2 a custom, relic, *etc* that remains from earlier times • **survivor** *noun* someone who remains alive: *the only survivor of the crash*

sus or **suss** *verb, slang* realize or find out • **have someone sussed** understand their character, motives, *etc*

susceptible *adj* **1** (with **to**) liable to be affected by: *susceptible to colds* **2** (with **to**) easily affected or influenced • **susceptibility** *noun*

sushi *noun* a Japanese dish of cakes of cold rice, slices of raw fish and raw vegetables

suspect *verb* **1** be inclined to think (someone) guilty: *I suspect her of the crime* **2** have doubts about: *I suspected his air of frankness* **3** guess: *I suspect that we're wrong* ◇ *noun* someone thought to be guilty of a crime *etc* ◇ *adj* arousing doubt; suspected

suspend *verb* **1** hang **2** keep from falling or sinking: *particles suspended in a liquid* **3** stop for a time: *suspend business* **4** take away a job, privilege, *etc* from (someone) for a time: *they suspended the student from classes*

suspender *noun* **1** an elastic strap worn to keep up stockings **2** (**suspenders**) *US* braces

suspense *noun* **1** a state of excited or nervous uncertainty **2** a state of being undecided

suspension *noun* **1** the act of suspending **2** the state of being suspended **3** the state of a solid which is mixed with a liquid or gas and does not sink or dissolve in it • **suspension bridge** *noun* a bridge that is suspended from cables hanging from towers

suspicion *noun* **1** a feeling of doubt or mistrust **2** an opinion or guess

suspicious *adj* **1** inclined to suspect or distrust **2** arousing suspicion • **suspiciously** *adv*

sustain *verb* **1** hold up; support **2** suffer (an injury *etc*) **3** give strength to: *the food will sustain you* **4** keep (something) going: *sustain a conversation* • **sustenance** *noun* food or nourishment

suttee *noun*, *hist* an Indian widow

who burned herself on her husband's funeral pyre

suture *noun* a stitch used to join the edges of a wound ◇ *verb* sew up a wound with stitches

suzerain /soo-zuh-rehn/ *noun* **1** a feudal lord **2** a supreme ruler • **suzerainty** *noun* supreme power

svelte *adj* having an attractively thin body; slender

SW *abbrev* south-west or south-western

swab *noun* **1** a piece of cotton wool used for cleaning a wound, absorbing blood, *etc* **2** a mop for cleaning a ship's deck ◇ *verb* (**swabbing**, **swabbed**) clean with a swab

swaddle *verb* wrap up (a young baby) tightly • **swaddling clothes** *plural noun*, *old* strips of cloth used to wrap up a young baby

swag *noun*, *informal* **1** stolen goods **2** *Aust* a bundle of possessions

swagger *verb* **1** walk proudly, swinging the arms and body **2** boast ◇ *noun* a proud walk or attitude

swain *noun*, *old* a young man, *esp* a boyfriend or fiancé

swallow¹ *verb* **1** pass (food or drink) down the throat into the stomach **2** (with **up**) make disappear **3** receive (an insult *etc*) without objection **4** keep back (tears, a laugh, *etc*) ◇ *noun* an act of swallowing

swallow² *noun* a bird with pointed wings and a forked tail

swamp *noun* an area of wet, marshy ground ◇ *verb* overwhelm: *swamped with work*

swan *noun* a large water bird with white feathers and a long neck • **swan song** *noun* the last work of a musician, writer, *etc*

swank *noun* boastful behaviour ◇ *verb* show off

swanky *adj* (**swankier**, **swankiest**)

informal very luxurious and expensive; top-class

swap *or* **swop** *verb* (**swapping** *or* **swopping**, **swapped** *or* **swopped**) give one thing in exchange for another: *swap addresses*

sward *noun, old* a patch of green turf

swarm *noun* **1** a large number of insects flying or moving together **2** a dense moving crowd ◇ *verb* **1** of insects: gather together in great numbers **2** move in crowds **3** be crowded with: *swarming with tourists* **4** (with **up**) climb up (a wall *etc*)

swarthy *adj* (**swarthier**, **swarthiest**) with a dark complexion

swashbuckling *adj* featuring exciting sword fights

swastika *noun* an ancient design of a cross with bent arms, taken up as a symbol of Nazism

swat *verb* (**swatting**, **swatted**) squash (a fly *etc*)

swatch *noun* a piece of fabric, carpet, *etc* used as a sample

swath /swoth/ *or* **swathe** /swehdh/ *noun* **1** a line of corn or grass cut by a scythe **2** a strip

swathe[1] *verb* wrap round with clothes or bandages

swathe[2] *another spelling of* **swath**

sway *verb* **1** swing or rock to and fro **2** bend in one direction or to one side **3** influence: *sway opinion* ◇ *noun* **1** a swaying movement **2** rule, power: *hold sway over*

swear *verb* (**swearing**, **swore**, **sworn**) **1** promise or declare solemnly **2** vow **3** say vulgar or taboo words **4** make (someone) take an oath: *to swear someone to secrecy* • **swearword** *noun* a word used in swearing • **sworn** *adj* holding steadily to an attitude *etc*: *they had been sworn friends since childhood/Richard and Wendy*

became sworn enemies • **swear by** have complete faith in and use regularly

sweat *noun* moisture secreted by the skin; perspiration ◇ *verb* **1** give out sweat **2** *informal* work hard • **sweater** *noun* a warm piece of clothing for the upper body; a pullover • **sweatshirt** *noun* a long-sleeved jersey made of soft, thick cotton • **sweatshop** *noun* a factory where people work long hours for little pay • **sweaty** *adj* wet or stained with sweat

swede *noun* a kind of large yellow turnip

sweep *verb* (**sweeping**, **swept**) **1** clean (a floor *etc*) with a brush or broom **2** (often with **up**) gather up (dust *etc*) by sweeping **3** carry (away, along, off, *etc*) with a long brushing movement **4** spread quickly throughout: *a new fad which is sweeping the country* **5** move quickly in a proud manner (*eg* from a room) **6** curve widely or stretch far ◇ *noun* **1** a sweeping movement **2** a wide long curving course **3** a chimney sweeper **4** a sweepstake • **sweeping** *adj* **1** of a statement *etc*: too general, allowing no exceptions, rash **2** of a victory *etc*: great, overwhelming

sweepstake *noun* a gambling system in which those who take part stake money which goes to the holder of the winning ticket

sweet *adj* **1** having the taste of sugar, not salty, sour or bitter **2** pleasing to the taste **3** pleasant to hear or smell **4** kind in a way that inspires affection ◇ *noun* **1** a small piece of sweet substance, *eg* chocolate, toffee, *etc* **2** something sweet served towards the end of a meal; a pudding • **sweetbreads** *plural noun* an animal's pancreas used for food • **sweetcorn** *noun* maize • **sweeten** *verb* make or become sweet • **sweetener** *noun* **1** an artificial substance used to sweeten food or drinks **2** *informal* a bribe • **sweetheart**

noun a lover • **sweetly** adv • **sweet-meat** noun, old a sugar-based morsel; a sweet • **sweetness** noun • **sweet pea** noun a sweet-smelling climbing flower grown in gardens • **sweet talk** noun flattery or persuasion • **sweet tooth** noun a liking for sweet-tasting things • **sweet william** noun a sweet-smelling type of garden flower

swell verb (**swelling, swelled, swollen**) **1** grow in size or volume **2** of the sea: rise into waves ◇ noun **1** an increase in size or volume **2** large, heaving waves **3** a gradual rise in the height of the ground ◇ adj, US informal excellent ◇ noun a dandy • **swelling** noun a swollen part of the body

swelter verb be uncomfortably hot • **sweltering** adj uncomfortably hot

swept past form of **sweep**

swerve verb turn quickly to one side ◇ noun a quick turn aside

swift adj moving quickly; rapid ◇ noun a bird similar to the swallow • **swiftly** adv • **swiftness** noun

swig noun, informal a large mouthful of a drink ◇ verb (**swigging, swigged**) informal gulp down

swill verb wash out ◇ noun partly liquid food given to pigs

swim verb (**swimming, swam, swum**) **1** move on or in water, using arms, legs, fins, etc **2** cross by swimming: swim the Channel **3** float, not sink **4** be dizzy **5** be covered (with liquid): meat swimming in grease ◇ noun an act of swimming • **swimmer** noun • **swimming bath** or **swimming pool** noun a large water-filled tank designed for swimming, diving in, etc • **swimming costume** or **swimsuit** noun a brief close-fitting garment for swimming in • **swimmingly** adv smoothly and successfully

swindle verb **1** cheat in order to obtain money from; defraud **2** get (money etc from someone) by cheating ◇ noun a deception in which

money is obtained • **swindler** noun

swine noun (plural **swine**) **1** old a pig **2** informal a contemptible person • **swineherd** noun, old someone who looks after pigs

swing verb (**swinging, swung**) **1** move to and fro; sway **2** move backwards and forwards on a hanging seat **3** turn or whirl round **4** walk quickly, moving the arms to and fro ◇ noun **1** a seat for swinging, hung on ropes etc from a support **2** a swinging movement • **swing bridge** noun a kind of bridge that swings open to let ships pass • **in full swing** going on busily

swingeing adj very great and damaging: swingeing cuts in taxation

Do not confuse with: **swinging**

swipe verb **1** strike with a sweeping blow **2** pass a plastic card through a reading device ◇ noun a sweeping blow

swirl verb sweep along with a whirling motion ◇ noun a whirling movement

swish verb **1** strike or brush against with a rustling sound **2** move making such a noise: swishing out of the room in her long dress ◇ noun a rustling sound or movement

switch noun (plural **switches**) **1** a small button or lever that operates something electrical **2** an act of switching **3** a change: a switch of loyalty **4** a thin stick ◇ verb **1** turn (off or on) by means of a switch **2** change, turn: switch jobs/hastily switching the conversation • **switchback** noun a road or railway with steep ups and downs or sharp turns • **switchblade** noun a flick knife • **switchboard** noun a board with equipment for making telephone connections

swither verb hesitate because of uncertainty; waver

swivel noun a joint that turns on a pin or pivot ◇ verb (**swivelling, swivelled**) turn on a swivel; pivot

swiz or **swizzle** noun, informal a swindle

swizzle stick noun a small stick used to stir drinks

swollen adj increased in size by swelling ◇ verb past participle of **swell**

swoon verb, old faint ◇ noun a fainting fit

swoop verb come down with a sweep, like a bird of prey ◇ noun a sudden downward rush • **at one fell swoop** in one single decisive action

swop another spelling of **swap**

sword noun a type of weapon with a long blade for cutting or piercing • **swordfish** noun a large type of fish with a long pointed upper jaw like a sword

swore past tense of **swear**

sworn past participle of **swear**

swot verb, informal study hard ◇ noun someone who studies hard

sybaritic adj 1 luxurious 2 fond of luxury

sycamore noun a tree with dark-green leaves and seeds with lobes like wings

sycophant noun someone who flatters others in order to gain favour or personal advantage • **sycophantic** adj

syllable noun a word or part of a word spoken with one breath (cheese has one syllable, but-ter two, mar-gar-ine three) • **syllabic** adj

syllabub noun a dessert of sweetened whipped cream and wine

syllabus noun (plural **syllabuses** or **syllabi**) a programme or list of lectures, classes, etc

syllogism noun a combination of two statements that leads to a third conclusion • **syllogistic** adj

sylph noun 1 a type of fairy supposed to inhabit the air 2 a slender, graceful woman • **sylphlike** adj

sylvan adj, old wooded

symbiosis noun a mutually beneficial partnership • **symbiotic** adj

symbol noun something that stands for or represents another thing • **symbolic** adj standing as a symbol of • **symbolism** noun the use of symbols to express ideas, esp in art and literature • **symbolist** noun & adj • **symbolize** verb be a symbol of

symmetrical adj having symmetry; not lopsided in appearance • **symmetrically** adv

symmetry noun the equality in size, shape and position of two halves on either side of a dividing line: spoiling the symmetry of the building

sympathetic adj feeling or showing sympathy • **sympathetically** adv • **sympathetic to** or **towards** inclined to be in favour of: sympathetic to the scheme

sympathize verb: **sympathize with** express or feel sympathy (for)

sympathy noun (plural **sympathies**) 1 a feeling of pity or sorrow for someone in trouble 2 agreement with, or understanding of, the feelings, attitudes, etc of others

symphony noun (plural **symphonies**) a long piece of classical music written for an orchestra of many different instruments

symposium noun (plural **symposiums** or **symposia**) 1 a meeting or conference for the discussion of some subject 2 a collection of essays dealing with a single subject

symptom noun an outward sign indicating the presence of a disease etc: symptoms of measles • **symptomatic** adj

synagogue *noun* a Jewish place of worship

synchronize *verb* **1** happen at the same time **2** cause to show the same time: *synchronize watches*

syncopate *verb, music* change the beat by accenting beats not usually accented • **syncopation** *noun*

syncope /*sing*-kuh-pi/ *noun* the contraction of a word by omitting a letter or syllable in the middle

syndicate *noun* a number of people who join together to manage some piece of business

syndrome *noun* a pattern of behaviour, events, *etc* characteristic of some problem or condition

synod *noun* a meeting of members of the clergy

synonym *noun* a word that has the same, or nearly the same, meaning as another, *eg* 'ass' and 'donkey', or 'brave' and 'courageous' • **synonymous** *adj* having the same meaning

synopsis *noun* (*plural* **synopses**) a short summary of the main points of a book, speech, *etc*

syntax *noun* rules for the correct combination of words to form sentences • **syntactic** *or* **syntactical** *adj*

synthesis *noun* **1** the act of making a whole by putting together its separate parts **2** the making of a substance by combining chemical elements

synthesize *verb* make (*eg* a drug) by synthesis

synthesizer *noun* a computerized instrument that creates electronic musical sounds

synthetic *adj* **1** made artificially to look like a natural product: *synthetic leather* **2** not natural, pretended: *synthetic charm* • **synthetically** *adv*

syphilis *noun* a highly contagious sexually transmitted disease • **syphilitic** *adj*

syphon *another spelling of* **siphon**

syringe *noun* a tubular instrument with a needle and plunger, used to extract blood, inject drugs, *etc* ◇ *verb* clean out with a syringe: *needing his ears syringed*

syrup *noun* **1** a thick sticky liquid made by boiling water or fruit juice with sugar **2** a purified form of treacle

system *noun* **1** an arrangement of several parts that work together: *railway system/solar system* **2** a way of organizing something: *democratic system of government* **3** a regular method of doing something **4** the body, or its parts, considered as a whole: *my system is run down* • **systemic** *adj* affecting the whole body • **systems analyst** *noun* a person who investigates the most effective way of processing data

systematic *adj* following a system; methodical • **systematically** *adv*

systole /*sis*-tuh-li/ *noun, med* a single contraction of the heart • **systolic** *adj*

Tt

ta *exclam, Brit informal* thanks

tab *noun* **1** a small tag or flap attached to something **2** a running total, *esp* of money owed; a tally

tabard *noun* a short sleeveless tunic

tabby *or* **tabby-cat** *noun* (*plural* **tabbies**) a striped cat

tabernacle *noun* a place of worship

table *noun* **1** a flat-topped piece of furniture for eating at, working at or putting things on **2** an arrangement of facts or figures in rows and columns: *multiplication tables* ◇ *verb* **1** make into a list or table **2** put forward for discussion: *table a motion* • **table-cloth** *noun* a cloth for covering a table • **tableland** *noun* a raised stretch of land with a level surface • **table linen** *noun* tablecloths and napkins • **table tennis** *noun* a form of tennis played across a table with small bats and a light ball

tableau *noun* (*plural* **tableaux**) a striking group or scene

table d'hôte /tah-bluh *doht*/ *noun* a meal of several courses at a fixed price

tablespoon *noun* a large size of spoon • **tablespoonful** *noun* (*plural* **tablespoonfuls**) the amount held in a tablespoon

tablet *noun* **1** a piece of solid medicine for swallowing; a pill **2** a small flat plate on which to write, paint, *etc* **3** a small flat piece, *eg* of soap or chocolate **4** a brittle sweet made with sugar and condensed milk

tabloid *noun* a small-sized newspaper, *esp* one with an informal or sensational style

taboo *adj* forbidden or disapproved of for social or religious reasons ◇ *noun* a taboo subject or behaviour

tabor /*teh*-buh/ *noun* a small kind of drum

tabular *adj* set in the form of a table

tabulate *verb* set out (information *etc*) in columns or rows

tachograph *noun* an instrument showing a vehicle's mileage, number of stops, *etc*

tachometer *noun* an instrument showing the speed of a vehicle's engine

tacit /*tas*-it/ *adj* understood but not spoken aloud, silent: *tacit agreement* • **tacitly** *adv*

taciturn *adj* tending not to say much; quiet • **taciturnity** *noun* • **taciturnly** *adv*

tack *noun* **1** a short sharp nail with a broad head **2** a sideways movement allowing a yacht to sail against the wind **3** a direction followed **4** a rough stitch to keep material in place while sewing ◇ *verb* **1** fasten with tacks **2** sew with tacks **3** of a yacht *etc*: move from side to side across the face of the wind • **change tack** change course or direction • **on the wrong tack** following the wrong train of thought

tackle *verb* **1** come to grips with; deal with **2** *football etc* try to stop, or take the ball from, another player ◇ *noun* **1** equipment, gear: *fishing tackle* **2** an act of tackling in sport **3** the ropes and rigging of a ship **4** ropes and pulleys for raising heavy weights

tacky¹ adj (**tackier, tackiest**) sticky

tacky² adj (**tackier, tackiest**) informal cheap-looking and badly made; vulgar

tact noun skill in dealing with people so as to avoid giving offence

tactful adj avoiding giving offence • **tactfully** adv • **tactfulness** noun

tactical adj 1 involving clever and successful planning 2 sensible in the circumstances; politic: tactical withdrawal

tactics plural noun 1 a way of acting in order to gain advantage 2 the art of coordinating military forces in action • **tactician** noun someone who uses tactics skilfully

tactile adj of or perceived through touch

tactless adj giving offence through lack of thought • **tactlessly** adv • **tactlessness** noun

tadpole noun a young frog or toad in its first stage of life

tae kwon do /tai kwon doh/ noun a Korean martial art similar to karate

taffeta /taf-i-tuh/ noun a thin, glossy fabric made mainly of silk

tag noun 1 a label: price tag 2 a familiar saying or quotation 3 a chasing game played by children (also called: **tig**) ◇ verb put a tag or tags on • **tag on to** or **tag after** follow closely and continually

tagliatelle /tal-yuh-tel-i/ noun pasta made in long ribbons

t'ai chi /tai chee/ noun a Chinese system of exercise and self-defence stressing the importance of balance and coordination

tail noun 1 an appendage sticking out from the end of the spine on an animal, bird or fish 2 an appendage on a machine etc: tail of an aeroplane 3 the stalk on a piece of fruit 4 (**tails**) the side of a coin opposite to the head 5 (**tails**) a tailcoat ◇ verb 1 informal follow and watch closely 2 remove the tails from (eg fish) • **tailback** noun a line of traffic stretching back from an obstruction • **tailboard** noun a movable board lowered to open the back of a lorry • **tailcoat** noun a coat with a divided tail, part of a man's evening dress • **tail end** noun the very end of a procession etc • **tailgate** noun, US a door at the back of a car that opens upwards • **tail light** noun, US a rear light on a vehicle • **tailspin** noun 1 a steep, spinning, downward dive of an aeroplane 2 informal a state of complete panic • **tailwind** noun a wind blowing from behind • **tail off** become less, fewer or worse • **turn tail** run away

tailor noun someone who cuts out and makes clothes ◇ verb 1 make and fit (clothes) 2 make to fit the circumstances; adapt: tailored to your needs • **tailor-made** adj exactly suited to requirements

taint verb 1 spoil by contact with something bad or rotten 2 corrupt ◇ noun a trace of decay or evil

tajine /ta-zheen/ noun a N African stew cooked in a clay pot

take verb (**taking, took, taken**) 1 get hold of; grasp 2 choose: take a card! 3 accept: do you take credit cards?/ please take a biscuit 4 have room for: my car only takes four people 5 eat, swallow: take your medicine 6 get or have regularly: doesn't take sugar 7 capture (a fort etc) 8 subtract: take two from eight 9 lead, carry, drive: take the children to school 10 put into practice; use: take care! 11 require: it'll take too much time 12 travel by: took the afternoon train 13 experience, feel: takes great pride in his work 14 photograph: took some shots inside the house 15 understand: took what I said the wrong way • **takeaway** noun 1 a meal prepared and bought in a restaurant or shop but taken away and eaten somewhere else **2** a restaurant or shop providing such meals • **take-off** noun **1** the act of leaving the ground **2** an unkind imitation • **takeover** noun the act of assuming control over an organization etc • **taking** adj inspiring affection ◇ noun (**takings**) money received from things sold • **take account of** consider • **take advantage of 1** make use of (an opportunity) **2** treat or use unfairly • **take after** be like in appearance or behaviour • **take care of** look after • **take down** note down • **take for** believe (mistakenly) to be: I took him for his brother • **take heed** pay careful attention • **take ill** become ill • **take in 1** include **2** receive **3** understand: didn't take in what you said **4** make smaller: take in a dress **5** cheat, deceive • **take leave of** dated say goodbye to • **take someone's life** kill them • **taken with** attracted to • **take off 1** remove (clothes etc) **2** imitate unkindly **3** of an aircraft: leave the ground • **take on 1** undertake (work etc) **2** accept (as an opponent): take you on at tennis • **take over** take control of • **take part in** share or help in • **take pity on** show pity for • **take place** happen • **take to 1** be attracted by **2** begin to do or use regularly: took to rising early • **take to heart** be deeply affected or upset by • **take to your heels** run away; flee • **take up 1** lift, raise **2** occupy (space, time, etc) **3** begin to learn or show interest in: take up playing the harp

talc noun **1** a soft mineral that is soapy to the touch **2** informal talcum powder • **talcum powder** noun a fine powder made from talc, used for rubbing on the body

tale noun **1** a story **2** an untrue story; a lie

talent noun **1** a special ability or skill: a talent for music **2** hist a measure of weight for gold or silver • **talented** adj skilled or gifted

talisman noun an object believed to have magic powers; a charm

talk verb **1** speak **2** gossip **3** give information ◇ noun **1** conversation **2** gossip **3** the subject of conversation: the talk is of revolution **4** a discussion or lecture: gave a talk on stained glass • **talkative** adj inclined to chatter • **talking-to** noun a scolding • **talk over** discuss • **talk round 1** persuade **2** discuss without coming to the main point • **talk shop** see **shop**

tall adj **1** high or higher than average **2** hard to believe: tall story • **tallness** noun • **tall order** noun a request to do something awkward or unreasonable

tallboy noun a tall kind of chest of drawers

tallow noun animal fat melted down to make soap, candles, etc

tally noun (plural **tallies**) **1** a record, eg of scores, work done or money owed **2** a ticket or label **3** old a notched stick for keeping a score ◇ verb (**tallies**, **tallying**, **tallied**) be consistent (with): his story doesn't tally with yours

tally-ho exclam a cry used by fox-hunters and humorously by people embarking on a task

Talmud noun the basic code of Jewish civil and canon law • **Talmudic** or **Talmudical** adj

talon noun a hooked claw of a bird of prey

tamari /ta-mah-ri/ noun a concentrated soy sauce

tamarind noun a tropical tree that produces long brown seed pods filled with a sweet-tasting pulp

tamarisk noun a bushy plant with thin branches, able to grow in dry conditions

tambourine noun a small one-sided drum with tinkling metal discs set into the sides

tame adj 1 of an animal: not wild, used to living with humans 2 not exciting enough ◊ verb make (esp an animal) tame

tam-o'-shanter noun, Scot a flat round hat with a full crown, often with a bobble on top

tamper verb: **tamper with** meddle with so as to damage or alter

tampon noun a plug of cotton wool inserted into the vagina to absorb blood during menstruation

tan verb (**tanning, tanned**) 1 make or become brown, eg by exposure to the sun 2 make (animal skin) into leather by treating with tannin ◊ noun 1 a suntan 2 a yellowish-brown colour

tandem noun a long bicycle with two seats and two sets of pedals one behind the other ◊ adv one behind the other • **in tandem** together

tandoori /tan-daw-ri/ noun a style of Indian cookery in which food is baked over charcoal in a clay oven

tang noun a strong taste, flavour or smell: the tang of lemons

tangent noun a straight line that touches a circle or curve without crossing it • **go off at a tangent** go off suddenly in another direction or line of thought

tangential adj not relevant; peripheral

tangerine noun a small orange with thin skin

tangible adj 1 able to be felt by touching 2 real, definite: tangible profits • **tangibly** adv

tangle verb 1 twist together in knots 2 make or become difficult or confusing ◊ noun 1 a twisted mass of knots 2 a confused situation

tango noun (plural **tangos**) a ballroom dance with long steps and pauses, originally from S America

tank noun 1 a large container for water, petrol, etc 2 a heavy armoured vehicle that moves on caterpillar wheels

tankard noun a large drinking mug

tanker noun 1 a ship or large lorry for carrying liquids, eg oil 2 an aircraft carrying fuel

tanner noun someone who works at tanning leather • **tannery** noun a place where leather is made

tannin noun a bitter-tasting substance found in tea, red wine, etc, also used in tanning and dyeing

Tannoy noun, trademark a public address system using loudspeakers

tantalize verb torment by offering something and keeping it out of reach • **tantalizing** adj

tantamount adj: **tantamount to** amounting to: tantamount to stealing

tantrum noun a fit of bad temper

Taoism /tow-izm/ noun an ancient Chinese philosophy emphasizing unity underlying all things • **Taoist** noun & adj

tap noun 1 a light touch or knock 2 a device with a valve for controlling the flow of liquid, gas, etc ◊ verb (**tapping, tapped**) 1 knock or strike lightly 2 start making use of; draw on 3 attach a listening device secretly to (a telephone) • **on tap** available for use

tap-dance noun a dance done with shoes that make a tapping sound ◊ verb perform a tap-dance

tape noun 1 a narrow band or strip used for sticking or tying 2 a piece of string over the finishing line on a racetrack 3 a tape measure 4 a strip of magnetic material for recording sound or pictures ◊ verb 1 fasten with tape 2 record on tape • **tape measure** noun a narrow strip of paper, plastic, etc used for measuring distance • **tape recorder** noun a kind of instrument for recording sound on magnetic tape • **tapeworm** noun a type of long worm sometimes found in the intestines of humans and animals • **have someone taped** have a good understanding of their character or worth

taper verb make or become thinner at one end ◇ noun **1** a long, thin kind of candle **2** a long waxed wick used for lighting oil lamps etc • **tapering** adj

tapestry noun (plural **tapestries**) a cloth with designs or figures woven into it, used to decorate walls or cover furniture

tapioca noun a starchy food obtained from the root of the cassava plant

tapir /teh-puh/ noun a kind of wild animal something like a large pig

tappet noun a lever transmitting motion from one part of an engine to another

tar noun **1** a thick, black, sticky liquid derived from wood or coal, used in roadmaking etc **2** dated informal a sailor ◇ verb (**tarring**, **tarred**) smear with tar • **tarred with the same brush (as)** having the same faults (as)

taramasalata /ta-ruh-ma-suh-lah-tuh/ noun a Middle-Eastern paste made from smoked cod's roe

tarantella noun a lively dance for pairs, originally from Naples

tarantula noun a type of large, poisonous spider

tardy adj (**tardier**, **tardiest**) slow or late • **tardiness** noun

tare[1] noun the weight of a goods vehicle when empty

tare[2] noun a weed

target noun **1** a mark to aim at in shooting, darts, etc **2** a result or sum that is aimed at: a target of £3000 **3** someone at whom unfriendly remarks are aimed: the target of her criticism

tariff noun **1** a list of prices **2** a list of taxes payable on goods brought into a country

tarmac noun the surface of a road or airport runway, made of tarmacadam ◇ verb surface with tarmacadam

tarmacadam noun a mixture of small stones and tar used to make road surfaces etc

tarn noun a small mountain lake

tarnish verb **1** of metal: (cause to) become dull or discoloured **2** spoil (a reputation etc)

tarot /ta-roh/ noun a type of fortune-telling using a special pack of cards

tarpaulin noun **1** strong waterproof cloth **2** a sheet of this material

tarragon noun a herb used in cooking

tarry[1] verb (**tarries**, **tarrying**, **tarried**) **1** stay behind, linger **2** be slow or late

tarry[2] adj like or covered with tar; sticky

tart noun **1** a sweet or savoury pie with no lid **2** informal a prostitute ◇ adj sharp, sour • **tartness** noun

tartan noun **1** fabric patterned with squares of different colours, traditionally used by Scottish Highland clans **2** one of these patterns: Macdonald tartan ◇ adj with a pattern of tartan

tartar noun **1** a substance that gathers on the teeth **2** a difficult or demanding person **3** a substance that forms inside wine casks • **cream of tartar** a white powder obtained from the tartar from wine casks, used in baking

task noun a set piece of work to be done • **task force** noun a group of people gathered together with the purpose of performing a special or specific task • **taskmaster** noun someone who sets and supervises tasks • **take to task** blame angrily; scold

tassel noun a hanging bunch of threads used to decorate a hat etc

taste verb **1** try by eating or drinking a sample **2** eat or drink some of: taste this soup **3** recognize (a flavour):

can you taste the chilli in it? **4** have a particular flavour: *tasting of garlic* **5** experience: *taste success* ◇ *noun* **1** the act or sense of tasting **2** a flavour **3** a small quantity of something **4** a liking: *taste for literature* **5** ability to judge what is suitable in behaviour, dress, *etc*, or what is fine or beautiful

tasteful *adj* showing good taste and judgement • **tastefully** *adv* • **tasteful-ness** *noun*

tasteless *adj* **1** without flavour **2** not tasteful; vulgar • **tastelessly** *adv* • **tastelessness** *noun*

tasty *adj* (**tastier, tastiest**) having a good flavour

tat *noun* cheap-looking and bad-ly made articles; rubbish • **tatty** *adj* shabby, tawdry

tatters *plural noun* torn, ragged piec-es • **tattered** *adj* ragged

tattie *noun, Scot* a potato

tattle *noun* gossip

tattoo *noun* **1** a coloured design on the skin, made by pricking with nee-dles **2** an outdoor military display with music *etc* **3** a beat of a drum ◇ *verb* prick coloured designs into the skin • **tattooed** *adj* marked with tattoos

taught *past form of* **teach**

taunt *verb* tease unkindly ◇ *noun* a jeer

taut *adj* **1** pulled tight **2** tense, strained • **tauten** *verb* make or become tight

tautology *noun* a form of repetition in which the same thing is said in dif-ferent ways, *eg* 'he looked *anxious* and *worried*' • **tautological** *adj*

tavern *noun, old* a pub

tawdry *adj* (**tawdrier, tawdriest**) **1** involving shameful or morally bad behaviour; sordid **2** cheap-looking and unattractively bright

tawny *adj* yellowish-brown

tax *noun* (*plural* **taxes**) **1** a charge made by the government on income, certain types of goods, *etc* **2** a strain, a burden: *severe tax on my patience* ◇ *verb* **1** require to pay tax **2** to put a strain on: *taxing her strength* • **taxa-tion** *noun* **1** the act or system of tax-ing **2** taxes • **taxpayer** *noun* someone who pays taxes • **tax with** *formal* accuse of

taxi *noun* (*plural* **taxis**) a vehicle that may be hired with its driver ◇ *verb* (**taxies, taxiing, taxied**) of an aero-plane: travel to or from the runway before or after take-off • **taxi rank** *noun* a place where taxis park to wait for hire

taxidermy *noun* the art of prepar-ing and stuffing the skins of animals to make them lifelike • **taxidermist** *noun* someone who does this work

taxonomy *noun* the science of clas-sifying plants and animals according to their differences and similarities • **taxonomic** *adj* • **taxonomist** *noun*

TB *abbrev* tuberculosis

T-cell *noun* a blood cell involved in the immune system

tea *noun* **1** a plant grown in India, China, *etc*, or its dried and prepared leaves **2** a drink made by infusing its dried leaves **3** any hot infusion: *beef tea/camomile tea* **4** an afternoon or early evening meal • **teacake** *noun* a light flat bun • **tea chest** *noun* a tall box of thin wood used to pack tea for export, often used as a packing case when empty • **teapot** *noun* a pot with a spout, for making and pouring tea • **teaspoon** *noun* a small spoon • **tea towel** *noun* a cloth for drying dishes

teach *verb* (**teaching, taught**) **1** give (someone) skill or knowledge **2** give knowledge of or training in (a sub-ject): *she teaches French* **3** be a teach-er: *decide to teach*

teacher *noun* someone employed to teach others in a school, or in a par-ticular subject: *guitar teacher*

teaching noun 1 the work of a teacher 2 guidance, instruction 3 (**teachings**) beliefs or rules of conduct that are preached or taught

teacup noun a medium-sized cup for drinking tea • **a storm in a teacup** see **storm**

teak noun 1 a hardwood tree from the East Indies 2 its very hard wood 3 a type of African tree

teal noun a small water bird like a duck

team noun 1 a side in a game: a football team 2 a group of people working together 3 two or more animals working together: team of oxen • **team spirit** noun willingness to work as part of a team • **team up with** join together with, usu in order to do something

---

Do not confuse with: **teem**

---

tear[1] noun 1 a drop of liquid from the eye 2 (**tears**) a state or spell of crying • **tear gas** noun gas that causes the eyes to stream with tears, used in crowd control etc • **in tears** weeping

tear[2] verb (**tearing, tore, torn**) 1 pull with force: tear apart/tear down 2 make a hole or split in (material etc) 3 hurt deeply 4 informal rush: tearing off down the road ◇ noun a hole or split made by tearing

tearful adj 1 inclined to cry 2 in tears; crying • **tearfully** adv

tease verb 1 irritate and upset on purpose 2 pretend to upset or annoy for fun: I'm only teasing 3 untangle (wool etc) with a comb 4 sort out (a problem or puzzle) ◇ noun someone who teases

teasel noun a type of prickly plant

teaser noun a difficult problem or puzzle

teat noun 1 the part of a mammal through which milk passes to its young 2 a rubber object shaped like this attached to a baby's feeding bottle

techie /tek-i/ noun, informal someone who is an expert in or very enthusiastic about new technology

technical adj 1 relating to a particular art or skill, esp a mechanical or industrial one: what is the technical term for this?/a technical expert 2 according to strict interpretations or rules: technical defeat • **technically** adv according to a strict interpretation or rule; strictly speaking

technicality noun (plural **technicalities**) a technical detail or point

technician noun someone trained in the practical side of an art

technique noun the way in which a process is carried out; a method

technology noun 1 science applied to practical (esp industrial) purposes 2 the practical skills of a particular civilization, period, etc • **technological** adj • **technologically** adv • **technologist** noun

teddy noun (plural **teddies**) 1 a stuffed toy bear (also called **teddy bear**) 2 a one-piece woman's undergarment

tedious adj boring • **tediously** adv • **tedium** noun

tee noun 1 the square of level ground from which a golf ball is driven 2 the peg or sand heap on which the ball is placed for driving • **tee up** place (a ball) on a tee

teem verb 1 be full: teeming with people 2 rain heavily

Do not confuse with: **team**

---

teenage adj suitable for, or typical of, people in their teens

teenager noun someone in their teens

teens plural noun the years of age from thirteen to nineteen

teeny adj (**teenier**, **teeniest**) informal tiny, minute

tee-shirt or **T-shirt** noun a short-sleeved shirt pulled on over the head

teeth plural of **tooth**

teethe verb of a baby: grow its first teeth • **teething troubles** plural noun **1** pain caused by growing teeth **2** difficulties encountered at the beginning of an undertaking

teetotal adj never drinking alcohol • **teetotaller** noun

tel abbrev telephone

tele- prefix **1** at a distance: telekinesis **2** making use of telecommunications: telebanking

telecommunications plural noun the sending of information by telephone, radio, television, etc

telegram noun a message sent by telegraph

telegraph noun a communications system in which messages are sent via a cable using groups of electrical signals to represent letters ◇ verb send (a message) by telegraph • **telegraphic** adj **1** of a telegraph **2** short, brief, concise

telekinesis noun the movement of objects from a distance through willpower, not touch

teleology noun the philosophy of viewing things in terms of their purpose, not their cause

telepathy noun communication between people without using sight, hearing, etc • **telepathic** adj

telephone noun an instrument for speaking over distances, using an electric current travelling along a wire, or radio waves ◇ verb send (a message) by telephone • **telephonist** noun an operator on a telephone switchboard

telephoto adj of a lens: used to photograph enlarged images of distant objects

teleprinter noun a typewriter that receives and prints out messages sent by telegraph

telesales noun the selling of goods or services by telephone

telescope noun a tubular instrument fitted with lenses that magnify distant objects ◇ verb **1** push or fit together so that one thing slides inside another **2** force together or inside each other; compress

teletex noun a high-speed means of transmitting data, similar to telex

teletext noun news and general information transmitted by television companies, viewable only on special television sets

televise verb broadcast on television: are they televising the football match?

television noun **1** the reproduction on a small screen of moving images sent from a distance **2** an apparatus for receiving these pictures

teleworker noun, dated someone who works from home and communicates with their employer by computer, fax, etc

telex noun **1** the sending of messages by means of teleprinters **2** a message sent in this way

tell verb (**telling**, **told**) **1** say or express in words: she's telling the truth **2** give the facts of (a story) **3** give information: can you tell me when it's 9 o'clock? **4** order, command: tell him to go away! **5** distinguish: I can't tell one wine from the other **6** give away a secret: promise not to tell **7** produce results: training will tell in the end • **teller** noun a bank clerk who receives and pays out money • **telling** adj having a marked effect: telling remark • **all told** considering all or everything • **tell off** informal scold • **tell on 1** have an effect on **2** give information about • **tell tales** give away information about the misdeeds of others

temerity noun the confidence to do something disrespectful or impolite; cheek

temp abbrev 1 temperature 2 temporary ◇ noun, informal a temporarily employed secretarial worker ◇ verb, informal work as a temp

temper noun 1 usual state of mind: of an even temper 2 a passing mood: in a good temper 3 a tendency to get angry easily 4 a fit of anger ◇ verb 1 bring (metal) to the right degree of hardness by heating and cooling 2 make less severe • **lose your temper** show anger

tempera noun a mixture of egg and water used to make a kind of paint

temperament noun someone's nature as it affects the way they feel and act; disposition • **temperamental** adj 1 of temperament 2 often changing mood 3 often breaking down

temperance noun the habit of not drinking much (or any) alcohol

temperate adj 1 moderate in temper, eating or drinking etc 2 of climate: neither very hot nor very cold

temperature noun 1 degree of heat or cold: today's temperature 2 a body heat higher than normal

tempest noun a storm with strong winds

tempestuous adj 1 very stormy and windy 2 violently emotional

template noun 1 a thin plate cut in a design for drawing round 2 a basic form used for making copies that are similar

temple¹ noun a building used for public worship; a church

temple² noun a small flat area on each side of the forehead

tempo noun (plural **tempos** or **tempi**) 1 the speed at which music is played 2 the speed or rate of an activity

temporal adj 1 relating to this world or this life only, not eternal or spiritual 2 relating to time

temporary adj lasting only for a time, not permanent

temporize verb, formal avoid or delay taking action in order to gain time

tempt verb 1 try to persuade or entice 2 attract 3 make inclined (to): tempted to phone him up • **temptation** noun 1 the act of tempting 2 the feeling of being tempted 3 something that tempts • **tempting** adj attractive

tempura /tem-paw-ruh/ noun a Japanese dish of fish, vegetables, etc fried quickly in batter

ten noun the number 10 ◇ adj 10 in number • **tenpin bowling** noun a game like skittles played by bowling a ball at ten pins standing at the end of a bowling lane

tenable adj 1 able to be defended; justifiable 2 of someone's position in a post: in which they can continue without the pressure to resign

tenacious adj 1 not easily defeated or dissuaded; persistent 2 keeping a firm hold or grip • **tenaciously** adv • **tenacity** noun

tenant noun someone who pays rent for the use of a house, land, etc • **tenancy** noun 1 the holding of a house, farm, etc by a tenant 2 the period of this holding • **tenanted** adj lived in by a tenant

tend verb 1 be likely or inclined to do something: these flowers tend to wilt 2 move or slope in a certain direction 3 take care of

tendency noun (plural **tendencies**) a leaning or inclination (towards): tendency to daydream

tender adj 1 soft, not hard or tough 2 easily hurt or damaged 3 hurting when touched 4 loving and gentle ◇ verb 1 offer (a resignation etc) formally 2 make a formal offer for a job

◇ *noun* **1** an offer to take on work, supply goods, *etc* for a fixed price **2** a small boat that carries stores for a large one **3** a truck for coal and water attached to a steam engine • **tenderfoot** *noun, dated* an inexperienced person • **tender-hearted** *adj* kind or sympathetic • **tenderize** *verb* soften (meat) before cooking • **legal tender** coins or notes that must be accepted when offered • **of tender years** very young

tendon *noun* a tough cord joining a muscle to a bone

tendril *noun* **1** a thin curling stem of a climbing plant which attaches itself to a support **2** a curling strand of hair *etc*

tenement *noun* a long, low-rise block of flats

tenet *noun* a principle or rule

tenner *noun, informal* a ten-pound note; ten pounds

tennis *noun* a game for two or four players using rackets to hit a ball to each other over a net • **tennis court** *noun* an area laid out for playing tennis

tenon *noun* a projecting part at the end of a piece of wood made to fit a **mortise**

tenor *noun* **1** a singing voice of the highest normal pitch for an adult male **2** a singer with this voice **3** the general course: *the even tenor of country life* **4** general meaning: *the tenor of the speech*

tense¹ *noun* the form of a verb that shows time of action, eg '*I was*' (**past tense**), '*I am*' (**present tense**), '*I shall be*' (**future tense**)

tense² *adj* **1** nervous or strained: *feeling tense/tense with excitement* **2** tightly stretched • **tensile** *adj* relating to stretching • **tension** *noun* **1** nervous feelings or behaviour **2** the state of being stretched

tent *noun* a movable shelter of canvas or other material, supported by poles and pegged to the ground

tentacle *noun* a long thin flexible part of an animal used to feel or grasp, eg the arm of an octopus • **tentacular** *adj*

tentative *adj* **1** experimental, initial: *a tentative offer* **2** uncertain, hesitating: *tentative smile* • **tentatively** *adv*

tenterhooks *plural noun*: **on tenterhooks** uncertain and very anxious about what will happen

tenth *adj* the last of ten items ◇ *noun* one of ten equal parts

tenuous *adj* slight or weak: *tenuous connection* • **tenuously** *adv*

tenure *noun* **1** the holding of property or a position of employment **2** the period, or terms or conditions of this

tepee *noun* a traditional Native American tent made of animal skins

tepid *adj* lukewarm

tequila /tuh-*kee*-luh/ *noun* a Mexican alcoholic drink made from the agave plant

tercentenary *noun* a 300th anniversary

term *noun* **1** a division of an academic or school year: *autumn term* **2** a word or expression: *dictionary of computing terms* **3** a length of time: *term of imprisonment* **4** (**terms**) the rules or conditions of an agreement: *what are their terms?* **5** (**terms**) fixed charges **6** (**terms**) footing, relationship: *on good terms with his neighbours* ◇ *verb* give a name to; call • **come to terms** reach an agreement or understanding • **come to terms with** be able to live with; accept • **in terms of** from the point of view of

termagant *noun, formal* a bad-tempered and noisy woman

terminal *noun* **1** an airport building containing arrival and departure areas

2 a bus station in a town centre running a service to a nearby airport **3** a point of connection in an electric circuit **4** a computer monitor connected to a network **5** a terminus ◊ *adj* **1** of an illness: fatal, incurable **2** of or growing at the end: *terminal bud*

terminate *verb* bring or come to an end • **termination** *noun*

terminology *noun* the special words or expressions used in a particular art, science, *etc*

terminus *noun* (*plural* **termini** *or* **terminuses**) **1** an end point on a railway, bus route, *etc* **2** *formal* the end

termite *noun* a pale-coloured wood-eating insect

tern *noun* a sea bird like a small gull

terpsichorean /turp-sik-uh-*ree*-un/ *adj, formal* relating to dancing

terrace *noun* **1** one of a series of raised level banks of earth on a hillside **2** a raised paved area at the side of a building **3** a connected row of houses ◊ *verb* form into a terrace or terraces

terracotta *noun* a brownish-red mixture of clay and sand used for tiles, pottery, *etc*

terra firma *noun* land as opposed to water

terrain *noun* an area of land considered in terms of its physical features: *the terrain is a bit rocky*

terrapin *noun* a small turtle living in ponds or rivers

terrarium *noun* an ornamental glass jar containing living plants *etc*

terrestrial *adj* **1** of or living on the earth **2** of television *etc* services: broadcast by transmitter, not by satellite or cable

terrible *adj* **1** causing great hardship or distress: *terrible disaster* **2** causing great fear: *a terrible sight* **3** *informal* very bad: *a terrible writer*

terribly *adv, informal* **1** badly: *sang terribly* **2** extremely: *terribly tired*

terrier *noun* a breed of small dog

terrify *verb* (**terrifies, terrifying, terrified**) frighten greatly • **terrific** *adj* **1** very frightening **2** *informal* very good, enjoyable, *etc*: *a terrific party*

territorial *adj* of or belonging to a territory • **territorial waters** *plural noun* seas close to, and considered to belong to, a country

territory *noun* (*plural* **territories**) **1** an area of land; a region **2** land under the control of a ruler or state **3** an area allocated to a salesman *etc* **4** a field of activity or interest

terror *noun* **1** very great fear **2** something that causes great fear **3** *informal* an uncontrollable child • **terrorize** *verb* frighten very greatly

terrorism *noun* the organized use of violence or intimidation for political or other ends • **terrorist** *noun* someone who practises terrorism

terse *adj* brief in an unfriendly way; brusque • **tersely** *adv* • **terseness** *noun*

tertiary *adj* third in position or order • **tertiary education** *noun* education at university or college level

tessera *noun* (*plural* **tesserae**) one of the small pieces making up a mosaic

test *noun* **1** a short examination **2** something done to check the performance or reliability of a machine *etc*: *ran tests on the new model* **3** a means of finding the presence of: *test for radioactivity* **4** an event that shows up a good or bad quality: *a test of courage* ◊ *verb* carry out tests on • **test match** *noun* a major sporting contest between two countries • **test pilot** *noun* a pilot who tests new aircraft • **test tube** *noun* a glass tube closed at one end, used in chemical tests

testament *noun* **1** a written statement **2** a will ● **Old Testament** and **New Testament** the two main divisions of the Christian Bible

testator *noun* the writer of a will ● **testatory** *adj* of a will or testament

testicle *noun* one of two sperm-producing glands enclosed in the male scrotum

testify *verb* (**testifies, testifying, testified**) **1** give evidence in a law court **2** make a solemn declaration of **3** (**testify to**) give evidence of; show: *testifies to his ignorance*

testimonial *noun* **1** a personal statement about someone's character, abilities, *etc* **2** a gift given in thanks for services given

testimony *noun* (*plural* **testimonies**) **1** the statement made by someone who testifies **2** evidence

testis *noun* (*plural* **testes**), *formal* a testicle

testosterone *noun* the main male sex hormone, secreted by the testicles

testy *adj* (**testier, testiest**) easily made angry; irritable ● **testily** *adv* ● **testiness** *noun*

tetanus *noun* (*also called*: **lockjaw**) a disease, caused *esp* by an infected wound, causing stiffening and spasms in the jaw muscles

tetchy *adj* (**tetchier, tetchiest**) bad-tempered; irritable ● **tetchily** *adv* ● **tetchiness** *noun*

tête-à-tête /tet-ah-*tet*/ *noun* a private talk between two people

tether *verb* **1** tie to a place with a rope *etc* **2** limit the freedom of ◇ *noun* a rope *etc* for tying an animal to restrict its movement

Teutonic /tyoo-*ton*-ik/ *adj* of, or typical of, German people or Germany

text *noun* **1** the written or printed part of a book, not the pictures, notes, *etc* **2** a printed or written ver-

sion of a speech, play, *etc* **3** a book used for study **4** the subject matter of a speech, essay, *etc* **5** a text message ◇ *verb* send a text message (to) ● **textbook** *noun* a book used for teaching, giving the main facts about a subject ● **texting** *noun* text messaging ● **text message** *noun* a typed message sent via a mobile phone ● **text messaging** *noun* sending typed messages by mobile phone

textile *noun* a woven cloth or fabric ◇ *adj* of weaving; woven

textual *adj* of or in a text ● **textually** *adv*

texture *noun* **1** the quality of a substance in terms of how it looks or feels: *rough texture/lumpy texture* **2** the quality of cloth resulting from weaving: *loose texture*

TGWU *abbrev* Transport and General Workers' Union

than *conj & prep* used in comparisons: *easier than I expected/better than me*

thane *noun, hist* a member of the aristocracy who was given land by the crown

thank *verb* express gratitude to (someone) for a favour, gift, *etc* ● **thankless** *adj* neither worthwhile nor appreciated: *thankless task* ● **thanks** *plural noun* gratitude; appreciation: *you'll get no thanks for it* ● **thanks to 1** with the help of: *we arrived on time, thanks to our friends* **2** owing to: *we were late, thanks to our car breaking down* ● **thank you** *or* **thanks** a polite expression used to thank someone

thankful *adj* grateful ● **thankfully** *adv* ● **thankfulness** *noun*

thanksgiving *noun* **1** a church service giving thanks to God **2** (**Thanksgiving**) *US* the fourth Thursday of November, a national holiday commemorating the first harvest of the Puritan settlers

that adj & pronoun (plural **those**) used to point out a thing or person etc (contrasted with: **this**): that woman over there/don't say that ◇ relative pronoun: the colours that he chose/the man that I spoke to ◇ adv to such an extent or degree: why were you that late? ◇ conj **1** used in reporting speech: she said that she was there **2** used to connect clauses: I heard that you were ill

thatch noun straw or reeds used to make the roof of a house ◇ verb cover with thatch

thaw verb **1** melt **2** of frozen food: defrost **3** become friendly after being hostile ◇ noun **1** the melting of ice and snow by heat **2** a change in the weather that causes this

the adj **1** referring to a particular person or thing: the boy in the park/I like the jacket I'm wearing **2** referring to all or any of a general group: the horse is of great use to man

theatre or US **theater** noun **1** a place for the public performance of plays etc **2** a room in a hospital for surgical operations **3** the acting profession

theatrical adj **1** of theatres or acting **2** over-dramatic • **theatricality** noun

thee pronoun, old you (sing) as the object of a sentence

theft noun stealing

their adj belonging to them: their car • **theirs** pronoun a thing or things belonging to them: the red car is theirs

---

Do not confuse with: **there**

---

theism /thee-izm/ noun belief in the existence of God • **theistic** or **theistical** adj

them pronoun, plural **1** people or things already spoken about (as the object of a verb): we've seen them **2**

those: one of them over in the corner ◇ pronoun, sing used to avoid giving the gender of the person being referred to: if anyone phones, ask them to leave their number

theme noun **1** the subject of a discussion, essay, etc **2** music a main melody that is repeated • **theme park** noun a large amusement park with exciting rides, often but not always based on a single theme • **theme song** or **theme tune** noun a tune that is repeated often in a film, television series, etc

themselves pronoun, plural **1** used reflexively: they tired themselves out walking **2** used for emphasis: they'll have to do it themselves

then adv **1** at that time: I didn't know you then **2** after that: and then where did you go? ◇ conj in that case; therefore: if you're busy, then don't come

thence adv, old from that time or place • **thenceforth** adv from that time onward

theocracy noun government of a state according to religious laws • **theocratic** adj

theodolite noun an instrument for measuring angles, used in surveying

theology noun the study of God and religion • **theologian** noun someone who studies theology • **theological** adj

theorem noun a mathematical or scientific statement that has been proved

theory noun (plural **theories**) **1** an explanation that has not been proved or tested **2** the underlying ideas in an art, science, etc, compared to practice or performance • **theoretical** adj of theory, not experience or practice • **theoretically** adv • **theorize** verb form theories

therapeutic adj **1** having a healing or beneficial effect **2** of therapy

therapist noun someone who gives

therapeutic treatment: *speech thera-pist*

therapy *noun* (*plural* **therapies**) treatment of disease or disorders

there *adv* at, in or to that place: *what did you do there?* ◇ *pronoun* used (with *be*) as a subject of a sentence or clause when the real subject follows the verb: *there is nobody at home* • **thereabouts** *adv* approximately • **thereafter** *adv* after that • **thereby** *adv* by that means • **therefore** *adv* for this or that reason • **thereof** *adv* of that • **thereupon** *adv* 1 because of this or that 2 immediately

---

Do not confuse with: **their**

---

therm *noun* a unit of heat used in measuring gas

thermal *adj* 1 of heat 2 of hot springs

thermodynamics *sing noun* the science of the relation between heat and mechanical energy

thermometer *noun* an instrument for measuring temperature

thermonuclear *adj* relating to the fusion of nuclei at high temperatures

Thermos *noun, trademark* a vacuum flask

thermostat *noun* a device for automatically controlling temperature in a room

thesaurus *noun* (*plural* **thesauri** or **thesauruses**) a reference book listing words and their synonyms

these *see* **this**

thesis *noun* (*plural* **theses**) 1 a long piece of written work on a topic, often part of a university degree 2 a statement of a point of view

thespian *noun, formal* an actor

they *pronoun, plural* some people or things already mentioned (used only as the subject of a verb): *they* followed the others ◇ *pronoun, sing* used to avoid giving the gender of the person being referred to: *anyone can come if they like*

thick *adj* 1 of fairly great width, not thin: *a thick slice/two metres thick* 2 of a mixture: flowing less easily than water; stiff: *a thick soup* 3 dense, difficult to see or pass through: *thick fog/thick woods* 4 of an accent: very strong 5 *informal* stupid 6 *informal* very friendly ◇ *noun* the thickest, most crowded or active part: *in the thick of the fight* • **thicken** *verb* make or become thick • **thicket** *noun* a group of close-set trees and bushes • **thickness** *noun* 1 the quality of being thick 2 the distance between opposite sides 3 a layer • **thickset** *adj* 1 having a thick sturdy body 2 closely set or planted • **thick-skinned** *adj* not sensitive or easily hurt

thief *noun* (*plural* **thieves**) someone who steals

thieve *verb* steal • **thieving** *noun* • **thievish** *adj* inclined to stealing

thigh *noun* the thick, fleshy part of the leg between the knee and the hip

thimble *noun* a small cap worn over the tip of a finger, used to push a needle while sewing

thin *adj* 1 not very wide between its two sides: *thin paper/thin slice* 2 slim, not fat 3 not dense or crowded: *thin population* 4 poor in quality: *thin wine* 5 of a voice: weak, not resonating 6 of a mixture: not stiff; watery: *a thin soup* ◇ *verb* (**thinning**, **thinned**) make or become thin or thinner • **thinness** *noun* • **thin-skinned** *adj* easily offended or upset

thine *adj, old* belonging to you (used before words beginning with a vowel or a vowel sound): *thine enemies* ◇ *pronoun, old* something belonging to you: *my heart is thine*

thing *noun* 1 an object that is not living 2 *informal* a person: *a nice* *old thing* **3** (**things**) belongings **4** an individual object, quality, idea, *etc*: *several things must be taken into consideration*

think *verb* (**thinking**, **thought**) **1** form ideas in the mind **2** believe, judge or consider: *I think that we should go* **3** (with **of**) intend: *she is thinking of resigning* • **think tank** *noun* a group of people who give expert advice and come up with ideas • **think better of** change your mind about • **think highly of** *or* **think much of** have a good opinion of • **think nothing of 1** have a poor opinion of **2** consider as easy or do willingly • **think out** work out in the mind

third *adj* the last of a series of three ◇ *noun* one of three equal parts • **third-rate** *adj* of very poor quality • **the third age** the age after retirement, early old age

thirst *noun* **1** a dry feeling in the mouth caused by lack of fluid **2** an eager desire (for): *thirst for knowledge* ◇ *verb* **1** feel thirsty **2** (with **for**) desire eagerly • **thirsty** *adj* **1** feeling thirst **2** eager (for) **3** of earth: parched, dry

thirteen *noun* the number 13 ◇ *adj* 13 in number • **thirteenth** *adj* the last of a series of thirteen ◇ *noun* one of thirteen equal parts

thirty *noun* the number 30 ◇ *adj* 30 in number • **thirtieth** *adj* the last of a series of thirty ◇ *noun* one of thirty equal parts

this *adj & pronoun* (*plural* **these**) **1** used to point out someone or something, *esp* one nearby (*contrasted with*: *that*): *look at this letter/take this instead* **2** to such an extent or degree: *this early*

thistle *noun* a prickly plant with purple flowers • **thistledown** *noun* the feathery bristles of the seeds of the thistle

thither *adv* to that place

thong *noun* **1** a thin strap of leather used to fasten something **2** a skimpy undergarment with a strap passing between the legs

thorax *noun* (*plural* **thoraxes** or **thoraces**) **1** the middle section of an insect's body **2** the chest in the human or animal body

thorn *noun* **1** a sharp prickle sticking out from the stem of a plant **2** a bush with thorns, *esp* the hawthorn • **thorny** *adj* **1** full of thorns; prickly **2** causing arguments or problems: *a thorny problem* • **a thorn in the flesh** a cause of constant irritation

thorough *adj* **1** complete, absolute: *a thorough muddle* **2** attending to every detail • **thoroughbred** *noun* an animal of pure breed • **thoroughfare** *noun* **1** a public street **2** a passage or way through: *no thoroughfare* • **thoroughgoing** *adj* thorough, complete • **thoroughly** *adv*

those *see* **that**

thou *pronoun, old* you (as the subject of a sentence)

though *conj* although: *though he disliked it, he ate it all* ◇ *adv, informal* however: *I wish I had gone, though*

thought *noun* **1** something that you think, an idea **2** the act of thinking **3** an opinion **4** consideration: *after much thought* ◇ *verb past form of* **think** • **thoughtful** *adj* **1** full of thought **2** thinking of others; considerate • **thoughtless** *adj* showing lack of thought; inconsiderate

thousand *noun* the number 1000 ◇ *adj* 1000 in number • **thousandth** *adj* the last of a series of a thousand ◇ *noun* one of a thousand equal parts

thrall *noun*: **in thrall 1** enchanted, fascinated **2** living as a slave

thrash *verb* **1** beat severely **2** move or toss violently (about) **3** (with **out**) discuss (a problem *etc*) thoroughly **4** thresh (grain) • **thrashing** *noun* a flogging; a beating

thread *noun* **1** a very thin line of cotton, wool, silk, *etc*, often twisted and drawn out **2** the ridge that goes in a spiral round a screw **3** a connected series of details in correct order ◇ *verb* **1** put a thread through a needle *etc* **2** make (your way) in a narrow space • **threadbare** *adj* of clothes: worn thin • **threadworm** *noun* a type of parasitic nematode

threat *noun* **1** a warning that you intend to hurt or punish someone **2** a warning of something bad that may come: *a threat of war* **3** something likely to cause harm: *a threat to our plans* • **threaten** *verb* **1** make a threat: *threatened to kill himself* **2** suggest the approach of something unpleasant **3** be a danger to

three *noun* the number 3 ◇ *adj* 3 in number

three-dimensional *adj* presented in such a way as to appear to have height, width and depth (often **3-D**)

threnody *noun, formal* a lament

thresh *verb* beat out (grain) from straw

threshold *noun* **1** a beginning: *on the threshold of a new era* **2** a doorway **3** a piece of wood or stone under the door of a building

threw *past tense of* **throw**

thrice *adv, old* three times

thrift *noun* careful management of money in order to save • **thrifty** *adj* careful about spending

thrill *noun* **1** an excited feeling **2** quivering or vibration ◇ *verb* **1** feel excitement **2** make excited • **thriller** *noun* an exciting story, often about crime and detection • **thrilling** *adj* very exciting

thrive *verb* **1** grow strong and healthy **2** do well or be successful

thro' *short for* **through**

throat *noun* **1** the back part of the mouth **2** the front part of the neck

throb *verb* (**throbbing**, **throbbed**) **1** of the heart *etc*: beat *esp* more strongly than normal **2** beat or vibrate rhythmically and regularly

throes *plural noun* great suffering or struggle • **in the throes of** in the middle of (a struggle, doing a task, *etc*)

thrombosis *noun* the forming of a clot in a blood vessel

throne *noun* **1** the seat of a monarch or bishop **2** a monarch or their power

throng *noun* a crowd ◇ *verb* **1** move in a crowd **2** fill (a place)

throttle *noun* a valve that controls the flow of fuel to an engine and so regulates speed, or the control that operates the valve ◇ *verb* choke by gripping the throat

through *prep* **1** entering from one direction and out in the other: *through the tunnel* **2** from end to end, or side to side, of: *all through the performance* **3** by way of: *related through his grandmother* **4** as a result of: *through his expertise* **5** *US* from (one date) to (another) inclusive: *Monday through Friday is five days* ◇ *adv* into and out, from beginning to end: *all the way through the tunnel* ◇ *adj* **1** without a break or change: *through train* **2** *informal* finished: *are you through with the newspaper?* **3** of a telephone call: connected: *I couldn't get through this morning* • **through-and-through** *adv* completely, entirely: *a gentleman through-and-through* • **throughout** *prep* **1** in all parts of: *throughout Europe* **2** from start to finish of: *throughout the journey* • **throughput** *noun* an amount of material put through a process • **through ticketing** *noun* a system where passengers travel on different transport networks using the same ticket

throw *verb* (**throwing**, **threw**, **thrown**) **1** send through the air with force **2** of a horse: make (a rider) fall to the ground **3** shape (pottery) on a wheel **4** give (a party) ◇ *noun* **1** the act of throwing **2** the distance a thing is thrown: *within a stone's throw of the house* ● **throwback** *noun* a reversion to an earlier form

thru *prep, US informal* through

thrush *noun* (*plural* **thrushes**) **1** a type of singing bird with a speckled breast **2** a type of infectious disease of the mouth, throat or vagina

thrust *verb* (**thrusting**, **thrust**) **1** push with force **2** make a sudden push forward with a pointed weapon **3** (with **on** or **upon**) force (something, yourself) upon ◇ *noun* **1** a stab **2** a pushing force

thud *noun* a dull, hollow sound like that made by a heavy body falling ◇ *verb* (**thudding**, **thudded**) move or fall with such a sound

thug *noun* a violent, brutal person

thumb *noun* the short, thick finger of the hand ◇ *verb* turn over (the pages of a book) with the thumb or fingers ● **thumbscrew** *noun, hist* an instrument of torture that squashed the thumbs ● **thumbs down** or **thumbs up** *noun* a show of disapproval or approval ● **rule of thumb** a practical method of doing something ● **under someone's thumb** under their control

thump *verb* **1** beat heavily **2** move or fall with a dull, heavy noise ◇ *noun* a heavy blow

thunder *noun* **1** the deep rumbling sound heard after a flash of lightning **2** any loud, rumbling noise ◇ *verb* **1** produce the sound of, or a sound like, thunder **2** shout out angrily ● **thunderbolt** *noun* **1** a flash of lightning followed by thunder **2** a very great and sudden surprise ● **thunderclap** *noun* a sudden roar of thunder ● **thunderous** *adj* very loud ● **thunderstruck** *adj* overcome by surprise ● **thundery** *adj* of weather: sultry and bringing thunder

Thursday *noun* the fifth day of the week

thus *adv* **1** in this or that manner: *he always talks thus* **2** to this degree or extent: *thus far* **3** because of this; therefore: *thus, we must go on*

thwart *verb* **1** hinder (someone) from carrying out a plan, intention, *etc* **2** prevent (an attempt *etc*) ◇ *noun* a cross seat for rowers in a boat

thy *adj, old* belonging to you: *thy wife and children*

thyme /taim/ *noun* a small sweet-smelling herb used for seasoning food

thyroid gland *noun* a large gland in the neck that influences the rate at which energy is used by the body

tiara *noun* a jewelled ornament for the head like a crown

tibia *noun* the bone of the shin, the larger of the two bones between the knee and ankle (*compare with*: **fibula**)

tic *noun* a twitch of muscles, *esp* of the face

tick¹ *noun* **1** a mark (✓) used to show that something is correct or has been dealt with **2** a small quick noise made regularly by a clock or watch **3** *informal* a moment: *I'll just be a tick* ◇ *verb* **1** mark with a tick **2** of a clock *etc*: produce regular ticks ● **ticking** *noun* the noise made by a clock *etc*

tick² *noun* a tiny blood-sucking mite

tick³ *noun* the cloth cover of a mattress or pillow

ticket *noun* **1** a card *etc* entitling the holder to travel, to be admitted to a theatre, *etc* **2** an official notice of a traffic offence, *eg* speeding

tickle *verb* **1** excite the surface nerves of a part of the body by touching lightly **2** please or amuse

ticklish *adj* **1** sensitive to tickling **2** not easy to deal with: *ticklish problem* ● **tickly** *adj* ticklish

tiddler *noun, informal* **1** a very small

fish **2** any small person or thing

tiddly adj (**tiddlier, tiddliest**) informal **1** tiny **2** slightly drunk

tiddlywinks sing noun a game in which small plastic discs (**tiddlywinks**) are flipped into a cup

tide noun **1** the regular rise and fall of the sea that happens twice each day **2** old time, season: Christmastide • **tidal** adj of the tide • **tidal wave** noun an enormous wave in the sea often caused by an earthquake etc • **tidemark** noun **1** a mark made by the tide at its highest point **2** informal a mark on the skin showing the furthest point of washing • **tide over** help to get over a difficulty for a time

tidings plural noun news

tidy adj (**tidier, tidiest**) **1** in good order; neat **2** informal fairly big: a tidy sum of money ◇ verb (**tidies, tidying, tidied**) make neat • **tidily** adv • **tidiness** noun

tie verb (**ties, tying, tied**) **1** fasten with a cord, string, etc **2** put a knot or bow in (string, shoelaces, etc) **3** join, unite **4** limit, restrict: tied to a tight schedule **5** score the same number of points (in a game etc), draw ◇ noun **1** a band of fabric worn round the neck, tied with a knot or bow **2** something that connects: ties of friendship **3** something that restricts or limits **4** an equal score in a competition **5** a game or match to be played • **tie-breaker** noun an extra question or part of a tied contest to decide a winner

tier /tee-uh/ noun a row of seats in a theatre etc, with others above or below it

tiff noun a slight quarrel

tig another name for **tag**

tiger noun a large animal of the cat family with a tawny coat striped with black • **tiger lily** noun a lily with large spotted flowers

tight adj **1** fitting too closely: these

jeans are a bit tight **2** firmly stretched, not loose **3** packed closely **4** informal short of money **5** informal drunk • **tight corner** noun an awkward situation • **tight-fisted** adj stingy • **tight-lipped** adj uncommunicative • **tightrope** noun a tightly stretched rope on which acrobats perform

tighten verb make or become tight or tighter

tights plural noun a close-fitting garment covering the feet, legs and body as far as the waist

tigress noun a female tiger

tile noun a flat piece of baked clay etc used in covering floors or roofs ◇ verb cover with tiles

till¹ noun a container or drawer for money in a shop ◇ verb cultivate (land); plough • **tillage** noun **1** the act of tilling **2** tilled land

till² see **until**

tiller noun the handle of a boat's rudder

tilt verb **1** fall into, or place in, a sloping position **2** hist joust **3** hist (with **at**) attack on horseback, using a lance ◇ noun **1** a slant **2** a thrust or jab • **at full tilt** with full speed and force

timber noun **1** wood for building etc **2** trees suitable for this **3** a wooden beam in a house or ship

timbre /tam-buh/ noun the quality of a musical sound or voice

time noun **1** the hour of the day **2** the period at which something happens **3** (often **times**) a particular period: in modern times **4** opportunity: no time to listen **5** a suitable or right moment: now is the time to ask **6** one of a number of occasions: he won four times **7** (**times**) multiplied by: two times four **8** the rhythm or rate of performance of a piece of music ◇ adj **1** of time **2** arranged to go off at a particular time: a time bomb ◇ verb **1** measure the minutes, seconds, *etc* taken to do anything **2** choose the time for (something) well, badly, *etc*: *time your entrance carefully* • **time-honoured** *adj* respected because it has lasted a long time • **timeless** *adj* **1** not belonging to any particular time **2** never ending: *timeless beauty* • **timely** *adj* coming at the right moment: *a timely reminder* • **timepiece** *noun, old* a clock or watch • **timeshare** *noun* a scheme by which someone buys the right to use a holiday home for a specified period each year • **timetable** *noun* a list showing times of classes, arrivals or departures of trains, *etc* • **at times** occasionally • **do time** *slang* serve a prison sentence • **in time** early enough • **on time** punctual • **the time being** the present time

timid *adj* easily frightened; shy • **timidity** *noun* • **timidly** *adv*

timorous *adj, formal* very timid • **timorously** *adv*

timpani *or* **tympani** *plural noun* kettledrums • **timpanist** *or* **tympanist** *noun* someone who plays timpani

tin *noun* **1** a silvery-white kind of metal **2** a box or can made of **tinplate**, thin iron covered with tin or other metal ◇ *verb* (**tinning**, **tinned**) pack (food *etc*) in tins • **tinfoil** *noun* a very thin sheet of *usu* aluminium used for wrapping • **tinny** *adj* **1** like tin **2** of sound: thin, high-pitched • **tinpot** *adj* of little importance

tincture *noun* **1** a slight tinge of colour **2** a characteristic quality **3** a medicine mixed in alcohol

tinder *noun* dry material easily set alight by a spark • **tinderbox** *noun*

tine *noun* a spike of a fork or of a deer's antler

tinge *verb* **1** colour slightly; tint **2** (with **with**) add a slight amount of (something) to ◇ *noun* a slight amount; a hint: *tinge of pink/tinge of sadness*

tingle *verb* **1** feel a sharp prickling sensation **2** feel a thrill of excitement ◇ *noun* a sharp prickle

tinker *noun* a mender of kettles, pans, *etc* ◇ *verb* **1** work casually or unskilfully **2** meddle (with)

tinkle *verb* make, or cause to make, a light ringing sound; clink ◇ *noun* a light ringing sound

tinnitus *noun* persistent ringing in the ears

Tin Pan Alley *noun, dated* the popular music industry, originally centred in 28th Street in New York

tinsel *noun* a sparkling, glittering material used for decoration

tint *noun* a variety or shade of a colour ◇ *verb* give slight colour to

tiny *adj* (**tinier, tiniest**) very small

tip *noun* **1** the top or point of something thin or tapering **2** a piece of useful information **3** a small gift of money to a waiter *etc* **4** a rubbish dump **5** *informal* a messy place ◇ *verb* (**tipping, tipped**) **1** (with **over**) overturn **2** (with **out** or **into**) empty out or into **3** (also with **off**) give a hint to **4** give a small gift of money **5** strike lightly • **tipster** *noun* someone who gives tips about horse racing

tipple *verb, informal* drink small amounts of alcohol regularly ◇ *noun* an alcoholic drink • **tippler** *noun*

tipsy *adj* (**tipsier, tipsiest**) rather drunk • **tipsiness** *noun*

tiptoe *verb* walk on your toes in order to go very quietly • **on tiptoe** standing or walking on your toes

tiptop *adj & adv, dated* excellent

tirade /tai-rehd/ *noun* a long angry or scolding speech

tiramisu /ti-ruh-mi-soo/ *noun* an Italian dessert consisting of layers of coffee-flavoured sponge and mascarpone cheese

tire[1] *verb* **1** make or become weary **2**

(with **of**) lose patience or interest in • **tired** adj **1** weary **2** (with **of**) bored with • **tireless** adj **1** never becoming weary **2** never resting • **tiresome** adj **1** making weary **2** long and dull **3** annoying: a tiresome child • **tiring** adj causing tiredness or weariness: a tiring journey

tire² US spelling of **tyre**

tiro or **tyro** noun (plural **tiros** or **tyros**) formal a beginner

tissue noun **1** a paper handkerchief **2** the substance of which body organs are made: muscle tissue **3** a mass of interrelated things, esp lies **4** finely woven cloth • **tissue paper** noun thin, soft paper used for wrapping

tit noun **1** a type of small bird: blue tit/great tit **2** a teat **3** slang a woman's breast • **tit for tat** something bad done to someone in repayment for something bad they did to you

titanic adj very large or great; enormous

titanium noun a light strong type of metal used in aircraft

titbit noun a tasty piece of food etc

titch noun, informal a tiny person

tithe noun, hist a tax paid to the church, a tenth part of someone's income or produce

titillate verb excite in a mildly erotic way • **titillating** adj • **titillation** noun

---

Do not confuse: **titillate** and **titivate**

---

titivate verb improve the appearance of

title noun **1** the name of a book, poem, etc **2** a word in front of a name to show rank or office (eg Sir, Lady, Major), or in addressing anyone formally (eg Mr, Mrs, Ms) **3** right or claim to money, an estate, etc • **titled** adj having a title that shows

noble rank • **title deed** noun a document that proves a right to ownership (of a house etc) • **title page** noun the page of a book on which are the title, author's name, etc • **title role** noun the part in a play that is the same as the title eg Hamlet

titter verb laugh in a quiet silly way; giggle ◊ noun a giggle

tittle-tattle noun gossip

titular adj **1** having a title without the duties of the position that goes with it **2** of a title

tizzy noun a state of confusion

TLA abbrev three-letter acronym

TLC abbrev tender loving care

TNT abbrev trinitrotoluene, a high explosive

to prep **1** showing the place or direction aimed for: going to the cinema/ emigrating to New Zealand **2** showing the indirect object in a phrase, sentence, etc: show it to me **3** used before a verb to indicate the infinitive: nice to meet you **4** showing that one thing belongs with another in some way: key to the door **5** about, concerning: what did he say to that? **6** showing a ratio, proportion, etc: odds are six to one against **7** showing the purpose or result of an action: tear it to pieces **8** compared with: nothing to what happened before ◊ adv almost closed: pull the door to • **to and fro** backwards and forwards

toad noun a type of amphibian like a frog

toadstool noun a mushroom-like fungus, often poisonous

toady noun (plural **toadies**) someone who flatters insincerely or obeys too willingly ◊ verb (**toadies**, **toadying**, **toadied**) give way to someone's wishes, or flatter them, to gain favour

toast verb **1** brown (bread) by heating at a fire or grill **2** drink to the success or health of (someone) ◊ noun **1**

bread toasted **2** the person to whom a toast is drunk **3** the drinking of a toast • **toaster** noun an electric machine for toasting bread • **toastmaster** noun the announcer of toasts at a public dinner • **toast rack** noun a stand with partitions for slices of toast

tobacco noun a type of plant whose dried leaves are used for smoking • **tobacconist** noun someone who sells tobacco, cigarettes, etc

toboggan noun a long light sledge ◇ verb go in a toboggan

today adv & noun **1** (on) this day **2** (at) the present time

toddle verb **1** walk unsteadily, with short steps **2** (with off) leave • **toddler** noun a young child just able to walk

toddy noun (plural **toddies**) a hot drink of whisky and honey

to-do noun (plural **to-dos**) a fuss or commotion

toe noun **1** one of the five finger-like parts of the foot **2** the front part of an animal's foot **3** the front part of a shoe, golf club, etc • **on your toes** alert, ready for action • **toe the line** do as you are told

toffee noun a kind of sweet made of sugar and butter • **toffee-nosed** adj, informal snobbish

tofu noun a paste of unfermented soya beans

toga noun, hist the loose outer garment worn by a citizen of ancient Rome

together adv **1** with each other, in place or time: let's stay together/three buses arrived together **2** in or into union or connection: glue the pages together **3** by joint action: together we can afford it

toggle noun a cylindrical fastening for a coat ◇ verb switch quickly between two positions, states, etc (esp between being on and off)

togs plural noun, informal clothes

toil verb **1** work hard and long **2** walk, move, etc with effort ◇ noun hard work • **toiler** noun

toilet noun **1** a receptacle for waste matter from the body, with a water supply for flushing this away **2** a room containing this **3** dated the act of washing yourself, dressing, and arranging your hair • **toiletries** plural noun soaps, cosmetics, etc • **toilet water** noun a lightly perfumed spirit-based liquid for the skin

toilette /twa-let/ noun washing and dressing

Toiseach /tee-shuxh/ noun the prime minister of the Republic of Ireland

token noun **1** a stamped piece of plastic etc, or a voucher, for use in place of money: bus token/book token **2** a mark or sign: a token of my friendship ◇ adj done for show only; insincere: token gesture

told past form of **tell**

tolerable adj **1** bearable **2** fairly good: tolerable player • **tolerably** adv

tolerance noun **1** fairness towards people with different beliefs, customs, etc from your own **2** ability to resist the effects of a drug etc • **tolerant** adj

tolerate verb **1** put up with; endure **2** allow • **toleration** noun

toll[1] noun a tax charged for crossing a bridge etc • **take a/its toll** cause damage or loss

toll[2] verb **1** sound (a large bell) slowly, as for a funeral **2** of a bell: be sounded slowly

tomahawk noun, hist a Native American light axe used as a weapon and tool

tomato noun (plural **tomatoes**) a juicy red-skinned vegetable cooked and also eaten raw in salads

tomb /toom/ *noun* **1** a grave **2** a burial vault or chamber

tombola *noun* a lottery with tickets drawn from a revolving drum

tomboy *noun* a girl who behaves in a way considered boyish

tombstone *noun* a stone placed over a grave in memory of the dead person

tomcat *noun* a male cat

tome *noun* a large heavy book

tomfoolery *noun, dated* silly behaviour

tomorrow *adv & noun* **1** (on) the day after today **2** (in) the future: *I'll do it tomorrow/the children of tomorrow*

tomtom *noun* **1** a tall thin drum hit with the hands **2** a deep drum in a drum kit

ton *noun* **1** a measure of weight equal to 2240 pounds, about 1016 kilograms **2** a unit of space in a ship equal to 100 cubic feet • **metric ton** or **metric tonne** 1000 kilogrammes

tone *noun* **1** quality of sound: *harsh tone* **2** *music* one of the larger intervals in a scale, *eg* between C and D **3** the quality of a voice expressing the mood of the speaker: *a gentle tone* **4** a shade of colour **5** muscle firmness or strength ◇ *verb* **1** (sometimes with **in**) fit in well **2** (with **down**) make or become softer **3** (with **up**) give strength to (muscles *etc*)

tongs *plural noun* an instrument for lifting things

tongue *noun* **1** the fleshy organ inside the mouth, used in tasting, speaking, and swallowing **2** a flap in a shoe **3** a long, thin strip of land **4** the tongue of an animal served as food **5** a language: *his mother tongue* • **tongue-tied** *adj* unable to speak clearly because of nervousness • **tongue twister** *noun* a phrase, sentence, *etc* not easy to say quickly, *eg* 'she sells sea shells'

tonic *noun* **1** a medicine that gives strength and energy **2** *music* the keynote of a scale **3** tonic water ◇ *adj* **1** of tones or sounds **2** of a tonic • **tonic water** *noun* carbonated water containing quinine

tonight *adv & noun* (on) the night of the present day

tonnage *noun* the space available in a ship, measured in tons

tonne *another spelling of* **ton**

tonsil *noun* one of a pair of soft fleshy lumps at the back of the throat • **tonsillitis** *noun* reddening of and pain in the tonsils

tonsure *noun* **1** the shaving of the top of the head of priests and monks **2** the part of the head so shaved

too *adv* **1** to a greater extent, in a greater quantity, *etc* than is wanted: *too hot to go outside/too many people in the room* **2** (with a negative) very, particularly: *not feeling too well* (ie not feeling very well) **3** also: *I'm feeling quite cold, too*

took *past tense of* **take**

tool *noun* an object used for doing a task, *esp* by hand • **toolbar** *noun* a bar on a computer screen showing features, functions, *etc* that the user can select

toot *noun* the sound of a car horn *etc* ◇ *verb* make a short, sharp sound

tooth *noun* (*plural* **teeth**) **1** any of the hard, bony objects sticking out of the gums, arranged in two rows in the mouth **2** any of the points on a saw, cogwheel, comb, *etc* • **toothache** *noun* pain in a tooth • **toothpaste** *noun* paste or powder for cleaning the teeth • **toothpick** *noun* a small sharp instrument for picking out food from between the teeth • **toothsome** *adj, dated* pleasant to the taste • **tooth and nail** fiercely and determinedly

top *noun* **1** the highest part of anything **2** the upper surface **3** the highest place or rank **4** a lid **5** a circus tent **6** a kind of spinning toy ◇ *adj* best, most important, or highest ◇ *verb* (**topping**, **topped**) **1** cover on the top **2** do better than **3** take off the top of **4** reach the top of • **topcoat** *noun* an overcoat • **top dog** *noun, informal* the most powerful or successful person in a group • **top hat** *noun* a man's tall silk hat • **top-heavy** *adj* having the upper part too heavy for the lower • **topmost** *adj* highest • **topnotch** *adj* of the highest quality • **top-secret** *adj* (of information *etc*) very secret

topaz *noun* a type of precious stone of various colours

topi *or* **topee** *noun* a helmet-like hat used as a protection against the sun

topiary *noun* the art of trimming bushes, hedges, *etc* into decorative shapes

topic *noun* a subject spoken or written about

topical *adj* concerned with present events • **topicalness** *noun*

topography *noun* the description of the features of the land in a certain region • **topographical** *adj*

topple *verb* become unsteady and fall

topsy-turvy *adj & adv* **1** turned upside down **2** completely different from the usual or expected way

torch *noun* (*plural* **torches**) **1** a small hand-held light with a switch and electric battery **2** a flaming piece of wood or coarse rope carried as a light in processions ◇ *verb, slang* set fire to deliberately

tore *past tense of* **tear²**

toreador *noun* a bullfighter mounted on horseback

torment *verb* **1** treat cruelly and make suffer **2** worry greatly **3** tease ◇ *noun* **1** great pain or suffering **2** a cause of these • **tormentor** *noun*

torn *past participle of* **tear²**

tornado *noun* (*plural* **tornadoes**) a violent whirling wind that causes great damage

torpedo *noun* (*plural* **torpedoes**) a large cylindrical missile fired by a ship or plane ◇ *verb* (**torpedoes**, **torpedoing**, **torpedoed**) hit or sink (a ship) with a torpedo

torpid *adj* lacking energy • **torpidity** *or* **torpor** *noun*

torque *noun* **1** a force causing rotation **2** a measure of the turning effect of such a force

torrent *noun* **1** a rushing stream **2** a heavy downpour of rain **3** a violent flow of words *etc*: *torrent of abuse* • **torrential** *adj* rushing or falling violently

torrid *adj* **1** very passionate: *torrid love affair* **2** of weather: extremely hot

torsion *noun* twisting motion

torso *noun* (*plural* **torsos**) the body excluding the head and limbs; the trunk

tortilla /taw-tee-yuh/ *noun* a Mexican flat round cake made from wheat or maize

tortoise *noun* a four-footed slow-moving reptile covered with a hard shell • **tortoiseshell** *noun* the shell of a kind of sea turtle, used in making ornamental articles ◇ *adj* **1** made of this shell **2** mottled brown, yellow and black: *a tortoiseshell cat*

tortuous *adj* **1** full of bends or diversions **2** annoyingly complicated

torture *verb* **1** treat someone cruelly as a punishment or to force them to confess something **2** cause to suffer ◇ *noun* **1** the act of torturing **2** great suffering

Tory *noun* (*plural* **Tories**) a member of the British Conservative Party

toss *verb* **1** throw up in the air **2**

throw up (a coin) to see which side falls uppermost **3** turn restlessly from side to side **4** of a ship: be thrown about by rough water • **toss-up** *noun* an equal choice or chance • **toss off 1** produce quickly **2** *slang* masturbate • **toss up** toss a coin

tot[1] *noun* **1** a little child **2** a small amount of alcoholic spirits

tot[2] *verb*: **tot up** add up

total *adj* **1** whole: *total number* **2** complete: *total wreck* ◇ *noun* **1** the entire amount **2** the sum of amounts added together ◇ *verb* (**totalling, totalled**) **1** add up **2** amount to **3** *slang* damage irreparably; wreck • **totally** *adv* completely

totalitarian *adj* governed by a single party that allows no opposition

totem *noun* an image of an animal or plant used as the badge or sign of a Native American tribe • **totem pole** *noun* a pole on which totems are carved and painted

totter *verb* **1** shake as if about to fall **2** stagger

toucan *noun* a type of S American bird with a very big beak

touch *verb* **1** feel (with the hand) **2** come or be in contact (with): *a leaf touched his cheek* **3** affect the feelings of; move: *the story touched those who heard it* **4** mark slightly with colour: *touched with gold* **5** reach the standard of: *I can't touch him at chess* **6** have anything to do with: *I wouldn't touch a job like that* **7** eat or drink: *he won't touch meat* **8** concern (someone): *an issue that touches us all* **9** *informal* persuade (someone) to lend you money: *I touched him for £10* ◇ *noun* **1** the act or feeling of touching **2** the sense of physical contact **3** a small quantity or degree: *a touch of salt* **4** of an artist, pianist, *etc*: skill or style **5** *sport* the ground beyond the edges of the pitch marked off by **touchlines** • **touch-and-go** *adj* very

uncertain: *it's touch-and-go whether we'll get it done on time* • **touching** *adj* causing emotion; moving • **touchstone** *noun* a test or standard of measurement of quality *etc* • **in** *or* **out of touch with** in, or not in, communication or contact with • **touch down** of an aircraft: land • **touch off** cause to happen • **touch on** mention briefly • **touch up** improve (a drawing or photograph *etc*) by making details clearer *etc*

touché /too-sheh/ *exclam* acknowledging a point scored in a game or argument

touchy *adj* (**touchier, touchiest**) very easily offended • **touchily** *adv* • **touchiness** *noun* • **touchy-feely** *adj, informal, derog* demonstrative and unafraid to express emotion through physical contact

tough *adj* **1** not easily damaged **2** of meat *etc*: hard to chew **3** of strong character **4** difficult to cope with or overcome: *tough opposition* • **toughen** *verb* become, or cause to become, tough

toupee /too-peh/ *noun* a small wig worn to cover a bald spot

tour *noun* a trip in which you visit various places for pleasure ◇ *verb* make a tour of • **tourism** *noun* the activities of tourists and of those who cater for their needs • **tourist** *noun* someone who travels for pleasure

tour de force *noun* an outstanding effort or accomplishment

tournament *noun* **1** a competition involving many contests and players **2** *hist* a meeting at which knights fought together on horseback

tourniquet /taw-ni-keh/ *noun* a bandage tied tightly round a limb to prevent loss of blood from a wound

tousled /towz-uld/ *adj* of hair: untidy and tangled

tout *verb* go about looking for

support, votes, buyers, *etc* ◇ *noun* **1** someone who does this **2** someone who gives tips to people who bet on horse races

tow *verb* pull (a car *etc*) with a rope attached to another vehicle ◇ *noun* **1** the act of towing **2** the rope used for towing • **towpath** *noun* a path alongside a canal *orig* used by horses that towed barges • **in tow** accompanying someone • **on tow** being towed

towards *or* **toward** *prep* **1** moving in the direction of (a place, person, *etc*): *walking towards the house* **2** to (a person, thing, *etc*): *his attitude towards his son* **3** as a help or contribution to: *I gave £5 towards the cost* **4** near, about (a time *etc*): *towards four o'clock*

towel *noun* a cloth for drying or wiping (eg the skin after washing) ◇ *verb* (**towelling**, **towelled**) rub dry with a towel • **towelling** *noun* a cotton cloth often used for making towels

tower *noun* a tall thin building or structure ◇ *verb* rise high (over, above) • **towering** *adj* **1** rising high **2** violent: *a towering rage*

town *noun* a place, larger than a village, that includes many buildings, houses, shops, *etc* • **town crier** *noun, hist* someone who made public announcements in a town • **town hall** *noun* the building where the official business of a town is done • **town planning** *noun* planning of the future development of a town

toxaemia /toks-ee-mi-uh/ *noun* blood poisoning

toxic *adj* **1** poisonous **2** caused by poison • **toxicology** *noun*

toxin *noun* a naturally-occurring poison

toy *noun* **1** an object for a child to play with **2** an object for amusement only • **toyboy** *noun, informal* a young male companion of an older woman • **toy with** consider casually

trace *noun* **1** a mark or sign left behind **2** a footprint **3** a small amount **4** a line drawn by an instrument recording a change (eg in temperature) **5** (**traces**) the straps by which a horse pulls a cart *etc* along ◇ *verb* **1** follow the tracks or course of **2** copy (a drawing *etc*) on transparent paper placed over it • **traceable** *adj* able to be traced (to) • **tracery** *noun* decorated stonework holding the glass in some church windows • **tracing** *noun* a traced copy

trachea /truh-*kee*-uh/ *noun* the windpipe

trachoma /truh-*koh*-muh/ *noun* an eye disease

track *noun* **1** a racecourse for runners, cyclists, *etc* **2** a railway line **3** a path or rough road **4** (**tracks**) marks left behind by someone or something that has passed **5** an endless band on which wheels of a tank *etc* travel ◇ *verb* follow (an animal) by its footprints and other marks left • **trackball** *noun* a rotating ball in a computer keyboard that controls cursor movement • **tracksuit** *noun* a warm suit worn while jogging, before and after an athletic performance *etc* • **keep** *or* **lose track of** keep or fail to keep aware of the whereabouts or progress of • **make tracks for** set off towards • **track down** search for (someone or something) until caught or found

tract *noun* **1** a stretch of land **2** a short pamphlet on a religious or political subject **3** a system made up of connected parts of the body: *the digestive tract*

tractable *adj* easily persuaded or influenced

traction *noun* **1** the force of pulling or dragging **2** medical treatment that involves holding limbs under the force of weights • **traction engine** *noun* a road steam engine

tractor *noun* a motor vehicle for agricultural work

trade noun 1 the buying and selling of goods 2 someone's occupation: a carpenter by trade ◇ verb 1 buy and sell 2 have business dealings (with) 3 deal (in) 4 exchange • **trademark** noun a registered mark or name put on goods to show that they are made by a certain company • **trader** noun someone who buys and sells • **tradesman** noun a workman in a skilled trade • **trade union** noun a group of workers of the same trade who join together to bargain with employers for fair wages etc • **trade unionist** noun a member of a trade union • **trade wind** noun a wind that blows towards the equator from the north-east and south-east • **trade in** give as part-payment for something else • **trade on** take advantage of, often unfairly

tradition noun 1 the handing down of customs, beliefs, stories, etc from generation to generation 2 a custom, belief, etc handed down in this way • **traditional** adj • **traditionalist** noun someone who believes in maintaining traditions

traffic noun 1 the vehicles that use roads or waterways 2 communication carried out on a communications network or system 3 dishonest dealings (eg in drugs) ◇ verb (**trafficking, trafficked**) deal dishonestly (in) • **traffic lights** plural noun lights of changing colours for controlling traffic at road junctions or street crossings

tragedy noun (plural **tragedies**) 1 a very sad event 2 a play about unhappy events and with a sad ending • **tragedian** noun • **tragic** adj 1 very sad 2 of tragedies • **tragically** adv

trail verb 1 draw along, in or through: trailing his foot through the water 2 hang down (from) or be dragged loosely behind 3 hunt (animals) by following footprints etc 4 walk wearily 5 of a plant: grow over the ground or a wall ◇ noun 1 an animal's track 2 a pathway through a wild region 3

something left stretching behind: a trail of dust • **trailer** noun 1 a vehicle pulled behind a car 2 a short film advertising a longer film to be shown at a later date

train noun 1 a railway engine with carriages or trucks 2 a part of a dress that trails behind the wearer 3 a line (of thought, events, etc) 4 a line of animals carrying people or baggage ◇ verb 1 prepare yourself by practice or exercise for a sporting event, job, etc 2 educate 3 exercise (animals or people) in preparation for a race etc 4 tame and teach (an animal) 5 (with **on** or **at**) aim, point (a gun, telescope, etc) at 6 make (a tree or plant) grow in a certain direction • **trainee** noun someone who is being trained • **trainer** noun someone who trains people or animals for a sport, circus, etc • **training** noun 1 preparation for a sport 2 experience or learning of the practical side of a job

traipse verb walk wearily

trait noun an aspect of someone's character: patience is one of his good traits

traitor noun 1 someone who goes over to the enemy's side, or gives away secrets to the enemy 2 someone who betrays trust • **traitorous** adj

trajectory noun (plural **trajectories**) the path of something moving through the air or through space

tram noun a short lightweight electric train that runs through streets on rails • **tramline** noun 1 a rail of a tramway 2 (**tramlines**) tennis the parallel lines marked at the sides of the court • **tramway** noun a system of tracks on which trams run

trammel verb (**trammelling, trammelled**) hinder ◇ noun something that hinders movement

tramp noun 1 a homeless person who lives on the streets by begging 2 a journey made on foot 3 a small cargo boat with no fixed route ◇ *verb* **1** walk with heavy footsteps **2** walk along, over, *etc*: *tramping the streets in search of a job*

trample *verb* **1** damage or injure by walking on **2** (*usu* with **on**) treat roughly or unfeelingly **3** tread heavily

trampoline *noun* a structure for gymnasts or children to bounce on, consisting of a sprung frame supporting an elastic sheet

trance *noun* a sleep-like or half-conscious state

tranquil *adj* quiet and peaceful • **tranquillity** *noun*

tranquillizer *noun* a drug to calm the nerves or cause sleep • **tranquillize** *verb* make calm

trans- *prefix* across, through: *transatlantic*

transact *verb* do (a piece of business) • **transaction** *noun* a piece of business

transatlantic *adj* **1** crossing the Atlantic Ocean: *transatlantic yacht race* **2** across or over the Atlantic: *transatlantic friends*

transcend *verb* **1** overcome (difficulties or disadvantages that hinder) **2** go beyond the limits of

transcribe *verb* **1** copy from one book into another or from one form of writing (*eg* shorthand) into another **2** adapt (a piece of music) for a particular instrument

transcript *noun* a written copy • **transcription** *noun* **1** the act of transcribing **2** a written copy

transept *noun* in a cross-shaped church, the part that goes across the long central part (the **nave**)

transexual *another spelling of* **transsexual**

transfatty acid *noun* (*also called* **transfat**) a type of fat found in margarine, produced by artificial hardening of vegetable oil

transfer *verb* (**transferring, transferred**) **1** remove to another place **2** hand over to another person ◇ *noun* **1** the act of transferring **2** a design or picture that can be transferred from one surface to another • **transferable** *adj* able to be transferred • **transference** *noun*

transfigure *verb* change greatly and for the better the form or appearance of • **transfiguration** *noun*

transfix *verb* **1** make unable to move or act, *eg* because of surprise: *transfixed by the sight* **2** pierce through

transform *verb* change in shape or appearance • **transformation** *noun* • **transformer** *noun* an apparatus for changing electrical energy from one voltage to another

transfusion *noun* a transfer of blood from one person to the body of another • **transfuse** *verb*

transgress *verb* break a rule, law, *etc* • **transgression** *noun* the act of breaking a rule, law, *etc*; a sin • **transgressor** *noun* someone who breaks a rule, law, *etc*

transient *adj* not lasting; passing • **transience** *noun*

transistor *noun* **1** a small device that controls the flow of an electric current **2** *dated* a portable radio set using these

transit *noun* **1** the carrying or movement of goods, passengers, *etc* from place to place **2** the passing of a planet between the sun and the earth • **transition** *noun* a change from one form, place, appearance, *etc* to another • **transitional** *adj* • **transitory** *adj* lasting only for a short time

transitive *adj, grammar* of a verb: having an object, *eg* the verb '*hit*' in 'he *hit* the ball'

translate *verb* **1** turn (something

said or written) into another language **2** develop or be converted (into): *will that enthusiasm translate into votes?* • **translation** *noun* **1** the act of translating **2** something translated • **translator** *noun* someone who translates

transliterate *verb* write (a word) in the letters of another alphabet

translucent *adj* allowing light to pass through, but not transparent • **translucence** *noun*

transmit *verb* (**transmitting, transmitted**) **1** send out signals that are received as programmes **2** pass on (a message, news, heat) • **transmission** *noun* **1** a radio or television broadcast **2** the act of transmitting • **transmitter** *noun* an instrument for transmitting (*esp* radio signals)

transmute *verb* change the form, substance or nature of

transnational *adj* relating to more than one nation

transom *noun* a beam across a window or the top of a door

transparency *noun* (*plural* **transparencies**) **1** the state of being transparent **2** a photograph printed on transparent material and viewed by shining light through it

transparent *adj* **1** able to be seen through **2** easily seen to be true or false: *a transparent excuse*

transpire *verb* **1** happen: *tell me what transpired* **2** let out (moisture *etc*) through pores of the skin or through the surface of leaves

transplant *verb* **1** lift and plant (a growing plant) in another place **2** remove (skin) and graft it on another part of the same body **3** remove (an organ) and graft it in another person or animal ◇ *noun* **1** the act of transplanting **2** a transplanted organ, plant, *etc* • **transplantation** *noun*

transport *verb* **1** carry from one place to another **2** overcome with strong feeling: *I was transported with delight* **3** *hist* send (a prisoner) to a prison in a different country ◇ *noun* **1** the act of transporting **2** any means of carrying persons or goods: *rail transport* **3** strong feeling: *transports of joy* • **transportation** *noun* **1** the act of transporting **2** means of transport **3** *hist* punishment of prisoners by sending them to a prison in a different country

transpose *verb* **1** cause (two things) to change places **2** change (a piece of music) from one key to another • **transposition** *noun*

transsexual *noun* someone who has become, or is in the process of becoming, a person of the opposite sex by having their sexual organs surgically changed

transubstantiation *noun* the changing of one substance into something different, *esp* the changing of communion wine and bread into the blood and body of Christ, or the belief that this happens

transverse *adj* lying, placed, *etc* across: *transverse beams in the roof*

transvestite *noun* someone who likes to wear clothes intended for the opposite sex

trap *noun* **1** a plan or trick for taking someone by surprise **2** a device for catching animals **3** a bend in a pipe which is kept full of water, for preventing the escape of air or gas **4** a carriage with two wheels ◇ *verb* (**trapping, trapped**) catch in a trap, or in such a way that escape is not possible • **trapdoor** *noun* a door in a floor or ceiling • **trapper** *noun* someone who makes a living by catching animals for their skins and fur

trapeze *noun* a swing used in performing gymnastic exercises or feats

trapezium *noun* a flat shape with four straight sides, two of which are parallel

trappings *plural noun* **1** clothes or ornaments suitable for a particular person or occasion **2** ornaments put on horses

Trappist *noun* a monk of an order whose members have taken a vow of silence

trash *noun* something of little worth ◇ *verb, informal* destroy • **trashy** *adj*

trauma *noun* **1** a very distressing experience that has a lasting emotional effect **2** *formal* injury to the body • **traumatic** *adj*

travail *noun, old* hard work

travel *verb* (**travelling, travelled**) **1** go on a journey **2** move **3** go along or across **4** visit foreign countries ◇ *noun* the act of travelling • **traveller** *noun* **1** someone who travels **2** *dated* a travelling representative of a business firm who tries to obtain orders for his firm's products

traverse *verb* go across or pass through ◇ *noun* **1** something that crosses or lies across **2** a going across a rock face *etc* **3** a zigzag track of a ship

travesty *noun* (*plural* **travesties**) a ridiculous distortion or imitation: *a travesty of justice*

trawl *verb* **1** fish by dragging a large net along the bottom of the sea **2** search (through) thoroughly • **trawler** *noun* a boat used for trawling

tray *noun* a flat piece of wood, metal, *etc* with a low edge, for carrying dishes

treachery *noun* (*plural* **treacheries**) the act of betraying those who have trusted you • **treacherous** *adj* **1** likely to betray **2** dangerous: *treacherous road conditions* • **treacherously** *adv*

treacle *noun* a thick dark syrup produced when sugar is refined

tread *verb* (**treading, trod, trodden**) **1** (with **on**) put your foot on **2** walk on or along ◇ *noun* **1** a step **2** the part of a tyre that touches the ground • **treadle** *noun* part of a machine that is worked by the foot • **treadmill** *noun* **1** *hist* a mill turned by the weight of people who were made to walk on steps fixed round a big wheel **2** any tiring routine work • **tread on someone's toes** offend or upset them • **tread water** keep yourself afloat in an upright position by moving your arms and legs

treason *noun* disloyalty to your own country or its government, *eg* by giving away its secrets to an enemy • **treasonable** *adj* consisting of, or involving, treason

treasure *noun* **1** a store of money, gold, *etc* **2** anything of great value or highly prized ◇ *verb* **1** value greatly **2** keep carefully because of its personal value: *she treasures the mirror her mother left her* • **treasurer** *noun* someone who has charge of the money of a club • **treasure-trove** *noun* something valuable of unknown ownership found and deemed to be the property of the Crown • **Treasury** *or* **treasury** *noun* the part of a government that has charge of the country's money

treat *verb* **1** behave towards: *I was treated very well in prison* **2** try to cure (someone) of a disease **3** try to cure (a disease) **4** write or speak about **5** buy (someone) a meal, drink, *etc* **6** try to arrange (a peace treaty *etc*) with ◇ *noun* something special (*eg* an outing) that gives a lot of pleasure: *they went to the theatre as a treat* • **treatment** *noun* **1** the act of treating (*eg* a disease) **2** remedy, medicine: *a new treatment for cancer* **3** the way in which someone or something is dealt with: *rough treatment*

treatise *noun* a long detailed essay

treaty *noun* (*plural* **treaties**) an agreement made between countries

treble *adj* **1** three times as much: *wood of treble thickness* **2** high in pitch: *treble note* ◇ *verb* become three times as much ◇ *noun* **1** the highest part in singing **2** a child who sings the treble part of a song

tree *noun* **1** the largest kind of plant, with a thick, firm wooden stem and branches **2** anything like a tree in shape

trefoil *noun* a three-part leaf or decoration

trek *noun* **1** a long or tiring journey **2** *old* a journey by wagon ◇ *verb* (**trekking, trekked**) **1** make a long hard journey **2** *old* make a journey by wagon

trellis *noun* (*plural* **trellises**) a network of strips for holding up growing plants

tremble *verb* **1** shake with cold, fear, or weakness **2** feel fear ◇ *noun* **1** the act of trembling **2** a fit of trembling

tremendous *adj* **1** very great or strong **2** *informal* very good; excellent • **tremendously** *adv, informal* very

tremolo *noun* (*plural* **tremolos**), *music* rapid repetition of the same note giving a trembling sound

tremor *noun* a shaking or quivering

tremulous *adj* **1** shaking **2** showing fear: *a tremulous voice*

trench *noun* (*plural* **trenches**) a long narrow ditch dug in the ground • **trenchcoat** *noun* a long raincoat with a belt

trenchant *adj* **1** hurting the feelings: *a trenchant remark* **2** of a policy *etc*: effective, vigorous

trend *noun* **1** a current fashion or taste **2** a general direction: *the trend of events* • **trendy** *adj, informal* fashionable

trepidation *noun* fear or nervousness

trespass *verb* **1** go illegally on private land *etc* **2** (with **on**) intrude: *trespassing on my free time* **3** sin ◇ *noun*

(*plural* **trespasses**) the act of trespassing • **trespasser** *noun*

tress *noun* (*plural* **tresses**) **1** a lock of hair **2** (**tresses**) long hair

trestle *noun* a wooden support with legs, used for holding up a table, platform, *etc*

trews *plural noun* tartan trousers

tri- *prefix* three: *trilateral*

trial *noun* **1** the act of testing or trying (eg something new) **2** a test **3** the judging (of a prisoner) in a court of law **4** suffering • **on trial 1** being tried (*esp* in a court of law) **2** for the purpose of trying out: *goods sent on trial* **3** being tested: *I'm still on trial with the company* • **trial and error** the trying of various methods or choices until the right one is found

triangle *noun* **1** a flat shape with three straight sides and three angles: △ **2** a triangular metal musical instrument, played by hitting with a small rod • **triangular** *adj* having the shape of a triangle

triathlon *noun* a sporting contest consisting of three events, *usu* swimming, cycling and running

tribe *noun* **1** a people who are all descended from the same ancestor **2** a group of families, *esp* of a wandering people ruled by a chief • **tribal** *adj* • **tribesman, tribeswoman** *noun*

tribulation *noun* great hardship or sorrow

tribunal *noun* **1** a group of people appointed to give judgement, *esp* on an appeal **2** a court of justice

tribune *noun, hist* a high official elected by the people in ancient Rome

tributary *noun* (*plural* **tributaries**) a stream that flows into a river or other stream

tribute *noun* **1** words or actions expressing praise or thanks: *a warm* *tribute to his courage* **2** money paid regularly by one nation or ruler to another in return for protection or peace

trice *noun*: **in a trice** in a very short time

triceps *noun* a muscle at the back of the arm that straightens the elbow

trick *noun* **1** a skilful action performed to puzzle and amuse **2** in card games, the cards picked up by the winner when each player has played a card ◇ *adj* meant to deceive: *trick photography* ◇ *verb* cheat by some quick or cunning action • **trickery** *noun* cheating • **trickster** *noun, dated* someone who deceives by tricks • **tricky** *adj* not easy to do

trickle *verb* **1** flow in small amounts **2** arrive or leave slowly and gradually: *replies are trickling in* ◇ *noun* a slow gradual flow

tricolour or *US* **tricolor** *noun* a flag with three bands of colour, *esp* the flag of France

tricycle *noun* a three-wheeled cycle

trident *noun* a three-pronged spear

tried past form of **try**

triennial *adj* **1** happening every third year **2** lasting for three years

tries see **try**

trifle *noun* **1** a pudding of whipped cream, sponge-cake, wine, *etc* **2** anything of little value **3** a small amount ◇ *verb* **1** (with **with**) act towards without sufficient respect: *in no mood to be trifled with* **2** amuse yourself in an idle way (with): *he trifled with her affections* **3** behave in a casual thoughtless manner

trifling *adj* very small in value or amount

trigger *noun* **1** a small lever on a gun pulled with the finger to cause the bullet to be fired **2** something that starts off a chain of events ◇ *verb* (with **off**) start, be the cause of, an important event, chain of events, *etc*

trigonometry *noun* the branch of mathematics concerned with the relationship between the sides and angles of triangles • **trigonometric** or **trigonometrical** *adj*

trilby *noun* (*plural* **trilbies**) a man's hat with an indented crown and narrow brim

trill *verb* sing, play or say in a quivering or bird-like way ◇ *noun* in music, a rapid repeating of two notes several times

trillion *noun* **1** a million million millions **2** (originally *US*) a million millions

trilobite *noun* a fossil whose body forms three long furrows

trilogy *noun* (*plural* **trilogies**) a group of three related plays, novels, *etc* by the same author, meant to be seen or read as a whole

trim *verb* (**trimming**, **trimmed**) **1** clip the edges or ends of: *trim the hedge* **2** decorate (*eg* a hat) **3** adjust and refine the position of (*eg* sails) ◇ *noun* **1** a neatening haircut **2** dress: *hunting trim* ◇ *adj* **1** tidy and in good order **2** slim

trimming *noun* **1** a decoration added to a dress, cake, *etc* **2** a piece of cloth, hair, *etc* cut off while trimming

Trinity *noun* in Christianity, the union of Father, Son and Holy Ghost in one God

trinket *noun* a small ornament of little value

trio *noun* (*plural* **trios**) **1** three performers **2** three people or things

trip *verb* (**tripping**, **tripped**) **1** (often with **up**) fall over **2** move with short, light steps **3** (with **up**) make a mistake ◇ *noun* a journey for pleasure or business • **tripper** *noun* someone who goes on a short pleasure trip

tripartite *adj* **1** in or having three parts **2** of an agreement: between three countries

tripe *noun* **1** part of the stomach of a cow or sheep used as food **2** *informal* nonsense

triple *adj* **1** made up of three **2** three times as large (as something else) ◇ *verb* make or become three times as large

triplet *noun* **1** one of three children or animals born of the same mother at one time **2** a set of three rhyming lines in a poem **3** *music* a group of three notes played in the time of two

triplicate *noun*: **in triplicate** in three copies

tripod *noun* a three-legged stand

triptych /*trip*-tik/ *noun* three painted panels forming a whole work of art

trisect *verb* cut into three • **trisection** *noun*

trite *adj* of a remark: used so often that it has little force or meaning

triumph *noun* **1** a great success or victory **2** celebration after a success: ride in triumph through the streets ◇ *verb* **1** win a victory **2** rejoice openly because of a victory • **triumphal** *adj* used in celebrating a triumph • **triumphant** *adj* feeling or showing great happiness because of a victory • **triumphantly** *adv*

trivet *noun* a metal tripod for resting something hot on

trivia *plural noun* unimportant details or facts

trivial *adj* of very little importance • **triviality** *noun* **1** something unimportant **2** trivialness • **trivialness** *noun* the state of being trivial

trod, **trodden** see **tread**

troglodyte *noun* a cave-dweller

troll *noun* a mythological giant or dwarf who lives in a cave

trolley *noun* (*plural* **trolleys**) **1** a small cart (*eg* as used by porters at railway stations) **2** a supermarket basket on wheels **3** a hospital bed on wheels for transporting patients **4** a table on wheels, used for serving tea *etc* • **trolley bus** *noun* a bus that gets its power from overhead wires

trollop *noun*, *dated derog* **1** a sexually promiscuous woman **2** a dirty untidy woman

trombone *noun* a brass wind instrument with a sliding tube that changes the notes

trompe l'oeil /tromp *luhy*/ *noun* an optical illusion

troop *noun* **1** (**troops**) soldiers **2** a collection of people or animals **3** a unit in cavalry *etc* ◇ *verb* go in a group: they all trooped out • **trooper** *noun* a horse-soldier • **troopship** *noun* a ship for carrying soldiers • **troop the colours** carry a regiment's flag past the lined-up soldiers of the regiment

trope *noun* a figure of speech

trophy *noun* (*plural* **trophies**) **1** a prize such as a silver cup won in a sports competition *etc* **2** something taken from an enemy and kept in memory of the victory

tropic *noun* **1** either of two imaginary circles running round the earth at about 23 degrees north (**Tropic of Cancer**) or south (**Tropic of Capricorn**) of the equator **2** (**tropics**) the hot regions near or between these circles ◇ *adj* (also **tropical**) **1** of the tropics **2** growing in hot countries: tropical fruit **3** very hot

trot *verb* (**trotting**, **trotted**) **1** of a horse: run with short, high steps **2** of a person: run slowly with short steps ◇ *noun* the pace of a horse or person when trotting • **trotters** *plural noun* the feet of pigs or sheep, *esp* when used as food

troth *noun*, *old* faith or fidelity

troubadour /troo-buh-daw/ noun, hist a travelling singer-musician, esp in medieval France

trouble verb 1 cause worry or sorrow to 2 cause inconvenience to 3 make an effort; bother (to): I didn't trouble to ring him ◇ noun 1 difficulty or problems 2 worry 3 something that causes difficulty 4 care and effort put into doing something 5 illness or injury • **troubleshooter** noun someone whose job is to solve difficulties (esp in a firm's business activities) • **troublesome** adj causing difficulty or problems

trough noun 1 a long open container for animals' food and water 2 an area of low atmospheric pressure 3 a dip between two sea waves

trounce verb 1 defeat heavily 2 punish or beat severely

troupe /troop/ noun a company of actors, dancers, etc • **trouper** noun a member of a troupe

trousers plural noun an outer garment for the lower part of the body that covers each leg separately • **trouser** adj of a pair of trousers: trouser leg

trousseau /troo-soh/ noun (plural **trousseaux** or **trousseaus**) a collection of clothes and linen that a woman keeps for her wedding and married life

trout noun a freshwater or sea fish with a speckled body

trowel noun 1 a small spade used in gardening 2 a similar tool with a flat blade, used for spreading mortar or plaster

troy weight noun a system of weights for weighing gold, gems, etc

truant noun someone who stays away from school without permission • **truancy** noun • **play truant** stay away from school without permission etc

truce noun a rest from fighting or quarrelling agreed to by both sides

truck noun 1 a large goods vehicle; a lorry 2 a wagon for carrying goods on a railway • **trucker** noun, US a lorry driver • **have no truck with** refuse to have dealings with

truculent adj fierce and threatening; aggressive • **truculence** noun

trudge verb walk with heavy steps, as if tired

true adj 1 correct, not invented or wrong: it's true that the earth is round 2 of a story etc: telling of something that really happened 3 accurate 4 faithful: a true friend 5 properly so called: the spider is not a true insect 6 rightful: the true heir 7 in the correct or intended position • **truism** noun a statement that is so clearly true that it is not worth making • **truly** adv

truffle noun a round fungus found underground and highly valued as a food

trug noun a shallow basket used in gardening

trump noun 1 a suit that has a higher value than cards of other suits 2 a card of this suit ◇ verb play a card that is a trump • **trump card** noun 1 a card that is a trump 2 something kept in reserve as a means of winning an argument etc • **trump up** make up • **turn up trumps** play your part well when things are difficult

trumpery noun (plural **trumperies**) something showy but worthless

trumpet noun 1 a brass musical instrument with a clear, high-pitched tone 2 the cry of an elephant ◇ verb 1 announce or promote loudly 2 to blow a trumpet

truncated adj 1 cut off at the top or end 2 shortened: a truncated version

truncheon noun a short heavy baton such as that used by police officers

trundle verb wheel or roll along slowly and heavily

trunk noun 1 the main stem of a tree

2 the body (not counting the head, arms, or legs) of a person or an animal **3** the long nose of an elephant **4** a large box or chest for clothes *etc* **5** *US* the luggage compartment of a car **6** (**trunks**) short pants worn by boys and men for swimming • **trunk call** *noun, dated* a telephone call to someone in another town • **trunk road** *noun, dated* a main road

truss *noun* (*plural* **trusses**) **1** a bundle (*eg* of hay, straw) **2** a system of beams to support a bridge **3** a supporting bandage for a hernia ◇ *verb* **1** tie tightly (up) **2** tie (up) the legs and wings of (a bird) ready for cooking

trust *noun* **1** belief in the ability, truthfulness or goodness of a thing or person **2** care or keeping: *the child was put in my trust* **3** an arrangement by which money or property is managed on behalf of someone **4** a number of business firms working closely together ◇ *verb* **1** have faith or confidence (in) **2** give (someone something) in the belief that they will use it well *etc*: *I can't trust your sister with my tennis racket* **3** feel confident (that): *I trust that you can find your way here* • **trustee** *noun* someone who keeps something in trust for another • **trustful** *adj* • **trusting** *adj* ready to trust, not suspicious • **trustworthy** *adj* • **trusty** *adj* able to be depended on • **take on trust** believe without checking or testing

truth *noun* **1** the facts **2** a true statement **3** the state of being true • **truthful** *adj* **1** telling the truth, not lying **2** of a statement: true • **truthfully** *adv* • **truthfulness** *noun*

try *verb* (**tries, trying, tried**) **1** make an effort (to do something) **2** test by using: *try this new soap* **3** test severely; strain: *you're trying my patience* **4** attempt to use, open, *etc*: *I tried the door but it was locked* **5** judge (a prisoner) in a court of law ◇ *noun* (*plural* **tries**) **1** an attempt **2** in rugby: a score

made by grounding the ball beyond the opponents' goal line • **trying** *adj* hard to bear; testing • **try on** put on (clothing) to see if it fits *etc* • **try out** test by using

tryst /trist/ *noun, old* an arrangement to meet someone, *esp* a lover, at a certain place

tsar *or* **tzar** *or* **czar** /zah/ *noun, hist* the emperor of pre-revolutionary Russia

tsarina *or* **tzarina** *or* **czarina** /zah-ree-nuh/ *noun, hist* **1** the wife of a tsar **2** an empress of Russia

tsetse /tet-si/ *noun or* **tsetse fly** an African biting fly that spreads dangerous diseases

T-shirt *another spelling of* **tee-shirt**

tsunami /tsoo-nah-mi/ *noun* a large sea wave caused by an earthquake

TT *abbrev* **1** Tourist Trophy, an annual motorcycle race on the roads of the Isle of Man **2** tuberculin tested **3** teetotal

tub *noun* **1** a large round container, *esp* wooden **2** a round container for ice-cream *etc*

tuba *noun* a large brass musical instrument giving a low note

tubby *adj* fat and round

tube *noun* **1** a hollow cylinder-shaped object through which liquid or gas passes **2** an organ of this kind in humans, animals, *etc* **3** a container from which a substance may be squeezed **4** an underground railway system **5** a cathode ray tube • **tubing** *noun* a length of tube • **tubular** *adj* shaped like a tube

tuber *noun* a swollen underground stem of a plant, *eg* a potato

tuberculosis *noun* an infectious disease affecting the lungs

TUC *abbrev* Trades Union Congress

tuck *verb* **1** fold or push (into or under a place) **2** gather (cloth) together into a fold **3** (with **in** or **up**) push bedclothes closely round (someone in bed) ◇ noun **1** a fold stitched in a piece of cloth **2** informal sweets, cakes, etc • **tuck shop** noun a shop in a school where sweets, cakes, etc are sold • **tuck in** informal to eat with enjoyment or greedily

Tuesday noun the third day of the week

tuft noun a bunch or clump of grass, hair, etc

tug verb (**tugging**, **tugged**) **1** pull hard **2** pull along ◇ noun **1** a strong pull **2** a tugboat • **tugboat** noun a small but powerful ship used for towing larger ones • **tug-of-war** noun a contest in which two sides, holding the ends of a strong rope, pull against each other

tuition noun **1** teaching **2** private coaching or teaching

tulip noun a cup-shaped flower grown from a bulb

tulle /tool/ noun a kind of cloth made of thin silk or rayon net

tumble verb **1** fall or come down suddenly and violently **2** roll about **3** do acrobatic tricks ◇ noun **1** a fall **2** a confused state • **tumbledown** adj falling to pieces • **tumbler** noun **1** a large drinking glass **2** an acrobat • **tumble to** understand suddenly

tumbrel or **tumbril** noun, hist a two-wheeled cart of the kind used to take victims to the guillotine during the French Revolution

tumescent adj swollen or enlarged

tummy noun (plural **tummies**) informal the stomach

tumour noun an abnormal growth in the body

tumult noun **1** a great noise made by a crowd **2** a confused or agitated state • **tumultuous** adj

tumulus noun an artificial mound of earth, esp over a tomb

tun noun a large cask, esp for wine

tuna noun (plural **tuna** or **tunas**) a large sea fish used as food

tundra noun a treeless Arctic plain with permanently frozen subsoil

tune noun **1** notes put together to form a melody **2** the music of a song ◇ verb **1** put (a musical instrument) in tune **2** adjust a radio set to a particular station **3** (sometimes with **up**) improve the working of an engine • **tuneful** adj having a pleasant tune • **tunefully** adv • **tuning fork** a steel fork that, when struck, gives a note of a certain pitch • **change your tune** change your opinions, attitudes, etc • **in tune 1** of a musical instrument: having each note adjusted to agree with the others or with the notes of other instruments **2** of a voice: having the same pitch as other voices or instruments **3** in agreement (with) • **to the tune of** to the sum of

tungsten noun a hard grey metal

tunic noun **1** a soldier's or police officer's jacket **2** hist a loose garment reaching to the knees, worn in ancient Greece and Rome **3** a similar modern garment: gym tunic

tunnel noun an underground passage, eg for a train ◇ verb (**tunnelling**, **tunnelled**) **1** make a tunnel **2** of an animal: burrow

turban noun **1** a long piece of cloth wound round the head, worn by Sikhs **2** a kind of hat resembling this

turbid adj of liquid: muddy, clouded

turbine noun an engine with curved blades, turned by the action of water, steam, hot air, etc

turbot noun a large flat sea fish used as food

turbulent adj **1** moving about irregularly and violently **2** likely to cause a disturbance or riot • **turbulence** noun irregular violent movement of air currents, *esp* when affecting the flight of aircraft

turd *noun* **1** a lump of faeces **2** *slang* a despicable person

tureen *noun* a large dish from which soup is served

turf *noun* **1** grass and the soil below it **2** (with **the**) the world of horse racing ◇ *verb* cover with turf • **turf out** *informal* force to leave; throw out

turgid *adj* of language: sounding grand but meaning little

turkey *noun* (*plural* **turkeys**) a large farmyard bird used as food

Turkish bath *noun* a type of hot air or steam bath in which someone is made to sweat heavily, is massaged and is then slowly cooled

turmeric *noun* a yellow spice made from the root of a plant of the ginger family, used in Asian cooking

turmoil *noun* a state of wild, confused movement or disorder

turn *verb* **1** go round: *wheels turning* **2** face or go in the opposite direction: *turned and walked away* **3** change direction: *the road turns sharply to the left* **4** direct (*eg* attention) **5** (with **on**) rotate or swing: *the door turns on its hinges* **6** become: *his hair turned white* **7** of leaves: to change colour **8** pass (the age of): *she must have turned 40* ◇ *noun* **1** the act of turning **2** a point where someone may change direction, *eg* a road junction: *take the first turn on the left* **3** a bend (*eg* in a road) **4** a spell of duty: *your turn to wash the dishes* **5** one of several acts making up a performance **6** a short stroll: *a turn along the beach* **7** a fit of dizziness, shock, *etc* • **turncoat** *noun* someone who betrays their party, principles, *etc* • **turning** *noun* a point where a road *etc* joins another • **turning point** *noun* a crucial point of change • **turnover** *noun* **1** rate of change or replacement (*eg* of workers in a firm *etc*) **2** the total amount of sales made by a firm during a certain time • **turnpike** *noun* **1** *hist* a gate across a road that opened when the user paid a toll **2** *US* a road on which a toll is paid • **turnstile** *noun* a gate that turns to allow only one person to pass at a time • **turntable** *noun* **1** a revolving platform for turning a railway engine round **2** the revolving part of a record player on which the record rests • **by turns** *or* **in turn** one after another in a regular order • **do someone a good** *or* **bad turn** act helpfully or unhelpfully towards someone • **to a turn** exactly, perfectly: *cooked to a turn* • **turn against** become hostile to • **turn down 1** say no to (*eg* an offer or request) **2** lessen (heat, volume of sound, *etc*) • **turn someone's head** fill them with pride or conceit • **turn in 1** go to bed **2** hand over to those in authority • **turn off 1** stop the flow of (a tap) **2** switch off the power for (a television *etc*) • **turn on 1** set running (*eg* water from a tap) **2** switch on power for (a television *etc*) **3** depend (on) **4** become angry with (someone) unexpectedly **5** *slang* arouse sexually • **turn out 1** force to leave; expel **2** make or produce **3** empty: *turn out your pockets* **4** of a crowd: gather for a special purpose **5** switch off (a light) **6** prove (to be): *he turned out to be right* • **turn to 1** set to work **2** go to for help *etc* • **turn up 1** appear or arrive **2** be found **3** increase (*eg* heat, volume of sound, *etc*)

turnip *noun* a large round vegetable with firm flesh

turpentine *noun* an oil from certain trees, used for mixing paints, cleaning paint brushes, *etc*

turpitude *noun, formal* wickedness

turquoise *noun* **1** a greenish-blue colour **2** a greenish-blue precious stone

turret *noun* **1** a small tower on a castle or other building **2** a structure for supporting guns on a warship

• **turreted** *adj* having turrets

turtle *noun* a kind of large tortoise that lives in water • **turtledove** *noun* a type of dove noted for its sweet, soft song • **turtleneck** *noun* a high, round neck on a sweater • **turn turtle** of a boat *etc*: turn upside down, capsize

tusk *noun* one of a pair of large teeth sticking out from the mouth of certain animals (*eg* elephants and walruses)

tussle *noun* a struggle or fight ◇ *verb* struggle

tussock *noun* a tuft of grass

tutelage /tyoo-tuh-lij/ *noun* the state of being protected by a guardian • **tutelary** *adj* protecting

tutor *noun* 1 a teacher of students in a university *etc* 2 a teacher employed privately to teach individual pupils ◇ *verb* teach • **tutorial** *noun* a meeting for study or discussion between tutor and students

tutti-frutti *noun* an Italian ice-cream containing nuts and various kinds of fruit

tutu *noun* a ballet dancer's short, stiff, spreading skirt

tuxedo *noun* (*plural* **tuxedos** or **tuxedoes**), *US* a dinner-jacket

TV *abbrev* television

twaddle *noun, informal* nonsense

twain *noun, old* two • **in twain** *old* in two; apart

twang *noun* 1 a tone of voice in which the words seem to come through the nose 2 a sound like that of a tightly-stretched string being plucked ◇ *verb* make such a sound

twat *noun, taboo slang* 1 the vagina 2 an idiot or despised person

tweak *verb* 1 pull with a sudden jerk 2 improve by making minor adjustments ◇ *noun* 1 a sudden jerk or pull 2 a minor adjustment made as an improvement

tweed *noun* 1 a woollen cloth with a rough surface 2 (**tweeds**) clothes made of this cloth ◇ *adj* made of tweed

tweezers *plural noun* small pincers for pulling out hairs, holding small things, *etc*

twelve *noun* the number 12 ◇ *adj* 12 in number • **twelfth** *adj* the last of a series of twelve ◇ *noun* one of twelve equal parts

twenty *noun* the number 20 ◇ *adj* 20 in number • **twentieth** *adj* the last of a series of twenty ◇ *noun* one of twenty equal parts

twerp *noun, informal* an idiot

twice *adv* two times

twiddle *verb* move absently with the fingers • **twiddle your thumbs** 1 turn your thumbs absently around one another 2 have nothing to do

twig *noun* a small branch of a tree

twilight *noun* 1 the faint light between sunset and night, or before sunrise 2 the time just before or after the peak of something: *the twilight of the dictatorship*

twill *noun* a kind of strong cloth with a ridged appearance

twin *noun* 1 one of two children or animals born to the same mother at the same birth 2 one of two things exactly the same ◇ *adj* 1 born at the same birth 2 very like another 3 made up of two parts or things which are alike • **twin bed** *noun* one of two matching single beds • **twinset** *noun* a matching cardigan and jumper

twine *noun* a strong kind of string made of twisted threads ◇ *verb* 1 wind or twist together 2 wind (about or around something)

twinge *noun* a sudden, sharp pain or unpleasant feeling

twinkle *verb* 1 of a star *etc*: shine with light that seems to vary in brightness 2 of eyes: shine with amusement *etc* ◇ *noun* the act or state of twinkling • **in a twinkling** in an instant

twirl *verb* **1** turn or spin round quickly and lightly **2** turn round and round with the fingers ◇ *noun* a spin round and round

twist *verb* **1** wind (threads) together **2** wind round or about something **3** make (*eg* a rope) into a coil **4** bend out of shape **5** bend or wrench painfully (*eg* your ankle) **6** make (*eg* facts) appear to have a meaning that is really false ◇ *noun* **1** the act of twisting **2** a painful wrench **3** something twisted: *a twist of tissue paper* • **twister** *noun, informal* **1** a tornado **2** *dated* a dishonest and unreliable person

twitch *verb* **1** jerk slightly and suddenly: *a muscle in his face twitched* **2** pull with a sudden light jerk ◇ *noun* **1** a muscle spasm **2** a sudden jerk

twitter *noun* **1** high, rapidly repeated sounds, as are made by small birds **2** a state of nervous excitement ◇ *verb* **1** of a bird: make a series of high quivering notes **2** of a person: to talk continuously

two *noun* the number 2 ◇ *adj* 2 in number • **two-faced** *adj* hypocritical • **twofold** *adj* double • **two-time** *verb* be sexually unfaithful to

tycoon *noun* a business man of great wealth and power

tyke *noun* a small cheeky or dirty child

tympani, tympanist *another spelling of* timpani, timpanist

type *noun* **1** kind **2** an example that has all the usual characteristics of its kind **3** printed lettering **4** a small metal block with a raised letter or sign, used for printing **5** a set of these ◇ *verb* print using a typewriter or keyboard • **typecast** *verb* give (an actor) parts very similar in character • **typescript** *noun* a typed script for a play *etc* • **typewriter** *noun* a machine with keys, used for printing letters on a sheet of paper • **typist** *noun* someone who works with a typewriter or word processor and does other secretarial or clerical tasks

typhoid *noun* an infectious disease caused by germs in infected food or drinking water

typhoon *noun* a violent storm of wind and rain in Eastern seas

typhus *noun* a dangerous fever carried by lice

typical *adj* having or showing the usual characteristics: *a typical Irishman/typical of her to be late* • **typically** *adv*

typify *verb* (**typifies, typifying, typified**) be a good example of: *typifying the English abroad*

typography *noun* the style or appearance of printed words • **typographer** *noun* someone who sets printing type • **typographical** *adj* • **typographically** *adv*

tyrannical *or* **tyrannous** *adj* cruel and domineering • **tyrannize** *verb* rule over harshly • **tyranny** *noun* cruel and oppressive government

tyrant *noun* a ruler who governs cruelly and oppressively

tyre *or US* **tire** *noun* a thick rubber cover round a motor or cycle wheel

tyro *another spelling of* tiro

tzar, tzarina *another spelling of* tsar, tsarina

Uu

ubiquitous *adj* **1** existing everywhere **2** being everywhere at once • **ubiquitously** *adv* • **ubiquity** *noun*

UCAS /yoo-kas/ *abbrev* Universities' Central Admissions Service

UDA *abbrev* Ulster Defence Association, an illegal Loyalist paramilitary organization operating in Northern Ireland

udder *noun* a bag-like part of a cow, goat, *etc* with teats which supply milk

UEFA /yoo-eh-fuh/ *abbrev* Union of European Football Associations

UFO *abbrev* unidentified flying object

Ugli *noun, trademark* a citrus fruit beilieved to be a cross between a grapefruit and a tangerine

ugly *adj* (**uglier, ugliest**) **1** unpleasant to look at or hear: *ugly sound* **2** threatening, dangerous: *gave me an ugly look* • **ugliness** *noun* • **ugly duckling** *noun* an unattractive or disliked person who later turns into a beauty, success, *etc*

UHF *abbrev* ultra high frequency

UHT *abbrev* **1** ultra-heat treated **2** ultra high temperature

uilean pipes /oo-li-un/ *plural noun* Irish bagpipes

ukelele /yoo-kuh-leh-lee/ *noun* a small stringed musical instrument played like a banjo

ulcer *noun* an open sore on the inside or the outside of the body • **ulcerated** *adj* having an ulcer or ulcers • **ulcerous** *adj*

ult *abbrev, dated* last month (from Latin *ultimo*): *we refer to your letter of 12th ult*

ulterior *adj* beyond what is admitted or seen: *ulterior motive*

ultimate *adj* last, final • **ultimately** *adv* finally, in the end

ultimatum *noun* (*plural* **ultimatums** *or* **ultimata**) a final demand sent with a threat to break off discussion, declare war, *etc* if it is not met

ultra- *prefix* **1** very: *ultra-careful* **2** beyond: *ultramicroscopic*

ultramarine *adj* of a deep blue colour

ultrasonic *adj* beyond the range of human hearing

ultraviolet *adj* having rays of slightly shorter wavelength than visible light

umber *noun* a mineral substance used to produce a brown paint

umbilical *adj* of the navel • **umbilical cord** *noun* a tube connecting an unborn mammal to its mother through the placenta

umbrage *noun* a feeling of offence or hurt: *took umbrage at my suggestion*

umbrella *noun* a portable object that protects against rain, consisting of a folding covered framework on a stick

umlaut /uum-lowt/ *noun* a symbol (¨) placed over a letter to modify its pronunciation

umpire *noun* **1** a sports official who sees that a game is played according to the rules **2** a judge asked to settle a dispute ◇ *verb* act as an umpire

umpteen *adj* many • **umpteenth** *adj*

UN *abbrev* United Nations

un- *prefix* **1** not: *unequal* **2** (with verbs) used to show the reversal of an action: *unfasten*

unabashed *adj* not ashamed or embarrassed

unable *adj* lacking enough strength, power, skill, *etc*

unaccountable *adj* not able to be explained • **unaccountably** *adv*

unaccustomed *adj* not used (to)

unadulterated *adj* not mixed with anything else

unanimous *adj* **1** all of the same opinion: *we were unanimous* **2** agreed to by all: *a unanimous decision* • **unanimity** *noun* • **unanimously** *adv*

unanswerable *adj* not able to be answered

unapproachable *adj* unfriendly and formal in manner

unarmed *adj* not armed

unassuming *adj* modest

unattached *adj* **1** not attached **2** not married or not in a long-term relationship

unaware *adj* not knowing: *unaware of the danger* • **unawares** *adv* **1** by surprise **2** unintentionally

unbalanced *adj* **1** lacking mental balance; deranged **2** not impartial; biased

unbearable *adj* too painful or bad to be endured

unbeknown *or* **unbeknownst** *adv* without the knowledge of (a person)

unbeliever *noun* someone who does not follow a certain religion

unbending *adj* not giving in or changing an opinion

unbounded *adj* extremely great:

unbounded enthusiasm

unbridled *adj* not kept under control: *unbridled fury*

unburden *verb*: **unburden yourself** tell your secrets or problems to someone else

uncalled *adj*: **uncalled for** quite unnecessary: *your remarks were uncalled for*

uncanny *adj* strange or mysterious • **uncannily** *adv*

uncared *adj*: **uncared for** not looked after properly

unceremonious *adj* done with no regard for politeness

uncertain *adj* **1** not certain; doubtful **2** not definitely known

uncharted *adj* **1** not shown on a map or chart **2** little known

uncle *noun* **1** the brother of your father or mother **2** the husband of your father's or mother's sister • **Uncle Sam** *noun, informal* the United States

unclean *adj* dirty or impure, *esp* from a religious point of view

uncomfortable *adj* not comfortable

uncommon *adj* not common, *esp* remarkably great • **uncommonly** *adv* very: *uncommonly well*

uncompromising *adj* not willing to give in or make concessions to others

unconditional *adj* with no conditions attached; absolute

unconscionable *adj* more than is reasonable: *made unconscionable demands*

unconscious *adj* **1** senseless, stunned (eg by an accident) **2** not aware (of) **3** not recognized by the person concerned: *unconscious prejudice against women* ◇ *noun* the deepest level of the mind

uncouth *adj* with rough manners or language; rude

uncover verb 1 remove a cover from 2 disclose

unction noun a ceremony anointing someone with oil • **unctuous** adj insincerely charming

uncut adj with no parts taken out; unedited

undaunted adj not scared or discouraged

undecided adj not yet decided

undeniable adj clearly true

under prep 1 directly below or beneath: under the bridge 2 less than: costing under £5 3 within the authority or command of: under General Montgomery 4 suffering: under attack 5 having, using: under a false name 6 in accordance with: under our agreement ◊ adv in or to a lower position, condition, etc • **go under** 1 sink beneath the surface of water 2 go out of business • **under age** younger than the legal or required age • **under way** in motion, started

under- prefix 1 below, beneath: underfloor 2 lower in position or rank: undersecretary 3 too little: undercharge

underachieve verb achieve less than your potential

underarm adv of bowling etc: with the arm kept below the shoulder

undercarriage noun the wheels of an aeroplane and their supports

underclothes plural noun underwear

undercoat noun 1 the layer of paint under the final coat 2 the kind of paint used under the final coat

undercover adj acting or done in secret: an undercover agent (ie a spy)

undercurrent noun 1 a flow or movement under the surface 2 a half-hidden feeling or tendency: an undercurrent of despair in her voice

undercut verb sell at a lower price than someone else

underdeveloped adj 1 not fully grown 2 of a country: lacking modern agricultural and industrial systems, and with a low standard of living

underdog noun the team or competitor considered less likely to win

underdone adj of food: not quite cooked

underestimate verb estimate at less than the real worth, value, etc

underfoot adv under the feet

undergo verb (**undergoes, undergoing, underwent, undergone**) 1 experience or endure 2 receive (eg as medical treatment)

undergraduate noun a university student who has not yet passed final examinations

underground adj 1 below the surface of the ground 2 operating in secret ◊ noun a railway that runs in tunnels beneath the surface of the ground

undergrowth noun shrubs or low plants growing amongst trees

underhand adj secretly deceitful; sly

underlay noun a protective layer beneath a carpet etc

underlie verb be the hidden cause or source of • **underlying** adj

underline verb 1 draw a line under 2 stress the importance of

underling noun someone of lower rank

undermine verb damage or weaken gradually

underneath adj & prep in a lower position (than); beneath: look underneath the table/wearing a jacket underneath his coat

undernourished adj not well nourished

underpants *plural noun* underwear covering the buttocks and upper legs

under par *adj* **1** not up to the usual level **2** unwell: *feeling under par*

underpass *noun* a road passing under another one

underpay *verb* pay too little

underpin *verb* be the underlying support or structure of

underplay *verb* describe as less important, impressive, *etc* than is true; play down

underprivileged *adj* not having normal living standards or rights

underrate *verb* think too little of; underestimate

underscore *verb* emphasize

undersell *verb* **1** sell for less than the true value **2** sell for less than someone else

undersigned *noun*: **the undersigned** the people whose names are written at the end of a letter or statement

undersized *adj* below the usual or required size

underskirt *noun* a thin skirt worn under another skirt

understand *verb* (**understanding, understood**) **1** see the meaning of **2** appreciate the reasons for: *I don't understand your behaviour* **3** have a thorough knowledge of: *do you understand economics?* **4** have the impression that: *I understood that you weren't coming* • **understandable** *adj*

understanding *noun* **1** the ability to see the full meaning of something **2** an agreement **3** condition: *on the understanding that we both pay half* **4** appreciation of other people's feelings, difficulties, *etc* ◇ *adj* able to understand other people's feelings; sympathetic

understatement *noun* a statement

that makes less of certain details than is actually the case • **understate** *verb*

understudy *noun* (*plural* **understudies**) an actor who learns the part of another actor and is able to take their place if necessary

undertake *verb* **1** promise (to do something) **2** take upon yourself (a task, duty, *etc*): *I undertook responsibility for the food* • **undertaker** *noun* someone whose job is to organize funerals • **undertaking** *noun* **1** something that is being attempted or done **2** a promise **3** the business of an undertaker

under-the-counter *adj* obtained or sold secretly and *usu* illegally

undertone *noun* **1** a soft voice **2** a partly hidden meaning, feeling, *etc*: *an undertone of discontent*

undertow *noun* a current below the surface of the water that moves in a direction opposite to the surface movement

undervalue *verb* value (something) below its real worth

underwater *adj* & *adv* under the surface of the water

underwear *noun* clothes worn next to the skin under other clothes

underweight *adj* under the usual or required weight

underwent *past tense of* **undergo**

underworld *noun* **1** the criminal world or level of society **2** the place where spirits go after death

underwriter *noun* someone who insures ships • **underwrite** *verb* **1** accept for insurance **2** accept responsibility or liability for

undesirable *adj* unpleasant or objectionable

undeveloped *adj* not developed

undies *plural noun*, *informal* underwear

undivided adj complete, total: undivided attention

undo verb (**undoes**, **undoing**, **undid**, **undone**) 1 unfasten (a coat, parcel, etc) 2 cancel the effect of; reverse: undoing all the good I did 3 old bring about the downfall of: alas, I am undone • **undoing** noun downfall

undoubted adj clearly true or existing • **undoubtedly** adv without doubt; certainly

undreamt-of adj not even imagined or dreamed of

undress verb take your clothes off

undue adj more than is necessary: undue expense • **unduly** adv

undulate verb 1 move as waves do 2 have a rolling, wavelike appearance • **undulating** adj • **undulation** noun

undying adj never fading: undying love

unearth verb find after a thorough search or much rummaging • **unearthly** adj 1 strange, as if not of this world 2 informal absurd, esp absurdly early: at this unearthly hour

uneasy adj nervous or worried • **uneasiness** noun

unedifying adj unpleasant because of its shameful nature

unemployed adj 1 without a job 2 formal not in use • **unemployment** noun 1 the state of being unemployed 2 the total number of unemployed people in a country • **the unemployed** unemployed people as a group

unenviable adj so unpleasant that nobody would want it: unenviable task

unequal adj 1 not equal; unfair: unequal distribution 2 lacking enough strength or skill: unequal to the job • **unequalled** adj better than all others

unequivocal adj clearly stated: unequivocal orders

unerring adj never making a mistake: unerring judgement

UNESCO /yoo-nes-koh/ abbrev United Nations Educational, Scientific and Cultural Organization

uneven adj 1 not smooth or level 2 not all of the same quality etc: this work is very uneven

unexceptionable adj impossible to object to or criticize

Do not confuse: **unexceptionable** and **unexceptional**

---

unexceptional adj not exceptional; ordinary

unexpected adj not expected; sudden

unexpurgated adj not censored

unfailing adj never failing or never likely to fail: unfailing accuracy

unfair adj not just

unfaithful adj 1 having a sexual relationship with someone who is not your regular sexual partner 2 failing to keep promises

unfasten verb undo the buttons etc of

unfathomable adj impossible to understand

unfeeling adj without sympathy or pity

unfettered adj not limited or controlled

unfit adj 1 not suitable 2 not good enough, or not in a suitable state (to, for): unfit for drinking/unfit to travel 3 not in good physical condition

unflagging adj not tiring or losing strength

unflappable adj always calm

unflinching adj not put off by pain, opposition, etc

unfold verb 1 spread out 2 of details

of a plot *etc*: become known

unforgettable *adj* unlikely to ever be forgotten; memorable

unfortunate *adj* **1** unlucky **2** regrettable: *unfortunate turn of phrase*

unfounded *adj* not based on fact; untrue

unfurl *verb* unfold (eg a flag)

ungainly *adj* physically awkward; clumsy

ungracious *adj* not polite

ungrateful *adj* not showing thanks for kindness

unguarded *adj* **1** without protection **2** thoughtless, careless: *unguarded remark*

unguent *noun* ointment

unhand *verb, old* let go of

unhappy *adj* (**unhappier, unhappiest**) **1** having negative feelings because something bad has happened; sad **2** unfortunate • **unhappily** *adv* • **unhappiness** *noun*

unhealthy *adj* **1** not well; ill **2** harmful to health: *unhealthy climate* **3** showing signs of not being well: *unhealthy complexion*

unheard-of *adj* not known to have happened before; unprecedented

unhinged *adj* mentally unbalanced; deranged

unholy *adj* **1** evil **2** outrageous

uni *noun, informal* a university

uni- *prefix* one, a single: *unicycle*

UNICEF /yoo-ni-sef/ *abbrev* United Nations Children's Fund

unicorn *noun* a mythological animal like a horse with one straight horn on its forehead

uniform *noun* the form of clothes worn by people in the armed forces, children at a certain school, *etc* ◇ *adj* the same in all parts or times • **uniformity** *noun* sameness

unify *verb* (**unifies, unifying, unified**) combine into one • **unification** *noun*

unilateral *adj* involving or done by only one person or group out of several • **unilateralism** *noun* the abandoning of nuclear weapons by one country, without waiting for others to do likewise • **unilateralist** *noun & adj*

uninhibited *adj* not worried about what others will think of your behaviour

uninitiated *adj* not having information that others have

uninterested *adj* not interested

Do not confuse with: **disinterested**

---

uninterrupted *adj* **1** continuing without a break **2** of a view: not blocked by anything

union *noun* **1** an organization that protects workers' rights; a trade union **2** a number of countries joined together **3** the act of joining together **4** partnership or marriage • **unionist** *noun* someone who supports the union of the United Kingdom • **unionize** *verb* encourage or force to join a trade union • **Union Jack** *noun* the flag of the United Kingdom

unique *adj* of which there is none similar or as good: *a unique sense of timing*

Do not confuse with: **rare**

---

unisex *adj* of or in a style suitable for either men or women

unison *noun* **1** the actions of people who all do or say something at the same time as each other **2** sameness of musical pitch • **in unison** all together

unit *noun* **1** a single thing, person or group, *esp* when considered as part of a larger whole: *army unit/storage unit*

2 a fixed amount or length used as a standard by which others are measured (eg metres, litres, centimetres, etc) **3** the number one ● **unitary** adj **1** forming a unit, not divided **2** using or based on units ● **unity** noun **1** complete agreement **2** the state of being one or a whole **3** the number one

unite verb **1** join together **2** act together ● **united** adj

universe noun all known things, including the earth and planets ● **universal** adj **1** relating to, or coming from, all people: *universal disapproval* **2** relating to the universe ● **universally** adv

university noun (plural **universities**) a college that teaches a wide range of subjects to a high level and awards degrees to students who pass its examinations

UNIX /yoo-niks/ noun a type of computer operating system designed to allow access to many users

unkempt adj untidy

unkind adj cruel

unleaded adj of petrol: not containing lead compounds

unleash verb allow to escape, develop or be expressed fully

unleavened adj of bread: not made to rise with yeast

unless conj if not: *unless he's here soon, I'm going (ie if he's not here soon)*

unlike prep **1** different from **2** not characteristic of: *it was unlike her not to phone* ◇ adj different

unlikely adj **1** not probable: *it's unlikely that it will rain today* **2** probably not true: *an unlikely tale*

unload verb **1** take the load from **2** remove the charge from a gun

unlooked-for adj not expected: *unlooked-for happiness*

unloose verb **1** set free; release **2** make loose or looser

unlucky adj (**unluckier**, **unluckiest**) **1** not lucky or fortunate **2** unsuccessful ● **unluckily** adv

unmanly adj lacking strength, courage or other qualities considered manly

unmask verb **1** show the true character of **2** bring to light (a plot etc)

unmatched adj without an equal

unmentionable adj too rude or embarrassing to be spoken of

unmistakable adj impossible to confuse with any other: *unmistakable handwriting*

unmitigated adj complete, absolute: *unmitigated disaster*

unmoved adj feeling no sympathy or other emotion: *unmoved by my pleas*

unnatural adj not natural, esp perverted or cruel

unnecessary adj not needed

unnerve verb cause to feel nervous or ill at ease

unobtrusive adj not obvious or conspicuous

unpack verb open (luggage) and remove the contents

unpalatable adj **1** not pleasing to the taste **2** not pleasant to have to face up to: *unpalatable facts*

unparalleled adj much better than before or than all others: *unparalleled success*

unpick verb take out sewing stitches from

unpleasant adj not pleasant; nasty

unprecedented adj never having happened before

unpremeditated adj done without having been planned: *unpremeditated murder*

unprepossessing adj not attractive or appealing

unpretentious *adj* not showy or affected

unprincipled *adj* having no moral principles

unprintable *adj* too obscene to print

unquestionable *adj* undoubted, certain

unravel *verb* (**unravelling, unravelled**) **1** take the knots or stitches out of **2** solve (a problem or mystery)

unreal *adj* **1** not real; imaginary **2** *informal* amazing, incredible

unremitting *adj* never stopping: *unremitting rain*

unrequited *adj* of love: not felt by the person loved

unrest *noun* a state of trouble or discontent, *esp* among a group of people

unrivalled *adj* without an equal

unruly *adj* **1** badly behaved **2** *dated* not obeying laws or rules • **unruliness** *noun*

unsavoury *adj* causing a feeling of disgust

unscathed *adj* not harmed

unscrew *verb* loosen (something screwed in)

unscrupulous *adj* having no scruples or principles

unseasonable *adj* **1** of weather: not usual for the time of year **2** not well-timed

unseat *verb* **1** remove from a political seat **2** throw from the saddle (of a horse)

unseemly *adj* not polite; improper: *unseemly haste*

unseen *adj* not seen • **sight unseen** (bought *etc*) without having been seen beforehand

unsettle *verb* make unrelaxed; disturb

unsettled *adj* **1** ill at ease **2** of weather: changeable **3** of a bill: unpaid

unsettling *adj* making you ill at ease

unsightly *adj* ugly

unsociable *adj* not willing to mix with other people

unsolicited *adj* not requested: *unsolicited advice*

unsophisticated *adj* **1** simple and uncomplicated **2** with little knowledge or experience of the modern world

unsound *adj* **1** not based on sound reasoning **2** insane

unspeakable *adj* too bad to describe in words: *unspeakable rudeness*

unstinting *adj* generous

unstoppable *adj* not able to be stopped

unstudied *adj* natural, not forced: *unstudied charm*

unsung *adj* not recognized as good: *an unsung Scots poet*

unsuspecting *adj* not aware of coming danger

unswerving *adj* sticking firmly to an intention, opinion or decision

untenable *adj* unjustifiable: *the government's position is untenable*

unthinkable *adj* **1** very unlikely **2** too bad to be thought of

untie *verb* **1** loosen the knot in **2** release from being tied-up

until *prep* up to the time of: *can you wait until Tuesday?* ◇ *conj* up to the time that: *keep walking until you come to the corner*

untimely *adj* **1** happening too soon: *untimely arrival* **2** not suitable to the occasion: *untimely remark*

unto *prep, old* to

untold *adj* **1** not yet told: *the untold story* **2** too great to be counted or measured: *untold riches*

untouchable *adj* **1** not to be touched **2** not able to be equalled or surpassed ◇ *noun, old* a Hindu of very low social caste

untoward *adj* **1** breaking social rules; improper **2** inconvenient

untrue *adj* **1** not true; false **2** *dated* unfaithful

untruth *noun* a lie • **untruthful** *adj*

unusual *adj* **1** not usual **2** rare, remarkable • **unusually** *adv*

unvarnished *adj* **1** not varnished **2** not exaggerated or changed; straightforward: *the unvarnished truth*

unveil *verb* **1** remove a cover from (a memorial *etc*) **2** cause to become known; disclose **3** remove a veil from

unwaged *adj* unemployed

unwarranted *adj* not justified or deserved

unwell *adj* not in good health

unwieldy *adj* not easily moved or handled • **unwieldiness** *noun*

unwind *verb* **1** wind off from a ball or reel **2** relax

unwitting *adj* **1** unintended: *unwitting insult* **2** unaware • **unwittingly** *adv*

unwonted *adj* unaccustomed, not usual: *unwonted cheerfulness*

unworthy *adj* **1** not deserving something **2** of little value or merit; worthless **3** below someone's usual standard, out of character: *that remark is unworthy of you*

unwritten *adj* **1** not written down **2** of a rule, law, *etc*: generally accepted

up *adv* **1** towards or in a higher or more northerly position: *walking up the hill/they live up in the Highlands* **2** completely, so as to finish: *drink up your tea* **3** to a larger size: *blow up a balloon* **4** as far as: *he came up to me and shook hands* **5** towards a big-

ger city *etc*, not necessarily one further north: *going up to London from Manchester* ◇ *prep* **1** towards or in the higher part of: *climbed up the ladder* **2** along: *walking up the road* ◇ *adj* (**upper**, **upmost** or **uppermost**) **1** ascending: *the up escalator* **2** ahead in score: *2 goals up* **3** richer: *£50 up on the deal* **4** risen: *the sun is up* **5** of a given length of time: ended: *your time is up* **6** *informal* wrong: *what's up with her today?* • **up-and-coming** *adj* likely to succeed • **on the up and up** getting steadily better all the time • **up and about 1** awake **2** out of bed after an illness • **ups and downs** times of good and bad luck • **up to 1** until: *up to the present* **2** capable of: *are you up to the job?* **3** falling as a responsibility to: *it's up to you to decide* **4** doing: *up to his tricks again* • **up to scratch** of the required standard • **up to speed** fully competent at a new job *etc*

upbeat *adj, informal* cheerful or optimistic

upbraid *verb* scold

upbringing *noun* the rearing of, or the training given to, a child

upcoming *adj* forthcoming

up-country *adv & adj* inland

update *verb* bring up to date ◇ *noun* **1** the act of updating **2** new information: *an update on yesterday's report*

upend *verb* turn upside down

upfront or **up-front** *adj* **1** speaking plainly and honestly; frank **2** foremost • **up front 1** of money: paid in advance **2** candidly, openly

upgrade *verb* **1** raise to a more important position **2** improve the quality of ◇ *noun, comput* a newer version of a software program

upheaval *noun* a violent disturbance or change

upheld *past form of* **uphold**

uphill *adj* **1** going upwards **2** difficult: *uphill struggle* ◇ *adv* upwards

uphold verb (**upholding**, **upheld**) 1 keep (eg a tradition) going 2 give support to

upholster verb fit (furniture) with springs, stuffing, covers, etc • **upholsterer** noun someone who upholsters furniture • **upholstery** noun covers, cushions, etc

upkeep noun 1 the act of keeping (eg a house or car) in a good state of repair 2 the cost of this

upland noun 1 high ground 2 (**uplands**) a hilly or mountainous region

uplift verb raise the spirits of; cheer up

upload verb, comput send data from your computer to another via the Internet, a local network, etc

up-market adj of high quality or price; luxury

upon prep 1 on the top of: upon the table 2 at or after the time of: upon completion of the task

upper adj higher or on the top ◇ noun 1 the part of a shoe etc above the sole 2 slang a drug that induces euphoria • **upper-case** adj of a letter: capital, eg A not a (contrasted with: **lower-case**) • **upper-class** adj belonging to the highest social class; aristocratic • **uppercut** noun a boxing punch that swings up from below • **upper hand** noun advantage or dominance • **uppermost** adj 1 most important or urgent 2 furthest up

uppity adj behaving in a superior way; haughty

upright adj 1 standing up; vertical 2 honest ◇ noun an upright post, piano, etc

uprising noun a revolt against a government etc

uproar noun a noisy disturbance • **uproarious** adj very noisy

uproot verb 1 tear up by the roots

2 leave your home and go to live in another place

upset verb (**upsetting**, **upset**) 1 make unhappy, angry, or worried 2 overturn 3 put out of order 4 ruin (plans etc) ◇ adj unhappy, angry, or worried ◇ noun 1 unhappiness, anger, or worry 2 something that causes these feelings

upshot noun a result or end of a matter: what was the upshot of all this?

upside-down adj & adv 1 with the top part underneath 2 in confusion

upstage adv away from the footlights on a theatre stage ◇ verb divert attention from (someone) to yourself

upstairs adv in or to the upper storey of a house etc ◇ noun the upper storey or storeys of a house ◇ adj in the upper storey or storeys: upstairs bedroom

upstanding adj 1 honest and respectable 2 formal standing up

upstart noun someone who does not show proper respect for more experienced or older people

upstream adv higher up a river or stream, towards the source

upsurge noun a sudden sharp increase

upswing noun a marked improvement, esp economically

uptake noun: **quick on the uptake** quick to understand

uptight adj nervous

up-to-date adj 1 familiar with the latest ideas, styles, etc 2 containing all recent facts etc: an up-to-date account • **up to date** 1 to the present time 2 aware of recent developments

upturn noun an improvement, esp economically

upward adj moving up; ascending • **upward** or **upwards** adv from a lower to a higher position • **upwardly** adv • **upwardly-mobile** adj moving to a higher social status • **upwards of** more than

uranium noun a radioactive metal

urban adj relating to a town or city (contrasted with: **rural**) • **urbanization** noun • **urbanize** verb make urban

urbane adj charming and relaxed in all social situations • **urbanity** noun

urchin noun a dirty, ragged child

urge verb 1 try to persuade: urging me to go home 2 advise or recommend: urge caution 3 drive (an animal) forwards ◇ noun a strong desire or impulse

urgent adj 1 requiring immediate attention 2 asking for immediate action • **urgency** noun • **urgently** adv

urine noun the waste liquid passed out of the body of animals and humans from the bladder • **urinary** adj • **urinate** verb pass urine from the bladder

urn noun 1 a vase for the ashes of a dead person 2 a metal drum with a tap, used for making and pouring out tea or coffee

ursine adj relating to bears

US or **USA** abbrev United States of America

us pronoun, plural used by a speaker or writer in referring to themselves together with other people (as the object in a sentence): when would you like us to come?

usable adj suitable for use

usage noun 1 the way something is used 2 the established way of using a word etc 3 custom, habit 4 treatment: rough usage

use verb /yooz/ 1 put to some purpose: use a knife to open it 2 bring into action: use your common sense 3 (often with **up**) expend all of (eg your patience or energy) 4 old treat: he used his wife cruelly ◇ noun /yoos/ 1 the act of using 2 value or suitability for a purpose: no use to anybody 3 the fact of being used: it's in use at the moment 4 custom • **no use** useless • **used to** 1 accustomed to 2 was or were in the habit of (doing something): we used to go there every year

used adj 1 not new: used cars 2 put to a purpose

useful adj serving a purpose; helpful • **usefully** adv • **usefulness** noun

useless adj having no use or effect • **uselessness** noun

user noun someone who uses anything, esp a computer • **user-friendly** adj easy to use

usher, **usherette** noun someone who shows people to their seats in a theatre etc • **usher** verb show or lead somewhere

USSR abbrev, hist Union of Soviet Socialist Republics

usual adj 1 done or happening most often: usual method 2 existing on most occasions: with his usual cheerfulness 3 ordinary ◇ noun a customary event, order, etc • **usually** adv on most occasions

usurp verb take possession of (eg a throne) by force • **usurper** noun

usury noun the lending of money with an excessively high rate of interest • **usurer** noun a moneylender who demands an excessively high rate of interest

utensil noun an instrument or container used in the home (eg a ladle, knife, pan)

uterus noun (plural **uteri**) the womb • **uterine** adj

utilitarian adj concerned with usefulness, rather than beauty, pleasure, etc

utility noun (plural **utilities**) 1

usefulness **2** a public service supplying water, gas, *etc*

utilize *verb* make use of • **utilization** *noun*

utmost *adj* **1** the greatest possible: *utmost care* **2** furthest • **do your utmost** make the greatest possible effort

utopia *noun* a perfect place; a paradise • **utopian** *adj*

utter[1] *verb* produce (words, a scream, *etc*) with the voice • **utterance** *noun* something said

utter[2] *adj* complete, total: *utter darkness* • **utterly** *adv* • **uttermost** *adj* greatest possible; utmost

U-turn *noun* a complete change in direction, policy, *etc*

UVA *abbrev* ultraviolet radiation

uvula *noun* the small piece of flesh hanging from the palate at the back of the mouth

uxorious *adj* of a man: extremely fond of his wife

Uzi /*oo*-zi/ *noun* a submachine-gun, *orig* used in Israel

Vv

v *abbrev* **1** against (from Latin *versus*) **2** see (from Latin *vide*) **3** verb **4** verse **5** volume

vacancy *noun* (*plural* **vacancies**) **1** a job that has not been filled **2** a room not already booked in a hotel *etc*

vacant *adj* **1** not occupied; empty **2** of an expression: showing no interest or intelligence • **vacantly** *adv*

vacate *verb* get out of; leave

vacation *noun* **1** a holiday **2** the act of vacating a place

vaccine *noun* a substance made from the germs that cause a disease, given to people and animals to try to prevent them catching that disease • **vaccinate** *verb* give a vaccine to • **vaccination** *noun*

vacillate *verb* move from one opinion to another; waver • **vacillation** *noun*

vacuous *adj* **1** empty-headed; stupid **2** having no meaning or purpose • **vacuously** *adv* • **vacuousness** *noun*

vacuum *noun* a space from which all, or almost all, the air has been removed • **vacuum cleaner** *noun* a machine that cleans carpets *etc* by sucking up dust • **vacuum flask** *noun* a container for keeping liquids hot or cold, with double walls enclosing a vacuum

vagabond *noun* **1** a person who never settles in one place; a wanderer **2** *old* a rogue

vagaries *plural noun* unexpected things: *vagaries of human nature*

vagina *noun* the passage connecting a woman's genitals to her womb • **vaginal** *adj* of the vagina

vagrant *noun* a homeless person who lives on the streets ◇ *adj* wandering • **vagrancy** *noun* the state of being a vagrant

vague *adj* **1** not clear or definite: *vague idea/vague shape* **2** not practical or efficient; forgetful • **vaguely** *adv*

vain *adj* **1** too concerned about yourself or your appearance **2** useless: *vain attempt* **3** meaningless: *vain promises* • **vainly** *adv* • **in vain** without success

vainglorious *adj, old* vainly boastful • **vaingloriously** *adv*

valance *noun* a decorative frill round the edge of a bed

vale *noun, formal* a valley

valediction *noun, formal* a farewell • **valedictory** *adj* saying farewell: *valedictory speech*

valency *noun* (*plural* **valencies**), *chemistry* the combining power of an atom or group with hydrogen (*eg* in water, H_2O, oxygen shows valency two)

valentine *noun* **1** a greetings card sent on St Valentine's Day, 14 February **2** the person it is sent to

valet *noun* /val-it/ or /val-eh/ a man's personal servant who looks after his clothes ◇ *verb* /val-it/ clean the interior of (someone else's car) as a service

valetudinarian *noun* someone who is over-anxious about their health

valiant *adj* brave • **valiantly** *adv*

valid *adj* 1 reasonable: *valid reason for not going* 2 legally in force: *valid passport* • **validate** *verb* make valid • **validity** *noun*

Valium *noun, trademark* a brand name for diazepam, a tranquillizing drug

valley *noun* (*plural* **valleys**) low land between hills, often with a river flowing through it

valorous *adj, formal* brave, courageous

valour *noun, formal* courage, bravery

valuable *adj* of great value • **valuables** *plural noun* articles of worth

value *noun* 1 monetary worth 2 purchasing power (of a coin *etc*) 3 importance 4 usefulness 5 *algebra* a number or quantity put as equal to an expression: *the value of x is 8* ◇ *verb* 1 give a monetary value to 2 think highly of • **valuation** *noun* 1 an estimated price or value 2 the act of valuing • **value-added tax** *noun* a government tax on articles and some services that people buy • **valueless** *adj* worthless • **valuer** *or* **valuator** *noun* someone trained to estimate the value of property

valve *noun* 1 a device allowing air, steam, or liquid to flow in one direction only 2 a small flap controlling the flow of blood in the body 3 an electronic component found in older television sets, radios, *etc*

vamp[1] *noun* a woman who sets out to attract men

vamp[2] *noun* the upper part of a boot or shoe ◇ *verb* 1 patch 2 play improvised music

vampire *noun* a dead person supposed to rise at night and suck the blood of sleeping people • **vampire bat** *noun* a S American bat that sucks blood

van[1] *noun* a road vehicle for carrying goods, smaller than a truck

van[2] *noun* a vanguard

vandal *noun* someone who pointlessly destroys or damages public buildings *etc* • **vandalism** *noun* the activities of a vandal • **vandalize** *verb* damage by vandalism

vane *noun* 1 a weathercock 2 the blade of a windmill, propeller, *etc*

vanguard *noun* 1 the leading group in a movement *etc* 2 the part of an army going in front of the main body

vanilla *noun* a sweet-scented flavouring obtained from the pods of a type of orchid

vanish *verb* 1 go out of sight 2 fade away to nothing

vanity *noun* (*plural* **vanities**) 1 excessive concern with yourself or your appearance 2 worthlessness 3 something vain and worthless

vanquish *verb* defeat

vantage point *noun* a position that gives a clear view

vapid *adj* lacking interest or imagination

vaporize *verb* change into vapour • **vaporizer** *noun* a device that sprays liquid very finely

vapour *noun* 1 the air-like or gas-like state of a substance that is usually liquid or solid: *water vapour* 2 mist or smoke in the air

variable, **variance**, **variation** *see* **vary**

varicose vein *noun* a swollen or enlarged vein, usually on the leg

variegated *adj* marked with different colours; multicoloured

variety *noun* (*plural* **varieties**) 1 the quality of being of many kinds, or of being different 2 a mixed collection: *a variety of books* 3 a sort, a type: *a variety of potato* 4 mixed theatrical entertainment including songs, comedy, *etc*

various adj 1 of different kinds: various shades of green 2 several: various attempts • **variously** adv

varlet noun, old a rascal

varnish noun a sticky liquid that gives a glossy surface to paper, wood, etc ◇ verb 1 paint with varnish 2 make superficially appealing

vary verb (**varies**, **varying**, **varied**) 1 make, be, or become different 2 make changes in (a routine etc) 3 differ or disagree • **variable** adj tending or able to change ◇ noun something that varies unpredictably • **variance** noun a state of differing or disagreeing • **variant** noun a different form or version ◇ adj in a different form • **variation** noun 1 a change 2 the extent of a difference or change: variations in temperature 3 music a repetition, in a slightly different form, of a main theme • **at variance** in disagreement

vascular adj relating to the blood vessels of animals or the tissues that transport sap in plants

vase /vahz/ or US /vehz/ noun a jar of pottery, glass, etc used as an ornament or for holding cut flowers

vasectomy noun (plural **vasectomies**) sterilization of a man by cutting, and removing part of, the sperm-carrying tubes

Vaseline noun, trademark a type of ointment made from petroleum

vassal noun, hist a tenant who held land from an overlord in return for certain services

vast adj of very great size or amount • **vastly** adv • **vastness** noun

VAT or **vat** abbrev value-added tax

vat noun a large tub or tank used eg for fermenting liquors and dyeing

vaudeville noun theatrical entertainment of dances and songs, usually comic

vault noun 1 an underground room 2 a strong room for storing valuables 3 an arched roof ◇ verb leap, supporting your weight on your hands, or on a pole

vaunt verb boast

VC abbrev Victoria Cross

VCR abbrev videocassette recorder

VD abbrev venereal disease

VDU abbrev visual display unit

veal noun meat from a calf

vector noun, math a quantity that has both direction and magnitude, represented by a straight line drawn from a given point

veer verb 1 change direction or course 2 change mood, opinions, etc

vegan /vee-gun/ noun a person who avoids all foods derived from animals

vegetable noun an edible part of a plant with a savoury taste, or the plant itself ◇ adj 1 of plants 2 made from or consisting of plants: vegetable dye/ vegetable oil

vegetarian noun someone who eats no meat, only vegetable and dairy foods ◇ adj consisting of, or eating, only vegetable or dairy foods

vegetate verb lead a dull, aimless life: sitting at home vegetating

vegetation noun 1 plants in general 2 the plants growing in a particular area

veggie adj & noun, informal vegetarian

vehement /vee-uh-munt/ adj emphatic and forceful in expressing opinions etc • **vehemence** noun • **vehemently** adv

vehicle noun 1 a means of transport used on land, esp one with wheels: motor vehicle 2 a means of conveying information, eg television or newspapers 3 a film, programme, etc devised as a way of showing off a performer's talent • **vehicular** adj

veil noun 1 a piece of cloth or netting worn to shade or hide the face 2 something that hides or covers up ◇ verb 1 cover with a veil 2 hide • take the veil become a nun

vein noun 1 one of the tubes that carry blood back to the heart 2 a small rib of a leaf 3 a thin layer of mineral in a rock 4 a streak in wood, stone, etc 5 a mood or personal characteristic: a vein of cheerfulness • veined adj marked with veins

Velcro noun, trademark a type of fastener made of two strips of specially treated fabric that interlock

veldt /velt/ noun, South African open grass-covered country with few or no trees

vellum noun 1 a fine parchment used for bookbinding, made from the skins of calves, kids, or lambs 2 thick, high-quality paper

velocity noun rate or speed of movement

velour /vuh-law/ noun a fabric with a soft, velvet-like surface

velvet noun 1 a fabric made from silk etc, with a thick, soft surface 2 velveteen ◇ adj 1 made of velvet 2 soft or smooth as velvet; silky • velvety adj soft, like velvet

velveteen noun a cotton fabric with a velvet-like pile

venal adj 1 willing to be bribed 2 done for a bribe; unworthy

Do not confuse with: **venial**

vend verb sell • vending machine noun a machine with sweets etc for sale, operated by putting coins in a slot • vendor noun someone who sells

vendetta noun a bitter long-lasting quarrel or feud

veneer noun 1 a thin surface layer of fine wood 2 a false outward show

hiding some bad quality: a veneer of good manners ◇ verb 1 cover a piece of wood with another thin piece of finer quality 2 give a good appearance to what is really bad

venerable adj worthy of respect because of age or wisdom

venerate verb respect or honour greatly • veneration noun 1 the act of venerating 2 great respect

venereal disease noun a disease contracted through sexual intercourse

Venetian blind noun a window blind formed of thin movable strips of metal or plastic hung on tapes

vengeance noun harm done to someone in return for harm they have done to you; revenge • with a vengeance with unexpected force or enthusiasm

vengeful adj seeking revenge • vengefully adv

venial adj of a sin: not very bad; pardonable (compare with: **cardinal**)

Do not confuse with: **venal**

venison noun meat from a deer

venom noun 1 poison 2 hatred or spite

venomous adj 1 poisonous 2 spiteful • venomously adv

vent noun 1 a small opening 2 a hole to allow air or smoke to pass through 3 an outlet 4 a slit at the bottom of the back of a coat etc ◇ verb express (strong emotion) in some way • give vent to express

ventilate verb 1 allow fresh air to pass through (a room etc) 2 old talk about; discuss • ventilation noun • ventilator noun a grating or other device for allowing in fresh air

ventral adj relating to the abdomen or belly

ventricle noun a small cavity in the brain or heart

ventriloquist noun someone who can speak without appearing to move their lips and can project their voice onto a puppet etc • **ventriloquism** noun

venture noun an undertaking that involves some risk: business venture ◇ verb **1** set off or set out **2** do or say something at the risk of causing annoyance: may I venture to suggest • **venturesome** adj • **venturous** adj

venue noun the place where an event happens

veracious adj, formal truthful • **veracity** noun truthfulness

Do not confuse with: **voracious**

veranda or **verandah** noun a kind of terrace with a roof supported by pillars, extending along the side of a house

verb noun the word that tells what someone or something does in a sentence, eg 'I sing'/'he had no idea'

verbal adj **1** of words **2** spoken, not written: verbal agreement **3** of verbs

verbatim /vuh-beh-tim/ adj in the exact words, word for word: a verbatim account

verbose adj using more words than necessary • **verbosity** noun

verdant adj, formal green with grass or leaves

verdict noun **1** the judge's decision at the end of a trial **2** someone's personal opinion on a matter

verdigris /vur-di-gree/ noun the greenish rust of copper, brass or bronze

verdure noun, formal green vegetation

verge noun **1** the grassy border along the edge of a road etc **2** edge, brink:

on the verge of a mental breakdown • **verge on** be close to: verging on the absurd

verger noun a church caretaker or other church official

verify verb (**verifies**, **verifying**, **verified**) show to be true; confirm • **verifiable** adj able to be verified • **verification** noun

verily adv, old truly, really

verisimilitude noun, formal closeness to real life; realism

veritable adj **1** true **2** real, genuine

verity noun, formal truth

vermicelli /vur-mi-chel-i/ noun a type of food like spaghetti but in much thinner pieces

vermilion noun a bright red colour

vermin plural noun animals or insects that are considered pests, eg rats, mice, fleas, etc • **verminous** adj full of vermin

vermouth /vur-muth/ noun a kind of drink containing white wine flavoured with wormwood

vernacular noun the ordinary spoken language of a country or district ◇ adj in the vernacular

vernal adj of the season of spring

verruca /vuh-roo-kuh/ noun a wart, especially on the foot

versatile adj **1** able to turn easily from one subject or task to another **2** useful in many different ways • **versatility** noun

verse noun **1** a number of lines of poetry forming a planned unit **2** poetry as opposed to prose **3** a short division of a chapter of the Bible • **versed in** skilled or experienced in

version noun **1** an account from one point of view **2** a form: another version of the same tune **3** a translation

verso noun the left-hand page of an open book (compare with: **recto**)

versus prep competing or considered against (short form: **v**)

vertebra noun (plural **vertebrae**) one of the bones of the spine

vertebrate noun an animal with a backbone

vertex noun (plural **vertices**) a point where two sloping lines or surfaces meet

vertical adj 1 standing upright 2 straight up and down • **vertically** adv

vertigo noun a whirling sensation when balance is disturbed; giddiness

verve noun lively spirit or enthusiasm

very adv 1 to a great extent or degree: seem very happy/walk very quietly 2 exactly: the very same ◇ adj 1 same, identical: the very people who claimed to support him voted against him 2 exactly what is wanted: the very man for the job 3 actual: in the very act of stealing 4 mere: the very thought of blood

vespers plural noun a church service in the evening

vessel noun 1 a ship 2 a container for liquid 3 a tube conducting fluids in the body: blood vessels

vest noun 1 an undergarment for the top half of the body 2 US a waistcoat ◇ verb give legally or officially: the power vested in me • **vested interest** noun a concern you have that something should be successful because you are involved in it, esp financially

vestibule noun an entrance hall

vestige noun an indication of something's existence; a trace

vestigial adj surviving only as a trace of former existence: vestigial wings

vestment noun a ceremonial garment, worn eg by a religious officer during a service

vestry noun (plural **vestries**) a room in a church in which vestments are kept

vet[1] noun, informal a veterinary surgeon

vet[2] verb (**vetting**, **vetted**) examine for suitability

vetch noun a plant of the pea family

veteran noun 1 someone who has given long service 2 an old soldier 3 US anyone who has served in the armed forces ◇ adj old, experienced

veterinarian noun, US a veterinary surgeon

veterinary adj relating to the treatment of animal diseases • **veterinary surgeon** noun a doctor who treats animals

veto /vee-toh/ noun (plural **vetoes**) 1 the power to forbid or block (a proposal) 2 an act of forbidding or blocking ◇ verb (**vetoes**, **vetoing**, **vetoed**) forbid, block

vex verb annoy

vexation noun 1 being annoyed 2 an annoying thing

vexatious adj, formal annoying

VHF abbrev very high frequency

via prep 1 passing through: travelling to Paris via London 2 by means of; using: via the Internet

viable adj practical enough to be done; practicable: viable proposition

viaduct noun a long bridge taking a railway or road over a river etc

viands plural noun, old food

vibrant adj full of energy; lively

vibrate verb 1 move back and forth very rapidly 2 of sound: echo • **vibration** noun 1 the act of vibrating 2 a rapid to-and-fro movement • **vibrator** noun an electrical device used for sexual stimulation • **vibratory** adj of vibration

vicar noun an Anglican priest in charge of a parish • **vicarage** noun the house of a vicar

vicarious adj 1 not experienced

personally but imagined through the experience of others: *vicarious thrill* **2** in place or on behalf of another person • **vicariously** *adv*

vice *noun* **1** a bad habit **2** immoral behaviour **3** a tool with two jaws for gripping objects firmly

vice- *prefix* second in rank to: *vice-chancellor/vice-president*

viceroy *noun* a governor acting on royal authority

vice versa *adv* the other way round: *I needed his help and vice versa (ie he needed mine)*

vicinity *noun* **1** neighbourhood **2** nearness

vicious *adj* **1** very violent **2** very spiteful • **vicious circle** *noun* a bad situation whose results cause it to get worse • **viciously** *adv* • **viciousness** *noun*

vicissitudes /vi-*sis*-i-tyoodz/ *plural noun, formal* changes of luck; ups and downs

victim *noun* **1** someone who is killed or harmed, intentionally or by accident: *victim of a brutal attack/victim of the financial situation* **2** an animal killed for sacrifice • **victimize** *verb* treat very unfairly

victor *noun* a winner of a contest *etc*

victorious *adj* successful in a battle or other contest

victory *noun* (*plural* **victories**) success in any battle, struggle or contest

victuals /*vit*-ulz/ *plural noun* food

video *adj* **1** relating to the recording and broadcasting of TV pictures and sound **2** relating to recording by video ◇ *noun* (*plural* **videos**) **1** a videocassette recorder **2** a recording on videotape **3** *US* television ◇ *verb* (**videos**, **videoing**, **videoed**) make a recording by video • **video game** *noun* an electronically operated game played

using a visual display unit • **video nasty** *noun* a pornographic or horror film on videotape • **videotape** *noun* magnetic tape for carrying pictures and sound

videocassette *noun* a cassette containing videotape • **videocassette recorder** *noun* a tape recorder using videocassettes for recording and playing back TV programmes

vie *verb* (**vies**, **vying**, **vied**): **vie with** compete with

view *noun* **1** a range or field of sight: *a good view* **2** a scene **3** an opinion ◇ *verb* **1** look at **2** watch (television) **3** consider • **viewpoint** *noun* **1** a place from which a scene is viewed **2** a personal opinion (also **point of view**) • **in view 1** in sight **2** in your mind as an aim • **in view of** taking into consideration • **on view** on show in public • **with a view to** with the purpose or intention of

vigil *noun* a time of watching or of keeping awake at night, often before a religious festival

vigilance *noun* watchfulness or alertness • **vigilant** *adj*

vigilante /vij-il-*an*-teh/ *noun* a private citizen who assumes the task of keeping order in a community

vignette /veen-*yet*/ *noun* **1** a small design or portrait **2** a short section of a film or book that is particularly interesting

vigorous *adj* **1** forceful: *vigorous defence* **2** strong and healthy • **vigorously** *adv*

vigour *noun* strength of body or mind; energy

Viking *noun, hist* a Norse invader of W Europe

vile *adj* **1** morally very bad; evil **2** disgusting • **vilely** *adv*

vilify *verb* (**vilifies**, **vilifying**, **vilified**) say very bad things about

villa *noun* a house in the country *etc* used for holidays

village *noun* a collection of houses not big enough to be called a town • **villager** *noun* someone who lives in a village

villain *noun* **1** a violent or wicked character **2** *informal* a criminal • **villainy** *noun* wickedness

villainous *adj* wicked

villein *noun, hist* a poor person forced to work for a lord; a serf

vindicate *verb* **1** clear from blame **2** justify

vindictive *adj* spiteful

vine *noun* **1** a climbing plant that produces grapes (also **grapevine**) **2** any climbing or trailing plant

vinegar *noun* a sour-tasting liquid made from wine, beer, *etc*, used for seasoning or pickling

vineyard /vin-yahd/ *noun* an area planted with grapevines

vintage *noun* **1** the gathering of ripe grapes **2** the grapes gathered **3** wine of a particular year, *esp* when of very high quality **4** time of origin or manufacture ◇ *adj* **1** of wine: of a particular year **2** very characteristic of an author, style, *etc*: *vintage Monty Python* • **vintage car** *noun* a car of a very early type, still able to run

vintner /vint-nuh/ *noun* a wine seller

vinyl *noun* a tough type of plastic

viola *noun* **1** a stringed instrument like a large violin **2** a member of the family of plants that includes violets and pansies

violate *verb* **1** break (a law, a treaty, *etc*) **2** harm sexually, *esp* rape **3** treat with disrespect **4** disturb or interrupt • **violation** *noun* • **violator** *noun*

violent *adj* **1** acting with great force: *violent storm* **2** caused by violence: *violent death* **3** uncontrollable: *violent temper* • **violence** *noun* great rough-

ness and force • **violently** *adv*

violet *noun* a kind of small bluish-purple flower

violin *noun* a musical instrument with four strings, held under the chin and played with a bow • **violinist** *noun* someone who plays the violin

VIP *abbrev* very important person

viper *noun* **1** an adder **2** a vicious or treacherous person

virago *noun* (*plural* **viragos**) a noisy, bad-tempered woman

viral *see* **virus**

virgin *noun* someone who has never had sexual intercourse • **the Virgin Mary** a name Christians give to the mother of Christ

virginal[1] *adj* of or like a virgin; chaste

virginal[2] *or* **virginals** *noun* an early type of musical instrument, with a keyboard

virile *adj* **1** of a man: having a lot of sexual energy **2** of a man: having manly qualities, *esp* physical strength • **virility** *noun*

virology *noun, med* the study of viruses

virtual *adj* in effect, though not in strict fact • **virtually** *adv* • **virtual reality** *noun* a computer simulation that gives the impression of being in a real situation

virtue *noun* **1** goodness of character and behaviour **2** a good quality, *eg* honesty, generosity, *etc* **3** a good point: *one virtue of plastic crockery is that it doesn't break* • **by virtue of** because of

virtuoso *noun* (*plural* **virtuosos**) a highly skilled artist, *esp* a musician • **virtuosity** *noun*

virtuous *adj* morally good • **virtuously** *adv*

virulent *adj* **1** of a disease: having a

rapidly harmful effect **2** full of poison **3** bitter, spiteful • **virulence** noun

virus noun (plural **viruses**) **1** a disease-causing organism smaller than a bacterium, or the disease it causes **2** comput a program that attaches to a computer system and can corrupt or destroy data stored on the hard disk • **viral** adj of a virus

visa noun a permit given by the authorities of a country to allow someone to stay for a time in that country

visage /viz-ij/ noun, formal the face or facial expression

vis-à-vis /veez-uh-vee/ prep in relation to, compared with

viscera /vis-uh-ruh/ plural noun the inner parts of the body • **visceral** adj **1** of the viscera **2** gory, bloody

viscid /vis-id/ adj viscous

viscount /vai-kownt/ noun a title of nobility next below an earl

viscountess noun a title of nobility next below a countess

viscous /vis-kus/ adj of a liquid: sticky, not flowing easily • **viscosity** noun

visible adj able to be seen • **visibility** noun **1** the clearness with which objects can be seen **2** the extent or range of vision as affected by fog, rain, etc • **visibly** adv

vision noun **1** the act or power of seeing **2** something seen in the imagination **3** a strange, supernatural sight **4** the ability to foresee likely future events

visionary adj seen in imagination only, not real ◊ noun (plural **visionaries**) someone who dreams up imaginative plans

visit verb **1** go to see; call on **2** stay with as a guest ◊ noun **1** a call at a person's house or at a place of interest etc **2** a short stay • **visitation** noun

1 a visit of an important official **2** a great misfortune, seen as a punishment from God • **visitor** noun someone who makes a visit

visor /vaiz-uh/ noun **1** a part of a helmet covering the face **2** a movable shade on a car's windscreen **3** a peak on a cap for shading the eyes

vista noun a view, esp one seen through a long, narrow opening

visual adj relating to, or received through, sight: visual aids • **visual display unit** noun a device like a television set, on which data from a computer's memory can be displayed

visualize verb form a clear picture of in the mind • **visualization** noun

vital adj **1** of the greatest importance: vital information **2** necessary to life **3** of life **4** vigorous, energetic: a vital personality • **vitality** noun **1** liveliness and energy **2** the ability to go on living • **vitalize** verb give life or vigour to • **vitally** adv • **vitals** plural noun, old parts of the body necessary for life

vitamin noun one of a group of substances necessary for health, occurring in different natural foods

vitiate verb, formal spoil or damage

vitreous adj of or like glass

vitrify verb (**vitrifies, vitrifying, vitrified**) make or become like glass

vitriol noun **1** sulphuric acid **2** hateful remarks

vitriolic adj hateful

vitro see **in vitro**

vituperate verb, formal be rude to; abuse • **vituperation** noun • **vituperative** adj abusive

viva /vai-vuh/ noun an oral examination ◊ verb examine orally

vivacious adj having an attractively lively personality • **vivaciously** adv • **vivacity** noun

vivarium noun a tank or other

enclosure for keeping living creatures

vivid adj **1** lifelike **2** extremely bright or colourful • **vividly** adv

vivisection noun the carrying out of experiments on living animals

vixen noun **1** a female fox **2** an ill-tempered woman

viz adv namely

vizier noun, hist a minister of state in some Eastern countries

vocabulary noun (plural **vocabularies**) **1** the range of words used by an individual or group **2** the words of a particular language **3** a list of words in alphabetical order, with their meanings

vocal adj **1** of the voice **2** expressing your opinions loudly and fully • **vocalist** noun a singer

vocation noun **1** an occupation or profession to which someone feels called to dedicate themselves **2** a strong inclination or desire to follow a particular course of action or work • **vocational** adj

vociferous adj expressing opinions loudly and forcefully • **vociferously** adv

vodka noun an alcoholic spirit made from grain or potatoes

vogue noun the fashion of the moment; popularity • **in vogue** in fashion

voice noun **1** the sound produced from the mouth in speech or song **2** ability to sing **3** an opinion ◇ verb express (an opinion) • **voicemail** noun a digital system for recording and storing telephone messages

void adj **1** containing nothing; empty **2** not valid ◇ noun an empty space • **void of** lacking completely

voile /voyl/ noun any very thin semi-transparent fabric

vol abbrev volume

volatile adj **1** of a liquid: quickly turning into vapour **2** easily becoming angry or violent

vol-au-vent /vol-oh-vonh/ noun a small round puff pastry case with a savoury filling

volcano noun (plural **volcanoes**) a mountain with an opening through which molten rock, ashes, etc are periodically thrown up from inside the earth • **volcanic** adj **1** relating to volcanoes **2** caused or produced by heat within the earth

vole noun a small rodent that lives near water

volition noun an act of will or choice: he did it of his own volition

volley noun (plural **volleys**) **1** a return of a ball in racquet sports, or kick in football, before it reaches the ground **2** a number of shots fired or missiles thrown at the same time **3** an outburst of abuse or criticism ◇ verb **1** return or kick (a ball) before it reaches the ground **2** shoot or throw in a volley • **volleyball** noun a team game in which players try to punch a ball over a high net before it hits the ground

volt noun the unit used in measuring the force of electricity • **voltage** noun electrical force measured in volts

volte-face /volt-fas/ noun a sudden complete reversal of opinion

voluble adj, formal speaking with a great flow of words • **volubility** noun

volume noun **1** a book, often one of a series **2** the amount of space taken up by anything **3** amount: volume of trade **4** loudness or fullness of sound • **voluminous** adj **1** wide and baggy **2** able to contain a lot

voluntary adj **1** done or acting by choice, not under compulsion **2** working without payment ◇ noun (plural **voluntaries**) a piece of organ music of the organist's choice played at a church service

volunteer *noun* someone who offers to do something of their own accord, often for no payment ◇ *verb* **1** act as a volunteer **2** give (information, an opinion, *etc*) unasked

voluptuous *adj* **1** of a woman: with a curvy figure that is sexually attractive **2** very or too fond of physical pleasure

vomit *verb* throw up the contents of the stomach through the mouth ◇ *noun* the matter thrown up by vomiting

voodoo *noun* a type of witchcraft originating in the W Indies and southern US

voracious *adj* **1** eating a lot of food; greedy: *voracious appetite* **2** extremely eager: *voracious reader* • **voracity** *noun*

Do not confuse with: **veracious**

---

vortex *noun* (*plural* **vortices** *or* **vortexes**) **1** a whirlpool **2** a whirlwind

votary *noun* (*plural* **votaries**) **1** someone who has made a vow **2** a devoted worshipper or admirer

vote *verb* **1** give your support to (a particular candidate, a proposal, *etc*) in a ballot or show of hands **2** decide by voting ◇ *noun* **1** an expression of opinion or support by voting **2** the right to vote • **voter** *noun* someone who votes

vouch *verb* (with **for**) say that you are sure of or can guarantee: *I can vouch for his courage* • **vouchsafe** *verb, old* give or grant (a reply, privilege, *etc*)

voucher *noun* a piece of printed paper that can be exchanged for money or goods

vow *noun* a solemn promise or declaration, *esp* one made to God ◇ *verb* **1** make a vow **2** threaten (revenge *etc*)

vowel *noun* **1** a sound made by the voice that does not require the use of the tongue, teeth or lips **2** the letters *a, e, i, o, u* (or various combinations of them), and sometimes *y*, which represent those sounds

vox pop *noun* **1** an interview with a member of the public (from Latin *vox populi*, voice of the people) **2** public or popular opinion

voyage *noun* a journey, usually by sea ◇ *verb* make a journey

voyeur /vwah-*yur*/ *noun* someone who gets sexual pleasure from watching other people secretly • **voyeurism** *noun* • **voyeuristic** *adj*

VSO *abbrev* Voluntary Service Overseas, an organization that arranges for people to do voluntary work in poor countries

vulgar *adj* **1** mentioning sex or bodily functions in a distasteful way; rude **2** showing a lack of good taste • **vulgarity** *noun* • **vulgarly** *adv* • **vulgar fraction** *noun* a fraction not written as a decimal, *eg* $\frac{1}{3}$ or $\frac{4}{5}$

vulnerable *adj* **1** liable to be hurt physically or emotionally **2** exposed to, or in danger of, attack • **vulnerability** *noun*

vulture *noun* a large bird that feeds mainly on the flesh of dead animals

vulva *noun* the opening of the vagina

Ww

wad *noun* 1 a lump of loose material, *eg* wool, cloth, paper, pressed together 2 a bunch of banknotes • **wadding** *noun* soft material, *eg* cotton wool, used for packing or padding

waddle *verb* walk with short steps moving from side to side, as a duck does ◊ *noun*

wade *verb* 1 walk through deep water or mud 2 get through with difficulty: *still wading through this book*

wader *noun* 1 a long-legged bird that wades in search of food 2 (**waders**) high waterproof boots worn by anglers for wading

wadi /*wod*-i/ *noun* a rocky river bed in N Africa, dry except in the rainy season

wafer *noun* 1 a very thin light biscuit 2 a very thin slice of anything

waffle *noun* 1 *US* a light, crisp cake made from batter and cooked in a **waffle-iron** 2 lengthy meaningless talk ◊ *verb* talk long and meaninglessly

waft *verb* carry or drift lightly through the air or over water

wag *verb* (**wagging**, **wagged**) move from side to side or up and down ◊ *noun* 1 an act of wagging 2 *dated* someone who is always joking • **waggish** *adj*, *dated* always joking

wage *noun* (often **wages**) payment for work ◊ *verb* carry on (a war *etc*)

wager *noun* a bet ◊ *verb* bet

waggle *verb* move from side to side in an unsteady manner ◊ *noun* an unsteady movement from side to side

wagon *or* **waggon** *noun* 1 a four-wheeled horse-drawn vehicle for carrying loads 2 an open railway carriage for goods 3 *US* a trolley for carrying food

wagtail *noun* a small black and white bird with a long tail that it wags up and down

waif *noun* an uncared-for or homeless child or animal • **waifs and strays** homeless children or animals

wail *verb* cry or moan in sorrow ◊ *noun* a sorrowful cry

wain *noun*, *old* a wagon

wainscot *noun* wood panelling on the lower part of a wall

waist *noun* the narrow part of the body, between the ribs and hips

waistcoat *noun* a short, sleeveless jacket, often worn under an outer jacket

wait *verb* 1 put off or delay action 2 (with **for**) remain in expectation or readiness for: *waiting for the bus to come* 3 be employed as a waiter or waitress ◊ *noun* a period spent waiting • **waiting list** *noun* a list of people waiting for something in order of priority • **waiting room** *noun* a room in which to wait at a railway station, clinic, *etc* • **wait on** 1 serve (someone) in a restaurant *etc* 2 act as a servant to

waiter, **waitress** *noun* someone whose job it is to serve people at table in a restaurant

waive *verb* officially ignore (a rule *etc*) or give up (a claim or right) • **waiver** *noun* 1 the act of waiving 2 a document indicating this

---

Do not confuse with: **wave** and **waver**

---

wake¹ verb (**waking**, **woke** or **waked**, **woken**) (often with **up**) stop sleeping ◇ noun **1** a night of watching beside a dead body **2** a feast or holiday • **wakeful** adj not sleeping or unable to sleep • **waking** adj being or becoming awake

wake² noun a streak of foamy water left in the track of a ship • **in the wake of** immediately behind or after

waken verb rouse or be roused from sleep; wake

walk verb **1** move along on foot **2** travel along (streets etc) on foot ◇ noun **1** an act of walking **2** a way of walking **3** a distance to be walked over: a short walk from here **4** a place for walking: a covered walk • **walkie talkie** noun, dated a portable radio set for sending and receiving messages • **walking stick** noun a stick used for support when walking • **walk of life** noun someone's rank or occupation • **walkover** noun an easy victory • **walkway** noun a path or passage for pedestrians • **walk the plank** hist be put to death by pirates by being made to walk off the end of a plank over a ship's side

Walkman noun, trademark a personal stereo

wall noun **1** a structure built of stone, brick, etc used to separate or enclose **2** the side of a building ◇ verb (with **in**, **off**, etc) enclose or separate with a wall • **off the wall** very unusual; eccentric

wallaby noun (plural **wallabies**) a small kind of kangaroo

wallet noun a small folding case for holding banknotes, credit cards, etc

wallflower noun **1** a sweet-smelling spring flower **2** someone who is continually without a partner at a dance etc

wallop verb, informal hit with a heavy blow ◇ noun

wallow verb roll about with enjoyment in water, mud, etc

wallpaper noun decorative paper used for covering interior walls ◇ verb cover with wallpaper

wally /wo-li/ noun (plural **wallies**), slang a stupid or inept person

walnut noun **1** a round crinkly nut **2** the tree that produces it, or the tree's hard golden-brown wood

walrus noun (plural **walruses**) a large seal-like animal with two long tusks

waltz noun (plural **waltzes**) **1** a ballroom dance for couples with a circling movement **2** music for this dance, with three beats to each bar ◇ verb dance a waltz

wan /won/ adj pale and ill-looking

wand noun a long slender rod used by a conjuror, magician, etc

wander verb **1** roam about with no definite purpose; roam **2** go astray **3** be mentally confused because of illness etc • **wanderer** noun

wanderlust noun a keen desire for travel

wane verb **1** become smaller (contrasted with: **wax**) **2** lose power or importance • **on the wane** becoming less, or less powerful

wangle verb get or achieve through craftiness, skilful planning, etc

wank verb, taboo slang masturbate ◇ noun an act of masturbating • **wanker** noun a worthless or contemptible person

wannabe /won-uh-bee/ noun, informal someone who desperately wants to be a particular thing: filmstar wannabes

want verb **1** wish for **2** need ◇ noun **1** poverty **2** lack • **wanted** adj looked for, esp by the police • **wanting** adj **1** not good enough **2** (with **in**) lacking: wanting in good taste

wanton adj done without thought or purpose; pointless: wanton cruelty

WAP abbrev Wireless Application Protocol, a system that enables the Internet to be accessed on a mobile phone

war noun an armed struggle, esp between nations ◇ verb (**warring**, **warred**) fight each other in a war • **war cry** noun words shouted aloud in battle, for encouragement • **warfare** noun the carrying on of war • **warhead** noun the part of a missile containing the explosive • **warlike** adj **1** fond of war **2** threatening war • **warrior** noun a great fighter • **warship** noun a ship armed with guns etc • **on the warpath** in a fighting or angry mood

warble verb sing like a bird; trill • **warbler** noun a type of songbird

ward noun **1** a hospital room containing a number of beds **2** one of the parts into which a town is divided for voting **3** someone who is in the care of a guardian ◇ verb (with **off**) defend yourself against (a blow etc) • **warden** noun **1** someone in charge of a hostel, college, or other large building **2** someone who guards a game reserve • **warder** noun a prison guard • **wardrobe** noun **1** a cupboard for clothes **2** someone's personal supply of clothes • **wardroom** noun a room for officers on a warship

-ware suffix manufactured material: earthenware/glassware • **warehouse** noun a building where goods are stored • **wares** plural noun goods for sale

warm adj **1** fairly hot **2** of clothes: keeping the wearer warm **3** of a person: friendly, loving ◇ verb make or become warm • **warm-blooded** adj having a blood temperature higher than that of the surrounding atmosphere • **warm-hearted** adj kind, generous • **warmth** noun

warn verb **1** tell (someone) beforehand about possible danger, misfortune, etc: I warned him about the icy roads **2** give cautionary advice to: I warned him not to be late • **warning** noun a remark, notice, etc that warns

warp verb **1** become twisted out of shape **2** distort: his previous experiences had warped his judgement ◇ noun the threads stretched lengthwise on a loom, crossed by the weft

warrant noun a certificate granting someone a right or authority: search warrant ◇ verb be a good enough reason for: the crime does not warrant such punishment • **warranted** adj guaranteed • **warranty** noun an assurance of the quality of goods being sold • **I warrant you** or **I'll warrant** I assure you

warren noun **1** a set of rabbit burrows **2** a building with many rooms and passages; a maze

wart noun a small hard growth on the skin • **warthog** noun a wild African pig

wary adj cautious • **warily** adv • **wariness** noun

was a past tense form of **be**

wash verb **1** clean with water, soap, etc **2** clean yourself with water etc **3** of water: flow over or against **4** sweep (away, along, etc) by force of water ◇ noun (plural **washes**) **1** an act of washing yourself **2** a streak of foamy water left behind by a moving boat **3** a liquid with which anything is washed **4** a thin coat of paint etc • **washbasin** noun a shallow sink for washing the hands and face • **washer** noun **1** someone or something that washes **2** a flat ring of metal, rubber, *etc* for keeping joints tight • **washerwoman** *noun, old* a woman who is paid to wash clothes • **washhand basin** *noun* a bathroom sink in which to wash your hands and face • **washing** *noun* **1** the act of cleaning with water and soap *etc* **2** clothes to be washed • **washing machine** *noun* an electric machine for washing clothes • **washing-up** *noun* dishes to be washed • **wash your hands of** have nothing further to do with • **wash up** wash the dishes

wasp *noun* a stinging flying insect with a slender yellow-and-black striped body

wassail /wos-ehl/ *verb, old* have a loud drinking session with friends

waste *verb* **1** spend (money, time, energy) in a needless or senseless way **2** decay or wear away gradually ◇ *noun* **1** unwanted things discarded as useless; rubbish **2** needless or senseless use; squandering **3** an expanse of water, snow, *etc* ◇ *adj* **1** thrown away as useless: *waste paper* **2** of land: uncultivated, barren and desolate • **wastage** *noun* **1** an amount wasted **2** loss through decay or squandering • **wasteful** *adj* using something needlessly or senselessly • **wastepaper basket** *noun* a basket for paper rubbish • **wastepipe** *noun* a pipe for carrying away dirty water or semi-liquid waste • **waster** or **wastrel** *noun* an idle, good-for-nothing person

watch *verb* **1** look at closely **2** (often with **over**) look after; mind **3** *old* stay awake ◇ *noun* (*plural* **watches**) **1** a small clock worn on the wrist or kept in a pocket **2** the act of keeping guard **3** someone who keeps guard **4** a sailor's period of duty on deck • **watchdog** *noun* **1** a dog that guards a building **2** an organization that monitors business practices *etc* • **watchful** *adj* alert and cautious • **watchfully** *adv* • **watchfulness** *noun* • **watchman** *noun* a man who guards a build-

ing *etc* at night • **watchword** *noun* a motto or slogan

water *noun* **1** a clear, tasteless liquid that falls as rain **2** a collection of this liquid in a lake, river, *etc* **3** urine ◇ *verb* **1** supply with water **2** dilute or mix with water **3** of the mouth: fill with saliva **4** of the eyes: fill with tears • **water biscuit** *noun* a thin savoury biscuit • **water butt** *noun* a large barrel for rain water • **water closet** *noun, old formal* a toilet • **watercolour** *noun* **1** paint that is mixed with water, not oil **2** a painting done with this paint • **watercourse** *noun* a stream, river or canal • **watercress** *noun* a plant that grows beside streams, with hot-tasting leaves eaten in salads • **waterfall** *noun* a place where a river falls from a height, often over a ledge of rock • **water ice** *noun* a dessert of crushed, fruit-flavoured ice • **water-lily** *noun* a plant that grows in ponds *etc*, with flat floating leaves and large flowers • **waterline** *noun* the level reached by the water on the hull of a boat • **waterlogged** *adj* of ground: too wet to walk on or play on • **water main** *noun* a large underground pipe carrying a public water supply • **watermark** *noun* a faint design on writing paper showing the maker's name, crest, *etc* • **watermelon** *noun* a large melon with red juicy flesh and a thick, green skin • **water mill** *noun* a mill driven by water • **water polo** *noun* a ball game played in a pool between teams of swimmers • **waterproof** *adj* not allowing water to pass through ◇ *noun* an overcoat made of waterproof material • **water rat** *noun* a kind of vole • **watershed** *noun* **1** a ridge separating the valleys of two rivers **2** a point after which something changes • **watertight** *adj* so closely fitted that water cannot leak through • **waterway** *noun* a channel along which ships can sail • **water wheel** *noun* a wheel turned by flowing water, used for powering something

• **waterworks** *plural noun* **1** a place that purifies and stores a town's water supply **2** *informal* the urinary system **3** *informal* tears • **watery** *adj* **1** full of water **2** of soup *etc*: too thin and tasteless

watt *noun* a unit of electric power • **wattage** *noun* electric power measured in watts

wattle *noun* **1** interwoven twigs and branches used for fences *etc* **2** a fleshy part hanging from the neck of a turkey **3** an Australian acacia tree

wave *noun* **1** a moving ridge on the surface of the water **2** a ridge or curve of hair **3** a vibration travelling through the air carrying light, sound, *etc* **4** a hand gesture for attracting attention, or saying hello or goodbye **5** a rush of an emotion (*eg* despair, enthusiasm, *etc*) ◇ *verb* **1** make a wave with the hand **2** move to and fro; flutter: *flags waving in the wind* **3** curl or curve • **waveband** *noun* the range of frequencies occupied by a particular type of broadcasting • **wavelength** *noun* the distance from one point on a wave or vibration to the next similar point • **wavy** *adj* having waves

---

Do not confuse with: **waive**

---

waver *verb* **1** be unsteady; wobble **2** be uncertain or undecided

wax *noun* **1** any of various fatty substances that are typically shiny and smooth, used *eg* for making candles **2** a fatty substance in the ear ◇ *adj* made of wax ◇ *verb* **1** rub with wax **2** grow, increase (*contrasted with*: **wane**) • **waxen** *adj* **1** of or like wax **2** pale • **waxworks** *plural noun* a museum displaying wax models of famous people • **waxy** *adj* of or like wax

way *noun* **1** an opening or passage: *the way out* **2** a road, path or course **3** room to go forward or pass: *block the way* **4** direction: *he went that way* **5** distance: *a long way* **6** condition: *in a bad way* **7** means, method: *there must be a way to do this* **8** manner: *in a clumsy way* **9** someone's own wishes or choice: *he always gets his own way* • **wayfarer** *noun, old* a traveller on foot • **waylay** *verb* wait for and stop (someone) • **-ways** *suffix* in the direction of: *lengthways/sideways* • **wayside** *noun* the edge of a road or path ◇ *adj* located by the side of a road • **wayward** *adj* behaving in a way that others cannot control and do not approve of • **by the way** incidentally • **by way of 1** travelling through **2** as if, with the purpose of: *by way of a favour* • **in the way** blocking progress • **make your way** go

WC *abbrev* water closet, *ie* a toilet

we *pronoun* used by a speaker or writer in mentioning themselves together with other people (as the subject of a verb): *we are having a party this weekend*

weak *adj* **1** not strong; feeble **2** lacking determination **3** easily overcome: *weak opposition* • **weaken** *verb* make or become weak • **weak-kneed** *adj* overcome with admiration or fear • **weakling** *noun* a person or animal lacking strength • **weakly** *adv* • **weakness** *noun* **1** lack of strength **2** a fault **3** a special fondness that cannot be resisted: *a weakness for chocolate*

weal *noun* a raised mark on the skin caused by a blow from a whip

wealth *noun* **1** riches **2** a large quantity: *wealth of information* • **wealthy** *adj* rich

wean¹ *verb* **1** make (a child or young animal) used to food other than the mother's milk **2** (with **from** or **off**) make (someone) gradually give up (a bad habit *etc*)

wean² /wehn/ *noun, Scot* a child

weapon *noun* **1** an object used for fighting, *eg* a sword, gun, *etc* **2** any means of attack

wear *verb* (**wearing, wore, worn**) **1** be dressed in **2** arrange in a particular way: *she wears her hair long* **3** have (a beard, moustache) on the face **4** damage or weaken by use, rubbing, *etc* **5** be damaged in this way **6** last: *wear well* ◇ *noun* **1** use by wearing: *formal wear* **2** damage by use **3** ability to last **4** clothes *etc*: *school wear* • **wearable** *adj* fit to be worn • **wearer** *noun* • **wearing** *adj* tiring • **wear and tear** damage owing to ordinary use • **wear off** pass away gradually • **wear on** become later: *the afternoon wore on* • **wear out 1** make or become unfit for further use **2** exhaust

weary *adj* (**wearier, weariest**) **1** having used up your strength or patience **2** tiring or boring ◇ *verb* (**wearies, wearying, wearied**) make or become tired, bored or impatient • **wearisome** *adj* causing tiredness, boredom or impatience • **weary of** tired of or bored with

weasel *noun* a small wild animal with a long slender body that lives on mice, birds, *etc*

weather *noun* atmospheric conditions, *eg* rain, sunshine or cloud ◇ *verb* **1** dry or wear away through exposure to the air **2** come safely through (a storm, difficulty, *etc*) • **weatherbeaten** *adj* showing signs of having been out in all weathers • **weathercock** or **weathervane** *noun* a flat piece of metal that swings in the wind to show its direction

weave *verb* (**weaving, wove, woven**) **1** pass threads over and under each other on a loom to form cloth **2** plait cane *etc* for basket-making **3** put together (a story, plan, *etc*) **4** move in and out between objects, or move from side to side: *weaving through the traffic* • **weaver** *noun* someone who weaves

Web *abbrev, comput* the World Wide Web • **webcam** *noun* a camera for filming live broadcasts on the Inter-

net • **webcast** *noun* a broadcast on the Internet • **weblog** *noun* a document containing personal observations posted on the Internet • **web page** *noun* one of the linked pages or files of a website • **website** *noun* the location on the World Wide Web of data relating to a particular person or organization

web *noun* **1** the net made by a spider; a cobweb **2** the skin between the toes of ducks, swans, frogs, *etc* **3** something woven • **webbed** *adj* of feet: having the toes joined by a web • **webbing** *noun* a type of strong, woven tape used for belts *etc* • **web-footed** or **web-toed** *adj* having webbed feet or toes

wed *verb* (**wedding, wedded**) marry • **wedlock** *noun* the state of being married

we'd *short for* we would, we should or we had

wedding *noun* **1** a marriage ceremony **2** *old* marriage

wedge *noun* **1** a piece of wood, metal, *etc* thick at one end with a thin edge at the other, used in splitting wood, forcing two surfaces apart *etc* **2** anything shaped like a wedge ◇ *verb* **1** fix or become fixed with a wedge **2** push or squeeze (in): *wedged in amongst the crowd*

Wednesday *noun* the fourth day of the week

wee[1] *verb, informal* urinate ◇ *noun* urine

wee[2] *adj, Scot* small

weed *noun* **1** a useless, troublesome plant **2** a weak, worthless person **3** (**weeds**) a widow's mourning clothes ◇ *verb* clear (a garden *etc*) of weeds • **weedy** *adj* **1** full of weeds **2** like a weed **3** thin and puny

week *noun* **1** the space of seven days from Sunday to Saturday **2** the working days of the week, not including

Saturday and Sunday • **weekday** noun any day except Saturday and Sunday • **weekend** noun the time from Saturday to Monday • **weekly** adj happening, or done, once a week ◇ adv once a week ◇ noun a newspaper or magazine that comes out once a week

weep verb 1 shed tears 2 ooze, drip: weeping wound • **weeping willow** noun a willow tree with drooping branches

weevil noun a small beetle that destroys grain, flour, etc

weft noun the threads on a loom that cross the warp

weigh verb 1 find out how heavy (something) is by putting it on a scale etc 2 have a certain heaviness: weighing 10 kilograms 3 raise (a ship's anchor) 4 of burdens etc: be troublesome 5 consider (a matter, a point) carefully • **weighbridge** noun a large scale for weighing vehicles • **weigh in** test your weight before a boxing match • **weigh out** measure out a quantity by weighing it on a scale

weight noun 1 the amount that anything weighs 2 a piece of metal weighing a certain amount: a 100 gramme weight 3 a load or burden 4 importance ◇ verb make heavy by adding or attaching a weight • **weightless** adj • **weightlessness** noun absence of the pull of gravity • **weighty** adj 1 heavy 2 important

weir noun a dam across a stream

weird adj 1 mysterious or supernatural 2 strange

welcome verb 1 receive (guests) with pleasure 2 accept gladly: I welcome the challenge ◇ noun an act of receiving guests ◇ adj 1 received with pleasure 2 much appreciated • **welcome to** permitted to do or take • **you're welcome!** used in reply to an expression of thanks

weld verb 1 join (pieces of metal) by pressure, with or without heating 2

join closely ◇ noun a joint made by welding • **welder** noun

welfare noun 1 wellbeing 2 financial support given by the government to people in need; benefits • **welfare state** noun a country with a health service, insurance against unemployment, pensions for those who cannot work etc

well adv (**better**, **best**) 1 in a good and correct manner: write well 2 thoroughly: well beaten 3 successfully: do well 4 conveniently: it fits in well with my plans ◇ adj in good health ◇ exclam expressing surprise, or used in explaining, narrating, etc ◇ noun 1 a spring of water 2 a shaft in the earth from which water, oil, etc is extracted 3 an enclosed space round which a staircase winds ◇ verb (often with **up**) rise up and gush: tears welled up in her eyes • **well-advised** adj wise • **wellbeing** noun general state of health, happiness and comfort • **well-bred** or **well-mannered** adj having good manners • **well-disposed** adj (with **to**) inclined to be in favour of • **well-informed** adj having or showing knowledge • **well-known** adj 1 famous 2 familiar • **well-meaning** adj having good intentions • **well-meant** adj kindly intended • **well-off** adj rich • **well-read** adj having read many good books • **well-to-do** adj rich • **well-wisher** noun someone who wishes someone success • **as well as** in addition to • **it is as well** or **it is just as well** it is fortunate or a good thing

we'll short for we will or we shall

wellingtons plural noun high rubber boots covering the lower part of the legs

welsh rarebit noun a dish made of cheese melted on toast

welt noun 1 a firm edging or band, eg on the wrist or waist of a garment 2 a weal

welter *noun* 1 a large but disordered mass; a jumble: *a welter of information* 2 great disorder or confusion ◇ *verb* roll about; wallow

wench *noun* (*plural* **wenches**), *old* a girl or young woman

wend *verb*: **wend your way** make your way slowly

went *past tense of* **go**

wept *past form of* **weep**

were *a past tense of* **be**

we're *short for* we are

werewolf /*wair*-wuulf/ *noun* a mythical creature that changes periodically from a human into a wolf

west *noun* the direction in which the sun sets, one of the four main points of the compass ◇ *adj* 1 in or to the west 2 of the wind: from the west ◇ *adv* in or towards the west • **westerly** *adj* 1 of the wind: coming from or facing the west 2 in or towards the west • **western** *adj* of the west ◇ *noun* a film or story about life among the early settlers in the western United States • **westward** *or* **westwards** *adj* & *adv* towards the west • **the Wild West** *hist* the western United States in the early days of its settlement

wet *adj* (**wetter, wettest**) 1 soaked or covered with water or other liquid 2 rainy: *a wet day* ◇ *noun* 1 water 2 rain ◇ *verb* (**wetting, wetted**) make wet • **wet suit** a suit that allows water to pass through but retains body heat

---

Do not confuse with: **whet**

---

whack *noun* a loud violent slap or blow ◇ *verb* slap or hit violently

whale *noun* a very large mammal living in the sea ◇ *verb* catch whales • **whalebone** *noun* a light bendable substance obtained from the upper jaw of certain whales • **whale oil** *noun* oil obtained from the blubber of a whale • **whaler** *noun* a ship engaged in catching whales

wharf *noun* (*plural* **wharfs** *or* **wharves**) a landing stage for loading and unloading ships

what *adj* & *pronoun* used to indicate something about which a question is being asked: *what day is this?/what are you doing?* ◇ *adj* any that: *give me what money you have* ◇ *conj* anything that: *I'll take what you can give me* ◇ *adj, adv* & *pronoun* used for emphasis in exclamations: *what ties he wears!/what rubbish!* • **whatever** *adj* & *pronoun* 1 anything (that): *show me whatever you have* 2 no matter what: *whatever happens* • **whatsoever** *adj* at all: *nothing whatsoever to do with me* • **what about?** used in asking whether the listener would like something: *what about a glass of milk?* • **what if?** what will or would happen if: *what if he comes back?* • **what with** because of: *what with having no exercise and being overweight, he had a heart attack*

wheat *noun* a grain from which many foods are made, eg bread and pasta • **wheatear** *noun* a small bird that visits Britain in summer • **wheaten** *adj* 1 made of wheat 2 wholemeal • **wheatgerm** *noun* the vitamin-rich embryo of wheat • **wheatmeal** *noun* meal made of wheat, *esp* wholemeal

wheedle *verb* beg or coax, often by flattery

wheel *noun* 1 a circular frame or disc turning on an axle, fitted to a vehicle to allow it to move along 2 a steering wheel of a car *etc* ◇ *verb* 1 move or push on wheels 2 turn round suddenly: *wheeled round in surprise* • **wheelbarrow** *noun* a handcart with one wheel in front, two handles and legs behind • **wheelchair** *noun* a chair on wheels for a disabled or infirm person • **wheelhouse** *noun* the shelter in which a ship's steering wheel is placed • **wheelie bin** *noun* a large dustbin on wheels • **wheelwright** noun someone who makes wheels and carriages

wheeze verb breathe with difficulty, making a whistling or croaking sound ◇ noun **1** the sound of difficult breathing **2** dated informal a joke

whelk noun a small shellfish used as food

whelp noun **1** a young lion **2** a puppy ◇ verb of a lion, dog, etc: give birth to young

when adv at what time: when did you arrive? ◇ adv & conj the time at which: I know when you left/I fell when I was coming in ◇ relative pronoun at which: at the time when I saw him ◇ conj seeing that, since: why walk when you have a car? • **whenever** adv & conj **1** at any given time: come whenever you're ready **2** at every time: I go whenever I get the chance

whence adv, old from what place: whence did you come? ◇ conj to the place from which: he's gone back whence he came • **whenceforth** adv & conj, old whence

where adv & conj to or in what place: where are you going?/I wonder where we are ◇ relative pronoun & conj (to the place) to which, or (in the place) in which: go where he tells you to go/it's still where it was • **whereupon** adv & conj at or after which time, event, etc • **wherever** adv to what place: wherever did you go? ◇ conj to any place: wherever you may go • **wherewithal** noun **1** the means of doing something **2** money

whereabouts noun the place where someone or thing is: I don't know her whereabouts ◇ adv & conj near or in what place: whereabouts is it?/I don't know whereabouts it is

whereas conj **1** when in fact: they thought I was lying, whereas I was telling the truth **2** but, on the other hand: he's tall, whereas I'm short

wherry noun (plural **wherries**) a type of shallow, light boat

whet verb (**whetting**, **whetted**) **1** make (desire, appetite, etc) keener **2** sharpen (a knife etc) by rubbing • **whetstone** noun a stone on which to sharpen blades

---

Do not confuse with: **wet**

---

whether conj **1** either if: whether you come or not **2** if: I don't know whether it's possible

which adj & pronoun **1** used to refer to a particular person or thing from a group: which colour do you like best?/which is yours? **2** the one that: show me which dress you would like ◇ relative pronoun referring to the person or thing just named: I bought the chair which you are sitting on • **whichever** adj & pronoun any (one), no matter which: I'll take whichever you don't want/I saw trees whichever way I turned

whiff noun a sudden puff or scent: whiff of perfume

while or **whilst** conj **1** during the time that: while I'm at the office **2** although: while I sympathize, I can't really help • **while** noun a space of time ◇ verb (with **away**) to pass (time) without boredom: he whiled away the time by reading

whim noun a sudden thought or desire • **whimsical** adj **1** amusing in a strange or rather old-fashioned way **2** done for fun • **whimsy** noun **1** whimsical quality **2** a whim

whimper verb cry with a low, whining voice ◇ noun a low, whining cry

whin noun gorse

whine verb **1** make a high-pitched, complaining cry **2** complain unnecessarily ◇ noun an unnecessary complaint

whinge verb (**whingeing**, **whinged**)

complain in a weak, annoying way ◇ *noun* a weak, annoying complaint • **whingeing** *adj* • **whinger** *noun*

whinny *verb* (**whinnies**, **whinnying**, **whinnied**) of a horse: neigh ◇ *noun* (*plural* **whinnies**) a neighing sound

whip *noun* 1 a lash with a handle, for punishing, urging on animals, *etc* 2 a member of parliament who sees that the members of their own party attend to give their vote when needed ◇ *verb* (**whipping**, **whipped**) 1 hit or drive with a lash 2 beat (eggs, cream, *etc*) into a froth 3 snatch (away, off, out, up, *etc*): *whipped out a revolver* 4 move fast, like a whip • **whip hand** *noun* the advantage in a fight, argument, *etc* • **whiplash** *noun* 1 the lash of a whip 2 a neck injury suffered *esp* in vehicle collisions • **whipper-snapper** *noun* a small, unimportant, impertinent person • **whipping** *noun* a beating with a whip

whippet *noun* a breed of racing dog like a small greyhound

whir another spelling of **whirr**

whirl *verb* 1 turn round quickly 2 carry (off, away, *etc*) quickly ◇ *noun* 1 a fast circling movement 2 great excitement or confusion: *in a whirl over the wedding arrangements* • **whirlpool** *noun* a place in a river or sea where the current moves in a circle • **whirlwind** *noun* a violent current of wind with a whirling motion

whirr *or* **whir** *noun* a sound of fast, continuous whirling ◇ *verb* (**whirring**, **whirred**) move or whirl with a buzzing noise

whisk *verb* 1 move quickly and lightly; sweep: *their car whisked past* 2 beat or whip (a mixture) ◇ *noun* a kitchen utensil for beating eggs or mixtures

whisker *noun* 1 a long bristle on the upper lip of a cat *etc* 2 (**whiskers**) hair on the sides of a man's face; sideburns

whisky *or Irish & US* **whiskey** *noun* (*plural* **whiskies** *or* **whiskeys**) an alcoholic spirit made from grain

whisper *verb* 1 speak very softly, using the breath only, not the voice 2 make a soft, rustling sound ◇ *noun* a soft sound made with the breath

whist *noun* a type of card game for four players

whistle *verb* 1 make a high-pitched sound by forcing breath through the lips or teeth 2 make such a sound with an instrument 3 move with such a sound, as does a bullet ◇ *noun* 1 the sound made by whistling 2 any instrument for whistling

whit *noun, dated* a tiny bit: *not a whit better*

white *adj* 1 of the colour of pure snow 2 pale or light-coloured: *white wine* 3 having a pale-coloured complexion ◇ *noun* 1 something white 2 someone with a pale-coloured complexion 3 the part of an egg surrounding the yolk • **white ant** *noun* a termite • **whitebait** *noun* the young of herring or sprats • **white elephant** *noun* something useless and costly or troublesome to maintain • **white-hot** *adj* having reached a degree of heat at which metals glow with a white light (hotter than **red-hot**) • **white knight** *noun* a company that comes to the aid of another facing an unwelcome takeover bid • **white-knuckle** *adj* causing extreme fear • **whiten** *verb* make or become white or whiter • **whiteness** *noun* • **white paper** *noun* a statement, printed on white paper, issued by the government for the information of parliament

whitewash *noun* a mixture of ground chalk and water, or lime and water, for whitening walls *etc* ◇ *verb* 1 put whitewash on 2 cover up the faults of and give a good appearance to

whither *adv & conj, old* to what place?

whiting noun a type of small fish related to the cod

whitlow noun an infected swelling beside the finger or toenail

Whitsun noun the week beginning with the seventh Sunday after Easter

whittle verb 1 pare or cut (wood etc) with a knife 2 (with **away** or **down**) make gradually less: whittled away his savings

whizz or **whiz** verb (**whizzing**, **whizzed**) 1 move with a hissing sound, like an arrow 2 move very fast • **whizz kid** noun someone who achieves rapid success while relatively young

WHO abbrev World Health Organization

who pronoun 1 used to refer to someone or some people unknown or unnamed (only as the subject of a verb): who is that woman in the green hat? 2 informal used as the object in a sentence (instead of **whom**): who did you choose? ◇ relative pronoun referring to the person or people just named: the woman who lives next door • **whodunit** or **whodunnit** noun, informal a detective novel or play • **whoever** pronoun any person or people

whole adj 1 complete 2 with nothing or no one missing; all 3 not broken 4 in good health ◇ noun the entire thing • **wholefood** noun food that is processed as little as possible or not at all • **wholehearted** adj enthusiastic and generous • **wholemeal** noun flour made from the entire wheat grain • **wholesome** adj giving health; healthy • **wholly** adv entirely, altogether • **on the whole** when everything is taken into account

wholesale noun the sale of goods in large quantities to a shop from which they can be bought in small quantities by ordinary buyers (compare with: **retail**) ◇ adj 1 buying or selling through wholesale 2 on a large scale: wholesale killing • **wholesaler** noun

who'll short for who will or who shall

whom pronoun 1 used to refer to someone or some people unknown or unnamed (only as the object of a sentence): whom did you see?/to whom am I speaking? 2 which person: do you know to whom I gave it? ◇ relative pronoun referring to the person or people just named: the person whom I liked best

whoop noun a loud cry of triumph or joy ◇ verb give a whoop • **whooping cough** noun an infectious disease in which violent bouts of coughing are followed by a whoop as the breath is drawn in

whore noun, informal derog a female prostitute

whortleberry noun the bilberry

whose adj & pronoun belonging to whom?: whose handwriting is this? ◇ relative pronoun of whom: the man whose wife I know

why adv & pronoun for which reason?: why did you not stay? • **the whys and wherefores** all the reasons or details

wick noun the twisted threads in a candle or lamp that draw the oil or grease up to the flame

wicked adj 1 morally very bad; evil 2 full of spite or hatred 3 slang excellent • **wickedly** adv • **wickedness** noun

wicker adj of a chair: made of woven willow twigs

wicket noun 1 cricket the set of three stumps, or one of these, at which the ball is bowled 2 cricket the ground between the bowler and the batsman 3 a small gate or door, esp in or beside a larger one

wide adj 1 broad, not narrow 2 stretching far 3 measuring a certain amount from side to side: five centimetres *wide* ◇ *adv* **1** off the target: *the shots went wide* **2** (often with **apart**) far apart: *hold your arms wide* • **wide awake** *adj* fully awake; alert • **wide boy** *noun, informal* a man who makes money in an unfair or dishonest way • **wide-eyed** *adj* with eyes wide open in surprise *etc* • **widely** *adv* **1** over a wide area; among many: *widely believed* **2** far apart • **widen** *verb* make or become wide • **wideness** *noun* • **wide open** *adj & adv* opened to the full extent • **widespread** *adj* spread over a large area or among many people: *a widespread belief* • **wide of the mark** not accurate

widow *noun* a woman whose husband is dead • **widower** *noun* a man whose wife is dead

width *noun* **1** measurement across, from side to side **2** large extent

wield *verb* **1** swing or handle (a cricket bat, sword, *etc*) **2** use (power, authority, *etc*)

wife *noun* (*plural* **wives**) **1** the woman to whom a man is married **2** a married woman

Wi-Fi /wai-fai/ *noun, trademark* a method of transmitting data between computers using radio waves

wig *noun* an artificial covering of hair for the head

wiggle *verb* move from side to side with jerky or twisting movements ◇ *noun* a jerky movement from side to side • **wiggly** *adj*

wigwam *noun, hist* a conical tent of skins made by some Native Americans

wild *adj* **1** of an animal: not tamed **2** of a plant: not cultivated in a garden **3** uncivilized **4** unruly or uncontrolled **5** of weather: stormy **6** in a very agitated state; frantic: *wild with anxiety* **7** of a guess *etc*: rash, inaccurate ◇ *noun* (usually **wilds**) an uncultivated or uncivilized region • **wild boar** *noun* a wild type of pig • **wild card** *noun* **1**

the right to compete in a tournament without fulfilling the usual entrance requirements **2** *comput* a symbol (*) used to represent any character or group of characters • **wild cat** *noun* a wild type of European cat • **wildcat** *adj* of a strike: not supported or permitted by trade union officials • **wildfire** *noun* lightning without thunder • **wildfowl** *noun* wild birds, *esp* those shot as game • **wild-goose chase** *noun* a troublesome and useless errand • **wildlife** *noun* wild animals and plants in their natural habitats • **like wildfire** very quickly

wilderness *noun* a wild, uncultivated or desolate region

wile *noun* a crafty trick or charming persuasive way of behaving • **wily** *adj*

will *verb* **1** (*past form* **would**) used to form future tenses of other verbs when the subject is **he**, **she**, **it**, **you** or **they**: *you will see me there* **2** *informal* often used for the same purpose when the subject is **I** or **we**: *I will tell you later* **3** used for emphasis, or to express a promise, when the subject is **I** or **we**: *I will do it if possible* (see also **shall**, **would**) **4** influence someone by exercising your will: *he willed her to win* **5** hand down (property *etc*) by will ◇ *noun* **1** determination: *the will to win* **2** a written statement about what is to be done with your property after your death **3** the power to choose or decide **4** desire: *against my will* **5** feeling towards someone: *a sign of goodwill* • **wilful** *adj* **1** intentional: *wilful damage* **2** fond of having your own way: *wilful child* • **willing** *adj* ready to do what is asked; eager • **at will** as or when you choose • **with a will** eagerly

will-o'-the-wisp *noun* a pale light sometimes seen by night over marshy places

willow *noun* **1** a tree with long slender branches **2** its wood, used in cricket bats • **willowy** adj slender and graceful

willy noun (plural **willies**) slang a penis

willy-nilly adv whether people want it or not

wilt verb **1** of a flower or plant: droop **2** lose strength

wily see **wile**

wimp noun, informal a physically weak or ineffectual person

wimple noun a folded veil worn around the head esp by nuns

win verb (**winning, won**) **1** gain by luck or in a contest **2** gain (the love of someone etc) by effort **3** come first in a contest **4** (often with **over**) gain the support or friendship of ◇ noun an act of winning; a victory • **winning** adj **1** victorious or successful **2** charming or attractive: winning smile • **winnings** plural noun money etc that has been won

wince verb shrink or start back in pain etc, flinch: her singing made me wince

winceyette noun a type of brushed cotton cloth

winch noun (plural **winches**) **1** a handle or crank for turning a wheel **2** a machine for lifting things, worked by winding a rope round a revolving cylinder • **winch up** lift up with a winch

wind¹ noun **1** a current of air **2** breath **3** air or gas in the stomach **4** the wind instruments in an orchestra ◇ verb put out of breath • **windfall** noun **1** an unexpected gain, eg a sum of money **2** a fruit blown from a tree • **wind instrument** noun a musical instrument sounded by the breath • **windjammer** noun a type of sailing ship • **windmill** noun a mill driven by sails that are moved by the wind, used for pumping water, grinding grain, etc • **windpipe** noun the tube leading from the mouth to the lungs • **wind-**

screen or US **windshield** noun a pane of glass in front of the driver of a vehicle • **windsurf** verb sail on a sailboard • **windsurfer** noun • **windsurfing** noun • **windswept** adj exposed to strong winds and showing the effects of it: windswept hair • **windward** adj & adv in the direction from which the wind blows • **windy** adj **1** of weather: with a strong wind blowing **2** of a place: exposed to strong winds • **get the wind up** informal become afraid • **get wind of** informal hear about in an indirect way

wind² /waind/ verb (**winding, wound**) **1** turn, twist or coil **2** (sometimes with **up**) screw up the spring of (a watch, clockwork toy, etc) **3** wrap closely • **winder** noun a key etc for winding a clock • **winding** adj curving or twisting • **wind up 1** bring or come to an end: wind up a meeting **2** informal annoy by teasing • **wind your way** make your way circuitously • **wound up** tense or agitated

windlass noun a machine for lifting up or hauling a winch

window noun **1** an opening in a wall, protected by glass, that lets in light and air **2** comput an enclosed rectangular area displayed on the VDU of a computer, used as an independent screen

wine noun **1** an alcoholic drink made from the fermented juice of grapes or other fruit **2** a rich dark red colour • **winepress** noun a machine that squeezes the juice out of grapes

wing noun **1** one of the arm-like limbs of a bird, bat or insect by means of which it flies **2** one of the two projections on the sides of an aeroplane **3** a part of a house built out to the side **4** the side of a stage, where actors wait to enter **5** a section of a political party: the left wing **6** in team sports, a player positioned at the edge of the field ◇ verb **1** wound (a bird) in the wing **2** soar • **wing commander** noun a high-ranking officer in the air force • **winged** *adj* **1** having wings **2** swift • **on the wing** flying • **under someone's wing** under the protection or care of someone

wink *verb* **1** open and close an eye quickly **2** give a hint by winking **3** of lights *etc*: flicker, twinkle ◇ *noun* **1** an act of winking **2** a hint given by winking • **forty winks** a short sleep

winkle *noun* (*also called*: **periwinkle**) a small edible shellfish • **winkle out** force or prise out gradually

winnow *verb* separate the chaff from the grain by tossing it up

winsome *adj, dated* charming

winter *noun* the coldest season of the year, following autumn ◇ *adj* relating to winter • **winter sports** *plural noun* sports done on snow or ice, eg skiing, tobogganing, *etc* • **wintry** *adj* **1** cold or frosty **2** expressing hostility; unfriendly: *a wintry look*

wipe *verb* **1** clean or dry by rubbing **2** (with **away**, **out**, **off** or **up**) clear away ◇ *noun* the act of cleaning by rubbing • **wiper** *noun* one of a pair of moving parts that wipe the windscreen of a car

wire *noun* **1** a thread-like length of metal **2** the metal thread used in communication by telephone *etc* **3** *informal* a telegram ◇ *adj* made of wire ◇ *verb* **1** supply (a building *etc*) with wires for carrying an electric current **2** *informal* send a telegram • **wireless** *adj* of communication: by radio waves ◇ *noun, old* a radio set • **wire netting** *noun* mesh made of wire • **wiry** *adj* **1** made of wire **2** of a person: thin but strong

wise *adj* **1** very knowledgeable **2** judging rightly; sensible • **wisdom** *noun* the quality of being wise • **wisdom tooth** *noun* one of the four large back teeth that appear after childhood • **-wise** *suffix* **1** in the manner or way of: *crabwise* **2** with reference

or regard to: *careerwise*

wish *verb* **1** feel or express a desire: *I wish he'd leave* **2** (often with **for**) long (for): *she wished for peace and quiet* **3** hope for on behalf of (someone): *wish someone luck* ◇ *noun* (*plural* **wishes**) **1** desire **2** a thing desired or wanted: *her great wish was to live abroad* **3** an expression of desire: *make a wish* **4** (**wishes**) expression of hope for another's happiness, good fortune, *etc*: *good wishes* • **wishbone** *noun* a forked bone in the breast of fowls • **wishful** *adj* wishing, eager • **wishful thinking** *noun* basing your belief on (false) hopes rather than known facts • **wish someone well** feel goodwill towards them

wishywashy *adj* **1** of liquid: thin and weak **2** lacking energy or liveliness **3** lacking colour

wisp *noun* a small tuft or strand: *a wisp of hair* • **wispy** *adj*

wistful *adj* thoughtful and rather sad: *a wistful glance* • **wistfully** *adv*

wit *noun* **1** the ability to express ideas amusingly **2** someone who can do this **3** (often **wits**) intelligence or common sense • **-witted** *suffix* having wits (of a certain kind): *slow-witted/quick-witted* • **witticism** *noun* a witty remark • **wittingly** *adv* knowingly • **witty** *adj* amusing • **at your wits' end** desperate because everything you have tried has failed • **keep your wits about you** keep alert • **to wit** namely

witch *noun* (*plural* **witches**) **1** a woman with magic powers obtained through evil spirits **2** an ugly old woman • **witchcraft** *noun* magic performed by a witch • **witch doctor** *noun* someone believed to have magic powers to cure illnesses *etc* • **witch-hazel** *noun* **1** a N American shrub **2** a healing lotion made from its bark and leaves

with *prep* **1** in the company of: *I was walking with my father* **2** by means of:

cut it with a knife **3** in the same direction as: *drifting with the current* **4** against: *fighting with his brother* **5** on the same side as: *played with Beckham* **6** having: *a man with a limp* **7** in the keeping of: *leave the keys with me*

withdraw *verb* (**withdrawing, withdrew, withdrawn**) **1** go back or away **2** take away or take out: *withdraw cash/withdraw troops* **3** take back (an insult *etc*) • **withdrawal** *noun* an act of withdrawing • **withdrawn** *adj* **1** of a place: lonely, isolated **2** of a person: unwilling to communicate with others

wither *verb* **1** dry up and decay **2** cause to feel very unimportant or embarrassed: *she withered him with a look* • **withering** *adj* **1** drying up and decaying **2** of a remark *etc*: very scornful or sarcastic • **withers** *plural noun* the ridge between the shoulder bones of a horse

withhold *verb* (**withholding, withheld**) refuse to give

within *prep* inside the limits of: *keep within the law* ◇ *adv* on the inside

without *prep* **1** in the absence of: *we went without you* **2** not having: *without a penny* **3** *formal* outside the limits of: *without the terms of the agreement* ◇ *adv, old* **1** on the outside **2** out-of-doors

withstand *verb* resist successfully

witness *noun* (*plural* **witnesses**) **1** someone who sees something happen **2** someone who gives evidence in a law court **3** *formal* proof or evidence ◇ *verb* **1** be present at and see **2** sign your name to confirm the authenticity of (someone else's signature) **3** give or be evidence • **witness box** *noun* the stand from which a witness in a law court gives evidence • **bear witness** give or be evidence of: *bear witness to his character*

wizard *noun* a man believed to have

the power of magic • **wizardry** *noun* magic

wizened *adj* very wrinkled with age: *a wizened old man*

WMD *abbrev* weapon(s) of mass destruction

woad *noun* **1** a blue dye **2** the plant from which it is obtained

wobble *verb* rock unsteadily from side to side ◇ *noun* an unsteady rocking • **wobbly** *adj* moving unsteadily

woe *noun* **1** grief or misery **2** a cause of sorrow; a trouble • **woebegone** *adj* sad-looking • **woeful** *adj* to be pitied; pitiful • **woefully** *adv*

wok *noun* an almost hemispherical pan used in Chinese cookery

wolf *noun* (*plural* **wolves**) a wild animal like a dog that hunts in packs ◇ *verb* eat greedily: *wolfing down his food* • **wolfhound** *noun* a large breed of dog once used to hunt wolves • **wolfish** *adj* like a wolf • **cry wolf** give a false alarm • **keep the wolf from the door** keep away hunger or poverty

wolverine *noun* a wild animal of the weasel family

woman *noun* (*plural* **women**) **1** an adult human female **2** human females in general **3** a domestic help • **womanhood** *noun* the state of being a woman • **womanish** *adj* of a man: effeminate • **womankind** *or* **womenkind** *noun* women generally • **womanly** *adj* like, or suitable for, a woman

womb /woom/ *noun* the part of a female mammal's body in which the young develop and stay till birth

wombat *noun* a small, beaver-like Australian animal with a pouch

women *plural of* **woman**

won *past form of* **win**

wonder *verb* **1** be curious or in doubt: *I wonder what will happen/I wonder whether to go or not* **2** feel surprise or amazement (at, that) ◇ *noun* **1** feelings of surprise and admiration produced by something unexpected and extraordinary **2** something strange, amazing or miraculous • **wonderful** *adj* **1** excellent **2** arousing wonder • **wonderland** *noun* a fairytale place • **wonderment** *noun, old* amazement • **wondrous** *adj, old* wonderful

wonky *adj* (**wonkier**, **wonkiest**) *informal* not properly steady or straight

wont *adj, old* accustomed (to do something) ◇ *noun* habit: *as is his wont*

won't *short for* will not

won ton *noun* a spicy Chinese dumpling, often served in soup

woo *verb* (**wooing**, **wooed**) **1** try to win the love of (someone) **2** try to gain the approval or business of • **wooer** *noun*

wood *noun* **1** a group of growing trees **2** the hard part of a tree, *esp* when cut for use • **woodbine** *noun* the honeysuckle • **woodchuck** *noun* a marmot • **woodcock** *noun* a game bird related to the snipe • **woodcut** *noun* **1** a picture engraved on wood **2** a print made from this engraving • **woodcutter** *noun* someone who fells trees, cuts up wood, *etc* • **wooded** *adj* covered with trees • **woodland** *noun* land covered with trees • **woodlouse** *noun* (*plural* **woodlice**) an insect with a jointed shell, found under stones *etc* • **woodpecker** *noun* a bird that pecks holes in the bark of trees with its beak, in search of insects • **wood spirit** *noun* methanol • **woodwind** *noun* wind instruments, made of wood or metal, *eg* the flute or clarinet • **woodwork** *noun* **1** the making of wooden articles **2** the wooden parts of a house, room, *etc* • **woodworm** *noun* the larva of a beetle that bores holes in wood and destroys it • **woody** *adj* **1** like wood **2** covered with trees

wooden *adj* **1** made of wood **2** not at all lively or natural: *a wooden speech* • **woodenly** *adv*

wool *noun* **1** the soft hair of sheep and other animals **2** yarn or cloth made of wool • **woolgathering** *noun, dated* daydreaming • **woollen** *adj* made of wool ◇ *noun* a knitted garment made of wool • **woolly** *adj* **1** made of, or like, wool **2** vague, hazy: *a woolly argument* ◇ *noun* a knitted woollen garment

word *noun* **1** a written or spoken sign representing a thing or an idea **2** (**words**) talk, remarks: *kind words* **3** news: *word of his death* **4** a promise: *break your word* ◇ *verb* choose words for: *he worded his refusal carefully* • **wording** *noun* choice or arrangement of words • **word processor** *noun* an electronic machine, or computer program, that can store, edit and print out text • **wordwrap** *noun, comput* the automatic placing of a word on a new line when it is too long to fit on the end of the existing line • **wordy** *adj* using too many words • **have words** *informal* quarrel • **in a word** in short • **take someone at their word** treat what they say as true • **take someone's word for something** trust that what they say is true • **word for word** in the exact words

wore *past tense of* **wear**

work *noun* **1** a physical or mental effort to achieve or make something **2** a job; employment: *out of work* **3** a task: *I've got work to do* **4** anything made or done **5** something produced by art, *eg* a book, musical composition, painting, *etc* **6** way of doing something: *poor work* **7** (**works**) a factory **8** (**works**) the mechanism (*eg* of a watch) **9** (**works**) deeds: *good works* ◇ *verb* **1** be engaged in physical or mental work **2** be employed **3** run or operate smoothly and efficiently **4** of a plan *etc*: be successful **5** get into a position slowly and gradually: *the screw worked loose* **6** organize or manage • **workable** *adj* able to be done • **workaday** *adj* ordinary and unexciting • **workaholic** *noun, informal* someone addicted to work • **worked up** *adj* angry, nervous or excited • **worker** *noun* someone who works at a job • **workforce** *noun* the number of workers in an industry, factory, *etc* • **working class** *noun* the social class the consists of people doing relatively junior, low-paid and *esp* manual jobs • **working-class** *adj* • **working day** *or* **working hours** *noun* a day or the hours that someone spends at work, on duty, *etc* • **working party** *noun* a group of people appointed to investigate a particular matter • **workman** *noun* someone who does a manual job, *esp* in the building trade • **workmanlike** *adj* done with skill • **workmanship** *noun* **1** the skill of a workman **2** way of making something • **workplace** *noun* an office, factory, *etc* • **workshop** *noun* a room or building where manufacturing, craftwork, *etc* is done • **work out 1** solve **2** discover as a result of deep thought **3** of a situation: turn out all right in the end

world *noun* **1** the earth and all things on it **2** the people of the world **3** any planet or star **4** the universe **5** a state of existence: *the next world* **6** a particular area of life or activity: *the insect world/the world of fashion* **7** a great deal: *a world of good* • **worldly** *adj* concerned with material things such as money, possessions, *etc*, not the soul or spirit • **worldwide** *adj* extending throughout the world ◇ *adv* throughout the world • **World Wide Web** *noun* the vast collection of data that can be accessed via the Internet

worm *noun* **1** a small crawling animal without a backbone, often living in soil **2** *informal* a low, contemptible person **3** something spiral-shaped, *eg* the thread of a screw **4** (**worms**) the condition of having threadworms *etc*

in the intestines **5** *comput* a kind of virus ◇ *verb* **1** move gradually and stealthily (in or into) **2** (with **out**) draw out (information) bit by bit

wormwood *noun* a plant with a bitter taste

worn *adj* damaged by use • **worn-out** *adj* exhausted

worry *verb* (**worries, worrying, worried**) **1** of a dog: shake or tear (something) with its teeth **2** annoy **3** make troubled and anxious **4** be troubled and anxious ◇ *noun* (*plural* **worries**) **1** anxiety **2** a cause of anxiety

worse *adj* **1** bad or evil to a greater degree **2** more ill ◇ *adv* badly to a greater degree, or more severely: *it's snowing worse than ever* • **worsen** *verb* make or become worse • **worse off 1** in a worse position **2** less wealthy

worship *verb* (**worshipping, worshipped**) **1** pay honour to (a god) **2** adore or admire deeply ◇ *noun* **1** a religious ceremony or service **2** deep reverence; adoration **3** a title used in addressing a mayor, provost, *etc* • **worshipful** *adj* **1** full of reverence **2** worthy of honour

worst *adj* bad or evil to the greatest degree ◇ *adv* badly to the greatest degree ◇ *verb* (**worsting, worsted**) defeat • **at worst** under the least favourable circumstances • **if the worst comes to the worst** if the worst possible circumstances occur

worsted[1] *noun* **1** a type of fine woollen yarn **2** a strong cloth made of this

worsted[2] *past form of* **worst**

worth *noun* **1** monetary value **2** importance or usefulness **3** excellence of character ◇ *adj* **1** equal in value to **2** deserving of: *worth considering* • **worthless** *adj* of no merit or value • **worthwhile** *adj* deserving time and effort • **worthy** *adj* **1** (often with **of**) deserving, suitable **2** of good character ◇ *noun, often derog* a highly

respected person: *local worthy*
• **worth your while** worth the trouble spent

would verb **1** the form of the verb **will** used to express a condition: *he would go if he could* **2** used for emphasis: *I tell you I would do it if possible* **3** old expressing a wish: *I would that he were gone*

would-be adj trying to be or pretending to be: *would-be actor/would-be socialist*

wound¹ /woond/ noun **1** a cut or injury caused by a weapon, in an accident, *etc* **2** an injury to someone's feelings ◇ verb **1** make a wound in **2** hurt the feelings of • **wounded** adj having a wound; injured

wound² /wownd/ *past form of* **wind²**

WPC abbrev Woman Police Constable

wrack /rak/ noun seaweed thrown onto the shore

wraith /rehth/ noun an apparition of a living person, often as a warning of death

wrangle verb quarrel noisily ◇ noun a noisy quarrel

wrap verb (**wrapping**, **wrapped**) **1** fold or roll round: *wrap it in tissue paper* **2** (with **up**) cover by folding or winding something round ◇ noun **1** a cloak or shawl **2** a flour tortilla wrapped around a savoury filling

wrapper noun a loose paper cover, *eg* round a book or sweet

wrath /rath/ or /roth/ noun violent anger • **wrathful** adj very angry

wreak verb **1** carry out: *wreak vengeance* **2** cause: *wreak havoc*

wreath noun **1** a ring of flowers or leaves **2** a curling wisp of smoke, mist, *etc*

wreathe verb form a circle round

wreck noun **1** destruction, *esp* of a ship by the sea **2** the remains of any-

thing destroyed, *esp* a ship **3** someone whose health or nerves are in bad condition ◇ verb destroy • **wreckage** noun the remains of something wrecked

wren noun a very small type of bird

wrench verb **1** pull with a violent, often twisting motion **2** sprain (your ankle *etc*) ◇ noun (*plural* **wrenches**) **1** a tool for gripping and turning nuts, bolts, *etc* **2** a violent twist **3** sadness caused by parting from someone or something

wrest verb, formal twist or take by force

wrestle verb **1** fight with someone, trying to bring them to the ground **2** (with **with**) think deeply about (a problem *etc*) • **wrestler** noun someone who wrestles as a sport • **wrestling** noun the sport in which two people fight to throw each other to the ground

wretch noun (*plural* **wretches**) **1** a person who is pitied: *a poor wretch* **2** a worthless or contemptible person

wretched /rech-id/ adj **1** very bad or very much disliked **2** of a very poor standard **3** very ill • **wretchedly** adv • **wretchedness** noun

wriggle verb **1** twist to and fro **2** move by doing this, as a worm does **3** escape (out of a difficulty *etc*)

-wright /-rait/ suffix a maker: *shipwright/playwright*

wring verb (**wringing**, **wrung**) **1** twist or squeeze (*esp* water out of wet clothes) **2** clasp and unclasp (your hands) in grief, anxiety, *etc* **3** cause pain to: *the story wrung everybody's heart* **4** obtain by force or great effort: *wrung a promise out of him* • **wringer** noun a machine for forcing water from wet clothes

wrinkle noun a small crease or fold on the skin or other surface ◇ verb make or become wrinkled • **wrinklie**

noun, informal derog an old person • **wrinkly** *adj*

wrist *noun* the joint by which the hand is joined to the arm

writ /rit/ *noun* a formal document giving an order, *esp* to appear in a law court

write *verb* (**writing, wrote, written**) **1** form letters with a pen, pencil, *etc* **2** put into writing: *write your name* **3** compose (a letter, a book, *etc*) **4** send a letter (to) **5** *comput* copy (a data file) • **write-off** *noun* a vehicle that has been damaged beyond repair • **write protect** *noun, comput* a method of ensuring that data on a disk can be read, but not altered • **writer** *noun* someone who writes; an author • **writing** *noun* a written text or texts • **write down** record in writing • **write off** regard as lost for ever • **write up** make a written record of

writhe /raidh/ *verb* twist or roll about, *eg* in pain

wrong *adj* **1** not correct **2** not right or fair; immoral **3** not what is intended: *take the wrong turning* **4** unsuitable: *the wrong weather for camping* **5** mistaken: *you are wrong if you think that* ◇ *noun* **1** whatever is not right or fair **2** a bad thing done to someone ◇ *verb* do a bad thing to • **wrongdoer** *noun* someone who does wrong • **wrongdoing** *noun* • **wrongful** *adj* not lawful or fair • **wrongly** *adv* • **go wrong 1** fail to work properly **2** make a mistake or mistakes • **in the wrong** guilty of injustice or error

wrote *past tense of* **write**

wroth /rohth/ *adj, old* angry

wrought /rawt/ *adj, old* made or manufactured ◇ *verb, old past form of* **work** • **wrought-iron** *noun* iron hammered, rather than cast, into shape • **wrought-up** *adj* agitated or anxious

wrung *past form of* **wring**

wry /rai/ *adj* **1** expressing humour in relation to something unpleasant: *wry remark* **2** twisted or turned to one side • **wryly** *adv*

WWW *or* **www** *abbrev* World Wide Web

WYSIWYG /wiz-i-wig/ *abbrev, comput* what you see (on the screen) is what you get (in the printout)

Xx

xenophobia *noun* hatred of foreigners or strangers • **xenophobe** *noun* someone who hates foreigners • **xenophobic** *adj*

Xerox *noun, trademark* **1** a photographic process used for copying documents **2** a copy made in this way ◇ *verb* copy by Xerox

Xmas *noun, informal* Christmas

X-rays *noun plural* rays that can pass through material impenetrable by light, and produce a photographic image of the object through which they have passed • **X-ray** *noun* a picture produced by X-rays on photographic film ◇ *verb* take a photographic image of with X-rays

xylophone *noun* a musical instrument consisting of a series of graded wooden plates that are struck with hammers

Yy

yacht /yot/ *noun* a sailing boat for racing or cruising • **yachtsman**, **yachtswoman** *noun*

yak *noun* a Tibetan long-haired ox

yam *noun* a tropical root vegetable similar to a potato

Yank or **Yankee** *noun, Brit informal derog* an American

yank *verb, informal* pull with a violent jerk ◇ *noun* a violent pull

yap *verb* (**yapping**, **yapped**) give a high-pitched bark

yard *noun* 1 a measure of length equal to 3 feet or 0.9144 of a metre 2 an enclosed space used for a particular purpose: *railway yard/shipbuilding yard* 3 *US* a garden

yardstick *noun* 1 a standard against which other things are judged 2 a yard-long measuring stick

yarn *noun* 1 wool, cotton, *etc* spun into thread 2 one of several threads forming a rope 3 a long, often improbable story

yarrow *noun* a strong-smelling plant with flat clusters of white flowers

yashmak *noun* a veil covering the lower half of the face, worn by Muslim women

yawl *noun* a small rowing boat or fishing boat

yawn *verb* 1 take a deep breath unintentionally with an open mouth, because of boredom or sleepiness 2 of a hole: be wide open; gape ◇ *noun* an open-mouthed deep breath

yd *abbrev* yard(s)

ye *pronoun, old* you

yea /jeh/ *adv, old* yes

year *noun* 1 the time taken by the earth to go once round the sun, about 365 days 2 the period from 1 January to 31 December 3 a period of twelve months starting at any point 4 (**years**) age: *wise for her years* • **yearling** *noun* a year-old animal • **yearly** *adj* happening once a year

yearn *verb* 1 feel a great desire 2 feel compassion • **yearning** *noun* an eager longing

yeast *noun* a substance that causes fermentation, used to make bread dough rise and in brewing

yell *verb* give a loud, shrill cry; scream ◇ *noun* a loud, shrill cry

yellow *noun* the colour of gold, egg-yolks, *etc* ◇ *adj* of this colour ◇ *verb* become yellow owing to ageing

yellowhammer *noun* a yellow bird of the finch family

yelp *verb* give a sharp bark or cry ◇ *noun* a sharp bark or cry

yen[1] *noun* the standard unit of Japanese currency

yen[2] *noun, informal* a strong desire; longing: *a yen to return to Scotland*

yeoman /yoh-mun/ *noun, hist* a farmer with his own land • **yeomanry** *noun, hist* farmers 2 a troop of cavalrymen serving voluntarily in the British army • **the Yeomen of the Guard** the company acting as bodyguard to the British king or queen on certain occasions

yes *exclam* expressing agreement

or consent ◇ *noun* **1** an expression of agreement or consent **2** a vote in favour

yesterday *adv & noun* **1** (on) the day before today **2** (in) the past

yet *adv* **1** by this time: *have you seen that film yet?* **2** before the matter is finished: *we may win yet* ◇ *conj* nevertheless: *I am defeated, yet I shall not surrender* • **yet another** and another one still • **yet more** still more

Yeti *noun* the Abominable Snowman

yew *noun* **1** a tree with dark green leaves and red berries **2** its wood

YHA *abbrev* Youth Hostels Association

yield *verb* **1** produce (a crop, results, *etc*) **2** give way to pressure or persuasion **3** stop fighting; surrender ◇ *noun* an amount produced; a crop • **yielding** *adj* giving way easily

yikes *exclam, Brit* goodness!, heavens!

ylang-ylang /ee-lang-ee-*lang*/ *noun* a SE Asian tree from whose flowers a fragrant oil is distilled

YMCA *abbrev* Young Men's Christian Association, or a hostel operated by it

yob *noun, informal* a bad-mannered aggressive youth

yodel *verb* (**yodelling, yodelled**) sing in a style involving frequent changes between an ordinary and a very high-pitched voice

yoga *noun* a Hindu system of philosophy and meditation involving special physical exercises

yoghurt *or* **yogurt** *noun* a semi-liquid food product made from fermented milk

yoke *noun* **1** a wooden frame joining oxen when pulling a plough or cart **2** a frame placed across the shoulders for carrying pails *etc* **3** something that limits freedom; a burden ◇ *verb* **1** put

a yoke on **2** join together

Do not confuse with: **yolk**

---

yokel *noun, derog* an unsophisticated country person; a bumpkin

yolk *noun* the yellow part of an egg

Do not confuse with: **yoke**

Yom Kippur *noun* the Day of Atonement, a Jewish day of fasting

yonder *adv, old* in that place (at a distance but within sight) ◇ *adj* that (object) over there: *by yonder tree*

yonks *plural noun, informal* a very long time; ages

yore *noun*: **of yore** *old* in times past

you *pronoun* the person(s) spoken to or written to, used as the *sing* or *plural* subject or object of a verb: *what did you say?/are you both free tomorrow?*

you'd *short for* you would, you should or you had

you'll *short for* you will or you shall

young *adj* **1** in early life **2** in the early part of growth ◇ *noun* **1** the offspring of animals **2** (**the young**) young people • **youngster** *noun* a young person

your *adj* belonging to you: *it's your life*

you're *short for* you are

yours *pronoun* belonging to you: *is this pen yours?* • **Yours, Yours faithfully, Yours sincerely** *or* **Yours truly** expressions used before a signature at the end of a letter

yourself *pronoun* (*plural* **yourselves**) **1** used reflexively: *don't trouble yourself* **2** used for emphasis: *you yourself can't go*

youth *noun* **1** the state of being young **2** the early part of life **3** a young man **4** young people in general • **youth**

hostel *noun* a hostel providing simple short-term accommodation

youthful *adj* **1** young **2** fresh and vigorous • **youthfully** *adv* • **youthfulness** *noun*

you've *short for* you have

Yo-yo *noun, trademark* a toy consisting of a reel that spins up and down on a string

yr *abbrev* year

yuan /yoo-*ahn*/ *noun* the main currency unit of The People's Republic of China

yucca *noun* a Mexican desert plant with thick spiky leaves

yucky *adj, informal* **1** disgusting **2** sentimental in a silly way

Yule *noun, old* Christmas • **Yuletide** *noun* Christmas time

yuppie *or* **yuppy** *noun* (*plural* **yuppies**) an ambitious young person in a well-paid professional job

YWCA *abbrev* Young Women's Christian Association, or a hostel operated by it

zabaglione /za-bal-yoh-ni/ noun custard made with egg yolks, sugar, and sweet wine

zany adj (**zanier, zaniest**) informal amusingly wild; crazy • **zanily** adv • **zaniness** noun

zap verb (**zapping, zapped**) informal 1 hit, shoot, destroy, etc suddenly 2 move rapidly; zip • **zapper** noun, informal a remote control for a TV etc

zeal noun great or excessive enthusiasm • **zealous** adj full of zeal • **zealously** adv

zealot /zel-ut/ noun a fanatical enthusiast

zebra noun a striped African animal of the horse family • **zebra crossing** a pedestrian street crossing painted in black and white stripes

zeitgeist /zait-gaist/ noun the attitudes and interests of people in the present period

zenith noun 1 the most successful point; the peak 2 the point of the heavens exactly overhead

zephyr /zef-uh/ noun, formal a soft, gentle breeze

zero noun 1 nothing or the sign for it (0) 2 the point (marked 0) from which a scale (eg on a thermometer) begins • **zero hour** noun the exact time when something has been arranged to take place • **zero option** noun a proposal to get rid of nuclear weapons if the opposing side does likewise • **zero-rated** adj of goods: not subject to VAT • **zero tolerance** noun a policy of allowing no leniency in the enforcement of the law or a rule

zest noun 1 great enjoyment 2 orange or lemon peel • **zestful** adj • **zestfully** adv

zigzag adj having sharp bends or angles ◇ verb (**zigzagging, zigzagged**) move in a zigzag direction

zimmer noun, trademark a hand-held metal frame used to give support in walking

zinc noun a bluish-white metal

zine /zeen/ noun, informal a special-interest magazine

zingy adj, informal very lively or interesting

zinnia noun a tropical American plant of the thistle family

zip noun 1 a fastening device for clothes, bags, etc, consisting of two rows of metal or nylon teeth that interlock when a sliding tab is pulled between them 2 a whizzing sound, eg made by a fast-flying object 3 informal energy, vigour ◇ verb (**zipping, zipped**) 1 fasten with a zip 2 fly past at speed 3 comput compress data so that it takes up less memory

zither noun a flat stringed musical instrument played with the fingers

zodiac noun an imaginary strip in space, divided into twelve equal parts • **signs of the zodiac** the divisions of the zodiac used in astrology, each named after a group of stars

zoetrope /zoh-i-trohp/ noun a rotating cylinder with pictures on the inside that appear to move when viewed through slots in the side

zombie *noun* 1 a corpse reanimated by witchcraft 2 a very slow or stupid person

zone *noun* 1 a section of a country, town, etc marked off for a particular purpose: *no-parking zone/smokeless zone* 2 any of the five main bands into which the earth's surface is divided according to temperature: *temperate zone* ◇ *verb* divide into zones

zonked *adj, slang* 1 exhausted 2 under the influence of alcohol or drugs

zoo *noun* a place where wild animals are kept and shown to the public

zoological *adj* 1 relating to animals 2 relating to zoos or containing a zoo: *zoological gardens*

zoology *noun* the science of animal life • **zoologist** *noun* someone who studies animal life

zoom *verb* 1 move with a loud, low buzzing noise 2 make such a noise 3 of an aircraft: climb sharply at high speed for a short time 4 of prices: increase sharply 5 use a zoom lens on a camera • **zoom lens** *noun* a photographic lens that makes a distant object appear gradually nearer without the camera being moved

Zoroastrianism *noun* an ancient Persian religion • **Zoroastrian** *adj*

zucchini /zoo-kee-ni/ *noun* (*plural* **zucchini** or **zucchinis**) *US* a courgette

zygote /zai-goht/ *noun* a cell formed when male and female reproductive cells fuse at the beginning of reproduction